Advertising and Promotion

AN INTEGRATED MARKETING COMMUNICATIONS PERSPECTIVE

SEVENTH EDITION

George E. Belch & Michael A. Belch

BOTH OF SAN DIEGO STATE UNIVERSITY

Boston Burr Ridge, IL Dubuque, IA Madison, WI New York

Bangkok Bogotá Caracas Kuala Lumpur Lisbon London

Milan Montreal New Delhi Santiago Seoul Singapore

ADVERTISING AND PROMOTION:
AN INTEGRATED MARKETING COMMUNICATIONS PERSPECTIVE
Published by McGraw-Hill/Irwin, a business unit of The McGraw-Hill Companies, Inc. 1221 Avenue of the Americas, New York, NY, 10020.

Some ancillaries, including electronic and print components, may not be available to customers outside the United States.

This book is printed on acid-free paper.

1 2 3 4 5 6 7 8 9 0 DOW/DOW 0 9 8 7 6

ISBN-13: 978-0-07-110589-7
ISBN-10: 0-07-110589-1

To Our Families:

Gayle, Danny, Derek

Melanie, Jessica, Milos

And a special dedication

To Mom

About the Authors

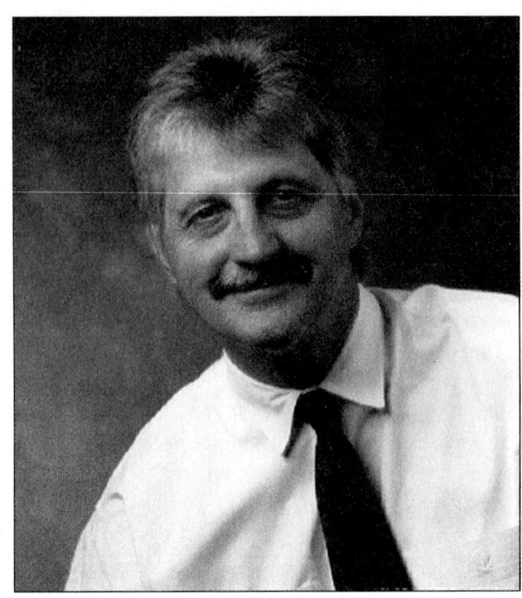

DR. GEORGE E. BELCH

George E. Belch is professor of marketing and chair of the marketing department at San Diego State University, where he teaches integrated marketing communications, strategic marketing planning, and consumer/customer behavior. Prior to joining San Diego State, he was a member of the faculty in the Graduate School of Management, University of California, Irvine. He received his PhD in marketing from the University of California, Los Angeles. Before entering academia, Dr. Belch was a marketing representative for the DuPont Company. He also worked as a research analyst for the DDB Worldwide advertising agency.

Dr. Belch's research interests are in the areas of consumer processing of advertising information as well as managerial aspects of integrated marketing communications. He has authored or coauthored more than 30 articles in leading academic journals including: *Journal of Marketing Research, Journal of Consumer Research, Journal of Advertising,* and *Journal of Business Research.* In 2000, he was selected as *Marketing Educator of the Year* by the Marketing Educators' Association for his career achievements in teaching and research. He also received the Distinguished Faculty Member Award for the College of Business Administration at San Diego State University in 2003.

Dr. Belch has taught in executive education and development programs for various universities around the world. He has also conducted seminars on integrated marketing communications as well as marketing planning and strategy for a number of multinational companies including Sprint, Microsoft, Qualcomm, MP3.com, Fluor Daniel, Square D Corporation, Armstrong World Industries, Sterling Software, Siliconix, and Texas Industries.

DR. MICHAEL A. BELCH

Michael (Mickey) A. Belch is a professor of marketing at San Diego State University and is also co-director of the Centre for Integrated Marketing Communications at San Diego State University. He received his undergraduate degree from Penn State University, his MBA from Drexel University, and his PhD from the University of Pittsburgh.

Before entering academia he was employed by the General Foods Corporation as a marketing representative, and has served as a consultant to numerous companies, including McDonalds, Whirlpool Corporation, Senco Products, GTI Corporation, IVAC, May Companies, Phillips-Ramsey Advertising and Public Relations, and Dailey & Associates Advertising. He has conducted seminars on integrated marketing and marketing management for a number of multinational companies and has also taught in executive education programs in France, Amsterdam, Spain, Chile, Argentina, Colombia, China, and Slovenia. He is the author or coauthor of more than 40 articles in academic journals in the areas of advertising, consumer behavior, and international marketing including: *Journal of Advertising, Journal of Advertising Research,* and *Journal of Business Research.* Dr. Belch is also a member of the editorial review board of the *Journal of Advertising.* He has also received outstanding teaching awards from undergraduate and graduate students numerous times.

Preface

The Changing World of Advertising and Promotion

Nearly everyone in the modern world is influenced to some degree by advertising and other forms of promotion. Organizations in both the private and public sectors have learned that the ability to communicate effectively and efficiently with their target audiences is critical to their success. Advertising and other types of promotional messages are used to sell products and services as well as to promote causes, market political candidates, and deal with societal problems such as alcohol and drug abuse. Consumers are finding it increasingly difficult to avoid the efforts of marketers, who are constantly searching for new ways to communicate with them.

Most of the people involved in advertising and promotion will tell you that there is no more dynamic and fascinating field to either practice or study. However, they will also tell you that the field is undergoing dramatic changes that are changing advertising and promotion forever. The changes are coming from all sides—clients demanding better results from their advertising and promotional dollars; lean but highly creative smaller ad agencies; sales promotion and direct-marketing firms, as well as interactive agencies, which want a larger share of the billions of dollars companies spend each year promoting their products and services; consumers who no longer respond to traditional forms of advertising; and new technologies that may reinvent the very process of advertising. We are experiencing perhaps the most dynamic and revolutionary changes of any era in the history of marketing, as well as advertising and promotion. These changes are being driven by advances in technology and developments that have led to the rapid growth of communications through interactive media, particularly the Internet.

For decades the advertising business was dominated by large, full-service Madison Avenue–type agencies. The advertising strategy for a national brand involved creating one or two commercials that could be run on network television, a few print ads that would run in general interest magazines, and some sales promotion support such as coupons or premium offers. However, in today's world there are a myriad of media outlets—print, radio, cable and satellite TV, and the Internet—competing for consumers' attention. Marketers are looking beyond the traditional media to find new and better ways to communicate with their customers. They no longer accept on faith the value of conventional advertising placed in traditional media. Major marketers such as Procter & Gamble, American Express, and McDonald's are moving away from a reliance on mass-media advertising and are spending more of their marketing communication budgets in specialized media that target specific markets. Companies are also spending more of their monies in other ways such as event marketing, sponsorships, cause-related promotions, and viral marketing. Advertising agencies are recognizing that they must change the way they do business.

In addition to redefining the role and nature of their advertising agencies, marketers are changing the way they communicate with consumers. They know they are operating in an environment where advertising messages are everywhere, consumers channel-surf past most commercials, and brands promoted in traditional ways often fail. New-age advertisers are redefining the notion of what an ad is and where it runs. Stealth messages are being woven into the culture and embedded into movies and TV shows or made into their own form of entertainment. Many experts argue that "branded content" is the wave of the future, and there is a growing movement to reinvent advertising and other forms of marketing communication to be more akin to entertainment. Companies such as American Express, Volkswagen, and Skyy Spirits are among those using branded entertainment as a way of reaching consumers. These companies create short films that can be viewed on their websites, arrange product placements, and integrate their products into movies and television shows to promote their products and services.

Marketers are also changing the ways they allocate their promotional dollars. Spending on sales promotion activities targeted at both consumers and the trade has surpassed advertising media expenditures for years and continues to rise. In his book *The End of Marketing as We Know It,* Sergio Zyman, the former head of marketing for Coca-Cola, declares traditional marketing is "not dying, but dead." He argues that advertising in general is overrated as part of the marketing mix and notes that all elements of the marketing mix communicate, such as brand names, packaging, pricing, and the way a product is distributed. The information revolution is exposing consumers to all types of communications, and marketers need to better understand this process.

A number of factors are impacting the way marketers communicate with consumers. The audiences that marketers seek, along with the media and methods for reaching them, have become increasingly fragmented. Advertising and promotional efforts have become more regionalized and targeted to specific audiences. Retailers have become larger and more powerful, forcing marketers to shift money from advertising budgets to sales promotion. Marketers expect their promotional dollars to generate immediate sales and are demanding more accountability from their agencies. The Internet revolution is well under way and the online audience is growing rapidly, not only in the United States but in most other countries as well. Many companies are coordinating all their communications efforts so that they can send cohesive messages to their customers. Some companies are building brands with little or no use of traditional media advertising. Many advertising agencies have acquired, started, or become affiliated with sales promotion, direct-marketing, interactive agencies, and public relations companies to better serve their clients' marketing communications needs. Their clients have become "media-neutral" and are asking that they consider whatever form of marketing communication works best to target market segments and build long-term reputations and short-term sales.

This text will introduce students to this fast-changing field of advertising and promotion. While advertising is its primary focus, it is more than just an introductory advertising text because there is more to most organizations' promotional programs than just advertising. The changes discussed above are leading marketers and their agencies to approach advertising and promotion from an integrated marketing communications (IMC) perspective, which calls for a "big picture" approach to planning marketing and promotion programs and coordinating the various communication functions. To understand the role of advertising and promotion in today's business world, one must recognize how a firm can use all the promotional tools to communicate with its customers.

To the Student: Preparing You for the New World of Advertising and Promotion

Some of you are taking this course to learn more about this fascinating field; many of you hope to work in advertising or some other promotional area. The changes in the industry have profound implications for the way today's student is trained and educated. You will not be working for the same kind of communication agencies that existed 5 or 10 years ago. If you work on the client side of the business, you will find that the way they approach advertising and promotion is changing dramatically.

Today's student is expected to understand all the major marketing communication functions: advertising, direct marketing, the Internet, interactive media, sales promotion, public relations, and personal selling. You will also be expected to know how to research and evaluate a company's marketing and promotional situation and how to use these various functions in developing effective communication strategies and programs. Marketers are also increasing their attention on the determination of return on investment (ROI) of various IMC tools as well as the problems companies face in attempting to make this evaluation. This book will help prepare you for these challenges.

As professors we were, of course, once students ourselves. In many ways we are perpetual students in that we are constantly striving to learn about and explain how advertising and promotion work. We share many of your interests and concerns and are often excited (and bored) by the same things. Having taught in the advertising and promotion area for a combined 50-plus years, we have developed an understanding of what makes a book in this field interesting to students. In writing this book, we have tried to remember how we felt about the various texts we used throughout the years and to incorporate the good things and minimize those we felt were of little use. We have tried not to overburden you with definitions, although we do call out those that are especially important to your understanding of the material.

We also remember that as students we were not really excited about theory. But to fully understand how integrated marketing communications works, it is necessary to establish some theoretical basis. The more you understand about how things are supposed to work, the easier it will be for you to understand why they do or do not turn out as planned.

Perhaps the question students ask most often is, How do I use this in the real world? In response, we provide numerous examples of how the various theories and concepts in the text can be used in practice. A particular strength of this text is the integration of theory with practical application. Nearly every day an example of advertising and promotion in practice is reported in the media. We have used many sources, such as *Advertising Age, Adweek, Brandweek, The Wall Street Journal, BusinessWeek, Fortune, Forbes, Sales & Marketing Management, Business 2.0, Promo,* and numerous online sites such as eMarketer, AdAge.com, MediaPost.com, and ClickZ News to find practical examples that are discussed throughout the text. We have spoken with hundreds of people about the strategies and rationale behind the ads and other types of promotions we use as examples. Each chapter begins with a vignette that presents an example of an advertising or promotional campaign or other interesting insights. Every chapter also contains several **IMC Perspectives** that present in-depth discussions of particular issues related to the chapter material and show how companies are using integrated marketing communications. **Global Perspectives** are presented throughout the text in recognition of the increasing importance of international marketing and the challenges of advertising and promotion and the role they play in the marketing programs of multinational marketers. **Ethical Perspectives** focus attention on important social issues and show how advertisers must take ethical considerations into account when planning and implementing advertising and promotional programs. **Diversity Perspectives** discuss the opportunities, as well as the challenges, associated with marketers' efforts to reach culturally and ethnically diverse target markets. There are also a number of **Career Profiles,** which highlight successful individuals working in various areas of the field of advertising and promotion.

Each chapter features beautiful four-color illustrations showing examples from many of the most current and best-integrated marketing communication campaigns being used around the world. We have included more than 350 advertisements and examples of numerous other types of promotion, all of which were carefully chosen to illustrate a particular idea, theory, or practical application. Please take time to read the opening vignettes to each chapter, the IMC, Global, Ethical, and Diversity Perspectives, and the Career Profiles and study the diverse ads and illustrations. We think they will stimulate your interest and relate to your daily life as a consumer and a target of advertising and promotion.

To the Instructor: A Text That Reflects the Changes in the World of Advertising and Promotion

Our major goal in writing the seventh edition of *Advertising and Promotion* was to continue to provide you with the most comprehensive and current text on the market for teaching advertising and promotion from an IMC perspective. This seventh edition focuses on the many changes that are occurring in areas of marketing communications and how they influence advertising and promotional strategies and tactics. We have done this by continuing with the *integrated marketing communications perspective* we introduced in the second edition. More and more companies are approaching advertising and promotion from an IMC perspective, coordinating the various promotional mix elements with other marketing activities that communicate with a firm's customers. Many advertising agencies are also developing expertise in direct marketing, sales promotion, event sponsorship, the Internet, and other areas so that they can meet all their clients' integrated marketing communication needs—and, of course, survive.

The text is built around an integrated marketing communications planning model and recognizes the importance of coordinating all of the promotional mix elements to develop an effective communications program. Although media advertising is often the most visible part of a firm's promotional program, attention must also be given to direct marketing, sales promotion, public relations, interactive media, and personal selling.

This text integrates theory with planning, management, and strategy. To effectively plan, implement, and evaluate IMC programs, one must understand the overall marketing process, consumer behavior, and communications theory. We draw from the extensive research in advertising, consumer behavior, communications, marketing, sales promotion, and other fields to give students a basis for understanding the marketing communications process, how it influences consumer decision making, and how to develop promotional strategies.

While this is an introductory text, we do treat each topic in some depth. We believe the marketing and advertising student of today needs a text that provides more than just an introduction to terms and topics. The book is positioned primarily for the introductory advertising, marketing communications, or promotions course as taught in the business/marketing curriculum. It can also be used in journalism/communications courses that take an integrated marketing communications perspective. Many schools also use the text at the graduate level. In addition to its thorough coverage of advertising, this text has chapters on sales promotion, direct marketing and marketing on the Internet, personal selling, and publicity/public relations. These chapters stress the integration of advertising with other promotional mix elements and the need to understand their role in the overall marketing program.

Organization of This Text

This book is divided into seven major parts. In Part One we examine the role of advertising and promotion in marketing and introduce the concept of integrated marketing communications. Chapter 1 provides an overview of advertising and promotion and its role in modern marketing. The concept of IMC and the factors that have led to its growth are discussed. Each of the promotional mix elements is defined, and an IMC planning model shows the various steps in the promotional planning process. This model provides a framework for developing the integrated marketing communications program and is followed throughout the text. Chapter 2 examines the role of advertising and promotion in the overall marketing program, with attention to the various elements of the marketing mix and how they interact with advertising and promotional strategy. We have also included coverage of market segmentation and positioning in this chapter so that students can understand how these concepts fit into the overall marketing programs as well as their role in the development of an advertising and promotional program.

In Part Two we cover the promotional program situation analysis. Chapter 3 describes how firms organize for advertising and promotion and examines the role of ad agencies and other firms that provide marketing and promotional services. We discuss how ad agencies are selected, evaluated, and compensated as well as the changes occurring in the agency business. Attention is also given to other types of marketing communication organizations such as direct marketing, sales promotion, and interactive agencies as well as public relations firms. We also consider whether responsibility for integrating the various communication functions lies with the client or the agency. Chapter 4 covers the stages of the consumer decision-making process and both the internal psychological factors and the external factors that influence consumer behavior. The focus of this chapter is on how advertisers can use an understanding of buyer behavior to develop effective advertising and other forms of promotion.

Part Three analyzes the communications process. Chapter 5 examines various communication theories and models of how consumers respond to advertising messages and other forms of marketing communications. Chapter 6 provides a detailed discussion of source, message, and channel factors.

In Part Four we consider how firms develop goals and objectives for their integrated marketing communications programs and determine how much money to spend trying to achieve them. Chapter 7 stresses the importance of knowing what to expect from advertising and promotion, the differences between advertising and communication objectives, characteristics of good objectives, and problems in setting objectives. We have also integrated the discussion of various methods for determining and allocating the promotional budget into this chapter. These first four sections of the text provide students with a solid background in the areas of marketing, consumer behavior, communications, planning, objective setting, and budgeting. This background lays the foundation for the next section, where we discuss the development of the integrated marketing communications program.

Part Five examines the various promotional mix elements that form the basis of the integrated marketing communications program. Chapter 8 discusses the planning and development of the creative strategy and advertising campaign and examines the creative process. In Chapter 9 we turn our attention to ways to execute the creative strategy and some criteria for evaluating creative work. Chapters 10 through 13 cover media strategy and planning and the various advertising media. Chapter 10 introduces the key principles of media planning and strategy and examines how a media plan is developed. Chapter 11 discusses the advantages and disadvantages of the broadcast media (TV and radio) as well as issues regarding the purchase of radio and TV time and audience measurement. Chapter 12 considers the same issues for the print media (magazines and newspapers). Chapter 13 examines the role of traditional support media such as outdoor and transit advertising, the yellow pages, and promotional products as well as the tremendous increase in the use of nontraditional branded entertainment strategies such as product placements and product integration.

In Chapters 14 through 17 we continue the IMC emphasis by examining other promotional tools that are used in the integrated marketing communications process. Chapter 14 looks at direct marketing. This chapter examines database marketing and the way by which companies communicate directly with target customers through various media including direct mail, infomercials, and direct-response TV commercials. Chapter 15 provides a detailed discussion of marketers' increasing use of interactive media, including the Internet and wireless technologies to market their products and services. We examine the increasing use of blogs, RSS, paid search, and other digital media strategies. We also give attention to how the Internet is used to implement various IMC activities including advertising, sales promotion, and even the selling of products and services. Chapter 16 examines the area of sales promotion including both consumer-oriented promotions and programs targeted to the trade (retailers, wholesalers, and other middlemen). Chapter 17 covers the role of publicity and public relations in IMC as well as corporate advertising. Basic issues regarding personal selling and its role in promotional strategy are presented in Chapter 18.

Part Six of the text consists of Chapter 19, where we discuss ways to measure the effectiveness of various elements of the integrated marketing communications program, including methods for pretesting and posttesting advertising messages and campaigns. In Part Seven we turn our attention to special markets, topics, and perspectives that are becoming increasingly important in contemporary marketing. In Chapter 20 we examine the global marketplace and the role of advertising and other promotional mix variables such as sales promotion, public relations, and the Internet in international marketing.

The text concludes with a discussion of the regulatory, social, and economic environments in which advertising and promotion operate. Chapter 21 examines industry self-regulation and regulation of advertising by governmental agencies such as the Federal Trade Commission, as well as rules and regulations governing sales promotion, direct marketing, and marketing on the Internet. Because advertising's role in society is constantly changing, our discussion would not be complete without a look at the criticisms frequently levied, so in Chapter 22 we consider the social, ethical, and economic aspects of advertising and promotion.

Chapter Features

The following features in each chapter enhance students' understanding of the material as well as their reading enjoyment.

Chapter Objectives

Objectives are provided at the beginning of each chapter to identify the major areas and points covered in the chapter and guide the learning effort.

Chapter Opening Vignettes

Each chapter begins with a vignette that shows the effective use of integrated marketing communications by a company or ad agency or discusses an interesting issue that is relevant to the chapter. These opening vignettes are designed to draw the students into the chapter by presenting an interesting example, development, or issue that relates to the material covered in the chapter. Companies, brands, and campaigns profiled in the opening vignettes include the Las Vegas Convention and Visitors Authority, Major League Baseball, the Apple iPod, the Crispin Porter & Bogusky advertising agency, Go Daddy.com, Nike, and Dove's Campaign for Real Beauty. Some of the chapter openers discuss current topics and issues such as the use of neuroscience to study the processing of advertising messages, measuring return-on-investment (ROI) for advertising and promotion, the growing popularity of celebrity magazines, and the controversy surrounding the growth in direct-to-consumer advertising of prescription drugs.

IMC Perspectives

These boxed items feature in-depth discussions of interesting issues related to the chapter material and the practical application of integrated marketing communications. Each chapter contains several of these insights into the world of integrated marketing communications. Some of the companies/brands whose IMC programs are discussed in these perspectives include AFLAC, LG Electronics, the U.S. Army, General Motors, AXE deodorant, Miller Lite beer, and ESPN. Issues such as the use of music to enhance the effectiveness of commercials, the repositioning of companies and brands, the fragmentation of media markets, the new age of micromarketing, and problems that companies have encountered when using contests and sweepstakes are also discussed in the IMC Perspectives.

Global Perspectives

These boxed sidebars provide information similar to that in the IMC Perspectives, with a focus on international aspects of advertising and promotion. Some of the companies/brands whose international advertising programs are covered in the Global Perspectives include MTV India, McDonald's, and Coca-Cola. Global Perspectives also discuss topics such as the Cannes International Advertising Awards, celebrities who appear in commercials in Japan while protecting their image in the United States, communication problems in international advertising, and the developing IMC programs to reach consumers in Third World countries.

Ethical Perspectives

These boxed items discuss the moral and/or ethical issues regarding practices engaged in by marketers and are also tied to the material presented in the particular chapter. Issues covered in the Ethical Perspectives include subliminal advertising, the battle between television networks and advertisers over tasteful advertising, and controversies arising from the increase in advertising of hard liquor on television and the use of video news releases as promotional tools.

Diversity Perspectives

These boxed items discuss topics related to the opportunities and challenges facing companies as they develop integrated marketing communications programs for markets that are becoming more ethnically diverse. The Diversity Perspectives include the rapid growth of the Hispanic market, issues involved in communicating with this important segment, and the emergence of Spanish-language television stations in the United States.

Career Profiles

Also included are Career Profiles of successful individuals working in the communications industry. The individuals featured in the Career Profiles include creative directors for R&R Partners as well as Deutsch LA, an account executive for the Margeotes Fertitta Powell advertising agency, the vice president of the Adcentive Group, the marketing manager for the San Diego Padres baseball team, the vice president of communications for the California Milk Advisory Board, the advertising manager for IBM Global Services, an assistant media buyer for the PHD advertising agency, the director of Internet marketing for KFMB television, and the senior marketing manager for the Dove Masterbrand.

Key Terms

Important terms are highlighted in boldface throughout the text and listed at the end of each chapter with a page reference. These terms help call students' attention to important ideas, concepts, and definitions and help them review their learning progress.

Chapter Summaries

These synopses serve as a quick review of important topics covered and a very helpful study guide.

Discussion Questions

Questions at the end of each chapter give students an opportunity to test their understanding of the material and to apply it. These questions can also serve as a basis for class discussion or assignments.

Four-Color Visuals

Print ads, photoboards, and other examples appear throughout the book. More than 400 ads, charts, graphs, and other types of illustrations are included in the text.

Changes in the Seventh Edition

We have made a number of changes in the seventh edition to make it as relevant and current as possible, as well as more interesting to students:

- **Updated Coverage of the Emerging Field of Integrated Marketing Communications** The seventh edition continues to place a strong emphasis on studying advertising and promotion from an integrated marketing communications perspective. We examine contemporary perspectives of integrated marketing communications that have been developed by those doing research and theory development in the area. We also consider developments that are impacting the way marketers communicate with consumers, such as the integration of brands and messages into television programs and other forms of entertainment and increased reliance on buzz marketing and other viral techniques. New technologies such as digital video recorders and the convergence of television, computers, and the Internet are changing the way companies are using advertising along with other marketing tools to communicate with their customers. In this new edition we examine how these cutting-edge developments are impacting the IMC program of marketers.
- **Updated Chapter on Support Media and Entertainment Marketing** The seventh edition continues to cover traditional support media including outdoor advertising, promotional products (advertising specialties), and the Yellow Pages. However, a restructuring of the presentation of these support media facilitates their understanding. New to this edition is the expansion of the discussion of branded entertainment. While branded entertainment techniques have been used by marketers in the past, the increase in both dollar expenditures and the various forms used has grown significantly over the past several years. The use of product placements has skyrocketed. TV shows such as *The Apprentice* have introduced a new form of product integration. Advertising in videogames and sponsored video-on-demand have also become more popular. In this new edition, we provide a state-of-the-art perspective on the use of entertainment marketing.
- **Updated Chapter on the Internet and Interactive Media** The seventh edition includes up-to-date information on the Internet and other forms of interactive media and how they are being used by marketers. We discuss a number of new Internet-based tools and strategies being used by marketers, including paid search, behavioral targeting, RSS, and others. We also discuss developments such as wireless communications as well as regulations affecting the use of the Internet and important issues such as privacy. This chapter discusses the latest developments in areas such as audience measurement and methods for determining the effectiveness of Internet advertising. Discussion of the emerging role of the Internet as an important integrated marketing communications tool and of the ways it is being used by marketers is integrated throughout the seventh edition.
- **New Diversity Perspectives** In the sixth edition we introduced a feature called Diversity Perspectives. These boxed items are designed to focus attention on the increase in the diversity of the consumer market in the United States. The 2000 census showed that the Hispanic market grew by 58 percent over the past decade, and another 35 percent increase is forecast over the next 10 years. Marketers are recognizing the importance of being able to communicate with a diverse market that includes Hispanics, African-Americans, Asian-Americans, and other ethnic groups. This feature focuses on the opportunities and challenges facing companies as they develop integrated marketing communications programs for markets that are becoming more ethnically diverse.
- **New Online Cases** A number of new short cases have been written for the seventh edition. The cases are available online and can be downloaded for classroom use and assignments. These cases are designed to build upon the material presented in the text and provide students with the opportunity to apply various IMC tools and concepts. The cases include companies and brands such as IBM, SoBe energy drinks, XM Satellite Radio, the Apple iPod, and the California Milk Advisory Board (the "Happy Cows" campaign). Cases from the previous edition have been updated and are also available online. These cases examine companies such as Gateway, Mazda, Chicken of the Sea International, Benetton, and the Partnership for a Drug Free America and the U.S. Office of National Drug Control Policy's War on Drugs.
- **New Chapter Opening Vignettes** *All* of the chapter opening vignettes in the seventh edition are new and were chosen for their currency and relevance to students. They demonstrate how various companies and advertising agencies use advertising and other IMC tools. They also provide interesting insights into some of the current trends and developments that are taking place in the advertising world.
- **New and Updated IMC Perspectives** All of the boxed items focusing on specific examples of how companies and their communications agencies are using integrated marketing communications are new or updated, and they provide insight into many of the most current and popular advertising and promotional campaigns being used by marketers. The IMC

Perspectives also address interesting issues related to advertising, sales promotion, direct marketing, marketing on the Internet, and personal selling.

- **New and Updated Global and Ethical Perspectives** Nearly all of the boxed items focusing on global and ethical issues of advertising and promotion are new; those retained from the sixth edition have been updated. The Global Perspectives examine the role of advertising and other promotional areas in international markets. The Ethical Perspectives discuss specific issues, developments, and problems that call into question the ethics of marketers and their decisions as they develop and implement their advertising and promotional programs.
- **New Career Profiles** The seventh edition has all new Career Profiles that discuss the career path of successful individuals working in various areas of advertising and promotion, including clients, advertising agencies, and the media. These profiles provide students with insight into various types of careers that are available in the area of advertising and promotion on the client and agency side as well as in media. They discuss the educational backgrounds of the individuals profiled, some of the responsibilities and requirements of their positions, and their career paths. This feature has been very popular among students, and in this edition we provide 10 new profiles. These profiles have been written by the individuals themselves and provide students with insight into the educational background of the persons profiled, how they got started in the field of advertising and promotion, their current responsibilities, and interesting aspects of their jobs as well as experiences.
- **Contemporary Examples** The field of advertising and promotion changes very rapidly, and we continue to keep pace with it. Wherever possible we updated the statistical information presented in tables, charts, and figures throughout the text. We reviewed the most current academic and trade literature to ensure that this text reflects the most current perspectives and theories on advertising, promotion, and the rapidly evolving area of integrated marketing communications. We also updated most of the examples and ads throughout the book. *Advertising and Promotion* continues to be the most contemporary text on the market, offering students as timely a perspective as possible.

Support Material

A high-quality package of instructional supplements supports the seventh edition. Nearly all of the supplements have been developed by the authors to ensure their coordination with the text. We offer instructors a support package that facilitates the use of our text and enhances the learning experience of the student.

Instructor's Manual

The instructor's manual is a valuable teaching resource that includes learning objectives, chapter and lecture outlines, answers to all end-of-chapter discussion questions, transparency masters, and further insights and teaching suggestions. Additional discussion questions are also presented for each chapter. These questions can be used for class discussion or as short-answer essay questions for exams.

Manual of Tests

A test bank of more than 1,500 multiple-choice questions has been developed to accompany the text. The questions provide thorough coverage of the chapter material, including opening vignettes and IMC, Global, Diversity, and Ethical Perspectives.

Computerized Test Bank

A computerized version of the test bank is available to adopters of the text.

Instructor CD-ROM

This exciting presentation CD-ROM allows the professor to customize a multimedia lecture with original material from the supplements package. It includes video clips, commercials, ads and art from the text, electronic slides and acetates, the computerized test bank, and the print supplements.

Electronic Slides

A disk containing nearly 300 PowerPoint slides is available to adopters of the seventh edition for electronic presentations. These slides contain lecture notes, charts, graphs, and other instructional materials.

Home Page

A home page on the Internet can be found at

www.mhhe.com/belch7e

It contains Web Exploration Links (hot links to other websites) as well as various other items of interest. For instructors, the home page will offer updates of examples, chapter opener vignettes and IMC, Global, and Ethical Perspectives; additional sources of advertising and promotion information; and downloads of key supplements. Adopters will be able to communicate directly with the authors through the site (contact your McGraw-Hill/ Irwin representative for your password).

Four-Color Transparencies

Each adopter may request a set of more than 100 four-color acetate transparencies that present print ads, photoboards, sales promotion offers, and other materials that do not appear in the text. (The same materials are available on the Instructor CD-ROM.) A number of important models or charts appearing in the text are also provided as color transparencies. Slip sheets are included with each transparency to give the instructor useful background information about the illustration and how it can be integrated into the lecture.

Video Supplements

A video supplement package has been developed specifically for classroom use with this text. The first set of videos contains more than 300 television and radio commercials that are examples of creative advertising. It can be used to help the instructor explain a particular concept or principle or give more insight into how a company executes its advertising strategy. Most of the commercials are tied to the chapter openings, IMC and Global Perspectives, or specific examples cited in the text. Insights and/or background information about each commercial are provided in the instructor's manual written specifically for the videos. The second set of videos contains longer segments on the advertising and promotional strategies of various companies and industries. We have produced three new video cases for the seventh edition. The companies or campaigns featured in the new video include the "What happens here, stays here . . ." campaign developed by R&R Partners for the Las Vegas Convention and Visitors Authority; the "Happy Cows" campaign developed by Deutsch LA for the California Milk Advisory Boards; and the integrated marketing campaign used by the San Diego Padres Major League Baseball team. We include three video cases from the sixth edition which examine the IMC campaigns developed for the U.S. Army, Skyy Spirits, and Chicken of the Sea International. Also included on the second set of video are segments featuring campaigns chosen as Ogilvy Award Winners by the Advertising Research Foundation and Reggie Award Winners by the Promotional Marketing Association. Short segments examining the use of celebrities in advertising and outdoor advertising in America are also included.

Acknowledgments

While this seventh edition represents a tremendous amount of work on our part, it would not have become a reality without the assistance and support of many other people. Authors tend to think they have the best ideas, approach, examples, and organization for writing a great book. But we quickly learned that there is always room for our ideas to be improved on by others. A number of colleagues provided detailed, thoughtful reviews that were immensely helpful in making this a better book. We are very grateful to the following individuals who worked with us on earlier editions. They include

David Allan, *St. Joseph's University*
Craig Andrews, *Marquette University*
Subir Bandyopadhyay, *University of Ottawa*
Michael Barone, *Iowa State University*
Jerri Beggs, *Illinois State University*
John Bennett, *University of Missouri*
Elizabeth Blair, *Ohio University*
Janice Blankenburg, *University of Wisconsin–Milwaukee*
Kathy Boyle, *University of Maryland*
Terry Bristol, *Oklahoma State University*
Beverly Brockman, *University of Alabama*
Lauranne Buchanan, *University of Illinois*
Jeffrey Buchman, *Fashion Institute*
Roy Busby, *University of North Texas*
Lindell Chew, *University of Missouri–St. Louis*
Catherine Cole, *University of Iowa*
Robert H. Ducoffe, *Baruch College*
Roberta Elins, *Fashion Institute of Technology*
Nancy Ellis, *Suffolk Community College*
Robert Erffmeyer, *University of Wisconsin–Eau Claire*
John Faier, *Miami University*
Raymond Fisk, *Oklahoma State University*
Alan Fletcher, *Louisiana State University*
Marty Flynn, *Suffolk Community College*
Judy Foxman, *Southern Methodist University*
Amy Frank, *Wingate University*
Jon B. Freiden, *Florida State University*
Stefanie Garcia, *University of Central Florida*
Geoff Gordon, *University of Kentucky*
Norman Govoni, *Babson College*
Donald Grambois, *Indiana University*
Stephen Grove, *Clemson University*
Robert Gulonsen, *Washington University*
Bill Hauser, *University of Akron*
Ron Hill, *University of Portland*
JoAnn Hopper, *Western Carolina University*
Paul Jackson, *Ferris State College*
Patricia Kennedy, *University of Nebraska*
Don Kirchner, *California State University–Northridge*
Paul Klein, *St. Thomas University*
Susan Kleine, *Arizona State University*
Patricia Knowles, *Clemson University*
Clark Leavitt, *Ohio State University*
Aron Levin, *Northern Kentucky University*
Lauren Lev, *Fashion Institute*
Tina Lowry, *Rider University*
Scott Mackenzie, *Indiana University*
Karen Machleit, *University of Cincinnati*
Elizabeth Moore-Shay, *University of Illinois*

Joe Msylivec, *Central Michigan University*
Darrel Muehling, *Washington State University*
John H. Murphy II, *University of Texas–Austin*
Carol Osborne, *USF Tampa*
Charles Overstreet, *Oklahoma State University*
Notis Pagiavlas, *University of Texas–Arlington*
Paul Prabhaker, *Depaul University, Chicago*
William Pride, *Texas A&M University*
Sanjay Putrevu, *Bryant University*
Joel Reedy, *University of South Florida*
Glen Reicken, *East Tennessee State University*
Scott Roberts, *Old Dominion University*
Michelle Rodriquez, *University of Central Florida*
Judith Sayre, *University of North Florida*
Andrea Scott, *Pepperdine University*
Elaine Scott, *Bluefield State College*
Carol Schibi, *State Fair Community College*
Denise D. Schoenbachler, *Northern Illinois University*
Eugene Secunda, *New York University*
Tanuja Singh, *Northern Illinois University*
Lois Smith, *University of Wisconsin*
Harlan Spotts, *Northeastern University*
Mary Ann Stutts, *Southwest Texas State University*
James Swartz, *California State University–Pomona*
Robert Taylor, *Radford University*
Brian Tietje, *Cal State Polytechnic*
Frank Tobolski, *DePaul University*
John Weitzel, *Western Michigan University*
Mike Weigold, *University of Florida–Gainesville*
Roy Winegar, *Grand Valley State University*
Terrence Witkowski, *California State University–Long Beach*
Elaine Young, *Champlain College*
Robert Young, *Northeastern University*

We are particularly grateful to the individuals who provided constructive comments on how to make this edition better: Craig Andrews, *Marquette University;* Christopher Cakebread, *Boston University;* Robert Cutter, *Cleveland State University;* Don Dickinson, *Portland State University;* Karen James, *Louisiana State University–Shreveport;* Robert Kent, *University of Delaware;* Herbert Jack Rotfield, *Auburn University;* Lisa Sciulli, *Indiana University of Pennsylvania;* Janice Taylor, *Miami University,* and Richard Wingerson, *Florida Atlantic University.* A very special thank-you goes to Roberta Elins and the faculty at the Fashion Institute of Technology, who provided many useful insights and interesting examples.

We would also like to acknowledge the cooperation we received from many people in the business, advertising, and media communities. This book contains several hundred ads, illustrations, charts, and tables that have been provided by advertisers and/or their agencies, various publications, and other advertising and industry organizations. Many individuals took time from their busy schedules to provide us with requested materials and gave us permission to use them. A special thanks to all of you.

A manuscript does not become a book without a great deal of work on the part of a publisher. Various individuals at Irwin/McGraw-Hill have been involved with this project over the past several years. Our sponsoring editor on the seventh edition, Barrett Koger, provided valuable guidance and was instrumental in making sure this was much more than just a token revision. A special thanks goes to Sarah Crago, our developmental editor, for all of her efforts and for being so great to work with. Thanks also to Christine Vaughan for doing a superb job of managing the production process. We also want to acknowledge the outstanding work of Charlotte Goldman for her help in obtaining permissions for most of the ads that appear throughout the book. Thanks to the other members of the product team, Adam Rooke, Jeremy Cheshareck, Joyce Chappetto, Debra Sylvester, and Damian Moshak, for all their hard work on this edition.

We would like to acknowledge the support we have received from the College of Business at San Diego State University. As always, a great deal of thanks goes to our families for putting up with us while we were revising this book. Once again we look forward to returning to normal. Finally, we would like to acknowledge each other for making it through this ordeal for the seventh time! Our mother to whom we dedicate this edition, will be happy to know that we still get along after all this—though it is definitely getting tougher and tougher.

George E. Belch
Michael A. Belch

Your guide through the exciting

Why It's a Powerful Learning Tool

The seventh edition continues to provide you with the most comprehensive and current text on the market in the area of advertising and promotion from an integrated marketing communications perspective. The following features in each chapter enhance students' understanding of the material as well as their reading enjoyment.

Chapter Openers

Chapter Objectives are provided at the beginning of each chapter to identify the major areas and points covered in the chapter and guide the learning effort. Each chapter also begins with a **Chapter Opening Vignette** that shows the effective use of integrated marketing communications by a company or ad agency or discusses an interesting issue that is relevant to the chapter. Some of the companies profiled in the opening vignettes include the Las Vegas Convention and Visitors Authority (LVCVA), the San Diego Padres, Apple, iPod, Dove, and Nike.

An Introduction to Integrated Marketing Communications

1

Chapter Objectives

1. To examine the marketing communication function and the growing importance of advertising and other promotional elements in the marketing programs of domestic and foreign companies.
2. To introduce the concept of integrated marketing communications (IMC) and consider how it has evolved.
3. To examine reasons for the increasing importance of the IMC perspective in planning and executing advertising and promotional programs.
4. To introduce the various elements of the promotional mix and consider their roles in an IMC program.
5. To examine how various marketing and promotional elements must be coordinated to communicate effectively.
6. To introduce a model of the IMC planning process and examine the steps in developing a marketing communications program.

What Happens in Las Vegas, Stays in Las Vegas

Las Vegas is one of the most popular destinations in the world. More than 37 million people visit the entertainment and gambling mecca each year including tourists from around the globe, businesspeople attending trade shows and conventions, and weekend visitors who come for three days of

partying. The daunting task of filling the city's nearly 130,000 hotel rooms each night and attracting new, as well as repeat, visitors to the city lies primarily with the Las Vegas Convention and Visitors Authority (LVCVA), which represents hotels, county, municipal, and private business association interests in the area. And for the past 25 years the LVCVA has worked closely with the advertising agency R & R Partners to help in the marketing of the city and to guide the branding of Las Vegas through its many incarnations.

While most people are aware of Las Vegas and its gaming heritage, the LVCVA and R & R Partners have been constantly challenged to position the city as a vibrant and contemporary player in the resort industry. Once known mainly for 24-hour gambling, all-you-can-eat buffets, and lounge shows, the new Las Vegas has evolved into a world-class shopping, dining, and entertainment destination. However, the city has also been facing greater competition as gambling and shows are now readily available in Atlantic City as well as in a myriad of riverboat and Native American gaming casinos that are only a few hours' drive or less from hundreds of cities across the country. Travelers and conventioneers interested in great dining and shopping could find these attractions in a variety of cities such as San Francisco, New Orleans, or New York.

In early 2000, Billy Vassiliadias, the CEO of R & R Partners, and Rossi Ralenkotter, the LVCVA president and CEO, reviewed agency research studies and came to the same conclusion. Las Vegas was losing its exclusivity, and the branding campaign for the city lacked a unifying idea that could break through all the clutter. They felt that they had done a good job of educating consumers about the new megaresorts and other attractions that had been built and helped transform Vegas from a gaming destination to an international gateway. However, the challenge was to find a unified way of marketing the city that would create a unique brand identity for Vegas that would resonate with and motivate a wide range of people.

R & R Partners approached the challenge by going back to basics and talking to consumers. The agency conducted qualitative account planning expeditions to Los Angeles, Las Vegas's primary feeder market, as well as major cities such as

world of advertising and promotion.

Chapter Pedagogy

Four-Color Visuals throughout the book consist of photoboards, commercial shots, charts, graphs, and over 400 print ads. **Key Terms** are highlighted in boldface throughout the text and listed at the end of each chapter with a page reference. **Chapter Summaries** serve as a quick review of important topics covered and as a study guide. **Discussion Questions** at the end of each chapter give students an opportunity to test their understanding of the material and to apply it. These questions can also serve as a basis for class discussion or assignments.

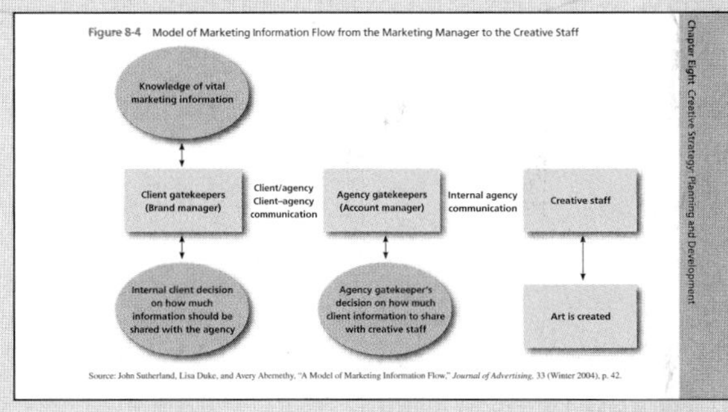
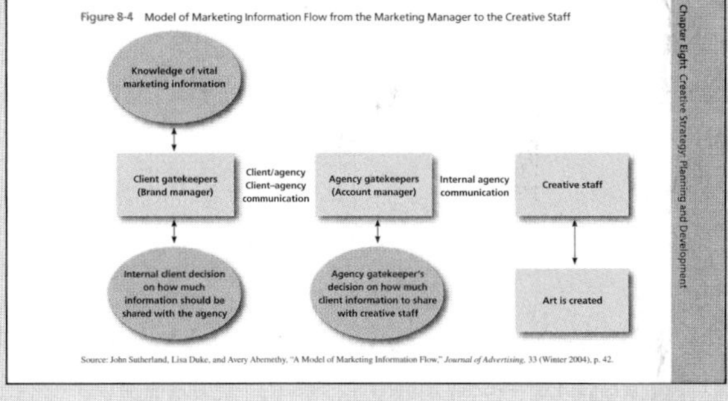
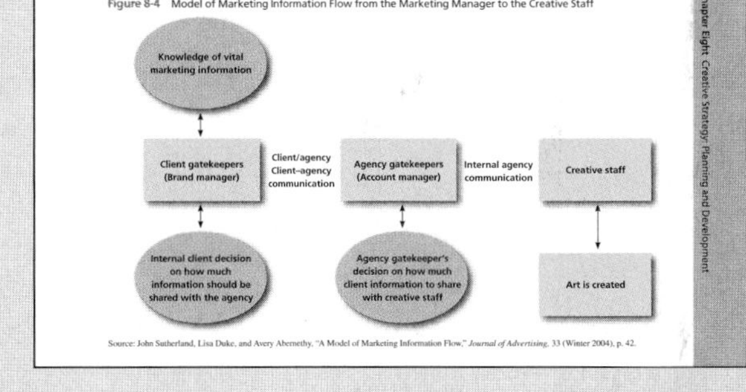

Summary

Promotion plays an important role in an organization's efforts to market its product, service, or ideas to its customers. Figure 2-1 shows a model for analyzing how promotions fit into a company's marketing program. The model includes a marketing strategy and analysis, target marketing, program development, and the target market. The marketing process begins with a marketing strategy that is based on a detailed situation analysis and guides for target market selection and development of the firm's marketing program.

In the planning process, the situation analysis requires that the marketing strategy be assumed. The promotional program is developed with this strategy as a guide. One of the key decisions to be made pertains to the target marketing process, which includes identifying, segmenting, targeting, and positioning to target markets. There are several bases for segmenting the market and various ways to position a product.

Once the target marketing process has been completed, marketing program decisions regarding product, price, distribution, and promotions must be made. All of these must be coordinated to provide an integrated marketing communications perspective, in which the positioning strategy is supported by one voice. Thus all product strategies, pricing strategies, and distribution choices must be made with the objective of contributing to the overall image of the product or brand. Advertising and promotion decisions, in turn, must be integrated with the other marketing-mix decisions to accomplish this goal.

Key Terms

strategic marketing plan, 41
market segments, 41
market opportunities, 41
competitive advantage, 43
target marketing, 44
market segmentation, 45
geographic segmentation, 47
demographic segmentation, 47
psychographic segmentation, 49
behavioristic segmentation, 49
80-20 rule, 50
benefit segmentation, 50
undifferentiated marketing, 51
differentiated marketing, 51
concentrated marketing, 51
positioning, 52
salient attributes, 53
repositioning, 55
product symbolism, 59
brand equity, 60
marketing channels, 62
resellers, 62
direct channels, 62
indirect channels, 63
promotional push strategy, 63
trade advertising, 63
promotional pull strategy, 63

Discussion Questions

1. Discuss the difference between a push and a pull strategy. What kinds of firms would be more likely to employ each strategy? Give examples.

2. The text describes a number of different positioning strategies. Give examples of products and/or brands that utilize each of these different strategies.

3. It has been said that benefit segmentation should be the starting

4. A number of companies have tried to reposition themselves in the marketplace. Some have been successful; others have not. Cite examples of both. What are the factors that you think led to their success or failure?

5. Companies price their products at different levels. Some are positioned as "price" products while others take on a position of "luxury goods." Describe how the price positioning of a product or

6. Recently, some marketers have noted that it is easier to develop communications programs to Generation X members than Generation Y. Briefly describe the characteristics of Gen X and Gen Y, and whether or not you believe this to be true.

7. As companies increase their efforts to target the Hispanic segment, they are likely to encounter differences from other subcultural groups. Discuss some of the differ-

Real Life Examples

The authors have used many sources to find practical examples to use throughout the text. In addition to the integration of the strategy and rationale behind the ads and other types of promotion that are used for current examples of industry practice, there are special in-depth discussions highlighted in boxed sections. **IMC Perspectives** present in-depth discussion of particular issues related to the chapter material and show how companies are using integrated marketing communications. **Global Perspectives** are presented throughout the text in recognition of the increasing importance of international marketing and the challenges of advertising and promotion and the role they play in the marketing programs of multinational marketers. **Ethical Perspectives** focus attention on important social issues and show how advertisers must take ethical considerations into account when planning and implementing advertising and promotional programs. **Diversity Perspectives** discuss the opportunities, as well as the challenges, associated with marketers' efforts to reach culturally and ethnically diverse target markets. There are also a number of **Career Profiles** which highlight successful individuals working in various areas of the field of advertising and promotion.

IMC PERSPECTIVE 5-2

LG Plans on Connecting with U.S. Consumers

154

CAREER PROFILE

Jenifer Barsell

Director of Marketing for the San Diego Padres

DIVERSITY PERSPECTIVE 2-1

Targeting to Hispanics—A Not-so-Minor Segment

46

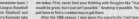

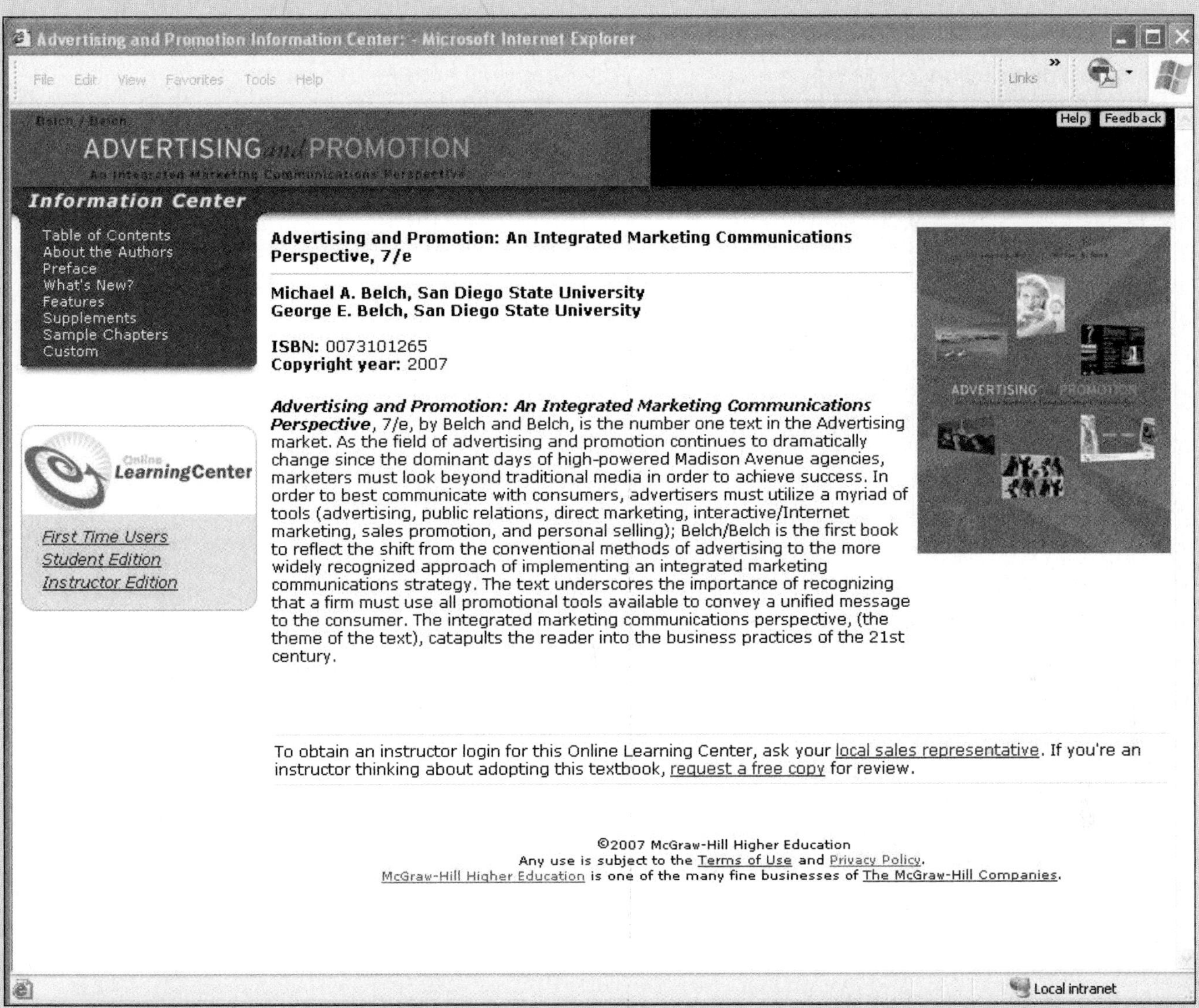

Online Learning Center

www.mhhe.com/belch07

For Instructors

The resources available online for instructors include downloadable versions of the Instructor's Manual, Video Instructor's Manual, Cases and case teaching notes, Video Clips, and notes for using the Campaign Planner.

For Students

A wealth of study tools is available for students at the site including self-assessing quizzes, an online Campaign Planner, key terms drills, and cases.

Contents in Brief

Contents

Part Four

Objectives and Budgeting for Integrated Marketing Communications Programs 190

Chapter Seven

Part Five

Developing the Integrated Marketing Communications Program 234

Chapter Eight

Chapter Nine

WEIDER
ALL NEW
PLATINUM
PROFESSIONAL
STRENGTH EQUIPMENT
AT HOME

ACTION SPORTS

Chapter Twenty-one

Chapter Twenty-two

Advertising and Promotion

AN INTEGRATED MARKETING COMMUNICATIONS PERSPECTIVE

An Introduction to Integrated Marketing Communications

1

Chapter Objectives

1. To examine the marketing communication function and the growing importance of advertising and other promotional elements in the marketing programs of domestic and foreign companies.
2. To introduce the concept of integrated marketing communications (IMC) and consider how it has evolved.
3. To examine reasons for the increasing importance of the IMC perspective in planning and executing advertising and promotional programs.
4. To introduce the various elements of the promotional mix and consider their roles in an IMC program.
5. To examine how various marketing and promotional elements must be coordinated to communicate effectively.
6. To introduce a model of the IMC planning process and examine the steps in developing a marketing communications program.

What Happens in Las Vegas, Stays in Las Vegas

Las Vegas is one of the most popular destinations in the world. More than 37 million people visit the entertainment and gambling mecca each year including tourists from around the globe, businesspeople attending trade shows and conventions, and weekend visitors who come for three days of partying. The daunting task of filling the city's nearly 130,000 hotel rooms each night and attracting new, as well as repeat, visitors to the city lies primarily with the Las Vegas Convention and Visitors Authority (LVCVA), which represents hotels, county, municipal, and private business association interests in the area. And for the past 25 years the LVCVA has worked closely with the advertising agency R & R Partners to help in the marketing of the city and to guide the branding of Las Vegas through its many incarnations.

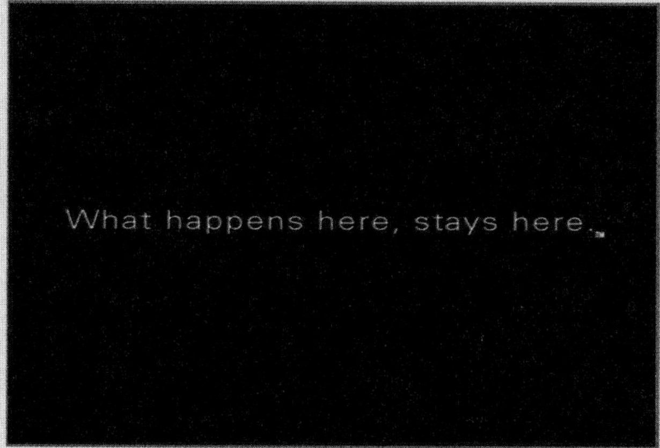
What happens here, stays here.

While most people are aware of Las Vegas and its gaming heritage, the LVCVA and R & R Partners have been constantly challenged to position the city as a vibrant and contemporary player in the resort industry. Once known mainly for 24-hour gambling, all-you-can-eat buffets, and lounge shows, the new Las Vegas has evolved into a world-class shopping, dining, and entertainment destination. However, the city has also been facing greater competition as gambling and shows are now readily available in Atlantic City as well as in a myriad of riverboat and Native American gaming casinos that are only a few hours' drive or less from hundreds of cities across the country. Travelers and conventioneers interested in great dining and shopping could find these attractions in a variety of cities such as San Francisco, New Orleans, or New York.

In early 2000, Billy Vassiliadias, the CEO of R & R Partners, and Rossi Ralenkotter, the LVCVA president and CEO, reviewed agency research studies and came to the same conclusion. Las Vegas was losing its exclusivity, and the branding campaign for the city lacked a unifying idea that could break through all the clutter. They felt that they had done a good job of educating consumers about the new megaresorts and other attractions that had been built and helped transform Vegas from a gaming destination to an international gateway. However, the challenge was to find a unified way of marketing the city that would create a unique brand identity for Vegas that would resonate with and motivate a wide range of people.

R & R Partners approached the challenge by going back to basics and talking to consumers. The agency conducted qualitative account planning expeditions to Los Angeles, Las Vegas's primary feeder market, as well as major cities such as

New York, Dallas, Miami, and Chicago. The research revealed that the biggest differentiator for Las Vegas was not the lavish hotels, casinos, restaurants, and night clubs. Vassiliadias noted that "the product, whether it was great dining or great properties, was this great canvas on which they paint their experience and that was truly the differentiator." From focus groups and other research, R & R learned that people love to come to Las Vegas to cut loose, have fun, and do things they wouldn't do back home—from overindulging in bars, restaurants, and casinos to staying out all night, everyone's expectations and experience is different.

The first campaign that R & R developed to appeal to these desires was called the Las Vegas Freedom party, which consisted of a series of spots encouraging people to escape the drudgery of everyday life and start their own party with a trip to Las Vegas. Several other campaign themes followed, including "What you want, when you want" and "Open 24 hours." While these campaigns circled and nibbled at the edges of the big idea, the real breakthrough came in 2003 when two of the agency's copywriters came up with the now famous tagline, "What happens here, stays here." This was a derivative of the traveling salesman's mantra, "What happens on the road, stays on the road." The next step was to decide how this slogan could be integrated with the "Only Vegas" umbrella theme that was being used to pitch convention and business travel.

R & R's creative department developed a series of commercials that used provocative "Only in Vegas" stories. The ads show situations that are unlikely to happen elsewhere and in ways that are open to several interpretations, from the mildly hedonistic to the downright sinful. Each commercial implies that something has happened to the character in Las Vegas that he or she may or may not want friends or family back home to know about. However, the commercials let the viewer project his or her own fantasy about Las Vegas and fill in the blanks. The story lines have included a nervous woman who blots out embarrassing portions of a postcard before mailing it; a newlywed who leaves her new husband in a wedding chapel to rush back to her convention; and a guy who requests a wake-up call to his cell phone because he doesn't know where he will be sleeping.

The first phase of the campaign began in January 2003 with a healthy dose of free publicity when the National Football League rejected the LVCVA's bid to buy a spot on the Super Bowl on the grounds that it did not want to be associated with gambling. From there, the edgy, sexy commercials took off and the campaign has become one of the most popular on television. *USA TODAY*'s consumer weekly Ad Track survey ranked the ads as the most effective campaign of the year in 2003. The campaign tagline, "What happens here, stays here," has achieved a pop culture status on par with Wendy's classic "Where's the beef?" and Budweiser's "Whassup?" The line has been used by Billy Crystal to close the Oscar's, in Jay Leno monologues, and was even used by First Lady Laura Bush as a retort to Leno's question about whether she saw the Chippendale dancers during a campaign visit to Vegas.

R & R Partners has leveraged the popular commercials into a fully integrated campaign that has included guerrilla marketing efforts around the Oscar and Grammy Awards, sponsorships, and public relations activities that have produced feature stories in a variety of popular media including CNN, National Public Radio, *USA TODAY,* the *New York Times,* and *Wall Street Journal* as well as a cover story in *Time* magazine. The campaign has also been recognized by the advertising and marketing industry as Billy Vassiliadias and Rossi Ralenkotter shared the 2004 Grand Marketer of the Year award, which is given by *Brandweek* magazine. However, most important to the LVCVA is the impact the campaign has had on the number of visitors to the city. In 2004, Las Vegas hosted a record-breaking 37.4 million visitors and the hotel occupancy rate averaged 89 percent. It appears that a lot is happening in Vegas, indeed.

Sources: Mike Beirne, "Playing for Keeps," *Brandweek,* October 11, 2004, pp. M6–11; Rich Thomaselli, "Las Vegas Ad Slogan Takes on Life of Its Own," *Advertising Age,* March 8, 2004, p. 6.

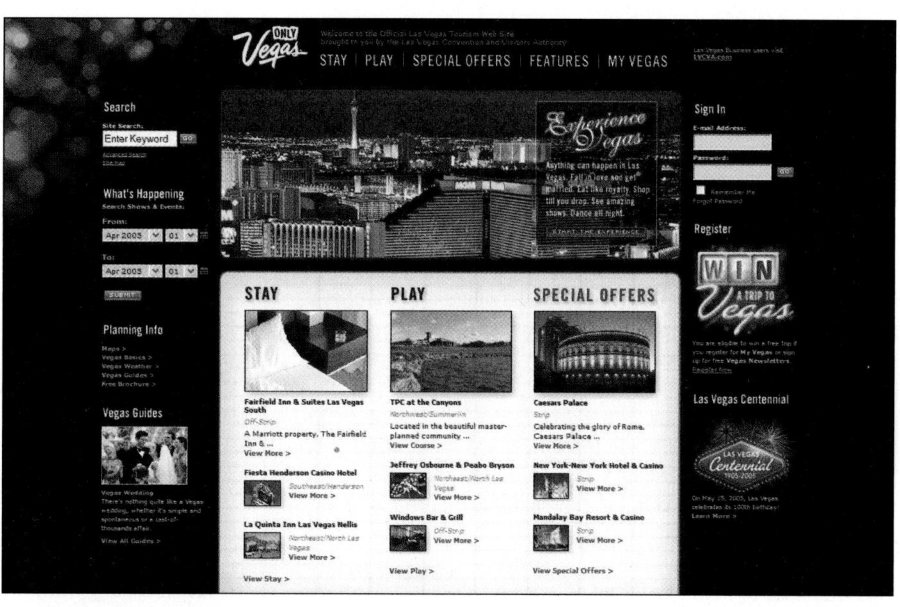

Exhibit 1-1 Consumers can get valuable information through the Las Vegas tourism website

The opening vignette illustrates how the roles of advertising and other forms of promotion are changing in the modern world of marketing. In the past, marketers such as the Las Vegas Convention and Visitors Authority (LVCVA) relied primarily on media advertising to tourists, travel agents, and convention planners to attract visitors to the city. However, today many companies are taking a different approach in developing their marketing communication programs. They integrate their advertising efforts with a variety of other communication tools such as websites on the Internet, direct marketing, sales promotion, publicity and public relations, entertainment marketing, and sponsorship of events. These companies recognize that there are many ways to reach their current and prospective customers and bring them into contact with their products and services. They also know that it is becoming increasingly difficult to reach their target audiences and communicate effectively with them. To deal with this challenge they are using a variety of communication tools and coordinating them to deliver a consistent message to their customers.

The various marketing communication tools developed by R & R Partners to promote Las Vegas exemplify how marketers are using an *integrated marketing communications* approach to reach their target audiences. The LVCVA runs ads in a variety of media including television, radio, magazines, newspapers, and billboards. Banner ads are run on various travel and entertainment-related websites on the Internet and linked to various search engines such as Google and Yahoo. The LVCVA has two distinct websites: one is designed to serve as a Vegas-branded consumer site that is experiential and entertaining while the other is more information-based and targets business audiences (Exhibit 1-1). Publicity is generated though press releases and public relations activities that have resulted in feature stories on Las Vegas in many magazines and television news and entertainment shows. The phrase "what happens here, stays here" has become part of popular culture and continually generates publicity for the city and reinforces the branding message. Using entertainment marketing is also a way the LVCVA promotes Las Vegas as various TV events have been broadcast from the city such as a live Fox TV New Year's Eve show and a Carson Daly MTV special. Direct marketing efforts are used to reach various audiences such as convention planners as well as several hundred thousand consumers in online and traditional databases. The LVCVA also maintains a staff of sales representatives who work to sell the city as a site for conventions, conferences, and other groups, as well as to travel agents.

Marketing communications is an integral part of the overall marketing program for most companies and organizations. However, these firms recognize that the way they must communicate with consumers and other relevant audiences to promote their products and services is changing rapidly. The fragmentation of mass markets, the rapid growth of the Internet and other new digital media, the emergence of global markets, economic uncertainties, and the changing lifestyles of consumers are all changing the way companies approach marketing as well as advertising and promotion. Developing marketing communication programs that are responsive to these changes is critical to the success of every company.

The Growth of Advertising and Promotion

Advertising and promotion are an integral part of our social and economic systems. In our complex society, advertising has evolved into a vital communications system for both consumers and businesses. The ability of advertising and other promotional methods to deliver carefully prepared

CAREER PROFILE

Randy Snow

Executive Vice President/Creative Director for R & R Partners

"Advertising? Why would you want to do that? How would you even get into it?" I used to hear that a lot. Growing up in the late 60s and early 70s in Reno, Nevada, I had a number of teachers and guidance counselors (not to mention two parents) react with puzzlement when I told them I thought advertising might be an interesting way to make a living. Mostly they smiled bemusedly and continued to steer me on a track to college and, they thought, to law school. After four years at the University of Nevada at Reno, I received a B.A. in journalism with a concentration in advertising and left dutifully the next fall for law school, where I lasted three days. Did I flunk out? No. You can't do that in three days. Even in law school. But it only took that long to figure out that, unless you are absolutely committed to earning the degree and becoming an attorney, you have no business being there. I had no business being there.

As suddenly as my law career died, my career in advertising began at the CBS affiliate in Reno where I joined the sales department . . . and failed miserably. However, while discovering that I would never make it as a media salesperson, I did find great enjoyment in writing and producing the ads I managed to sell. From there, my circuitous route to the present began. First, a position at a small, five-person agency in Reno where I did literally everything including servicing the clients, planning and buying media, writing and producing the ads, and even collecting the bills. I made almost no money, but the experience was invaluable. Having a working knowledge of every aspect of the advertising business has served me well ever since.

After that, it was on to the client side and a two-year stint in the advertising and public relations department of a major hotel-casino. I learned public relations, dealt with celebrities, worked with an agency, and spent a lot of nights, weekends, and holidays working in a business that never takes a day off. It was a great learning experience, but over time, the job evolved into something that had less and less to do with the side of the business I enjoyed. It was time to go and so I went back to the agency side, where I've been ever since. I returned to the agency side as somewhat of a hybrid account executive/copywriter. But it seemed inevitable that I would eventually tilt in the direction of my aptitude and merged exclusively onto the creative highway. Since then, it's been a slow, but steady, move up the creative ladder. It began with a job as creative director at a Reno-based firm called DRGM, followed by a move to Las Vegas in 1989 (still with DRGM), followed by a move to R & R Partners in 1993 and my first introduction to the Las Vegas Convention and Visitors Authority (LVCVA) account.

Since then, it's been almost 13 years of writing, producing, and nurturing along a lot of work for a wide variety of clients. Chief among them has been the LVCVA. Although I have had the opportunity to work with a variety of clients in a number of fields, there has never been a day when the LVCVA is far from my mind. They have been, and continue to be, our agency's biggest client, as well as our best client. There is an old saying that "every client gets the advertising they deserve." In the case of the LVCVA, that is absolutely true. They have pushed us to our greatest heights through a desire to break the mold and a willingness to trust the advertising we create for them.

For me, the culmination of that desire and trust came with the creation of our current television campaign for the brand featuring the tagline, "What happens here, stays here." Today, the campaign slogan has become part of popular culture and is quoted by celebrities, politicians, broadcasters, and ordinary people all over the world. It may seem as though it would have been an easy tagline to approve. However, at the time, no destination or travel client had done advertising so provocative and honest. Although I did not personally come up with the line, I will always be proud that I was the creative director who approved it, honed it, and helped shepherd it through the process of approval and execution.

I will always be proud that I was the creative director who approved it . . .

My only disappointment lies in the irony that the further I move up the ladder in the agency's creative hierarchy, the less creative work I actually do. Today, I spend almost all of my time managing, guiding, nurturing, cajoling, poking, and prodding the creative directors, writers, art directors, and designers on my staff. I have no complaints with that, but my first true love will always be found in the writing, the imagining, and the producing of the work itself. It's what I always wanted to do.

messages to target audiences has given them a major role in the marketing programs of most organizations. Companies ranging from large multinational corporations to small retailers increasingly rely on advertising and promotion to help them market products and services. In market-based economies, consumers have learned to rely on advertising and other forms of promotion for information they can use in making purchase decisions.

Evidence of the increasing importance of advertising and promotion comes from the growth in expenditures in these areas. In 1980, advertising expenditures in the United States were $53 billion, and $49 billion was spent on sales promotion techniques such as product samples, coupons, contests, sweepstakes, premiums, rebates, and allowances and discounts to retailers. By 2005, over $276 billion was spent on local and national advertising, while spending on sales promotion programs targeted toward consumers and retailers increased to nearly $300 billion.[1] Companies bombarded the U.S. consumer with messages and promotional offers, collectively spending more than $30 a week on every man, woman, and child in the country—nearly 50 percent more per capita than in any other nation.

Promotional expenditures in international markets have grown as well. Advertising expenditures outside the United States increased from $55 billion in 1980 to nearly $294 billion by 2005.[2] Both foreign and domestic companies spend billions more on sales promotion, personal selling, direct marketing, event sponsorships, and public relations, all important parts of a firm's marketing communications program.

The tremendous growth in expenditures for advertising and promotion reflects in part the growth of the U.S. and global economies and the efforts of expansion-minded marketers to take advantage of growth opportunities in various regions of the world. The growth in expenditures also reflects the fact that marketers around the world recognize the value and importance of advertising and promotion. Promotional strategies play an important role in the marketing programs of companies as they attempt to communicate with and sell their products to their customers. To understand the roles advertising and promotion play in the marketing process, let us first examine the marketing function.

What Is Marketing?

Before reading on, stop for a moment and think about how you would define marketing. Chances are that each reader of this book will come up with a somewhat different answer, since marketing is often viewed in terms of individual activities that constitute the overall marketing process. One popular conception of marketing is that it primarily involves sales. Other perspectives view marketing as consisting of advertising or retailing activities. For some of you, market research, pricing, or product planning may come to mind.

While all of these activities are part of marketing, it encompasses more than just these individual elements. For nearly two decades, the American Marketing Association (AMA), the organization that represents marketing professionals in the United States and Canada, defined marketing as *the process of planning and executing the conception, pricing, promotion, and distribution of ideas, goods, and services to create exchanges that satisfy individual and organizational objectives.*[3] This definition of marketing focused on **exchange** as a central concept in marketing and the use of the basic marketing activities to create and sustain relationships with customers.[4] For exchange to occur there must be two or more parties with something of value to one another, a desire and ability to give up that something to the other party, and a way to communicate with each other. Advertising and promotion play an important role in the exchange process by informing customers of an organization's product or service and convincing them of its ability to satisfy their needs or wants.

Not all marketing transactions involve the exchange of money for a product or service. Nonprofit organizations such as various causes, charities, religious groups, the arts, and colleges and universities (probably including the one you are attending) receive millions of dollars in donations every year. Nonprofits often use ads like the one in Exhibit 1-2 to solicit contributions from the public. Donors generally do not receive any material benefits for their contributions; they donate in exchange for intangible social and psychological satisfactions such as feelings of goodwill and altruism.

Exhibit 1-2 Nonprofit organizations use advertising to solicit contributions and support

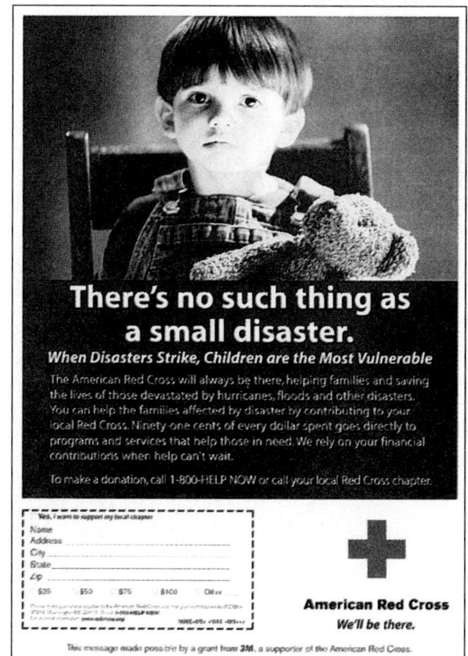

While many still view exchange as the core phenomenon or domain for study in marketing, there is also agreement among most academicians and practitioners that the discipline is rapidly changing. To reflect these changes, the AMA adopted a revised definition of **marketing** in 2004, which is as follows:

> Marketing is an organizational function and a set of processes for creating, communicating and delivering value to customers and for managing customer relationships in ways that benefit the organization and its stakeholders.[5]

This revised definition is viewed as being more strategic in nature as well as more reflective of the role marketing plays in the functioning of an organization. It also recognizes the important role marketing plays in the process of building and sustaining relationships with customers and delivering value to them.

Marketing Focuses on Relationships and Value

Today, most markets are seeking more than just a one-time exchange or transaction with customers. The focus of market-driven companies is on developing and sustaining *relationships* with their customers. Successful companies recognize that creating, communicating, and delivering *value* to their customers is extremely important. **Value** is the customer's perception of all of the benefits of a product or service weighed against all the costs of acquiring and consuming it.[6] Benefits can be functional (the performance of the product), experiential (what it feels like to use the product), and/or psychological (feelings such as self-esteem or status that result from owning a particular brand). Costs include the money paid for the product or service as well as other factors such as acquiring information about the product/service, making the purchase, learning how to use it, maintaining the product, and disposing of it.

The focus on customer relationships and value has led many companies to emphasize **relationship marketing,** which involves creating, maintaining, and enhancing long-term relationships with individual customers as well as other stakeholders for mutual benefit.[7]

The movement toward relationship marketing is due to several factors. First, companies recognize that customers have become much more demanding. Consumers desire *superior customer value,* which includes quality products and services that are competitively priced, convenient to purchase, delivered on time, and supported by excellent customer service. They also want personalized products and services that are tailored to their specific needs and wants. Advances in information technology, along with flexible manufacturing systems and new marketing processes, have led to **mass customization,** whereby a company can make a product or deliver a service in response to a particular customer's needs in a cost-effective way.[8] New technology is making it possible to configure and personalize a wide array of products and services including computers, automobiles, clothing, cosmetics, jewelry, and mortgages. Consumers can log on to the Dell website and build their own computers or to NikeiD.com to design personalized athletic shoes and other products (Exhibit 1-3).

Exhibit 1-3
Consumers can personalize athletic shoes and other products on Nike's website

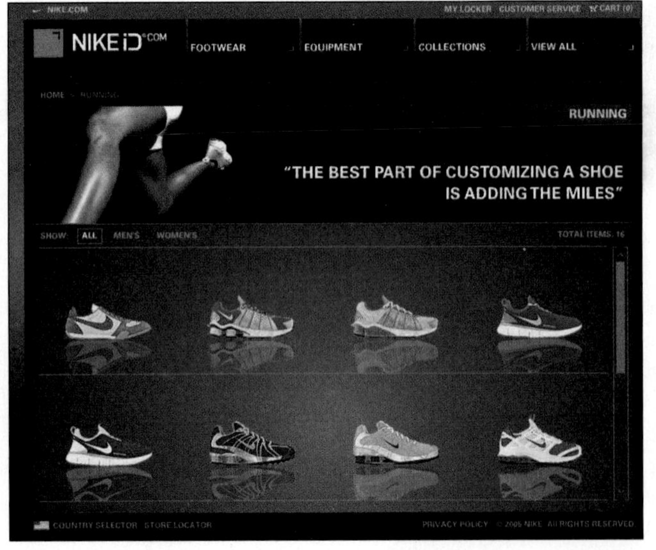

Another reason why marketers are emphasizing relationships is that it is more cost effective to retain customers than to acquire new ones. Marketers are giving more attention to the lifetime value of a customer because studies have shown that reducing customer defections by just 5 percent can increase future profit by as much as 30 to 90 percent.[9] As companies focus more attention on customer retention, many are developing **customer relationship management (CRM)** programs, which involve the systematic tracking of consumers' preferences and behaviors and modifying the product or service offer as much as possible to meet individual needs and wants.[10] Information technology, particularly database systems, is an integral part of CRM programs as companies must capture information about their customer and adjust elements of their marketing programs to better meet their needs and wants. Marketing communications is also an important part of customer relationship management as companies strive to create more personalized and meaningful one-to-one communications with customers and manage their contacts and interactions with them.

The Marketing Mix

Marketing facilitates the exchange process and the development of relationships by carefully examining the needs and wants of consumers, developing a product or service that satisfies these needs, offering it at a certain price, making it available through a particular place or channel of distribution, and developing a program of promotion or communication to create awareness and interest. These four Ps—product, price, place (distribution), and promotion—are elements of the **marketing mix.** The basic task of marketing is combining these four elements into a marketing program to facilitate the potential for exchange with consumers in the marketplace.

The proper marketing mix does not just happen. Marketers must be knowledgeable about the issues and options involved in each element of the mix. They must also be aware of how these elements can be combined to form an effective marketing program that delivers value to consumers. The market must be analyzed through consumer research, and the resulting information must be used to develop an overall marketing strategy and mix.

The primary focus of this book is on one element of the marketing mix: the promotional variable. However, the promotional program must be part of a viable marketing strategy and be coordinated with other marketing activities. A firm can spend large sums on advertising or sales promotion, but it stands little chance of success if the product is of poor quality, is priced improperly, or does not have adequate distribution to consumers. Marketers have long recognized the importance of combining the elements of the marketing mix into a cohesive marketing strategy. Many companies also recognize the need to integrate their various marketing communications efforts, such as media advertising, direct marketing, sales promotion, Internet marketing, event sponsorships, and public relations, to achieve more effective marketing communications.

Integrated Marketing Communications

For many years, the promotional function in most companies was dominated by mass-media advertising. Companies relied primarily on their advertising agencies for guidance in nearly all areas of marketing communication. Most marketers did use additional promotional and marketing communication tools, but sales promotion and direct-marketing agencies as well as package design firms were generally viewed as auxiliary services and often used on a per-project basis. Public relations agencies were used to manage the organization's publicity, image, and affairs with relevant publics on an ongoing basis but were not viewed as integral participants in the marketing communications process.

Many marketers built strong barriers around the various marketing and promotional functions and planned and managed them as separate practices, with different budgets, different views of the market, and different goals and objectives. These companies failed to recognize that the wide range of marketing and promotional tools must be coordinated to communicate effectively and present a consistent image to target markets.

The Evolution of IMC

During the 1980s, many companies began taking a broader perspective of marketing communication and seeing the need for a more strategic integration of their promotional tools. The decade was characterized by the rapid development of areas such as sales promotion, direct marketing, and public relations, which began challenging advertising's role as the dominant form of marketing communication. These firms began moving toward the process of **integrated marketing communications (IMC),** which involves coordinating the various promotional elements and other marketing activities that communicate with a firm's customers.[11] As marketers embraced the concept of integrated marketing communications, they began asking their ad agencies to coordinate the use of a variety of promotional tools rather than relying primarily on media advertising. A number of companies also began to look beyond traditional advertising agencies and use other types of promotional specialists to develop and implement various components of their promotional plans.

Many agencies responded to the call for synergy among the promotional tools by acquiring PR, sales promotion, and direct-marketing companies and touting themselves as IMC agencies that offer one-stop shopping for all their clients' promotional needs.[12] Some agencies became involved in these nonadvertising areas to gain control over their clients' promotional programs and budgets and struggled to offer any real value beyond creating advertising. However, the advertising industry soon recognized that IMC was more than just a fad. Terms such as *new advertising, orchestration,* and *seamless communication* were used to describe the concept of integration.[13] A task force from the American Association of Advertising Agencies (the "4As") developed one of the first definitions of integrated marketing communications:

> a concept of marketing communications planning that recognizes the added value of a comprehensive plan that evaluates the strategic roles of a variety of communication disciplines—for example, general advertising, direct response, sales promotion, and public relations—and combines these disciplines to provide clarity, consistency, and maximum communications impact.[14]

The 4As' definition focuses on the process of using all forms of promotion to achieve maximum communication impact. However, advocates of the IMC concept argued for an even broader perspective that considers *all sources of brand or company contact* that a customer or prospect has with a product or service.[15] They noted that the process of integrated marketing communications calls for a "big-picture" approach to planning marketing and promotion programs and coordinating the various communication functions. It requires that firms develop a total marketing communications strategy that recognizes how all of a firm's marketing activities, not just promotion, communicate with its customers.

Exhibit 1-4 Montblanc uses a variety of marketing mix elements including price, product design, brand name, and distribution strategy to create a high-quality, upscale image for its watches

Consumers' perceptions of a company and/or its various brands are a synthesis of the bundle of messages they receive or contacts they have, such as media advertisements, price, package design, direct-marketing efforts, publicity, sales promotions, websites, point-of-purchase displays, and even the type of store where a product or service is sold. The integrated marketing communications approach seeks to have all of a company's marketing and promotional activities project a consistent, unified image to the marketplace. It calls for a centralized messaging function so that everything a company says and does communicates a common theme and positioning. For example, Montblanc uses classic design and a distinctive brand name as well as high price to position its watches, pens, and other products as high-quality, high-status products. This upscale image is enhanced by the company's strategy of distributing its products only through boutiques, jewelry stores, and other exclusive shops including its own stores. Notice how this image is reflected in the Montblanc ad shown in Exhibit 1-4.

Many companies have adopted this broader perspective of IMC. They see it as a way to coordinate and manage their marketing communication programs to ensure that they send customers a consistent message about the company and/or its brands. For these companies, integration represents an improvement over the traditional method of treating the various marketing and promotion elements as virtually separate activities. However, this perspective of IMC has been challenged on the basis that it focuses primarily on the tactical coordination of various communication tools with the goal of making them look and sound alike.[16] It has been criticized as an "inside-out marketing" approach that is a relatively simple matter of bundling promotional mix elements together so they have one look and speak with one voice.[17] As IMC continues to evolve, both academicians as well as practitioners are recognizing that a broader perspective is needed that views the discipline from a more strategic perspective.

A Contemporary Perspective of IMC

As marketers become more sophisticated and develop a better understanding of IMC, they are recognizing that it involves more than just coordinating the various elements of their marketing and communications programs into a "one look, one voice" approach. As IMC evolves, it is being recognized as a business process that helps companies identify the most appropriate and effective methods for communicating and building relationships with customers and other stakeholders. Don Schultz of Northwestern University has developed what many think is a more appropriate definition of IMC, as follows:

> Integrated marketing communication is a strategic business process used to plan, develop, execute and evaluate coordinated, measurable, persuasive brand communications programs over time with consumers, customers, prospects, employees, associates and other targeted relevant external and internal audiences. The goal is to generate both short-term financial returns and build long-term brand and shareholder value.[18]

There are several important aspects of this definition of IMC. First, it views IMC as an ongoing strategic business process rather than just tactical integration of various communication activities. It also recognizes that there are a number of relevant audiences that are an important part of the process. Externally these include customers, prospects, suppliers, investors, interest groups, and the general public. It also views internal audiences such as employees as an important part of the IMC process. Schultz also notes that this definition reflects the increasing emphasis that is being placed on the demand for accountability and measurement of the *outcomes* of marketing communication programs as well as marketing in general.

Many companies are realizing that communicating effectively with customers and other stakeholders involves more than just the tactical use of the traditional marketing communication tools. These firms, along with many advertising agencies, are embracing IMC and incorporating it into their marketing and business practices. It is true, however, that not all companies have moved beyond the stage of simply bundling promotional mix elements together and made the organization changes and investment that are needed for true integration. Moreover, some academics and practitioners have questioned whether IMC is just another "management fashion" whose influence will be transitory.[19] Critics of IMC argue that it merely reinvents and renames existing ideas and concepts and that it questions its significance for marketing and advertising thought and practice.[20]

While the debate over the value and relevance of IMC is likely to continue, proponents of the concept far outnumber the critics. IMC is proving to be a permanent change that offers significant value to marketers in the rapidly changing communications environment they are facing in the new millennium. IMC has been described as one of the "new-generation" marketing approaches being used by companies to better focus their efforts in acquiring, retaining, and developing relationships with customers and other stakeholders.[21] Some scholars have stated that IMC is undoubtedly the major communications development of the last decade of the 20th century.[22] We will now discuss some of the reasons for the growing importance of IMC.

Reasons for the Growing Importance of IMC

The IMC approach to marketing communications planning and strategy is being adopted by both large and small companies and has become popular among firms marketing consumer products and services as well as business-to-business marketers. There are a number of reasons why marketers are adopting the IMC approach. A fundamental reason is that they understand the value of strategically integrating the various communications functions rather than having them operate autonomously. By coordinating their marketing communications efforts, companies can avoid duplication, take advantage of synergy among promotional tools, and develop more efficient and effective marketing communications programs. Advocates of IMC argue that it is one of the easiest ways for a company to maximize the return on its investment in marketing and promotion.[23]

The move to integrated marketing communications also reflects an adaptation by marketers to a changing environment, particularly with respect to consumers, technology, and media. Major changes have occurred among consumers with respect to demographics, lifestyles, media use, and buying and shopping patterns. For example, cable TV and more recently digital satellite systems have vastly expanded the number of channels available to households. According to Nielsen Media Research, the average U.S. household receives 100 TV channels, compared with 27 in 1994. Every day more and more consumers are surfing the Internet's World Wide Web. There are now more than 800 million Internet users around the world including nearly 200 million in the United States. In the United States, 67 percent of U.S. households are connected to the Internet and over half of these homes have high-speed broadband access.[24] Every day more consumers are surfing the Internet's World Wide Web. Online services such as America Online, Yahoo!, and Microsoft Network provide information and entertainment as well as the opportunity to shop for and order a vast array of products and services. Marketers are responding by developing websites on which they can advertise their products and services interactively as well as transact sales. For example, travelers can use American Airlines' AA.com website to plan flights, check for special fares, purchase tickets, and reserve seats, as well as make hotel and car-rental reservations (Exhibit 1-5).

Even as new technologies and formats create new ways for marketers to reach consumers, they are affecting the more traditional media. Television, radio, magazines, and newspaper audiences are becoming more fragmented and reaching smaller and more selective audiences. IMC Perspective 1-1 discusses how technology is leading to greater fragmentation of media and how the focus of marketers is shifting from mass to micromarketing.

In addition to the decline in audience size for many media, marketers are facing the problem of consumers being less responsive to traditional advertising. Many consumers are turned off by advertising; they are tired of being bombarded with sales messages. This is leading many marketers to look for alternative ways to communicate with their target audiences.

Exhibit 1-5 Travelers can use American Airlines' website to purchase tickets and reserve seats

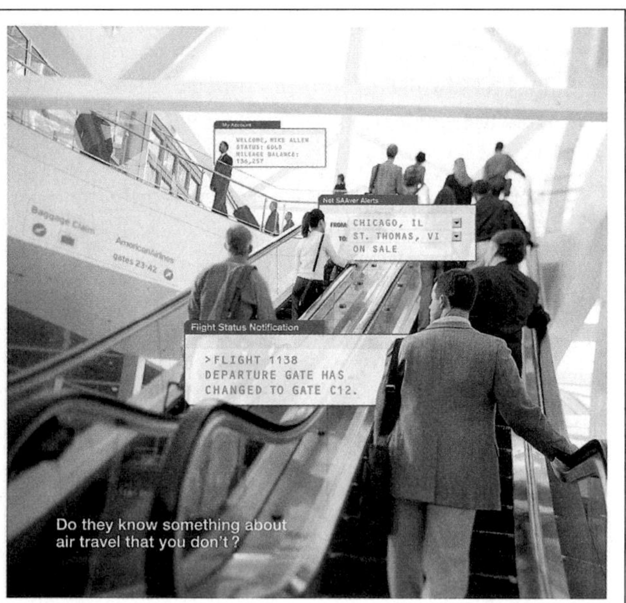

My Account
WELCOME, MIKE ALLEN
STATUS: GOLD
MILEAGE BALANCE:
136,257
Net SAAver Alerts
FROM CHICAGO, IL
TO ST. THOMAS, VI
ON SALE
Baggage Claim
AmericanAirlines
gates 23-42
Flight Status Notification
>FLIGHT 1138
DEPARTURE GATE HAS
CHANGED TO GATE C12.
Do they know something about
air travel that you don't?

> Introducing the new AA.com
Log on to the new AA.com and you'll know how to travel in a whole new way. You'll know that the My Account feature allows you to personalize information and store travel preferences to speed booking. You'll know how to manage your AAdvantage account and receive Net SAAver Alerts to as many as 30 of your favorite cities. You'll know that Flight Status Notification delivers the latest gate and flight time updates to your cell phone, pager, PDA or e-mail. And you'll know you can use and earn AAdvantage miles online for everything from booking flights to purchasing upgrades. But there's a lot more you'll know. So add to your knowledge base by simply logging on to the new AA.com today. AmericanAirlines

For example, marketers often hire product placement firms or negotiate directly with major studios and production companies to get their brands into movies and television shows. MGM/United Artists has created special scenes in its James Bond movies to feature automobiles such as the BMW Z3 and Aston Martin V12 Vanquish sports car. The NBC hit series *The Apprentice* has built entire episodes around having the competitors work on tasks involving products such as Nestlé's Taster's Choice instant coffee, Pepsi Edge soda, Mattel toys, and Crest Vanilla Mint toothpaste. Companies pay as much as $2 million to have their brands featured on the show.[25]

Marketers must consider that many of those in Generation Y, the age cohort born between 1979 and 1994 (which includes most college students), are very skeptical of traditional advertising. Having grown up in an even more media-saturated and brand conscious world than their parents did, they respond to advertising differently and prefer to encounter marketing messages in different places and from different sources. Marketers recognize that to penetrate the skepticism and to capture the attention of the Gen Ys they have to bring their messages to these people in different ways. Many companies are turning to a stealth-type of strategy known as *buzz marketing* whereby brand come-ons become part of popular culture, and consumers themselves are lured into spreading the

IMC PERSPECTIVE 1-1

The New Age of Micromarketing

For years, major consumer products companies such as McDonald's, Procter & Gamble, and Coca-Cola spent most of their advertising and promotion budgets on mass media, including television and magazines. However, over the past five years these companies have been relying less and less on TV commercials and print ads to sell their products. McDonald's now spends only a third of its U.S. marketing budget on television compared to two-thirds in 2000. A number of other consumer product giants such as General Motors and Unilever have also been moving away from the mass-marketing approach and focusing more on well-defined and targeted market segments.

For these companies, as well as many others, the evolution from mass to micromarketing is a fundamental change driven as much by necessity as by opportunity. They recognize that the consumer market is much more diverse and commercially self-indulgent than it was even five years ago. The country has fragmented into a myriad of market segments that are defined not only by demography, but by increasingly nuanced product preferences. The mass audience assembled by network television and augmented by other mass media is fragmenting at an accelerating rate. Viewing audiences are defecting from network television to other forms of entertainment such as DVDs, cable, the Internet, and video games. New technologies such as digital-video recorders allow viewers to skip commercials altogether. The proliferation of digital and wireless communication is spreading the mass audience of old across hundreds of narrowcast cable TV and radio channels, thousands of specialized magazines, and millions of video game consoles, personal digital assistants, and cell phone screens.

A few decades ago, an advertiser could reach 80 percent of U.S. women during an evening by running commercials on the three major networks of CBS, NBC, and ABC. To achieve this level of reach today, a company would have to run ads on 100 television channels. More than three-quarters of U.S. households now have cable or satellite, and the average home receives more than 100 TV channels. Collectively, cable channels now have more prime-time viewers than the four broadcast networks, with a 52 percent share to broadcast's 44 percent. However, the audiences attracted by even the largest cable stations such as ESPN and CNN are still much smaller than those of the broadcast networks.

The media fragmentation is not confined to television as the print media have also become increasingly specialized. There are approximately 6,200 consumer magazines published in the United States and only 10 percent are general-interest titles, compared to 30 percent two decades ago. Moreover, general-interest magazines such as *Time* and *Newsweek* offer demographically targeted editions as well as ad-customized versions of its national edition. There have been weeks when *Time* has produced as many as 20,000 ad-customized versions of the magazine. The Internet is rapidly coming of age as an important advertising medium with online versions of nearly every television station, newspaper, and magazine in the country. The Web offers marketers tremendous opportunities for targeting based on numerous dimensions. The crude banner and pop-up ads that initially defined Internet advertising are giving way to more refined formats such as "paid search," which is the fastest growing form of online advertising. Online search giants Google and Yahoo are adding refinements that will make it possible for paid-search advertisers to target Internet users by region or city.

To respond to the media fragmentation, marketers are increasing their spending on media that are more targeted and can reach specific market segments. McDonald's now uses much of the money that used to pay for commercials on network television and spends it on more specialized media that targets specific markets. To reach young men, which are one of its prime target markets, McDonald's advertises on Footlocker's in-store video network and pays for closed-circuit sports programming piped into Hispanic bars. The company reaches mothers through ads in women's magazines such as *O: The Oprah Magazine* and *Marie Claire* and on websites such as iVillage and Yahoo. The company's chief marketing officer, Larry Light, has stated, "We are a big marketer. We are not a mass marketer."

McDonald's is not the only company that has moved away from mass marketing. For many years Procter & Gamble was considered the quintessential mass marketer. However, today the company is becoming much more selective in its use of television advertising to back brands such as Tide, Crest, Pampers, and Old Spice. In a recent speech to the American Association of Advertising Agencies Media Conference, Procter & Gamble's Global Marketing Officer Jim Stengel took the industry to task for clinging to an outdated media model that is not in touch with today's consumer. Stengel stated that "there must be—and is—life beyond the 30-second spot," and called on the advertising industry to embrace and develop new media.

There appears to be no stopping the fragmentation of the consumer market as well as the proliferation of media. The success of marketing communication programs will depend on how well companies make the transition from the fading age of mass marketing to the new era of micromarketing. Many companies are learning that it no longer makes economic sense to send an advertising message to the many in hopes of persuading the few.

Sources: Anthony Bianco, "The Vanishing Mass Market," *BusinessWeek*, July 12, 2004, pp. 61–68; Jeff Neff and Lisa Sanders, "It's Broken," *Advertising Age*, February 16, 2004, pp. 1, 30.

	Old	New
Consumers	Couch potatoes passively receive whatever the networks broadcast	Empowered media users control and shape the content, thanks to TiVo, iPod, and the Internet
Aspirations	To keep up with the crowd	To stand out from the crowd
TV choice	Three networks plus a PBS station, maybe	Hundreds of channels, plus video on demand
Magazines	Age of the big glossies: *Time, Life, Look,* and *Newsweek*	Age of the special interest: A magazine for every hobby and affinity group
Ads	Everyone hums the Alka-Seltzer jingle	Talking to a group of one: Ads go ever narrower
Brands	Rise of the big, ubiquitous brands, from Coca-Cola to Tide	Niche brands, product extensions, and mass customization mean lots of new variations

message. The positive word of mouth generated through buzz marketing campaigns has been an integral part of successful IMC campaigns used to launch brands such as the Chrysler PT Cruiser and Ford Focus automobiles.[26]

The integrated marketing communications movement is also being driven by changes in the ways companies market their products and services. A major reason for the growing importance of the IMC approach is the ongoing revolution that is changing the rules of marketing and the role of the traditional advertising agency.[27] Major characteristics of this marketing revolution include:

- *A shifting of marketing dollars from media advertising to other forms of promotion, particularly consumer- and trade-oriented sales promotions.* Many marketers feel that traditional media advertising has become too expensive and is not cost-effective. Also, escalating price competition in many markets has resulted in marketers' pouring more of their promotional budgets into price promotions rather than media advertising.
- *A movement away from relying on advertising-focused approaches, which emphasize mass media such as network television and national magazines, to solve communication problems.* Many companies are turning to lower-cost, more targeted communication tools such as event marketing and sponsorships, direct mail, sales promotion, and the Internet as they develop their marketing communications strategies.
- *A shift in marketplace power from manufacturers to retailers.* Due to consolidation in the retail industry, small local retailers are being replaced by regional, national, and international chains. Large retailers such as Wal-Mart are using their clout to demand larger promotional fees and allowances from manufacturers, a practice that often siphons money away from advertising. Moreover, new technologies such as checkout scanners give retailers information on the effectiveness of manufacturers' promotional programs. This is leading many marketers to shift their focus to promotional tools that can produce short-term results, such as sale promotion.
- *The rapid growth and development of database marketing.* Many companies are building databases containing customer names; geographic, demographic, and psychographic profiles; purchase patterns; media preferences; credit ratings; and other characteristics. Marketers are using this information to target consumers through a variety of direct-marketing methods such as telemarketing, direct mail, and direct-response advertising, rather than relying on mass media. Advocates of the approach argue that database marketing is critical to the development and practice of effective IMC.[28]
- *Demands for greater accountability from advertising agencies and changes in the way agencies are compensated.* Many companies are moving toward incentive-based systems whereby compensation of their ad agencies is based, at least in part, on objective measures such as sales, market share, and profitability. Demands for accountability are motivating many agencies to consider a variety of communication tools and less expensive alternatives to mass-media advertising.
- *The rapid growth of the Internet, which is changing the very nature of how companies do business and the ways they communicate and interact with consumers.* The Internet revolution is well under way, and the Internet audience is growing rapidly. The Internet is an interactive medium that is becoming an integral part of communication strategy, and even business strategy, for many companies.

This marketing revolution is affecting everyone involved in the marketing and promotional process. Companies are recognizing that they must change the ways they market and promote their products and services. They can no longer be tied to a specific communication tool (such as media advertising); rather, they should use whatever contact methods offer the best way of delivering the message to their target audiences. Ad agencies continue to reposition themselves as offering more than just advertising expertise; they strive to convince their clients that they can manage all or any part of clients' integrated communications needs. Most agencies recognize that their future success depends on their ability to understand all areas of promotion and help their clients develop and implement integrated marketing communications programs.

The Role of IMC in Branding

One of the major reasons for the growing importance of integrated marketing communications over the past decade is that it plays a major role in the process of developing and sustaining brand identity and equity. As branding expert Kevin Keller notes, "Building and properly managing brand equity has become a priority for companies of all sizes, in all types of industries, in all types of markets."[29] With more and more products and services competing for consideration by customers who have less and less time to make choices, well-known brands have a major competitive advantage in today's marketplace. Building and maintaining brand identity and equity require the creation of well-known brands that have favorable, strong, and unique associations in the mind of the consumer.[30] Companies recognize that brand equity is as important an asset as factories, patents, and cash because strong brands have the power to command a premium price from consumers as well as investors. Figure 1-1 shows the world's most valuable brands, as measured by Interbrand, a leading brand consultancy company.

Figure 1-1 The World's 10 Most Valuable Brands

Rank	Brand	Brand Value (Billions)
1	Coca-Cola	$67.52
2	Microsoft	59.94
3	IBM	53.38
4	General Electric	46.99
5	Intel	35.59
6	Nokia	26.45
7	Walt Disney Co.	26.44
8	McDonald's Corp.	26.01
9	Toyota Motor Corp.	24.84
10	Marlboro	21.19

Source: *BusinessWeek*, August 1, 2005, p. 90.

Brand identity is a combination of many factors, including the name, logo, symbols, design, packaging, and performance of a product or service as well as the image or type of associations that comes to mind when consumers think about a brand. It encompasses the entire spectrum of consumers' awareness, knowledge, and image of the brand as well as the company behind it. It is the sum of all points of encounter or contact that consumers have with the brand, and it extends beyond the experience or outcome of using it. These contacts can also result from various forms of integrated marketing communications activities used by a company, including mass-media advertising, sales promotion offers, sponsorship activities at sporting or entertainment events, websites on the Internet, and direct-mail pieces such as letters, brochures, catalogs, or videos. Consumers can also have contact with or receive information about a brand in stores at the point of sale; through articles or stories they see, hear, or read in the media; or through interactions with a company representative, such as a salesperson. IMC Perspective 1-2 discusses how many companies are finding new ways to build brand equity as the relationship between consumers and brands changes.

Marketers recognize that in the modern world of marketing there are many different opportunities and methods for *contacting* current and prospective customers to provide them with information about a company and/or brands. The challenge is to understand how to use the various IMC tools to make such contacts and deliver the branding message effectively and efficiently. A successful IMC program requires that marketers find the right combination of communication tools and techniques, define their role and the extent to which they can or should be used, and coordinate their use. To accomplish this, the persons responsible for the company's communication efforts must have an understanding of the IMC tools that are available and the ways they can be used.

The Promotional Mix: The Tools for IMC

Promotion has been defined as the coordination of all seller-initiated efforts to set up channels of information and persuasion in order to sell goods and services or promote an idea.[31] While implicit communication occurs through the various elements of the marketing mix, most of an organization's communications with the marketplace take place as part of a carefully planned and controlled promotional program. The basic tools used to accomplish an organization's communication objectives are often referred to as the **promotional mix** (Figure 1-2).

IMC PERSPECTIVE 1-2

Finding New Ways to Build Brands

Consider for a moment what consumers' reactions would be to a pair of running or basketball shoes if the Nike name or "swoosh" was taken off of them or to a can of cola without the Coke or Pepsi name. Would a Godiva chocolate by any other name taste as sweet? Do plain blue jeans carry the same cachet as those bearing the Diesel or 7 For All Mankind label? There was a time when consumers were proudly declaring their independence from the appeal of name-brand products in favor of more practical generics and private labels. However, in today's marketplace the appeal of brand names is greater than ever and marketers recognize that building and reinforcing the image of their brands is a key to profitability and growth.

While companies are well aware of the importance of branding, they are learning that the ways of building strong brands are changing. Marketers are finding that they can no longer build and maintain brand equity merely by spending large sums of money on media advertising. Brands are becoming less about the actual product and more about how people relate to them. Consumers today demand more than just product quality or performance as many view brands as a form of self-expression.

The relationship between brands and their customers has become much more complex. One reason for this is that today's consumer knows much more about brands and the companies that make them than ever. The value chain of companies has become increasingly visible, and consumers often select brands based on the social, economic, and environmental records and policies of the companies that make them. Cynicism about corporations is at an all-time high, and many companies must work hard to gain consumer trust and confidence. Companies are also finding it more difficult to control their brand image as the Internet provides consumers with a wealth of information about their products and services that can be easily accessed and shared. They can use the Internet to make price and quality comparisons or to learn what others think about various brands as well as to learn about their experiences or satisfaction with them.

For many companies, mass-media advertising has long been the cornerstone of their brand-building efforts. However, astute marketers are finding new ways to build relationships with customers. Many companies are moving from an advertising-focused model that relies on one-way communication to an interactive model whereby consumers can easily communicate with them as well as with other customers. Some companies are offering consumers the opportunity to customize products and services through their websites. Firms such as Dell, eBay, and Amazon.com are using mass customization to bind consumers more tightly to their brands. In Britain, Coca-Cola has launched the myCokeMusic.com website where surfers can legally download more than 250,000 songs and mix their own tracks and submit them for a review by their peers.

Companies are also recognizing that an effective way to build brand equity is by letting consumers experience their products. Apple Computer has opened nearly 100 retail stores where consumers can come in and experience products such as iPods and personal computers first hand. Sony is expanding its Sony Style stores and expects to have 60 in the United States alone in the next few years. The stores are part of the company's effort to show off its products in the best possible light and to polish its brand name in the minds of consumers. Companies such as Starbucks recognize that they are selling more than just a product. The company's chairman, Howard Schultz, notes that "the product is the experience" as people go to Starbucks for the hip, relaxed ambiance, the music, and the service they receive from the baristas who often remember their favorite coffee drink. Starbucks positions its stores as a community gathering place where people can get together and enjoy a cup of coffee as well as conversation.

Marketers are also turning to entertainment as a way of connecting with consumers. They are making their brands part of reality TV shows such as *The Apprentice, Extreme Makeover Home Edition,* or *Queer Eye for the Straight Guy.* A number of companies are using a new approach called "advertainment," which is a cross between advertising and entertainment. Some are creating branded entertainment in the form of short films that they show on their websites. Skyy Spirits and BMW were the first to use this genre and a number of other companies such as Levi Strauss, American Express, Coca-Cola, and DKNY that have created entertainment content that has been shown on their websites.

Consumers' passion for brands shows no sign of waning and, in fact, may be getting stronger. However, marketers must recognize that brands are shifting from being mere product identifiers to personal identifiers and the ways they connect consumers to them is changing. As branding guru Larry Light notes, the key to all successful brands is that they stand for something and are much more than simply trademarks or logos.

Sources: Diane Brady, "Cult Brands," *BusinessWeek,* August 2, 2004, pp. 64–67; Linda Tischler, "The Good Brand," *Fast Company,* August 2004, pp. 47–49.

Figure 1-2 Elements of the Promotional Mix

Traditionally the promotional mix has included four elements: advertising, sales promotion, publicity/public relations, and personal selling. However, in this text we view direct marketing as well as interactive media as major promotional-mix elements that modern-day marketers use to communicate with their target markets. Each element of the promotional mix is viewed as an integrated marketing communications tool that plays a distinctive role in an IMC program. Each may take on a variety of forms. And each has certain advantages.

Advertising

Advertising is defined as any paid form of nonpersonal communication about an organization, product, service, or idea by an identified sponsor.[32] The *paid* aspect of this definition reflects the fact that the space or time for an advertising message generally must be bought. An occasional exception to this is the public service announcement (PSA), whose advertising space or time is donated by the media.

The *nonpersonal* component means that advertising involves mass media (e.g., TV, radio, magazines, newspapers) that can transmit a message to large groups of individuals, often at the same time. The nonpersonal nature of advertising means that there is generally no opportunity for immediate feedback from the message recipient (except in direct-response advertising). Therefore, before the message is sent, the advertiser must consider how the audience will interpret and respond to it.

Advertising is the best-known and most widely discussed form of promotion, probably because of its pervasiveness. It is also a very important promotional tool, particularly for companies whose products and services are targeted at mass consumer markets such as automobile manufacturers, packaged goods, and drug companies. More than 200 companies spend over $100 million on advertising and promotion in the United States each year. Figure 1-3 shows the advertising expenditures of the 25 leading national advertisers.

Several reasons explain why advertising is such an important part of many marketers' IMC programs. First, advertising is still the most cost-effective way to reach large audiences. The average 30-second commercial on the four major networks during evening prime-time programming reaches 6 million households.

Figure 1-3 25 Leading Advertisers in the United States, 2004

Rank	Advertiser	Ad Spending (Millions)
1	General Motors Corp.	$3,997
2	Procter & Gamble	3,919
3	Time Warner	3,283
4	Pfizer	2,957
5	SBC Communications	2,686
6	DaimlerChrylser	2,462
7	Ford Motor Co.	2,458
8	Walt Disney Co.	2,241
9	Verizon Communications	2,197
10	Johnson & Johnson	2,175
11	GlaxoSmithKline	1,828
12	Sears Holdings Corp.	1,823
13	Toyota Motor Corp.	1,821
14	General Electric Co.	1,819
15	Sony Corp.	1,539
16	Nissan Motor Corp.	1,529
17	Altria Group	1,399
18	McDonald's Corp.	1,388
19	L'Oreal	1,341
20	Unilever	1,319
21	Novartis	1,284
22	PepsiCo	1,262
23	Home Depot	1,255
24	Merck & Co.	1,250
25	U.S. Government	1,228

Source: *Advertising Age,* June 27, 2005, p. S-2.

Advertising.
The way great brands get to be great brands.
American Advertising Federation aaf.org

Exhibit 1-6 The American Advertising Federation promotes the value of advertising

The cost per thousand households reached in 2004 was $19.85. Popular shows such as *American Idol* and *Desperate Housewives* can reach as many as 25 to 30 million viewers each week. Thus, for marketers who are interested in building or maintaining brand awareness and reaching a mass audience at one time, there is no effective substitute for network television.[33]

Advertising is also a valuable tool for building company or brand equity as it is a powerful way to provide consumers with information as well as to influence their perceptions. Advertising can be used to create favorable and unique images and associations for a brand which can be very important for companies selling products or services that are difficult to differentiate on the basis of functional attributes. Brand image plays an important role in the purchase of many products and services, and advertising is still recognized as one of the best ways to build a brand. Exhibit 1-6 shows an ad from a campaign run by the American Advertising Federation promoting the value of advertising.

The nature and purpose of advertising differ from one industry to another and/or across situations. Companies selling products and services to the consumer market generally rely heavily on advertising to communicate with their target audiences as do retailers and other local merchants. However, advertising can also be done by an industry to stimulate demand for a product category such as beef or milk. Advertising is also used extensively by companies who compete in the business and professional markets to reach current and potential customers. For example, business-to-business marketers use advertising to perform important functions such as building awareness of the company and its products, generating leads for the sales force, and reassuring customers about the purchase they have made. Exhibit 1-7 shows an example of an ad from a campaign being run by the German-based firm Degussa, the largest specialty chemical company in the world, to help build awareness and an identity for the company. Figure 1-4 describes the most common types of advertising.

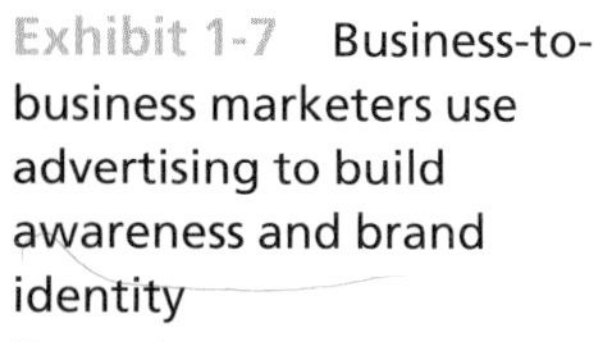
Exhibit 1-7 Business-to-business marketers use advertising to build awareness and brand identity

Direct Marketing

One of the fastest-growing sectors of the U.S. economy is **direct marketing,** in which organizations communicate directly with target customers to generate a response and/or a transaction. Traditionally, direct marketing has not been considered an element of the promotional mix. However, because it has become such an integral part of the IMC program of many organizations and often involves separate objectives, budgets, and strategies, we view direct marketing as a component of the promotional mix.

Direct marketing is much more than direct mail and mail-order catalogs. It involves a

Figure 1-4 Classifications of Advertising

ADVERTISING TO CONSUMER MARKETS

National Advertising
Advertising done by large companies on a nationwide basis or in most regions of the country. Most of the ads for well-known companies and brands that are seen on prime-time TV or in other major national or regional media are examples of national advertising. The goals of national advertisers are to inform or remind consumers of the company or brand and its features, benefits, advantages, or uses and to create or reinforce its image so that consumers will be predisposed to purchase it.

Retail/Local Advertising
Advertising done by retailers or local merchants to encourage consumers to shop at a specific store, use a local service, or patronize a particular establishment. Retail or local advertising tends to emphasize specific patronage motives such as price, hours of operation, service, atmosphere, image, or merchandise assortment. Retailers are concerned with building store traffic, so their promotions often take the form of direct-action advertising designed to produce immediate store traffic and sales.

Primary- versus Selective-Demand Advertising
Primary-demand advertising is designed to stimulate demand for the general product class or entire industry. Selective-demand advertising focuses on creating demand for a specific company's brands. Most advertising for products and services is concerned with stimulating selective demand and emphasizes reasons for purchasing a particular brand.

An advertiser might concentrate on stimulating primary demand when, for example, its brand dominates a market and will benefit the most from overall market growth. Primary-demand advertising is often used as part of a promotional strategy to help a new product gain market acceptance, since the challenge is to sell customers on the product concept as much as to sell a particular brand. Industry trade associations also try to stimulate primary demand for their members' products, among them cotton, milk, orange juice, pork, and beef.

ADVERTISING TO BUSINESS AND PROFESSIONAL MARKETS

Business-to-Business Advertising
Advertising targeted at individuals who buy or influence the purchase of industrial goods or services for their companies. Industrial goods are products that either become a physical part of another product (raw material or component parts), are used in manufacturing other goods (machinery), or are used to help a company conduct its business (e.g., office supplies, computers). Business services such as insurance, travel services, and health care are also included in this category.

Professional Advertising
Advertising targeted to professionals such as doctors, lawyers, dentists, engineers, or professors to encourage them to use a company's product in their business operations. It might also be used to encourage professionals to recommend or specify the use of a company's product by end-users.

Trade Advertising
Advertising targeted to marketing channel members such as wholesalers, distributors, and retailers. The goal is to encourage channel members to stock, promote, and resell the manufacturer's branded products to their customers.

Exhibit 1-8 The Bose Corporation uses direct-response advertising to promote its audio products

variety of activities, including database management, direct selling, telemarketing, and direct-response ads through direct mail, the Internet, and various broadcast and print media. Some companies, such as Tupperware, Discovery Toys, and Amway, do not use any other distribution channels, relying on independent contractors to sell their products directly to consumers. Companies such as L.L. Bean, Lands' End, and J. Crew have been very successful in using direct marketing to sell their clothing products. Dell has become the market leader in the computer industry by selling a full line of personal computers through direct marketing.

One of the major tools of direct marketing is **direct-response advertising,** whereby a product is promoted through an ad that encourages the consumer to purchase directly from the manufacturer. Traditionally, direct mail has been the primary medium for direct-response advertising, although television and magazines have become increasingly important media. For example, Exhibit 1-8 shows a direct-response ad for the Bose Corporation's Acoustic Waveguide products. Direct-response advertising and other forms of direct marketing have become very popular over the past two decades, owing primarily to changing lifestyles, particularly the increase in two-income households. This has meant more discretionary income but less time for in-store shopping. The availability of credit cards and toll-free phone numbers has also facilitated the purchase of products from direct-response ads. More recently, the rapid growth of the Internet is fueling the growth of direct marketing. The convenience of shopping through catalogs or on a company's website and placing orders by mail, by phone, or online has led the tremendous growth of direct marketing.

Direct-marketing tools and techniques are also being used by companies that distribute their products through traditional distribution channels or have their own sales force. Direct marketing plays a big role in the integrated marketing communications programs of consumer-product companies and business-to-business marketers. These companies spend large amounts of money each year developing and maintaining databases containing the addresses and/or phone numbers of present and prospective customers. They use telemarketing to call customers directly and attempt to sell them products and services or qualify them as sales leads. Marketers also send out direct-mail pieces ranging from simple letters and flyers to detailed brochures, catalogs, and videotapes to give potential customers information about their products or services. Direct-marketing techniques are also used to distribute product samples.

Interactive/Internet Marketing

Over the past decade we have been experiencing perhaps the most dynamic and revolutionary changes of any era in the history of marketing, as well as advertising and promotion. These changes are being driven by advances in technology and developments that have led to dramatic growth of communication through interactive media, particularly the Internet. **Interactive media** allow for a back-and-forth flow of information whereby users can participate in and modify the form and content of the information they receive in real time. Unlike traditional forms of marketing communications such as advertising, which are one-way in nature, the new media allow users to perform a variety of functions such as receive and alter information and images, make inquiries, respond to questions, and, of course, make purchases. In addition to the Internet, other forms of interactive media include CD-ROMs, kiosks, interactive television, and digital cell phones.

Many companies are now making text messaging a part of their integrated campaigns. For example, when Frito-Lay introduced its new Doritos Black Pepper Jack brand of tortilla chips, the integrated "if not Now when?" (inNw?) campaign included a text message component.[34] Ads were run inviting consumers to send the text message "inNw?" to Doritos to learn more about the product. Those opting in would receive a message back in a few seconds informing them that they could win cool prizes if they knew what "inNw" meant. If a correct message was messaged back, the texter was sent a message with a potential winner code, which they could take to a dedicated website and enter it to see if they won a prize (Exhibit 1-9).

Exhibit 1-9 Text messaging was part of the integrated campaign for Doritos Black Pepper Jack

The interactive medium that is having the greatest impact on marketing is the Internet. While the Internet is changing the ways companies design and implement their entire business and marketing strategies, it is also affecting their marketing communications programs. Millions of companies, ranging from large multinational corporations to small local businesses, have developed websites to promote their products and services, by providing current and potential customers with information as well as to entertain and interact with them. The Internet is actually a multifaceted promotional tool. On one hand, it is an advertising medium as many companies advertise their products and services on the websites of other companies and/or organizations or pay to link their banner ads or websites to search engines such as Google and Yahoo. The Internet can also be viewed as a marketing communications tool in its own right as it is a medium that can be used to execute all of the elements of the promotional mix. In addition to advertising on the Web, marketers offer sales promotion incentives such as coupons, contests, and sweepstakes online, and they use the Internet to conduct direct marketing, personal selling, and public relations activities more effectively and efficiently.

The interactive nature of the Internet is one of its major advantages. This capability enables marketers to gather valuable personal information from customers and prospects and to adjust their offer accordingly, in some cases in real time. Unlike traditional media, which are essentially one-way forms of communication, digital media such as the Internet allow for two-way communication. Another major advantage of the Internet is that it offers the capability to more closely and precisely measure the effects of advertising and other types of promotion. There are a number of metrics that can be generated when consumers visit websites, which allow marketers to determine how consumers are responding to their campaigns and the return on investment they are getting from their promotional dollars.

Companies recognize the advantages of the Internet and the various ways it can be used. However, a number of companies are also developing campaigns that integrate their Web strategies with other aspects of their IMC programs such as media advertising. An excellent example of this is the "Perspectives" campaign developed by Wieden & Kennedy for Sharp Electronics to introduce its new Aquos liquid crystal display television. Sharp created a website that was the focal point of the IMC program and had the agency develop advertisements that would spark consumers' interest and drive them to the site. The agency created a mysterious TV commercial showing a strange scene of a man driving an orange car along a country road and suddenly losing control of the vehicle when he swerves to avoid an attractive woman. The car ends up in a swimming pool of a chateau, startling an elderly man who is relaxing in the water. The spot ends by showing the car submerging into the water as the moretosee.com Web address appears on the screen (Exhibit 1-10). Once on the site consumers could participate in trying to solve the mystery. The site contained video clips, character blogs relating various events, chat rooms in which site visitors could work together to solve the mystery, as well as various audio and video clues. The campaign was very effective in driving traffic to the website where consumers could learn more about the Aquos TV.[35]

Exhibit 1-10 Sharp's campaign for the new Aquos TV creatively integrated the use of advertising and the Internet

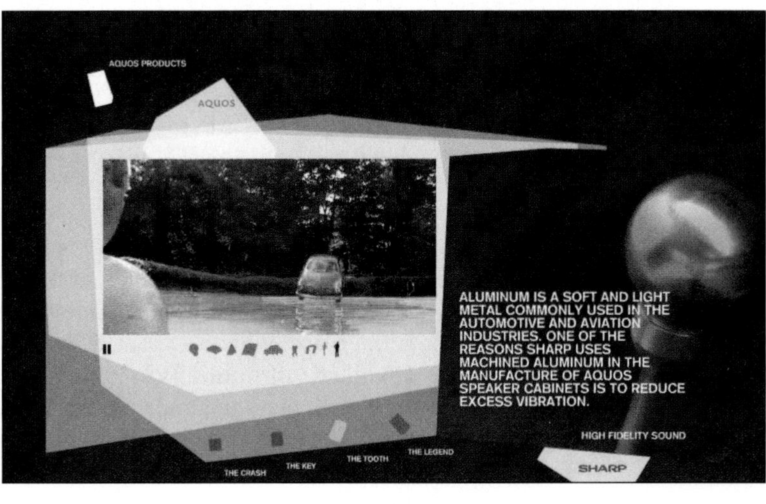

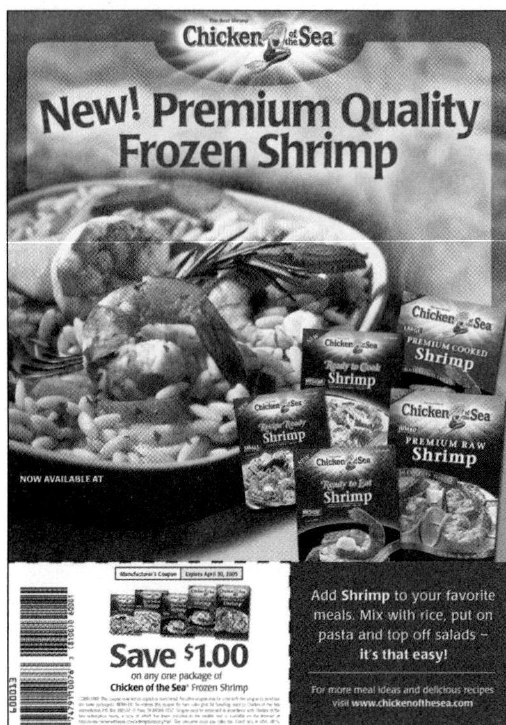

Exhibit 1-11 Coupons are a popular consumer-oriented sales promotion tool

Sales Promotion

The next variable in the promotional mix is **sales promotion,** which is generally defined as those marketing activities that provide extra value or incentives to the sales force, the distributors, or the ultimate consumer and can stimulate immediate sales. Sales promotion is generally broken into two major categories: consumer-oriented and trade-oriented activities.

Consumer-oriented sales promotion is targeted to the ultimate user of a product or service and includes couponing, sampling, premiums, rebates, contests, sweepstakes, and various point-of-purchase materials (Exhibit 1-11). These promotional tools encourage consumers to make an immediate purchase and thus can stimulate short-term sales. *Trade-oriented sales promotion* is targeted toward marketing intermediaries such as wholesalers, distributors, and retailers. Promotional and merchandising allowances, price deals, sales contests, and trade shows are some of the promotional tools used to encourage the trade to stock and promote a company's products.

Among many consumer packaged-goods companies, sales promotion is often 60 to 70 percent of the promotional budget.[36] In recent years many companies have shifted the emphasis of their promotional strategy from advertising to sales promotion. Reasons for the increased emphasis on sales promotion include declining brand loyalty and increased consumer sensitivity to promotional deals. Another major reason is that retailers have become larger and more powerful and are demanding more trade promotion support from companies.

Promotion and *sales promotion* are two terms that often create confusion in the advertising and marketing fields. As noted, promotion is an element of marketing by which firms communicate with their customers; it includes all the promotional-mix elements we have just discussed. However, many marketing and advertising practitioners use the term more narrowly to refer to sales promotion activities to either consumers or the trade (retailers, wholesalers). In this book, *promotion* is used in the broader sense to refer to the various marketing communications activities of an organization.

Publicity/Public Relations

Another important component of an organization's promotional mix is publicity/public relations.

Publicity

Publicity refers to nonpersonal communications regarding an organization, product, service, or idea not directly paid for or run under identified sponsorship. It usually comes in the form of a news story, editorial, or announcement about an organization and/or its products and services. Like advertising, publicity involves nonpersonal communication to a mass audience, but unlike advertising, publicity is not directly paid for by the company. The company or organization attempts to get the media to cover or run a favorable story on a product, service, cause, or event to affect awareness, knowledge, opinions, and/or behavior. Techniques used to gain publicity include news releases, press conferences, feature articles, photographs, films, and videotapes.

An advantage of publicity over other forms of promotion is its credibility. Consumers generally tend to be less skeptical toward favorable information about a product or service when it comes from a source they perceive as unbiased. For example, the success (or failure) of a new movie is often determined by the reviews it receives from film critics, who are viewed by many moviegoers as objective evaluators. Another advantage of publicity is its low cost, since the company is not paying for time or space in a mass medium such as TV, radio, or newspapers. While an organization may incur some costs in developing publicity items or maintaining a staff to do so, these expenses will be far less than those for the other promotional programs.

Publicity is not always under the control of an organization and is sometimes unfavorable. Negative stories about a company and/or its products can be very damaging. For example, recently the packaged food industry has received a great deal of negative publicity regarding the nutritional value of their products as well as their marketing practices, particularly to young people. Companies such as Kraft Foods' General Mills, PepsiCo, and others have been the target of criticism by consumer activists who have argued that these companies contribute to the obesity problem in the United States by advertising unhealthy foods to children.[37] McDonald's also had to deal with the negative publicity that was generated by the success of the documentary film *Super Size Me,* in which filmmaker Morgan Spurlock chronicled his decline in health while eating all of his meals at McDonald's for 30 days in a row.[38]

Exhibit 1-12 Advertising is often used to enhance a company's corporate image

Public Relations It is important to recognize the distinction between publicity and public relations. When an organization systematically plans and distributes information in an attempt to control and manage its image and the nature of the publicity it receives, it is really engaging in a function known as public relations. **Public relations** is defined as "the management function which evaluates public attitudes, identifies the policies and procedures of an individual or organization with the public interest, and executes a program of action to earn public understanding and acceptance."[39] Public relations generally has a broader objective than publicity, as its purpose is to establish and maintain a positive image of the company among its various publics.

Public relations uses publicity and a variety of other tools—including special publications, participation in community activities, fund-raising, sponsorship of special events, and various public affairs activities—to enhance an organization's image. Organizations also use advertising as a public relations tool. For example, the Toyota ad shown in Exhibit 1-12 discusses how the company builds vehicles in the United States, which creates more than 200,000 jobs.

Traditionally, publicity and public relations have been considered more supportive than primary to the marketing and promotional process. However, many firms have begun making PR an integral part of their predetermined marketing and promotional strategies. PR firms are increasingly touting public relations as a communications tool that can take over many of the functions of conventional advertising and marketing.[40]

Personal Selling

The final element of an organization's promotional mix is **personal selling,** a form of person-to-person communication in which a seller attempts to assist and/or persuade prospective buyers to purchase the company's product or service or to act on an idea. Unlike advertising, personal selling involves direct contact between buyer and seller, either face-to-face or through some form of telecommunications such as telephone sales. This interaction gives the marketer communication flexibility; the seller can see or hear the potential buyer's reactions and modify the message accordingly. The personal, individualized communication in personal selling allows the seller to tailor the message to the customer's specific needs or situation.

Personal selling also involves more immediate and precise feedback because the impact of the sales presentation can generally be assessed from the customer's reactions. If the feedback is unfavorable, the salesperson can modify the message. Personal selling efforts can also be targeted to specific markets and customer types that are the best prospects for the company's product or service.

IMC Involves Audience Contacts

The various promotional mix elements are the major tools that marketers use to communicate with current and/or prospective customers as well as other relevant audiences. However, many companies are taking an *audience contact* perspective in developing their IMC programs whereby they consider all of the potential ways of reaching their target audience and presenting the company or brand in a favorable manner. They recognize that there are a variety of ways customers may come into contact with a company or brand. These contacts can range from simply seeing or hearing an ad for a brand to actually having the opportunity to use or experience a brand at a company-sponsored event.

A key aspect of integrated marketing communications is that it encourages marketers to consider a variety of communication tools and how they can be used to deliver messages about their company or brands. Figure 1-5 shows the various ways by which consumers can come into contact with a company or brand. Marketers must determine how valuable each of these contact tools are for communicating with their target audience and how they can be combined to form an effective IMC program. This is generally done by starting with the target audience and determining which IMC tools will be most effective in reaching, informing, and persuading them and ultimately influencing their behavior. IMC Perspective 1-3 discusses how companies such as American Express are moving away from media advertising and using a variety of other contact points.

It is the responsibility of those involved in the marketing communications process to determine how the various contact tools will be used to reach the target audience and help achieve the company's marketing objectives. The IMC program is generally developed with specific goals and objectives in mind and is the end product of a detailed marketing and promotional planning process. We will now look at a model of the process that companies follow in developing and executing their IMC programs.

The IMC Planning Process

In developing an integrated marketing communications strategy, a company combines the various promotional-mix elements, balancing the strengths and weaknesses of each to produce an effective communications program. **Integrated marketing communications management** involves the process of planning, executing, evaluating, and controlling the use of the various promotional-mix elements to effectively communicate with target audiences. The marketer must consider which promotional tools to use and how to integrate them to achieve marketing and communication objectives.

Figure 1-5 IMC Audience Contact Tools

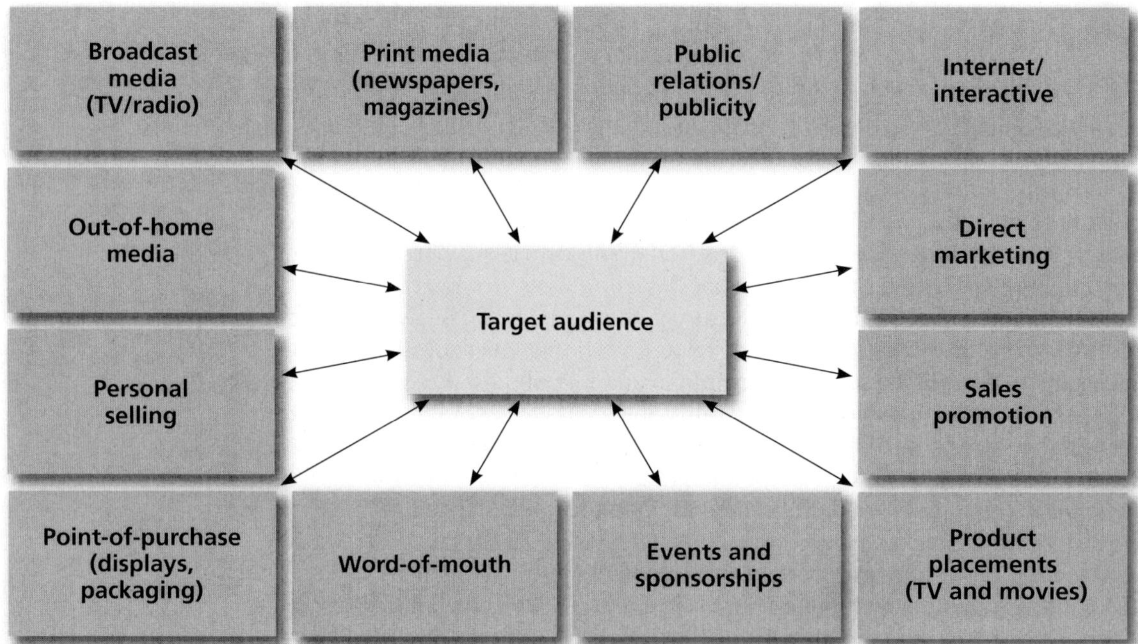

IMC PERSPECTIVE 1-3

American Express Moves Beyond TV to Connect with Consumers

A decade ago, American Express Co. spent 80 percent of its annual advertising and promotion budget on television advertising. However, by 2004, TV accounted for only about a third of its budget and print spending has remained flat over the past 10 years. So what is American Express doing with the estimated $673 million it spends to promote its credit cards each year? The financial services company is on the forefront of experimenting with an array of new ways to connect with consumers that include short films for the Internet, artistic exhibits, sponsorship of concerts and events, and promoting its brands on reality shows.

In March 2004, the company launched the first of two four-minute films featuring longtime company spokesman Jerry Seinfeld and an animated version of *Superman* exclusively on the American Express website. The humorous films were designed to depict the benefits of card membership by showing situations where Superman is powerless and the comedian comes to the rescue with an American Express card. Within a few weeks the first of *The Adventures of Seinfeld and Superman* "webisodes" had drawn more than 2 million viewers, and people returned to the website after the second online short was released two months later. To support the sequel launch and reach a wider audience for the films, the first short aired on NBC prior to the encore airing of the *Friends* finale in May.

American Express (AmEx) also extended the campaign by entering into a partnership with the TBS cable television network whereby the first webisode was aired in its entirety following the much anticipated premiere of the hit series *Sex and the City* on the network. The following week, TBS aired a sneak preview of the second webisode, which directed viewers to the American Express website where they could watch the film in its entirety as well as view the first film and behind-the-scenes clips and interviews. In addition to the films, the AmEx website also offered viewers an interactive experience whereby they could discover special features in Seinfeld's virtual apartment as well as learn more about the services provided to American Express cardholders.

American Express's shift away from television began in 1999, with the introduction of Blue, a new credit card that was targeted toward Gen Xers. The goal was to establish a technology position for the new card which offered a "smart-chip" feature as well as revolving credit. Research showed that television was not the best way to reach the card's tech-savvy, nomadic target market. Rather than launching the Blue campaign with a high-profile approach such as advertising during the Super Bowl, AmEx staged a concert in New York's Central Park. The "American Express Brings You Central Park in Blue" concert featured Sheryl Crow and Friends, who included Eric Clapton, Stevie Nicks, Chrissie Hynde, Keith Richards, and the Dixie Chicks. The event had national appeal and impact as consumers could experience the concert through the first-ever "trimulcast" on Fox TV, 60 radio stations, and the Internet at a special blueconcerts.com website.

American Express has continued to use nontraditional ways to promote the Blue card. In February 2004, the company transformed the Los Angeles House of Blues jazz club into the "House of Blue." Images of the see-through card were beamed onto the building's facade. The event featured performances by Elvis Costello, Stevie Wonder, and Counting Crows while waitresses decked out in blue shorts and blue wigs served azure cocktails. AmEx has also used more stealthy, lifestyle-driven methods to promote the card such as placing Blue-labeled water bottles at health clubs and printing Blue ads on millions of popcorn bags. AmEx's new model appears to be working as the five-year-old Blue card is the most successful new product launch in the company's history.

American Express has also taken advantage of the burgeoning interest in reality TV shows by becoming involved in the sponsorship of several programs including *The Restaurant* on NBC and *Blow Out* on Bravo. The company received plugs for its Open: Small Business Network brand on the reality shows. The company sponsored an online forum showcasing Jonathan Antin, the celebrity hairstylist who is the star of the Bravo reality series that was designed to help small business owners share their experiences and opinions. In another endeavor to reach consumers in a unique way, the company toured a museum-style exhibit that included images from its vintage print advertisements. The exhibit, which was displayed in a variety of public venues, featured photos of celebrity cardholders such as Tom Hanks, Woody Allen, and Sammy Davis Jr. that were taken by famed photographer Annie Leibovitz. To ensure traffic and buzz about the exhibit, AmEx alerted local hotel concierges, which helped generate long lines to view the photographs.

American Express chief marketing officer John Hayes has noted that he has not sworn off television altogether but rather is looking for better ways to reach consumers and become involved in things they value. In a speech to the sales force of the NBC television network, Hayes warned, "Your business model needs to adapt and to change. It used to be that we bought the time, shipped you the commercials, had lunch or a glass of wine together once in awhile; you took care of the quality of the programming and we made sure the check did not bounce. We all sat back, checked the ratings, watched our business grow . . . those days are woefully over."

Sources: Ann M. Mack, "Buddy Movies," *Mediaweek*, November 22, 2004, pp. 14–16; Suzanne Vranica, "For Big Marketers Like AmEx, TV Ads Lose Starring Role," *The Wall Street Journal*, May 17, 2004, pp. B1, 3.

Companies also must decide how to distribute the total marketing communications budget across the various promotional-mix elements. What percentage of the budget should be allocated to advertising, sales promotion, the Internet, sponsorships, and personal selling?

As with any business function, planning plays an important role in the development and implementation of an effective integrated marketing communications program. This process is guided by an **integrated marketing communications plan** that provides the framework for developing, implementing, and controlling the organization's IMC program. Those involved with the IMC program must decide on the role and function of the specific elements of the promotional mix, develop strategies for each element, determine how they will be integrated, plan for their implementation, and consider how to evaluate the results achieved and make any necessary adjustments. Marketing communications is but one part of, and must be integrated into, the overall marketing plan and program.

A model of the IMC planning process is shown in Figure 1-6. The remainder of this chapter presents a brief overview of the various steps involved in this process.

Review of the Marketing Plan

The first step in the IMC planning process is to review the marketing plan and objectives. Before developing a promotional plan, marketers must understand where the company (or the brand) has been, its current position in the market, where it intends to go, and how it plans to get there. Most of this information should be contained in the **marketing plan,** a written document that describes the overall marketing strategy and programs developed for an organization, a particular product line, or a brand. Marketing plans can take several forms but generally include five basic elements:

1. A detailed situation analysis that consists of an internal marketing audit and review and an external analysis of the market competition and environmental factors.
2. Specific marketing objectives that provide direction, a time frame for marketing activities, and a mechanism for measuring performance.
3. A marketing strategy and program that include selection of target market(s) and decisions and plans for the four elements of the marketing mix.
4. A program for implementing the marketing strategy, including determining specific tasks to be performed and responsibilities.
5. A process for monitoring and evaluating performance and providing feedback so that proper control can be maintained and any necessary changes can be made in the overall marketing strategy or tactics.

For most firms, the promotional plan is an integral part of the marketing strategy. Thus, the promotional planners must know the roles advertising and other promotional-mix elements will play in the overall marketing program. The promotional plan is developed similarly to the marketing plan and often uses its detailed information. Promotional planners focus on information in the marketing plan that is relevant to the promotional strategy.

Promotional Program Situation Analysis

After the overall marketing plan is reviewed, the next step in developing a promotional plan is to conduct the situation analysis. In the IMC program, the situation analysis focuses on the factors that influence or are relevant to the development of a promotional strategy. Like the overall marketing situation analysis, the promotional program situation analysis includes both an internal and an external analysis.

Internal Analysis The **internal analysis** assesses relevant areas involving the product/service offering and the firm itself. The capabilities of the firm and its ability to develop and implement a successful promotional program, the organization of the promotional department, and the successes and failures of past programs should be reviewed. The analysis should study the relative advantages and disadvantages of performing the promotional functions in-house as opposed to hiring an external agency (or agencies). For example, the internal analysis may indicate the firm is not capable of planning, implementing, and managing certain areas of the promotional program. If this is the case, it would be wise to look for assistance from an advertising agency or some other promotional facilitator. If the organization is already using an ad agency, the focus will be on the quality of the agency's work and the results achieved by past and/or current campaigns.

In this text we will examine the functions ad agencies perform for their clients, the agency selection process, compensation, and considerations in evaluating agency performance. We will also discuss the role and function of other promotional facilitators such as sales promotion firms, direct-marketing companies, public relations agencies, and marketing and media research firms.

Another aspect of the internal analysis is assessing the strengths and weaknesses of the firm or the brand from an image perspective. Often the image a firm brings to the market will have a significant impact on the way the firm can advertise and promote itself as well as its various products and services. Companies or brands that are new to the market or those for whom perceptions are negative may have to concentrate on their images, not just the benefits or attributes of the specific product or service. On the other hand, a firm with a strong reputation and/or image is already a step ahead when it comes to marketing its products or services. For example, Starbucks has an outstanding image that is a result of the quality of its coffee and other products as well as its reputation as a socially responsible company. The company is recognized as a good citizen in its dealings with communities, employees, suppliers, and the environment. Starbucks recognizes that being recognized as a socially responsible company is an important part of its tremendous growth and success. The company publishes a Corporate Social Responsibility Annual Report each year that describes its social, environmental, and economic impacts on the communities in which it does business (Exhibit 1-13).

The internal analysis also assesses the relative strengths and weaknesses of the product or service; its advantages and disadvantages; any unique selling points or benefits it may have; its packaging, price, and design; and so on. This information is particularly important to the creative personnel who must develop the advertising message for the brand.

Figure 1-7 is a checklist of some of the areas one might consider when performing analyses for promotional planning purposes. Addressing internal areas may require information the company does not have available internally and must gather as part of the external analysis.

External Analysis The **external analysis** focuses on factors such as characteristics of the firm's customers, market segments, positioning strategies, and competitors, as shown in Figure 1-7. An important part of the external analysis is a detailed consideration of customers' characteristics and buying patterns, their decision processes, and factors influencing their purchase decisions. Attention must also be given to consumers' perceptions and attitudes, lifestyles, and criteria for making purchase decisions. Often, marketing research studies are needed to answer some of these questions.

Exhibit 1-13 Starbucks has a very strong brand image and reputation as a socially responsible company

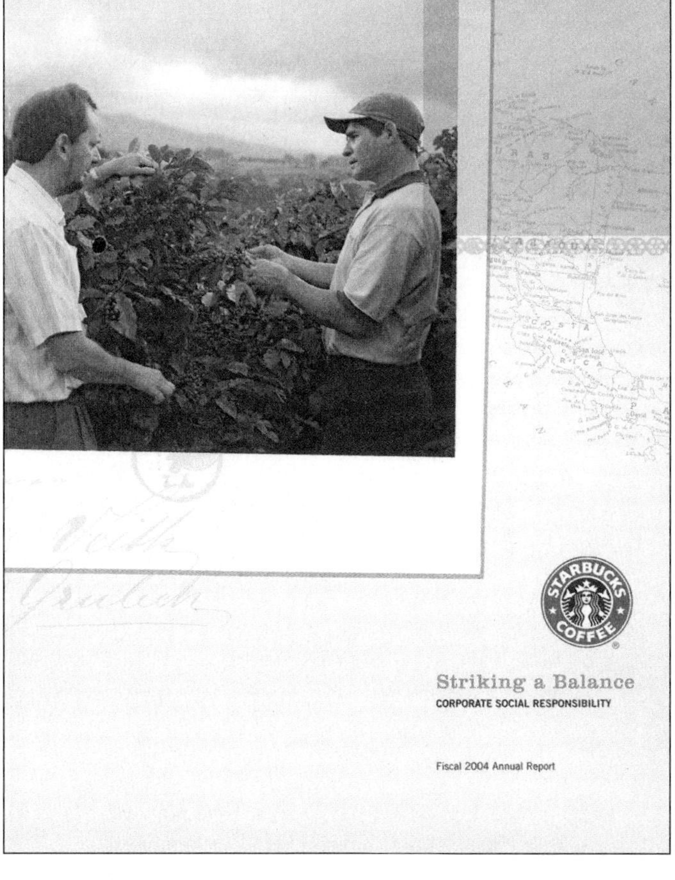

Figure 1-6 An Integrated Marketing Communications Planning Model

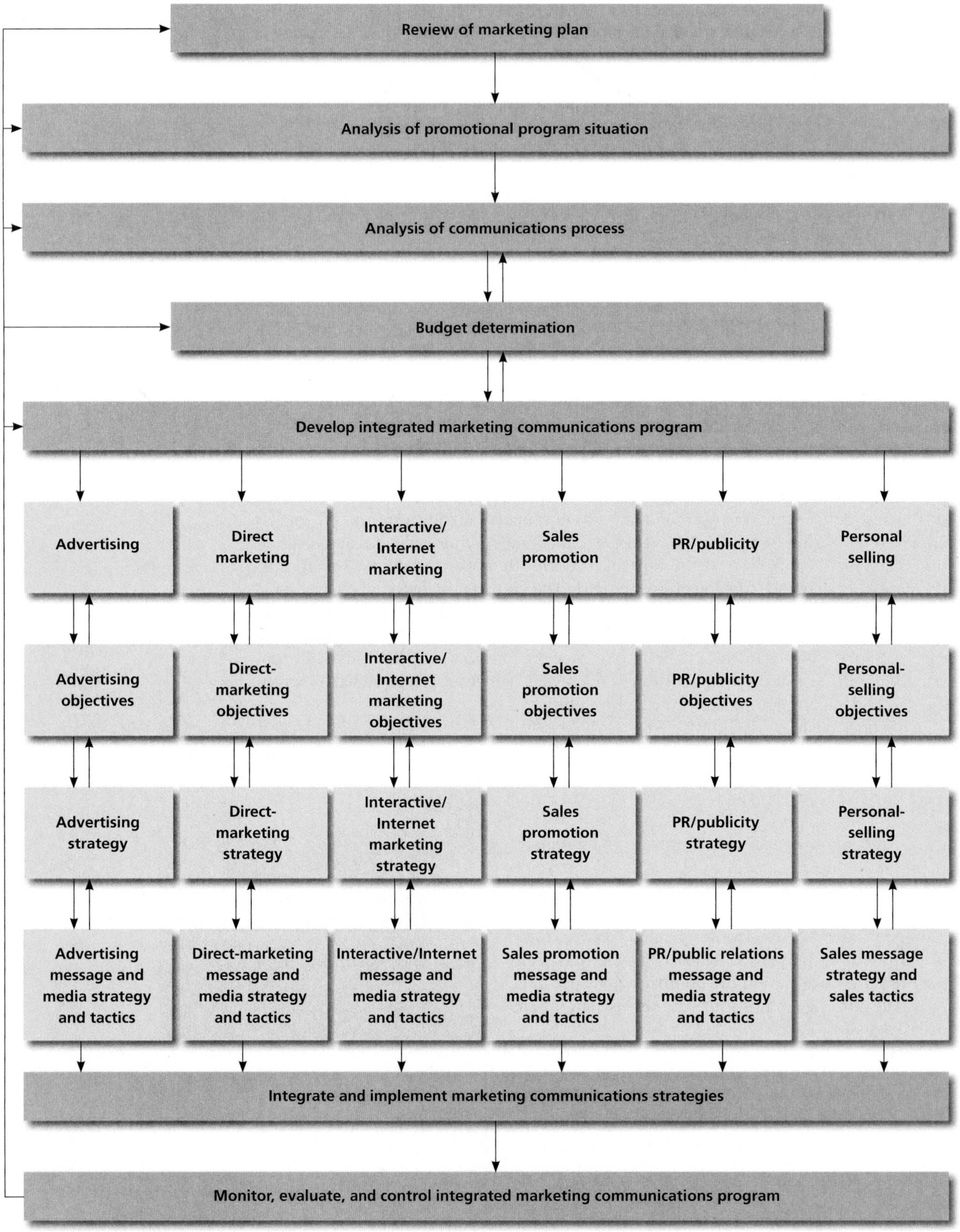

Review of marketing plan

Analysis of promotional program situation

Analysis of communications process

Budget determination

Develop integrated marketing communications program

Advertising	Direct marketing	Interactive/Internet marketing	Sales promotion	PR/publicity	Personal selling
Advertising objectives	Direct-marketing objectives	Interactive/Internet marketing objectives	Sales promotion objectives	PR/publicity objectives	Personal-selling objectives
Advertising strategy	Direct-marketing strategy	Interactive/Internet marketing strategy	Sales promotion strategy	PR/publicity strategy	Personal-selling strategy
Advertising message and media strategy and tactics	Direct-marketing message and media strategy and tactics	Interactive/Internet message and media strategy and tactics	Sales promotion message and media strategy and tactics	PR/public relations message and media strategy and tactics	Sales message strategy and sales tactics

Integrate and implement marketing communications strategies

Monitor, evaluate, and control integrated marketing communications program

Review of Marketing Plan
Examine overall marketing plan and objectives
Role of advertising and promotion
Competitive analysis
Assess environmental influences

Analysis of Promotional Program Situation

Internal analysis
- Promotional department organization
- Firm's ability to implement promotional program
- Agency evaluation and selection
- Review of previous program results

External analysis
- Consumer behavior analysis
- Market segmentation and target marketing
- Market positioning

Analysis of Communications Process
Analyze receiver's response processes
Analyze source, message, channel factors
Establish communications goals and objectives

Budget Determination
Set tentative marketing communications budget
Allocate tentative budget

Develop Integrated Marketing Communications Program

Advertising
- Set advertising objectives
- Determine advertising budget
- Develop advertising message
- Develop advertising media strategy

Direct marketing
- Set direct-marketing objectives
- Determine direct-marketing budget
- Develop direct-marketing message
- Develop direct-marketing media strategy

Interactive/Internet marketing
- Set interactive/Internet marketing objectives
- Determine interactive/Internet marketing budget
- Develop interactive/Internet message
- Develop interactive/Internet media strategy

Sales promotion
- Set sales promotion objectives
- Determine sales promotion budget
- Determine sales promotion tools and develop messages
- Develop sales promotion media strategy

Public relations/publicity
- Set PR/publicity objectives
- Determine PR/publicity budget
- Develop PR/publicity messages
- Develop PR/publicity media strategy

Personal selling
- Set personal-selling and sales objectives
- Determine personal-selling/sales budget
- Develop sales message
- Develop selling roles and responsibilities

Integrate and Implement Marketing Communications Strategies
Integrate promotional-mix strategies
Create and produce ads
Purchase media time and space
Design and implement direct-marketing programs
Design and distribute sales promotion materials
Design and implement public relations/publicity programs
Design and implement interactive/Internet marketing programs

Monitor, Evaluate, and Control Integrated Marketing Communications Program
Evaluate promotional program results/effectiveness
Take measures to control and adjust promotional strategies

Figure 1-7 Areas Covered in the Situation Analysis

Internal Factors	External Factors
Assessment of Firm's Promotional Organization and Capabilities	***Customer Analysis***
Organization of promotional department	Who buys our product or service?
Capability of firm to develop and execute promotional programs	Who makes the decision to buy the product?
Determination of role and function of ad agency and other promotional facilitators	Who influences the decision to buy the product?
Review of Firm's Previous Promotional Programs and Results	How is the purchase decision made? Who assumes what role?
Review previous promotional objectives	What does the customer buy? What needs must be satisfied?
Review previous promotional budgets and allocations	Why do customers buy a particular brand?
Review previous promotional-mix strategies and programs	Where do they go or look to buy the product or service?
Review results of previous promotional programs	When do they buy? Any seasonality factors?
Assessment of Firm or Brand Image and Implications for Promotion	What are customers' attitudes toward our product or service?
Assessment of Relative Strengths and Weaknesses of Product or Service	What social factors might influence the purchase decision?
What are the strengths and weaknesses of product or service?	Do the customers' lifestyles influence their decisions?
What are its key benefits?	How is our product or service perceived by customers?
Does it have any unique selling points?	How do demographic factors influence the purchase decision?
Assessment of packaging, labeling, and brand image	***Competitive Analysis***
How does our product or service compare with competition?	Who are our direct and indirect competitors?
	What key benefits and positioning are used by our competitors?
	What is our position relative to the competition?
	How big are competitors' ad budgets?
	What message and media strategies are competitors using?
	Environmental Analysis
	Are there any current trends or developments that might affect the promotional program?

A key element of the external analysis is an assessment of the market. The attractiveness of various market segments must be evaluated and the segments to target must be identified. Once the target markets are chosen, the emphasis will be on determining how the product should be positioned. What image or place should it have in consumers' minds?

This part of the promotional program situation analysis also includes an in-depth examination of both direct and indirect competitors. While competitors were analyzed in the overall marketing situation analysis, even more attention is devoted to promotional aspects at this phase. Focus is on the firm's primary competitors: their specific strengths and weaknesses; their segmentation, targeting, and positioning strategies; and the promotional strategies they employ. The size and allocation of their promotional budgets, their media strategies, and the messages they are sending to the marketplace should all be considered.

The external phase also includes an analysis of the marketing environment and current trends or developments that might affect the promotional program. For example, food and beverage marketers have had to respond to the overall trend toward greater nutritional awareness and an increased interest in low-carb products that has resulted from the popularity of the carbohydrate restricting diets such as Atkins and South Beach.[41] Some companies responded to the trend by introducing low-carb products while others touted the fact that their existing brands were already low in carbohydrates (Exhibit 1-14). Many food companies have also addressed the trend by providing more nutritional information for their products on their websites.

Analysis of the Communications Process

This stage of the promotional planning process examines how the company can effectively communicate with consumers in its target markets. The promotional planner must think about the process consumers will go through in responding to marketing communications. The response process for products or services for which consumer decision making is characterized by a high level of interest is often different from that for low-involvement or routine purchase decisions. These differences will influence the promotional strategy.

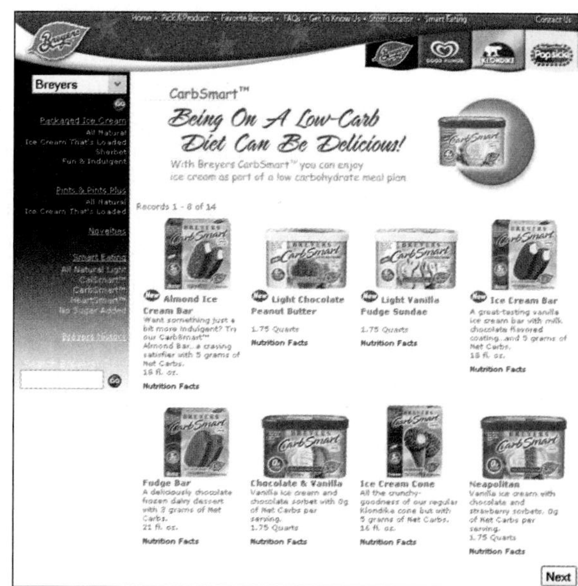

Exhibit 1-14 Breyers promotes its low-carb ice cream products

Communication decisions regarding the use of various source, message, and channel factors must also be considered. The promotional planner should recognize the different effects various types of advertising messages might have on consumers and whether they are appropriate for the product or brand. Issues such as whether a celebrity spokesperson should be used and at what cost may also be studied. Preliminary discussion of media-mix options (print, TV, radio, newspaper, direct marketing, Internet) and their cost implications might also occur at this stage.

An important part of this stage of the promotional planning process is establishing communication goals and objectives. In this text, we stress the importance of distinguishing between communication and marketing objectives. **Marketing objectives** refer to what is to be accomplished by the overall marketing program. They are often stated in terms of sales, market share, or profitability.

Communication objectives refer to what the firm seeks to accomplish with its promotional program. They are often stated in terms of the nature of the message to be communicated or what specific communication effects are to be achieved. Communication objectives may include creating awareness or knowledge about a product and its attributes or benefits; creating an image; or developing favorable attitudes, preferences, or purchase intentions. Communication objectives should be the guiding force for development of the overall marketing communications strategy and of objectives for each promotional-mix area.

Budget Determination

After the communication objectives are determined, attention turns to the promotional budget. Two basic questions are asked at this point: What will the promotional program cost? How will the money be allocated? Ideally, the amount a firm needs to spend on promotion should be determined by what must be done to accomplish its communication objectives. In reality, promotional budgets are often determined using a more simplistic approach, such as how much money is available or a percentage of a company's or brand's sales revenue. At this stage, the budget is often tentative. It may not be finalized until specific promotional-mix strategies are developed.

Developing the Integrated Marketing Communications Program

Developing the IMC program is generally the most involved and detailed step of the promotional planning process. As discussed earlier, each promotional-mix element has certain advantages and limitations. At this stage of the planning process, decisions have to be made regarding the role and importance of each element and their coordination with one another. As Figure 1-4 shows, each promotional-mix element has its own set of objectives and a budget and strategy for meeting them. Decisions must be made and activities performed to implement the promotional programs. Procedures must be developed for evaluating performance and making any necessary changes.

For example, the advertising program will have its own set of objectives, usually involving the communication of some message or appeal to a target audience. A budget will be determined, providing the advertising manager and the agency with some idea of how much money is available for developing the ad campaign and purchasing media to disseminate the ad message.

Two important aspects of the advertising program are development of the message and the media strategy. Message development, often referred to as *creative strategy*, involves determining the basic appeal and message the advertiser wishes to convey to the target audience. This process, along with the ads that result, is to many students the most fascinating aspect of promotion. *Media strategy* involves determining which communication channels will be used to deliver the advertising message to the target audience. Decisions must be made regarding which types of media will be used (e.g., newspapers, magazines, radio, TV, outdoor, Internet) as well as specific media selections (e.g., a particular magazine or TV program). This task requires careful evaluation of the media options' advantages and limitations, costs, and ability to deliver the message effectively to the target market.

Once the message and media strategies have been determined, steps must be taken to implement them. Most large companies hire advertising agencies to plan and produce their messages and to evaluate and purchase the media that will carry their ads. However, most agencies work very closely with their clients as they develop the ads and select media, because it is the advertiser that ultimately approves (and pays for) the creative work and media plan.

A similar process takes place for the other elements of the IMC program as objectives are set, an overall strategy is developed, message and media strategies are determined, and steps are taken to implement them. While the marketer's advertising agencies may be used to perform some of the other IMC functions, they may also hire other communication specialists such as direct-marketing and interactive and/or sales promotion agencies, as well as public relations firms.

Monitoring, Evaluation, and Control

The final stage of the IMC planning process is monitoring, evaluating, and controlling the promotional program. It is important to determine how well the IMC program is meeting communications objectives and helping the firm accomplish its overall marketing goals and objectives. The IMC planner wants to know not only how well the promotional program is doing but also why. For example, problems with the advertising program may lie in the nature of the message or in a media plan that does not reach the target market effectively. The manager must know the reasons for the results in order to take the right steps to correct the program.

This final stage of the process is designed to provide managers with continual feedback concerning the effectiveness of the IMC program, which in turn can be used as input into the planning process. As Figure 1-6 shows, information on the results achieved by the IMC program is used in subsequent promotional planning and strategy development.

Perspective and Organization of This Text

Traditional approaches to teaching advertising, promotional strategy, or marketing communications courses have often treated the various elements of the promotional mix as separate functions. As a result, many people who work in advertising, sales promotion, direct marketing, interactive/Internet, or public relations tend to approach marketing communications problems from the perspective of their particular specialty. An advertising person may believe marketing communications objectives are best met through the use of media advertising; a promotional specialist argues for a sales promotion program to motivate consumer response; a public relations person advocates a PR campaign to tackle the problem. These orientations are not surprising, since each person has been trained to view marketing communications problems primarily from one perspective.

In the contemporary business world, however, individuals working in marketing, advertising, and other promotional areas are expected to understand and use a variety of marketing communications tools, not just the one in which they specialize. Ad agencies no longer confine their services to the advertising area. Many are involved in sales promotion, public relations, direct marketing, event sponsorship, Internet/interactive, and other marketing communications areas. Individuals working on the client or advertiser side of the business, such as brand, product, or promotional managers, are developing marketing programs that use a variety of marketing communications methods.

This text views advertising and promotion from an integrated marketing communications perspective. We will examine all the promotional-mix elements and their roles in an organization's integrated marketing communications efforts. Although media advertising may be the most visible part of the communications program, understanding its role in contemporary marketing requires attention to other promotional areas such as the Internet and interactive marketing, direct marketing, sales promotion, public relations, and personal selling. Not all the promotional-mix areas are under the direct control of the advertising or marketing communications manager. For example, personal selling is typically a specialized marketing function outside the control of the advertising or promotional department. Likewise, publicity/public relations is often assigned to a separate department. All these departments should, however, communicate to coordinate all the organization's marketing communications tools.

The purpose of this book is to provide you with a thorough understanding of the field of advertising and other elements of a firm's promotional mix and show how they are combined to form an integrated marketing communications program. To plan, develop, and implement an effective IMC program, those involved must understand marketing, consumer behavior, and the communications process. The first part of this book is designed to provide this foundation by examining the roles of advertising and other forms of promotion in the marketing process. We examine the process of market segmentation and positioning and consider their part in developing an IMC strategy. We also discuss how firms organize for IMC and make decisions regarding ad agencies and other firms that provide marketing and promotional services.

We then focus on consumer behavior considerations and analyze the communications process. We discuss various communications models of value to promotional planners in developing strategies and establishing goals and objectives for advertising and other forms of promotion. We also consider how firms determine and allocate their marketing communications budget.

After laying the foundation for the development of a promotional program, this text will follow the integrated marketing communications planning model presented in Figure 1-6. We examine each of the promotional-mix variables, beginning with advertising. Our detailed examination of advertising includes a discussion of creative strategy and the process of developing the advertising message, an overview of media strategy, and an evaluation of the various media (print, broadcast, and support media). The discussion then turns to the other areas of the promotional mix: direct marketing, interactive/Internet marketing, sales promotion, public relations/publicity, and personal selling. Our examination of the IMC planning process concludes with a discussion of how the program is monitored, evaluated, and controlled. Particular attention is given to measuring the effectiveness of advertising and other forms of promotion.

The final part of the text examines special topic areas and perspectives that have become increasingly important in contemporary marketing. We will examine the area of international advertising and promotion and the challenges companies face in developing IMC programs for global markets as well as various countries around the world. The text concludes with an examination of the environment in which integrated marketing communications operates, including the regulatory, social, and economic factors that influence, and in turn are influenced by, an organization's advertising and promotional program.

Summary

Advertising and other forms of promotion are an integral part of the marketing process in most organizations. Over the past decade, the amount of money spent on advertising, sales promotion, direct marketing, and other forms of marketing communication has increased tremendously, both in the United States and in foreign markets. To understand the role of advertising and promotion in a marketing program, one must understand the role and function of marketing in an organization. The basic task of marketing is to combine the four controllable elements, known as the marketing mix, into a comprehensive program that facilitates exchange with a target market. The elements of the marketing mix are the product or service, price, place (distribution), and promotion.

For many years, the promotional function in most companies was dominated by mass-media advertising. However, more and more companies are recognizing the importance of integrated marketing communications, coordinating the various marketing and promotional elements to achieve more efficient and effective communication programs. A number of factors underlie the move toward IMC by marketers as well as ad agencies and other promotional facilitators. Reasons for the growing importance of the integrated marketing communications perspective include a rapidly changing environment with respect to consumers, technology, and media. The IMC movement is also being driven by changes in the ways companies market their products and services. A shift in marketing dollars from advertising to sales promotion, the rapid growth and development of database marketing, and the fragmentation of media markets are among the key changes taking place.

Promotion is best viewed as the communication function of marketing. It is accomplished through a promotional mix that includes advertising, personal selling, publicity/public relations, sales promotion, direct marketing, and interactive/Internet marketing. The inherent advantages and disadvantages of each of these promotional-mix elements influence the roles they play in the overall marketing program. In developing the IMC program, the marketer must decide which tools to use and how to combine them to achieve the organization's marketing and communication objectives.

Promotional management involves coordinating the promotional-mix elements to develop an integrated program of effective marketing communication. The model of the IMC planning process in Figure 1-6 contains a number of steps: a review of the marketing plan; promotional program situation analysis; analysis of the communications process; budget determination; development of an integrated marketing communications program; integration and implementation of marketing communications strategies; and monitoring, evaluation, and control of the promotional program.

Key Terms

exchange, 7
marketing, 8
value, 8
relationship marketing, 8
mass customization, 8
customer relationship management, 8
marketing mix, 9
integrated marketing communications (IMC), 9
promotion, 15
promotional mix, 15
advertising, 17
direct marketing, 18
direct-response advertising, 20
interactive media, 20
sales promotion, 22
publicity, 22
public relations, 23
personal selling, 23
integrated marketing communications management, 24
integrated marketing communications plan, 26
marketing plan, 26
internal analysis, 27
external analysis, 27
marketing objectives, 31
communication objectives, 31

Discussion Questions

1. The opening vignette to the chapter discusses the success the Las Vegas Convention and Visitors Authority has enjoyed with the "Only in Vegas" campaign. Why do you think this campaign has been so successful? How long do you think the LVCVA will be able to continue using this campaign theme?

2. Discuss how integrated marketing communications differs from traditional advertising and promotion. What are some of the reasons more marketers are taking an IMC perspective to their advertising and promotional programs?

3. Compare the new definition of integrated marketing communications developed by Don Shultz with the original definition that was developed by the American Association of Advertising Agencies. How do they differ?

4. Discuss the role integrated marketing communications plays in relationship marketing. How might the mass customization of advertising and other forms of marketing communications be possible?

5. Discuss the changes which are leading to the fragmentation of media markets. How are marketers responding to media fragmentation?

6. Discuss the role integrated marketing commuincations plays in the branding building process. How are marketers changing the ways they go about building strong brands?

7. Discuss the role of the Internet in the integrated marketing communications program of a company. How can the Internet be used to execute the various elements of the promotional mix?

8. What is meant by primary versus selective demand advertising? Provide examples of each. Discuss when a marketer might focus on primary demand stimulation versus selective demand stimulation.

9. What is meant by customer contact points? Select a company or brand and discuss the various contact points which marketers can use to reach consumers of this product or service.

10. Why is it important for those who work in marketing to understand and appreciate all the various integrated marketing communication tools and how they can be used?

The Role of IMC in the Marketing Process

2

Chapter Objectives

1. To understand the marketing process and the role of advertising and promotion in an organization's integrated marketing program.
2. To know the various decision areas under each element of the marketing mix and how they influence and interact with advertising and promotional strategy.
3. To understand the concept of target marketing in an integrated marketing communications program.
4. To recognize the role of market segmentation and its use in an integrated marketing communications program.
5. To understand the use of positioning and repositioning strategies.

Major League Baseball and Marketing—A Great Team

PLAY DOWNTOWN
SAN DIEGO Padres
SATISFY YOUR FIVE SENSES
RANDY JONES
SMELL... THE FRESHLY CUT GRASS
TASTE... THE GRILLED HOT DOGS
HEAR... THE CRACK OF THE BAT
FEEL... THE EXCITEMENT
SEE... IT ALL

Baseball—the national pastime—is not only a major league sport; it's also major league when it comes to integrated marketing. While taking some hits to its image lately, the sport continues to remain attractive to fans (40.5 million tickets had been sold for the 2005 season by February 28, 2005) and to corporations lined up to get involved in various ways. Chevrolet is the "official vehicle of Major League Baseball"; Wheaties is the "official breakfast cereal." Home Depot has a deal, as do DHL delivery service, MasterCard, Ameriquest, Anheuser-Busch, Gillette, Nike, Pepsi, and numerous others.

Individual teams also have marketing partnerships. Consider the San Diego Padres as just one example. In 2004, the Padres moved into their brand new stadium, $450 million Petco Park, in downtown San Diego. To get their name on the stadium, the specialty retailer of premium pet food, supplies, and services signed a 22-year stadium sponsorship deal for an estimated $60 million dollars. Petco is elated with the deal, noting that the family atmosphere in the park is directly in line with their corporate objectives to see Petco and the San Diego community thrive. It is a winning combination for the Padres as well, as partnering with a nationally known family-products company does wonders for the team image.

Other companies think the same way, and although they do not have their name on the stadium, they are involved in a variety of other ways. For example, US Bank sponsors the Jr. Padres, where kids under the age of 13 get promotional items like T-shirts and beach towels with a membership, as well as a loyalty program that allows them to earn points toward other awards for attending the games. Numerous companies have signage inside the stadium including Toyota, Union 76, Sycuan Casino, and Cox Cable among others. Still more are involved with Padres' special promotions and/or events, which include promotional or premium gift days and event days. Gift days involve giving fans in attendance free gifts such as ball caps, jackets, and sports bags, whereas event days include camera nights, concerts, fireworks and action sports events, and so on. Local and/or national businesses such as Cox Communications, Coca Cola, and MasterCard pay the Padres to cosponsor the gift days by putting their names on the promotional items and being mentioned in the advertising. The event days (or nights) are planned well in advance, sometimes as early as at the end of the previous season. Both types of activities are supported throughout the season, and most home games have a promotion associated with them

Besides advertising and promotions, other IMC elements are employed throughout the season as well. Public relations activities constitute a major part of the communications effort according to Padres' Executive Vice President of Communication Jeff Overton. Whereas in the past, public relations activities were limited to game notes and media guides, they are now integrated throughout the communications effort, through a variety of means—all of which are designed to create goodwill and enhance the image of the ball club in the San Diego community. Community involvement and openness with the media by on-field talent is encouraged to create a special relationship between the fans and the players. The Padres, as well as Major League Baseball itself, recognize how vital public relations is to a team's success.

In addition to public relations, *The Friar Wire*—an e-mail newsletter—keeps fans up-to-date on Padres' happenings. The team's website (operated by MLB) also provides information regarding upcoming games, events, and baseball news for those living in the San Diego area, as well as "out-of-market" fans. And, of course, you can buy tickets there as well.

Padres en Espanol (Padres in Spanish) is part of the multicultural commitment to the Hispanic community living in San Diego, as well as Mexico (Petco Park is approximately 17 miles from Tijuana, Mexico). The *Padres en Espanol* section of the website is entirely in Spanish and provides the same information as the site in English. All printed team materials are bilingual, and all games are broadcast on TV and radio in Spanish. There is a Padres' store in Tijuana that sells tickets and Padres' merchandise. With an Hispanic population of 345,000 (27 percent of the population) in the City of San Diego alone, this segment offers very attractive market potential to the team.

Clearly, the San Diego Padres, as well as all other Major League Baseball teams, employ a variety of IMC elements to reach their target markets. When it comes to marketing, these teams and MLB are definitely in the major leagues.

Sources: Brian Steinberg and Suzanne Vranica, "Sticking with the National Pastime; Marketers Line Up to Bat for Major League Baseball Despite Steroid Controversy," *The Wall Street Journal,* March 30, 2005, p. B3; Barry Janoff, "MLB, Sponsors Map '05 Plans; Kmart, UD Score with Pistons," *Brandweek,* December 13, 2004, p. 12; Gideon Fidelzeid, *PRweek,* April 5, 2004, p. 8.

The Padres MLB example is just one example of how companies and organizations use marketing strategies that will be discussed in this chapter. These include the identification of market opportunities, market segmentation, target marketing and positioning, and marketing program development. Baseball marketers' recognition of the importance of a strong brand image coupled with a strong IMC program reflects the solid marketing orientation required to be successful in today's marketplace.

In this chapter, we take a closer look at how marketing strategies influence the role of promotion and how promotional decisions must be coordinated with other areas of the marketing mix. In turn, all elements of the marketing mix must be consistent in a strategic plan that results in an integrated marketing communications program. We use the model in Figure 2-1 as a framework for analyzing how promotion fits into an organization's marketing strategy and programs.

This model consists of four major components: the organization's marketing strategy and analysis, the target marketing process, the marketing planning program development (which includes the promotional mix), and the target market. As the model shows, the marketing process begins with the development of a marketing strategy and analysis in which the company decides the product or service areas and particular markets where it wants to compete. The company must then coordinate the various elements of the marketing mix into a cohesive marketing program that will reach the target market effectively. Note that a firm's promotion program is directed not only to the final buyer but also to the channel or "trade" members that distribute its products to the ultimate consumer. These channel members must be convinced there is a demand for the company's products so they will carry them and will aggressively merchandise and promote them to consumers. Promotions play an important role in the marketing program for building and maintaining demand not only among final consumers but among the trade as well.

As noted in Chapter 1, all elements of the marketing mix—price, product, distribution, and promotions—must be integrated to provide consistency and maximum communications impact. Development of a marketing plan is instrumental in achieving this goal.

As Figure 2-1 shows, development of a marketing program requires an in-depth analysis of the market. This analysis may make extensive use of marketing research as an input into the planning process. This input, in turn, provides the basis for the development of marketing strategies in regard to product, pricing, distribution, and promotion decisions. Each of these steps requires a detailed analysis, since this plan serves as the road map to follow in achieving marketing goals. Once the detailed market analysis has been completed and marketing objectives have been established, each element in the marketing mix must contribute to a comprehensive integrated marketing program. Of course, the promotional program element (the focus of this text) must be combined with all other program elements in such a way as to achieve maximum impact.

Figure 2-1 Marketing and Promotions Process Model

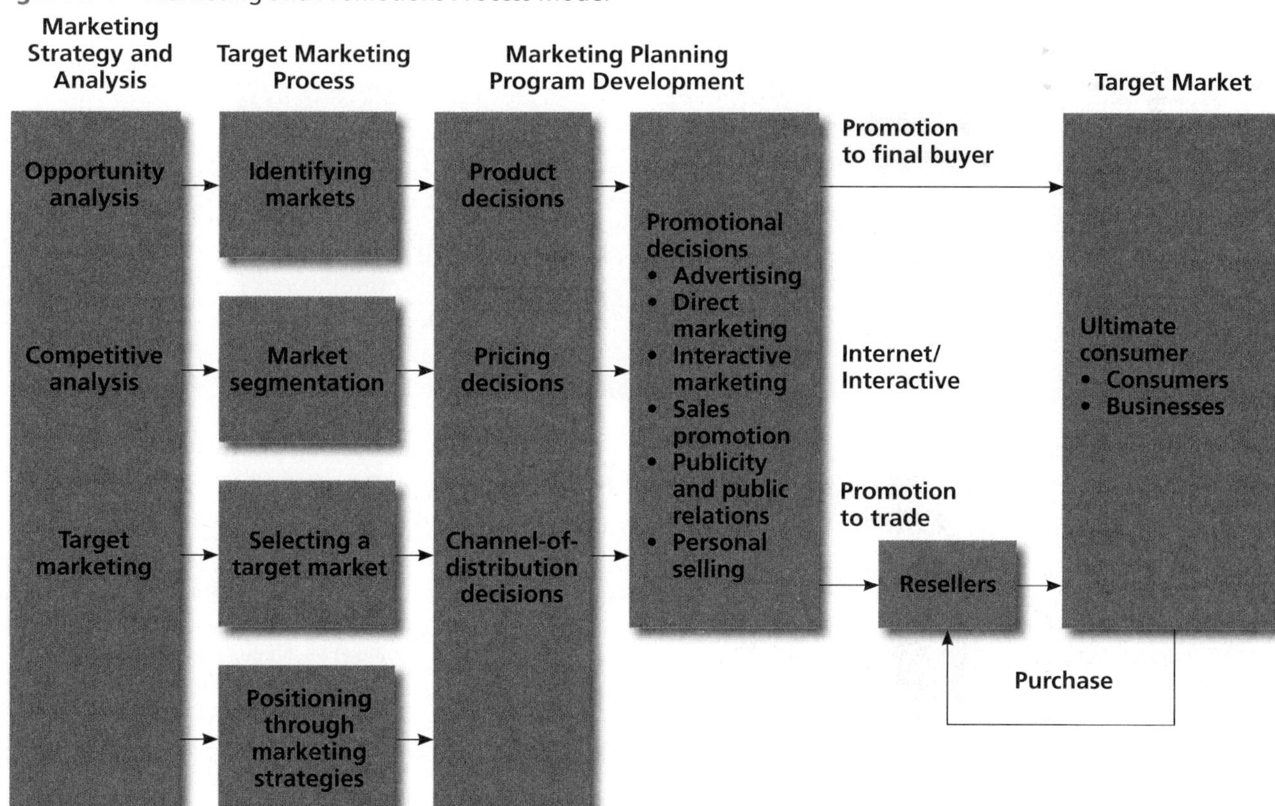

CAREER PROFILE

Jenifer Barsell

Director of Marketing for the San Diego Padres

Growing up in San Diego, the Padres were my hometown team. I can vividly remember attending my first Major League Baseball game at Jack Murphy Stadium (now Qualcomm Stadium) and watching Tony Gwynn, Garry Templeton, and Terry Kennedy take the field. I went off to college at California State University, Chico, to pursue an undergraduate degree in business and then an MBA, but I never stopped cheering for the Friars. More than 20 years after seeing my first big-league ballgame, I was hired as a 27-year-old intern in the Padres marketing department. I was quite a bit older than most of the interns, but I didn't let it bother me because I was determined to make sports marketing my career. Prior to this internship I had worked in the accounting field, but quickly determined it was not what I wanted to do for the rest of my life.

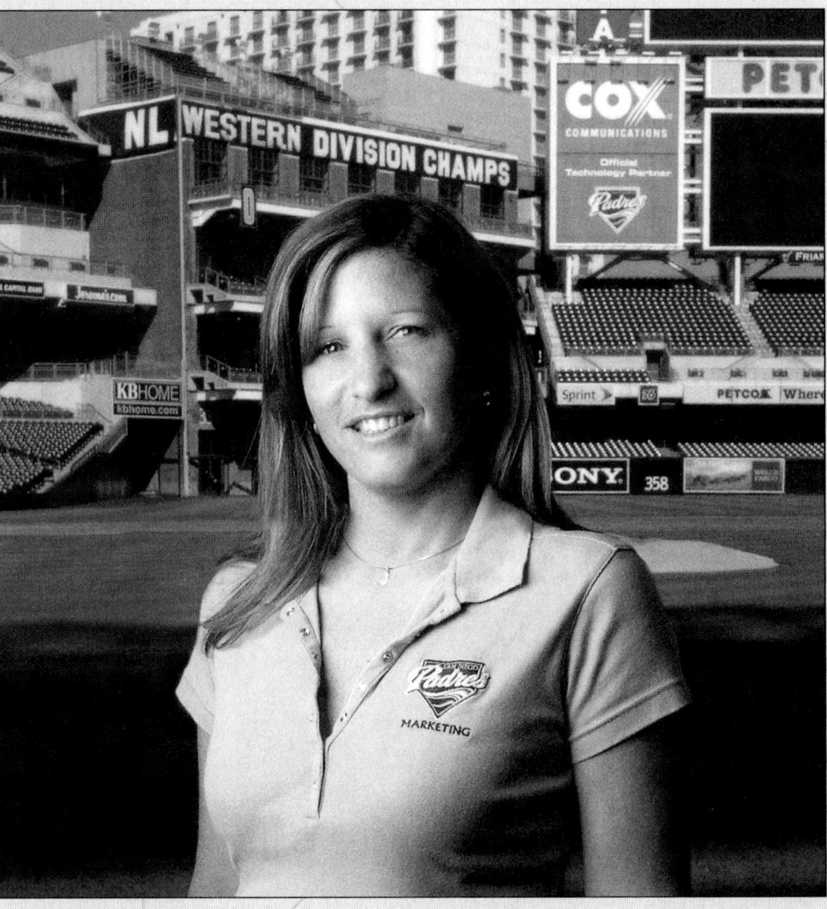

Before obtaining the internship with the Padres, I interned in the athletic department at San Diego State University and worked game days for the San Diego Chargers football team. I was also a member of the Super Bowl Host Committee where I assisted with the planning and marketing of many events surrounding Super Bowl XXXII, which was held in San Diego. I began working for the Padres in 1998; and what a thrilling time I had during that first season as the team made it all the way to the World Series where we lost to the New York Yankees. The Padres had been to the World Series only once previously, in 1984, and it was very exciting to be a part of a championship team.

While the club was busy winning the National League Championship that season, we were very busy off the field as well, campaigning for a proposition on the November ballot that would provide funding for a new downtown ballpark for San Diego and the Padres. It was a busy year to say the least, but that season taught me many lessons I still carry with me today. First, never limit your thinking with thoughts like "that would be great, but it just isn't possible." Anything is possible. You just have to find a creative way to get there.

After the 1998 season, I was given the opportunity I had been waiting for. I was hired as the new advertising manager for the Padres. My responsibilities included managing our advertising agency in areas such as creative and media buying. Prior to the 2000 season, I was promoted to director of advertising and market research. Making the jump from intern to director in just two years is something that I am extremely proud of achieving. I am now the director of marketing for the Padres and am responsible for overseeing its overall branding, advertising, media buying, Latino Marketing, ballpark graphics, fan loyalty, publications, website, market research, and kids club. Integrated marketing is very important to Major League Baseball teams, such as the Padres, as we use a variety of communication tools to attract fans, build relationships with them, and work with the community.

A number of things have happened during my time with the Padres that I am proud to be a part of, including the rebranding of the club prior to the 2004 season, which included the unveiling of new team logos and uniforms. I was also heavily involved with the opening of San Diego's beautiful new downtown ballpark, PETCO Park, which drew over 3 million fans during its first season. It has been, and continues to be, a great ride that I enjoy every day when I arrive at the ballpark. I knew that getting into sports marketing was going to be difficult and that I would have to make sacrifices. However, I am doing exactly what I want to do. As a fan and a member of the Padres family, I am excited to be here. And it will be even better when the Padres make their third trip to the World Series and finally win it all!

> "Anything is possible. You just have to find a creative way to get there."

Marketing Strategy and Analysis

Any organization that wants to exchange its products or services in the marketplace successfully should have a **strategic marketing plan** to guide the allocation of its resources. A strategic marketing plan usually evolves from an organization's overall corporate strategy and serves as a guide for specific marketing programs and policies. For example, a few years ago Abercrombie & Fitch decided to reposition the brand as part of the overall corporate effort to attract a younger audience. As we noted earlier, marketing strategy is based on a situation analysis—a detailed assessment of the current marketing conditions facing the company, its product lines, or its individual brands. From this situation analysis, a firm develops an understanding of the market and the various opportunities it offers, the competition, and the **market segments** or target markets the company wishes to pursue. We examine each step of the marketing strategy and *planning* in this chapter.

Opportunity Analysis

A careful analysis of the marketplace should lead to alternative market opportunities for existing product lines in current or new markets, new products for current markets, or new products for new markets. **Market opportunities** are areas where there are favorable demand trends, where the company believes customer needs and opportunities are not being satisfied, and where it can compete effectively. For example, the branded athletic footwear market continues to increase, with worldwide brand sales increasing by 21.5 percent in 2004, exceeding $8.3 billion in the United States alone.[1] Athletic-shoe companies such as Nike, Reebok, and others see the shoe market as an opportunity to broaden their customer base both domestically and internationally (Exhibit 2-1). To capitalize on this growth, companies spend millions of dollars on advertising alone. In the first 9 months of 2004, New Balance spent "only" $12.0 million, Reebok spent $35.2 million, Adidas $70.8 million, and Nike spent over $192 million to reach this market.[2,3] Changes in lifestyles have seen changes in the market for trail, running, basketball, and "lifestyle" shoes such as slip-ons .

A company usually identifies market opportunities by carefully examining the marketplace and noting demand trends and competition in various market segments. A market can rarely be viewed as one large homogeneous group of customers; rather, it consists of many heterogeneous groups, or segments. In recent years, many companies have recognized the importance of tailoring their marketing to meet the needs and demand trends of different market segments.

For example, different market segments in the personal computer (PC) industry include the home, education, science, and business markets. These segments can be even further divided. The business market consists of both small companies and large corporations; the education market can range from elementary schools to colleges and universities. A company that is marketing its products in the auto industry must decide in which particular market segment or segments it wishes to compete. This decision depends on the amount and nature of competition the brand will face in a particular market. For example, a number of companies that have been successful in the luxury-car segment have now introduced SUVs. Lincoln, Cadillac, Lexus, BMW, Mercedes, and Porsche now offer models in this line. Honda and Toyota are now competing in the hybrid car market, while GM plans to introduce four new models in 2006 in an attempt to compete in various niche markets.[4] A competitive analysis is an important part of marketing strategy development and warrants further consideration.

Exhibit 2-1 The market for athletic shoes continues to grow

Exhibit 2-2 Pepsi's Sparkling Aquafina is just one of many new beverages to hit the market

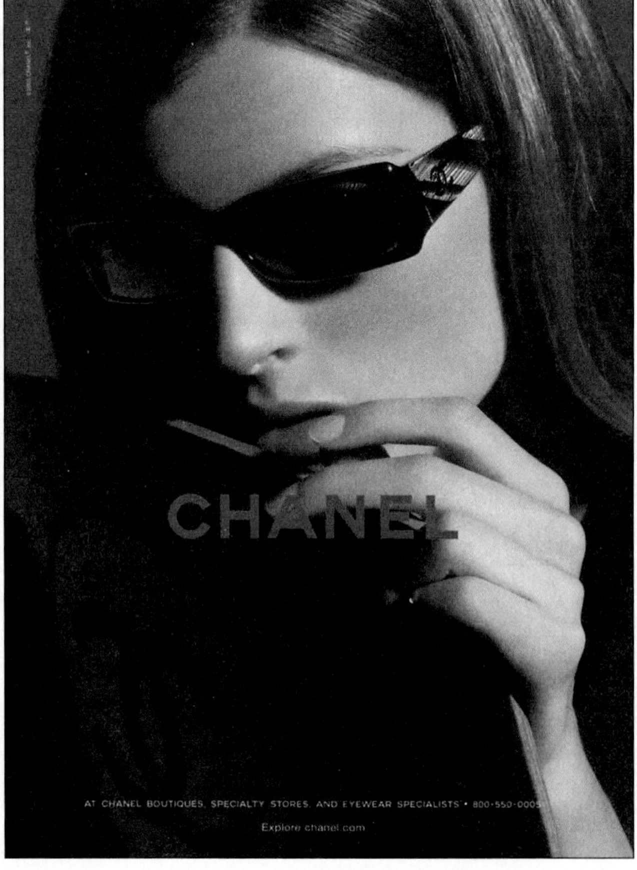

Exhibit 2-3 Chanel is just one of many companies competing in the luxury goods market

Competitive Analysis

In developing the firm's marketing strategies and plans for its products and services, the manager must carefully analyze the competition to be faced in the marketplace. This may range from direct brand competition (which can also include its own brands) to more indirect forms of competition, such as product substitutes. For example, as a result of shrinking cola sales, both Coke and Pepsi planned to launch more than two dozen new products in 2005.[5] Besides competing head to head in the soda market with products like Coke, Diet Coke, Diet Coke with Lemon, and more, versus Pepsi, Diet Pepsi, Pepsi Twist, Pepsi Blue, and Pepsi Vanilla, the companies face competition from other drinks including bottled water, juices, and teas (Exhibit 2-2).

At a more general level, marketers must recognize they are competing for the consumer's discretionary income, so they must understand the various ways potential customers choose to spend their money. For example, recently the U.S. market has seen significant growth in the high-end luxury market, with more consumers spending more of their money on luxury goods than ever before.[6] High-end products from Coach, Tiffany's, and Ralph Lauren are all benefiting from this change in consumer spending habits. Interestingly, it is not just the wealthy who are purchasing these very expensive products, but the middle class is doing so as well. Leading marketers apply labels such as the "massification of luxury," "luxflation," or the "new luxury" segments (Exhibit 2-3).[7]

An important aspect of marketing strategy development is the search for a **competitive advantage,** something special a firm does or has that gives it an edge over competitors. Ways to achieve a competitive advantage include having quality products that command a premium price, providing superior customer service, having the lowest production costs and lower prices, or dominating channels of distribution. Competitive advantage can also be achieved through advertising that creates and maintains product differentiation and brand equity, an example of which was the long-running advertising campaign for Michelin tires, which stressed security as well as performance. The strong brand images of Colgate toothpaste, Campbell's soup, Nike shoes, Sony, and McDonald's give them a competitive advantage in their respective markets.

Exhibit 2-4 Capital One has increased its efforts to enhance its brand image

Recently, there has been concern that some marketers have not been spending enough money on advertising to allow leading brands to sustain their competitive edge. Advertising proponents have been calling for companies to protect their brand equity and franchises by investing more money in advertising instead of costly trade promotions. Some companies, recognizing the important competitive advantage strong brands provide, have been increasing their investments in them. Hallmark and McDonald's are just two of many examples. Hallmark used tie-ins and product placements in the movie *Polar Express,* as well as in-theater advertising and consumer promotions, to go along with their traditional media advertising as part of its estimated $138 million advertising and promotional budget, in an attempt to enhance its brand equity. Capital One has also increased its marketing efforts (Exhibit 2-4).[8]

Competitors' marketing programs have a major impact on a firm's marketing strategy, so they must be analyzed and monitored. The reactions of competitors to a company's marketing and promotional strategy are also very important. Competitors may cut price, increase promotional spending, develop new brands, or attack one another through comparative advertising. One of the more intense competitive rivalries is the battle between Coca-Cola and Pepsi. A number of other intense competitive rivalries exist in the marketplace, including Hertz and Avis and Ford and GM among others.

A final aspect of competition is the growing number of foreign companies penetrating the U.S. market and taking business from domestic firms. In products ranging from beer to cars to electronics, imports are becoming an increasingly strong form of competition with which U.S. firms must contend. As we move to a more global economy, U.S. companies must not only defend their domestic markets but also learn how to compete effectively in the international marketplace, as well.

Target Market Selection

After evaluating the opportunities presented by various market segments, including a detailed competitive analysis, the company may select one, or more, as a target market. This target market becomes the focus of the firm's marketing effort, and goals and objectives are set according to where the company wants to be and what it hopes to accomplish in this market. As noted in Chapter 1, these goals and objectives are set in terms of specific performance variables such as sales, market share, and profitability. The selection of the target market (or markets) in which the firm will compete is an important part of its marketing strategy and has direct implications for its advertising and promotional efforts.

Recall from our discussion of the integrated marketing communications planning program that the situation analysis is conducted at the beginning of the promotional planning process. Specific objectives—both marketing and communications—are derived from the situation analysis, and the promotional-mix strategies are developed to achieve these objectives. Marketers rarely go after the entire market with one product, brand, or service offering. Rather, they pursue a number of different strategies, breaking the market into segments and targeting one or more of these segments for marketing and promotional efforts. This means different objectives may be established, different budgets may be used, and the promotional-mix strategies may vary, depending on the market approach used.

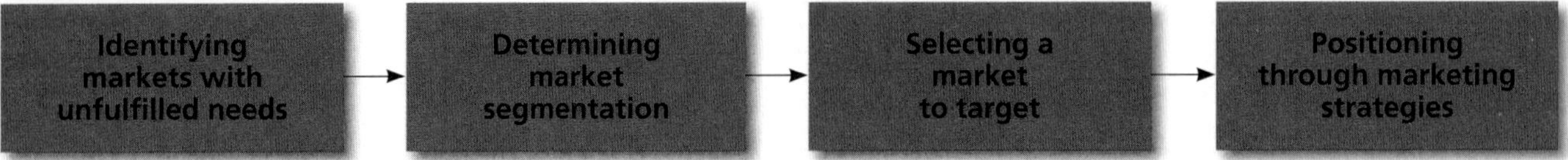

Figure 2-2 The Target Marketing Process

The Target Marketing Process

Because few, if any, products can satisfy the needs of all consumers, companies often develop different marketing strategies to satisfy different consumer needs. The process by which marketers do this (presented in Figure 2-2) is referred to as **target marketing** and involves four basic steps: identifying markets with unfulfilled needs, segmenting the market, targeting specific segments, and positioning one's product or service through marketing strategies.

Identifying Markets

When employing a target marketing strategy, the marketer identifies the specific needs of groups of people (or segments), selects one or more of these segments as a target, and develops marketing programs directed to each. This approach has found increased applicability in marketing for a number of reasons, including changes in the market (consumers are becoming much more diverse in their needs, attitudes, and lifestyles); increased use of segmentation by competitors; and the fact that more managers are trained in segmentation and realize the advantages associated with this strategy. Perhaps the best explanation, however, comes back to the basic premise that you must understand as much as possible about consumers to design marketing programs that meet their needs most effectively.

Target market identification isolates consumers with similar lifestyles, needs, and the like, and increases our knowledge of their specific requirements. The more marketers can establish this common ground with consumers, the more effective they will be in addressing these requirements in their communications programs and informing and/or persuading potential consumers that the product or service offering will meet their needs.

Let's use the beer industry as an example. Years ago, beer was just beer, with little differentiation, many local distributors, and few truly national brands. The industry began consolidating; many brands were assumed by the larger brewers or ceased to exist. As the number of competitors decreased, competition among the major brewers increased. To compete more effectively, brewers began to look at different tastes, lifestyles, and so on, of beer drinkers and used this information in their marketing strategies. This process resulted in the identification of many market segments, each of which corresponds to different customers' needs, lifestyles, and other characteristics.

As you can see in Figure 2-3, the beer market has become quite segmented, offering superpremiums, premiums, populars (low price), imports, lights (low calorie), and malts. Low-alcohol and nonalcoholic brands have also been introduced, as has draft beer in bottles and cans. And there are now imported lights, superpremium drafts, dry beers, ice beers, low-carbohydrate beers, and on and on. As you can see in Exhibit 2-5, to market to these various segments, Grupo Modelo pursues a strategy whereby it offers a variety of products from which consumers can choose, varying the marketing mix for each. Each appeals to a different set of needs. Taste is certainly one; others include image, cost, and the size of one's waistline. A variety of other reasons for purchasing are also operating, including the consumer's social class, lifestyle, and economic status.

Marketers competing in nearly all product and service categories are constantly searching for ways to segment

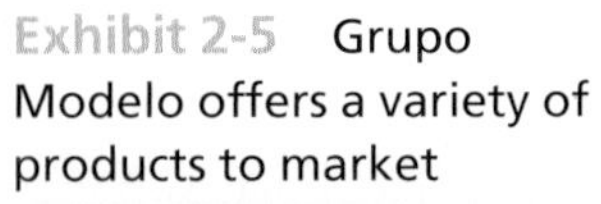
Exhibit 2-5 Grupo Modelo offers a variety of products to market

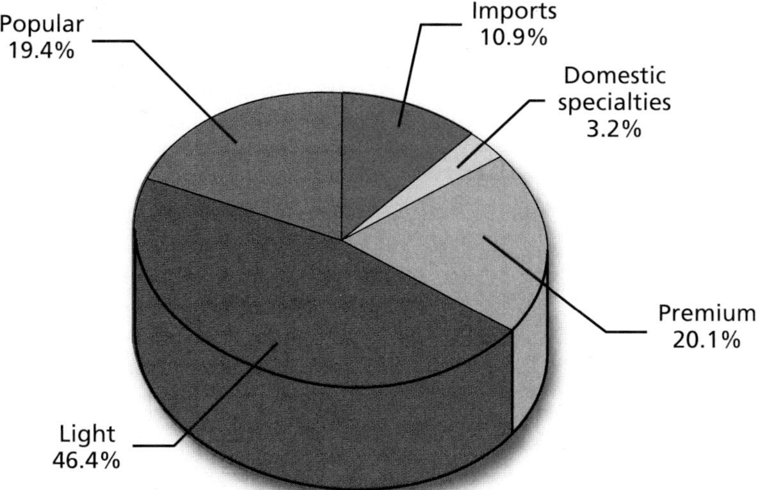

Figure 2-3 Market Breakdown by Product in the Beer Industry

their markets in an attempt to better satisfy customers' needs. Diversity Perspective 2-1 discusses the increasing emphasis being placed on marketing to Hispanic groups. The remainder of this section discusses ways to approach this task.

Market Segmentation

It is not possible to develop marketing strategies for every consumer. Rather, the marketer attempts to identify broad classes of buyers who have the same needs and will respond similarly to marketing actions. As noted by Eric N. Berkowitz, Roger A. Kerin, and William Rudelius, **market segmentation** is "dividing up a market into distinct groups that (1) have common needs and (2) will respond similarly to a marketing action."[9] The segmentation process involves five distinct steps:

1. Finding ways to group consumers according to their needs.
2. Finding ways to group the marketing actions—usually the products offered—available to the organization.
3. Developing a market-product grid to relate the market segments to the firm's products or actions.
4. Selecting the target segments toward which the firm directs its marketing actions.
5. Taking marketing actions to reach target segments.

The more marketers segment the market, the more precise is their understanding of it. But the more the market becomes divided, the fewer consumers there are in each segment. Thus, a key decision is, How far should one go in the segmentation process? Where does the process stop? As you can see by the strategy taken in the beer industry, it can go far!

In planning the promotional effort, managers consider whether the target segment is substantial enough to support individualized strategies. More specifically, they consider whether this group is accessible. Can it be reached with a communications program? For example, you will see in Chapter 10 that in some instances there are no media that can efficiently be used to reach some targeted groups. Or the promotions manager may identify a number of segments but be unable to develop the required programs to reach them. The firm may have insufficient funds to develop the required advertising campaign, inadequate sales staff to cover all areas, or other promotional deficiencies. After determining that a segmentation strategy is in order, the marketer must establish the basis on which it will address the market. The following section discusses some of the bases for segmenting markets and demonstrates advertising and promotions applications.

DIVERSITY PERSPECTIVE 2-1

Targeting to Hispanics—A Not-so-Minor Segment

Since 1991, the U.S. Hispanic market has grown 85 percent to more than 41.3 million people, compared to only an 18 percent growth in the rest of the population. The buying power of this market has tripled over the past 15 years as well, reaching $686 billion (the rest of the population has grown by less than one half as much), and projections are that it will grow an additional 45 percent to $992 billion by the end of the decade. As might be expected, marketers are raging a fierce battle for their business, now spending an estimated $4 billion a year in advertising to reach this segment.

Whereas in the past the Hispanic market received only minor attention by large companies, it now has become the focal point for a number of consumer marketing companies. These companies realize the sales potential existing in this segment, and the future growth that is expected, and are targeting Hispanics through a variety of means. Consider just a few examples:

- Procter & Gamble (P&G) has formed an ethnic marketing division responsible for managing 12 brands targeted to this segment. In an attempt to reach new mothers to sell them Pampers, television commercials in both English and Spanish were created. The diapers—along with other P&G products such as Crest and Tide—were included in sample packs distributed to mothers when discharged from the hospital. P&G also publishes a Martha Stewart type of magazine titled *Avanzando con Tu Familia* (Helping Your Family Move Ahead) targeting 1 million recent immigrants throughout the United States, distributes coupons, conducts grassroots marketing activities, engages in in-store sampling, and supports the Hispanic Scholarship Fund. Of the 12 brands, six are the number-one brands in their categories among Hispanics, far exceeding the success of Colgate-Palmolive and Unilever's Hispanic targeted efforts. P&G expects to triple its Hispanic advertising and promotional budget in 2005.

- Hershey Foods has also increased its efforts to reach the Hispanic segment by announcing a major deal with popular Mexican singer Thalia Sodi to represent a variety of Hershey's products in the U.S. general and Hispanic markets. Since she began to sing in both Spanish and English, Thalia has become a very popular crossover artist with nine albums on the market, and already has her own clothing lines at Kmart and Kohl's stores. Hershey's efforts may have been driven, in part, by the success experienced in this segment by its rival, M & M Mars.

- Perhaps inspired by the popularity of Budweiser's "Whassup" commercials, Coors Brewing Company developed their own Spanish version of the campaign targeted to young Latino males. Instead of "Whassup," the key slang word is *guey!* (pronounced "gway") that roughly translates to "dude." However, depending on the inflection, the word could take on a number of macho meanings including "Want a beer?," "Check out those girls," and/or "Wow." The advertising campaign was targeted to Hispanic males watching U.S. sports (like the NBA) on English-speaking TV as well as Spanish-speaking programs.

- Automobile companies including GM, Chrysler, and Nissan also target this segment. Toyota has its own Spanish-language website. In early 2005, the automobile company announced its first interactive game on the site, in an attempt to "enhance the brand and reach the younger Hispanic market all the while gaining 'hand raisers' information" according to Teri Hill, car advertising manager of Toyota. The game is considered a good way to expand the efforts beyond traditional TV and print media to reach this segment and to encourage visitors to explore the site. The game—*El Invicto* (The Undefeated)—involves soccer—a very popular Hispanic sport—and goal-keepers whose job is to protect a Toyota Corolla parked next to the net. If the ball hits the auto, the game immediately ends, with the instruction that "Remember that love for your Corolla comes first" reinforced. The campaign was supported using banner ads on other high-traffic Spanish-language portals and websites, including AOL Latino, MSN Latino, and Univision.

- Others targeting this segment include Citibank, Heineken, Dr. Scholls, and Johnson & Johnson. Coca Cola—after slashing its ad budget targeting Hispanics by 48 percent in 2003— reversed itself in 2005, promising to spend an additional $350 million to $400 million to reach this segment, considering it to be one of their three most important growth segments for North America.

The minority Hispanic market is now receiving major marketing efforts!

Sources: Sean Gregory, "Diapers for Fatima," *Time Inside Business,* February 2005, pp. B6–B11; Jean Halliday, "Toyota Launches Spanish-Language Digital Game," www.adage.com, April 6, 2005, pp. 1–2; Laurel Wentz, "Coors Launches Hispanic Version of a 'Whassup' Ad," www.adage.com, May 6, 2004, pp. 1–2; Laurel Wentz, "Hershey Foods to Sign Latin Singer Thalia," www.adage.com, April 8, 2004, pp. 1–2.

Bases for Segmentation As shown in Figure 2-4, several methods are available for segmenting markets. Marketers may use one of the segmentation variables or a combination of approaches. Consider the market segmentation strategy that might be employed to market snow skis. The consumer's lifestyle—active, fun-loving, enjoys outdoor sports—is certainly important. But so are other factors, such as age (participation in downhill skiing drops off significantly at about age 30) and income (have you seen the price of a lift ticket lately?), as well as marital status. Let us review the bases for segmentation and examine some promotional strategies employed in each.

Exhibit 2-6 Big Red markets to a specific geographic region

Geographic Segmentation In the **geographic segmentation** approach, markets are divided into different geographic units. These units may include nations, states, counties, or even neighborhoods. Consumers often have different buying habits depending on where they reside. For example, General Motors, among other car manufacturers, considers California a very different market from the rest of the United States and has developed specific marketing programs targeted to the consumers in that state. Other companies have developed programs targeted at specific regions. Exhibit 2-6 shows an ad for Big Red, just one of the regional soft-drink "cult" brands—along with Cheerwine (the Carolinas), Vernors (Michigan), and Moxie (New England)—that have found success by marketing in regional areas (in this case, Texas). One company—Olde Brooklyn Beverage Company—has even gone so far as to promote a brand based on a specific section of New York City, differentiating it from bigger brands by promoting the product's "Brooklyn Attitude."

Demographic Segmentation Dividing the market on the basis of demographic variables such as age, sex, family size, education, income, and social class is called **demographic segmentation.** Secret deodorant and the Lady Schick shaver are products that have met with a great deal of success by using the demographic variable of sex as a basis for segmentation. iVillage, a website targeting women, may be one of the most successful websites on the Internet (Exhibit 2-7).

Although market segmentation on the basis of demographics may seem obvious, companies discover that they need to focus more attention on a specific demographic group. For example, Ikea—noting that more than 70 percent of its shoppers are women—has enhanced its store environment to be more "women friendly," as has the Home Depot, which has recently introduced "Do It Herself" workshops (Exhibit 2-8).[10] Harley-Davidson recently announced strategies to broaden its appeal to younger riders and women who are now in their fifties or older or are from the baby-boomer generation, the cohort born between 1946 and 1964.[11] Some magazines like *Modern Maturity* are targeted to an estimated 76 million people who are in the "Be Generation." *Segunda Juventud* targets 50+ Hispanics (Exhibit 2-9 on page 49).

Exhibit 2-7 iVillage initiated a website targeted at women

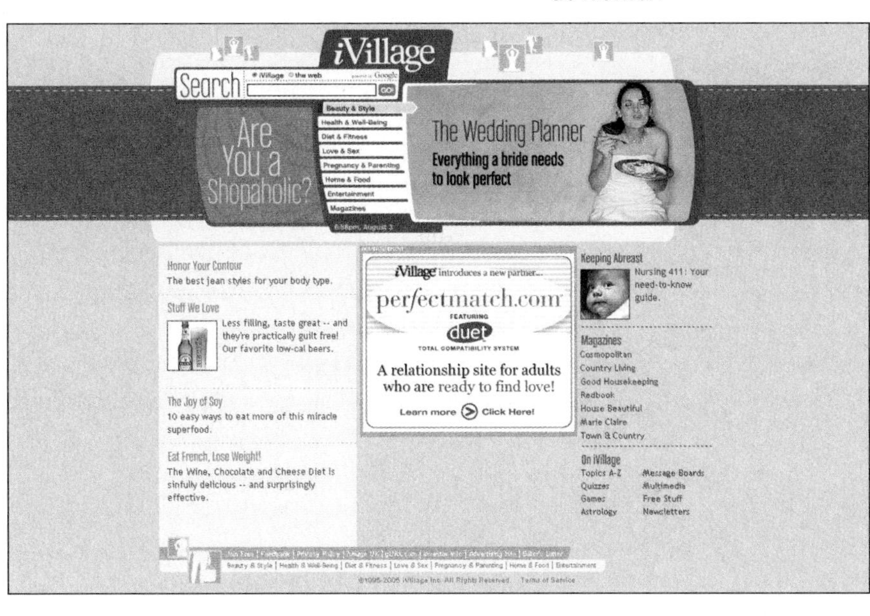

Other products that have successfully employed demographic segmentation include Oil of Olay (sex), Doan's Pills (age), Procter & Gamble (race), Mercedes-Benz and BMW cars (income), and Banquet prepackaged dinners (family size).

While demographics may still be the most common method of segmenting markets, it is important to recognize that other factors may be the underlying basis for homogeneity

Figure 2-4 Some Bases for Market Segmentation

Main Dimension	Segmentation Variables	Typical Breakdowns
Customer Characteristics		
Geographic	Region	Northeast; Midwest; South; West; etc.
	City size	Under 10,000; 10,000–24,999; 25,000–49,999; 50,000–99,999; 100,000–249,999; 250,000–499,999; 500,000–999,999; 1,000,000 or more
	Metropolitan area	Metropolitan statistical area (MSAs)
	Density	Urban; suburban; small town; rural
Demographic	Gender	Male; female
	Age	Under 6 yrs; 6–11 yrs; 12–17 yrs; 18–24 yrs; 25–34 yrs; 35–44 yrs; 45–54 yrs; 55–64 yrs; 65–74 yrs; 75 yrs plus
	Race	African-American; Asian; Hispanic; White/Caucasian; etc.
	Life stage	Infant; preschool; child; youth; collegiate; adult; senior
	Birth era	Baby boomer (1949–1964); Generation X (1965–1976); baby boomlet/Generation Y (1977–present)
	Household size	1; 2; 3–4; 5 or more
	Residence tenure	Own home; rent home
	Marital status	Never married; married; separated; divorced; widowed
Socioeconomic	Income	<$15,000; $15,000–$24,999; $25,000–$34,999; $35,000–$49,999; $50,000–$74,999; $75,000–$99,999; $100,000+
	Education	Some high school or less; high school graduate (or GED); etc.
	Occupation	Managerial and professional specialty; technical, sales, and administrative support; service; farming, forestry, and fishing
Psychographic	Personality	Gregarious; compulsive; introverted; aggressive; ambitious
	Values (VALS)	Actualizers; fulfilleds; achievers; experiencers; believers; strivers; makers; strugglers
	Lifestyle (Claritas)	Settled in; white picket fence; and 46 other household segments
Buying Situations		
Outlet type	In-store	Department; specialty; outlet; convenience; supermarket; superstore/mass merchandiser; catalog
	Direct	Mail order/catalog; door-to-door; direct response; Internet
Benefits sought	Product features	Situation specific; general
	Needs	Quality; service; price/value; financing; warranty; etc.
Usage	Usage rate	Light user; medium user; heavy user
	User status	Nonuser; ex-user; prospect; first-time user; regular user
Awareness and intentions	Product knowledge	Unaware; aware; informed; interested; intending to buy; purchaser; rejection
Behavior	Involvement	Minimum effort; comparison; special effort

and/or consumer behavior. The astute marketer will identify additional bases for segmenting and will recognize the limitations of demographics.

Psychographic Segmentation Dividing the market on the basis of personality and/or lifestyles is referred to as **psychographic segmentation.** While there is some disagreement as to whether personality is a useful basis for segmentation, lifestyle factors have been used effectively. Many consider lifestyle the most effective criterion for segmentation.

The determination of lifestyles is usually based on an analysis of the activities, interests, and opinions (AIOs) of consumers. These lifestyles are then correlated with the consumers' product, brand, and/or media usage. For many products and/or services, lifestyles may be the best discriminator between use and nonuse, accounting for differences in food, clothing, and car selections, among numerous other consumer behaviors.[12]

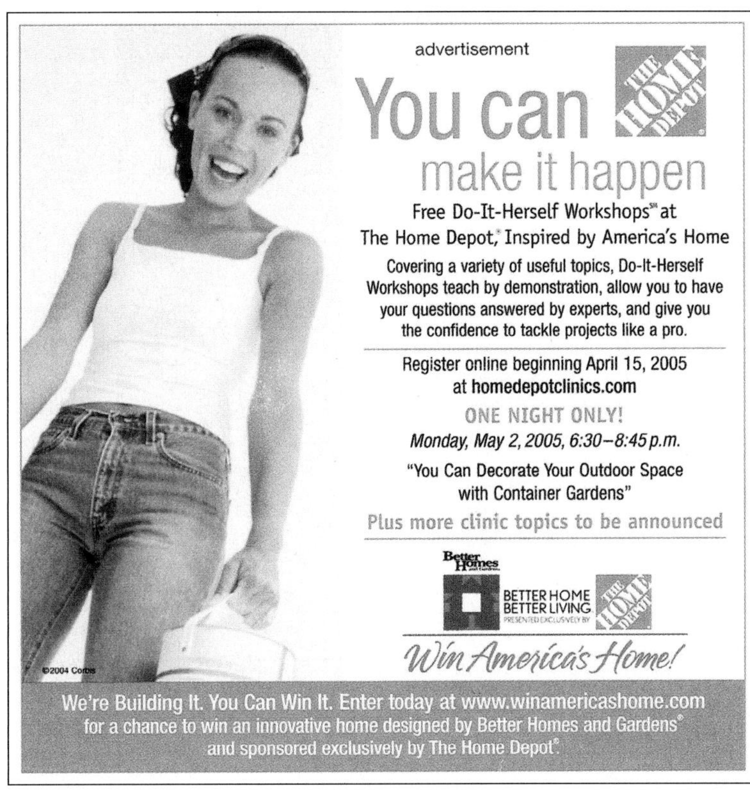

Exhibit 2-8 Home Depot reaches out to the female market

Psychographic segmentation has been increasingly accepted with the advent of the values and lifestyles (VALS) program. Although marketers employed lifestyle segmentation long before VALS and although a number of alternatives—for example, PRIZM—are available, VALS remains one of the more popular options. Developed by the Stanford Research Institute (SRI), VALS has become a very popular method for applying lifestyle segmentation. VALS 2 divides Americans into eight lifestyle segments that exhibit distinctive attitudes, behaviors, and decision-making patterns.[13] SRI believes that when combined with an estimate of the resources the consumer can draw on (education, income, health, energy level, self-confidence, and degree of consumerism), the VALS 2 system is an excellent predictor of consumer behaviors. A number of companies now employ lifestyle segmentation including GM, which defines the target market for the Hummer as "highly adventurist, entrepreneurial and free-spirited achievers,"[14] and *Redbook* magazine, which targets young marrieds, focusing its content on the changes that take place in one's lifestyle when they get married. Companies like Nestle's, Clinique, and Hyundai, among others, have increased their ad expenditures in the magazine as a result.

Behavioristic Segmentation Dividing consumers into groups according to their usage, loyalties, or buying responses to a product is **behavioristic segmentation.** For example, product or brand usage, degree of use (heavy versus light), and/or brand loyalty are combined with demographic and/or psychographic criteria to develop profiles of market segments. In the case of usage, the marketer assumes that nonpurchasers of a brand or product who have the same characteristics as purchasers hold greater potential for adoption than nonusers with different characteristics. A profile (demographic or psychographic) of the user is developed, which serves as the basis for promotional strategies designed to attract new users. For example, teenagers share certain similarities in their consumption behaviors. Those who do not currently own an Apple iPod are more likely to be potential buyers than people in other age groups. (Apple has successfully extended the appeal of its new computers to adopters of the iPod.)

Exhibit 2-9 *Segunda Juventud* targets the 50+ Hispanic segment

Degree of use relates to the fact that a few consumers may buy a disproportionate amount of many products or brands. Industrial marketers

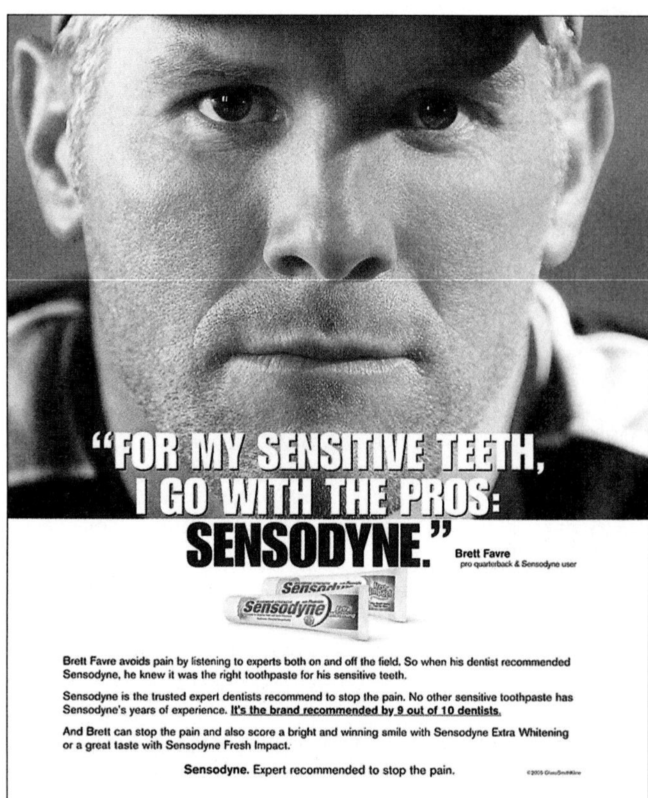

Exhibit 2-10 Sensodyne offers a benefit to those with sensitive teeth

refer to the **80-20 rule,** meaning 20 percent of their buyers account for 80 percent of their sales volume. Again, when the characteristics of these users are identified, targeting them allows for a much greater concentration of efforts and less wasted time and money. The same heavy-half strategy is possible in the consumer market as well. The majority of purchases of many products (e.g., soaps and detergents, shampoos, cake mixes, beer, dog food, colas, bourbon, and toilet tissue—yes, toilet tissue!) are accounted for by a small proportion of the population. Perhaps you can think of some additional examples.

Benefit Segmentation In purchasing products, consumers are generally trying to satisfy specific needs and/or wants. They are looking for products that provide specific benefits to satisfy these needs. The grouping of consumers on the basis of attributes sought in a product is known as **benefit segmentation** and is widely used.

Consider the purchase of a wristwatch. While you might buy a watch for particular benefits such as accuracy, water resistance, or stylishness, others may seek a different set of benefits. Watches are commonly given as gifts for birthdays, Christmas, and graduation. Certainly some of the same benefits are considered in the purchase of a gift, but the benefits the purchaser derives are different from those the user will obtain. Ads that portray watches as good gifts stress different criteria to consider in the purchase decision. The next time you see an ad or commercial for a watch, think about the basic appeal and the benefits it offers.

Another example of benefit segmentation can be seen in the toothpaste market. Some consumers want a product with fluoride (Crest, Colgate); others prefer one that freshens their breath (Close-Up, Aqua-Fresh). More recent benefit segments offer tartar control (Crest) and plaque reduction (Viadent) or toothpaste for people with sensitive teeth (Sensodyne) (Exhibit 2-10). The Den-Mat Corp. introduced Rembrandt whitening toothpaste for consumers who want whiter teeth, and other brands followed with their own whitening attributes (Crest's Extra Whitening, Colgate's Sparkling White).

The Process of Segmenting a Market

The segmentation process develops over time and is an integral part of the situation analysis. It is in this stage that marketers attempt to determine as much as they can about the market: What needs are not being fulfilled? What benefits are being sought? What characteristics distinguish among the various groups seeking these products and services? A number of alternative segmentation strategies may be used. Each time a specific segment is identified, additional information is gathered to help the marketer understand this group.

For example, once a specific segment is identified on the basis of benefits sought, the marketer will examine lifestyle characteristics and demographics to help characterize this group and to further its understanding of this market. Behavioristic segmentation criteria will also be examined. In the purchase of ski boots, for example, specific benefits may be sought—flexibility or stiffness—depending on the type of skiing the buyer does. All this information will be combined to provide a complete profile of the skier.

A number of companies now offer research services to help marketing managers define their markets and develop strategies targeting them. The VALS and PRIZM systems discussed earlier are just a few of the services offered; others use demographic, socioeconomic, and geographic data to cluster consumer households into distinct "microgeographic" segments. One of these companies, Claritas, provides demographic and psychographic profiles of geographic areas as small as census track, block group, or zip code +4. Users of the system include retailers such as Ace Hardware, travel-related companies (Alamo Car Rental), and financial services (GMAC Services) among others. (See Exhibit 2-11.)

PRIZM Social Groups

HIGH / $ / LOW

URBAN	SUBURBAN	SECOND CITY	TOWN AND COUNTRY
U1 URBAN UPTOWN 04 Young Digerati 07 Money & Brains 16 Bohemian Mix 26 The Cosmopolitans 29 American Dreams	S1 ELITE SUBURBS 01 Upper Crust 02 Blue Blood Estates 03 Movers & Shakers 06 Winner's Circle	C1 SECOND CITY SOCIETY 10 Second City Elite 12 Brite Lites, Li'l City 13 Upward Bound	T1 LANDED GENTRY 05 Country Squires 09 Big Fish, Small Pond 11 God's Country 20 Fast-Track Families 25 Country Casuals
U2 MIDTOWN MIX 31 Urban Achievers 40 Close-In Couples 54 Multi-Culti Mosaic	S2 THE AFFLUENTIALS 08 Executive Suites 14 New Empty Nests 15 Pools & Patios 17 Beltway Boomers 18 Kids & Cul-de-Sacs 19 Home Sweet Home	C2 CITY CENTERS 24 Up-and-Comers 27 Middleburg Managers 34 White Picket Fences 35 Boomtown Singles 41 Sunset City Blues	T2 COUNTRY COMFORT 23 Greenbelt Sports 28 Traditional Times 32 New Homesteaders 33 Big Sky Families 37 Mayberry-ville
U3 URBAN CORES 59 Urban Elders 61 City Roots 65 Big City Blues 66 Low-Rise Living	S3 MIDDLEBURBS 21 Gray Power 22 Young Influentials 30 Suburban Sprawl 36 Blue-Chip Blues 39 Domestic Duos	C3 MICRO-CITY BLUES 47 City Startups 53 Mobility Blues 60 Park Bench Seniors 62 Hometown Retired 63 Family Thrifts	T3 MIDDLE AMERICA 38 Simple Pleasures 42 Red, White & Blues 43 Heartlanders 45 Blue Highways 50 Kid Country, USA 51 Shotguns & Pickups
	S4 INNER SUBURBS 44 New Beginnings 46 Old Glories 49 American Classics 52 Suburban Pioneers		T4 RUSTIC LIVING 48 Young & Rustic 55 Golden Ponds 56 Crossroads Villagers 57 Old Milltowns 58 Back Country Folks 64 Bedrock America

Exhibit 2-11 Claritas provides cluster profiles for marketers

Selecting a Target Market

The outcome of the segmentation analysis will reveal the market opportunities available. The next phase in the target marketing process involves two steps: (1) determining how many segments to enter and (2) determining which segments offer the most potential.

Determining How Many Segments to Enter

Three market coverage alternatives are available. **Undifferentiated marketing** involves ignoring segment differences and offering just one product or service to the entire market. For example, when Henry Ford brought out the first assembly-line automobile, all potential consumers were offered the same basic product: a black Ford. For many years, Coca-Cola offered only one product version. While this standardized strategy saves the company money, it does not allow the opportunity to offer different versions of the product to different markets.

Differentiated marketing involves marketing in a number of segments, developing separate marketing strategies for each. The Michelob Ultra ads in Exhibit 2-12 reflect Anheuser-Busch's use of this strategy. Notice how the two ads differ given slightly different target markets and media.

While an undifferentiated strategy offers reduced costs through increased production, it does not allow for variety or tailoring to specific needs. Through differentiation, products—or advertising appeals—may be developed for the various segments, increasing the opportunity to satisfy the needs and wants of various groups.

The third alternative, **concentrated marketing,** is used when the firm selects one segment and attempts to capture a large share of this market. Volkswagen used this strategy in the 1950s when it was the only major automobile company competing in the economy-car segment in the United States. While Volkswagen has now assumed a

Exhibit 2-12 Michelob Ultra varies their ads for different media

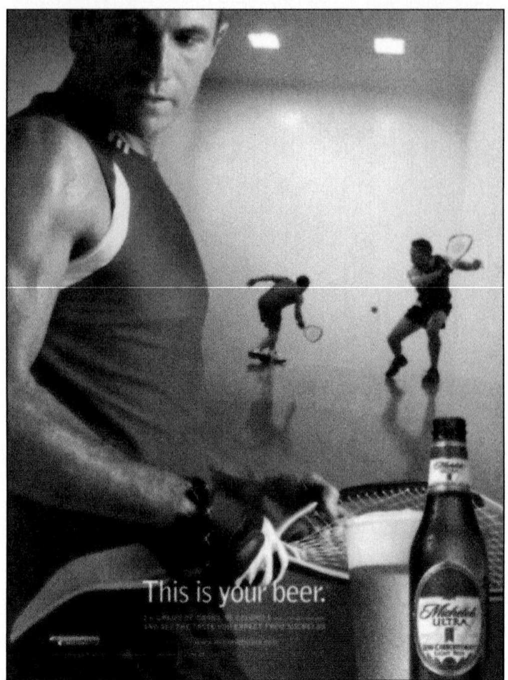

more differentiated strategy, other companies have found the concentrated strategy effective. For example, Maxwell Business Systems has focused its business exclusively on providing software for job cost accounting/MIS systems for government contractors through its JAMIS product line (Exhibit 2-13), where L'Oreal competes in the cosmetics and beauty segment.

Determining Which Segments Offer Potential The second step in selecting a market involves determining the most attractive segment. The firm must examine the sales potential of the segment, the opportunities for growth, the competition, and its own ability to compete. Then it must decide whether it can market to this group. Stories abound of companies that have entered new markets only to find their lack of resources or expertise would not allow them to compete successfully. For example, Royal Crown (RC) Cola has often been quite successful in identifying new segment opportunities but because of limited resources has been less able to capitalize on them than Coke and Pepsi. RC was the first to bring to market diet colas and caffeine-free colas, but it has not been able to establish itself as a market leader in either market. After selecting the segments to target and determining that it can compete, the firm proceeds to the final step in Figure 2-2: the market positioning phase.

Exhibit 2-13 Maxwell Business Systems pursues a concentrated marketing strategy with JAMIS

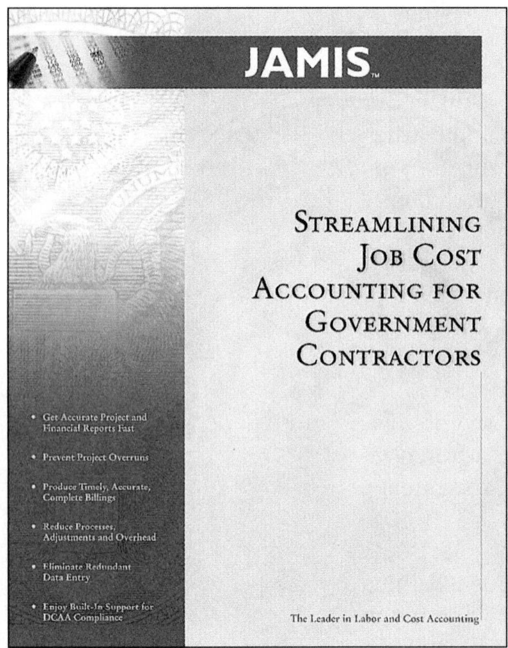

Market Positioning

Positioning has been defined as "the art and science of fitting the product or service to one or more segments of the broad market in such a way as to set it meaningfully apart from competition."[15] As you can see, the position of the product, service, or even store is the image that comes to mind and the attributes consumers perceive as related to it. This communication occurs through the message itself, which explains the benefits, as well as the media strategy employed to reach the target group. Take a few moments to think about how some products are positioned and how their positions are conveyed to you. For example, what comes to mind when you hear the name Mercedes, Dr Pepper, or Sony? What about department stores such as Neiman Marcus, Sears, and JCPenney? Now think of the ads for each of these products and companies. Are their approaches different from their competitors'? When and where are these ads shown?

Approaches to Positioning Positioning strategies generally focus on either the consumer or the competition. While both approaches involve the association of product benefits with consumer needs, the former does so by linking the product with the benefits the consumer will derive or creating a favorable brand image, as shown in Exhibit 2-14. The latter approach positions the product by comparing it and the benefit it offers with the competition. Products like Scope mouthwash (positioning itself as better tasting than Listerine) and Malt-o-Meal cereals (positioned as a better value than its competitors) have employed this strategy successfully (Exhibit 2-15).

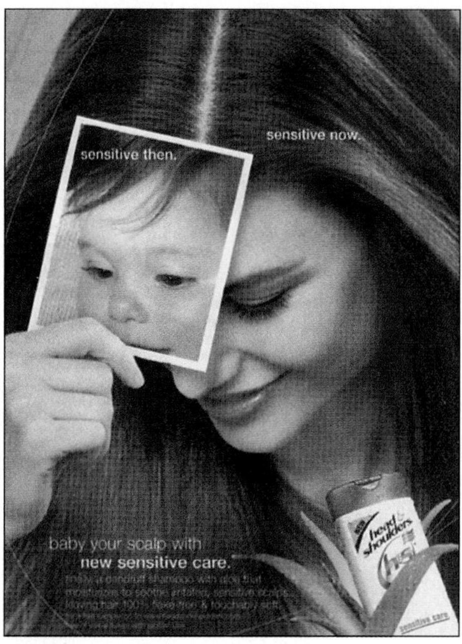

Exhibit 2-14 Positioning that focuses on the consumer

Many advertising practitioners consider market positioning the most important factor in establishing a brand in the marketplace. David Aaker and John Myers note that the term *position* has been used to indicate the brand's or product's image in the marketplace.[16] Jack Trout and Al Ries suggest that this brand image must contrast with competitors. They say, "In today's marketplace, the competitors' image is just as important as your own. Sometimes more important."[17] Jack Trout notes that a good branding strategy cannot exist without positioning. Trout further states that branding is about the process of building a brand, while positioning is about putting that brand in the mind of the consumer.[18] Thus, *positioning,* as used in this text, relates to the image of the product and or brand relative to competing products or brands. The position of the product or brand is the key factor in communicating the benefits it offers and differentiating it from the competition. Let us now turn to strategies marketers use to position a product.

Developing a Positioning Strategy To create a position for a product or service, Trout and Ries suggest that managers ask themselves six basic questions:[19]

1. What position, if any, do we already have in the prospect's mind? (This information must come from the marketplace, not the managers' perceptions.)
2. What position do we want to own?
3. What companies must be outgunned if we are to establish that position?
4. Do we have enough marketing money to occupy and hold the position?
5. Do we have the guts to stick with one consistent positioning strategy?
6. Does our creative approach match our positioning strategy?

A number of positioning strategies might be employed in developing a promotional program. David Aaker and J. Gary Shansby discuss six such strategies: positioning by product attributes, price/quality, use, product class, users, and competitor.[20] Aaker and Myers add one more approach, positioning by cultural symbols.[21]

Positioning by Product Attributes and Benefits A common approach to positioning is setting the brand apart from competitors on the basis of the specific characteristics or benefits offered. Sometimes a product may be positioned on more than one product benefit. Marketers attempt to identify **salient attributes** (those that are important to consumers and are the basis for making a purchase decision). For example, when Apple first introduced its computers, the key benefit stressed was ease of use—an effective strategy, given the complexity of computers in the market at that time. More recently, there have been a number of new products positioned as offering zero or low carbohydrates, including sodas, beers, and other foods (Exhibit 2-16).

Exhibit 2-15 Positioning that focuses on the competition

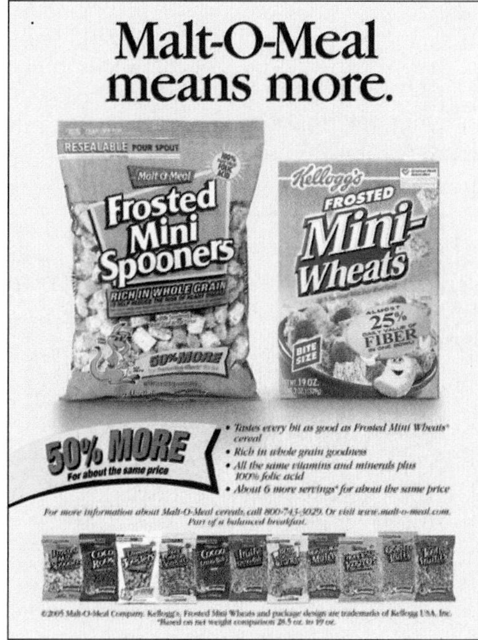

Positioning by Price/Quality Marketers often use price/quality characteristics to position their brands. One way they do this is with ads that reflect the image of a high-quality brand where cost, while

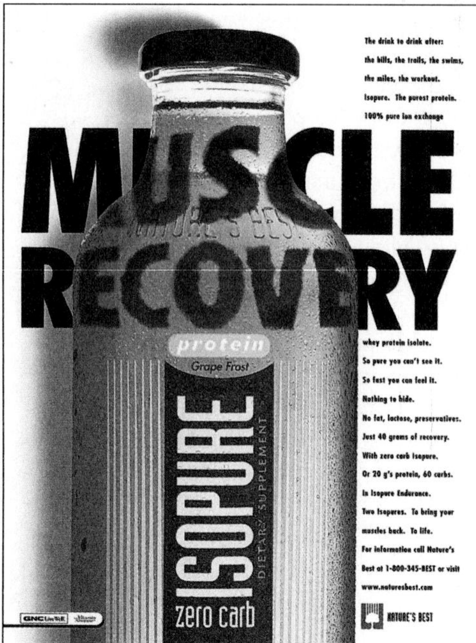

Exhibit 2-16 Isopure positions itself as a zero-carb muscle recovery drink

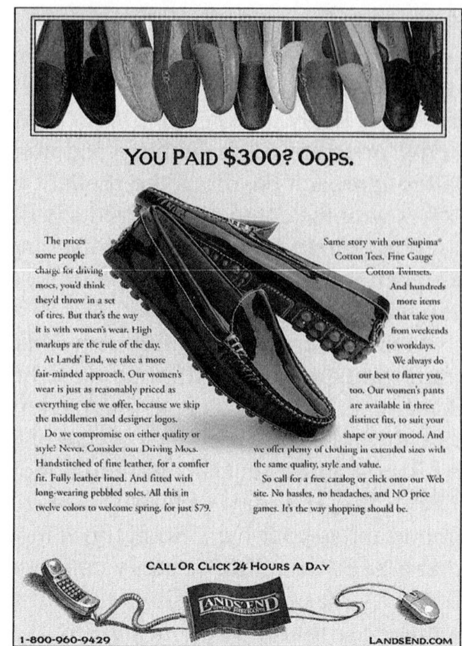

Exhibit 2-17 Lands' End positions its brand as having high quality for the right price

not irrelevant, is considered secondary to the quality benefits derived from using the brand. Premium brands positioned at the high end of the market use this approach to positioning.

Another way to use price/quality characteristics for positioning is to focus on the quality or value offered by the brand at a very competitive price. For example, the Lands' End ad shown in Exhibit 2-17 uses this strategy by suggesting that quality need not be unaffordable. Remember that although price is an important consideration, the product quality must be comparable to, or even better than, competing brands for the positioning strategy to be effective.

Positioning by Use or Application Another way to communicate a specific image or position for a brand is to associate it with a specific use or application. For example, Black & Decker introduced the Snakelight as an innovative solution to the problem of trying to hold a flashlight while working. A TV commercial showed various uses for the product, while creative packaging and in-store displays were used to communicate the uses.

While this strategy is often used to enter a market on the basis of a particular use or application, it is also an effective way to expand the usage of a product. For example, Arm & Hammer baking soda has been promoted for everything from baking to relieving heartburn to eliminating odors in carpets and refrigerators (Exhibit 2-18).

Exhibit 2-18 Arm & Hammer baking soda demonstrates numerous product uses

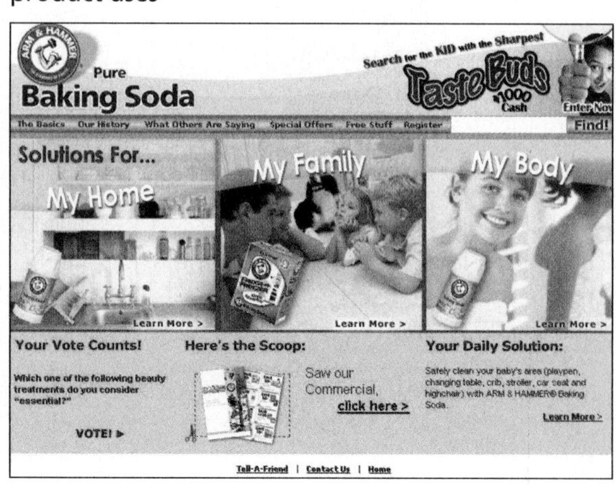

Positioning by Product Class Often the competition for a product comes from outside the product class. For example, airlines know that while they compete with other airlines, trains and buses are also viable alternatives. Amtrak has positioned itself as an alternative to airplanes, citing cost savings, enjoyment, and other advantages. Manufacturers of music CDs must compete with MP3 players; many margarines position themselves against butter. Rather than positioning against another brand, an alternative strategy is to position oneself against another product category. The California Avocado Information Bureau recently launched a major IMC campaign to more strongly position itself as a fruit (as opposed to a vegetable). The print, radio, outdoor, and online campaign took a humorous approach, positioning the avocado as a "fun fruit," while at the same time demonstrating the healthy advantages relative to other fruits and vegetables, and providing numerous products for which it might become an alternative including cream cheese, butter, and dips (Exhibit 2-19). A recent Mountain High yogurt ad positions the product as a substitute for other baking ingredients.

Exhibit 2-19 The California Avocado Information Bureau positions by product class

Positioning by Product User Positioning a product by associating it with a particular user or group of users is yet another approach. An example would be the Valvoline ad shown in Exhibit 2-20. This campaign emphasizes identification or association with a specific group, in this case, people who receive pleasure from working on their cars.

Positioning by Competitor Competitors may be as important to positioning strategy as a firm's own product or services. As Trout and Ries observe, the old strategy of ignoring one's competition no longer works.[22] (Advertisers used to think it was a cardinal sin to mention a competitor in their advertising.) In today's market, an effective positioning strategy for a product or brand may focus on specific competitors. This approach is similar to positioning by product class, although in this case the competition is within the same product category. Perhaps the best-known example of this strategy was Avis, which positioned itself against the car-rental leader, Hertz, by stating, "We're number two, so we try harder." The Malt-o-Meal ad shown earlier (Exhibit 2-15) is an example of positioning a brand against the competition. When positioning by competitor, a marketer must often employ another positioning strategy as well to differentiate the brand.

Exhibit 2-20 Valvoline positions by product user

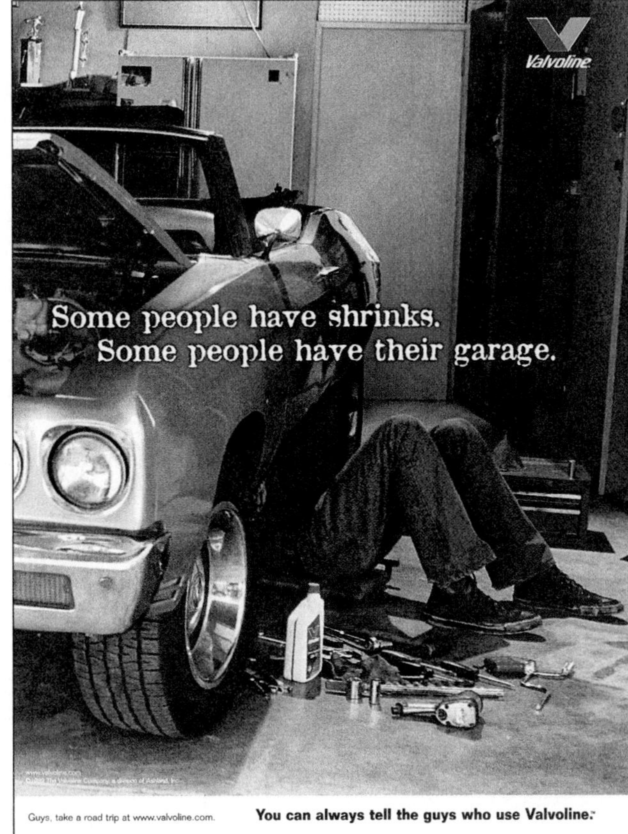

Positioning by Cultural Symbols Aaker and Myers include an additional positioning strategy in which cultural symbols are used to differentiate brands. Examples are the Jolly Green Giant, the Keebler elves, Speedy Alka-Seltzer, the Pillsbury Doughboy, Buster Brown, Ronald McDonald, Chiquita Banana, and Mr. Peanut. Each of these symbols has successfully differentiated the product it represents from competitors' (Exhibit 2-21).

Repositioning One final positioning strategy involves altering or changing a product's or brand's position. **Repositioning** a product usually occurs because of declining or stagnant sales or because of anticipated opportunities in other market positions. Repositioning is often difficult to accomplish because of entrenched perceptions about and attitudes toward the product or brand. Many companies' attempts to change their positions have met with little or no success. For example, Kmart and Sears—historically strong retail giants—both experienced declining sales for decades until dethroned by Wal-Mart in the early 1990s. Oldsmobile's Aurora saw declining sales during this time as well. All three have attempted to reposition themselves to a level of higher quality, appealing to younger and more well-to-do customers, with limited success. The Oldsmobile line was discontinued, Kmart filed for bankruptcy, and Sears has had difficulty shedding its image as stodgy and old-fashioned.[23] (In late 2004, Sears and Kmart joined together as one company.) Buick has repositioned in an attempt to reach a younger market (using Tiger Woods, in his twenties, as a spokesperson), while La-Z-Boy is attempting to move away from its blue-collar image to a more affluent one.

IMC Perspective 2-1 describes how other companies have fared in their repositioning attempts.

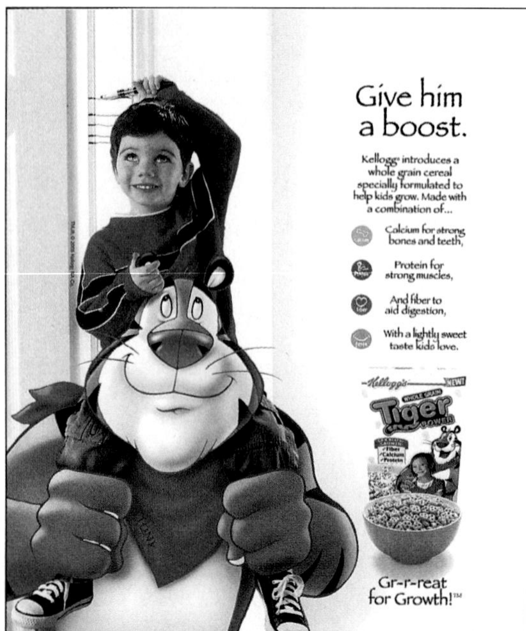

Give him a boost.
Kellogg's introduces a whole grain cereal specially formulated to help kids grow. Made with a combination of...
Calcium for strong bones and teeth,
Protein for strong muscles,
And fiber to aid digestion,
With a lightly sweet taste kids love.
Kellogg's
NEW!
Tiger
Fiber
Calcium
Protein
Gr-r-reat for Growth!™

Exhibit 2-21 Tony the Tiger has become a cultural symbol

Determining the Positioning Strategy

Having explored the alternative positioning strategies available, the marketer must determine which strategy is best suited for the firm or product and begin developing the positioning platform. As you remember from the promotional planning process in Chapter 1, the input into this stage will be derived from the situation analysis—specifically, the marketing research conducted therein. Essentially, the development of a positioning platform can be broken into a six-step process:[24]

1. *Identifying competitors.* This process requires broad thinking. Competitors may not be just those products and/or brands that fall into our product class or with which we compete directly. For example, a red wine competes with other red wines of various positions. It may also compete with white, sparkling, and nonalcoholic wines. Malt liquors provide an alternative, as do beer and other alcoholic drinks. Other nonalcoholic drinks may come into consideration at various times and/or in certain situations. The marketer must consider all likely competitors, as well as the diverse effects of use and situations on the consumer.

2. *Assessing consumers' perceptions of competitors.* Once we define the competition, we must determine how they are perceived by consumers. Which attributes are important to consumers in evaluating a product and/or brand? As you might expect, for many products, consumers consider a wide variety of attributes or product benefits—most if not all of which are important. Much of marketing firms' research is directed at making such determinations. Consumers are asked to take part in focus groups and/or complete surveys indicating which attributes are important in their purchase decisions. For example, attributes considered important in the selection of a bank may include convenience, teller friendliness, financial security, and a host of other factors. This process establishes the basis for determining competitive positions.

3. *Determining competitors' positions.* After identifying the relevant attributes and their relative importance to consumers, we must determine how each competitor (including our own entry) is positioned with respect to each attribute. This will also show how the competitors are positioned relative to each other. Consumer research is required to make this assessment.

4. *Analyzing the consumers' preferences.* Our discussion of segmentation noted various factors that may distinguish among groups of consumers, including lifestyles, purchase motivations, and demographic differences. Each of these segments may have different purchase motivations and different attribute importance ratings. One way to determine these differences is to consider the *ideal brand* or *product,* defined as the object the consumer would prefer over all others, including objects that can be imagined but do not exist. Identifying the ideal product can help us identify different ideals among segments or identify segments with similar or the same ideal points.

5. *Making the positioning decision.* Going through the first four steps should let us decide which position to assume in the marketplace. Such a decision is not always clear and well defined, however, and research may provide only limited input. In that case, the marketing manager or groups of managers must make some subjective judgments. These judgments raise a number of questions:

- *Is the segmentation strategy appropriate?* Positioning usually entails a decision to segment the market. Consider whether the market segment sought will support

IMC PERSPECTIVE 2-1

Changing the Look of Mr. Peanut and Mr. Goodwrench and the Images of Some Others

Most (if not all) of you may be too young to remember Mr. Peanut or Mr. Goodwrench. The former—Mr. Peanut—first appeared on a billboard in Times Square in New York City in 1942, as a "dignified dandy"—complete with top hat and cane—the cultural icon representing Planter's Peanuts. Mr. Goodwrench is not quite as old, having debuted as the trusty auto mechanic for General Motors in the 1970s, but has not been seen in a television commercial for over a decade. These two well-known corporate symbols join the Maytag repairman (the appliance repairman with nothing to do) as examples of attempts by companies to revive and/or make over their symbolic images. Each of these icons has been given a new persona to reflect what their companies consider to be more up-to-date representations, while maintaining the positioning they are meant to represent.

Mr. Peanut has received a more contemporary look (he still has the top hat and cane), appearing in commercials showing him doing chin-ups to keep in shape or dancing on the Planter's website. Mr. Goodwrench—a "buttoned-up white man" when he appeared in the 1970s—now has a number of images. Depending on the medium and the target market, he could be black, white, Asian, or even a Ms. Goodwrench—whatever it takes to represent a GM dealership technician. And the new Mr. Goodwrench is sometimes funny, while the original was as serious as his job demanded.

Although these three images have received only minor overhauls, a number of other brands have taken more dramatic efforts at repositioning themselves. The Old Spice brand of cologne that you are familiar with has a very different image than it did 68 years ago when it first hit the market. The current campaign (initiated in the 1990s) attempts to reach active young men with sports-themed commercials and a more modern bright red label. The commercials of your parents' age depicted bravado young sailors rushing to shore to the tune of an instrumental jingle, and the package design was white with much larger lettering. A number of brand extensions have also contributed to the broadened brand image.

Birkenstocks and Stride-Rite shoes have also been repositioned. The Birkenstock brand has been synonymous with stability, comfort, and endurance—and with hippies—since its introduction in the 1960s. The new Birkenstock wearer is a hip, well-educated urbanite with an eye for design and the money to indulge in whims—at least that's what image the company wants to have. Stride-Rites—previously positioned as sensible shoes for kids—now portray an upscale and fun image, and the company has moved from rational purchase appeals to more emotional ones with their campaign theme "Life's waiting. Let's go." The quality image remains, augmented by fashion and emotional connections.

Finally, there is Häagen-Dazs. Yes, the premium-price line of ice cream, sorbet, and frozen yogurt is getting a face-lift as well. The longtime image of sybaritic indulgence is giving way to a remake of the brand that focuses on the pedigree of its ingredients rather than of the consumers who buy it. The repositioning will attempt to make the brand less intimidating and appealing to a wider variety of shoppers—not just the preppies, yuppies, and other upscale buyers many associate with Häagen-Dazs. The focus is now on elegant simplicity—as opposed to ostentatious puffery—and "approachable luxury," says David Ritterbush, vice president of marketing for super premium brands. Mr. Ritterbush notes that the change was necessary to stay current, as the market has changed since the 1960s when the brand was first introduced.

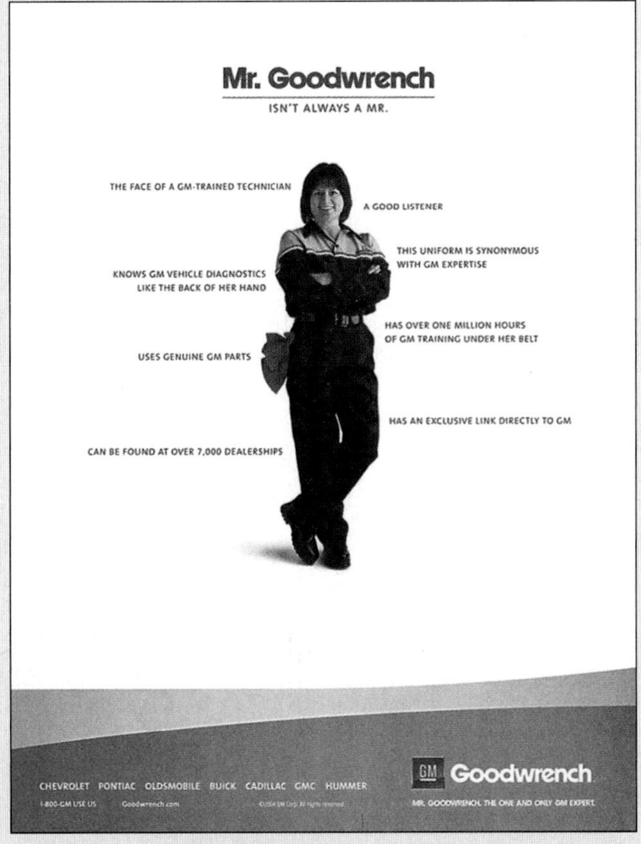

These are just a few of the many examples of companies' attempts to make slight changes in their images as well as major repositioning changes. Each of the above examples demonstrates that repositioning is not just a strategy to save or revive failing brands. Rather, these examples show that even successful brands need to remain current.

Sources: Theresa Howard, "GM Revives Mr. Goodwrench Ads, Throwing In Comedic Twist," *USA Today,* December 6, 2004, p. 10B; Stuart Elliott, "The Scoop on New Ads for Häagen-Dazs," New York Times.com, June 15, 2004, pp. 1–9; Stuart Elliott, "Thoroughly Modern Mr. Peanut," New York Times.com, March 24, 2004, p. 7; Sandra O'Loughlin, "Hip Shoes, Not for Hippies," *Brandweek,* November 3, 2003, p. 18; Christine Bittar, "Old Spice Does New Tricks," *Brandweek,* June 2, 2003, pp. 17–18.

an entry and whether it is in the best interests of the company to deemphasize the remaining market. When a specific position is chosen, consumers may believe this is what the product is for. Those not looking for that specific benefit may not consider the brand. If the marketer decides on an undifferentiated strategy, it may be possible to be general in the positioning platform. For example, Toyota's slogan, "Moving forward," allows receivers to project their feelings about the brand—all of which (hopefully) involve a positive image of Toyota.

• *Are there sufficient resources available to communicate the position effectively?* It is very expensive to establish a position. One ad, or even a series of ads, is not likely to be enough. The marketer must commit to a long-range effort in all aspects of the marketing campaign to make sure the objectives sought are obtained. Too often, the firm abandons a position and/or advertising campaign long before it can establish a position successfully. The repositioning effort of JCPenney is an excellent example of sticking with a campaign. The efforts to create a more upscale image began in the 1990s and has continued ever since. In contrast, Sears has switched campaigns so often in the past few years that it has been impossible to establish a distinct position in the consumer's mind. Further, once a successful position is attained, it is likely to attract competitors. It may become expensive to ward off "me-too" brands and continue to hold on to the brand distinction.

• *How strong is the competition?* The marketing manager must ask whether a position sought is likely to be maintained, given the strengths of the competition. For example, General Foods (now Kraft-GF) often made it a practice not to be the first entry into a market. When competitors developed new markets with their entries, General Foods would simply improve on the product and capture a large percentage of the market share. This leads to two basic questions: First, if our firm is first into the market, will we be able to maintain the position (in terms of quality, price, etc.)? Second, if a product is positioned as finest quality, it must be. If it is positioned as lowest cost, it has to be. Otherwise, the position claimed is sure to be lost.

• *Is the current positioning strategy working?* There is an old saying, "If it ain't broke, don't fix it." If current efforts are not working, it may be time to consider an alternative positioning strategy. But if they are working, a change is usually unwise. Sometimes executives become bored with a theme and decide it is time for a change, but this change causes confusion in the marketplace and weakens a brand's position. Unless there is strong reason to believe a change in positioning is necessary, stick with the current strategy.

6. *Monitoring the position.* Once a position has been established, we want to monitor how well it is being maintained in the marketplace. Tracking studies measure the image of the product or firm over time. Changes in consumers' perceptions can be determined, with any slippage immediately noted and reacted to. At the same time, the impact of competitors can be determined.

Before leaving this section, you might stop to think for a moment about the positioning (and repositioning) strategies pursued by different companies. Any successful product that comes to mind probably occupies a distinct market position.

Developing the Marketing Planning Program

The development of the marketing strategy and selection of a target market(s) tell the marketing department which customers to focus on and what needs to attempt to satisfy. The next stage of the marketing process involves combining the various elements of the marketing mix into a cohesive, effective marketing program. Each marketing-mix element is multidimensional and includes a number of decision areas. Likewise, each must consider and contribute to the overall IMC program. We now examine product, price, and distribution channels and how each influences and interacts with the promotional program.

Product Decisions

An organization exists because it has some product, service, or idea to offer consumers, generally in exchange for money. This offering may come in the form of a physical product (such as a soft drink, pair of jeans, or car), a service (banking, airlines, or legal assistance), a cause (United Way, March of Dimes), or even a person (a political candidate). The product is anything that can be marketed and that, when used or supported, gives satisfaction to the individual.

A *product* is not just a physical object; it is a bundle of benefits or values that satisfies the needs of consumers. The needs may be purely functional, or they may include social and psychological benefits. For example, the campaign for Michelin tires discussed earlier stresses the quality built into Michelin tires (value) as well as their performance and durability (function). The term **product symbolism** refers to what a product or brand means to consumers and what they experience in purchasing and using it.[25] For many products, strong symbolic features and social and psychological meaning may be more important than functional utility.[26] For example, designer clothing such as Versace, Gucci, and Prada is often purchased on the basis of its symbolic meaning and image, particularly by teenagers and young adults. Advertising plays an important role in developing and maintaining the image of these brands (Exhibit 2-22).

Product planning involves decisions not only about the item itself, such as design and quality, but also about aspects such as service and warranties as well as brand name and package design. Consumers look beyond the reality of the product and its ingredients. The product's quality, branding, packaging, and even the company standing behind it all contribute to consumers' perceptions.[27] In an effective IMC program, advertising, branding, and packaging are all designed to portray the product as more than just a bundle of attributes. All are coordinated to present an image or positioning of the product that extends well beyond its physical attributes. Think for a minute about the ads for Nike; the product benefits and attributes are usually not even mentioned—yet information about the brand is communicated effectively.

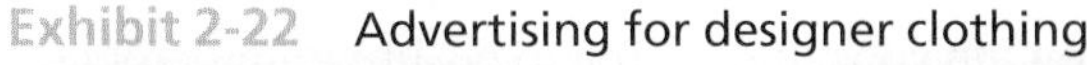
Exhibit 2-22 Advertising for designer clothing

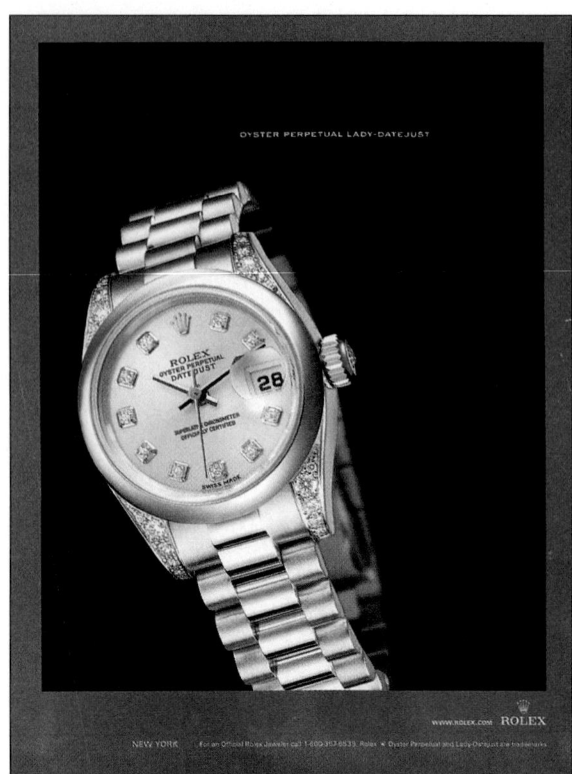

Exhibit 2-23 Rolex creates strong brand equity through advertising

Branding Choosing a brand name for a product is important from a promotional perspective because brand names communicate attributes and meaning. Marketers search for brand names that can communicate product concepts and help position the product in customers' minds. Names such as Safeguard (soap), I Can't Believe It's Not Butter! (margarine), Easy-Off (oven cleaner), Arrid (antiperspirant), and Spic and Span (floor cleaner) all clearly communicate the benefits of using these products and at the same time create images extending beyond the names themselves. (What about La-Z-Boy?)

One important role of advertising in respect to branding strategies is creating and maintaining **brand equity,** which can be thought of as an intangible asset of added value or goodwill that results from the favorable image, impressions of differentiation, and/or the strength of consumer attachment to a company name, brand name, or trademark. Brand equity allows a brand to earn greater sales volume and/or higher margins than it could without the name, providing the company with a competitive advantage. The strong equity position a company and/or its brand enjoys is often reinforced through advertising. For example, Rolex watches command a premium price because of their high quality as well as the strong brand equity they have developed through advertising (Exhibit 2-23).

Packaging Packaging is another aspect of product strategy that has become increasingly important. Traditionally, the package provided functional benefits such as economy, protection, and storage. However, the role and function of the package have changed because of the self-service emphasis of many stores and the fact that more and more buying decisions are made at the point of purchase. One study estimated that as many as two-thirds of all purchases made in the supermarket are unplanned. The package is often the consumer's first exposure to the product, so it must make a favorable first impression. A typical supermarket has more than 30,000 items competing for attention. Not only must a package attract and hold the consumer's attention, but it must also communicate information on how to use the product, divulge its composition and content, and satisfy any legal requirements regarding disclosure. Moreover, many firms design the package to carry a sales promotion message such as a contest, sweepstakes, or premium offer.

Many companies view the package as an important way to communicate with consumers and create an impression of the brand in their minds. In other instances packages can extend the brand by offering new uses. For example, Listerine's PocketPaks (Exhibit 2-24) have created new opportunities for the mouthwash. Design factors such as size, shape, color, and lettering all contribute to the appeal of a package and can be as important as a commercial in determining what goes from the store shelf to the consumer's shopping cart. Many products use packaging to create a distinctive brand image and identity. The next time you walk by a perfume counter, stop to look at the many unique package designs (see Exhibit 2-25). Packaging can also serve more functional purposes. For example, M&M's new packaging protects the candy and makes it easy to dispense (Exhibit 2-26).

Exhibit 2-24 Listerine communicates through effective packaging

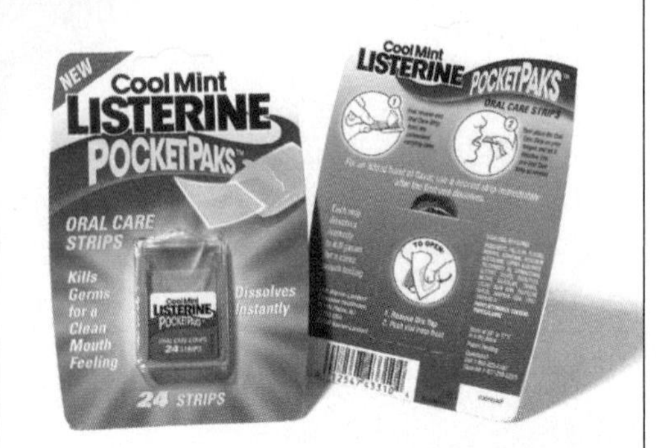

Price Decisions

The *price variable* refers to what the consumer must give up to purchase a product or service. While price is discussed in terms of the dollar amount exchanged for an item, the cost of a product to the consumer includes time, mental activity, and behavioral effort.[28] The marketing manager is usually concerned with establishing a price level, developing pricing policies, and monitoring competitors' and consumers' reactions to prices in the marketplace. A firm must consider a number of factors in determining the price it charges for its product or service, including costs, demand factors, competition, and perceived value. From an IMC perspective, the price must be consistent with the perceptions of the product, as well as the communications strategy. Higher prices, of course, will communicate a higher product quality, while lower prices reflect bargain or "value" perceptions. A product positioned as highest quality but carrying a lower price than competitors will only confuse consumers. In other words, the price, the advertising, and the distribution channels must present one unified voice speaking to the product's positioning.

Exhibit 2-25 The packaging creates product image

Relating Price to Advertising and Promotion Factors such as product quality, competition, and advertising all interact in determining what price a firm can and should charge. The relationship among price, product quality, and advertising was examined in one study using information on 227 consumer businesses from the Profit Impact of Marketing Strategies (PIMS) project of the Strategic Planning Institute.[29] Several interesting findings concerning the interaction of these variables emerged from this study:

- Brands with high relative advertising budgets were able to charge premium prices, whereas brands that spent less than their competitors on advertising charged lower prices.
- Companies with high-quality products charged high relative prices for the extra quality, but businesses with high quality and high advertising levels obtained the highest prices. Conversely, businesses with low quality and low advertising charged the lowest prices.
- The positive relationship between high relative advertising and price levels was stronger for products in the late stage of the product life cycle, for market leaders, and for low-cost products (under $10).
- Companies with relatively high prices and high advertising expenditures showed a higher return on investment than companies with relatively low prices and high advertising budgets.
- Companies with high-quality products were hurt the most, in terms of return on investment, by inconsistent advertising and pricing strategies.

The study concluded that pricing and advertising strategies go together. High relative ad expenditures should accompany premium prices, and low relative ad expenditures should be tailored to low prices. These results obviously support the IMC perspective that one voice must be conveyed.

Exhibit 2-26 Packaging may also add product benefits

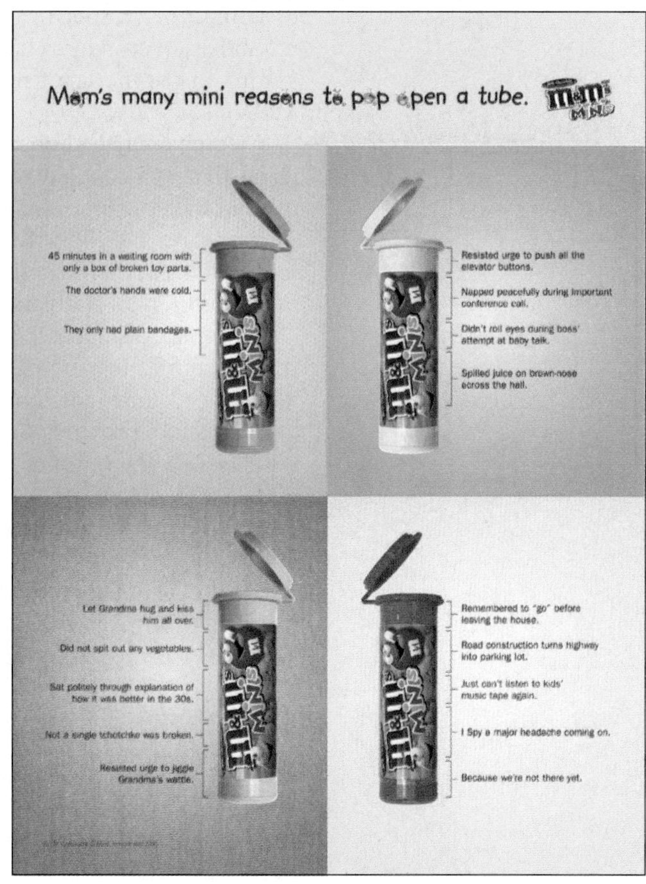

Distribution Channel Decisions

As consumers, we generally take for granted the role of marketing intermediaries or channel members. If we want a six-pack of soda or a box of detergent, we can buy it at a supermarket, a convenience store, or even a drugstore. Manufacturers understand the value and importance of these intermediaries.

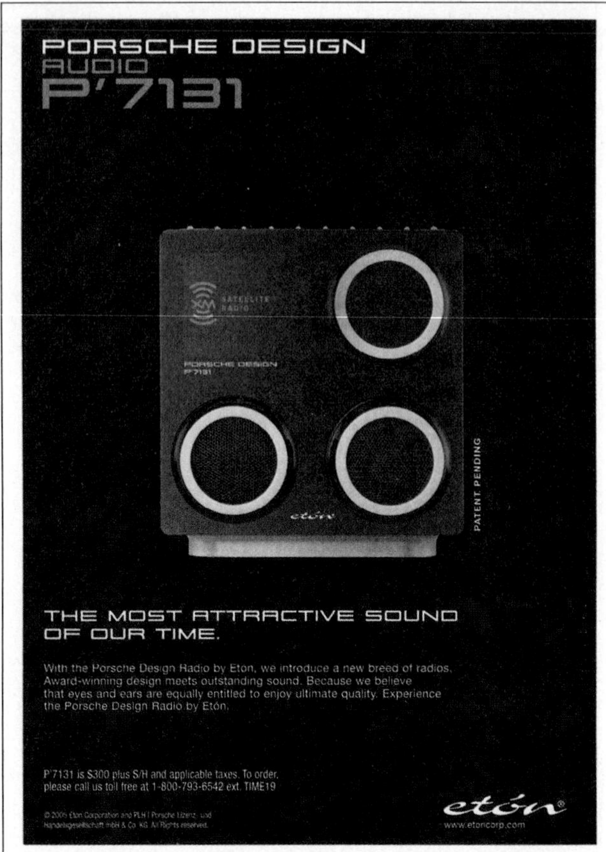

Exhibit 2-27 Some products compete on the basis of quality rather than price

One of a marketer's most important marketing decisions involves the way it makes its products and services available for purchase. A firm can have an excellent product at a great price, but it will be of little value unless it is available where the customer wants it, when the customer wants it, and with the proper support and service. **Marketing channels,** the place element of the marketing mix, are "sets of interdependent organizations involved in the process of making a product or service available for use or consumption."[30]

Channel decisions involve selecting, managing, and motivating intermediaries such as wholesalers, distributors, brokers, and retailers that help a firm make a product or service available to customers. These intermediaries, sometimes called **resellers,** are critical to the success of a company's marketing program.

The distribution strategy should also take into consideration the communication objectives and the impact that the channel strategy will have on the IMC program. Stewart and colleagues discuss the need for "integrated channel management," which "reflects the blurring of the boundaries of the communications and distribution functions."[31] Consistent with the product and pricing decisions, where the product is distributed will send a communications message. Does the fact that a product is sold at Neiman Marcus or Saks convey a different message regarding its image than if it were distributed at Kmart or Wal-Mart? If you think about it for a moment, the mere fact that the product is distributed in these channels communicates an image about it in your mind. Stewart gives examples of how channel elements contribute to communication—for example, grocery store displays, point-of-purchase merchandising, and shelf footage. The distribution channel in a well-integrated marketing program serves as a form of reminder advertising. The consumer sees the brand name and recalls the advertising. (Think about the last time you passed a McDonald's. Did it remind you of any of McDonald's ads?)

A company can choose not to use any channel intermediaries but, rather, to sell to its customers through **direct channels.** This type of channel arrangement is sometimes used in the consumer market by firms using direct-selling programs, such as Avon, Tupperware, and Mary Kay, or firms that use direct-response advertising, telemarketing, or the Internet to sell their products. Direct channels are also frequently used by manufacturers of industrial products and services, which are often selling expensive and complex products that require extensive negotiations and sales efforts, as well as service and follow-up calls after the sale. The ad for Porsche Design Audio shown here reflects the higher cost and quality associated with the brand (Exhibit 2-27).

Chapter 15 provides a discussion of the role of the Internet in an IMC program. As will be seen, the Internet is relied upon by many companies as a direct channel of distribution, since they offer products and services for sale on their websites. Amazon.com and Barnesandnoble.com are just two of the many examples of such efforts.

Most consumer-product companies distribute through **indirect channels,** usually using a network of wholesalers (institutions that sell to other resellers) and/or retailers (which sell primarily to the final consumer).

Developing Promotional Strategies: Push or Pull?

Most of you are aware of advertising and other forms of promotion directed toward ultimate consumers or business customers. We see these ads in the media and are often part of the target audience for the promotions. In addition to developing a consumer marketing mix, a company must have a program to motivate the channel members. Programs designed to persuade the trade to stock, merchandise, and promote a manufacturer's products are part of a **promotional push strategy.** The goal of this strategy is to push the product through the channels of distribution by aggressively selling and promoting the item to the resellers, or trade.

Promotion to the trade includes all the elements of the promotional mix. Company sales representatives call on resellers to explain the product, discuss the firm's plans for building demand among ultimate consumers, and describe special programs being offered to the trade, such as introductory discounts, promotional allowances, and cooperative ad programs. The company may use **trade advertising** to interest wholesalers and retailers and motivate them to purchase its products for resale to their customers. Trade advertising usually appears in publications that serve the particular industry.

A push strategy tries to convince resellers they can make a profit on a manufacturer's product and to encourage them to order the merchandise and push it through to their customers. Sometimes manufacturers face resistance from channel members who do not want to take on an additional product line or brand. In these cases, companies may turn to a **promotional pull strategy,** spending money on advertising and sales promotion efforts directed toward the ultimate consumer. The goal of a pull strategy is to create demand among consumers and encourage them to request the product from the retailer. Seeing the consumer demand, retailers will order the product from wholesalers (if they are used), which in turn will request it from the manufacturer. Thus, stimulating demand at the end-user level pulls the product through the channels of distribution.

Whether to emphasize a push or a pull strategy depends on a number of factors, including the company's relations with the trade, its promotional budget, and demand for the firm's products. Companies that have favorable channel relationships may prefer to use a push strategy and work closely with channel members to encourage them to stock and promote their products. A firm with a limited promotional budget may not have the funds for advertising and sales promotion that a pull strategy requires and may find it more cost-effective to build distribution and demand by working closely with resellers. When the demand outlook for a product is favorable because it has unique benefits, is superior to competing brands, or is very popular among consumers, a pull strategy may be appropriate. Companies often use a combination of push and pull strategies, with the emphasis changing as the product moves through its life cycle.

The Role of Advertising and Promotion

As shown in the marketing model in Figure 2-1, the marketing program includes promotion both to the trade (channel members) and to the company's ultimate customers. Marketers use the various promotional-mix elements—advertising, sales promotion, direct marketing, publicity/public relations, and personal selling—to inform consumers about their products, their prices, and places where the products are available. Each promotional-mix variable helps marketers achieve their promotional objectives, and all variables must work together to achieve an integrated marketing communications program.

To this point, we have discussed the various elements of the marketing plan that serves as the basis for the IMC program. The development and implementation of an IMC program is based on a strong foundation that includes market analysis, target marketing and positioning, and coordination of the various marketing-mix elements. Throughout the following chapters of this text, we will explore the role of various IMC elements in helping to achieve marketing objectives.

Summary

Promotion plays an important role in an organization's efforts to market its product, service, or ideas to its customers. Figure 2-1 shows a model for analyzing how promotions fit into a company's marketing program. The model includes a marketing strategy and analysis, target marketing, program development, and the target market. The marketing process begins with a marketing strategy that is based on a detailed situation analysis and guides for target market selection and development of the firm's marketing program.

In the planning process, the situation analysis requires that the marketing strategy be assumed. The promotional program is developed with this strategy as a guide. One of the key decisions to be made pertains to the target marketing process, which includes identifying, segmenting, targeting, and positioning to target markets. There are several bases for segmenting the market and various ways to position a product.

Once the target marketing process has been completed, marketing program decisions regarding product, price, distribution, and promotions must be made. All of these must be coordinated to provide an integrated marketing communications perspective, in which the positioning strategy is supported by one voice. Thus all product strategies, pricing strategies, and distribution choices must be made with the objective of contributing to the overall image of the product or brand. Advertising and promotion decisions, in turn, must be integrated with the other marketing-mix decisions to accomplish this goal.

Key Terms

strategic marketing plan, 41
market segments, 41
market opportunities, 41
competitive advantage, 43
target marketing, 44
market segmentation, 45
geographic segmentation, 47
demographic segmentation, 47
psychographic segmentation, 49
behavioristic segmentation, 49
80-20 rule, 50
benefit segmentation, 50
undifferentiated marketing, 51
differentiated marketing, 51
concentrated marketing, 51
positioning, 52
salient attributes, 53
repositioning, 55
product symbolism, 59
brand equity, 60
marketing channels, 62
resellers, 62
direct channels, 62
indirect channels, 62
promotional push strategy, 63
trade advertising, 63
promotional pull strategy, 63

Discussion Questions

1. Discuss the difference between a push and a pull strategy. What kinds of firms would be more likely to employ each strategy? Give examples.

2. The text describes a number of different positioning strategies. Give examples of products and/or brands that utilize each of these different strategies.

3. It has been said that benefit segmentation should be the starting point for determining market segments to target, and that other segmentation strategies may just be descriptors of the segment. Discuss whether you agree or disagree with this position, citing specific examples to support your case.

4. A number of companies have tried to reposition themselves in the marketplace. Some have been successful; others have not. Cite examples of both. What are the factors that you think led to their success or failure?

5. Companies price their products at different levels. Some are positioned as "price" products while others take on a position of "luxury goods." Describe how the price positioning of a product or brand leads to different strategies for each of the other marketing variables of product, distribution, and promotion.

6. Recently, some marketers have noted that it is easier to develop communications programs to Generation X members than Generation Y. Briefly describe the characteristics of Gen X and Gen Y, and whether or not you believe this to be true.

7. As companies increase their efforts to target the Hispanic segment, they are likely to encounter differences from other subcultural groups. Discuss some of the differences that they might expect to notice in the Hispanic subculture.

8. Changing lifestyles can create both opportunities and threats for the marketer. Provide an example of a change in lifestyle that poses a threat to marketers, and one that provides an opportunity. Give an example of a product or brand that has been affected in both of these ways.

9. A number of approaches to segmentation have been cited in the text. Provide examples of companies and/or brands that employ each.

10. Describe how the positioning strategy adopted for a brand would need to be supported by all other elements of the marketing mix.

Organizing for Advertising and Promotion: The Role of Ad Agencies and Other Marketing Communication Organizations

3

Chapter Objectives

1. To understand how companies organize for advertising and other aspects of integrated marketing communications.
2. To examine methods for selecting, compensating, and evaluating advertising agencies.
3. To explain the role and functions of specialized marketing communications organizations.
4. To examine various perspectives on the use of integrated services and responsibilities of advertisers versus agencies.

Crispin Porter and Bogusky: The Agency That Is Hotter Than South Beach on a Saturday Night

If you ask most people in the world of marketing and advertising where they would expect to find the hottest ad agency in the industry, chances are they would name a city such as New York, Los Angeles, or Chicago. It is unlikely that many would mention Miami, as the city is better known for its beaches and art deco than for its ad agencies. However, Miami is quickly moving onto the advertising community's radar screen as it is the home of the ad world's most buzzed-about agency: Crispin Porter and Bogusky (CP+B). While hot agencies come and go, many believe that CP+B bears watching as they have been grabbing attention with campaigns for clients such as Virgin Atlantic Airways, the Mini-Cooper, Molson, and Burger King.

CP+B actually began as a small agency in Miami called Crispin Advertising in 1965. During the early 1990s, CP+B created ads that swept local award shows such as a Sunglass Hut billboard featuring a gigantic pair of shades and the headline "What to Wear to a Nude Beach." Many of its clients in Miami had small ad budgets, and CP+B began placing ads in odd places such as on shopping carts, on trash dumpsters, and park benches. Agency partner Alex Bogusky notes that "we found ways to cheat a little and still get noticed." However, it also was the foundation of CP+B's nontraditional approach to advertising, which includes guerilla tactics, unconventional uses of media, and holistic marketing strategies that integrate everything from product design to packaging to event marketing.

For more than a decade CP+B worked on local accounts and struggled to get hold of a client that could draw national attention. A major turning point came in 1997 when CP+B developed an antismoking campaign for the State of Florida that was targeted to teens. The campaign began with street-level research as agency staffers went out at night and talked to local teenagers and learned that conventional antismoking appeals made rebellious kids want to smoke even more. Rather than using traditional methods such as slick TV commercials, CP+B decided to use guerilla marketing tactics and promote an "anti-brand" that teens could latch on to. CP+B called the campaign "Truth" and created a corporate logo for it that was scattered across Florida on posters, leaflets, T-shirts, stickers, and other gear. They also rented trucks and trains to traverse the state and staged impromptu live events where the Truth material was distributed. A Truth website was created and served as information central for the entire campaign.

The Truth campaign was very effective as smoking among teens in Florida declined an average of 38 percent between 1998 and 2002. It also helped put CP+B on the map as the American Legacy Foundation decided to use Truth as the basis of a national antismoking campaign. CP+B was partnered with Boston agency Arnold Worldwide to bring the message to teens on a much larger scale that included commercials on the Super Bowl. The Truth campaign is widely regarded as one of the most successful youth smoking prevention programs in the world.

CP+B really grabbed the attention of the advertising community in 2002 with the award-winning campaign that was created to introduce the Mini Cooper automobile. The tiny British car was launched with an equally small advertising budget so CP+B used little TV spending and relied on magazine and billboard ad and public relations stunts that generated millions of dollars worth of buzz for the Mini. CP+B generated buzz by placing actual Minis in a variety of odd places such as on top of SUVs that toured the country and removing seats from sports stadiums to display the cars at Major League Baseball and NFL games. Street props were created that included a coin-operated ride in the shape of a Mini and product placements in TV shows and movies, including a starring role for the car in the hit movie *The Italian Job.*

Many of CP+B's clients still have modest ad budgets, and the agency has continued to find unique ways to grab consumers' attention. The agency uses traditional TV commercials sparingly, which is close to heresy in an industry that grew fat by spending millions of their clients' dollars to run television spots. While many advertising agencies have been promising for years to become less reliant on TV ads and to provide other ways to reach consumers, CP+B is one of the few that has delivered. Alex Bogusky, the agency's executive creative director, challenges those working on an account to begin with a blank slate and answer the question, "What if there were no TV and no magazines—how would we make this brand famous?" If someone brings him an idea for a TV commercial right away, Bogusky says he won't even look at it.

CP+B solicits ideas for ads from everyone in the agency, including media and account services people, who are kept out of the creative loop at most agencies. The agency's goal is to find the best places to reach the target audience and the most interesting vehicles to carry the message, even if they have to be invented. For Molson beer, the agency wanted to trigger conversation among men in bars, which CP+B did by stamping individualized pickup lines on the labels of the bottles.

In 2004, Crispin won its biggest client yet when Burger King shifted its $300 million account giving the agency its first opportunity to work for a major mass marketer. Burger King presented CP+B with perhaps its biggest challenge as the fast-food chain's customer traffic and sales had declined over the past five years, and the company had changed advertising campaigns, as well as agencies, four times in as many years. However, if the Burger King account was at all intimidating it did not show up in the advertising as CP+B responded with some highly creative messages designed to rebuild BK's brand image among its primary target audience of young males. The branding effort included one of the most talked about campaigns in years called "Subservient Chicken," which began as an online viral marketing program that drew more than 14 million unique visitors to a website where they could give a command to a guy dressed up in a chicken suit, all in support of Burger King's new chicken sandwich. The campaign was later extended to other media, including TV, print, and a 10-minute film that ran on DirectTV. CP+B's creative work has helped contribute to a turnaround at Burger King as the company's store traffic is up for the first time since 1997, and sales growth is also up significantly.

CP+B continues to be as hot as South Beach on a Saturday night. In 2004, they were selected as "Agency of the Year" by *Advertising Age,* the industry's leading trade publication. However, Crispin plans to remain in Miami and ignore the temptation to open offices in major corporate centers such as New York. The agency's partners believe that being far removed from the big agencies and media giants has allowed them to evolve as an independent species that does things differently. CP+B has put itself, as well as Miami, on the advertising community's radar screen.

Sources: Warren Berger, "Dare-Devils," *Business 2.0,* April 2004, pp. 111–116; "Crispin Ups Ante," *Advertising Age,* January 10, 2005, pp. S1, 2; Mae Anderson, "Dissecting 'Subservient Chicken,'" *Adweek.com,* March 7, 2005.

Developing and implementing an integrated marketing communications program is usually a complex and detailed process involving the efforts of many persons. As consumers, we generally give little thought to the individuals or organizations that create the clever advertisements that capture our attention or the contests or sweepstakes we hope to win. But for those involved in the marketing process, it is important to understand the nature of the industry and the structure and functions of the organizations involved. As can be seen from the opening vignette, the advertising and promotions business is changing as marketers search for better ways to communicate with their customers. These changes are impacting the way marketers organize for marketing communications, as well as their relationships with advertising agencies and other communication specialists.

This chapter examines the various organizations that participate in the IMC process, their roles and responsibilities, and their relationship to one another. We discuss how companies organize internally for advertising and promotion. For most companies, advertising is planned and executed by an outside ad agency. Many large agencies offer a variety of other IMC capabilities, including public relations, Internet/interactive, sales promotion, and direct marketing. Thus, we will devote particular attention to the ad agency's role and the overall relationship between company and agency.

Other participants in the promotional process (such as direct-marketing, sales promotion, and interactive agencies and public relations firms) are becoming increasingly important as more companies take an integrated marketing communications approach to promotion. We examine the role of these specialized marketing communications organizations in the promotional process as well. The chapter concludes with a discussion of whether marketers are best served by using the integrated services of one large agency or the separate services of a variety of communications specialists.

Participants in the Integrated Marketing Communications Process: An Overview

Before discussing the specifics of the industry, we'll provide an overview of the entire system and identify some of the players. As shown in Figure 3-1, participants in the integrated marketing communications process can be divided into five major groups: the advertiser (or client), advertising agencies, media organizations, specialized communication services, and collateral services. Each group has specific roles in the promotional process.

The advertisers, or **clients,** are the key participants in the process. They have the products, services, or causes to be marketed, and they provide the funds that pay for advertising and promotions. The advertisers also assume major responsibility for developing the marketing program and making the final decisions regarding the advertising and promotional program to be employed. The organization may perform most

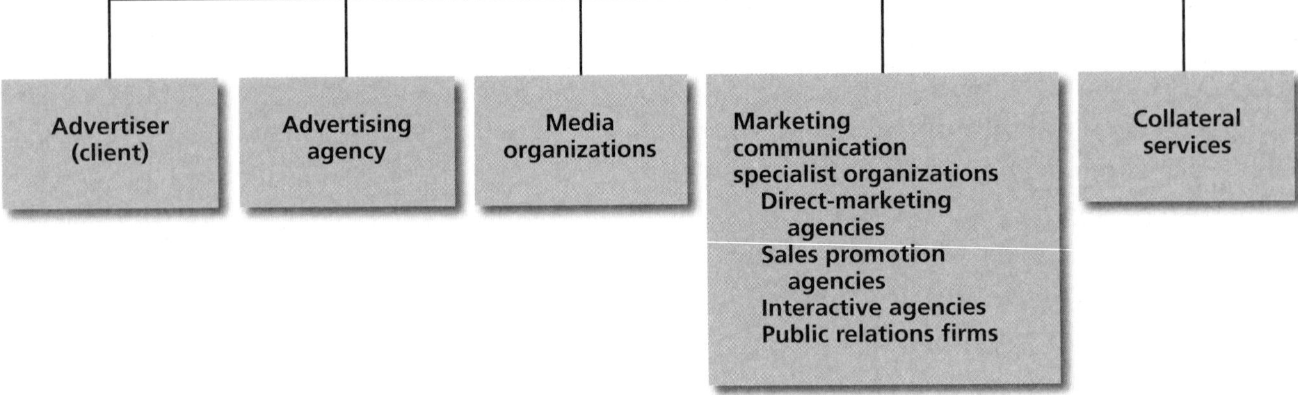
Advertiser (client)
Advertising agency
Media organizations
Marketing communication specialist organizations
Direct-marketing agencies
Sales promotion agencies
Interactive agencies
Public relations firms
Collateral services

Figure 3-1 Participants in the Integrated Marketing Communications Process

of these efforts itself, either through its own advertising department or by setting up an in-house agency.

However, many organizations use an **advertising agency,** an outside firm that specializes in the creation, production, and/or placement of the communications message and that may provide other services to facilitate the marketing and promotions process. Many large advertisers retain the services of a number of agencies, particularly when they market a number of products. For example, Kraft Foods uses as many as eight advertising agencies for its various brands, while Procter & Gamble uses five primary ad agencies and two major media buying services companies. Many large companies often use additional agencies that specialize in creating ads for specific ethnic markets. For example, in addition to its primary agency of record, Toyota Motor Corporation uses three additional agencies in the United States to create ads for the African-American, Hispanic, and Asian-American markets. More and more, ad agencies are acting as partners with advertisers and assuming more responsibility for developing the marketing and promotional programs.

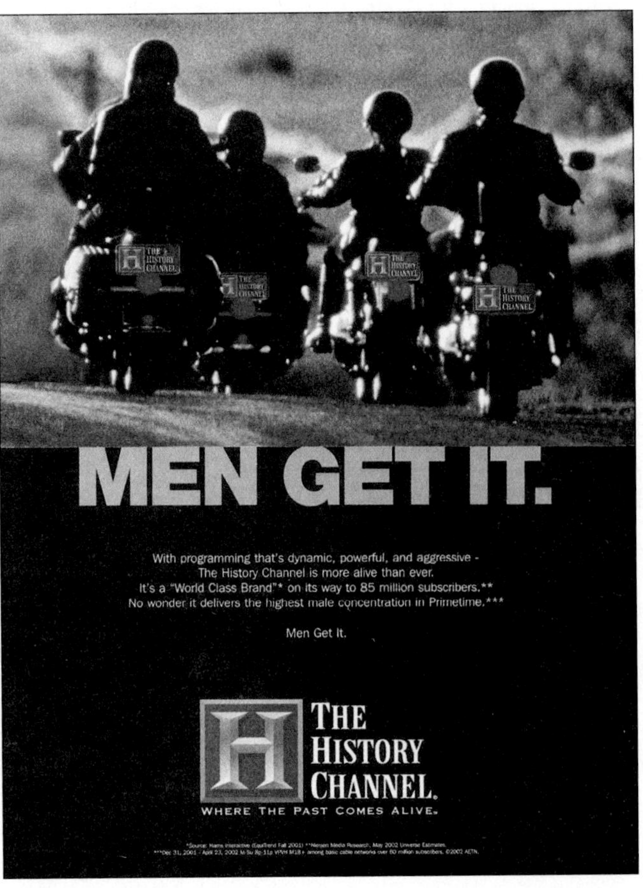
MEN GET IT.
With programming that's dynamic, powerful, and aggressive -
The History Channel is more alive than ever.
It's a "World Class Brand"* on its way to 85 million subscribers.**
No wonder it delivers the highest male concentration in Primetime.***
Men Get It.
THE HISTORY CHANNEL.
WHERE THE PAST COMES ALIVE.

Exhibit 3-1 The History Channel advertises its ability to reach male television viewers

Media organizations are another major participant in the advertising and promotions process. The primary function of most media is to provide information or entertainment to their subscribers, viewers, or readers. But from the perspective of the promotional planner, the purpose of media is to provide an environment for the firm's marketing communications message. The media must have editorial or program content that attracts consumers so that advertisers and their agencies will want to buy time or space with them. Exhibit 3-1 shows an ad run in advertising trade publications promoting the value of *The History Channel* magazine as a media vehicle for reaching men. While the media perform many other functions that help advertisers understand their markets and their customers, a medium's primary objective is to sell itself as a way for companies to reach their target markets with their messages effectively.

The next group of participants are organizations that provide **specialized marketing communications services.** They include direct-marketing agencies, sales promotion agencies, interactive agencies, and public relations firms. These organizations provide services in their areas of expertise. A direct-response agency develops and implements direct-marketing programs, while sales promotion agencies develop promotional programs such as contests and sweepstakes, premium offers, or sampling programs. Interactive agencies are being retained to develop websites for the Internet and help marketers as they move deeper into the realm of interactive media. Public relations firms are used to generate and manage publicity for a company and its products and services as well as to focus on its relationships and communications with its relevant publics.

The final participants shown in the promotions process of Figure 3-1 are those that provide **collateral services,** the wide range of support functions used by advertisers, agencies, media organizations, and specialized marketing communications firms. These individuals and companies perform specialized functions the other participants use in planning and executing advertising and other promotional functions. We will now examine the role of each participant in more detail. (Media organizations will be examined in Chapters 10 through 14.)

Organizing for Advertising and Promotion in the Firm: The Client's Role

Virtually every business organization uses some form of marketing communications. However, the way a company organizes for these efforts depends on several factors, including its size, the number of products it markets, the role of advertising and promotion in its marketing mix, the advertising and promotion budget, and its marketing organization structure. Many individuals throughout the organization may be involved in the advertising and promotion decision-making process. Marketing personnel have the most direct relationship with advertising and are often involved in many aspects of the decision process, such as providing input to the campaign plan, agency selection, and evaluation of proposed programs. Top management is usually interested in how the advertising program represents the firm, and this may also mean being involved in advertising decisions even when the decisions are not part of its day-to-day responsibilities.

While many people both inside and outside the organization have some input into the advertising and promotion process, direct responsibility for administering the program must be assumed by someone within the firm. Many companies have an advertising department headed by an advertising or communications manager operating under a marketing director. An alternative used by many large multiproduct firms is a decentralized marketing (brand management) system. A third option is to form a separate agency within the firm, an in-house agency. Each of these alternatives is examined in more detail in the following sections.

The Centralized System

In many organizations, marketing activities are divided along functional lines, with advertising placed alongside other marketing functions such as sales, marketing research, and product planning, as shown in Figure 3-2. The **advertising manager** is responsible for all promotions activities except sales (in some companies this individual

Figure 3-2 The Advertising Department under a Centralized System

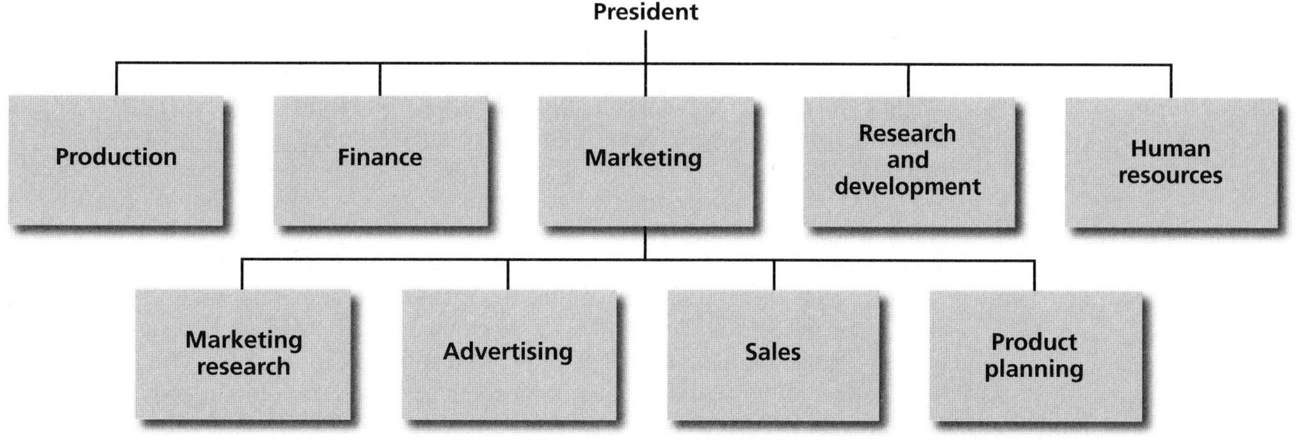

has the title of Marketing Communications Manager). In the most common example of a **centralized system,** the advertising manager controls the entire promotions operation, including budgeting, coordinating creation and production of ads, planning media schedules, and monitoring and administering the sales promotions programs for all the company's products or services.

The specific duties of the advertising or marketing communications manager depend on the size of the firm and the importance it places on promotional programs. Basic functions the manager and staff perform include the following.

Planning and Budgeting

The advertising department is responsible for developing advertising and promotions plans that will be approved by management and recommending a promotions program based on the overall marketing plan, objectives, and budget. Formal plans are submitted annually or when a program is being changed significantly, as when a new campaign is developed. While the advertising department develops the promotional budget, the final decision on allocating funds is usually made by top management.

Administration and Execution

The manager must organize the advertising department and supervise and control its activities. The manager also supervises the execution of the plan by subordinates and/or the advertising agency. This requires working with such departments as production, media, art, copy, and sales promotion. If an outside agency is used, the advertising department is relieved of much of the executional responsibility; however, it must review and approve the agency's plans.

Coordination with Other Departments

The manager must coordinate the advertising department's activities with those of other departments, particularly those involving other marketing functions. For example, the advertising department must communicate with marketing research and/or sales to determine which product features are important to customers and should be emphasized in the company's communications. Research may also provide profiles of product users and nonusers for the media department before it selects broadcast or print media. The advertising department may also be responsible for preparing material the sales force can use when calling on customers, such as sales promotion tools, advertising materials, and point-of-purchase displays.

Coordination with Outside Agencies and Services

Many companies have an advertising department but still use many outside services. For example, companies may develop their advertising programs in-house while employing media buying services to place their ads and/or use collateral services agencies to develop brochures, point-of-purchase materials, and so on. The department serves as liaison between the company and any outside service providers and also determines which ones to use. Once outside services are retained, the manager will work with other marketing managers to coordinate their efforts and evaluate their performances.

A centralized organizational system is often used when companies do not have many different divisions, product or service lines, or brands to advertise. For example, airlines such as Southwest, American, and Continental have centralized advertising departments. Many companies prefer a centralized advertising department because developing and coordinating advertising programs from one central location facilitates communication regarding the promotions program, making it easier for top management to participate in decision making. A centralized system may also result in a more efficient operation because fewer people are involved in the program decisions, and as their experience in making such decisions increases, the process becomes easier.

At the same time, problems are inherent in a centralized operation. First, it is difficult for the advertising department to understand the overall marketing strategy for the brand. The department may also be slow in responding to specific needs and problems of a product or brand. As companies become larger and develop or acquire new products, brands, or even divisions, the centralized system may become impractical.

The Decentralized System

In large corporations with multiple divisions and many different products, it is very difficult to manage all the advertising, promotional, and other functions through a centralized department. These types of companies generally have a **decentralized system,** with separate manufacturing, research and development, sales, and marketing departments for various divisions, product lines, or businesses. Many companies that use a decentralized system, such as Procter & Gamble, Unilever, and Nestlé, assign each product or brand to a **brand manager** who is responsible for the total management of the brand, including planning, budgeting, sales, and profit performance. (The term *product manager* is also used to describe this position.) The brand manager, who may have one or more assistant brand managers, is also responsible for the planning, implementation, and control of the marketing program.[1]

Under this system, the responsibilities and functions associated with advertising and promotions are transferred to the brand manager, who works closely with the outside advertising agency and other marketing communications specialists as they develop the promotional program.[2] In a multiproduct firm, each brand may have its own ad agency and may compete against other brands within the company, not just against outside competitors. For example, Exhibit 3-2 shows ads for Tide and ERA, which are both Procter & Gamble products that compete for a share of the laundry detergent market.

As shown in Figure 3-3, the advertising department is part of marketing services and provides support for the brand managers. The role of marketing services is to assist the brand managers in planning and coordinating the integrated marketing communications program. In some companies, the marketing services group may include sales promotion. The brand managers may work with sales promotion people to develop budgets, define strategies, and implement tactical executions for both trade and consumer promotions. Marketing services may also provide other types of support services, such as package design and merchandising.

Some companies may have an additional layer(s) of management above the brand managers to coordinate the efforts of all the brand managers handling a related group of products. An example is the organizational structure of Procter & Gamble, shown in Figure 3-4. This system—generally referred to as a **category management system**—includes category managers as well as brand and advertising managers. The category manager oversees management of the entire product category and focuses on the strategic role of the various brands in order to build profits and market share.[3]

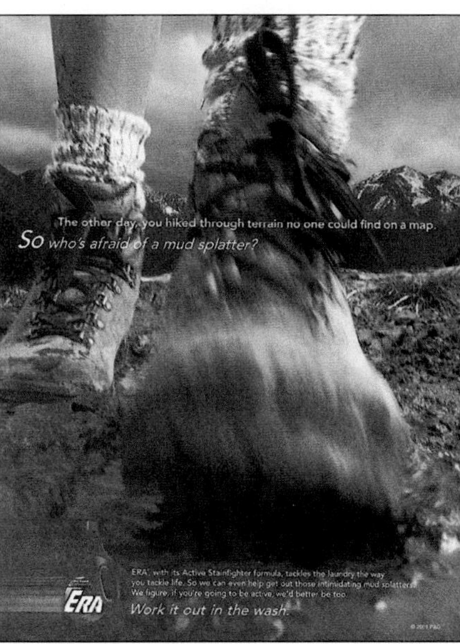

Exhibit 3-2 Many of Procter & Gamble's brands compete against each other

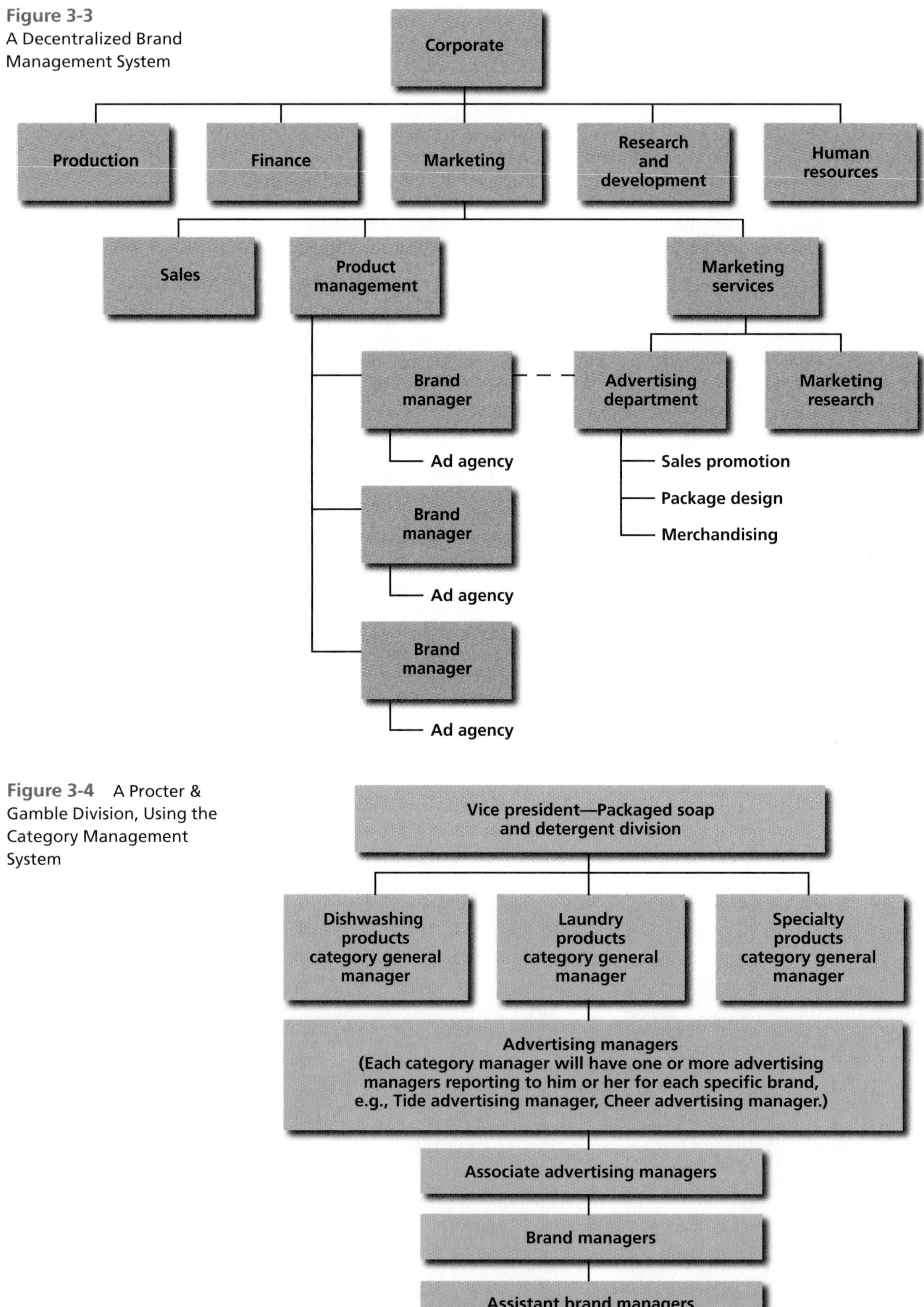

Figure 3-3 A Decentralized Brand Management System

Figure 3-4 A Procter & Gamble Division, Using the Category Management System

The advertising manager may review and evaluate the various parts of the program and advise and consult with the brand managers. This person may have the authority to override the brand manager's decisions on advertising. In some multiproduct firms that spend a lot on advertising, the advertising manager may coordinate the work of the various agencies to obtain media discounts for the firm's large volume of media purchases.

An advantage of the decentralized system is that each brand receives concentrated managerial attention, resulting in faster response to both problems and opportunities. The brand managers have full responsibility for the marketing program, including the identification of target markets as well as the development of integrated marketing communications programs that will differentiate the brand.[4] The brand manager system is also more flexible and makes it easier to adjust various aspects of the advertising and promotional program, such as creative platforms and media and sales promotion schedules.[5]

There are some drawbacks to the decentralized approach. Brand managers often lack training and experience. The promotional strategy for a brand may be developed by a brand manager who does not really understand what advertising or sales promotion can and cannot do and how each should be used. Brand managers may focus too much on short-run planning and administrative tasks, neglecting the development of long-term programs.

Another problem is that individual brand managers often end up competing for management attention, marketing dollars, and other resources, which can lead to unproductive rivalries and potential misallocation of funds. The manager's persuasiveness may become a bigger factor in determining budgets than the long-run profit potential of the brands. These types of problems were key factors in Procter & Gamble's decision to switch to a category management system.

Finally, the brand management system has been criticized for failing to provide brand managers with authority over the functions needed to implement and control the plans they develop.[6] Some companies have dealt with this problem by expanding the roles and responsibilities of the advertising and sales promotion managers and their staff of specialists. The staff specialists counsel the individual brand managers, and advertising or sales promotion decision making involves the advertising and/or sales promotion manager, the brand manager, and the marketing director. IMC Perspective 3-1 discusses why General Motors, which is the largest advertiser in the United States, decided to drop its brand management system and give division marketing directors more control of the advertising and promotion for its various models.

In-House Agencies

Some companies, in an effort to reduce costs and maintain greater control over agency activities, have set up their own advertising agencies internally. An **in-house agency** is an advertising agency that is set up, owned, and operated by the advertiser. Some in-house agencies are little more than advertising departments, but in other companies they are given a separate identity and are responsible for the expenditure of large sums of advertising dollars. Large advertisers that use in-house agencies include Calvin Klein, Avon, Revlon, and Benetton. Many companies use in-house agencies exclusively; others combine in-house efforts with those of outside agencies. For example, retail giant Target has an internal creative department that handles the design of its weekly circulars, direct-mail pieces, in-store displays, promotions, and other marketing materials. However, the retailer uses outside agencies to develop most of its branding and image-oriented ads and for specific TV and print assignments. Other retailers such as Benetton and Banana Republic also have in-house advertising departments that work with outside agencies (Exhibit 3-3).

A major reason for using an in-house agency is to reduce advertising and promotion costs. Companies with very large advertising budgets pay a substantial amount to outside agencies in the form of media commissions. With an internal structure, these commissions go to the in-house agency. An in-house agency can also provide related work such as sales presentations and sales force materials, package design, and public relations at a lower cost than outside agencies. A study by M. Louise Ripley found that creative and media services were the most likely functions to be performed outside, while merchandising and sales promotion were the most likely to be performed in-house.[7]

IMC PERSPECTIVE 3-1

General Motors Does Away with Brand Management

The goal of General Motors (GM) founder Alfred P. Sloan was to "build a car for every purse and purpose," and for many years GM created some of the strongest brand names in the auto industry including Cadillac, Pontiac, Chevrolet, Oldsmobile, Buick, and more recently Saturn and Hummer. However, during the 1980s and early 1990s, fuzzy advertising and marketing, as well as look-alike models from competing GM divisions, helped blur the identity of many of these brands. The problem was compounded by a system where dozens of managers in marketing, sales, and planning would work on various aspects of marketing for many different models. Moreover, GM's traditional divisional managers had too many responsibilities and could not give enough attention to the individual brands.

In 1996, GM decided to address these problems by implanting a brand management system for the purpose of again creating strong identities for its more than 40 brands of cars, trucks, minivans, and sport utility vehicles. While the use of brand management was new to GM, the organizational system had been around since 1927 when Procter & Gamble pioneered the concept by assigning a manager to work exclusively on Camay soap. Since then the practice of making a single manager a brand's internal champion with responsibility for all of its marketing had become commonplace in most large consumer, as well as industrial product, companies.

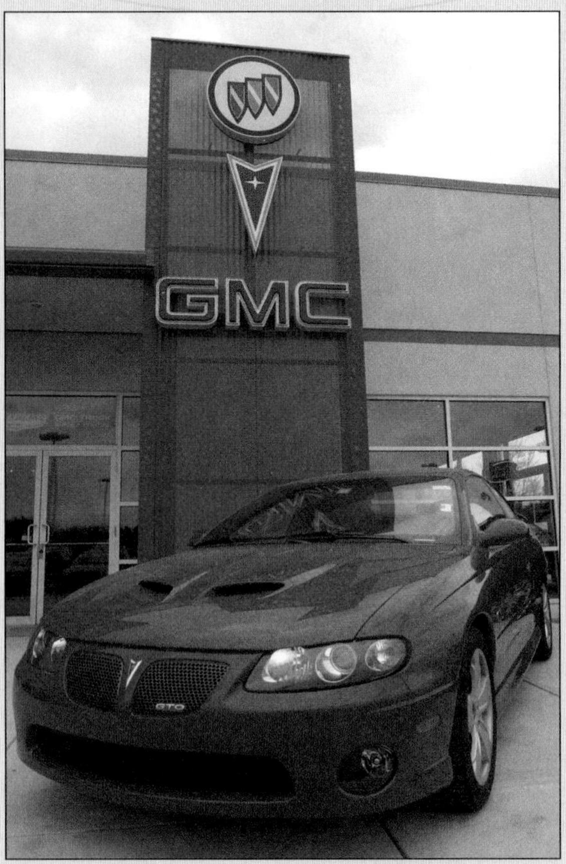

To put the new system into practice, GM named over 40 brand managers, including a number of outsiders from packaged goods companies such as Nabisco and Procter & Gamble. The brand managers worked under the general managers of the various GM divisions including Pontiac, Cadillac, Buick, Oldsmobile, Chevrolet, and GMC but were accountable for the sales success of individual brands such as the Chevrolet Malibu, Cadillac Seville, or Buick Century. They were also responsible for developing positioning platforms that would appeal to specific target markets based on analyses of their needs as well as conceiving, implementing, and managing advertising and promotion campaigns that would differentiate their brands.

When GM first implemented brand management, it was considered a success as the new system brought common processes and practices and helped eliminate duplicated marketing efforts across the various divisions. The system was credited with playing a major role in increasing sales of numerous GM models such as the Pontiac Grand Prix and Chevy Malibu. Under the brand management system, 30 key models had their own taglines and the advertising often barely mentioned the GM division. Moreover, many believed that the system was helping GM achieve its goal of creating strong brand images for its vehicles and getting consumers to pay full price rather than waiting for incentives such as rebates or low-interest financing.

While some GM executives were happy with the brand management system, others were becoming less and less enamored with it as the new millennium began. One concern was that the practice of developing distinct taglines for each individual model and barely mentioning the division name was confusing consumers. Another concern was that the system was placing too much emphasis on consumer research, which would dictate the decision-making process. Many felt that relying too much on consumer input for future vehicle designs would not work because of the long lead time to develop the products. As one executive noted, "The whole world rotated by the time the vehicle came out." Yet another problem was that the brand managers were never really given the authority that was called for in the original plan in areas such as product development, design, manufacturing, and pricing as the divisional executives who worked with engineers and manufacturing staff retained control.

In early 2002, GM announced that it was evolving its brand management system, and the definition of a brand no longer would apply to individual models but rather to divisions, which was the way the rest of the industry had done it for years. While new models would still receive dedicated advertising and promotion launches, they would use the division's brand umbrella theme. For example, ads for all Cadillac models use the "Break Through" tagline. In May 2002, GM eliminated the brand manager title and executives in these positions were retitled marketing directors. Instead of being assigned to individual models, the marketing directors were assigned to a group of vehicles that share a common engineering platform.

In early 2004, GM put the final nail in the coffin of its brand management effort when it announced a restructuring of the marketing staff at its vehicle division. Marketing directors who handled multiple nameplates were eliminated as were marketing teams that were aligned by model lines. They were replaced by a single marketing director and marketing team for each division, which has responsibility for advertising, promotion, and marketing for all models. The reorganization gives marketing directors more control of the IMC programs in that advertising directors now report to them rather than general managers of the divisions. Under the old system advertising directors had more power than marketing directors.

The reorganization may make things a little easier for the various advertising agencies that handle GM's brands as they incurred high overhead costs supporting each vehicle's brand team with account teams and other staff. GM is the largest advertiser in the United States as the company spends more than $3 billion per year on advertising and promotion. The company is hoping that the reorganization will help establish stronger identities for its various divisions as well as differentiate its various models. Ultimately GM hopes the new system will help the company regain some of the market share it has lost over the past two decades as its share of the highly competitive U.S. market has declined from 45 percent in 1980 to 25 percent in 2005. It appears that brand management was not the answer at GM and the company is looking for better ways to create a line of well-defined brands that Alfred Sloan would be proud of.

Sources: Jean Halliday, "GM Puts Final Nail in Coffin of Brand-Management Effort," *Advertising Age,* April 5, 2004, p. 8; Jean Halliday, "GM's Brand Management Evolves," *Automotive News,* June 24, 2002, p. M4; Kathleen Kerwin, "GM Warms Up the Branding Iron," *Business Week,* September 23, 1996, pp. 153–154.

Saving money is not the only reason companies use in-house agencies. Time savings, bad experiences with outside agencies, and the increased knowledge and understanding of the market that come from working on advertising and promotion for the product or service day by day are also reasons. Companies can also maintain tighter control over the process and more easily coordinate promotions with the firm's overall marketing program. Some companies use an in-house agency simply because they believe it can do a better job than an outside agency could.[8]

Opponents of in-house agencies say they can give the advertiser neither the experience and objectivity of an outside agency nor the range of services. They argue that outside agencies have more highly skilled specialists and attract the best creative talent

Exhibit 3-3 Benetton's in-house agency works with outside agencies to develop ads

Figure 3-5 Comparison of Advertising Organization Systems

Organizational system	Advantages	Disadvantages
Centralized	• Facilitated communications • Fewer personnel required • Continuity in staff • Allows for more top-management involvement	• Less involvement with and understanding of overall marketing goals • Longer response time • Inability to handle multiple product lines
Decentralized	• Concentrated managerial attention • Rapid response to problems and opportunities • Increased flexibility	• Ineffective decision making • Internal conflicts • Misallocation of funds • Lack of authority
In-house agencies	• Cost savings • More control • Increased coordination	• Less experience • Less objectivity • Less flexibility

and that using an external firm gives a company a more varied perspective on its advertising problems and greater flexibility. Outside agencies also can provide greater strategic planning capabilities, outside perspectives on customers, and more creative experience with certain media such as television.[9] In-house personnel may become narrow or grow stale while working on the same product line, but outside agencies may have different people with a variety of backgrounds and ideas working on the account. Flexibility is greater because an outside agency can be dismissed if the company is not satisfied, whereas changes in an in-house agency could be slower and more disruptive.

The cost savings of an in-house agency must be evaluated against these considerations. For many companies, high-quality advertising is critical to their marketing success and should be the major criterion in determining whether to use in-house services. Companies like Rockport and Redken Laboratories have moved their in-house work to outside agencies in recent years. Redken cited the need for a "fresh look" and objectivity as the reasons, noting that management gets too close to the product to come up with different creative ideas. Companies often hire outside agencies as they grow and their advertising budgets and needs increase. For example, Gateway hired a full-service outside agency to handle its advertising as the personal computer company experienced rapid growth during the 90s.[10]

The ultimate decision as to which type of advertising organization to use depends on which arrangement works best for the company. The advantages and disadvantages of the three systems are summarized in Figure 3-5. We now turn our attention to the functions of outside agencies and their roles in the promotional process.

Advertising Agencies

Many major companies use an advertising agency to assist them in developing, preparing, and executing their promotional programs. An ad agency is a service organization that specializes in planning and executing advertising programs for its clients. More than 13,000 U.S. and international agencies are listed in the *Standard Directory of Advertising Agencies* (the "Red Book"); however, most are individually owned small businesses employing fewer than five people. The U.S. ad agency business is highly concentrated. Nearly two-

Rank	Agency	Headquarters	Gross Income (Millions)
1	JWT* [WPP]	New York	$476.5
2	Leo Burnett Worldwide* [Publicis]	Chicago	362.7
3	McCann-Erickson Worldwide* [Interpublic]	New York	320.8
4	BBDO Worldwide* [Omnicom]	New York	272.0
5	Ogilvy & Mather Worldwide* [WPP]	New York	249.3
6	DDB Worldwide Communications* [Omnicom]	New York	248.1
7	Grey Worldwide* [WPP]	New York	231.9
8	Foote Cone & Belding Worldwide* [Interpublic]	New York	225.1
9	Y&R* [WPP]	New York	192.5
10	Publicis Worldwide* [Publicis]	New York	184.7
11	Saatchi & Saatchi* [Publicis]	New York	179.8
12	Deutsch* [Interpublic]	New York	165.1
13	Euro RSCG Worldwide* [Havas]	New York	161.4
14	Campbell-Ewald* [Interpublic]	Warren, Mich.	143.0
15	Doner	Southfield, Mich.	141.3
16	Richards Group	Dallas	134.0
17	TBWA Worldwide* [Omnicom]	New York	122.6
18	Lowe Worldwide* [Interpublic]	New York	120.9
19	Hill, Holliday, Connors, Cosmopulos* [Interpublic]	Boston	105.9
20	RPA	Santa Monica, Calif.	99.3
21	Campbell Mithun* [Interpublic]	Minneapolis	94.8
22	Arnold Worldwide* [Havas]	Boston	92.9
23	Dailey & Associates* [Interpublic]	West Hollywood, Calif.	90.3
24	Zimmerman & Partners* [Omnicom]	Ft. Lauderdale, Fla.	90.3
25	Cramer-Krasselt	Chicago	83.7

Source: *Advertising Age,* May 2, 2005, p. S-2.

Figure 3-6 Top 25 Agencies Ranked by U.S. Core Advertising Revenue, 2004

thirds of the domestic **billings** (the amount of client money agencies spend on media purchases and other equivalent activities) are handled by the top 500 agencies. In fact, just 10 U.S. agencies handle nearly 30 percent of the total volume of business done by the top 500 agencies in the United States. The top agencies also have foreign operations that generate substantial billings and income. The top 25 agencies, ranked by their U.S. gross incomes, are listed in Figure 3-6. The table shows that the advertising business is also geographically concentrated, with 14 of the top 25 agencies headquartered in New York City. Nearly 40 percent of U.S. agency business is handled by New York–based agencies. Other leading advertising centers in the United States include Boston, Chicago, Los Angeles, Detroit, and Minneapolis.[11] IMC Perspective 3-2 discusses how New York City remains the center of the advertising industry in the United States while other cities such as Chicago and San Francisco are losing some of their luster.

IMC PERSPECTIVE 3-2

New York City: Still the Big Apple of the Advertising Industry

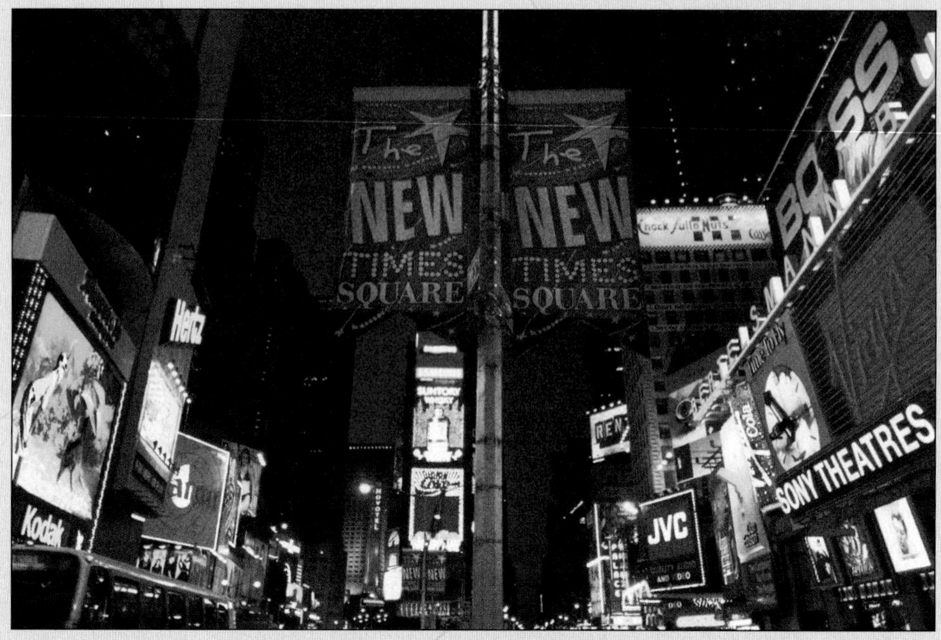

There is a famous *New Yorker* magazine illustration of a map of the United States that shows Manhattan in the foreground, then a vast empty space west of the Hudson River extending all the way to California. Some might argue that the illustration is indicative of the advertising industry in the United States, as New York City has long been the center of the agency business. New York City–based agencies account for nearly four times the annual billings of Chicago, which ranks second in total billings. In any given year, anywhere from 60 to 75 percent of the top 25 agencies are headquartered in New York City or the surrounding area. Of the top five agency holding companies, two are based in New York City while two others have their U.S. headquarters in the surrounding area. In addition to advertising agencies, nine of the top 10 media specialist companies are in the Big Apple as are the majority of the top direct marketing, interactive, and marketing services agencies.

There are a number of reasons why New York City is the center of the advertising business in the United States, including the fact that many of the major companies with large advertising budgets are based in the city or in a surrounding area. In 2005, 43 of the companies ranked in the Fortune 500 were headquartered in New York City while another 45 or so of the top firms were located nearby in suburbs or in cities in Connecticut or New Jersey. Nearly all of these top companies market their products and services around the world and prefer to have their global accounts stewarded from media-centric Manhattan. New York is the leading media center as all of the major television and radio networks are based in the city as are many magazines and news organizations. New York City is also, like Paris and London, a place where fashion, film, entertainment, publishing, and the arts all come together. As one agency executive notes, "Advertising has always looked to these other fields for inspiration. But now people outside advertising are savvy to that, too. If you're in a pop-culture backwater and you're not tapped into it, then you're screwed because not only are your competitors clued into it, your consumers are, too." Many of the top young creative talent in the world of advertising feed on the energy of New York and find it an inspiring place to live and work.

While many advertising agencies as well as other types of marketing communication companies are soaking up the energy of New York City, other cities such as Chicago and San Francisco are losing ground as advertising centers. Chicago is still a major advertising center and holds a prominent, although distant second, place behind New York in terms of total client billings. Many of the major megamarketers in the Midwest including Sears, Kraft Foods, Kellogg's, McDonald's, General Motors, and Anheuser-Busch use Chicago agencies such as Leo Burnett, DDB Worldwide, and Burrell Communications as well as direct marketing firms such as Draft. Chicago agencies have always had a great deal of stability as many of their clients have been traditional packaged-goods marketers such as Helene Curtis, Kimberly-Clark, and Kraft rather than technology companies or dot-coms. However, Chicago agencies have often had to deal with the stigma of lagging behind agencies in New York and other cities in terms of creativity. One reason given for this is that much of the elite junior and senior creative talent is drawn to New York where there are more creatively focused shops. There are also fewer creative boutiques and midsized agencies in Chicago, which is where some of the most innovative and creative work often originates.

The chief creative officer of one Chicago agency notes that the city is never going to be viewed as a top creative market as it has built an image of being hardworking and responsible with its creative work and a reputation of being a solid, straightforward place to do advertising. Of course, many advertising people on Michigan Avenue might disagree with the claim that Madison Avenue is the center of the advertising universe or that their work is not as creative. They could cite some of the outstanding ads created by Leo Burnett for Altoids or campaigns developed by DDB for Anheuser-Busch brands such as Budweiser and Bud Light as examples. However, many will argue that Chicago enjoyed its golden age one or two decades ago when agencies like Leo Burnett, Foote Cone & Belding, and Needham Harper & Steers were pumping out award-winning campaigns for big brands such as Hallmark Cards, Kellogg's, and others.

Another city that has lost some of its luster as an advertising center in recent years is San Francisco. For many years the city on the left coast was a center of advertising creativity, owing to its combination of top-rate opportunities for advertising professionals along with an appealing lifestyle. At the beginning of the new millennium, there were 14 hot creative shops in San Francisco. However, by 2005 only seven were still in business, and some of these have downsized as they have lost key accounts. The advertising industry in the Bay area was shaken by the dot-com bust and the fact that many of the surviving companies such as Yahoo! and E*Trade Financial Corp. have moved their accounts from San Francisco–based agencies.

A number of other San Francisco–based companies that have traditionally used in-town agencies are also straying, including Chevron, Visa International, and Electronic Arts. Foote Cone & Belding (FCB), San Francisco, which was once the largest agency in the West, has downsized in recent years as a result of losing key accounts such as Levi Strauss & Co. The only San Francisco agency on *Advertising Age*'s top 100 list is Goodby, Silverstein & Partners whose clients include Saturn, Hewlett-Packard, and the California Milk Processor Board for whom it has created the popular "Got Milk?" campaign. The former head of FCB has noted that most San Francisco agencies may have to position themselves as regional shops because they will not have the staff and depth needed to pitch national accounts.

While major cities such as New York and Chicago still dominate the advertising industry, the onetime view of individual cities as creative meccas may be changing. Creative work is coming from agencies in many other cities such as Crispin Porter + Bogusky in Miami; Wieden & Kennedy in Portland, Oregon; Fallon Worldwide in Minneapolis; and GSD&M in Austin, Texas. However, it does appear that the shift toward a media-centric, pop culture–obsessed society as well as an increasingly global economy is helping the Big Apple to regain its status as the center of the advertising universe.

Sources: Alice Z. Cuneo, "Not So Golden Anymore," *Advertising Age*, January 24, 2005, pp. 1, 53; Kate Macarthur, "Chicago Blues," *Advertising Age*, September 10, 2001, pp. 1, 7; Anthony Vagnoni, "NYC: Cool (Again)," *Advertising Age*, April 12, 1999, pp. 1, 2.

During the late 1980s and into the 90s, the advertising industry underwent major changes as large agencies merged with or acquired other agencies and support organizations to form large advertising organizations, or superagencies. These **superagencies** were formed so that agencies could provide clients with integrated marketing communications services worldwide. Some advertisers became disenchanted with the superagencies and moved to smaller agencies that were flexible and more responsive.[12] However, during the mid-90s the agency business went through another wave of consolidation as a number of medium-size agencies were acquired and became part of large advertising organizations such as Omnicom Group, WPP Group, and the Interpublic Group of Cos. Many of the mid-size agencies were acquired by or forged alliances with larger agencies because their clients wanted an agency with international communications capabilities and their alignment with larger organizations gave them access to a network of agencies around the world. The consolidation of the agency business continued into the new millennium as large agencies such as Fallon Worldwide, Leo Burnett, Saatchi & Saatchi, and Kaplan Thaler were acquired by the giant French holding company Publicis Groupe. By 2005, the top four holding companies—Omnicom, WPP, Interpublic, and Publicis—accounted for 57 percent of the publicly reported advertising and marketing revenue in the United States.[13]

Many of the advertising organizations and major agencies have been acquiring companies specializing in areas such as interactive communications, public relations, direct marketing, and sales promotion so that they can offer their clients an ever-broader range of integrated marketing communication services.[14] Recently the activity of the advertising holding companies has moved in a new direction as they have begun pursuing alliances with talent agencies. An agreement negotiated between the Screen Actors Guild and the Association of Talent Agents in 2002 allows outside investors such as advertising agencies to own stakes in talent agencies that seek and negotiate work on behalf of actors, directors, and writers as well as some athletes.[15] By having a stake in the talent business, ad agencies can negotiate deals with current, as well as up-and-coming, celebrities for their clients.

The Ad Agency's Role

The functions performed by advertising agencies might be conducted by the clients themselves through one of the designs discussed earlier in this chapter, but most large companies use outside firms. This section discusses some reasons advertisers use external agencies.

Reasons for Using an Agency

Probably the main reason outside agencies are used is that they provide the client with the services of highly skilled individuals who are specialists in their chosen fields. An advertising agency staff may include artists, writers, media analysts, researchers, and others with specific skills, knowledge, and experience who can help market the client's products or services. Many agencies specialize in a particular type of business and use their knowledge of the industry to assist their clients. For example, Mentus Inc. is an agency that specializes in integrated marketing communications for the high-technology, e-commerce, and bioscience industries (Exhibit 3-4).

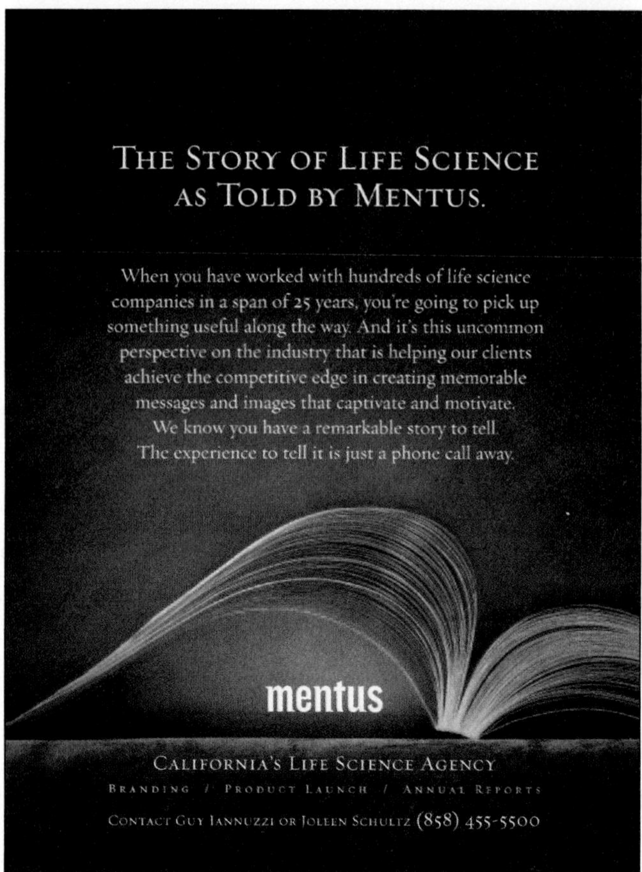

Exhibit 3-4 Mentus Communications specializes in creating ads for high-tech companies

An outside agency can also provide an objective viewpoint of the market and its business that is not subject to internal company policies, biases, or other limitations. The agency can draw on the broad range of experience it has gained while working on a diverse set of marketing problems for various clients. For example, an ad agency that is handling a travel-related account may have individuals who have worked with airlines, cruise ship companies, travel agencies, hotels, and other travel-related industries. The agency may have experience in this area or may even have previously worked on the advertising account of one of the client's competitors. Thus, the agency can provide the client with insight into the industry (and, in some cases, the competition).

Types of Ad Agencies

Since ad agencies can range in size from a one- or two-person operation to large organizations with over 1,000 employees, the services offered and functions performed will vary. This section examines the different types of agencies, the services they perform for their clients, and how they are organized.

Full-Service Agencies

Many companies employ what is known as a **full-service agency,** which offers its clients a full range of marketing, communications, and promotions services, including planning, creating, and producing the advertising; performing research; and selecting media. A full-service agency may also offer nonadvertising services such as strategic market planning; sales promotions, direct marketing, and interactive capabilities; package design; and public relations and publicity.

The full-service agency is made up of departments that provide the activities needed to perform the various advertising functions and serve the client, as shown in Figure 3-7.

Account Services

Account services, or account management, is the link between the ad agency and its clients. Depending on the size of the client and its advertising budget, one or more account executives serve as liaison. The **account executive** is responsible for understanding the advertiser's marketing and promotions needs and interpreting them to agency personnel. He or she coordinates agency efforts in planning, creating, and producing ads. The account executive also presents agency recommendations and obtains client approval.

As the focal point of agency-client relationships, the account executive must know a great deal about the client's business and be able to communicate this to specialists in the agency working on the account.[16] The ideal account executive has a strong marketing background as well as a thorough understanding of all phases of the advertising process.

Marketing Services

Over the past two decades, use of marketing services has increased dramatically. One service gaining increased attention is research, as agencies realize that to communicate effectively with their clients' customers, they must have a good understanding of the target audience. As shown in Chapter 1, the advertising planning process begins with a thorough situation analysis, which is based on research and information about the target audience.

Most full-service agencies maintain a *research department* whose function is to gather, analyze, and interpret information that will be useful in developing advertising for their clients. This can be done through primary research—where a study is designed, executed, and interpreted by the research department—or through the use of

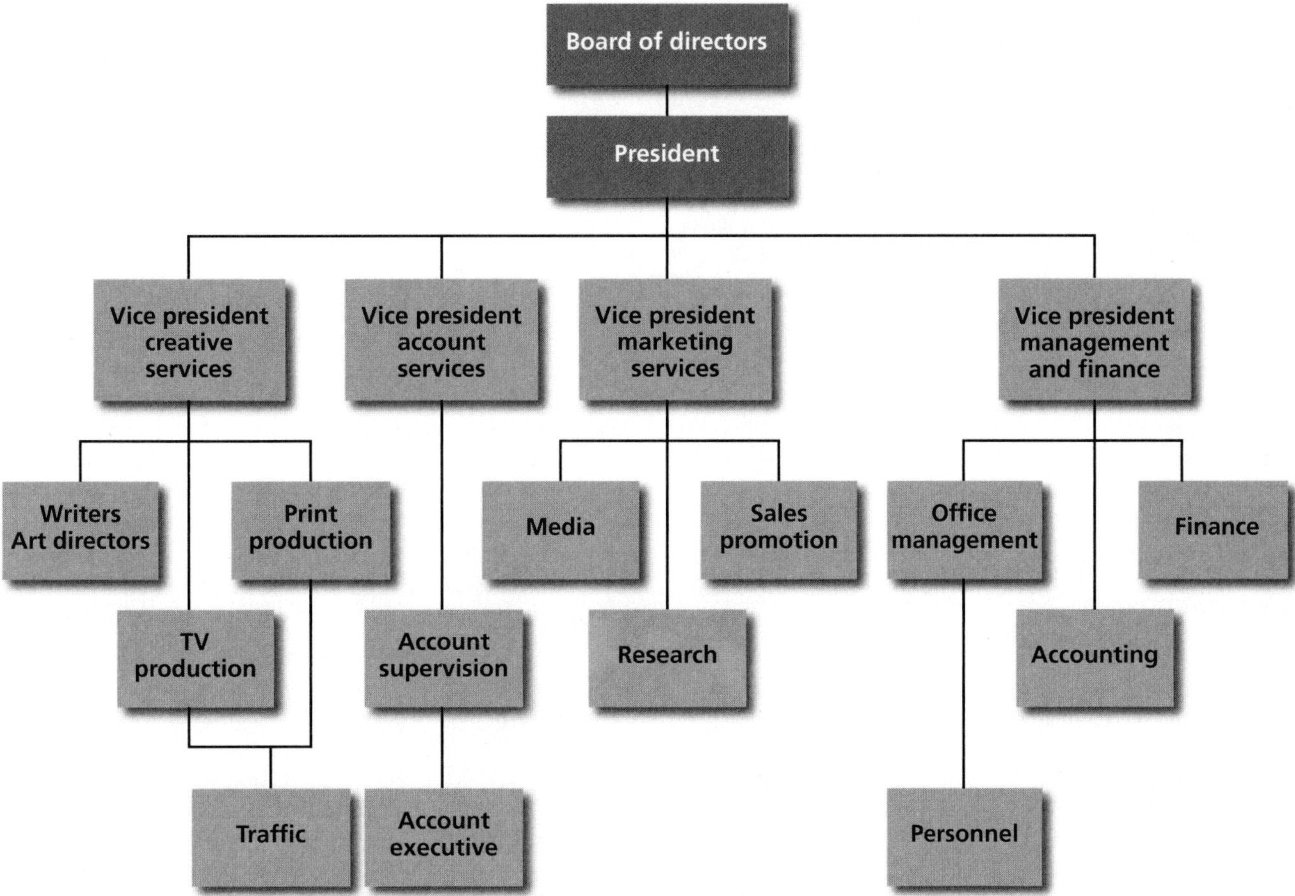

Figure 3-7 Full-Service Agency Organizational Chart

secondary (previously published) sources of information. Sometimes the research department acquires studies conducted by independent syndicated research firms or consultants. The research staff then interprets these reports and passes on the information to other agency personnel working on that account. The research department may also design and conduct research to pretest the effectiveness of advertising the agency is considering. For example, copy testing is often conducted to determine how messages developed by the creative specialists are likely to be interpreted by the receiving audience.

In many large agencies, the marketing services department may include **account planners** who are individuals that gather information that is relevant to the client's product or service and can be used in the development of the creative strategy as well as other aspects of the IMC campaign. Account planners work with the client as well as other agency personnel including the account executives, creative team members, media specialists, and research department personnel to gather information about the target audience. They organize all of the information and make recommendations regarding advertising and promotion strategy that can be used by the creative department as well as by others in the agency.

The *media department* of an agency analyzes, selects, and contracts for space or time in the media that will be used to deliver the client's advertising message. The media department is expected to develop a media plan that will reach the target market and effectively communicate the message. Since most of the client's ad budget is spent on media time and/or space, this department must develop a plan that both communicates with the right audience and is cost-effective.

Media specialists must know what audiences the media reach, their rates, and how well they match the client's target market. The media department reviews information on demographics, magazine and newspaper readership, radio listenership, and consumers' Internet and TV viewing patterns to develop an effective media plan. The media buyer implements the media plan by purchasing the actual time and space.

CAREER PROFILE

Dan Kohler

Account Director, Margeotes Fertitta Powell

If there's one thing I've learned in my 11-plus-year career in advertising, it's that opportunities are yours to create: All it takes is a willingness to speak up and take little risks. At one crazy point of my life, I thought I was going to be an accountant. Yes, a full-fledged CPA. You see, I had majored in accounting at Indiana University, and by the time I graduated, the job offers were on the table. During the process of thinking through which "Big 6" firm would offer the best home for me, I came upon the startling realization that perhaps none of them would provide me with the proper outlet for the creative side of my personality. So with a sigh of reluctance, I decided to switch career paths upon college graduation. The next obvious question was: What to do? I had always enjoyed my marketing and advertising classes—especially the creative, problem-solving aspects. The right-to-left-brain ratio was there, and so I decided to channel all energies into finding a job at an advertising agency.

I landed my first job not at an agency, but at a company called Life Fitness, working in their market research department. My job was to unearth insights about various pieces of exercise equipment by talking with consumers. I didn't realize it at the time, but that first job provided a frame of reference on some basic components of account planning. Shortly thereafter, I leveraged my "expertise" with numbers to position myself as a star media department candidate and was able to snag my first agency job at Hal Riney & Partners in Chicago. As an assistant media planner, I worked on accounts such as Progressive Insurance and John Deere & Company.

After about a year, when I really started understanding the roles different departments in the agency play, I decided that account management was where I belonged. From strategic and creative development all the way through getting a commercial on air, account managers could plunge into everything, all while driving the client relationship. I loved the fact that the account planner is kind of the "hub of the wheel." So one early morning, I decided to take a little risk and place a call to the agency president to set up a meeting to talk about my career. In that meeting he said to me, "We're pitching this business and I'd like for you to get involved. If we win it, you're the assistant account executive." I gladly took up the challenge and did what it took to help prepare the agency for the pitch. I even participated in the pitch meeting itself. Soon thereafter, I had a new title on my business card and the president became my first mentor.

In order to continue growing, you need to be willing to shake things up and keep challenging yourself.

When working at an agency it is important to remember that although you spend most of your time focused on your own accounts, you really work for the agency as a whole. While at Riney I made sure to get involved with as much as possible, and got to know everyone in the agency. After four years as an account person, I was promoted several times and built up solid marketing and advertising experience working on clients such as Subway Sandwiches, Budget Rent a Car, Midway Video Games, RollingStone.com, and new business.

With that under my belt, I decided to take a chance and try out a new lifestyle, climate, and advertising market. I moved to Los Angeles to join Dailey and Associates, working on the Kauffman and Broad account. After a year, I moved to Deutsch Advertising, where I was hired to work on the AIG SunAmerica account and new business. The first pitch I was involved with was for the California Milk Advisory Board (CMAB) account. I was extremely impressed with the quality of the client and the work that the agency developed on their behalf. When the agency won the CMAB advertising assignment, I quickly set up a meeting with the general manager of the agency requesting that I be assigned to the account. And thus began an extremely rewarding six-year tenure at Deutsch. The benefit of working for a mid-sized agency is that you realize the value of working on large world-class brands without the layers that can limit exposure to agency upper management. At Deutsch I was given the opportunity to interface with many of the heads of departments on a regular basis—especially while working on new business assignments. While there, I also added Burger King and the Partnership for a Drug-Free America to my client repertoire. These experiences gave me the understanding and exposure tantamount in my growing into the account person I am today.

The latest opportunity I created has taken me across the country to Manhattan, where I recently joined Margeotes Fertitta Powell to help run the Coca-Cola and Perry apparel accounts. It all ties back to risk taking—in order to continue growing, you need to be willing to shake things up and keep challenging yourself. It's ongoing.

The media department is becoming an increasingly important part of the agency business. An agency's ability to negotiate prices and effectively use the vast array of media vehicles, as well as other sources of customer contact, is becoming as important as its ability to create ads. Some of the major agencies and/or their holding companies have formed independent media services companies to better serve their clients. For example, Starcom MediaVest Group is a subsidiary of the Publicis Groupe and has a network of over 100 offices in 67 countries, while McCann Erickson Worldwide formed Universal McCann, which is now one of the primary media specialist agencies for the Interpublic Group. Other large media specialist companies include MindShare, which is owned by the WPP Group, and OMD Worldwide, which is owned by the Omnicom Group. These media specialist firms serve the media needs of the agencies that are part of their parent holding companies but may also offer media services to other clients as well. A number of large advertisers have consolidated their media buying with these large media specialist companies to save money and improve media efficiency. For example, General Motors consolidated its nearly $3.5 billion national and regional media buying account with Starcom MediaVest in 2005 while MindShare handles all of the global media planning and buying for American Express.[17]

The research and media departments perform most of the functions that full-service agencies need to plan and execute their clients' advertising programs. Some agencies offer additional marketing services to their clients to assist in other promotional areas. An agency may have a sales promotion department, or merchandising department, that specializes in developing contests, premiums, promotions, point-of-sale materials, and other sales materials. It may have direct-marketing specialists and package designers, as well as a PR/publicity department. Many agencies have developed interactive media departments to create websites for their clients. The growing popularity of integrated marketing communications has prompted many full-function agencies to develop capabilities and offer services in these other promotional areas. Traditional advertising agencies are recognizing that they must develop integrated marketing capabilities that extend beyond media advertising.

Creative Services

The creative services department is responsible for the creation and execution of advertisements. The individuals who conceive the ideas for the ads and write the headlines, subheads, and body copy (the words constituting the message) are known as **copywriters.** They may also be involved in determining the basic appeal or theme of the ad campaign and often prepare a rough initial visual layout of the print ad or television commercial.

While copywriters are responsible for what the message says, the *art department* is responsible for how the ad looks. For print ads, the art director and graphic designers prepare *layouts,* which are drawings that show what the ad will look like and from which the final artwork will be produced. For TV commercials, the layout is known as a *storyboard,* a sequence of frames or panels that depict the commercial in still form.

Members of the creative department work together to develop ads that will communicate the key points determined to be the basis of the creative strategy for the client's product or service. Writers and artists generally work under the direction of the agency's creative director, who oversees all the advertising produced by the organization. The director sets the creative philosophy of the department and may even become directly involved in creating ads for the agency's largest clients.

Once the copy, layout, illustrations, and mechanical specifications have been completed and approved, the ad is turned over to the *production department.* Most agencies do not actually produce finished ads; they hire printers, engravers, photographers, typographers, and other suppliers to complete the finished product. For broadcast production, the approved storyboard must be turned into a finished commercial. The production department may supervise the casting of people to appear in the ad and the setting for the scenes as well as choose an independent production studio. The department may hire an outside director to turn the creative concept into a commercial. For example, several companies, including Nike and Kmart, have used film director Spike Lee to direct their commercials; Airwalk shoes has used John Glen, who directed many of the James Bond films, for its TV spots. Copywriters, art directors, account managers, people from research and planning, and representatives from the client side may all participate in production decisions, particularly when large sums of money are involved.

Creating an advertisement often involves many people and takes several months. In large agencies with many clients, coordinating the creative and production processes can be a major problem. A *traffic department* coordinates all phases of production to see that the ads are completed on time and that all deadlines for submitting the ads to the media are met. The traffic department may be located in the creative services area of the agency, or be part of media or account management, or be separate.

Management and Finance

Like any other business, an advertising agency must be managed and perform basic operating and administrative functions such as accounting, finance, and human resources. It must also attempt to generate new business. Large agencies employ administrative, managerial, and clerical people to perform these functions. The bulk of an agency's income (approximately 64 percent) goes to salary and benefits for its employees. Thus, an agency must manage its personnel carefully and get maximum productivity from them.

Agency Organization and Structure

Full-function advertising agencies must develop an organizational structure that will meet their clients' needs and serve their own internal requirements. Most medium-size and large agencies are structured under either a departmental or a group system. Under the **departmental system,** each of the agency functions shown in Figure 3-7 is set up as a separate department and is called on as needed to perform its specialty and serve all of the agency's clients. Ad layout, writing, and production are done by the creative department, marketing services is responsible for any research or media selection and purchases, and the account services department handles client contact. Some agencies prefer the departmental system because it gives employees the opportunity to develop expertise in servicing a variety of accounts.

Many large agencies use the **group system,** in which individuals from each department work together in groups to service particular accounts. Each group is headed by an account executive or supervisor and has one or more media people, including media planners and buyers; a creative team, which includes copywriters, art directors, artists, and production personnel; and one or more account executives. The group may also include individuals from other departments such as marketing research, direct marketing, or sales promotion. The size and composition of the group varies depending on the client's billings and the importance of the account to the agency. For very important accounts, the group members may be assigned exclusively to one client. In some agencies, they may serve a number of smaller clients. Many agencies prefer the group system because employees become very knowledgeable about the client's business and there is continuity in servicing the account.

Other Types of Agencies and Services

Not every agency is a large full-service agency. Many smaller agencies expect their employees to handle a variety of jobs. For example, account executives may do their own research, work out their own media schedule, and coordinate the production of ads written and designed by the creative department. Many advertisers, including some large companies, are not interested in paying for the services of a full-service agency but are interested in some of the specific services agencies have to offer. Over the past few decades, several alternatives to full-service agencies have evolved, including creative boutiques and media buying services.

Creative Boutiques

Creative boutiques are small ad agencies that provide only creative services and have long been an important part of the advertising industry. These specialized agencies have creative personnel such as writers and artists on staff but do not have media, research, or account planning capabilities. Creative boutiques have developed in response to some companies' desires to use only the creative services of an outside agency while maintaining control of other marketing communication functions internally. While most creative boutiques work directly

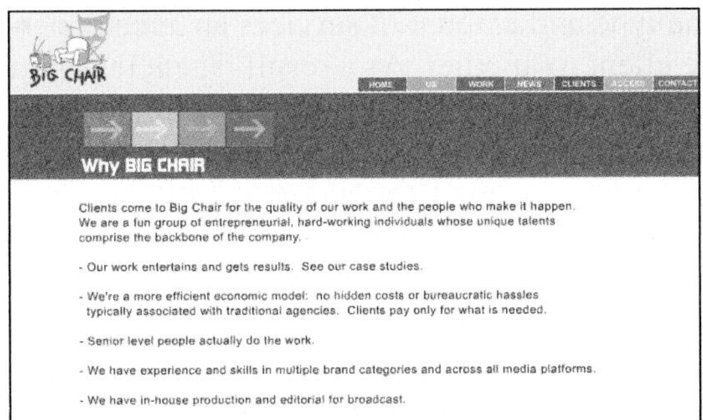

Exhibit 3-5 Big Chair Creative Group is a very successful creative boutique

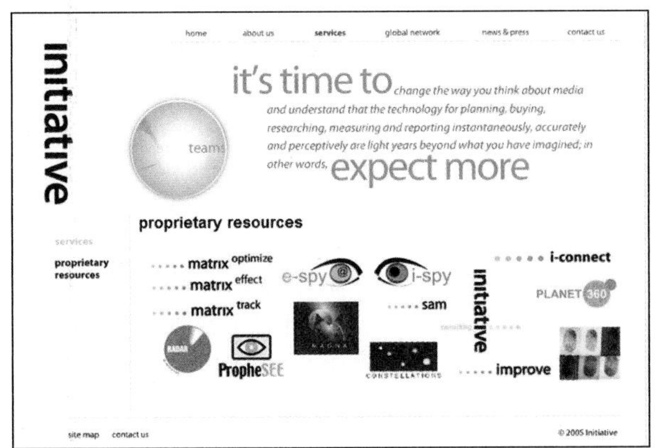

Exhibit 3-6 Initiative is one of the leading media specialist companies

for companies, full-service agencies often subcontract work to them when they are very busy or want to avoid adding full-time employees to their payrolls. They are usually compensated on a project or hourly fee basis.

Many creative boutiques have been formed by members of the creative departments of full-service agencies who leave the firm and take with them clients who want to retain their creative talents. An advantage of these smaller agencies is their ability to turn out inventive creative work quickly and without the cumbersome bureaucracy and politics of larger agencies. Many companies also prefer working directly with a smaller creative boutique because they can get more attention and better access to creative talent than they would at a larger agency. An example of a successful creative boutique is Big Chair Creative Group, which is a New York–based agency whose clients include magazines such as *Time, Vibe,* and *Sports Illustrated* as well as brands such as Smirnoff Ice and Lever 2000 soap (Exhibit 3-5).

Creative boutiques will continue to be an important part of the advertising industry. However, they face challenges as many find themselves competing against larger agencies for business, particularly when there are cutbacks in advertising spending. Moreover, many clients want the range of services that large agencies provide as they are often looking for business-building ideas rather than just creative work.[18]

Media Specialist Companies

Media specialist companies are companies that specialize in the buying of media, particularly radio and television time. The task of purchasing advertising media has grown more complex as specialized media proliferate, so media buying services have found a niche by specializing in the analysis and purchase of advertising time and space. Agencies and clients usually develop their own media strategies and hire the buying service to execute them. Some media buying services do help advertisers plan their media strategies. Because media buying services purchase such large amounts of time and space, they receive large discounts and can save the small agency or client money on media purchases. Media buying services are paid a fee or commission for their work.

Media buying services have been experiencing strong growth in recent years as clients seek alternatives to full-service agency relationships. Many companies have been unbundling agency services and consolidating media buying to get more clout from their advertising budgets. Nike, Maytag, and Gateway are among those that have switched some or all of their media buying from full-service agencies to independent media buyers. As noted earlier, many of the major agencies have formed independent media services companies that handle the media planning and buying for their clients and also offer their services separately to companies interested in a more specialized or consolidated approach to media planning, research, and/or buying. The rise of the independent media-buying services, operating outside the structure of the traditional ad agency media department, and the divestment of these departments from the agency system are two of the most significant developments that have occurred in the advertising industry in recent years. Exhibit 3-6 shows how Initiative, which is one of the largest media specialist companies, promotes its services.

Agency Compensation

As you have seen, the type and amount of services an agency performs vary from one client to another. As a result, agencies use a variety of methods to get paid for their services. Agencies are typically compensated in three ways: commissions, some type of fee arrangement, or percentage charges.

Commissions from Media

The traditional method of compensating agencies is through a **commission system,** where the agency receives a specified commission (usually 15 percent) from the media on any advertising time or space it purchases for its client. (For outdoor advertising, the commission is 16⅔ percent.) This system provides a simple method of determining payments, as shown in the following example.

Assume an agency prepares a full-page magazine ad and arranges to place the ad on the back cover of a magazine at a cost of $100,000. The agency places the order for the space and delivers the ad to the magazine. Once the ad is run, the magazine will bill the agency for $100,000, less the 15 percent ($15,000) commission. The media will also offer a 2 percent cash discount for early payment, which the agency may pass along to the client. The agency will bill the client $100,000 less the 2 percent cash discount on the net amount, or a total of $98,300, as shown in Figure 3-8. The $15,000 commission represents the agency's compensation for its services.

Appraisal of the Commission System

While the commission system was the primary agency compensation method for many years, it has always been controversial. Critics of the commission system have long argued that it encourages agencies to recommend high-priced media to their clients to increase their commission level. The system has also been criticized on the grounds that it ties agency compensation to media costs, which have been skyrocketing over the past decade. Still others charge that the system encourages agencies to recommend mass-media advertising and avoid noncommissionable IMC tools such as direct mail, sales promotion, public relations, or event sponsorships, unless they are requested by the clients.

Defenders of the commission system argue that it is easy to administer and keeps the emphasis in agency compensation on nonprice factors such as the quality of the advertising developed for clients. Proponents of the system argue that agency services are proportional to the size of the commission, since more time and effort are devoted to the large accounts that generate high revenue for the agency. They also note that the system is more flexible than it appears as agencies often perform other services for large clients at no extra charge as a way of justifying the large commission they receive.

Companies began moving away from the commission system during the 1990s, and most companies no longer use it as the basis for compensating their agencies. A 2004 study of agency compensation conducted by the Association of National Advertisers (ANA) found that only 10 percent of major advertisers still paid commissions to their agencies, down from 21 percent in 2000.[19] Among those companies that do pay commissions, most do not pay the traditional 15 percent. Many advertisers have gone to a **negotiated commission** system whereby the commissions average from 8 to 10 percent or are based on a sliding scale that becomes lower as the clients' media expenditures increase. Agencies are also relying less on media commissions for their income

Figure 3-8 Example of Commission System Payment

Media Bills Agency		Agency Bills Advertiser	
Costs for magazine space	$100,000	Costs for magazine space	$100,000
Less 15% commission	−15,000	Less 2% cash discount	−1,700
Cost of media space	85,000	Advertiser pays agency	$ 98,300
Less 2% cash discount	−1,700		
Agency pays media	$ 83,300	Agency income	$ 15,000

as their clients expand their IMC programs to include other forms of promotion and cut back on mass-media advertising. The amount of agency income coming from media commissions is declining as many companies are now using other methods of agency compensation such as fees and performance-based incentives.

Fee, Cost, and Incentive-Based Systems

Since many believe the commission system is not equitable to all parties, many agencies and their clients have developed some type of fee arrangement or cost-plus agreement for agency compensation. Some are using incentive-based compensation, which is a combination of a commission and a fee system.

Fee Arrangement

There are two basic types of fee arrangement systems. In the straight or **fixed-fee method,** the agency charges a basic monthly fee for all of its services and credits to the client any media commissions earned. Agency and client agree on the specific work to be done and the amount the agency will be paid for it. Sometimes agencies are compensated through a **fee-commission combination,** in which the media commissions received by the agency are credited against the fee. If the commissions are less than the agreed-on fee, the client must make up the difference. If the agency does much work for the client in noncommissionable media, the fee may be charged over and above the commissions received.

Both types of fee arrangements require that the agency carefully assess its costs of serving the client for the specified period, or for the project, plus its desired profit margin. To avoid any later disagreement, a fee arrangement should specify exactly what services the agency is expected to perform for the client. Fee arrangements have become the primary type of agreement used by advertisers with their agencies, accounting for 74 percent of the compensation plans in the recent ANA survey. Blended compensation plans that include fees and commissions were used by 8 percent of the companies surveyed.

Cost-Plus Agreement

Under a **cost-plus system,** the client agrees to pay the agency a fee based on the costs of its work plus some agreed-on profit margin (often a percentage of total costs). This system requires that the agency keep detailed records of the costs it incurs in working on the client's account. Direct costs (personnel time and out-of-pocket expenses) plus an allocation for overhead and a markup for profits determine the amount the agency bills the client.

Fee agreements and cost-plus systems are commonly used in conjunction with a commission system. The fee-based system can be advantageous to both the client and the agency, depending on the size of the client, advertising budget, media used, and services required. Many clients prefer fee or cost-plus systems because they receive a detailed breakdown of where and how their advertising and promotion dollars are being spent. However, these arrangements can be difficult for the agency, as they require careful cost accounting and may be difficult to estimate when bidding for an advertiser's business. Agencies are also reluctant to let clients see their internal cost figures.

Incentive-Based Compensation

Many clients these days are demanding more accountability from their agencies and tying agency compensation to performance through some type of **incentive-based system.** While there are many variations, the basic idea is that the agency's ultimate compensation level will depend on how well it meets predetermined performance goals. These goals often include objective measures such as sales or market share as well as more subjective measures such as evaluations of the quality of the agency's creative work. Companies using incentive-based systems determine agency compensation through media commissions, fees, bonuses, or some combination of these methods. The use of performance incentives varies by the size of the advertiser, with large advertisers the most likely to use them. Figure 3-9 shows the various performance criteria used along with the basis for the incentive and the use of performance incentives by advertiser size.

Recognizing the movement toward incentive-based systems, most agencies have agreed to tie their compensation to performance.[20] Agency executives note that pay for

Figure 3-9 Use of Performance Incentives by Advertisers

Performance Criteria Used for Incentive Systems	
Sales goals	73%
Market share	29
Profit	25
Brand/ad awareness	50
Brand perceptions	23
Copy test results	25
Performance reviews	58
Other criteria	11
Basis for Incentive	
Agency performance	14%
Company performance	17
Both agency and company performance	69
Performance incentive use by size of advertiser	
Under $4 million	13%
$4 million–$20 million	10
$20 million–$100 million	33
More than $100 million	44

Source: Association of National Advertisers: Trend in Compensation Survey: 2000.

performance works best when the agency has complete control over a campaign. Thus, if a campaign fails to help sell a product or service, the agency is willing to assume complete responsibility and take a reduction in compensation. On the other hand, if sales increase, the agency can receive greater compensation for its work.

Percentage Charges

Another way to compensate an agency is by adding a markup of **percentage charges** to various services the agency purchases from outside providers. These may include market research, artwork, printing, photography, and other services or materials. Markups usually range from 17.65 to 20 percent and are added to the client's overall bill. Since suppliers of these services do not allow the agency a commission, percentage charges cover administrative costs while allowing a reasonable profit for the agency's efforts. (A markup of 17.65 percent of costs added to the initial cost would yield a 15 percent commission. For example, research costs of $100,000 × 17.65% = $100,000 + $17,650 = $117,650. The $17,650 markup is about 15 percent of $117,650.)

The Future of Agency Compensation

As you can see, there is no one method of agency compensation to which everyone subscribes. Companies have continued to make significant changes in their agency compensation plans over the past decade. One of the most significant findings from the ANA survey is the rapid rise in incentive-based compensation agreements as more than 38 percent of advertisers are using some type of performance-based system versus only 13 percent in the early 1990s. Companies with large advertising budgets are even more likely to use incentive-based systems as the ANA survey found that 56 percent of marketers with $100 million-plus ad budgets use incentives versus only 18 percent of marketers with budgets below $15 million.[21]

As more companies adopt IMC approaches, they are reducing their reliance on traditional media advertising, and this is leading to changes in the way they compensate their agencies. For example, Procter & Gamble (P&G), which is the world's largest advertiser, no longer uses the commission system to compensate its agencies. In 2000, P&G implemented a major change in its compensation structure by moving from a commission-based system to a sales-based incentive system. P&G made the change to encourage its agencies to focus less on expensive commissionable media such as television and magazines and to make use of other IMC tools such as direct mail, event marketing, public relations, and the Internet.[22] In 2004, P&G announced that it was very satisfied with its incentive-based compensation system and was extending it to media agencies and other marketing services providers.[23] A number of other major advertisers, including Colgate-Palmolive, Unilever, General Motors, Nissan, and Ford, also use some form of incentive-based compensation system. General Motors made the change to encourage its agencies to look beyond traditional mass-media advertising and to develop more creative ways of reaching automobile customers.[24]

Many companies are changing their compensation systems as they move away from traditional mass media and turn to a wider array of communication tools. Companies are also making their agencies more accountable for the fees they charge them for their services as well as for the way they spend their advertising dollars. IMC Perspective 3-3 discusses the changes that are occurring in the agency business.

IMC PERSPECTIVE 3-3

The Times Are a Changing on Madison Avenue

For many years Madison Avenue was a world unto itself. Advertising agencies were compensated based on a 15 percent commission on the media purchases they made for their clients: every time an ad appeared on television, played on radio, or was placed in a magazine, the cash registers rang on Madison Avenue. Agencies were dominated by "creatives" who came up with big ideas that could be translated into TV, print, radio, or billboard ads that would be run through these mass media to be seen or heard by the millions of consumers comprising the mass markets. The industry was inspired by men such as David Ogilvy, Bill Bernbach, and Leo Burnett who became legendary figures as a result of their creative genius and the iconic ad campaigns they developed for brands such as Marlboro, Maytag, Avis, and many others.

However, by the late 1980s, the ad industry began to change. Many of the world's largest agencies recognized that their clients were shifting more of their promotional budgets away from traditional media advertising to other forms of marketing communication such as direct marketing, public relations, sales promotion, and event sponsorship. In response to this trend, many of these agencies began acquiring expertise in these areas that they could point to when touting their IMC capabilities. However, an even greater change was occurring as the new generation of top agency executives were trained in finance, corporate strategy, and mergers and acquisitions rather than copywriting. During the late 1980s and early 90s, a wave of consolidation swept through Madison Avenue as large agencies merged with or acquired other agencies and formed large holding companies such as WPP Group, Omnicom Group, Interpublic Group, and Publicis Groupe. They also bought support organizations such as public relations firms, direct marketing firms, event marketers, and Internet start-ups and brought them into their holding companies.

During the late 90s, the ad industry prospered, in large part due to the advertising frenzy driven by the Internet bubble, and many agencies were still able to get many of their clients to agree to pay them based on a percentage of their media billings. However, at the beginning of the new millennium, the advertising business crashed headlong into the worst advertising recession since the Great Depression. Global ad spending dropped by 7 percent in 2001 to $440 billion and agencies laid off 40,000 employees—19 percent of their workforce. The recession resulted in more change on Madison Avenue in four years than the industry has seen in four decades.

Over the past five years, major advertisers such as Chrysler, General Motors, and Unilever have done away with commissions entirely. The vast majority of clients now compensate their agencies by paying fees based on the agency's labor costs. To make matters more complicated, some companies now have their procurement officers negotiate contracts with their advertising agencies rather than their marketing or advertising managers. Many agencies are finding the procurement people to be much more difficult to negotiate with on issues such as their allocation of labor costs, employee salaries, overhead, and reasonable profit. The agencies argue that procurement departments really do not understand the advertising business and the role they play in brand-building. Some agencies have tried to take a stand against clients who view them as vendors rather than marketing partners. However, other agencies are often willing to accept lower margins to gain new business, which has resulted in a loss of pricing power for many agencies. The intervention of procurement departments into the advertising process is also receiving a cold reception from many marketing executives who argue that the advertising process is different from sourcing raw materials for manufacturing. They note that creating ideas is different from creating widgets and also express concern over procurement executives trying to take over the agency selection process.

Many agencies are finding that their clients are also changing the way they choose to spend their marketing dollars. Some companies believe that agencies are still relying too much on television and print media and need to embrace new forms of digital media such as the Internet, PDAs, personal video recorders, cellular phones, and video games. There is also a shift in the balance of power occurring within agencies. The ad industry is no longer dominated by the creatives as the media buying has become a more important and powerful area. Many of the holding companies have spun off their media divisions into freestanding firms that handle only media buying. Large media-buying firms, such as WPP Group's MindShare or Publicis Groupe's Starcom MediaVest, can use their size and clout to extract better media prices and cost savings for their clients. These media companies are also the major source of growth for their parent companies since clients have negotiated very thin margins in other areas.

The ascension of the media buyers into the powerful position in the advertising business is disrupting the old guard on Madison Avenue. The CEO of Carat North America, one of the largest media-buying companies, has stated, "We're getting to the point where the media plan is done first, and the creative is done behind it. This is a radical vision for the advertising business that would have been unheard of five years ago. We used to be the dorks. Now we're driving the whole advertising process." Of course not everyone in the agency business agrees with this position, nor do they like what is happening to the agency business. Donny Deutsch, CEO of Deutsch, Inc. in New York and perhaps the best known of the contemporary admen, notes that "a lot of the great independent spirit that has driven this industry has gone by the wayside," and he fumes over media buyers who claim they understand the business better than their creative peers.

While agency executives may not like the changes that are occurring in the world of advertising, most recognize that they have little choice but to adapt to the changes. Most clients no longer want traditional marketing approaches that rely on mass-media advertising. As a CEO of one agency notes, "Historically, agencies pushed clients. Today, clients are pushing agencies. The same-old, same-old is not being accepted."

Sources: Stuart Elliott, "Advertisers Want Something Different," *The New York Times,* www.nytimes.com, May 23, 2005; Bradley Johnson, "Procurement, Marketing Don't See Eye to Eye," *Advertising Age,* May 9, 2005, pp. 3, 82; Devin Leonard, "Nightmare on Madison Avenue," *Fortune,* June 28, 2004, pp. 92–108.

Evaluating Agencies

Given the substantial amounts of money being spent on advertising and promotion, demand for accountability of the expenditures has increased. Regular reviews of the agency's performance are necessary. The agency evaluation process usually involves two types of assessments, one financial and operational and the other more qualitative. The **financial audit** focuses on how the agency conducts its business. It is designed to verify costs and expenses, the number of personnel hours charged to an account, and payments to media and outside suppliers. The **qualitative audit** focuses on the agency's efforts in planning, developing, and implementing the client's advertising programs and considers the results achieved.

The agency evaluation is often done on a subjective, informal basis, particularly in smaller companies where ad budgets are low or advertising is not seen as the most critical factor in the firm's marketing performance. However some companies have developed formal, systematic evaluation systems, particularly when budgets are large and the advertising function receives much emphasis. The top management of these companies wants to be sure money is being spent efficiently and effectively. As the costs of advertising and other forms of promotion rise, more companies are adopting formal procedures for evaluating the performance of their agencies.

One example of a formal agency evaluation system is that used by Whirlpool, which markets a variety of consumer products. Whirlpool management meets once a year with the company's agencies to review their performance. Whirlpool managers complete an advertising agency performance evaluation, part of which is shown in Exhibit 3-7. These reports are compiled and reviewed with the agency at each annual meeting. Whirlpool's evaluation process covers six areas of performance. The company and the agency develop an action plan to correct areas of deficiency.

Exhibit 3-7 Whirlpool's Ad Agency Performance Evaluation

CREATIVE SERVICES

	Always 4	Often 3	Occasionally 2	Seldom 1	Never 0	NA	Marks Scored
1. Agency produces fresh ideas and original approaches							
2. Agency accurately interprets facts, strategies and objectives into usable advertisements and plans							
3. Creative group is knowledgeable about company's products, markets and strategies							
4. Creative group is concerned with good advertising communications and develops campaigns and ads that exhibit this concern							
5. Creative group produces on time							
6. Creative group performs well under pressure							
7. Creative group operates in a businesslike manner to control production costs and other creative charges							
8. Agency presentations are well organized with sufficient examples of proposed executions							
9. Creative group participates in major campaign presentations							
10. Agency presents ideas and executions not requested but felt to be good opportunities							
11. Agency willingly accepts ideas generated by other locations/agency offices vs. being over-protective of its own creative product							
12. Other areas not mentioned							
13. Agency demonstrates commitment to client's business							
14. Agency creative proposals are relevant and properly fulfill creative brief							

Value—(marks)

Rating:			
Excellent	90–100%	Total marks scored	
Good	80–89%		
Average	70–79%	Total possible marks	
Fair	60–69%		
Poor	below 60%	Score	

ACCOUNT REPRESENTATION & SERVICE

	Always 4	Often 3	Occasionally 2	Seldom 1	Never 0	NA	Marks Scored
1. Account representatives act with personal initiative							
2. Account representatives anticipate needs in advance of direction by client (ie: are proactive)							
3. Account group takes direction well							
4. Agency is able to demonstrate results of programs implemented							
5. Account representatives function strategically rather than as creative advisors only							
6. Account representatives are knowledgeable about competitive programs and share this information along with their recommendations in a timely manner							
7. Account representatives respond to client requests in a timely fashion							
8. Account group operates in a business-like manner to control costs							
9. Agency recommendations are founded on sound reasoning and supported factually, and appropriately fit within budget constraints							
10. Agency is able to advise the client on trends and developments in technology							
11. Account representatives demonstrate a high degree of professionalism in both written and oral communication							
12. Agency presents ideas and executions not requested but felt to be good opportunities							
13. Agency makes reasoned recommendations on allocation of budgets							
14. Agency demonstrates commitment to client's business							
15. There is a positive social relationship between client and agency							

Value—(marks)

Rating:			
Excellent	90–100%	Total marks scored	
Good	80–89%		
Average	70–79%	Total possible marks	
Fair	60–69%		
Poor	below 60%	Score	

Companies develop evaluation procedures that emphasize different areas. For example, R. J. Reynolds emphasizes creative development and execution, marketing counsel and ideas, promotion support, and cost controls, without any mention of sales figures. Sears focuses on the performance of the agency as a whole in an effort to establish a partnership between the agency and the client. These and other evaluation methods are being used more regularly by advertisers. As fiscal controls tighten, clients will require more accountability from their providers and adopt formal evaluation procedures.

Gaining and Losing Clients

The evaluation process described above provides valuable feedback to both the agency and the client, such as indicating changes that need to be made by the agency and/or the client to improve performance and make the relationship more productive. Many agencies have had very long-lasting relationships with their clients. For example, General Electric has been with the BBDO Worldwide agency for over 80 years. Other well-known companies or brands that have had long-lasting relationships include Marlboro/Leo Burnett (50 years), McDonald's/DDB Worldwide (37 years), and Kellog's/Leo Burnett (56 years). Exhibit 3-8 shows an ad run by Dr Pepper/Seven Up Inc. celebrating its long-term relationship with the Young & Rubicam agency.

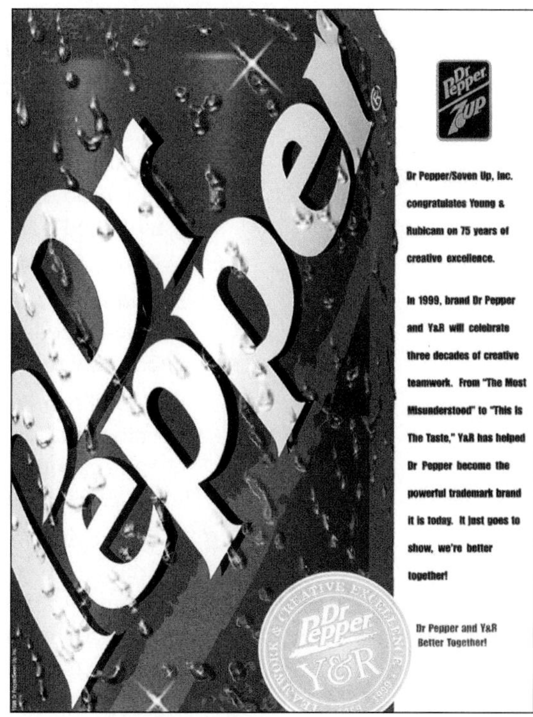

Exhibit 3-8 Young & Rubicam has been the agency for Dr Pepper for more than three decades

While many successful agency-client relationships go on for years, loyalty to a single agency is becoming less common as marketers seeks new ways of connecting with consumers.[25] In recent years, a number of long-standing client relationships have been terminated. In late 2004, PepsiCo moved its Diet Pepsi account from BBDO to DDB Worldwide citing concerns over the creative work that was being done for the brand. Advertising for Diet Pepsi had been handled by BBDO since the brand was introduced in the 1960s. Although BBDO continues to handle advertising for other PepsiCo soft drink brands such as Pepsi-Cola, Mountain Dew, and Sierra Mist, the move is an example of how clients are willing to change agencies for underperforming brands.[26]

Some companies switch agencies quite often in search of better creative work or for a variety of other reasons such as reorganizations that lead to changes in top management, changes in marketing or advertising strategy, or conflicts that might arise from mergers and acquisitions among both clients and agencies. For example, Gateway has changed agencies seven times in the past 10 years as the company has undergone changes in its top management as well as its business strategy (Exhibit 3-9).

There are a number of reasons clients switch agencies. Understanding these potential problems can help the agency avoid them.[27] In addition, it is important to understand the process agencies go through in trying to win new clients.

YOU'RE ALWAYS TOLD TO "DO MORE WITH LESS"
Here's something that returns the favor.
Gateway
RAID 5 UPGRADE
XEON

Exhibit 3-9 Gateway has changed agencies a number of times over the past decade

Why Agencies Lose Clients

Some of the more common reasons agencies lose clients follow:

- *Poor performance or service.* The client becomes dissatisfied with the quality of the advertising and/or the service provided by the agency.
- *Poor communication.* The client and agency personnel fail to develop or maintain the level of communication necessary to sustain a favorable working relationship.

- *Unrealistic demands by the client.* The client places demands on the agency that exceed the amount of compensation received and reduce the account's profitability.
- *Personality conflicts.* People working on the account on the client and agency sides do not have enough rapport to work well together.
- *Personnel changes.* A change in personnel at either the agency or the advertiser can create problems. New managers may wish to use an agency with which they have established ties. Agency personnel often take accounts with them when they switch agencies or start their own.
- *Changes in size of the client or agency.* The client may outgrow the agency or decide it needs a larger agency to handle its business. If the agency gets too large, the client may represent too small a percentage of its business to command attention.
- *Conflicts of interest.* A conflict may develop when an agency merges with another agency or when a client is part of an acquisition or merger. In the United States, an agency cannot handle two accounts that are in direct competition with each other. In some cases, even indirect competition will not be tolerated.
- *Changes in the client's corporate and/or marketing strategy.* A client may change its marketing strategy and decide that a new agency is needed to carry out the new program. As more companies adapt an integrated marketing communications approach, they are looking for agencies that have integrated capabilities and can handle more than just their media advertising.
- *Declining sales.* When sales of the client's product or service are stagnant or declining, advertising may be seen as contributing to the problem. A new agency may be sought for a new creative approach.
- *Conflicting compensation philosophies.* Disagreement may develop over the level or method of compensation. As more companies move toward incentive-based compensation systems, disagreement over compensation is becoming more commonplace.
- *Changes in policies.* Policy changes may result when either party reevaluates the importance of the relationship, the agency acquires a new (and larger) client, or either side undergoes a merger or acquisition.

If the agency recognizes these warning signs, it can try to adapt its programs and policies to make sure the client is satisfied. Some of the situations discussed here are unavoidable, and others are beyond the agency's control. But to maintain the account, problems within the agency's control must be addressed.

The time may come when the agency decides it is no longer in its best interest to continue to work with the client. Personnel conflicts, changes in management philosophy, and/or insufficient financial incentives are just a few of the reasons for such a decision. Then the agency may terminate the account relationship.

How Agencies Gain Clients

Competition for accounts in the agency business is intense, since most companies have already organized for the advertising function and only a limited number of new businesses require such services each year. While small agencies may be willing to work with a new company and grow along with it, larger agencies often do not become interested in these firms until they are able to spend at least $1 million per year on advertising. Many of the top 15 agencies won't accept an account that spends less than $5 million per year. Once that expenditure level is reached, competition for the account intensifies.

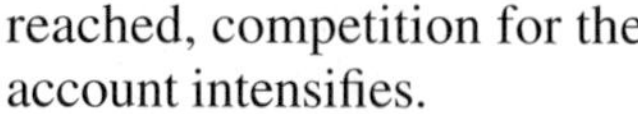

In large agencies, most new business results from clients that already have an agency but decide to change their relationships. Thus, agencies must constantly search and compete for new clients. Some of the ways they do this follow.

Referrals Many good agencies obtain new clients as a result of referrals from existing clients, media representatives, and even other agencies. These agencies maintain good working relationships with their clients, the media, and outside parties that might provide business to them.

Solicitations One of the more common ways to gain new business is through direct solicitation. In smaller agencies, the president may solicit new accounts. In most large agencies, a new business development group seeks out and establishes contact with new clients. The group is responsible for writing solicitation letters, making cold calls, and following up on leads. The cutbacks in ad spending by many companies during the recent recession have resulted in many agencies' pitching their services on an unsolicited basis to marketers who are satisfied with their agencies. Senior executives recognize that new business is the lifeblood of their agencies and are encouraging their business development teams to pursue advertisers who have not even put their accounts up for review.[28]

Presentations A basic goal of the new business development group is to receive an invitation from a company to make a presentation. This gives the agency the opportunity to sell itself—to describe its experience, personnel, capabilities, and operating procedures, as well as to demonstrate its previous work.

The agency may be asked to make a speculative presentation, in which it examines the client's marketing situation and proposes a tentative communications campaign. Because presentations require a great deal of time and preparation and may cost the agency a considerable amount of money without a guarantee of gaining the business, many firms refuse to participate in "creative shootouts." They argue that agencies should be selected on the basis of their experience and the services and programs they have provided for previous clients. Nevertheless, most agencies do participate in this form of solicitation, either by choice or because they must do so to gain accounts.

Due in part to the emphasis on speculative presentations, a very important role has developed for *ad agency review consultants,* who specialize in helping clients choose ad agencies. These consultants are often used to bring an objective perspective to the agency review process and to assist advertisers who may lack the resources, experience, or organizational consensus needed to successfully conduct a review. The use of search consultants is increasing as studies have shown that they are used in 30 to 40 percent of the agency reviews where the ad budget for the account is worth $10 million or more.[29] Because their opinions are respected by clients, the entire agency review process may be structured according to their guidelines. However, one study found that while many companies use search consultants to help them with their reviews, they do not always have a direct influence on the final decision regarding which agency they hire.[30]

Public Relations Agencies also seek business through publicity/public relations efforts. They often participate in civic and social groups and work with charitable organizations pro bono (at cost, without pay) to earn respect in the community. Participation in professional associations such as the American Association of Advertising Agencies and the Advertising Research Foundation can also lead to new contacts. Successful agencies often receive free publicity throughout the industry as well as in the mass media.

Image and Reputation Perhaps the most effective way an agency can gain new business is through its reputation. Agencies that consistently develop excellent campaigns are often approached by clients. Agencies may enter their work in award competitions or advertise themselves to enhance their image in the marketing community. In some cases the clients themselves may provide valuable testimonials. For example, Exhibit 3-10 shows an ad from IBM congratulat-

Exhibit 3-10 IBM congratulates its agency for developing an award-winning campaign

ing its agency, Ogilvy & Mather, for winning the Grand EFFIE in the annual competition sponsored by the New York American Marketing Association that recognizes the most effective advertising campaigns.

Specialized Services

Many companies assign the development and implementation of their promotional programs to an advertising agency. But several other types of organizations provide specialized services that complement the efforts of ad agencies. Direct-response agencies, sales promotion agencies, and public relations firms are important to marketers in developing and executing IMC programs in the United States as well as international markets. Let us examine the functions these organizations perform.

Direct-Marketing Agencies

One of the fastest-growing areas of IMC is direct marketing, where companies communicate with consumers through telemarketing, direct mail, television, the Internet, and other forms of direct-response advertising. As this industry has grown, numerous direct-response agencies have evolved that offer companies their specialized skills in both consumer and business markets. Many of the top direct-marketing agencies such as Rapp Collins Worldwide, Draft, Wunderman, and OgilvyOne are subsidiaries of large agency holding companies. However, there are also a number of independent direct-marketing agencies including those that serve large companies as well as smaller firms that handle the needs of local companies (Exhibit 3-11).

Direct-marketing agencies provide a variety of services, including database management, direct mail, research, media services, and creative and production capabilities. While direct mail is their primary weapon, many direct-response agencies are expanding their services to include such areas as infomercial production and database management. Database development and management is becoming one of the most important services provided by direct-response agencies. Many companies are using database marketing to pinpoint new customers and build relationships and loyalty among existing customers.

A typical direct-response agency is divided into three main departments: account management, creative, and media. Some agencies also have a department whose function is to develop and manage databases for their clients. The account managers work with their clients to plan direct-marketing programs and determine their role in the overall integrated marketing communications process. The creative department consists of copywriters, artists, and producers. Creative is responsible for developing the direct-response message, while the media department is concerned with its placement.

Like advertising agencies, direct-response agencies must solicit new business and have their performance reviewed by their existing clients, often through formal assessment programs. Most direct-response agencies are compensated on a fee basis.

Exhibit 3-11 Protocol promotes its direct-marketing services

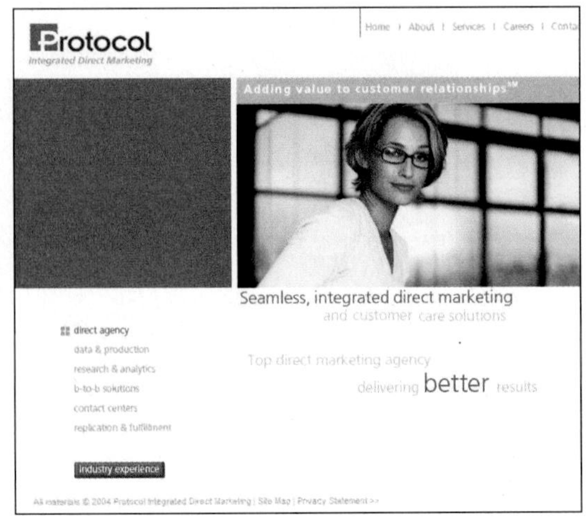

Sales Promotion Agencies

Developing and managing sales promotion programs such as contests, sweepstakes, refunds and rebates, premium and incentive offers, and sampling programs is a very complex task. Most companies use a **sales promotion agency** to develop and administer these programs. Some large ad agencies have created their own sales promotion department or acquired a sales promotion firm. However, most sales promotion agencies are independent companies that specialize in providing the services needed to plan, develop, and execute a variety of sales promotion programs.

Sales promotion agencies often work in conjunction with the client's advertising and/or direct-response agencies to coordinate their efforts with the advertising and direct-marketing programs. Services provided by large sales promotion agencies include promotional planning, creative, research, tie-in coordination, fulfillment, premium design and manufacturing, catalog production, and contest/sweepstakes management. Many sales promotion agencies are also developing direct/database marketing and telemarketing to expand their integrated marketing services capabilities. Sales promotion agencies are generally compensated on a fee basis. Exhibit 3-12 shows a page from the website of Don Jagoda Associates, one of the leading sales promotion agencies.

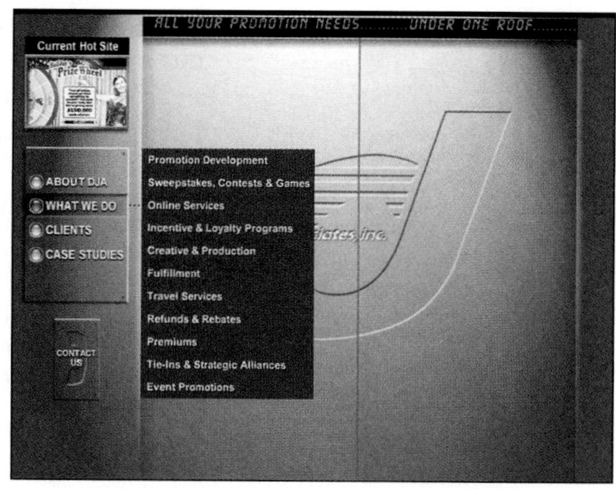

Exhibit 3-12 Don Jagoda Associates is one of the leading promotional agencies

Public Relations Firms

Many large companies use both an advertising agency and a PR firm. The **public relations firm** develops and implements programs to manage the organization's publicity, image, and affairs with consumers and other relevant publics, including employees, suppliers, stockholders, government, labor groups, citizen action groups, and the general public. The PR firm analyzes the relationships between the client and these various publics, determines how the client's policies and actions relate to and affect these publics, develops PR strategies and programs, implements these programs using various public relations tools, and evaluates their effectiveness.

The activities of a public relations firm include planning the PR strategy and program, generating publicity, conducting lobbying and public affairs efforts, becoming involved in community activities and events, preparing news releases and other communications, conducting research, promoting and managing special events, and managing crises. As companies adopt an IMC approach to promotional planning, they are increasingly coordinating their PR activities with advertising and other promotional areas. Many companies are integrating public relations and publicity into the marketing communications mix to increase message credibility and save media costs.[31] Public relations firms are generally compensated by retainer. We will examine their role in more detail in Chapter 17.

Interactive Agencies

With the rapid growth of the Internet and other forms of interactive media, a new type of specialized marketing communications organization has evolved—the interactive agency. Many marketers are using **interactive agencies** that specialize in the development and strategic use of various interactive marketing tools such as websites for the Internet, banner ads, CD-ROMs, text messages, search engine optimization, and kiosks. They recognize that the development of successful interactive marketing programs requires expertise in technology as well as areas such as creative website design, database marketing, digital media, and customer relationship management. Many traditional advertising agencies have established interactive capabilities, ranging from a few specialists within the agency to an entire interactive division.

Exhibit 3-13 iDeutsch developed the website and various online promotions for the California Milk Advisory Board

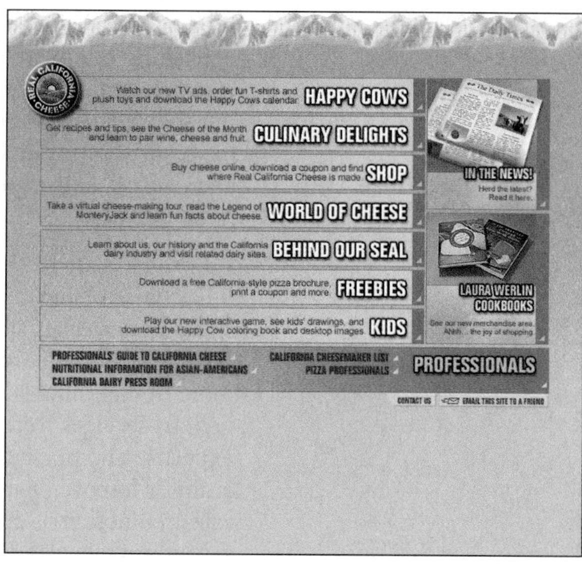

Some of the largest interactive agencies such as EuroRSCG 4D and Ogilvy Interactive are affiliates of major agencies, while others such as Agency.com, Organic, and R/GA are owned by major holding companies. Many agencies work closely with their interactive affiliates in developing integrated marketing campaigns for their clients. For example, iDeutsch, the interactive arm of the Deutsch agency, has developed the websites and online campaigns for clients such as Snapple, Almay, and the California Milk Advisory Board; the parent agency handles the off-line campaign in traditional media for these companies (Exhibit 3-13).

While many agencies have or are developing interactive capabilities, a number of marketers are turning to more specialized interactive agencies to develop websites and interactive media. They feel these companies have more expertise in designing and developing websites as well as managing and supporting them. Interactive agencies range from smaller companies that specialize in website design and creation to full-service interactive agencies that provide all the elements needed for a successful Internet/interactive marketing program. These services include strategic consulting regarding the use of the Internet and online branding, technical knowledge, systems integration, and the development of electronic commerce capabilities.

Full-service interactive agencies, such as Agency.com, have created successful Internet marketing programs for a number of companies, including Nike, MetLife, Hewlett-Packard, McDonald's, and British Airways. For example, Agency.com developed the website and various online promotions that support the global brand positioning strategy for British Airways. As the Internet becomes an increasingly important marketing tool, more companies will be turning to interactive agencies to help them develop successful interactive marketing programs. The number of interactive agencies will continue to grow, as will their importance in the development and implementation of Internet-based strategies and initiatives.

Collateral Services

The final participants in the promotional process are those that provide various collateral services. They include marketing research companies, package design firms, consultants, photographers, printers, video production houses, and event marketing services companies.

Marketing Research Companies

One of the more widely used collateral service organizations is the marketing research firm. Companies are increasingly turning to marketing research to help them understand their target audiences and to gather information that will be of value in designing and evaluating their advertising and promotions programs. Even companies with their own marketing research departments often hire outside research agencies to perform some services. Marketing research companies offer specialized services and can gather objective information that is valuable to the advertiser's promotional programs. They conduct *qualitative* research such as in-depth interviews and focus groups, as well as *quantitative* studies such as market surveys.

Integrated Marketing Communications Services

You have seen that marketers can choose from a variety of specialized organizations to assist them in planning, developing, and implementing an integrated marketing communications program. But companies must decide whether to use a different organization for each marketing communications function or consolidate them with a large advertising agency that offers all of these services under one roof.

As noted previously in the chapter, during the 1980s and '90s, many of the large agencies realized that their clients were shifting their promotional dollars away from traditional advertising to other forms of promotion and began developing IMC capabilities. Some did this through mergers and acquisitions and became superagencies consisting of advertising, public relations, sales promotion, and direct-response agencies. Many large agencies are continuing to expand their IMC capabilities by acquiring specialists in various fields. All the major agency holding companies either own or have substantial investments in interactive, sales promotion, and direct-marketing agencies as well as public relations firms.

Pros and Cons of Integrated Services

It has been argued that the concept of integrated marketing is nothing new, particularly in smaller companies and communication agencies that have been coordinating a variety of promotional tools for years. And larger advertising agencies have been trying to gain more of their clients' promotional business for over 20 years. However, in the past, the various services were run as separate profit centers. Each was motivated to push its own expertise and pursue its own goals rather than develop truly integrated marketing programs. Moreover, the creative specialists in many agencies resisted becoming involved in sales promotion or direct marketing. They preferred to concentrate on developing magazine ads or television commercials rather than designing coupons or direct-mail pieces.

Proponents of integrated marketing services contend that past problems are being solved and the various individuals in the agencies and subsidiaries are learning to work together to deliver a consistent message to the client's customers. They argue that maintaining control of the entire promotional process achieves greater synergy among each of the communications program elements. They also note that it is more convenient for the client to coordinate all of its marketing efforts—media advertising, direct mail, special events, sales promotions, and public relations—through one agency. An agency with integrated marketing capabilities can create a single image for the product or service and address everyone, from wholesalers to consumers, with one voice.

But not everyone wants to turn the entire IMC program over to one agency. Opponents say the providers become involved in political wrangling over budgets, do not communicate with each other as well and as often as they should, and do not achieve synergy. They also claim that agencies' efforts to control all aspects of the promotional program are nothing more than an attempt to hold on to business that might otherwise be lost to independent providers. They note that synergy and economies of scale, while nice in theory, have been difficult to achieve and competition and conflict among agency subsidiaries have been a major problem.[32]

Many companies use a variety of vendors for communication functions, choosing the specialist they believe is best suited for each promotional task, be it advertising, sales promotion, or public relations. While many ad agencies are working to master integration and compete against one another, they still must compete against firms that offer specialized services. As marketing consultant Jack Trout notes, "As long as there are a lot of specialized players, integrating an agency will be tricky. Specialists walk in the door and say 'this is all we do and we're good at it,' which is a hell of an argument. An agency that has all marketing operations in-house will never be perceived as the best in breed."[33]

Responsibility for IMC: Agency versus Client

Surveys of advertisers and agency executives have shown that both groups believe integrated marketing is important to their organizations' success and that it will be even more important in the future.[34] However, marketers and agency executives have very different opinions regarding who should be in charge of the integrated marketing communications process. Many advertisers prefer to set strategy for and coordinate their own IMC campaigns, but some agency executives see this as their domain.

While agency executives believe their shops are capable of handling the various elements an integrated campaign requires, many marketers, particularly larger firms, disagree. Marketing executives say the biggest obstacle to implementing IMC is the lack of people with the broad perspective and skills to make it work. Internal turf battles, agency egos, and fear of budget reductions are also cited as major barriers to successful integrated marketing campaigns.[35] A recent study of agency and marketing executives regarding integrated marketing found that the most challenging aspect of integration is ensuring that the strategy is executed consistently in all forms along with measuring the success of different aspects of an IMC campaign. The survey also found that compensation of integrated programs is a problem as each communication discipline has a different cost structure.[36]

Many ad agencies are adding more resources to offer their clients a full line of services. They are expanding their agencies' capabilities in interactive and multimedia advertising, database management, direct marketing, public relations, and sales promotion. However, many marketers still want to set the strategy for their IMC campaigns and seek specialized expertise, more quality and creativity, and greater control and cost efficiency by using multiple providers.

Most marketers do recognize that ad agencies will no longer stick primarily to advertising and will continue to expand their IMC capabilities. There is an opportunity for agencies to broaden their services beyond advertising—but they will have to develop true expertise in a variety of integrated marketing communications areas. They will also have to create organizational structures that make it possible for individuals with expertise in a variety of communications areas to work well together both internally and externally. One thing is certain: as companies continue to shift their promotional dollars away from media advertising to other IMC tools, agencies will continue to explore ways to keep these monies under their roofs.

Summary

The development, execution, and administration of an advertising and promotions program involve the efforts of many individuals, both within the company and outside it. Participants in the integrated marketing communications process include the advertiser or client, ad agencies, media organizations, specialized marketing communications firms, and providers of collateral services.

Companies use three basic systems to organize internally for advertising and promotion. Centralized systems offer the advantages of facilitated communications, lower personnel requirements, continuity in staff, and more top-management involvement. Disadvantages include a lower involvement with overall marketing goals, longer response times, and difficulties in handling multiple product lines.

Decentralized systems offer the advantages of concentrated managerial attention, more rapid responses to problems, and increased flexibility, though they may be limited by ineffective decision making, internal conflicts, misallocation of funds, and a lack of authority. In-house agencies, while offering the advantages of cost savings, control, and increased coordination, have the disadvantage of less experience, objectivity, and flexibility.

Many firms use advertising agencies to help develop and execute their programs. These agencies may take on a variety of forms, including full-service agencies, creative boutiques, and media buying services. The first offers the client a full range of services (including creative, account, marketing, and financial and management services); the other two specialize in creative services and media buying, respectively. Agencies are compensated through commission systems, percentage charges, and fee- and cost-based systems. Recently, the emphasis on agency accountability has increased. Agencies are being evaluated on both financial and qualitative aspects, and some clients are using incentive-based compensation systems that tie agency compensation to performance measures such as sales and market share.

In addition to using ad agencies, marketers use the services of other marketing communication specialists, including direct-marketing agencies, sales promotion agencies, public relations firms, and interactive agencies. A marketer must decide whether to use a different specialist for each promotional function or have all of its integrated marketing communications done by an advertising agency that offers all of these services under one roof.

Recent studies have found that most marketers believe it is their responsibility, not the ad agency's, to set strategy for and coordinate IMC campaigns. The lack of a broad perspective and specialized skills in nonadvertising areas is seen as the major barrier to agencies' increased involvement in integrated marketing communications.

Key Terms

clients, 69
advertising agency, 70
media organizations, 70
specialized marketing communications services, 70
collateral services, 71
advertising manager, 71
centralized system, 72
decentralized system, 73
brand manager, 73
category management system, 73
in-house agency, 75
billings, 79
superagencies, 81
full-service agency, 82
account executive, 82
account planners, 83
copywriters, 85
departmental system, 86
group system, 86
creative boutique, 86
media specialist companies, 87
commission system, 88
negotiated commission, 88
fixed-fee method, 89
fee-commission combination, 89
cost-plus system, 89
incentive-based system, 89
percentage charges, 90
financial audit, 92
qualitative audit, 92
direct-marketing agency, 96
sales promotion agency, 96
public relations firm, 97
interactive agencies, 97

Discussion Questions

1. The opening vignette discusses the Crispin Porter and Bogusky agency and how they have become one of the hottest agencies in the advertising industry. Discuss the reasons CP+B has become such a hot agency. How do they approach advertising differently than traditional agencies?

2. Discuss the responsibilities of an advertising or marketing communications manager in a company that uses a centralized organizational system versus a company that uses a decentralized system.

3. IMC Perspective 3-1 discusses the recent decision by General Motors to drop the use of a brand management system. Analyze GM's decision to eliminate brand managers. Do you think the new system they have implemented works better and helps the company establish stronger identities for its various brands and models?

4. Discuss the pros and cons of using an in-house advertising agency. What are some of the reasons why companies might change from using an in-house agency and hire an outside agency?

5. IMC Perspective 3-2 discusses how the advertising agency business is heavily concentrated in New York City and the surrounding area. Why do New York–based agencies dominate the industry? How might agencies outside of New York compete for companies' advertising and marketing communications business?

6. Why might a company choose to use a creative boutique rather than a larger, full-service agency? Find an example of a company that uses a creative boutique and discuss why the decision to use a smaller agency may be appropriate for this firm.

7. Discuss the role of media specialist companies. Why are marketers likely to use a media specialist company to handle their media buying and planning versus the media department of an agency?

8. Discuss the changes that are occurring in the way advertising agencies are compensated and the factors that underlie these changes.

9. Discuss the reasons why advertising agencies lose accounts. Find an example of a company that changed advertising agencies and identify the factors that led them to switch to another agency.

10. Discuss the pros and cons for a marketer having one company handle all of its integrated marketing communication needs versus using specialized marketing communication firms to handle the various components of the program.

Perspectives on Consumer Behavior

4

Chapter Objectives

1. To understand the role consumer behavior plays in the development and implementation of advertising and promotional programs.
2. To understand the consumer decision-making process and how it varies for different types of purchases.
3. To understand various internal psychological processes, their influence on consumer decision making, and implications for advertising and promotion.
4. To recognize the various approaches to studying the consumer learning process and their implications for advertising and promotion.
5. To recognize external factors such as culture, social class, group influences, and situational determinants and how they affect consumer behavior.
6. To understand alternative approaches to studying consumer behavior.

Mapping the Mind: Smart Marketing or Orwellian Intrusion?

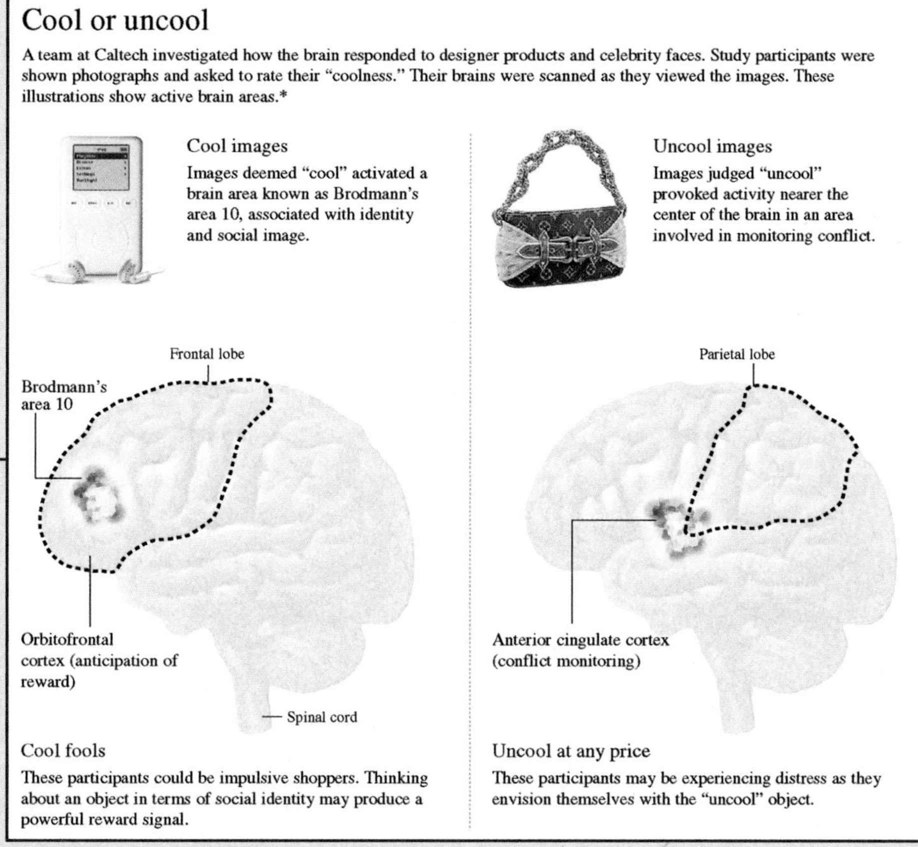

Cool or uncool
A team at Caltech investigated how the brain responded to designer products and celebrity faces. Study participants were shown photographs and asked to rate their "coolness." Their brains were scanned as they viewed the images. These illustrations show active brain areas.*
Cool images
Images deemed "cool" activated a brain area known as Brodmann's area 10, associated with identity and social image.
Uncool images
Images judged "uncool" provoked activity nearer the center of the brain in an area involved in monitoring conflict.
Frontal lobe
Brodmann's area 10
Orbitofrontal cortex (anticipation of reward)
Spinal cord
Parietal lobe
Anterior cingulate cortex (conflict monitoring)
Cool fools
These participants could be impulsive shoppers. Thinking about an object in terms of social identity may produce a powerful reward signal.
Uncool at any price
These participants may be experiencing distress as they envision themselves with the "uncool" object.

In their never-ending search to learn more about why consumers buy, marketers seemingly will stop at nothing. From surveys to focus groups to mind-probing interviews that put consumers in a near hypnotic state, market researchers have employed anthropologists, sociologists, economists, psychologists, and now neuroscientists to learn the "why of buy." For the most part, these efforts have been more of an art than a science—until now.

It has been estimated that by the time the average American reaches the age of 65, he or she will have been exposed to approximately 136,692,500 ads of various forms, and will have watched over 2 million television commercials. Consumers are overwhelmed by commercial messages, and advertisers know it. That's why they want to know more about which ads you see, recall, and remember, and what you think about when you see them. In an attempt to gain this understanding, marketers have turned to neuroscience, and are conducting research experiments designed to see what is happening inside of your brain.

Using technologies originally designed for the medical field such as positron emission tomography (PET) and functional magnetic resonance imaging (fMRI), the scientists have teamed up with marketers to examine physiological reactions to ads and brands through brain scan imaging. By monitoring the brain activity directly, scientists are learning how consumers make up their minds by measuring chemical activity and/or changes in the magnetic fields of the brain even though the consumers themselves may not know how or why they make these decisions. Some of these scientists believe that exposure to marketing messages may even alter the brain, just as learning to read or play the piano might.

But what is it they are looking for? In one study participants wore goggles while attached to a medical imaging scanner and watched as products such as iPods, chairs, and coffeepots and name brands such as Versace, Oakley, Evian, and Honda among others flashed in front of them inside the goggles. Two scientists observed the differences in brain activity that each product and brand evoked. In a similar study, faces of well-known celebrities were shown, with brain activity measured, followed by a 14-page questionnaire. The results? Uma Thurman—*cool.* Barbra Streisand—*uncool.* Justin Timberlake—*uncool.* Patrick Swayze—*very uncool.*

Another study conducted at the Neuroimaging Lab at Baylor College of Medicine repeated the Pepsi Challenge while observing participants through an fMRI. The results showed that when no brand names were known, subjects preferred Pepsi: The response was five times stronger than that of Coke. But when subjects were told which brands they were tasting, nearly all of the subjects said they preferred Coke. It was obvious that volunteers were responding to the influence of the Coke brand. Anette Asp and Steve Quartz, two researchers at Caltech, note that there are "branded brains," and that based on their neurological patterns people can be classified in broad psychological categories. At one extreme are the "cool fools" who tend to be compulsive or impulsive shoppers who respond to celebrities and "cool" brands with bursts of brain activity. At the other end are those who tend to be more anxious, apprehensive, or even neurotic and who react intensely to unstylish items. Still others purchase out of fear or anxiety that they may not be seen as sufficiently stylish.

Marketers argue that understanding the brain will help make marketing efforts more effective and that this knowledge could even help solve some societal problems. For example, the results could provide insight into why the antidrug campaign has not been effective. Others, however, are not so sure. Some believe the results are blown out of proportion and provide less insight than the marketers have claimed. Susan Linn, a Harvard psychologist, believes that it does work and worries that neuromarketing will make advertising too effective. Commerical Alert, an anticonsumerism activist group, says that use of the research will only increase the ills created by modern marketing. The group, founded by Ralph Nader and Gary Ruskin, refer to the research as "Orwellian," and have asked the Senate Committee on Commerce, Science, and Transportation to investigate the practice. They fear that consumers may increase their consumption of alcohol, tobacco, and gambling, and that children are particularly at risk of manipulation.

While analysts disagree over the effectiveness and value of monitoring brain activity, the research goes on. As noted by Linn, "We're now talking about marketers actually invading people's minds and that's just plain creepy." Not everyone agrees.

Sources: Robert Lee Hotz, "Searching for the Why of Buy," *Los Angeles Times,* February 27, 2005, pp. A1, 26–27; Randy Dotinga, "Advertisers Tap Brain Science," www.wired.com, May 31, 2005, pp. 1–2; Scott LaFee, "Through Neuroimaging, Marketers Hope to Peer Inside Consumers' Minds," *San Diego Union Tribune,* signonsandiego.com, July 28, 2004, pp. 1–8; Edwin Colyer, "The Science of Branding," Brandchannel.com, March 15, 2004, pp. 1–3.

The introduction to this chapter demonstrates the importance marketers place on research designed to understand consumers' behaviors. The lead-in examines just one of the many methodologies being employed for this purpose. What is important for marketers to know is how and why consumers' needs develop, what they are, and who is likely to use the product or service. Specifically, marketers will study consumer behaviors in an attempt to understand the many factors that lead to and impact purchase decisions. Those who develop advertising and other promotional strategies begin by identifying relevant markets and then analyzing the relationship between target consumers and the product/service or brand. Often, in an attempt to gain insights, marketers will employ techniques borrowed from other disciplines. Research methods used in psychology, anthropology, sociology, and, now, neuroscience are becoming more popular in businesses as managers attempt to explore consumers' purchasing motives. The motives for purchasing, attitudes, and lifestyles need to be understood before effective marketing strategies can be formulated.

These are just a few of the aspects of consumer behavior that promotional planners must consider in developing integrated marketing communications programs. As you will see, consumer choice is influenced by a variety of factors.

It is beyond the scope of this text to examine consumer behavior in depth. However, promotional planners need a basic understanding of consumer decision making, factors that influence it, and how this knowledge can be used in developing promotional strategies and programs. We begin with an overview of consumer behavior.

An Overview of Consumer Behavior

A challenge faced by all marketers is how to influence the purchase behavior of consumers in favor of the product or service they offer. For companies like Visa, this means getting consumers to charge more purchases on their credit cards. For BMW, it means getting them to purchase or lease a car; for business-to-business marketers like Xerox or FedEx, it means getting organizational buyers to purchase more of their office products or use their services. While their ultimate goal is to influence consumers' purchase behavior, most marketers understand that the actual purchase is only part of an overall process.

Consumer behavior can be defined as the process and activities people engage in when searching for, selecting, purchasing, using, evaluating, and disposing of products and services so as to satisfy their needs and desires. For many products and services, purchase decisions are the result of a long, detailed process that may include an extensive information search, brand comparisons and evaluations, and other activities. Other purchase decisions are more incidental and may result from little more than seeing a product prominently displayed at a discount price in a store. Think of how many times you have made impulse purchases in stores.

Marketers' success in influencing purchase behavior depends in large part on how well they understand consumer behavior. Marketers need to know the specific needs customers are attempting to satisfy and how they translate into purchase criteria. They need to understand how consumers gather information regarding various alternatives and use this information to select among competing brands. They need to understand how customers make purchase decisions. Where do they prefer to buy a product? How are they influenced by marketing stimuli at the point of purchase? Marketers also need to understand how the consumer decision process and reasons for purchase vary among different types of customers. For example, purchase decisions may be influenced by the personality or lifestyle of the consumer.[1] Notice how the ad shown in Exhibit 4-1 reflects the various roles in the life of the target audience members. IMC Perspective 4-1 describes how marketers target specific demographic and lifestyle groups.

Exhibit 4-1 Ashworth appeals to the active lifestyle

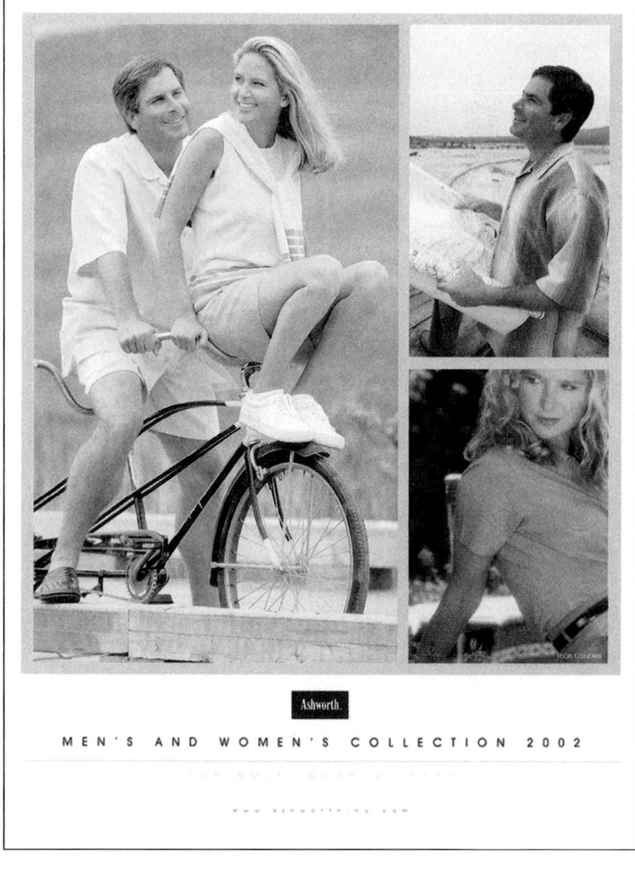

The conceptual model in Figure 4-1 will be used as a framework for analyzing the consumer decision process. We will discuss what occurs at the various stages of this model and how advertising and promotion can be used to influence decision making. We will also examine the influence of various psychological concepts, such as motivation, perception, attitudes, and integration processes. Variations in the consumer decision-making process will be explored, as will perspectives regarding consumer learning and external influences on the consumer decision process. The chapter concludes with a consideration of alternative means of studying consumer behavior.

IMC PERSPECTIVE 4-1

Tweens, Twixters, Bratty Boomers, X, and Y: Marketers Try to Figure It Out

You have probably heard of the baby boomers—the 78 million Americans born between 1946 and 1964, and generation X—the 60 million born between 1965 and 1979. There is a good chance you are in the age cohort known as generation Y (sometimes called millennials or echo boomers) along with 60 to 70 million others born between 1979 and 1995. Now meet the twixters and the tweens.

Let's start with the twixters. According to social scientists, a permanent shift in lifestyles has taken place in the United States. In the past, one would advance from childhood to adolescence and then to adulthood, but now some seem to make a stop along the way—somewhere between the ages 18 to 25, but sometimes older. At this age, the life cycle seems to pause for a while, transitioning into a never-never land between the free life of adolescence and the responsibilities of adulthood. The name "twixters" has been assigned to this group indicating their betwixt and between stage. They aren't quite kids but they aren't yet moving on to be adults (compared to 1970, almost twice as many of this age live at home with their parents). What is certain is that they do not move on. What is not so certain is who is responsible for their not doing so: themselves or society. They take longer to finish college, most of them owe money when they do, and they maintain very close relationships with their parents (some would say coddled or over-protected). Good jobs are hard to find once they graduate, and housing costs are astronomical. Twixters are faced with an overwhelming number of choices in life—from 40 kinds of coffee at the grocery store, to 200 or more TV stations, to 15 million personal ads on Match.com. Relative to others their age, they spend more than average on eating out, clothes, and entertainment. They are more idealistic, say that they are enjoying life, and maintain close social relationships through e-mail, text messaging, online communities, cocktail and dinner parties, and group functions.

Marketers consider twixters to be an attractive and potentially lucrative target market. Game Boys, iPods, electronics, flat-screen TVs, and designer clothing brands are their products of choice. They can afford them because they have higher disposable income while living at home with their parents. Many advertisers don't want them to grow up—or leave home.

Another lifestyle segment of interest to marketers has been referred to by at least one author as the "bratty boomers." Cliff Banks, writing for WardsAuto.com, warns auto dealers to be careful of the last wave of the gen Y cohort—the group that in five to 10 years will be their prime customers as well as their employees. Banks notes that this group is going to change the way vehicles are marketed and how they are managed as employees. Jim Farley, vice president of Scion, Toyota Motor Corp., targeted to this segment and has spent the past few years hanging out with this crowd at Scion events. He considers them to be polite, closely tied to their families, and environmentally conscious. At the same time, they are savvy, worldly, sometimes rebellious, and many feel entitled. Farley notes that they have little patience, particularly those who have been given so much already by their parents—many of whom have created expectations through their own possessions such as BMWs and Lexuses. They are entering the buying world with more wealth and buying influence than any group in history according to a study by Harris Interactive.

What does all this mean to the marketer? Toyota has found that traditional means of advertising to this generation do not work, and the company spends only 30 percent of its budget on these media. The other 70 percent is spent on lifestyle events and taking the car to the market. There is no price negotiating because it creates mistrust. Most cars are configured by the customer at a kiosk at the dealership or on the Internet, averaging $1,200 on accessories. Customized cars must be ready the next day. More than 60 percent of interactions take place online, though Toyota is considering opening its dealerships 24 hours a day because this group expects service when *they* want it—not during traditional times.

And then there are the tweens. We know less about them because they are young (ages 8 to 14), but of no less importance given that they spend an estimated $38 billion per year, and their parents spend another $126 billion on them. Research shows that they are consumer savvy and understand the intent of advertising to sell them something. Yet most of them are not adverse to advertising: 43 percent think it is funny; 39 percent find it informative; and 35 percent say it is entertaining and/or interesting. At the same time 52 percent of tweens say they don't watch commercials if they are repeats or are boring. Perhaps the best way to reach this group is through celebrities and by using product placements, as 72 percent admit that seeing a favorite character using a brand makes them more interested in it. With spending by this group on the increase, we will want to learn more as they grow.

Three age groups. Three distinct lifestyles. Some similarities and major differences in buying behaviors. No wonder some say consumer research will never go away!

Sources: Cliff Banks, "Here Come the Bratty Boomers," WardsAuto.com, January 26, 2005, pp. 1–4; Lev Grossman, "Grow Up? Not So Fast," *Time*, January 25, 2005, pp. 43–53; Laura DeMarco, "Change Rate X," *San Diego Union Tribune*, October 11, 2004, pp. D1, 5; David G. Kennedy, "Coming of Age in Consumerism," *American Demographics*, April 2004, p. 14.

A. Stages in the Consumer Decision-Making Process

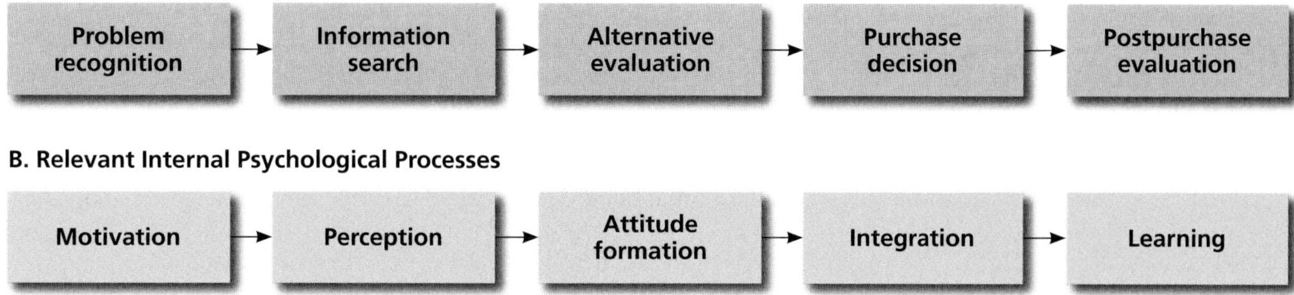

Figure 4-1 A Basic Model of Consumer Decision Making

The Consumer Decision-Making Process

As shown in Figure 4-1, the consumer's purchase decision process is generally viewed as consisting of stages through which the buyer passes in purchasing a product or service. This model shows that decision making involves a number of internal psychological processes. Motivation, perception, attitude formation, integration, and learning are important to promotional planners, since they influence the general decision-making process of the consumer. We will examine each stage of the purchase decision model and discuss how the various subprocesses influence what occurs at this phase of the consumer behavior process. We will also discuss how promotional planners can influence this process.

Problem Recognition

Figure 4-1 shows that the first stage in the consumer decision-making process is **problem recognition,** which occurs when the consumer perceives a need and becomes motivated to solve the problem. The problem recognition stage initiates the subsequent decision processes.

Problem recognition is caused by a difference between the consumer's *ideal state* and *actual state.* A discrepancy exists between what the consumer wants the situation to be like and what the situation is really like. (Note that *problem* does not always imply a negative state. A goal exists for the consumer, and this goal may be the attainment of a more positive situation.)

Sources of Problem Recognition

The causes of problem recognition may be very simple or very complex and may result from changes in the consumer's current and/or desired state. These causes may be influenced by both internal and external factors.

Out of Stock Problem recognition occurs when consumers use their existing supply of a product and must replenish their stock. The purchase decision is usually simple and routine and is often resolved by choosing a familiar brand or one to which the consumer feels loyal.

Dissatisfaction Problem recognition is created by the consumer's dissatisfaction with the current state of affairs and/or the product or service being used. For example, a consumer may think her ski boots are no longer comfortable or stylish enough. Advertising may be used to help consumers recognize when they have a problem and/or need to make a purchase. The Nasonex ad shown in Exhibit 4-2 helps viewers realize that allergy season is coming and that Nasonex helps relieve congestion.

Exhibit 4-2 Nasonex reminds consumers of problems with allergies

New Needs/Wants Changes in consumers' lives often result in new needs and wants. For example, changes in one's financial situation, employment status, or lifestyle may create new needs and trigger problem recognition. As you will see, when you graduate from college and begin your professional career, your new job may necessitate a change in your wardrobe. (Good-bye blue jeans and T-shirts, hello suits and ties.)

Not all product purchases are based on needs. Some products or services sought by consumers are not essential but are nonetheless desired. A **want** has been defined as a felt need that is shaped by a person's knowledge, culture, and personality.[2] Many products sold to consumers satisfy their wants rather than their basic needs.

Related Products/Purchases Problem recognition can also be stimulated by the purchase of a product. For example, the purchase of a new iPod may lead to the recognition of a need for accessories, such as a dock, attachment for the car, or a carrying case. The purchase of a personal computer may prompt the need for software programs, upgrades, printers, and so on.

Marketer-Induced Problem Recognition Another source of problem recognition is marketers' actions that encourage consumers not to be content with their current state or situation. Ads for personal hygiene products such as mouthwash, deodorant, and foot sprays may be designed to create insecurities that consumers can resolve through the use of these products. Marketers change fashions and clothing designs and create perceptions among consumers that their wardrobes are out of style. The Got Milk ad in Exhibit 4-3 informs parents of kids' special needs for calcium.

Marketers also take advantage of consumers' tendency toward *novelty-seeking behavior,* which leads them to try different brands. Consumers often try new products or brands even when they are basically satisfied with their regular brand. Marketers encourage brand switching by introducing new brands into markets that are already saturated and by using advertising and sales promotion techniques such as free samples, introductory price offers, and coupons.

New Products Problem recognition can also occur when innovative products are introduced and brought to the attention of consumers. Marketers are constantly introducing new products and services and telling consumers about the types of problems they solve. For example, the T-Mobile ad shown in Exhibit 4-4 introduces a new mobile technology that allows the businessperson to continue to stay connected to e-mail while out of the office.

Exhibit 4-3 This ad for Got Milk reminds parents that kids have special needs for calcium

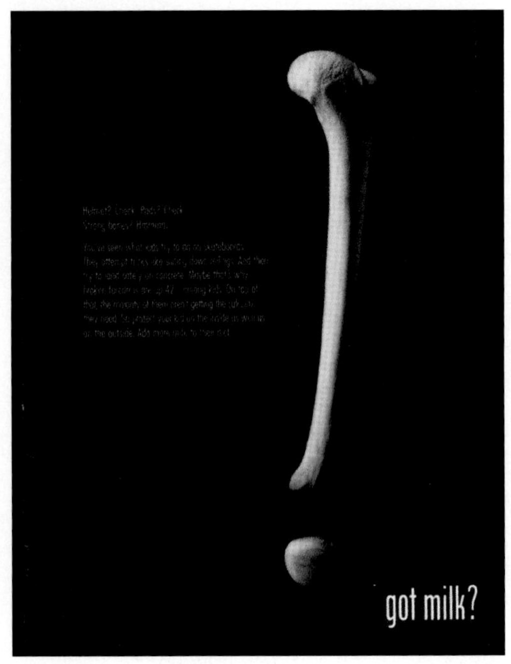

Marketers' attempts to create problem recognition among consumers are not always successful. Consumers may not see a problem or need for the product the marketer is selling. A main reason many consumers were initially reluctant to purchase personal computers was that they failed to see what problems owning one would solve. One way PC manufacturers successfully activated problem recognition was by stressing how a computer helps children improve their academic skills and do better in school.

Examining Consumer Motivations

Marketers recognize that while problem recognition is often a basic, simple process, the way a consumer perceives a problem and becomes motivated to solve it will influence the remainder of the decision process. For example, one consumer may perceive the need to purchase a new watch from a functional perspective and focus on reliable, low-priced alternatives. Another consumer may see the purchase of a watch as more of a fashion statement and focus on the design and image of various brands. To better understand the reasons underlying consumer purchases, marketers devote considerable attention to examining **motives**—that is, those factors that compel a consumer to take a particular action.

Hierarchy of Needs One of the most popular approaches to understanding consumer motivations is based on the classic theory of human motivation popularized many years ago by psychologist Abraham Maslow.[3] His **hierarchy of needs** theory postulates five basic levels of human needs, arranged in a hierarchy based on their importance. As shown in Figure 4-2, the five needs are (1) *physiological*—the basic level of primary needs for things required to sustain life, such as food, shelter, clothing, and sex; (2) *safety*—the need for security and safety from physical harm; (3) *social/love and belonging*—the desire to have satisfying relationships with others and feel a sense of love, affection, belonging, and acceptance; (4) *esteem*—the need to feel a sense of accomplishment and gain recognition, status, and respect from others; and (5) *self-actualization*—the need for self-fulfillment and a desire to realize one's own potential.

Exhibit 4-4 T-Mobile phones introduce the innovative use of BlackBerry

According to Maslow's theory, the lower-level physiological and safety needs must be satisfied before the higher-order needs become meaningful. Once these basic needs are satisfied, the individual moves on to attempting to satisfy higher-order needs such as self-esteem. In reality, it is unlikely that people move through the needs hierarchy in a stairstep manner. Lower-level needs are an ongoing source of motivation for consumer purchase behavior. However, since basic physiological needs are met in most developed countries, marketers often sell products that fill basic physiological needs by appealing to consumers' higher-level needs. For example, in marketing its washcloths, Huggies focuses on the love between parent and child (social needs) in addition to the gentleness of the product (Exhibit 4-5).

While Maslow's need hierarchy has flaws, it offers a framework for marketers to use in determining what needs they want their products and services to be shown satisfying. Advertising campaigns can then be designed to show how a brand can fulfill these needs. Marketers also recognize that different market segments emphasize different need levels. For example, a young single person may be attempting to satisfy

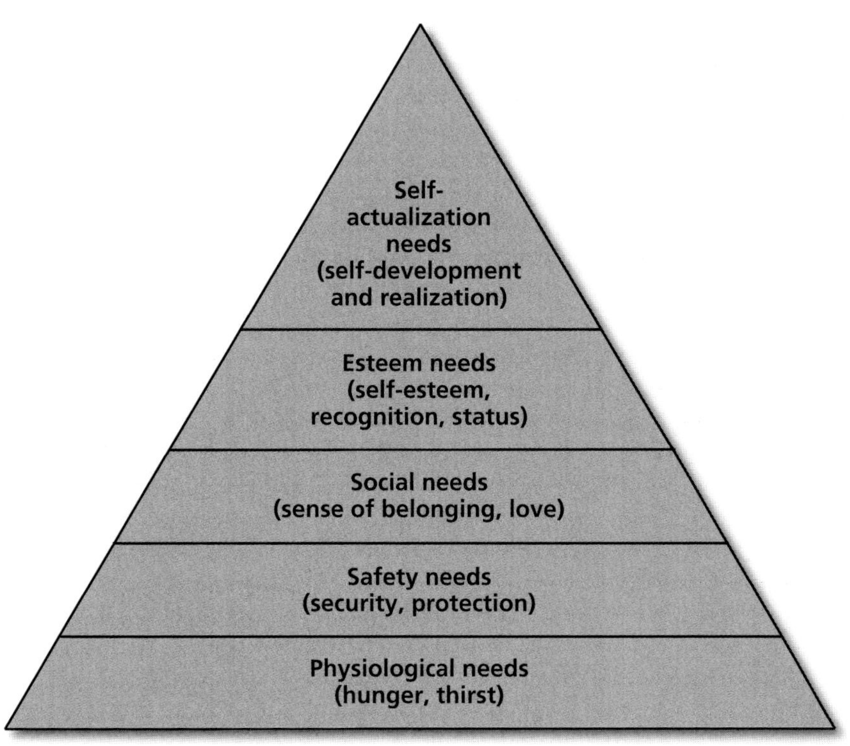

Figure 4-2 Maslow's Hierarchy of Needs

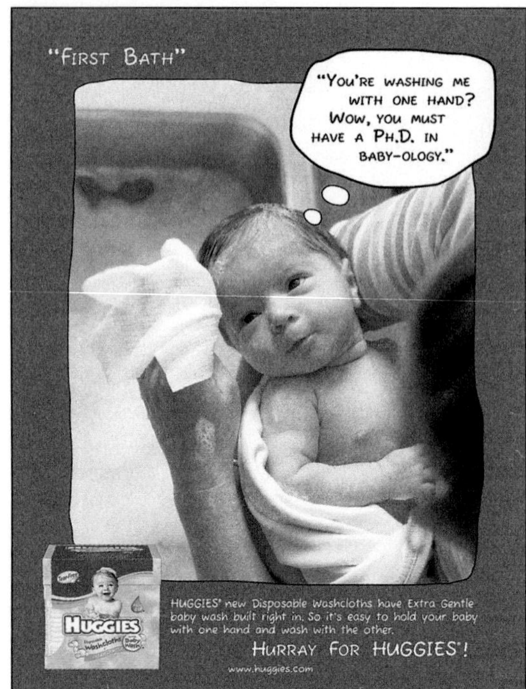

Exhibit 4-5 Huggies appeals to needs for love and belonging in this ad

social or self-esteem needs in purchasing a car, while a family with children will focus more on safety needs. Chrysler used ads like the one in Exhibit 4-6 to position its cars as meeting the security needs of consumers.

Psychoanalytic Theory A somewhat more controversial approach to the study of consumer motives is the **psychoanalytic theory** pioneered by Sigmund Freud.[4] Although his work dealt with the structure and development of personality, Freud also studied the underlying motivations for human behavior. Psychoanalytic theory had a strong influence on the development of modern psychology and on explanations of motivation and personality. It has also been applied to the study of consumer behavior by marketers interested in probing deeply rooted motives that may underlie purchase decisions.

Those who attempt to relate psychoanalytic theory to consumer behavior believe consumers' motivations for purchasing are often very complex and unclear to the casual observer—and to the consumers themselves. Many motives for purchase and/or consumption may be driven by deep motives one can determine only by probing the subconscious.

Among the first to conduct this type of research in marketing, Ernest Dichter and James Vicary were employed by a number of major corporations to use psychoanalytic techniques to determine consumers' purchase motivations. The work of these researchers and others who continue to use this approach assumed the title of **motivation research.**

Motivation Research in Marketing Motivation researchers use a variety of methodologies to gain insight into the underlying causes of consumer behavior. Methods employed include in-depth interviews, projective techniques, association tests, and focus groups in which consumers are encouraged to bring out associations related to products and brands (see Figure 4-3). As one might expect, such associations often lead to interesting insights as to why people purchase. For example:

Exhibit 4-6 Chrysler uses an appeal to security needs

- A man's purchase of a high-priced fur for his wife proves his potency.[5]
- Consumers prefer large cars because they believe such cars protect them from the "jungle" of everyday driving.[6]
- A man buys a convertible as a substitute mistress.
- Women like to bake cakes because they feel like they are giving birth to a baby.
- Women wear perfume to "attract a man" and "glorify their existence."
- Men like frankfurters better than women do because cooking them (frankfurters, not men!) makes women feel guilty. It's an admission of laziness.
- When people shower, their sins go down the drain with the soap as they rinse.[7]

As you can see from these examples, motivation research has led to some very interesting, albeit controversial, findings and to much skepticism from marketing managers. However, major corporations and advertising agencies continue to use motivation research to help them market their products.

Problems and Contributions of Psychoanalytic Theory and Motivation Research Psychoanalytic theory has been criticized as being too vague, unresponsive to the external environment, and too reliant on

In-depth interviews
Face-to-face situations in which an interviewer asks a consumer to talk freely in an unstructured interview using specific questions designed to obtain insights into his or her motives, ideas, or opinions.

Projective techniques
Efforts designed to gain insights into consumers' values, motives, attitudes, or needs that are difficult to express or identify by having them project these internal states upon some external object.

Association tests
A technique in which an individual is asked to respond with the first thing that comes to mind when he or she is presented with a stimulus; the stimulus may be a word, picture, ad, and so on.

Focus groups
A small number of people with similar backgrounds and/or interests who are brought together to discuss a particular product, idea, or issue.

Figure 4-3 Some of the Marketing Research Methods Used to Probe the Mind of the Consumer

the early development of the individual. It also uses a small sample for drawing conclusions. Because of the emphasis on the unconscious, results are difficult if not impossible to verify, leading motivation research to be criticized for both the conclusions drawn and its lack of experimental validation. Since motivation research studies typically use so few participants, there is also concern that it really discovers the idiosyncracies of a few individuals and its findings are not generalizable to the whole population.

Still, it is difficult to ignore the psychoanalytic approach in furthering our understanding of consumer behavior. Its insights can often be used as a basis for advertising messages aimed at buyers' deeply rooted feelings, hopes, aspirations, and fears. Such strategies are often more effective than rationally based appeals.

Some corporations and advertising agencies have used motivation research to gain further insights into how consumers think. Examples include the following:[8]

- Chrysler had consumers sit on the floor, like children, and use scissors to cut words out of magazines to describe a car.[9]
- McCann-Erickson asked women to draw and describe how they felt about roaches. The agency concluded that many women associated roaches with men who had abandoned them and that this was why women preferred roach killers that let them see the roaches die.
- Saatchi & Saatchi used psychological probes to conclude that Ronald McDonald created a more nurturing mood than did the Burger King (who was perceived as more aggressive and distant).
- Foote, Cone & Belding gave consumers stacks of photographs of faces and asked them to associate the faces with the kinds of people who might use particular products.
- The advertising agency Marcus Thomas, LLC conducted in-depth one-on-one interviews and used projective techniques to determine underlying motivations for choosing one cardiovascular care facility over another.

While often criticized, motivation research has also contributed to the marketing discipline. The qualitative nature of the research is considered important in assessing how and why consumers buy. Focus groups and in-depth interviews are valuable methods for gaining insights into consumers' feelings, and projective techniques are often the only way to get around stereotypical or socially desirable responses. In addition,

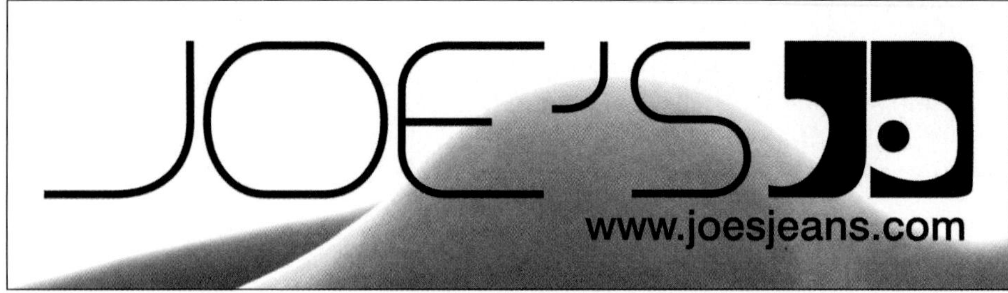

Exhibit 4-7 Joes Jeans uses sex appeal in its advertising

motivation research is the forerunner of psychographics (discussed in Chapter 2).

Finally, we know that buyers are sometimes motivated by symbolic as well as functional drives in their purchase decisions. At least one study has shown that two-thirds of all prime-time TV shows present an average of 5.2 scenes per hour that contain talk about sex. Thus, we see the use of sexual appeals and symbols in ads like Exhibit 4-7.

Information Search

The second stage in the consumer decision-making process is *information search.* Once consumers perceive a problem or need that can be satisfied by the purchase of a product or service, they begin to search for information needed to make a purchase decision. The initial search effort often consists of an attempt to scan information stored in memory to recall past experiences and/or knowledge regarding various purchase alternatives.[10] This information retrieval is referred to as **internal search.** For many routine, repetitive purchases, previously acquired information that is stored in memory (such as past performance or outcomes from using a brand) is sufficient for comparing alternatives and making a choice.

If the internal search does not yield enough information, the consumer will seek additional information by engaging in **external search.** External sources of information include:

- *Personal sources,* such as friends, relatives, or co-workers.
- *Marketer-controlled (commercial) sources,* such as information from advertising, salespeople, or point-of-purchase displays and the Internet.
- *Public sources,* including articles in magazines or newspapers and reports on TV.
- *Personal experience,* such as actually handling, examining, or testing the product.

Determining how much and which sources of external information to use involves several factors, including the importance of the purchase decision, the effort needed to acquire information, the amount of past experience relevant, the degree of perceived risk associated with the purchase, and the time available. For example, the selection of a movie to see on a Friday night might entail simply talking to a friend or checking the movie guide in the daily newspaper. A more complex purchase such as a new car might use a number of information sources—perhaps a review of *Road & Track, Motortrend,* or *Consumer Reports;* discussion with family members and friends; and test-driving of cars. At this point in the purchase decision, the information-providing aspects of advertising are extremely important.

Perception

Knowledge of how consumers acquire and use information from external sources is important to marketers in formulating communication strategies. Marketers are particularly interested in (1) how consumers sense external information, (2) how they select and attend to various sources of information, and (3) how this information is interpreted and given meaning. These processes are all part of **perception,** the process by which an individual receives, selects, organizes, and interprets information to create a meaningful picture of the world.[11] Perception is an individual process; it depends on internal factors such as a person's beliefs, experiences, needs, moods, and expectations. The perceptual process is also influenced by the characteristics of a stimulus (such as its size, color, and intensity) and the context in which it is seen or heard (Exhibit 4-8).

Sensation

Perception involves three distinct processes. **Sensation** is the immediate, direct response of the senses (taste, smell, sight, touch, and hearing) to a stimulus such as an ad, package, brand name, or point-of-purchase display. Perception uses these senses to create a representation of the stimulus. Marketers recognize that it is important to understand consumers' physiological reactions to marketing stimuli. For example, the visual elements of an ad or package design must attract consumers' favorable attention.

Marketers sometimes try to increase the level of sensory input so that their advertising messages will get noticed. For example, marketers of colognes and perfumes often use strong visuals as well as scent strips to appeal to multiple senses and attract the attention of magazine readers. Some advertisers have even inserted microcomputer chips into their print ads to play a song or deliver a message.

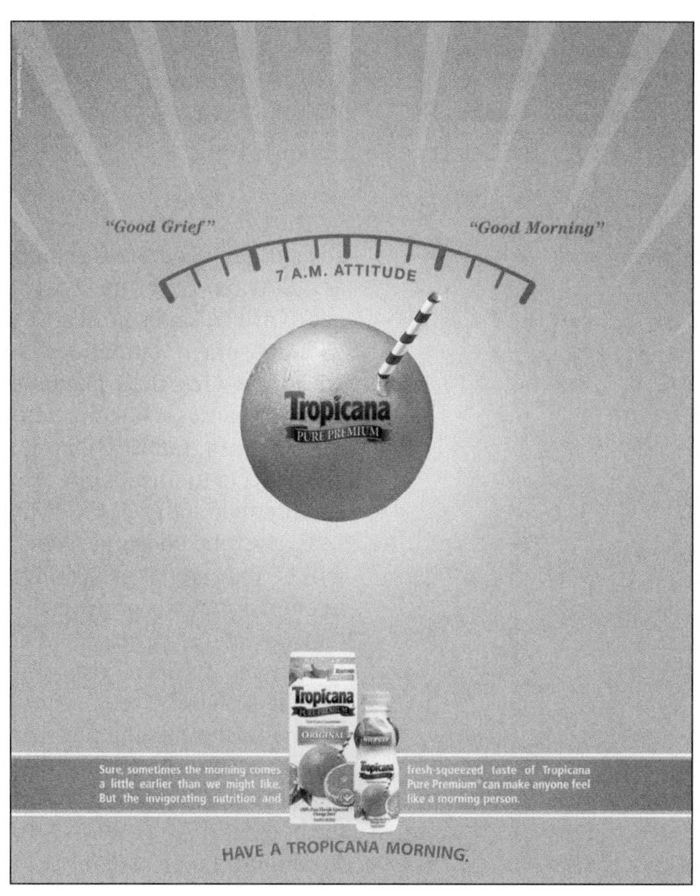

Exhibit 4-8 Tropicana uses color to focus attention on orange juice

Selecting Information

Sensory inputs are important but are only one part of the perceptual process. Other determinants of whether marketing stimuli will be attended to and how they will be interpreted include internal psychological factors such as the consumer's personality, needs, motives, expectations, and experiences. These psychological inputs explain why people focus attention on some things and ignore others. Two people may perceive the same stimuli in very different ways because they select, attend, and comprehend differently. An individual's perceptual processes usually focus on elements of the environment that are relevant to his or her needs and tune out irrelevant stimuli. Think about how much more attentive you are to advertising for personal computers, tires, or stereos when you are in the market for one of these products (a point that is made by the message from the American Association of Advertising Agencies in Exhibit 4-9).

Interpreting the Information

Once a consumer selects and attends to a stimulus, the perceptual process focuses on organizing, categorizing, and interpreting the incoming information. This stage of the perceptual process is very individualized and is influenced by internal psychological factors. The interpretation and meaning an individual assigns to an incoming stimulus also depend in part on the nature of the stimulus. For example, many ads are objective, and their message is clear and straightforward. Other ads are more ambiguous, and their meaning is strongly influenced by the consumer's individual interpretation.

Selectivity occurs throughout the various stages of the consumer's perceptual process. Perception may be viewed as a filtering process in which internal and external factors influence what is received and how it is processed and interpreted. The sheer number and complexity of the marketing stimuli a person is exposed to in any given day require that this filtering occur. **Selective perception** may occur at the exposure, attention, comprehension, or retention stage of perception, as shown in Figure 4-4.

Exhibit 4-9 This ad reminds consumers of how advertising responds to their needs

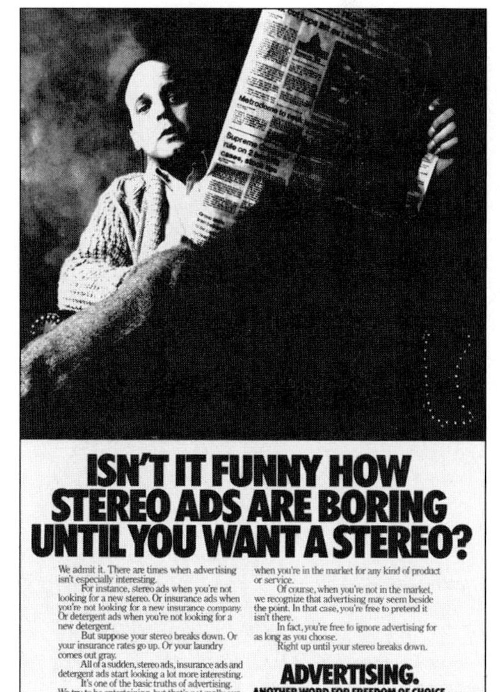

ISN'T IT FUNNY HOW STEREO ADS ARE BORING UNTIL YOU WANT A STEREO?
We admit it. There are times when advertising isn't especially interesting.
For instance, stereo ads when you're not looking for a new stereo. Or insurance ads when you're not looking for a new insurance company. Or detergent ads when you're not looking for a new detergent.
But suppose your stereo breaks down. Or your insurance rates go up. Or your laundry comes out gray.
All of a sudden, stereo ads, insurance ads and detergent ads start looking a lot more interesting.
It's one of the basic truths of advertising. We try to be entertaining, but that's not really our job. Our job is to help you make the right choices when you're in the market for any kind of product or service.
Of course, when you're not in the market, we recognize that advertising may seem beside the point. In that case, you're free to pretend it isn't there.
In fact, you're free to ignore advertising for as long as you choose.
Right up until your stereo breaks down.
ADVERTISING.
ANOTHER WORD FOR FREEDOM OF CHOICE.
American Association of Advertising Agencies

Selective Perception

Selective exposure occurs as consumers choose whether or not to make themselves available to information. For example, a viewer of a television show may change channels or leave the room during commercial breaks.

Selective attention occurs when the consumer chooses to focus attention on certain stimuli while excluding others. One study of selective attention estimated that the typical consumer is exposed to nearly 1,500

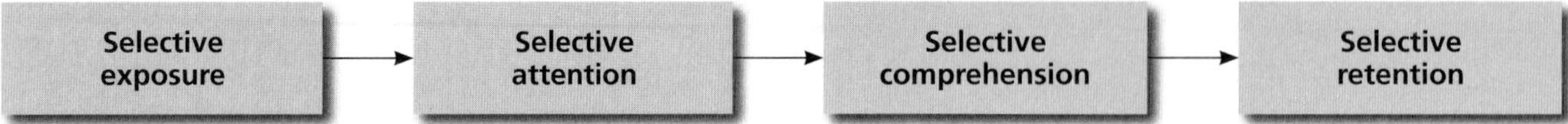

Figure 4-4 The Selective Perception Process

ads per day yet perceives only 76 of these messages.[12] Other estimates range as high as 4,000 exposures per day. This means advertisers must make considerable effort to get their messages noticed. Advertisers often use the creative aspects of their ads to gain consumers' attention. For example, some advertisers set their ads off from others by showing their products in color against a black-and-white background. This creative tactic has been used in advertising for many products, among them Cherry 7UP, Nuprin, Pepto-Bismol, and Tropicana. Notice how the color red is used in the ad for VO5 to attract attention while also focusing on the product line, packaging, and brand identity in Exhibit 4-10.

Even if the consumer does notice the advertiser's message, there is no guarantee it will be interpreted in the intended manner. Consumers may engage in **selective comprehension,** interpreting information on the basis of their own attitudes, beliefs, motives, and experiences. They often interpret information in a manner that supports their own position. For example, an ad that disparages a consumer's favorite brand may be seen as biased or untruthful, and its claims may not be accepted.

The final screening process shown in Figure 4-4 is **selective retention,** which means consumers do not remember all the information they see, hear, or read even after attending to and comprehending it. Advertisers attempt to make sure information will be retained in the consumer's memory so that it will be available when it is time to make a purchase. **Mnemonics** such as symbols, rhymes, associations, and images that assist in the learning and memory process are helpful. Many advertisers use telephone numbers that spell out the company name and are easy to remember. Eveready put pictures of its pink bunny on packages to remind consumers at the point of purchase of its creative advertising.

Subliminal Perception

Advertisers know consumers use selective perception to filter out irrelevant or unwanted advertising messages, so they employ various creative tactics to get their messages noticed. One controversial tactic advertisers have been accused of using is appealing to consumers' subconscious. **Subliminal perception** refers to the ability to perceive a stimulus that is below the level of conscious awareness. Psychologists generally agree it is possible to perceive things without being consciously aware of them.

Exhibit 4-10 Color is used to attract attention to VO5

As you might imagine, the possibility of using hidden persuaders such as subliminal audio messages or visual cues to influence consumers might be intriguing to advertisers but would not be welcomed by consumers. The idea of marketers influencing consumers at a subconscious level has strong ethical implications. Ethical Perspective 4-1 discusses researchers' mixed opinions as to whether motivation research and subliminal advertising are likely to be effective in influencing consumer behavior.

Alternative Evaluation

After acquiring information during the information search stage of the decision process, the consumer moves to alternative evaluation. In this stage, the consumer compares the various brands or products and services he or she has identified as being capable of solving the consumption problem and satisfying the needs or motives that initiated the decision process. The various brands identified as purchase options to be considered during the alternative evaluation process are referred to as the consumer's *evoked set.*

ETHICAL PERSPECTIVE 4-1

Psychoanalytic Theory, Subliminal Advertising, and Morphological Research: Appealing to the Consumer's Subconscious

It has been nearly half a century since Vance Packard's famous book *The Hidden Persuaders* shocked the world. In his book, Packard accused advertisers of using research techniques like "depth interviews" and "motivation research" to develop messages that appealed to consumers' subconscious. These appeals led consumers to be persuaded to make purchases without consciously being aware why they made their choices. At about the same time, James Vicary, a motivational researcher, introduced the concept of subliminal advertising, reporting that he had increased the sales of popcorn and Coke by subliminally flashing the messages "eat popcorn" and "drink Coca-Cola" across the screen. Wilson Bryant Key further fueled the fires with his books claiming that subliminal advertising was, indeed, manipulating consumer behaviors.

As you might imagine, a rash of research studies, articles, and books designed to explore motivation research and subliminal advertising soon followed in an attempt to determine the veracity of these techniques. In a series of extensive reviews on the topic (1982, 1988), Timothy Moore concluded that there was no evidence to support the fact that subliminal messages can affect consumers' motivations, perceptions, or attitudes. Studies by Joel Saegart and Jack Haberstroh supported Moore's position. For a long period of time subliminal advertising, motivation research, and the application of psychoanalytic theory to consumer behaviors seemed to go away, with members of society and academia apparently losing interest. But while the theories went away, they never really disappeared.

In 1994, after a review of the literature Kathryn Theus concluded that "certain themes might be effectively applied by advertising or marketing specialists." Later research conducted in Australia concluded that subliminally implanted sexy images led to greater recall of ads among hypnotized subjects. Cooper and Copper also weighed in noting that subliminal stimuli embedded in the TV show *The Simpsons* made viewers thirsty. Then, in the 2000 Bush–Gore presidential campaign, the Republicans were accused of subliminally implanting the word *rats* into ads to attach the meaning to Al Gore. Once again, motivation research was back in the spotlight.

In an article in *The Journal of Advertising Research* in 2004, Dirk Zeims suggests that unfortunately, the contributions of motivation research have recently been ignored or forgotten completely. Zeims contends that "such fundamental insights are essential for practical merchandising and for advertising because the arguments used by advertisements only work when they take up the unconscious mechanism" (p. 211). He suggests continuing the tradition of psychoanalytic theory through morphological market psychology—a combination of Gestalt psychology and psychoanalysis—which explores the hidden psychological meanings of products and brands when considered along with their more obvious functional attributes.

Zeims cites two examples of the morphological approach in practice. The first describes an analysis of purchasing paper towels. The functional promises provided in the ads promote their use in cleaning, focusing on the attributes of firmness and saturation potential. Morphological analyses revealed an even broader motivation for purchase: "They were attributed with the magical potential to undo little accidents that occur [in] everyday life." Symbolically speaking, paper towels help soak up all the accidents and irregularities of everyday life, and help consumers pretend that some everyday conflicts never happened. As a result, paper towels can be used to resolve conflicts within the family.

The second example involves the use of mobile phones. Functionally the phones are convenient and make communications easier. From a morphological perspective their use speaks to a deeper desire on the part of the consumer to "expand their importance and possess all encompassing powers. They can interfere with anyone, from everywhere. They can contact people from a distance and control them" (p. 212). Zeims contends that it is the omnipresence and omnipotence that cell phones offer that is the true motivation for purchasing them. Zeims also discusses unconscious motivations underlying the Visa, MasterCard, and Victoria's Secret appeals.

According to morphological research, the approach broadens the horizon of motivational research conducted in the past and enables marketers to create better advertisements by uncovering important unconscious psychological processes. This leads to more effective advertisements, whose appeals go beyond the functional attributes of a product.

Like subliminal advertising, morphological research has its supporters and its skeptics. Because the purchase motives reside in the subconscious, no one can be sure they actually exist. On the other hand, they can't be sure that they do not exist either!

Sources: Dirk Zeims, "The Morphological Approach for Unconscious Consumer Motivation Research," *Journal of Advertising Research,* June 2004, pp. 210–215; Joel Cooper and Grant Copper, "Subliminal Motivation: A Story Revisited," *Journal of Applied Social Psychology* 32, no. 11 (November 2002), pp. 2213–2228; "Hypnosis Reveals Ad Effects," *Adweek Asia,* January 29, 1999, p. 4; "Breaking French Connection," *Ad Age,* March 22, 1999, p. 52; Kathryn Theus, "Subliminal Advertising and the Psychology of Processing Unconcsious Stimuli: A Review of Research," *Psychology & Marketing* 11, no. 3, 1994, pp. 271–90; Timothy Moore, "Subliminal Advertising: What You See Is What You Get," *Journal of Marketing* 46, no. 2 (Spring 1982), pp. 38–47; Timothy Moore, "The Case against Subliminal Manipulation," *Psychology and Marketing* 5, no. 4 (Winter 1988), pp. 297–316; Kalpana Srinivasan, "FCC Ends Probe on Republican Ad," www.individual.com, March 12, 2001, pp. 1–2; George E. Condon Jr. and Toby Eckert, "Flap over 'RATS' Latest to Plague Bush's Drive," *San Diego Tribune,* September 13, 2000, p. A1.

SPOKANE OFFERS SUCCESS AND A PLACE TO ENJOY IT.
THE SPOKESMAN-REVIEW

Exhibit 4-11 Spokane wants to be in the evoked set of business locations

The Evoked Set The evoked set is generally only a subset of all the brands of which the consumer is aware. The consumer reduces the number of brands to be reviewed during the alternative evaluation stage to a manageable level. The exact size of the evoked set varies from one consumer to another and depends on such factors as the importance of the purchase and the amount of time and energy the consumer wants to spend comparing alternatives.

The goal of most advertising and promotional strategies is to increase the likelihood that a brand will be included in the consumer's evoked set and considered during alternative evaluation. Marketers use advertising to create *top-of-mind awareness* among consumers so that their brands are part of the evoked set of their target audiences. Popular brands with large advertising budgets use *reminder advertising* to maintain high awareness levels and increase the likelihood they will be considered by consumers in the market for the product. Marketers of new brands or those with a low market share need to gain awareness among consumers and break into their evoked sets. The ad promoting Spokane as a better place to live and do business (Exhibit 4-11) shows this strategy being used in a different context from products and brands. The ad presents the many benefits of Spokane and encourages prospective businesses to consider it in their evoked set of places to locate or relocate.

Advertising is a valuable promotional tool for creating and maintaining brand awareness and making sure a brand is included in the evoked set. However, marketers also work to promote their brands in the actual environment where purchase decisions are made. Point-of-purchase materials and promotional techniques such as in-store sampling, end-aisle displays, or shelf tags touting special prices encourage consumers to consider brands that may not have initially been in their evoked set.

Evaluative Criteria and Consequences Once consumers have identified an evoked set and have a list of alternatives, they must evaluate the various brands. This involves comparing the choice alternatives on specific criteria important to the consumer. **Evaluative criteria** are the dimensions or attributes of a product or service that are used to compare different alternatives. Evaluative criteria can be objective or subjective. For example, in buying an automobile, consumers use objective attributes such as price, warranty, and fuel economy as well as subjective factors such as image, styling, and performance.

Evaluative criteria are usually viewed as product or service attributes. Many marketers view their products or services as *bundles of attributes,* but consumers tend to think about products or services in terms of their *consequences* instead. J. Paul Peter and Jerry Olson define consequences as specific events or outcomes that consumers experience when they purchase and/or consume a product or service.[13] They distinguish between two broad types of consequences. **Functional consequences** are concrete outcomes of product or service usage that are tangible and directly experienced by consumers. The taste of a soft drink or a potato chip, the acceleration of a car, and the clarity of a fax transmission are examples of functional consequences. **Psychosocial consequences** are abstract outcomes that are more intangible, subjective, and personal, such as how a product makes you feel or how you think others will view you for purchasing or using it.

Marketers should distinguish between product/service attributes and consequences, because the importance and meaning consumers assign to an attribute are usually determined by its consequences for them. Moreover, advertisers must be sure consumers understand the link between a particular attribute and a consequence. For example, the Ping golf ad in Exhibit 4-12 focuses on the consequences of using the Ping G-2 golf club to hit the ball long and straight.

Product/service attributes and the consequences or outcomes consumers think they will experience from a particular brand are very important, for they are often the basis on which consumers form attitudes and purchase intentions and decide among various choice alternatives. Two subprocesses are very important during the alternative evaluation stage: (1) the process by which consumer attitudes are created, reinforced, and changed and (2) the decision rules or integration strategies consumers use to compare brands and make purchase decisions. We will examine each of these processes in more detail.

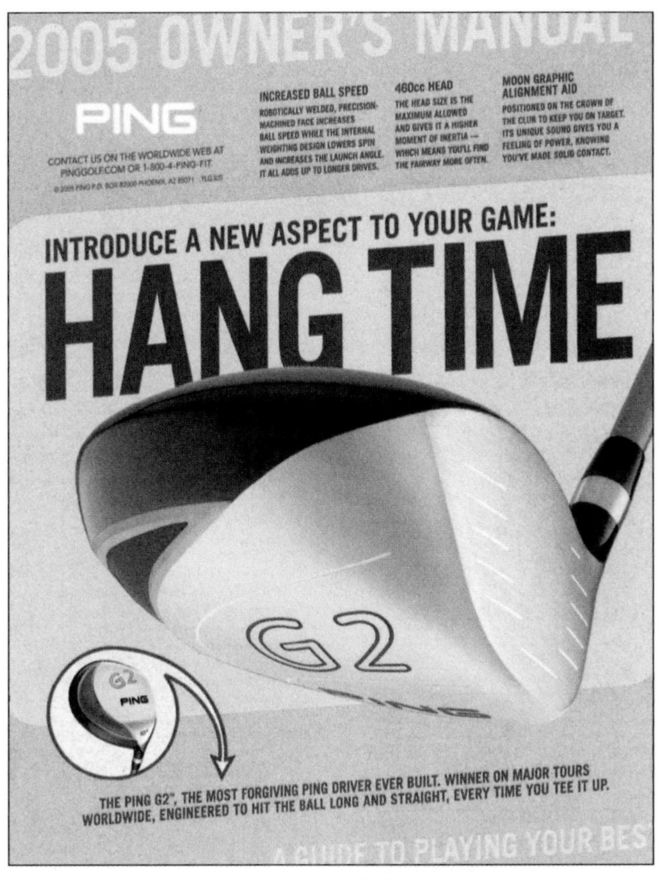

Exhibit 4-12 This ad emphasizes the positive consequences of using a Ping G-2 driver

Attitudes

Attitudes are one of the most heavily studied concepts in consumer behavior. According to Gordon Allport's classic definition, "attitudes are learned predispositions to respond to an object."[14] More recent perspectives view attitudes as a summary construct that represents an individual's overall feelings toward or evaluation of an object.[15] Consumers hold attitudes toward a variety of objects that are important to marketers, including individuals (celebrity endorsers such as Tiger Woods or Andre Agassi), brands (Cheerios, Kix), companies (Intel, Microsoft), product categories (beef, pork, tuna), retail stores (Wal-Mart, Sears), or even advertisements (Nike ads).

Attitudes are important to marketers because they theoretically summarize a consumer's evaluation of an object (or brand or company) and represent positive or negative feelings and behavioral tendencies. Marketers' keen interest in attitudes is based on the assumption that they are related to consumers' purchase behavior. Considerable evidence supports the basic assumption of a relationship between attitudes and behavior.[16] The attitude-behavior link does not always hold; many other factors can affect behavior.[17] But attitudes are very important to marketers. Advertising and promotion are used to create favorable attitudes toward new products/services or brands, reinforce existing favorable attitudes, and/or change negative attitudes. An approach to studying and measuring attitudes that is particularly relevant to advertising is multiattribute attitude models.

Multiattribute Attitude Models

Consumer researchers and marketing practitioners have been using multiattribute attitude models to study consumer attitudes for two decades.[18] A **multiattribute attitude model** views an attitude object, such as a product or brand, as possessing a number of attributes that provide the basis on which consumers form their attitudes. According to this model, consumers have beliefs about specific brand attributes and attach different levels of importance to these attributes. Using this approach, an attitude toward a particular brand can be represented as

$$A_B = \sum_{i=1}^{n} B_i \times E_i$$

where A_B = attitude toward a brand

B_i = beliefs about the brand's performance on attribute i

E_i = importance attached to attribute i

n = number of attributes considered

For example, a consumer may have beliefs (B_i) about various brands of toothpaste on certain attributes. One brand may be perceived as having fluoride and thus preventing cavities, tasting good, and helping control tartar buildup. Another brand may not be perceived as having these attributes, but consumers may believe it performs well on other attributes such as freshening breath and whitening teeth.

To predict attitudes, one must know how much importance consumers attach to each of these attributes (E_i). For example, parents purchasing toothpaste for their children may prefer a brand that performs well on cavity prevention, a preference that leads to a more favorable attitude toward the first brand. Teenagers and young adults

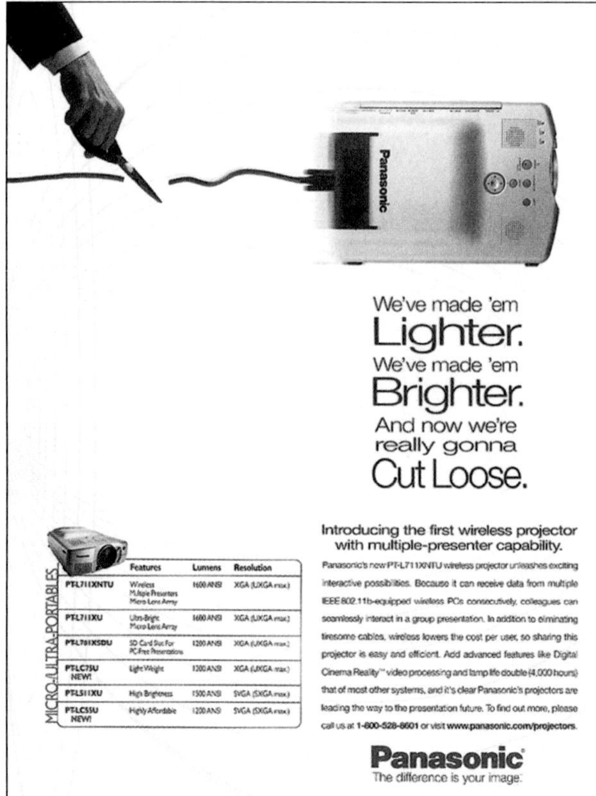

Panasonic
We've made 'em
Lighter.
We've made 'em
Brighter.
And now we're
really gonna
Cut Loose.
Introducing the first wireless projector with multiple-presenter capability.
Panasonic's new PT-L711XNTU wireless projector unleashes exciting interactive possibilities. Because it can receive data from multiple IEEE 802.11b-equipped wireless PCs consecutively, colleagues can seamlessly interact in a group presentation. In addition to eliminating tiresome cables, wireless lowers the cost per user, so sharing this projector is easy and efficient. Add advanced features like Digital Cinema Reality™ video processing and lamp life double (4,000 hours) that of most other systems, and it's clear Panasonic's projectors are leading the way to the presentation future. To find out more, please call us at 1-800-528-8601 or visit www.panasonic.com/projectors.
MICRO-/ULTRA-PORTABLES
Features Lumens Resolution
PT-L711XNTU Wireless Multiple Presenters Micro Lens Array 1600 ANSI XGA (UXGA max)
PT-L711XU Ultra-Bright Micro Lens Array 1600 ANSI XGA (UXGA max)
PT-L701XSDU SD Card Slot For PC-Free Presentations 1200 ANSI XGA (UXGA max)
PT-LC75U NEW! Light Weight 1200 ANSI XGA (UXGA max)
PT-LS11XU High Brightness 1500 ANSI SVGA (SXGA max)
PT-LC55U NEW! Highly Affordable 1200 ANSI SVGA (SXGA max)
Panasonic
The difference is your image.

Exhibit 4-13 Panasonic adds a new attribute for customers to consider

may prefer a brand that freshens their breath and makes their teeth white and thus prefer the second brand.

Consumers may hold a number of different beliefs about brands in any product or service category. However, not all of these beliefs are activated in forming an attitude. Beliefs concerning specific attributes or consequences that are activated and form the basis of an attitude are referred to as **salient beliefs.** Marketers should identify and understand these salient beliefs. They must also recognize that the saliency of beliefs varies among different market segments, over time, and across different consumption situations.

Attitude Change Strategies

Multiattribute models help marketers understand and diagnose the underlying basis of consumers' attitudes. By understanding the beliefs that underlie consumers' evaluations of a brand and the importance of various attributes or consequences, the marketer is better able to develop communication strategies for creating, changing, or reinforcing brand attitudes. The multiattribute model provides insight into several ways marketers can influence consumer attitudes, including:

- Increasing or changing the strength or belief rating of a brand on an important attribute (Southwest Airlines has the most on-time arrivals).
- Changing consumers' perceptions of the importance or value of an attribute (demonstrating safety in Mercedes' ads).
- Adding a new attribute to the attitude formation process (Ragu's organically grown tomato sauce).
- Changing perceptions of belief ratings for a competing brand (Volvo's ads that show Volvo as stylish).

The first strategy is commonly used by advertisers. They identify an attribute or consequence that is important and remind consumers how well their brand performs on this attribute. In situations where consumers do not perceive the marketer's brand as possessing an important attribute or the belief strength is low, advertising strategies may be targeted at changing the belief rating. Even when belief strength is high, advertising may be used to increase the rating of a brand on an important attribute. BMW's "The Ultimate Driving Machine" campaign is a good example of a strategy designed to create a belief and reinforce it through advertising.

Exhibit 4-14 This turkey ad compares its product to beef and chicken

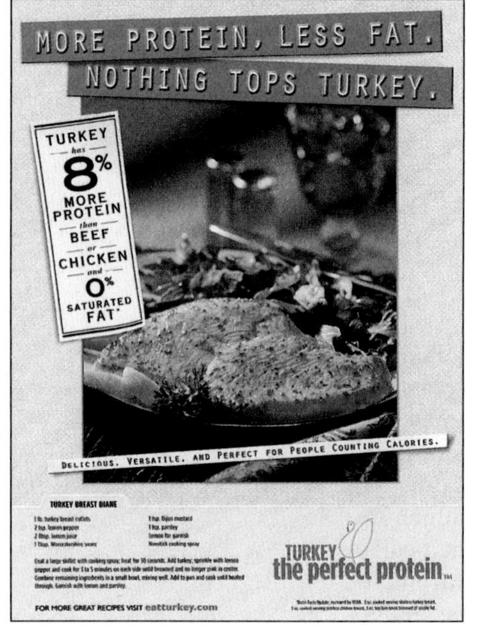

MORE PROTEIN, LESS FAT.
NOTHING TOPS TURKEY.
TURKEY has 8% MORE PROTEIN than BEEF or CHICKEN and 0% SATURATED FAT*
DELICIOUS, VERSATILE, AND PERFECT FOR PEOPLE COUNTING CALORIES.
TURKEY BREAST DIANE
TURKEY the perfect protein
FOR MORE GREAT RECIPES VISIT eatturkey.com

Marketers often attempt to influence consumer attitudes by changing the relative importance of a particular attribute. This second strategy involves getting consumers to attach more importance to the attribute in forming their attitude toward the brand. Marketers using this strategy want to increase the importance of an attribute their particular brand has.

The third strategy for influencing consumer attitudes is to add or emphasize a new attribute that consumers can use in evaluating a brand. Marketers often do this by improving their products or focusing on additional benefits or consequences associated with using the brand. Exhibit 4-13 shows how Panasonic introduced its projector focusing on weight, brightness, and wireless in an attempt to influence consumers' attitudes.

A final strategy marketers use is to change consumer beliefs about the attributes of competing brands or product categories. This strategy has become much more common with the increase in comparative advertising, where marketers compare their brands to competitors' on specific product attributes. An example of this is the turkey industry ad shown in Exhibit 4-14, where turkey is compared to chicken and beef.

Integration Processes and Decision Rules

Another important aspect of the alternative evaluation stage is the way consumers combine information about the characteristics of brands to arrive at a purchase decision. **Integration processes** are the way product knowledge, meanings, and beliefs are combined to evaluate two or more alternatives.[19] Analysis of the integration process focuses on the different types of *decision rules* or strategies consumers use to decide among purchase alternatives.

Consumers often make purchase selections by using formal integration strategies or decision rules that require examination and comparison of alternatives on specific attributes. This process involves a very deliberate evaluation of the alternatives, attribute by attribute. When consumers apply such formal decision rules, marketers need to know which attributes are being considered so as to provide the information the consumers require.

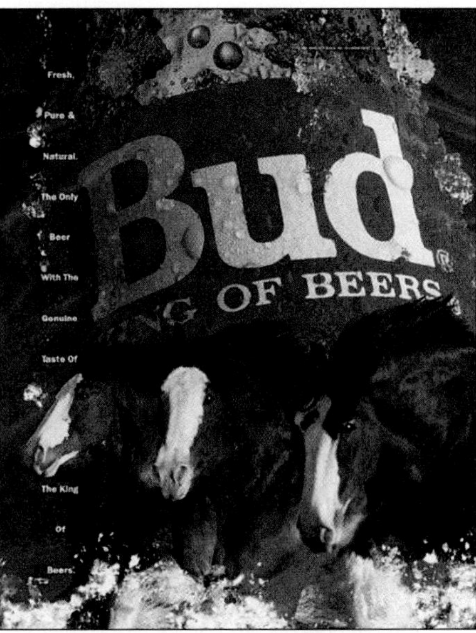

Exhibit 4-15 Market leaders such as Budweiser can appeal to consumer affect

Sometimes consumers make their purchase decisions using more simplified decision rules known as **heuristics.** Peter and Olson note that heuristics are easy to use and are highly adaptive to specific environmental situations (such as a retail store).[20] For familiar products that are purchased frequently, consumers may use price-based heuristics (buy the least expensive brand) or promotion-based heuristics (choose the brand for which I can get a price reduction through a coupon, rebate, or special deal).

One type of heuristic is the **affect referral decision rule,**[21] in which consumers make a selection on the basis of an overall impression or summary evaluation of the various alternatives under consideration. This decision rule suggests that consumers have affective impressions of brands stored in memory that can be accessed at the time of purchase. How many times have you gone into a store and made purchases based on your overall impressions of the brands rather than going through detailed comparisons of the alternatives' specific attributes?

Marketers selling familiar and popular brands may appeal to an affect referral rule by stressing overall affective feelings or impressions about their products. Market leaders, whose products enjoy strong overall brand images, often use ads that promote the brand as the best overall. Allstate's "The Good Hands People," Rice-A-Roni's "The San Francisco Treat," Jeep's "There's only one," and Budweiser's "The king of beers" are all examples of this strategy (Exhibit 4-15).

Purchase Decision

At some point in the buying process, the consumer must stop searching for and evaluating information about alternative brands in the evoked set and make a *purchase decision.* As an outcome of the alternative evaluation stage, the consumer may develop a **purchase intention** or predisposition to buy a certain brand. Purchase intentions are generally based on a matching of purchase motives with attributes or characteristics of brands under consideration. Their formation involves many of the personal subprocesses discussed in this chapter, including motivation, perception, attitude formation, and integration.

A purchase decision is not the same as an actual purchase. Once a consumer chooses which brand to buy, he or she must still implement the decision and make the actual purchase. Additional decisions may be needed, such as when to buy, where to buy, and how much money to spend. Often, there is a time delay between the formation of a purchase intention or decision and the actual purchase, particularly for highly involved and complex purchases such as automobiles, personal computers, and consumer durables.

For nondurable products, which include many low-involvement items such as consumer package goods, the time between the decision and the actual purchase may be short. Before leaving home, the consumer may make a shopping list that includes specific brand names because the consumer has developed **brand loyalty**—a preference for a particular brand that results in its repeated purchase. Marketers strive to develop and maintain brand loyalty among consumers. They use reminder advertising to keep their brand names in front of consumers, maintain prominent shelf positions and displays in stores, and run periodic promotions to deter consumers from switching brands.

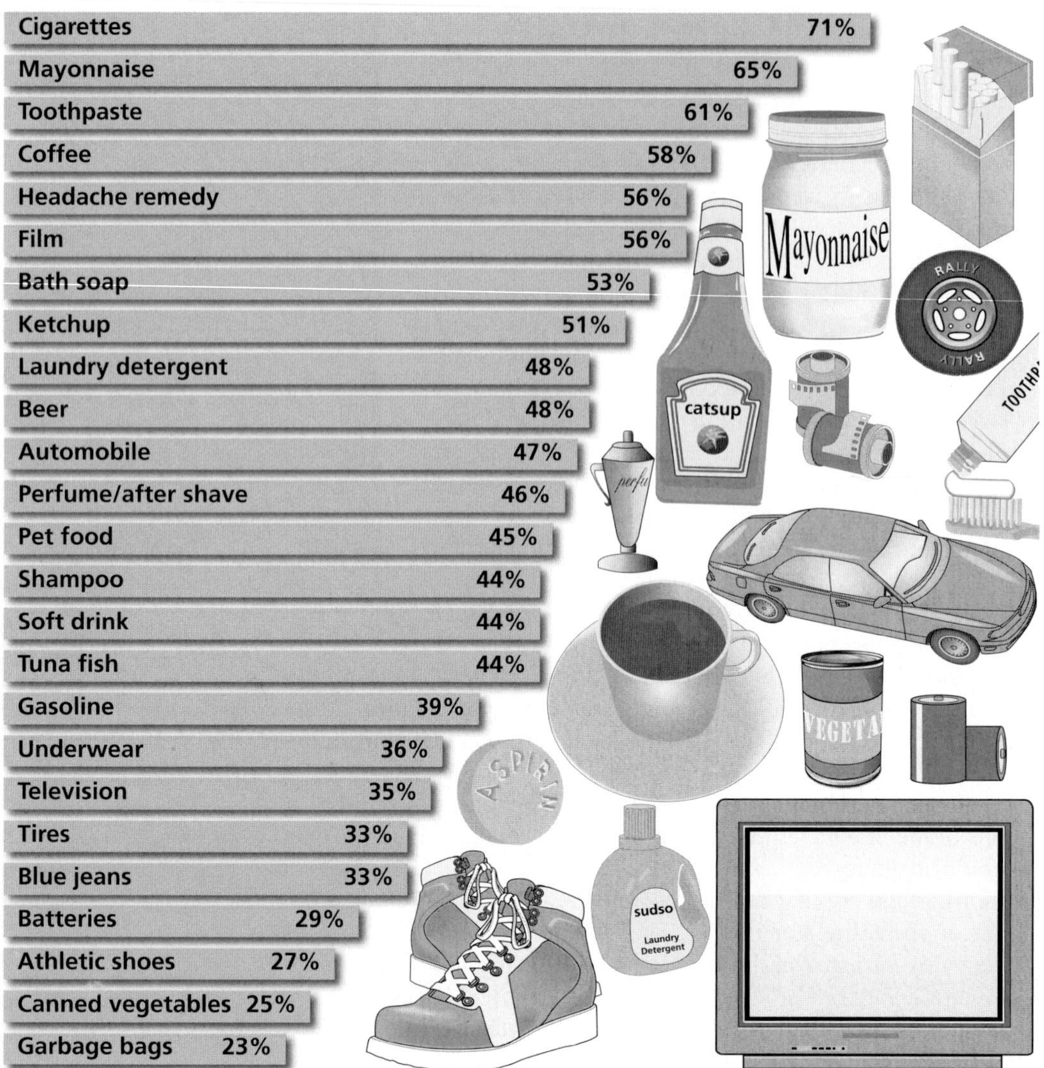

Figure 4-5 Faithful or Fickle? Percentage of Users of These Products Who Are Loyal to One Brand

Maintaining consumers' brand loyalty is not easy. Competitors use many techniques to encourage consumers to try their brands, among them new product introductions and free samples. As Figure 4-5 shows, for many products fewer than 50 percent of consumers are loyal to one brand. Marketers must continually battle to maintain their loyal consumers while replacing those who switch brands.

Purchase decisions for nondurable, convenience items sometimes take place in the store, almost simultaneous with the purchase. Marketers must ensure that consumers have top-of-mind awareness of their brands so that they are quickly recognized and considered. These types of decisions are influenced at the actual point of purchase. Packaging, shelf displays, point-of-purchase materials, and promotional tools such as on-package coupons or premium offers can influence decisions made through constructive processes at the time of purchase.

Postpurchase Evaluation

The consumer decision process does not end with the purchase. After using the product or service, the consumer compares the level of performance with expectations and is either satisfied or dissatisfied. *Satisfaction* occurs when the consumer's expectations are either met or exceeded; *dissatisfaction* results when performance is below expectations. The postpurchase evaluation process is important because the feedback acquired from actual use of a product will influence the likelihood of future purchases. Positive performance means the brand is retained in the evoked set and increases the likelihood it will be purchased again. Unfavorable outcomes may lead the consumer to form negative attitudes toward the brand, lessening the likelihood it will be purchased again or even eliminating it from the consumer's evoked set.

Another possible outcome of purchase is **cognitive dissonance,** a feeling of psychological tension or postpurchase doubt that a consumer experiences after making a difficult purchase choice. Dissonance is more likely to occur in important decisions where the consumer must choose among close alternatives (especially if the unchosen alternative has unique or desirable features that the selected alternative does not have).

Consumers experiencing cognitive dissonance may use a number of strategies to attempt to reduce it. They may seek out reassurance and opinions from others to confirm the wisdom of their purchase decision, lower their attitudes or opinions of the unchosen alternative, deny or distort any information that does not support the choice they made, or look for information that does support their choice. An important source of supportive information is advertising; consumers tend to be more attentive to advertising for the brand they have chosen.[22] Thus, it may be important for companies to advertise to reinforce consumer decisions to purchase their brands.

Marketers must recognize the importance of the postpurchase evaluation stage. Dissatisfied consumers who experience dissonance not only are unlikely to repurchase the marketer's product but may also spread negative word-of-mouth information that deters others from purchasing the product or service. The best guarantee of favorable postpurchase evaluations is to provide consumers with a quality product or service that always meets their expectations. Marketers must be sure their advertising and other forms of promotion do not create unreasonable expectations their products cannot meet.

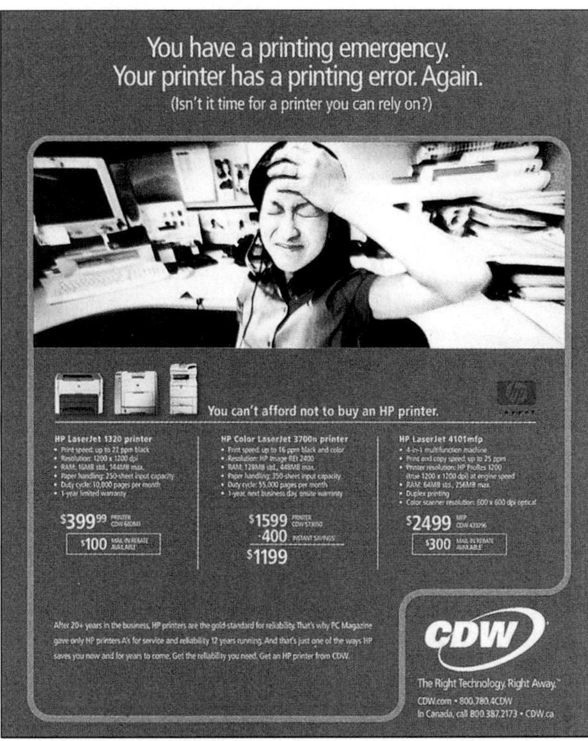

Exhibit 4-16
CDW attempts to capitalize on consumer dissatisfaction

Marketers have come to realize that postpurchase communication is also important. Some companies send follow-up letters and brochures to reassure buyers and reinforce the wisdom of their decision. Many companies have set up toll-free numbers or e-mail addresses for consumers to call if they need information or have a question or complaint regarding a product. Marketers also offer liberalized return and refund policies and extended warranties and guarantees to ensure customer satisfaction. Some have used customers' postpurchase dissatisfaction as an opportunity for gaining new business, as is reflected in Exhibit 4-16.

Variations in Consumer Decision Making

The preceding pages describe a general model of consumer decision making. But consumers do not always engage in all five steps of the purchase decision process or proceed in the sequence presented. They may minimize or even skip one or more stages if they have previous experience in purchasing the product or service or if the decision is of low personal, social, or economic significance. To develop effective promotional strategies and programs, marketers need some understanding of the problem-solving processes their target consumers use to make purchase decisions.[23]

Many of the purchase decisions we make as consumers are based on a habitual or routine choice process. For many low-priced, frequently purchased products, the decision process consists of little more than recognizing the problem, engaging in a quick internal search, and making the purchase. The consumer spends little or no effort engaging in external search or alternative evaluation.

Marketers of products characterized by a routine response purchase process need to get and/or keep their brands in the consumer's evoked set and avoid anything that may result in their removal from consideration. Established brands that have strong market share position are likely to be in the evoked set of most consumers. Marketers of these brands want consumers to follow a routine choice process and continue to purchase their products. This means maintaining high levels of brand awareness through reminder advertising, periodic promotions, and prominent shelf positions in retail stores.

Marketers of new brands or those with a low market share face a different challenge. They must find ways to disrupt consumers' routine choice process and get them

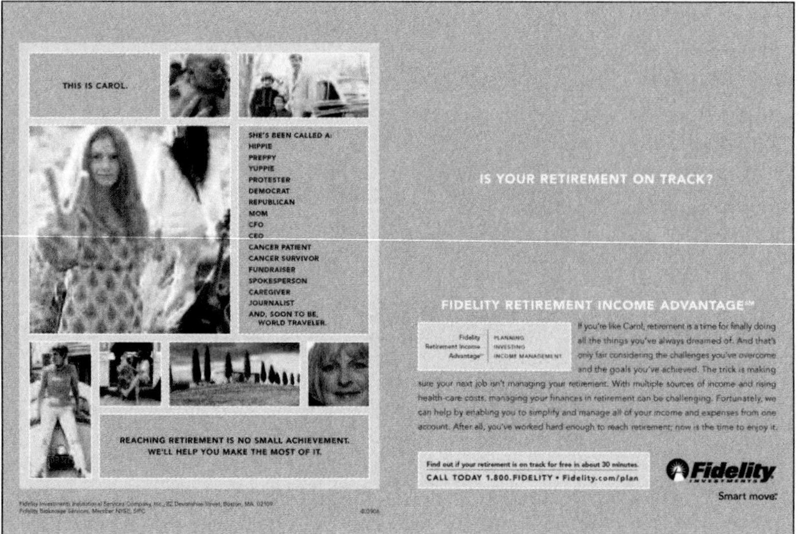

Exhibit 4-17 This ad for Fidelity Investments shows how marketers can appeal to consumers engaging in extended problem solving

to consider different alternatives. High levels of advertising may be used to encourage trial or brand switching, along with sales promotion efforts in the form of free samples, special price offers, high-value coupons, and the like.

A more complicated decision-making process may occur when consumers have limited experience in purchasing a particular product or service and little or no knowledge of the brands available and/or the criteria to use in making a purchase decision. They may have to learn what attributes or criteria should be used in making a purchase decision and how the various alternatives perform on these dimensions. For products or services characterized by problem solving, whether limited or extensive, marketers should make information available that will help consumers decide. Advertising that provides consumers with detailed information about a brand and how it can satisfy their purchase motives and goals is important. Marketers may also want to give consumers information at the point of purchase, through either displays or brochures. Distribution channels should have knowledgeable salespeople available to explain the features and benefits of the company's product or service and why it is superior to competing products.

The Fidelity Investments ad in Exhibit 4-17 is a good example of how advertising can appeal to consumers who may be engaging in extended problem solving when considering retirement investing. Notice how the ad communicates with consumers who may be concerned about their plan for retirement. The ad helps the consumer by offering expert advice and planning a variety of options. The ad also makes more detailed information available by offering a toll-free number and a website.

The Consumer Learning Process

The discussion of the decision process shows that the way consumers make a purchase varies depending on a number of factors, including the nature of the product or service, the amount of experience they have with the product, and the importance of the purchase. One factor in the level of problem solving to be employed is the consumer's *involvement* with the product or brand. Chapter 5 examines the meaning of involvement, the difference between low- and high-involvement decision making, and the implications of involvement for developing advertising and promotional strategies.

Our examination of consumer behavior thus far has looked at the decision-making process from a *cognitive orientation.* The five-stage decision process model views the consumer as a problem solver and information processor who engages in a variety of mental processes to evaluate various alternatives and determine the degree to which they might satisfy needs or purchase motives. There are, however, other perspectives regarding how consumers acquire the knowledge and experience they use in making purchase decisions. To understand these perspectives, we examine various approaches to learning and their implications for advertising and promotion.

Consumer learning has been defined as "the process by which individuals acquire the purchase and consumption knowledge and experience they apply to future related behavior."[24] Two basic approaches to learning are the behavioral approach and cognitive learning theory.

Behavioral Learning Theory

Behavioral learning theories emphasize the role of external, environmental stimuli in causing behavior; they minimize the significance of internal psychological processes. Behavioral learning theories are based on the *stimulus–response orientation* (S–R), the premise that learning occurs as the result of responses to external stimuli in the environment. Behavioral learning theorists believe learning occurs through the connection between a stimulus and a response. We will examine the basic principles of two behavioral learning theory approaches: classical conditioning and operant conditioning.

Classical Conditioning

Classical conditioning assumes that learning is an *associative process* with an already existing relationship between a stimulus and a response. Probably the best-known example of this type of learning comes from the studies done with animals by the Russian psychologist Pavlov.[25] Pavlov noticed that at feeding times, his dogs would salivate at the sight of food. The connection between food and salivation is not taught; it is an innate reflex reaction. Because this relationship exists before the conditioning process, the food is referred to as an *unconditioned stimulus* and salivation is an *unconditioned response.* To see if salivation could be conditioned to occur in response to another neutral stimulus, Pavlov paired the ringing of a bell with the presentation of the food. After a number of trials, the dogs learned to salivate at the sound of the bell alone. Thus, the bell became a **conditioned stimulus** that elicited a **conditioned response** resembling the original unconditioned reaction.

Two factors are important for learning to occur through the associative process. The first is contiguity, which means the unconditioned stimulus and conditioned stimulus must be close in time and space. In Pavlov's experiment, the dog learns to associate the ringing of the bell with food because of the contiguous presentation of the two stimuli. The other important principle is *repetition,* or the frequency of the association. The more often the unconditioned and conditioned stimuli occur together, the stronger the association between them will be.

Applying Classical Conditioning

Learning through classical conditioning plays an important role in marketing. Buyers can be conditioned to form favorable impressions and images of various brands through the associative process. Advertisers strive to associate their products and services with perceptions, images, and emotions known to evoke positive reactions from consumers. Many products are promoted through image advertising, in which the brand is shown with an unconditioned stimulus that elicits pleasant feelings. When the brand is presented simultaneously with this unconditioned stimulus, the brand itself becomes a conditioned stimulus that elicits the same favorable response.

Figure 4-6 provides a diagram of this process, and the ad for Lancôme in Exhibit 4-18 shows an application of this strategy. Notice how this ad associates Lancôme with the freshness and moisture of grapes. The brand's positioning plays off this association.

Classical conditioning can also associate a product or service with a favorable emotional state. A study by Gerald Gorn used this approach to examine how background music in ads influences product choice.[26] He found that subjects were more likely to choose a product when it was presented against a background of music they liked rather than music they disliked. These results suggest the emotions generated by a commercial are important because they may become associated with the advertised product through classical conditioning. Kellaris and colleagues also showed that music that was congruent with the message enhanced both ad recall and recognition.[27] Richard Yalch also has demonstrated that music can be used effectively as a mnemonic device to enhance the

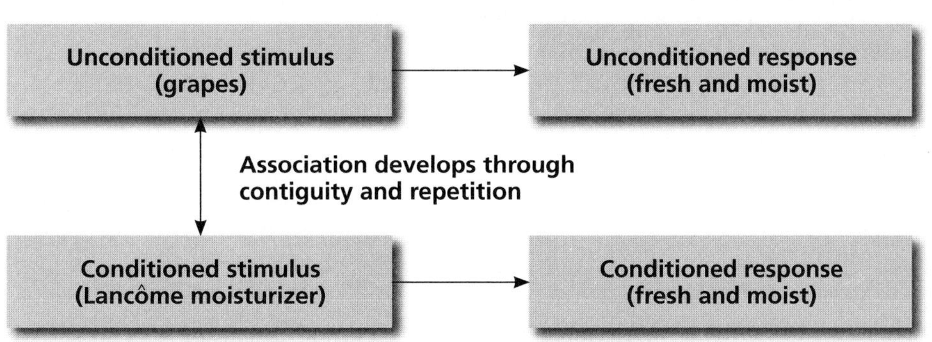

Figure 4-6 The Classical Conditioning Process

Exhibit 4-18 Lancôme associates its product with the moisture of grapes

recall of advertising slogans. Advertisers often attempt to pair a neutral product or service stimulus with an event or situation that arouses positive feelings, such as humor, an exciting sports event, or popular music.

Operant Conditioning

Classical conditioning views the individual as a passive participant in the learning process who simply receives stimuli. Conditioning occurs as a result of exposure to a stimulus that occurs before the response. In the **operant conditioning** approach, the individual must actively *operate* or act on some aspect of the environment for learning to occur. Operant conditioning is sometimes referred to as *instrumental conditioning* because the individual's response is instrumental in getting a positive reinforcement (reward) or negative reinforcement (punishment).

Reinforcement, the reward or favorable consequence associated with a particular response, is an important element of instrumental conditioning. Behavior that is reinforced strengthens the bond between a stimulus and a response. Thus, if a consumer buys a product in response to an ad and experiences a positive outcome, the likelihood that the consumer will use this product again increases. If the outcome is not favorable, the likelihood of buying the product again decreases.

The principles of operant conditioning can be applied to marketing, as shown in Figure 4-7. Companies attempt to provide their customers with products and services that satisfy their needs and reward them to reinforce the probability of repeat purchase. Reinforcement can also be implied in advertising; many ads emphasize the benefits or rewards a consumer will receive from using a product or service. Reinforcement also occurs when an ad encourages consumers to use a particular product or brand to avoid unpleasant consequences. For example, the ad for Energizer batteries in Exhibit 4-19 shows how using this product will help avoid negative consequences—that is, being without a working cell phone when you need it.

Two concepts that are particularly relevant to marketers in their use of reinforcement through promotional strategies are schedules of reinforcement and shaping. Different **schedules of reinforcement** result in varying patterns of learning and behavior. Learning occurs most rapidly under a *continuous reinforcement schedule,* in which

Figure 4-7 Instrumental Conditioning in Marketing

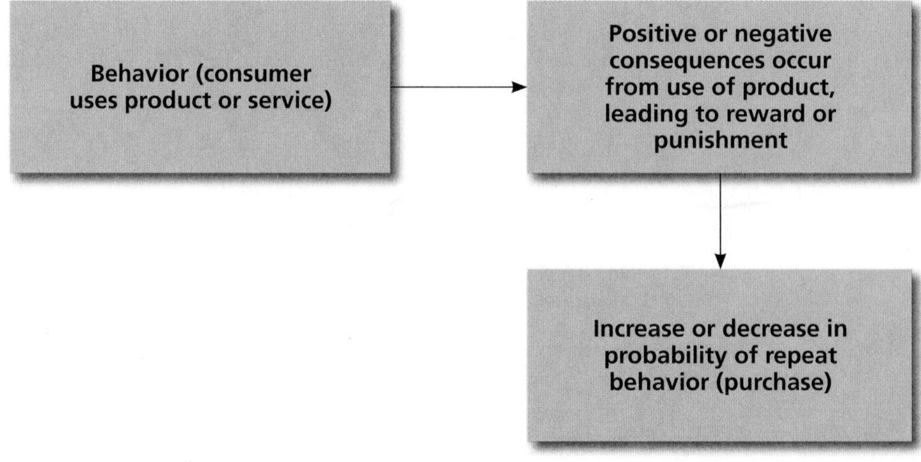

every response is rewarded—but the behavior is likely to cease when the reinforcement stops. Marketers must provide continuous reinforcement to consumers or risk their switching to brands that do.

Learning occurs more slowly but lasts longer when a *partial* or *intermittent reinforcement schedule* is used and only some of the individual's responses are rewarded. Promotional programs have partial reinforcement schedules. A firm may offer consumers an incentive to use the company's product. The firm does not want to offer the incentive every time (continuous reinforcement), because consumers might become dependent on it and stop buying the brand when the incentive is withdrawn. A study that examined the effect of reinforcement on bus ridership found that discount coupons given as rewards for riding the bus were as effective when given on a partial schedule as when given on a continuous schedule.[28] The cost of giving the discount coupons under the partial schedule, however, was considerably less.

Reinforcement schedules can also be used to influence consumer learning and behavior through a process known as **shaping,** the reinforcement of successive acts that lead to a desired behavior pattern or response. Rothschild and Gaidis argue that shaping is a very useful concept for marketers:

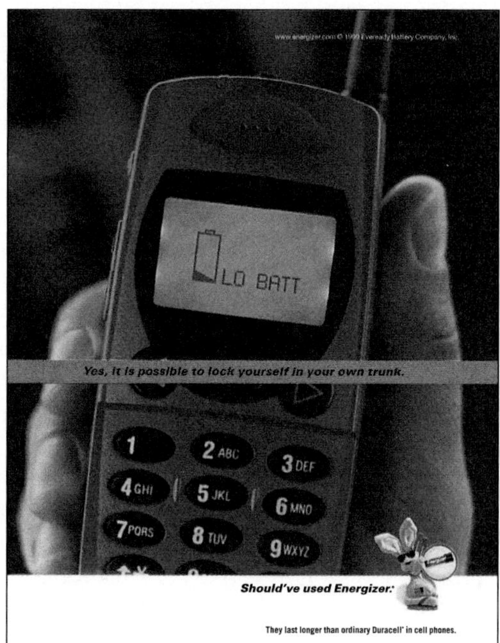

Exhibit 4-19 This Energizer batteries ad shows how to avoid negative consequences

> Shaping is an essential process in deriving new and complex behavior because a behavior cannot be rewarded unless it first occurs; a stimulus can only reinforce acts that already occur. New, complex behaviors rarely occur by chance in nature. If the only behavior to be rewarded were the final complex sought behavior, one would probably have to wait a long time for this to occur by chance. Instead, one can reward simpler existing behaviors; over time, more complex patterns evolve and these are rewarded. Thus the shaping process occurs by a method of successive approximations.[29]

In a promotional context, shaping procedures are used as part of the introductory program for new products. Figure 4-8 provides an example of how samples and discount coupons can be used to introduce a new product and take a consumer from trial to repeat purchase. Marketers must be careful in their use of shaping procedures: If they drop the incentives too soon, the consumer may not establish the desired behavior; but if they overuse them, the consumer's purchase may become contingent on the incentive rather than the product or service.

Terminal Goal: Repeat Purchase Behavior

Approximation Sequence	Shaping Procedure	Reinforcement Applied
Induce product trial	Free samples distributed; large discount coupon	Product performance; coupon
Induce purchase with little financial obligation	Discount coupon prompts purchase with little cost; coupon good for small discount on next purchase enclosed	Product performance; coupon
Induce purchase with moderate financial obligation	Small discount coupon prompts purchase with moderate cost	Product performance
Induce purchase with full financial obligation	Purchase occurs without coupon assistance	Product performance

Figure 4-8 Application of Shaping Procedures in Marketing

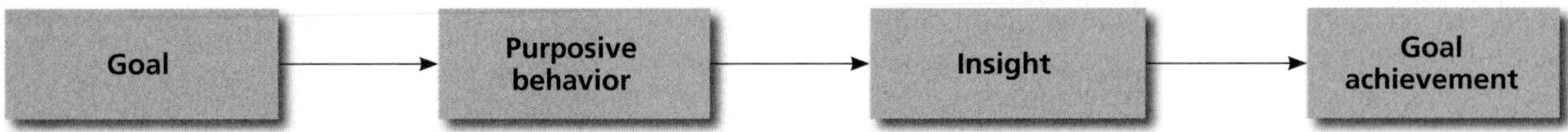

Figure 4-9 The Cognitive Learning Process

Cognitive Learning Theory

Behavioral learning theories have been criticized for assuming a mechanistic view of the consumer that puts too much emphasis on external stimulus factors. They ignore internal psychological processes such as motivation, thinking, and perception; they assume that the external stimulus environment will elicit fairly predictable responses. Many consumer researchers and marketers disagree with the simplified explanations of behavioral learning theories and are more interested in the complex mental processes that underlie consumer decision making. The cognitive approach to studying learning and decision making has dominated the field of consumer behavior in recent years. Figure 4-9 shows how cognitive theorists view the learning process.

Since consumer behavior typically involves choices and decision making, the cognitive perspective has particular appeal to marketers, especially those whose product/service calls for important and involved purchase decisions. Cognitive processes such as perception, formation of beliefs about brands, attitude development and change, and integration are important to understanding the decision-making process for many types of purchases. The subprocesses examined during our discussion of the five-stage decision process model are all relevant to a cognitive learning approach to consumer behavior.

Environmental Influences on Consumer Behavior

The consumer does not make purchase decisions in isolation. A number of external factors have been identified that may influence consumer decision making. They are shown in Figure 4-10 and examined in more detail in the next sections.

Culture

The broadest and most abstract of the external factors that influence consumer behavior is **culture,** or the complexity of learned meanings, values, norms, and customs shared by members of a society. Cultural norms and values offer direction and guidance to members of a society in all aspects of their lives, including their consumption behavior. It is becoming increasingly important to study the impact of culture on con-

Figure 4-10 External Influences on Consumer Behavior

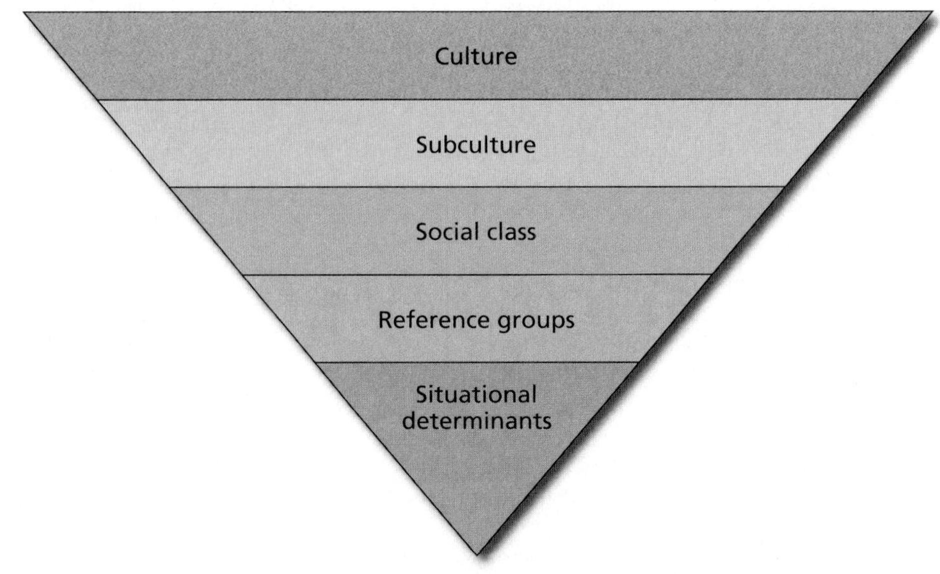

sumer behavior as marketers expand their international marketing efforts. Each country has certain cultural traditions, customs, and values that marketers must understand as they develop marketing programs.

Marketers must also be aware of changes that may be occurring in a particular culture and the implications of these changes for their advertising and promotional strategies and programs. American culture continually goes through many changes that have direct implications for advertising. Marketing researchers monitor these changes and their impact on the ways companies market their products and services.

While marketers recognize that culture exerts a demonstrable influence on consumers, they often find it difficult to respond to cultural differences in different markets. The subtleties of various cultures are often difficult to understand and appreciate, but marketers must understand the cultural context in which consumer purchase decisions are made and adapt their advertising and promotional programs accordingly.

Subcultures

Within a given culture are generally found smaller groups or segments whose beliefs, values, norms, and patterns of behavior set them apart from the larger cultural mainstream. These **subcultures** may be based on age, geographic, religious, racial, and/or ethnic differences. A number of subcultures exist within the United States. The three largest racial/ethnic subcultures are African-Americans, Hispanics, and various Asian groups. These racial/ethnic subcultures are important to marketers because of their size, growth, purchasing power, and distinct purchasing patterns. Marketers develop specific marketing programs for various products and services for these target markets. The ads in Exhibit 4-20 are just two of the many specifically designed to appeal to U.S. subcultures—in these cases, blacks and Hispanics. Many others can easily be found that target teens, generations X and Y, the elderly, and so on.

Social Class

Virtually all societies exhibit some form of stratification whereby individuals can be assigned to a specific social category on the basis of criteria important to members of that society. **Social class** refers to relatively homogeneous divisions in a society into which people sharing similar lifestyles, values, norms, interests, and behaviors can be grouped. While a number of methods for determining social class exist, class structures in the United States are usually based on occupational status, educational attainment, and income. Sociologists generally agree there are three broad levels of social classes in the United States: the upper (14 percent), middle (70 percent), and lower (16 percent) classes.[30]

Exhibit 4-20
Ads targeted to subcultures

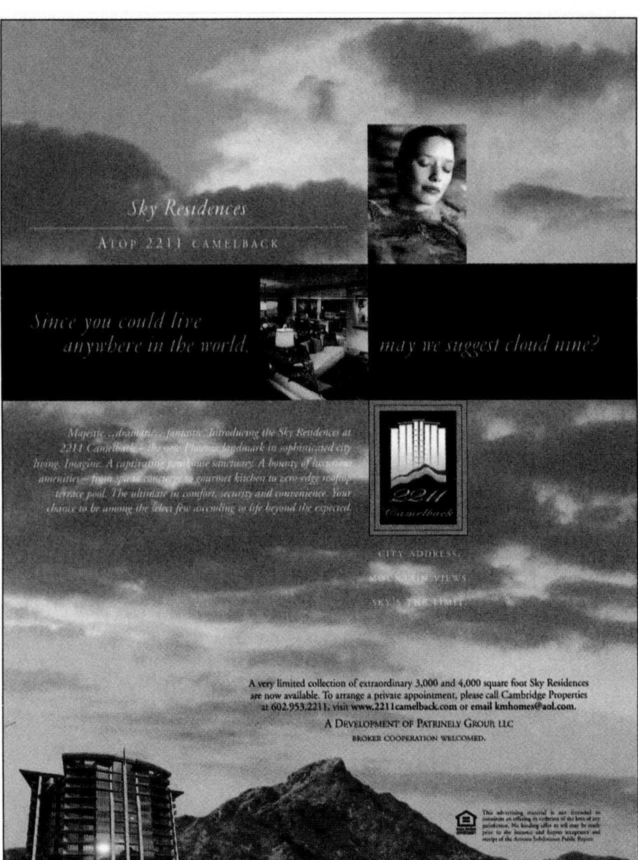

Exhibit 4-21
Sky Residence targets upper classes

Social class is an important concept to marketers, since consumers within each social stratum often have similar values, lifestyles, and buying behavior. Thus, the various social class groups provide a natural basis for market segmentation. Consumers in the different social classes differ in the degree to which they use various products and services and in their leisure activities, shopping patterns, and media habits. Marketers respond to these differences through the positioning of their products and services, the media strategies they use to reach different social classes, and the types of advertising appeals they develop. The ad for Sky Residences in Exhibit 4-21 shows how a product attempts to appeal to the upper classes in both copy and illustration.

Reference Groups

Think about the last time you attended a party. As you dressed for the party, you probably asked yourself (or someone else) what others would be wearing. Your selection of attire may have been influenced by those likely to be present. This simple example reflects one form of impact that groups may exert on your behavior.

A group has been defined as "two or more individuals who share a set of norms, values, or beliefs and have certain implicitly or explicitly defined relationships to one another such that their behavior is interdependent."[31] Groups are one of the primary factors influencing learning and socialization, and group situations constitute many of our purchase decisions.

A **reference group** is "a group whose presumed perspectives or values are being used by an individual as the basis for his or her judgments, opinions, and actions." Consumers use reference groups as a guide to specific behaviors, even when the groups are not present.[32] In the party example, your peers—although not present—provided a standard of dress that you referred to in your clothing selection. Likewise, your college classmates, family, and co-workers, or even a group to which you aspire, may serve as referents, and your consumption patterns will typically conform to the expectations of the groups that are most important to you.

Marketers use reference group influences in developing advertisements and promotional strategies. The ads in Exhibit 4-22 are examples of *aspirational* reference groups (to which we might like to belong) and *disassociative* groups (to which we do not wish to belong), respectively.

Family Decision Making: An Example of Group Influences

In some instances, the group may be involved more directly than just as a referent. Family members may serve as referents to each other, or they may actually be involved in the purchase decision process—acting as an individual buying unit. As shown in Figure 4-11, family members may assume a variety of roles in the decision-making process.[33] Each role has implications for marketers.

First, the advertiser must determine who is responsible for the various roles in the decision-making process so messages can be targeted at that person (or those people). These roles will also dictate media strategies, since the appropriate magazines, newspapers, or TV or radio stations must be used. Second, understanding the decision-making process and the use of information by individual family members is critical to the design of messages and choice of promotional program elements. In sum, to create an effective promotional program, a marketer must have an overall understanding of how the decision process works and the role that each family member plays.

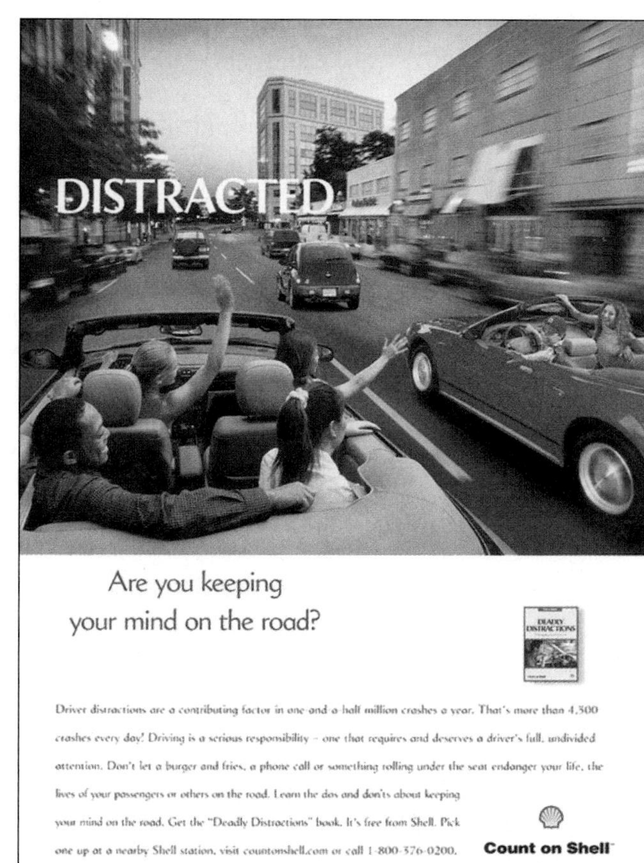

Exhibit 4-22 The ad on the left shows an aspirational reference group; the one on the right stresses a disassociative reference group

Situational Determinants

The final external factor is the purchase and usage situation. The specific situation in which consumers plan to use the product or brand directly affects their perceptions, preferences, and purchasing behaviors.[34] Three types of **situational determinants** may have an effect: the specific usage situation, the purchase situation, and the communications situation.

The initiator. The person responsible for initiating the purchase decision process,for example, the mother who determines she needs a new car.

The information provider. The individual responsible for gathering information to be used in making the decision, for example, the teenage car buff who knows where to find product information in specific magazines or collects it from dealers.

The influencer. The person who exerts influence as to what criteria will be used in the selection process. All members of the family may be involved. The mother may have her criteria, whereas others may each have their own input.

The decision maker(s). That person(s) who actually makes the decision. In our example, it may be the mother alone or in combination with another family member.

The purchasing agent. The individual who performs the physical act of making the purchase. In the case of a car, a husband and wife may decide to choose it together and sign the purchase agreement.

The consumer. The actual user of the product. In the case of a family car, all family members are consumers. For a private car, only the mother might be the consumer.

Figure 4-11 Roles in the Family Decision-Making Process

Usage refers to the circumstance in which the product will be used. For example, purchases made for private consumption may be thought of differently from those that will be obvious to the public. The *purchase* situation more directly involves the environment operating at the time of the purchase. Time constraints, store environments, and other factors may all have an impact. The *communications* situation is the condition in which an advertising exposure occurs (in a car listening to the radio, with friends, etc.). This may be most relevant to the development of promotional strategies, because the impact on the consumer will vary according to the particular situation. For example, a consumer may pay more attention to a commercial that is heard alone at home than to one heard in the presence of friends, at work, or anywhere distractions may be present. If advertisers can isolate a particular time when the listener is likely to be attentive, they will probably earn his or her undivided attention.

In sum, situational determinants may either enhance or detract from the potential success of a message. To the degree that advertisers can assess situational influences that may be operating, they will increase the likelihood of successfully communicating with their target audiences.

Alternative Approaches to Consumer Behavior

In addition to the perspectives discussed, consumer researchers complement these psychological approaches with perspectives driven from other scientific disciplines, such as economics, sociology, anthropology, philosophy, semiotics, neuroscience, or history. These cross-disciplinary perspectives have broadened the realm of methodologies used to study consumers and have provided additional insights into consumer decision processes. Global Perspective 4-1 demonstrates an effective utilization of cultural anthropology.

New Methodologies

Whereas psychologists often study consumer responses to advertising and other forms of communication in controlled settings, where environmental variables can be kept constant, sociologists and anthropologists study behavior in context. For this reason, they often employ qualitative methodologies such as individual interviews, participant observation studies, and/or ethnographies. These methods help capture the social, cultural, and environmental influences that may affect consumer behavior.

The humanities have also been a source of new methodologies for consumer research. Historians and semioticians focus their analyses on the advertising messages and other forms of communications themselves. These researchers examine the significance of communications from a linguistic or historical perspective. Research methods such as semiotic and structural analyses examine the symbolic meanings of advertising and different facets of consumption.

New Insights

These alternative perspectives and methodologies provide additional insights and expand our knowledge of consumers. For example, the cultural significance of advertising messages in shaping cultures and triggering communities is now better understood. Likewise, marketers now have a better understanding of how advertising campaigns like "Got Milk" become popular and help shape our culture. Thanks to the many interpretive analyses of advertisements over recent years, we are also more aware of the influence of advertising images on society.

Some consumer researchers believe that cross-disciplinary research is better suited for the study of consumers because it takes into account their complexity and multidimensionality. When considered along with psychological research, these alternative approaches help us better understand the impact of communications.

GLOBAL PERSPECTIVE 4-1

Cultural Anthropologists Help Sell Deodorant

In the highly lucrative and competitive deodorant market, companies are always looking for the edge that will give them an advantage over competitors. Unilever may just have found it, and they call it *ethnography*. The European-based company hired a U.S.-based research organization specializing in cultural anthropology to observe young males between the ages of 18 and 22 and their friends in their everyday environs to learn more about their likes, dislikes, activities, and decision-making behaviors. The 28 young men—from Los Angeles and Pittsburgh—were videotaped, and then the tapes were analyzed to gain insights through the participants' own descriptions of their activities while being observed in everyday facets of their lives.

Once the tapes were finished, executives from Unilever, their advertising and public relations agencies, and their event specialist agency met to take a "deep dive" into the young men's psyches. More specifically, the executives wanted to understand the participant's mating life, that is, what he is about, why he does what he does, what excites him, and what he fears. Not surprisingly, much of the young men's lives focused on sex. Their interest was not just dating: They preferred to go to parties with other male friends and "hook up." Relationships were avoided whenever possible, as were the words *boyfriends* and *girlfriends*. They just wanted to have sex. The anthropologists even typed the males into groups based upon their characteristics into classifications such as "pimp daddy," "player," "sweetheart," and "shy guy."

So what does this have to do with marketing deodorant? A lot! Based upon these findings the basis for the integrated marketing campaign theme was developed—"Wear this deodorant and you'll pick up chicks!" Simply put, using AXE products (deodorant, body spray, shower gel, and more) will help you in your mating attempts. (In Ireland and Australia, the product is called Lynx, though the same theme is used.) The television commercials focus on spontaneous sexual encounters and the need to be ready at any time, while protected (and enhanced) by AXE. The AXE man is always ready. The commercials have won the Gold Lion—the top award given at the Cannes Film Festival for international advertising quality—two of the past four years, and 10 times overall. The advertising campaign theme is also maintained through other integrated strategies.

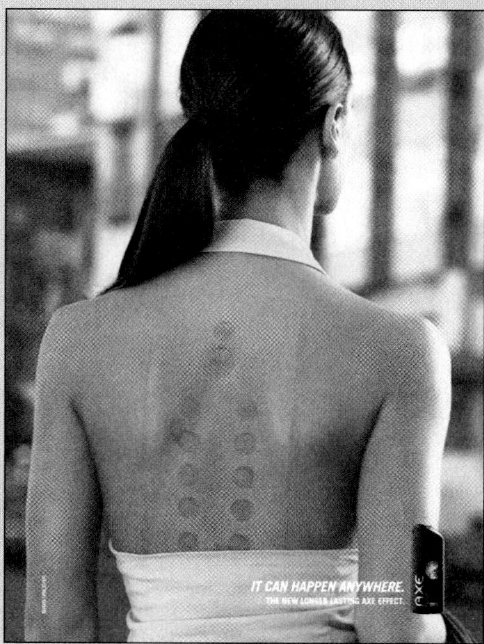

IT CAN HAPPEN ANYWHERE.
THE NEW LONGER LASTING AXE EFFECT.
AXE

In Colombia, female AXE patrols visit bars and nightclubs, frisking guys and spraying them with body spray. The "AXE angels" (also female) pass out samples at various events including the MTV Video Awards. The viral marketing campaign launched a fake website including videos, fake recordings of phone calls, and pictures. A one-hour TV program, *The AXE House Party: Hundreds of Girls, Rock Stars, and a Beach House,* was developed and aired as a television special on the cable channel TNN. Invitations to the party were passed out by street teams, through public relations activities, and via an ad campaign that directed consumers to the website for a chance to win an invitation. The promotion won a Promotional Marketing Association Reggie Award for excellence.

Print and online promotions were also used to promote the seduction skills used in an online digital fantasy game called Mojo Master. The game, which cost over a million dollars to produce, challenges young men armed with AXE deodorant body spray, shower gel, deodorant stick, and invisible solid to pick up girls. Each time one of the products is used it enhances the male's "mojo," and helps him enhance his "attraction meter." If one is good enough, he qualifies to use the AXE fragrance. What are the girls in the game like? "Absolutely stunning," says the director of the company that developed the game.

But can ethnography lead to successful product marketing? Consider the following: *The AXE House Party* generated attention from MTV, VH-1, *Rolling Stone,* and *Jimmy Kimmel Live.* In the four weeks following the promotion, brand awareness among 11 to 24 year olds increased 22 percent, and market share jumped from 3 percent to 3.7 percent. In regard to the bottom line, the campaign's results are equally impressive: (1) First launched in 1983, the products are now marketed in more than 60 countries; (2) the AXE brand is number one in several European and Latin American markets as well as in Asia and the United States, where it has been marketed only since 2003; (3) sales are almost seven times those of the competitive Old Spice brand introduced at the same time; and (4) sales of the body spray in the United States in 2004 were over $60 million, making it the category leader. In this case, ethnography and IMC seem to have produced a winning combination.

Sources: Ian Herbert, "Spray It, Don't Say It," *U.S. News & World Report,* May 30, 2005, p. 58; Kris Oser, "AXE's Latest Sex Ad Is a Digital Game," www.Adage.com, May 20, 2005, pp. 1–3; Christine Bittar, "Bringing Down the House: AXE Shakes Its Groove Thang," *Brandweek,* March 22, 2004, p. R4; Jack Neff, "Analyzing AXE Man," *Advertising Age,* June 21, 2004, pp. 4–5.

Summary

This chapter introduced you to the field of consumer behavior and examined its relevance to promotional strategy. Consumer behavior is best viewed as the process and activities that people engage in when searching for, selecting, purchasing, using, evaluating, and disposing of products and services to satisfy their needs and desires. A five-stage model of the consumer decision-making process consists of problem recognition, information search, alternative evaluation, purchase, and postpurchase evaluation. Internal psychological processes that influence the consumer decision-making process include motivation, perception, attitude formation and change, and integration processes.

The decision process model views consumer behavior primarily from a cognitive orientation. The chapter considered other perspectives by examining various approaches to consumer learning and their implications for advertising and promotion. Behavioral learning theories such as classical conditioning and operant (instrumental) conditioning were discussed. Problems with behavioral learning theories were noted, and the alternative perspective of cognitive learning was discussed.

The chapter also examined relevant external factors that influence consumer decision making. Culture, subculture, social class, reference groups, and situational determinants were discussed, along with their implications for the development of promotional strategies and programs. The chapter concluded with an introduction to alternative perspectives on the study of consumer behavior (also called interpretive, postmodern, or postpositivist perspectives).

Key Terms

consumer behavior, 105
problem recognition, 107
want, 108
motives, 108
hierarchy of needs, 109
psychoanalytic theory, 110
motivation research, 110
internal search, 112
external search, 112
perception, 112
sensation, 112
selective perception, 113
selective exposure, 113
selective attention, 113
selective comprehension, 114
selective retention, 114
mnemonics, 114
subliminal perception, 114
evaluative criteria, 116
functional consequences, 116
psychosocial consequences, 116
multiattribute attitude model, 117
salient beliefs, 118
integration processes, 119
heuristics, 119
affect referral decision rule, 119
purchase intention, 119
brand loyalty, 119
cognitive dissonance, 121
classical conditioning, 123
conditioned stimulus, 123
conditioned response, 123
operant conditioning, 124
reinforcement, 124
schedules of reinforcement, 124
shaping, 125
culture, 126
subcultures, 127
social class, 127
reference group, 128
situational determinants, 129

Discussion Questions

1. Global Perspective 4-1 discusses the use of cultural anthropology to understand consumer behaviors. Why is it necessary for marketers to use alternative approaches to consumer behavior?

2. Discuss both sides of the argument (pro or con) for using neuroscience in consumer research.

3. Explain how a consumer's lifestyle may impact consumer behavior.

4. Explain how the screening processes involved in selective perception might impact a viewer of television commercials.

5. Describe how subliminal perception could be used by marketers to the detriment of consumers.

6. A number of factors may lead to problem recognition among consumers. Discuss the various causes of problem recognition, and give an example of each.

7. Explain the concept of an *evoked set.* Why is this concept important to marketers? Give examples of an evoked set, and how marketers might attempt to influence consumers to gain consideration.

8. Jerry Olson and J. Paul Peter define two broad categories of evaluative consequences. Describe each of these and provide examples.

9. Figure 4-10 details a number of external influences on consumer behavior. Describe each of these influences, explaining how it might have an impact on consumer behavior, and provide an example of each.

10. In the text it was indicated that families may influence the consumer decision-making process. Describe how various family members may assume the different roles described in Figure 4-11. Also explain how these roles might change depending upon the product under consideration.

The Communication Process

5

Chapter Objectives

1. To understand the basic elements of the communication process and the role of communications in marketing.
2. To examine various models of the communication process.
3. To analyze the response processes of receivers of marketing communications, including alternative response hierarchies and their implications for promotional planning and strategy.
4. To examine the nature of consumers' cognitive processing of marketing communications.

Buzz Marketing: The New Word of Mouth

Consumers have long had a love/hate relationship with advertising. We enjoy watching music- and celebrity-laden commercials that are often more entertaining, humorous, and/or interesting than the programs they are sponsoring. We purchase magazines such as *Glamour, Vogue,* and *Maxim,* which contain as many ad pages as, if not more than, articles. But many consumers are

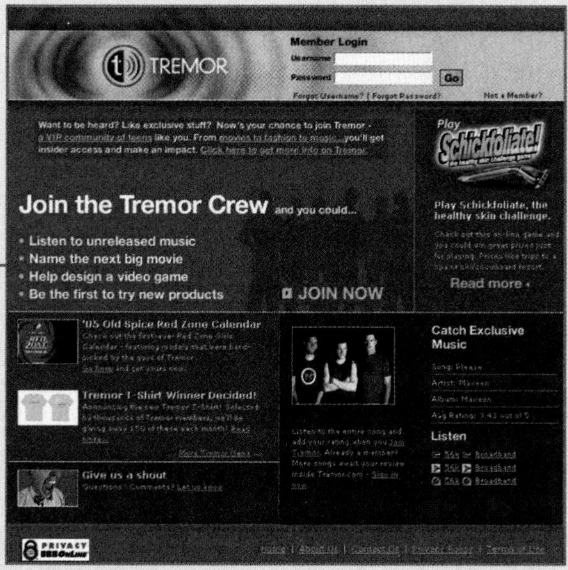

tired of being bombarded with sales messages and are turned off by advertising. This is especially true of generation Y, the age cohort born between 1979 and 1994, which is 60 million strong. The millennials, as the generation Y cohort is sometimes called, are three times the size of their gen X predecessors and the biggest group to hit the American market since the 72 million baby boomers who are their parents. Having grown up in an even more media-saturated, brand-conscious world than their parents, they can be extremely difficult to reach and influence through traditional advertising. Even when they do catch TV commercials or print ads, these jaded consumers often ignore the marketing message.

Marketers recognize that to penetrate the skepticism and capture the attention of the gen Ys they have to bring their messages to these consumers in a different way. To do so, many companies are turning to a stealthy strategy known as *buzz marketing,* in which brand come-ons become part of popular culture and consumers themselves are lured into spreading the message. They turn their brands into carefully guarded secrets that they reveal to only a knowing few in each community. Each carefully cultivated recipient of the brand message becomes a powerful carrier, spreading the word to yet more carriers, who tell a few more, and so on. The goal of the marketer is to find the trendsetters in each community and push them into talking about their product to their friends and admirers. As one ad agency executive notes, "Ultimately, the brand benefits because an accepted member of the social circle will always be far more credible than any communication that could come directly from the brand."

Buzz marketing is just one of the new names for what used to be known simply as "word of mouth" as terms such as *consumer-generated marketing* and *viral marketing* are also used to describe the process. The use of word-of-mouth marketing is really nothing new: Marketers of beer and liquor have long understood the value of bartenders hyping their brands while pharmaceutical companies have always encouraged physicians to talk up their products. However, what is new is the number of companies that are now using buzz marketing and also the sophisticated ways they are going about it. The practice includes a variety of techniques such as handing out product samples, providing products to influential people and encouraging them to talk about the brand to others, building Web communities so customers can chat about their product experiences online, and even hiring actors to talk up a brand in public places.

Procter & Gamble (P&G), the company that ironically is the world's largest advertiser, has assembled a stealth sales force of 250,000 teens, between the ages of 13 to 19, into a marketing arm called Tremor. Their mission is to help marketers reach other teens and plant information about their brands in places where it is difficult to gain access, such as homes, schools, and social gatherings. These teens are selected and organized by P&G, which looks for kids with a wide social circle and a gift of gab. The company uses e-mail invitations and Web banner ads to recruit new members and offers them a chance to register to win a free product, like a DVD player or iPod. As part of the registration process they are asked to report how many friends, family members, and acquaintances they communicate with every day. Only the most gregarious prospects, about 10 percent of the respondents, are invited to join the Tremor network, which is billed as a way for kids to influence companies and find out about cool new products before their friends do.

Procter & Gamble keeps the Tremorites interested by giving them free samples, coupons, and the thrill of being an "insider." In return, they deliver endorsements for everything from movies to milk to motor oil in school cafeterias, at sleepovers, and by cell phone and e-mail. However, P&G does not pay the teens to participate and they are free to form their own opinions about the products and the information they receive. While a third of Tremor's activities are devoted to P&G products such as Pantene shampoo, CoverGirl cosmetics, and Pringles potato chips, they have also been used to promote other brands such as Valvoline motor oil, Vanilla Coke, and Sony's Net MD digital music player. P&G charges around $1 million to use Tremor for a national campaign and does more than 20 per year in the United States.

A number of other major marketers have used buzz marketing techniques to create a cutting-edge cool image for their brands. When Ford launched the Focus subcompact car a few years ago, the company recruited 120 trendsetters in five key markets and gave each a Focus to drive for six months. Their duties were simply to be seen with the car, to hand out Focus-themed trinkets to anyone who expressed interest in it, and to keep a record of where they took the car. Ford also tapped into the youth market by sponsoring music festivals and aligning the Focus with cutting-edge fashion designers. Toyota used a buzz campaign to help launch its new Scion automobile line, which is targeted directly at millennials who are trendsetters and influencers. The strategy includes promoting the brand to the hip-hop underground culture by promoting it in such hangouts as "cool" nightclubs, art exhibits, local hip-hop or electronica concerts, and aftermarket shows.

While the use of buzz and viral marketing campaigns is becoming more prevalent, experts note that the techniques are very resistant to manipulation, and marketers must be careful about how they use them. Several companies, including Sony Ericcson Mobile Communications, Mazda, and Dr Pepper/7UP, have had buzz marketing campaigns backfire when consumers recognized that the companies were artificially trying to promote buzz for their brands. In fact, the Word of Mouth Marketing Association, a year-old trade group, recently announced a new set of rules and guidelines for word-of-mouth advertising. Under the guidelines, marketers must make sure that people talking up products or services disclose whom they are working for. They also must use real consumers, not actors, to discuss what they really believe about a product.

Some experts note that the growing popularity of buzz marketing could well cause its downfall. Once everyone does it, it's no longer buzz; it's simply obscure and annoying advertising. And when consumers recognize that companies are trying to create a buzz for their brand, they are likely to be turned off to the technique. By then, of course, marketers will have found yet another stealthy way to deliver their sales messages.

Sources: Lillie Guyer, "Scion Connects in Out of Way Places," *Advertising Age,* February 21, 2005, p. 38; Suzanne Vranica, "Getting Buzz Marketers to Fess Up," *The Wall Street Journal,* February 9, 2005, p. B9; Melanie Wells, "Kid Nabbing," *Forbes,* February 2, 2004, pp. 84–88; Garry Khermouch and Jeff Green, "Buzz Marketing," *BusinessWeek,* July 30, 2001, pp. 50–56.

The function of all elements of the integrated marketing communications program is to communicate. An organization's IMC strategy is implemented through the various communications it sends to current or prospective customers as well as other relevant publics. Organizations send communications and messages in a variety of ways, such as through advertisements, brand names, logos and graphic systems, websites, press releases, package designs, promotions, and visual images. As you can see from the opening vignette, marketers are also recognizing the power of word-of-mouth communication and turning to nontraditional marketing campaigns to generate buzz about their products or services.

The way marketers communicate with their target audiences depends on many factors, including how much current and/or potential customers know and what they think about a company or brand and the image it hopes to create. Those involved in the planning and implementation of an IMC program need to understand the communication process and what it means in terms of how they create, deliver, manage, and evaluate messages about a company or brand. Developing an effective marketing communications program is far more complicated than just choosing a product feature or attribute to emphasize. Marketers must understand how consumers will perceive and interpret their messages and how these reactions will shape consumers' responses to the company and/or its product or service.

This chapter reviews the fundamentals of communication and examines various perspectives and models regarding how consumers respond to advertising and promotional messages. Our goal is to demonstrate how valuable an understanding of the communication process can be in planning, implementing, and evaluating the marketing communications program.

The Nature of Communication

Communication has been variously defined as the passing of information, the exchange of ideas, or the process of establishing a commonness or oneness of thought between a sender and a receiver.[1] These definitions suggest that for communication to occur, there must be some common thinking between two parties and information must be passed from one person to another (or from one group to another). As you will see in this chapter, establishing this commonality in thinking is not always as easy as it might seem; many attempts to communicate are unsuccessful.

The communication process is often very complex. Success depends on such factors as the nature of the message, the audience's interpretation of it, and the environment in which it is received. The receiver's perception of the source and the medium used to transmit the message may also affect the ability to communicate, as do many other factors. Words, pictures, sounds, and colors may have different meanings to different audiences, and people's perceptions and interpretations of them vary. For example, if you ask for a soda on the East Coast or West Coast, you'll receive a soft drink such as Coke or Pepsi. However, in parts of the Midwest and South, a soft drink is referred to as pop. If you ask for a soda, you may get a glass of pop with ice cream in it. Marketers must understand the meanings that words and symbols take on and how they influence consumers' interpretation of products and messages.

Language is one of the major barriers to effective communication, as there are different languages in different countries, different languages or dialects within a single country, and more subtle problems of linguistic nuance and vernacular. This can be particularly challenging to companies marketing their products in foreign countries, as discussed in Global Perspective 5-1. The growth of bilingual, multicultural ethnic markets in the United States is also creating challenges for domestic marketers. For example, while many marketers are recognizing the importance of appealing to the Hispanic market, they find that communicating with this fast-growing segment can be very challenging. They have to decide whether to use ads with a Hispanic-focused creative, dub or remake general market campaigns into Spanish, or run English-language ads and hope that they will be picked up by bilingual Hispanics. Many companies are creating ads specifically for the Hispanic market. Exhibit 5-1 shows an outdoor ad the California Milk Processor Board developed to target Hispanic

Exhibit 5-1 This outdoor ad for milk targets Hispanic consumers by appealing to love for family

GLOBAL PERSPECTIVE 5-1

Communication Problems in International Marketing

Communication is a major problem facing companies that market their product and services in foreign countries. Language is one of the main barriers to effective communication, as there can be different languages or dialects within a single country, and more subtle problems of linguistic nuance and vernacular. For example, China has many languages and dialects, with differences great enough that people from different regions of the country often cannot understand each other. As another example, about 40 percent of the Canadian population does not use English as its preferred language. Of the non-English speakers, about 60 percent speak French with the balance spread among a dozen or so other languages.

Mistranslations and faulty word choices have often created problems for companies in foreign markets. International marketers must also be aware of the connotation of the words, signs, symbols, and expressions they use as brand names or logos or in various forms of promotion. Also, advertising copy, slogans, and symbols do not always transfer well into other languages. This not only impedes communication but also sometimes results in embarrassing blunders that can damage a company's or a brand's credibility or image and thereby cost it customers.

There are several widely cited examples of translation problems. For example, when Coca-Cola introduced its brand into China, the Chinese characters sounded like *Coca-Cola* but meant "bite the wax tadpole." With the help of a language specialist, the company substituted four Mandarin characters that retained the Coca-Cola sound but mean "can happy, mouth happy." Then there is the classic story of when General Motors (GM) and Chevrolet introduced its Nova to Latin America: The car did not do well because "no va" means "won't go" in Spanish. However, GM denied that the name was a problem, noting that the brand did pretty well in these markets and that in grammatical terms, "no va" is *not* how a Spanish speaker would describe a dead car. Perdue Farms also ran into problems years ago with the translation of its slogan "It takes a tough man to make a tender chicken" into Spanish. The translated version was "It takes a sexually aroused man to make a chicken affectionate."

Company and brand names can also get lost in translation. Before launching *Good Housekeeping* magazine in Japan, the Hearst Corporation experimented with a number of Japanese translations of the title. The closest word in Japanese, *kaji,* means "domestic duties," which can be interpreted as work performed by servants. Hearst decided to retain the English name for the magazine, but the word *Good* appears on the cover in much larger type than the word *Housekeeping.* When Toyota launched a new version of its popular MR roadster, the company changed the name of the car to the MR2 in the United States and other countries. However, the French version of the new name, "M-R-deux," when spoken with a breezy accent sounds a lot like *merde,* which is French for crap. Mercedes-Benz also ran into a problem in 2005 when the company shortened the name of its Grand Sports Tourer to the sleek, succinct GST. However, in Canada, GST is the acronym for the widely loathed goods and services tax, which presents Canadians with the prospect of calculating the GST on the GST!

Many multinational companies are trying to develop global brands that can be marketed internationally using the same brand name and advertising campaigns. However, they must be careful that brand names, advertising slogans, signs, symbols, and other forms of marketing communication don't lose something in the translation. There are several things international marketers can do to avoid joining the top 10 list of language blunders. The first line of defense is to hire a translation service to review the material and make sure there are no problems. However, experts note that relying on translators alone may not be foolproof as they may not be steeped in current slang or the subtleties of a language. The experts recommend that translated materials be read by a linguistically mixed staff as well as by contacts in the local market who know dialects and slang. For example, at the international branding consulting firm Landor Associates, new brand names or ad slogans trigger native-speaker checks in eight languages.

While the use of translators and native-speaker checks can help to identify language problems, they do not solve the problem of how well an ad campaign translates into another culture. The vice president of marketing for the direct marketing agency Infocore notes that ad campaign concepts will never translate perfectly into another culture, which is a problem that many marketers do not want to acknowledge. He cites two basic problems including multinational ad agencies being constrained by managers who do not want to surrender power to strangers in foreign markets, and the "don't mess with the creative" mantra of marketers who assume that the magic of a campaign that works in one culture can be grafted onto another.

Time and again, problems with brand names, ad slogans, and visual signs and symbols have come back to haunt even the best of marketers. As Simon Anholt, a British marketing and branding expert, notes: "Language is in many respects such a silly little thing, but it has the power to bring marketing directors to their knees. That's where the terror lies."

Sources: Mark Laswell, "Lost in Translation," *Business 2.0,* August 2004, pp. 68–70; Kevin Reagan, "In Asia, Think Globally Communicate Locally," *Marketing News,* July 19, 1999, pp. 12, 14; Yumiko Ono, "Will Good Housekeeping Translate into Japanese?" *The Wall Street Journal,* December 30, 1997, p. B1.

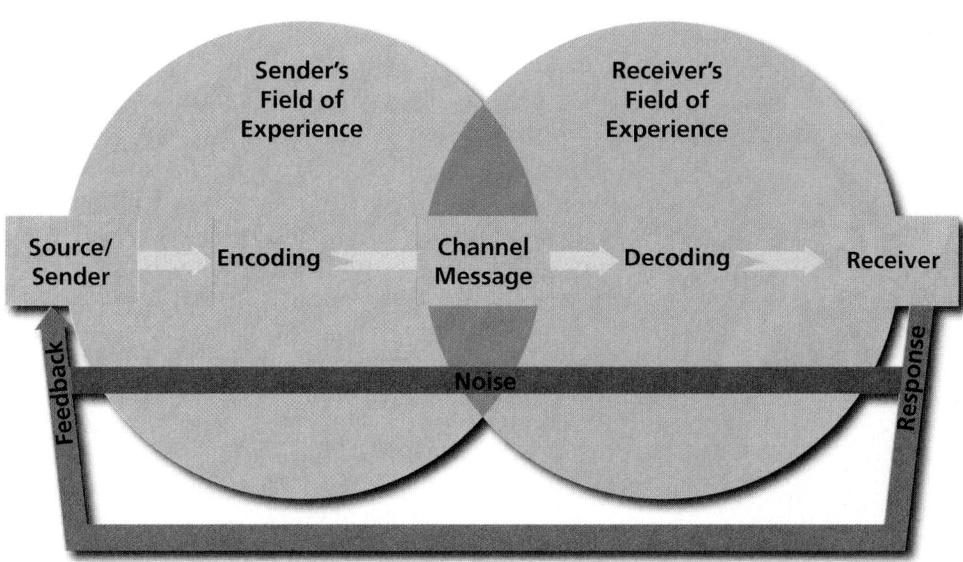

Figure 5-1 A Model of the Communication Process

consumers. Notice how the message in the ad (Family, Love and Milk) addresses commitment to family, which is a strong traditional Latino value.

A Basic Model of Communication

Over the years, a basic model of the various elements of the communication process has evolved, as shown in Figure 5-1.[2] Two elements represent the major participants in the communication process, the sender and the receiver. Another two are the major communication tools, message and channel. Four others are the major communication functions and processes: encoding, decoding, response, and feedback. The last element, noise, refers to any extraneous factors in the system that can interfere with the process and work against effective communication.

Source Encoding

The sender, or **source,** of a communication is the person or organization that has information to share with another person or group of people. The source may be an individual (say, a salesperson or hired spokesperson, such as a celebrity, who appears in a company's advertisements) or a nonpersonal entity (such as the corporation or organization itself). For example, the source of many ads is the company, since no specific spokesperson or source is shown. However, in the Rolex ad shown in Exhibit 5-2, Olympic gold medalist Picabo Street is also a source since she appears as a spokesperson for the company.

Exhibit 5-2 Picabo Street is a source in this Rolex ad

Because the receiver's perceptions of the source influence how the communication is received, marketers must be careful to select a communicator the receiver believes is knowledgeable and trustworthy or with whom the receiver can identify or relate in some manner. (How these characteristics influence the receiver's responses is discussed further in Chapter 6.)

The communication process begins when the source selects words, symbols, pictures, and the like, to represent the message that will be delivered to the receiver(s). This process, known as **encoding,** involves putting thoughts, ideas, or information into a symbolic form. The sender's goal is to encode the message in such a way that it will be understood by the receiver. This means using words, signs, or symbols that are familiar to the target audience. Many symbols have universal meaning, such as the familiar circle with a line through it to denote no parking, no smoking, and so forth. Many companies also have highly recognizable symbols—such as McDonald's golden arches, Nike's swoosh, or the Coca-Cola trademark—that are known to consumers around the world.

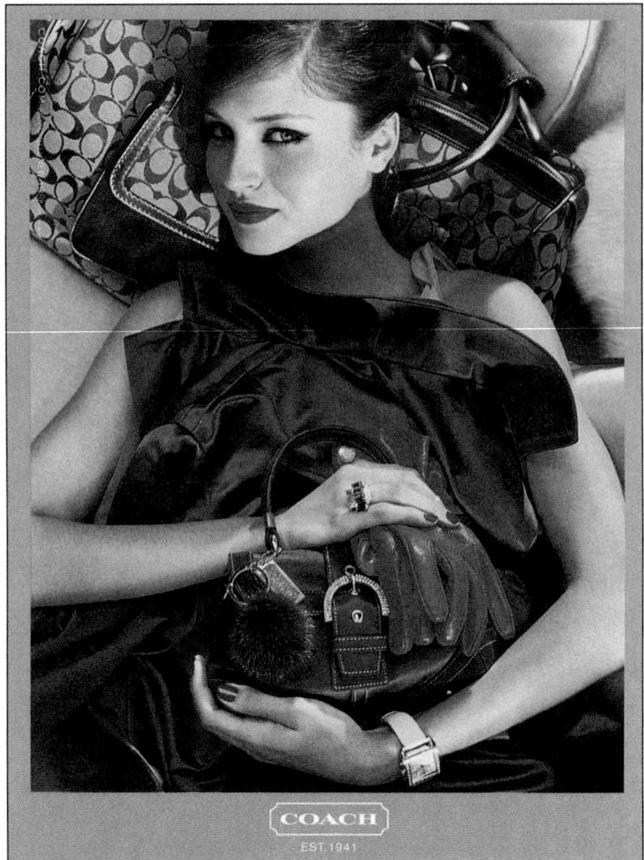

Exhibit 5-3 The image projected by an ad often communicates more than words

Message

The encoding process leads to development of a **message** that contains the information or meaning the source hopes to convey. The message may be verbal or nonverbal, oral or written, or symbolic. Messages must be put into a transmittable form that is appropriate for the channel of communication being used. In advertising, this may range from simply writing some words or copy that will be read as a radio message to producing an expensive television commercial. For many products, it is not the actual words of the message that determine its communication effectiveness but rather the impression or image the ad creates. Notice how the Coach ad shown in Exhibit 5-3 uses only a picture to deliver its message. However, the use of the brand name and picture is an effective way to communicate Coach's intended message of the eloquent simplicity as well as classic design and American style of its handbags.

To better understand the symbolic meaning that might be conveyed in a communication, advertising and marketing researchers have begun focusing attention on **semiotics,** which studies the nature of meaning and asks how our reality—words, gestures, myths, signs, symbols, products/services, theories—acquires meaning.[3] Semiotics is important in marketing communications since products and brands acquire meaning through the way they are advertised and consumers use products and brands to express their social identities. Consumer researcher Michael Solomon notes: "From a semiotic perspective, every marketing message has three basic components: an object, a sign or symbol and an interpretant. The object is the product that is the focus of the message (e.g., Marlboro cigarettes). The sign is the sensory imagery that represents the intended meanings of the object (e.g., the Marlboro cowboy). The interpretant is the meaning derived (e.g., rugged, individualistic, American)."[4]

Marketers may use individuals trained in semiotics and related fields such as cultural anthropology to better understand the conscious and subconscious meanings the nonverbal signs and symbols in their ads transmit to consumers. For example, Levi Strauss & Co.'s former agency, TBWA/Chiat/Day, hired a cultural anthropologist to help it better understand the image and meaning of clothing and fashion among young consumers. As part of the process, the agency research team recruited hip-looking young people in the streets of the East Village section of New York City, an area picked because they felt it is the best reflection of today's youth life. Those chosen were handed a piece of red cardboard and a white marker and asked to "write down something you believe in; something that's true about you or your world." The process provided the agency with insight into the teen market and was the impetus for an ad campaign featuring teenagers holding placards inscribed with their philosophical messages.[5] Exhibit 5-4 shows the thinking behind the various elements of one of the ads used in the campaign as explained by Sean Dee, the director of the Levi's brand.

Some advertising and marketing people are skeptical about the value of semiotics. They question whether social scientists read too much into advertising messages and are overly intellectual in interpreting them. However, the meaning of an advertising message or other form of marketing communication lies not in the message but with the people who see and interpret it. Moreover, consumers behave on the basis of meanings they ascribe to marketplace stimuli. Thus, marketers must consider the meanings consumers attach to the various signs and symbols. Semiotics may be helpful in analyzing how various aspects of the marketing program—such as advertising messages, packaging, brand names, and even the nonverbal communications of salespeople (gestures, mode of dress)—are interpreted by receivers.[6]

Channel

The **channel** is the method by which the communication travels from the source or sender to the receiver. At the broadest level, channels of communication are of two

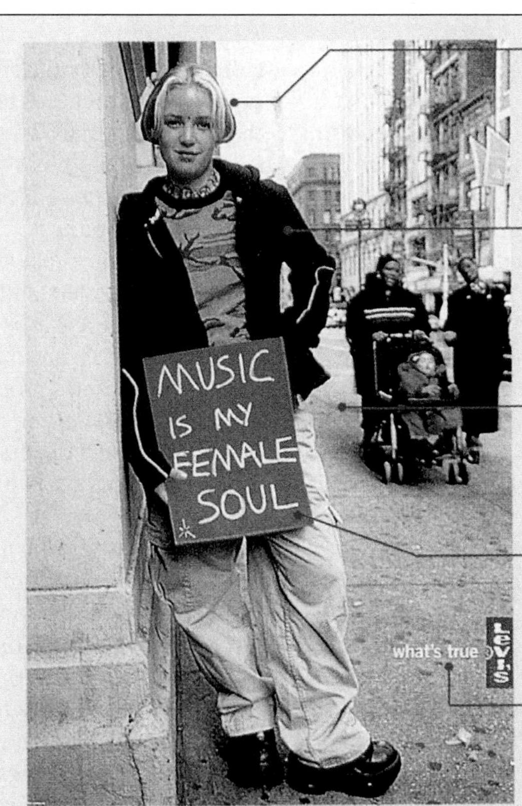

THE MODEL: A premed student at New York University
"We wanted people who are not defined by what they do but by what they are. We chose her because she looks like a Levi's type. She's young. She has her own point of view. She's sexy, but in an understated way. She's not trying too hard. She's definitely got something about her."

THE CLOTHES: Levi's cargo pants, her own T-shirt, zip-up sweatshirt, combat boots, and accessories
"It's important that she wore what she wanted. We're not trying to create a Levi's uniform; that wouldn't be very 'real.' We didn't use a professional stylist or a hairdresser; that wouldn't be real."

THE SETTING: Manhattan's East Village
"We picked New York City because it's the best reflection of today's youth life. We drove around the grittiest parts of the city. The people in the background [of this image] give it a street feel; it's obviously not staged in a studio."

THE STATEMENT: "Music is my female soul"
"It's hard for people to believe, but the [language] came totally from the kids; there was no prompting. . . . We liked the music theme [in this statement] because we do a lot to promote original music; we see music as being *the* voice of the young people."

THE TAG LINE: "What's true"
"The challenge with youth marketing these days is not to dictate to kids. This [line] is both a statement and a question. Is what we're saying true? Or is it a declaration? It works because it's provocative and ambiguous."

Exhibit 5-4 Semiotic analysis is used to describe the various elements of this Levi's ad

types, personal and nonpersonal. *Personal channels* of communication are direct interpersonal (face-to-face) contact with target individuals or groups. Salespeople serve as personal channels of communication when they deliver their sales message to a buyer or potential customer. Social channels of communication such as friends, neighbors, associates, co-workers, or family members are also personal channels. They often represent **word-of-mouth communication,** a powerful source of information for consumers.[7]

As noted in the opening vignette to the chapter, many companies are working to generate positive word-of-mouth discussion for their companies or brands. Knowing that the average consumer often listens to what others say about a brand, marketers will target specific groups of influential consumers such as trendsetters or loyal customers. A recent study conducted by David Godes and Diane Mayzlin on the effects of a word-of-mouth campaign for a chain store examined the characteristics of the most successful "agents" so that firms could better understand at whom they should target their buzz marketing efforts.[8] They found that agents who were not loyal customers of the store were more effective at generating sales through word of mouth than were loyal customers. The explanation offered for these somewhat counterintuitive findings is that loyal customers have already told their friends and acquaintances about a product and are already generating positive word of mouth. On the other hand, nonloyal customers may be more responsive to buzz marketing campaigns designed to encourage them to spread the word about a product. However, marketers still have to identify the best generators of buzz among both loyal and nonloyal customers such as those who are considered opinion leaders by their peers and "social butterflies," who have a high propensity to meet new people and connect with friends.

Nonpersonal channels of communication are those that carry a message without interpersonal contact between sender and receiver. Nonpersonal channels are generally referred to as the **mass media** or mass communications, since the message is sent to many individuals at one time. For example, a TV commercial broadcast on a prime-time show may be seen by 10 million households in a given evening. Nonpersonal channels of communication consist of two major types, print and broadcast. Print media include newspapers, magazines, direct mail, and billboards; broadcast media include radio and television.

Receiver/Decoding

The **receiver** is the person(s) with whom the sender shares thoughts or information. Generally, receivers are the consumers in the target market or audience who read, hear, and/or see the marketer's message and decode it. **Decoding** is the process of transforming the sender's message back into thought. This process is heavily influenced by the receiver's frame of reference or **field of experience,** which refers to the experiences, perceptions, attitudes, and values he or she brings to the communication situation.

For effective communication to occur, the message decoding process of the receiver must match the encoding of the sender. Simply put, this means the receiver understands and correctly interprets what the source is trying to communicate. As Figure 5-1 showed, the source and the receiver each have a frame of reference (the circle around each) that they bring to the communication situation. Effective communication is more likely when there is some *common ground* between the two parties. (This is represented by the overlapping of the two circles.) The more knowledge the sender has about the receivers, the better the sender can understand their needs, empathize with them, and communicate effectively.

While this notion of common ground between sender and receiver may sound basic, it often causes great difficulty in the advertising communications process. Marketing and advertising people often have very different fields of experience from the consumers who constitute the mass markets with whom they must communicate. Most advertising and marketing people are college-educated and work and/or reside in large urban areas such as New York, Chicago, or Los Angeles. Yet they are attempting to develop commercials that will effectively communicate with millions of consumers who have never attended college, work in blue-collar occupations, and live in rural areas or small towns. The executive creative director of a large advertising agency described how advertising executives become isolated from the cultural mainstream: "We pull them in and work them to death. And then they begin moving in sushi circles and lose touch with Velveeta and the people who eat it."[9]

Another factor that can lead to problems in establishing common ground between senders and receivers is age. IMC Perspective 5-1 discusses the youth bias in advertising and whether advertisers ignore older consumers.

Advertisers spend millions of dollars every year to understand the frames of reference of the target markets who receive their messages. They also spend much time and money pretesting messages to make sure consumers understand and decode them in the manner the advertiser intended.

Noise

Throughout the communication process, the message is subject to extraneous factors that can distort or interfere with its reception. This unplanned distortion or interference is known as **noise.** Errors or problems that occur in the encoding of the message, distortion in a radio or television signal, or distractions at the point of reception are examples of noise. When you are watching your favorite commercial on TV and a problem occurs in the signal transmission, it will obviously interfere with your reception, lessening the impact of the commercial.

Noise may also occur because the fields of experience of the sender and receiver don't overlap. Lack of common ground may result in improper encoding of the message—using a sign, symbol, or words that are unfamiliar or have different meaning to the receiver. The more common ground there is between the sender and the receiver, the less likely it is this type of noise will occur.

Response/Feedback

The receiver's set of reactions after seeing, hearing, or reading the message is known as a **response.** Receivers' responses can range from nonobservable actions such as storing information in memory to immediate action such as dialing a toll-free number to order a product advertised on television. Marketers are very interested in **feedback,** that part of the receiver's response that is communicated back to the sender. Feedback, which may take a variety of forms, closes the loop in the communications flow and lets the sender monitor how the intended message is being decoded and received.

IMC PERSPECTIVE 5-1

Do Advertisers Ignore Older Consumers?

A few years ago, a battle raged between two of the major television networks, CBS and ABC, over *The Late Show with David Letterman,* which airs in the late-fringe time slot on CBS. ABC was trying to lure Letterman's show away from CBS to replace *Nightline,* the news show hosted by Ted Koppel, which has been airing in its late-fringe time slot since 1980. When Koppel announced that he would leave *Nightline* at the end of 2005, a number of media buyers suggested that ABC would be smart to put an entertainment show in the time slot so they could reach the coveted 18- to 49-year-old age "demo." While *Nightline* averages a 1.1 program rating among 18- to 49-year-olds, Letterman gets a 1.6 rating; NBC's *Tonight Show with Jay Leno* leads both of them with a 2.1 rating for the demo. Although the differences in the numbers may not seem that great, they have a huge impact on the amount the networks can charge for commercial time and the advertising revenue they generate. Whereas NBC brought in $386 million from the late-fringe segment in 2004, CBS generated $251 million, and ABC pulled in the smallest amount with $206 million.

Observers note that the battle over ratings among the 18 to 49 demo in the late-fringe segment is just another example of advertisers' fixation with reaching younger consumers while paying less attention to those over the age of 50. Ironically, the 18- to 49-year-old demo was initially developed to reach the baby boom generation when they were younger and in their peak buying years. Madison Avenue has been focused on the younger adult target market for decades, and the media have become obsessed with the under-50 demo as well. For example, all of the major TV networks, including ABC, NBC, CBS, and Fox, have been filling their prime-time programming with shows aimed at people in their 20s, 30s, and 40s, such as *Desperate Housewives, The Apprentice,* and *24.*

Media experts want to purchase commercial time on shows that reach younger consumers with the hope that they will also get older people as well—while the opposite is rarely the case. People over 50 watch more television and are easier for the networks to reach than the younger demo, which is busy with work and family and is tempted by a myriad of entertainment options. The advertising president of Fox Broadcasting notes: "If you target young, you're going to get younger viewers and keep your older ones. But if you target old that is what you are going to get—older viewers." The networks also realize they can charge a premium for commercials airing on shows that capture 18- to 49-year-old viewers because this group is so coveted by such advertisers as movie studios, automobile manufacturers, financial services companies, and beer and computer manufacturers.

Another area where advertising is often seen as having a youth bias is among agency personnel. A study conducted for the Association of Advertising Agencies International found that professionals who work in advertising agencies are also much younger than the U.S. adult population. Nearly 40 percent of ad agency professional staff are between the ages of 30 to 39 while only 20 percent of the adult population is in its 30s. The youth bias is particularly evident in the creative departments as agency employment drops like a rock after age 40, particularly among those involved in creating the ads. As a result, agencies rarely have creative professionals with a true understanding of life after age 50, not to mention life after 60 or 70.

Many older consumers do not like being ignored by advertisers. For example, the American Association of Retired Professionals

IF THIS IS YOUR APPROACH TO RETIREMENT,
THIS IS YOUR BEER.
Lose the carbs. Not the taste.
Michelob ULTRA

(AARP), which is a very powerful organization dedicated to addressing the needs and interests of persons 50 and older, recently drew attention to the issue in an ad campaign built around a photo of a morgue, complete with toe-tagged cadavers. The slogan used in the ad was "When you turn 50 doctors don't pronounce you dead—marketers do." The group publisher of AARP magazines notes that advertisers are terrified of seeming too friendly to the gray-haired set as they fear that they might alienate their younger audience.

Advertisers who are unable to connect with the so-called mature market may be squandering opportunities to reach a valuable market. More than half of the nation's wealth is in the hands of people over 50, and they spend an estimated $2 trillion a year on products and services. Moreover, the number of Americans in their 50s will grow by 40 percent over the next 10 years. Many wonder why advertisers remain focused on younger consumers when spending power is becoming progressively more concentrated among those aged 50 and older. One reason may be the conventional wisdom among marketers that younger people spend more on cars, electronics, furniture, appliances, and other items and are more willing to switch brands and try new products and services. There is also the problem of advertisers not wanting to have their products and services perceived as being for older consumers for fear of damaging their brand image among younger consumers.

Many advertisers are beginning to recognize the potential and power of older consumers and are making more of an effort to reach them. Cadillac and Audi have incorporated the music of such 1970's rock icons as Led Zeppelin, Jimi Hendrix, and David Bowie into their TV commercials to strike a chord with aging baby boomers. Anheuser-Busch introduced Michelob Ultra, a low-calorie, lower carbohydrate beer aimed at consumers over 50 after its research showed that many boomers stopped drinking beer in order to stay trim. However, many believe that good ads targeted at older consumers are still too few and far between and the youth bias in advertising is a problem. They note that the best hope for those over 50 to become relevant again lies in the marketing people who are growing and maturing themselves and will recognize that they ought to follow the green—which is quickly going gray.

Sources: Meg James, "Over 50 and Out of Favor," *The Los Angeles Times,* May 10, 2005, pp. A1, 10; Claire Atkinson, "Media Buyers: Put 'Nightline' to Bed," *Advertising Age,* April 4, 2005, pp. 1, 63; Hillary Chura, "Boomers Hope to Break Age-Old Ad Myth," *Advertising Age,* May 13, 2002, p. 16.

For example, in a personal-selling situation, customers may pose questions, comments, or objections or indicate their reactions through nonverbal responses such as gestures and frowns.[10] The salesperson has the advantage of receiving instant feedback through the customer's reactions. But this is generally not the case when mass media are used. Because advertisers are not in direct contact with the customers, they must use other means to determine how their messages have been received. While the ultimate form of feedback occurs through sales, it is often hard to show a direct relationship between advertising and purchase behavior. So marketers use other methods to obtain feedback, among them customer inquiries, store visits, coupon redemptions, and reply cards. Research-based feedback analyzes readership and recall of ads, message comprehension, attitude change, and other forms of response. With this information, the advertiser can determine reasons for success or failure in the communication process and make adjustments.

Successful communication is accomplished when the marketer selects an appropriate source, develops an effective message or appeal that is encoded properly, and then selects the channels or media that will best reach the target audience so that the message can be effectively decoded and delivered. In Chapter 6, we will examine the source, message, and channel decisions and see how promotional planners work with these controllable variables to develop communication strategies. Since these decisions must consider how the target audience will respond to the promotional message, the remainder of this chapter examines the receiver and the process by which consumers respond to advertising and other forms of marketing communications.

Analyzing the Receiver

To communicate effectively with their customers, marketers must understand who the target audience is, what (if anything) it knows or feels about the company's product or service, and how to communicate with the audience to influence its decision-making process. Marketers must also know how the market is likely to respond to various sources of communication or different types of messages. Before they make decisions regarding source, message, and channel variables, promotional planners must understand the potential effects associated with each of these factors. This section focuses on the receiver of the marketing communication. It examines how the audience is identified and the process it may go through in responding to a promotional message. This information serves as a foundation for evaluating the controllable communication variable decisions in the next chapter.

Identifying the Target Audience

The marketing communication process really begins with identifying the audience that will be the focus of the firm's advertising and promotional efforts. The target audience may consist of individuals, groups, niche markets, market segments, or a general public or mass audience (Figure 5-2). Marketers approach each of these audiences differently.

The target market may consist of *individuals* who have specific needs and for whom the communication must be specifically tailored. This often requires person-to-person communication and is generally accomplished through personal selling. Other forms of communication, such as advertising, may be used to attract the audience's attention to the firm, but the detailed message is carried by a salesperson who can respond to the specific needs of the individual customer. Life insurance, financial services, and real estate are examples of products and services promoted this way.

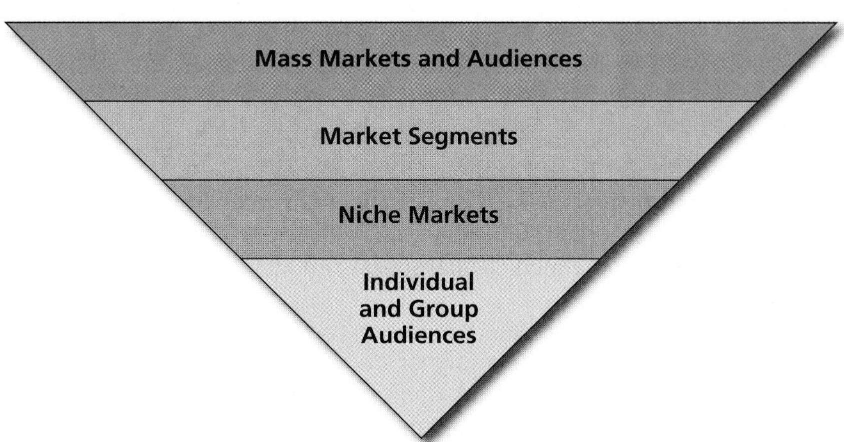

Figure 5-2 Levels of Audience Aggregation

A second level of audience aggregation is represented by the *group.* Marketers often must communicate with a group of people who make or influence the purchase decision. For example, organizational purchasing often involves buying centers or committees that vary in size and composition. Companies marketing their products and services to other businesses or organizations must understand who is on the purchase committee, what aspect of the decision each individual influences, and the criteria each member uses to evaluate a product. Advertising may be directed at each member of the buying center, and multilevel personal selling may be necessary to reach those individuals who influence or actually make decisions.

Marketers look for customers who have similar needs and wants and thus represent some type of market segment that can be reached with the same basic communication strategy. Very small, well-defined groups of customers are often referred to as *market niches.* They can usually be reached through personal-selling efforts or highly targeted media such as direct mail. The next level of audience aggregation is *market segments,* broader classes of buyers who have similar needs and can be reached with similar messages. As we saw in Chapter 2, there are various ways of segmenting markets and reaching the customers in these segments. As market segments get larger, marketers usually turn to broader-based media such as newspapers, magazines, and TV to reach them.

Marketers of most consumer products attempt to attract the attention of large numbers of present or potential customers (*mass markets*) through mass communication such as advertising or publicity. Mass communication is a one-way flow of information from the marketer to the consumer. Feedback on the audience's reactions to the message is generally indirect and difficult to measure.

TV advertising, for example, lets the marketer send a message to millions of consumers at the same time. But this does not mean effective communication has occurred. This may be only one of several hundred messages the consumer is exposed to that day. There is no guarantee the information will be attended to, processed, comprehended, or stored in memory for later retrieval. Even if the advertising message is processed, it may not interest consumers or may be misinterpreted by them. Studies by Jacob Jacoby and Wayne D. Hoyer have shown that nearly 20 percent of all print ads and even more TV commercials are miscomprehended by readers.[11]

Unlike personal or face-to-face communications, mass communications do not offer the marketer an opportunity to explain or clarify the message to make it more effective. The marketer must enter the communication situation with knowledge of the target audience and how it is likely to react to the message. This means the receiver's response process must be understood, along with its implications for promotional planning and strategy.

The Response Process

Perhaps the most important aspect of developing effective communication programs involves understanding the *response process* the receiver may go through in moving toward a specific behavior (like purchasing a product) and how the promotional efforts of the marketer influence consumer responses. In many instances, the marketer's only objective may be to create awareness of the company or brand name, which may trigger interest in the product. In other situations, the marketer may want to convey detailed information to change consumers' knowledge of and attitudes toward the brand and ultimately change their behavior.

Traditional Response Hierarchy Models

A number of models have been developed to depict the stages a consumer may pass through in moving from a state of not being aware of a company, product, or brand to actual purchase behavior. Figure 5-3 shows four of the best-known response hierarchy models. While these response models may appear similar, they were developed for different reasons.

The **AIDA model** was developed to represent the stages a salesperson must take a customer through in the personal-selling process.[12] This model depicts the buyer as passing successively through attention, interest, desire, and action. The salesperson must first get the customer's attention and then arouse some interest in the company's product or service. Strong levels of interest should create desire to own or use the product. The action stage in the AIDA model involves getting the customer to make a purchase commitment and closing the sale. To the marketer, this is the most important stage in the selling process, but it can also be the most difficult. Companies train their sales reps in closing techniques to help them complete the selling process.

Perhaps the best known of these response hierarchies is the model developed by Robert Lavidge and Gary Steiner as a paradigm for setting and measuring advertising objectives.[13] Their **hierarchy of effects model** shows the process by which advertising works; it assumes a consumer passes through a series of steps in sequential order from initial awareness of a product or service to actual purchase. A basic premise of this model is that advertising effects occur over a period of time. Advertising communication may not lead to immediate behavioral response or purchase; rather, a series of effects must occur, with each step fulfilled before the consumer can move to the next stage in the hierarchy. As we will see in Chapter 7, the hierarchy of effects model has become the foundation for objective setting and measurement of advertising effects in many companies.

The **innovation adoption model** evolved from work on the diffusion of innovations.[14] This model represents the stages a consumer passes through in adopting a new product or service. Like the other models, it says potential adopters must be moved through a series of steps before taking some action (in this case, deciding to adopt a new product). The steps preceding adoption are awareness, interest, evaluation, and trial. The

Figure 5-3 Models of the Response Process

	Models			
Stages	**AIDA model**[a]	**Hierarchy of effects model**[b]	**Innovation adoption model**[c]	**Information processing model**[d]
Cognitive stage	Attention	Awareness Knowledge	Awareness	Presentation Attention Comprehension
Affective stage	Interest Desire	Liking Preference Conviction	Interest Evaluation	Yielding Retention
Behavioral stage	Action	Purchase	Trial Adoption	Behavior

challenge facing companies introducing new products is to create awareness and interest among consumers and then get them to evaluate the product favorably. The best way to evaluate a new product is through actual use so that performance can be judged. Marketers often encourage trial by using demonstration or sampling programs or allowing consumers to use a product with minimal commitment (Exhibit 5-5). After trial, consumers either adopt the product or reject it.

Exhibit 5-5 Sampling or demonstration programs encourage trial of new products such as disposable contact lenses

The final hierarchy model shown in Figure 5-3 is the **information processing model** of advertising effects, developed by William McGuire.[15] This model assumes the receiver in a persuasive communication situation like advertising is an information processor or problem solver. McGuire suggests the series of steps a receiver goes through in being persuaded constitutes a response hierarchy. The stages of this model are similar to the hierarchy of effects sequence; attention and comprehension are similar to awareness and knowledge, and yielding is synonymous with liking. McGuire's model includes a stage not found in the other models: retention, or the receiver's ability to retain that portion of the comprehended information that he or she accepts as valid or relevant. This stage is important since most promotional campaigns are designed not to motivate consumers to take immediate action but rather to provide information they will use later when making a purchase decision.

Each stage of the response hierarchy is a dependent variable that must be attained and that may serve as an objective of the communication process. As shown in Figure 5-4, each stage can be measured, providing the advertiser with feedback regarding the effectiveness of various strategies designed to move the consumer to purchase. The information processing model may be an effective framework for planning and evaluating the effects of a promotional campaign.

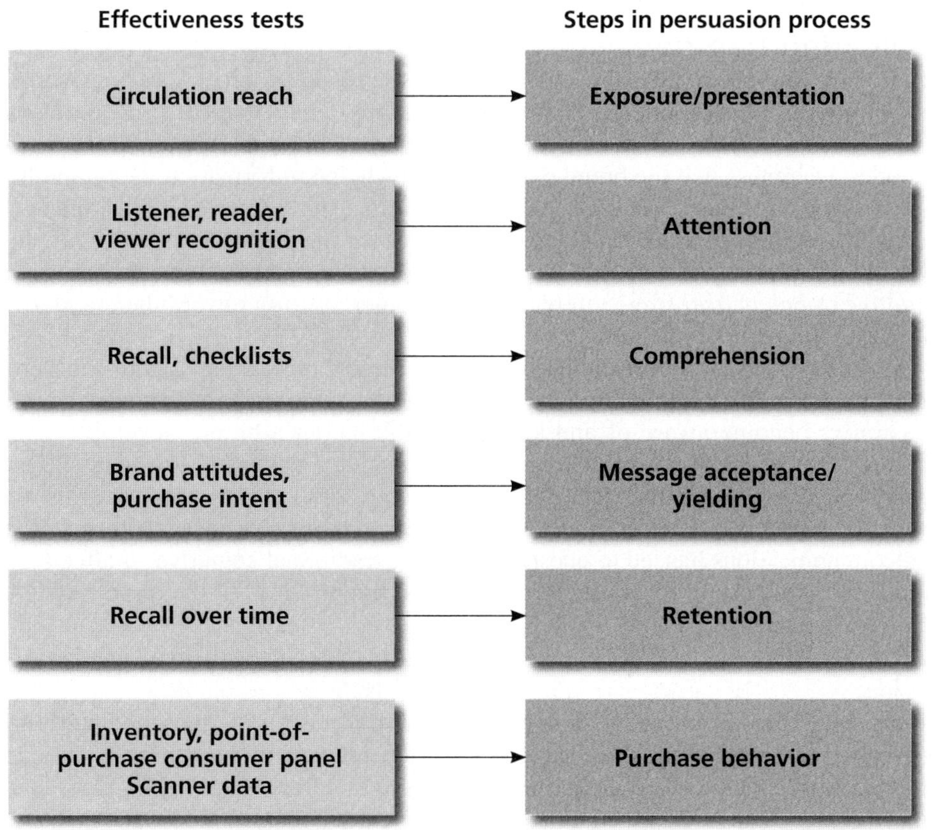

Figure 5-4 Methods of Obtaining Feedback in the Response Hierarchy

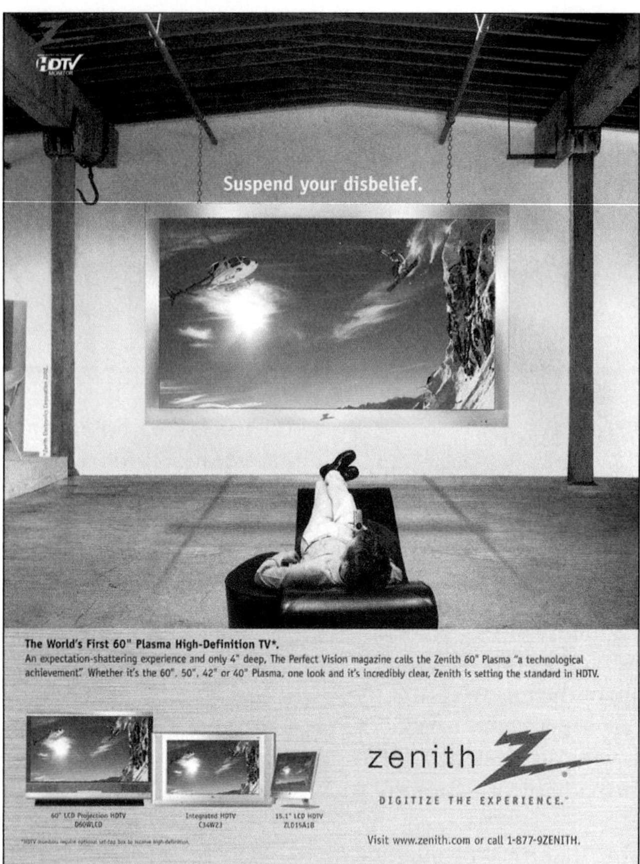

HDTV
Suspend your disbelief.
The World's First 60" Plasma High-Definition TV*.
An expectation-shattering experience and only 4" deep, The Perfect Vision magazine calls the Zenith 60" Plasma "a technological achievement." Whether it's the 60", 50", 42" or 40" Plasma, one look and it's incredibly clear, Zenith is setting the standard in HDTV.
60" LCD Projection HDTV D60WLCD
Integrated HDTV C34W23
15.1" LCD HDTV ZLD15A1B
zenith
DIGITIZE THE EXPERIENCE.
Visit www.zenith.com or call 1-877-9ZENITH.

Exhibit 5-6 Advertising for innovative new products such as HDTV must make consumers aware of their features and benefits

Implications of the Traditional Hierarchy Models

The hierarchy models of communication response are useful to promotional planners from several perspectives. First, they delineate the series of steps potential purchasers must be taken through to move them from unawareness of a product or service to readiness to purchase it. Second, potential buyers may be at different stages in the hierarchy, so the advertiser will face different sets of communication problems. For example, a company introducing an innovative product like Zenith's plasma high-definition television (HDTV) may need to devote considerable effort to making people aware of the product, how it works, and its benefits (Exhibit 5-6). Marketers of a mature brand that enjoys customer loyalty may need only supportive or reminder advertising to reinforce positive perceptions and maintain the awareness level for the brand.

The hierarchy models can also be useful as intermediate measures of communication effectiveness. The marketer needs to know where audience members are on the response hierarchy. For example, research may reveal that one target segment has low awareness of the advertiser's brand, whereas another is aware of the brand and its various attributes but has a low level of liking or brand preference.

For the first segment of the market, the communication task involves increasing the awareness level for the brand. The number of ads may be increased, or a product sampling program may be used. For the second segment, where awareness is already high but liking and preference are low, the advertiser must determine the reason for the negative feelings and then attempt to address this problem in future advertising.

When research or other evidence reveals a company is perceived favorably on a particular attribute or performance criterion, the company may want to take advantage of this in its advertising.

Evaluating Traditional Response Hierarchy Models

As you saw in Figure 5-3, the four models presented all view the response process as consisting of movement through a sequence of three basic stages. The *cognitive stage* represents what the receiver knows or perceives about the particular product or brand. This stage includes awareness that the brand exists and knowledge, information, or comprehension about its attributes, characteristics, or benefits. The *affective stage* refers to the receiver's feelings or affect level (like or dislike) for the particular brand. This stage also includes stronger levels of affect such as desire, preference, or conviction. The *conative* or *behavioral stage* refers to the consumer's action toward the brand: trial, purchase, adoption, or rejection.

All four models assume a similar ordering of these three stages. Cognitive development precedes affective reactions, which precede behavior. One might assume that consumers become aware of and knowledgeable about a brand, develop feelings toward it, form a desire or preference, and then make a purchase. While this logical progression is often accurate, the response sequence does not always operate this way.

Over the past two decades, considerable research in marketing, social psychology, and communications has led to questioning of the traditional cognitive → affective → behavioral sequence of response. Several other configurations of the response hierarchy have been theorized.

Alternative Response Hierarchies

Michael Ray has developed a model of information processing that identifies three alternative orderings of the three stages based on perceived product differentiation and product involvement.[16] These alternative response hierarchies are the standard learning, dissonance/attribution, and low-involvement models (Figure 5-5).

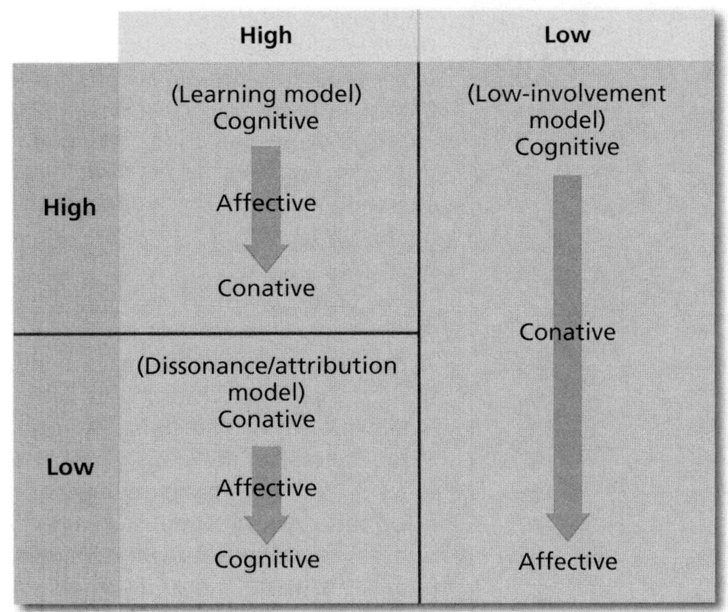

Figure 5-5 Alternative Response Hierarchies: The Three-Orders Model of Information Processing

The Standard Learning Hierarchy

In many purchase situations, the consumer will go through the response process in the sequence depicted by the traditional communication models. Ray terms this a **standard learning model,** which consists of a learn → feel → do sequence. Information and knowledge acquired or *learned* about the various brands are the basis for developing affect, or *feelings,* that guide what the consumer will *do* (e.g., actual trial or purchase). In this hierarchy, the consumer is viewed as an active participant in the communication process who gathers information through active learning.

Ray suggests the standard learning hierarchy is likely when the consumer is highly involved in the purchase process and there is much differentiation among competing brands. High-involvement purchase decisions such as those for industrial products and services and consumer durables like personal computers, printers, cameras, appliances, and cars are areas where a standard learning hierarchy response process is likely. Ads for products and services in these areas are usually very detailed and provide customers with information that can be used to evaluate brands and help them make a purchase decision. Notice how the Subaru Tribeca SUV ad shown in Exhibit 5-7 appeals to the various steps in the standard learning hierarchy with the "Think. Feel. Drive." theme and copy that relates to each stage.

Exhibit 5-7 This Subaru ad addresses the various stages in the standard learning hierarchy

The Dissonance/Attribution Hierarchy

A second response hierarchy proposed by Ray involves situations where consumers first behave, then develop attitudes or feelings as a result of that behavior, and then learn or process information that supports the behavior. This **dissonance/attribution model,** or do → feel → learn, occurs in situations where consumers must choose between two alternatives that are similar in quality but are complex and may have hidden or unknown attributes. The consumer may purchase the product on the basis of a recommendation by some nonmedia source and then

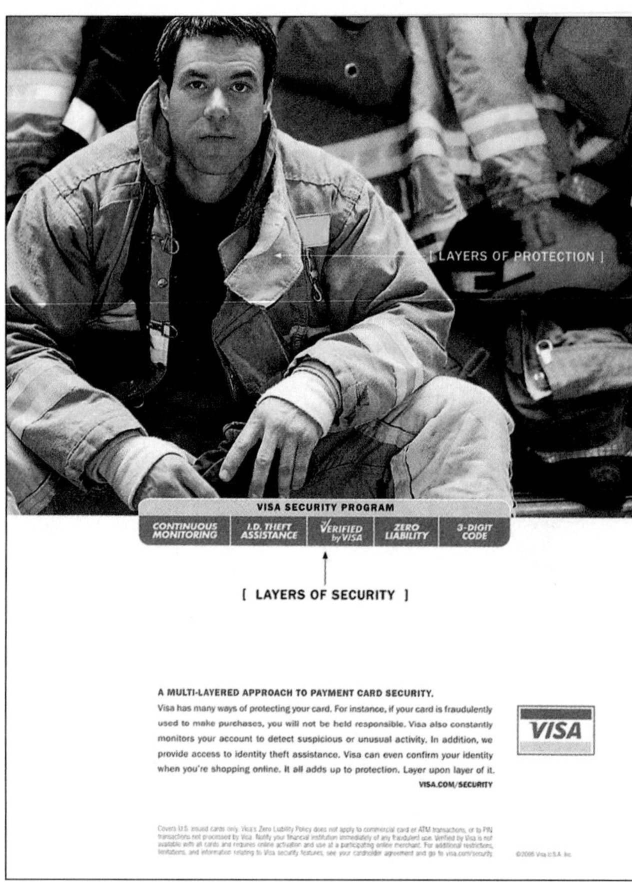

Exhibit 5-8 This ad reinforces the wisdom of the decision to use a Visa credit card

attempt to support the decision by developing a positive attitude toward the brand and perhaps even developing negative feelings toward the rejected alternative(s). This reduces any *postpurchase dissonance* or anxiety the consumer may experience resulting from doubt over the purchase (as discussed in Chapter 4). Dissonance reduction involves *selective learning,* whereby the consumer seeks information that supports the choice made and avoids information that would raise doubts about the decision.

According to this model, marketers need to recognize that in some situations, attitudes develop *after* purchase, as does learning from the mass media. Ray suggests that in these situations the main effect of the mass media is not the promotion of original choice behavior and attitude change but rather the reduction of dissonance by reinforcing the wisdom of the purchase or providing supportive information. For example, the ad shown in Exhibit 5-8 reinforces consumers' decision to use a Visa credit card by reassuring them of the various layers of security the company provides to its cardholders.

As with the standard learning model, this response hierarchy is likely to occur when the consumer is involved in the purchase situation; it is particularly relevant for postpurchase situations. For example, a consumer may purchase tires recommended by a friend and then develop a favorable attitude toward the company and pay close attention to its ads to reduce dissonance.

Some marketers resist this view of the response hierarchy because they can't accept the notion that the mass media have no effect on the consumer's initial purchase decision. But the model doesn't claim the mass media have no effect—just that their major impact occurs after the purchase has been made. Marketing communications planners must be aware of the need for advertising and promotion efforts not just to encourage brand selection but to reinforce choices and ensure that a purchase pattern will continue.

The Low-Involvement Hierarchy

Perhaps the most intriguing of the three response hierarchies proposed by Ray is the **low-involvement hierarchy,** in which the receiver is viewed as passing from cognition to behavior to attitude change. This learn → do → feel sequence is thought to characterize situations of low consumer involvement in the purchase process. Ray suggests this hierarchy tends to occur when involvement in the purchase decision is low, there are minimal differences among brand alternatives, and mass-media (especially broadcast) advertising is important.

The notion of a low-involvement hierarchy is based in large part on Herbert Krugman's theory explaining the effects of television advertising.[17] Krugman wanted to find out why TV advertising produced a strong effect on brand awareness and recall but little change in consumers' attitudes toward the product. He hypothesized that TV is basically a low-involvement medium and the viewer's perceptual defenses are reduced or even absent during commercials. In a low-involvement situation, the consumer does not compare the message with previously acquired beliefs, needs, or past experiences. The commercial results in subtle changes in the consumer's knowledge structure, particularly with repeated exposure. This change in the consumer's knowledge does not result in attitude change but is related to learning something about the advertised brand, such as a brand name, ad theme, or slogan. According to Krugman, when the consumer enters a purchase situation, this information may be sufficient to trigger a purchase. The consumer will then form an attitude toward the purchased brand as a result of experience with it. Thus, in the low-involvement situation the response sequence is as follows:

Message exposure under low involvement →

Shift in cognitive structure → Purchase →

Positive or negative experience → Attitude formation

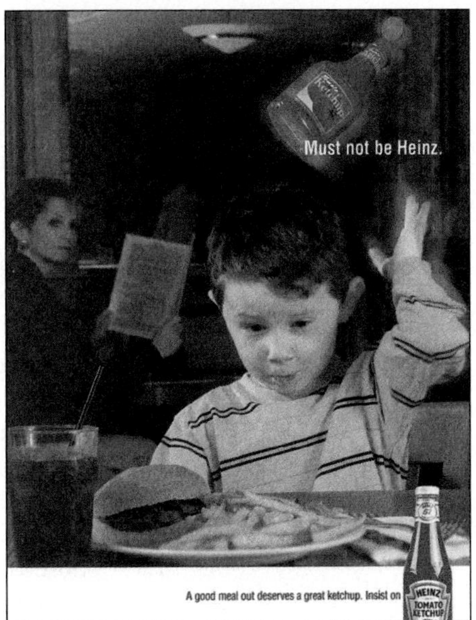

Exhibit 5-9 Advertising promoting taste quality has helped Heinz dominate the ketchup market

In the low-involvement hierarchy, the consumer engages in *passive learning* and *random information catching* rather than active information seeking. The advertiser must recognize that a passive, uninterested consumer may focus more on nonmessage elements such as music, characters, symbols, and slogans or jingles than actual message content. The advertiser might capitalize on this situation by developing a catchy jingle that is stored in the consumer's mind without any active cognitive processing and becomes salient when he or she enters the actual purchase situation.

Advertisers of low-involvement products also repeat simple product claims such as a key copy point or distinctive product benefit. A study by Scott Hawkins and Stephen Hoch found that under low-involvement conditions, repetition of simple product claims increased consumers' memory of and belief in those claims.[18] They concluded that advertisers of low-involvement products might find it more profitable to pursue a heavy repetition strategy than to reach larger audiences with lengthy, more detailed messages. For example, Heinz has dominated the ketchup market for over 20 years by repeatedly telling consumers that its brand is the thickest and richest. Heinz has used a variety of advertising campaigns over the years. However, they all have communicated the same basic message that Heinz is the best and most preferred brand of ketchup (Exhibit 5-9).

Low-involvement advertising appeals prevail in much of the advertising we see for frequently purchased consumer products: Wrigley's Doublemint gum invites consumers to "Double your pleasure." Bounty paper towels claim to be the "quicker picker-upper." Oscar Mayer uses the catchy jingle, "I wish I were an Oscar Mayer wiener." Each of these appeals is designed to help consumers make an association without really attempting to formulate or change an attitude.

Another popular creative strategy used by advertisers of low-involvement products is what advertising analyst Harry McMahan calls *VIP,* or *visual image personality.*[19] Advertisers often use symbols like the Pillsbury doughboy, Morris the cat, Tony the tiger, and Mr. Clean to develop visual images that will lead consumers to identify and retain ads. Eveready began using the pink bunny in ads for its Energizer batteries in 1989, and he has helped sales of the brand keep going and going for nearly 17 years (Exhibit 5-10).

Implications of the Alternative Response Models

Advertising and consumer researchers recognize that not all response sequences and behaviors are explained adequately by either the traditional or the alternative response hierarchies. Advertising is just one source of information consumers use in learning about products, forming attitudes, and/or making a purchase decision. Consumers are likely to integrate information from advertising and other forms of marketing communication as well as direct experience in forming judgments about a brand. For example, a study by Robert Smith found that advertising can lessen the negative effects of an unfavorable trial experience on brand evaluations when the ad is processed before the trial. However, when a negative trial experience precedes exposure to an ad, cognitive evaluations of the ad are more negative.[20] More recent research has also shown that advertising can affect consumers' objective sensory interpretation of their experiences with a brand and what they remember about it.[21]

Exhibit 5-10 The Energizer bunny is a popular personality symbol for the brand

The various response models offer an interesting perspective on the ways consumers respond to advertising and other forms of marketing communications. They also provide insight into promotional strategies marketers might pursue in different situations. A review of these alternative models of the response process shows that the traditional standard learning model does not always apply. The notion of a highly involved consumer who engages in active information processing and learning and acts on the basis of higher-order beliefs and a well-formed attitude may be inappropriate for some types of purchases. Sometimes consumers make a purchase decision on the basis of general awareness resulting from repetitive exposure to advertising, and attitude development occurs after the purchase, if at all. The role of advertising and other forms of promotion may be to induce trial, so consumers can develop brand preferences primarily on the basis of their direct experience with the product.

From a promotional planning perspective, it is important that marketers examine the communication situation for their product or service and determine which type of response process is most likely to occur. They should analyze involvement levels and product/service differentiation as well as consumers' use of various information sources and their levels of experience with the product or service. Once the manager has determined which response sequence is most likely to operate, the integrated marketing communications program can be designed to influence the response process in favor of the company's product or service. Several planning models have been developed that consider involvement levels as well as other factors including response processes and motives that underlie the attitude formation and subsequent brand choice.[22] These models can be of value to managers as they develop strategies for advertising and other forms of marketing communication. We will now examine a popular planning model developed by the Foote Cone & Belding advertising agency, which theorizes that advertising and other promotional tools work differently depending on the type of product involved and the decision process sequence that consumers are likely to follow.

The FCB Planning Model

An interesting approach to analyzing the communication situation comes from the work of Richard Vaughn of the Foote Cone & Belding advertising agency. Vaughn and his associates developed an advertising planning model by building on traditional response theories such as the hierarchy of effects model and its variants and research on high and low involvement.[23] They added the dimension of thinking versus feeling processing at each involvement level by bringing in theories regarding brain specialization. The right/left brain theory suggests the left side of the brain is more capable of rational, cognitive thinking, while the right side is more visual and emotional and engages more in the affective (feeling) functions. Their model, which became known as the FCB grid, delineates four primary advertising planning strategies—informative, affective, habit formation, and satisfaction—along with the most appropriate variant of the alternative response hierarchies (Figure 5-6).

Vaughn suggests that the *informative strategy* is for highly involving products and services where rational thinking and economic considerations prevail and the standard learning hierarchy is the appropriate response model. The *affective strategy* is for highly involving/feeling purchases. For these types of products, advertising should stress psychological and emotional motives such as building self-esteem or enhancing one's ego or self-image.

The *habit formation strategy* is for low-involvement/thinking products with such routinized behavior patterns that learning occurs most often after a trial purchase. The response process for these products is consistent with a behavioristic learning-by-doing model (remember our discussion of operant conditioning in Chapter 4?). The *self-satisfaction strategy* is for low-involvement/feeling products where appeals to sensory pleasures and social motives are important. Again, the do → feel or do → learn hierarchy is operating, since product experience is an important part of the learning process. Vaughn acknowledges that some minimal level of awareness (passive learning) may precede purchase of both types of low-involvement products, but

Figure 5-6 The Foote Cone & Belding (FCB) Grid

	Thinking	Feeling
High involvement	**1. Informative (thinker)** Car–house–furnishings–new products model: Learn–feel–do (economic?) **Possible implications** Test: Recall, Diagnostics Media: Long copy format, Reflective vehicles Creative: Specific information, Demonstration	**2. Affective (feeler)** Jewelry–cosmetics–fashion apparel–motorcycles model: Feel–learn–do (psychological?) **Possible implications** Test: Attitude change, Emotional arousal Media: Large space, Image specials Creative: Executional, Impact
Low involvement	**3. Habit formation (doer)** Food–household items model: Do–learn–feel (responsive?) **Possible implications** Test: Sales Media: Small space ads, 10-second I.D.s, Radio; POS Creative: Reminder	**4. Self-satisfaction (reactor)** Cigarettes–liquor–candy model: Do–feel–learn (social?) **Possible implications** Test: Sales Media: Billboards, Newspapers, POS Creative: Attention

deeper, active learning is not necessary. This is consistent with the low-involvement hierarchy discussed earlier (learn → do → feel).

The FCB grid provides a useful way for those involved in the advertising planning process, such as creative specialists, to analyze consumer–product relationships and develop appropriate promotional strategies. Consumer research can be used to determine how consumers perceive products or brands on the involvement and thinking/feeling dimensions.[24] This information can then be used to develop effective creative options such as using rational versus emotional appeals, increasing involvement levels, or even getting consumers to evaluate a think-type product on the basis of feelings. For example, in recent years appliance companies have been touting the design and image of their products as much as functionality in their advertising. One company that has taken a unique approach to its advertising is Whirlpool whose "Just Imagine" campaign featured Household Goddesses—five ethereal female figures who use water, fire, or air to take control of their environments while promoting various Whirlpool appliances (Exhibit 5-11). The campaign, which originated in Europe and was then adapted to the U.S. market, is designed to connect with the modern "supermoms," working women who have a very demanding and busy lifestyle and want control of their lives. The goal of the ads is to strike an emotional chord with women by showing them as strong females in control of their environment who can be made even stronger through the latest technology found in Whirlpool appliances. The campaign used stylish and dramatic commercials to get consumers to notice Whirlpool appliances and make them believe the brand is in tune with their changing needs and values. IMC Perspective 5-2 discusses how another company, LG Electronics, is using a variety of IMC tools to develop a brand image and to connect with consumers on an emotional level as it enters the U.S. market.

Exhibit 5-11
Whirlpool's advertising connects with consumers on an emotional as well as a rational level

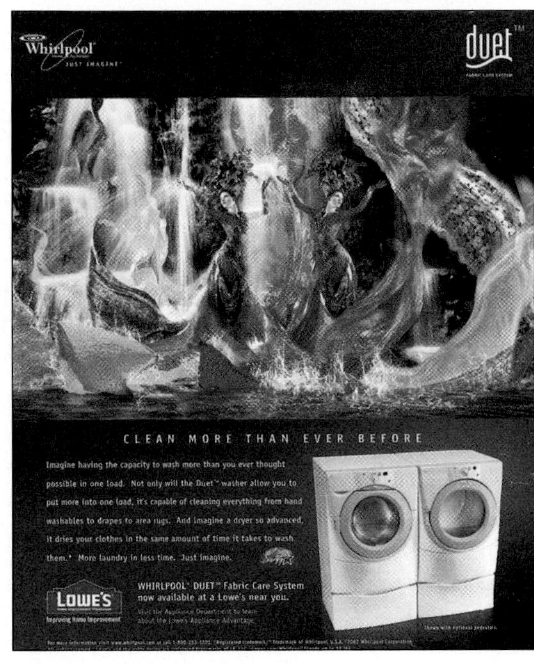

IMC PERSPECTIVE 5-2

LG Plans on Connecting with U.S. Consumers

MUSIC. VIDEO.
Easy As...Rockin' As...Smart as LG.
Carry the ultimate audio-visual experience in your pocket with the VX8100 from LG. Stream, download and play multimedia content on-demand, and enhance your listening experience with powerful stereo speakers that can fill a room with music. It's the true integration of sound and vision.
Available at Verizon Wireless.
LG
Life's Good
www.LGUSA.com

For many years, the consumer electronics market was dominated by Japanese companies including Sony, Panasonic, Fujitsu, and Mitsubishi. However, these companies, as well as others such as Philips Electronics from the Netherlands and U.S.-based Motorola, find themselves up against two other formidable competitors from a country that is rapidly emerging as a major force in a variety of areas. If you are thinking that country is China, think again, as the country is South Korea, the home of two of the fastest growing consumer electronic firms in the world—Samsung Electronics and LG Electronics. While Samsung is currently the better known of the two companies, LG is quickly gaining ground on its Korean counterpart and is taking steps to become a market leader, particularly in the United States.

The company began in 1958 as Goldstar and shortened its name to LG in 1995 to broaden its global appeal. LG is already the world's top manufacturer of household air conditioners, the number-three appliance manufacturer, and a global leader in such products as plasma display panels (PDP) and liquid crystal displays for TVs. Most Americans have probably already used an LG Electronics product, but the name on it was Gateway, Dell, Apple, IBM, or Verizon as the company has made products for these other companies for many years. Now LG is aggressively pursuing market share under its own brand name in the United States, which is the world's largest consumer electronics market, by positioning itself as a manufacturer of stylish, cutting-edge, performance-driven products.

As LG makes its push into the U.S. market, its management recognizes the importance of connecting with consumers on an emotional level and not just promoting the functionality of its products. LG's branding platform in the United States uses the same slogan that the company uses around the world, "Life's Good," which underscores the company's commitment to delivering products that enhance the human experience and help make life better. In 2004, LG initiated a major integrated marketing communications program designed to increase recognition of the company in the United States and to position the company as a digital convergence leader. The company's effort to expand its U.S. footprint began with the unveiling of a $10 million light emitting diode (LED) billboard screen on Times Square in New York City. Another major branding initiative took place at the giant Consumer Electronics show in Las Vegas where LG's happy face logo and phones were plastered on banners a quarter mile in any direction from the convention center. LG was also the lead sponsor of the Freemont Street Experience in downtown Las Vegas, which featured a 90-foot-high, four-block-long electronic canopy where spectacular light and sound shows and live concerts were staged.

The company was a sponsor at the Sundance Film festival where its PDP products were prominently displayed at high-profile venues frequented by celebrities and trendsetters and also has underwritten the restoration of the landmark Wiltern Theater in Los Angeles, which has been renamed the Wiltern LG and features some of the company's most exciting new digital display technologies. Also in 2004, the company launched a five-year, multi-million-dollar sponsorship of action sports, which includes a marketing campaign promoting the new LG Mobile Phone Sports Championships with season-ending competitions for skateboarding, freestyle BMX, motocross, and in-line skating.

A major focus of LG's efforts in the U.S. market is on the marketing of its cellular telephones, an area where the company's world-class designers have helped the company develop a reputation for stylish, functional mobile phones that are becoming very popular among hip, young consumers. Jon Maron, the director of marketing for LG Electronics MobileComm, notes that "increasingly mobile phones are becoming indispensable elements of our lives, representing much more than just a means of voice communication. LG is leading the charge to develop high-quality, feature-packed phones that represent hubs of communication, entertainment and information."

In mid-2005, LG launched an integrated marketing campaign designed to differentiate its phones from its competitors, to educate consumers in the various ways in which its phones fit into their lives, and to provide cross-promotional opportunities with LG wireless carriers and retail partners. The campaign is based on the theme "six degrees" and illustrates the many ways in which LG phones ensure that consumers are constantly in touch with their worlds. The creative marketing features images of trendy, fashionable young adults using LG phones in both traditional and innovative ways such as listening to music, text messaging, and accessing the Internet, all of which illustrate how LG mobile phones can fit into the lives of consumers, keeping them connected, entertained, and informed. The campaign began with spots airing in more than 1,000 movie theaters nationwide and print ads in national and regional print media such as *Entertainment Weekly, Rolling Stone, Jane, Maxim,* and *ESPN Magazine.* The print and cinema ads were followed by spots airing on a variety of network and cable TV outlets.

The "six degrees" integrated campaign also included a Concierge program that provided celebrity influencers with special fittings by experts with the latest LG products as well as customized point-of-sale displays accentuating the advertising theme. The online elements included a Web-based community for LG customers to share tips and reviews of LG products and to enter online promotions and contests as well as online games incorporating LG products and themes, including a game based on the Fox television hit series *24.*

LG's chief executive, Kim Ssang Su, has noted that the company is no longer content with being a second-tier player and wants to be a global market leader. Success in cellular handsets is an important part of the company's strategy as LG managers believe that once consumers have an LG phone in their hands, they're more likely to consider the brand when they are purchasing a TV, refrigerator, or DVD player. While LG is likely to face stiff competition from competitors who defend their market share, it appears that its rivals now have another fast-moving Korean company to contend with. And one that understands the importance of connecting with consumers.

Sources: "LG Electronics MobileCom Launches Integrated Marketing and Advertising Campaign," press release, www.biz.yahoo.com, May 31, 2005; Moon Ihlwan, "Korea's LG May Be the Next Samsung," *BusinessWeek,* January 24, 2005, pp. 51–52; Beth Snyder Bulik, "LG's $100 Mil Charge Apes Samsung Tack," *Advertising Age,* June 21, 2004 pp. 1, 33.

Cognitive Processing of Communications

The hierarchical response models were for many years the primary focus of approaches for studying the receivers' responses to marketing communications. Attention centered on identifying relationships between specific controllable variables (such as source and message factors) and outcome or response variables (such as attention, comprehension, attitudes, and purchase intentions). This approach has been criticized on a number of fronts, including its black-box nature, since it can't explain what is causing these reactions.[25] In response to these concerns, researchers began trying to understand the nature of cognitive reactions to persuasive messages. Several approaches have been developed to examine the nature of consumers' cognitive processing of advertising messages.

The Cognitive Response Approach

One of the most widely used methods for examining consumers' cognitive processing of advertising messages is assessment of their **cognitive responses,** the thoughts that occur to them while reading, viewing, and/or hearing a communication.[26] These thoughts are generally measured by having consumers write down or verbally report their reactions to a message. The assumption is that these thoughts reflect the recipient's cognitive processes or reactions and help shape ultimate acceptance or rejection of the message.

The cognitive response approach has been widely used in research by both academicians and advertising practitioners. Its focus has been to determine the types of responses evoked by an advertising message and how these responses relate to attitudes toward the ad, brand attitudes, and purchase intentions. Figure 5-7 depicts the three basic categories of cognitive responses researchers have identified—product/message, source-oriented, and ad execution thoughts—and how they may relate to attitudes and intentions.

Exhibit 5-12 Consumers often generate support arguments in response to ads for quality products

Product/Message Thoughts

The first category of thoughts comprises those directed at the product or service and/or the claims being made in the communication. Much attention has focused on two particular types of responses, counterarguments and support arguments.

Counterarguments are thoughts the recipient has that are opposed to the position taken in the message. For example, consider the ad for Ultra Tide shown in Exhibit 5-12. A consumer may express disbelief or disapproval of a claim made in an ad. ("I don't believe that any detergent could get that stain out!") Other consumers who see this ad may generate **support arguments,** or thoughts that affirm the claims made in the message. ("Ultra Tide looks like a really good product—I think I'll try it.")

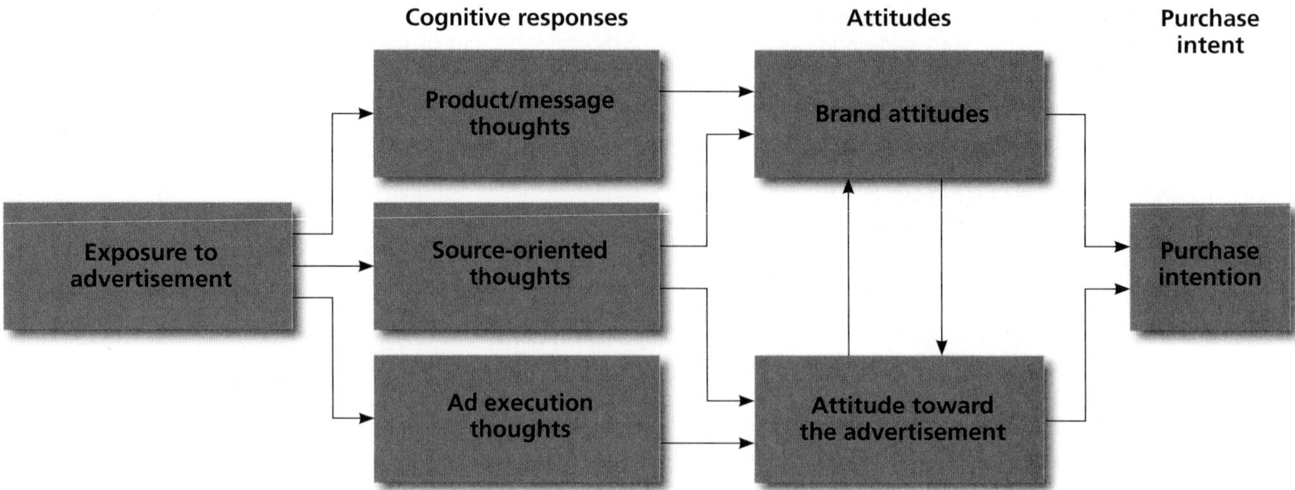

Figure 5-7 A Model of Cognitive Response

The likelihood of counterarguing is greater when the message makes claims that oppose the receiver's beliefs. For example, a consumer viewing a commercial that attacks a favorite brand is likely to engage in counterarguing. Counterarguments relate negatively to message acceptance; the more the receiver counterargues, the less likely he or she is to accept the position advocated in the message.[27] Support arguments, on the other hand, relate positively to message acceptance. Thus, the marketer should develop ads or other promotional messages that minimize counterarguing and encourage support arguments.

Source-Oriented Thoughts A second category of cognitive responses is directed at the source of the communication. One of the most important types of responses in this category is **source derogations,** or negative thoughts about the spokesperson or organization making the claims. Such thoughts generally lead to a reduction in message acceptance. If consumers find a particular spokesperson annoying or untrustworthy, they are less likely to accept what this source has to say.

Of course, source-related thoughts are not always negative. Receivers who react favorably to the source generate favorable thoughts, or **source bolsters.** As you would expect, most advertisers attempt to hire spokespeople their target audience likes so as to carry this effect over to the message. Considerations involved in choosing an appropriate source or spokesperson will be discussed in Chapter 6.

Ad Execution Thoughts The third category of cognitive responses shown in Figure 5-7 consists of the individual's thoughts about the ad itself. Many of the thoughts receivers have when reading or viewing an ad do not concern the product and/or message claims directly. Rather, they are affective reactions representing the consumer's feelings toward the ad. These thoughts may include reactions to ad execution factors such as the creativity of the ad, the quality of the visual effects, colors, and voice tones. **Ad execution-related thoughts** can be either favorable or unfavorable. They are important because of their effect on attitudes toward the advertisement as well as the brand.

In recent years, much attention has focused on consumers' affective reactions to ads, especially TV commercials.[28] **Attitude toward the ad** (A → ad) represents the receivers' feelings of favorability or unfavorability toward the ad. Advertisers are interested in consumers' reactions to the ad because they know that affective reactions are an important determinant of advertising effectiveness, since these reactions may be transferred to the brand itself or directly influence purchase intentions. One study found that people who enjoy a commercial are twice as likely as those who are neutral toward it to be convinced that the brand is the best.[29]

Consumers' feelings about the ad may be just as important as their attitudes toward the brand (if not more so) in determining an ad's effectiveness.[30] The importance of affective reactions and feelings generated by the ad depends on several factors, among

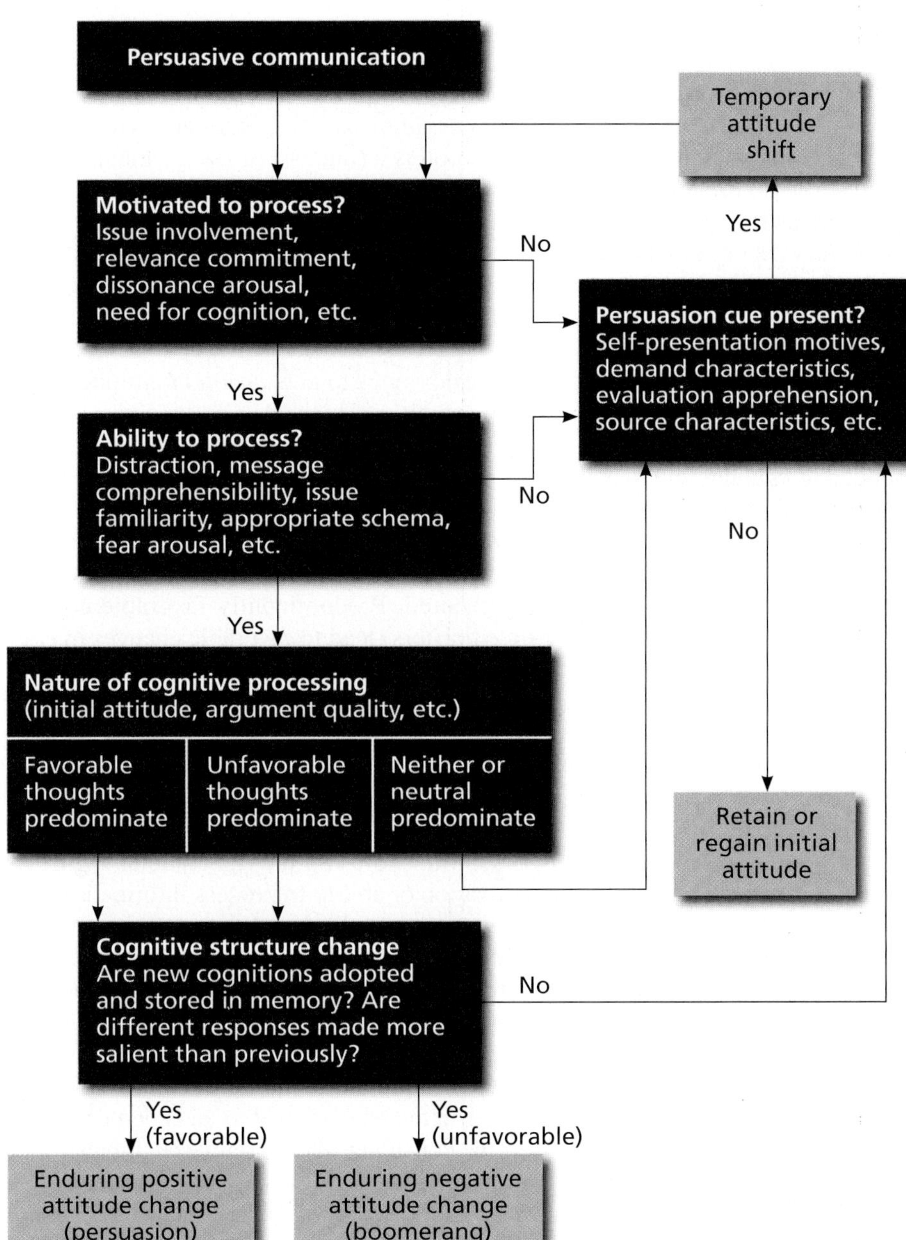

Figure 5-8 The Elaboration Likelihood Model of Persuasion

them the nature of the ad and the type of processing engaged in by the receiver.[31] Many advertisers now use emotional ads designed to evoke feelings and affective reactions as the basis of their creative strategy. The success of this strategy depends in part on the consumers' involvement with the brand and their likelihood of attending to and processing the message.

We end our analysis of the receiver by examining a model that integrates some of the factors that may account for different types and levels of cognitive processing of a message.

The Elaboration Likelihood Model

Differences in the ways consumers process and respond to persuasive messages are addressed in the **elaboration likelihood model (ELM)** of persuasion, shown in Figure 5-8.[32] The ELM was devised by Richard Petty and John Cacioppo to explain the process by which persuasive communications (such as ads) lead to persuasion by influencing *attitudes.* According to this model, the attitude formation or change process depends on the amount and nature of *elaboration,* or processing, of relevant information that occurs in response to a persuasive message. High elaboration means the receiver engages in careful consideration, thinking, and evaluation of the information or arguments contained in the message. Low elaboration occurs when the receiver does not engage in active information processing or thinking but rather makes inferences about the position being advocated in the message on the basis of simple positive or negative cues.

The ELM shows that elaboration likelihood is a function of two elements, motivation and ability to process the message. *Motivation* to process the message depends on such factors as involvement, personal relevance, and individuals' needs and arousal levels. *Ability* depends on the individual's knowledge, intellectual capacity, and opportunity to process the message. For example, an individual viewing a humorous commercial or one containing an attractive model may be distracted from processing the information about the product.

According to the ELM, there are two basic routes to persuasion or attitude change. Under the **central route to persuasion,** the receiver is viewed as a very active, involved participant in the communication process whose ability and motivation to attend, comprehend, and evaluate messages are high. When central processing of an advertising message occurs, the consumer pays close attention to message content and scrutinizes the message arguments. A high level of cognitive response activity or processing occurs, and the ad's ability to persuade the receiver depends primarily on the receiver's evaluation of the quality of the arguments presented. Predominantly favorable cognitive responses (support arguments and source bolsters) lead to favorable changes in cognitive structure, which lead to positive attitude change, or persuasion.

Conversely, if the cognitive processing is predominantly unfavorable and results in counterarguments and/or source derogations, the changes in cognitive structure are unfavorable and *boomerang,* or result in negative attitude change. Attitude change that occurs through central processing is relatively enduring and should resist subsequent efforts to change it.

Under the **peripheral route to persuasion,** shown on the right side of Figure 5-8, the receiver is viewed as lacking the motivation or ability to process information and is not likely to engage in detailed cognitive processing. Rather than evaluating the information presented in the message, the receiver relies on peripheral cues that may be incidental to the main arguments. The receiver's reaction to the message depends on how he or she evaluates these peripheral cues.

The consumer may use several types of peripheral cues or cognitive shortcuts rather than carefully evaluating the message arguments presented in an advertisement.[33] Favorable attitudes may be formed if the endorser in the ad is viewed as an expert or is attractive and/or likable or if the consumer likes certain executional aspects of the ad such as the way it is made, the music, or the imagery. Notice how the ad in Exhibit 5-13 for Maxfli golf balls contains several positive peripheral cues, including a popular celebrity endorser (golfer Fred Couples) and excellent visual imagery. These cues might help consumers form a positive attitude toward the brand even if they do not process the message portion of the ad.

Exhibit 5-13 This ad contains peripheral cues, most notably a celebrity endorser

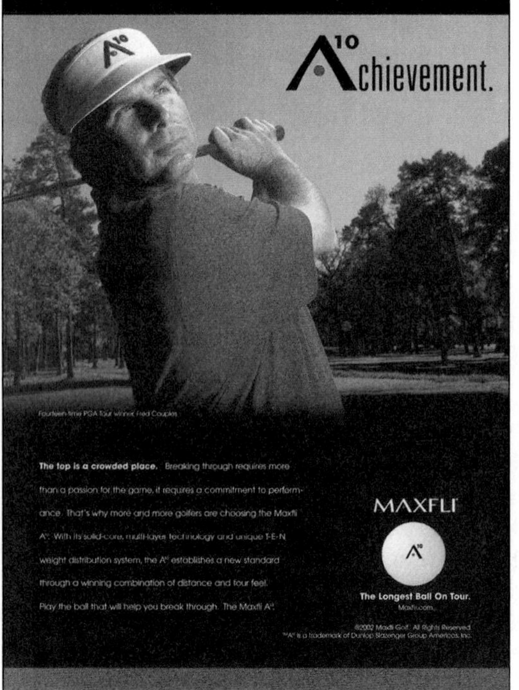

Peripheral cues can also lead to rejection of a message. For example, ads that advocate extreme positions, use endorsers who are not well liked or have credibility problems, or are not executed well (such as low-budget ads for local retailers) may be rejected without any consideration of their information or message arguments. As shown in Figure 5-9, the ELM views attitudes resulting from peripheral processing as temporary. So favorable attitudes must be maintained by continual exposure to the peripheral cues, such as through repetitive advertising.

Implications of the ELM

The elaboration likelihood model has important implications for marketing communications, particularly with respect to involvement. For example, if the involvement level of consumers in the target audience is high, an ad or sales presentation should contain strong arguments that are difficult for the message recipient to refute or counterargue. If the involvement level of the target audience is low, peripheral cues may be more important than detailed message arguments.

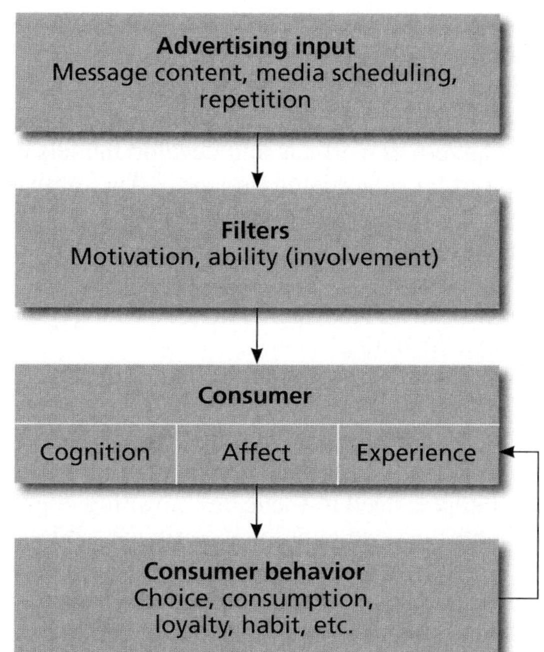

Figure 5-9 A Framework for Studying How Advertising Works

An interesting test of the ELM showed that the effectiveness of a celebrity endorser in an ad depends on the receiver's involvement level.[34] When involvement was low, a celebrity endorser had a significant effect on attitudes. When the receiver's involvement was high, however, the use of a celebrity had no effect on brand attitudes; the quality of the arguments used in the ad was more important.

The explanation given for these findings was that a celebrity may serve as a peripheral cue in the low-involvement situation, allowing the receiver to develop favorable attitudes based on feelings toward the source rather than engaging in extensive processing of the message. A highly involved consumer, however, engages in more detailed central processing of the message content. The quality of the message claims becomes more important than the identity of the endorser.

The ELM suggests that the most effective type of message depends on the route to persuasion the consumer follows. Many marketers recognize that involvement levels are low for their product categories and consumers are not motivated to process advertising messages in any detail. That's why marketers of low-involvement products often rely on creative tactics that emphasize peripheral cues and use repetitive advertising to create and maintain favorable attitudes toward their brand.

Summarizing the Response Process and the Effects of Advertising

As you have seen from our analysis of the receiver, the process consumers go through in responding to marketing communications can be viewed from a number of perspectives. Vakratsas and Ambler recently reviewed more than 250 journal articles and books in an effort to better understand how advertising works and affects the consumer.[35] On the basis of their review of these studies, they concluded that although effects hierarchies have been actively employed for nearly 100 years, there is little support for the concept of a hierarchy of effects in the sense of temporal sequence. They note that in trying to understand the response process and the manner in which advertising works, there are three critical intermediate effects between advertising and purchase (Figure 5-9). These include *cognition,* the "thinking" dimension of a person's response; *affect,* the "feeling" dimension; and *experience,* which is a feedback dimension based on the outcomes of product purchasing and usage. They conclude that individual responses to advertising are mediated or filtered by factors such as motivation and ability to process information, which can radically alter or change the individual's response to advertising. They suggest that the effects of advertising should be evaluated using these three dimensions, with some intermediate variables being more important than others, depending on factors such as the product category, stage of the product life cycle, target audience, competition, and impact of other marketing-mix components.

Other researchers have been critical of the hierarchy models as well. For example, Hall argues that advertisers need to move away from explicit and implicit reliance on hierarchical models of advertising effects and develop models that place affect and experience at the center of the advertising process.[36] The implication of these criticisms is that marketers should focus on cognition, affect, and experience as critical variables that advertising may affect. However, they should not assume a particular sequence of responses but, rather, engage in research and analysis to better understand how advertising and other forms of promotion may affect these intermediate variables in various product/market situations.

While a number of issues and concerns regarding hierarchy of effects models have been noted, many believe that they are of value to advertising practice and research. For example, Thomas Barry contends that despite their limitations, hierarchical models do help predict behavior. He notes that these models also provide insight into whether advertising strategies need to focus on impacting cognition, affect, and/or behavior based on audience or segmentation experiences and they provide valuable planning, training, and conceptual frameworks.[37]

Those responsible for planning the IMC program need to learn as much as possible about their target audience and how it may respond to advertising, along with other forms of marketing communication. For example, William Weilbacher has noted that marketing communications programs include more than just advertising.[38] Consumers are continually immersed in brand-sponsored communications that include public relations, a broad range of sales promotion activities, websites, direct marketing, event sponsorships, movie and TV show product placements, and other forms of marketing communication. He argues that hierarchy models must move beyond just explaining the effects of advertising and consider how, and with what effects, consumers synthesize information from all the various integrated marketing communications activities for a brand. The various models discussed in this chapter are important as they present the basic elements of communication and provide insight into how consumers process and respond to advertising and other IMC tools. It is vital to understand the communications process as it provides a foundation for studying and evaluating integrated marketing communications. Those involved in various aspects of IMC find that understanding the communications process helps them make better decisions in planning, implementing, and evaluating their marketing communication programs.

Summary

The function of all elements of the IMC program is to communicate, so promotional planners must understand the communication process. This process can be very complex; successful marketing communications depend on a number of factors, including the nature of the message, the audience's interpretation of it, and the environment in which it is received. For effective communication to occur, the sender must encode a message in such a way that it will be decoded by the receiver in the intended manner. Feedback from the receiver helps the sender determine whether proper decoding has occurred or whether noise has interfered with the communication process.

Promotional planning begins with the receiver or target audience, as marketers must understand how the audience is likely to respond to various sources of communication or types of messages. For promotional planning, the receiver can be analyzed with respect to both its composition (i.e., individual, group, or mass audiences) and the response process it goes through. A number of models of the response process have been developed including the AIDA, hierarchy of effects, innovation adoption, and information processing model. Different orderings of the traditional response hierarchy include the standard learning, dissonance/attribution, and low-involvement models.

The cognitive response approach examines the thoughts evoked by a message and how they shape the receiver's ultimate acceptance or rejection of the communication. The elaboration likelihood model of attitude formation and change recognizes two forms of message processing, the central and peripheral routes to persuasion, which are a function of the receiver's motivation and ability to process a message. There are three critical intermediate effects between advertising and purchase including cognition, affect, and experience. Those responsible for planning the IMC program should learn as much as possible about their target audience and how it may respond to advertising and other forms of marketing communications.

Key Terms

communication, 137
source, 139
encoding, 139
message, 140
semiotics, 140
channel, 140
word-of-mouth communication, 141
mass media, 141
receiver, 142
decoding, 142
field of experience, 142
noise, 142
response, 142
feedback, 142
AIDA model, 146
hierarchy of effects model, 146
innovation adoption model, 146
information processing model, 147
standard learning model, 149
dissonance/attribution model, 149
low-involvement hierarchy, 150
cognitive responses, 155
counterarguments, 155
support arguments, 155
source derogations, 156
source bolsters, 156
ad execution-related thoughts, 156
attitude toward the ad, 156
elaboration likelihood model (ELM), 157
central route to persuasion, 158
peripheral route to persuasion, 158

Discussion Questions

1. The opening vignette to the chapter discusses how marketers are using buzz marketing to generate word of mouth for their brands. Discuss the pros and cons of buzz marketing techniques. Do you think buzz marketing may lose its impact over time?

2. Discuss some of the ways marketers can deal with communication problems such as mistranslations when developing advertising messages in different languages.

3. Discuss how semiotics can be of value to the study of IMC. Select a marketing stimulus such as an advertisement, package, or other relevant marketing symbol and conduct a semiotic analysis of it.

4. IMC Perspective 5-1 suggests that ageism is a problem in advertising in a number of ways. Do you agree with the position that many advertisers ignore older consumers? Evaluate both sides of this argument.

5. Discuss how the innovation adoption model could be used by a company such as Apple in planning the introduction of a new product such as the iPod Nano.

6. Discuss how marketers of low-involvement products such as soft drinks or paper towels would use various IMC tools differently than a marketer of a high-involvement product such as a personal computer or automobile.

7. Choose one of the four advertising planning strategies identified by the FCB grid shown in Figure 5-6. Find an example of an advertisement that you feel is a good example of this ad planning strategy and explain why.

8. IMC Perspective 5-2 discusses how LG Electronics is building its brand image in the U.S. market. Evaluate LG's use of various integrated marketing tools to build an image for its mobile phones and other products.

9. Explain what is meant by a central versus peripheral route to persuasion and the factors that might determine when each might be used by consumers in response to an advertisement or other form of marketing communication.

10. Evaluate the arguments for and against the use of hierarchical response models for planning advertising and overall IMC programs.

Source, Message, and Channel Factors

6

Chapter Objectives

1. To study the major variables in the communication system and how they influence consumers' processing of promotional messages.
2. To examine the considerations involved in selecting a source or communicator of a promotional message.
3. To examine different types of message structures and appeals that can be used to develop a promotional message.
4. To consider how the channel or medium used to deliver a promotional message influences the communication process.

Paris Hilton Heats Things Up for Carl's Jr.

The Carl's Jr. fast-food hamburger chain originated in southern California in 1941 and now has more than 1,000 stores throughout the western United States. Carl's Jr. is now part of CKE Restaurants, Inc. (CKE), which also includes the Hardee's, La Salsa Fresh Mexican Grill, and Green Burrito restaurant brands. However, as a regional player in the fast-food business, Carl's Jr. and the other brands have nowhere near the number of locations, sales, or market share of its major competitors such as McDonald's, Burger King, and Wendy's. Having lower sales means that Carl's also has less money to spend on advertising, so the company has to get more bang for its advertising buck. As Claudia Caplan, the chief marketing officer for Mendelsohn Zien Advertising, the agency for Carl's Jr., notes: "We're never going to have McDonald's or Burger King's budget. Whatever we do has to have an effect that is multiplied over several platforms. It needs to be more than just a television commercial."

In May 2005 the agency found a way to create a TV commercial that indeed was more than just a commercial and could be leveraged over several platforms when it created a spot featuring Paris Hilton. The granddaughter of hotel magnate Barron Hilton, Paris became an Internet legend when a sex videotape shot by a boyfriend showed up on the Web. She later starred in the Fox reality show *The Simple Life,* which featured the 24-year-old heiress and a friend living on a farm and doing ordinary jobs. Although many in the "celebrity business" argue that she has become famous merely for being famous, Hilton has also built herself into a multi-million-dollar empire and brand. She has written a book, cut an album, had a starring role in a movie, and has a popular jewelry line with Amazon.com as well as a namesake fragrance.

When Carl's Jr. and its sister chain Hardee's, which has more than 2,000 restaurants throughout the Midwest and Southeast, decided to introduce a new menu item called the Spicy BBQ Six Dollar Burger, the company and its agency decided that featuring Paris Hilton in the commercial would be a great way to launch it. The commercial featured Hilton wearing a designer swimsuit and cavorting with a water hose as she washes a black Bentley automobile. After a sensuous sudsing of the car and herself, she takes a bite of the new hamburger as the image fades to a tagline echoing the two-word mantra, "That's hot." The spot is set to a sultry version of Cole Porter's classic song, "I Love Paris in the Springtime."

CKE's executive vice president of marketing, Brad Haley, noted that "Paris was chosen to star in the ad because she is an intriguing cultural icon and the 'it girl' of the moment. She fascinates Carl's Jr.'s most loyal customers, young hungry guys, as well as young hungry girls. The ad plays more like a music video than a typical television commercial. And the message is very simple: Paris, the situation and the Spicy BBQ Six Dollar Burger are hot." Carl's Jr. and its agency also found ways to leverage the Paris Hilton commercial across multiple platforms. Knowing the media's infatuation with Hilton, they were able to generate an extensive amount of publicity for the spot. About a week before airing the commercial, Carl's Jr. issued a press release revealing its plans to use Hilton in a racy spot to promote the Spicy BBQ Burger. Nearly 80 stories appeared in local and national media as rumors began about the spot and were picked up by the Associated Press. The commercial premiered on *Entertainment Tonight* with a sneak preview that included behind-the-scenes footage from the filming of the ad. The spot, along with a special video, were made available via satellite immediately after its debut and photos were provided to the media on a website.

The platform for the commercial also included the Internet. Two days after the debut of the ad, Carl's Jr. and Hardee's launched a website (www.spicyparis.com) showcasing the Paris Hilton commercial as well as footage and still shots from the filming of the spot along with a special Internet-only version of the ad. Visitors immediately flooded the site, which was unequipped to handle the unexpected traffic volume, and the host servers crashed for four hours. The website also included interviews with Hilton along with company and agency executives as well as promotional offers and downloads such as pictures and screen savers of various scenes from the spot.

While the ad featuring Hilton initially was used only for Carl's Jr. and was limited to western markets, it immediately began generating controversy across the country. The president of Morality in Media argued that the spot was "too hot for TV" while the research director for the Parents Television Council stated that "this commercial is basically soft-core porn and inappropriate for television." Both groups urged the Federal Communications Commission to ban the commercial, which brought even more attention to the controversy and generated millions of dollars worth of free media coverage as well as more visitors to the websites. Brad Haley of Carl's Jr. estimated that the publicity would rival the $16 million media budget for the TV campaign. A month after the ad debuted for Carl's Jr., the company began using the spot in the Midwest and Southeast to promote Hardee's Spicy BBQ Thickburger, which spurred another round of protests, as well as publicity.

Marketing and advertising experts have debated the value of the Paris Hilton ad. Critics argued that while the spot might be remembered and generate a short-term spike in sales, it could ultimately damage the image of Carl's Jr. and Hardee's because the restaurants have to attract the mainstream market, which includes families. However, Claudia Caplan noted that the agency designed the commercial to play off Hilton's existing notoriety and to grab the attention of 18- to 34-year-old men, which is the core demographic market for the restaurants. In the 10 years that Mendelsohn Zien has handled the advertising for Carl's Jr., the agency has become well-known for pushing the envelope to appeal to this core target market. Although some believe that they may have pushed a little too far this time, others argue that the use of Paris Hilton in the campaign for the Spicy BBQ Burger was very astute marketing and a great way to leverage a relatively small advertising budget.

Sources: Kate Macarthur, "Don't Read This Story—It's a PR Ploy," *Advertising Age,* May 30, 2005, pp. 1, 53; Meg James, "Critics Are Saying 'That's Too Hot' of Sexy Carl's Jr. Ad," *Los Angeles Times,* May 24, 2005, p. C1; "Explosive Response to Paris Hilton Ad Crashes Carl's Jr. Web Site," press release, Carlsjr.com, May 23, 2005.

In this chapter, we analyze the major variables in the communication system: the source, the message, and the channel. We examine the characteristics of sources, how they influence reactions to promotional messages, and why one type of communicator is more effective than another. We then focus on the message itself and how structure and type of appeal influence its effectiveness. Finally, we consider how factors related to the channel or medium affect the communication process.

Promotional Planning through the Persuasion Matrix

To develop an effective advertising and promotional campaign, a firm must select the right spokesperson to deliver a compelling message through appropriate channels or media. Source, message, and channel factors are controllable elements in the communications model. The **persuasion matrix** (Figure 6-1) helps marketers see how each controllable element interacts with the consumer's response process.[1] The matrix has two sets of variables. *Independent variables* are the controllable components of the communication process, outlined in Chapter 5; *dependent variables* are the steps a receiver goes through in being persuaded. Marketers can choose the person or source who delivers the message, the type of message appeal used, and the channel or medium. And although they can't control the receiver, they can select their target audience. The destination variable is included because the initial message recipient may pass on information to others, such as friends or associates, through word of mouth.

Promotional planners need to know how decisions about each independent variable influence the stages of the response hierarchy so that they don't enhance one stage at the expense of another. A humorous message may gain attention but result in decreased comprehension if consumers fail to process its content. Many ads that use humor, sexual appeals, or celebrities capture consumers' attention but result in poor recall of the brand name or message. The following examples, which correspond to the numbers in Figure 6-1, illustrate decisions that can be evaluated with the persuasion matrix.

1. *Receiver/comprehension: Can the receiver comprehend the ad?* Marketers must know their target market to make their messages clear and understandable. A less educated person may have more difficulty interpreting a complicated message. Jargon may be unfamiliar to some receivers. The more marketers know about the target market, the more they see which words, symbols, and expressions their customers understand.

2. *Channel/presentation: Which media will increase presentation?* A top-rated, prime-time TV program is seen by nearly 12 million households each week. Popular magazines such as *TV Guide* and *Reader's Digest* reach nearly 10 million homes with

Figure 6-1 The Persuasion Matrix

	Independent variables: The communication components				
Dependent variables: Steps in being persuaded	Source	Message	Channel	Receiver	Destination
Message presentation			(2)		
Attention	(4)				
Comprehension				(1)	
Yielding		(3)			
Retention					
Behavior					

each issue. But the important point is how well they reach the marketer's target audience. CNN's financial show *Lou Dobbs Moneyline* reaches only around a million viewers each weekday evening, but its audience consists mostly of upscale businesspeople who are prime prospects for expensive cars, financial services, and business-related products.

3. *Message/yielding: What type of message will create favorable attitudes or feelings?* Marketers generally try to create agreeable messages that lead to positive feelings toward the product or service. Humorous messages often put consumers in a good mood and evoke positive feelings that may become associated with the brand being advertised. Music adds emotion that makes consumers more receptive to the message. Many advertisers use explicit sexual appeals designed to arouse consumers or suggest they can enhance their attractiveness to the opposite sex. Some marketers compare their brands to the competition.

4. *Source/attention: Who will be effective in getting consumers' attention?* The large number of ads we are bombarded with every day makes it difficult for advertisers to break through the clutter. Marketers deal with this problem by using sources who will attract the target audience's attention—actors, athletes, rock stars, or attractive models. For example, Carl's Jr. commercial discussed in the opening vignette used Paris Hilton to break through the clutter and attract the attention of TV viewers.

Source Factors

The source component is a multifaceted concept. When Tiger Woods appears in a commercial for Nike, is the source Woods himself, the company, or some combination of the two? And, of course, consumers get information from friends, relatives, and neighbors; in fact, personal sources may be the most influential factor in a purchase decision. Word-of-mouth information transmitted from one individual to another is often perceived as more reliable and trustworthy than that received through more formal marketing channels such as advertising. As was discussed in Chapter 5, marketers are using buzz and stealth marketing methods to generate favorable word-of-mouth discussion and recommendations for their products and services.[2]

We use the term **source** to mean the person involved in communicating a marketing message, either directly or indirectly. A *direct source* is a spokesperson who delivers a message and/or demonstrates a product or service, like tennis star Andre Agassi who endorses Head tennis rackets in Exhibit 6-1. An *indirect source,* say, a model, doesn't actually deliver a message but draws attention to and/or enhances the appearance of the ad. Some ads use neither a direct nor an indirect source; the source is the organization with the message to communicate. Since most research focuses on individuals as a message source, our examination of source factors follows this approach.

Exhibit 6-1 Tennis star Andre Agassi serves as a spokesperson for Head

Companies are very careful when selecting individuals to deliver their selling messages. Many firms spend huge sums of money for a specific person to endorse their product or company. They also spend millions recruiting, selecting, and training salespeople to represent the company and deliver sales presentations. They recognize that the characteristics of the source affect the sales and advertising message.

Marketers try to select individuals whose traits will maximize message influence. The source may be knowledgeable, popular, and/or physically attractive; typify the target audience; or have the power to reward or punish the receiver in some manner. Herbert Kelman developed three basic categories of source attributes: credibility, attractiveness, and power.[3] Each influences the recipient's attitude or behavior through a different process (see Figure 6-2).

Source Credibility

Credibility is the extent to which the recipient sees the source as having relevant knowledge, skill, or experience and trusts the

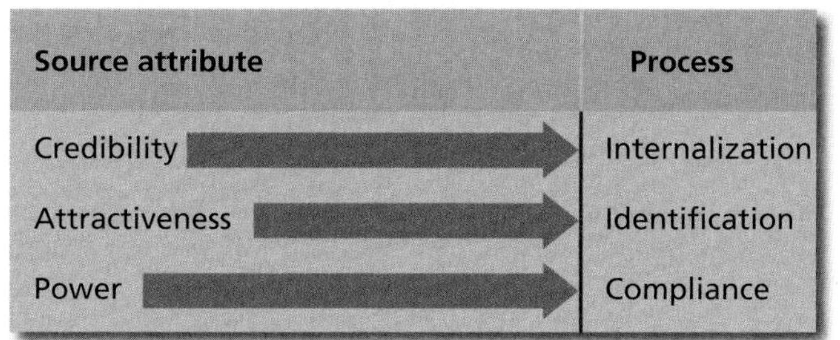

Source attribute
Process
Credibility
Internalization
Attractiveness
Identification
Power
Compliance

Figure 6-2 Source Attributes and Receiver Processing Modes

source to give unbiased, objective information. There are two important dimensions to credibility, expertise and trustworthiness.

A communicator seen as knowledgeable—someone with expertise—is more persuasive than one with less expertise. But the source also has to be trustworthy—honest, ethical, and believable. The influence of a knowledgeable source will be lessened if audience members think he or she is biased or has underlying personal motives for advocating a position (such as being paid to endorse a product).

One of the most reliable effects found in communications research is that expert and/or trustworthy sources are more persuasive than sources who are less expert or trustworthy.[4] Information from a credible source influences beliefs, opinions, attitudes, and/or behavior through a process known as **internalization,** which occurs when the receiver adopts the opinion of the credible communicator since he or she believes information from this source is accurate. Once the receiver internalizes an opinion or attitude, it becomes integrated into his or her belief system and may be maintained even after the source of the message is forgotten.

A highly credible communicator is particularly important when message recipients have a negative position toward the product, service, company, or issue being promoted, because the credible source is likely to inhibit counterarguments. As discussed in Chapter 5, reduced counterarguing should result in greater message acceptance and persuasion.

Applying Expertise

Because attitudes and opinions developed through an internalization process become part of the individual's belief system, marketers want to use communicators with high credibility. Companies use a variety of techniques to convey source expertise. Sales personnel are trained in the product line, which increases customers' perceptions of their expertise. Marketers of highly technical products recruit sales reps with specialized technical backgrounds in engineering, computer science, and other areas to ensure their expertise.

Spokespeople are often chosen because of their knowledge, experience, and expertise in a particular product or service area. Endorsements from individuals or groups recognized as experts, such as doctors or dentists, are also common in advertising (Exhibit 6-2). The importance of using expert sources was shown in a study by Roobina Ohanian, who found that the perceived expertise of celebrity endorsers was more important in explaining purchase intentions than their attractiveness or trustworthiness. She suggests that celebrity spokespeople are most effective when they are knowledgeable, experienced, and qualified to talk about the product they are endorsing.[5]

Exhibit 6-2 Dove promotes the fact that it is recommended by experts in skin care

Applying Trustworthiness

While expertise is important, the target audience must also find the source believable. Finding celebrities or other figures with a trustworthy image is often difficult. Many trustworthy public figures hesitate to endorse products because of the potential impact on their reputation and image. It has been suggested that former CBS news anchor Walter Cronkite, who has repeatedly been rated one of the most trusted people in America, could command millions of dollars as a product spokesperson. Global Perspective 6-1 discusses how some American celebrities protect their image by endorsing products in Japan rather than in the United States.

GLOBAL PERSPECTIVE 6-1

Celebrities Sell Out—But Only in Japan

While many celebrities make huge sums of money endorsing products and serving as advertising spokespeople, some big stars won't appear in ads in the United States as they don't want fans to think they've sold out. There has also long been a feeling among actors and actresses that appearing in commercials might devalue their image among the powerful Hollywood producers and directors. However, this has been changing in recent years as even some of the biggest names in entertainment have decided to cash in on their celebrity and appear in commercials. For example, Nicole Kidman was paid $8 million to appear in commercials for the Chanel No. 5 fragrance line for one year while Catherine Zeta-Jones is getting $20 million for four years to appear for the wireless service provider T-Mobile. And Brad Pitt was paid an estimated $1 million for one airing of a Heineken commercial during the 2005 Super Bowl that showed him dodging paparazzi on his way to pick up a six-pack of the Dutch beer.

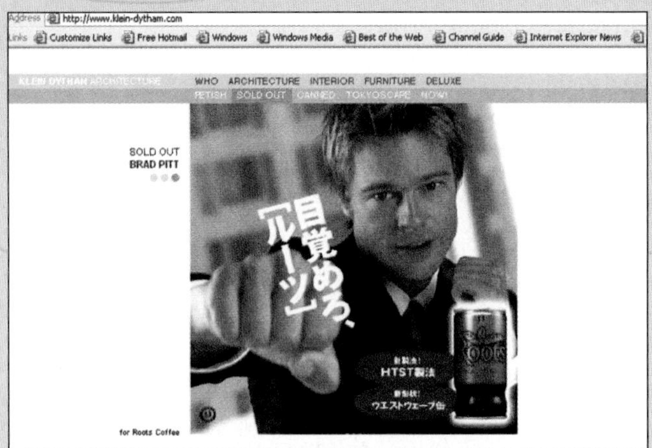

While some of the A-list celebrities still resist the temptation to cash in on their fame in the United States, they are only too happy to appear in ads in foreign countries. And nowhere are ads starring American celebrities more prevalent than in Japan. Even the rich and famous have trouble saying no to Japanese advertisers who will pay them between $1 million to $3 million for a few hours' work to make 10-second spots that their Western fans across the Pacific will never see. In Japan, celebrities make more money for less work and because the commercials will never air in the United States, they think they can make the money without looking like they are selling their artistic souls.

Megastars such as Charlize Theron, Brad Pitt, Sean Connery, and Harrison Ford are paid millions for appearing in Japanese commercials. Theron has appeared in an ad for Honda and for Lux bath products, while Ford received several million dollars for appearing sweaty and bare-chested in Kirin beer commercials and print ads. Pitt has appeared in ads for canned coffee and blue jeans, former Beatle Ringo Starr has promoted an apple drink, and David Bowie has advertised Vittel water. Sometimes celebrities are forced to change their images or personalities to suit the advertising style of Japanese companies and the tastes of audiences in Japan. Japanese commercials have a totally different feel than those in the United States and Europe and have often been described as "tacky" or "cheesy" by Western standards. For example, one ad showed actor Dennis Hopper sitting in a tub with a rubber ducky to promote a brand of shampoo and body wash while, in another, Sean Connery was shown carrying a ham into a room to a James Bond tune. Many of the commercials show a myriad of images of the celebrities during the short spots, putting even the best music video editors to shame.

There are several reasons why Japanese companies are willing to shell out huge sums of money for these stars. Many Japanese are fascinated by American culture and its celebrities, and endorsement of a brand by a star gives it a certain international cachet. Also, Japanese advertising emphasizes style and mood rather than substance; consumers expect to be entertained rather than bored by product information or testimonials. Because most Japanese commercials last only 10 seconds, advertisers think that an instantly recognizable Western celebrity who can capture viewers' attention is well worth the money. Some movie studios also encourage celebrities to do commericals in Japan because it boosts their visibility and helps the marketing of their films in Japan and other Asian markets.

While many celebrities are cashing in on endorsement deals in Japan, they still try to protect their image at home. For example, the stars commonly have nondisclosure clauses in their contracts, specifying that the ads cannot be shown—or sometimes even discussed (oops!)—outside of Japan. However, with the growth of the Internet, such blatant moneymaking is no longer a secret. A small Canadian Web company, Zero One Design, is dedicated to showing U.S. celebrities pitching products in Japan at gaijinagogo.com and a Vancouver-based English teacher runs the spots on his Japander.com website. Recently, several celebrities, including Arnold Schwarzenegger, Meg Ryan, and Leonardo DiCaprio, threatened legal action against the sites for showing their commercials, arguing that they infringed on the star's intellectual property rights.

Audiences also saw how stars sometimes appear in Japanese commercials through the Oscar-winning film *Lost in Translation,* in which Bill Murray plays an out-of-luck, self-loathing actor who goes to Japan to advertise whiskey. The actors and actresses who actually appear in ads in Japan are hardly down and out. However, they are used to getting their way, and most want the knowledge of their Japanese endorsements to stay across the Pacific. Sorry about that.

Sources: Sasha Haines-Stiles, "And Hello, A-Listers!," *Forbes,* July 4, 2005, p. 60; Hugh Davies, "Pitt's Five Million Reasons to Do a Beer Advert," news.telegraph.co.uk, May 2, 2005; Debra Lau, "Movie Stars Moonlight in Japan," Forbes.com, March 14, 2001.

Advertisers use various techniques to increase the perception that their sources are trustworthy. Hidden cameras are used to show that the consumer is not a paid spokesperson and is making an objective evaluation of the product. Disguised brands are compared. (Of course, the sponsor's brand always performs better than the consumer's regular brand, and he or she is always surprised.) Advertisers also use the overheard-conversation technique to enhance trustworthiness. This involves creating a situation in a commercial where a person is shown overhearing a conversation in which favorable claims are made about a product or service. Most consumers are skeptical of these techniques, so they may have limited value in enhancing perceptions of an advertiser's credibility.

Marketers can also deal with the source-trustworthiness issue by using other IMC tools such as publicity. Information received from sources such as newscasters is often very influential because these individuals are perceived as unbiased and thus more credible, even though they are often presenting stories that stem from press releases. In some situations celebrities may appear on news programs or talk shows and promote an upcoming cause or event such as the release of a new movie or music CD. With the increase in stealth marketing techniques, many consumers are becoming wary of endorsements made by celebrities on news programs and talk shows. For example, a *New York Times* article revealed that drug companies were making payments to celebrities or their favorite charities in return for the celebrities' touting the companies' pharmaceutical products on news and talk shows. As a result of the controversy from the article, CNN and the major broadcast networks announced that they would disclose any such financial deals during an interview.[6]

Concerns over potential bias in touting a product or service can involve more than celebrities. Several so-called consumer advocates and product experts have been criticized for giving favorable reviews and/or promoting specific products on local and national TV news programs and other shows without disclosing that they were being paid by the companies to mention their brands. Concern has been expressed over the practice as most television shows present the information presented by trend and fashion gurus or individuals with expertise in areas such as consumer electronics as unbiased and based solely on their expertise. However, the presentation is misleading to consumers if the experts have been paid to mention the products.[7]

Using Corporate Leaders as Spokespeople Another way of enhancing source credibility is to use the company president or chief executive officer as a spokesperson in the firm's advertising. Many companies believe the use of their president or CEO is the ultimate expression of the company's commitment to quality and customer service. For some firms, the use of a president or CEO in their ads can help create an identity and personality for the company and/or brand. For example, Richard Branson's irreverence and zeal for life have helped personify the image of Virgin's empire of megastores, airlines, mobile phones, and soft drinks. Branson has been used occasionally in ads for various Virgin brands. As the executive director of global brand consulting firm Enterprise IG notes: "The CEO is the absolute bottom line for a company. There's a lot of power in that."[8] There have been cases where ad campaigns featuring CEOs have not only increased sales but also helped turn the company leaders into celebrities.[9] Lee Iacocca appeared in more than 60 commercials for Chrysler Corp. and became a national business hero for guiding the successful turnaround of the company. In 2005 Chrysler brought back Iacocca to be the pitchman in ads for its "Employee Pricing Plus" program. One of the most popular corporate spokespersons ever was Dave Thomas, the founder of Wendy's fast-food restaurants. Thomas appeared in more than 800 ads for Wendy's between 1989 and early 2002 when he passed away[10] (Exhibit 6-3). Other well-known corporate leaders who sometimes appear in ads for their companies include Dell computer founder Michael Dell; August Busch IV, CEO of

Exhibit 6-3 Dave Thomas was a very effective spokesperson for Wendy's for many years

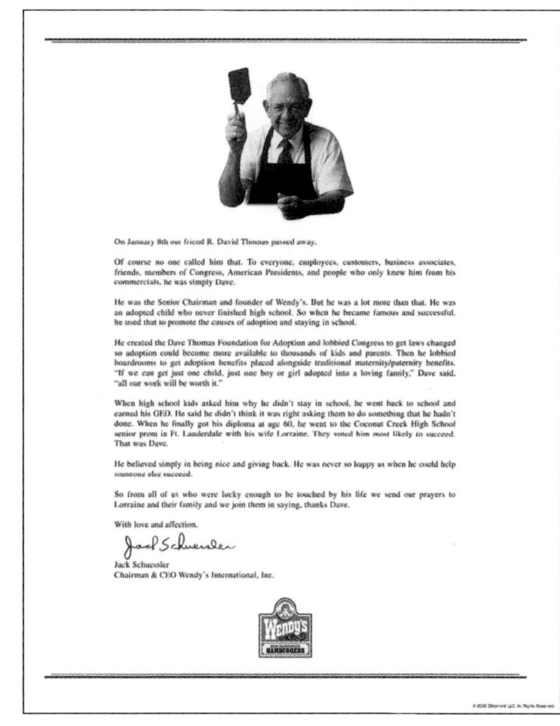

Anheuser-Busch; and Peter Coors, who is the former CEO of the Coors Brewing Co. The practice of using company founders, owners, and presidents as advertising spokespersons is particularly prevalent among small and mid-size companies such as retailers and auto dealers serving local markets. For these companies, the decision to have the owner or president become a quasi actor has to do with advertising budgets too small to accommodate professional actors or announcers, who may charge thousands of dollars to tape a few commercials.

Many marketing and advertising experts question the strategy of using company presidents or owners in ads and note that it is often ego rather than logic that results in their use.[11] The experts suggest that businesspeople should get in front of the camera only if they exude credibility and possess the intangible quality of provoking a warm, fuzzy feeling in viewers. Another concern is that creating an image or culture around the CEO can make the corporate brand image more vulnerable if the individual becomes involved in any type of controversy such as a labor dispute, political issue, or personal problem. Critics of the practice also note that CEO spokespeople who become very popular may get more attention than their company's product/service or advertising message. And if a firm's image becomes too closely tied to a popular leader, there can be problems if that person leaves the company. For example, Wendy's had a difficult time replacing Dave Thomas, who had become an advertising icon and was the voice and personality of the company.[12]

Major corporations are likely to continue to use their top executives in their advertising, particularly when they have celebrity value that helps enhance the firm's image. Some research suggests the use of a company president or CEO can improve attitudes and increase the likelihood that consumers will inquire about a company's product or service.[13] Defenders of the practice argue that the use of top executives or business owners in ads is an effective way of projecting an image of trust and honesty and, more important, the idea that the company isn't run by some faceless corporate monolith. As one expert notes: "These guys come into people's living rooms every night and, over the course of weeks and years, become like members of the family. It gets to the point that when you think of a certain product category, you think of the guy you see all the time on TV."[14]

Limitations of Credible Sources

Several studies have shown that a high-credibility source is not always an asset, nor is a low-credibility source always a liability. High- and low-credibility sources are equally effective when they are arguing for a position opposing their own best interest.[15] A very credible source is more effective when message recipients are not in favor of the position advocated in the message.[16] However, a very credible source is less important when the audience has a neutral position, and such a source may even be less effective than a moderately credible source when the receiver's initial attitude is favorable.[17]

Another reason a low-credibility source may be as effective as a high-credibility source is the **sleeper effect,** whereby the persuasiveness of a message increases with the passage of time. The immediate impact of a persuasive message may be inhibited because of its association with a low-credibility source. But with time, the association of the message with the source diminishes and the receiver's attention focuses more on favorable information in the message, resulting in more support arguing. However, many studies have failed to demonstrate the presence of a sleeper effect.[18] Many advertisers hesitate to count on the sleeper effect, since exposure to a credible source is a more reliable strategy.[19]

Source Attractiveness

A source characteristic frequently used by advertisers is **attractiveness,** which encompasses similarity, familiarity, and likability.[20] *Similarity* is a supposed resemblance between the source and the receiver of the message, while *familiarity* refers to knowledge of the source through exposure. *Likability* is an affection for the source as a result of physical appearance, behavior, or other personal traits. Even when the sources are not athletes or movie stars, consumers often admire their physical appearance, talent, and/or personality.

Source attractiveness leads to persuasion through a process of **identification,** whereby the receiver is motivated to seek some type of relationship with the source and thus adopts similar beliefs, attitudes, preferences, or behavior. Maintaining this position depends on the source's continued support for the position as well as the receiver's continued identification with the source. If the source changes position, the receiver may also change. Unlike internalization, identification does not usually integrate information from an attractive source into the receiver's belief system. The receiver may maintain the attitudinal position or behavior only as long as it is supported by the source or the source remains attractive.

Marketers recognize that receivers of persuasive communications are more likely to attend to and identify with people they find likable or similar to themselves. Similarity and likability are the two source characteristics marketers seek when choosing a communicator.

Applying Similarity

Marketers recognize that people are more likely to be influenced by a message coming from someone with whom they feel a sense of similarity.[21] If the communicator and receiver have similar needs, goals, interests, and lifestyles, the position advocated by the source is better understood and received. Similarity is used in various ways in marketing communications. Companies select salespeople whose characteristics match well with their customers'. A sales position for a particular region may be staffed by someone local who has background and interests in common with the customers. Global marketers often hire foreign nationals as salespeople so customers can relate more easily to them.

Companies may also try to recruit former athletes to sell sporting goods or beer, since their customers usually have a strong interest in sports. Several studies have shown that customers who perceive a salesperson as similar to themselves are more likely to be influenced by his or her message.[22]

Similarity is also used to create a situation where the consumer feels empathy for the person shown in the commercial. In a slice-of-life commercial, the advertiser usually starts by presenting a predicament with the hope of getting the consumer to think, "I can see myself in that situation." This can help establish a bond of similarity between the communicator and the receiver, increasing the source's level of persuasiveness. Many companies feel that the best way to connect with consumers is by using regular-looking, everyday people with whom the average person can easily identify. For example, some of the most popular commercials in previous years have been those from the "Whassup?" campaign for Budweiser beer. In these ads the agency cast a group of real-life friends from Philadelphia, rather than actors, who greet each other with an exaggerated "Whassup?" when they speak with one another or get together to watch a game and enjoy a Bud.

Exhibit 6-4 Maria Sharapova has endorsement contracts with a number of companies including Nike, Canon, Motorola, and Tag Heuer

Applying Likability: Using Celebrities

Advertisers recognize the value of using spokespeople who are admired: TV and movie stars, athletes, musicians, and other popular public figures. It is estimated that nearly 20 percent of all TV commercials feature celebrities, and advertisers pay hundreds of millions of dollars for their services. The top celebrity endorser is golfer Tiger Woods, who makes an estimated $80 million a year from endorsement contracts with Nike, American Express, Accenture, Buick, and several other companies. Former basketball star Michael Jordan is still one of the highest-paid and most sought after endorsers among athletes along with soccer star David Beckham and cyclist Lance Armstrong. For women, the top endorser is tennis star Maria Sharapova, who has endorsement deals with a number of companies including Nike, Canon, Tag Heuer, and Colgate-Palmolive[23] (Exhibit 6-4). Other top female endorsers include actress and singers Jennifer Lopez and Jessica Simpson, tennis players Venus and Serena Williams, and golfer Annika Sørenstram.

Why do companies spend huge sums to have celebrities appear in their ads and endorse their products? They think celebrities have *stopping power.* That is, they draw attention to advertising messages in a very cluttered media environment. Marketers think a popular celebrity will favorably influence consumers' feelings, attitudes, and purchase behavior. And they believe celebrities can enhance the target audience's perceptions of the product in terms of image and/or performance. For example, a well-known athlete may convince potential buyers that the product will enhance their own performance.

A number of factors must be considered when a company decides to use a celebrity spokesperson, including the dangers of overshadowing the product and being overexposed, the target audience's receptivity, and risks to the advertiser.

Overshadowing the Product How will the celebrity affect the target audience's processing of the advertising message? Consumers may focus their attention on the celebrity and fail to notice the brand. Advertisers should select a celebrity spokesperson who will attract attention and enhance the sales message, yet not overshadow the brand. For example, Chrysler Corp. chose singer Celine Dion to appear in ads for various brands including the Pacifica sport wagon, Crossfire sports coupe, and Town & Country minivan and also signed on as the sponsor of her Las Vegas show "A New Day." She starred in a number of lavish TV commercials that were part of Chrysler's "Drive & Love" campaign, which was developed to give Chrysler a more upscale image and help achieve a premium positioning for the brand. However, the campaign was not successful as it was believed that her celebrity persona overshadowed the products and did more to sell her than the cars.[24]

Overexposure Consumers are often skeptical of endorsements because they know the celebrities are being paid.[25] This problem is particularly pronounced when a celebrity endorses too many products or companies and becomes overexposed. For example, cyclist Lance Armstrong has endorsement contracts with nearly 20 different companies, including Discovery Communications, Nike, PowerBar, General Mills, Oakley, and many others, and has limited his endorsements so he does not become overexposed.[26] Advertisers can protect themselves against overexposure with an exclusivity clause limiting the number of products a celebrity can endorse. However, such clauses are usually expensive, and most celebrities agree not to endorse similar products anyway. Many celebrities, knowing their fame is fleeting, try to earn as much endorsement money as possible, yet they must be careful not to damage their credibility by endorsing too many products. For example, singer/actress Cher damaged her credibility as an advertising spokesperson by appearing in too many infomercials. When she realized that appearing in so many infomercials was devastating to her acting career as well, she ceased doing them.[27]

Target Audiences' Receptivity One of the most important considerations in choosing a celebrity endorser is how well the individual matches with and is received by the advertiser's target audience. Many former athletes such as golfer Arnold Palmer and tennis player Chris Everett are still effective endorsers because they have very favorable images among aging baby boomers and seniors. Basketball star LeBron James is a very effective spokesperson for several companies and brands including Nike and Sprite and has tremendous name recognition and is very popular among younger consumers who are heavy consumers of athletic shoes and soft drinks.[28] Figure 6-3 shows the results of a recent consumer survey that asked younger and older adults which traits are extremely important to them in determining whether an endorsement will influence their opinions of a product.[29]

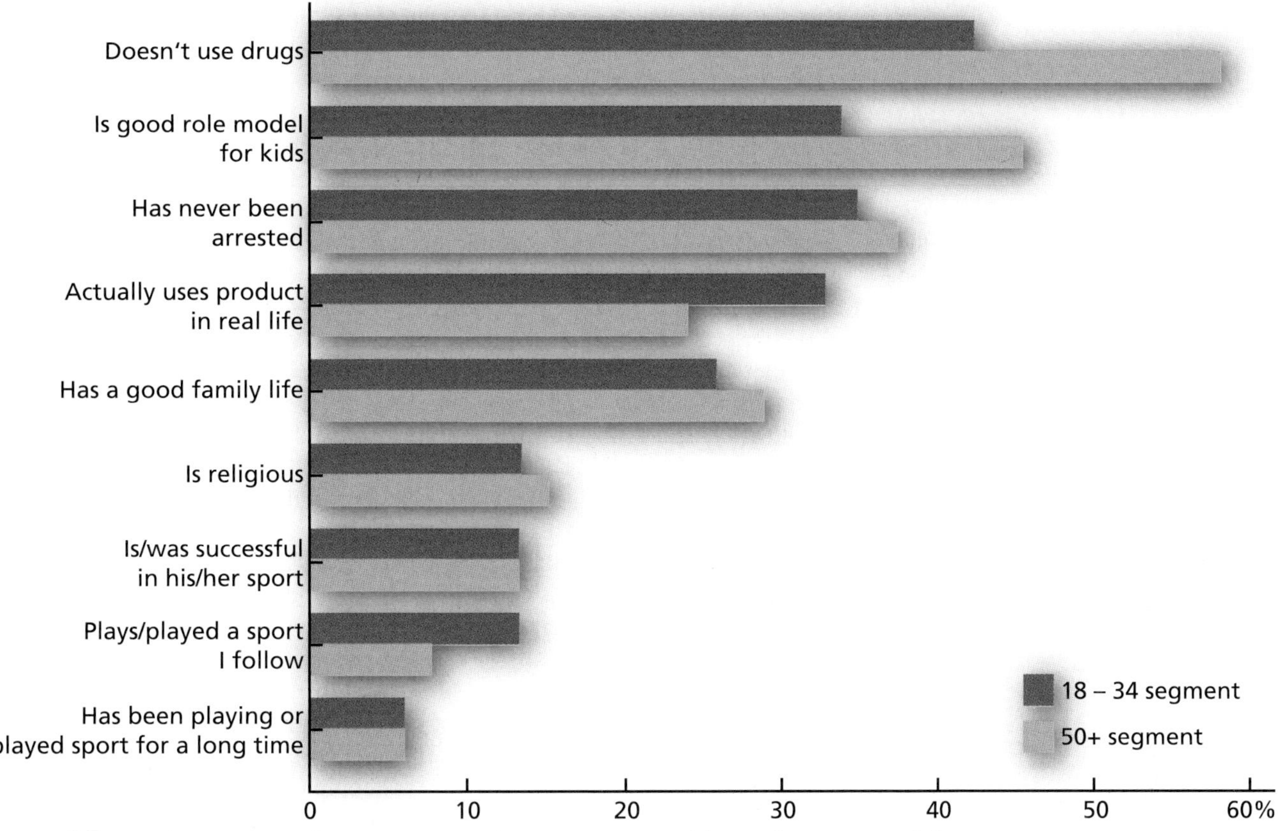

Figure 6-3 Endorser Traits That Are Extremely Important to Older and Younger Adults

Consumers who are particularly knowledgeable about a product or service or have strongly established attitudes may be less influenced by a celebrity than those with little knowledge or neutral attitudes. One study found that college-age students were more likely to have a positive attitude toward a product endorsed by a celebrity than were older consumers.[30] The teenage market has generally been very receptive to celebrity endorsers, as evidenced by the frequent use of entertainers and athletes in ads targeted to this group for products such as apparel, cosmetics, and beverages. However, many marketers are finding that teenage consumers are more skeptical and cynical toward the use of celebrity endorsers and respond better to ads using humor, irony, and unvarnished truth.[31] Some marketers targeting teenagers have responded to this by no longer using celebrities in their campaigns or by poking fun at their use.

Some companies avoid the use of celebrities entirely as they have determined that the market they are targeting is really not influenced by their endorsements. For example, New Balance has become the number-two athletic footwear company behind Nike without the aid of celebrity endorsers. Its core customers are between the ages of 25 and 49 and are older and more mature than the youth and teen market that most athletic shoe companies target. The company has an across-the-board policy against hiring athletes to endorse its products and has run several ad campaigns through the years that poke fun at its competitors for paying exorbitant amounts of money to athletes to wear their shoes. In early 2005, New Balance launched its "For Love or Money" campaign that suggests that some professional athletes play more for money than for love of the game (Exhibit 6-5). New Balance CEO Jim Davis says, "We don't see any value in paying someone $20 million to promote our shoes. We prefer to channel that money into putting out a better shoe."[32]

Exhibit 6-5 New Balance prefers not to use athletes to endorse its shoes

Risk to the Advertiser A celebrity's behavior may pose a risk to a company.[33] A number of entertainers and athletes have been involved in activities that could embarrass the companies whose products they endorsed. For example, Hertz used O. J. Simpson as its spokesperson for 20 years and lost all that equity when he was accused of murdering his ex-wife and her friend. Pepsi had a string of problems with celebrity endorsers; it severed ties with Mike Tyson, after his wife accused him of beating her, and with singer Michael Jackson, after he was accused of having sex with a 12-year-old boy. Pepsi dropped a TV commercial featuring Madonna when some religious groups and consumers objected to her "Like a Prayer" video and threatened to boycott Pepsi products. More recently, several companies, including McDonald's and Coca-Cola, terminated endorsement contracts with basketball star Kobe Bryant when he was charged with sexual assault. Other companies, such as Nike and Upper Deck, have long-term contracts with Bryant but have not been using him as an endorser. Even though the charges against Bryant were dropped, sports-marketing experts have noted that it will take him years, if he is ever able to repair his image and again become a marketable pitchman.[34]

Marketers are recognizing that the use of celebrity endorsers can be a very expensive and high-risk strategy because what the celebrities do in their personal lives can impact their image and the way they are viewed by the public. Some companies may face a dilemma in selecting celebrity endorsers: While they prefer them to be upright, they still want them to have an edge or be somewhat irreverent to be able to connect with consumers. This may be particularly true for companies marketing their products to younger consumers.

To avoid problems, companies often research a celebrity's personal life and background. Many endorsement contracts include a morals clause allowing the company to terminate the contract if a controversy arises. Several companies, including luxury brands Burberry and Chanel as well as fashion retailer H&M, canceled their contracts with supermodel Kate Moss in the wake of a British tabloid photo which showed her using cocaine.[35] However, marketers should remember that adding morals clauses to their endorsement contracts only gets them out of a problem; it does not prevent it. Thus, it is important that they carefully consider the character of a celebrity as well as the potential risk associated with using him or her as a spokesperson or endorser for the company or one of its brands.[36]

Understanding the Meaning of Celebrity Endorsers Advertisers must try to match the product or company's image, the characteristics of the target market, and the personality of the celebrity.[37] The image celebrities project to consumers can be just as important as their ability to attract attention. An interesting perspective on celebrity endorsement was developed by Grant McCracken.[38] He argues that credibility and attractiveness don't sufficiently explain how and why celebrity endorsements work and offers a model based on meaning transfer (Figure 6-4).

Figure 6-4 Meaning Movement and the Endorsement Process

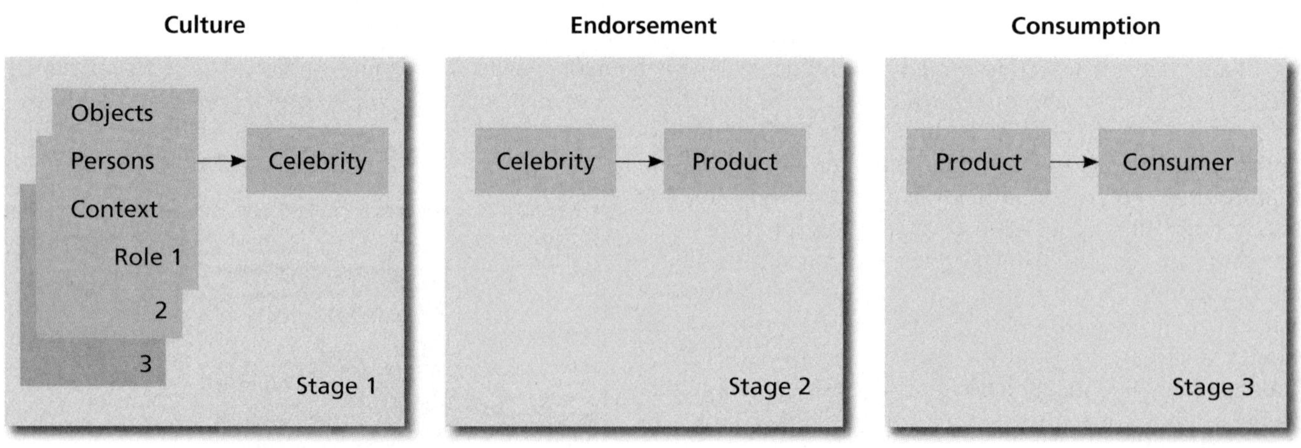

According to this model, a celebrity's effectiveness as an endorser depends on the culturally acquired meanings he or she brings to the endorsement process. Each celebrity contains many meanings, including status, class, gender, and age as well as personality and lifestyle. In explaining stage 1 of the meaning transfer process, McCracken notes:

> Celebrities draw these powerful meanings from the roles they assume in their television, movie, military, athletic, and other careers. Each new dramatic role brings the celebrity into contact with a range of objects, persons, and contexts. Out of these objects, persons, and contexts are transferred meanings that then reside in the celebrity.[39]

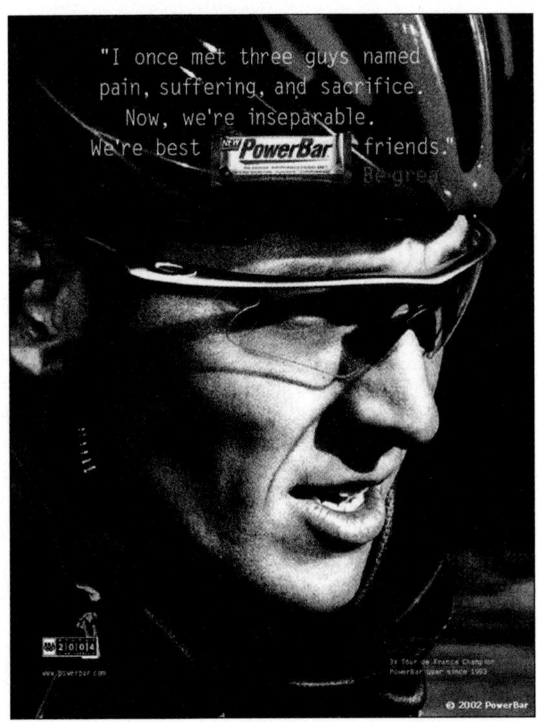

Exhibit 6-6 Cyclist Lance Armstrong helps position PowerBar as a product that provides energy to athletes

Examples of celebrities who have acquired meanings include actor Bill Cosby as the perfect father (from his role on *The Cosby Show*), actor Jerry Seinfeld as the quirky comedian (from his role on the sitcom *Seinfeld*), and singer/actress Jessica Simpson as an attractive, ditzy blonde (from her MTV reality show *Newlyweds: Nick & Jessica* and the movie *The Dukes of Hazzard*). Cyclist Lance Armstrong has developed a very favorable image as a fierce competitor and an All-American superhero by winning the grueling Tour de France cycling race seven times after overcoming a life-threatening form of testicular cancer.

McCracken suggests celebrity endorsers bring their meanings and image into the ad and transfer them to the product they are endorsing (stage 2 of the model in Figure 6-4). For example, PowerBar, the leading brand of energy performance bars, takes advantage of Armstrong's image as a competitor and champion with great determination in ads such as the one shown in Exhibit 6-6. He is also an effective endorser for the product since he competes in a very grueling and demanding sport where the benefits of sustained energy are very important.

In the final stage of McCracken's model, the meanings the celebrity has given to the product are transferred to the consumer. By using Armstrong in its ads, PowerBar hopes to enhance its image as a product that can provide extra energy to athletes and enhance their performance. McCracken notes that this final stage is complicated and difficult to achieve. The way consumers take possession of the meaning the celebrity has transferred to a product is probably the least understood part of the process.

The meaning transfer model has some important implications for companies using celebrity endorsers. Marketers must first decide on the image or symbolic meanings important to the target audience for the particular product, service, or company. They must then determine which celebrity best represents the meaning or image to be projected. An advertising campaign must be designed that captures that meaning in the product and moves it to the consumer. Marketing and advertising personnel often rely on intuition in choosing celebrity endorsers for their companies or products, but some companies conduct research studies to determine consumers' perceptions of celebrities' meaning. Global Perspective 6-2 discusses how NBA basketball star Yao Ming has become a very effective endorser for companies trying to enter China and how his management team conducted research to determine how his image might appeal to the values of Chinese consumers.

Marketers may also pretest ads to determine whether they transfer the proper meaning to the product. When celebrity endorsers are used, the marketer should track the campaign's effectiveness. Does the celebrity continue to be effective in communicating the proper meaning to the target audience? Celebrities who are no longer in the limelight may lose their ability to transfer any significant meanings to the product.

As we have seen, marketers must consider many factors when choosing a celebrity to serve as an advertising spokesperson for the company or a particular brand. Studies have shown that advertising and marketing managers take these various factors into account when choosing a celebrity endorser.[40] Among the most important factors are the celebrity's match with the target audience and the product/service or brand, the overall image of the celebrity, the cost of acquiring the celebrity, trustworthiness, the risk of controversy, and the celebrity's familiarity and likability among the target audience.

GLOBAL PERSPECTIVE 6-2

Yao Mania Helps Marketers Enter China

China is a very big country with more than four times the population of the United States. Yet many companies have found it very difficult to enter this market as war and communism have conspired to keep the Chinese poor and Westerners out for centuries. This is rapidly changing, however, as the Chinese government is opening the doors to outside companies and the standard of living in the country is improving. China has the world's fastest growing economy and may soon pass the United States to become the largest consumer market across the globe. Nearly all of the multinational companies are entering China, and many view sports as the way to court the estimated 300 million young Chinese consumers who are emerging as a critical market for their global marketing campaigns. A number of companies using sports to connect with Chinese consumers are doing so through the most popular athlete in China—a 7 foot 5 inch, 25-year-old basketball star who actually plays in the United States.

Yao Ming has been playing for the Houston Rockets of the National Basketball Association (NBA) since 2002 when he was the first player chosen in the NBA draft. Although he was ready to start his global journey several years earlier, Chinese officials were hesitant to let him move to the United States and play in the NBA. Ming was considered a national treasure, and they wanted him to play at home until they understood the American landscape and were sure he was ready to play in the NBA. They huddled with international scouts to determine whether he would be the top pick in the NBA draft, what team he would go to, how much he would get paid, and, most important, if he would embarrass the Chinese people against NBA competition. When Houston was awarded the top pick in the 2002 draft, Chinese officials decided it was a good place for Ming to play. The Rockets paid Yao's professional team a $350,000 transfer fee and the deal called for Ming to give at least 50 percent of his salary to various Chinese sporting bodies while continuing to play for the Chinese national team in international competitions, such as the Olympics.

Before leaving for the NBA, Yao made Erik Zhang, a distant cousin who was an MBA student at the University of Chicago, his official representative. Zhang recognized Yao's tremendous potential as an endorser as he was at the lucrative nexus of American corporate marketing dollars and Chinese consumers. To help turn Yao Ming into a pitchman, Zhang recruited the deputy dean of faculty at the University of Chicago Graduate School of Business, a sports agent and a marketing director. One of the first steps taken by Team Yao, as the group is known, was to commission a University of Chicago business school class to prepare a marketing study on Yao Ming. The MBA students conducted extensive surveys and focus groups in five Chinese cities, including Shanghai and Beijing, to examine the core values of the 400 million urban Chinese consumers on whom the marketers would focus. They found that words such as *hardworking, self-confidence, respect, talent, heroism,* and *lightheartedness* were used to describe values that are important to these Chinese urbanites. Their study also found that Ming rated higher than other Chinese celebrities on those qualities and was by far China's most popular celebrity.

Even before Team Yao began using their findings to market his appeal as an endorser, a number of American companies were knocking on the door. Apple Computer cast Ming opposite the diminutive Verne Troyer, who plays Mini-Me in the Austin Powers movies, in an ad for its notebook computer. Apple CEO Steve Jobs noted that "we chose him because we just thought he was hipper than other people around." Ming made his English-speaking debut in a popular Visa commercial that showed him going back and forth with a slick sales clerk in a souvenir shop in New York City when he asked if he could write a check. McDonald's signed Ming to a global endorsement deal as has PepsiCo and Garmin International, which is using him as part of a branding and advertising campaign promoting its satellite navigation products.

While many companies are using Ming in ad campaigns that run in the United States and other countries, his greatest potential is in helping them market their products in China. Chinese fans cannot get enough of Yao as TV ratings spike dramatically when his Rockets games are shown in China, and viewing parties are often held to watch his televised games. Tickets for two Rockets games that were played in Shanghai and Beijing at the beginning of the 2004–05 season sold out in hours, and courtside seats went for $2,500, more than twice the annual income of an average Chinese citizen.

The company that may benefit the most from Ming's popularity in China is Reebok, which signed him to a multiyear endorsement deal for an estimated $90 million when his contract with Nike expired in 2003. Reebok has launched a Yao Ming signature shoe line and hopes that he can help the company capture 25 percent of what will become a $1.5 billion sports apparel market in China over the next several years. Several other companies are also using Ming to promote their products in China including Anheuser-Busch and Eastman Kodak, which reported a 30 percent increase in digital-printing volume following a promotion featuring him.

Team Yao has been structuring his endorsement deals with an eye toward the 2008 Olympics, to be held in Beijing. The hope is that he will be reaching his basketball prime just as the world's attention is focused on him and his country.

So what does Ming think about all of the attention he has been receiving? He says he really doesn't care and just wants to endorse products he actually uses and to appear in ads that make him look cool. He has said: "I think it's all pretty boring. I'd much rather be playing basketball." The companies that are using Yao to help market their products probably do not find it at all boring. However, they do want him to be playing basketball so that hundreds of millions of consumers in China, as well as in other countries, can be watching—and buying the products he endorses.

Sources: Peter Wonacott, "Yao-Mania: Hoop Star's China Visit Evokes Beatles, 1964," *The Wall Street Journal,* October 15, 2004, pp. B1, 7; Josh Tyrangiel, "The Center of Attention," *Time,* February 10, 2003, pp. 68–70; Elliott Teaford, "Yao Switches from Nike to Reebok," *Los Angeles Times,* October 24, 2003, p. D7.

While some advertising and marketing executives rely on their own intuition and gut feeling, many turn to research that measures a celebrity's familiarity and appeal among their target audience as well as other factors. Many companies and their advertising agencies rely on Q-scores that are commercially available from the New York–based firm Marketing Evaluations, Inc. To determine its Q-scores for sport personalities, actors, actresses, and entertainers, the company surveys a representative national panel of consumers several times a year. Respondents are asked to indicate whether they have ever seen or heard of the performer or sports personality and, if they have, to rate him or her on a scale that includes one of my favorites, very good, good, fair, or poor. The *familiarity score* indicates what percentage of people has heard of the person while the *one of my favorites score* is an absolute measure of the appeal or popularity of the celebrity. The well-known *Q-score* is calculated by taking the percentage of respondents who indicate that a person is "one of my favorites" and then dividing that number by the percentage of respondents who indicate they have heard of that person. This score thus answers the question, How appealing is the person among those who do know him or her? The average Q-score for performers is generally around 18 and about 17 for sports personalities. Marketing Evaluation's Q-scores are also broken down on the basis of various demographic criteria such as a respondent's age, income, occupation, education, and race so that marketers have some idea of how a celebrity's popularity varies among different groups of consumers.

In addition to Q-scores, marketers are also using information provided by other firms to match celebrities with their products. Hollywood-Madison Group, a firm that arranges celebrity endorsements, has poured over 13 years of research into its Fame Index, which is a database listing more than 10,000 celebrities by 250 criteria such as age, sex, residence, career highlights, charity affiliations, fears, interests, and addictions. The database is updated daily with information from the Internet, magazines, newspaper articles, and television.[41]

Applying Likability: Decorative Models Advertisers often draw attention to their ads by featuring a physically attractive person who serves as a passive or decorative model rather than as an active communicator. Research suggests that physically attractive communicators generally have a positive impact and generate more favorable evaluations of both ads and products than less attractive models.[42] The gender appropriateness of the model for the product being advertised and his or her relevance to the product are also important considerations.[43] Products such as cosmetics or fashionable clothing are likely to benefit from the use of an attractive model, since physical appearance is very relevant in marketing these items.

Some models draw attention to the ad but not to the product or message. Studies show that an attractive model facilitates recognition of the ad but does not enhance copy readership or message recall. Thus, advertisers must ensure that the consumer's attention will go beyond the model to the product and advertising message.[44] Marketers must also consider whether the use of highly attractive models might negatively impact advertising effectiveness. Several recent studies have shown that some women experience negative feelings when comparing themselves with beautiful models used in ads and the images of physical perfection they represent.[45]

Some companies have developed marketing campaigns that undermine the traditional approach to beauty care advertising by telling women, as well as young girls, that they're beautiful just the way they are. For example, Unilever's Dove brand has long eschewed the use of supermodels in its ads and used everyday women and girls who resemble its typical consumers. The company recently developed an interesting global integrated marketing campaign designed to appeal to everyday women.[46] The "Campaign for Real Beauty" includes magazine ads, extensive public relations, and a website (www.campaignforrealbeauty.com) where women can discuss beauty-related issues (Exhibit 6-7). Dove has taken a social advocacy approach in the campaign, which it proclaims "aims to change the status quo and offer in its place a broader, healthier, more democratic view of beauty."[47]

Exhibit 6-7 Dove's "Campaign for Real Beauty" uses everyday women rather than supermodels in its ads

Source Power

The final characteristic in Kelman's classification scheme is **source power.** A source has power when he or she can actually administer rewards and punishments to the receiver. As a result of this power, the source may be able to induce another person(s) to respond to the request or position he or she is advocating. The power of the source depends on several factors. The source must be perceived as being able to administer positive or negative sanctions to the receiver *(perceived control)* and the receiver must think the source cares about whether or not the receiver conforms *(perceived concern).* The receiver's estimate of the source's ability to observe conformity is also important *(perceived scrutiny).*

When a receiver perceives a source as having power, the influence process occurs through a process known as **compliance.** The receiver accepts the persuasive influence of the source and acquiesces to his or her position in hopes of obtaining a favorable reaction or avoiding punishment. The receiver may show public agreement with the source's position but not have an internal or private commitment to this position. Persuasion induced through compliance may be superficial and last only as long as the receiver perceives that the source can administer some reward or punishment.

Power as a source characteristic is very difficult to apply in a nonpersonal influence situation such as advertising. A communicator in an ad generally cannot apply any sanctions to the receiver or determine whether compliance actually occurs. An indirect way of using power is by using an individual with an authoritative personality as a spokesperson. For example, for many years Take Pride in America used the late actor Charles Bronson, whose movie roles earned him an image as a rugged tough guy, in public service campaigns commanding people not to pollute or damage public lands (Exhibit 6-8).

Exhibit 6-8 Actor Charles Bronson's authoritative image made him an effective source

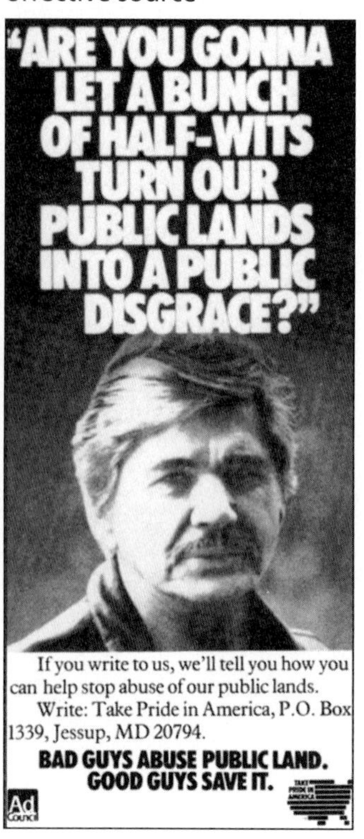

The use of source power applies more in situations involving personal communication and influence. For example, in a personal selling situation, the sales rep may have some power over a buyer if the latter anticipates receiving special rewards or favors for complying with the salesperson. Some companies provide their sales reps with large expense accounts to spend on customers for this very purpose. Representatives of companies whose product demand exceeds supply are often in a position of power; buyers may comply with their requests to ensure an adequate supply of the product. Sales reps must be very careful in their use of a power position, since abusing a power base to maximize short-term gains can damage long-term relationships with customers.

Message Factors

The way marketing communications are presented is very important in determining their effectiveness. Promotional managers must consider not only the content of their persuasive messages but also how this information will be structured for presentation and what type of message appeal will be used. Advertising, in all media except radio, relies heavily on visual as well as verbal information. Many options are available with respect to the design and presentation of a message. This section examines the structure of messages and considers the effects of different types of appeals used in advertising.

Message Structure

Marketing communications usually consist of a number of message points that the communicator wants to get across. An important aspect of message strategy is knowing the best way to communicate these points and overcome any opposing viewpoints audience members may hold. Extensive research has been conducted on how the structure of a persuasive message can influence its effectiveness, including order of presentation, conclusion drawing, message sidedness, refutation, and verbal versus visual message characteristics.

Order of Presentation

A basic consideration in the design of a persuasive message is the arguments' order of presentation. Should the most important message points be placed at the beginning of the message, in the middle, or at the end? Research on learning and memory generally indicates that items presented first and last are remembered better than those presented in the middle (see Figure 6-5).[48] This suggests that a communicator's strongest arguments should be presented early or late in the message but never in the middle.

Presenting the strongest arguments at the beginning of the message assumes a **primacy effect** is operating, whereby information presented first is most effective. Putting the strong points at the end assumes a **recency effect,** whereby the last arguments presented are most persuasive.

Whether to place the strongest selling points at the beginning or the end of the message depends on several factors. If the target audience is opposed to the communicator's position, presenting strong points first can reduce the level of counterarguing. Putting weak arguments first might lead to such a high level of counterarguing that strong arguments that followed would not be believed. Strong arguments work best at the beginning of the message if the audience is not interested in the topic, so they can arouse interest in the message. When the target audience is predisposed toward the communicator's position or is highly interested in the issue or product, strong arguments can be saved for the end of the message. This may result in a more favorable opinion as well as better retention of the information.

The order of presentation can be critical when a long, detailed message with many arguments is being presented. Most effective sales presentations open and close with strong selling points and bury weaker arguments in the middle. For short communications, such as a 15- or 30-second TV or radio commercial, the order may be less critical. However, many product and service messages are received by consumers with low

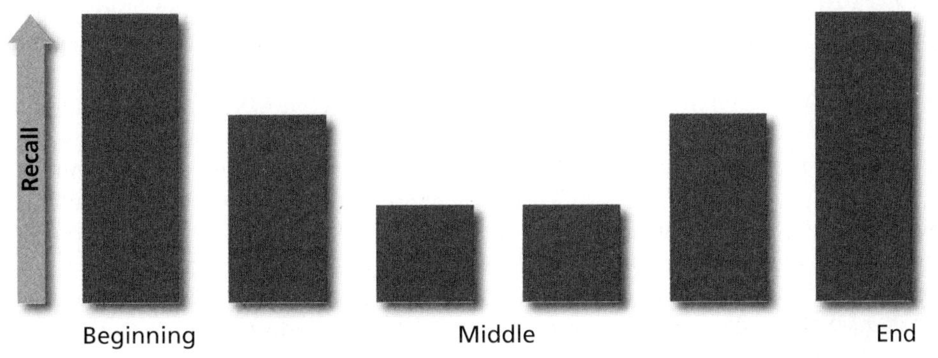

Figure 6-5 Ad Message Recall as a Function of Order of Presentation

involvement and minimal interest. Thus, an advertiser may want to present the brand name and key selling points early in the message and repeat them at the end to enhance recall and retention. Order of presentation is also an important consideration in other forms of marketing communication. For example, many press releases use the "pyramid style" of writing, whereby most of the important information is presented up front to ensure that it is read since editors often cut from the end of articles.

Conclusion Drawing Marketing communicators must decide whether their messages should explicitly draw a firm conclusion or allow receivers to draw their own conclusions. Research suggests that, in general, messages with explicit conclusions are more easily understood and effective in influencing attitudes. However, other studies have shown that the effectiveness of conclusion drawing may depend on the target audience, the type of issue or topic, and the nature of the situation.[49]

More highly educated people prefer to draw their own conclusions and may be annoyed at an attempt to explain the obvious or to draw an inference for them. But stating the conclusion may be necessary for a less educated audience, who may not draw any conclusion or may make an incorrect inference from the message. Marketers must also consider the audience's level of involvement in the topic. For highly personal or ego-involving issues, message recipients may want to make up their own minds and resent any attempts by the communicator to draw a conclusion. One study found that open-ended ads (without explicit conclusions) were more effective than closed-ended arguments that did include a specific conclusion—but only for involved audiences.[50]

Whether to draw a conclusion for the audience also depends on the complexity of the topic. Even a highly educated audience may need assistance if its knowledge level in a particular area is low. Does the marketer want the message to trigger immediate action or a more long-term effect? If immediate action is an objective, the message should draw a definite conclusion. This is a common strategy in political advertising, particularly for ads run close to election day. When immediate impact is not the objective and repeated exposure will give the audience members opportunities to draw their own conclusions, an open-ended message may be used.

Drawing a conclusion in a message may make sure the target audience gets the point the marketer intended. But many advertisers believe that letting customers draw their own conclusions reinforces the points being made in the message. For example, a health services agency in Kentucky found that open-ended ads were more memorable and more effective in getting consumers to use health services than were ads stating a conclusion. Ads that posed questions about alcohol and drug abuse and left them unanswered resulted in more calls by teenagers to a help line for information than did a message offering a resolution to the problem.[51] The ad for Silk Soymilk in Exhibit 6-9 is a very good example of an open-ended message. The question in the headline encourages consumers to be open to the idea of drinking soymilk.

Exhibit 6-9 This ad makes effective use of an open-ended approach

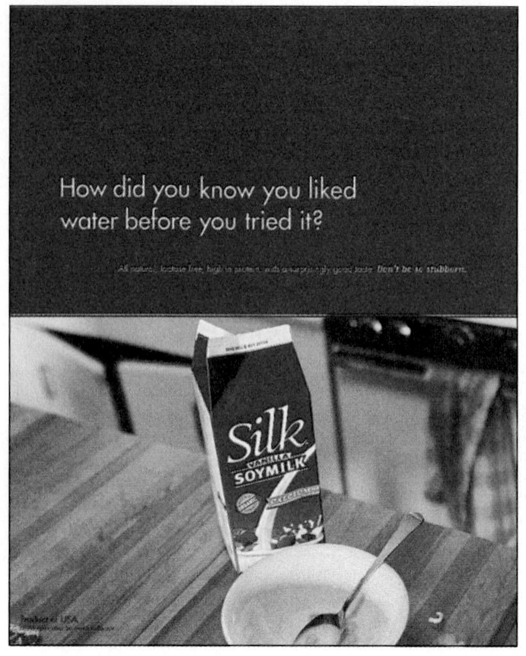

Message Sidedness Another message structure decision facing the marketer involves message sidedness. A **one-sided message** mentions only positive attributes or benefits. A **two-sided message** presents both good and bad points. One-sided messages are most effective when the target audience already holds a favorable opinion about the topic. They also work better with a less educated audience.[52]

Two-sided messages are more effective when the target audience holds an opposing opinion or is highly educated. Two-sided messages may enhance the credibility of the source.[53] A better-educated audience usually knows there are opposing arguments, so a communicator who presents both sides of an issue is likely to be seen as less biased and more objective.

Most advertisers use one-sided messages. They are concerned about the negative effects of acknowledging a weakness in their brand or don't want to say anything positive about their competitors. There are exceptions, however. Sometimes advertisers compare brands on several attributes and do not show their product as being the best on every one.

In some situations marketers may focus on a negative attribute as a way of enhancing overall perceptions of the product. For example, W. K. Buckley Limited has become one of the leading brands of cough syrup in Canada by using a blunt two-sided slogan, "Buckley's Mixture. It tastes awful. And it works." Ads for the brand poke fun at the cough syrup's terrible taste but also suggest that the taste is a reason why the product is effective (Exhibit 6-10). Buckley's is using the humorous two-sided message strategy in the U.S. market as well.[54]

Exhibit 6-10 Buckley's Cough Syrup uses a two-sided message to promote the product's effectiveness

Refutation In a special type of two-sided message known as a **refutational appeal,** the communicator presents both sides of an issue and then refutes the opposing viewpoint. Since refutational appeals tend to "inoculate" the target audience against a competitor's counterclaims, they are more effective than one-sided messages in making consumers resistant to an opposing message.[55]

Refutational messages may be useful when marketers wish to build attitudes that resist change and must defend against attacks or criticism of their products or the company. For example, Exhibit 6-11 shows an ad used by the Almond Board of California to refute nutritional concerns about almonds regarding their fat content. Market leaders, who are often the target of comparative messages, may find that acknowledging competitors' claims and then refuting them can help build resistant attitudes and customer loyalty.

Verbal versus Visual Messages Thus far our discussion has focused on the information, or verbal, portion of the message. However, the nonverbal, visual elements of an ad are also very important. Many ads provide minimal amounts of information and rely on visual elements to communicate. Pictures are commonly used in advertising to convey information or reinforce copy or message claims.

Both the verbal and visual portions of an ad influence the way the advertising message is processed.[56] Consumers may develop images or impressions based on visual elements such as an illustration in an ad or the scenes in a TV commercial. In some cases, the visual portion of an ad may reduce its persuasiveness, since the processing stimulated by the picture may be less controlled and consequently less favorable than that stimulated by words.[57]

Exhibit 6-11 A refutational appeal is used to address nutritional concerns about almonds

Pictures affect the way consumers process accompanying copy. A recent study showed that when verbal information was low in imagery value, the use of pictures providing examples increased both immediate and delayed recall of product attributes.[58] However, when the verbal information was already high in imagery value, the addition of pictures did not increase recall. Advertisers often design ads where the visual image supports the verbal appeal to create a compelling impression in the consumer's mind. Notice how the ad for the Rain-X Self-Dry Car Wash System uses a clever visual image to communicate the key attribute of the product (Exhibit 6-12).

Sometimes advertisers use a different strategy; they design ads in which the visual portion is incongruent with or contradicts the verbal information presented. The logic behind this strategy is that the use of an unexpected picture or visual image will grab consumers' attention and get them to engage in more effortful or elaborative processing.[59] A number of studies have shown that the use of a visual that is inconsistent with the verbal content leads to more recall and greater processing of the information presented.[60]

Message Appeals

One of the advertiser's most important creative strategy decisions involves the choice of an appropriate appeal. Some ads are designed to appeal to the rational, logical aspect of the consumer's decision-making process; others appeal to feelings in an attempt to evoke some emotional reaction. Many believe that effective advertising combines the practical reasons for purchasing a product with emotional values. In this section we will examine several common types of message appeals, including comparative advertising, fear, and humor.

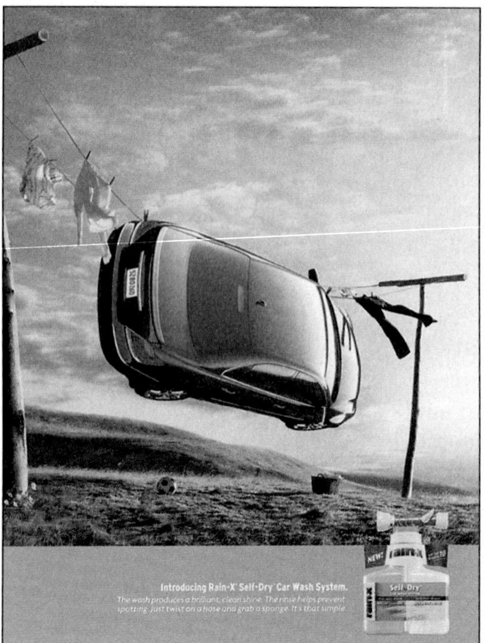

Exhibit 6-12 Visual images are often designed to support verbal appeals

Comparative Advertising

Comparative advertising is the practice of either directly or indirectly naming competitors in an ad and comparing one or more specific attributes.[61] This form of advertising became popular after the Federal Trade Commission (FTC) began advocating its use in 1972. The FTC reasoned that direct comparison of brands would provide better product information, giving consumers a more rational basis for making purchase decisions. Television networks cooperated with the FTC by lifting their ban on comparative ads, and the result was a flurry of comparative commercials.

Initially, the novelty of comparative ads resulted in greater attention. But since they have become so common, their attention-getting value has probably declined. Some studies show that recall is higher for comparative than noncomparative messages, but comparative ads are generally not more effective for other response variables, such as brand attitudes or purchase intentions.[62] Advertisers must also consider how comparative messages affect credibility. Users of the brand being attacked in a comparative message may be especially skeptical about the advertiser's claims.

Comparative advertising may be particularly useful for new brands, since it allows a new market entrant to position itself directly against the more established brands and to promote its distinctive advantages. Direct comparisons can help position a new brand in the evoked, or choice, set of brands the customer may be considering.

Comparative advertising is often used for brands with a small market share. They compare themselves to an established market leader in hopes of creating an association and tapping into the leader's market. For example, Savin Corp. used comparative ads for a number of years that were aimed directly at Xerox, the market leader in the copier industry. The campaign was very effective in convincing decision makers at small and mid-size companies that Savin should be considered as an alternative to Xerox as well as other copier companies such as Canon, Konica, and Mita (Exhibit 6-13). Market leaders, on the other hand, often hesitate to use comparison ads, as most believe they have little to gain by featuring competitors' products in their ads. There are exceptions, of course; Coca-Cola resorted to comparative advertising in response to challenges made by Pepsi that were reducing Coke's market share. And recently Anheuser-Busch has been using comparative ads attacking archrival Miller Brewing Co., which has been gaining market share at the expense of Budweiser and other brands. IMC Perspective 6-1 discusses how Miller has effectively used comparative advertising for its Miller Lite brand.

Exhibit 6-13 Savin used a comparative ad to position itself against Xerox

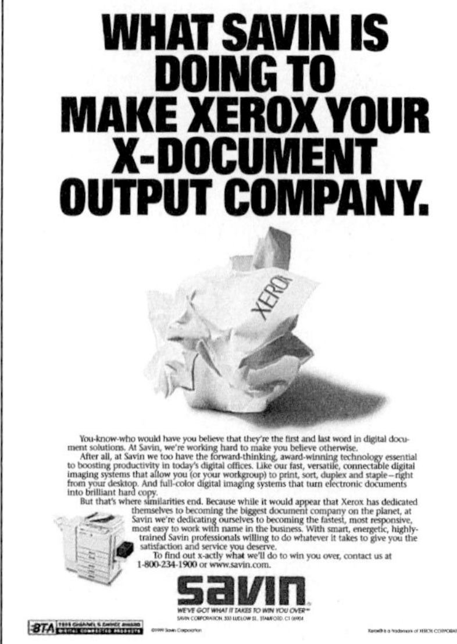

Another area where comparative messages are quite commonly used is political advertising. Political advertising is viewed as an important component of political speech and thus enjoys more First Amendment protection than commercial speech and less regulation by either government or self-policing agencies. Thus, it has become quite common for political ads to contain negative, one-sided attacks on an opposing candidate's weaknesses such as character flaws, voting record, public misstatements, broken promises, and the like.[63] The goal of these ads is to discredit the character, record, or position of an opponent and create doubt in voters' minds about his or her ability to govern effectively. A major reason why negative political ads are used successfully is that voters often tend to weight negative information more heavily than positive information when forming impressions of political candidates.[64]

IMC PERSPECTIVE 6-1

Miller Lite Finds the Right Advertising Formula

One of the most memorable and successful advertising campaigns of all times was the "Tastes Great, Less Filling" theme, which began in 1974, for Miller Lite beer. The campaign used humorous commercials featuring famous (and not so famous) ex-athletes and other celebrities arguing over whether the brand's main appeal was its great taste or the fact that it contained fewer calories than regular beer and was less filling. The campaign ran for 17 years and helped make Miller Lite the second best-selling beer in the United States for many years, as well as making light beer a legitimate segment of the beer market.

In the late 1980s, Miller began taking the campaign in a new direction as the ads began moving away from the use of ex-athletes. Although the tagline was still being used, the commercials used rock bands, old movie and party scenes, the Miller Lite girls, and other images to appeal to a broader and younger market. Miller Lite also faced strong competition in the light beer market from other brands such as Bud Light and Coors Light. Despite not entering the market until 1982, Anheuser-Busch had grown Bud Light into a strong brand and Coors Light had replaced the flagship brand as the company's best-selling product. By the early 1990s, Miller Lite continued to lose market share and the company dropped the "Taste Great, Less Filling" campaign. What followed was a six-year odyssey of advertising flip-flops that included adolescent humor and far-out wit to lure young male beer drinkers. But spots featuring cowboys singing goodbye to their beer on the way to the bathroom didn't help sell a lot of Miller Lite.

In 1999, Miller dusted off the 24-year-old formula of having people debate the merits of the brand. The new ad theme was the "Great Taste of a True Pilsner Beer" and pitted celebrities against one another in mock arguments over whether Miller Lite tastes great because it's smooth or because of its choice hops. Miller marketing people hoped the celebrity bickering approach would work a second time over Lite's taste and ingredients, which is what the company thought really mattered to beer drinkers.

ALL TOGETHER NOW...
"MORE TASTE THAN BUD LIGHT
WITH HALF THE CARBS."
Miller
Lite
Great Taste. Less Filling.
Miller
Good call.

Over the next several years, other campaigns were used including an attempt to revive the 30-year-old "Miller Time" tagline that was used in the 1970s for the Miller High Life brand. The new ads modified the theme to "Grab a Miller Lite. It's Miller Time" and featured guys bonding over beer, sexy women, and humorous vignettes. In 2002, the ads took the bonding concept in a slightly different direction with a campaign featuring ads that focus on real consumer insights and storytelling. The slogan was modified to "Life is best told over a great-tasting Miller Lite at a place called Miller Time."

In 2002, the Miller Brewing Co. was purchased by South African Breweries PLC and the management team decided that the only way Miller was going to gain market was to take on industry leader Anheuser-Busch, which sells 49 percent of the beer in the United States. A decision was made to position Miller Lite and Miller Genuine draft as challenger brands to attack the number-one brand with comparative ads. In 2003, ads began pitching Miller Lite as the low-carb alternative to market leader Bud Light. One very effective spot showed a close-up shot of the beer with a voiceover and text explaining that Miller Lite has fewer than half of the carbs of Bud Light. Another campaign hailed Miller as the "President of Beers," in a jab at Budweiser's longtime "King of Beers" tagline. The ads urged drinkers to "vote" for Miller beers and mocked such Anheuser-Busch icons as the Clydesdales. Later that year, the company launched the "Good Call" campaign for Miller Lite and Genuine Draft. The ads hammered home the message that Miller beers are better-tasting alternatives and sometimes attacked Bud Light and Budweiser directly. When Anheuser-Busch introduced Budweiser Select, a low-carb extension of the Budweiser brand, Miller ran ads suggesting that it was just a Miller Lite wannabe.

The comparative advertising campaign for Miller Lite was very successful as Miller Lite sales increased by 10.5 percent in 2004, reaching their highest level in a decade. The sales increase was particularly significant given that overall beer sales increased by less than 1 percent for the year and Bud Light sales increased by only 3.7 percent. Generally market leaders do not respond against challengers who attack them in comparative ads; however, Anheuser-Busch decided to respond by running ads pointing out that Miller Brewing Co. was owned by a foreign company since the new SABMiller is based in London. In early 2005, Anheuser-Busch began running ads with a patriotic theme and contained lines such as "This is America's Beer. This is Anheuser-Busch." Print ads hailed Anheuser-Busch as the "American Beer Company."

Miller Brewing Co. is still faced with the challenge of trying to revive other brands in its portfolio such as Genuine Draft, High Life, and Milwaukee's Best. Many expect that the company will continue to challenge the industry Goliath by creating comparative ads for these brands as well.

Sources: James B. Arndorfer, "If You Love Your Country, Drink Bud," *Advertising Age,* March 28, 2005, pp. 1, 122; Adrienne Carter, "Making Lite of the King," *BusinessWeek,* March 28, 2005, p. 105; James B. Arndorfer, "Miller Turnaround Hits One-Year Mark for Surging Lite Line," *Advertising Age,* August 23, 2004, p. 6.

However, studies have shown that the use of "attack advertising" by politicians can result in negative perceptions of both candidates.[65]

Fear Appeals

Fear is an emotional response to a threat that expresses, or at least implies, some sort of danger. Ads sometimes use **fear appeals** to evoke this emotional response and arouse individuals to take steps to remove the threat. Some, like the antidrug ads used by the Partnership for a Drug-Free America, stress physical danger that can occur if behaviors are not altered. Others—like those for deodorant, mouthwash, or dandruff shampoos—threaten disapproval or social rejection.

How Fear Operates Before deciding to use a fear appeal–based message strategy, the advertiser should consider how fear operates, what level to use, and how different target audiences may respond. One theory suggests that the relationship between the level of fear in a message and acceptance or persuasion is curvilinear, as shown in Figure 6-6.[66] This means that message acceptance increases as the amount of fear used rises—to a point. Beyond that point, acceptance decreases as the level of fear rises.

This relationship between fear and persuasion can be explained by the fact that fear appeals have both facilitating and inhibiting effects.[67] A low level of fear can have facilitating effects; it attracts attention and interest in the message and may motivate the receiver to act to resolve the threat. Thus, increasing the level of fear in a message from low to moderate can result in increased persuasion. High levels of fear, however, can produce inhibiting effects; the receiver may emotionally block the message by tuning it out, perceiving it selectively, or denying its arguments outright. Figure 6-6 illustrates how these two countereffects operate to produce the curvilinear relationship between fear and persuasion.

A study by Anand-Keller and Block provides support for this perspective on how fear operates.[68] They examined the conditions under which low- and high-fear appeals urging people to stop smoking are likely to be effective. Their study indicated that a communication using a low level of fear may be ineffective because it results in insufficient motivation to elaborate on the harmful consequences of engaging in the destructive behavior (smoking). However, an appeal arousing high levels of fear was ineffective because it resulted in too much elaboration on the harmful consequences. This led to defensive tendencies such as message avoidance and interfered with processing of recommended solutions to the problem.

Another approach to the curvilinear explanation of fear is the protection motivation model.[69] According to this theory, four cognitive appraisal processes mediate the individual's response to the threat: appraising (1) the information available regarding the severity of the perceived threat, (2) the perceived probability that the threat will occur, (3) the perceived ability of a coping behavior to remove the threat, and (4) the individual's perceived ability to carry out the coping behavior.

Figure 6-6 Relationship between Fear Levels and Message Acceptance

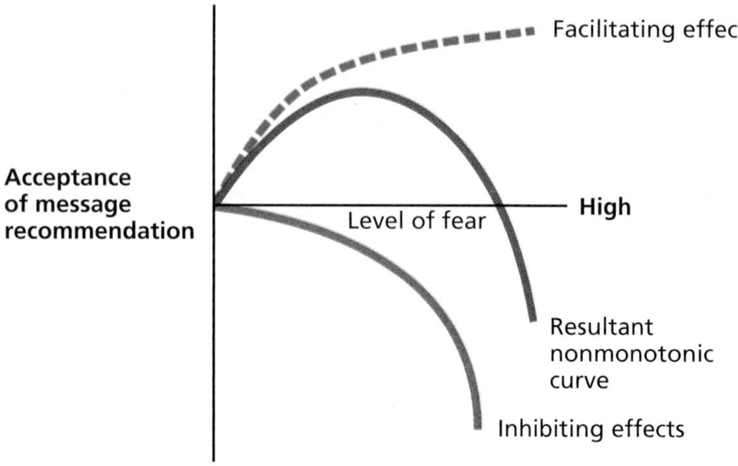

This model suggests that both the cognitive appraisal of the information in a fear appeal message and the emotional response mediate persuasion. An audience is more likely to continue processing threat-related information, thereby increasing the likelihood that a coping behavior will occur.

The protection motivation model suggests that ads using fear appeals should give the target audience information about the severity of the threat, the probability of its occurrence, the effectiveness of a coping response, and the ease with which the response can be implemented.[70] For example, the Havrix ad in Exhibit 6-14 discusses how tourists can pick up hepatitis A when traveling to high-risk areas outside the United States and describes the severity of the problem. However, the ad reduces anxiety by offering a solution to the problem—a vaccination with Havrix.

It is also important to consider how the target audience may respond. Fear appeals are more effective when the message recipient is self-confident and prefers to cope with dangers rather than avoid them.[71] They are also more effective among nonusers of a product than among users. Thus, a fear appeal may be better at keeping nonsmokers from starting than persuading smokers to stop.

In reviewing research on fear appeals, Herbert Rotfeld has argued that some of the studies may be confusing different types of threats and the level of potential harm portrayed in the message with fear, which is an emotional response.[72] He concludes that the relationship between the emotional responses of fear or arousal and persuasion is not curvilinear but rather is monotonic and positive, meaning that higher levels of fear do result in greater persuasion. However, Rotfeld notes that not all fear messages are equally effective, because different people fear different things. Thus they will respond differently to the same threat, so the strongest threats are not always the most persuasive. This suggests that marketers using fear appeals must consider the emotional responses generated by the message and how they will affect reactions to the message.

Exhibit 6-14 This ad uses a mild fear appeal but reduces anxiety by offering a solution to the problem

Humor Appeals

Humorous ads are often the best known and best remembered of all advertising messages. Many advertisers, including FedEx, Little Caesar's pizza, Pepsi, and Budweiser, have used humor appeals effectively. Humor is usually presented through radio and TV commercials as these media lend themselves to the execution of humorous messages. However, humor is occasionally used in print ads as well. The clever Altoids gum ad shown in Exhibit 6-15 is a very good example of how humor can be used effectively in print. This award-winning magazine ad was used to attract attention and generate curiosity about the new brand.

Advertisers use humor for many reasons. Humorous messages attract and hold consumers' attention. They enhance effectiveness by putting consumers in a positive mood, increasing their liking of the ad itself and their feeling toward the product or service. And humor can distract the receiver from counterarguing against the message.[73]

Exhibit 6-15 This clever ad is an example of how humor can be executed in print media

PREPARE YOURSELF
ALTOIDS
Chewing Gum
PEPPERMINT
THE CURIOUSLY STRONG GUM
curious? altoids.com

Critics argue that funny ads draw people to the humorous situation but distract them from the brand and its attributes. Also, effective humor can be difficult to produce and some attempts are too subtle for mass audiences. And, there is concern that humorous ads may wear out faster than serious appeals. **Wearout** refers to the tendency of a television or radio commercial to lose its effectiveness when it is seen and/or heard repeatedly.[74] Wearout may occur if consumers no longer pay attention to a commercial after several exposures or become annoyed at seeing or hearing an ad multiple times. Some experts argue that humorous ads wear out faster than other formats because once the consumer gets the joke, the ad becomes boring. However, advocates of humor argue that funny ads are effective longer as consumers will respond more favorably to a well-executed humorous ad than a serious message.[75]

Clearly, there are valid reasons both for and against the use of humor in advertising. Not every product or service lends itself to a humorous approach. A number of studies

Figure 6-7 Summary of Top Ad Agency Research and Creative Directors' Opinions Regarding Humor

- Humor does aid awareness and attention, which are the objectives best achieved by its use.
  - Humor may harm recall and comprehension in general.
  - Humor may aid name and simple copy registration.
  - Humor may harm complex copy registration.
  - Humor may aid retention.
- Humor does not aid persuasion in general.
  - Humor may aid persuasion to switch brands.
  - Humor creates a positive mood that enhances persuasion.
- Humor does not aid source credibility.
- Humor is generally not very effective in bringing about action/sales.
- Creatives are more positive on the use of humor to fulfill all the above objectives than research directors are.
- Radio and TV are the best media in which to use humor; direct mail and newspapers are least suited.
- Consumer nondurables and business services are best suited to humor; corporate advertising and industrial products are least suited.
- Humor should be related to the product.
- Humor should not be used with sensitive goods or services.
- Audiences that are younger, better educated, upscale, male, and professional are best suited to humor; older, less educated, and downscale groups are least suited to humor appeals.

have found that the effectiveness of humor depends on several factors, including the type of product and audience characteristics.[76] For example, humor has been more prevalent and more effective with low-involvement, feeling products than high-involvement, thinking products.[77] An interesting study surveyed the research and creative directors of the top 150 advertising agencies.[78] They were asked to name which communications objectives are facilitated through the appropriate situational use of humor in terms of media, product, and audience factors. The general conclusions of this study are shown in Figure 6-7.

Channel Factors

The final controllable variable of the communication process is the channel, or medium, used to deliver the message to the target audience. While a variety of methods are available to transmit marketing communications, as noted in Chapter 5 they can be classified into two broad categories, personal and nonpersonal media.

Personal versus Nonpersonal Channels

There are a number of basic differences between personal and nonpersonal communications channels. Information received from personal influence channels is generally more persuasive than information received via the mass media. Reasons for the differences are summarized in the following comparison of advertising and personal selling:

> From the standpoint of persuasion, a sales message is far more flexible, personal, and powerful than an advertisement. An advertisement is normally prepared by persons having minimal personal contact with customers. The message is designed to appeal to a large number of persons. By contrast, the message in a good sales presentation is not determined in advance. The salesman has a tremendous store of knowledge about his product or service and selects appropriate items as the interview progresses. Thus, the salesman can adapt this to the thinking and needs of the customer or prospect at the time of the sales call. Furthermore, as objections arise and are voiced by the buyer, the salesman can treat the objections in an appropriate manner. This is not possible in advertising.[79]

Effects of Alternative Mass Media

The various mass media that advertisers use to transmit their messages differ in many ways, including the number and type of people they reach, costs, information processing requirements, and qualitative factors. The mass media's costs and efficiency in exposing a target audience to a communication will be evaluated in Chapters 10 through 12. However, we should recognize differences in how information is processed and how communications are influenced by context or environment.

Differences in Information Processing

There are basic differences in the manner and rate at which information from various forms of media is transmitted and can be processed. Information from ads in print media, such as newspapers, magazines, or direct mail, is *self-paced;* readers process the ad at their own rate and can study it as long as they desire. In contrast, information from the broadcast media of radio and television is *externally paced;* the transmission rate is controlled by the medium.

The difference in the processing rate for print and broadcast media has some obvious implications for advertisers. Self-paced print media make it easier for the message recipient to process a long, complex message. Advertisers often use print ads when they want to present a detailed message with a lot of information. Broadcast media are more effective for transmitting shorter messages or, in the case of TV, presenting pictorial information along with words.

While there are limits to the length and complexity of broadcast messages, advertisers can deal with this problem. One strategy is to use a radio or TV ad to get consumers' attention and direct them to specific print media for a more detailed message. For example, home builders use radio ads to draw attention to new developments and direct listeners to the real estate section of the newspaper for more details. Some advertisers develop broadcast and print versions of the same message. The copy portion is similar in both media, but the print ad can be processed at a rate comfortable to the receiver.

Effects of Context and Environment

Interpretation of an advertising message can be influenced by the context or environment in which the ad appears. Communication theorist Marshall McLuhan's thesis, "The medium is the message," implies that the medium communicates an image that is independent of any message it contains.[80] A **qualitative media effect** is the influence the medium has on a message. The image of the media vehicle can affect reactions to the message. For example, an ad for a high-quality men's clothing line might have more of an impact in a fashion magazine like *GQ* than in *Sports Afield.* Airlines, destination resorts, and travel-related services advertise in publications such as *Travel & Leisure* partly because the articles, pictures, and other ads help to excite readers about travel (Exhibit 6-16).

Exhibit 6-16 *Travel & Leisure* magazine creates an excellent reception environment for travel-related ads

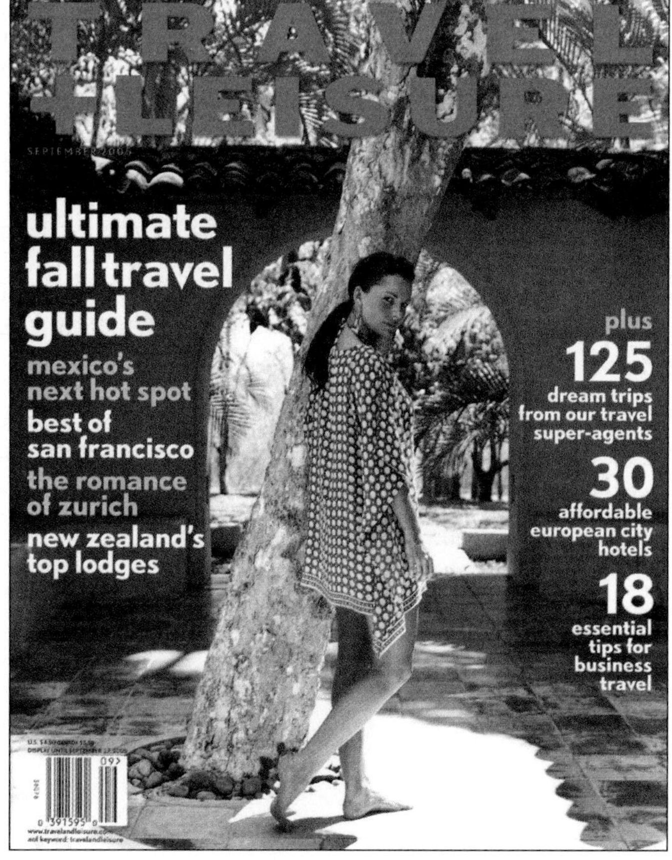

A media environment can also be created by the nature of the program in which a commercial appears. One study found that consumers reacted more positively to commercials seen during a happy TV program than a sad one.[81] Advertisers pay premium dollars to advertise on popular programs that create positive moods, like the Olympic Games and Christmas specials. Conversely, advertisers tend to avoid programs that create a negative mood among viewers or may be detrimental to the company or its products.

Many companies won't advertise on programs with excessive violence or sexual content. As a corporate policy, Coca-Cola never advertises on TV news programs because it thinks bad news is inconsistent with Coke's image as an upbeat, fun product. A study by Andrew Aylesworth and Scott MacKenzie found that commercials placed in programs that induce negative moods are processed less systematically than ads placed in programs that put viewers in positive moods.[82] They suggest that media buyers might be well advised to follow the conventional wisdom of placing their ads during "feel-good" programming, especially if the message is intended to work through a central route to persuasion. However, messages intended to operate through a peripheral route to persuasion might be more effective if they are shown during more negative programs, where presumably viewers will not analyze the ad in detail because of their negative mood state.

Clutter

Another aspect of the media environment, which is important to advertisers, is the problem of **clutter,** which has been defined as the amount of advertising in a medium.[83] However, for television, clutter is often viewed as including all the nonprogram material that appears in the broadcast environment—commercials, promotional messages for shows, public service announcements (PSAs), and the like. Clutter is of increasing concern to advertisers since there are so many messages in various media competing for the consumer's attention. Half of the average magazine's pages contain ads and in some publications the ratio of ads to editorial content is even higher. On average, around a quarter of a broadcast hour on TV is devoted to commercials, while most radio stations carry an average of 10 to 12 minutes of commercial time per hour. The high level of advertising often annoys consumers and makes it difficult for ads to communicate effectively.

Clutter has become a major concern among television advertisers as a result of increases in nonprogram time and the trend toward shorter commercials. While the 30-second commercial replaced 60-second spots as the industry standard in the 1970s, many advertisers are now using 15-second spots. The advertising industry continues to express concern over the highly cluttered viewing environment on TV, as the amount of clutter increased as much as 30 percent during the 1990s and another 8 percent since 2000. Studies have found that commercial clutter on the four major networks has been increasing as the average amount of nonprogramming time ranges from nearly 17 minutes per hour during prime time to 21 minutes per hour during daytime.[84] A recent study found that the average length of a commercial break during prime time on the major networks is just over three minutes. Thus, a viewer watching three hours of prime-time programs on the major networks would be subjected to 130 commercials, programming promotions, and public service announcements (PSAs).[85] Clutter levels are even higher on many cable networks and during syndicated programs. The problem is even greater during popular shows, to which the networks add more commercials because they can charge more. And, of course, advertisers and their agencies perpetuate the problem by pressuring the networks to squeeze their ads into top-rated shows with the largest audiences.

Advertisers and agencies want the networks to commit to a minimum amount of program time and then manage the nonprogram portion however they see fit. If the networks wanted to add more commercials, it would come out of their promos, PSAs, or program credit time. The problem is not likely to go away, however, and advertisers will continue to search for ways to break through the clutter, such as using humor, celebrity spokespeople, or novel, creative approaches.[86]

Summary

This chapter focused on the controllable variables that are part of the communication process—source, message, and channel factors. Decisions regarding each of these variables should consider their impact on the various steps of the response hierarchy the message receiver passes through. The persuasion matrix helps assess the effect of controllable communication decisions on the consumer's response process.

Selection of the appropriate source or communicator to deliver a message is an important aspect of communications strategy. Three important attributes are source credibility, attractiveness, and power. Marketers enhance message effectiveness by hiring communicators who are experts in a particular area and/or have a trustworthy image. The use of celebrities to deliver advertising messages has become very popular; advertisers hope they will catch the receivers' attention and influence their attitudes or behavior through an identification process. The chapter discusses the meaning a celebrity brings to the endorsement process and the importance of matching the image of the celebrity with that of the company or brand.

The design of the advertising message is a critical part of the communication process. There are various options regarding message structure, including order of presentation of message arguments, conclusion drawing, message sidedness, refutation, and verbal versus visual traits. The advantages and disadvantages of different message appeal strategies were considered, including comparative messages and emotional appeals such as fear and humor.

Finally, the channel or medium used to deliver the message was considered. Differences between personal and nonpersonal channels of communication were discussed. Alternative mass media can have an effect on the communication process as a result of information processing and qualitative factors. The context in which an ad appears and the reception environment are important factors to consider in the selection of mass media. Clutter has become a serious problem for advertisers, particularly on TV, where commercials have become shorter and more numerous.

Key Terms

persuasion matrix, 165
source, 166
credibility, 166
internalization, 167
sleeper effect, 170
attractiveness, 170
identification, 171
source power, 178
compliance, 178
primacy effect, 179
recency effect, 179
one-sided message, 180
two-sided message, 180
refutational appeal, 181
comparative advertising, 182
fear appeals, 184
wearout, 185
qualitative media effect, 187
clutter, 188

Discussion Questions

1. The opening vignette to the chapter discusses how Carl's Jr. and Hardee's used Paris Hilton in a campaign to introduce the new Spicy BBQ Six Dollar Burger. Evaluate the pros and cons of the decision by CKE Restaurants to use her in the IMC campaign. How might they evaluate the impact of the campaign featuring Hilton?

2. Discuss how marketers can use the persuasion matrix shown in Figure 6-1 to plan their integrated marketing communication programs. Choose a TV commercial or print ad and use the persuasion matrix to evaluate how it might influence consumers' response process.

3. Discuss the various components of source credibility. Find an example of an ad or some other form of marketing communication that uses these source characteristics.

4. Discuss the ethics of celebrities endorsing products in foreign countries such as Japan but not in the United States to protect their image. Do you think celebrities hurt their image by endorsing products and/or appearing in ads? Why or why not?

5. Evaluate the decision by athletic shoe company New Balance not to pay athletes to endorse its products or appear in its ads. Do you think this is a good business decision? Support your position.

6. A number of companies such as McDonald's and Coca-Cola terminated their endorsement contracts with basketball star Kobe Bryant when he was accused of sexual assault. Since the charges against Bryant were dropped, do you think he can be used again as an endorser? Why or why not?

7. Find a celebrity who is currently appearing in an ad for a particular company or brand and use McCracken's meaning transfer model (shown in Figure 6-4) to analyze the use of this individual as a spokesperson.

8. What is meant by a primacy versus recency effect? When might an advertiser want to try and achieve its type of effect?

9. What is a refutational appeal? Under what conditions might a marketer create a refutational message?

10. IMC Perspective 6-1 discusses how the Miller Brewing Co. has successfully used comparative advertising for its Miller Lite brand to compete against Bud Light. Why do you think the comparative ads for Miller Lite have been successful? Evaluate the decision by Anheuser Busch to counter with comparative advertising.

11. What is meant by a qualitative media effect? Select a magazine and discuss the nature of the media environment in that publication.

Establishing Objectives and Budgeting for the Promotional Program

7

Chapter Objectives

1. To recognize the importance and value of setting specific objectives for advertising and promotion.
2. To understand the role objectives play in the IMC planning process and the relationship of promotional objectives to marketing objectives.
3. To know the differences between sales and communications objectives and the issues regarding the use of each.
4. To recognize some problems marketers encounter in setting objectives for their IMC programs.
5. To understand the process of budgeting for IMC.
6. To understand theoretical issues involved in budget setting.
7. To know various methods of budget setting.

The Search for the Holy Grail: Marketers Seek the Elusive ROI

It seems that as long as there has been advertising, there has been someone who is determined to figure out whether the monies being spent are worth it or not. The now famous John Wanamaker quote, "I know that 50 percent of my money is wasted, I just don't know which 50 percent," has pretty much summed up advertisers' perspective on the relationship between advertising and sales. Until now that is.

While marketers have never really been content to spend on advertising without knowing whether it was working or not, they seemed to have resigned themselves to the fact that it was extremely difficult—if not impossible—to determine the return on their investment. However, as the number of media options has increased dramatically over the past few years, so too has the demand for accountability. The availability of more data, increasingly sophisticated measurement tools, and the belief that traditional media are not as effective as in the past, combined with the ability of direct marketing and—to a lesser degree—sales promotion to show the impact of various expenditures, have increased pressures on managers. These managers must demonstrate the same ability to demonstrate impact for other media including advertising, product placements, and guerrilla tactics. It simply comes down to an attempt to determine how much to spend and where to spend it.

As noted by Joe Mandese, editor of *MediaPost* online advertising and media directory, "Three new letters—ROI—have officially joined the lexicon of media planning and buying terms." Mandese notes that according to a study conducted by the Advertising Research Foundation, "Nearly half of advertisers and agencies altered their 2005 media buying plans based on some form of ROI—or return on investment—analysis." Further, the vast majority of both advertisers and agency personnel said there would be an increased emphasis on determining ROI in the future. Marketers now want to know the actual return on investment of each dollar spent, and they want a view of likely returns on future campaigns. Martyn Straw, chief strategy officer of BBDO Worldwide, who specializes in determining ROI for his clients, attributes much of this emphasis to the fact that "marketing has gone from being a cost or expense to being an investment," and investments, he notes, demand accountability.

While all of this sounds good in theory, the fact remains that measuring ROI is not as simple as it seems. Part of the reason is the fact that the primary criteria often used to make this determination are not always agreed upon or easy to measure. For the advertiser, the primary focus is usually on the impact of the expenditures on sales and/or market share. Media planners often focus on factors such as cost efficiencies or "fit" with the media content. This lack of a uniform set of metrics makes it difficult to determine effectiveness. Further complicating the process is the fact that different media are used to achieve different objectives.

Mark LaNeve, head of North American marketing and advertising for General Motors Corporation, cites customer tracking as the top priority of communications. LaNeve notes that GM no longer advertises just because "it feels good," and there are no more sponsored golf tournaments unless the sponsoring brand collects a number of customer profiles through test drives. He credits such measures (among others) in assisting GM to cut the marketing expenditures for Cadillac in half while increasing sales and market share over the past three years. Yet LaNeve also notes that while he "knows with 98 percent certainty what the payoff of a direct marketing campaign will be before committing a cent," he admits the impact of image-building TV and print ads remains "a mystery or educated guess." It is this "holy grail" of measurement—figuring out the impact of traditional mass advertising—that has him, as well as almost everyone else, stumped. In fact, no one is ready to step up to the plate and claim that they can determine the ROI associated with mass advertising. And not everyone agrees that ROI is the answer.

Rishad Tobaccowala, chief innovation officer of media agency Publicis Groupe Media, contends that there is an altered media landscape driven by the "arrogance of ROI," and that too much time and effort is being spent on cutting costs and measuring inputs (cost of media, cost of eyeballs) as opposed to determining the costs of outcomes. He says that marketers are too focused on these variables because they can control and measure them. The result of this orientation, Tobaccowala notes, will be to drive talent from the industry, starve innovation, and—most important—"take the industry further down the path of measuring the wrong data." He calls for measurement systems that will deliver the company's success in the future, and that will lead to an investment in tomorrow rather than how to cut costs today. No wonder they call it the search for the holy grail. Will anyone even know if they do find it?

Sources: Rishad Tobaccowala, "Counterpoint," *Point,* May 2005, p. 6; Joe Mandese, "Half of Media Buys Driven by ROI, TV, Online Dominate," *MediaPost,* April 20, 2005, pp. 1–3. Diane Brady and David Kiley, "Making Marketing Measure Up," *BusinessWeek,* December 13, 2004, pp. 112–113.

The lead-in to this chapter reports on one of the prime issues facing marketers today—determining the return on investment (ROI) of expenditures on advertising and promotion. As you can see, there is no 100 percent agreement on how to measure ROI, or even what should be measured. As this chapter will demonstrate, the success of a program can and should be measured by both marketing and communications objectives. This chapter will examine how the goals for the integrated marketing communications program follow the company's overall marketing strategy and how these goals determine and are determined by the promotional budget.

Unfortunately, many companies have difficulty with the most critical step in the promotional planning process—setting realistic objectives that will guide the development of the IMC program. Complex marketing situations, conflicting perspectives regarding what advertising and other promotional mix elements are expected to accomplish, and uncertainty over resources make the setting of marketing communications objectives "a job of creating order out of chaos."[1] While the task of setting objectives can be complex and difficult, it must be done properly, because specific goals and objectives are the foundation on which all other promotional decisions are made. Budgeting for advertising and other promotional areas, as well as creative and media strategies and tactics, evolves from these objectives. They also provide a standard against which performance can be measured.

Setting specific objectives should be an integral part of the planning process. However, many companies either fail to use specific marketing communications objectives or set ones that are inadequate for guiding the development of the promotional plan or measuring its effectiveness. Many marketers are uncertain as to what integrated marketing communications should be expected to contribute to the marketing program. The goal of their company's advertising and promotional program is simple: to generate sales. They fail to recognize the specific tasks that advertising and other promotional mix variables must perform in preparing customers to buy a particular product or service.

As we know, advertising and promotion are not the only marketing activities involved in generating sales. Moreover, it is not always possible or necessary to measure the effects of advertising in terms of sales. For example, the Ford ad in Exhibit 7-1 is designed to promote the company's support in the fight against breast cancer.

Consider the Honda ad shown in Exhibit 7-2. What objectives (other than generating sales) might the company have for this ad? How might its effectiveness be measured?

This chapter examines the nature and purpose of objectives and the role they play in guiding the development, implementation, and evaluation of an IMC program. Attention is given to the various types of objectives appropriate for different situations. We will also examine the budget-setting process and the interdependence of objective setting and budgeting.

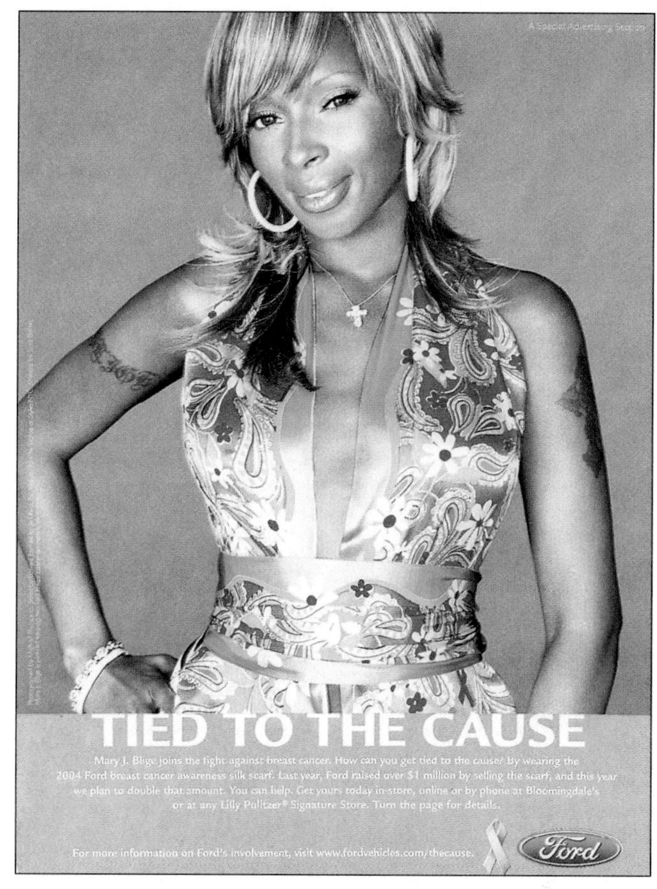

Exhibit 7-1 The objective of this ad is to demonstrate Ford's support for a cause

The Value of Objectives

Perhaps one reason many companies fail to set specific objectives for their integrated marketing communications programs is that they don't recognize the value of doing so. Another may be disagreement as to what the specific objectives should be. Advertising and promotional objectives are needed for several reasons, including the functions they serve in communications, planning and decision making, and measurement and evaluation.

Communications

Specific objectives for the IMC program facilitate coordination of the various groups working on the campaign. Many people are involved in the planning and development of an integrated marketing communications program on the client side as well as in the various promotional agencies. The advertising and promotional program must be coordinated within the company, inside the ad agency, and between the two. Any other parties involved in the promotional campaign, such as public relations and/or sales promotion firms, research specialists, or media buying services, must also know what the company hopes to accomplish through its marketing communications program. Many problems can be avoided if all parties have written, approved objectives to guide their actions and serve as a common base for discussing issues related to the promotional program.

Planning and Decision Making

Specific promotional objectives also guide development of the integrated marketing communications plan. All phases of a firm's promotional strategy should be based on the established objectives, including budgeting, creative, and media decisions as well as supportive programs such as direct marketing, public relations/publicity, sales promotion, and/or reseller support.

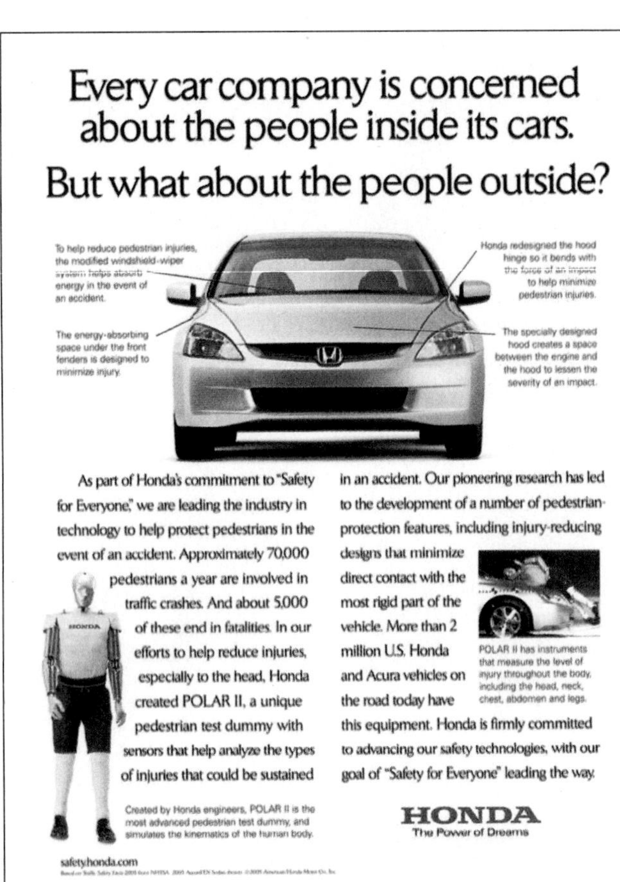

Every car company is concerned about the people inside its cars.
But what about the people outside?
To help reduce pedestrian injuries, the modified windshield-wiper system helps absorb energy in the event of an accident.
Honda redesigned the hood hinge so it bends with the force of an impact to help minimize pedestrian injuries.
The energy-absorbing space under the front fenders is designed to minimize injury.
The specially designed hood creates a space between the engine and the hood to lessen the severity of an impact.
As part of Honda's commitment to "Safety for Everyone," we are leading the industry in technology to help protect pedestrians in the event of an accident. Approximately 70,000 pedestrians a year are involved in traffic crashes. And about 5,000 of these end in fatalities. In our efforts to help reduce injuries, especially to the head, Honda created POLAR II, a unique pedestrian test dummy with sensors that help analyze the types of injuries that could be sustained in an accident. Our pioneering research has led to the development of a number of pedestrian-protection features, including injury-reducing designs that minimize direct contact with the most rigid part of the vehicle. More than 2 million U.S. Honda and Acura vehicles on the road today have this equipment. Honda is firmly committed to advancing our safety technologies, with our goal of "Safety for Everyone" leading the way.
POLAR II has instruments that measure the level of injury throughout the body, including the head, neck, chest, abdomen and legs.
Created by Honda engineers, POLAR II is the most advanced pedestrian test dummy, and simulates the kinematics of the human body.
HONDA
The Power of Dreams
safety.honda.com

Exhibit 7-2 Honda's objectives for this ad may be other than sales

Meaningful objectives can also be a useful guide for decision making. Promotional planners are often faced with a number of strategic and tactical options in terms of choosing creative options, selecting media, and allocating the budget among various elements of the promotional mix. Choices should be made based on how well a particular strategy matches the firm's promotional objectives.

Measurement and Evaluation of Results

An important reason for setting specific objectives is that they provide a benchmark against which the success or failure of the promotional campaign can be measured. Without specific objectives, it is extremely difficult to determine what the firm's advertising and promotion efforts accomplished. One characteristic of good objectives is that they are *measurable;* they specify a method and criteria for determining how well the promotional program is working. By setting specific and meaningful objectives, the promotional planner provides a measure(s) that can be used to evaluate the effectiveness of the marketing communications program. Most organizations are concerned about the return on their promotional investment, and comparing actual performance against measurable objectives is the best way to determine if the return justifies the expense.

Determining Promotional Objectives

Integrated marketing communications objectives should be based on a thorough situation analysis that identifies the marketing and promotional issues facing the company or a brand. The situation analysis is the foundation on which marketing objectives are determined and the marketing plan is developed. Promotional objectives evolve from the company's overall marketing plan and are rooted in its marketing objectives. Advertising and promotion objectives are not the same as marketing objectives (although many firms tend to treat them as synonymous).

Marketing versus Communications Objectives

Marketing objectives are generally stated in the firm's marketing plan and are statements of what is to be accomplished by the overall marketing program within a given time period. Marketing objectives are usually defined in terms of specific, measurable outcomes such as sales volume, market share, profits, or return on investment. Good marketing objectives are *quantifiable;* they delineate the target market and note the time frame for accomplishing the goal (often one year). For example, a copy machine company may have as its marketing objective "to increase sales by 10 percent in the small-business segment of the market during the next 12 months." To be effective, objectives must also be *realistic* and *attainable.*

A company with a very high market share may seek to increase its sales volume by stimulating growth in the product category. It might accomplish this by increasing consumption by current users or encouraging nonusers to use the product. Some firms have as their marketing objectives expanding distribution and sales of their product in certain market areas. Companies often have secondary marketing objectives that are related to actions they must take to solve specific problems and thus achieve their primary objectives.

Once the marketing communications manager has reviewed the marketing plan, he or she should understand where the company hopes to go with its marketing program, how it intends to get there, and the role advertising and promotion will play. Marketing goals defined in terms of sales, profit, or market share increases are usually not appropriate promotional objectives. They are objectives for the entire marketing program, and achieving them depends on the proper coordination and execution of all the marketing-mix elements, including not just promotion but product planning and production, pricing, and distribution. For example, a company may be very successful in its promotional program, creating interest and/or trial for a product. But what if the product is unavailable when the consumer goes to buy it, or what if, once in the store, the consumer feels the product is overpriced and decides not to buy? Should the promotional program be blamed when the product's poor performance is due to other marketing strategies or tactics?

Integrated marketing communications objectives are statements of what various aspects of the IMC program will accomplish. They should be based on the particular communications tasks required to deliver the appropriate messages to the target audience. Managers must be able to translate general marketing goals into communications goals and specific promotional objectives. Some guidance in doing this may be available from the marketing plan, as the situation analysis should provide important information on

- The market segments the firm wants to target and the target audience (demographics, psychographics, and purchase motives).
- The product and its main features, advantages, benefits, uses, and applications.
- The company's and competitors' brands (sales and market share in various segments, positioning, competitive strategies, promotional expenditures, creative and media strategies, and tactics).
- Ideas on how the brand should be positioned and specific behavioral responses being sought (trial, repurchase, brand switching, and increased usage).

Sometimes companies do not have a formal marketing plan, and the information needed may not be readily available. In this case, the promotional planner must attempt to gather as much information as possible about the product and its markets from sources both inside and outside the company.

After reviewing all the information, the promotional planner should see how integrated marketing communications fits into the marketing program and what the firm hopes to achieve through advertising and other promotional elements. The next step is to set objectives in terms of specific communications goals or tasks.

Many promotional planners approach promotion from a communications perspective and believe the objective of advertising and other promotional mix elements is usually to communicate information or a selling message about a product or service. Other managers argue that sales or some related measure, such as market share, is the only meaningful goal for advertising and promotion and should be the basis for setting objectives. These two perspectives have been the topic of considerable debate and are worth examining further.

Sales versus Communications Objectives

Sales-Oriented Objectives

To many managers, the only meaningful objective for their promotional program is sales. They take the position that the basic reason a firm spends money on advertising and promotion is to sell its product or service. Promotional spending represents an investment of a firm's scarce resources that requires an economic justification. Rational managers generally compare investment options on a common financial basis, such as return on investment (ROI). As discussed in the chapter lead-in, determining the specific return on advertising and promotional dollars is often a quite difficult task. However, many managers believe that monies spent on advertising and other forms of promotion should produce measurable results, such as increasing sales volume by a certain percentage or dollar

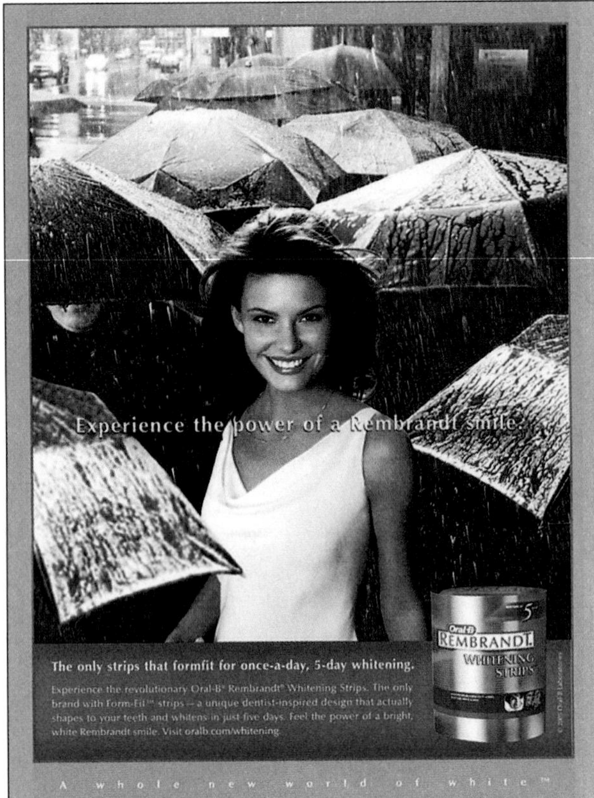

Exhibit 7-3 Growth in the tooth-whitening market led to numerous brand extensions

amount or increasing the brand's market share. They believe objectives (as well as the success or failure of the campaign) should be based on the achievement of sales results. For example, two of the largest three oral care manufacturers (Unilever and Colgate-Palmolive) joined Procter & Gamble in the marketing of at-home tooth-whitening kits (Exhibit 7-3). Unilever spent $20 million on Mentadent and Colgate allocated $60 million on Simply White in their product launches. Colgate's objective was to get $100 million in sales in the first year (the total category sales are estimated at $500 million and were expected to reach $700 million in the United States alone).[2] The rapid growth of the category has led to a number of line extensions and new entries as can be seen in Exhibit 7-3.

As a result, they have increased their efforts to make agencies more accountable for their performances. In turn, some agencies have developed their own tools to attempt to provide more ROI information in regard to how their integrated communications programs are performing. Grey Global Group, Interpublic Group, and J. Walter Thompson are just a few of the agencies that are boasting of their ability to measure their client's ROIs. McCann-Erickson's World Group Fusion 2.0 system has been adopted by many of its clients including General Motors, Microsoft, and Pfizer.[3]

Some managers prefer sales-oriented objectives to make the individuals involved in advertising and promotion think in terms of how the promotional program will influence sales. Or they may confuse marketing objectives with advertising and promotional objectives. For example, in recent years the major U.S. cereal manufacturers have focused on goals designed to stimulate sales. When cereal sales dropped in the mid-1990s, Post Cereals and General Mills both slashed their prices in an attempt to increase sales. Kellogg's immediately followed suit. Much of the money used to fund the price cuts came from decreases in advertising and promotions spending. By the end of 1998 an estimated $1.5 billion had been cut from advertising budgets. Yet sales continued to fall, profits dropped, and still no brand-share gains were recorded. The sales of ready-to-eat cereals continued their decline into 2004.[4] Interestingly, the few bright spots came from heavily advertised brands. Kellogg's Smart Start and Special K brands showed sales increases of 72 and 22 percent, respectively, in the first quarter of 2002, when their advertising budgets were significantly increased.[5] The increases continued as a result of more brand differentiated advertising, putting Kellogg's back into the leadership position.[6] For Kellogg's and Post the goal was to increase sales and market share versus store brands. This goal not only became the basis of the marketing plan but carried over as the primary objective of the promotional program. The success of the advertising and promotional campaign was judged only by attainment of these goals.

Problems with Sales Objectives Given Kellogg's and Post's failures to reverse their sales declines, does this mean the advertising and promotional program was ineffective? (For Kellogg's the new advertising seemed to work.) Or does it mean the price cuts didn't work? It might help to compare this situation to a football game and think of advertising as a quarterback. The quarterback is one of the most important players on the team but can be effective only with support from the other players. If the team loses, is it fair to blame the loss entirely on the quarterback? Of course not. Just as the quarterback is but one of the players on the football team, promotion is but one element of the marketing program, and there are many other reasons why the targeted sales level was not reached. The quarterback can lead his team to victory only if the linemen block, the receivers catch his passes, and the running backs help the offense establish a balanced attack of running and passing. Even if the quarterback plays an outstanding game, the team can still lose if the defense gives up too many points.

In the business world, poor sales results can be due to any of the other marketing-mix variables, including product design or quality, packaging, distribution, or pricing.

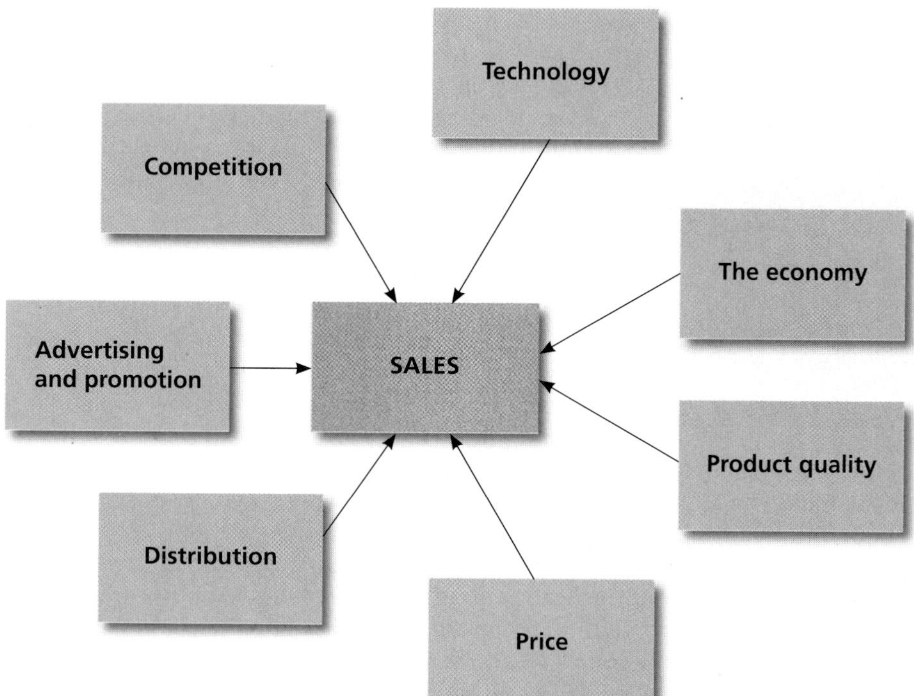

Figure 7-1 Factors Influencing Sales

Advertising can make consumers aware of and interested in the brand, but it can't make them buy it, particularly if it is not readily available or is priced higher than a competing brand. As shown in Figure 7-1, sales are a function of many factors, not just advertising and promotion. There is an adage in marketing that states, "Nothing will kill a poor product faster than good advertising." Taken with the other factors shown in Figure 7-1, this adage demonstrates that all the marketing elements must work together if a successful plan is to be implemented.

Another problem with sales objectives is that the effects of advertising often occur over an extended period. Many experts recognize that advertising has a lagged or **carryover effect;** monies spent on advertising do not necessarily have an immediate impact on sales.[7] Advertising may create awareness, interest, and/or favorable attitudes toward a brand, but these feelings will not result in an actual purchase until the consumer enters the market for the product, which may occur later. A review of econometric studies that examined the duration of cumulative advertising effects found that for mature, frequently purchased, low-priced products, advertising's effect on sales lasts up to nine months.[8] Models have been developed to account for the carryover effect of advertising and to help determine the long-term effect of advertising on sales.[9] The carryover effect adds to the difficulty of determining the precise relationship between advertising and sales.

Another problem with sales objectives is that they offer little guidance to those responsible for planning and developing the promotional program. The creative and media people working on the account need some direction as to the nature of the advertising message the company hopes to communicate, the intended audience, and the particular effect or response sought. As you will see shortly, communications objectives are recommended because they provide operational guidelines for those involved in planning, developing, and executing the advertising and promotional program.

Where Sales Objectives Are Appropriate

While there can be many problems in attempting to use sales as objectives for a promotional campaign, there are situations where sales objectives are appropriate. Certain types of promotion efforts are direct action in nature; they attempt to induce an immediate behavioral response from the prospective customer. A major objective of most sales promotion

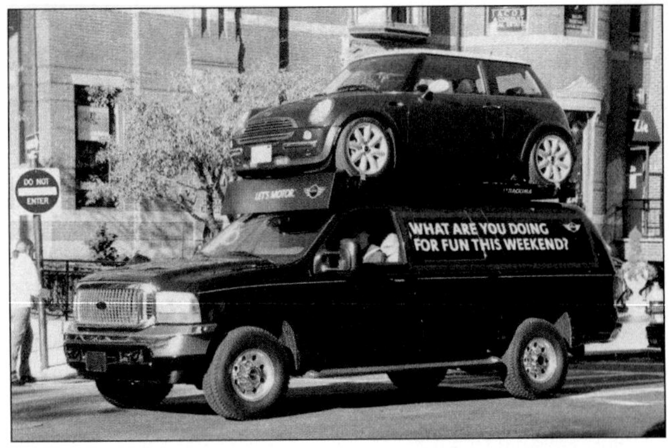

Exhibit 7-4 MINI USA used a nontraditional, integrated campaign to relaunch the MINI brand in the U.S. market

programs is to generate short-term increases in sales. The "ads" in Exhibit 7-4 were part of BMW Group's nontraditional integrated marketing campaign that simultaneously relaunched the MINI brand, introduced two new models—the MINI Cooper and MINI Cooper S—and established a new automotive segment (MINI is the smallest car on the American road) to the American public. Over 5.3 million Classic MINIs were sold worldwide from 1959 to 2000 but only 10,000 Classic MINIs were sold in the United States from 1960 to 1967. Over the years, MINI became a British automotive icon, with milkmen, rock stars, and royalty alike behind the wheel. Since the SUV dominated the American marketplace, the spirit of the MINI brand values and extremely low brand awareness necessitated the development of a nontraditional campaign that would uniquely position the MINI brand and break through the cluttered automotive advertising environment. In the prelaunch phase, MINIs were stacked on top of SUVs that toured the country to bring attention to the brand. Then, seats were removed from sports stadiums in Oakland, California, and New Orleans, and MINIs were put on display at Major League Baseball and National Football League football games. At these events, wallet cards were handed out encouraging interested parties to visit the MINIUSA.com website to create their own customized MINI and sign up to become a "MINI Insider." For launch, traditional media (magazine and out-of-home) were used in nontraditional ways and complemented by extensive public relations activities. The campaign yielded over 115,000 "MINI Insider" registrants on the website and record click-through rates on outbound e-mail campaigns. Thousands of MINIs were preordered even before the car was available in dealer showrooms, putting MINI well on track to reach its sales goal of 20,000 units.[10] (By 2003 sales had reached 36,000 units.[11])

Direct-response advertising is one type of advertising that evaluates its effectiveness on the basis of sales. Merchandise is advertised in material mailed to customers, in newspapers and magazines, through the Internet, or on television. The consumer purchases the merchandise by mail, on the Net, or by calling a toll-free number. The direct-response advertiser generally sets objectives and measures success in terms of the sales response generated by the ad. For example, objectives for and the evaluation of a direct-response ad on TV are based on the number of orders received each time a station broadcasts the commercial. Because advertising is really the only form of communication and promotion used in this situation and response is generally immediate, setting objectives in terms of sales is appropriate. The SkyTel interactive messaging system shown in Exhibit 7-5 is an example of a product sold through direct-response advertising.

Exhibit 7-5 Sales results are an appropriate objective for direct-response advertising

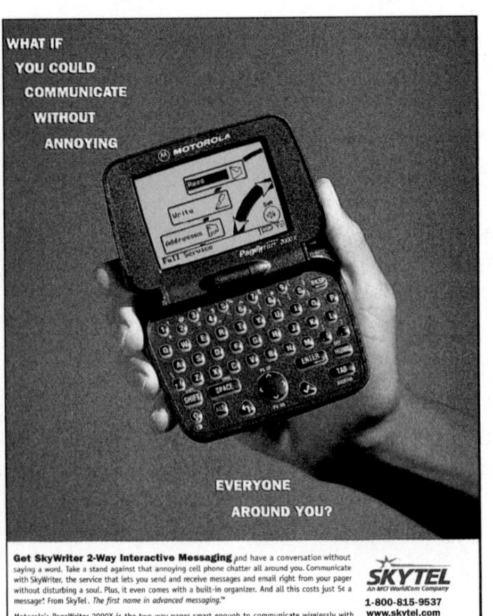

Retail advertising, which accounts for a significant percentage of all advertising expenditures, is another area where the advertiser often seeks a direct response, particularly when sales or special events are being promoted. The ad for Pier 1 import's back to school sale shown in Exhibit 7-6 is designed to attract consumers to stores during the sales period (and to generate sales volume). Pier 1 import's management can determine the effectiveness of its promotional effort by analyzing store traffic and sales volume during sale days and comparing them to figures for nonsale days. But retailers may also allocate advertising and promotional dollars to image-building campaigns designed to create and enhance favorable perceptions of their stores. In this case, sales-oriented objectives would not be appropriate; the effectiveness of the campaign would be based on its ability to create or change consumers' image of the store.

Sales-oriented objectives are also used when advertising plays a dominant role in a firm's marketing program and other factors are relatively stable. For example, many packaged-goods companies compete in mature markets with established channels of distribution, stable competitive prices and promotional budgets, and products of similar quality. They view advertising and sales promotion as the key determinants of a brand's sales or market share, so it may be possible to isolate the effects of these promotional mix variables.[12] Many companies have accumulated enough market knowledge with their advertising, sales promotion, and direct-marketing programs to have considerable insight into the sales levels that should result from their promotional efforts. Referring to the cereal companies mentioned earlier, Mark Baynes, vice president of Kellogg's Morning Foods Division, attributes Kellogg's recent turnabout in sales to effective advertising, brand repositioning, and more emotional appeals that generate interest.[13] Thus, many companies believe it is reasonable to set objectives and evaluate the success of their promotional efforts in terms of sales results.

Advertising and promotional programs tend to be evaluated in terms of sales, particularly when expectations are not being met. Marketing and brand managers under pressure to show sales results often take a short-term perspective in evaluating advertising and sales promotion programs. They are often looking for a quick fix for declining sales or loss of market share. They ignore the pitfalls of making direct links between advertising and sales, and campaigns, as well as ad agencies, may be changed if sales expectations are not being met. As discussed in Chapter 3, many companies want their agencies to accept incentive-based compensation systems tied to sales performance. Thus, while sales may not be an appropriate objective in many advertising and promotional situations, managers are inclined to keep a close eye on sales and market share figures and make changes in the promotional program when these numbers become stagnant, or decline.

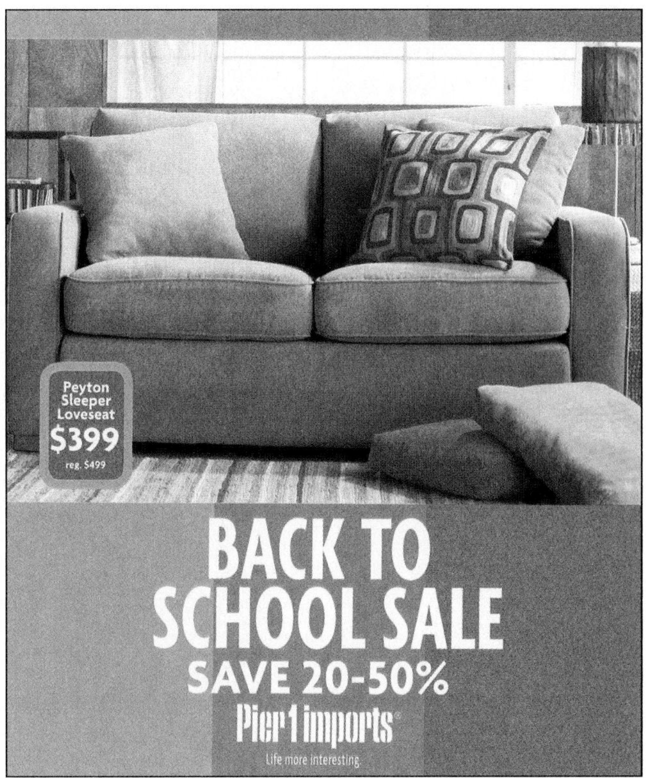

Exhibit 7-6 Retail ads often seek sales objectives

Exhibit 7-7 Philips creates an image for its products

Communications Objectives

Some marketers do recognize the problems associated with sales-oriented objectives. They recognize that the primary role of an IMC program is to communicate and that planning should be based on communications objectives. Advertising and other promotional efforts are designed to achieve such communications as brand knowledge and interest, favorable attitudes and image, and purchase intentions. Consumers are not expected to respond immediately; rather, advertisers realize they must provide relevant information and create favorable predispositions toward the brand before purchase behavior will occur.

For example, the ad for Philips in Exhibit 7-7 is designed to inform consumers of the company's focus on technology that makes sense and is simple. While there is no call for immediate action, the ad creates favorable impressions about the company by creating a distinct image. Consumers will consider this image when they enter the market for products in this category.

Figure 7-2 Effect of Advertising on Consumers: Movement from Awareness to Action

Related behavioral dimensions	Movement toward purchase	Example of types of promotion or advertising relevant to various steps
Conative The realm of motives. Ads stimulate or direct desires.	**Purchase**	Point-of-purchase Retail store ads Deals "Last-chance" offers Price appeals Testimonials
	Conviction	
Affective The realm of emotions. Ads change attitudes and feelings.	**Preference**	Competitive ads Argumentative copy
	Liking	"Image" copy Status, glamour appeals
Cognitive The realm of thoughts. Ads provide information and facts.	**Knowledge**	Announcements Descriptive copy Classified ads Slogans Jingles Skywriting
	Awareness	Teaser campaigns

Advocates of communications-based objectives generally use some form of the hierarchical models discussed in Chapter 5 when setting advertising and promotion objectives. In all these models, consumers pass through three successive stages: cognitive, affective, and conative. As consumers proceed through the three stages, they move closer to making a purchase. Figure 7-2 shows the various steps in the Lavidge and Steiner hierarchy of effects model as the consumer moves from awareness to purchase, along with examples of types of promotion or advertising relevant to each step.

Communications Effects Pyramid

Advertising and promotion perform communications tasks in the same way that a pyramid is built, by first accomplishing lower-level objectives such as awareness and knowledge or comprehension.[14] Subsequent tasks involve moving consumers who are aware of or knowledgeable about the product or service to higher levels in the pyramid (Figure 7-3). The initial stages, at the base of the pyramid, are easier to accomplish than those toward the top, such as trial and repurchase or regular use. Thus, the percentage of prospective customers will decline as they move up the pyramid. Figure 7-4 shows how a company introducing a new brand of shampoo targeted at 18- to 34-year-old females might set its IMC objectives using the communications effects pyramid.

The communications pyramid can also be used to determine promotional objectives for an established brand. The promotional planner must determine where the target audience lies with respect to the various blocks in the pyramid. If awareness levels for

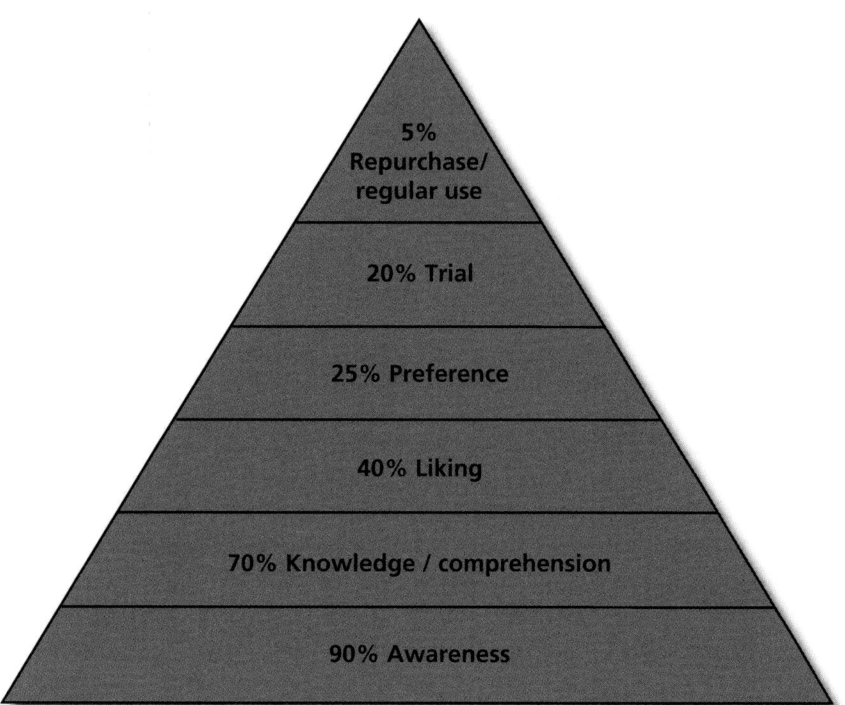

Figure 7-3 Communications Effects Pyramid

a brand and knowledge of its features and benefits are low, the communications objective should be to increase them. If these blocks of the pyramid are already in place, but liking or preference is low, the advertising goal may be to change the target markets' image of the brand and move consumers through to purchase. A number of companies including GM and Sprint have their own versions of communications pyramids that they use for planning.

Problems with Communications Objectives

Not all marketing and advertising managers accept communications objectives; some say it is too difficult to translate a sales goal into a specific communications objective. But at some point a sales goal must be transformed into a communications objective. If the marketing plan

Figure 7-4 Setting Objectives Using the Communications Effects Pyramid

Product: Backstage Shampoo

Time period: Six months

Objective 1: Create awareness among 90 percent of target audience. Use repetitive advertising in newspapers, magazines, TV and radio programs. Simple message.

Objective 2: Create interest in the brand among 70 percent of target audience. Communicate information about the features and benefits of the brand—i.e., that it contains no soap and improves the texture of the hair. Use more copy in ads to convey benefits.

Objective 3: Create positive feelings about the brand among 40 percent and preference among 25 percent of the target audience. Create favorable attitudes by conveying information, promotions, sampling, etc. Refer consumer to website for more information, beauty tips, etc.

Objective 4: Obtain trial among 20 percent of the target audience. Use sampling and cents-off coupons along with advertising and promotions. Offer coupons through website.

Objective 5: Develop and maintain regular use of Backstage Shampoo among 5 percent of the target audience. Use continued-reinforcement advertising, fewer coupons and promotions. Increase communications efforts to professionals.

Figure 7-5 Factors Related to Success of Advertising for New Products

- **Communicating that something is different about the product.** Successful introductory commercials communicated some point of difference for the new product.
- **Positioning the brand difference in relation to the product category.** Successful commercials positioned their brand's difference within a specific product category. For example, a new breakfast product was positioned as the "crispiest cereal" and a new beverage as the "smoothest soft drink."
- **Communicating that the product difference is beneficial to consumers.** Nearly all of the successful commercials linked a benefit directly to the new product's difference.
- **Supporting the idea that something about the product is different and/or beneficial to consumers.** All the successful commercials communicated support for the product's difference claim or its relevance to consumers. Support took the form of demonstrations of performance, information supporting a uniqueness claim, endorsements, or testimonials.

for an established brand has an objective of increasing sales by 10 percent, the promotional planner will eventually have to think in terms of the message that will be communicated to the target audience to achieve this. Possible objectives include the following:

- Increasing the percentage of consumers in the target market who associate specific features, benefits, or advantages with our brand.
- Increasing the number of consumers in the target audience who prefer our product over the competition's.
- Encouraging current users of the product to use it more frequently or in more situations.
- Encouraging consumers who have never used our brand to try it.

In some situations, promotional planners may gain insight into communications objectives' relationship to sales from industry research. Evalucom, Inc., conducted a study of commercials for new products. Some succeeded in stimulating anticipated levels of sales; others did not. Figure 7-5 shows four factors the study identified that affect whether a commercial for a new product is successful in generating sales.

In attempting to translate sales goals into specific communications objectives, promotional planners often are not sure what constitutes adequate levels of awareness, knowledge, liking, preference, or conviction. There are no formulas to provide this information. The promotional manager will have to use his or her personal experience and that of the brand or product managers, as well as the marketing history of this and similar brands. Average scores on various communications measures for this and similar products should be considered, along with the levels achieved by competitors' products. This information can be related to the amount of money and time spent building these levels as well as the resulting sales or market share figures.

At some point, sales-oriented objectives must be translated into what the company hopes to communicate and to whom it hopes to communicate it. For example, in the highly competitive office supply industry Boise Cascade has been around for over 35 years. In a market where differentiation is difficult to achieve due to the fact that many companies make the same products at about equal prices, Boise lacked personality. The company needed to change the consumers' focus from price to the advantages provided by its knowledge and experience in the industry. After identifying the target market as women 18 to 54 with a high school diploma, the company combined with its agency to develop a "personality test" that customers and potential customers could take to learn more about their personalities and interactive styles. In addition, participants could learn more about the styles of co-workers, relatives, and so on, to improve communications. The "You've Got to Have Personality" campaign was designed in an attempt to have participants learn more about themselves as well as Boise Cascade. Initially using advertising, direct mail, the Internet, and sales promotions, the program was later extended to include trade shows and other promotions. The results were obvious—a 30 percent increase in Web traffic and a 250 percent jump in visitors to the company's online magazine. Most important, recognition of the Boise name increased, a personality was established, and sales of the products promoted in the "Personality" flyer increased 15.8 percent over the previous year.[15] IMC Perspective 7-1 examines the communications objectives used in an award-winning IMC campaign by Molson beer.

Many marketing and promotional managers recognize the value of setting specific communications objectives and their important role as operational guidelines to the planning, execution, and evaluation of the promotional program. Communications objectives are the criteria used in the DAGMAR approach to setting advertising goals and objectives, which has become one of the most influential approaches to the advertising planning process.

DAGMAR: An Approach to Setting Objectives

In 1961, Russell Colley prepared a report for the Association of National Advertisers titled *Defining Advertising Goals for Measured Advertising Results* (DAGMAR).[16] In it, Colley developed a model for setting advertising objectives and measuring the results of an ad campaign. The major thesis of the **DAGMAR** model is that communications effects are the logical basis for advertising goals and objectives against which success or failure should be measured. Colley's rationale for communications-based objectives was as follows:

> Advertising's job, purely and simply, is to communicate to a defined audience information and a frame of mind that stimulates action. Advertising succeeds or fails depending on how well it communicates the desired information and attitudes to the right people at the right time and at the right cost.[17]

Under the DAGMAR approach, an advertising goal involves a **communications task** that is specific and measurable. A communications task, as opposed to a marketing task, can be performed by, and attributed to, advertising rather than to a combination of several marketing factors. Colley proposed that the communications task be based on a hierarchical model of the communications process with four stages:

- *Awareness*—making the consumer aware of the existence of the brand or company.
- *Comprehension*—developing an understanding of what the product is and what it will do for the consumer.
- *Conviction*—developing a mental disposition in the consumer to buy the product.
- *Action*—getting the consumer to purchase the product.

As discussed earlier, other hierarchical models of advertising effects can be used as a basis for analyzing the communications response process. Some advertising theorists prefer the Lavidge and Steiner hierarchy of effects model, since it is more specific and provides a better way to establish and measure results.[18]

While the hierarchical model of advertising effects was the basic model of the communications response process used in DAGMAR, Colley also studied other specific tasks that advertising might be expected to perform in leading to the ultimate objective of a sale. He developed a checklist of 52 advertising tasks to characterize the contribution of advertising and serve as a starting point for establishing objectives.

Characteristics of Objectives

A second major contribution of DAGMAR to the advertising planning process was its definition of what constitutes a good objective. Colley argued that advertising objectives should be stated in terms of concrete and measurable communications tasks, specify a target

IMC PERSPECTIVE 7-1

Changing the Brand Image to Make Friends and Increase Sales

Does achieving communications objectives lead to an increase in sales? The answer to this question is maybe or maybe not, as sales are a function of a number of factors beyond just advertising and promotion. At the same time, there is more and more evidence of a strong relationship between the two. Take the case (not a case!) of Molson Canadian beer for example.

Although it is the number-one-selling domestic beer in Canada, Molson Canadian saw its market share in the United States drop during the 1990s. Import beers as a category had experienced rapid growth during this time, but Molson's sales dropped by about 50 percent due largely to lack of attention from Miller Brewing Company, which owned the rights to the product in the United States. In order to save the brand, and turn the declining sales trend around, Molson bought back the rights from Miller and embarked on a communications strategy to reposition Molson Canadian.

The new strategy began with an in-depth research study of the beer-drinking culture of the target market—males 21 to 27. The research team visited clubs, restaurants, bars, and virtually anywhere else these guys could buy a bottle of imported beer. They watched what the men drank, how they held the bottle, the difference between "Wednesday night beers" (with the guys) and "Friday night beers" (with the ladies), even where the beer was placed on the bar or table in front of them. Their conclusion? Guys go to bars to meet women, and beer, like clothing, is used as a signal to make them more attractive to the opposite sex. Beer labels, like designer labels, are a badge to show who they are. Unfortunately for Molson, the Molson Canadian brand had no badge. Essentially the label had no identity, evoked no meaning or relevance, and, worst of all, provided no assistance in making them more attractive to the opposite sex.

Based on this information, the brand team at Molson established two goals: (1) make the label mean something; and (2) give it relevance to males by helping them build confidence and succeed in their quest to meet women. To do this, a second label, dubbed the Twin Label, was added to the bottles to serve as a signaling device to women by communicating something about the bottle holder. In all, 232 different labels were developed in categories including pickup lines, icebreakers, comebacks, and other statements reflecting strength and physical prowess. The Twin Labels effort was supported with an advertising campaign called "Friends," which ran print ads in *Cosmopolitan, Maxim, Stuff,* and *FHM,* the former to let women know that Molson men were caring and sensitive, the latter three (all men's magazines) to inform the target audience that they are programming women to have a favorable impression of the Molson drinker. The ads suggested that the men save the labels to use the next time they buy a woman a drink. Other "phony" materials—pictures of adoring grandparents, orphans admiring the man's largesse, and puppy and kitten pictures—were available on the Molson U.S. website. So, too, were business cards for luxury yachts, private-jet charters, and other items that could be used to impress women. Television commercials communicated the same message ending with the tagline "Let your Molson do the talking," with a mild disclaimer to male beer fans that Molson would not really help them get women.

The efforts earned Molson and their agency a Jay Chiat Planning Gold and Grand Prix award from the American Association of Advertising Agencies (AAAA). But, did it work? Molson tracked the opinions of the target audience to determine if their efforts had an impact on the brand image. Beer drinkers were asked to finish the following sentence, "Molson is for __________." After six months there was a 23 percent increase among those who said "Young people in their 20s," a 36 percent increase among those who said "Guys who are successful with the ladies," and a 17 percent increase among those who said "Guys who go out on the town a lot." The number of men who had never tried Molson but said they would consider trying it increased by 26 percent. "But what about sales?" you ask. Depending on who you talk to, sales increased by somewhere between 32.5 percent and 48 percent as a result of the campaign.

However, not everyone is impressed. The Marin Institute, an industry watchdog, says the ads violated the industry trade group's (The Beer Institute's) voluntary advertising code, and were neither responsible nor in good taste. The watchdog group said the ads promoted lying and deception, and were offensive and cynical. Molson's response? A company spokesperson said the ads did not promote deception but promoted the brand in a humorous light, noting further that "No one really takes it seriously." Except for the sales.

Sources: Stan Sutter, "Scandal, Beer and Vaughn," *Marketing,* March 22–28, 2005, p. 3; Christopher Lawton, "In Molson Ads, Tips to Get Girls Turns Some Off," *The Wall Street Journal,* July 28, 2004, p. B1; "Gold and Grand Prix Nontraditional Advertising Communications," American Association of Advertising Agencies, 2004, pp. 99–105.

audience, indicate a benchmark starting point and the degree of change sought, and specify a time period for accomplishing the objective(s).

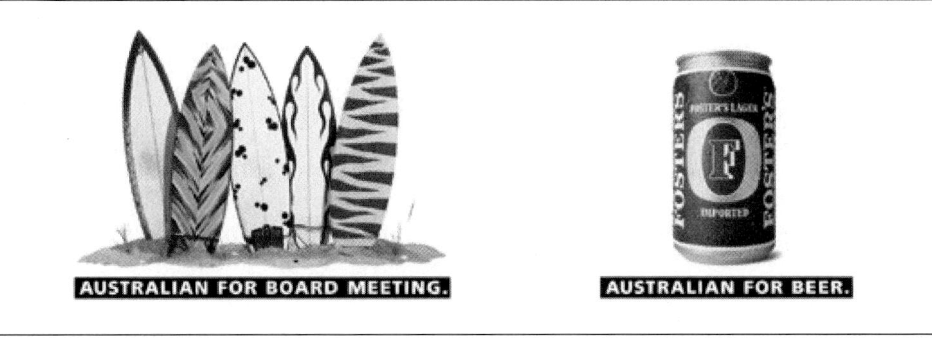

Exhibit 7-8 Foster's Beer delivers a very successful campaign

Concrete, Measurable Tasks The communications task specified in the objective should be a precise statement of what appeal or message the advertiser wants to communicate to the target audience. Advertisers generally use a copy platform to describe their basic message. The objective or copy platform statement should be specific and clear enough to guide the creative specialists who develop the advertising message. For example, Foster's Beer, after a successful introduction, saw sales decline significantly. Knowing that to reverse the downward trend something significant had to be done, Fosters developed an entirely new positioning campaign with the following objectives:

- Strengthen the brand's image.
- Maximize brand presence.
- Broaden the market base beyond traditional import beer drinkers.
- Increase sales.

Using a variety of tools including billboards, videos, point-of-sale promotions, and spot television (Exhibit 7-8), the program doubled its unaided awareness scores, tripled trial, and increased brand awareness by 40 percent. In addition, beer sales doubled in test markets, and overall beer sales increased by 12.1 percent in the first year of the campaign.[19]

According to DAGMAR, the objective must also be measurable. There must be a way to determine whether the intended message has been communicated properly. For example, as was shown in IMC Perspective 7-1, all of the key objectives Molson wished to communicate were accomplished.

Target Audience Another important characteristic of good objectives is a well-defined target audience. The primary target audience for a company's product or service is described in the situation analysis. It may be based on descriptive variables such as geography, demographics, and psychographics (on which advertising media selection decisions are based) as well as on behavioral variables such as usage rate or benefits sought. Figure 7-6 demonstrates the objective-setting process involved in

Target Market:	Qualified prospective employees; geographically located in San Jose, Seattle, and Boston (around MIT)	
Positioning:	Google Labs as a choice destination for the best and brightest in the IT world to practice innovation	
Objectives:	To sort out from thousands of applications only those most qualified candidates, thus saving time and money and attracting the best employees	
Budget:	$948,000.00	
Media:	Outdoor:	Billboards
	Print:	Tech, science, and professional journals; college newspapers
	Internet:	Linux online blog; home site Web pages
	Public Relations:	CBS's *60 Minutes; ABC World News Tonight, The Wall Street Journal;* 200 other media
Results:	2,500 qualified applicants; 300 percent increase in applications	

Figure 7-6 Google Labs Objective Setting

Google's search for qualified job applicants. Notice how the target audience was defined using criteria other than those just mentioned.

Benchmark and Degree of Change Sought

To set objectives, one must know the target audience's present status concerning response hierarchy variables such as awareness, knowledge, image, attitudes, and intentions and then determine the degree to which consumers must be changed by the advertising campaign. Determining the target market's present position regarding the various response stages requires **benchmark measures.** Often a marketing research study must be conducted to determine prevailing levels of the response hierarchy. In the case of a new product or service, the starting conditions are generally at or near zero for all the variables, so no initial research is needed.

Establishing benchmark measures gives the promotional planner a basis for determining what communications tasks need to be accomplished and for specifying particular objectives. For example, a preliminary study for a brand may reveal that awareness is high but consumer perceptions and attitudes are negative. The objective for the campaign must then be to change the target audience's perceptions of and attitudes toward the brand. In the case of Google, the objectives were to dispel the image that Google was a finished product that needed only minor changes, therefore offering little challenge or innovative opportunities.

Quantitative benchmarks are not only valuable in establishing communications goals and objectives but essential for determining whether the campaign was successful. Objectives provide the standard against which the success or failure of a campaign is measured. An ad campaign that results in a 90 percent awareness level for a brand among its target audience cannot really be judged effective unless one knows what percentage of the consumers were aware of the brand before the campaign began. A 70 percent precampaign awareness level would lead to a different interpretation of the campaign's success than would a 30 percent level.

Specified Time Period

A final consideration in setting advertising objectives is specifying the time period in which they must be accomplished. Appropriate time periods can range from a few days to a year or more. Most ad campaigns specify time periods from a few months to a year, depending on the situation facing the advertiser and the type of response being sought. For example, awareness levels for a brand can be created or increased fairly quickly through an intensive media schedule of widespread, repetitive advertising to the target audience. Repositioning of a product requires a change in consumers' perceptions and takes much more time. The repositioning of Marlboro cigarettes from a feminine brand to one with a masculine image, for instance, took several years.

Assessment of DAGMAR

The DAGMAR approach to setting objectives has had considerable influence on the advertising planning process. Many promotional planners use this model as a basis for setting objectives and assessing the effectiveness of their promotional campaigns. DAGMAR also focused advertisers' attention on the value of using communications-based rather than sales-based objectives to measure advertising effectiveness and encouraged the measurement of stages in the response hierarchy to assess a campaign's impact. Colley's work has led to improvements in the advertising and promotional planning process by providing a better understanding of the goals and objectives toward which planners' efforts should be directed. This usually results in less subjectivity and leads to better communication and relationships between client and agency.

Criticisms of DAGMAR

While DAGMAR has contributed to the advertising planning process, it has not been totally accepted by everyone in the advertising field. A number of problems have led to questions regarding its value as a planning tool:[20]

- *Problems with the response hierarchy.* A major criticism of the DAGMAR approach is its reliance on the hierarchy of effects model. The fact that consumers do not always go through this sequence of communications effects before making a purchase has been recognized, and alternative response models have been developed.[21] DAGMAR MOD II recognizes that the appropriate response model depends on the situation and emphasizes identifying the sequence of decision-making steps that apply in a buying situation.[22]

- *Sales objectives.* Another objection to DAGMAR comes from those who argue that the only relevant measure of advertising objectives is sales. They have little tolerance for ad campaigns that achieve communications objectives but fail to increase sales. Advertising is seen as effective only if it induces consumers to make a purchase.[23] The problems with this logic were addressed in our discussion of communications objectives.
- *Practicality and costs.* Another criticism of DAGMAR concerns the difficulties involved in implementing it. Money must be spent on research to establish quantitative benchmarks and measure changes in the response hierarchy. This is costly and time-consuming and can lead to considerable disagreement over method, criteria, measures, and so forth. Many critics argue that DAGMAR is practical only for large companies with big advertising and research budgets. Many firms do not want to spend the money needed to use DAGMAR effectively.
- *Inhibition of creativity.* A final criticism of DAGMAR is that it inhibits advertising creativity by imposing too much structure on the people responsible for developing the advertising. Many creative personnel think the DAGMAR approach is too concerned with quantitative assessment of a campaign's impact on awareness, brand-name recall, or specific persuasion measures. The emphasis is on passing the numbers test rather than developing a message that is truly creative and contributes to brand equity.

Problems in Setting Objectives

Although the DAGMAR model suggests a logical process for advertising and promotion planning, most advertisers and their agencies fail to follow these basic principles. They fail to set specific objectives for their campaigns and/or do not have the proper evidence to determine the success of their promotional programs. A classic study conducted by Stewart H. Britt examined problems with how advertisers set objectives and measure their accomplishment.[24] The study showed that most advertising agencies did not state appropriate objectives for determining success and thus could not demonstrate whether a supposedly successful campaign was really a success. Even though these campaigns may have been doing something right, they generally did not know what it was.

Although this study was conducted in 1969, the same problems exist in advertising today. A more recent study examined the advertising practices of business-to-business marketers to determine whether their ads used advertising objectives that met Colley's four DAGMAR criteria.[25] Entries from the annual Business/Professional Advertising Association Gold Key Awards competition, which solicits the best marketing communications efforts from business-to-business advertisers, were evaluated with respect to their campaigns' objectives and summaries of results. Most of these advertisers did not set concrete advertising objectives, specify objective tasks, measure results in terms of stages of a hierarchy of effects, or match objectives to evaluation measures. The authors concluded: "Advertising practitioners have only partially adopted the concepts and standards of objective setting and evaluation set forth 25 years ago."[26]

Improving Promotional Planners' Use of Objectives

As we have seen, it is important that advertisers and their agencies pay close attention to the objectives they set for their campaigns. They should strive to set specific and measurable objectives that not only guide promotional planning and decision making but also can be used as a standard for evaluating performance. Unfortunately, many companies do not set appropriate objectives for their integrated marketing communications programs.

Many companies fail to set appropriate objectives because top management has only an abstract idea of what the firm's IMC program is supposed to be doing. In a study by the American Business Press that measured the attitudes of chairs, presidents, and other senior managers of business-to-business advertising companies, more than half of the 427 respondents said they did not know whether their advertising was working and less than 10 percent thought it was working well.[27] This study showed overwhelmingly that top management did not even know what the company's advertising was supposed to do, much less how to measure it.

Few firms will set objectives that meet all the criteria set forth in DAGMAR. However, promotional planners should set objectives that are specific and measurable and go beyond basic sales goals. Even if specific communications response elements are not always measured, meeting the other criteria will sharpen the focus and improve the quality of the IMC planning process.

Setting Objectives for the IMC Program

One reason so much attention is given to advertising objectives is that for many companies advertising has traditionally been the major way of communicating with target audiences. Other promotional mix elements such as sales promotion, direct marketing, and publicity are used intermittently to support and complement the advertising program.

Another reason is that traditional advertising-based views of marketing communications planning, such as DAGMAR, have dominated the field for so long. These approaches are based on a hierarchical response model and consider how marketers can develop and disseminate advertising messages to move consumers along an effects path. This approach, shown in Figure 7-7, is what professor Don Schultz calls *inside-out planning.* He says, "It focuses on what the marketer wants to say, when the marketer wants to say it, about things the marketer believes are important about his or her brand, and in the media forms the marketer wants to use."[28]

Schultz advocates an *outside-in planning* process for IMC that starts with the customer and builds backward to the brand. This means that promotional planners study the various media customers and prospects use, when the marketer's messages might be most relevant to customers, and when they are likely to be most receptive to the message.

A similar approach is suggested by Professor Tom Duncan, who argues that IMC should use **zero-based communications planning,** which involves determining what tasks need to be done and which marketing communications functions should be used and to what extent.[29] This approach focuses on the task to be done and searches for the best ideas and media to accomplish it. Duncan suggests that an effective IMC program should lead with the marketing communications function that most effectively addresses the company's main problem or opportunity and should use a promotional

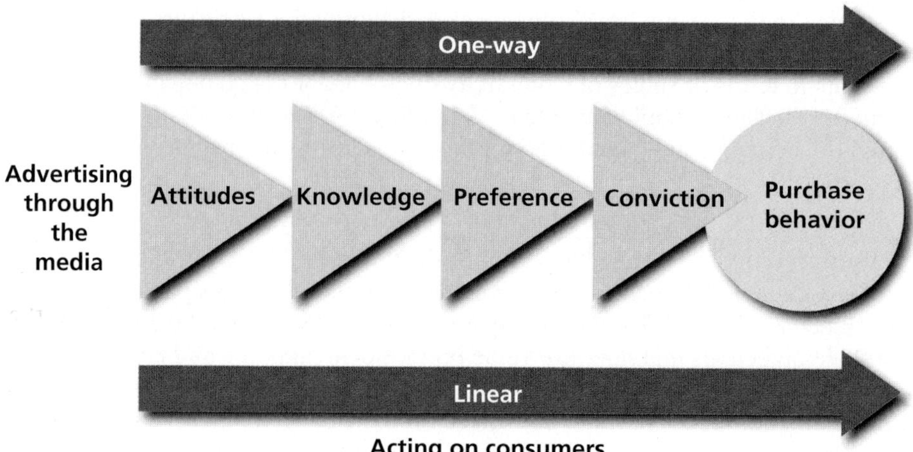

Figure 7-7 Traditional Advertising-Based View of Marketing Communications

mix that draws on the strengths of whichever communications functions relate best to the particular situation.

Many of the considerations for determining advertising objectives are relevant to setting goals for other elements of the integrated marketing communications program. The promotional planner should determine what role various sales promotion techniques, publicity and public relations, direct marketing, and personal selling will play in the overall marketing program and how they will interact with advertising as well as with one another.

For example, the marketing communications program for the San Diego Zoological Society has a number of objectives. First, it must provide funding for the society's programs and maintain a large and powerful base of supporters for financial and political strength. The program must educate the public about the society's various programs and maintain a favorable image on a local, regional, national, and even international level. A major objective of the IMC program is drawing visitors to the two attractions (Exhibit 7-9).

Exhibit 7-9 The San Diego Zoo attempts to attract visitors through a variety of media

To achieve these objectives, the San Diego Zoological Society and its advertising agency developed an IMC program. As can be seen in Figure 7-8, this program employed a variety of integrated marketing communication tools. When setting objectives for these promotional elements, planners must consider what the firm hopes to communicate through the use of this element, among what target audience, and during what time period. As with advertising, results should be measured and evaluated against the original objectives, and attempts should be made to isolate the effects of each promotional element. Objectives for marketing communications elements other than advertising are discussed more thoroughly in Part Five of the text.

Establishing and Allocating the Promotional Budget

If you take a minute to look back at Figure 1-4 in Chapter 1, you will see that while the arrows from the review of the marketing plan and the promotional situation analysis to analysis of the communications process are *unidirectional,* the flow between the communications analysis and budget determination is a *two-way interaction.* What this means is that while establishing objectives is an important part of the planning process, the limitations of the budget are important too. No organization has an unlimited budget, so objectives must be set with the budget in mind.

Often when we think of promotional expenditures of firms, we think only about the huge amounts being spent. We don't usually take the time to think about how these monies are being allocated and about the recipients of these dollars. The budgeting decisions have a significant impact not only on the firm itself but also on numerous others involved either directly or indirectly. The remainder of this chapter provides insight into some underlying theory with respect to budget setting, discusses how companies budget for promotional efforts, and demonstrates the inherent strengths and weaknesses associated with these approaches. Essentially, we focus on two primary budgeting decisions: establishing a budget amount and allocating the budget.

Establishing the Budget

The size of a firm's advertising and promotions budget can vary from a few thousand dollars to more than a billion. When companies like Procter & Gamble and General Motors spend more than 2 billion dollars per year to promote their products, they expect such expenditures to accomplish their stated objectives. The budget decision is no less critical to a firm spending only a few thousand dollars; its ultimate success or failure may depend on the monies spent. One of the most critical decisions facing the marketing manager is how much to spend on the promotional effort.

Advertising

Objectives: Drive attendance to Zoo and Wild Animal Park. Uphold image and educate target audience and inform them of new attractions and special events and promotions.

Audience: Members and nonmembers of Zoological Society. Households in primary and secondary geographic markets consisting of San Diego County and 5 other counties in southern California. Tertiary markets of 7 western states. Tourist and group sales markets.

Timing: As allowed and determined by budget. Mostly timed to coincide with promotional efforts.

Tools/media: Television, radio, newspaper, magazines, direct mail, outdoor, tourist media (television and magazine).

Sales Promotions

Objectives: Use price, product, and other variables to drive attendance when it might not otherwise come.

Audience: Targeted, depending on co-op partner, mostly to southern California market.

Timing: To fit needs of Zoo and Wild Animal Park and cosponsoring partner.

Tools/media: Coupons, sweepstakes, tours, broadcast tradeouts, direct mail: statement stuffers, fliers, postcards, online ticket discounts.

Public Relations

Objectives: Inform, educate, create, and maintain image for Zoological Society and major attractions; reinforce advertising message.

Audience: From local to international, depending on subject, scope, and timing.

Timing: Ongoing, although often timed to coincide with promotions and other special events. Spur-of-the-moment animal news and information such as acquisitions, births, etc.

Tools/media: Coverage by major news media, articles in local, regional, national and international newspapers, magazines and other publications such as visitors' guides, tour books and guides, appearances by Zoo spokesperson Joanne Embery on talk shows (such as "The Tonight Show"), zoo newsletter, adopt an animal program, support conservation program.

Cause Marketing/Corporate Sponsorships/Events Underwriting

Objectives: To provide funding for Zoological Society programs and promote special programs and events done in cooperation with corporate sponsor. Must be win-win business partnership for Society and partner.

Audience: Supporters of both the Zoological Society and the corporate or product/service partner.

Timing: Coincides with needs of both partners, and seasonal attendance generation needs of Zoo and Wild Animal Park.

Tools: May involve advertising, publicity, discount co-op promotions, ticket trades, hospitality centers. Exposure is directly proportional to amount of underwriting by corporate sponsor, both in scope and duration, education programs, Conservation and Research for Endangered Species (CRES).

Direct Marketing

Objectives: Maintain large powerful base of supporters for financial and political strength.

Audience: Local, regional, national and international. Includes children's program (Koala Club), seniors (60+), couples, single memberships, and incremental donor levels.

Timing: Ongoing, year-round promotion of memberships.

Tools: Direct mail and on-grounds visibility.

Group Sales

Objectives: Maximize group traffic and revenue by selling group tours to Zoo and Wild Animal Park.

Audience: Conventions, incentive groups, bus tours, associations, youth, scouts, schools, camps, seniors, clubs, military, organizations, domestic and foreign travel groups.

Timing: Targeted to drive attendance in peak seasons or at most probable times such as convention season.

Tools: Travel and tourism trade shows, telemarketing, direct mail, trade publication advertising.

Internet

Objectives: Provide information regarding the zoo, programs, memberships and public relations activities.

Audience: All audiences interested in acquiring more information about the zoo.

Timing: Ongoing, updated frequently over time.

Tools: Website, zoo blog, including videos, shop zoo and zoo e-newsletter calendar.

Figure 7-8 The San Diego Zoo Sets Objectives for Various Promotional Elements

Unfortunately, many managers fail to realize the value of advertising and promotion. They treat the communications budget as an expense rather than an investment. Instead of viewing the dollars spent as contributing to additional sales and market share, they see budget expenses as cutting into profits. As a result, when times get tough, the advertising and promotional budget is the first to be cut—even though there is strong evidence that exactly the opposite should occur, as Exhibit 7-10 argues. Moreover, the decision is not a one-time responsibility. A new budget is formulated every year, each time a new product is introduced, or when either internal or external factors necessitate a change to maintain competitiveness.

While it is one of the most critical decisions, budgeting has perhaps been the most resistant to change. A comparison of advertising and promotional texts over the past 10 years would reveal the same methods for establishing budgets. The theoretical basis for this process remains rooted in economic theory and marginal analysis. (Advertisers also use an approach based on **contribution margin**—the difference between the total revenue generated by a brand and its total variable costs. But, as Robert Steiner says, *marginal analysis* and *contribution margin* are essentially synonymous terms.)[30] We begin our discussion of budgeting with an examination of these theoretical approaches.

> # In A Recession, The Best Defense Is A Good Offense.
>
> It's a recession. Your instincts demand that you cut the ad budget. But, as the McGraw-Hill Research[1] analysis of business-to-business advertising expenditures during the 1981-82 recession shows, it's those with the courage to maintain or increase advertising in a recession who reap a major sales advantage over their competitors who panic and fall back into a defensive posture. And this advantage continues to expand long after the recession is over.
>
> **Effects of Advertising in a Recession on Sales (Indices)**
>
> | | 1980 | 1981 | 1982 | 1983 | 1984 | 1985 |
> |---|---|---|---|---|---|---|
> | *Companies that Eliminated or Decreased Advertising in Both 1981 and 1982* | 100 | 96 | 88 | 89 | 106 | 119 |
> | *Companies that Maintai~ed or Increased Advertising in Both 1981 and 1982* | 100 | 137 | 159 | 195 | 283 | 375 |
>
> McGraw-Hill Research, 1986.
>
> Recessions last an average of 11 months, but any advertising decision made during one can have permanent repercussions. The McGraw-Hill study demonstrates that nervous advertisers lose ground to the brave and can't gain it back. In 1980, according to the chart seen here, sales indices were identical, but by 1985 the brave had racked up a 3.2 to 1 sales advantage. A similar study done by McGraw-Hill during the 1974-75 recession corroborates the 1980's research.
>
> A recession is the single greatest period in which to make short- and long-term gains. And, surprisingly, increasing advertising modestly during one has much the same effect on your profits as cutting advertising does. According to The Center for Research & Development's October 1990 study of consumer advertising during a recession, advertisers who yield "to the natural inclination to cut spending in an effort to increase profits in a recession find that it doesn't work."[2] This study, relying on the PIMS[3] database, also uncovered that aggressive recessionary advertisers picked up 4.5 *times* as much market share gain as their overcautious competitors, leaving them in a far better position to exploit the inevitable recovery and expansion.
>
> Chevrolet countered its competitors during the 1974-75 recession by aggressively beefing up its ad spending and attained a two percent market share increase. Today, two share points in the automotive industry are worth over $4 billion. Delta Airlines and Revlon also boosted ad spending in the 1974-75 recession and achieved similar results.
>
> Continuous advertising sustains market leadership. And it's far easier to sustain momentum than it is to start it up again. Consider this list of market category leaders: Campbell's, Coca-Cola, Ivory, Kellogg, Kodak, Lipton and Wrigley. This is the leadership list for 1925. And 1990. These marketers have maintained a relentless commitment to their brands in both good times and bad. Kellogg had the guts to pump up its ad spending during the Great Depression and cemented a market leadership it has yet to relinquish.
>
> These are the success stories. Space and diplomacy don't allow the mention of the names of those who lacked gusto and chose to cut their ad spending in recessionary times.
>
> But if you would like to learn more about how advertising can help make the worst of times the best of times, please write to Department C, American Association of Advertising Agencies, 666 Third Avenue, New York, New York 10017, enclosing a check for five dollars. You will receive a booklet covering the pertinent research done on all the U.S. recessions since 1923. Please allow 4 to 6 weeks for delivery.
>
> [1] McGraw-Hill Research, 1986. [2] The Center for Research and Development ©1990. [3] Profit Impact of Market Strategies. The Strategic Planning Institute, Cambridge, MA.
>
> AAAA

Exhibit 7-10 The AAAA promotes the continued use of advertising in a recession

Theoretical Issues in Budget Setting

Most of the models used to establish advertising budgets can be categorized as taking an economic or a sales response perspective.

Marginal Analysis Figure 7-9 graphically represents the concept of **marginal analysis.** As advertising/promotional expenditures increase, sales and gross margins also increase to a point, but then they level off. Profits are shown to be a result of the gross margin minus advertising expenditures. Using this theory to establish its budget, a firm would continue to spend advertising/promotional dollars as long as the marginal revenues created by these expenditures exceeded the incremental advertising/promotional costs. As shown on the graph, the optimal expenditure level is the point where marginal costs equal the marginal revenues they generate (point *A*). If the sum of the advertising/promotional expenditures exceeded the revenues they generated, one would conclude the appropriations were too high and scale down the budget. If revenues were higher, a higher budget might be in order. (We will see later in this chapter that this approach can also be applied to the allocation decision.)

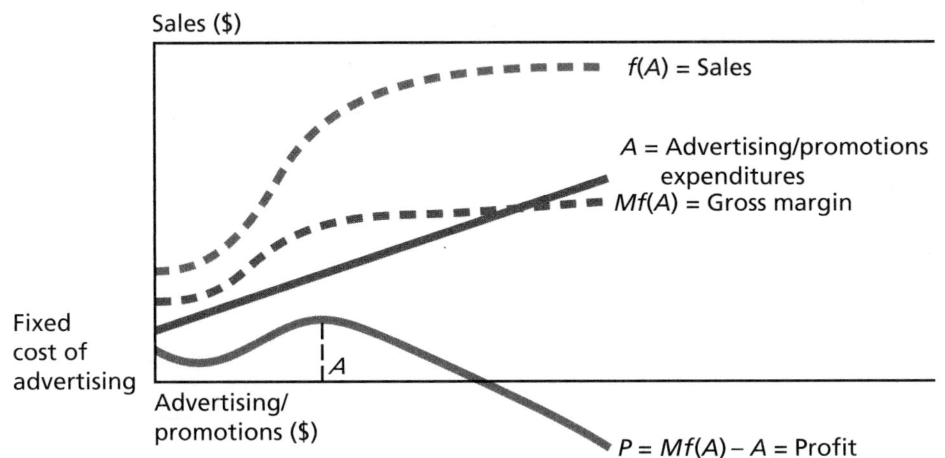

Figure 7-9 Marginal Analysis

While marginal analysis seems logical intuitively, certain weaknesses limit its usefulness. These weaknesses include the assumptions that (1) sales are a direct result of advertising and promotional expenditures and this effect can be measured and (2) advertising and promotion are solely responsible for sales. Let us examine each of these assumptions in more detail.

1. *Assumption that sales are a direct measure of advertising and promotions efforts.* Earlier in this chapter we discussed the fact that the advertiser needs to set communications objectives that contribute to accomplishing overall marketing objectives but at the same time are separate. One reason for this strategy is that it is often difficult, if not impossible, to demonstrate the effects of advertising and promotions on sales. In studies using sales as a direct measure, it has been almost impossible to establish the contribution of advertising and promotion. As noted by Frank Bass, "There is no more difficult, complex, or controversial problem in marketing than measuring the influence of advertising on sales."[31] In the words of David Aaker and James Carman, "Looking for the relationship between advertising and sales is somewhat worse than looking for a needle in a haystack."[32] Thus, to try to show that the size of the budget will directly affect sales of the product is misleading. A more logical approach would be to examine the impact of various budgets on the attainment of communications objectives.

As we saw in the discussion of communications objectives, sales are not the only goal of the promotional effort. Awareness, interest, attitude change, and other communications objectives are often sought, and while the bottom line may be to sell the product, these objectives may serve as the basis on which the promotional program is developed.

2. *Assumption that sales are determined solely by advertising and promotion.* This assumption ignores the remaining elements of the marketing mix—price, product, and distribution—which do contribute to a company's success. Environmental factors may also affect the promotional program, leading the marketing manager to assume the advertising was or was not effective when some other factor may have helped or hindered the accomplishment of the desired objectives.

Overall, you can see that while the economic approach to the budgeting process is a logical one, the difficulties associated with determining the effects of the promotional effort on sales and revenues limit its applicability. Marginal analysis is seldom used as a basis for budgeting (except for direct-response advertising).

Sales Response Models You may have wondered why the sales curve in Figure 7-9 shows sales leveling off even though advertising and promotions efforts continue to increase. The relationship between advertising and sales has been the topic of much research and discussion designed to determine the shape of the response curve.

Almost all advertisers subscribe to one of two models of the advertising/sales response function: the concave-downward function or the S-shaped response curve.

- *The concave-downward function.* After reviewing more than 100 studies of the effects of advertising on sales, Julian Simon and Johan Arndt concluded that the effects of advertising budgets follow the microeconomic law of diminishing returns.[33] That is, as the amount of advertising increases, its incremental value decreases. The logic is that those with the greatest potential to buy will likely act on the first (or earliest) exposures, while those less likely to buy are not likely to change as a result of the advertising. For those who may be potential buyers, each additional ad will supply little or no new information that will affect their decision. Thus, according to the **concave-downward function model,** the effects of advertising quickly begin to diminish, as shown in Figure 7-10A. Budgeting under this model suggests that fewer advertising dollars may be needed to create the optimal influence on sales.
- *The S-shaped response function.* Many advertising managers assume the **S-shaped response curve** (Figure 7-10B), which projects an S-shaped response function to the budget outlay (again measured in sales). Initial outlays of the advertising budget have little impact (as indicated by the essentially flat sales curve in range A). After a certain

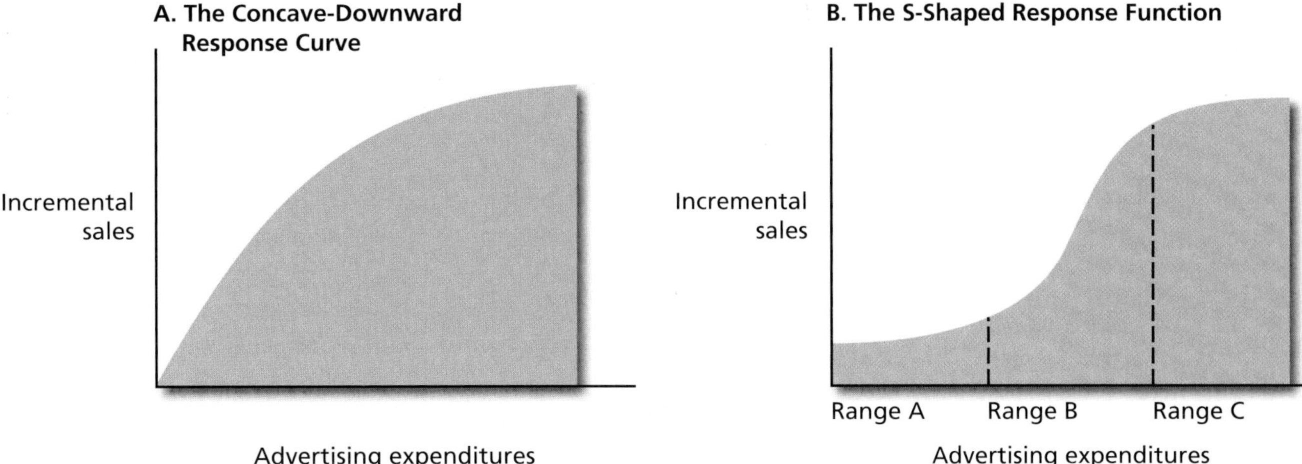

Figure 7-10 Advertising Sales/Response Functions

budget level has been reached (the beginning of range B), advertising and promotional efforts begin to have an effect, as additional increments of expenditures result in increased sales. This incremental gain continues only to a point, however, because at the beginning of range C additional expenditures begin to return little or nothing in the way of sales. This model suggests a small advertising budget is likely to have no impact beyond the sales that may have been generated through other means (for example, word of mouth). At the other extreme, more does not necessarily mean better: Additional dollars spent beyond range B have no additional impact on sales and for the most part can be considered wasted. As with marginal analysis, one would attempt to operate at that point on the curve in area B where the maximum return for the money is attained.

Weaknesses in these sales response models render them of limited use to practitioners for direct applications. Many of the problems seen earlier—the use of sales as a dependent variable, measurement problems, and so on—limit the usefulness of these models. At the same time, keep in mind the purpose of discussing such models. Even though marginal analysis and the sales response curves may not apply directly, they give managers some insight into a theoretical basis of how the budgeting process should work. Some empirical evidence indicates the models may have validity. One study, based on industry experience, has provided support for the S-shaped response curve; the results indicate that a minimum amount of advertising dollars must be spent before there is a noticeable effect on sales.[34]

The studies discussed in earlier chapters on learning and the hierarchy of effects also demonstrate the importance of repetition on gaining awareness and on subsequent higher-order objectives such as adoption. Thus, while these models may not provide a tool for setting the advertising and promotional budget directly, we can use them to guide our appropriations strategy from a theoretical basis. As you will see later in this chapter, such a theoretical basis has advantages over many of the methods currently being used for budget setting and allocation.

Additional Factors in Budget Setting While the theoretical bases just discussed should be considered in establishing the budget appropriation, a number of other issues must also be considered. A weakness in attempting to use sales as a *direct* measure of response to advertising is that various situational factors may have an effect. In one comprehensive study, 20 variables were shown to affect the advertising/sales ratio. Figure 7-11 lists these factors along with some others identified in later studies and their relationships.[35] For a product characterized by emotional buying motives, hidden product qualities, and/or a strong basis for differentiation, advertising would have a noticeable impact on sales (see Exhibit 7-11). Products characterized as large-dollar purchases and those in the maturity or decline stages of

Figure 7-11 Factors Influencing Advertising Budgets

Factor	Relationship of Advertising/ Sales	Factor	Relationship of Advertising/ Sales	Factor	Relationship of Advertising/ Sales
Product Factors		Maturity	—	***Strategy Factors***	
Basis for differentiation	+	Decline	—	Regional markets	—
Hidden product qualities	+	Inelastic demand	+	Early stage of brand life cycle	+
Emotional buying motives	+	Market share	—	High margins in channels	—
Durability	—	Competition:		Long channels of distribution	+
Large dollar purchase	—	Active	+	High prices	+
Purchase frequency	Curvilinear	Concentrated	+	High quality	+
Market Factors		Pioneer in market	—	Media strategy	+
Stage of product life cycle:		***Customer Factors***		Creative strategy	+
Introductory	+	Industrial products users	—	Promotional strategy	+
Growth	+	Concentration of users	+	***Cost Factors***	
				High profit margins	+

Note: + relationship means the factor leads to a positive effect of advertising on sales; — relationship indicates little or no effect of advertising on sales.

Exhibit 7-11 A strong basis for differentiation could show a noticeable effect of advertising on sales

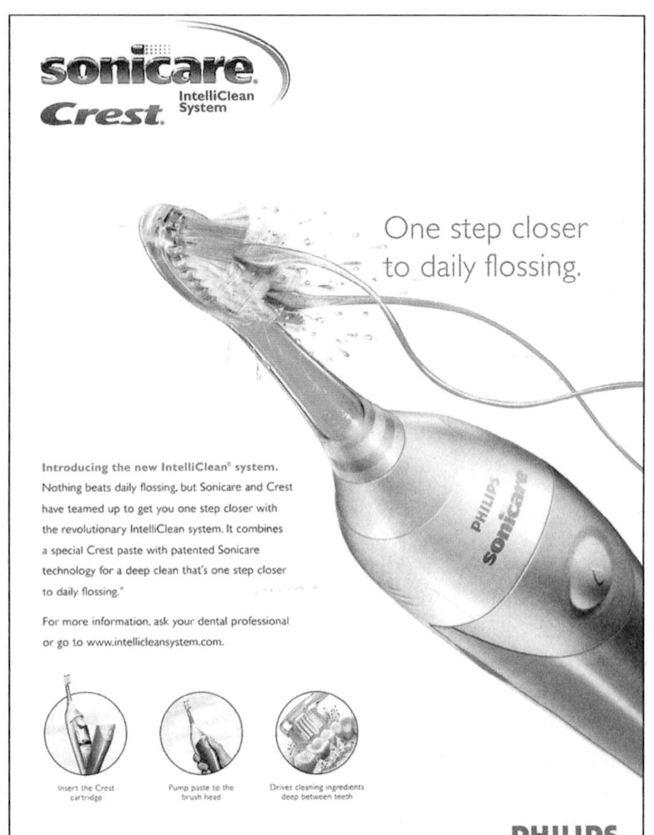

the product would be less likely to benefit. A study released by Deutsche Bank in 2004 examined 23 household, personal care, food, and beverage brands over a three-year period. The study concluded that 18 percent of these generated a positive ROI in the first year, and 45 percent saw their investment pay off long term as a result of TV advertising. Substantially new products had strong positive returns, while TV ads for those in the mature or declining stages of the product life cycle did not—though strong creative copy could lead to positive ROI even for mature brands (see Exhibit 7-12). The study also concluded that the effects could vary by industry, as pharmaceutical ads had a 6 to 10 percent higher ROI than package goods.[36] The study showed that other factors involving the market, customer, costs, and strategies employed have different effects.

The results of this study are interesting but limited, since they relate primarily to the percentage of sales dollars allocated to advertising and the factors influencing these ratios. As we will see later in this chapter, the percentage-of-sales method of budgeting has inherent weaknesses in that the advertising and sales effects may be reversed. So we cannot be sure whether the situation actually led to the advertising/sales relationship or vice versa. Thus, while these factors should be considered in the budget appropriation decision, they should not be the sole determinants of where and when to increase or decrease expenditures.

The *Advertising Age* Editorial Sounding Board consists of 92 executives of the top 200 advertising companies in the United States (representing the client side) and 130 executives of the 200 largest advertising agencies and 11 advertising consultants (representing the agency side). A survey of the board yielded the factors shown in Figure 7-12 that are important in budget setting.

Overall, the responses of these two groups reflect in part their perceptions as to factors of importance in how budgets are set. To understand the differences in the relative importance of these factors, it is important to understand the approaches currently employed in budget setting. The next section examines these approaches.

Exhibit 7-12 Even though it is a mature brand, Gatorade showed positive ROI in the 2004 study by Deutsche Bank

Budgeting Approaches

The theoretical approaches to establishing the promotional budget are seldom employed. In smaller firms, they may never be used. Instead, a number of methods developed through practice and experience are implemented. This section reviews some of the more traditional methods of setting budgets and the relative advantages and disadvantages of each. First, you must understand two things: (1) Many firms employ more than one method, and (2) budgeting approaches vary according to the size and sophistication of the firm.

Top-Down Approaches

The approaches discussed in this section may be referred to as **top-down approaches** because a budgetary amount is established (usually at an executive level) and then the monies are passed down to the various departments (as shown in Figure 7-13). These budgets are essentially predetermined and have no true theoretical basis. Top-down methods include the affordable method, arbitrary allocation, percentage of sales, competitive parity, and return on investment (ROI).

The Affordable Method In the **affordable method** (often referred to as the "all-you-can-afford method"), the firm determines the amount to be spent in various areas such as production and operations. Then it allocates what's left to advertising and promotion, considering this to be the amount it can afford. The task to be performed by the advertising/promotions function is not considered, and the likelihood of under- or overspending is high, as no guidelines for measuring the effects of various budgets are established.

Strange as it may seem, this approach is common among small firms. Unfortunately, it is also used in large firms, particularly those that are not marketing-driven and do not understand the role of advertising and promotion. For example, many high-tech firms focus on new product development and engineering and assume that the product, if good enough, will sell itself. In these companies, little money may be left for performing the advertising and promotions tasks.

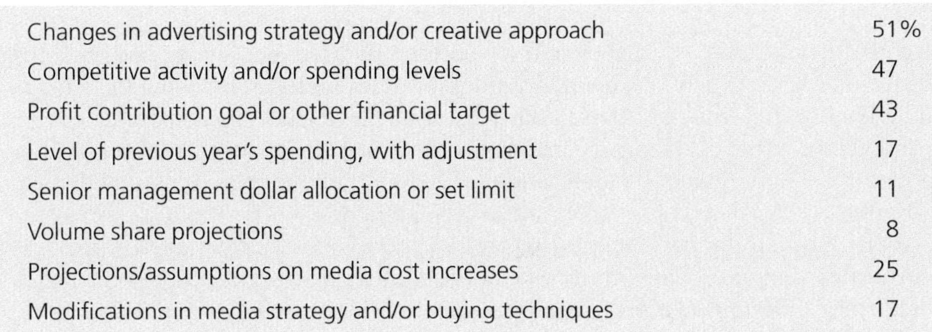

Factor	%
Changes in advertising strategy and/or creative approach	51%
Competitive activity and/or spending levels	47
Profit contribution goal or other financial target	43
Level of previous year's spending, with adjustment	17
Senior management dollar allocation or set limit	11
Volume share projections	8
Projections/assumptions on media cost increases	25
Modifications in media strategy and/or buying techniques	17

Figure 7-12 Factors Considered in Budget Setting

Figure 7-13 Top-Down versus Bottom-Up Approaches to Budget Setting

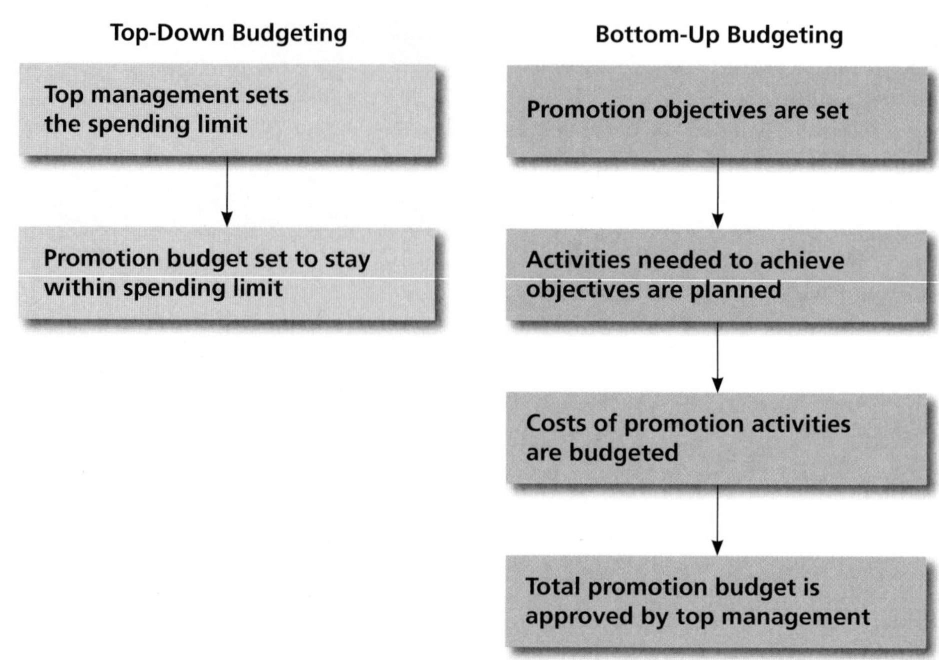

The logic for this approach stems from "We can't be hurt with this method" thinking. That is, if we know what we can afford and we do not exceed it, we will not get into financial problems. While this may be true in a strictly accounting sense, it does not reflect sound managerial decision making from a marketing perspective. Often this method does not allocate enough money to get the product off the ground and into the market. In terms of the S-shaped sales response model, the firm is operating in range A. Or the firm may be spending more than necessary, operating in range C. When the market gets tough and sales and/or profits begin to fall, this method is likely to lead to budget cuts at a time when the budget should be increased.

Arbitrary Allocation Perhaps an even weaker method than the affordable method for establishing a budget is **arbitrary allocation,** in which virtually no theoretical basis is considered and the budgetary amount is often set by fiat. That is, the budget is determined by management solely on the basis of what is felt to be necessary. In a discussion of how managers set advertising budgets, Melvin Salveson reported that these decisions may reflect "as much upon the managers' psychological profile as they do economic criteria."[37] While Salveson was referring to larger corporations, the approach is no less common in small firms and nonprofit organizations.

The arbitrary allocation approach has no obvious advantages. No systematic thinking has occurred, no objectives have been budgeted for, and the concept and purpose of advertising and promotion have been largely ignored. Other than the fact that the manager believes some monies must be spent on advertising and promotion and then picks a number, there is no good explanation why this approach continues to be used. Yet budgets continue to be set this way, and our purpose in discussing this method is to point out only that it is used—not recommended.

Percentage of Sales Perhaps the most commonly used method for budget setting (particularly in large firms) is the **percentage-of-sales method,** in which the advertising and promotions budget is based on sales of the product. Management determines the amount by either (1) taking a percentage of the sales dollars or (2) assigning a fixed amount of the unit product cost to promotion and multiplying this amount by the number of units sold. These two methods are shown in Figure 7-14.

A variation on the percentage-of-sales method uses a percentage of projected future sales as a base. This method also uses either a straight percentage of projected sales or a unit cost projection. In the straight-percentage method, sales are projected for the coming year based on the marketing manager's estimates. The

Method 1: Straight Percentage of Sales		
2002	Total dollar sales	$1,000,000
	Straight % of sales at 10%	$100,000
2003	Advertising budget	$100,000
Method 2: Percentage of Unit Cost		
2002	Cost per bottle to manufacturer	$4.00
	Unit cost allocated to advertising	1.00
2003	Forecasted sales, 100,000 units	
2003	Advertising budget (100,000 × $1)	$100,000

Figure 7-14 Alternative Methods for Computing Percentage of Sales for Eve Cologne

budget is a percentage of these sales, often an industry standard percentage like those presented in Figure 7-15.

One advantage of using future sales as a base is that the budget is not based on last year's sales. As the market changes, management must factor the effect of these changes on sales into next year's forecast rather than relying on past data. The resulting budget is more likely to reflect current conditions and be more appropriate.

Figure 7-15 reveals that the percentage allocated varies from one industry to the next. Some firms budget a very small percentage (for example, 0.2 percent in life insurance), and others spend a much higher proportional amount (18.7 percent in health services). Actual dollar amounts spent vary markedly according to the company's total sales figure. Thus, a smaller percentage of sales in the construction machinery industry may actually result in significantly more advertising dollars being spent.

Proponents of the percentage-of-sales method cite a number of advantages. It is financially safe and keeps ad spending within reasonable limits, as it bases spending on the past year's sales or what the firm expects to sell in the upcoming year. Thus, there will be sufficient monies to cover this budget, with increases in sales leading to budget increases and sales decreases resulting in advertising decreases. The percentage-of-sales method is simple, straightforward, and easy to implement. Regardless of which basis—past or future sales—is employed, the calculations used to arrive at a budget are not difficult. Finally, this budgeting approach is generally stable. While the budget may vary with increases and decreases in sales, as long as these changes are not drastic the manager will have a reasonable idea of the parameters of the budget.

At the same time, the percentage-of-sales method has some serious disadvantages, including the basic premise on which the budget is established: sales. Letting the level of sales determine the amount of advertising and promotions dollars to be spent reverses the cause-and-effect relationship between advertising and sales. It treats advertising as an expense associated with making a sale rather than an investment. As shown in Figure 7-16 on page 220, companies that consider promotional expenditures an investment reap the rewards.

A second problem with this approach was actually cited as an advantage earlier: stability. Proponents say that if all firms use a similar percentage, that will bring stability to the marketplace. But what happens if someone varies from this standard percentage? The problem is that this method does not allow for changes in strategy either internally or from competitors. An aggressive firm may wish to allocate more monies to the advertising and promotions budget, a strategy that is not possible with a percentage-of-sales method unless the manager is willing to deviate from industry standards.

The percentage-of-sales method of budgeting may result in severe misappropriation of funds. If advertising and promotion have a role to perform in marketing a product, then allocating more monies to advertising will, as shown in the S-shaped curve, generate incremental sales (to a point). If products with low sales have smaller promotion budgets, this will hinder sales progress. At the other extreme, very successful products may have excess budgets, some of which may be better appropriated elsewhere.

Figure 7-15 2005 Advertising-to-Sales Ratios for the 200 Largest Ad-Spending Industries

Industry	SIC	Ad as % Sales	Ad as % Margin	Annual Ad Growth %
ABRASIVE,ASBESTOS,MISC MINRL	3290	3.7	16	9.8
ACCIDENT & HEALTH INSURANCE	6321	0.4	1.8	5.1
AGRICULTURAL CHEMICALS	2870	1.9	4.3	2.9
AGRICULTURAL SERVICES	0700	1.2	4.9	15.3
AGRICULTURE PRODUCTION-CROPS	0100	0.5	3.2	–10.3
AIR COURIER SERVICES	4513	0.8	2.9	5.5
AIR TRANSPORT, SCHEDULED	4512	1	7.3	1
AIR-COND,HEATING,REFRIG EQ	3585	1.3	4.7	5.8
AIRCRAFT	3721	0.1	0.7	0
AMUSEMENT PARKS	7996	9.6	20.7	4
APPAREL & OTHER FINISHED PDS	2300	4.8	11.3	4.8
APPAREL AND ACCESSORY STORES	5600	3.7	8.2	5.3
AUTO AND HOME SUPPLY STORES	5531	2.5	5.4	15.4
AUTO DEALERS, GAS STATIONS	5500	1	6.3	8.2
AUTO RENT & LEASE,NO DRIVERS	7510	2.2	6.7	6.7
AUTO REPAIR,SERVICES,PARKING	7500	2.6	10.2	-21.3
BEVERAGES	2080	7.5	12.1	5.6
BIOLOGICAL PDS,EX DIAGNSTICS	2836	1.6	2.2	10.4
BLANKBOOKS,BINDERS,BOOKBIND	2780	5.9	9.4	4.6
BLDG MATL,HARDWR,GARDEN-RETL	5200	3.7	9.4	17.1
BOOKS: PUBG, PUBG & PRINTING	2731	7.3	15.4	0.4
BTLD & CAN SOFT DRINKS,WATER	2086	2.8	5.8	14.1
BUSINESS SERVICES, NEC	7389	1.5	4.6	–0.5
CABLE AND OTHER PAY TV SVCS	4841	2.3	5.2	15.9
CACULATE,ACCT MACH,EX COMP	3578	0.5	1.6	2.1
CAN FRUIT,VEG,PRESRV,JAM,JEL	2033	2.4	8.3	18.4
CAN,FROZN,PRESRV FRUIT & VEG	2030	3.9	9.9	–1.2
CATALOG, MAIL-ORDER HOUSES	5961	3.6	15	10.2
CEMENT, HYDRAULIC	3241	0.5	1.3	15.6
CHEMICALS & ALLIED PDS-WHSL	5160	0.9	4.9	1.3
CHEMICALS & ALLIED PRODUCTS	2800	3.4	6.7	9.9
CIGARETTES	2111	1.6	4.8	–3.1
CMP INTEGRATED SYS DESIGN	7373	1.1	2.5	2.9
CMP PROCESSING,DATA PREP SVC	7374	2.8	7.4	3.7
CMP PROGRAMMING,DATA PROCESS	7370	3.3	8.5	4.5
COMMERCIAL PRINTING	2750	0.4	1.8	–0.3
COMMUNICATIONS SERVICES, NEC	4899	2.8	6.8	9.5
COMPUTER & OFFICE EQUIPMENT	3570	1.2	4.1	11.7
COMPUTER COMMUNICATION EQUIP	3576	1.6	2.2	9.5
COMPUTER PERIPHERAL EQ, NEC	3577	3	6	11.7
COMPUTER STORAGE DEVICES	3572	0.3	0.8	–2.5
COMPUTERS & SOFTWARE-WHSL	5045	0.2	1.1	–3.5
CONGLOMERATE	9997	0.4	1.1	–2.1
CONSTRUCTION MACHINERY & EQ	3531	0.3	1	8.9
CONVENIENCE STORES	5412	1.7	4.4	11.2
CONVRT PAPR,PAPRBRD,EX BOXES	2670	1.2	3	0
CREDIT REPORTING AGENCIES	7320	1.1	2.1	6.8
CUTLERY, HANDTOOLS,GEN HRDWR	3420	9.1	16.3	8.6
DAIRY PRODUCTS	2020	1.3	6.6	15.9
DEPARTMENT STORES	5311	4.4	13.6	0.8
DISTILLED AND BLENDED LIQUOR	2085	10.4	36.5	3.8
DOLLS AND STUFFED TOYS	3942	10.9	22.3	2.4
DRUG & PROPRIETARY STORES	5912	0.8	4.1	11.3
DRUGS AND PROPRIETARY-WHSL	5122	0	0.4	4.8
DURABLE GOODS-WHOLESALE	5000	0.2	2.3	21.7
EATING PLACES	5812	2.9	13	7
EDUCATIONAL SERVICES	8200	8.1	15.6	10.1
ELEC MEAS & TEST INSTRUMENTS	3825	0.6	1.1	–8.3
ELECTR, OTH ELEC EQ, EX CMP	3600	2.7	7.3	6.4
ELECTRIC & OTHER SERV COMB	4931	0.3	0.9	–4.7
ELECTRIC HOUSEWARES AND FANS	3634	3.8	13.1	–2.9
ELECTRIC LIGHTING, WIRING EQ	3640	1	2.9	4.5
ELECTRICAL INDL APPARATUS	3620	2.8	7.6	8.5
ELECTROMEDICAL APPARATUS	3845	0.8	1.1	10.6
ELECTRONIC COMPONENTS, NEC	3679	0.7	1.7	10.1
ELECTRONIC COMPUTERS	3571	0.9	3.5	5.9
ELECTRONIC PARTS,EQ-WHSL,NEC	5065	0.3	2.1	15.4
EMPLOYMENT AGENCIES	7361	2.9	7.1	–1.4
ENGINES AND TURBINES	3510	1.3	4.9	15.3
EQUIP RENTAL & LEASING, NEC	7359	2.5	3.9	–2.4
FAMILY CLOTHING STORES	5651	2.2	6	6.4
FARM MACHINERY AND EQUIPMENT	3523	0.7	2.6	4.7
FINANCE LESSORS	6172	0.3	0.5	10.1
FIRE, MARINE, CASUALTY INS	6331	1	5	15.7
FOOD AND KINDRED PRODUCTS	2000	11.9	22.3	8.1
FOOTWEAR, EXCEPT RUBBER	3140	4.3	9.8	5
FURNITURE STORES	5712	7.2	18.1	9.3
GAMES,TOYS,CHLD VEH,EX DOLLS	3944	9.9	21.4	8.3
GENERAL INDL MACH & EQ, NEC	3569	1.1	2.2	–3.5
GRAIN MILL PRODUCTS	2040	4.5	18	10.4
GROCERIES & RELATED PDS-WHSL	5140	2.4	12.1	8
GROCERY STORES	5411	1	3.8	3.7
HARDWR, PLUMB, HEAT EQ-WHSL	5070	0.1	0.4	14
HEALTH SERVICES	8000	18.7	44	2.5
HELP SUPPLY SERVICES	7363	0.4	1.8	2.6
HOBBY, TOY, AND GAME SHOPS	5945	4	11.5	12.3
HOME FURNITURE & EQUIP STORE	5700	3.4	8.2	12.5
HOME HEALTH CARE SERVICES	8082	1.4	3.1	12
HOSPITAL & MEDICAL SVC PLANS	6324	0.5	2.2	15.3
HOTELS AND MOTELS	7011	2.3	10.4	6.6
HOUSEHOLD APPLIANCES	3630	1.6	6.3	3.1
HOUSEHOLD AUDIO & VIDEO EQ	3651	5.3	35.9	8.8
HOUSEHOLD FURNITURE	2510	3.9	13.8	11
ICE CREAM & FROZEN DESSERTS	2024	4.9	41.9	14.3
IN VITRO,IN VIVO DIAGNOSTICS	2835	6.6	14	15
INDL COML FANS,BLOWRS,OTH EQ	3564	2.9	8.7	10.3
INDL INORGANIC CHEMICALS	2810	0.2	0.5	8.8
INDUSTRIAL MEASUREMENT INSTR	3823	0.7	1.1	17.8
INDUSTRIAL ORGANIC CHEMICALS	2860	1.4	5.9	11.4
INS AGENTS,BROKERS & SERVICE	6411	2	3.2	33.3
INVESTMENT ADVICE	6282	1.9	3.5	3.3
JEWELRY STORES	5944	4.9	11.6	6.6

Figure 7-15 Concluded

Industry	SIC	Ad as % Sales	Ad as % Margin	Annual Ad Growth %	Industry	SIC	Ad as % Sales	Ad as % Margin	Annual Ad Growth %
KNIT OUTERWEAR MILLS	2253	3.3	9.3	4.4	PHOTOGRAPHIC EQUIP & SUPPLY	3861	2.4	5.6	1.8
LAB ANALYTICAL INSTRUMENTS	3826	0.7	1.3	7.2	PLASTC,SYNTH MATLS;EX GLASS	2820	0.2	0.8	0
LEATHER AND LEATHER PRODUCTS	3100	1.7	2.5	5.4	PLASTICS PRODUCTS, NEC	3089	1.2	4	-3.6
LIFE INSURANCE	6311	0.2	1.6	8.2	POULTRY SLAUGHTER & PROCESS	2015	2.1	7.2	20.7
LUMBER & OTH BLDG MATL-RETL	5211	2.8	7.5	11	PREPACKAGED SOFTWARE	7372	2.4	3.1	2.1
LUMBER, PLYWD, MILLWORK-WHSL	5031	0.8	7.2	6.2	PRIM SMELT,REFIN NONFER METL	3330	0.2	0.7	10.7
MALT BEVERAGES	2082	8.8	16.5	10	PROF & COML EQ & SUPPLY-WHSL	5040	3.2	7.7	8.2
MANAGEMENT CONSULTING SVCS	8742	1.5	5.2	2.2	RADIO BROADCASTING STATIONS	4832	5.4	15.8	2
MEAT PACKING PLANTS	2011	1.2	10.7	2.5	RADIO, TV BROADCAST, COMM EQ	3663	1.1	2.9	8
MED, DENTAL, HOSP EQ-WHSL	5047	0.5	2.1	9.8	RADIO,TV,CONS ELECTR STORES	5731	3	10.7	5.5
MENS,BOYS FRNSH, WORK CLTHNG	2320	4	9.2	6.5	RADIOTELEPHONE COMMUNICATION	4812	3.1	5.9	9.1
METAL MINING	1000	0.2	0.4	13.1	REAL ESTATE	6500	8.8	20.6	14
METALWORKING MACHINERY & EQ	3540	6.6	17.3	6.3	REAL ESTATE AGENTS & MGRS	6531	2.4	8.7	15.6
MILLWORK,VENEER,PLYWOOD	2430	1.8	9	7.8	REAL ESTATE INVESTMENT TRUST	6798	3.6	9.4	5.8
MISC AMUSEMENT & REC SERVICE	7990	2.3	5.7	2.1	REFUSE SYSTEMS	4953	0.3	0.9	22.5
MISC BUSINESS CREDIT INSTN	6159	0.5	0.6	9.8	RETAIL STORES, NEC	5990	4.3	10	5.9
MISC BUSINESS SERVICES	7380	1	1.9	1.7	RUBBER AND PLASTICS FOOTWEAR	3021	9.4	20.3	7.9
MISC CHEMICAL PRODUCTS	2890	1.5	4.1	4.5	SECURITY & COMMODITY BROKERS	6200	1.7	4.2	2.7
MISC ELEC MACHY,EQ,SUPPLIES	3690	5.8	16.1	15.9	SECURITY BROKERS & DEALERS	6211	1	2.1	-4.3
MISC FABRICATED METAL PRODS	3490	5.2	14.9	8.4	SEMICONDUCTOR,RELATED DEVICE	3674	2.2	4	14.8
MISC FOOD PREPS, KINDRED PDS	2090	2.2	5.4	15.6	SHIP & BOAT BLDG & REPAIRING	3730	1.1	4	-0.8
MISC MANUFACTURNG INDUSTRIES	3990	1.6	2.9	1.3	SHOE STORES	5661	2.4	6.9	4.9
MISC NONDURABLE GOODS-WHSL	5190	1.9	8.9	19	SOAP,DETERGENT,TOILET PREPS	2840	10	18.5	12.2
MISC SHOPPING GOODS STORES	5940	4	11.7	13.4	SOCIAL SERVICES	8300	11.4	88.6	-11.1
MISC TRANSPORTATION EQUIP	3790	1	4.7	22.7	SPEC OUTPATIENT FACILITY,NEC	8093	2.4	3.2	55.6
MISCELLANEOUS PUBLISHING	2741	2.5	3.7	36.1	SPECIAL CLEAN,POLISH PREPS	2842	10.7	20.6	8.6
MISCELLANEOUS RETAIL	5900	0.7	3	14.1	SPECIAL INDUSTRY MACHY, NEC	3559	0.4	0.8	5.9
MORTGAGE BANKERS & LOAN CORR	6162	2.3	3.5	12.6	SPORTING & ATHLETIC GDS, NEC	3949	5.9	14.8	7.4
MOTION PIC, VIDEOTAPE PRODTN	7812	13.7	32	5.5	SRCH,DET,NAV,GUID,AERO SYS	3812	1.1	5.8	9.8
MOTION PICTURE THEATERS	7830	1.3	5.5	-14.3	STEEL WORKS & BLAST FURNACES	3312	0.3	0.8	14.9
MOTOR VEHICLE PART,ACCESSORY	3714	0.4	2.1	5.7	SUBDIVIDE, DEV, EX CEMETERY	6552	0.8	1.1	11.6
MOTOR VEHICLES & CAR BODIES	3711	2.3	9.6	7.6	SUGAR & CONFECTIONERY PRODS	2060	5.9	15.6	9.5
NEWSPAPER:PUBG, PUBG & PRINT	2711	11.1	24.1	4.8	SURGICAL,MED INSTR,APPARATUS	3841	0.3	0.5	9.1
OFFICES OF MEDICAL DOCTORS	8011	4.9	13.1	11.7	TELE & TELEGRAPH APPARATUS	3661	1.2	2.6	6.3
OPERATIVE BUILDERS	1531	0.8	3	11.7	TELEVISION BROADCAST STATION	4833	10.7	32.9	6.6
OPHTHALMIC GOODS	3851	4.5	6.5	9.1	TIRES AND INNER TUBES	3011	2.3	9	11.8
ORTHO,PROSTH,SURG APPL,SUPLY	3842	1.5	2.4	9.9	TOBACCO PRODUCTS	2100	4.4	5.4	3.5
PAINTS, VARNISHES, LACQUERS	2851	2	5	6.8	TRANSPORTATION SERVICES	4700	14.2	26.8	12.7
PAPER & PAPER PRODUCTS-WHSL	5110	1.4	6.4	20.7	TRUCKING, EXCEPT LOCAL	4213	0.4	3	13.9
PAPER AND ALLIED PRODUCTS	2600	1.3	4.9	-3	TRUCKING,COURIER SVC,EX AIR	4210	0.2	1.3	-5.8
PAPER MILLS	2621	3.2	16.9	6.8	VARIETY STORES	5331	0.9	3.2	5.9
PATENT OWNERS AND LESSORS	6794	5.6	8	12.5	VIDEO TAPE RENTAL	7841	3.1	5.1	5.3
PERFUME,COSMETIC,TOILET PREP	2844	7.9	17.5	8	WATCHES, CLOCKS AND PARTS	3873	9.8	17.5	13.1
PERIODICAL:PUBG,PUBG & PRINT	2721	4.1	11.5	-10.3	WATER TRANSPORTATION	4400	7.8	20.6	7.9
PERSONAL CREDIT INSTITUTIONS	6141	0.4	1	2.8	WINE,BRANDY & BRANDY SPIRITS	2084	2.2	7	-6.2
PERSONAL SERVICES	7200	3.6	10.7	8	WMNS,MISS,CHLD,INFNT UNDGRMT	2340	4.6	11.4	10.9
PETROLEUM REFINING	2911	0.1	0.4	9.7	WOMEN'S CLOTHING STORES	5621	3.7	9.1	7.7
PHARMACEUTICAL PREPARATIONS	2834	4.6	6	10.1	WOMENS,MISSES,JRS OUTERWEAR	2330	2.6	4.7	7.8
PHONE COMM EX RADIOTELEPHONE	4813	2.4	4.2	5.9	WOOD HSHLD FURN, EX UPHOLSRD	2511	30.4	84.5	-17.6

SOURCE: Advertising Ratios & Budgets, 29th edition (Ratios are 2005 values).

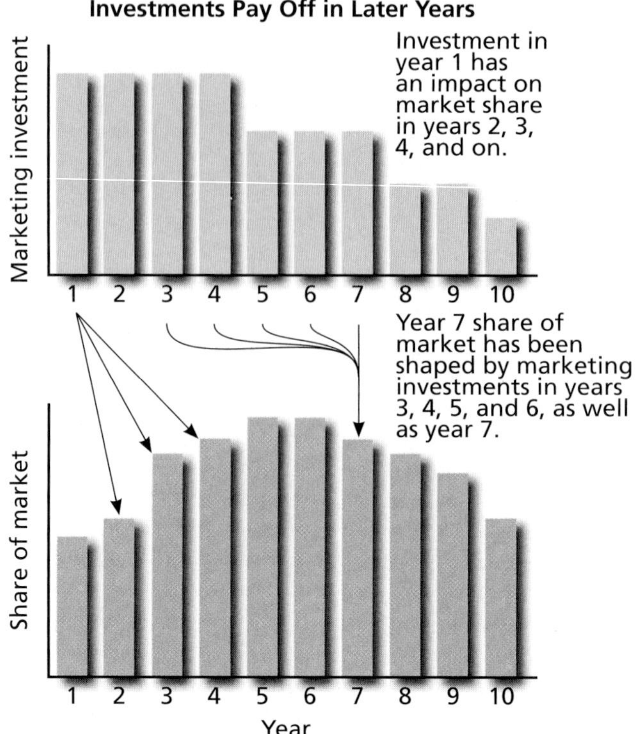

Figure 7-16 Investments Pay Off in Later Years

The percentage-of-sales method is also difficult to employ for new product introductions. If no sales histories are available, there is no basis for establishing the budget. Projections of future sales may be difficult, particularly if the product is highly innovative and/or has fluctuating sales patterns.

Finally, if the budget is contingent on sales, decreases in sales will lead to decreases in budgets when they most need to be increased. Continuing to cut the advertising and promotion budgets may just add impetus to the downward sales trend. On the other hand, some of the more successful companies have allocated additional funds during hard times or downturns in the cycle of sales. Companies that maintain or increase their ad expenditures during recessions achieve increased visibility and higher growth in both sales and market share (compared to those that reduce advertising outlays). For example, Sunkist can attribute at least some of its success in maintaining its strong image to the fact that it has maintained consistent levels of advertising expenditures over 80 years, despite recessions.[38]

While the percentage-of-future-sales method has been proposed as a remedy for some of the problems discussed here, the reality is that problems with forecasting, cyclical growth, and uncontrollable factors limit its effectiveness.

Competitive Parity If you asked marketing managers if they ever set their advertising and promotions budgets on the basis of what their competitors allocate, they would probably deny it. Yet if you examined the advertising expenditures of these companies, both as a percentage of sales and in respect to the media where they are allocated, you would see little variation in the percentage-of-sales figures for firms within a given industry. Such results do not happen by chance alone. Companies that provide competitive advertising information, trade associations, and other advertising industry periodicals are sources for competitors' expenditures. Larger corporations often subscribe to services such as Competitive Media Reporting, which estimates the top 1,000 companies' advertising in 10 media and in total. Smaller companies often use a **clipping service,** which clips competitors' ads from local print media, allowing the company to work backward to determine the cumulative costs of the ads placed.

In the **competitive parity method,** managers establish budget amounts by matching the competition's percentage-of-sales expenditures. The argument is that setting budgets in this fashion takes advantage of the collective wisdom of the industry. It also takes the competition into consideration, which leads to stability in the marketplace by minimizing marketing warfare. If companies know that competitors are unlikely to match their increases in promotional spending, they are less likely to take an aggressive posture to attempt to gain market share. This minimizes unusual or unrealistic ad expenditures.

The competitive parity method has a number of disadvantages, however. For one, it ignores the fact that advertising and promotions are designed to accomplish specific objectives by addressing certain problems and opportunities. Second, it assumes that because firms have similar expenditures, their programs will be equally effective. This assumption ignores the contributions of creative executions and/or media allocations, as well as the success or failure of various promotions. Further, it ignores possible advantages of the firm itself; some companies simply make better products than others. A study by Yoo and Mandhachitara indicates that a competitive parity strategy must consider the fact that a competitor's advertising can actually benefit one's own firm, and that one competitor's gain is not always the other's loss. As shown in Figure 7-17 there are four different situations to determine how the competitive budgets may impact sales—only one of which involved the zero-sum scenario.[39]

Also, there is no guarantee that competitors will continue to pursue their existing strategies. Since competitive parity figures are determined by examination of competitors' previous years' promotional expenditures (short of corporate espionage), changes in market emphasis and/or spending may not be recognized until the competition has already established an advantage. Further, there is no guarantee that a competitor will not increase or decrease its own expenditures, regardless of what other companies do. Finally, competitive parity may not avoid promotional wars. Coke versus Pepsi and Anheuser-Busch versus Miller have been notorious for their spending wars, each responding to the other's increased outlays.

In summary, few firms employ the competitive parity method as a sole means of establishing the promotional budget. This method is typically used in conjunction with the percentage-of-sales or other methods. It is never wise to ignore the competition; managers must always be aware of what competitors are doing. But they should not just emulate them in setting goals and developing strategies.

Return on Investment (ROI) In the percentage-of-sales method, sales dictate the level of advertising appropriations. But advertising causes sales. In the marginal

Figure 7-17 Competitors' Advertising Outlays Do Not Always Hurt

Figure 7-18 Aegis Rated ROI of Various Media

Medium	The Measurement Challenge	ROI Measurability
Direct Response	Direct mail, telemarketing, and other forms are the most measurable of media listed here. Direct can have a synergistic effect, especially for pharma, telecom, and financial services.	5
Sales Promotion	Offers such as coupons and discounts generate a lot of consumer response and therefore a bounty of data. The data lend themselves to measurement, especially for package goods via syndicated scanner data. Free-standing inserts generate much valuable data.	5
Internet	The Internet can be very influential for big-ticket purchases like cars. Very measurable,with the cautionary note that "Internet is a very broad net," ranging from search engines to ads in content to websites such as in the auto market, where such marques as Saab get lots of hits, and all should be looked at separately. The goal is to understand how the consumer in interacting online with the brand.	5
TV	While promotions have very pronounced, short-term effects that allow precise measurement, TV has a more subtle and gradual effect that may show greater variability. But ROI can be measured with a high degree of accuracy, and there's no excuse for TV not to show a measurable effect. MMA clients have been using a lot more analysis to create a better mix between :15s and :30s, and better allocation across dayparts.	4.5
Print	The experts can slice and dice print by weekly vs. monthly publications, by targeted vs. general market, by promotional ads vs. equity-building. Print promotional materials, like free-standing inserts, are a separate—and much more measurable—matter. As with all other media, accuracy and timing of the data are crucial in determining how measurable the medium is. Print can play a strong role in expanding the reach of the media mix.	4.5
Public Relations	There are companies that specialize in the measurement of PR campaigns' quality; they can measure the number of impressions delivered—via positive or negative PR—for a brand name or category. PR can have a measurable impact on sales (think trans fats in food). The problem: Many marketers aren't buying these PR data.	4
Video Games	Whether the game is played online or offline is crucial. An ad embedded in a game cartridge is very hard to measure because there's no way to know how often it's played. Though there's no denying "True Crime's" Nick Kang is a big hit. With online games, there are great data available through the Internet.	Online Offline

analysis and S-shaped curve approaches, incremental investments in advertising and promotions lead to increases in sales. The key word here is *investment.* In the **ROI budgeting method,** advertising and promotions are considered investments, like plant and equipment. Thus, the budgetary appropriation (investment) leads to certain returns. Like other aspects of the firm's efforts, advertising and promotion are expected to earn a certain return. As noted in the lead-in to this chapter, ROI has received a great deal of attention by practitioners over the past few years, with many still disagreeing as to how it should be measured. Figure 7-18 reports the results of *Advertising Age*'s request of the Aegis Group rating of how various media perform under this criterion (5 = best).

While the ROI method looks good on paper, the reality is that it is rarely possible to assess the returns provided by the promotional effort—at least as long as sales continue to be the basis for evaluation. Thus, while managers are certain to ask how much return they are getting for such expenditures, the question remains unanswered and, as shown in the chapter introduction, depends on the criteria used to determine effectiveness. ROI remains a difficult method to employ.

Summary of Top-Down Budgeting Methods You are probably asking yourself why we even discussed these budgeting methods if they are not recommended for use

Figure 7-18 Concluded

Medium	The Measurement Challenge	ROI Measurability
Radio	The available data typically aren't as strong as those for its traditional-media colleagues of TV and print, and this hampers radio.	3
Cinema	Movie advertising can be measured by the number of impressions delivered, much like outdoor or kiosk advertising would be measured.	3
Sponsored Events	Measurability depends on whether sponsorship is likely to spark short-term effect. A major recurring event like the Olympics is very measurable. Others can be difficult to measure short term. Measurement can be complex because events have so many pieces, including how the event is advertised, the PR buzz, signage, and the recollection of the event itself.	3
Product Placement	There are companies that measure quality of placement as well as the quantity of exposures. Treated much like TV advertising, with the caveat that not every product placement is the same. Fox's "American Idol" is a great example: AT&T Wireless's tie-in, which involved voting by text message, is interactive—even part of the entertainment—while Paula Abdul drinking from a Coke cup is not. (P.S. AT&T Wireless, now owned by Cingular, isn't an MMA client.) So the question becomes: How do you score the quality of placement?	3
Outdoor	Available data are limited due to the nature of outdoor advertising; there's no syndicated vendor that sells the needed data on outdoor. And outdoor lacks "variance"—the billboard is up X number of months and seen by an unchanging X number of people each day.	2
Guerrilla Marketing	Hard to measure if the variable you're using is sales. If 10,000 people at an event get free T-shirts, it's difficult to measure the effect on the 400,000 people living in that market. Because guerrilla can encompass so many different kinds of tactics, getting useful data can be a problem—it depends on how measurable the response is. Marketers' ROI expectations for guerrilla are lower than for other media, so the urgency to measure is less. Not to mention they spend a lot less on guerrilla than on traditional media like TV.	1

Source: From *Advertising Age,* June 20, 2005, pp. 5–6. Used with permission.

or have severe disadvantages that limit their effectiveness. But you must understand the various methods used in order to recognize their limitations, especially since these flawed methods are commonly employed by marketers. Research conducted over a number of years by various researchers indicates that the affordable, competitive parity, percentage of sales, and objective and task methods are the most commonly employed budgeting methods. As noted, the emphasis on ROI has dramatically increased over the past few years.[40,41,42,43,44] Tradition and top management's desire for control are probably the major reasons why top-down methods continue to be popular.

Build-Up Approaches

The major flaw associated with the top-down methods is that these judgmental approaches lead to predetermined budget appropriations often not linked to objectives and the strategies designed to accomplish them. A more effective budgeting strategy would be to consider the firm's communications objectives and budget what is deemed necessary to attain these goals. As noted earlier, the promotional planning model shows the budget decision as an interactive process, with the communications objectives on one hand and the promotional mix alternatives on the other. The idea is to budget so these promotional mix strategies can be implemented to achieve the stated objectives.

Objective and Task Method It is important that objective setting and budgeting go hand in hand rather than sequentially. It is difficult to establish a budget without specific objectives in mind, and setting objectives without regard to how much money is available makes no sense. For example, a company may wish to create awareness among *X* percent of its target market. A minimal budget amount will be required to accomplish this goal, and the firm must be willing to spend this amount.

The **objective and task method** of budget setting uses a **buildup approach** consisting of three steps: (1) defining the communications objectives to be accomplished, (2) determining the specific strategies and tasks needed to attain them, and (3) estimating the costs associated with performance of these strategies and tasks. The total budget is based on the accumulation of these costs.

Implementing the objective and task approach is somewhat more involved. The manager must monitor this process throughout and change strategies depending on how well objectives are attained. As shown in Figure 7-19, this process involves several steps:

1. *Isolate objectives.* When the promotional planning model is presented, a company will have two sets of objectives to accomplish—the marketing objectives for the product and the communications objectives. After the former are established, the task involves determining what specific communications objectives will be designed to accomplish these goals. Communications objectives must be specific, attainable, and measurable, as well as time limited.

2. *Determine tasks required.* A number of elements are involved in the strategic plan designed to attain the objectives established. (These strategies constitute the remaining chapters in this text.) These tasks may include advertising in various media, sales promotions, and/or other elements of the promotional mix, each with its own role to perform.

3. *Estimate required expenditures.* Buildup analysis requires determining the estimated costs associated with the tasks developed in the previous step. For example, it involves costs for developing awareness through advertising, trial through sampling, and so forth.

4. *Monitor.* As you will see in Chapter 19 on measuring effectiveness, there are ways to determine how well one is attaining established objectives. Performance should be monitored and evaluated in light of the budget appropriated.

5. *Reevaluate objectives.* Once specific objectives have been attained, monies may be better spent on new goals. Thus, if one has achieved the level of consumer awareness sought, the budget should be altered to stress a higher-order objective such as evaluation or trial.

The major advantage of the objective and task method is that the budget is driven by the objectives to be attained. The managers closest to the marketing effort will have specific strategies and input into the budget-setting process.

The major disadvantage of this method is the difficulty of determining which tasks will be required and the costs associated with each. For example, specifically what tasks are needed to attain awareness among 50 percent of the target market? How much will it cost to perform these tasks? While these decisions are easier to determine for certain objectives—for example, estimating the costs of sampling required to stimulate trial in a defined market area—it is not always possible to know exactly what is required and/or how much it will cost to complete the job. This process is easier if there is past experience to use as

Figure 7-19 The Objective and Task Method

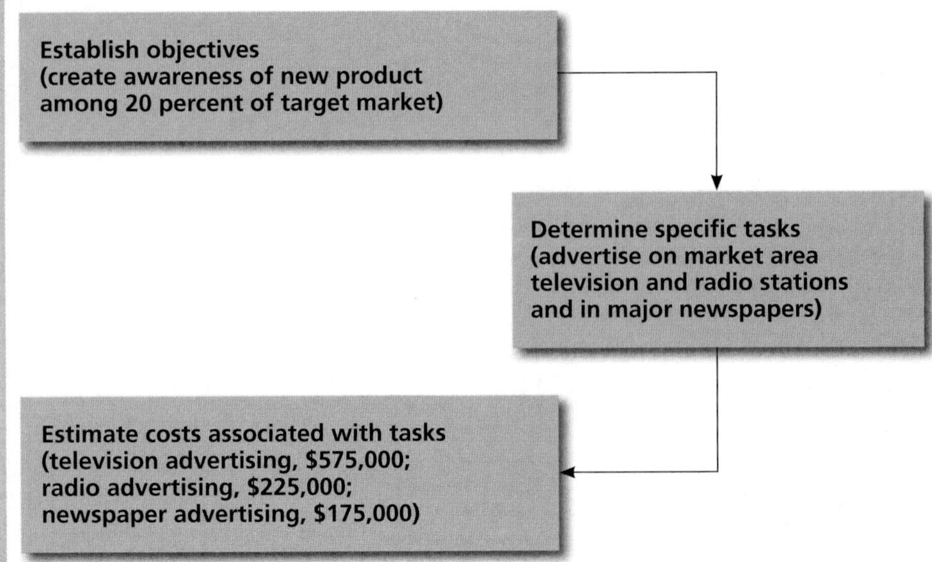

a guide, with either the existing product or a similar one in the same product category. But it is especially difficult for new product introductions. As a result, budget setting using this method is not as easy to perform or as stable as some of the methods discussed earlier. Given this disadvantage, many marketing managers have stayed with those top-down approaches for setting the total expenditure amount.

The objective and task method offers advantages over methods discussed earlier but is more difficult to implement when there is no track record for the product. The following section addresses the problem of budgeting for new product introductions.

Payout Planning The first months of a new product's introduction typically require heavier-than-normal advertising and promotion appropriations to stimulate higher levels of awareness and subsequent trial. After studying more than 40 years of Nielsen figures, James O. Peckham estimated that the average share of advertising to sales ratio necessary to launch a new product successfully is approximately 1.5:2.0.[45] This means that a new entry should be spending at approximately twice the desired market share, as shown in the two examples in Figure 7-20. For example, in the food industry, brand 101 gained a 12.6 percent market share by spending 34 percent of the total advertising dollars in this category. Likewise, brand 401 in the toiletry industry had a 30 percent share of advertising dollars to gain 19.5 percent of sales.

To determine how much to spend, marketers often develop a **payout plan** that determines the investment value of the advertising and promotion appropriation. The basic idea is to project the revenues the product will generate, as well as the costs it will incur, over two to three years. Based on an expected rate of return, the payout plan will assist in determining how much advertising and promotions expenditure will be necessary when the return might be expected. A three-year payout plan is shown in Figure 7-21. The product would lose money in year 1, almost break even in year 2, and finally begin to show substantial profits by the end of year 3.

The advertising and promotion figures are highest in year 1 and decline in years 2 and 3. This appropriation is consistent with Peckham's findings and reflects the additional outlays needed to make as rapid an impact as possible. (Keep in mind that shelf space is limited, and store owners are not likely to wait around for a product to become successful.) The budget also reflects the firm's guidelines for new product expenditures, since companies generally have established deadlines by which the product must begin to show a profit. Finally, keep in mind that building market share may be more difficult than maintaining it—thus the substantial dropoff in expenditures in later years.

Figure 7-20 Share of Advertising/Sales Relationship (Two-Year Summary)

A. New Brands of Food Products

Brand	Average share of advertising	Attained share of sales	Ratio of share of advertising to share of sales
101	34%	12.6%	2.7
102	16	10.0	1.6
103	8	7.6	1.1
104	4	2.6	1.5
105	3	2.1	1.4

B. New Brands of Toiletry Products

Brand	Average share of advertising	Attained share of sales	Ratio of share of advertising to share of sales
401	30%	19.5%	1.5
402	25	16.5	1.5
403	20	16.2	1.2
404	12	9.4	1.3
405	16	8.7	1.8
406	19	7.3	2.6
407	14	7.2	1.9
408	10	6.0	1.7
409	7	6.0	1.2
410	6	5.9	1.0
411	10	5.9	1.7
412	6	5.2	1.2

Figure 7-21 Example of Three-Year Payout Plan ($ Millions)

	Year 1	Year 2	Year 3
Product sales	15.0	35.50	60.75
Profit contribution (@ $0.50/case)	7.5	17.75	30.38
Advertising/promotions	15.0	10.50	8.50
Profit (loss)	(7.5)	7.25	21.88
Cumulative profit (loss)	(7.5)	(0.25)	21.63

While the payout plan is not always perfect, it does guide the manager in establishing the budget. When used in conjunction with the objective and task method, it provides a much more logical approach to budget setting than the top-down approaches previously discussed. Yet on the basis of the studies reported on earlier, payout planning does not seem to be a widely employed method.

Quantitative Models Attempts to apply *quantitative models* to budgeting have met with limited success. For the most part, these methods employ **computer simulation models** involving statistical techniques such as multiple regression analysis to determine the relative contribution of the advertising budget to sales. Because of problems associated with these methods, their acceptance has been limited, and quantitative models have yet to reach their potential. As requirements for accountability continue to increase, more sophisticated models may be forthcoming. Specific discussion of these models is beyond the scope of this text, however. Such methods do have merit but may need more refinement before achieving widespread success.

Summary of Budgeting Methods There is no universally accepted method of setting a budget figure. Weaknesses in each method may make it unfeasible or inappropriate. As earlier studies have shown, the use of the objective and task method continues to stay high, whereas less sophisticated methods vary in their rates of adoption. More advertisers are also employing the payout planning approach.

In a study of how managers make decisions regarding advertising and promotion budgeting decisions, George Low and Jakki Mohr interviewed 21 managers in eight consumer-product firms. Their research focused on the decision processes and procedures used to set spending levels on the factors that influence the allocation of advertising and promotion dollars.

On the basis of their results (shown in Figure 7-22), the authors concluded that the budget-setting process is still a perplexing issue to many managers and that institutional pressures led to a greater proportion of dollars being spent on sales promotions than managers would have preferred. In addition, the authors concluded that to successfully develop and implement the budget, managers must (1) employ a comprehensive strategy to guide the process, avoiding the piecemeal approach often employed, (2) develop a strategic planning framework that employs an integrated marketing communications philosophy, (3) build in contingency plans, (4) focus on long-term objectives, and (5) consistently evaluate the effectiveness of programs.[46]

By using these approaches in combination with the percentage-of-sales methods, these advertisers are likely to arrive at a more useful, accurate budget. For example, many firms now start the budgeting process by establishing the objectives they need to accomplish and then limit the budget by applying a percentage-of-sales or another method to decide whether or not it is affordable. Competitors' budgets may also influence this decision.

Allocating the Budget

Once the budget has been appropriated, the next step is to allocate it. The allocation decision involves determining which markets, products, and/or promotional elements will receive which amounts of the funds appropriated.

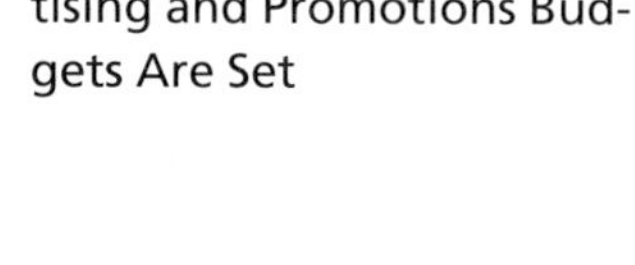

Figure 7-22 How Advertising and Promotions Budgets Are Set

The Nature of the Decision Process

- Managers develop overall marketing objectives for the brand.
- Financial projections are made on the basis of the objectives and forecasts.
- Advertising and promotions budgets are set on the basis of quantitative models and managerial judgment.
- The budget is presented to senior management, which approves and adjusts the budgets.
- The plan is implemented (changes are often made during implementation).
- The plan is evaluated by comparing the achieved results with objectives.

Factors Affecting Budget Allocations

- The extent to which risk taking is encouraged and/or tolerated.
- Sophistication regarding the use of marketing information.
- Managerial judgment.
- Use of quantitative tools.
- Brand differentiation strategies.
- Brand equity.
- The strength of the creative message.
- Retailer power.
- Short- versus long-term focus.
- Top-down influences.
- Political sales force influences.
- Historical inertia.
- Ad hoc changes.

Allocating to IMC Elements

As noted earlier, advertisers are shifting some of their budget dollars away from traditional advertising media and into sales promotions targeted at both the consumer and the trade. Direct marketing, the Internet, entertainment marketing, and other promotional tools are also receiving increased attention and competing for more of the promotional budget as discussed in IMC Perspective 7-2. Figure 7-23 demonstrates where the advertising expenditures were allocated in 2004. (Keep in mind that these numbers report on advertising in traditional media and the Internet and do not take into consideration other IMC elements such as public relations, direct marketing, and other nontraditional media.) Figure 7-24 represents a forecast as to where these monies may be spent in 2005. As you can see, the largest percentage increases are expected to be on the Internet, in Spanish, and on cable TV. While there are a number of reasons for these allocations, the fact that they are targeted media is certainly one contributing factor. The advantage of more target selectivity has led to an increased emphasis

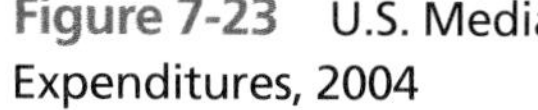

Figure 7-23 U.S. Media Expenditures, 2004

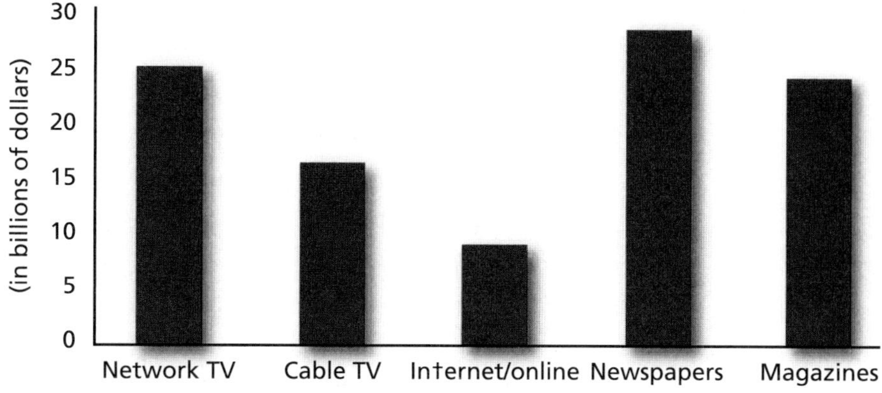

- **$141 billion on all forms of advertising (2004)**
- **Network TV (18%) $25 billion**
- **Cable TV (12%) $17 billion**
- **Internet/online (6%) $9 billion**
- **Newspapers (20%) $28 billion**
- **Magazines (17%) $24 billion**

Source: TNS Media Intelligence, *New York Times*, May 2005.

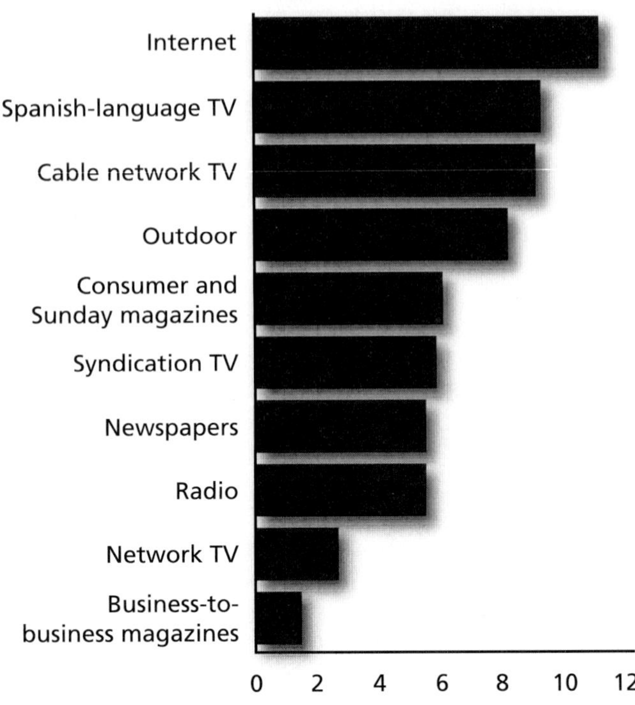

Source: TNS Media Intelligence.

Figure 7-24 U.S. Advertising Spending 2005 Forecast (% Increase from 2004)

on direct marketing, while a variety of new media have given marketers new ways to reach prospective customers. Rapidly rising media costs, the ability of sales promotions to motivate trial, maturing of the product and/or brand, and the need for more aggressive promotional tools have also led to shifts in strategy.[47] (We will discuss the reasons for these changes in subsequent chapters.)

Some marketers have also used the allocation decision to stretch their advertising dollar and get more impact from the same amount of money. For example, IBM has continued to trim its advertising expenditures every year since 1999. While still exceeding $1.4 billion per year, this number is down over $350 million since 1999. The company has taken a number of steps including consolidating and cutting division expenditures, reducing agency fees, producing less campaigns, and relying more on targeted media. IBM feels confident that the cuts will not hurt them because they have spent over $14 billion on one consistent campaign since 1995.[48] Other companies have re-evaluated as well, including Procter & Gamble, American Express, and McDonald's—all of whom have reallocated significant portions of their budgets from traditional to nontraditional media.

Client/Agency Policies

Another factor that may influence budget allocation is the individual policy of the company or the advertising agency. The agency may discourage the allocation of monies to sales promotion, preferring to spend them on the advertising area. The agency may take the position that these monies are harder to track in terms of effectiveness and may be used improperly if not under its control. (In many cases commissions are not made on this area, and this fact may contribute to the agency's reluctance.)[49]

The orientation of the agency or the firm may also directly influence where monies are spent. Many ad agencies are managed by officers who have ascended through the creative ranks and are inclined to emphasize the creative budget. Others may have preferences for specific media. For example, some agencies position themselves as experts in cable TV programming and often spend more client money in this medium. Others tend to spend more monies on the Internet. Both the agency and the client may favor certain aspects of the promotional program, perhaps on the basis of past successes, that will substantially influence where dollars are spent.

Market Size

While the budget should be allocated according to the specific promotional tools needed to accomplish the stated objectives, the *size* of the market will affect the decision. In smaller markets, it is often easier and less expensive to reach the target market. Too much of an expenditure in these markets will lead to saturation and a lack of effective spending. In larger markets, the target group may be more dispersed and thus more expensive to reach. Think about the cost of purchasing media in Chicago or New York City versus a smaller market like Columbus, Ohio, or Birmingham, Alabama. The former would be much more costly and would require a higher budget appropriation.

Market Potential

For a variety of reasons, some markets hold more potential than others. Marketers of snow skis would find greater returns on their expenditures in Denver, Colorado, than in Fort Lauderdale, Florida. Imported Mexican beers sell better in the border states (Texas, Arizona, California) than in the Midwest. A disproportionate number of imported cars are sold in California and New England.

IMC PERSPECTIVE 7-2

Which Medium Should Get the Bulk of the Budget? Ask Jaguar, Zellers, Pontiac, or Taco Bell and You May Get a Different Answer

Imagine a group of kids trying to divvy up a limited amount of candy. Now imagine the same kids grown up working in a corporation with a limited budget for IMC. It is not a pretty sight. Everyone argues why they should get the larger share. In comes Mom (or the boss) who, in an attempt to instill some reason, demands that a logical basis for dividing the candy (or money) be established. Such is the scenario being played out in marketing and communications departments throughout the world on almost a daily basis. The difference (if there is one) is that the decision involves the determination as to where to spend the media budget and to justify this expenditure.

Unfortunately for advertisers, when they ask consumers where they heard about the organization, the most common answer is "I don't remember." Thus, it is difficult to establish the cause-and-effect relationship between media and purchase behaviors. Companies haven't given up, however, and continue to search for the answer. Jaguar Land Rover believes they have gained insight into the relationship between their advertising and sales revenues by hiring a company named Who's Calling. When a potential prospect calls a Jaguar or Land Rover dealership, Who's Calling records the call and captures the name and address of the caller, then maps where they live. The information is provided to the dealer, who can then see which ad, billboard, direct marketing, or other program was running in this area at the time. According to the dealers, Who's Calling allows them to pinpoint which marketing strategies are generating the most leads, leading to greater advertising and promotional efficiencies. Jaguar Land Rover believes in its advertising.

Zellers stores of Canada believe that public relations (PR) provides the best ROI. When Zellers launched their new Hillary Duff clothing line, dubbed "Stuff by Hillary Duff," they focused on the use of PR. Utilizing a press conference, fashion show, one-on-one personal interviews with Duff, and an intensive media relations follow-up, the PR program netted more than 50 million consumer impressions including 40 separate articles about the launch in newspapers and teen/tween publications; coverage on 40 distinct Internet sites; and TV coverage on the news, teen programs, and *Entertainment Tonight.* Duff also appeared on the cover of *TV Guide* during launch week—all of this at an extremely low cost per person reached. Zellers votes for PR.

But not so fast. General Motors (GM) likes the idea of product integration for their money. An April 2005 episode of *The Apprentice* required participants to create a marketing brochure for the new Pontiac Solstice. While actual dollar figures for the branded entertainment deal were not disclosed, estimates are that it cost GM about $2 million. So, what did they get in return? During the program, visits to Pontiac.com increased by 1,400 percent over a typical Thursday night. Over the next three days, 966,110 unique visitors, an increase of 580 percent, came to the site. It took only 41 minutes to sell the first 1,000 cars to come off the assembly line, with another 35,197 registrations to buy within the next three days.

Let's not forget about good old TV advertising. Taco Bell says that just by running two spots on the NFL's AFC Championship Game they were able to show a 14 percent increase in sales. This is an increase that the fast-food company says is not unusual for this time of year. And, let's not forget the Paris Hilton commercial for Carl's Junior, which led to an increase in website visits and sales of burgers.

The direct response people and other media advocates would like to throw in their two cents, but space here does not permit. We will just have to trust them!

Sources: Jean Halliday and Marc Graser, "GM's Apprentice Task Reaps Eye-Popping ROI," *Advertising Age,* April 25, 2005, p. 8; Paul-Mark Rendon and Michelle Halpern, "Public Relations ROI," *Marketing,* January 31, 2005, pp. 13–14; Coreen Bailor, "Marketing ROI Makes Jaguar Land Rover Purr," *Customer Relationship Management,* December 2004, p. 57; Wayne Friedman, "ROI Measurement Still Falls Short," *Television Week,* January 31, 2005, p. 19.

When particular markets hold higher potential, the marketing manager may decide to allocate additional monies to them. (Keep in mind that just because a market does not have high sales does not mean it should be ignored. The key is *potential*—and a market with low sales but high potential may be a candidate for additional appropriations.)

There are several methods for estimating marketing potential. Many marketers conduct research studies to forecast demand and/or use secondary sources of information such as those provided by government agencies or syndicated services like Dun & Bradstreet, A. C. Nielsen, and Audits and Surveys. One source for consumer goods information is the *Survey of Buying Power,* published annually by *Sales & Marketing Management* magazine. The survey contains population, income, and retail sales data for states, counties, metropolitan statistical areas, and cities in the United States and Canada with populations of 40,000 or more.

Market Share Goals Two studies in the *Harvard Business Review* discussed advertising spending with the goal of maintaining and increasing market share.[50] John Jones compared the brand's share of market with its share of advertising voice (the total value of the main media exposure in the product category). Jones classified the brands as "profit taking brands, or underspenders" and "investment brands, those whose share of voice is clearly above their share of market." His study indicated that for those brands with small market shares, profit takers are in the minority; however, as the brands increase their market share, nearly three out of five have a proportionately smaller share of voice.

Jones noted that three factors can be cited to explain this change. First, new brands generally receive higher-than-average advertising support. Second, older, more mature brands are often "milked"—that is, when they reach the maturity stage, advertising support is reduced. Third, there's an advertising economy of scale whereby advertising works harder for well-established brands, so a lower expenditure is required. Jones concluded that for larger brands, it may be possible to reduce advertising expenditures and still maintain market share. Smaller brands, on the other hand, have to continue to maintain a large share of voice.

James Schroer addressed the advertising budget in a situation where the marketer wishes to increase market share. His analysis suggests that marketers should:

- Segment markets, focusing on those markets where competition is weak and/or underspending instead of on a national advertising effort.
- Determine their competitors' cost positions (how long the competition can continue to spend at the current or increased rate).
- Resist the lure of short-term profits that result from ad budget cuts.
- Consider niching strategies as opposed to long-term wars.

Figure 7-25 shows Schroer's suggestions for spending priorities in various markets.

Economies of Scale in Advertising Some studies have presented evidence that firms and/or brands maintaining a large share of the market have an advantage

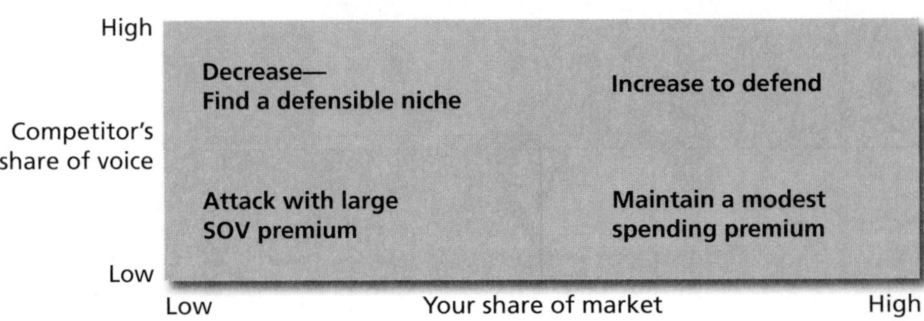

Figure 7-25 The Share of Voice (SOV) Effect and Ad Spending: Priorities in Individual Markets

over smaller competitors and thus can spend less money on advertising and realize a better return.[51] Larger advertisers can maintain advertising shares that are smaller than their market shares because they get better advertising rates, have declining average costs of production, and accrue the advantages of advertising several products jointly. In addition, they are likely to enjoy more favorable time and space positions, cooperation of middlepeople, and favorable publicity. These advantages are known as **economies of scale.**

Reviewing the studies in support of this position and then conducting research over a variety of small package products, Kent Lancaster found that this situation did not hold true and that in fact larger brand share products might actually be at a disadvantage.[52] His results indicated that leading brands spend an average of 2.5 percentage points more than their brand share on advertising. More specifically, his study concluded:

1. There is no evidence that larger firms can support their brands with lower relative advertising costs than smaller firms.
2. There is no evidence that the leading brand in a product group enjoys lower advertising costs per sales dollar than do other brands.
3. There is no evidence of a static relationship between advertising costs per dollar of sales and the size of the advertiser.

The results of this and other studies suggest there really are no economies of scale to be accrued from the size of the firm or the market share of the brand.[53]

Organizational Characteristics

In a review of the literature on how allocation decisions are made between advertising and sales promotion, George Low and Jakki Mohr concluded that organizational factors play an important role in determining how communications dollars are spent.[54] The authors note that the following factors influence the allocation decision. These factors vary from one organization to another, and each influences the relative amounts assigned to advertising and promotion:

- The organization's structure—centralized versus decentralized, formalization, and complexity.
- Power and politics in the organizational hierarchy.
- The use of expert opinions (for example, consultants).
- Characteristics of the decision maker (preferences and experience).
- Approval and negotiation channels.
- Pressure on senior managers to arrive at the optimal budget.

One example of how these factors might influence allocations relates to the level of interaction between marketing and other functional departments, such as accounting and operations. The authors note that the relative importance of advertising versus sales promotion might vary from department to department. Accountants, being dollars-and-cents minded, would argue for the sales impact of promotions, while operations would argue against sales promotions because the sudden surges in demand that might result would throw off production schedules. The marketing department might be influenced by the thinking of either of these groups in making its decision.

The use of outside consultants to provide expert opinions might also affect the allocation decision. Trade journals, academic journals, and even books might also be valuable inputs into the decision maker's thinking. In sum, it seems obvious that many factors must be taken into account in the budget allocation decision. Market size and potential, specific objectives sought, and previous company and/or agency policies and preferences all influence this decision.

Summary

This chapter has examined the role of objectives in the planning and evaluation of the IMC program and how firms budget in an attempt to achieve these objectives. Specific objectives are needed to guide the development of the promotional program, as well as to provide a benchmark against which performance can be measured and evaluated. Objectives serve important functions as communications devices, as a guide to planning the IMC program and deciding on various alternatives, and for measurement and evaluation.

Objectives for IMC evolve from the organization's overall marketing plan and are based on the roles various promotional mix elements play in the marketing program. Many managers use sales or a related measure such as market share as the basis for setting objectives. However, many promotional planners believe the role of advertising and other promotional mix elements is to communicate because of the various problems associated with sales-based objectives. They use communications-based objectives like those in the response hierarchy as the basis for setting goals.

Much of the emphasis in setting objectives has been on traditional advertising-based views of marketing communications. However, many companies are moving toward zero-based communications planning, which focuses on what tasks need to be done, which marketing communication functions should be used, and to what extent. Many of the principles used in setting advertising objectives can be applied to other elements in the promotional mix.

As you have probably concluded, the budget decision is not typically based on supporting experiences or strong theoretical foundations. Nor is it one of the more soundly established elements of the promotional program. The budgeting methods used now have some major problems. Economic models are limited, often try to demonstrate the effects on sales directly, and ignore other elements of the marketing mix. Some of the methods discussed have no theoretical basis and ignore the roles advertising and promotion are meant to perform.

One possible way to improve the budget appropriation is to tie the measures of effectiveness to communications objectives rather than to the broader-based marketing objectives. Using the objective and task approach with communications objectives may not be the ultimate solution to the budgeting problem, but it is an improvement over the top-down methods. Marketers often find it advantageous to employ a combination of methods.

As with determining the budget, managers must consider a number of factors when allocating advertising and promotions dollars. Market size and potential, agency policies, and the preferences of management itself may influence the allocation decision.

Key Terms

- marketing objectives, 194
- integrated marketing communications objectives, 195
- carryover effect, 197
- DAGMAR, 203
- communications task, 203
- benchmark measures, 206
- zero-based communications planning, 208
- contribution margin, 211
- marginal analysis, 211
- concave-downward function model, 212
- S-shaped response curve, 212
- top-down approaches, 215
- affordable method, 215
- arbitrary allocation, 216
- percentage-of-sales method, 216
- clipping service, 220
- competitive parity method, 220
- ROI budgeting method, 222
- objective and task method, 224
- buildup approach, 224
- payout plan, 225
- computer simulation models, 226
- economies of scale, 231

Discussion Questions

1. As noted in the chapter, there is an increased emphasis on the determination of ROI. Discuss some of the reasons leading to this increase in attention. Why is it so difficult to measure ROI?

2. Chapter 7 differentiates between communications objectives and sales objectives. Explain the difference. What are examples of communications objectives? From where are these objectives derived?

3. Exhibit 7-10 reflects the AAAA's contention that advertisers should not cut their budgets during a time of recession. Explain why advertisers usually do make cuts in marketing communications budgets during a recession. Is this likely to be an effective or ineffective strategy? Explain why.

4. Figure 7-17 reflects the results of a study conducted by Yoo and Mandhachitara that shows that advertising spending and effects may differ in different competitive environments. Explain each of the four scenarios presented in Figure 7-17 and give examples of brands in each of these cells.

5. IMC Perspective 7-2 notes that different companies believe that various media are more important than others for their marketing purposes. Discuss the various perspectives taken by these companies, and explain why everyone may not agree on the same level of importance for media.

6. The lead-in to the chapter discusses the fact that the companies that spend the most on advertising do not necessarily achieve the highest brand value for their products. Sometimes, those who spend very little are able to achieve this objective. Explain what factors may lead to these results. Provide examples.

7. Some marketers feel that the cereal companies have focused too much on sales objectives, creating a situation in which price cutting and couponing have become essential to selling the product. Do you think that these companies may be able to reverse this situation? Describe some of the options available to the cereal manufacturers.

8. Figure 7-1 notes the numerous factors that influence sales. Provide examples of products and/or services that have been directly influenced by each of these factors.

9. What is DAGMAR? Explain how marketers might use DAGMAR in establishing objectives. What are some of the problems associated with the use of DAGMAR?

10. Discuss the two sales response models described in the text. Explain the differences between the two models. Provide examples of types of products that might follow each of these response curves.

Creative Strategy: Planning and Development

8

Chapter Objectives

1. To discuss what is meant by advertising creativity and examine the role of creative strategy in advertising.
2. To examine creative strategy development and the roles of various client and agency personnel involved in it.
3. To consider the process that guides the creation of advertising messages and the research inputs into the stages of the creative process.
4. To examine various approaches used for determining major selling ideas that form the basis of an advertising campaign.

Great Advertising Helps the iPod Become a Cultural Icon

In January 2004 at the annual state-of-the-company keynote address, Apple CEO Steve Jobs cued the tape of Apple's famous "1984" commercial that was used to launch the Macintosh computer and considered by many the best TV ad ever made. The classic spot was based on the concept of Big Brother (understood to symbolize IBM) from George Orwell's classic novel *1984* and used stark images of Orwell's dystopia and a dramatic scene of a young woman throwing a mallet through a movie screen to destroy the controlling force. The "1984" spot was shown only one time on television during the 1984 Super Bowl, but it became the most talked-about commercial ever. However, there was something different about the ad that Jobs showed to celebrate the 20th anniversary of the "1984" commercial; the hammer-carrying woman who ultimately destroyed Big Brother carried something extra around her waist—an Apple iPod. Job's wanted to send a message that the iPod was more than a clever device that holds a lot of songs and provides owners the opportunity to customize their music listening experience. The iPod is a world-changing product that has become a cultural phenomenon and an indispensable part of the lifestyle for the millions of people who own one.

The iPod was introduced to the market in October 2001 with a high-profile ad campaign that included commercials set to music by the then little-known band Jet. The initial tagline for the campaign was "iPod. Think Different," which was based on previous ads that had been used for Apple computers. In 2002, the iPod was promoted using the "Switchers" campaign, which was used across the entire line of Apple products and encouraged consumers to switch from Windows-based computers to Macintoshes and other Apple machines. In the fall of 2003, Apple's agency, TBWA/Chiat/Day Los Angeles, launched the Silhouettes campaign for iPod. The agency's legendary creative director, Lee Clow, and his team recognized that the most visible iPod icon was the device's white earphones and cord—a cue that was taken from watching a user dance his way across an intersection while listening to music. The creative team came away with the graphic idea of using a black silhouetted figure with the highlighted cord and earphones in white, surrounded by a background of bright neon colors. Commercials for the iPod show the silhouettes dancing to music from such groups as the Black Eyed Peas and N.E.R.D. One spot showed a young man listening to his iPod while walking past a wall of iPod print ads, which are themselves dancing to music from the Vines, only to return to their stationary form when he turns the device off. The campaign also included print ads, billboards, and posters featuring the black silhouettes of people listening to music with a white iPod against a bright single-color background.

A year after the Silhouettes campaign was launched, Apple extended it in a unique direction by entering into a cross promotion with the rock band U2, a collaboration hatched by the band's lead singer Bono and Steve Jobs, who are longtime friends. A television commercial featured a silhouetted image of Bono singing the introduction to the band's hit "Vertigo." As part of the promotion, U2's new album *How to Dismantle an Atomic Bomb* was released exclusively on Apple's iTunes Music Store and topped the sales charts for weeks after its release. Apple also developed a special black-and-red U2 version of the iPod, which included "The Complete U2," a digital box set containing 446 songs, the latest U2 album, rare live cuts, remixes, and 40 unreleased songs from the group.

The marketing campaign for the iPod has also included online ads and promotions with companies such as PepsiCo and AOL. PepsiCo ran a 100-million song giveaway promotion whereby codes for free songs were placed in the bottle caps of Pepsi, Diet Pepsi, and Sierra Mist soft drinks. A number of other major brands including Volkswagen, BMW, Hewlett-Packard, Bose, and Motorola have also entered into co-branding and joint promotional efforts that have capitalized on the popularity of the iPod. BMW ran an "iPod your BMW" campaign that included print ads and a special website. Volkswagen's agency created the "Pods Unite" campaign offering purchasers of VW Beetles a free iPod with a customer-engraved "Drivers Wanted" logo and a $100 coupon for use at Apple retail stores.

More than 4 million iPods have been sold since the product was first introduced. Apple's iTunes online music store commands 70 percent of the legal download music market. Many artists credit the company with helping to save the recording industry by providing a way to have music downloaded legitimately. An entire economy has evolved around the iPod as more than 1,000 peripheral devices, from carrying cases to cables, have been developed to add to its functionality, and companies are lining up to ally themselves with the device and to capitalize on its popularity and brand equity. Revenue from the sale of iPods and the iTunes music downloads helped Apple Computer generate profits in 2004, and the company's stock price has more than doubled over the past two years. Moreover, other Apple products are benefiting from the halo effect of the device as younger consumers whose first exposure to the company has been through the iPod are now considering other Apple products.

The Silhouettes campaign has contributed significantly to success of the brand as the iPod ads have become instantly recognizable for their imagery as well as for their music. In 2004, the campaign won the Grand Prize Kelly Award from the Magazine Publishers of America for creative excellence and effectiveness. In 2005, TBWA/Chiat/Day won the Grand Prize at the Effie Awards, which are sponsored by the New York American Marketing Association. The Effies are considered one of the most significant awards in the industry as they recognize effective advertising and marketing campaigns that have achieved results in the marketplace. Apple plans to keep the iPod at the forefront of popular culture and to borrow the buzz from the product to help generate sales of other brands. Great creative work such as the Silhouettes campaign will help the iPod maintain its status as a cultural icon.

Sources: Marie Anderson, "Grand Effie Goes to TBWA/C/D," *Adweek.com,* June 8, 2005; Thomas Mucha, "Silhouettes and Synergy," *Business 2.0,* January/February 2005, p. 62; Beth Snyder Bulik, "The iPod Economy," *Advertising Age,* October 18, 2004, pp. 1, 37; Scott Van Camp, "They March to His Rhythm," *Brandweek,* October 11, 2004, pp. M36–41.

One of the most important components of an integrated marketing communications program is the advertising message. While the fundamental role of an advertising message is to communicate information, it does much more. The commercials we watch on TV or hear on radio and the print ads we see in magazines and newspapers are a source of entertainment, motivation, fascination, fantasy, and sometimes irritation as well as information. Ads and commercials appeal to, and often create or shape, consumers' problems, desires, and goals. From the marketer's perspective, the advertising message is a way to tell consumers how the product or service can solve a problem or help satisfy desires or achieve goals. Advertising can also be used to create images or associations and position a brand in the consumer's mind as well as transform the experience of buying and/or using a product or service. Many consumers who have never driven or even ridden in a BMW perceive it as "the ultimate driving machine" (Exhibit 8-1). Many people feel good about sending Hallmark greeting cards because they have internalized the company's advertising theme, "when you care enough to send the very best."

Exhibit 8-1 Excellent advertising helps create an image for BMW automobiles as "the ultimate driving machine"

One need only watch an evening of commercials or peruse a few magazines to realize there are a myriad of ways to convey an advertising message. Underlying all of these messages, however, are a **creative strategy** that determines what the advertising message will say or communicate and **creative tactics** for how the message strategy will be executed. In this chapter, we focus on advertising creative strategy. We consider what is meant by creativity, particularly as it relates to advertising, and examine a well-known approach to creativity in advertising.

We also examine the creative strategy development process and various approaches to determining the *big idea* that will be used as the central theme of the advertising campaign and translated into attention-getting, distinctive, and memorable messages. Creative specialists are finding it more and more difficult to come up with big ideas that will break through the clutter and still satisfy the concerns of their risk-averse clients. Yet their clients are continually challenging them to find the creative message that will strike a responsive chord with their target audience.

Some of you may not be directly involved in the design and creation of ads; you may choose to work in another agency department or on the client side of the business. However, because creative strategy is often so crucial to the success of the firm's promotional effort, everyone involved in the promotional process should understand the creative strategy and tactics that underlie the development of advertising campaigns and messages, as well as the creative options available to the advertiser. Also, individuals on the client side as well as agency people outside the creative department must work with the creative specialists in developing the advertising campaign, implementing it, and evaluating its effectiveness. Thus, marketing and product managers, account representatives, researchers, and media personnel must appreciate the creative process and develop a productive relationship with creative personnel.

The Importance of Creativity in Advertising

For many students, as well as many advertising and marketing practitioners, the most interesting aspect of advertising is the creative side. We have all at one time or another been intrigued by an ad and admired the creative insight that went into it. A great ad is a joy to behold and often an epic to create, as the cost of producing a TV commercial can exceed $1 million. Many companies see this as money well spent. They realize that the manner in which the advertising message is developed and executed is often critical to the success of the promotional program, which in turn can influence the effectiveness of the entire marketing program. Procter & Gamble, Levi Strauss, Apple Computer, General Motors, Coca-Cola, PepsiCo, Nike, McDonald's, and many other companies spend millions of dollars each year to produce advertising messages and hundreds of millions more to purchase media time and space to run them. While these companies make excellent products, they realize creative advertising is also an important part of their marketing success.

Good creative strategy and execution can often be central to determining the success of a product or service or reversing the fortunes of a struggling brand. Conversely, an advertising campaign that is poorly conceived or executed can be a liability. Many companies have solid marketing and promotional plans and spend substantial amounts of money on advertising, yet have difficulty coming up with a creative campaign that will differentiate them from their competitors. However, just because an ad or commercial is creative or popular does not mean it will increase sales or revive a declining brand. Many ads have won awards for creativity but failed to increase sales. In some instances, the failure to generate sales has cost the agency the account. For example, many advertising people believe some of the best ads of all time were those done for Alka-Seltzer in the 1960s and 70s, including the classic "Mama Mia! That's a spicy meatball!" and "I can't believe I ate the whole thing." While the commercials won numerous creative awards, Alka-Seltzer sales still declined and the agencies lost the account.[1] In the late 90s, Nissan asked its agency to change the popular "Enjoy the ride" campaign that was widely praised for its amusing, creative executions but was not helping increase sales.[2] Nissan dealers complained that the ads did not focus enough attention on the product, and asked its agency to focus more on the cars. Recently Nissan launched a new advertising campaign using "Shift" as the umbrella tagline.[3] The new campaign uses a combination of emotional and product-focused ads that are designed to strengthen Nissan's brand image while showing its revitalized product line, which includes the new 350Z sports car (see Exhibit 8-2).

Many advertising and marketing people have become ambivalent toward, and in some cases even critical of, advertising awards.[4] They argue that agency creative people are often more concerned with creating ads that win awards than ones that sell their clients' products. Other advertising people believe awards are a good way to recognize creativity that often does result in effective advertising. Global Perspective 8-1 discusses how the emphasis on creative awards has shifted to the international arena with awards like the Cannes Lions.

Exhibit 8-2 In Nissan's new ads, the cars are once again the stars

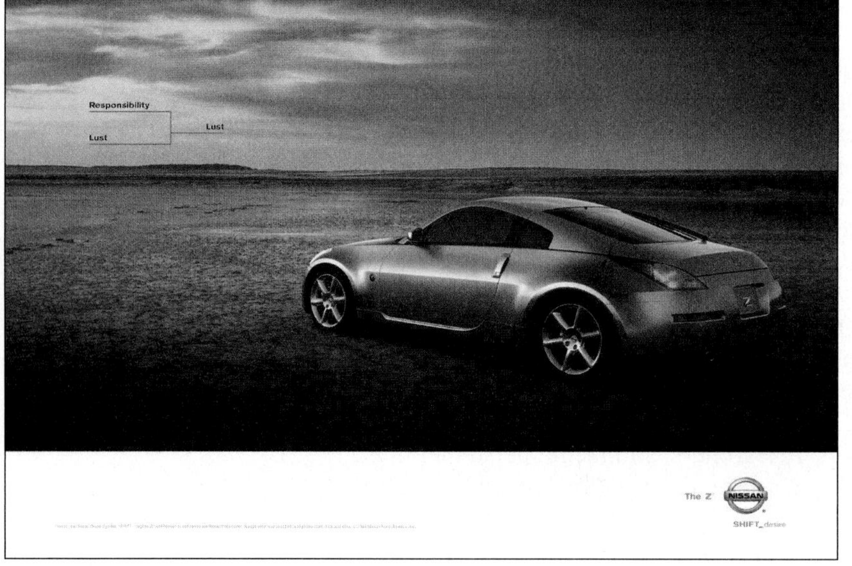

As we saw in Chapter 7, the success of an ad campaign cannot always be judged in terms of sales. However, many advertising and marketing personnel, particularly those on the client side, believe advertising must ultimately lead the consumer to purchase the product or service. Finding a balance between creative advertising and effective advertising is difficult. To better understand this dilemma, we turn to the issue of creativity and its role in advertising.

GLOBAL PERSPECTIVE 8-1

Cannes Festival Continues to Be the Olympic Games of Advertising

For many years the most coveted prize for creativity in advertising was a Clio award. However, the Clios lost much of their prestige after financial problems resulted in the cancellation of their 1992 awards ceremony. Although the Clio Festival is an increasingly popular awards competition, the Clios have not quite yet regained their former status as the advertising industry's premier award for creative excellence. There are a number of other popular and well-recognized U.S.-based advertising award competitions that recognize outstanding creative work. These include the Kelly Awards given by the Magazine Publishers of America; the Best Awards, sponsored by *Advertising Age;* the One Show sponsored by the One Club for Art & Copy; the Effies, which are given each year by the New York American Marketing Association; and the Creative Excellence in Business Advertising (CEBA) Awards, which are sponsored by American Business Media.

While these contests remain very popular in the United States, on a global level the Cannes Lions International Advertising Festival is now widely considered the most prestigious advertising award competition. Inspired by the movie industry's more famous Cannes Film Festival, the Cannes Lions is considered by many to be the "Olympics of Advertising." The Cannes competition receives entries from agencies around the world hoping to win Lions (the name of the award) in each of the major categories: film (television), press and poster (print and outdoor ads), Cyber (online marketing and ads for websites) advertising, media planning/buying, and direct marketing. The competition recently added several new awards: the Titanium Lion, which is given for innovative work across integrated media, and the Radio Lion, which was initiated in 2005.

Agencies from the United States generally focus their entries on the TV part of the competition where they fare much better than in the print category, which is usually dominated by agencies from Europe whose style of advertising is considered more popular among the Cannes jury. Such was the case in the 2005 Cannes competition as U.S. agencies failed to win any Gold Lions in the poster competition and only gold, silver, and three bronzes in the print category. The film category rescued U.S. agencies from what threatened to be a bad year at Cannes, as they won five of 18 Gold Lions in the category and a total of 27 overall. However, the Grand Prix award for the world's best TV commercial went to the United Kingdom agency Wieden & Kennedy, London, which created "Grrr"—a 90-second cinema and TV spot for Honda. The "Grrr" commercial, a whimsical and psychedelic animated spot created to promote Honda's first diesel engine, was inspired by a professed hatred of the type of motor by the company's chief engineer, who agreed to create one only if he could start from scratch. The commercial begins with the question "Can hate be good?" and follows clanking diesel engines flying around a candy-colored kingdom full of animals taking swipes at disruptive engines as the whistling tune jingle cheerily suggests, "Hate something. Change something. Make Something betterrr."

One of the other big winners at the 2005 competition was the U.S. agency Crispin, Porter & Bogusky (CP+B) from Miami, which won a Cyber Lions Grand Prix for the "Come Clean" website that was developed for Method, an environmentally friendly household products brand. The campaign won rave reviews as an example of how the Web could be used for brand building as visitors to ComeClean.com can type in confessions that appear on a woman's hand and get washed away with a Method soaping. Simultaneously, a female voice gives the user a witty personalized scolding for the wrongdoings. CP+B also won a Titanium Lion for an integrated campaign developed for the Mini Cooper automobile. The "Counterfeit" campaign warned about fake Mini Coopers and directed people to a website where they could buy a real DVD about fictitious counterfeit cars and use their mouse to slap buyers who had been duped into buying suspiciously cheap Minis.

Agencies from the United States dominated the new radio Lions contest by winning one of the two Golds and two of the eight Silver Lions awarded. DDB Worldwide, Chicago, won the first-ever Radio Lions Grand Prix for the long-running "Real Men of Genius" campaign developed for Bud Light beer.

Although many advertising people in the United States are critical of creative advertising awards, the Cannes competition attracted nearly 5,000 entries in 2005 from 75 countries, so someone must think they are important. And don't try to downplay their importance in advertising-crazy countries like Brazil and Argentina, where agency creative directors are treated like rock stars, or in Europe, where agency leaders are seen as titans of industry, on par with top CEOs. Agencies such as TBWA Worldwide, Paris, which won the Agency of the Year prize, know that the prestige of a Cannes award enhances their image and helps attract new business to their agency.

52nd International Advertising Festival
CANNES LIONS 2005
19 - 25 JUNE

Sources: Laurel Wentz, "At Cannes, the Lions say 'Grrr'," *Advertising Age,* June 27, 2005, pp. 1, 55; Ann-Christine Diaz, "Crispin Porter and DDB Brasil Each Win Cyber Grand Prix," *AdAge.com,* June 22, 2005; Mae Anderson, "Born of Hate," *Adweek,* June 20, 2005, pp. 28, 29.

Advertising Creativity

What Is Creativity?

Creativity is probably one of the most commonly used terms in advertising. Ads are often called creative. The people who develop ads and commercials are known as creative types. And advertising agencies develop reputations for their creativity. Perhaps so much attention is focused on the concept of creativity because many people view the specific challenge given to those who develop an advertising message as being creative. It is their job to turn all of the information regarding product features and benefits, marketing plans, consumer research, and communication objectives into a creative concept that will bring the advertising message to life. This begs the question: What is meant by *creativity* in advertising?

Different Perspectives on Advertising Creativity

Perspectives on what constitutes creativity in advertising differ. At one extreme are people who argue that advertising is creative only if it sells the product. An advertising message's or campaign's impact on sales counts more than whether it is innovative or wins awards. At the other end of the continuum are those who judge the creativity of an ad in terms of its artistic or aesthetic value and originality. They contend creative ads can break through the competitive clutter, grab the consumer's attention, and have some impact.

As you might expect, perspectives on advertising creativity often depend on one's role. A study by Elizabeth Hirschman examined the perceptions of various individuals involved in the creation and production of TV commercials, including management types (brand managers and account executives) and creatives (art director, copywriter, commercial director, and producer).[5] She found that product managers and account executives view ads as promotional tools whose primary purpose is to communicate favorable impressions to the marketplace. They believe a commercial should be evaluated in terms of whether it fulfills the client's marketing and communicative objectives. The perspective of those on the creative side was much more self-serving, as Hirschman noted:

> In direct contrast to this client orientation, the art director, copywriter, and commercial director viewed the advertisement as a communication vehicle for promoting their own aesthetic viewpoints and personal career objectives. Both the copywriter and art director made this point explicitly, noting that a desirable commercial from their standpoint was one which communicated their unique creative talents and thereby permitted them to obtain "better" jobs at an increased salary.[6]

In her interviews, Hirschman also found that brand managers were much more risk-averse and wanted a more conservative commercial than the creative people, who wanted to maximize the impact of the message.

What constitutes creativity in advertising is probably somewhere between the two extremes. To break through the clutter and make an impression on the target audience, an ad often must be unique and entertaining. As noted in Chapter 5, research has shown that a major determinant of whether a commercial will be successful in changing brand preferences is its "likability," or the viewer's overall reaction.[7] TV commercials and print ads that are well designed and executed and generate emotional responses can create positive feelings that are transferred to the product or service being advertised. Many creative people believe this type of advertising can come about only if they are given considerable latitude in developing advertising messages. But ads that are creative only for the sake of being creative often fail to communicate a relevant or meaningful message that will lead consumers to purchase the product or service.

Everyone involved in planning and developing an advertising campaign must understand the importance of balancing the "it's not creative unless it sells" perspective with the novelty/uniqueness and impact position. Marketing and brand managers or account executives must recognize that imposing too many sales- and marketing-oriented communications objectives on the creative team can result in mediocre advertising, which is often ineffective in today's competitive, cluttered media environment. At the same time, the creative specialists must recognize that the goal of advertising is to assist in selling the product or service and good advertising must communicate in a manner that helps the client achieve this goal.

Advertising creativity is the ability to generate fresh, unique, and appropriate ideas that can be used as solutions to communications problems. To be *appropriate* and effective, a creative idea must be relevant to the target audience. Many ad agencies recognize the importance of developing advertising that is creative and different yet communicates relevant information to the target audience. Figure 8-1 shows the perspective on creativity that the former D'Arcy, Masius Benton & Bowles agency developed to guide its creative efforts and help achieve superior creativity consistently. The agency viewed a creative advertising message as one that is built around a creative core or power idea and uses excellent design and execution to communicate information that interests the target audience. It used these principles in doing outstanding creative work for Procter & Gamble's Charmin and Pampers brands, Norelco, and many other popular brands for many years.

Exhibit 8-3 Absolut vodka creates ads specifically for the publications in which they appear, such as this one for *Los Angeles Magazine*

Advertising creativity is not the exclusive domain of those who work on the creative side of advertising. The nature of the business requires creative thinking from everyone involved in the promotional planning process. Agency people, such as account executives, media planners, researchers, and attorneys, as well as those on the client side, such as marketing and brand managers, must all seek creative solutions to problems encountered in planning, developing, and executing an advertising campaign. An excellent example of creative synergy between the media and creative departments of an agency, as well as with the client, is seen in the TBWA/Chiat/Day agency and its relationship with Absolut vodka. The creative strategy for the brand plays off the distinctive shape of its bottle and depicts it with visual puns and witty headlines that play off the Absolut name. The agency and client recognized they could carry the advertising campaign further by tailoring the print ads for the magazines or regions where they appear. Absolut's media schedule includes over 100 magazines, among them various consumer and business publications. The creative and media departments work together selecting magazines and deciding on the ads that will appeal to the readers of each publication. The creative department is often asked to create media-specific ads to run in a particular publication. Exhibit 8-3 shows an Absolut ad that was developed specifically for *Los Angeles Magazine.*

Planning Creative Strategy

The Creative Challenge

Those who work on the creative side of advertising often face a real challenge. They must take all the research, creative briefs, strategy statements, communications objectives, and other input and transform them into an advertising message. Their job is to write copy, design layouts and illustrations, or produce commercials that effectively communicate the central theme on which the campaign is based. Rather than simply stating the features or benefits of a product or service, they must put the advertising message into a form that will engage the audience's interest and make the ads memorable.[8]

The job of the creative team is challenging because every marketing situation is different and each campaign or advertisement may require a different creative approach. Numerous guidelines have been developed for creating effective advertising,[9] but there is no magic formula. As copywriter Hank Sneiden notes in his book *Advertising Pure and Simple:*

> Rules lead to dull stereotyped advertising, and they stifle creativity, inspiration, initiative, and progress. The only hard and fast rule that I know of in advertising is that there are no

Figure 8-1 D'Arcy, Masius Benton & Bowles's Universal Advertising Standards

1. *Does this advertising position the product simply and with unmistakable clarity?*

   The target audience for the advertised product or service must be able to see and sense in a flash *what* the product is for, *whom* it is for, and *why* they should be interested in it.

   Creating this clear vision of how the product or service fits into their lives is the first job of advertising. Without a simple, clear, focused positioning, no creative work can begin.

2. *Does this advertising bolt the brand to a clinching benefit?*

   Our advertising should be built on the most compelling and persuasive consumer benefit—not some unique-but-insignificant peripheral feature.

   Before you worry about how to say it, you must be sure you are saying *the right thing.* If you don't know what the most compelling benefit is, you've got to find out before you do anything else.

3. *Does this advertising contain a Power Idea?*

   The Power Idea is the vehicle that transforms the strategy into a dynamic, creative communications concept. It is the core creative idea that sets the stage for brilliant executions to come. The ideal Power Idea should:

   - Be describable in a simple word, phrase, or sentence without reference to any final execution.
   - Be likely to attract the prospect's attention.
   - Revolve around the clinching benefit.
   - Allow you to brand the advertising.
   - Make it easy for the prospect to vividly experience our client's product or service.

4. *Does this advertising design in Brand Personality?*

   The great brands tend to have something in common: the extra edge of having a Brand Personality. This is something beyond merely identifying what the brand does for the consumer; all brands *do* something, but the great brands also *are* something.

   A brand can be whatever its designers want it to be—and it can be so from day one.

5. *Is this advertising unexpected?*

   Why should our clients pay good money to wind up with advertising that looks and sounds like everybody else's in the category? They shouldn't.

   We must dare to be different, because sameness is suicide. We can't be outstanding unless we first stand out.

   The thing is not to *emulate* the competition but to *annihilate* them.

6. *Is this advertising single-minded?*

   If you have determined the right thing to say and have created a way to say it uncommonly well, why waste time saying anything else?

   If we want people to remember one big thing from a given piece of advertising, let's not make it more difficult than it already is in an overcommunicated world.

   The advertising should be all about that one big thing.

7. *Does this advertising reward the prospect?*

   Let's give our audience something that makes it easy—even pleasurable—for our message to penetrate: a tear, a smile, a laugh. An emotional stimulus is that special something that makes them want to see the advertising again and again.

8. *Is this advertising visually arresting?*

   Great advertising you remember—and can play back in your mind—is unusual to look at: compelling, riveting, a nourishing feast for the eyes. If you need a reason to strive for arresting work, go no further than Webster: "Catching or holding the attention, thought, or feelings. Gripping. Striking. Interesting."

9. *Does this advertising exhibit painstaking craftsmanship?*

   You want writing that is really written. Visuals that are designed. Music that is composed.

   Lighting, casting, wardrobe, direction—all the components of the art of advertising are every bit as important as the science of it. It is a sin to nickel-and-dime a great advertising idea to death.

   Why settle for good, when there's great? We should go for the absolute best in concept, design, and execution.

   This is our craft—the work should sparkle.

   "Our creative standards are not a gimmick. They're not even revolutionary. Instead, they are an explicit articulation of a fundamental refocusing on our company's only reason for being.

   "D'Arcy's universal advertising standards are the operating link between our vision today—and its coming reality."

rules. No formulas. No right way. Given the same problem, a dozen creative talents would solve it a dozen different ways. If there were a sure-fire formula for successful advertising, everyone would use it. Then there'd be no need for creative people. We would simply program robots to create our ads and commercials and they'd sell loads of product—to other robots.[10]

Taking Creative Risks

Many creative people follow proven formulas when creating ads because they are safe. Clients often feel uncomfortable with advertising that is too different. Bill Tragos, former chair of TBWA, the advertising agency noted for its excellent creative work for Absolut vodka, Evian, and many other clients, says, "Very few clients realize that the reason that their work is so bad is that they are the ones who commandeered it and directed it to be that way. I think that at least 50 percent of an agency's successful work resides in the client."[11]

Many creative people say it is important for clients to take some risks if they want breakthrough advertising that gets noticed. One agency that has been successful in getting its clients to take risks is Wieden & Kennedy, best known for its excellent creative work for companies such as Nike, Microsoft, and ESPN (see Exhibit 8-4). The agency's founders believe a key element in its success has been a steadfast belief in taking risks when most agencies and their clients have been retrenching and becoming more conservative.[12] The agency can develop great advertising partly because clients like Nike are willing to take risks and go along with the agency's priority system, which places the creative work first and the client–agency relationship second. The agency has even terminated relationships with large clients like Gallo when they interfered too much with the creative process. Several major advertisers including Procter & Gamble and Coca-Cola have added Wieden & Kennedy to their agency roster in efforts to increase the creativity of their advertising.[13]

An example of a company that has begun taking more creative risks with its advertising is Wrigley. For many years the company, which has long dominated the market for chewing gum, was very conservative with its advertising and relied on more traditional, attribute-focused messages. However, in recent years Wrigley has taken a more dynamic approach to its marketing by introducing new products and using an edgier creative approach in its ads.[14] Exhibit 8-5 shows a clever ad used to introduce the new Cool Green Apple flavor of Wrigley's Extra, which is the leading brand of sugar-free gum.

Not all companies or agencies agree that advertising has to be risky to be effective, however. Many marketing managers are more comfortable with advertising that simply communicates product or service features and benefits and gives the consumer a reason to buy. They see their ad campaigns as multi-million-dollar investments whose goal is to sell the product rather than finance the whims of their agency's creative staff.[15] They argue that some creative people have lost sight of advertising's bottom line: Does it sell? IMC Perspective 8-1 discusses the ongoing debate over the artsy, image-oriented approach to advertising taken by many creative types versus the more hard-sell approach that many clients prefer.

The issue of how much latitude creative people should be given and how much risk the client should be willing to take is open to considerable debate. However, clients and agency personnel generally agree that the ability to develop novel yet appropriate approaches to communicating with the customer makes the creative specialist valuable—and often hard to find.

Exhibit 8-4 Wieden & Kennedy's belief in taking risks has led to creative advertising for clients such as Nike

IMC PERSPECTIVE 8-1

The Perpetual Debate: Creative versus Hard-Sell Advertising

For decades there has been a perpetual battle over the role of advertising in the marketing process. The war for the soul of advertising has been endlessly fought between those who believe ads should move people and those who just want to move product. On one side are the "suits" or "rationalists," who argue that advertising must sell the product or service, and that the more selling points or information in the ad, the better its chance of moving the consumer to purchase. On the other side are the "poets" or proponents of creativity who argue that advertising has to build an emotional bond between consumers and brands or companies that goes beyond product advertising. The debate over the effectiveness of creative or artistic advertising is not new. The rationalists have taken great delight in pointing to long lists of creative and award-winning campaigns over the years that have failed in the marketplace. Some note that even legendary adman David Ogily, who many consider the greatest copyright of all time, once said, "If it doesn't sell, it's not creative."

The "poets" argue that the most important thing good advertising does is make an emotional connection with consumers. They note that consumers do not want to be bombarded by ads; they want to be entertained and inspired. Indeed, a recent survey of regular TV viewers found that 64 percent look for ways to avoid commercials rather than watch them. Thus, advertising has to be creative and enjoyable so that consumers will not zap it, yet still be able to help sell a product or service. It is the second part of this mandate that causes concern among the "suits." They note that there were many creative campaigns that moved consumers' emotions but were terminated because they did not increase sales and/or market share and put accounts and reputations on the line.

A number of major advertisers have dismissed agencies that earned critical acclaim and awards for their creative work but failed to move the sales needle including Levis Strauss, Norwegian Cruise Lines, and Gateway. Norwegian Cruise Lines' marketing director, Nina Cohen, described the sensual "It's different out here" campaign produced by Goodby, Silverstein & Partners in the mid-1990s as gorgeous but irrelevant. She noted that "while there are some creative icons out there who feel they have some higher voice to answer to, as clients, we're the ones you have to answer to." However, co-creative director Jeff Goodby considered his agency's creative work for Norwegian both beautiful and effective and argues that the impact of creative and entertaining advertising on sales isn't always quantifiable for good reason. He notes, "It's where the magic happens in advertising, and you can never predict that. It's dangerous to be suspicious of that." Many of the "poets" on the creative side agree with Goodby and like to cite the teaching of legendary adman Bill Bernbach, who preached that persuasion is an art, not a science, and its success is dependent on a complex mix of intangible human qualities that can be neither measured nor predicted.

Most of the "poets" who support advertising that connects on an emotional level insist that selling product is as much a priority for them as it is for those on the rational side of the debate. One top agency executive notes, "We've proven that this kind of advertising works, otherwise we wouldn't be in business, us or the agencies that practice the craft at this level." However, Brent Bouchez, former executive creative director at the Bozzell agency, argues that the "poets" are losing sight of the fact that advertising is about selling things and being really creative in advertising means solving problems and building interesting brands that people want to buy. He notes, "It's time we stopped teaching young creative people to consider it a victory if the logo in an ad is hard to find, or if the product doesn't appear in the commercial at all. It's time we stopped using 'break through the clutter' as an excuse to say nothing about what it is we're selling or why you should buy it."

It is unlikely there will ever be peace between the warring factions as long as there are "rationalists" and "poets" who make a point of arguing over which approach works best. Steve Hayden, vice chairman of Ogilvy Worldwide, says, "It's the ad industry's reflection of the essential Platonic–Aristotelian split in the world, pitting two groups of people against each other who usually can't agree which end is up." However, Nina Cohen, who has worked on both the agency and the client side of the business, is bewildered by the intense opinions held by people on each side and asks, "Aren't we all here to do the same thing?"—meaning to build brands and business. While the answer is, of course, yes, the debate over how to do it is likely to continue.

Sources: Jonathon Cranin, "Has Advertising Gone the Way of the Costra Nostra?" *Advertising Age,* June 6, 2005, p. 28; Brent Bouchez, "Trophies Are Meaningless," *Advertising Age,* July 30, 2001; Anthony Vagnoni, "Creative Differences," *Advertising Age,* November 17, 1997, pp. 1, 28, 30.

Creative Personnel

The image of the creative advertising person perpetuated in novels, movies, and TV shows is often one of a freewheeling, freethinking, eccentric personality. The educational background of creative personnel is often in nonbusiness areas such as art, literature, music, humanities, or journalism, so their interests and perspectives tend to differ from those of managers with a business education or background. Creative people tend to be more abstract and less structured, organized, or conventional in their approach to a problem, relying on intuition more often than logic. For example, Arthur Kover conducted a study of advertising copywriters and found that they work without guidance from any formal theories of communication. However, those interviewed in his study did have similar informal, implicit theories that guide them in creating ads. These theories are based on finding ways to break through the ad clutter, open the consciousness of consumers, and connect with them to deliver the message.[16]

Advertising creatives are sometimes stereotyped as odd, perhaps because they dress differently and do not always work the conventional 9-to-5 schedule. Of course, from the perspective of the creatives, it is the marketing or brand managers and account executives (the "suits") who are strange. In many agencies, you can't tell the creative personnel from the executives by their dress or demeanor. Yet the differences between creative and managerial personalities and perspectives must be recognized and tolerated so that creative people can do their best work and all those involved in the advertising process can cooperate.

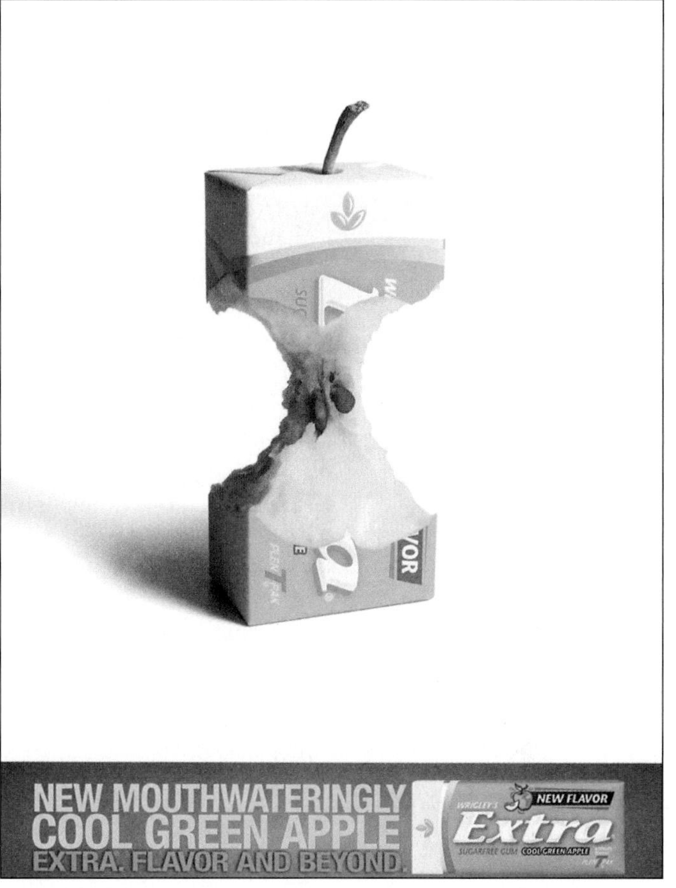

Exhibit 8-5 Wrigley's takes more of a creative risk with its new ads

Most agencies thrive on creativity, for it is the major component in the product they produce. Thus, they must create an environment that fosters the development of creative thinking and creative advertising. Clients must also understand the differences between the perspectives of the creative personnel and marketing and product managers. While the client has ultimate approval of the advertising, the opinions of creative specialists must be respected when advertising ideas and content are evaluated. (Evaluation of the creative's ideas and work is discussed in more detail in Chapter 9.)

The Creative Process

Some advertising people say creativity in advertising is best viewed as a process and creative success is most likely when some organized approach is followed. This does not mean there is an infallible blueprint to follow to create effective advertising; as we saw earlier, many advertising people reject attempts to standardize creativity or develop rules. However, most do follow a process when developing an ad.

One of the most popular approaches to creativity in advertising was developed by James Webb Young, a former creative vice president at the J. Walter Thompson agency. Young said, "The production of ideas is just as definite a process as the production of Fords; the production of ideas, too, runs an assembly line; in this production the mind follows an operative technique which can be learned and controlled; and that its effective use is just as much a matter of practice in the technique as in the effective use of any tool."[17] Young's model of the creative process contains five steps:

1. *Immersion.* Gathering raw material and information through background research and immersing yourself in the problem.
2. *Digestion.* Taking the information, working it over, and wrestling with it in the mind.
3. *Incubation.* Putting the problems out of your conscious mind and turning the information over to the subconscious to do the work.

4. *Illumination.* The birth of an idea—the "Eureka! I have it!" phenomenon.
5. *Reality or verification.* Studying the idea to see if it still looks good or solves the problem; then shaping the idea to practical usefulness.

Young's process of creativity is similar to a four-step approach outlined much earlier by English sociologist Graham Wallas:

1. *Preparation.* Gathering background information needed to solve the problem through research and study.
2. *Incubation.* Getting away and letting ideas develop.
3. *Illumination.* Seeing the light or solution.
4. *Verification.* Refining and polishing the idea and seeing if it is an appropriate solution.

Models of the creative process are valuable to those working in the creative area of advertising, since they offer an organized way to approach an advertising problem. Preparation or gathering of background information is the first step in the creative process. As we saw in earlier chapters, the advertiser and agency start by developing a thorough understanding of the product or service, the target market, and the competition. They also focus on the role of advertising in the marketing and promotional program.

These models do not say much about how this information will be synthesized and used by the creative specialist because this part of the process is unique to the individual. In many ways, it's what sets apart the great creative minds and strategists in advertising. However, many agencies are now using a process called *account planning* to gather information and help creative specialists as they go through the creative process of developing advertising.

Account Planning

To facilitate the creative process, many agencies now use **account planning,** which is a process that involves conducting research and gathering all relevant information about a client's product or service, brand, and consumers in the target audience. Account planning began in Great Britain during the 1960s and 70s and has spread to agencies in the United States as well as throughout Europe and Asia. The concept has become very popular in recent years as many agencies have seen the successful campaigns developed by agencies that are strong advocates of account planning.[18] One such agency is Goodby, Silverstein & Partners, which has used account planning to develop highly successful campaigns for clients such as Saturn, Hewlett-Packard, Sega, and Nike, as well as the popular "Got milk?" ads for the California Milk Processor Board.

Jon Steel, a former vice president and director of account planning at the agency's San Francisco office, has written an excellent book on the process titled *Truth, Lies & Advertising: The Art of Account Planning.*[19] He notes that the account planner's job is to provide the key decision makers with all the information they require to make an intelligent decision. According to Steel, "Planners may have to work very hard to influence the way that the advertising turns out, carefully laying out a strategic foundation with the client, handing over tidbits of information to creative people when, in their judgment, that information will have the greatest impact, giving feedback on ideas, and hopefully adding some ideas of their own."

Account planning plays an important role during creative strategy development by driving the process from the customers' point of view. Planners will work with the client as well as other agency personnel, such as the creative team and media specialists. They discuss how the knowledge and information they have gathered can be used in the development of the creative strategy as well as other aspects of the advertising campaign. Account planners are usually responsible for all the research (both qualitative and quantitative) conducted during the creative strategy development process. In the following section we examine how various types of research and information can provide input to the creative process of advertising. This information can be gathered by account planners or others whose job it is to provide input to the process.

Inputs to the Creative Process: Preparation, Incubation, Illumination

Background Research

Only the most foolish creative person or team would approach an assignment without first learning as much as possible about the client's product or service, the target market, the competition, and any other relevant background information. The creative specialist should also be knowledgeable about general trends, conditions, and developments in the marketplace, as well as research on specific advertising approaches or techniques that might be effective. The creative specialist can acquire background information in numerous ways. Some informal fact-finding techniques have been noted by Sandra Moriarty:

- Reading anything related to the product or market—books, trade publications, general interest articles, research reports, and the like.
- Asking everyone involved with the product for information—designers, engineers, salespeople, and consumers.
- Listening to what people are talking about. Visits to stores, malls, restaurants, and even the agency cafeteria can be informative. Listening to the client can be particularly valuable, since he or she often knows the product and market best.
- Using the product or service and becoming familiar with it. The more you use a product, the more you know and can say about it.
- Working in and learning about the client's business to understand better the people you're trying to reach.[20]

To assist in the preparation, incubation, and illumination stages, many agencies provide creative people with both general and product-specific preplanning input. **General preplanning input** can include books, periodicals, trade publications, scholarly journals, pictures, and clipping services, which gather and organize magazine and newspaper articles on the product, the market, and the competition, including the latter's ads. This input can also come from research studies conducted by the client, the agency, the media, or other sources.

Another useful general preplanning input concerns trends, developments, and happenings in the marketplace. Information is available from a variety of sources, including local, state, and federal governments, secondary research suppliers, and various industry trade associations, as well as advertising and media organizations. For example, advertising industry groups like the American Association of Advertising Agencies and media organizations like the National Association of Broadcasters (NAB) and Magazine Publishers of America (MPA) publish research reports and newsletters that provide information on market trends and developments and how they might affect consumers. Those involved in developing creative strategy can also gather relevant and timely information by reading publications like *Adweek, Advertising Age, Brandweek,* and *The Wall Street Journal* (see Exhibit 8-6).

Exhibit 8-6 Advertising industry publications are excellent sources of information on market trends

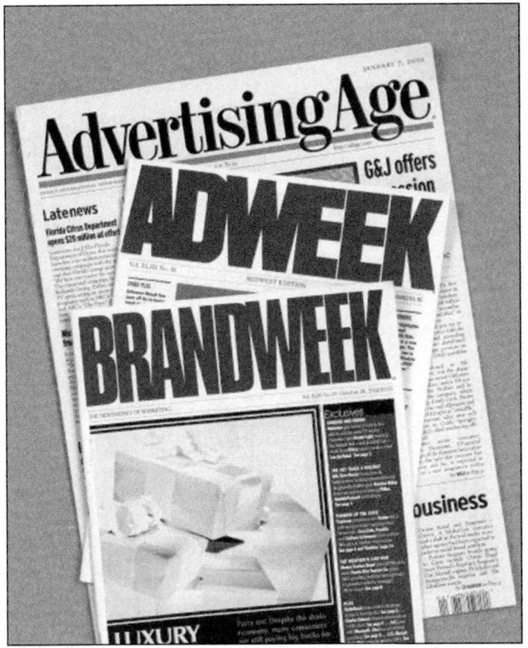

Product/Service-Specific Research

In addition to getting general background research and preplanning input, creative people receive **product/service-specific preplanning input.** This information generally comes in the form of specific studies conducted on the product or service, the target audience, or a combination of the two. Quantitative and qualitative consumer research such as attitude studies, market structure, and positioning studies such as perceptual mapping and lifestyle research, focus group interviews, and demographic and psychographic profiles of users of a particular product, service, or brand are examples of product-specific preplanning input.

Many product- or service-specific studies helpful to the creative team are conducted by the client or the agency. A number of years ago, the BBDO ad agency developed an approach called **problem detection** for finding ideas around which creative strategies could be based.[21] This research technique involves asking consumers familiar with a product (or service) to generate an exhaustive list of things that bother them or problems they encounter when using it. The consumers rate these problems in order of importance and evaluate various brands in terms of their association with each problem. A problem detection study can provide valuable input for product improvements, reformulations, or new products. It can also give the creative people ideas regarding attributes or features to emphasize and guidelines for positioning new or existing brands.

Some agencies conduct psychographic studies annually and construct detailed psychographic or lifestyle profiles of product or service users. DDB Worldwide conducts a large-scale psychographic study each year that taps into the minds of 4,000 consumers to measure their activities, interests, opinions, and attitudes as well as their usage of a wide range of products and services. The information is used to construct a psychographic profile of the target audiences for whom they are developing ads as well as to gain insight into general consumer trends.

A number of advertising agencies conduct branding research to help better identify clients' customers and how they connect to their brands. Agencies use this research to determine how a brand is perceived among consumers, and these insights, in turn, are used to develop more effective advertising campaigns.[22] DDB Worldwide provides clients with branding insights through a technique called Brand Capital, which contains information on more than 500 brands. The proprietary branding research is based on a global marketing study consisting of quantitative surveys conducted among 14,000 consumers in 14 countries. The agency uses the information from the Brand Capital study to compare the desired self-image and lifestyles of consumers who love a brand with those who have a less strong connection. Young & Rubicam has developed a proprietary tool for building and managing a brand it refers to as BrandAsset Valuator. The technique uses measures of four factors including brand differentiation, relevance, esteem, and knowledge to identify core issues for the brand and to evaluate current brand performance and potential. The Leo Burnett agency relies on its Brand Belief System to guide its global brand building philosophy and practice. This system focuses on the development of the brand believer bond, which is at the core of the relationship between a brand and its believers and considers four fundamental questions.

Nearly all of the major agencies are conducting branding research and/or developing models or systems that they can use to gain better insight into consumers and develop more effective campaigns for their clients. The importance of building and maintaining strong brands is likely to become even greater in the future. This will put even more pressure on agencies to develop new and better tools and techniques that can be used to guide their clients' advertising campaigns.

Qualitative Research Input

Many agencies, particularly larger ones with strong research departments, have their own research programs and specific techniques they use to assist in the development of creative strategy and provide input to the creative process. In addition to the various quantitative research studies, qualitative research techniques such as in-depth interviews or focus groups can provide the creative team with valuable insight at the early stages of the creative process. **Focus groups** are a research method whereby consumers (usually 10 to 12 people) from the target market are led through a discussion regarding a particular topic. Focus groups give insight as to why and how consumers use a product or service, what is important to them in choosing a particular brand, what they like and don't like about various products or services, and any special needs they might have that aren't being satisfied. A focus group session might also include a discussion of types of ad appeals to use or evaluate the advertising of various companies.

Focus group interviews bring the creative people and others involved in creative strategy development into contact with the customers. Listening to a focus group gives copywriters, art directors, and other creative specialists a better sense of who the target audience is, what the audience is like, and who the creatives need to write, design, or direct to in creating an advertising message. Focus groups can also be used to evaluate the viability of different creative approaches under consideration and suggest the best direction to pursue.[23]

Another form of qualitative input that has become popular among advertising agencies is **ethnographic research,** which involves observing consumers in their natural environment.[24] Some agencies send anthropologists or trained researchers into the field to study and observe consumers in their homes, at work, or at play. For example, the Ogilvy & Mather agency has a research unit called the Discovery Group, which moves into consumers' homes, follows consumers in their leisure pursuits, or trails them as they move through their daily lives.[25] For Ogilvy client Miller Brewing Co., Discovery staffers traveled around the country filming Miller drinkers, as well as those drinking competitive brands. They used the tapes to study group dynamics and how the dynamics changed while people were drinking. The agency used the insights gained from the study to help develop a new advertising campaign for Miller Lite beer. Many marketing and agency researchers prefer ethnographic research over the use of focus groups, as the latter technique has a number of limitations. Strong personalities can often wield undue influence in focus groups, and participants often will not admit, or may not even recognize, their behavior patterns and motivations. However, ethnographic studies can cost more to conduct and are more difficult to administer. IMC Perspective 8-2 discusses an interesting perspective from Malcolm Gladwell, the author of several best-selling and influential books, on how focus groups might stifle efforts by advertising creatives.

Generally, creative people are open to any research or information that will help them understand the client's target market better and assist in generating creative ideas. The advertising industry is recognizing the importance of using research to guide the creative process. The Advertising Research Foundation recently initiated the David Ogilvy Awards, named after the advertising legend who founded Ogilvy & Mather. These awards are presented to teams of advertising agencies, client companies, and research companies in recognition of research that has been used successfully to determine the strategy and effectiveness of ad campaigns. For example, the California Milk Processor Board, which is a past winner of the David Ogilvy Award, has used both quantitative and qualitative research in developing the popular "Got milk?" advertising campaign. Focus groups and survey research studies were conducted to help understand companion foods that are consumed with milk and how consumers react to the effect of "milk deprivation," which is the key idea behind the humorous ads in the campaign (see Exhibit 8-7).[26]

Inputs to the Creative Process: Verification, Revision

The verification and revision stage of the creative process evaluates ideas generated during the illumination stage, rejects inappropriate ones, refines and polishes those that remain, and gives them final expression. Techniques used at this stage include directed focus groups to evaluate creative concepts, ideas, or themes; message communication studies; portfolio tests; and evaluation measures such as viewer reaction profiles.

Exhibit 8-7 Research helped in the development of the popular "Got Milk?" campaign

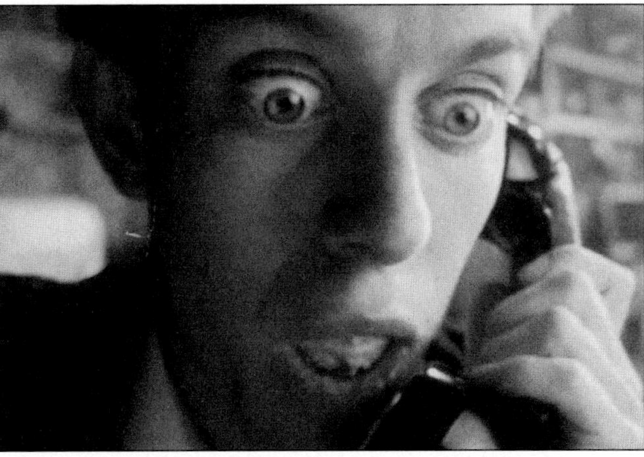

IMC PERSPECTIVE 8-2

Do Focus Groups Stifle Advertising Creativity?

Focus group interviews with consumers are one of the widely used research techniques used by marketers as well as their advertising agencies. The process of having a group that usually consists of 8 to 12 people interact with one another and discuss their thoughts and feelings is widely used to gain more insight into a problem or issue as well as to probe attitudes and reasons for purchase behavior. Focus groups are also often used to evaluate consumers' opinions and reactions to advertising concepts as well as the ads themselves. However, agency creative personnel have long expressed concern over the idea of having their ideas and work critiqued by consumers. They argue that it interferes with the creative process and limits their ability to develop innovative and breakthrough advertising messages. And now they are getting support from one of the most influential marketing thinkers as well as from a number of other advertising and marketing executives.

Malcolm Gladwell is the author of the best-selling book *The Tipping Point* and has gained guru status among marketers for his insights into the epidemic-like spread of trends and the power of word-of-mouth influence. In the book, which has become required reading among those working in advertising and marketing, Gladwell analyzes the process by which social change occurs and describes how a small number of consumers can ignite a trend, if they are the right ones. However, it is Gladwell's new book, *Blink: The Power of Thinking Without Thinking,* that is being lauded by advertising creatives. In *Blink,* Gladwell examines the content and origin of instantaneous impressions, and the book centers on the premise that decisions made quickly can be as good as those made after much deliberation.

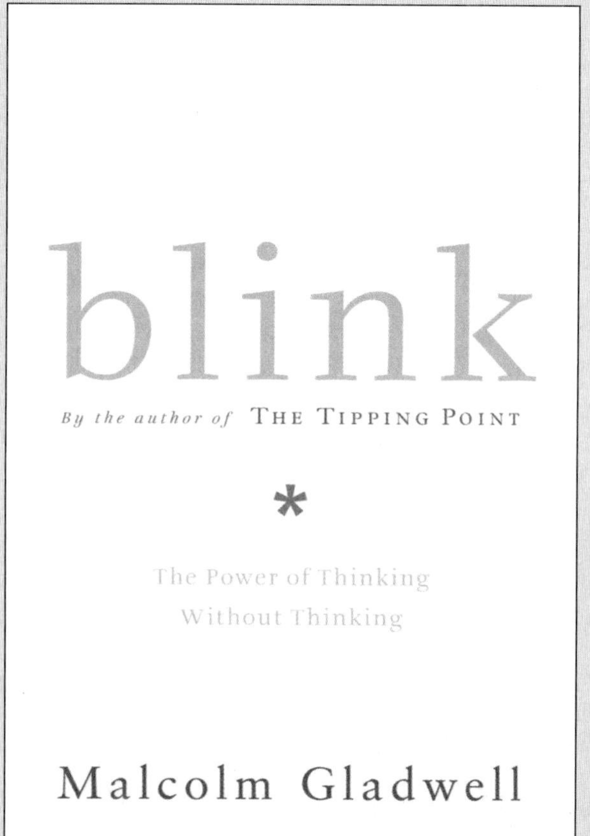

Of particular relevance to those working in the creative realm of advertising is Gladwell's argument that the unique insights that drive innovation and great advertising campaigns are not gained through traditional market research techniques such as consumer surveys and focus groups. He notes that we live in a society dedicated to the idea that we're always better off when we gather as much information as possible and spend as much time as possible in deliberation. However, Gladwell states, "There is very little psychological justification for the notion that you can find out what people think about an idea—particularly a revolutionary new idea—by asking them. I can only hope that my book can be used as ammunition on the part of creatives to protect their work from the numbing effect of market research."

A number of marketing and advertising executives agree wholeheartedly with Gladwell's position regarding focus groups. For example, Lucas Jenson, the market-research manager for Ben & Jerry's ice cream, notes that the Unilever division has not done a focus group in three years. Instead he has sent up an internal "Get Connected" program in which employees are rewarded for gaining insights in a variety of nontraditional ways such as reading a book such as *Blink,* answering a consumer letter, and meeting with "Chunk Spelunkers," who are hard-core customers who have signed up online for Ben & Jerry's "Chunk Mail." Another executive who agrees with Gladwell is Ed Razek, chief creative officer at Limited Brands' Victoria's Secret. He notes that customers cannot tell you what they want because they really haven't seen it, yet.

Other major marketers are forgoing traditional market research as they develop advertising and marketing campaigns. For example, when Nike was launching its new line of skateboarding footwear, the company did not conduct research among the notoriously individualistic skateboarders. Instead, the company went directly to industry insider Keven Imamura, editor of *TransWorld Stance,* which is a popular magazine among skaters. Imamura notes that "Nike relied on me to get inside the head of a skateboarder, since focus groups of skateboarders would be nothing we'd want to be a part of." Procter & Gamble (P&G) is another company that is changing its approach to market research. While P&G still uses traditional market research to ask consumers about the pros and cons of its products, the world's largest consumer products company also assigns employees to spend hours with women, watching them do laundry, clean floors, apply makeup, and change diapers.

Gladwell supports the use of observational, ethnographic research; he argues that it is the highly artificial, formulaic efforts that thwart creativity and the better judgment of marketers and advertisers. Of course, many agency creative personnel agree with him. One agency executive notes, "Creatives largely agree they don't want more focus testing, some because they agree it's not the most valid way of assessing work and some because they don't like what they hear." Another notes that "creativity is very intangible and to the extent that we try to make it science we destroy it in some manner. . . . Twenty years ago there was a lot of intuition that went into this business and since then we've needed more and more proof for our clients of our ideas."

Not everyone in the advertising and marketing world agrees with Gladwell's position that focus groups and other forms of market research fail to verify anything but the status quo. For example, Roger Adams, the executive director of advertising and marketing and a customer relationship manager at General Motors, is still a believer in focus groups but cautions that their success does depend on how you use them. Many marketers note that companies have improved at conducting focus groups and controlling for factors that may sway groups members a certain way. Proponent of focus groups argue that they still have a role to play if they are used wisely because they involve consumers in collecting ideas, brainstorming, and learning what they think is still a good idea. Just don't try telling this to the creatives.

Sources: Sarah Ellison, "P&G Chief's Turnaround Recipe: Find Out What Women Want," *The Wall Street Journal,* June 1, 2005, pp. A1, 16; Stephanie Thompson, "'Tipping Point' Guru Takes on Focus Groups," *Advertising Age,* January 24, 2005, pp. 4, 54; Malcolm Gladwell, *Blink: The Power of Thinking Without Thinking,* New York: Little, Brown and Company, 2004.

At this stage of the creative process, members of the target audience may be asked to evaluate rough creative layouts and to indicate what meaning they get from the ad, what they think of its execution, or how they react to a slogan or theme. The creative team can gain insight into how a TV commercial might communicate its message by having members of the target market evaluate the ad in storyboard form. A **storyboard** is a series of drawings used to present the visual plan or layout of a proposed commercial. It contains a series of sketches of key frames or scenes along with the copy or audio portion for each scene (see Exhibit 8-8).

Testing a commercial in storyboard form can be difficult because storyboards are too abstract for many consumers to understand. To make the creative layout more realistic and easier to evaluate, the agency may produce an **animatic,** a videotape of the storyboard along with an audio soundtrack. Storyboards and animatics are useful for research purposes as well as for presenting the creative idea to other agency personnel or to the client for discussion and approval.

At this stage of the process, the creative team is attempting to find the best creative approach or execution style before moving ahead with the campaign themes and going into actual production of the ad. The verification/revision process may include more formal, extensive pretesting of the ad before a final decision is made. Pretesting and related procedures are examined in detail in Chapter 19.

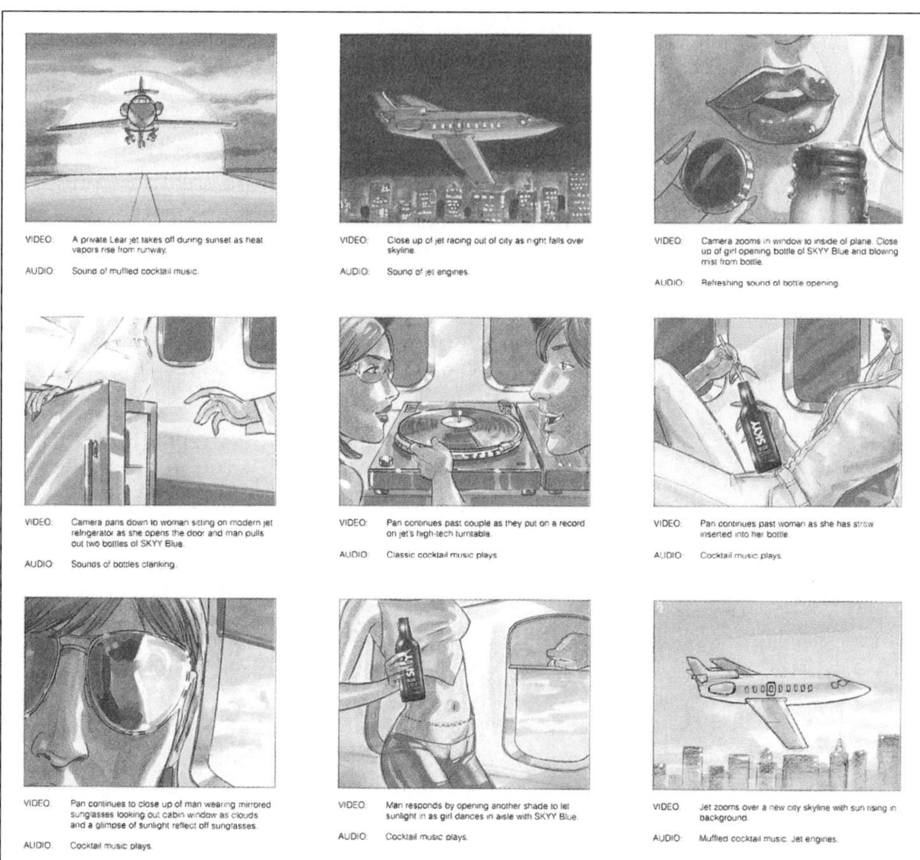

Exhibit 8-8 Marketers can gain insight into consumers' reactions to a commercial by showing them a storyboard

Creative Strategy Development

Advertising Campaigns

Most ads are part of a series of messages that make up an IMC or **advertising campaign,** which is a set of interrelated and coordinated marketing communication activities that center on a single theme or idea that appears in different media across a specified time period. Determining the unifying theme around which the campaign will be built is a critical part of the creative process, as it sets the tone for the individual ads and other forms of marketing communications that will be used. A **campaign theme** should be a strong idea, as it is the central message that will be communicated in all the advertising and other promotional activities.

Advertising campaign plans are short-term in nature and, like marketing and IMC plans, are done on an annual basis. However, the campaign themes are usually developed with the intention of being used for a longer time period. Unfortunately, many campaign themes last only a short time, usually because they are ineffective or market conditions and/or competitive developments in the marketplace change.

While some marketers change their campaign themes often, a successful campaign theme may last for years. Philip Morris has been using the "Marlboro country" campaign for over 40 years, General Mills has positioned Wheaties cereal as the "Breakfast of Champions" for decades, and BMW has used the "ultimate driving machine" theme since 1974. Even though BMW has changed agencies several times over the past three decades, the classic tagline has been retained. Figure 8-2 lists the top 10 advertising slogans of the past century, as selected by *Advertising Age.*

Like any other area of the marketing and promotional process, the creative aspect of advertising and the development of the campaign theme is guided by specific goals and objectives. A creative strategy that focuses on what must be communicated will guide the selection of the campaign theme and the development of all messages used in the ad campaign. The creative strategy is based on several factors, including identification of the target audience; the basic problem, issue, or opportunity the advertising must address; the major selling idea or key benefit the message needs to communicate; and any supportive information that needs to be included in the ad. Once these factors are determined, a creative strategy statement should describe the message appeal and execution style that will be used. Many ad agencies outline these elements in a document known as the copy or creative platform.

Copy Platform

The written **copy platform** specifies the basic elements of the creative strategy. Different agencies may call this document a *creative platform* or *work plan, creative brief, creative blueprint,* or *creative contract.* The account representative or manager assigned to the account usually prepares the copy platform. In larger agencies, an individual from research or the strategic account planning department may write it. People from the agency team or group assigned to the account, including creative personnel as well as representatives from media and research, have input. The advertising manager and/or the marketing and brand managers from the client side ultimately approve the copy platform. Figure 8-3 shows a sample copy-platform outline that can be used to guide the creative process. Just as there are different names for the copy platform, there are variations in the outline and format used and in the level of detail included.

Several components of the copy platform were discussed in previous chapters. For example, Chapter 7 examined the DAGMAR model and showed how the setting of advertising objectives requires specifying a well-defined target audience and developing a communication task statement that spells out what message must be com-

Figure 8-2 Top 10 Advertising Slogans of the Century

Company or Brand	Campaign Theme
1. DeBeers	Diamonds are forever
2. Nike	Just do it
3. Coca-Cola	The pause that refreshes
4. Miller Lite	Tastes great, less filling
5. Avis	We try harder
6. Maxwell House	Good to the last drop
7. Wheaties	Breakfast of champions
8. Clairol	Does she . . . or doesn't she
9. Morton Salt	When it rains it pours
10. Wendy's	Where's the beef?

1. Basic problem or issue the advertising must address.
2. Advertising and communications objectives.
3. Target audience.
4. Major selling idea or key benefits to communicate.
5. Creative strategy statement (campaign theme, appeal, and execution technique to be used).
6. Supporting information and requirements.

Figure 8-3 Copy Platform Outline

municated to this audience. Determining what problem the product or service will solve or what issue must be addressed in the ad helps in establishing communication objectives for the campaign to accomplish. Two critical components of the copy platform are the development of the major selling idea and creative strategy development. These two steps are often the responsibility of the creative team or specialist and form the basis of the advertising campaign theme.

Many copy platforms also include supporting information and requirements (brand identifications, disclaimers, and the like) that should appear in any advertising message. This information may be important in ensuring uniformity across various executions of the ads used in a campaign or in meeting any legal requirements.

Obtaining information regarding customers, the product or service, and the market that can be used in developing the copy platform is an important part of the creative planning process. While it is important that this basic information is provided to agency creatives, this may not always occur due to breakdowns in communication on the client as well as the agency side or between the two. John Sutherland, Lisa Duke, and Avery Abernethy developed a model of the flow of marketing information from clients to the agency creative staff, shown in Figure 8-4.[27] The model shows that there are five major communication interfaces and decision points where gatekeepers can impede the flow of information to agency creatives.

Figure 8-4 Model of Marketing Information Flow from the Marketing Manager to the Creative Staff

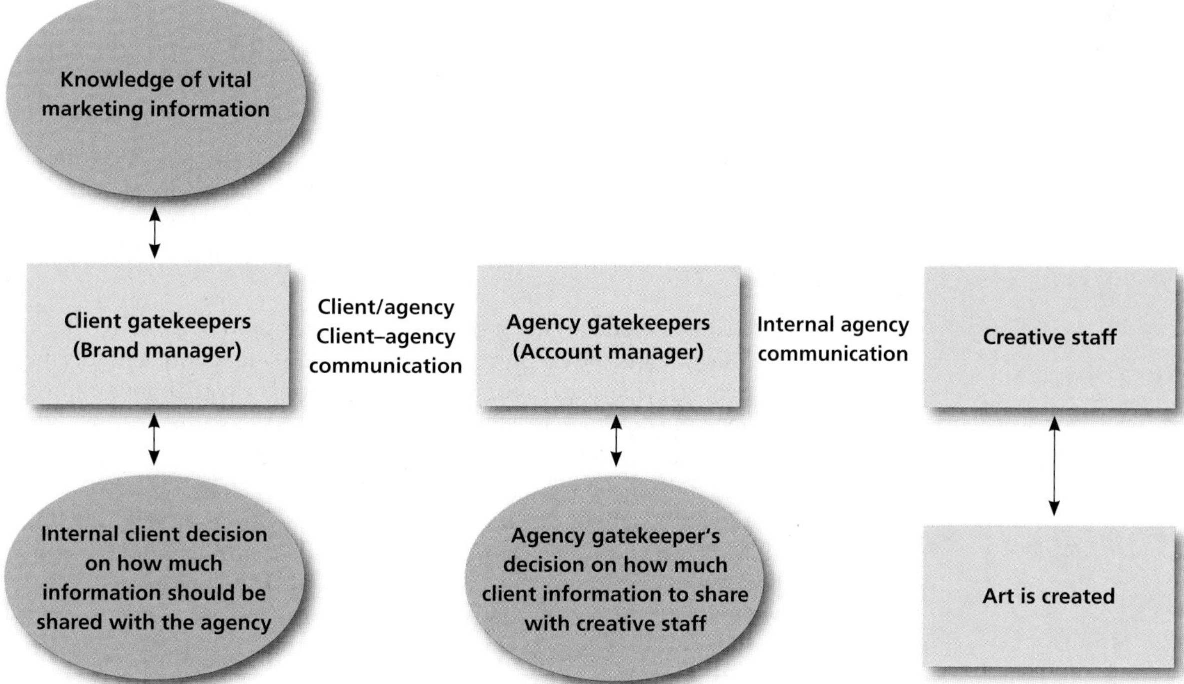

Source: John Sutherland, Lisa Duke, and Avery Abernethy, "A Model of Marketing Information Flow," *Journal of Advertising*, 33 (Winter 2004), p. 42.

A great deal of attention has been paid to the client–agency communication interface that occurs between the brand manager and/or advertising manager on the client side and the account manager on the agency side. Communication problems can occur between clients and their agencies, which can make the job of the creative staff much more difficult. However, this model shows that there are four other potential communication interface failure points, including (1) the client or client gatekeeper lacking knowledge of some or all of the information needed for effective advertising, (2) the client deciding not to share with the agency all of the available information that is relevant to creating effective advertising, (3) the agency gatekeeper(s) deciding not to share with creative staffers all of the client information they receive, and (4) internal agency communication failures which may result in the creative staff not receiving all of the relevant information received from the client.

Sutherland, Duke, and Abernethy recently conducted an extensive survey of agency creative directors, copywriters, and art directors on the specific types of marketing information that is made available to them for use in developing and executing a creative strategy. They identified six specific types of marketing information including the demographic profile of the target audience, customer product usage information, client's product performance information, competitors' product performance information, marketing strategy information, and the main selling point supplied by the client. Their study showed that agency creative personnel often lack the information needed to effectively design and execute creative strategies. They found that information in these specific categories was provided to creatives only around one-half to two-thirds of the time. Even the most basic target demographic profile was not provided 30 percent of the time. This study indicates that there is a gap in the information that creative personnel need to develop effective advertising and what they are being provided and points to the need for better communication between clients and agencies.

The information contained in the copy platform provides the creative staff with important background information and the basic elements of the overall advertising strategy. The next step in the creative process is the development of the message strategy and begins with the search for the *big idea* that will build on the strategy and bring it to life. One of the major challenges for the creative team is determining the major selling idea that will be used as the basis of the campaign. We will examine some approaches often used for determining the major selling idea and campaign theme.

The Search for the Major Selling Idea

An important part of creative strategy is determining the central theme that will become the **major selling idea** of the ad campaign. As A. Jerome Jeweler states in his book *Creative Strategy in Advertising:*

> The major selling idea should emerge as the strongest singular thing you can say about your product or service. This should be the claim with the broadest and most meaningful appeal to your target audience. Once you determine this message, be certain you can live with it; be sure it stands strong enough to remain the central issue in every ad and commercial in the campaign.[28]

Some advertising experts argue that for an ad campaign to be effective it must contain a big idea that attracts the consumer's attention, gets a reaction, and sets the advertiser's product or service apart from the competition's. Well-known adman John O'Toole describes the *big idea* as "that flash of insight that synthesizes the purpose of the strategy, joins the product benefit with consumer desire in a fresh, involving way, brings the subject to life, and makes the reader or audience stop, look, and listen."[29]

Of course, the real challenge to the creative team is coming up with the big idea to use in the ad. Many products and services offer virtually nothing unique, and it can be difficult to find something interesting to say about them. The late David Ogilvy, generally considered one of the most creative advertising copywriters ever to work in the business, has stated:

> I doubt if more than one campaign in a hundred contains a big idea. I am supposed to be one of the more fertile inventors of big ideas, but in my long career as a copywriter I have not had more than 20, if that.[30]

While really great ideas in advertising are difficult to come by, there are many big ideas that became the basis of very creative, successful advertising campaigns. Classic examples include "We try harder," which positioned Avis as the underdog car-rental company that provided better service than Hertz; the "Pepsi generation" theme and subsequent variations like "the taste of a new generation" and "GenerationNext"; the "Be all you can be" theme used in recruitment ads for the U.S. Army; and Wendy's "Where's the beef?" which featured the late, gravelly voiced Clara Peller delivering the classic line that helped make the fast-food chain a household name. More recent big ideas that have resulted in effective advertising campaigns include the "Intel inside" campaign for Intel microprocessors that go in personal computers; Nike's "Just do it"; the "Like a rock" theme for Chevrolet trucks; BMW's "Ultimate driving machine"; and the "Got milk" and milk moustache themes used to promote milk consumption. Some of the big ideas that are used in the IMC campaign of companies are no longer being developed for execution through traditional mass media. As discussed in IMC Perspective 8-3, many companies are taking advantage of the expanded creative opportunities that are available on the Internet and are integrating traditional media with online elements and using a new genre of advertising known as *advertainment.*

Exhibit 8-9 United Technologies "punks" ad is an excellent example of a big idea in business-to-business advertising

Big ideas are important in business-to-business advertising as well. For example, United Technologies Corp., a company that provides high-technology products to aerospace and building-systems industries throughout the world, recently began a major advertising campaign to increase awareness of the firm and its various subsidiaries. One of the first advertisements in the campaign was the eye-catching ad shown in Exhibit 8-9, which uses the headline "the punks who killed heavy metal," with the headline atop of what vaguely looks like a movie blood splotch. The copy explains that the punks are actually scientists (notice the white pocket protectors) from the company's research center and touts their role in developing metal foams—materials much lighter than traditional metals—that will help make a variety of UTC products, from helicopters to jet engines to elevators, lighter and more economical to operate. The ad was very effective in cutting through the clutter of corporate advertising in publications such as the *The Wall Street Journal, Barron's* and *BusinessWeek.*

It is difficult to pinpoint the inspiration for a big idea or to teach advertising people how to find one. However, several approaches can guide the creative team's search for a major selling idea and offer solutions for developing effective advertising. Some of the best-known approaches follow:

- Using a unique selling proposition.
- Creating a brand image.
- Finding the inherent drama.
- Positioning.

Unique Selling Proposition

The concept of the **unique selling proposition (USP)** was developed by Rosser Reeves, former chair of the Ted Bates agency, and is described in his influential book *Reality in Advertising.* Reeves noted three characteristics of unique selling propositions:

1. Each advertisement must make a proposition to the consumer. Not just words, not just product puffery, not just show-window advertising. Each advertisement must say to each reader: "Buy this product and you will get this benefit."
2. The proposition must be one that the competition either cannot or does not offer. It must be unique either in the brand or in the claim.
3. The proposition must be strong enough to move the mass millions, that is, pull over new customers to your brand.[31]

Reeves said the attribute claim or benefit that forms the basis of the USP should dominate the ad and be emphasized through repetitive advertising. An example of advertising based on a USP is the campaign for Colgate's new Total toothpaste (Exhibit 8-10).The brand's unique ingredients make it the only toothpaste that provides long-lasting protection and has been proved effective in fighting cavities between brushings.

IMC PERSPECTIVE 8-3

Many Creative Campaigns Now Involve the Internet

Traditionally when planning a new campaign for a client, most agencies would have their creative teams conceive and develop advertising for mass-media channels such as television, radio, and/or print. The online component would be an add-on that played a supportive role such as providing additional information about a brand, promotional offers, or a place to watch commercials. However, the interactive element is increasingly becoming the centerpiece or starting point of a campaign, and some of the best creative work is being done by those working in online advertising.

Many in the advertising industry point to the campaign created by Fallon Worldwide for BMW as the milestone event that launched a new genre of advertising known as *advertainment.* Fallon worked with the Hollywood production company Anonymous Content to create a series of short files called *The Hire,* featuring British actor Clive Owen as a James Bond-type driver who takes costars such as Madonna, Mickey Rourke, and Stellan Skarsgaard for the ride of their lives in a BMW. A special website, BMWFilms.com, was created to show the films. A number of other companies have turned to the advertainment genre to promote their products including Skyy Spirits, Levi's, and Amazon.

Some argue that the tipping point for online creativity came with the immensely popular Subservient Chicken campaign that Crispin, Porter + Bogusky created for Burger King as well as online promotion for Microsoft's Halo 2 video game for its Xbox gaming system, which used a prelaunch teaser website. The viral push, which did not include one word of English and required gamers to crack a secret code to translate the language, helped presell 1 million game units before they even hit retailers' shelves.

A number of factors may explain why the online element is becoming the focal point of many campaigns. First, for many companies the Web is where the people are. Marketers recognize that consumers are spending more time on the Internet than they are with traditional media. Surveys show that 58 percent of broadband Internet users spend more time online than watching television and nearly a quarter of Internet users have decreased their TV viewing. The second major reason is that there are much more creative opportunities available through online advertising versus traditional media. Commercials are not limited to the traditional 15- or 30-second spots because films created for viewing online can be of any length. There are also very few rules or restrictions for online advertising, there are no networks to censor what is shown or said, and marketers do not have to worry as much about various regulatory or media watchdog groups policing their ads.

Online ads are also becoming increasingly popular because they provide consumers with the opportunity to interact with or even create the message. For example, athletic shoe brand Converse created an award-winning campaign that was built around the Converse Gallery website (Conversegallery.com), which featured fifty 24-second films about the sneakers that were created by consumers rather than creative directors. Consumers sent in films showing their Converse sneakers playing the piano and starring in action-adventure films. The co-creative director at Butler, Shine Sterns & Partners, the agency that created the campaign, notes, "The magic of that kind of work is you can get your consumers involved in the campaign the way you can't in other media."

Some companies are also creating campaigns that integrate traditional media advertising with online elements and get consumers involved by generating curiosity. One of the first companies to do this successfully was Nike, which developed the "Whatever" campaign to introduce the Air Cross Trainer II shoes. The ads featured star athletes such as sprinter Marion Jones in dramatic situations, and as each spot ended, the words "Continued at Whatever.Nike.com" appeared on the screen. When viewers visited the site they could select from six possible endings to the commercial, read information on the sports and athletes featured in the ads, and even purchase the shoes. The technique was also used recently by Sharp Electronics, which turned to Haxan Films, the creator of the campaign for the *Blair Witch Project,* to become involved with the introduction of its Aquos liquid crystal display televisions. Haxan worked with Sharp's ad agency, Wieden & Kennedy, to help create TV ads designed to drive viewers to a website to participate in solving a mystery as it unfolds. The online component included video clips, blogs, and interaction between the characters on the site and visitors.

Win two front-row
seats to excitement.
The Hire
The Ultimate Driving Machine
Win a 2002 Z3 roadster like the one seen in The Hire by filling out and returning the attached card. Answer all of the trivia questions correctly and you'll be entered to win.
THE HIRE

As more companies use the Internet as the centerpiece of their IMC campaigns, more attention is being given to how to do so successfully. Those creating ads and other online content note that the best interactive work should engage its audience without demanding too much for it, be viral, tie back to the brand promise, and be something consumers will actually seek out. It must also give the consumer the feeling he or she is discovering his own entertainment experience. And now that many technology barriers such as bandwidth limits are being overcome, creative experts note that the technology should serve the idea rather than the other way around. With technology becoming increasingly able to support their ideas, marketers will be developing campaigns that move almost seamlessly from online to offline as well as including other digital technologies such as text messaging to mobile phones and electronic billboards. Many companies are demanding more out-of-the-box thinking from their advertising when it comes to creativity. This may mean moving beyond the TV screen and onto the computer monitor.

Sources: Catherine P. Taylor, "What Comes Next?" *Adweek*, May 30, 2005, pp. 74–75; Kris Oser, "Web Wizards Take the Lead in Creative Process," *Advertising Age*, December 6, 2004, p. 6; Kris Oser, "Microsoft's Halo2 Soars on Viral Push," *Advertising Age*, October 25, 2004, p. 46; Michael McCarthy, "Ads Go Hollywood with Short Films," *USA Today*, June 20, 2002, p. 3B.

For Reeves's approach to work, there must be a truly unique product or service attribute, benefit, or inherent advantage that can be used in the claim. The approach may require considerable research on the product and consumers, not only to determine the USP but also to document the claim. As we shall see in Chapter 21, the Federal Trade Commission objects to advertisers' making claims of superiority or uniqueness without providing supporting data. Also, some companies have sued their competitors for making unsubstantiated uniqueness claims.[32]

Advertisers must also consider whether the unique selling proposition affords them a *sustainable competitive advantage* that competitors cannot easily copy. In the packaged-goods field in particular, companies quickly match a brand feature for feature, so advertising based on USPs becomes obsolete. For example, a few years ago Procter & Gamble invented a combination shampoo and conditioner to rejuvenate its struggling Pert brand. The reformulated brand was called Pert Plus and its market share rose from 2 to 12 percent, making it the leading shampoo. But competing brands like Revlon and Suave quickly launched their own two-in-one formula products.[33]

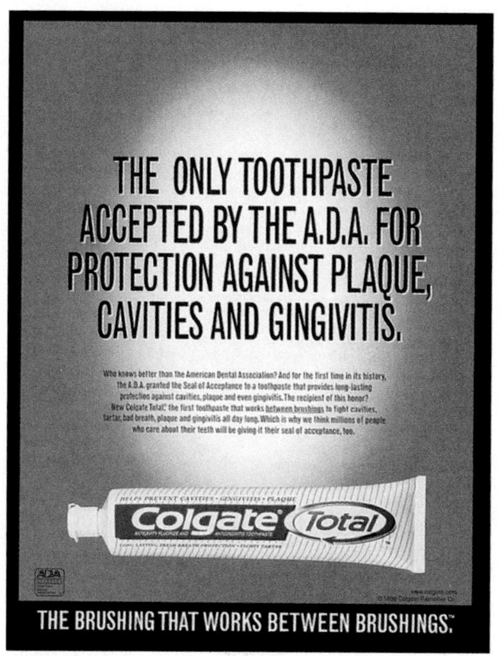

Exhibit 8-10 This Colgate Total ad uses a unique selling proposition

Creating a Brand Image

In many product and service categories, competing brands are so similar that it is very difficult to find or create a unique attribute or benefit to use as the major selling idea. Many of the packaged-goods products that account for most of the advertising dollars spent in the United States are difficult to differentiate on a functional or performance basis. The creative strategy used to sell these products is based on the development of a strong, memorable identity for the brand through **image advertising.**

David Ogilvy popularized the idea of brand image in his famous book *Confessions of an Advertising Man.* Ogilvy said that with image advertising, "every advertisement should be thought of as a contribution to the complex symbol which is the brand image." He argued that the image or personality of the brand is particularly important when brands are similar:

> The greater the similarity between brands, the less part reason plays in brand selection. There isn't any significant difference between the various brands of whiskey, or cigarettes, or beer. They are all about the same. And so are the cake mixes and the detergents and the margarines. The manufacturer who dedicates his advertising to building the most sharply defined personality for his brand will get the largest share of the market at the highest profit. By the same token, the manufacturers who will find themselves up the creek are those shortsighted opportunists who siphon off their advertising funds for promotions.[34]

Image advertising has become increasingly popular and is used as the main selling idea for a variety of products and services, including soft drinks, liquor, cigarettes, cars, airlines, financial services, perfume/colognes, and clothing. Many consumers wear designer jeans or Ralph Lauren polo shirts or drink certain brands of beer or soft drinks because of the image of these brands. The key to successful image advertising is developing an image that will appeal to product users. For example, in 2005 Reebok initiated a $50 million global ad campaign using the "I am what I am" theme,

Exhibit 8-11 Reebok's "I am what I am" campaign creates an image of the brand as about being yourself

which, uses image advertising to promote the number-two athletic shoe company as the brand for young consumers.[35] The campaign is designed to create an image for Reebok as a brand that is about being yourself rather than trying to become something you are not. The ads feature a variety of celebrity personalities including tennis star Andy Roddick, rappers Jay-Z and 50 Cent, NBA stars Yao Ming and Allan Iverson, and film star Lucy Liu. The image-oriented ads feature a portrait of the celebrity next to a visual symbol of an aspect of the star's private life and a quote about his or her life (see Exhibit 8-11).

Finding the Inherent Drama

Another approach to determining the major selling idea is finding the **inherent drama** or characteristic of the product that makes the consumer purchase it. The inherent drama approach expresses the advertising philosophy of Leo Burnett, founder of the Leo Burnett agency in Chicago. Burnett said inherent drama "is often hard to find but it is always there, and once found it is the most interesting and believable of all advertising appeals."[36] He believed advertising should be based on a foundation of consumer benefits with an emphasis on the dramatic element in expressing those benefits.

Burnett advocated a down-home type of advertising that presents the message in a warm and realistic way. Some of the more famous ads developed by his agency using the inherent-drama approach are for McDonald's, Maytag appliances, Kellogg cereals, and Hallmark cards. Notice how the Hallmark commercial shown in Exhibit 8-12 uses this approach to deliver a poignant message.

Positioning

The concept of *positioning* as a basis for advertising strategy was introduced by Jack Trout and Al Ries in the early 1970s and has become a popular basis of creative development.[37] The basic idea is that advertising is used to establish or "position" the product or service in a particular place in the consumer's mind. Positioning is done for companies as well as for brands. Many of the top brands in various product and service categories have retained their market leadership because they have established and maintained a strong position or identity in the minds of consumers.[38] For example, Crest has built and maintained the success of its toothpaste based on the position of cavity prevention while BMW's positioning of its car as the "ultimate driving machine" transcends and helps to differentiate its entire product line. Positioning is also done for companies as well as for brands. For example, the ad shown in Exhibit 8-13 is part of "the other IBM" campaign that is designed to position the company as a provider of business consulting and more than just a technology provider. The integrated campaign, which includes print ads, television and online ads, sponsorships, and a micro website, is designed to reveal a side of IBM that has been largely unknown to many potential business consulting and services clients.[39]

LEO BURNETT COMPANY, INC.
AS FILMED AND RECORDED (4/96) "Report Card" 2:00

HALLMARK CARDS, INC.
HMHF6359

1. (MUSIC: UNDER THROUGHOUT)

2. MAXX: Hi, Mom, I'm home!
MOM: Hi. Is your coat on the floor?
MAXX: No...

3. MAXX: Can I go over to Lee's house?
MOM: Do you have any homework?
MAXX: Yeah.
MOM: After you finish it you can go.

4. MAXX: Cool.
MOM: Did you turn in your milk money?
MAXX: Yeah.

5. Hey--who moved my lunar module?

6. MOM: Maxx, what's this?
MAXX: Did Amy move my lunar module?
MOM: Maxx?

7. MAXX: It's something from Mrs. Bennett.
MOM: What'd she give you a card for?
MAXX: Cause I was nice to somebody.

8. MOM: Who were you nice to?
MAXX: Scott.
MOM: Who's Scott?

9. MAXX: The boy who comes to school just once in a while cause he's sick.
MOM: Was he at the school play?
MAXX: Nope, can we get an armadillo?

10. MOM: How were you nice to him?

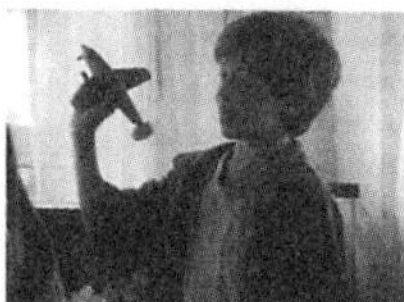

11. MAXX: Well, Mrs. Bennett always has me sit next to him. Scott can't go out for recess and stuff so I stay in and play Yahtzee with him.

12. MOM: I didn't know you were doing that.
MAXX: I like him. It's no big deal.
Could I see your card?

13. MAXX: Sure. MOM: (READING): "You didn't have to do what you did. And that's what made it so special." Maxx? Do you know what this means?

14. MAXX: Kinda.
MOM: It means you should be very proud of yourself. I know I am.

15. MAXX: Mom?
MOM: Yeah?
MAXX: You're squooshing me.

Exhibit 8-12 This Hallmark commercial uses an inherent-drama approach

Exhibit 8-13 This ad is part of a campaign that positions IBM as a provider of business consulting and services

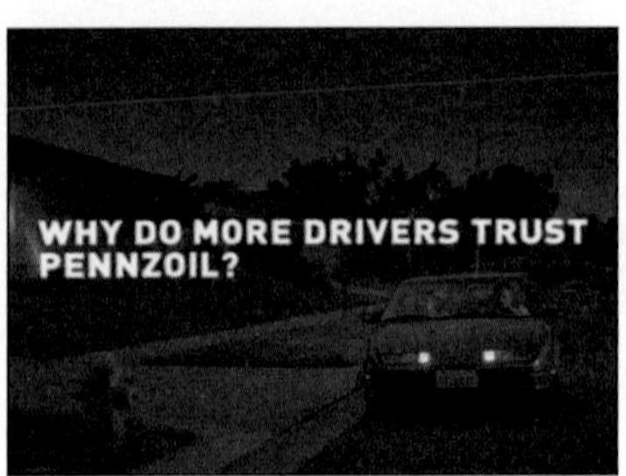

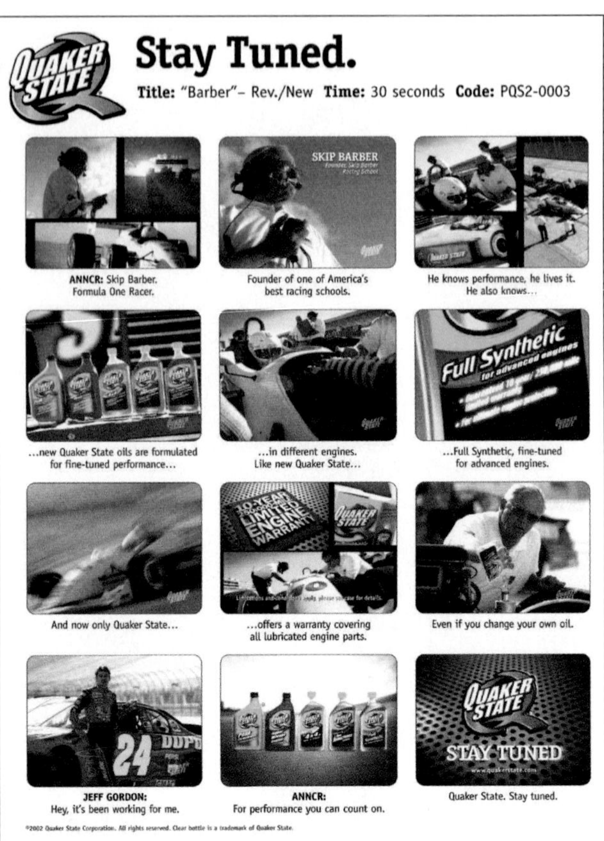

Exhibit 8-14 Advertising for Pennzoil and Quaker State positions the brands differently

Trout and Ries originally described positioning as the image consumers had of the brand in relation to competing brands in the product or service category, but the concept has been expanded beyond direct competitive positioning. As discussed in Chapter 2, products can be positioned on the basis of product attributes, price/quality, usage or application, product users, or product class. Any of these can spark a major selling idea that becomes the basis of the creative strategy and results in the brand's occupying a particular place in the minds of the target audience. Since positioning can be done on the basis of a distinctive attribute, the positioning and unique selling proposition approaches can overlap. Positioning approaches have been used as the foundation for a number of successful creative strategies.

Positioning is often the basis of a firm's creative strategy when it has multiple brands competing in the same market. For example, the two top-selling brands of motor oil, Pennzoil and Quaker State, were merged into the same company when the two companies merged a few years ago. The Pennzoil–Quaker State Co. creates separate identities for the two brands by positioning them differently.[40] Pennzoil is positioned as a brand that stands for protection, while Quaker State uses a performance positioning. Advertising for Pennzoil uses the "we're driving protection" tagline, while Quaker State ads use the "stay tuned" theme (see Exhibit 8-14).

The USP, brand image, inherent-drama, and positioning approaches are often used as the basis of the creative strategy for ad campaigns. These creative styles have become associated with some of the most successful creative minds in advertising and their agencies.[41] However, many other creative approaches are available.

Some of the more contemporary advertising visionaries who have had a major influence on modern-day advertising include Hal Riney of Hal Riney & Partners, Lee Clow and Jay Chiat of TBWA/Chiat/Day, Dan Wieden of Wieden & Kennedy, and Jeff Goodby and Rich Silverstein of Goodby, Silverstein & Partners. In describing today's creative leaders, Anthony Vagnoni of *Advertising Age* writes:

> The modern creative kings don't write books, rarely give interviews or lay out their theories on advertising. They've endorsed no set of rules, professed no simple maxims like Mr. Ogilvy's famous "When you don't have anything to say, sing it." If pronouncements and books are out the window, what's replaced them is a conscious desire to lift the intelligence level of advertising. Today's leaders see advertising as an uplifting social force, as a way to inspire and entertain.[42]

Goodby and Silverstein note: "Advertising works best when it sneaks into people's lives, when it doesn't look or feel like advertising. It's about treating people at their best, as opposed to dealing with them at their lowest common denominator." They describe their creative formula as doing intelligent work that the public likes to see and that, at the same time, has a sales pitch.[43] Lee Clow says, "No rule book will tell you how to target the masses anymore. The best of us understand the sociocultural realities of people and how they interact with the media. If we didn't, we couldn't make the kinds of messages that people would be able to connect with."[44]

Specific agencies are by no means limited to any one creative approach. For example, the famous "Marlboro country" campaign, a classic example of image advertising, was developed by Leo Burnett Co. Many different agencies have followed the unique selling proposition approach advocated by Rosser Reeves at Ted Bates. The challenge to the creative specialist or team is to find a major selling idea—whether it is based on a unique selling proposition, brand image, inherent drama, position in the market, or some other approach—and use it as a guide in developing an effective creative strategy.

Summary

The creative development and execution of the advertising message are a crucial part of a firm's integrated marketing communications program and are often the key to the success of a marketing campaign. Marketers generally turn to ad agencies to develop, prepare, and implement their creative strategy since these agencies are specialists in the creative function of advertising. The creative specialist or team is responsible for developing an effective way to communicate the marketer's message to the customer. Other individuals on both the client and the agency sides work with the creative specialists to develop the creative strategy, implement it, and evaluate its effectiveness.

The challenge facing the writers, artists, and others who develop ads is to be creative and come up with fresh, unique, and appropriate ideas that can be used as solutions to communications problems. Creativity in advertising is a process of several stages, including preparation, incubation, illumination, verification, and revision. Various sources of information are available to help the creative specialists determine the best campaign theme, appeal, or execution style.

Creative strategy development is guided by specific goals and objectives and is based on a number of factors, including the target audience, the basic problem the advertising must address, the objectives the message seeks to accomplish, and the major selling idea or key benefit the advertiser wants to communicate. These factors are generally stated in a copy platform, which is a work plan used to guide development of the ad campaign. An important part of creative strategy is determining the major selling idea that will become the central theme of the campaign. There are several approaches to doing this, including using a unique selling proposition, creating a brand image, looking for inherent drama in the brand, and positioning.

Key Terms

creative strategy, 237
creative tactics, 237
advertising creativity, 241
account planning, 246
general preplanning input, 247
product/service-specific preplanning input, 247
problem detection, 247
focus groups, 248
ethnographic research, 249
storyboard, 251
animatic, 251
advertising campaign, 252
campaign theme, 252
copy platform, 252
major selling idea, 254
unique selling proposition (USP), 255
image advertising, 257
inherent drama, 258

Discussion Questions

1. The opening vignette discusses the tremendous success of the Apple iPod. Discuss the role advertising has played in the marketing of the iPod. Do you think the iPod would have been as successful without the award-winning "Silhouettes" campaign?

2. Explain what is meant by creative strategy and creative tactics in advertising. Find an example of an advertising campaign and evaluate the creative strategy and tactics used in the ads.

3. Advertising creativity is viewed as the ability to generate unique and appropriate ideas that can be used as solutions to communication problems. This definition suggests that a creative ad is one that is novel but also relevant or appropriate. Find an example of an advertisement (either a print ad or TV commercial) that is novel but not necessarily relevant to the product or service. Discuss why the client would have approved this ad.

4. What is your opinion of advertising awards, such as the Cannes Lions, that are based solely on creativity? If you were a marketer, would you take these creative awards into consideration in your agency evaluation process? Why or why not?

5. Television commercials are often developed that rely on unusual creative tactics and have very little relevance to the product or service being advertised. Creative personnel in agencies defend the use of the strange messages by noting that they are novel and provide a way to break through the clutter. Evaluate the pros and cons of this argument.

6. IMC Perspective 8-1 discusses the debate over creative versus hard-sell advertising. Discuss the arguments for and against each perspective. Which do you support? Who should be responsible for judging the creativity of an ad—clients or agency creative personnel?

7. IMC Perspective 8-2 discusses how Malcom Gladwell has proposed that the unique insights that drive innovative and great advertising campaigns are not gained through traditional marketing research techniques such as focus groups. Evaluate Gladwell's argument that focus groups may inhibit the creative process.

8. Assume that you have been hired as an account planner by an advertising agency and assigned to work on the advertising campaign for a new brand of bottled water. Describe the various types of general and product-specific preplanning input you might provide to the creative team.

9. Briefly describe the five major communication interfaces and decision points in the model of marketing information flow shown in Figure 8-4. Discuss how breakdowns in communication can occur at each interface and how this might negatively impact the creative process.

10. Find an example of an ad or campaign that you think reflects one of the approaches used to develop a major selling idea such as unique selling proposition, brand image, inherent drama, or positioning. Discuss how the major selling idea is reflected in this ad or campaign.

Creative Strategy: Implementation and Evaluation

9

Chapter Objectives

1. To analyze various types of appeals that can be used in the development and implementation of an advertising message.
2. To analyze the various creative execution styles that advertisers can use and the advertising situations where they are most appropriate.
3. To analyze various tactical issues involved in the creation of print advertising and TV commercials.
4. To consider how clients evaluate the creative work of their agencies and discuss guidelines for the evaluation and approval process.

Happy Cows Help Sell Real California Cheese

When asked to name the leading dairy state in the United States, it is likely that most consumers would name Wisconsin or another midwestern state. However, they might be surprised to learn that the nation's leading dairy state is actually California, which is the production leader in just about every product category including milk, butter, and ice cream. And much to the dismay of the cheese heads in Wisconsin, the Golden State will soon become the top cheese producer thanks in part to a creative advertising campaign featuring cows who, like many people, are happy to be living in California.

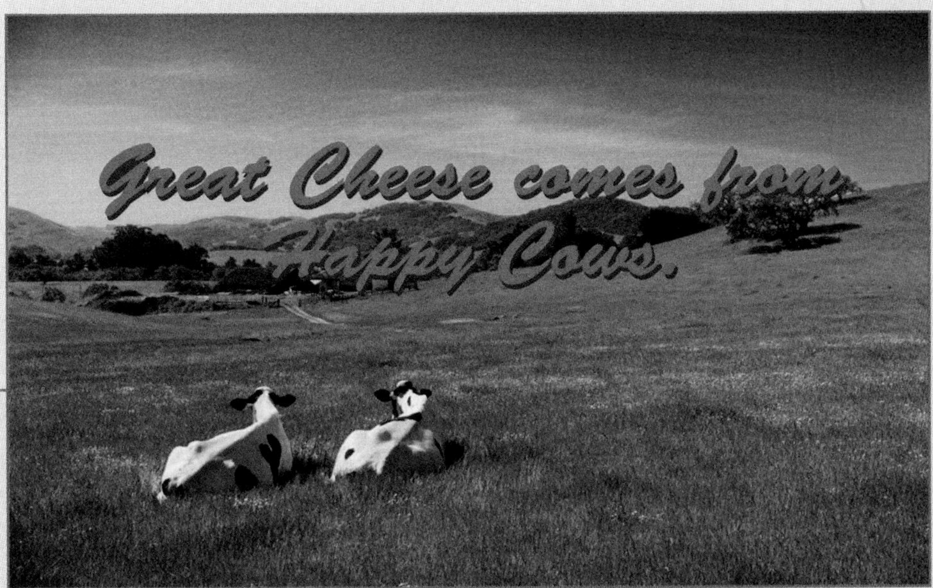

More than two decades ago the California Milk Advisory Board (CMAB), which is a state agency responsible for promoting California dairy products, developed a long-range strategic plan designed to make the state a leading producer of cheese. One of the first steps taken by the CMAB to implement its strategy was to create a distinct and compelling identity that would be the focal point of an integrated marketing communications program. The CMAB created the Real California Cheese seal as a certification mark to identify natural cheese made in California from California milk. The seal is placed on the many styles and varieties of cheeses from California cheesemakers who qualify for and use the seal on their packaging. The seal is also used in all forms of advertising, on all Real California Cheese coupons and promotions, on point-of-sale materials at retail stores, and even on restaurant menus and table tents.

The placement of the seal in all of the elements of consumer communications reinforces the message and maximizes awareness of the trademark. However, the CMAB also relies on advertising and other IMC tools to create a fondness and preference for cheese with the Real California Cheese seal. From 1995 to 2000, the CMAB ran a very popular campaign using the tagline "It's the Cheese," which made humorous exaggerated claims that the real reason people come to California is the cheese. However, after running the campaign for five years the CMAB decided that it was time to take a new and creative approach and also to strengthen its message by telling consumers why California cheese is so good.

In 2000, the CMAB hired a new agency, Deutsch LA, which took on the task of developing a new creative strategy to promote California cheese. The agency's executive creative director, Eric Hirshberg, and his creative team decided that rather than focusing on the cheese, the campaign would revolve around the idea that California cheese is better because it comes from "happy" cows. The tagline developed for the campaign was "Great Cheese Comes from Happy Cows. Happy Cows Come from California." The humorous ads feature cows that seem to talk, think, and process the world just as people do. They enjoy California's best-known features such as sunny skies, a lack of snow, and beautiful scenery. One restriction the agency put on the cows is that they have to seem human with human thoughts; they should not do things cows wouldn't do—like riding surf boards.

Different executions of the humorous commercials have been created, including one that features a cow still traumatized whenever she recalls the blizzards she endured while living in the Midwest and another that features a couple of bulls lusting after a cow who is showering in a sprinkler as "Lady," Styx's hit song from the '70s, plays in the background. In another spot, two cows lounging in a pasture are pestered by a manic rooster who wants to know the secret to their mellow attitude.

Deutsch has extended the campaign to other media including outdoor venues, radio, and the Internet. The success of the TV commercials has paved the way for Deutsch to add radio to the creative mix because people can visualize the cows when listening to 60-second radio spots. The popular radio commercials feature bantering between Janice and Diane, two of the star cows from the TV commercials.

A major component of the integrated marketing communications campaign is the website that Deutsch has created (www.realcaliforniacheese.com), which is handled by the agency's interactive arm, iDeutsch. The website is consistent with the mission, personality, and look of the Happy Cows campaign and includes links to the commercials, as well as cheese recipes, nutritional information, interactive games for kids, promotional offers, and even a merchandise store where consumers can buy Happy Cow merchandise such as Janice and Diane plush toys and puppets. The website gets more than 25,000 visitors per month and is extremely popular among consumers who have become fans of the Happy Cows campaign.

Prior to 2004, the CMAB ran the Happy Cows campaign primarily in markets where Real California Cheese had a major presence. In 2004, Real California Cheese achieved national distribution in several major retail accounts as well as in the food service industry, and the advertising and promotional efforts were expanded to a national level. The advertising campaign has won numerous creative awards, and the ads have achieved the agency's goal of establishing an emotional bond between consumers and the contented California bovines. However, the real success of the campaign is seen in the numbers as California cheese production has increased more than 400 percent over the past two decades, which is three times faster than overall U.S. cheese production growth during this period. The campaign has helped position California to soon become the country's leading cheese producer—in addition to having the happiest cows.

Sources: "How California Created the Dairy Industry of the Future," California Milk Advisory Board 2005; Michelle Greenwald, "It's the Cheese: Real California Cheese Case Study," *Columbia University, Graduate School of Business Case Study,* 2005; Gregory Solman, "Deutsch's 'Happy Cows' Keep CMAB Content," *Adweek.com,* August 18, 2003.

In Chapter 8, we discussed the importance of advertising creativity and examined the various steps in the creative process. We focused on determining what the advertising message should communicate. This chapter focuses on *how* the message will be executed. It examines various appeals and execution styles that can be used to develop the ad and tactical issues involved in the design and production of effective advertising messages. We conclude by presenting some guidelines clients can use to evaluate the creative work of their agencies.

Appeals and Execution Styles

The **advertising appeal** refers to the approach used to attract the attention of consumers and/or to influence their feelings toward the product, service, or cause. An advertising appeal can also be viewed as "something that moves people, speaks to their wants or needs, and excites their interest."[1] The **creative execution style** is the way a particular appeal is turned into an advertising message presented to the consumer. According to William Weilbacher:

> The appeal can be said to form the underlying content of the advertisement, and the execution the way in which that content is presented. Advertising appeals and executions are usually independent of each other; that is, a particular appeal can be executed in a variety of ways and a particular means of execution can be applied to a variety of advertising appeals. Advertising appeals tend to adapt themselves to all media, whereas some kinds of executional devices are more adaptable to some media than others.[2]

Advertising Appeals

Hundreds of different appeals can be used as the basis for advertising messages. At the broadest level, these approaches are generally broken into two categories: informational/rational appeals and emotional appeals. In this section, we focus on ways to use rational and emotional appeals as part of a creative strategy. We also consider how rational and emotional appeals can be combined in developing the advertising message.

Informational/Rational Appeals

Informational/rational appeals focus on the consumer's practical, functional, or utilitarian need for the product or service and emphasize features of a product or service and/or the benefits or reasons for owning or using a particular brand. The content of these messages emphasizes facts, learning, and the logic of persuasion.[3] Rational-based appeals tend to be informative, and advertisers using them generally attempt to convince consumers that their product or service has a particular attribute(s) or provides a specific benefit that satisfies their needs. Their objective is to persuade the target audience to buy the brand because it is the best available or does a better job of meeting consumers' needs. For example, the Nordica ad shown in Exhibit 9-1 uses a rational appeal to explain the features and benefits of its Beast Synergy System ski collection.

Exhibit 9-1 Nordica uses a rational appeal to advertise the features of its skis and bindings

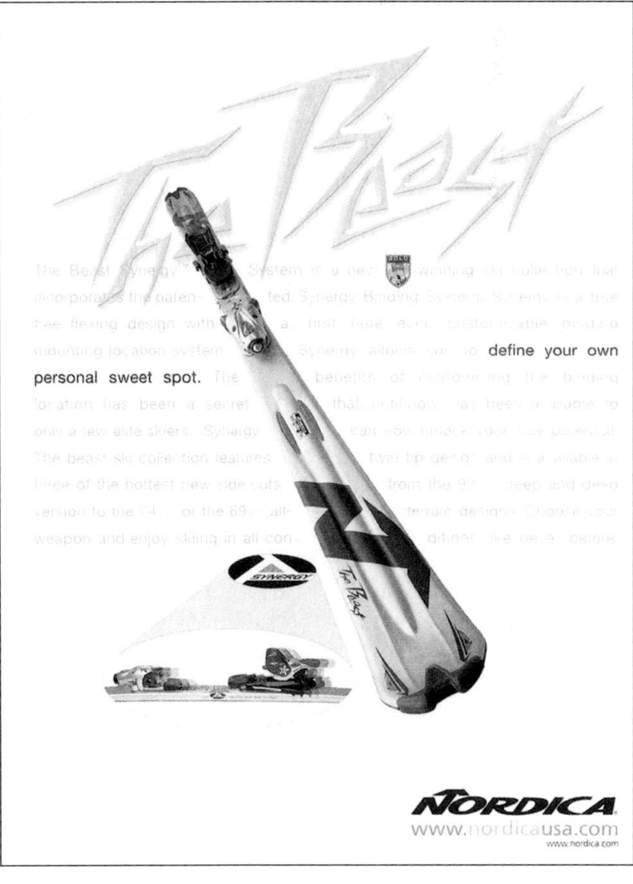

Many rational motives can be used as the basis for advertising appeals, including comfort, convenience, economy, health, and sensory benefits such as touch, taste, and smell. Other rational motives or purchase criteria commonly used in advertising include quality, dependability, durability, efficiency, efficacy, and performance. The particular features, benefits, or evaluative criteria that are important to consumers and can serve as the basis of an informational/rational appeal vary from one product or service category to another as well as among various market segments.

Weilbacher identified several types of advertising appeals that fall under the category of rational approaches, among them feature, competitive advantage, favorable price, news, and product/service popularity appeals.

Ads that use a *feature appeal* focus on the dominant traits of the product or service. These ads tend to be highly informative and present the customer with a number of important product attributes or features that will lead to favorable attitudes and can be used as the basis for a rational purchase decision. Technical and high-involvement products such as automobiles often use this type of advertising appeal. However, a feature appeal can be used for a variety of products and services. For example, Exhibit 9-2 shows an ad for MacGregor golf clubs that focuses on the features and benefits of the club's V-Foil speed technology.

CAREER PROFILE

Eric Hirshberg, Executive Creative Director

Deutsch LA

There's a widely held belief among advertising creative people that in order to build a great portfolio of work, one must jump from agency to agency every couple of years. While I'm sure this theory has its merits, I've never subscribed to it. If you track the great work over the years, you will find that it is much more connected to certain agencies than to individual creative people. Thus, I have always strived to be a part of cultures I believe in and that are committed to doing great work. As a result, I have worked at only two agencies in my career.

The first one was a small, creatively well-regarded boutique called Fattal & Collins in Los Angeles. Although the work I did there was on a relatively small scale, campaigns I did for clients like ABC, Sega, Gold's Gym, Infiniti Motors, the LA City Fire Department, and Century City Shopping Center found their ways into the award show annuals and generated some buzz. I became the creative director of the agency at the somewhat young age of 26. Working at Fattal & Collins afforded me the opportunity to reach a leadership position far earlier than I would have had I taken a more traditional route. It also afforded me the ability to form my own philosophies and style, as opposed to learning at the feet of the establishment like everyone else did. It also put me in a position to interview with Donny Deutsch for the job of opening up Deutsch LA.

"I have had a great career in advertising and take pride in the recognition I have received from my peers."

Donny Deutsch was another individual who made his way in advertising outside of the agency establishment. So he decided that instead of sending out one of his top officers from his thriving New York office to open up Deutsch LA, he would take a chance on local, up-and-coming talent that had not yet made the big time and give them their shot. At the time, I was working closely with another individual, Mike Sheldon, who was our director of client services. Mike and I had forged a great chemistry and partnership and pitched ourselves to Donny as a team. The three of us immediately hit it off. Donny liked my work. He also liked the fact that we knew how to pitch and win new business and that we had managed to penetrate the automotive category—a key for any LA agency. Donny has since told me that the key to my getting the job was not my resume or portfolio, but simply that he saw something in me—a fire in the belly, a passion, a wide-eyed optimism, and a certain amount of naiveté—that he liked. He hired both Mike and me to co-head Deutsch LA and to start it basically from scratch.

We started in a 5,000-square-foot loft above a movie theater with about 10 employees. After making a few key hires, we immediately turned our attention to new business. We then went on what can only be described as a new business tear, the likes of which the advertising business in LA (or anywhere else for that matter) has rarely seen. We won a number of new accounts including Baskin Robbins, LA Cellular, Mitsubishi Motors, Expedia.com, Sun America, California Cheese, DIRECTV, and more. In the span of five years, Deutsch LA was a 300-person agency with about $800 million in billings, and a nationally admired creative reputation. Looking back on it, I honestly don't know how we did it.

Even more important to me than the agency's meteoric growth was the fact that for each client we won, we were doing creative work that was always attention-getting, effective, and, in some cases, truly groundbreaking. The agency has gone on to do great work for other clients such as Coors Light, Old Navy, PacifiCare, TGIFriday's, and Chevrolet to name a few. But it was those first few years that really established our agency brand.

All of this has, of course, led to more than a few nice industry accolades. We were named National Agency of the Year by *Adweek* in 1998, 1999, 2001, and 2002 and the West Coast Agency of the Year in 2000. We have also won our share of creative awards from the likes of The One Show, Communication Arts, the National Addys, *Adweek*'s Best Spots of the Decade, and the Best of Show Honors at The Belding Awards in 2002. The agency's creative work has been equally well received by the business community. *The Wall Street Journal* named our "Wingman" campaign for Coors Light one of the three best of 2004. *Automotive News* named our work for Mitsubishi its Campaign of the Year in 2002. *Women's Wear Daily* surveyed the most memorable fashion ads of 2004 and our work for Old Navy generated four spots in the top ten, including the number one and number three slots. Our work has also been profiled in *The New York Times, The Wall Street Journal,* and *USA Today* as well as on *The Today Show* and *The CBS Morning News.* For my efforts, I was named the Creative Leader of the Year by the Western States Advertising Agency Association in 2002.

When you develop the kind of reputation we have, the phone rings from time to time with some interesting extracurricular projects. I was asked to work as an advisor for John Kerry's presidential debate prep team; and a small group of us at Deutsch contributed to the candidate winning all three debates in the polls. I was also approached by Jon Bon Jovi to help launch Bon Jovi's latest album and re-brand the band in the process. I ended up conceiving and directing a VH-1 top ten video and Deutsch put together a non-traditional campaign to launch the album, creating, not just advertising, everything from album art to tour merchandise.

On a personal level, I am happily married to my wife Tara and am a proud father. I'm also a passionate, lifelong singer/songwriter and last year released an independent CD called "Wish I Was Here," which was called "a peek behind the male veil" by indie pop queen Liz Phair.

Exhibit 9-2 MacGregor Golf uses a feature appeal to promote its clubs

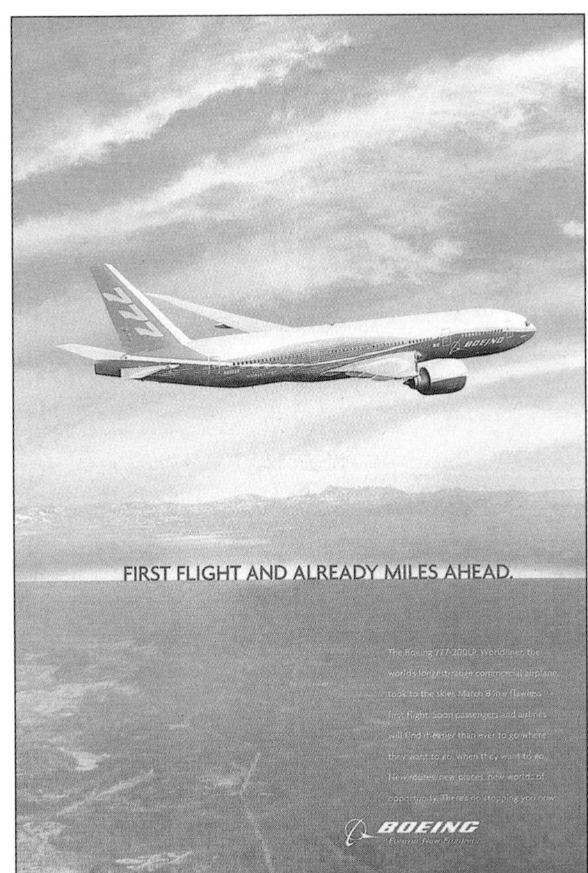

Exhibit 9-3 Boeing uses a news appeal to promote its 777-200LR Worldliner

When a *competitive advantage appeal* is used, the advertiser makes either a direct or an indirect comparison to another brand (or brands) and usually claims superiority on one or more attributes. This type of appeal was discussed in Chapter 6 under "Comparative Advertising."

A *favorable price appeal* makes the price offer the dominant point of the message. Price appeal advertising is used most often by retailers to announce sales, special offers, or low everyday prices. Price appeal ads are often used by national advertisers during recessionary times. Many fast-food chains have made price an important part of their marketing strategy through promotional deals and "value menus" or lower overall prices, and their advertising strategy is designed to communicate this. Many other types of advertisers use price appeals as well, such as airlines and car-rental companies.

News appeals are those in which some type of news or announcement about the product, service, or company dominates the ad. This type of appeal can be used for a new product or service or to inform consumers of significant modifications or improvements. This appeal works best when a company has important news it wants to communicate to its target market. Exhibit 9-3 shows an ad using a news appeal that was run by Boeing to announce the first flight of the company's new Boeing 777-200LR Worldliner, which is the world's longest range commercial airplane. The ad was run a few days after the inaugural flight to create interest and excitement in the new plane, which can connect any two cities in the world with nonstop service.

Product/service popularity appeals stress the popularity of a product or service by pointing out the number of consumers who use the brand, the number who have switched to it, the number of experts who recommend it, or its leadership position in the market. The main point of this advertising appeal is that the wide use of the brand proves its quality or value and other customers should consider using it. The ad for

Exhibit 9-4 This Neutrogena ad uses a product popularity appeal

Neutrogena's Healthy Skin Anti-Wrinkle cream shown in Exhibit 9-4 uses a product popularity appeal by noting that it is the brand most recommended by dermatologists as well as the sales leader in the category.

Emotional Appeals

Emotional appeals relate to the customers' social and/or psychological needs for purchasing a product or service. Many consumers' motives for their purchase decisions are emotional, and their feelings about a brand can be more important than knowledge of its features or attributes. Advertisers for many products and services view rational, information-based appeals as dull. Many advertisers believe appeals to consumers' emotions work better at selling brands that do not differ markedly from competing brands, since rational differentiation of them is difficult.[4]

Many feelings or needs can serve as the basis for advertising appeals designed to influence consumers on an emotional level, as shown in Figure 9-1. These appeals are based on the psychological states or feelings directed to the self (such as pleasure or excitement), as well as those with a more social orientation (such as status or recognition). The ad for Kellogg's Nutri-Grain cereal bars shown in Exhibit 9-5 appeals to emotional motives such as self-esteem and respect by using a clever visual image to suggest what might happen to women who eat pastry in the morning. The "Respect yourself" campaign has been very effective in positioning Nutri-Grain as a healthy alternative for those who don't take time to eat breakfast.

Advertisers can use emotional appeals in many ways in their creative strategy. Kamp and Macinnis note that commercials often rely on the concept of *emotional integration,* whereby they portray the characters in the ad as experiencing an emotional benefit or outcome from using a product or service.[5] Ads using humor, sex, and other appeals that are very entertaining, arousing, upbeat, and/or exciting can affect the emotions of consumers and put them in a favorable frame of mind. Many TV advertisers use poignant ads that bring a lump to viewers' throats. Hallmark, Nike, Kodak, and Oscar Mayer often create commercials that evoke feelings of warmth, nostalgia, and/or sentiment. Marketers use emotional appeals in hopes that the positive feeling they evoke will transfer to the brand and/or company. Research shows that positive mood states and feelings created by advertising can have a favorable effect on consumers' evaluations of a brand.[6] Studies also show that emotional advertising is better remembered than nonemotional messages.[7]

McDonald's changed its advertising strategy and is putting more emotion in its commercials to evoke a feel-good connection with consumers. McDonald's believes the emotional ads take advantage of the chain's unique bond with consumers, which is a significant point of differentiation in the highly competitive fast-food business. In 2003, McDonald's began using the "I'm Lovin It" theme which has been the basis for a global IMC campaign

Figure 9-1 Bases for Emotional Appeals

Personal States or Feelings		Social-Based Feelings
Safety	Arousal/stimulation	Recognition
Security	Sorrow/grief	Status
Fear	Pride	Respect
Love	Achievement/accomplishment	Involvement
Affection	Self-esteem	Embarrassment
Happiness	Actualization	Affiliation/belonging
Joy	Pleasure	Rejection
Nostalgia	Ambition	Acceptance
Sentiment	Comfort	Approval
Excitement		

that is designed to enhance consumers' emotional attachment to the fast-food chain. The campaign has been very successful and has helped the company achieve strong sales growth over the past two years.[8]

Another reason for using emotional appeals is to influence consumers' interpretations of their product usage experience. One way of doing this is through what is known as transformational advertising. A **transformational ad** is defined as "one which associates the experience of using (consuming) the advertised brand with a unique set of psychological characteristics which would not typically be associated with the brand experience to the same degree without exposure to the advertisement."[9]

Transformational ads create feelings, images, meanings, and beliefs about the product or service that may be activated when consumers use it, transforming their interpretation of the usage experience. Christopher Puto and William Wells note that a transformational ad has two characteristics:

1. It must make the experience of using the product richer, warmer, more exciting, and/or more enjoyable than that obtained solely from an objective description of the advertised brand.
2. It must connect the experience of the advertisement so tightly with the experience of using the brand that consumers cannot remember the brand without recalling the experience generated by the advertisement.[10]

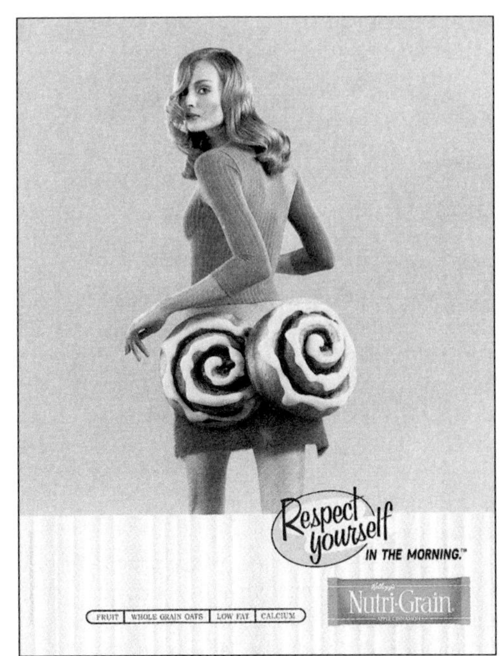

Exhibit 9-5 Nutri-Grain appeals to consumers' self-esteem and respect in this clever ad

Transformational advertising can help differentiate a product or service by making the consumption experience more enjoyable by suggesting the type of experiences consumers might have when they consume the product or service. This type of advertising is often used by companies in the travel industry to help consumers envision the experience or feeling they might have when they take a trip such as a cruise or visit a particular destination.

Image advertising, which is designed to give a company or brand a unique association or personality, is often transformational in nature. It is designed to create a certain feeling or mood that is activated when a consumer uses a particular product or service. For example, the Lambesis agency has created a unique image for Skyy vodka by creating ads that associate the brand with cinematic-based cocktail moments (see Exhibit 9-6). IMC Perspective 9-1 discusses how the agency is using a different transformational advertising approach based on image attributes of sophistication and style to introduce Skyy90, a new line extension to compete in the ultra-premium segment of the vodka market against brands such as Grey Goose and Ketel One.

Exhibit 9-6 Advertising for Skyy vodka uses a cinematic theme to create an image for the brand

Combining Rational and Emotional Appeals

In many advertising situations, the decision facing the creative specialist is not whether to choose an emotional or a rational appeal but, rather, determining how to combine the two approaches. As noted copywriters David Ogilvy and Joel Raphaelson have stated:

> Few purchases of any kind are made for entirely rational reasons. Even a purely functional product such as laundry detergent may offer what is now called an emotional benefit—say, the satisfaction of seeing one's children in bright, clean clothes. In some product categories the rational element is small. These include soft drinks, beer, cosmetics, certain personal care products, and most old-fashioned products. And who hasn't experienced the surge of joy that accompanies the purchase of a new car?[11]

IMC PERSPECTIVE 9-1

Skyy Goes After the Ultra-Premium Market

The last decade has been a great time for marketers of vodka as the product category has experienced strong growth and one wave of chic new brands has been followed by another. Consumption of vodka has increased steadily since 1998, and the vodka category is double the size of the next distilled spirits segment, rum. Ironically, a bland-tasting product that was best known for helping Russians make it through a cold, bleak winter has become a status symbol for many trendy twenty- and thirtysomethings in America. Marketers have tried to capitalize on the growing popularity of vodka and the growth of the "cocktail culture" that has brought more young adults to the spirits market by creating a distinct image for their brands and getting consumers to think of them as cutting-edge, edgy, and hip.

While a myriad of new vodka brands have been introduced over the past decade, one of the most successful has been Skyy, which has overtaken Stolichnaya as the number-two super-premium vodka in the United States. Skyy trails only Absolut, a brand which achieved iconic status through ads that focused on the distinctive shape of the bottle with visual puns and witty headlines. Skyy Spirits was founded in 1992 by Maurice Kanbar, who developed it as a premium brand for older connoisseurs, like himself, desirous of the perfect martini. Kanbar developed a four-stage distillation process that extracts many of the congers, which are natural impurities that remain in alcohol after distillation and may contribute to headaches. He created what he believed to be the purest of vodkas.

Much of Skyy's initial growth was driven by word of mouth. The company successfully placed its eye-catching blue bottle into swanky Hollywood parties and nightclubs known for attracting a hip crowd. Skyy quickly generated a buzz on the nightclub circuit, where word spread that its quadruple-distilled formula reduced the likelihood of hangovers. The company spent much of its limited marketing budget on sponsoring independent film festivals and producing artsy short films that were shown at these events. Skyy also uses the Internet to feature these films as a way of expanding its presence on the Web and shows them as part of the festivals and movie premieres that it sponsors.

Image advertising has also become an important part of Skyy's brand-building efforts. The Lambesis agency took over the account in 1998 and created the "Skyy Cinema" campaign to target 21- to 34-year-old urban, metro consumers. The high-impact ads do not contain any copy but rather rely on stylish, seductive visuals that set up various noir-inspired story lines but leave the actual scenarios up to the mind of the viewer. All of the ads establish Skyy's distinctive cobalt blue bottle as the "star" and showcase the brand as a catalyst for a great cocktail moment. The campaign has helped Skyy vodka sales increase from 3,000 cases in 1993 to nearly 2 million cases in 2004.

While sales of Skyy continue to increase, the new growth segment in the vodka category is the ultra-premium category where brands such as Grey Goose, Ketel One, Belvedere, and Level (which is made by Absolut) dominate. Vodka drinkers are willing to pay upward of $30 a bottle or $14 or more a drink for these brands because they think their vodka martinis and cosmopolitans taste better or they are drinking the trendiest brands. To compete in this market, Skyy has introduced a brand extension called Skyy90, which is being positioned as the world's first modern luxury vodka with taste by design. The advertising and other communications for the brand focus on the art of modern luxury and how the same principles of design used in modern art, architecture, and technology have guided Skyy's master distiller in the creation of Skyy90. The objective is to create an image for Skyy90 as the brand for those who desire the taste of modern luxury by associating it with sophistication and style.

All photography, illustrations, and copy for Skyy90 reflect a higher aesthetic and integrate modern luxury icons and environments. The Skyy90 bottle was designed to echo simple and pure design principles and serve as an expression of modern luxury. Lambesis has also created a mini website (SKYY90.com) for Skyy90 that has an ultra-modern tone, feel, and style and provides information on the ingredients, facilities, innovative processes, and technology that are involved in distilling the brand.

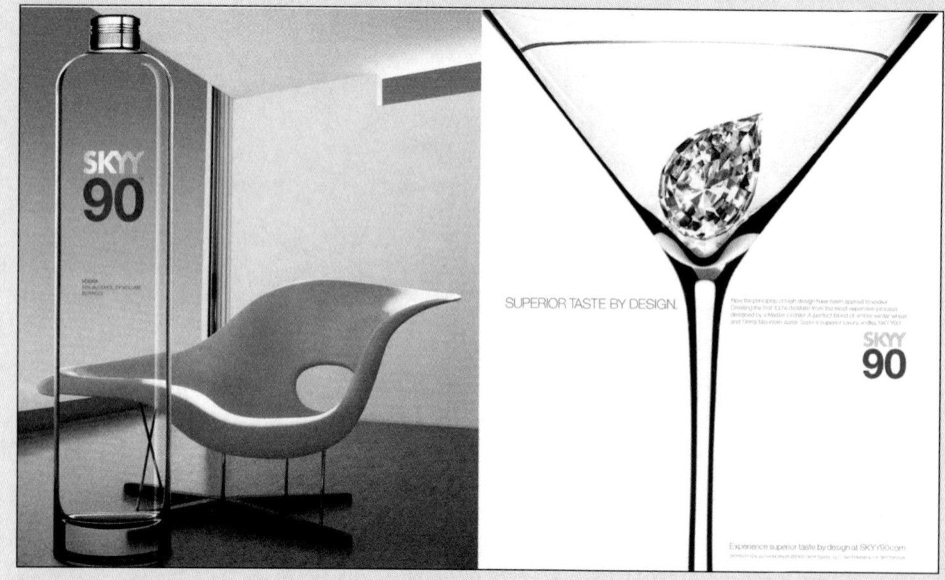

Skyy Sprits recognizes that it will face stiff competition in the ultra-premium category where brands such as Grey Goose and Ketel One spend more than $18 million and $10 million per year, respectively, on advertising. Grey Goose, the market leader in the segment, advertises the brand as the world's best-tasting vodka and saw its sales increase by 27 percent in 2004. High-priced luxury brands are becoming popular across all spirit product categories, including tequila, scotch, and rum as consumers trade up to more expensive drinks. The company hopes to grab its share of ultra-premium vodka sales with its unique positioning of Skyy90 and from its association with the core Skyy brand.

Sources: Christopher Lawton, "Stolichnaya Marketer Takes Shot at Dated Ads for Grey Goose," *The Wall Street Journal,* April, 15, 2005, p. B5; James B. Arndorfer, "Spirits Makers Raise the Bar on Lux Brands," *Advertising Age,* November 1, 2004, pp. 4, 62; Kenneth Hein, "Strategy: Skyy Sets the Stage in Sultry Cinematic Scenes," *Adweek,* June 17, 2002; Theresa Howard, "Marketers of the Next Generation: Teresa Zepeda," *Brandweek,* November 8, 1999, pp. 38–21.

Consumer purchase decisions are often made on the basis of both emotional and rational motives, and attention must be given to both elements in developing effective advertising. Note how the ad for the Suzuki Reno shown in Exhibit 9-7 appeals to both rational and emotional motives as it points out specific product features as well as noting how the car's styling and design make if different from other vehicles.

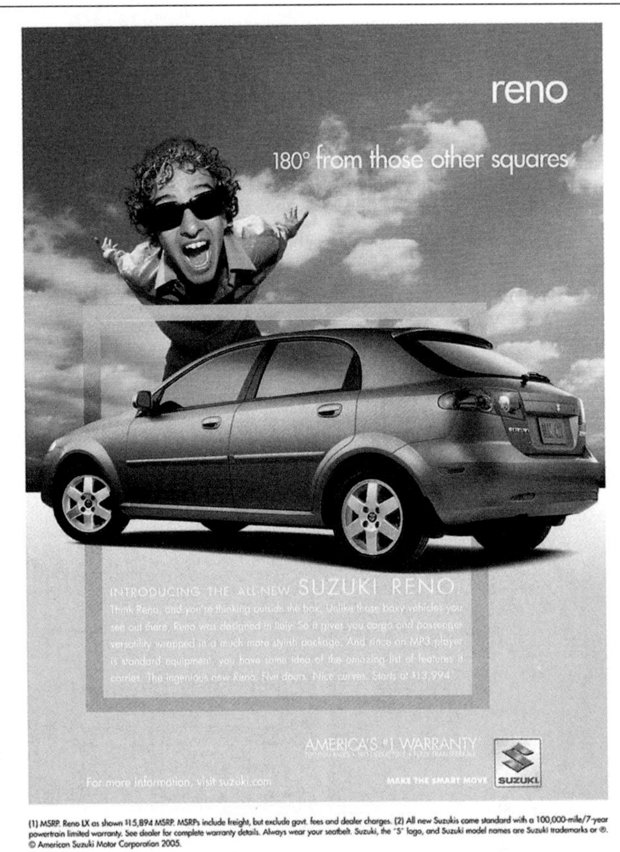

Exhibit 9-7 Suzuki addresses both rational and emotional motives in this ad

Advertising researchers and agencies have given considerable thought to the relationship between rational and emotional motives in consumer decision making and how advertising influences both. McCann-Erickson Worldwide, in conjunction with advertising professor Michael Ray, developed a proprietary research technique known as *emotional bonding.* This technique evaluates how consumers feel about brands and the nature of any emotional rapport they have with a brand compared to the ideal emotional state they associate with the product category.[12]

The basic concept of emotional bonding is that consumers develop three levels of relationships with brands, as shown in Figure 9-2. The most basic relationship indicates how consumers *think* about brands in respect to product benefits. This occurs, for the most part, through a rational learning process and can be measured by how well advertising communicates product information. Consumers at this stage are not very brand loyal, and brand switching is common.

At the next stage, the consumer assigns a *personality* to a brand. For example, a brand may be thought of as self-assured, aggressive, and adventurous, as opposed to compliant and timid. The consumer's judgment of the brand has moved beyond its attributes or delivery of product/service benefits. In most instances, consumers judge

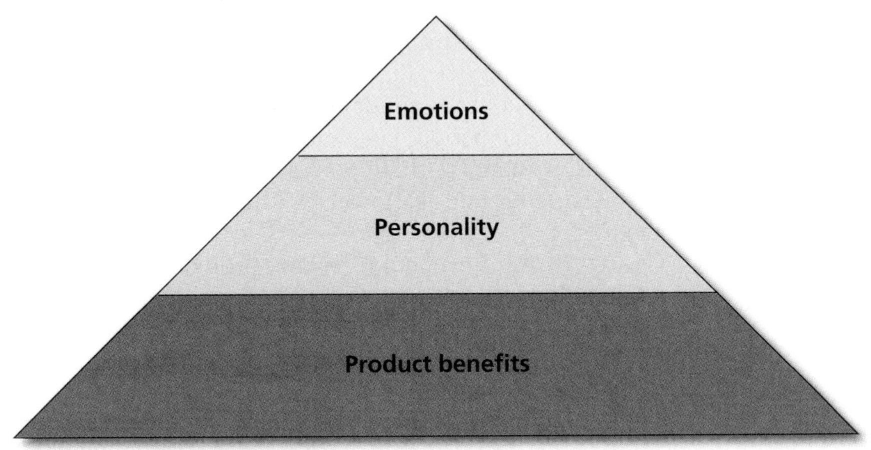

Figure 9-2 Levels of Relationships with Brands

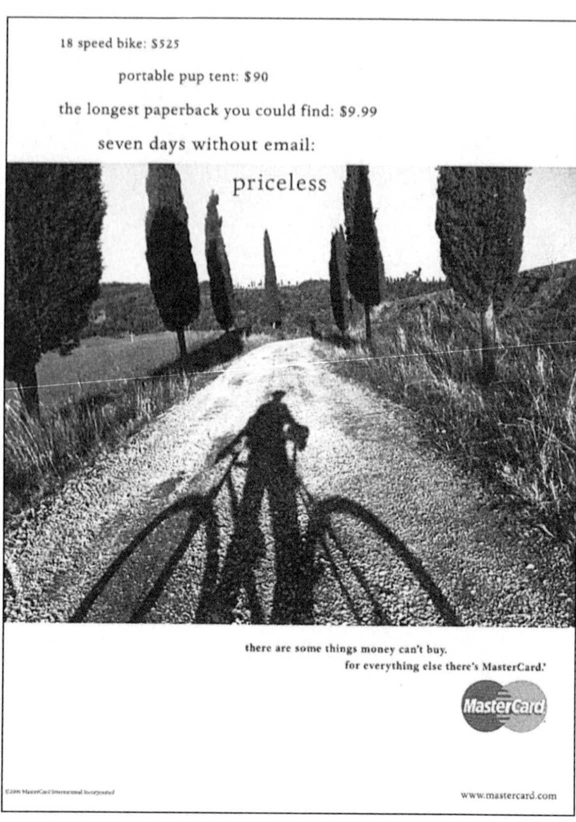

18 speed bike: $525
portable pup tent: $90
the longest paperback you could find: $9.99
seven days without email:
priceless
there are some things money can't buy.
for everything else there's MasterCard.
MasterCard
www.mastercard.com

Exhibit 9-8 MasterCard's "Priceless" campaign creates an emotional bond with consumers

Exhibit 9-9 Altoids uses reminder advertising to build brand awareness

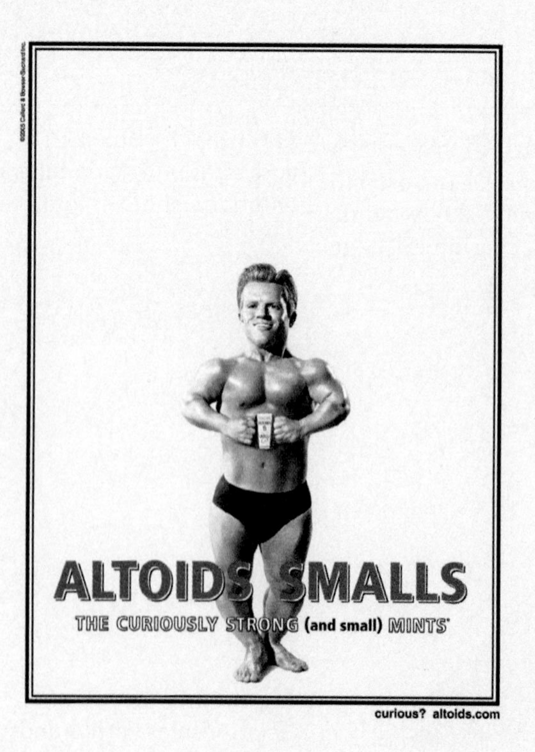

the personality of a brand on the basis of an assessment of overt or covert cues found in its advertising.

ALTOIDS SMALLS
THE CURIOUSLY STRONG (and small) MINTS
curious? altoids.com

McCann-Erickson researchers believe the strongest relationship that develops between a brand and the consumer is based on feelings or emotional attachments to the brand. Consumers develop *emotional bonds* with certain brands, which result in positive psychological movement toward them. The marketer's goal is to develop the greatest emotional linkage between its brand and the consumer. McCann-Erickson believes advertising can develop and enrich emotional bonding between consumers and brands. McCann and its subsidiary agencies use emotional bonding research to provide strategic input into the creative process and determine how well advertising is communicating with consumers. McCann-Erickson used emotional bonding research as the basis for the "Priceless" campaign for MasterCard International, which has been extremely successful. When the agency took over the account in the late '90s, MasterCard had become the third card in the consumer's wallet behind Visa and American Express. The challenge was to reposition the brand and create an emotional bond between consumers and MasterCard while retaining the brand's functional appeal. The idea behind the campaign is that good spenders use credit cards to acquire things that are important to them and enrich their daily lives. The creative execution involves showing a shopping list of items that could be purchased for a certain dollar amount and one key item that could not and thus was deemed "Priceless." The tagline "There are some things money can't buy. For everything else there's MasterCard," positions the card as the way to pay for everything that matters. An entire integrated marketing campaign has been built around the "Priceless" campaign theme that includes sponsorships with Major League Baseball, the National Hockey League, and the PGA golf tour. Contests and sweepstakes have also been part of the campaign. The campaign now runs in 80 countries and has won numerous creative awards. Exhibit 9-8 shows one of the print ads from the campaign.

Additional Types of Appeals

Not every ad fits neatly into the categories of rational or emotional appeals. For example, ads for some brands can be classified as **reminder advertising,** which has the objective of building brand awareness and/or keeping the brand name in front of consumers. Well-known brands and market leaders often use reminder advertising. For example, Altoids breath mints runs reminder ads to build national brand awareness and communicate its quirky "curiously strong" message to consumers (Exhibit 9-9). Products and services that have a seasonal pattern to their consumption also use reminder advertising, particularly around the appropriate period. For example, marketers of candy products often increase their media budgets and run reminder advertising around Halloween, Valentine's Day, Christmas, and Easter.

Advertisers introducing a new product often use **teaser advertising,** which is designed to build curiosity, interest, and/or excitement about a product or brand by talking about it but not actually showing it. Teasers, or *mystery ads* as they are sometimes called, are also used by marketers to draw attention to upcoming advertising campaigns and generate interest and publicity for them.

Teaser ads also are often used for new movies or TV shows and for major product launches. They are especially popular among automotive advertisers for introducing a new model or announcing significant changes in a vehicle. For example, Porsche used teaser ads to generate interest in and excitement for the Cayenne SUV when it was introduced to the U.S. market in 2002 (Exhibit 9-10). The ads used the theme "Cayenne: The next Porsche" and were part of an integrated campaign that included a website telling the story of the new Cayenne, from development through testing to its unveiling.[13]

Teaser campaigns can generate interest in a new product, but advertisers must be careful not to extend them too long or they will lose their effectiveness.[14] As one advertising executive says, "Contrary to what we think, consumers don't hold seminars about advertising. You have to give consumers enough information about the product in teaser ads to make them feel they're in on the joke."[15]

Many ads are not designed to sell a product or service but rather to enhance the image of the company or meet other corporate goals such as soliciting investment or recruiting employees. These are generally referred to as corporate image advertising and are discussed in detail in Chapter 17.

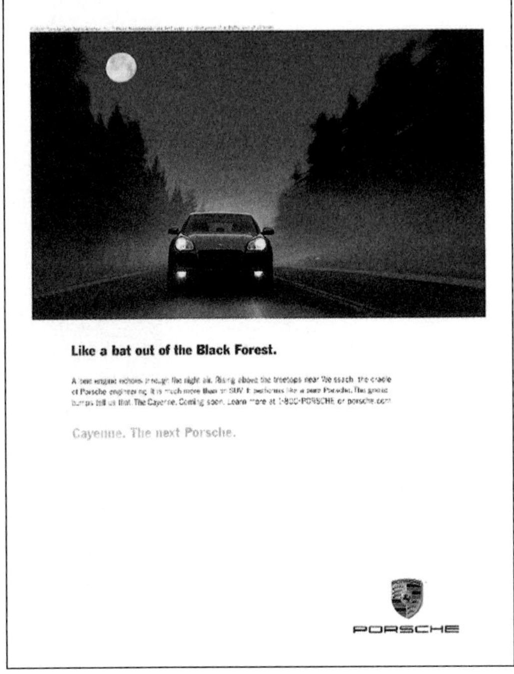

Like a bat out of the Black Forest.
Cayenne. The next Porsche.
PORSCHE

Exhibit 9-10 Porsche used teaser ads to create interest in the new Cayenne SUV

Advertising Execution

Once the specific advertising appeal that will be used as the basis for the advertising message has been determined, the creative specialist or team begins its execution. *Creative execution* is the way an advertising appeal is presented. While it is obviously important for an ad to have a meaningful appeal or message to communicate to the consumer, the manner in which the ad is executed is also important.

One of the best-known advocates of the importance of creative execution in advertising was William Bernbach, founder of the Doyle Dane Bernbach agency. In his famous book on the advertising industry, *Madison Avenue,* Martin Mayer notes Bernbach's reply to David Ogilvy's rule for copywriters that "what you say in advertising is more important than how you say it." Bernbach replied, "Execution can become content, it can be just as important as what you say. A sick guy can utter some words and nothing happens; a healthy vital guy says them and they rock the world."[16] Bernbach was one of the revolutionaries of his time who changed advertising creativity on a fundamental level by redefining how headlines and visuals were used, how art directors and copywriters worked together, and how advertising could be used to arouse feelings and emotions.

An advertising message can be presented or executed in numerous ways:

- Straight sell or factual message
- Scientific/technical evidence
- Demonstration
- Comparison
- Testimonial
- Slice of life
- Animation
- Personality symbol
- Imagery
- Dramatization
- Humor
- Combinations

We now examine these formats and considerations involved in their use.

Straight Sell or Factual Message

One of the most basic types of creative executions is the straight sell or factual message. This type of ad relies on a straightforward presentation of information concerning the product or service. This execution is often used with informational/rational appeals, where the focus of the message is the product or service and its specific attributes and/or benefits.

Straight-sell executions are commonly used in print ads. A picture of the product or service occupies part of the ad, and the factual copy takes up the rest of the space.

Exhibit 9-11 Hitachi uses a straight-sell execution style in this ad

They are also used in TV advertising, with an announcer generally delivering the sales message while the product/service is shown on the screen. Ads for high-involvement consumer products as well as industrial and other business-to-business products generally use this format. The ad for the Hitachi CineForm Series plasma TV, which is shown in Exhibit 9-11, is part of a campaign that uses an informative, straight-sell execution to communicate the product's features and benefits.

Scientific/Technical Evidence

In a variation of the straight sell, scientific or technical evidence is presented in the ad. Advertisers often cite technical information, results of scientific or laboratory studies, or endorsements by scientific bodies or agencies to support their advertising claims. For example, an endorsement from the American Council on Dental Therapeutics on how fluoride helps prevent cavities was the basis of the campaign that made Crest the leading brand on the market. The ad for Eagle One's NanoWax shown in Exhibit 9-12 uses this execution style to position the brand as the most technologically advanced car wax available.

Exhibit 9-12 This ad uses scientific evidence to promote Eagle One NanoWax

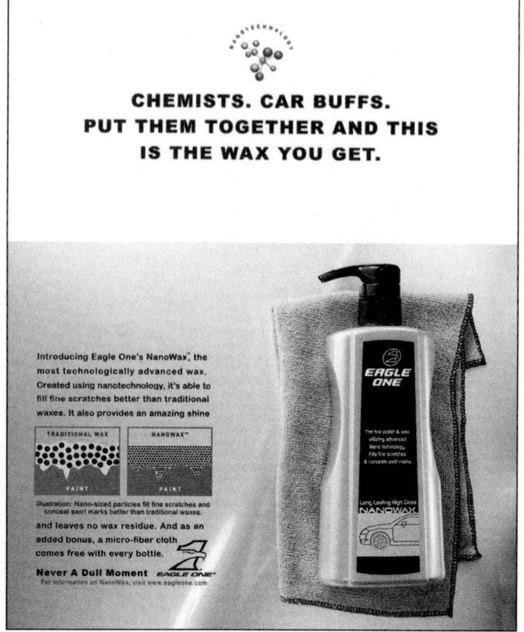

Demonstration

Demonstration advertising is designed to illustrate the key advantages of the product/service by showing it in actual use or in some staged situation. Demonstration executions can be very effective in convincing consumers of a product's utility or quality and of the benefits of owning or using the brand. TV is particularly well suited for demonstration executions, since the benefits or advantages of the product can be shown right on the screen. Although perhaps a little less dramatic than TV, demonstration ads can also work in print. The Mentadent toothpaste ad shown in Exhibit 9-13 uses this technique to demonstrate how the brand's Liquid Calcium technology replenishes the surface enamel to whiten teeth and guard against stains.

Comparison

Brand comparisons can also be the basis for the advertising execution. The comparison execution approach is increasingly popular among advertisers, since it offers a direct way of communicating a brand's particular advantage over its competitors or positioning a new or lesser-known brand with industry leaders. Comparison executions are often used to execute competitive advantage appeals, as discussed earlier.

Testimonial

Many advertisers prefer to have their messages presented by way of a testimonial, where a person praises the product or service on the basis of his or her personal experience with it. Testimonial executions can have ordinary satisfied customers discuss their own experiences with the brand and the benefits of using it. This approach can be very effective when the person delivering the testimonial is someone with whom the target audience can identify or who has an interesting story to tell. The testimonial must be based on actual use of the product or service to avoid legal problems, and the spokesperson must be credible.

Apple Computer made effective use of testimonials as part of its "Switch" campaign, which features computer users from various walks of life discussing why they switched from Windows-based machines to Macintoshes (Exhibit 9-14). The people giving the testimonials in the ads are from various walks of life, including a writer, publisher, programmer, and Windows network administrator, and were chosen from a group of some 10,000 former PC users who wrote the company to proclaim their love for Apple. As part of the campaign Apple created a website that includes testimonials from PC users who switched to Macs and provides more detailed information for those considering switching.

A related execution technique is the *endorsement,* where a well-known or respected individual such as a celebrity or expert in the product or service area speaks on behalf of the company or the brand. When endorsers promote a company or its products or services, the message is not necessarily based on their personal experiences.

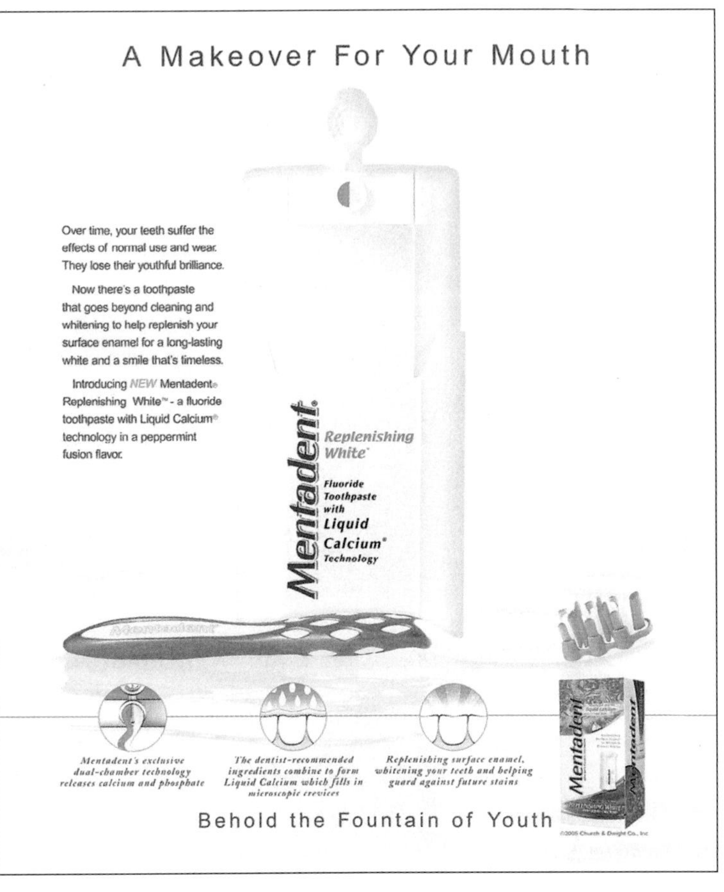

Exhibit 9-13 This ad uses a demonstration execution to explain the benefits of Mentadent

Slice of Life A widely used advertising format, particularly for packaged-goods products, is the slice-of-life execution, which is generally based on a problem/solution approach. This type of ad portrays a problem or conflict that consumers might face in their daily lives. The ad then shows how the advertiser's product or service can resolve the problem.

Slice-of-life executions are often criticized for being unrealistic and irritating to watch because they are often used to remind consumers of problems of a personal nature, such as dandruff, bad breath, body odor, and laundry problems. Often these ads come across as contrived, silly, phony, or even offensive to consumers. However, many advertisers still prefer this style because they believe it is effective at presenting a situation to which most consumers can relate and at registering the product feature or benefit that helps sell the brand. For many years, Procter & Gamble was known for its reliance on slice-of-life advertising executions as many of the company's commercials used either the slice-of-life or testimonial format. However, P&G has begun using humor, animation, and other less traditional execution styles and now relies less on slice-of-life or testimonials.[17]

Slice-of-life or problem/solution execution approaches are not limited to consumer-product advertising. Many business-to-business marketers use this type of advertising to demonstrate how their products and services can be used to solve business problems.[18]

Some business-to-business marketers use a variation of the problem/solution execution that is sometimes referred to as *slice-of-death advertising.*[19] This execution style is used in conjunction with a fear appeal, as the focus is on the negative consequences that result when businesspeople make the

Exhibit 9-14 Apple's "Switch" campaign makes effective use of testimonials

"My PC wasn't Plug-n-Play.
It was Plug-n-Get-Mad."
apple.com/switch

Exhibit 9-15 Listerine uses a slice-of-life execution to introduce a new flavor

wrong decision in choosing a supplier or service provider. For example, FedEx has used this type of advertising for nearly three decades through humorous, but to-the-point, commercials that show what might happen when important packages and documents aren't received on time.

Execution is critical in using the technique effectively as these ads are designed to be dramatizations of a supposedly real-life situation that consumers might encounter. Getting viewers to identify with the situation and/or characters depicted in the ad can be very challenging. Since the success of slice-of-life ads often depends on how well the actors come across and execute their roles, professional actors are often used to achieve credibility and to ensure that the commercial is of high quality. Smaller companies and local advertisers often do not have ad budgets large enough to hire the talent or to pay for the production quality needed to effectively create slice-of-life spots. Thus, this execution technique is more likely to be used by companies with ad budgets that are large enough to fund the use of professional talent and production of quality commercials.

Many marketers like to use the slice-of-life genre as they believe it can be an effective way of addressing a problem or issue and offering a solution. For example, Listerine used a slice-of-life commercial effectively to introduce a new Natural Citrus flavor of the popular mouthwash.[20] The spot was designed to address the problem that some consumers have with the intense taste of the original flavor of the product. The spot opens with a mother returning home from the store with two surprises: danish and Listerine. However, when her husband and two kids see the mouthwash they run and hide. The mother then tells them it is Natural Citrus Listerine, which tastes less intense. The humorous spot ends with the father coming out of a kitchen cupboard and pots and pans dangling as one of the boys climbs down from the top of the kitchen island as the voiceover says, "You can handle it. Germs can't" (see Exhibit 9-15).

Animation

An advertising execution approach that has become popular in recent years is animation. With this technique, animated scenes are drawn by artists or created on the computer, and cartoons, puppets, or other types of fictional characters may be used. Cartoon animation is especially popular for commercials targeted at children. Animated cartoon characters have also been used in many campaigns including Green Giant vegetables (the Jolly Green Giant) and Keebler cookies (the Keebler elves). Another successful example of animation execution was the ad campaign developed for the California Raisin Advisory Board. A technique called Claymation was used to create the dancing raisin characters used in these ads.

The use of animation as an execution style may increase as creative specialists discover the possibilities of computer-generated graphics and other technological innovations.[21]

Some advertisers have begun using ads that mix animation with real people. Nike has used this technique to develop several creative, entertaining commercials. One featured Michael Jordan and Bugs Bunny trouncing a foursome of bullies on the basketball court and was the inspiration for the movie *Space Jam*. The agency for Star-Kist tuna also used this technique when the company brought its animated Charlie the Tuna character out of retirement to appear in commercials for the brand. While the old "Sorry Charlie" commercials portrayed Charlie as not being good enough for Star-Kist, the new ads used him in a different way, such as giving a courtroom address arguing that not all tunas are created equal and asking for jurors to judge for themselves (see Exhibit 9-16).

Exhibit 9-16 This Star-Kist commercial mixes an animated character with real people.

Personality Symbol Another type of advertising execution involves developing a central character or personality symbol that can deliver the advertising message and with which the product or service can be identified. This character can be a person, like Mr. Whipple, who asked shoppers, "Please don't squeeze the Charmin," or the Maytag repairman, who sits anxiously by the phone but is never needed because the company's appliances are so reliable.

Personality figures can also be built around animated characters and animals. As discussed in Chapter 5, personality symbols such as Morris the cat, Tony the tiger, and Charlie the tuna have been used for decades to promote 9-Lives cat food, Kellogg's Frosted Flakes, and Star-Kist tuna, respectively. Other popular personality symbols that have been used more recently include the Energizer bunny, Geico insurance's gecko, and Frank and Louie—the talking lizards who appeared in ads for Budweiser beer. IMC Perspective 9-2 discusses how advertising featuring the Aflac duck has been very successful in raising awareness, as well as sales, for the supplemental insurance company over the past five years.

Imagery You have probably noticed that some ads contain little or no information about the brand or company and are almost totally visual. These advertisements use imagery executions whereby the ad consists primarily of visual elements such as pictures, illustrations, and/or symbols rather than information. An imagery execution is used when the goal is to encourage consumers to associate the brand with the symbols, characters, and/or situation shown in the ad. Imagery ads are often the basis for emotional appeals that are used to advertise products or services where differentiation based on physical characteristics is difficult, such as soft drinks, liquor, designer clothing, and cosmetics. However, image is important for all types of products and services as marketers want the target audience to hold a favorable set of psychosocial associations for their company or brand.

An imagery execution may be based on *usage imagery* by showing how a brand is used or performs and the situation in which it is used. For example, advertising for trucks and SUVs often shows the vehicles navigating tough terrain or in challenging situations such as towing a heavy load. Notice how the clever Jeep ad shown in Exhibit 9-17 uses only the image of the vehicle on the bottom of a snowboard to associate the vehicle with the outdoors and adventuresome activities. This type of execution can also be based on *user imagery* where the focus is on the type of person who uses the brand. Ads for cosmetics often use very attractive models in the hope of getting consumers to associate his or her physical

Exhibit 9-17 This ad associates the Jeep Wrangler with images of the outdoors and adventure

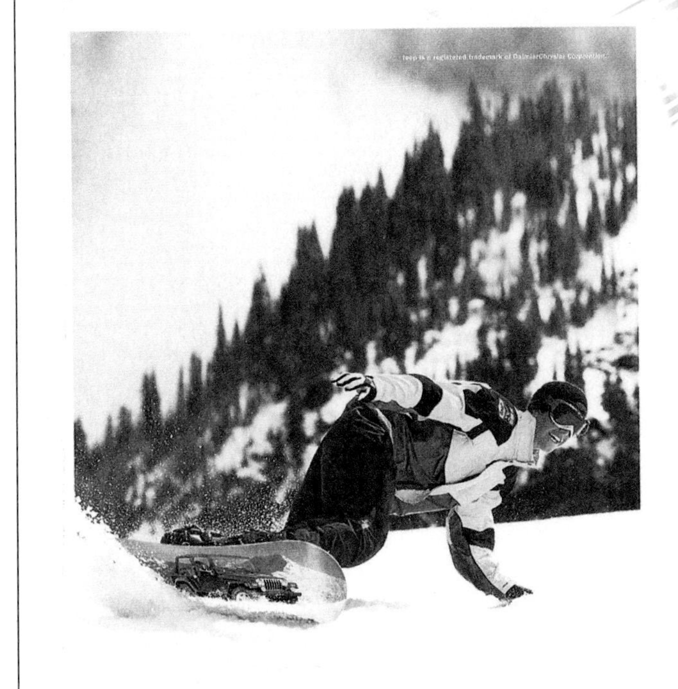

IMC PERSPECTIVE 9-2

A Sassy Duck Keeps Sales Quackin' for Aflac

If it looks like a duck, walks like a duck, and talks like a duck it must be either: (a) a duck or (b) the central character in one of the most effective advertising campaigns in recent years. From the perspective of Aflac (American Family Life Assurance Company of Columbus), the answer is *b* as the company has developed a memorable advertising campaign around the idea of showing a Pekin duck belting out his signature Aflac quack as people talk about insurance. Aflac is the number one provider of guaranteed renewable insurance in the United States. The company's various insurance plans, which supplement primary health and life coverage, are sold through agents who work with customers in putting together a program that best meets their needs. However, advertising plays an important role in making consumers aware of the company and interested in learning more about its insurance plans. A clever ad campaign based on humorous commercials featuring the Aflac duck has helped make the company one of the most recognizable names in the insurance business.

The campaign was born in late 1999 when Aflac chairman and CEO Daniel Amos and his advertising committee gave their agency, the Kaplan Thaler Group, the charge of creating a campaign that differentiated its advertising from other insurers, while increasing the company's name recognition. The company was facing a competitive situation in which a large number of insurance and financial services ads were competing for viewers' attention. Also, because the company name was often mispronounced, Aflac wanted to create a mnemonic device that would reinforce name awareness and recall.

A few days before they were to present campaign ideas to the company, the agency's creative team had hit a wall. However, during a lunch break, creative director Eric David spent time walking around the block saying the Aflac brand name over and over, until he realized he was quacking like a duck. David recognized that he was on to something and presented the idea to his creative partner Tom Amico, who agreed that the acronym sounded similar to a quacking duck. The pair also agreed that using a duck in the advertising would be a good way to get people to remember the company name. From there they created a humorous campaign based around the theme of a white, sassy Pekin duck with a bright yellow beak who waddles into a variety of odd situations and belts out his signature "*Aaa-flaaack*" quack as people talk about insurance.

It only took David and Amico a short time to develop the idea for the first Aflac television commercial, which was called "Park Bench," starring the duck. The spot features two businessmen having lunch in a park when a bicyclist crashes behind them, and their conversation turns to injury and missing work and the need for supplemental insurance. One of the men explains supplemental insurance to the other but cannot remember the name of the company that provides it. A nearby frustrated duck keeps quacking the Aflac name but is ignored by the man as he struggles to remember the name. The spot first aired on December 31, 1999, and within six days Aflac had received more hits on its website than it had in the entire previous year.

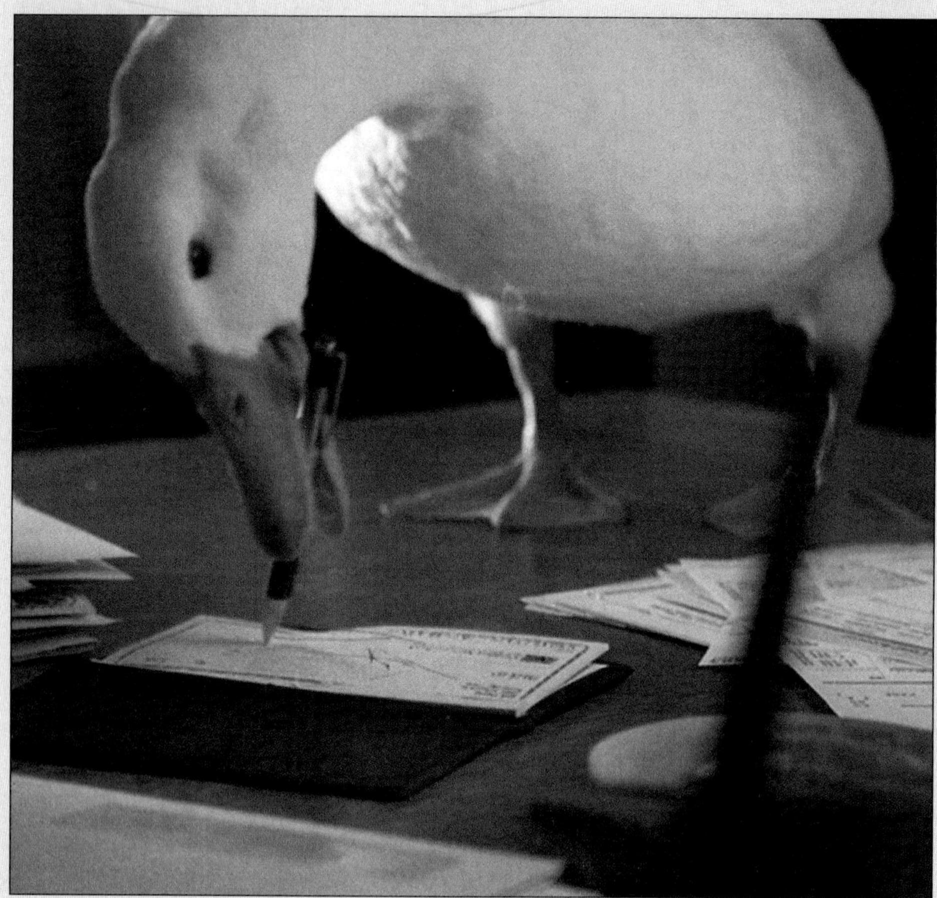

Since the campaign featuring the duck began, Aflac has gone from a virtually unknown company to one of the most recognized brands of insurance. The company's name awareness has skyrocketed from 12 percent to over 90 percent, and the campaign has helped to generate sales leads for Aflac agents as well as help the company to recruit new agents. However, the campaign has done more than boost awareness as Aflac's sales have increased by nearly 30 percent over the past five years. More than 20 commercials have been created for the campaign, some of which have featured celebrities such as Yogi Berra, Chevy Chase, the Amazing Kreskin, and Donald Trump's wife Melania.

The duck has also become a very popular personality symbol. The company receives numerous e-mails and telephone calls about the duck and has even begun selling a variety of duck gear items on its website (www.aflac.com), including a stuffed version of the duck, which quacks "Aflac" when squeezed. The Aflac duck has become part of popular culture and has been featured on the CNBC network, *The Tonight Show with Jay Leno, Saturday Night Live,*

Lemony Snicket's A Series of Unfortunate Events, and more. In 2004, the duck edged out Ronald McDonald to join the Madison Avenue Advertising Walk of Fame as one of America's favorite advertising icons. The publicity has had a synergistic effect with the ad campaign and helped augment awareness and interest in the company. Aflac plans to keep using the iconic duck and has even integrated him into the company's redesigned corporate logo to take advantage of the tremendous equity that has resulted from the ads and other elements of the IMC campaign.

Sources: Suzanne Vranica, "Aflac Partly Muzzles Iconic Duck," *The Wall Street Journal,* December 2, 2004, p. B8; Kathleen Sampey, "Melania Trump to Make Aflac Ad Debut," *Adweek.com,* April 26, 2005; "Big Ideas for Ducks and Their Keepers," *Adweek.com,* October 13, 2003; Theresa Howard, "Aflac Duck Gives Wings to Insurer's Name Recognition," *USA Today,* May 17, 2001, p. B9.

attractiveness with the brand (see Exhibit 9-18). Most Nike ads have very little copy and rely primarily on images of athletes achieving success by using the company's products. Image executions rely heavily on visual elements such as photography, color, tonality, and design to communicate the desired image to the consumer. Marketers who rely on image executions have to be sure that the usage or user imagery with which they associate their brand evokes the right feelings and reactions from the target audience.

Dramatization Another execution technique particularly well suited to television is dramatization, where the focus is on telling a short story with the product or service as the star. Dramatization is somewhat akin to slice-of-life execution in that it often relies on the problem/solution approach, but it uses more excitement and suspense in telling the story. The purpose of using drama is to draw the viewer into the action it portrays. Advocates of drama note that when it is successful, the audience becomes lost in the story and experiences the concerns and feelings of the characters.[22] According to Sandra Moriarty, there are five basic steps in a dramatic commercial:

> First is exposition, where the stage is set for the upcoming action. Next comes conflict, which is a technique for identifying the problem. The middle of the dramatic form is a period of rising action where the story builds, the conflict intensifies, the suspense thickens. The fourth step is the climax, where the problem is solved. The last part of a drama is the resolution, where the wrap-up is presented. In advertising that includes product identification and call to action.[23]

The real challenge facing the creative team is how to encompass all these elements in a 30-second commercial. A good example of the dramatization execution technique is the ad for Zerex antifreeze in Exhibit 9-19, which shows a woman's sense of relief when her car starts at the airport on a cold winter night. The ad concludes with a strong identification slogan, "The temperature never drops below Zerex," that connects the brand name to its product benefit.

Humor Like comparisons, humor was discussed in Chapter 6 as a type of advertising appeal, but this technique can also be used as a way of presenting other advertising appeals. Humorous executions are particularly well suited to television or radio, although some print ads attempt to use this style. The pros and cons of using humor as an executional technique are similar to those associated with its use as an advertising appeal.

Exhibit 9-18 This bebe ad uses an attractive model to create a favorable image for the brand

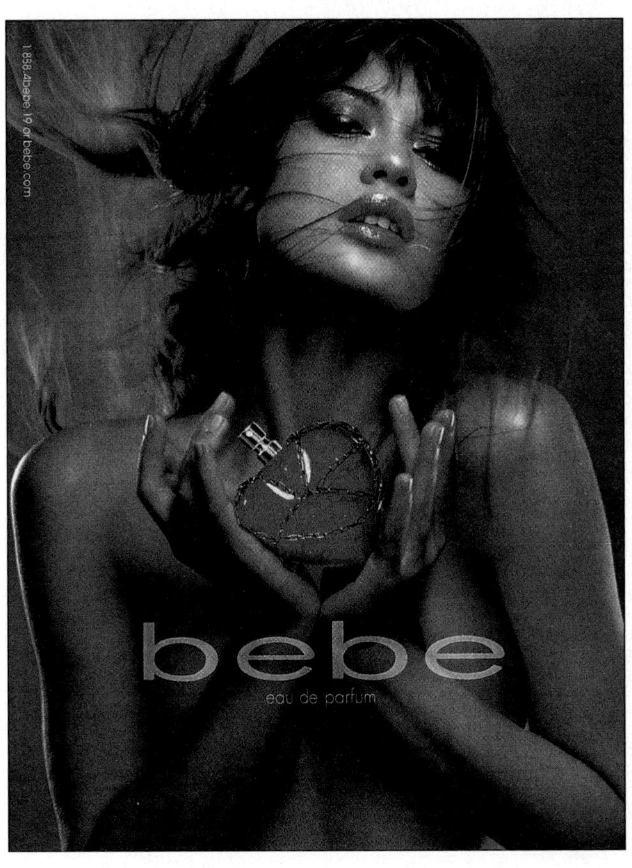

Combinations Many of the execution techniques can be combined to present the advertising message. For example, animation is often used to create personality symbols or present a fantasy. Slice-of-life ads are often used to demonstrate a product or service. Comparisons are sometimes made using a humorous approach. FedEx uses humorous executions of the slice-of-death genre depicting businesspeople experiencing dire consequences when they use another delivery service and an important document doesn't arrive on time. It is the responsibility of the creative specialist(s) to determine whether more than one execution style should be used in creating the ad.

Creative Tactics

Our discussion thus far has focused on the development of creative strategy and various appeals and execution styles that can be used for the advertising message.

Once the creative approach, type of appeal, and execution style have been determined, attention turns to creating the actual advertisement. The design and production of advertising messages involve a number of activities, among them writing copy, developing illustrations and other visual elements of the ad, and bringing all of the pieces together to create an effective message. In this section, we examine the verbal and visual elements of an ad and discuss tactical considerations in creating print ads and TV commercials.

Creative Tactics for Print Advertising

The basic components of a print ad are the headline, the body copy, the visual or illustrations, and the layout (the way they all fit together). The headline and body copy portions of the ad are the responsibility of the copywriters; artists, often working under the direction of an art director, are responsible for the visual presentation. Art directors also work with the copywriters to develop a layout, or arrangement of the various components of the ad: headlines, subheads, body copy, illustrations, captions, logos, and the like. We briefly examine the three components of a print ad and how they are coordinated.

Exhibit 9-19 This ZEREX ad uses a dramatization execution

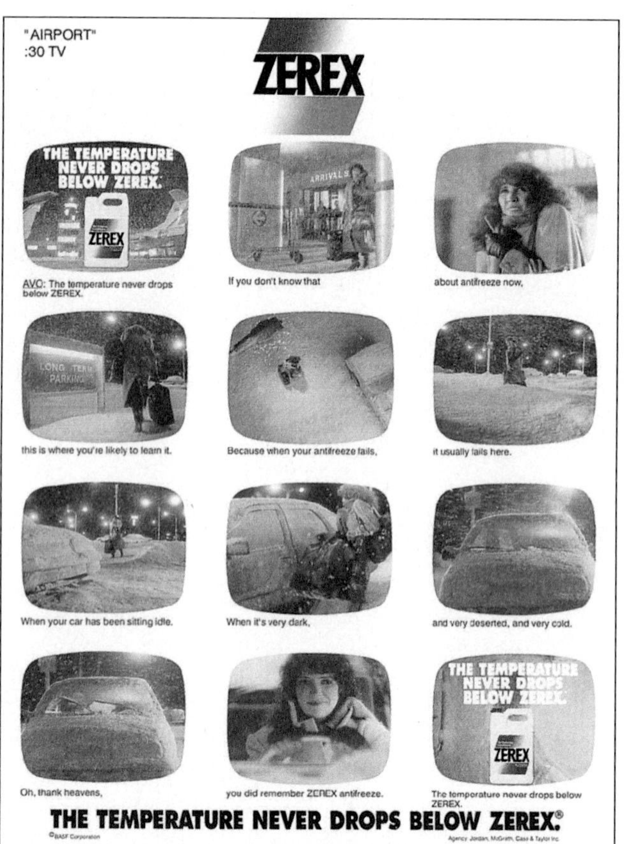

Headlines The **headline** is the words in the leading position of the ad—the words that will be read first or are positioned to draw the most attention.[24] Headlines are usually set in larger type and are often set apart from the body copy or text portion of the ad to give them prominence. Most advertising people consider the headline the most important part of a print ad.

The most important function of a headline is attracting readers' attention and interesting them in the rest of the message. While the visual portion of an ad is obviously important, the headline often shoulders most of the responsibility of attracting readers' attention. Research has shown the headline is generally the first thing people look at in a print ad, followed by the illustration. Only 20 percent of readers go beyond the headline and read the body copy.[25] So in addition to attracting attention, the headline must give the reader good reason to read the copy portion of the ad, which contains more detailed and persuasive information about the product or service. To do this, the headline must put forth the main theme, appeal, or proposition of the ad in a few words. Some print ads contain little if any body copy, so the headline must work with the illustration to communicate the entire advertising message.

Headlines also perform a segmentation function by engaging the attention and interest of consumers who are most likely to buy a particular product or service. Advertisers begin the segmentation process by choosing to advertise in certain types of publications (e.g., a travel, general-interest, or fashion magazine). An effective headline goes even further in selecting good prospects for the product by addressing their specific needs, wants, or interests. For example, the headline in the ad for Dell's Latitude computer shown in Exhibit 9-20 catches the attention of businesspeople who are interested in a notebook computer with excellent performance and long battery life.

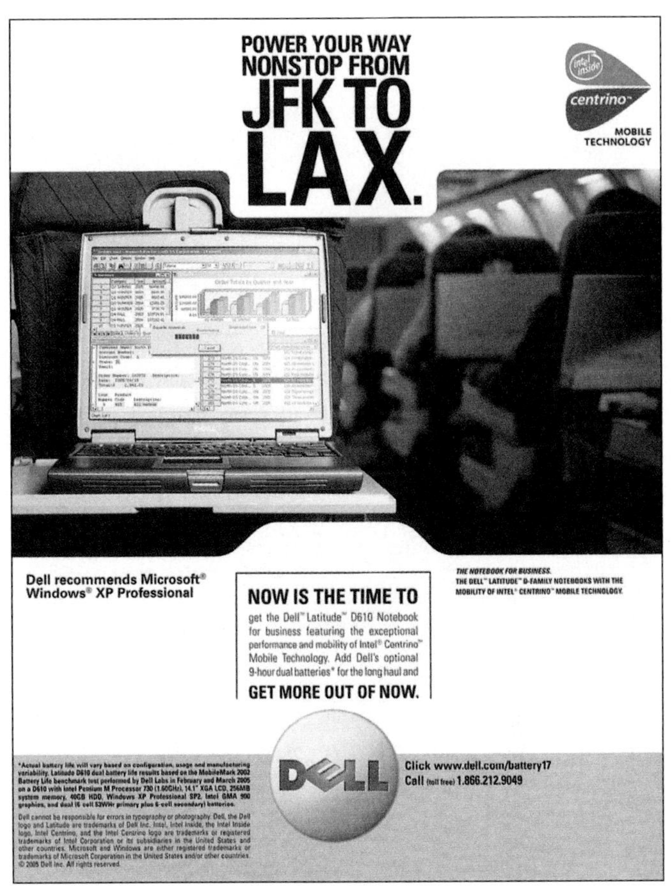

Exhibit 9-20 The headline of this ad catches the attention of business travelers

Types of Headlines There are numerous headline possibilities. The type used depends on several factors, including the creative strategy, the particular advertising situation (e.g., product type, media vehicle(s) being used, timeliness), and its relationship to other components of the ad, such as the illustration or body copy. Headlines can be categorized as direct and indirect. **Direct headlines** are straightforward and informative in terms of the message they are presenting and the target audience they are directed toward. Common types of direct headlines include those offering a specific benefit, making a promise, or announcing a reason the reader should be interested in the product or service.

Indirect headlines are not straightforward about identifying the product or service or getting to the point. But they are often more effective at attracting readers' attention and interest because they provoke curiosity and lure readers into the body copy to learn an answer or get an explanation. Techniques for writing indirect headlines include using questions, provocations, how-to statements, and challenges.

Indirect headlines rely on their ability to generate curiosity or intrigue so as to motivate readers to become involved with the ad and read the body copy to find out the point of the message. This can be risky if the headline is not provocative enough to get the readers' interest. Advertisers deal with this problem by using a visual appeal that helps attract attention and offers another reason for reading more of the message. For example, the ad for the Lexus GS sports sedan shown in Exhibit 9-21 uses a question as the headline that invites consumers to read the copy to learn more about the features of the car and decide how to categorize it. The visual portion of the ad supports the positioning theme by showing the GS 430 being driven on a windy road.

Subheads While many ads have only one headline, it is also common to see print ads containing the main head and one or more secondary heads, or **subheads.** Subheads are usually smaller than the main headline but larger than the body copy. They may appear above or below the main headline or within the body copy. The Cambridge SoundWorks ad shown in Exhibit 9-22 uses subheads within the body copy.

Subheads are often used to enhance the readability of the message by breaking up large amounts of body copy and highlighting key sales points. Their content reinforces the headline and advertising slogan or theme.

Body Copy

The main text portion of a print ad is referred to as the **body copy** (or sometimes just *copy*). While the body copy is usually the heart of the advertising message, getting the target audience to read it is often difficult. The copywriter faces a dilemma: The body copy must be long enough to communicate the advertiser's message yet short enough to hold readers' interest.

Body copy content often flows from the points made in the headline or various subheads, but the specific content depends on the type of advertising appeal and/or

Exhibit 9-21 This ad uses a question-style headline and strong visual image that motivate consumers to read the copy

Exhibit 9-22 This ad uses subheads to make the copy easier to read

execution style being used. For example, straight-sell copy that presents relevant information, product features and benefits, or competitive advantages is often used with the various types of rational appeals discussed earlier in the chapter. Emotional appeals often use narrative copy that tells a story or provides an interesting account of a problem or situation involving the product.

Advertising body copy can be written to go along with various types of creative appeals and executions—comparisons, price appeals, demonstrations, humor, dramatizations, and the like. Copywriters choose a copy style that is appropriate for the type of appeal being used and effective for executing the creative strategy and communicating the advertiser's message to the target audience.

Visual Elements

The third major component of a print ad is the visual element. The illustration is often a dominant part of a print ad and plays an important role in determining its effectiveness. The visual portion of an ad must attract attention, communicate an idea or image, and work in a synergistic fashion with the headline and body copy to produce an effective message. In some print ads, the visual portion of the ad is essentially the message and thus must convey a strong and meaningful image. For example, the award-winning ad for Sims Snowboards shown in Exhibit 9-23 uses a powerful visual image. In a scene reminiscent of the protestor blocking military vehicles in Beijing's Tiananmen Square during the 1989 student uprising, a snowboarder stands in the path of snow-grooming machines (which pack the snow, to the distress of snowboarders). The single line of copy, "In a courageous act of solidarity, a lone snowboarder stands up for freedom," reinforces the message presented by the visual image.

Many decisions have to be made regarding the visual portion of the ad: what identification marks should be included (brand name, company or trade name, trademarks, logos); whether to use photos or hand-drawn or painted illustrations; what colors to use (or even perhaps black and white or just a splash of color); and what the focus of the visual should be.

Exhibit 9-23 This ad for Sims Snowboards uses a strong visual image and a layout that resembles a newspaper page

Layout While each individual component of a print ad is important, the key factor is how these elements are blended into a finished advertisement. A **layout** is the physical arrangement of the various parts of the ad, including the headline, subheads, body copy, illustrations, and any identifying marks. The layout shows where each part of the ad will be placed and gives guidelines to the people working on the ad. For example, the layout helps the copywriter determine how much space he or she has to work with and how much copy should be written. The layout can also guide the art director in determining the size and type of photos. In the ad for Sims Snowboards shown in Exhibit 9-23, the layout is designed to make the ad look like it was reprinted from a newspaper page. Notice how this theme is carried through in the copy, which reads like a newspaper photo caption and ends with "Story on 2C." Layouts are often done in rough form and presented to the client so that the advertiser can visualize what the ad will look like before giving preliminary approval. The agency should get client approval of the layout before moving on to the more costly stages of print production.

Creative Tactics for Television

As consumers, we see so many TV commercials that it's easy to take for granted the time, effort, and money that go into making them. Creating and producing commercials that break through the clutter on TV and communicate effectively is a detailed, expensive process. On a cost-per-minute basis, commercials are the most expensive productions seen on television.

TV is a unique and powerful advertising medium because it contains the elements of sight, sound, and motion, which can be combined to create a variety of advertising appeals and executions. Unlike print, the viewer does not control the rate at which the message is presented, so there is no opportunity to review points of interest or reread things that are not communicated clearly. As with any form of advertising, one of the first goals in creating TV commercials is to get the viewers' attention and then maintain it. This can be particularly challenging because of the clutter and because people often view TV commercials while doing other things (reading a book or magazine, talking).

Like print ads, TV commercials have several components. The video and audio must work together to create the right impact and communicate the advertiser's message.

Video The video elements of a commercial are what is seen on the TV screen. The visual portion generally dominates the commercial, so it must attract viewers' attention and communicate an idea, message, and/or image. A number of visual elements may have to be coordinated to produce a successful ad. Decisions have to be made regarding the product, the presenter, action sequences, demonstrations, and the like, as well as the setting(s), the talent or characters who will appear in the commercial, and such other factors as lighting, graphics, color, and identifying symbols.

Audio The audio portion of a commercial includes voices, music, and sound effects. Voices are used in different ways in commercials. They may be heard through the direct presentation of a spokesperson or as a conversation among various people appearing in the commercial. A common method for presenting the audio portion of a commercial is through a **voiceover,** where the message is delivered or action on the screen is narrated or described by an announcer who is not visible. A trend among major advertisers is to have celebrities with distinctive voices do the voiceovers for their commercials.[26] Actor Richard Dreyfuss does the voiceovers in some Honda commercials, Jeff Goldblum does Apple Computers, and mega-stars such as Julia Roberts and Robert Redford have done ads for America Online and United Airlines, respectively.

Music is also an important part of many TV commercials and can play a variety of roles.[27] In many commercials, the music provides a pleasant background or helps create the appropriate mood. Advertisers often use **needledrop,** which Linda Scott describes as follows:

> Needledrop is an occupational term common to advertising agencies and the music industry. It refers to music that is prefabricated, multipurpose, and highly conventional. It is, in that sense, the musical equivalent of stock photos, clip art, or canned copy. Needledrop is an inexpensive substitute for original music; paid for on a one-time basis, it is dropped into a commercial or film when a particular normative effect is desired.[28]

In some commercials, music is much more central to the advertising message. It can be used to get attention, break through the advertising clutter, communicate a key selling point, help establish an image or position, or add feeling.[29] For example, music can work through a classical conditioning process to create positive emotions that become associated with the advertised product or service. Music can also create a positive mood that makes the consumer more receptive toward the advertising message.[30]

Because music can play such an important role in the creative strategy, many companies have paid large sums for the rights to use popular songs in their commercials. There are two kinds of works to which companies negotiate rights when licensing music for use in commercials. The *musical composition* includes the music notes and the words, while the *master recording* includes the voice(s) of the original artist.[31] The latter is usually much more expensive to buy, so advertisers will often negotiate for the rights to use the music and have it performed by someone with a similar voice. Rights to music can be held by various parties, such as the original artist, the artist's estate, or a music publishing company. For example, the rights to songs done by the late reggae star Bob Marley are held by his estate, while the rights to songs by the Beatles are controlled by a music publishing company. Nortel Networks licensed the composition rights to use the classic Beatles song "Come Together" (which it had performed by a different artist) and used the music as the central theme in a global advertising campaign.[32] While it is less expensive to rerecord the music, some advertisers are willing to pay millions of dollars to use the voices of the original artists in their commercials. IMC Perspective 9-3 discusses how marketers also have made songs an important part of their commercials in recent years and are starting to make their names part of the songs.

Music can be used as part of a commercial or as the basis for it. The Coca-Cola Co. recently remade its famous 1971 musical ad known as "Hilltop" (for its Italian backdrop), which featured a large international cast of young people singing "I'd like to teach the world to sing in perfect harmony/ I'd like to buy the world a Coke and keep it company." The new version is called "Chilltop" and was shot on the roof of a building in Philadelphia. Hip-hop artist G. Love and a cast of young people gather on the rooftop at sunset to sing a new set of lyrics to the familiar tune, which draws on the tagline for a campaign used to introduce Coke Zero. The updated lyrics are, "I'd like to teach the world to chill, take time to stop and smile/I'd like to buy the world a Coke and chill with it awhile." The commercial is part of a campaign for the new product aimed at the "go-go" lifestyle of 18- to 24-year-olds and positions Coke Zero as the perfect beverage to drink to take a moment and recenter yourself.[33]

Another important musical element in both TV and radio commercials is **jingles,** catchy songs about a product or service that usually carry the advertising theme and a simple message. For example, Doublemint gum has used the well-known "Double your pleasure, double your fun with Doublemint, Doublemint gum" for years. The jingle is very memorable and serves as a good reminder of the product's minty flavor. Oscar Mayer has used the popular jingles for some of its products, such as the bologna song ("My bologna has a first name/ It's O-S-C-A-R") and the Oscar Mayer wiener song ("I'd love to be an Oscar Mayer wiener"), as the basis of integrated marketing programs. The company's fleet of wienermobiles travel the country as part of the Oscar Mayer Talent Search, where local auditions are held in search of children who will continue the 30-year tradition of singing the catchy bologna and wiener jingles.[34]

In some commercials, jingles are used more as a form of product identification and appear at the end of the message. Jingles are often composed by companies that specialize in writing commercial music for advertising. These jingle houses work with the creative team to determine the role music will play in the commercial and the message that needs to be communicated. Figure 9-3 shows the 10 jingles selected by *Advertising Age* as the best of the past century.

While the use of jingles dates back to the 1950s, they are used less frequently today than in the past as many advertisers are using current and classic pop songs in their ads. The director of music at the Leo Burnett agency notes that companies using jingles must be careful, noting that "we are living in a world of iPods, MTV, and video and jingles sound corny."[35] However, despite these concerns, many marketers still use jingles. For example, Procter & Gamble (P&G) recently created a new jingle to tout the virtues of Charmin's new megaroll toilet paper. The company is also taking its jingle beyond radio and TV commercials by embedding sound chips in store shelves, which play the song when consumers walk by, and using it at events and promotions. A P&G brand manager has stated that the company believes that jingles still work, noting that "if they are humming it, they are buying it."[36] Jingles are also still commonplace in the advertising done by local advertisers as these companies view them as an effective way to keep their company name and/or advertising in the minds of their customers and prospects.

Planning and Production of TV Commercials

One of the first decisions that has to be made in planning a TV commercial is the type of appeal and execution style that will be used. Television is well suited to both rational and emotional advertising appeals or combinations of the two. Various execution styles used with rational appeals, such as a straight sell or announcement, demonstration, testimonial, or comparison, work well on TV.

Advertisers recognize that they need to do more than talk about, demonstrate, or compare their products or services. Their commercials have to break through the clutter and grab viewers' attention; they must often appeal to emotional, as well as rational, buying motives. Television is essentially an entertainment medium, and many advertisers recognize that their commercials are most successful when they entertain as well as inform. Many of the most popular advertising campaigns are characterized by commercials with strong entertainment value, like the humorous "Got milk" ads, musical spots for the Gap, the many stylish and engaging Nike ads, and Volkswagen's "Drivers Wanted" campaign, which explores drivers' life experiences with their VWs.[37]

Figure 9-3 Top 10 Jingles of the Century

Jingle	Company or Brand
1. You deserve a break today	McDonald's
2. Be all that you can be	U.S. Army
3. Pepsi Cola Hits the Spot	Pepsi Cola
4. M'm, M'm Good	Campbell's Soup
5. See the USA in your Chevrolet	Chevrolet
6. I wish I was an Oscar Mayer Wiener	Oscar Mayer
7. Double your pleasure, double your fun	Wrigley's Doublemint gum
8. Winston tastes good like a cigarette should	Winston
9. It's the Real Thing	Coca-Cola
10. Brylcreem—A little dab'll do ya	Brylcreem

IMC PERSPECTIVE 9-3

Advertisers Marry Music with Their Products, and Vice Versa

While music has always been an important part of television commercials, more and more advertisers are using popular songs in their ads that resonate with consumers and help keep their products and services top-of-mind. Songs from artists and rock groups such as Madonna, Sting, Bob Seger, Led Zeppelin, the Rolling Stones, and the Beatles serve as the backdrop in commercials for just about everything, including cars, beer, fast food, computers, and insurance. Nike pioneered the commercial use of music from major artists in 1987 when it featured the original recording of the classic Beatles' song "Revolution" in ads for its shoes. Cadillac struck a multi-million-dollar deal with Led Zeppelin to use the legendary band's song "Rock and Roll" for the relaunch of its"Break Through" advertising campaign in 2002.

There are a number of reasons why companies are paying large sums of money to use popular songs in their commercials. Music plays an important role in setting the tone for a commercial and can be used for entertainment, to target an audience, and/or to create an emotional or nostalgic connection with the viewer. When advertisers marry the right song with the right product, they can strike a responsive chord with consumers, which gets them to attend to the commercial and can help differentiate the company or brand. For example, ads for Chevrolet trucks began using Bob Seger's hit song "Like a Rock" in 1991, and the agency made it the tagline for one of the most successful and long-lasting campaigns in automotive advertising. The manager for Chevy trucks says, "It is not just a marketing campaign. It captures the soul of the brand. It is how to build a truck, it is how to run a company."

Other companies have also used the lyrics of a song to help deliver their advertising message. Microsoft paid a reported $12 million to the Rolling Stones for the use of its song "Start Me Up," which was featured in ads for its Windows 95 operating system. Six years later the company used the song from another megastar when it tapped Madonna for a multimillion deal to use the Material Girl's Grammy Award–winning song "Ray of Light" to introduce its new XP software. The creative director at McCann-Erickson, in San Francisco, which created the ad campaign, noted that the lyrics of the song were exactly what the agency was looking for to use in commercials for a technology product like the XP software. The upbeat electric song uses phrases like "faster than the speeding light she's flying." Some advertisers find certain songs helpful in creating the mood they desire in their commercials. Hewlett-Packard used the song "Picture Book" by the British band the Kinks in a commercial for its digital photography as the lyrics and melody worked well in the nostalgic spot, which featured images of still photographs coming to life.

For many years, popular singers and rock groups would not allow their songs to be used in commercials and some are still unwilling to do so. Rumor has it that Cadillac originally wanted to use the classic Doors' song "Break on Through (to the Other Side)" in its commercials, but the surviving members of the group turned them down. Neil Young steadfastly refuses to let his music be used in ads. However, many artists have learned that the benefits, exposure, and money often far outweigh an outdated concern over selling out to the advertising world. As it becomes more difficult to become part of a station's playlist, many musicians are finding that commercials can actually help them sell their music. For example, Sting sold the rights to his song "Desert Rose" to Jaguar for use in a commercial in 2000. The song, which did not fit well with radio playlists, lingered on *Billboard*'s top 100 list but didn't become a hit until the commercials started airing. "Start the Commotion" by the Wiseguys was released in 1999 but didn't hit *Billboard*'s top 40 list until it was featured in a commercial for the Mitsubishi Eclipse two years later. The song "Jerk It Out" by the Caesars was released in 2003 but did not generate significant sales until it was featured in an iPod ad two years later.

With more companies than ever using music in their ads, there is concern that the practice has gotten out of hand. Some critics note that watching TV commercials these days is almost like turning the radio dial as more songs from every kind of era and every kind of artist can be heard. Record companies are struggling to find new sources of revenue to offset weak CD sales and are pushing hard to get advertisers to use existing pop songs in their ads instead of jingles.

There is also concern over a growing trend of product placements in song lyrics as some marketers are making deals with artists to have brand names mentioned in their songs. Seagram's gin was mentioned in a number of songs by various hip-hop artists such as Petey Pablo's "Freek-a-Leek," which included the lyric "Now I got to give a shout out to Seagram gin, cause I'm drinkin' it and they payin' me for it." Busta Rhymes recently recorded a song titled "Pass the Courvoisier," while Hypnotiq, which is a new liquor that is a blend of vodka, fruit, and cognac, has been named in songs by a number of artists, including R. Kelly, Missy Elliot, Lil' Kim, and Usher. McDonald's received widespread derision when it announced that it would pay hip-hop artists for mentioning Big Macs.

As more artists become open to the idea of having their music used in commercials, as well as the money that accompanies it, we will quite likely hear our favorite songs become part of the pitch for a variety of products and services. And even if we choose to tune out the ads, there is a good chance we may still hear the brand names being mentioned in the songs. Someone in an urban music chatroom recently wrote, "Big Mac rhymes with heart attack, do you think they'd give me money for that?" Guess he isn't lovin' it. Nor are many other music fans.

Sources: Justin Ames and Rusell Simmons, "How to Put Some Bling into Your Brand," *Irish Times*, July 30, 2005, p. 7; Domenic Priore, "The Band Play On: When Marketing Gives Music a Lift," *Brandweek*, July 25, 2005, pp. 26, 27; Donnal De Marc, "TV Ads Go Pop," *Washington Times*, May 12, 2002, p. A1.

Some of the most popular commercials in recent years have been those used by Citibank to promote its Citi Identity Theft Solutions Service. The ads use humor to show how identify theft can damage the financial lives of victims. The commercials feature the victim speaking with the voices of the identity thieves, who talk about how much fun they had with the victim's credit cards and bank accounts. However, the thieves' voices are humorously out of place; for example, a rough-sounding thug's voice comes out of the mouth of an older woman as she cleans her pool. The voice notes how he is wanted in four states and used the woman's credit to purchase a new pickup with a V-8, 500 horsepower, and mudflaps with naked ladies on them. Another spot shows a woman in a hair salon speaking with the voice of a computer geek who has used her account to buy a variety of high-tech products such as a plasma TV. The creative strategy has also been executed successfully in print as shown by the ad in Exhibit 9-24. The ads are very effective as they use humor to address an important but emotional issue and encourage consumers to take advantage of the company's identity theft prevention services.[38]

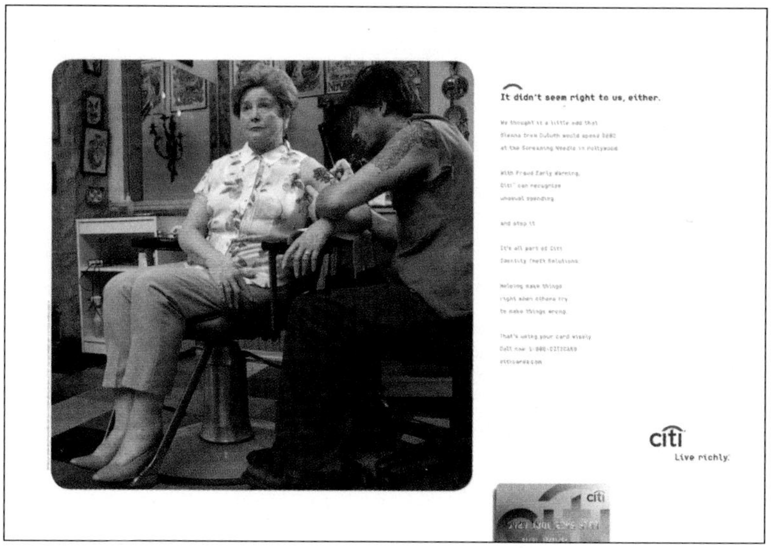

Exhibit 9-24 Citibank's identity theft commercials are very popular and effective

TV is particularly well suited to drama; no other advertising medium can touch emotions as well. Various emotional appeals such as humor, fear, and fantasy work well on TV, as do dramatizations and slice-of-life executions.

Planning the Commercial The various elements of a TV commercial are brought together in a **script,** a written version of a commercial that provides a detailed description of its video and audio content. The script shows the various audio components of the commercial—the copy to be spoken by voices, the music, and sound effects. The video portion of the script provides the visual plan of the commercial—camera actions and angles, scenes, transitions, and other important descriptions. The script also shows how the video corresponds to the audio portion of the commercial.

Once the basic script has been conceived, the writer and art director get together to produce a storyboard, a series of drawings used to present the visual plan or layout of a proposed commercial. The storyboard contains still drawings of the video scenes and descriptions of the audio that accompanies each scene. Like layouts for print ads, storyboards provide those involved in the production and approval of the commercial with a good approximation of what the final commercial will look like. In some cases an animatic (a videotape of the storyboard along with the soundtrack) may be produced if a more finished form of the commercial is needed for client presentations or pretesting.

Production Once the storyboard or animatic of the commercial is approved, it is ready to move to the production phase, which involves three stages:

1. *Preproduction*—all the work and activities that occur before the actual shooting/recording of the commercial.
2. *Production*—the period during which the commercial is filmed or videotaped and recorded.
3. *Postproduction*—activities and work that occur after the commercial has been filmed and recorded.

The various activities of each phase are shown in Figure 9-4. Before the final production process begins, the client must usually review and approve the creative strategy and the various tactics that will be used in creating the advertising message.

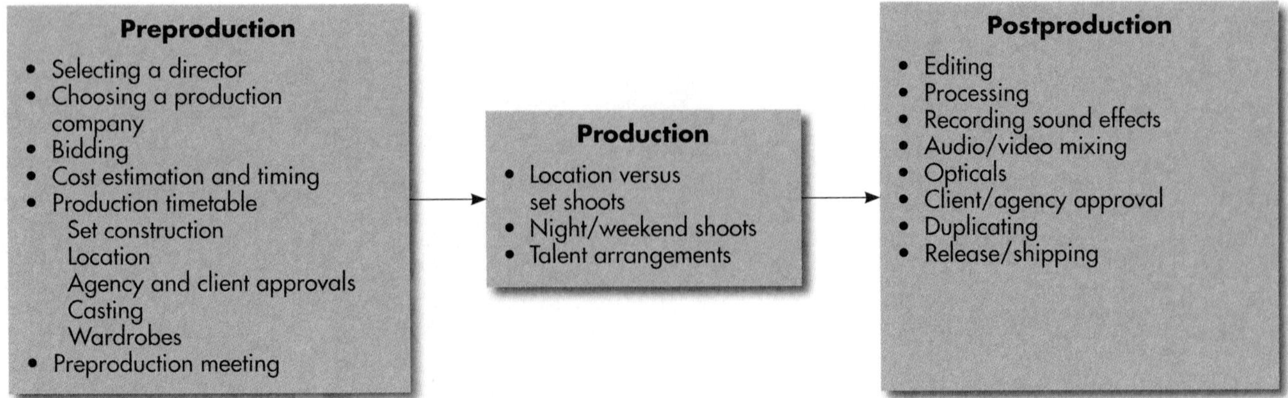

Figure 9-4 The Three Phases of Production for Commercials

Client Evaluation and Approval of Creative Work

While the creative specialists have much responsibility for determining the advertising appeal and execution style to be used in a campaign, the client must evaluate and approve the creative approach before any ads are produced. A number of people on the client side may be involved in evaluating the creative work of the agency, including the advertising or communications manager, product or brand managers, marketing director or vice president, representatives from the legal department, and sometimes even the president or chief executive officer (CEO) of the company or the board of directors.

The amount of input each of these individuals has in the creative evaluation and approval process varies depending on the company's policies, the importance of the product to the company, the role of advertising in the marketing program, and the advertising approach being recommended. For example, the Chiat/Day agency had to convince Apple's board of directors to air the famous "1984" commercial used to introduce the Macintosh personal computer. Apple's board thought the commercial, which was based on the concept of Big Brother from George Orwell's classic novel *1984,* was too controversial and might be detrimental to its image, particularly in the business market. The spot used stark images of Orwell's dystopia, and a dramatic scene of a young woman throwing a mallet through a movie screen to destroy a controlling force, purportedly symbolizing its major competitor IBM (see Exhibit 9-25). The agency convinced Apple's board to run the commercial during the 1984 Super Bowl, which is the only time it ever appeared as a commercial on TV, and the impact was tremendous. The spot was the focus of attention in the media and was the talk of the marketing and advertising industries. A few years ago, *TV Guide* named the "1984" spot the greatest television commercial of all time.

Earlier in this chapter, we noted that Procter & Gamble has been moving away from testimonials and slice-of-life advertising executions to somewhat riskier and more lively forms of advertising. But the company remains conservative and has been slow to adopt the avant-garde ads used by many of its competitors. Agencies that do the advertising for various P&G brands recognize that quirky executions that challenge the company's subdued corporate culture are not likely to be approved.[39] As discussed in the previous chapter, Wrigley was always very conservative in its advertising for its various brands of gum. However, since Bill Wrigley, Jr., took over the company in 1999 following the death of his more traditional father, the company has allowed its ad agency to take more creative risks and use more edgy advertising.[40]

In many cases, top management is involved in selecting an ad agency and must approve the theme and creative strategy for the campaign. Evaluation and approval of the individual ads proposed by the agency often rest with the advertising and product managers who are primarily responsible for the brand. The account executive and a

Exhibit 9-25 Apple's famous "1984" commercial almost never made it to television

member of the creative team present the creative concept to the client's advertising and product and/or marketing managers for their approval before beginning production. A careful evaluation should be made before the ad actually enters production, since this stage requires considerable time and money as suppliers are hired to perform the various functions required to produce the actual ad.

The client's evaluation of the print layout or commercial storyboard can be difficult, since the advertising or brand manager is generally not a creative expert and must be careful not to reject viable creative approaches or accept ideas that will result in inferior advertising. However, personnel on the client side can use the guidelines discussed next to judge the efficacy of creative approaches suggested by the agency.

Guidelines for Evaluating Creative Output

Advertisers use numerous criteria to evaluate the creative approach suggested by the ad agency. In some instances, the client may want to have the rough layout or storyboard pretested to get quantitative information to assist in the evaluation. However, the evaluation process is usually more subjective; the advertising or brand manager relies on qualitative considerations. Basic criteria for evaluating creative approaches are discussed next:

- *Is the creative approach consistent with the brand's marketing and advertising objectives?* One of the most important factors the client must consider is whether the creative appeal and execution style recommended by the agency are consistent with the marketing strategy for the brand and the role advertising and promotion have been assigned in the overall marketing program. This means the creative approach must be compatible with the image of the brand and the way it is positioned in the marketplace and should contribute to the marketing and advertising objectives.
- *Is the creative approach consistent with the creative strategy and objectives? Does it communicate what it is supposed to?* The advertising appeal and execution must meet the communications objectives laid out in the copy platform, and the ad must say what the advertising strategy calls for it to say. Creative specialists can lose sight of what the advertising message is supposed to be and come up with an approach that fails to execute the advertising strategy. Individuals responsible for approving the ad should ask the creative specialists to explain how the appeal or execution style adheres to the creative strategy and helps meet communications objectives.
- *Is the creative approach appropriate for the target audience?* Generally, much time has been spent defining, locating, and attempting to understand the target audience for the advertiser's product or service. Careful consideration should be given to whether the ad appeal or execution recommended will appeal to, be understood by, and communicate effectively with the target audience. This involves studying all elements of the ad and how the audience will respond to them. Advertisers do not want to approve advertising that they believe will receive a negative reaction from the target audience. For example, it has been suggested that advertising targeted to older consumers should use models who are 10 years younger than the average age of the target audience, since most people feel younger than their chronological age.[41] Advertisers also face a considerable challenge developing ads for the teen market because

CAREER PROFILE

Nancy Fletcher

Vice President of Communications, California Milk Advisory Board

I was planning to major in business when I took a public relations class during my junior year at Cal State, Fullerton. I really took an interest in it and before long I switched my major to communications. A year later, I was awarded an internship with GTE, where I had an invaluable experience learning about corporate communications and public affairs. During my senior year of college, I interned with Burson-Marsteller in Los Angeles and ended up staying on when I graduated. Los Angeles was very exciting during the 1984 Summer Olympics and I gained experience working for a number of corporate clients, including M&M Mars, Suzuki, and the AT&T Torch Run.

I moved to Fleishman-Hillard (FH) in Los Angeles in 1985, where I worked primarily on consumer product publicity for accounts like American Honda and Ralston-Purina. The nice thing about working for a large agency is the exposure to many different accounts. I started up a travel group that began by handling the grand opening publicity for hotels in Las Vegas, such as Excalibur, Luxor, and the MGM Grand. We later grew this business by adding a major airline, international hotel chain, and a Mexican resort to our roster. The agency then gave me the opportunity to open a new office in San Francisco in 1993. While there I led the corporate account for Levi Strauss & Co., where I managed global communications programs utilizing our FH offices in Europe, Asia, and throughout the United States.

In 1995, the California Milk Advisory Board (CMAB) was launching a major program to promote Real California Cheese and I was asked to come on board to manage the public relations aspects of the campaign as well as promote all California dairy products. I was intrigued by the opportunity to be on the ground floor for a burgeoning program and I was ready to develop an in-depth understanding of one industry. I also had the chance to act as spokesperson for California's entire dairy industry, which was and still is the largest in the nation. Needless to say, I jumped at the opportunity.

> I was intrigued by the opportunity to be on the ground floor for a burgeoning program

It's been incredibly rewarding to develop a program that has elevated the image of an entire industry and gives well-deserved recognition to California's 2,100 dairy families. Over the past decade, we've developed and implemented a long-term integrated marketing communications strategy based around Real California Cheese that balances public relations, advertising, the use of our website, and retail and foodservice promotions. Thanks to our efforts, California's cheesemakers have been featured in such publications as *The Washington Post, BusinessWeek,* and *The New York Times,* as well as numerous television programs, and California's Happy Cows have become household icons. Simultaneously, California cheese and dairy production has increased at a breakneck rate, while specialty cheeses from California have won more and more cheese contests at home and abroad.

The importance of public relations in an integrated marketing campaign is often underestimated, in large part because there's no control over the frequency of the message getting out. However, messages delivered through the media are given much greater credibility than traditional advertising—by consumers as well as the trade. Getting a reporter to do a story on the California dairy industry can take months, but when that article hits a publication like *The New York Times* the impact is enormous.

I believe it's important to keep in mind that public relations isn't one thing or one way of doing things—it encompasses many communications strategies and tools that help define a client's image, stimulate consumer demand, and produce results. A reporter who just wrote an article on cheese isn't likely to write another one on the same topic soon, so we have to be creative in developing new angles for different media. We develop trend stories for feature media, provide new recipes to food editors, pitch lifestyle and travel stories, and promote our industry's success in the business section. By reaching more and more consumers through different segments of trusted media, we broaden our consumer base, drive production, and give our cheesemakers impetus to continue offering a broad and growing selection of high-quality cheeses.

I've learned that by thinking creatively and strategically, a great deal can be accomplished. At the CMAB, we've stuck to our long-term strategy of using a well-planned and well-executed integrated marketing campaign while maintaining the flexibility to adapt to changing conditions. We raise the awareness of California dairy products with advertising, foster a credible message with public relations, and encourage wider distribution with retail and foodservice promotions. And with all of these components working hand in hand, we've delivered tremendous results. And we also have a great deal of fun in the process!

teenagers' styles, fashions, language, and values change so rapidly. They may find they are using an advertising approach, a spokesperson, or even an expression that is no longer popular among teens. Diversity Perspective 9-1 discusses issues advertisers must consider in developing messages for Hispanics, who are a very fast-growing market segment.

• *Does the creative approach communicate a clear and convincing message to the customer?* Most ads are supposed to communicate a message that will help sell the brand. Many ads fail to communicate a clear and convincing message that motivates consumers to use a brand. While creativity is important in advertising, it is also important that the advertising communicate information attributes, features and benefits, and/or images that give consumers a reason to buy the brand. The Golf Pride ad shown in Exhibit 9-26 is an example of how advertising can be creative yet still communicate important product benefits. The ad uses a humorous appeal by showing a snowman staring at a golfer as he gets ready to eat breakfast. *Snowman* is a term used by golfers for a score of an eight on a hole (which is very bad) in reference to the character's resemblance to the shape of the number 8. The visual image is likely to attract the attention of golfers while the copy explains how they can improve their performance by regripping their clubs with Golf Pride grips.

• *Does the creative execution keep from overwhelming the message?* A common criticism of advertising, and TV commercials in particular, is that so much emphasis is placed on creative execution that the advertiser's message gets overshadowed. Many creative, entertaining commercials have failed to register the brand name and/or selling points effectively. For example, Aflac had to modify the commercials using its iconic duck character after several research studies showed that many consumers were not exactly sure what Aflac insurance was. Consumers indicated that the advertising didn't explain what supplemental insurance is and what Aflac does, so recent ads focus more attention on explaining the product and the company.[42]

With the increasing amount of clutter in most advertising media, it may be necessary to use a novel creative approach to gain the viewer's or reader's attention. However, the creative execution cannot overwhelm the message. Clients must walk a fine line: Make sure the sales message is not lost, but be careful not to stifle the efforts of the creative specialists and force them into producing dull, boring advertising.

• *Is the creative approach appropriate for the media environment in which it is likely to be seen?* Each media vehicle has its own specific climate that results from the nature of its editorial content, the type of reader or viewer it attracts, and the nature of the ads it contains. Consideration should be given to how well the ad fits into the media environment in which it will be shown. For example, the Super Bowl has become a showcase for commercials. People who care very little about advertising know how much a 30-second commercial costs and pay as much attention to the ads as to the game itself, so many advertisers feel compelled to develop new ads for the Super Bowl or to save new commercials for the game.

• *Is the ad truthful and tasteful?* Marketers also have to consider whether an ad is truthful, as well as whether it might offend consumers. For example, the Quizno's sandwich chain briefly ran an ad campaign in 2004 featuring the Spongemonkeys, micelike creatures with bulging eyes who screamed, "We love the subs!" The vermin were created by an animator, and the ads were aimed at making the brand cool and generating buzz among 18- to 24-year-olds. However, consumer reactions to the commercials featuring the creatures were extremely negative, and many of the franchisees encouraged consumers to contact the

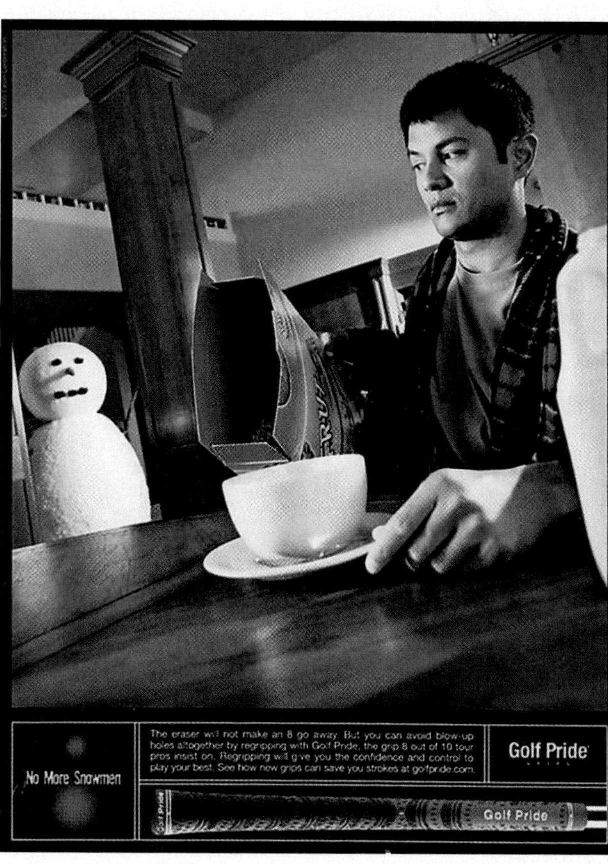

Exhibit 9-26 This humorous Golf Pride ad is creative and communicates an important product benefit

DIVERSITY PERSPECTIVE 9-1

Communicating with the Hispanic Market

As companies look for ways to increase their sales, many turn their attention to the Hispanic market, which is growing faster than other racial or ethnic groups in the country. The results from the 2000 Census show that over the past decade, the Hispanic market grew by 58 percent, compared with only 3 percent for the non-Hispanic white segment. Another 35 percent jump in the Hispanic market is forecast over the next 10 years. Revised figures released by the U.S. Census Bureau in June 2005 put the total U.S. Hispanic population at 41.3 million, and many believe the official count has been underreported. Moreover, the ranks of Hispanic teenagers are projected to swell to 18 percent of the U.S. teen population over the next decade, up from 12 percent in 2000. Nearly one in five children born in the United States today is of Latin American descent, and more than half of all children in Los Angeles alone are born to Latina mothers.

Marketers are recognizing the importance of appealing to the Hispanic market as they spent an estimated $3.3 billion advertising to this segment in 2005. However, they are also finding that communicating with this fast-growing segment can be very challenging and requires more than creating an ad in Spanish with tried-and-true Hispanic themes. They have to decide whether to use ads with a Hispanic-focused creative, to dub or remake general-market campaigns into Spanish, or to run English-language ads and trust that they will be picked up by bilingual Hispanics. Contributing to the challenge is the fact that Hispanics, and teens in particular, often live in two worlds: one rich in traditional Latino values such as a strong commitment to family and religion, and the other in which they eagerly participate in mainstream teen America. They bounce between hip-hop and Rock en Espanol; they watch *Buffy the Vampire Slayer* with their friends and Spanish telenovelas (nighttime soap operas) with their parents. They blend Mexican rice with spaghetti sauce and spread peanut butter and jelly on tortillas.

Advertising and marketing executives have different perspectives on how to best reach this young bicultural group. For example, the California Milk Processor Board (CMPB) conducted research on targeting English versions of its popular "Got milk?" commercials to Hispanic teens and found that they reacted enthusiastically to the ads. The CMPB had considered doing the ads in Spanglish (a combination of English and Spanish) but found that the language was not a major issue for teens because they reacted to ideas, not language. However, a study of Hispanic teens by the Roslow Research Group found that advertising to bilingual Hispanics in Spanish is significantly more effective than advertising to them in English. Some marketers are moving from using Spanish translations of their general-market TV commercials into developing ads specifically for the Hispanic market. For example, Dunkin' Donuts created a Spanish-language commercial and found that it led to a 61 percent increase in ad recall in this market.

Dr Pepper recently began focusing more attention on the Hispanic market and has been very systematic and deliberate in doing so. The company began the process by hiring a Hispanic marketing manager and then retaining a Hispanic agency based in San Antonio. While planning its first campaign for the Hispanic market, they were faced with the problem of finding a concept that works with both acculturated Hispanics who grew up drinking Dr Pepper and recent immigrants, for whom it is essentially a new product. Acculturated Hispanics drink 62 percent more Dr Pepper than the general population so the company's goal is to retain their loyalty while also pursuing the huge growth opportunity among the unacculturated immigrants.

The agency conducted research among both groups and found that there were Dr Pepper lovers and people with no relationship with the brand. The challenge was to find a bridge between the two groups so the company could proceed with one campaign. The research revealed that the common bond was Dr Pepper's unique taste, which is easily distinguished from rival cola brands such as Coke and Pepsi that taste similar. A TV commercial was developed that shows those familiar with Dr Pepper acting as advocates for the brand. The spot shows blindfolded teens in a laboratory sipping canned soft drinks through a straw and rejecting each with a bored "no." However, when given Dr Pepper, they recognize it instantly and refuse to give the cans back to the researchers. Radio advertising is also an important part of the campaign, and a series of commercials were created in both acculturated and unacculturated versions. All of the ads end with the tagline "inconfundible" or "unmistakable."

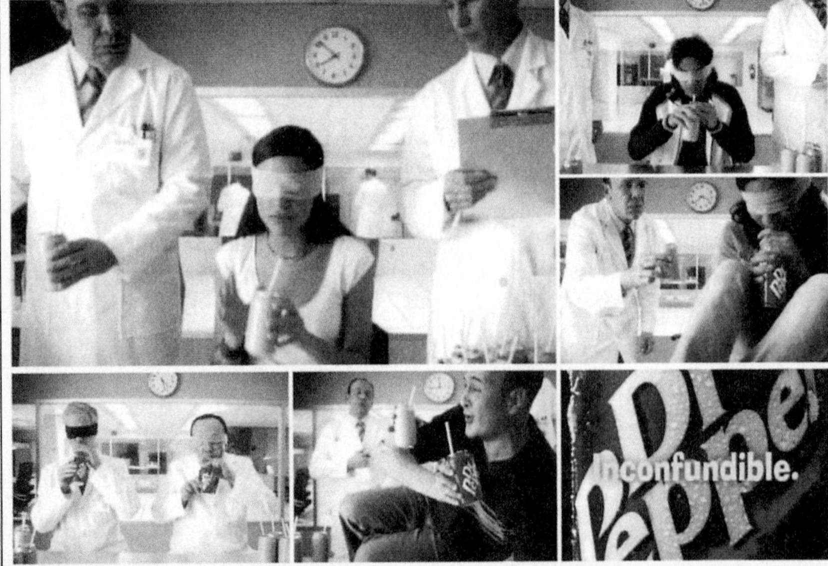

Given the tremendous growth of the Hispanic population, marketers will be giving more attention to this market. This will mean doing more original creative work to communicate better with Hispanics, running more ads in Spanish-language media, and doing more research to gain strategic insights into the Hispanic consumers they are counting on to fuel their growth.

Sources: Laurel Wentz, "Getting Hispanics to Be a Pepper, Too," *Advertising Age,* June 20, 2005, p. 27; Laurel Wentz, "Dunkin' Donuts Creates Spanish-Language Spot," *Advertising Age,* September 6, 2004, p. 15; Becky Ebenkamp, "A House Lacking in Lactose? Intolerable," *Brandweek,* January 21, 2002, p. 23.

corporate office to distance themselves from the ads. While the company noted that the campaign achieved its goal of generating buzz, many consumers were turned off by the appearance of the ads in commercials for a food product. After a few months, the company decided to drop the ads and run commercials focusing more on its menu items and product benefits.[43] The ultimate responsibility for determining whether an ad deceives or offends the target audience lies with the client. It is the job of the advertising or brand manager to evaluate the approach suggested by the creative specialists against company standards. The firm's legal department may be asked to review the ad to determine whether the creative appeal, message content, or execution could cause any problems for the company. It is much better to catch any potential legal problems before the ad is shown to the public.

The advertising manager, brand manager, or other personnel on the client side can use these basic guidelines in reviewing, evaluating, and approving the ideas offered by the creative specialists. There may be other factors specific to the firm's advertising and marketing situation. Also, there may be situations where it is acceptable to deviate from the standards the firm usually uses in judging creative output. As we shall see in Chapter 19, the client may want to move beyond these subjective criteria and use more sophisticated pretesting methods to determine the effectiveness of a particular approach suggested by the creative specialist or team.

Summary

In this chapter, we examined how the advertising message is implemented and executed. Once the creative strategy that will guide the ad campaign has been determined, attention turns to the specific type of advertising appeal and execution format to carry out the creative plan. The appeal is the central message used in the ad to elicit some response from consumers or influence their feelings. Appeals can be broken into two broad categories, rational and emotional. Rational appeals focus on consumers' practical, functional, or utilitarian need for the product or service; emotional appeals relate to social and/or psychological reasons for purchasing a product or service. Numerous types of appeals are available to advertisers within each category.

The creative execution style is the way the advertising appeal is presented in the message. A number of common execution techniques were examined in the chapter, along with considerations for their use. Attention was also given to tactical issues involved in creating print and TV advertising. The components of a print ad include headlines, body copy, illustrations, and layout. We also examined the video and audio components of TV commercials and various considerations involved in the planning and production of commercials.

Creative specialists are responsible for determining the advertising appeal and execution style as well as the tactical aspects of creating ads. However, the client must review, evaluate, and approve the creative approach before any ads are produced or run. A number of criteria can be used by advertising, product, or brand managers and others involved in the promotional process to evaluate the advertising messages before approving final production.

Key Terms

Discussion Questions

1. The opening vignette discusses the "Happy Cows" campaign that was developed for the California Milk Advisory Board to promote Real California Cheese. Analyze the various components of this campaign from an IMC perspective. Why do you think the campaign has been so successful?

2. Discuss the difference between an advertising appeal and a creative execution style. Find several ads and analyze the particular appeal and execution style used in each.

3. Discuss some of the various social and psychological states or needs that can be used as the basis for emotional advertising appeals. Find examples of ads that use social and psychological needs as the basis for their advertising appeals.

4. What is meant by transformational advertising? Analyze the cinematic-themed ad for Skyy vodka shown in Exhibit 9-6 as well as the advertising for the Skyy 90 line extension discussed in IMC Perspective 9-1 from a transformational advertising perspective.

5. What is meant by emotional bonding? Discuss how this concept can be used in developing an advertising campaign for a brand.

6. Discuss the use of slice-of-life execution techniques in advertising. For what types of products and services might this execution technique work best?

7. IMC Perspective 9-2 discusses how the campaign featuring the Aflac duck has been very successful in increasing brand name awareness. Why do you think this campaign has been so successful? What challenges does Aflac face by continuing to use the duck as the focal point of the campaign?

8. Discuss the role of headlines and subheads in print advertisements. Find examples of print ads that use various types of direct and indirect headlines.

9. Discuss the role of music in advertising. Why might companies/brands such as Microsoft, Cadillac and Nike pay such large sums of money for the rights to use popular songs in their commercials?

10. What are some of the factors marketers must consider in developing advertising for the Hispanic market? Do you think marketers should advertise to bilingual Hispanics in English or Spanish?

Media Planning and Strategy

10

Chapter Objectives

1. To understand the key terminology used in media planning.
2. To know how a media plan is developed.
3. To know the process of developing and implementing media strategies.
4. To be familiar with sources of media information and characteristics of media.

The Media Landscape in 2020: A Brave New World?

Can you guess which TV show was ranked number one for two straight years and still today has some of its episodes ranked in the top 10 highest Neilsen ratings? You probably guessed *Friends, M*A*S*H, Seinfeld,* or maybe *Dallas.* The *Beverly Hillbillies* no doubt, was not one of your first choices (in fact, you probably have never heard of this show). Nevertheless, the sitcom featuring the Clampetts (an Ozark hillbilly family that accidentally struck it rich when patriarch Jed, while hunting, shot the ground and struck oil and moved the family to Beverly Hills, California) achieved TV ratings that may never be seen again.

As you no doubt know, however, numbers can be deceiving. Was the *Beverly Hillbillies* that good? Probably not. But the program aired on CBS from 1962 to 1971—a time when there were only three major networks; cable and satellite TV were in the distant future. If you wanted to watch TV, you had three choices, and the *Beverly Hillbillies* just happened to be the best one. Mass media was king. (GM spent almost its entire TV budget on one program—*The Dinah Shore Chevy Show.*) It seemed that almost everyone watched TV, read a newspaper, and listened to the radio. There was no Internet, no wireless, and no satellite radio. There were few specialized magazines and iPods weren't even a dream. Erwin Ephron, a media consultant, estimates that in the 1980s a media planner had approximately 1,250 TV scheduling options to consider. By the 1990s, with 100 national broadcast and cable networks in existence, the number of combinations that could go into a TV advertising schedule was 1.25 quadrillion!

It's a very different media landscape out there now, and it doesn't appear that it's going to get better for mass media in the foreseeable future. Since the 1970s, prime-time network ratings and newspaper circulation figures have been in a decline. At the same time, there has been a proliferation of new advertising forms, resulting in a virtual bombardment of communications targeted to consumers. Some marketers estimate that the consumer is exposed to over 4,000 advertising messages a day, from what seems to be an unlimited variety of sources. In addition, consumers have created their own media through blogs and podcasts, creating publicity (good and bad) for companies and their products, and providing yet more information.

So what does all this mean? First of all, the way that marketers attempt to reach consumers has undergone a major transformation. Companies can no longer rely solely on television to reach their markets. Expenditures in traditional media (such as TV) are being moved to other media forms. Many of the largest TV commercial buyers have reduced their TV buys. Pepsi re-launched its Pepsi One product with no TV advertising. Reebok has shifted much of its budget to new media, and Heineken announced that they would spend no more money on television in the U.K., moving their ad dollars to sponsorships and other media. Branded entertainment—placing products in entertainment vehicles through short videos, product placements, product integrations, and so forth—has become the new media darling. Nissan, Toyota, and Volkswagen have shifted millions of dollars to this form of advertising. CBS has approached advertisers in an attempt to have them sponsor video on demand (VOD) offerings as a way of generating revenue lost from the decline of traditional commercials.

Even the way companies buy, schedule, and attempt to measure media effectiveness is changing. Terms like *reach, frequency,* and *CPM* are giving way to *ROI, stickiness,* and *recency.* Advertisers can no longer afford to throw out messages to the mass market hoping someone will watch. Consumers now "graze" through media as opposed to being engrossed in them; they multitask and prefer to see commercial messages when they want them—not when the advertiser wants to show them. The use of demographics to define audiences has given way to determining consumers' interests as a basis for media buys.

When 2020 comes around, will there no longer be television advertising? Will newspapers and general interest magazines no longer exist? Will all advertising be focused on narrow market segments and be "on demand"? Probably not. As noted by David Poltrack, executive vice president of research at CBS-TV, "Unless someone can come up with a more effective way of introducing a new product than broad-based advertising exposure, I think that business [advertising] is always going to be there." Maybe it's just wishful thinking.

Sources: Joe Mandese, "Hitting the Wall," *MEDIA,* October 2005, pp. 26–33; Karl Greenberg, "Auto Mobility," *Brandweek,* March 21, 2005, pp. SR 1–4; Daren Fonda, "Prime-Time Peddling," *Time,* May 30, 2005, pp. 50–51; Wayne Friedman, "Nissan, Toyota Rev Up Branded Content," mediapost.com, October 10, 2005, pp. 1–2; Wayne Friedman, "CBS Seeks Video Search, On-Demand Deals," mediapost.com, November 23, 2005, pp. 1–2.

The discussion in this chapter's opening vignette demonstrates some of the many changes taking place in the media environment. Perhaps at no other time in history have so many changes taken place that significantly alter the media decision process. As a result, media planning has become more complex than ever before. As you will see in the following chapters, these changes offer the marketer opportunities not previously available, but they also require in-depth knowledge of all the alternatives. Integrated marketing communications programs are no longer a luxury; they are a necessity. Media planners must now consider new options as well as recognize the changes that are occurring in traditional sources. New and evolving media contribute to the already difficult task of media planning. Planning when, where, and how the advertising message will be delivered is a complex and involved process. The primary objective of the media plan is to develop a framework that will deliver the message to the target audience in the most efficient, cost-effective manner possible—that will communicate what the product, brand, and/or service can do.

This chapter presents the various methods of message delivery available to marketers, examines some key considerations in making media decisions, and discusses the development of media strategies and plans. Later chapters will explore the relative advantages and disadvantages of the various media and examine each in more detail.

An Overview of Media Planning

The media planning process is not an easy one. Options include mass media such as television, newspapers, radio, and magazines (and the choices available within each of these categories—see Figure 10-1) as well as out-of-the-home media such as outdoor advertising, transit advertising, and electronic billboards. A variety of support media such as direct marketing, the Internet, promotional products, and others such as sales promotions, and in-store point-of-purchase options must also be considered. A proliferation of new media, including branded entertainment and interactive media, has also provided the marketer with many options to consider.

Figure 10-1 The Traditional Media Landscape

Medium	Number
TV stations	3,510
Broadcast networks (TV and cable)	100
Radio stations	13,898
Satellite radio stations	2
Consumer magazines	5,340
Newspapers (daily and weekly)	8,100

Source: *Mediaweek*, May 16, 2005.

While at first glance the choices among these alternatives might seem relatively straightforward, this is rarely the case. Part of the reason media selection becomes so involved is the nature of the media themselves. TV combines both sight and sound, an advantage not offered by other media. Magazines can convey more information and may keep the message available to the potential buyer for a much longer time. Newspapers also offer their own advantages, as do outdoor, direct media, and each of the others. The Internet offers many of the advantages of other media but is also limited in its capabilities. The characteristics of each alternative must be considered, along with many other factors. This process becomes even more complicated when the manager has to choose between alternatives within the same medium—for example, between *Time* and *Newsweek* or between *Grey's Anatomy* and *CSI.*

Many companies, large and small, have come to realize the importance of a sound media strategy. They are focusing additional attention on the integration of creative work and media, as well as the use of multiple media vehicles to achieve the optimal impact. For example, Buick, which has advertised on *Desperate Housewives* since its inception, has had its products integrated into the program's scripts and has launched an Internet campaign on AOL to promote the integration. The auto manufacturer also sponsors four-minute recaps of the show each week online, as well as video highlights. Other auto companies, like Toyota and Hyundai, are launching advertising and promotional campaigns more in line with the TV shows on which they will appear, as well as seeking new ways to get their products seen[1] (Exhibit 10-1).

The product and/or service being advertised affects the media planning process. As demonstrated in Figure 10-2, firms have found some media more useful than others in conveying their messages to specific target audiences. For example, GM and Procter & Gamble spend heavily on broadcast media, while others like Time Warner and Verizon allocate higher percentages of the budget to the Internet. The result is placement of advertising dollars in these preferred media—and significantly different media strategies.

Some Basic Terms and Concepts

Before beginning our discussion of media planning, we review some basic terms and concepts used in the media planning and strategy process.

Media planning is the series of decisions involved in delivering the promotional message to the prospective purchasers and/or users of the product or brand. Media planning is a process, which means a number of decisions are made, each of which may be altered or abandoned as the plan develops.

The media plan is the guide for media selection. It requires development of specific **media objectives** and specific **media strategies** (plans of action) designed to attain

Exhibit 10-1 Some companies are focusing more attention on product placement

Figure 10-2 Leading National Advertisers, Ranked by Total U.S. Advertising Spending, 2004—$ Millions

Rank				Total U.S. Ad Spending				U.S. Measured Media Spending Breakout						
2004	2003	Advertiser	Headquarters	2004	% CHG	Estimated Unmeasured	Measured Media	Magazine	Newspaper	Outdoor	TV	Radio	Internet	Yellow Pages
1	1	General Motors Corp.	Detroit	$3,997.4	6.3	$1,199.8	$2,797.6	$500.9	$461.2	$48.3	$1,619.3	$62.4	$66.1	$39.4
2	2	Procter & Gamble Co.	Cincinnati	3,919.7	17.0	914.1	3,005.6	665.6	124.9	3.6	2,158.4	41.0	12.2	0.0
3	3	Time Warner	New York	3,283.1	6.8	1,344.9	1,938.2	364.6	377.6	70.9	888.2	91.7	145.3	0.0
4	4	Pfizer	New York	2,957.3	10.3	1,896.1	1,061.1	258.1	29.8	0.8	721.1	27.4	23.9	0.0
5	5	SBC Communications	San Antonio, Texas	2,686.8	3.4	850.8	1,835.9	50.6	814.0	20.5	779.6	105.9	56.3	8.9
6	6	DaimlerChrysler	Auburn Hills, Mich./ Stuttgart, Germany	2,462.1	3.2	651.5	1,810.6	367.7	166.8	23.8	1,185.8	13.0	40.3	13.3
7	7	Ford Motor Co.	Dearborn, Mich.	2,458.0	11.4	814.8	1,643.3	395.1	179.5	17.8	942.1	26.6	61.2	21.0
8	9	Walt Disney Co.	Burbank, Calif.	2,241.5	10.1	851.5	1,390.0	181.9	258.5	39.7	808.7	47.9	53.3	0.0
9	13	Verizon Communications	New York	2,197.3	31.4	669.3	1,528.0	36.3	648.2	41.4	564.1	101.7	124.6	11.9
10	10	Johnson & Johnson	New Brunswick, N.J.	2,175.7	10.9	783.1	1,392.5	343.9	38.4	1.0	956.7	23.2	29.4	0.0

these objectives. Once the decisions have been made and the objectives and strategies formulated, this information is organized into the media plan.

The **medium** is the general category of available delivery systems, which includes broadcast media (like TV and radio), print media (like newspapers and magazines), direct mail, outdoor advertising, and other support media. The **media vehicle** is the specific carrier within a medium category. For example, *Time* and *Newsweek* are print vehicles; *CSI* and *60 Minutes* are broadcast vehicles. As you will see in later chapters, each vehicle has its own characteristics as well as its own relative advantages and disadvantages. Specific decisions must be made as to the value of each in delivering the message.

Reach is a measure of the number of different audience members exposed at least once to a media vehicle in a given period of time. **Coverage** refers to the potential audience that might receive the message through a vehicle. Coverage relates to potential audience; reach refers to the actual audience delivered. (The importance of this distinction will become clearer later in this chapter.) Finally, **frequency** refers to the number of times the receiver is exposed to the media vehicle in a specified period. While there are numerous more media planning terms that are important and commonly used (for a useful reference see *Advertising Media A to Z*),[2] we will begin our discussion with these as they are critical to your understanding of the planning process.

The Media Plan

The media plan determines the best way to get the advertiser's message to the market. In a basic sense, the goal of the media plan is to find that combination of media that enables the marketer to communicate the message in the most effective manner to the largest number of potential customers at the lowest cost.

The activities involved in developing the media plan and the purposes of each are presented in Figure 10-3. As you can see, a number of decisions must be made throughout this process. As the plan evolves, events may occur that necessitate changes. Many advertisers find it necessary to alter and update their objectives and strategies frequently.

Problems in Media Planning

Unfortunately, the media strategy decision has not become a standardized task. A number of problems contribute to the difficulty of establishing the plan and reduce its effectiveness. These problems include insufficient information, inconsistent terminologies, time pressures, and difficulty measuring effectiveness.

Insufficient Information

While a great deal of information about markets and the media exists, media planners often require more than is available. Some data are just not measured, either because they cannot be or because measuring them would be too expensive. For example, continuous measures of radio listenership exist, but only periodic listenership studies are reported due to sample size and cost constraints. There are problems with some measures of audience size in TV and print as well, as demonstrated by IMC Perspective 10-1.

The timing of measurements is also a problem; some audience measures are taken only at specific times of the year. (For example, **sweeps periods** in February, May, July, and November are used for measuring TV audiences and setting advertising rates.) This information is then generalized to succeeding months, so future planning decisions must be made on past data that may not reflect current behaviors. Think about planning for TV advertising for the fall season. There are no data on the audiences of new shows, and audience information taken on existing programs during the summer may not indicate how these programs will do in the fall because summer viewership is generally much lower. While the advertisers can review these programs before they air, all markets do not have actual audience figures.

The lack of information is even more of a problem for small advertisers, who may not be able to afford to purchase the information they require. As a result, their decisions are based on limited or out-of-date data that were provided by the media themselves, or no data at all.

Figure 10-3 Activities Involved in Developing the Media Plan

The situation analysis

Purpose: To understand the marketing problem. An analysis is made of a company and its competitors on the basis of:

1. Size and share of the total market.
2. Sales history, costs, and profits.
3. Distribution practices.
4. Methods of selling.
5. Use of advertising.
6. Identification of prospects.
7. Nature of the product.

The marketing strategy plan

Purpose: To plan activities that will solve one or more of the marketing problems. Includes the determination of:

1. Marketing objectives.
2. Product and spending strategy.
3. Distribution strategy.
4. Which elements of the marketing mix are to be used.
5. Identification of "best" market segments.

The creative strategy plan

Purpose: To determine what to communicate through advertisements. Includes the determination of:

1. How product can meet consumer needs.
2. How product will be positioned in advertisements.
3. Copy themes.
4. Specific objectives of each advertisement.
5. Number and sizes of advertisements.

Setting media objectives

Purpose: To translate marketing objectives and strategies into goals that media can accomplish.

Determining media strategy

Purpose: To translate media goals into general guidelines that will control the planner's selection and use of media. The best strategy alternatives should be selected.

Selecting broad media classes

Purpose: To determine which broad class of media best fulfills the criteria. Involves comparison and selection of broad media classes such as newspapers, magazines, radio, television, and others. The analysis is called intermedia comparisons. Audience size is one of the major factors used in comparing the various media classes.

Selecting media within classes

Purpose: To compare and select the best media within broad classes, again using predetermined criteria. Involves making decisions about the following:

1. If magazines were recommended, then which magazines?
2. If television was recommended, then
   a. Broadcast or cable television?
   b. Network or spot television?
   c. If network, which program(s)?
   d. If spot, which markets?
3. If radio or newspapers were recommended, then
   a. Which markets shall be used?
   b. What criteria shall buyers use in making purchases of local media?

Media use decisions—broadcast

1. What kind of sponsorship (sole, shared, participating, or other)?
2. What levels of reach and frequency will be required?
3. Scheduling: On which days and months are commercials to appear?
4. Placement of spots: In programs or between programs?

Media use decisions—print

1. Number of ads to appear and on which days and months.
2. Placements of ads: Any preferred position within media?
3. Special treatment: Gatefolds, bleeds, color, etc.
4. Desired reach or frequency levels.

Media use decisions—other media

1. Billboards
   a. Location of markets and plan of distribution.
   b. Kinds of outdoor boards to be used.
2. Other media: Decisions peculiar to those media.

IMC PERSPECTIVE 10-1

The Ratings Controversy: Will It Ever Be Resolved?

So long as there have been broadcast media, there have been companies attempting to measure the audiences these media reach. And, it seems, for just as long there has been controversy as to the accuracy of these measures. Although this controversy is not limited to the broadcast industry—outdoor ads, newspapers, and magazines have also had their critics—it seems that television and radio get the lion's share of the attention. And, it seems that it just doesn't want to go away!

The latest battles involve both radio and television, the two major players in the ratings industry (Arbitron and Nielsen), a couple of upstarts, the largest radio company (Clear Channel Communications), and the U.S. government (Senate and House committees). While all involved agree that there are problems with the existing systems and that improvements are necessary, there is little more that they agree upon. Let's look at the issues, starting with radio.

Arbitron—the sole provider of radio ratings in the United States—has used diaries—in which listeners record their listening times in a diary—for more than 40 years to determine how many people are listening. While advertisers and their agencies have questioned the accuracy of this methodology, they considered it acceptable enough to use in their media planning. But times have changed. An increased emphasis on ROI, the growth of Clear Channel Communications (which now owns more than 1,100 stations), and advances in technology have led to cries for change. Add to this the concern over losing revenue to nontraditional media, and people begin to listen. At the request of broadcasters, the Radio Advertising Bureau commissioned a study by Forrester Research to ask advertisers and agency executives what the impact of a newer technology would mean to them. The new technology, currently being test-marketed by Arbitron, is a portable people meter (a device worn like a pager) that detects inaudible codes embedded in radio (as well as TV) programming. Called the Personal People Meter (PPM) it automatically detects listening habits, eliminating some of the problems associated with keeping diaries. The results of the survey look promising, as Forrester estimates that adoption of the PPM would lead to a 3 percent increase in revenue—about $414 million per year. Continuation of the diary method would supposedly lead to a decline of 2 percent or $282 million.

But wait. Everyone isn't convinced: Two large radio groups, Radio One and Cox Radio, refused to participate in Arbitron's next test-market study, calling the system "flawed and hypothetical," and not worthy of consideration. Clear Channel is also considering using a competitor to Arbitron, a company called Naviguage, which combines global positioning technology with continuous tracking of listenership. Unfortunately, Naviguage tracks only listening in vehicles—not in the home—a less-than-perfect methodology according to its opponents.

Television's woes in tracking ratings continue as well. Nielsen Media Research, the provider of TV ratings, has also been under attack. Like Arbitron, Nielsen has used the diary method to collect ratings and (also like Arbitron) wants to move away from this methodology through the use of local people meters (LPMs). Nielsen has continuously increased the number of markets using meters, currently in 56 of the 210 measured TV markets. However, not everyone is convinced that this is such a good idea. While proponents argue that the meter methodology is superior to the diary method, opponents are particularly upset with the LPMs used in some markets to assess the viewing habits of minorities. According to these opponents, the fault rates (representing the percentage of boxes not counted at one time) are too high, inaccurately representing minority viewership.

A task force, called the Independent Task Force on Television Measurement, was created by Nielsen and a New York congressman to evaluate the new system. At the same time, four Republican senators proposed legislation that would form a Media Ratings Council (MRC) whose responsibility would be to evaluate and arbitrate these disagreements. Nielsen, along with other politicians, media companies, and advertisers, vigorously opposes the MRC legislation, arguing that it would limit Nielsen's ability to introduce new and improved measurement systems. Meanwhile, the standard rating system used in the past continues to be the basis for determining viewership.

So while everyone seems to agree that the status quo is not acceptable, no one seems to agree on what the new standard should be. Say tuned for future developments.

Sources: Joe Mandese, "TV, Radio, Outdoor Ratings Poised for Transformation, New Alliances," Mediapost.com, July 22, 2005, pp. 1–3; Katy Bachman and Paul Heine, "Ads Would Grow with PPM," Mediaweek.com, July 25, 2005, p. 1; "Nielsen Task Force Urges Senate to Drop TV Ratings Legislation," MediaPost.com, July 21, 2005, p. 1.

Inconsistent Terminologies Problems arise because the cost bases used by different media often vary and the standards of measurement used to establish these costs are not always consistent. For example, print media may present cost data in terms of the cost to reach a thousand people (cost per thousand, or CPM), broadcast media use the cost per ratings point (CPRP), and outdoor media use the number of showings. The advent of the Internet brought about a whole new lexicon of terminologies. Audience information that is used as a basis for these costs has also been collected by different methods. Finally, terms that actually mean something different (such as *reach* and *coverage*) may be used synonymously, adding to the confusion.

In 2005, a joint task force composed of members of the National Association of Advertisers (AAAA) and the Advertising Research Foundation (ARF) launched an initiative to determine a better way to measure consumer exposure to an advertisement. The group unveiled an initiative that would significantly change the way exposure was measured, essentially replacing the use of frequency (the number of exposures to an ad) with engagement, a measure they said would better reflect the growing number of media choices available to consumers. Although the committee agreed on backing the new term, others were not so willing, asking for a more precise definition of *engagement.* The committee agreed to further examine and validate the concept.[3]

Time Pressures It seems that advertisers are always in a hurry—sometimes because they need to be; other times because they think they need to be. Actions by a competitor—for example, the cutting of airfares by one carrier—require immediate response. But sometimes a false sense of urgency dictates time pressures. In either situation, media selection decisions may be made without proper planning and analysis of the markets and/or media.

Difficulty Measuring Effectiveness Because it is so hard to measure the effectiveness of advertising and promotions in general, it is also difficult to determine the relative effectiveness of various media or media vehicles. (Recall the discussion of ROI from Chapter 7.) While progress is being made in this regard, the media planner may have little more than an estimate of or a good guess at the impact of these alternatives.

Because of these problems, not all media decisions are quantitatively determined. Sometimes managers have to assume the image of a medium in a market with which they are not familiar, anticipate the impact of recent events, or make judgments without full knowledge of all the available alternatives.

While these problems complicate the media decision process, they do not render it an entirely subjective exercise. The remainder of this chapter explores in more detail how media strategies are developed and ways to increase their effectiveness.

Developing the Media Plan

The promotional planning model in Chapter 1 discussed the process of identifying target markets, establishing objectives, and formulating strategies for attaining them. The development of the media plan and strategies follows a similar path, except that the focus is more specifically keyed to determining the best way to deliver the message. The process, shown in Figure 10-4, involves a series of stages: (1) market analysis, (2) establishment of media objectives, (3) media strategy development and implementation, and (4) evaluation and follow-up. Each of these is discussed in turn, with specific examples. The website for this text contains an actual media plan, which we refer to throughout the remainder of the chapter to exemplify each phase further.

Market Analysis and Target Market Identification

The situation analysis stage of the overall promotional planning process involves a complete review of internal and external factors, competitive strategies, and the like. In the development of a media strategy, a market analysis is again performed, although this time the focus is on the media and delivering the message. The key questions at this stage are these: To whom shall we advertise (who is the target market)? What internal and external factors may influence the media plan? Where (geographically) and when should we focus our efforts?

Figure 10-4 Developing the Media Plan

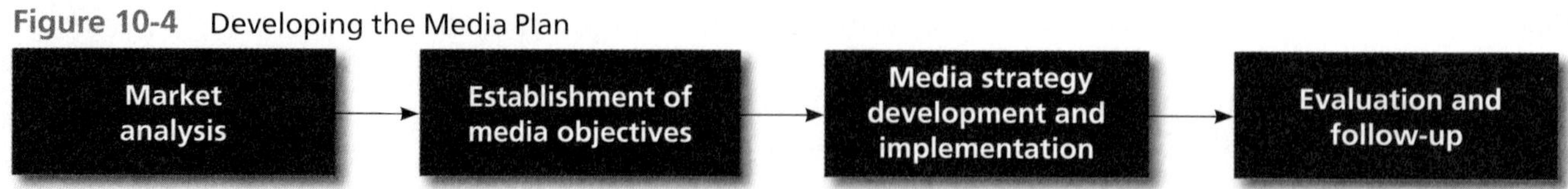

To Whom Shall We Advertise?

While a number of target markets might be derived from the situation analysis, to decide which specific groups to go after, the media planner may work with the client, account representative, marketing department, and creative directors. A variety of factors can assist media planners in this decision. Some will require primary research, whereas others will be available from published (secondary) sources.

The Simmons Market Research Bureau (SMRB) provides secondary information: syndicated data on audience size and composition for approximately 200 magazine titles, every network and cable TV show, all major newspapers, and the top 75 Internet sites, as well as data on usage of over 450 product categories and services. This information comes in the form of raw numbers, percentages, and indexes. As seen in Figure 10-5, information is given on (1) the number of adults in the United States by each category under consideration; (2) the number of users; (3) the percentage of users falling into each category (for example, the percentage who are female); (4) the percentage of each category that uses the product (for example, the percentage of all females using); (5) an index number; and (6) the same information classified by heavy, medium, and light users. Both Simmons and its major competitor, Mediamark Research Inc. (MRI), also provide lifestyle information and media usage characteristics of the population.

Media planners are often more concerned with the percentage figures and index numbers than with the raw numbers. This is largely due to the fact that they may have their own data from other sources, both primary and secondary; the numbers provided may not be specific enough for their needs; or they question the numbers provided because of the methods by which they were collected. The total (raw) numbers provided by Simmons and MRI are used in combination with the media planner's own figures.

On the other hand, the **index number** is considered a good indicator of the potential of the market. This number is derived from the formula

$$\text{Index} = \frac{\text{Percentage of users in a demographic segment}}{\text{Percentage of population in the same segment}} \times 100$$

An index number over 100 means use of the product is proportionately greater in that segment than in one that is average (100) or less than 100. For example, the MRI data in Figure 10-6 show that people in the age groups 18–24 and 25–34, respectively, are more likely to use videogame systems than those in the other age segments, as are those with a household income of $60,000–$74,999. Many occupational groups are users, though executives are least likely to be. Attended college also has a higher index. Depending on their overall strategy, marketers may wish to use this information to determine which groups are now using the product and target them or to identify a group that is currently using the product less and attempt to develop that segment.

Figure 10-5 Market Research Profile of Cola Users

		Filter Sample '(000)	Total Sample 21452 202447 Regular Cola (Not Diet)-Drink? YES	Heavy Users	Medium Users	Light Users
	Sample		13820	415	2521	9802
	'(000)		141102	5610.93	28022.6	97006
	Vertical		100.00%	100.00%	100.00%	100.00%
	Horizontal		69.70%	2.77%	13.84%	47.92%
	Index		100	100	100	100
SEX: MALE	Sample	9538	6634	235	1324	4666
	'(000)	97199.5	71224.6	3238.06	15000.3	48607.6
	Vertical	48.01%	50.48%	57.71%	53.53%	50.11%
	Horizontal	100.00%	73.28%	3.33%	15.43%	50.01%
	Index	100	105	120	111	104
SEX: FEMALE	Sample	11914	7186	180	1197	5136
	'(000)	105248	69877.4	2372.87	13022.4	48398.4
	Vertical	51.99%	49.52%	42.29%	46.47%	49.89%
	Horizontal	100.00%	66.39%	2.26%	12.37%	45.99%
	Index	100	95	81	89	96
AGE: 18–24	Sample	2017	1550	97	388	968
	'(000)	26148.3	20700.6	1522.87	4904.96	13146.1
	Vertical	12.92%	14.67%	27.14%	17.50%	13.55%
	Horizontal	100.00%	79.17%	5.82%	18.76%	50.28%
	Index	100	114	210	136	105
AGE: 25–34	Sample	2918	2176	67	446	1501
	'(000)	38580.7	30089.7	1430.86	6509.51	19703.8
	Vertical	19.06%	21.33%	25.50%	23.23%	20.31%
	Horizontal	100.00%	77.99%	3.71%	16.87%	51.07%
	Index	100	112	134	122	107
AGE: 35–44	Sample	4547	3042	79	564	2162
	'(000)	45760.3	32541.8	805.978	6585.31	22802.8
	Vertical	22.60%	23.06%	14.36%	23.50%	23.51%
	Horizontal	100.00%	71.11%	1.76%	14.39%	49.83%
	Index	100	102	64	104	104
AGE: 45–54	Sample	4722	2979	80	547	2132
	'(000)	36552.8	24895.1	976.554	5069.16	17142.1
	Vertical	18.06%	17.64%	17.40%	18.09%	17.67%
	Horizontal	100.00%	68.11%	2.67%	13.87%	46.90%
	Index	100	98	96	100	98
AGE: 55–64	Sample	3110	1907	45	318	1390
	'(000)	22980.8	14994.6	469.025	2617.5	10849.2
	Vertical	11.35%	10.63%	8.20%	9.34%	11.18%
	Horizontal	100.00%	65.25%	2.00%	11.39%	47.21%
	Index 100	94	72	82	99	
AGE: 65+	Sample	4138	2166	47	258	1649
	'(000)	32424.2	17880.1	414.636	2336.19	13362
	Vertical	16.02%	12.67%	7.39%	8.34%	13.77%
	Horizontal	100.00%	55.14%	1.28%	7.21%	41.21%
	Index	100	79	46	52	86
AGE: 18–34	Sample	4935	3726	164	834	2468
	'000)	64729	50790.4	2953.74	11414.5	32849.9
	Vertical	31.97%	36.00%	52.64%	40.73%	33.86%
	Horizontal	100.00%	78.47%	4.56%	17.63%	50.75%
	Index	100	113	165	127	106
AGE: 18–49	Sample	11918	8336	287	1671	5764
	'(000)	129634	96569.7	4349.01	20484.1	64875.3
	Vertical	64.03%	68.44%	77.51%	73.10%	66.88%
	Horizontal	100.00%	74.49%	3.36%	15.80%	50.05%
	Index	100	107	121	114	104
AGE: 35–49	Sample	6983	4610	123	837	3295
	'(000)	64905.3	45779.4	1395.28	9069.66	32025.4
	Vertical	32.06%	32.44%	24.87%	32.37%	33.01%
	Horizontal	100.00%	70.53%	2.15%	13.97%	49.34%
	Index	100	101	78	101	103
AGE: 25–54	Sample	12187	8197	226	1557	5795
	'(000)	120894	87526.6	3213.4	18164	59648.7
	Vertical	59.72%	62.03%	57.27%	64.82%	61.49%
	Horizontal	100.00%	72.40%	2.66%	15.03%	49.34%
	Index	100	104	96	109	103
AGE: 50+	Sample	9534	5484	128	850	4038
	'(000)	72812.9	44532.3	1261.92	7538.5	32130.7
	Vertical	35.97%	31.56%	22.49%	26.90%	33.12%
	Horizontal	100.00%	61.16%	1.73%	10.35%	44.13%
	Index	100	88	63	75	92
HIGH SCHOOL - 12 YEARS (GRADUATED)	Sample	6330	4334	156	828	3067
	'(000)	69022.9	50021.6	2343.45	10345.5	33973.3
	Vertical	34.09%	35.15%	41.77%	36.92%	35.02%
	Horizontal	100.00%	72.47%	3.40%	14.99%	49.22%
	Index	100	104	123	108	103
COLLEGE- 4 YEARS (GRADUATED)	Sample	3494	2145	37	345	1569
	'(000)	25136.4	16638.5	281.425	2964.29	12050.7
	Vertical	12.42%	11.79%	5.02%	10.58%	12.42%
	Horizontal	100.00%	66.19%	1.12%	11.79%	47.94%
	Index	100	95	40	85	100
DID NOT GRADUATE HIGH SCHOOL	Sample	2196	1527	78	325	1021
	'(000)	32884.4	24128.2	1528.37	5285.51	15608.2
	Vertical	16.24%	17.10%	27.24%	18.86%	16.09%
	Horizontal	100.00%	73.37%	4.65%	16.07%	47.46%
	Index	100	105	168	116	99
ATTENDED COLLEGE (1–3 YEARS)	Sample	4915	3201	84	574	2297
	'(000)	42788.9	29502.1	970.031	5565.53	20926
	Vertical	21.14%	20.91%	17.29%	19.86%	21.57%
	Horizontal	100.00%	68.95%	2.27%	13.01%	48.91%
	Index	100	99	82	94	102
Employed Male	Sample	6863	4962	173	1020	3477
	'(000)	69831.6	53300.2	2421.39	11075.3	36505.1
	Vertical	34.49%	37.77%	43.16%	39.52%	37.63%
	Horizontal	100.00%	76.33%	3.47%	15.86%	52.28%
	Index	100	110	125	115	109

Base: All adults	Total (000)	Project (000)	Percent Across	Percent Down	Index
Total	211,845	14,945	8.5	100.0	100
Age 18–24	27,492	5,007	21.9	33.5	258
Age 25–34	39,096	5,842	14.9	32.6	176
Age 35–44	44,333	3,155	7.1	17.6	84
Age 45–54	40,026	1,964	4.9	10.9	58
Age 55–64	26,743	585	2.2	3.3	26
Age 65+	34,155	392	1.1	2.2	14
Adults 18–34	66,588	11,849	17.8	66.0	210
Adults 18–49	132,201	16,030	12.1	89.3	143
Adults 25–54	123,455	10,962	8.9	61.1	105
Men 18–34	33,202	8,265	24.9	46.1	294
Men 18–49	65,359	10,811	16.5	60.2	195
Men 25–54	60,686	7,168	11.8	39.9	139
Women 18–34	33,386	3,583	10.7	20.0	127
Women 18–49	66,841	5,219	7.8	29.1	92
Women 25–54	62,769	3,794	6.0	21.1	71
Educ: graduated college plus	51,950	3,198	6.2	17.8	73
Educ: attended college	57,213	6,043	10.6	33.7	125
Educ: graduated high school	67,355	5,861	8.7	32.7	103
Educ: did not graduate high school	35,327	2,843	8.0	15.8	95
Educ: post graduate	17,196	742	4.3	4.1	51
Educ: no college	102,682	8,704	8.5	48.5	100
Occupation: professional	22,111	1,621	7.3	9.0	87
Occupation: executive/admin/managerial	20,682	1,299	6.3	7.2	74
Occupation: clerical/sales/technical	38,455	4,028	10.5	22.4	124
Occupation: precision/crafts/repair	14,379	1,484	10.3	8.3	122
Occupation: other	39,596	4,778	12.1	26.6	142
HHI $150,000+	14,089	929	6.6	5.2	78
HHI $75,000–$149,999	51,008	4,078	8.0	22.7	94
HHI $60,000–$74,999	24,052	2,178	9.1	12.1	107
HHI $50,000–$59,999	18,915	1,447	7.6	8.1	90

Figure 10-6 Principal Users of Videogames—MRI Report

While the index is helpful, it should not be used alone. Percentages and product usage figures are also needed to get an accurate picture of the market. Just because the index for a particular segment of the population is very high, that doesn't always mean it is an attractive segment to target. The high index may be a result of a low denominator (a very small proportion of the population in this segment). In Figure 10-7, the 18- to 24-year-old age segment has the highest index, but it also has both the lowest product usage and the lowest population percentage. A marketer who relied solely on the index would be ignoring a full 82 percent of product users.

Keep in mind that while Simmons and MRI provide demographic, geographic, and psychographic information, other factors may be more useful in defining specific markets. As noted by Joe Mandese, interests and activities may be more relevant for media buying.[4]

Age Segment	Population in Segment (%)	Product Use in Segment (%)	Index
18–24	15.1	18.0	119
25–34	25.1	25.0	100
35–44	20.6	21.0	102
45+	39.3	36.0	91

Figure 10-7 How High Indexes Can Be Misleading

What Internal and External Factors Are Operating?

Media strategies are influenced by both internal and external factors operating at any given time. *Internal factors* may involve the size of the media budget, managerial and administrative capabilities, or the organization of the agency, as demonstrated in Figure 10-8. *External factors* may include the economy (the rising costs of media), changes in technology (the availability of new media), competitive factors, and the like. While some of this information may require primary research, much information is available through secondary sources, including magazines, syndicated services, and even the daily newspaper.

One service's competitive information was shown in Figure 10-2. The Competitive Media Reporting Service provides media spending figures for various brands competing in the same market. Competitive information is also available from many other sources, as shown in Appendix A to this chapter.

Where to Promote?

The question of where to promote relates to geographic considerations. As noted in Chapter 7, companies often find that sales are stronger in one area of the country or the world than another and may allocate advertising expenditures according to the market potential of an area. For years, Whirlpool has had a much greater brand share of the appliance market in the East and Midwest than in the Southeast and West. The

Figure 10-8 Organizing the Media Buying Department

While various firms and ad agencies have different ways of organizing the media buying department, three seem to be the most common. The first form employs a product/media focus, the second places more emphasis on the market itself, and the third organizes around media classes alone:

- **Form 1** In this organizational arrangement, the media buyers and assistant media buyers are responsible for a product or group of products and/or brands. Their media planner both plans and buys for these products/brands in whichever geographic areas they are marketed. For example, if the agency is responsible for the advertising of Hart skis, the media planners determine the appropriate media in each area for placing the ads for these skis. The logic underlying this approach is that the planner knows the product and will identify the best media and vehicles for promoting it.
- **Form 2** In this approach, the market is the focal point of attention. Media planners become "experts" in a particular market area and are responsible for planning and buying for all products/brands the firm and/or agency markets in those areas. For example, a planner may be responsible for the Memphis, Tennessee, market. If the agency has more than one client who wishes to market in this area, media selection for all of the brands/products is the responsibility of the same person. The logic is that his or her knowledge of the media and vehicles in the area allows for a more informed media choice. The nonquantitative characteristics of the media get more attention under this approach.
- **Form 3** Organizing around a specific class of media—for example, print or broadcast—is a third alternative. The purchasing and development unit handles all the agency print or broadcast business. Members of the media department become specialists who are brought in very early in the promotional planning process. Planners perform only planning functions, while buyers are responsible for all purchases. The buying function itself may be specialized with specific responsibilities for specialty advertising, national buys, local buys, and so on. Knowledge of the media and the audience each serves is considered a major benefit. Also, people who handle all the media buys can negotiate better deals.

As to which strategy works best, who's to say? Each has been in use for some time. The second approach requires that the agency be big enough and have enough clients to support the geographic assignment. The third alternative seems to be the most common design.

CAREER PROFILE

Lisa Steiner

Assistant Broadcast Negotiator, PHD Network, a Division of Omnicom Group

Whoever thought that you could make a living by simply watching TV? Sounds like the perfect profession. My recent graduation from San Diego State University led to just that, as I stumbled across a media buying job and into an advertising career. I was hired on as an assistant broadcast negotiator for a prominent media service agency, PHD. Our department specializes in purchasing commercial time in spot, syndicated, and cable television as well as spot radio. We represent several clients including Daimler Chrysler and Mitsubishi. It's exciting to have the opportunity to work on so many high-profile accounts.

PHD is a worldwide agency with several locations. Our office in Los Angeles covers most markets in the western region of the United States. I specifically assist two negotiators who buy commercial airtime from stations in the San Francisco and Sacramento, California, markets.

One of the many exciting parts of my job is learning about the products that we purchase from the stations. My favorite time of year comes in June and July when the stations send their sales reps to our office to present the upcoming fall line-up. This means that we get to see the season premieres of all new programs before they are offered to the public. Once the buyers are familiar with the available inventory, they will begin to estimate ratings for these shows. Predicting the success of a particular program can be extremely challenging, especially if it is brand new, because it has no history to evaluate. Buyers will analyze several different rating books and use many formulas to predict these ratings. But it isn't always so mathematical. They will also consider many trends, such as a program's current popularity or competing programs in a particular time period. Market conditions play a major role in predicting these numbers as well.

Negotiations are also a major part of media buying. Buyers and sales reps will debate their estimated ratings and costs until agreements are reached. It is vital for the buyer to have done a thorough analysis of available research prior to negotiations, so that they can defend their estimates based on facts. It is the ultimate goal of the buyer to get the client the most exposure for the least amount of money. It is also important to remember that in the end, it is the buyer who has to explain the results to the client.

"We get to see the season premieres of all new programs before they are offered to the public."

My primary role as an assistant is to monitor and maintain the buy schedule after the order has been placed with the station. It is inevitable that some inventory on the original buy will not be available. Oftentimes a station will bump us out of a spot; for example, a presidential speech causes the regularly scheduled program to be missed or maybe a baseball game ran late. Nonetheless, the station will offer us a "make good" in an attempt to replace a spot that was missed. I get to decide if we want to accept or reject the offer.

The majority of my time as an assistant is spent resolving what are called "discrepancies." A spot is considered "discrepant" if it did not run according to our ordered schedule. It is my job to find which spots aired incorrectly, and then I determine if these spots are efficient in helping us reach our goal. I decide to accept these spots if they delivered at least our estimated rating, and I will credit a spot if it under-delivered the rating. If they didn't air our ordered spots at all, then I need to get the station to make them good within the next month. It all comes down to how closely our overall estimated numbers match up to the overall actual number. Monitoring each spot helps us to be more accurate.

As a recent college graduate, I am lucky to have found my niche so quickly. Media buying perfectly fits my personality because I am extremely detail-oriented and enjoy working with numbers. I find it exciting to work with broadcast media, not to mention attending endless lunches and dinners—even sporting events and concerts. In the past year I have been exposed to a world of endless opportunities, not only in media buying, but in the entire industry of advertising communications. But like anything else, expect long hours and a lot of hard work. As I lay the foundation for my career, I am excited to see what lies ahead. However, thus far, the most important lesson that media buying has taught me is that if you can learn to estimate accurately, you are bound to achieve your goal.

question is, where will the ad dollars be more wisely spent? Should Whirlpool allocate additional promotional monies to those markets where the brand is already the leader to maintain market share, or does more potential exist in those markets where the firm is not doing as well and there is more room to grow? Perhaps the best answer is that the firm should spend advertising and promotion dollars where they will be the most effective—that is, in those markets where they will achieve the desired objectives. Unfortunately, as we have seen so often, it is not always possible to measure directly the impact of promotional efforts. At the same time, certain tactics can assist the planner in making this determination.

Using Indexes to Determine Where to Promote In addition to the indexes from Simmons and MRI, three other indexes may also be useful:

1. The **survey of buying power index,** published annually by *Sales & Marketing Management* magazine, is conducted for every major metropolitan market in the United States and is based on a number of factors, including population, effective buying income, and total retail sales in the area. Each of these factors is individually weighted to drive a buying power index that charts the potential of a particular metro area, county, or city relative to the United States as a whole. The resulting index gives media planners insight into the relative value of that market, as shown in Figure 10-9. When used in combination with other market information, the survey of buying power index helps the marketer determine which geographic areas to target.
2. The **brand development index (BDI)** helps marketers factor the rate of product usage by geographic area into the decision process.

$$\text{BDI} = \frac{\text{Percentage of brand to total U.S. sales in the market}}{\text{Percentage of total U.S. population in the market}} \times 100$$

The BDI compares the percentage of the brand's total U.S. sales in a given market area with the percentage of the total population in the market to determine the sales potential for that brand in that market area. An example of this calculation is shown in Figure 10-10. The higher the index number, the more market potential exists. In this case, the index number indicates this market has high potential for brand development.

3. The **category development index (CDI)** is computed in the same manner as the BDI, except it uses information regarding the product category (as opposed to the brand) in the numerator:

$$\text{CDI} = \frac{\text{Percentage of product category total sales in market}}{\text{Percentage of total U.S. population in market}} \times 100$$

The CDI provides information on the potential for development of the total product category rather than specific brands. When this information is combined with the BDI, a much more insightful promotional strategy may be developed. For example, consider the market potential for coffee in the United States. One might first look at how well the product category does in a specific market area. In Utah and Idaho, for example, the category potential is low (see Figure 10-11). The marketer analyzes the BDI to find how the brand is doing relative to other brands in this area. This information can then be used in determining how well a particular product category and a particular brand are performing and figuring what media weight (or quantity of advertising) would be required to gain additional market share, as shown in Figure 10-12.

While these indexes provide important insights into the market potential for the firm's products and/or brands, this information is supplemental to the overall strategy determined earlier in the promotional decision-making process. In fact, much of this information may have already been provided to the media planner. Since it may be used more specifically to determine the media weights to assign to each area, this decision ultimately affects the budget allocated to each area as well as other factors such as reach, frequency, and scheduling.

Figure 10-9 Survey of Buying Power Index

Metro Area	Population					Effective Buying Income				Retail Sales				Buying Power Index	
County	1/1/01 Total Pop. (000s)	1/1/06 Total Pop. (000s)	% Change 2001–2006	1/1/06 Total Hshlds. (000s)	% Change 2001–2006	2005 Total EBI ($000)	% Change 2000–2005	Average Household EBI ($) 2000	Average Household EBI ($) 2005	2006 Total Retail Sales ($000)	% Change 2001–2006	Retail Sales per Household ($) 2001	Retail Sales per Household ($) 2006	2001	2006
OREGON															
CORVALLIS	78.7	81.1	3.0	30.9	4.4	1,854,799	30.6	47,993	60,026	992,224	31.9	25,423	32,111	.0253	.0263
BENTON	78.7	81.1	3.0	30.9	4.4	1,854,799	30.6	47.993	60,026	992,224	31.9	25,423	32,111	.0253	.0263
EUGENE-SPRINGFIELD	**326.0**	**343.0**	**5.2**	**137.7**	**6.4**	**6,555,563**	**25.9**	**40,234**	**47,608**	**5,760,107**	**20.8**	**36,864**	**41,831**	**.1118**	**.1124**
LANE	326.0	343.0	5.2	137.7	6.4	6,555,563	25.9	40,234	47,608	5,760,107	20.8	36,864	41,831	.1118	.1124
MEDFORD-ASHLAND	183.9	198.5	7.9	80.2	9.4	3,698,500	28.2	39,366	46,116	5,323,418	36.8	53,074	66,377	.0725	.0769
JACKSON	183.9	198.5	7.9	80.2	9.4	3,698,500	28.2	39,366	46,116	5,323,418	36.8	53,074	66,377	.0725	.0769
PORTLAND-VANCOUVER	**1,948.3**	**2,125.2**	**9.1**	**835.6**	**9.9**	**52,817,163**	**35.6**	**51,205**	**63,209**	**36,596,371**	**26.1**	**38,160**	**43,797**	**.7474**	**.7940**
CLACKAMAS	342.9	372.6	8.7	141.7	9.8	10,102,780	35.8	57,611	71,297	4,621,412	12.8	31,730	32,614	.1288	.1343
COLUMBIA	44.0	48.9	11.1	18.4	12.2	973,958	34.4	44,179	52,933	421,167	36.4	18,823	22,890	.0126	.0136
MULTNOMAH	666.2	688.8	3.4	287.1	3.9	15,876,995	26.6	45,390	55,301	16,090,416	32.2	44,054	56,045	.2665	.2751
WASHINGTON	455.4	507.4	11.4	198.4	12.6	14,049,490	40.1	56,921	70,814	9,554,319	19.0	46,041	48,661	.1945	.2076
YAMHILL	86.5	97.3	12.5	33.8	14.2	1,949,382	36.9	48,097	57,674	960,790	15.2	28,169	28,426	.0265	.0281
CLARK, WASH	353.3	410.2	16.1	156.2	17.4	9,864,558	45.3	51,050	63,153	4,848,267	38.4	26,332	31,039	.1185	.1353
PORTLAND-SALEM CONSOLIDATED AREA	**2,300.7**	**2,507.5**	**9.0**	**979.9**	**9.9**	**60,054,928**	**35.0**	**49,892**	**61,287**	**42,004,281**	**26.1**	**37,370**	**42,866**	**.8604**	**.9116**
SALEM	**352.4**	**382.3**	**8.5**	**144.3**	**10.1**	**7,237,765**	**30.6**	**42,276**	**50,158**	**5,407,910**	**25.8**	**32,784**	**37,477**	**.1130**	**.1176**
MARION	289.1	312.2	8.0	118.1	9.7	5,934,535	30.2	42,308	50,250	5,193,924	26.5	38,135	43,979	.0976	.1014
POLK	63.3	70.1	10.7	26.2	12.0	1,303,230	32.2	42,130	49,742	213,986	12.2	8,153	8,167	.0154	.0162
TOTAL METRO COUNTIES	**2,536.0**	**2,719.9**	**7.3**	**1,072.5**	**8.2**	**62,299.232**	**32.0**	**47,640**	**58,088**	**49,231,763**	**25.5**	**39,590**	**45,904**	**.9515**	**.9919**
TOTAL STATE	**3,464.9**	**3,702.3**	**6.9**	**1,465.3**	**8.0**	**78,533,444**	**30.3**	**44,416**	**53,595**	**62,519,210**	**24.5**	**37,014**	**42,666**	**1.2320**	**1.2726**

Source: *Sales & Marketing Management.*

$$BDI = \frac{\text{Percentage of brand sales in South Atlantic region}}{\text{Percentage of U.S. population in South Atlantic region}} \times 100$$

$$= \frac{50\%}{16\%} \times 100$$

$$= 312$$

Figure 10-10 Calculating BDI

$$CDI = \frac{\text{Percentage of product category sales in Utah/Idaho}}{\text{Percentage of total U.S. population in Utah/Idaho}} \times 100$$

$$= \frac{1\%}{1\%} \times 100$$

$$= 100$$

$$BDI = \frac{\text{Percentage of total brand sales in Utah/Idaho}}{\text{Percentage of total U.S. population in Utah/Idaho}} \times 100$$

$$= \frac{2\%}{1\%} \times 100$$

$$= 200$$

Figure 10-11 Using CDI and BDI to Determine Market Potential

	High BDI	Low BDI
High CDI	High market share Good market potential	Low market share Good market potential
Low CDI	High market share Monitor for sales decline	Low market share Poor market potential

High BDI and high CDI	This market usually represents good sales potential for both the product category and the brand.
High BDI and low CDI	The category is not selling well, but the brand is; probably a good market to advertise in but should be monitored for declining sales.
Low BDI and high CDI	The product category shows high potential but the brand is not doing well; the reasons should be determined.
Low BDI and low CDI	Both the product category and the brand are doing poorly; not likely to be a good place for advertising.

Figure 10-12 Using BDI and CDI Indexes

Establishing Media Objectives

Just as the situation analysis leads to establishment of marketing and communications objectives, the media situation analysis should lead to determination of specific media objectives. The media objectives are not ends in themselves. Rather, they are designed to lead to the attainment of communications and marketing objectives. Media objectives are the goals for the media program and should be limited to those that can be accomplished through media strategies. An example of media objectives is this: Create awareness in the target market through the following:

- Use broadcast media to provide coverage of 80 percent of the target market over a six-month period.

- Reach 60 percent of the target audience at least three times over the same six-month period.
- Concentrate heaviest advertising in winter and spring, with lighter emphasis in summer and fall.

Developing and Implementing Media Strategies

Having determined what is to be accomplished, media planners consider how to achieve these objectives. That is, they develop and implement media strategies, which evolve directly from the actions required to meet objectives and involve the criteria in Figure 10-13.

The Media Mix

A wide variety of media and media vehicles are available to advertisers. While it is possible that only one medium and/or vehicle might be employed, it is much more likely that a number of alternatives will be used. The objectives sought, the characteristics of the product or service, the size of the budget, and individual preferences are just some of the factors that determine what combination of media will be used.

As an example, consider a promotional situation in which a product requires a visual demonstration to be communicated effectively. In this case, TV may be the most effective medium. If the promotional strategy calls for coupons to stimulate trial, print media may be necessary. For in-depth information, the Internet may be best.

By employing a media mix, advertisers can add more versatility to their media strategies, since each medium contributes its own distinct advantages (as demonstrated in later chapters). By combining media, marketers can increase coverage, reach, and frequency levels while improving the likelihood of achieving overall communications and marketing goals.

Target Market Coverage

The media planner determines which target markets should receive the most media emphasis. Developing media strategies involves matching the most appropriate media to this market by asking, "Through which media and media vehicles can I best get my message to prospective buyers?" The issue here is to get coverage of the market, as shown in Figure 10-14. The optimal goal is full market coverage, shown in the second pie chart. But this is a very optimistic scenario. More realistically, conditions shown in the third and fourth charts are most likely to occur. In the third chart, the coverage of the media does not allow for coverage of the entire market, leaving some potential customers without exposure to the message. In the fourth chart, the marketer is faced with a problem of overexposure (also called **waste coverage**), in which the media coverage exceeds the targeted audience. If media coverage reaches people who are not sought as buyers and are not potential users, then it is wasted. (This term is used for coverage that reaches people who are not potential buyers and/or users. Consumers may not be part of the intended target market but may still be considered as potential—for example, those who buy the product as a gift for someone else.)

Figure 10-13 Criteria Considered in the Development of Media Plans

- The media mix
- Target market coverage
- Geographic coverage
- Scheduling
- Reach versus frequency
- Creative aspects and mood
- Flexibility
- Budget considerations

The goal of the media planner is to extend media coverage to as many of the members of the target audience as possible while minimizing the amount of waste coverage. The situation usually involves trade-offs. Sometimes one has to live with less coverage than desired; other times, the most effective media expose people not sought. In this instance, waste coverage is justified because the media employed are likely to be the most effective means of delivery available and the cost of the waste coverage is exceeded by the value gained from their use.

When watching football games on TV, you may have noticed commercials for stock brokerage firms such as Charles Schwab, Ameritrade, and E*Trade. Not all viewers are candidates for stock market services, but a very high percentage of potential cus-

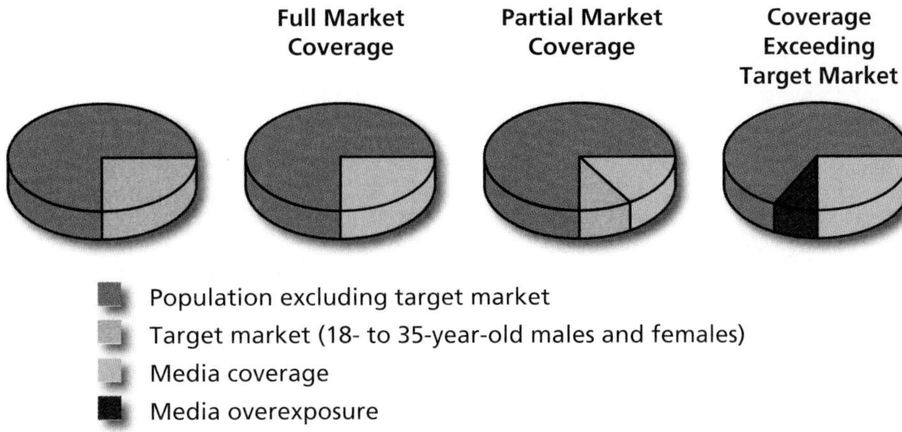

Figure 10-14 Marketing Coverage Possibilities

tomers can be reached with this strategy. So football programs are considered a good media buy because the ability to generate market coverage outweighs the disadvantages of high waste coverage.

Figure 10-15 shows how information provided by MRI can be used to match media to target markets. It profiles magazines read and TV shows watched by the videogame users identified in Figure 10-6. (You can practice using index numbers here.) From Figure 10-15, you can see that TechTV, Spike TV, *Allure,* and *American Photo* would likely be wise selections, whereas Turner Classic Movies, *American Legion,* or *Atlantic Monthly* would be less likely to lead to the desired exposures.

Geographic Coverage

Snow skiing is much more popular in some areas of the country than in others. It would not be the wisest of strategies to promote skis in those areas where interest is not high, unless you could generate an increase in interest. It may be possible to promote an interest in skiing in the Southeast, but a notable increase in sales of ski equipment is not very likely, given the market's distance from snow. The objective of weighting certain geographic areas more than others makes sense, and the strategy of exerting more promotional efforts and dollars in those areas follows naturally.

Scheduling

Obviously, companies would like to keep their advertising in front of consumers at all times as a constant reminder of the product and/or brand name. In reality, this is not possible for a variety of reasons (not the least of which is the budget). Nor is it necessary. The primary objective of *scheduling* is to time promotional efforts so that they will coincide with the highest potential buying times. For some products these times are not easy to identify; for others they are very obvious. Three scheduling methods available to the media planner—continuity, flighting, and pulsing—are shown in Figure 10-16 on page 317.

Continuity refers to a continuous pattern of advertising, which may mean every day, every week, or every month. The key is that a regular (continuous) pattern is developed without gaps or nonadvertising periods. Such strategies might be used for advertising for food products, laundry detergents, or other products consumed on an ongoing basis without regard for seasonality.

A second method, **flighting,** employs a less regular schedule, with intermittent periods of advertising and nonadvertising. At some time periods there are heavier promotional expenditures, and at others there may be no advertising. Many banks, for example, spend no money on advertising in the summer but maintain advertising throughout the rest of the year. Snow skis are advertised heavily between October and April; less in May, August, and September; and not at all in June and July.

Pulsing is actually a combination of the first two methods. In a pulsing strategy, continuity is maintained, but at certain times promotional efforts are stepped up. In the beer industry, advertising continues throughout the year but may increase at holiday

		Total (000)	Proj (000)	Pct across	Pct down	Index
Science Channel		7,235	902	12.5	5.0	147
Sci-Fi Channel		28,480	3,541	12.4	19.7	147
Soap Net	*	5,223	404	7.7	2.3	91
Speed Channel		9,569	1,347	14.1	7.5	166
Spike TV		13,779	1,994	14.5	11.1	171
Style	*	4,789	451	9.4	2.5	111
Sundance	*	2,655	330	12.4	1.8	145
Superstation WGN		21,877	2,186	10.0	12.2	118
TBS		63,229	6,783	10.7	37.8	127
TechTV		3,659	787	21.5	4.4	254
TLC (The Learning Channel)		41,792	4,056	9.7	22.6	115
Toon Disney		13,680	1,409	10.3	7.9	122
The Travel Channel		25,026	2,023	8.1	11.3	95
TNT (Turner Network Television)		58,108	5,654	9.7	31.5	115
TCM (Turner Classic Movies)		23,695	1,528	6.4	8.5	76
TV Guide Channel		20,835	1,848	8.9	10.3	105
TV Land		21,342	1,782	8.3	9.9	99
USA Network		56,210	6,118	10.9	34.1	128
VH1		25,537	4,259	16.7	23.7	197
VH1 Classic		3,760	552	14.7	3.1	173
The Weather Channel		73,917	5,568	7.5	31.0	89
WE: Women's Entertainment		11,333	1,072	9.5	6.0	112
AARP The Magazine		25,002	644	2.6	3.6	112
Allure	*	4,301	479	11.1	2.7	131
American Baby		6,735	783	11.6	4.4	137
American Hunter	*	3,912	455	11.6	2.5	137
American Legion	*	3,449	99	2.9	0.6	34
American Photo	*	1,356	256	18.9	1.4	223
American Rifleman	*	4,529	483	10.7	2.7	126
American Way	*	1,218	85	7.0	0.5	82
American Woodworker	*	4,132	325	7.9	1.8	93
Architectural Digest	*	4,746	210	4.4	1.2	52
Arthritis Today	*	3,014	155	5.1	0.9	61
Arthur Frommer's Budget Travel	*	1,666	98	5.9	0.5	69
Atlantic Monthly	*	1,366	37	2.7	0.2	32
Attache	*	13,21	112	8.5	0.6	101
Automobile	*	3,343	518	15.5	2.9	183

* Denotes sample size less than 50

Figure 10-15 MRI Provides Media Usage of Videogame Buyers

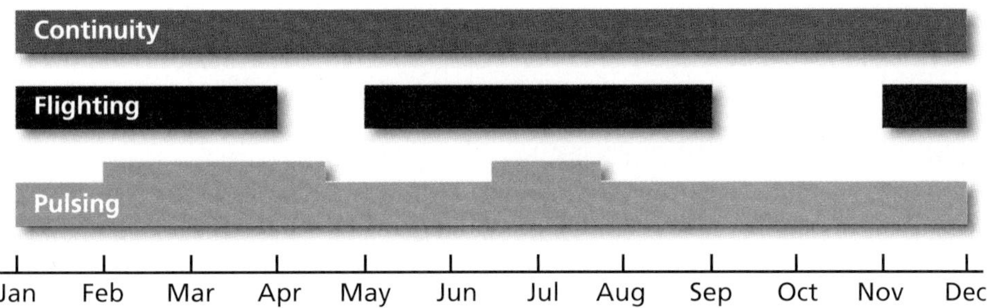

Figure 10-16 Three Methods of Promotional Scheduling

periods such as Memorial Day, Labor Day, or the Fourth of July. The scheduling strategy depends on the objectives, buying cycles, and budget, among other factors. There are certain advantages and disadvantages to each scheduling method, as shown in Figure 10-17. One recent and comprehensive study (acclaimed by many in the TV research community as "the most comprehensive study ever to shed light on scheduling") indicates that continuity is more effective than flighting. On the basis of the idea that it is important to get exposure to the message as close as possible to when the consumer is going to make the purchase, the study concludes that advertisers should continue weekly schedules as long as possible.[5] The key here may be the "as long as possible" qualification. Given a significant budget, continuity may be more of an option than it is for those with more limited budgets.

Reach versus Frequency

Since advertisers have a variety of objectives and face budget constraints, they usually must trade off reach and frequency. They must decide whether to have the message be seen or heard by more people (reach) or by fewer people more often (frequency).

How Much Reach Is Necessary?

Thinking back to the hierarchies discussed in Chapter 5, you will recall that the first stage of each model requires awareness of the

	Continuity
Advantages	Serves as a constant reminder to the consumer Covers the entire buying cycle Allows for media priorities (quantity discounts, preferred locations, etc.)
Disadvantages	Higher costs Potential for overexposure Limited media allocation possible

	Flighting
Advantages	Cost efficiency of advertising only during purchase cycles May allow for inclusion of more than one medium or vehicle with limited budgets
Disadvantages	Weighting may offer more exposure and advantage over competitors Increased likelihood of wearout Lack of awareness, interest, retention of promotional message during nonscheduled times Vulnerability to competitive efforts during nonscheduled periods

	Pulsing
Advantages	All of the same as the previous two methods
Disadvantages	Not required for seasonal products (or other cyclical products)

Figure 10-17 Characteristics of Scheduling Methods

product and/or brand. The more people are aware, the more are likely to move to each subsequent stage. Achieving awareness requires reach—that is, exposing potential buyers to the message. New brands or products need a very high level of reach, since the objective is to make all potential buyers aware of the new entry. High reach is also desired at later stages of the hierarchy. For example, at the trial stage of the adoption hierarchy, a promotional strategy might use cents-off coupons or free samples. An objective of the marketer is to reach a larger number of people with these samples, in an attempt to make them learn of the product, try it, and develop favorable attitudes toward it. (In turn, these attitudes may lead to purchase.)

The problem arises because there is no known way of determining how much reach is required to achieve levels of awareness, attitude change, or buying intentions, nor can we be sure an ad placed in a vehicle will actually reach the intended audience. (There has been some research on the first problem, which will be discussed in the section below on effective reach.)

If you buy advertising time on *60 Minutes,* will everyone who is tuned to the program see the ad? No. Many viewers will leave the room, be distracted during the commercial, and so on, as shown in Figure 10-18 (which also provides a good example of the difference between reach and coverage). If I expose everyone in my target group to the message once, will this be sufficient to create a 100 percent level of awareness? The answer again is no. This leads to the next question: What frequency of exposure is necessary for the ad to be seen and to have an impact?

What Frequency Level Is Needed?

With respect to media planning, *frequency* carries a slightly different meaning. (Remember when we said one of the problems in media planning is that terms often take on different meanings?) Here frequency is the number of times one is exposed to the media vehicle, not necessarily to the ad itself. While one study has estimated the actual audience for a commercial may be as much as 30 percent lower than that for the program, not all researchers agree.[6] Figure 10-18 demonstrates that depending on the program, this number may range from 12 to 40 percent.

Most advertisers do agree that a 1:1 exposure ratio does not exist. So while your ad may be placed in a certain vehicle, the fact that a consumer has been exposed to that vehicle does not ensure that your ad has been seen. As a result, the frequency level

Figure 10-18 Who's Still There to Watch the Ads?

How many viewers actually watch a commercial? R. D. Percy & Co. reports that its advanced people meters, equipped with heat sensors that detect viewers present, indicate that spots retain, on average, 82 percent of the average-minute ratings for the quarter hour. During early morning news programs, "commercial efficiency" (as Percy calls it) is lower because so many people are bustling about, out of the room (blue), but the rate rises at night.

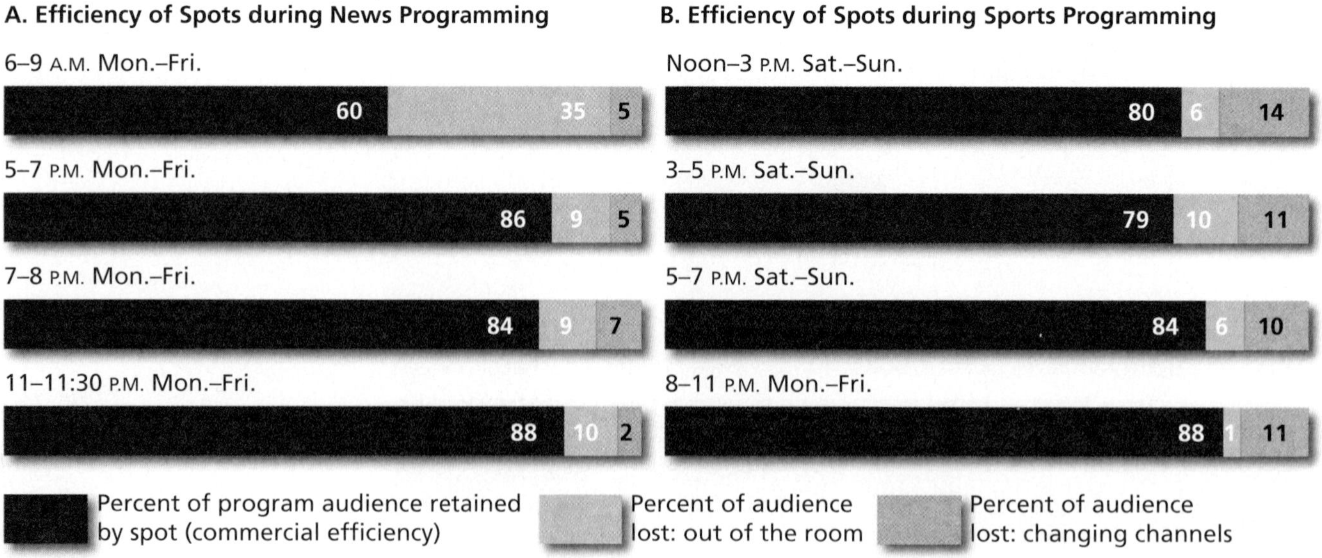

A. Efficiency of Spots during News Programming

	Percent of program audience retained by spot (commercial efficiency)	Percent of audience lost: out of the room	Percent of audience lost: changing channels
6–9 A.M. Mon.–Fri.	60	35	5
5–7 P.M. Mon.–Fri.	86	9	5
7–8 P.M. Mon.–Fri.	84	9	7
11–11:30 P.M. Mon.–Fri.	88	10	2

B. Efficiency of Spots during Sports Programming

	Percent of program audience retained by spot (commercial efficiency)	Percent of audience lost: out of the room	Percent of audience lost: changing channels
Noon–3 P.M. Sat.–Sun.	80	6	14
3–5 P.M. Sat.–Sun.	79	10	11
5–7 P.M. Sat.–Sun.	84	6	10
8–11 P.M. Mon.–Fri.	88	1	11

expressed in the media plan overstates the actual level of exposure to the ad. This overstatement has led some media buyers to refer to the reach of the media vehicle as "opportunities to see" an ad rather than actual exposure to it.

Because the advertiser has no sure way of knowing whether exposure to a vehicle results in exposure to the ad, the media and advertisers have adopted a compromise: One exposure to the vehicle constitutes reach, given that this exposure must occur for the viewer even to have an opportunity to see the ad. Thus, the exposure figure is used to calculate reach and frequency levels. But this compromise does not help determine the frequency required to make an impact. The creativity of the ad, the involvement of the receiver, noise, and many other intervening factors confound any attempts to make a precise determination.

At this point, you may be thinking, "If nobody knows this stuff, how do they make these decisions?" That's a good question, and the truth is that the decisions are not always made on hard data. Says Joseph Ostrow, executive vice president/director of communications services with Young and Rubicam, "Establishing frequency goals for an advertising campaign is a mix of art and science but with a definite bias toward art."[7] Let us first examine the process involved in setting reach and frequency objectives and then discuss the logic of each.

Establishing Reach and Frequency Objectives

It is possible to be exposed to more than one media vehicle with an ad, resulting in repetition (frequency). If one ad is placed on one TV show one time, the number of people exposed is the reach. If the ad is placed on two shows, the total number exposed once is **unduplicated reach.** Some people will see the ad twice. The reach of the two shows, as depicted in Figure 10-19, includes a number of people who were reached by both shows (C). This overlap is referred to as **duplicated reach.**

Both unduplicated and duplicated reach figures are important. Unduplicated reach indicates potential new exposures, while duplicated reach provides an estimate of frequency. Most media buys include both forms of reach. Let us consider an example.

A measure of potential reach in the broadcast industry is the TV (or radio) **program rating.** This number is expressed as a percentage. For an estimate of the total number of homes reached, multiply this percentage times the number of homes with TV sets. For example, if there are 109.5 million homes with TV sets in the United States and the program has a rating of 30, then the calculation is 0.30 times 109.5, or 32.85 million homes. (We go into much more detail on ratings and other broadcast terms in Chapter 11.)

A. Reach of One TV Program

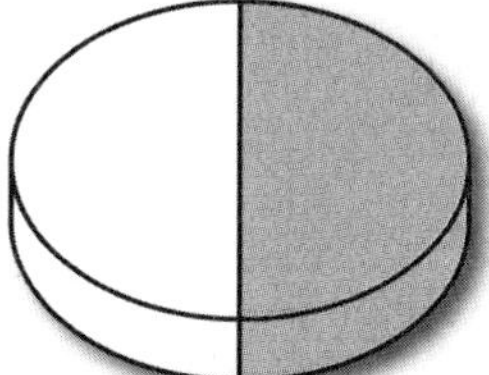

Total market audience reached

B. Reach of Two Programs

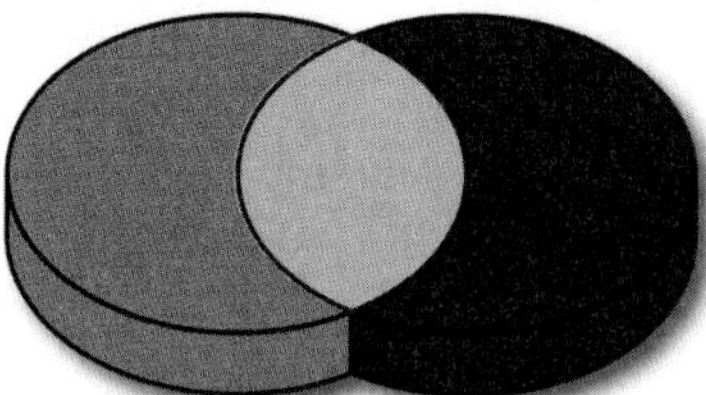

Total market audience reached

C. Duplicated Reach

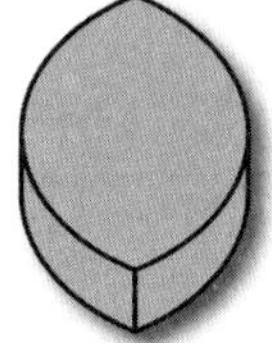

Total market reached with both shows

D. Unduplicated Reach

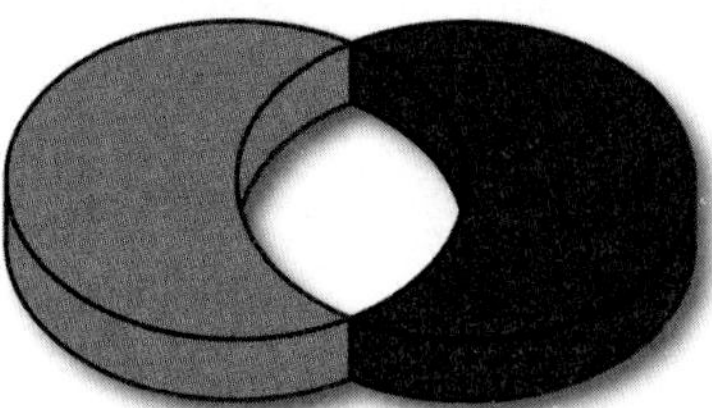

Total reach less duplicated reach

Figure 10-19 Representation of Reach and Frequency

Using Gross Ratings Points The media buyer typically uses a numerical indicator to know how many potential audience members may be exposed to a series of commercials. A summary measure that combines the program rating and the average number of times the home is reached during this period (frequency of exposure) is a commonly used reference point known as **gross ratings points (GRPs):**

$$\text{GRP} = \text{Reach} \times \text{Frequency}$$

GRPs are based on the total audience the media schedule may reach; they use a duplicated reach estimate. **Target ratings points (TRPs)** refer to the number of people in the primary target audience the media buy will reach—and the number of times. Unlike GRP, TRP does not include waste coverage.

Given that GRPs do not measure actual reach, the advertiser must ask: How many GRPs are needed to attain a certain reach? How do these GRPs translate into effective reach? For example, how many GRPs must one purchase to attain an unduplicated reach of 50 percent, and what frequency of exposure will this schedule deliver? The following example may help you to understand how this process works.

First you must know what these ratings points represent. A purchase of 100 GRPs could mean 100 percent of the market is exposed once or 50 percent of the market is exposed twice or 25 percent of the market is exposed four times, and so on. As you can see, this information must be more specific for the marketer to use it effectively. To know how many GRPs are necessary, the manager needs to know how many members of the intended audience the schedule actually reaches. The graph in Figure 10-20 helps make this determination.

In Figure 10-20, a purchase of 100 TRPs on one network would yield an estimated reach of 32 percent of the total households in the target market. This figure would climb to 37.2 percent if two networks were used and 44.5 percent with three. Working backward through the formula for GRPs, the estimate of frequency of exposure—3.125, 2.688, and 2.247, respectively—demonstrates the trade-off between reach and frequency.

As an example of a media buy, Denny's purchased 1,300 GRPs in a 10-week period to introduce a new Grand Slam promotion. This purchase employed TV spots in 28 markets and was estimated to reach 40 percent of the target audience an average of 17 times. To determine if this was a wise media buy, we need to know whether this was an effective reach figure. Certainly, reaching 40 percent of the target market is attractive. But why was the frequency level so high? And was it likely to be effective? In other words, does this level of GRPs affect awareness, attitudes, and purchase intentions?

A number of researchers have explored this issue. David Berger, vice president and director of research at Foote, Cone & Belding, has determined that 2,500 GRPs are likely to lead to roughly a 70 percent probability of high awareness, 1,000 to 2,500 would yield about a 33 percent probability, and less than 1,000 would probably result in almost no awareness.[8] David Olson obtained similar results and further showed that as awareness increased, trial of the product would also increase, although at a significantly slower rate.[9] In both cases, it was evident that high numbers of GRPs were required to make an impact.

Figure 10-20 Estimates of Reach for Network TRPs

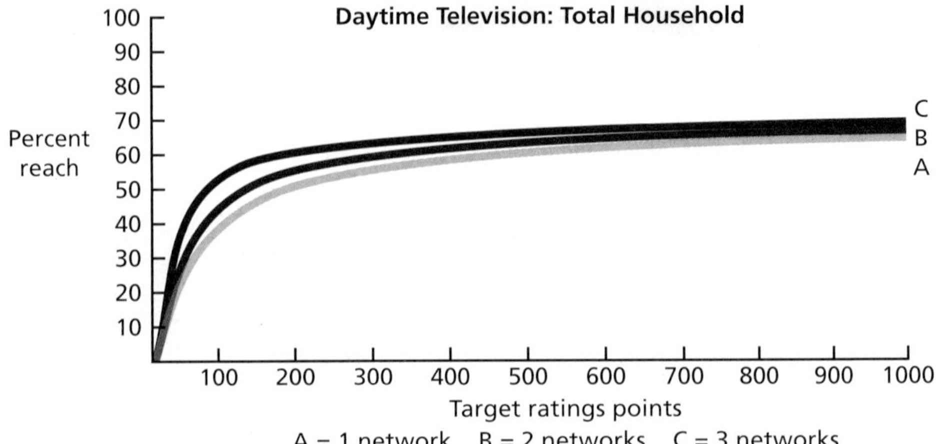

1. One exposure of an ad to a target group within a purchase cycle has little or no effect in most circumstances.
2. Since one exposure is usually ineffective, the central goal of productive media planning should be to enhance frequency rather than reach.
3. The evidence suggests strongly that an exposure frequency of two within a purchase cycle is an effective level.
4. Beyond three exposures within a brand purchase cycle or over a period of four or even eight weeks, increasing frequency continues to build advertising effectiveness at a decreasing rate but with no evidence of decline.
5. Although there are general principles with respect to frequency of exposure and its relationship to advertising effectiveness, differential effects by brand are equally important.
6. Nothing we have seen suggests that frequency response principles or generalizations vary by medium.
7. The data strongly suggest that wearout is not a function of too much frequency; it is more of a creative or copy problem.

Figure 10-21 The Effects of Reach and Frequency

Figure 10-21 summarizes the effects that can be expected at different levels of exposure, on the basis of research in this area. A number of factors may be operating, and direct relationships may be difficult to establish.[10] In addition to the results shown in Figure 10-21, Joseph Ostrow has shown that while the number of repetitions increases awareness rapidly, it has much less impact on attitudinal and behavioral responses.[11]

You can imagine how expensive it was for Denny's to purchase 1,300 gross ratings points on TV. Now that you have additional information, we will ask again, "Was this a good buy?"

Determining Effective Reach

Since marketers have budget constraints, they must decide whether to increase reach at the expense of frequency or increase the frequency of exposure but to a smaller audience. A number of factors influence this decision. For example, a new product or brand introduction will attempt to maximize reach, particularly unduplicated reach, to create awareness in as many people as possible as quickly as possible. At the same time, for a high-involvement product or one whose benefits are not obvious, a certain level of frequency is needed to achieve effective reach.

Effective reach represents the percentage of a vehicle's audience reached at each effective frequency increment. This concept is based on the assumption that one exposure to an ad may not be enough to convey the desired message. As we saw earlier, no one knows the exact number of exposures necessary for an ad to make an impact, although advertisers have settled on three as the minimum. Effective reach (exposure) is shown in the shaded area in Figure 10-22 in the range of 3 to 10 exposures. Fewer than 3 exposures is considered insufficient reach, while more than 10 is considered overexposure and thus ineffective reach. This exposure level is no guarantee of effective communication; different messages may require more or fewer exposures. For example, Jack Myers, president of Myers Reports, argues that the three-exposure theory was valid in the 1970s when consumers were exposed to approximately 1,000 ads per day. Now that they are exposed to 3,000 to 5,000 per day, three exposures may not be enough. Adding in the fragmentation of television, the proliferation of magazines, and the advent of a variety of alternative media leads Myers to believe that 12 exposures may be the *minimum* level of frequency required. Also, Jim Surmanek, president/CEO of Media Analysis Plus, contends that the complexity of the message, message length, and recency of exposure also impact this figure.[12]

Since they do not know how many times the viewer will actually be exposed, advertisers typically purchase GRPs that lead to more than three exposures to increase the likelihood of effective reach and frequency. Surmanek also argues that effective reach can be as low as one exposure, if the exposure is very recent or close to the purchase occasion (thus, recency is more important than frequency). He contends that more exposures are necessary when the message is complex and requires several exposures to be understood.[13]

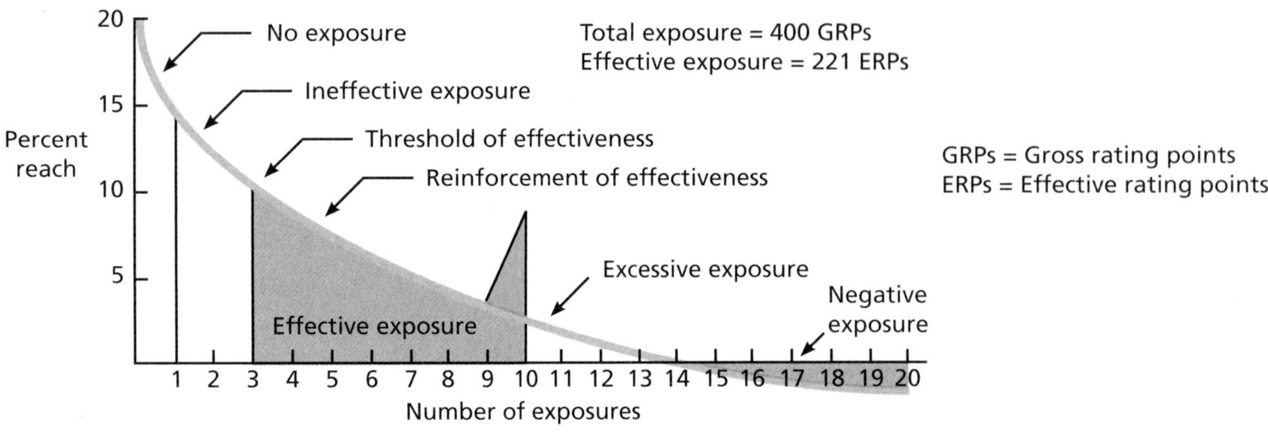

Figure 10-22 Graph of Effective Reach

Determining effective reach is further complicated by the fact that when calculating GRPs, advertisers use a figure that they call **average frequency,** or the average number of times the target audience reached by a media schedule is exposed to the vehicle over a specified period. The problem with this figure is revealed in the following scenario:

Consider a media buy in which:

50 percent of audience is reached 1 time.

30 percent of audience is reached 5 times.

20 percent of audience is reached 10 times.

Average frequency = 4

In this media buy, the average frequency is 4, which is slightly more than the number established as effective. Yet a full 50 percent of the audience receives only one exposure. Thus, the average-frequency number can be misleading, and using it to calculate GRPs might result in underexposing the audience.

Although GRPs have their problems, they can provide useful information to the marketer. A certain level of GRPs is necessary to achieve awareness, and increases in GRPs are likely to lead to more exposures and/or more repetitions—both of which are necessary to have an effect on higher-order objectives. Perhaps the best advice for purchasing GRPs is offered by Ostrow, who recommends the following strategies:[14]

1. Instead of using average frequency, the marketer should decide what minimum frequency goal is needed to reach the advertising objectives effectively and then maximize reach at that frequency level.
2. To determine effective frequency, one must consider marketing factors, message factors, and media factors. (See Figure 10-23.)

In summary, the reach-versus-frequency decision, while critical, is very difficult to make. A number of factors must be considered, and concrete rules do not always apply. The decision is often more of an art than a science.

Creative Aspects and Mood

The context of the medium in which the ad is placed may also affect viewers' perceptions. A specific creative strategy may require certain media. Because TV provides both sight and sound, it may be more effective in generating emotions than other media; magazines may create different perceptions from newspapers. In developing a media strategy, marketers must consider both creativity and mood factors. Let us examine each in more detail.

Creative Aspects It is possible to increase the success of a product significantly through a strong creative campaign. But to implement this creativity, you

Marketing Factors

- *Brand history.* Is the brand new or established? New brands generally require higher frequency levels.
- *Brand share.* An inverse relationship exists between brand share and frequency. The higher the brand share, the lower the frequency level required.
- *Brand loyalty.* An inverse relationship exists between loyalty and frequency. The higher the loyalty, the lower the frequency level required.
- *Purchase cycles.* Shorter purchasing cycles require higher frequency levels to maintain top-of-mind awareness.
- *Usage cycle.* Products used daily or more often need to be replaced quickly, so a higher level of frequency is desired.
- *Competitive share of voice.* Higher frequency levels are required when a lot of competitive noise exists and when the goal is to meet or beat competitors.
- *Target group.* The ability of the target group to learn and to retain messages has a direct effect on frequency.

Message or Creative Factors

- *Message complexity.* The simpler the message, the less frequency required.
- *Message uniqueness.* The more unique the message, the lower the frequency level required.
- *New versus continuing campaigns.* New campaigns require higher levels of frequency to register the message.
- *Image versus product sell.* Creating an image requires higher levels of frequency than does a specific product sell.
- *Message variation.* A single message requires less frequency; a variety of messages requires more.
- *Wearout.* Higher frequency may lead to wearout. This effect must be tracked and used to evaluate frequency levels.
- *Advertising units.* Larger units of advertising require less frequency than smaller ones to get the message across.

Media Factors

- *Clutter.* The more advertising that appears in the media used, the more frequency is needed to break through the clutter.
- *Editorial environment.* The more consistent the ad is with the editorial environment, the less frequency is needed.
- *Attentiveness.* The higher the level of attention achieved by the media vehicle, the less frequency is required. Low-attention-getting media require more repetitions.
- *Scheduling.* Continuous scheduling requires less frequency than does flighting or pulsing.
- *Number of media used.* The fewer media used, the lower the level of frequency required.
- *Repeat exposures.* Media that allow for more repeat exposures (for example, monthly magazines) require less frequency.

Figure 10-23 Factors Important in Determining Frequency Levels

must employ a medium that will support such a strategy. For example, the campaign for Lancome moisturizer shown in Chapter 4 used print media to communicate the message effectively. Hallmark, among many others, has effectively used TV to create emotional appeals. In some situations, the media strategy to be pursued may be the driving force behind the creative strategy, as the media and creative departments work closely together to achieve the greatest impact with the audience of the specific media.

Mood Certain media enhance the creativity of a message because they create a mood that carries over to the communication. For example, think about the moods created by the following magazines: *Gourmet, Skiing, Travel,* and *House Beautiful.* Each of these special-interest vehicles puts the reader in a particular mood. The promotion of fine wines, ski boots, luggage, and home products is enhanced by this mood. What different images might be created for your product if you advertised it in the following media?

The New York Times versus the *National Enquirer*

Architectural Digest versus *Reader's Digest*

A highly rated prime-time TV show versus an old rerun

Television versus the Internet

The message may require a specific medium and a certain media vehicle to achieve its objectives. Likewise, certain media and vehicles have images that may carry over to the perceptions of messages placed within them.

Flexibility

An effective media strategy requires a degree of flexibility. Because of the rapidly changing marketing environment, strategies may need to be modified. If the plan has not built in some flexibility, opportunities may be lost and/or the company may not be able to address new threats. Flexibility may be needed to address the following:

1. *Market opportunities.* Sometimes a market opportunity arises that the advertiser wishes to take advantage of. For example, wine companies have attempted to capitalize on the increasing interest in this drink created by changing trends in the U.S. marketplace. The development of a new advertising medium may offer an opportunity that was not previously available.
2. *Market threats.* Internal or external factors may pose a threat to the firm, and a change in media strategy is dictated. For example, a competitor may alter its media strategy to gain an edge. Failure to respond to this challenge could create problems for the firm.
3. *Availability of media.* Sometimes a desired medium (or vehicle) is not available to the marketer. Perhaps the medium does not reach a particular target segment or has no time or space available. There are still some geographic areas that certain media do not reach. Even when the media are available, limited advertising time or space may have already been sold or cutoff dates for entry may have passed. Alternative vehicles or media must then be considered.
4. *Changes in media or media vehicles.* A change in the medium or in a particular vehicle may require a change in the media strategy. For example, the advent of cable TV opened up new opportunities for message delivery, as will the introduction of interactive media. The Internet has led many consumer companies to adopt this medium while a number of new technologies have provided additional options. In the first 6 months of 2004 alone, 76 new special-interest magazines were launched.[15] Likewise, a drop in ratings or a change in editorial format may lead the advertiser to use different programs or print alternatives.

Fluctuations in these factors mean the media strategy must be developed with enough flexibility to allow the manager to adapt to specific market situations.

Budget Considerations

One of the more important decisions in the development of media strategy is cost estimating. The value of any strategy can be determined by how well it delivers the message to the audience with the lowest cost and the least waste. We have already explored a number of factors, such as reach, frequency, and availability that affect this decision. The marketer tries to arrive at the optimal delivery by balancing cost with each of these. As the following discussion shows, understanding cost figures may not be as easy as it seems.

Advertising and promotional costs can be categorized in two ways. The **absolute cost** of the medium or vehicle is the actual total cost required to place the message. For example, a full-page four-color ad in *Newsweek* magazine costs about $210,000. **Relative cost** refers to the relationship between the price paid for advertising time or space and the size of the audience delivered; it is used to compare media vehicles. Relative

	Time	*Newsweek*
Per-page cost	$234,000	$210,000
Circulation	4.0 million	3.1 million
Calculation of CPM	$\frac{234{,}000 \times 1{,}000}{4{,}000{,}000}$	$\frac{210{,}000 \times 1{,}000}{3{,}100{,}000}$
CPM	$58.5	$67.74

Figure 10-24 Cost per Thousand Computations: *Time* versus *Newsweek*

costs are important because the manager must try to optimize audience delivery within budget constraints. Since a number of alternatives are available for delivering the message, the advertiser must evaluate the relative costs associated with these choices. The way media costs are provided and problems in comparing these costs across media often make such evaluations difficult.

Determining Relative Costs of Media

To evaluate alternatives, advertisers must compare the relative costs of media as well as vehicles within these media. Unfortunately, the broadcast, print, and out-of-home media do not always provide the same cost breakdowns, nor necessarily do vehicles within the print media. Following are the cost bases used:

1. **Cost per thousand (CPM).** For years the magazine industry has provided cost breakdowns on the basis of cost per thousand people reached. The formula for this computation is

$$\text{CPM} = \frac{\text{Cost of ad space (absolute cost)}}{\text{Circulation}} \times 1{,}000$$

Figure 10-24 provides an example of this computation for two vehicles in the same medium—*Time* and *Newsweek*—and shows that (all other things being equal) *Time* is a more cost-effective buy, even though its absolute cost is higher. (We will come back to "all other things being equal" in a moment.)

2. **Cost per ratings point (CPRP).** The broadcast media provide a different comparative cost figure, referred to as cost per ratings point or *cost per point (CPP),* based on the following formula:

$$\text{CPRP} = \frac{\text{Cost of commercial time}}{\text{Program rating}}$$

An example of this calculation for a spot ad in a local TV market is shown in Figure 10-25. It indicates that *Survivor* would be more cost-effective than *CSI.*

3. **Daily inch rate.** For newspapers, cost effectiveness is based on the daily inch rate, which is the cost per column inch of the paper. Like magazines, newspapers now use the cost-per-thousand formula discussed earlier to determine relative costs. As shown in Figure 10-26, the *Pittsburgh Post Gazette* costs significantly more to advertise in than does the *Cleveland Plain Dealer* (again, all other things being equal).

As you can see, it is difficult to make comparisons across various media. What is the broadcast equivalent of cost per thousand or the column inch rate? In an attempt to

	CSI	*Survivor*
Cost per spot ad	$10,000	$7,500
Rating	18	17
Reach (households)	197,100	186,150
Calculation	$10,000/18	$7,500/17
CPRP (CPP)	$555	$441

Figure 10-25 Comparison of Cost per Ratings Point: *CSI* versus *Survivor* in a Local TV Market

Figure 10-26 Comparative Costs in Newspaper Advertising

	Pittsburgh Post Gazette	Cleveland Plain Dealer
Cost per page	\$33,924	\$44,352
Cost per inch	257	352
Circulation	238,860	354,309
Calculation	$\text{CPM} = \frac{\text{Page cost} \times 1{,}000}{\text{Circulation}}$	
	$= \frac{\$33{,}924 \times 1{,}000}{238{,}860}$	$\frac{\$44{,}352 \times 1{,}000}{354{,}309}$
	\$142.02	\$125.18

standardize relative costing procedures, the broadcast and newspaper media have begun to provide costs per thousand, using the following formulas:

$$\text{Television: } \frac{\text{Cost of 1 unit of time} \times 1{,}000}{\text{Program rating}} \qquad \text{Newspapers: } \frac{\text{Cost of ad space} \times 1{,}000}{\text{Circulation}}$$

While the comparison of media on a cost-per-thousand basis is important, intermedia comparisons can be misleading. The ability of TV to provide both sight and sound, the longevity of magazines, and other characteristics of each medium make direct comparisons difficult. The media planner should use the cost-per-thousand numbers but must also consider the specific characteristics of each medium and each media vehicle in the decision.

The cost per thousand may overestimate or underestimate the actual cost effectiveness. Consider a situation where some waste coverage is inevitable. The circulation (using the *Time* magazine figures to demonstrate our point) exceeds the target market. If the people reached by this message are not potential buyers of the product, then having to pay to reach them results in too low a cost per thousand, as shown in scenario A of Figure 10-27. We must use the potential reach to the target market—the destination sought—rather than the overall circulation figure. A medium with a much higher cost per thousand may be a wiser buy if it is reaching more potential receivers. (Most

Figure 10-27 Cost per Thousand Estimates

Scenario A: Overestimation of Efficiency

Target market	18–49
Magazine circulation	4,000,000
Circulation to target market	65% (2,600,000)
Cost per page	\$234,000

$$\text{CPM} = \frac{\$234{,}000 \times 1{,}000}{4{,}000{,}000} = \$58.5$$

$$\text{CPM (actual target audience)} = \frac{\$234{,}000 \times 1{,}000}{2{,}600{,}000} = \$90.00$$

Scenario B: Underestimation of Efficiency

Target market	All age groups, male and female
Magazine circulation	4,000,000
Cost per page	\$234,000
Pass-along rate	3* (33% of households)

$$\text{CPM (based on readers per copy)} = \frac{\text{Page cost} \times 1{,}000}{\text{Circulation} + 3(1{,}320{,}000)} = \frac{234{,}000 \times 1{,}000}{7{,}960{,}000}$$

$$= \$29.40$$

*Assuming pass-along was valid.

media buyers rely on **target CPM,** or **TCPM,** which calculates CPMs based on the target audience, not the overall audience.)

CPM may also underestimate cost efficiency. Magazine advertising space sellers have argued for years that because more than one person may read an issue, the actual reach is underestimated. They want to use the number of **readers per copy** as the true circulation. This would include a **pass-along rate,** estimating the number of people who read the magazine without buying it. Scenario B in Figure 10-27 shows how this underestimates cost efficiency. Consider a family in which a father, mother, and two teenagers read each issue of *Time.* Assume such families constitute 33 percent of *Time*'s circulation base. While the circulation figure includes only one magazine, in reality there are four potential exposures in these households, increasing the total reach to 7.96 million.

While the number of readers per copy makes intuitive sense, it has the potential to be extremely inaccurate. The actual number of times the magazine changes hands is difficult to determine. How many people in a fraternity read each issue of *Sports Illustrated* or *Maxim* that is delivered? How many people in a sorority or on a dorm floor read each issue of *Cosmopolitan* or *Vanity Fair?* How many of either group read each issue of *BusinessWeek?* While research is conducted to make these determinations, pass-along estimates are very subjective and using them to estimate reach is speculative. These figures are regularly provided by the media, but managers are selective about using them. At the same time, the art of media buying enters, for many magazines' managers have a good idea how much greater the reach is than their circulation figures provided.

In addition to the potential for over- or underestimation of cost efficiencies, CPMs are limited in that they make only *quantitative* estimates of the value of media. While they may be good for comparing very similar vehicles (such as *Time* and *Newsweek*), they are less valuable in making intermedia comparisons, for example, CPM for magazines versus Internet banner ads. We have already noted some differences among media that preclude direct comparisons.

You can see that the development of a media strategy involves many factors. Ostrow may be right when he calls this process an art rather than a science, as so much of it requires going beyond the numbers. IMC Perspective 10-2 demonstrates how involved successful media plans can be.

Evaluation and Follow-Up

All plans require some evaluation to assess their performance. The media plan is no exception.

In outlining the planning process, we stated that objectives are established and strategies developed for them. Having implemented these strategies, marketers need to know whether or not they were successful. Measures of effectiveness must consider two factors: (1) How well did these strategies achieve the media objectives? (2) How well did this media plan contribute to attaining the overall marketing and communications objectives? If the strategies were successful, they should be used in future plans. If not, their flaws should be analyzed.

The problem with measuring the effectiveness of media strategies is probably obvious to you at this point. At the outset of this chapter, we suggested the planning process was limited by problems with measurements and lack of consistent terminology (among others). While these problems limit the degree to which we can assess the relative effectiveness of various strategies, it is not impossible to make such determinations. Sometimes it is possible to show that a plan has worked. Even if the evaluation procedure is not foolproof, it is better than no attempt. We will discuss more about measuring effectiveness in Chapter 19.

Characteristics of Media

To this point, we have discussed the elements involved in the development of media strategy. One of the most basic elements in this process is the matching of media to markets. In the following chapters, you will see that each medium has its own characteristics that make it better or worse for attaining specific objectives. First, Figure 10-28 provides an overall comparison of media and some of the characteristics by which they are evaluated. This is a very general comparison, and the various media options must be analyzed for each situation. Nevertheless, it is a good starting point and serves as a lead-in to subsequent chapters.

IMC PERSPECTIVE 10-2

What Excellent Media Plans Look Like

Each year *Adweek* and *Mediaweek* select the best media plans of the year. The selection is made by a number of top executives of advertising and media agencies, with category winners including "Best media plan spending more than $25 million, between $10 to $25 million," and so on. As the winners for 2004 indicate, the winning media plans involve a lot more than just advertising. The following are just a few of the examples of the winners.

Dyson—Spending More Than $25 Million

Vacuum cleaners are for housewives, right? Not according to MediaCom, the agency working on the Dyson vacuum cleaner account. When you are purchasing a $400 product for the home, you must market to men as well, they said. Dyson, a British company that has marketed its product in the United States only since 2002, has already surpassed the Hoover Company in dollar volume sales, due largely to its technology and innovativeness. Nevertheless, creating interest in a vacuum cleaner, especially one that costs around $400, is not an easy task. However, it was those unique selling points that gave the agency the opportunity to consider marketing the program through entertainment programs. The first effort was a product integration on the Discover Channel program *Big!* where craftsmen create big products out of small ones. In this case, a 16-foot-tall Dyson was built and inducted into the *Guiness Book of Records.* Dyson received 60 minutes of exposure and so much interest that they turned it into a sales tape that was sent out to 150 offices around the world. Other integration opportunities to reach both men and women included NBC's *Friends, Will & Grace,* and *ER,* ABC's *Extreme Makeover: Home Edition,* and Style Network's *Clean House.* But integrations are not the only way to create awareness, so traditional advertising spots were also purchased on *Everybody Loves Raymond, The West Wing,* and *Desperate Housewives* as well as on select cable programs on HGTV, Food Network, and the Turner networks. The print list included *Metropolitan Home* and *O: The Oprah Magazine, The New Yorker, Cargo,* and *Out,* most of which aligned quite well with the target audience. Outdoor ads were placed in New York and San Francisco, as was a public relations effort on the Great American Clean Out Day in Central Park. But did it work? Dyson thinks so, as awareness and recall of the product "skyrocketed" and sales increased by more than 300 percent. In addition, the unpaid placements including NBC's *Friends, Will & Grace,* and *ER* extended the reach well beyond the media buy itself.

Engineered to easily navigate
the most complex obstacle course ever created.
Your living room.
the ball dyson
The new Dyson Ball turns and maneuvers unlike any other vacuum. And, of course, it doesn't lose suction.
Test-drive one today. 1-866-693-9766 or dyson.com

Chrysler Crossfire—Spending $10 to $25 Million

In search of the "big idea" to make a splash for Chrysler's new Crossfire, media agency PHD knew they needed something out of the ordinary. What could be more out of the ordinary than *The Apprentice?* The relationship with the NBC program started out with category exclusive ads on the program, and various forms of product integration (the winner won a Crossfire), as well as mentions and segment sponsorships on *The Today Show,* which featured a recap of the previous night's episode and interviews with the voted-off contestant. In addition, an interactive sweepstakes on the NBC website, billboard advertising, Web ads, radio spots, and live events featuring the Crossfire were also part of the plan. Chrysler was the exclusive sponsor of *The Apprentice* website. But it didn't stop there. As part of *The Apprentice* deal, PHD and NBC joined together to promote the show with lobby cards in 4,000 Regal Cinema theater lobbies, promotional signs in all Trump hotels, and other grassroots efforts. Co-branded advertisements with nine magazines and 84 radio stations followed, as did one-third page ads in *BusinessWeek, Entertainment Weekly, Forbes, Fortune, Newsweek, People, Time, US News & World Report,* and *US Weekly,* promoting the final episode. The results: 50 million impressions on the website, 1.1 million (348,000 unique) entries into the sweepstakes, 1,600 live reads promoting the sponsorship on radio, and a sales increase of 266 percent. Not bad.

GM Planworks—Spending Less Than $10 Million

Perhaps one of the most effective campaigns of 2004 was for yet another car company—this time GM's Pontiac. While GM Planworks received the award, the plan was actually a joint effort of a number of participants including Pontiac's advertising agency Leo Burnett's chemistri, Vigilante—an urban marketing agency, a number of Internet search engines, and the producers of *The Oprah Winfrey Show.* Like Chrysler with its Crossfire, GM wanted to make a splash with the introduction of its new Pontiac G6. Planning actually began a full year ahead of the introduction, with the goal of reaching an audience that consisted of 60 percent females. Noting the success that the Apple iPod enjoyed after an appearance on the *Oprah* show, the planning group believed that this medium could work for them as well, but they wanted to make it an "event" not just an appearance on the show. Tying in to their previous theme of "Wildest Dreams," in which average people get a once-in-a-lifetime opportunity, Pontiac decided to give away 276 cars on the season premiere show to needy viewers ranging from school teachers to housewives. Convincing Oprah Winfrey was the easy part. Working with all of the other media to promote the show without giving away the secret that the cars would be given away was the hard part. Among those sworn to secrecy were the audience members who received the cars three days before the program aired; the search engines including Google, Yahoo!, America Online, and MSN (links were made using the words *Oprah, Giveaway,* and *Pontiac,* but did not review the program); and all of those involved with the show itself. The results exceeded everyone's expectations. David Letterman, Jay Leno, news reports, and seemingly every U.S. newspaper talked about the event. *TV Guide* awarded the giveaway as the "Top TV Moment" of 2004. The cost to GM of $8.5 million resulted in an estimated $100 million worth of publicity. A survey showed that 87 percent of adults were aware of the promotion, which drove 600 percent more traffic to the Pontiac website with a click-through rate of 17 percent—the highest in Pontiac's history. And, most important, it sold cars!

Google—Spending Less Than $1 Million

The winner in the less than $1 million category was Google and the work performed by its agency Crispin, Porter+Bogusky. This plan was previously discussed in Chapter 7.

Sources: Tony Case, "GM Planworks," *Mediaweek,* June 20, 2005, pp. 10, 14; John Consoli, "PHD," *Mediaweek,* June 20, 2005, pp. 6, 8; Eric Schmuckler, "Mediacom," *Mediaweek,* June 20, 2005, pp. 3–4.

Figure 10-28 Media Characteristics

Media	Advantages	Disadvantages
Television	Mass coverage High reach Impact of sight, sound, and motion High prestige Low cost per exposure Attention getting Favorable image	Low selectivity Short message life High absolute cost High production costs Clutter
Radio	Local coverage Low cost High frequency Flexible Low production costs Well-segmented audiences	Audio only Clutter Low attention getting Fleeting message
Magazines	Segmentation potential Quality reproduction High information content Longevity Multiple readers	Long lead time for ad placement Visual only Lack of flexibility
Newspapers	High coverage Low cost Short lead time for placing ads Ads can be placed in interest sections Timely (current ads) Reader controls exposure Can be used for coupons	Short life Clutter Low attention-getting capabilities Poor reproduction quality Selective reader exposure
Outdoor	Location specific High repetition Easily noticed	Short exposure time requires short ad Poor image Local restrictions
Direct mail	High selectivity Reader controls exposure High information content Opportunities for repeat exposures	High cost/contact Poor image (junk mail) Clutter
Internet and interactive media	User selects product information User attention and involvement Interactive relationship Direct selling potential Flexible message platform	Limited creative capabilities Websnarl (crowded access) Technology limitations Few valid measurement techniques Limited reach

Summary

This chapter has presented an overview of the determination of media objectives, development of the media strategy, and formalization of objectives and strategy in the form of a media plan. Sources of media information, characteristics of media, and key media decisions were also discussed.

The media strategy must be designed to supplement and support the overall marketing and communications objectives. The objectives of this plan are designed to deliver the message the program has developed.

The basic task involved in the development of media strategy is to determine the best matching of media to the target market, given the constraints of the budget. The media planner attempts to balance reach and frequency and to deliver the message to the intended audience with a minimum of waste coverage. At the same time, a number of additional factors affect the media decision. Media strategy development has been called more of an art than a science because while many quantitative data are available, the planner also relies on creativity and nonquantifiable factors.

This chapter discussed many factors, including developing a proper media mix, determining target market and geographic coverage, scheduling, and balancing reach and frequency. Creative aspects, budget considerations, the need for flexibility in the schedule, and the use of computers in the media planning process were also considered.

The chapter also introduced a number of resources available to the media planner. A summary chart of advantages and disadvantages of various media was provided.

Key Terms

media planning, 301
media objectives, 301
media strategies, 301
medium, 303
media vehicle, 303
reach, 303
coverage, 303
frequency, 303
sweeps periods, 303
index number, 307
survey of buying power index, 311
brand development index (BDI), 311
category development index (CDI), 311
waste coverage, 314
continuity, 315
flighting, 315
pulsing, 315
unduplicated reach, 319
duplicated reach, 319
program rating, 319
gross ratings points (GRPs), 320
target ratings points (TRPs), 320
effective reach, 321
average frequency, 322
absolute cost, 324
relative cost, 324
cost per thousand (CPM), 325
cost per ratings point (CPRP), 325
daily inch rate, 325
target CPM (TCPM), 327
readers per copy, 327
pass-along rate, 327

Discussion Questions

1. Explain the differences between CPM and TCPM. Give examples of a company or product that might select one of the methods versus the other.

2. The chapter discusses some of the many changes taking place in the media environment. Discuss some of the reasons that marketers might be shifting advertising dollars to less traditional media. Does this mean that TV advertising will no longer exist in the future?

3. Describe what is meant by readers per copy. Why is this different from CPM? Discuss some of the advantages and disadvantages of using both.

4. As noted in the chapter, there is a trade-off between reach and frequency for advertisers with a limited budget. Explain what this means. Under which circumstances would a planner wish to emphasize reach? Frequency?

5. One well-known media planner has noted that media buying is a combination of art and science with a definite bias toward art. Explain what this means and give examples of circumstances of situations in which this might be the case.

6. Describe the three methods of promotional scheduling. Give examples of products and/or services that might employ each method.

7. The text notes that one problem in media planning is that ratings information is gathered during sweeps periods. Explain what sweeps periods are, and why this might pose a problem.

8. Figure 10-28 notes some of the advantages and disadvantages associated with various media options. Referring to Figure 10-28, provide examples of products and/or services that might most benefit from the use of each medium.

9. Describe what is meant by waste coverage. The decision must often be made between waste coverage and undercoverage. Give examples when the marketer might have to choose between the two, and when it may be acceptable to live with waste coverage.

10. Figure 10-5 provides a profile of the cola user. Using the indices, describe the profile of the cola user. Now describe the profile of the heavy cola user.

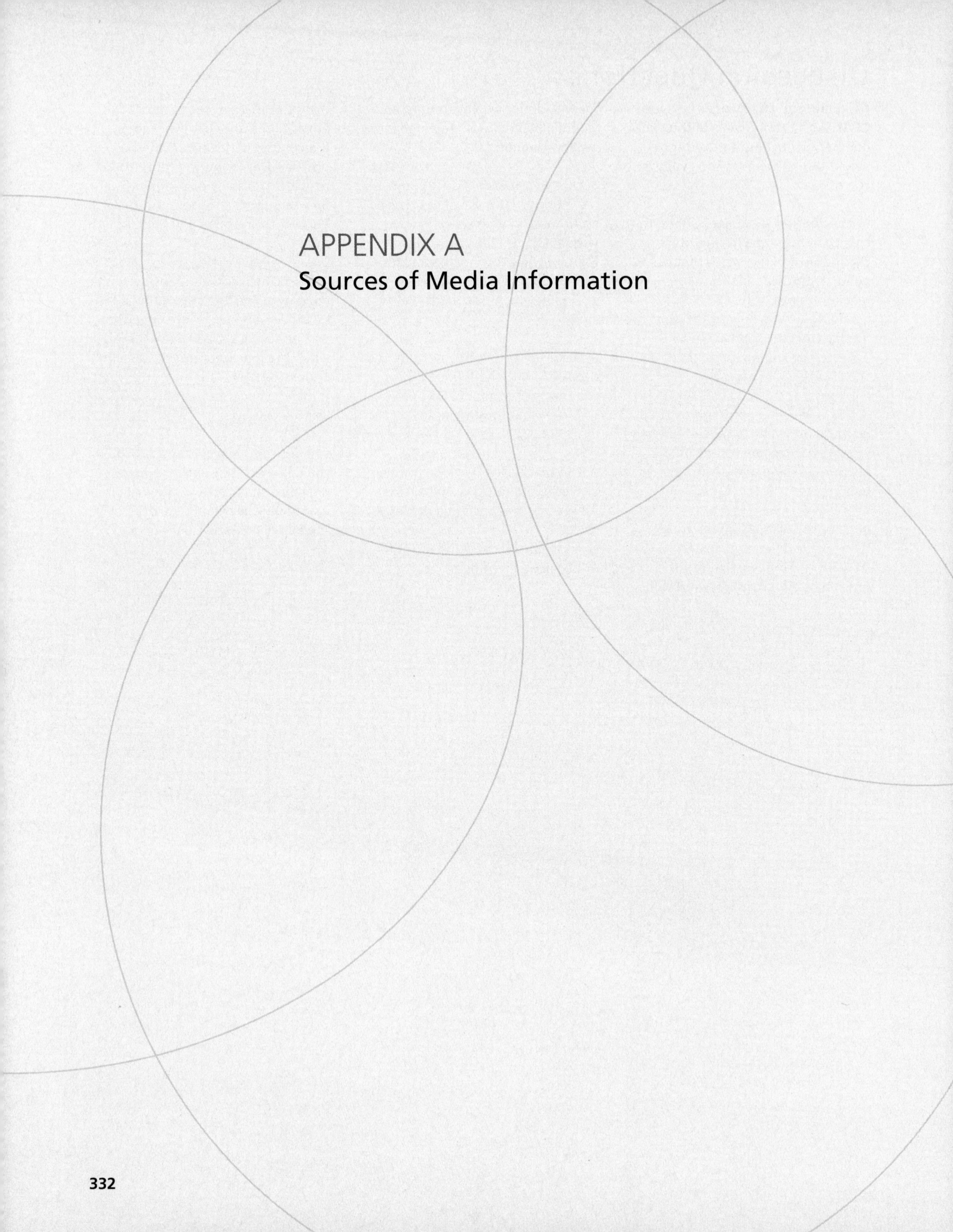

APPENDIX A
Sources of Media Information

APPENDIX A

Sources of Media Information

Cross-reference guide to advertising media sources

	General Information	Competitive Activities	Market Information (Geographic)	Audience Information (Target Groups)	Advertising Rates
Nonmedia information (general marketing)	1, 10, 15, 16, 20, 21, 22	1	10, 11, 15, 16, 18, 19, 21, 24	15, 16, 20	
Multimedia or intermedia	1, 15, 16, 20	1, 13	18	2, 24	2
Daily newspapers	9			5, 9, 15, 16, 20	2, 23
Weekly newspapers	9				23
Consumer magazines	3, 14	13	3	3, 15, 16, 20	2, 23
Farm publications				5, 25	2, 23
Business publications			6, 8	6, 25	2, 23
Network television		7, 13		15, 16, 17, 20	2
Spot television		7, 13		15, 16, 17, 20	2, 23
Network radio		7		12, 15, 16, 17, 20, 26	2
Spot radio				4, 5, 12, 17, 20	2, 23

1. *Advertising Age*
2. Advertising agency media estimating guides
3. Magazine Publishers Association (MPA)
4. Arbitron Ratings Company
5. Audit Bureau of Circulations (ABC)
6. Business/Professional Advertising Association (B/PAA) Media Data
7. Broadcast Advertisers Reports (BAR)
8. Business Publications Audit of Circulation (BPA)
9. Newspaper Association of America (NAA)
10. *State and Metropolitan Area Data Book*
11. *Editor & Publisher Market Guide*
12. Survey of World Advertising Expenditures, Stach/Inra/Hooper
13. Competitive Media Reporting
14. Magazine Publishers Association of America (MPA)
15. Mediamark Research, Inc. (MRI)
16. Mendelsohn Media Research, Inc. (MMR)
17. Nielsen Media Research Company
18. Prizm
19. *Sales & Marketing Management Survey of Buying Power*
20. Simmons Market Research Bureau: *Study of Media and Markets*
21. *Standard Directory of Advertisers*
22. *Standard Directory of Advertising Agencies*
23. Standard Rate and Data Service
24. Telmar
25. Verified Audit Circulation Corporation (VAC)

Evaluation of Broadcast Media

11

Chapter Objectives

1. To examine the structure of the television and radio industries and the role of each medium in the advertising program.

2. To consider the advantages and limitations of TV and radio as advertising media.

3. To explain how advertising time is purchased for the broadcast media, how audiences are measured, and how rates are determined.

4. To consider future trends in TV and radio and how they will influence the use of these media in advertising.

Bring Back the Good Old Days of Television

Nearly 80 percent of the commercials shown during the decade were 60 seconds in length, and the time that networks could make available for advertising was limited to 9 minutes during prime time. In most households the husband was the breadwinner while the wife stayed home and raised the children. Thus, the daytime game shows and soap operas became very popular shows for reaching women. In the evening the family could be easily reached by popular network programs such as the *Ed Sullivan Show, The Beverly Hillbillies,* or *Disney's Wonderful World of Color.*

During the 1970s things began to change. The number of U.S. households with televisions increased from 55 million in 1965 to nearly 70 million in 1975, and the percentage of TV households able to receive 10 or more stations increased to 31 percent. However, the networks' share of the prime-time audience was still over 90 percent. One important change that occurred in the '70s was the emergence of the 30-second commercial; more than 90 percent of the spots airing on network TV were using the shorter format by 1975. During this decade, advertisers increasingly turned to television as it was regarded as the most effective and efficient medium for advertising to mass markets. Competition for the limited amount of network time, along with an inflationary economy, led to a dramatic increase in TV advertising rates—the

Television has been the dominant form of entertainment in most households for more than a half a century and advertising has been the lifeblood of the industry for nearly as long. Ever since Bulova ran the first TV ad in 1941 at a cost of $10.00, the commercial has been considered the quintessential form of advertising for many marketers. However, television advertising has gone through many changes over the past 40 years and is currently facing a number of challenges that may significantly change its role as the preeminent advertising medium.

In the 1960s and '70s, television was dominated by the three major networks. In 1965, only 8 percent of U.S. households with television could receive as many as 10 channels on their primarily black-and-white TV set, and the three major networks (ABC, CBS, and NBC) had nearly 95 percent of the prime-time viewing audience.

cost of a prime-time TV spot increased by more than 200 percent from 1970 to 1982.

The size of the television-viewing audience and popularity of the medium continued to increase throughout the 1970s and into the '80s as cable became more prevalent in U.S. homes and increased the number of channel options. By the end of the '80s, more than half of the homes in the country were wired for cable, and many of these could receive up to 30 channels. Cable networks such as CNN, MTV, ESPN, Nickelodeon, and many others were becoming very popular, and the three major networks' share of the television viewing audience was steadily declining. The number of ads on network TV had nearly tripled by 1990 to more than 6,000 per week as networks and TV stations responded to demand by making more time available for commercials. Adding to the clutter problem was the growing popularity of 15-second commercials, which accounted for nearly a third of the network commercials by the early '90s.

During the '90s, cable TV penetration continued to grow as cable operators wired nearly 70 million homes by the end of the decade, making it the dominant form of television access. New access mediums also began to emerge, including direct broadcast satellite (DBS) services such as DirecTV and Primestar. Subscribers to satellite services purchased a small dish and paid a monthly programming fee to receive as many as 200 channels of movies, news, music, and sports in crisp digital video and CD-quality sound. Cable operators responded by increasing the number of channels available to their subscribers, and cable networks promoted the opportunities they offered for "narrowcasting" or reaching very specialized audiences such as sports fans, news junkies, or music buffs. The network television–viewing audience continued to decline during the '90s, eroding an average of 2 percent a year, and cable stations were collectively commanding nearly as many prime-time viewers as the four major networks, which now included Fox.

Although some analysts expressed concern over the decline in network viewers, many media companies that owned the major networks had already responded by purchasing some of the popular cable networks. For example, the Walt Disney Company purchased both ABC and ESPN while Viacom acquired MTV and VH1 in addition to CBS. Moreover, demand for television advertising time continued to increase during the '90s as more companies turned to TV to deliver their advertising messages. The cost of reaching 1,000 homes in prime time jumped from $7.64 to nearly $15 by 1999. Television advertising had survived several major challenges including the Internet and the VCR boom. While the Internet gained in popularity during the late '90s, the viability of the Web as an advertising medium was limited by low bandwidth from dial-up connections as broadband penetration was less than 10 percent. And although many households owned VCRs, they were used primarily to watch movies rather than to record shows and fast-forward through the commercials.

Although television's combination of reach and impact helped it retain its role as the king of advertising media at the turn of the century, the situation changed very quickly over the past 5 years. At the beginning of the decade, TiVo launched the first digital video recorder (DVR), a device that digitally records television shows and saves them on a massive hard drive. While DVRs are essentially hard-disk replacements for VCRs, they are easier to use and offer consumers many more features. These include the users' being able to program the device to record and store certain types of shows and to easily fast-forward through commercials when playing back the recorded show. In addition to TiVo and its competitors, many cable companies are now making low-cost DVRs available to consumers who subscribe to their digital cable service. Cable operators are also offering video-on-demand (VOD) services whereby digital cable subscribers have access to content stored on the cable companies' servers such as movies, games, catalogs, and even home shopping.

Estimates are that by 2007, nearly 34 million U.S. households will have VOD and more than 20 million will own DVRs. These technologies make it even easier for consumers to view TV programs on their own schedule, to skip ads at will, or to watch commercial-free television. Compounding the problem is the rapid growth of broadband Internet access, which has catapulted to nearly 60 percent of U.S. homes. Consumers are spending more and more time on the Internet, and young people in particular spend more time surfing the Web than they do watching television. Many companies such as DaimlerChrysler, Procter & Gamble, PepsiCo, and Coca-Cola are moving some of the monies they have traditionally spent on cable and network TV to online advertising on various portals such as MSN, Google, and Yahoo.

Although television has survived challenges to its role as the king of advertising media in the past, many analysts believe that it may not be as easy this time around. Media experts note that network television faces major problems if it continues to operate on the same basic model. While consumers' love affair with television as a form of entertainment is still strong, they want to watch what they want and when they want, and this often does not include commercials. This means that marketers will continue to look for alternatives to the 30- (or is it 15-) second TV commercial. No wonder so many in the industry yearn for the good old days!

Sources: Stephanie N. Mehta, "How the Web Will Save the Commercial," *Fortune,* August 8, 2005, pp. 57–60; Eric Schmitt, "The :30 Is on Its Last Legs; Now's the Time to Rewire TV Ad Industry," *Advertising Age,* April 11, 2005, p. 46; Bob Garfield, "The Chaos Scenario," *Advertising Age,* April 4, 2005, pp. 1, 57–59.

The changes that are occurring in the television industry are important as they are having a profound impact on the primary form of entertainment in most households as well as the largest advertising medium. TV has virtually saturated households throughout the United States and most other countries and has become a mainstay in the lives of most people. The average American household watches over eight hours of TV a day, and the tube has become the predominant source of news and entertainment for many people. Over 90 percent of the TV households in the United States have a VCR, and many have entertainment centers with big-screen TVs, DVD players, DVRs, and surround sound. On any given evening during the prime-time hours of 8 to 11 P.M., more than 100 million people are watching TV. Popular shows like *CSI: Miami, Desperate Housewives,* and *American Idol* average more than 20 million viewers. The large numbers of people who watch television are important to the TV networks and stations because they can sell time on these programs to marketers who want to reach that audience with their advertising messages. Moreover, the qualities that make TV a great medium for news and entertainment also encourage creative ads that can have a strong impact on customers.

Radio is also an integral part of our lives. Many of us wake up to clock radios in the morning and rely on radio programs to inform and/or entertain us while we drive to work or school. For many people, radio is a constant companion in their cars, at home, even at work. The average American listens to the radio nearly three hours each day.[1] Like TV viewers, radio listeners are an important audience for marketers.

In this chapter, we examine the broadcast media of TV and radio, including the general characteristics of each as well as their specific advantages and disadvantages. We examine how advertisers use TV and radio as part of their advertising and media strategies, how they buy TV and radio time, and how audiences are measured and evaluated for each medium. We also examine the factors that are changing the role of TV and radio as advertising media.

Television

It has often been said that television is the ideal advertising medium. Its ability to combine visual images, sound, motion, and color presents the advertiser with the opportunity to develop the most creative and imaginative appeals of any medium. However, TV does have certain problems that limit or even prevent its use by many advertisers.

Advantages of Television

TV has numerous advantages over other media, including creativity and impact, coverage and cost effectiveness, captivity and attention, and selectivity and flexibility.

Creativity and Impact Perhaps the greatest advantage of TV is the opportunity it provides for presenting the advertising message. The interaction of sight and sound offers tremendous creative flexibility and makes possible dramatic, lifelike representations of products and services. TV commercials can be used to convey a mood or image for a brand as well as to develop emotional or entertaining appeals that help make a dull product appear interesting.

Television is also an excellent medium for demonstrating a product or service. For example, print ads are effective for showing a car and communicating information regarding its features, but only a TV commercial can put you in the driver's seat and give you the sense of actually driving, as shown by the Porsche commercial in Exhibit 11-1.

Coverage and Cost Effectiveness Television advertising makes it possible to reach large audiences. Nearly everyone, regardless of age, sex, income, or educational level, watches at least some TV. Most people do so on a regular basis. According to Nielsen Media Research estimates, nearly 280 million people age 2 or older live in the nation's 110.2 million TV households, nearly 77 percent of whom are 18 or older.[2]

Marketers selling products and services that appeal to broad target audiences find that TV lets them reach mass markets, often very cost efficiently. The average prime-time TV show reaches 7 million homes; a top-rated show like *ER* may reach nearly 15 million homes and perhaps twice that many viewers. In 2005, the average cost per thousand (CPM) homes reached was nearly $20 for network evening shows and $4.59 for daytime weekly shows.[3]

Exhibit 11-1 This TV commercial helps viewers feel the sensation of driving a sports car

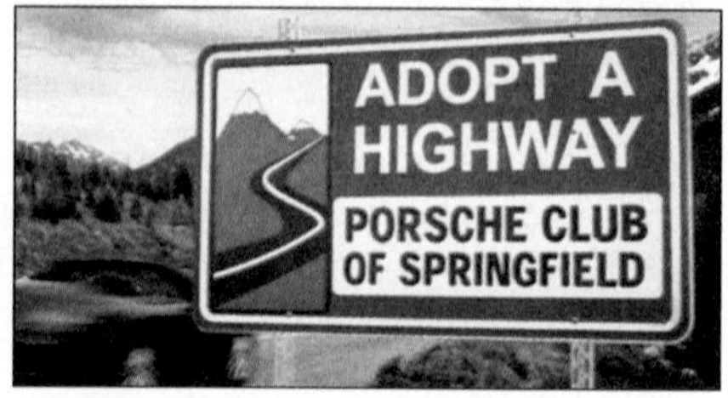

Rank	Company	Measured TV Advertising (millions)
1	Procter & Gamble	$833.6
2	General Motors	753.5
3	Johnson & Johnson	521.6
4	Ford Motor Co.	497.6
5	Time Warner	451.9
6	Pfizer	417.8
7	Walt Disney Co.	417.6
8	SBC Communications	396.2
9	PepsiCo	379.5
10	DaimlerChrysler	359.4

Figure 11-1 Top 10 Network TV Advertisers, 2004

Source: "Special Report Leading National Advertisers," *Advertising Age,* June 27, 2005. p. S-20.

Because of its ability to reach large audiences in a cost-efficient manner, TV is a popular medium among companies selling mass-consumption products. Companies with widespread distribution and availability of their products and services use TV to reach the mass market and deliver their advertising messages at a very low cost per thousand. Television has become indispensable to large consumer packaged-goods companies, carmakers, and major retailers. Companies like General Motors and Ford spend nearly two-thirds of their media budgets on various forms of TV—network, spot, cable, and syndicated programs—while PepsiCo and Coca-Cola spend more than 80 percent. Figure 11-1 shows the top 10 network television advertisers and their expenditures.

Captivity and Attention Television is basically intrusive in that commercials impose themselves on viewers as they watch their favorite programs. Unless we make a special effort to avoid commercials, most of us are exposed to thousands of them each year. The increase in viewing options and the penetration of VCRs, DVDs, DVRs, remote controls, and other automatic devices have made it easier for TV viewers to avoid commercial messages. Studies of consumers' viewing habits found that as much as a third of program audiences may be lost during commercial breaks.[4] However, the remaining viewers are likely to devote some attention to many advertising messages. As discussed in Chapter 5, the low-involvement nature of consumer learning and response processes may mean TV ads have an effect on consumers simply through heavy repetition and exposure to catchy slogans and jingles.

Selectivity and Flexibility Television has often been criticized for being a nonselective medium, since it is difficult to reach a precisely defined market segment through the use of TV advertising. But some selectivity is possible due to variations in the composition of audiences as a result of program content, broadcast time, and geographic coverage. For example, Saturday morning TV caters to children; Saturday and Sunday afternoon programs are geared to the sports-oriented male; and weekday daytime shows appeal heavily to homemakers.

With the growth of cable TV, advertisers refine their coverage further by appealing to groups with specific interests such as sports, news, history, the arts, or music, as well as specific demographic groups. Exhibit 11-2 shows an ad promoting Comedy Central and its ability to reach the young, affluent consumers.

Advertisers can also adjust their media strategies to take advantage of different geographic markets through local or spot ads in specific market areas. Ads can be scheduled to run repeatedly or to take advantage of special occasions. For example,

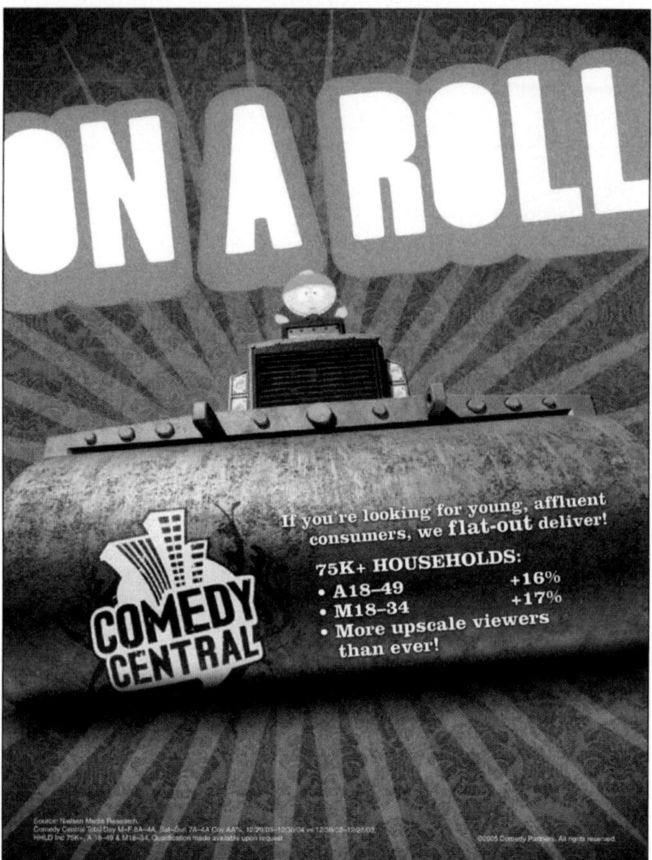

Exhibit 11-2 Comedy Central promotes its ability to reach an important demographic segment

companies such as Anheuser-Busch and Gillette are often major sponsors during baseball's World Series, which allows them to advertise heavily to men who constitute the primary market for their products.

Limitations of Television

Although television is unsurpassed from a creative perspective, the medium has several disadvantages that limit or preclude its use by many advertisers. These problems include high costs, the lack of selectivity, the fleeting nature of a television message, commercial clutter, limited viewer attention, and distrust of TV ads.

Costs

Despite the efficiency of TV in reaching large audiences, it is an expensive medium in which to advertise. The high cost of TV stems not only from the expense of buying airtime but also from the costs of producing a quality commercial. Production costs for a national brand 30-second spot average nearly $400,000 and can reach over a million for more elaborate commercials.[5] Many advertisers also develop commercials specifically for certain ethnic markets such as African-Americans and Hispanics.[6] More advertisers are using media-driven creative strategies that require production of a variety of commercials, which drive up their costs. Even local ads can be expensive to produce and often are not of high quality. The high costs of producing and airing commercials often price small- and medium-size advertisers out of the market.

Lack of Selectivity

Some selectivity is available in television through variations in programs and cable TV. But advertisers who are seeking a very specific, often small, target audience find the coverage of TV often extends beyond their market, reducing its cost effectiveness (as discussed in Chapter 10). Geographic selectivity can be a problem for local advertisers such as retailers, since a station bases its rates on the total market area it reaches. For example, stations in Pittsburgh, Pennsylvania, reach viewers in western and central Pennsylvania, eastern Ohio, northern West Virginia, and even parts of Maryland. The small company whose market is limited to the immediate Pittsburgh area may find TV an inefficient media buy, since the stations cover a larger geographic area than the merchant's trade area.

Audience selectivity is improving as advertisers target certain groups of consumers through the type of program or day and/or time when they choose to advertise. However, TV still does not offer as much audience selectivity as radio, magazines, newspapers, or direct mail for reaching precise segments of the market.

Fleeting Message

TV commercials usually last only 30 seconds or less and leave nothing tangible for the viewer to examine or consider. Commercials have become shorter and shorter as the demand for a limited amount of broadcast time has intensified and advertisers try to get more impressions from their media budgets. Thirty-second commercials became the norm in the mid-1970s, and in September 1986, the three major networks began accepting 15-second spots across their full schedules (except during children's viewing time). Since 1987, these shorter spots have been accounting for about a third of all network commercials and 10 percent of nonnetwork commercial activity. Thirty-second spots remain the dominant commercial length, accounting for nearly 60 percent of network spots and nearly 80 percent of nonnetwork ads.[7]

An important factor in the decline in commercial length has been the spiraling inflation in media costs over the past decade. With the average cost of a prime-time spot reaching over $120,000, many advertisers see shorter commercials as the only way to keep their media costs in line. A 15-second spot typically sells for half the price of a 30-second spot. By using 15- or even 10-second commercials, advertisers think they can run additional spots to reinforce the message or reach a larger audience. Many advertisers believe shorter commercials can deliver a message just as effectively as longer spots for much less money.

Several years ago, many advertising people predicted 15-second spots would become the dominant commercial unit. However, the growth in the use of 15-second commercials peaked at 38 percent in 1989 and has declined slightly since then. The decline may be due to several factors, including creative considerations, lower prices for network time, and a desire by the networks to restrict clutter.[8]

Clutter The problems of fleeting messages and shorter commercials are compounded by the fact that the advertiser's message is only one of many spots and other nonprogramming material seen during a commercial break, so it may have trouble being noticed. One of advertisers' greatest concerns with TV advertising is the potential decline in effectiveness because of such *clutter.*

The next time you watch TV, count the number of commercials, promotions for the news or upcoming programs, or public service announcements that appear during a station break and you will appreciate why clutter is a major concern. With all of these messages competing for our attention, it is easy to understand why the viewer comes away confused or even annoyed and unable to remember or properly identify the product or service advertised.

While the use of shorter commercials by advertisers has contributed to the problem, clutter also increases when the networks and individual stations run promotional announcements for their shows, make more time available for commercials, and redistribute time to popular programs. For many years, the amount of time available for commercials was restricted by the Code Authority of the National Association of Broadcasters to 9.5 minutes per hour during prime time and 12 minutes during nonprime time. The Justice Department suspended the code in 1982 on the grounds that it violated antitrust law. At first the networks did not alter their time standards, but in recent years they have increased the number of commercial minutes in their schedules. The networks argue that they must increase commercial inventory or raise their already steep rates. Advertisers and agencies have been pressuring the networks to cut back on the commercials and other sources of clutter.

Limited Viewer Attention When advertisers buy time on a TV program, they are not purchasing guaranteed exposure but rather the opportunity to communicate a message to large numbers of consumers. But there is increasing evidence that the size of the viewing audience shrinks during a commercial break. People leave the room to go to the bathroom or to get something to eat or drink, or they are distracted in some other way during commercials.

Getting consumers to pay attention to commercials has become an even greater challenge in recent years. The increased presence of VCRs and remote controls has led to the problems of zipping and zapping. **Zipping** occurs when customers fast-forward through commercials as they play back a previously recorded program. A study by Nielsen Media Research found that while 80 percent of recorded shows are actually played back, viewers zip past more than half of the commercials.[9] Another study found that most viewers fully or partially zipped commercials when watching a prerecorded program.[10]

Zapping refers to changing channels to avoid commercials. Nearly all television sets come with remote controls, which enable viewers to switch channels easily. An observational study conducted by John Cronin found as much as a third of program audiences may be lost to electronic zapping when commercials appear.[11] A Nielsen study found that most commercial zapping occurs at the beginning and, to a lesser extent, the end of a program. Zapping at these points is likely to occur because commercial breaks are so long and predictable. Zapping has also been fueled by the emergence

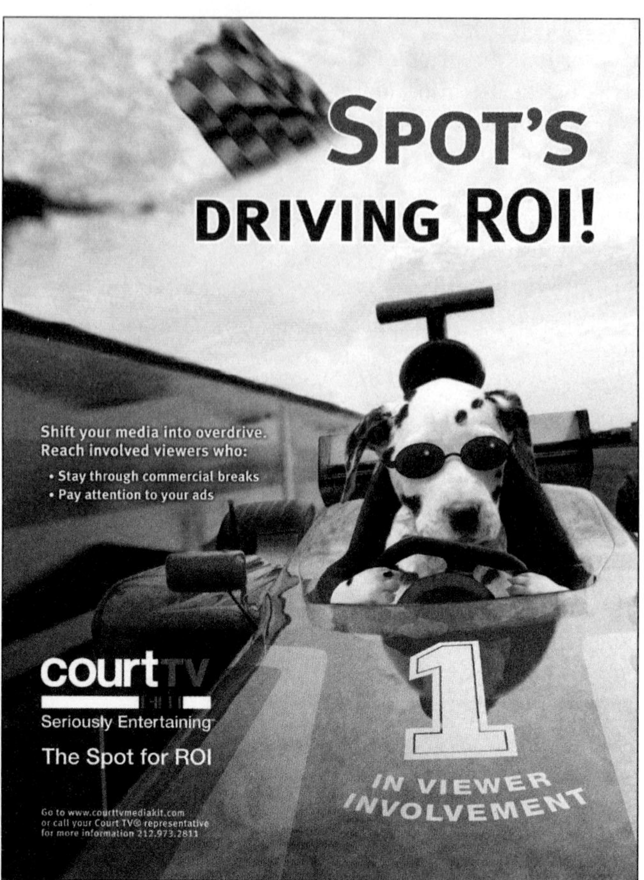

Exhibit 11-3 Court TV promotes its ability to retain viewers during commercial breaks

of 24-hour continuous-format programming on cable channels such as CNN, MTV, and ESPN. Viewers can switch over for a few news headlines, sports scores, or a music video and then switch back to the program. Research shows that young adults zap more than older adults and that men are more likely to zap than women.[12]

How to inhibit zapping? The networks also use certain tactics to hold viewers' attention, such as previews of the next week's show or short closing scenes at the end of a program. Some programs start with action sequences before the opening credits and commercials. One way is to increase viewers' involvement with the program, which means they will be less likely to switch channels during commercial breaks. Exhibit 11-3 shows an ad for Court TV promoting how higher involvement with its programming results in more retention during commercial breaks. Some advertisers believe that producing different executions of a campaign theme is one way to maintain viewers' attention. Others think the ultimate way to zap-proof commercials is to produce creative advertising messages that will attract and hold viewers' attention. However, this is easier said than done, as many consumers just do not want to watch commercials. As more viewers gain access to remote controls and the number of channels increases, the zapping problem is likely to continue.

A study on zapping among viewers of the five major commercial channels in the Netherlands was conducted by Lex van Meurs.[13] He found that during commercial breaks, 29 percent of the audience stopped watching television or switched away to another channel. This loss of viewers was partially compensated for by an average increase of 7 percent of new viewers who zapped in from another channel. The study also found that people stop viewing TV during a commercial break because they have a reason to stop watching television altogether or they want to find out what is being shown on other channels. The number of people zapping in and out during breaks was not caused by the type of products being advertised or by specific characteristics of the commercials. Another recent study, by Alan Tse and Ruby Lee, found that zapping during commercial breaks was very prevalent among TV viewers in Hong Kong and that zappers recalled fewer of the brands advertised than did nonzappers. They also found that most of the brands that were recalled by zappers were placed near the end of the commercial break, which is when viewers would be likely to be returning to a program.[14]

Advances in technology are likely to continue to lead to changes in television viewing habits, which will impact the number of consumers who watch TV commercials.[15] IMC Perspective 11-1 discusses how new technologies such as digital video recorders and video on demand are becoming a major threat to the television industry's traditional advertising-based business model.

Distrust and Negative Evaluation

To many critics of advertising, TV commercials personify everything that is wrong with the industry. Critics often single out TV commercials because of their pervasiveness and the intrusive nature of the medium. Consumers are seen as defenseless against the barrage of TV ads, since they cannot control the transmission of the message and what appears on their screens. Viewers dislike TV advertising when they believe it is offensive, uninformative, or shown too frequently or when they do not like its content.[16] Studies have shown that of the various forms of advertising, distrust is generally the highest for TV commercials.[17] Also, concern has been raised about the effects of TV advertising on specific groups, such as children or the elderly.[18]

IMC PERSPECTIVE 11-1

DVRs, VOD, and IPTV Will Change the Future of Television Advertising

Television programs have always been shown in time slots, with viewers watching whatever is on at that particular time. Advertisers are used to this world of synchronous viewing and they buy TV ad time based on Nielsen ratings, which measure how many people are watching various programs. However, several new technologies are available to make it easier for television viewers to watch shows on their own time. These time-shifting technologies include digital video recorders (DVRs) and video on demand (VOD), and they have the potential to destroy the central role of the TV schedule and allow consumers to view programs on their own clock and to skip ads at will.

TiVo Inc. introduced the first DVR in 1999. The device digitally records television shows over the air or piped into a home from standard cable or satellite feeds and saves them on a massive multi-gigabyte internal hard drive that can hold 40 hours or more of programming. TiVo owners subscribe to a monthly service that allows them to easily search and record shows and then view them on their own schedule. Users can also browse an on-screen program guide, select the show they want to watch, or schedule a recording with a touch of a button on their remote control rather than punching in times and channels. The device also allows users to record shows based on their own search criteria, such as keywords, genres, actors, or directors. And perhaps the most popular feature of the device is that it allows users to fast-forward through commercials during playback.

While TiVo had 3.6 million subscribers by 2005, other companies also make DVRs and cable operators now integrate digital recording technology into their set-top boxes. Satellite television operators also have been providing TiVos DVRs as well as their own DVRs to new subscribers who agree to pay a monthly service fee for DVR service. As prices for digital video recorders and service continue to drop, the number of households with DVRs is expected to increase rapidly. In 2005, 8 percent of U.S. homes had DVR devices, but the percentage is expected to increase to 40 percent by 2009.

As DVRs become more popular, the television networks and stations are likely to face major challenges from advertisers who are concerned that households with the devices will record shows and skip through the commercials when they play them back. Their concerns appear to be well founded as several studies have shown that as much as 80 percent of viewed prime-time programming is time-shifted in households having DVRs, and 70 percent of the ads are being skipped when the programs are viewed. Advertisers are obviously concerned over the prospect of having fewer TV viewers see their ads as well as paying to reach viewers who record shows and fast-forward through the commercials.

In addition to digital video recording, television-viewing patterns are also being affected by the availability of another time-shifting technology, video on demand (VOD), which is being offered by cable operators as well as by some satellite television companies. VOD systems allow users to select and watch video content as part of an interactive television system. Many of these systems allow the user to pause, fast-forward, or rewind the program just as they might do on a VCR or DVR. Some cable operators are offering free on-demand content while others are charging for access to the programming. For example, Comcast, the nation's

largest cable operator, offers its digital cable customers hundreds of hours of free programming whenever they want to call it up. The programming includes instructional shows on poker, short videos of singles looking for mates, and weekly highlights of the best soccer goals from around the world. Content is also available from National Geographic, the History Channel, Nickelodeon, MTV, and the Cartoon network as well as NBC and CBS. And the company sells VOD content such as movies. Estimates are that by 2007 nearly 97 percent of the country's 34 million digital cable subscribers will have VOD, and the number will increase to 44 million by 2009.

The growing popularity of DVRs and VOD poses a major threat to television advertising's traditional business model. Marketers are already searching for ways around the problem of consumers zipping through commercials such as inserting pop-ups that appear as the ad is being fast-forwarded and can be clicked on for viewing. Many advertising experts note that agencies will have to get more creative and develop more interesting ads that consumers will want to watch rather than skip. They also note that marketers need to take advantage of some of the capability of DVR systems to collect large amounts of demographic data that networks and agencies can use to tightly target and telegraph ads to specific audiences. DVR services could take certain commercials out of a program and replace them with ads that are of more interest to specific types of TV viewers or ads that include contests or other incentives that will encourage consumers not to skip them.

While VOD is clearly a threat to the traditional TV ad business, many companies view it as the ultimate invitation marketing tool as it provides them the opportunity to create their own branded "watch it when you want" content. For example, General Motors is already airing segments that offer close-ups of its vehicles while Coca-Cola has signed on as the primary sponsor of a live-music service Concert Channel where it will be able to use a variety of advertising formats beyond the traditional 30-second spot including 10-second interstices and long-form ads. Companies with long-running and popular ad campaigns such as Nike could make their entire ad archive available via VOD so consumers could watch them whenever they want.

While DVRs and VOD are already affecting the way many households utilize television, efforts are already under way to merge them with the Internet through a new technology called Internet Protocol TV (IPTV). IPTV transforms video content into digital files and makes TV a two-way experience that allows viewers to interact with their screen. IPTV will make possible the long-awaited convergence of television with the Internet. Technology gurus predict that in 10 years everything we watch on television will be high definition, interactive, and delivered via the Internet. Experts note that advertisers, as well as marketers, must find ways to respond to such new technologies as DVRs, VOD, and IPTV. Those who fail to do so may find their businesses and careers DOA.

Sources: Stephanie N. Mehta, "How the Web Will Save the Commercial," *Fortune,* August 8, 2005, pp. 57–60; Claire Atkinson, "Can VOD Save TV?" *Advertising Age,* April 18, 2005, pp. 1, 44–46; Kim Gerard, "Saving TiVo," *Business 2.0,* September 2004, pp. 92–100.

Buying Television Time

A number of options are available to advertisers that choose to use TV as part of their media mix. They can purchase time in a variety of program formats that appeal to various types and sizes of audiences. They can purchase time on a national, regional, or local basis. Or they can sponsor an entire program, participate in the sponsorship, or use spot announcements during or between programs.

The purchase of TV advertising time is a highly specialized phase of the advertising business, particularly for large companies spending huge sums of money. Large advertisers that do a lot of TV advertising generally use agency media specialists or specialized media buying services to arrange the media schedule and purchase TV time. Decisions have to be made regarding national or network versus local or spot purchases, selection of specific stations, sponsorship versus participation, different classes of time, and appropriate programs. Local advertisers may not have to deal with the first decision, but they do face all the others.

Network versus Spot

A basic decision for all advertisers is allocating their TV media budgets to network versus local or spot announcements. Most national advertisers use network schedules to provide national coverage and supplement this with regional or local spot purchases to reach markets where additional coverage is desired.

Network Advertising

A common way advertisers disseminate their messages is by purchasing airtime from a **television network.** A network assembles a series of affiliated local TV stations, or **affiliates,** to which it supplies programming and services. These affiliates, most of which are independently owned, contractually agree to preempt time during specified hours for programming provided by the networks and to carry the national advertising within the program. The networks share the advertising revenue they receive during these time periods with the affiliates. The affiliates are also free to sell commercial time in nonnetwork periods and during station breaks in the preempted periods to both national and local advertisers.

The three traditional major networks are NBC, ABC, and CBS. The Fox Broadcasting Co. broadcasts its programs over a group of affiliated independent stations and has become the fourth major network. A number of Fox's prime-time programs, such as *The O.C.* and *24,* have become very popular, particularly among the 18-to-49 age group that is often targeted by advertisers. Fox has also become a major player in sports programming with its contracts to broadcast sporting events such as NFL football and Major League Baseball.

Two additional competitors in network television have emerged over the past five years. WB is a network that was originally financed by Time Warner and, following the merger with AOL, is now part of the AOL–Time Warner media conglomerate. WB reaches a national audience through its affiliates, and its programming includes comedy, drama, and talk shows such as *Gilmore Girls* and *7th Heaven.* The other new network is United Paramount Network (UPN), which has more than 100 affiliates and now has five nights a week of prime-time programming that includes shows such as *America's Next Top Model* and *WWE Smackdown* (Exhibit 11-4). In addition to WB,

UPN, and the four major networks, there are also several Spanish-language networks in the United States.[19] Diversity Perspective 11-1 discusses how Spanish-language television networks such as Univision and Telemundo are becoming increasingly popular and provide advertisers a way to reach the fast-growing Hispanic market.

The networks have affiliates throughout the nation for almost complete national coverage. When an advertiser purchases airtime from one of these four national networks, the commercial is transmitted across the nation through the affiliate station network. Network advertising truly represents a mass medium, as the advertiser can broadcast its message simultaneously throughout the country.

A major advantage of network advertising is the simplification of the purchase process. The advertiser has to deal with only one party or media representative to air a commercial nationwide. The networks also offer the most popular programs and generally control prime-time programming. Advertisers interested in reaching huge nationwide audiences generally buy network time during the prime viewing hours of 8 to 11 P.M. eastern time.

The major drawback is the high cost of network time, particularly on the four major networks. Figure 11-2 shows cost estimates for a 30-second spot on the networks' prime-time shows during the fall 2005 television season.[20] Many of the popular prime-time shows charge $200,000 or more for a 30-second spot; the highest-rated shows, like *Desperate Housewives* and *CSI,* can command nearly half a million dollars. Thus, only advertisers with large budgets can afford to use network advertising on a regular basis.

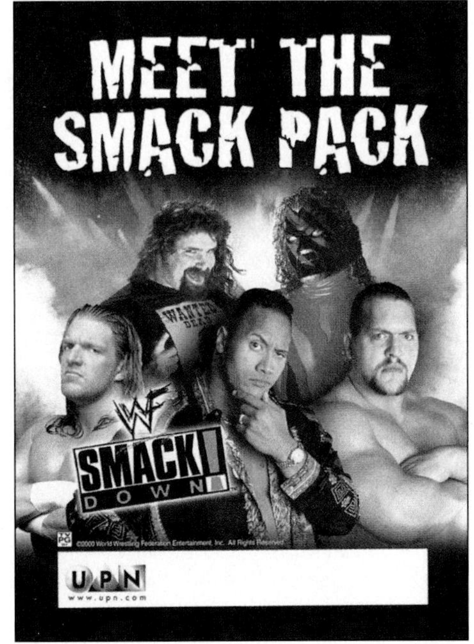

Exhibit 11-4 UPN is one of the newest television networks

Figure 11-2 What TV Shows Cost: Estimated Price of a 30-Second Spot on the Major Networks: Fall 2005

SUNDAY

Network	7 p.m. (ET)		8 p.m.		9 p.m.		10 p.m.
ABC	America's Funniest Home Videos $86,302		Extreme Makeover: Home Ed. $342,000		Desperate Housewives $439,499		Grey's Anatomy $352,569
CBS	60 Minutes $109,980		Cold Case $130,978		CBS Sunday Movie $94,200		
NBC	Dateline $64,490		West Wing $120,000		Law & Order: Criminal Intent $141,870		Crossing Jordan $154,563
FOX	Animation $79,300	King of the Hill $143,700	The Simpsons $340,700	War at Home $148,461	Family Guy $166,378	American Dad $218,000	No Fox programming
WB	Reba $36,000	Reba $36,000	Charmed $63,200		Blue Collar TV $58,500	Blue Collar TV $55,000	No WB programming

MONDAY

Network	8 p.m.		9 p.m.		10 p.m.
ABC	Wife Swap/The Bachelor[1] $92,850/$100,000		Mon. Nt. Football/Emily/Jake[1] $346,500/$108,000/$91,000		MNF/What About Brian[1] $346,500/$176,000
CBS	King of Queens $182,800	Met Your Mother $151,630	Two & Half Men $327,000	Out of Practice $292,000	CSI: Miami $229,000
NBC	Surface $116,003		Las Vegas $155,400		Medium $228,950
FOX	Arrested Dev./Hse.[1] $175,550/N.R.	Kitchen Con. $59,432	Prison Break/24[1] $160,669/$309,000		No Fox programming
UPN	One on One $41,500	All of Us $32,066	Girlfriends $52,975	Half and Half $46,450	No UPN programming
WB	7th Heaven $92,100		Just Legal $57,200		No WB programming

TUESDAY

Network	8 p.m.		9 p.m.		10 p.m.
ABC	According to Jim $192,900	Rodney $132,600	Commander in Chief $182,580		Boston Legal $191,100
CBS	NCIS $133,300		The Amazing Race $210,900		Close to Home $144,800
NBC	The Biggest Loser $130,748		My Name is Earl $189,536	The Office $217,000	Law & Order: SVU $191,776
FOX	Bones/American Idol[1] $101,328/$496,866		House/Bones[1] $204,533/$210,000		No Fox programming
UPN	America's Next Top Model (r) $32,669		Sex, Lies and Secrets $24,751		No UPN programming
WB	Gilmore Girls $112,900		Supernatural $115,056		No WB programming

WED.

Network	8 p.m.		9 p.m.		10 p.m.
ABC	George Lopez $134,389	Freddie $153,900	Lost $333,166		Invasion $217,000
CBS	Still Standing $107,800	Yes, Dear $119,150	Criminal Minds $128,400		CSI: New York $163,000
NBC	The Apprentice: Martha $163,146		E-Ring $149,500		Law & Order $178,314
FOX	That '70s Show $133,040	Stacked $181,000	Head Cases/Idol $153,250/$518,466		No Fox programming
UPN	America's Next Top Model $62,319		Veronica Mars $51,500		No UPN programming
WB	One Tree Hill $100,456		Related $58,476		No WB programming

THURSDAY

Network	8 p.m.		9 p.m.		10 p.m.
ABC	Alias $112,650		The Night Stalker $120,050		Prime Time Live $119,376
CBS	Survivor: Guatemala $351,000		CSI: Crime Scene Investigation $478,000		Without a Trace $265,700
NBC	Joey $149,475	Will & Grace $238,266	The Apprentice $299,600		ER $344,166
FOX	The O.C. $172,200		Reunion $130,000		No Fox programming
UPN	Hates Chris $140,900	Eve $47,750	Cuts $30,174	Love, Inc. $28,424	No UPN programming
WB	Smallville $71,776		Everwood $55,000		No WB programming

FRIDAY

Network	8 p.m.		9 p.m.		10 p.m.
ABC	Supernanny $96,576		Hope & Faith $154,450	Hot Properties $120,650	20/20 $119,000
CBS	Ghost Whisperer $83,701		Threshold $80,250		Numbers $111,340
NBC	Three Wishes $82,700		Dateline $73,692		Inconceivable $136,000
FOX	Bernie Mac N.R.	Malcolm $129,000	The Gate $76,600		No Fox programming
UPN	WWE Smackdown $22,000				No UPN programming
WB	What I Like $37,900	Twins $54,400	Reba $62,350	Living W/ Fran $40,798	No WB programming

SATURDAY

Network	8 p.m.		9 p.m.		10 p.m.
ABC	ABC Movie of the Week $94,300				
CBS	Crime Time Saturday $62,500		Crime Time Saturday $93,100		48 Hours Mystery $87,800
NBC	NBC Saturday Night Movie $53,175				
FOX	Cops $69,397	Cops $64,977	America's Most Wanted $69,150		No Fox programming

DIVERSITY PERSPECTIVE 11-1

Spanish-Language Networks Take On the Big Four

The television industry has grown accustomed to fierce battles among the major networks for viewers as ABC, CBS, NBC, and Fox continually go head-to head with one another. Whereas the major networks are accustomed to battling each other as well as the cable networks, they are also facing competition from the two largest Spanish-language television networks in the United States—Univision and Telemundo. The two companies dominate the battle to lure the eyeballs of the 40 million Hispanics in the United States, a market segment whose buying power is expected to exceed $1 trillion by 2010. Hispanics now represent 14 percent of the total U.S. population and are the fastest growing market within the country. According to Nielsen Media Research estimates, there are over 11 million Hispanic-American television households in the United States and approximately 90 percent speak some Spanish at home. Language usage has an important impact on their choice of TV programs and a substantial share of viewing in these homes is to Spanish-language television. Moreover, Hispanics tend to be younger, have larger families, and watching TV is often a shared family experience.

Univision Communications, based in Los Angeles, is the leading Spanish-language media company in the United States. It owns Univision Network, which covers 98 percent of Hispanic households in the United States and commands two-thirds of the audience watching Spanish-language TV. The company also owns Galavision, which is available to 6.5 million Hispanic cable subscribers and offers news, sports, variety/lifestyle, and comedy programming; Univision Radio, which is the leading Spanish-language radio broadcaster in the United States; and Univision.com, which is the most visited Spanish-language Internet portal in the United States. In 2002 Univision Communications launched a second broadcast network, TeleFutura, which counter-programs against Univision and Galavision, airing alternative genres during every daypart. TeleFutura has captured 11 percent of the estimated 6 million prime-time Spanish-language TV viewers. Programming on Univision's core network is full of *novellas* or soap operas produced by Mexico's Grupo Televisa; these programs are very popular among Hispanics of Mexican descent, who make up nearly two-thirds of the Latino population in the United States. Its programming also includes soccer matches, variety, news, talk, and music shows.

Univision's big rival is Telemundo, based in Hialeah, Florida, which was purchased by General Electric Co.'s NBC network in late 2001. Telemundo has seen its ratings rise for the past four years with programming that includes novellas in prime time, and sports, movies, and comedies on the weekend. In 2002, Telemundo entered into a deal to broadcast NBA and WNBA games in Spanish. Since it is part of NBC, Telemundo can promote its shows heavily on the network, which will also give it the Spanish TV rights to other programs such as the Billboard Latin Music Awards, the Olympics, and Miss Universe contests.

Univision and Telemundo are battling each other over the fastest-growing media market in the United States: Ad spending on Hispanic television reached nearly $1.5 billion in 2005 and is growing nearly 10 percent a year, while advertising revenues in mainstream network television have shown little or no increases. A major reason for this growth is that major advertisers such as Procter & Gamble, General Motors, Sears, Wal-Mart, Ford Motor Company, McDonald's, and many others are developing ads specifically for the Hispanic market, and they recognize that Spanish-language TV networks are the best way to reach this fast-growing market with these commercial messages. The two networks provide marketers the most effective way to reach foreign-born Hispanics who watch primarily Spanish-language TV. It is estimated that some 5 million Hispanic adults prefer Spanish-language prime-time television.

Whereas Univision and Telemundo are very popular among Spanish-dominant Hispanics, the networks are also becoming increasingly popular among young bilingual Hispanics. Univision, in particular, has gained on the Big Four networks. During the 2004–2005 television seasons, Univision ranked number one among 18- to 34-year-old viewers that advertisers pay a premium to reach on 52 nights. On two-thirds of the evenings, it ranked higher than at least one of the Big Four. On one Monday night, the Univision novella *Rubi* drew 3.1 million adults between the ages of 18 to 34, nearly a million more than Fox's *24* and CBS's *Everybody Loves Raymond*. Univision already has surpassed the major networks in several big-city markets as its stations in Los Angeles, New York, Miami, Houston, and Dallas had higher prime-time ratings in the coveted 18 to 34 age category than their ABC, CBS, NBC, and Fox counterparts during recent ratings periods.

While Univision and Telemundo are likely to continue their battle for Hispanic TV viewers, both networks recognize they can and must continue to grow by attracting viewers from the Big Four.

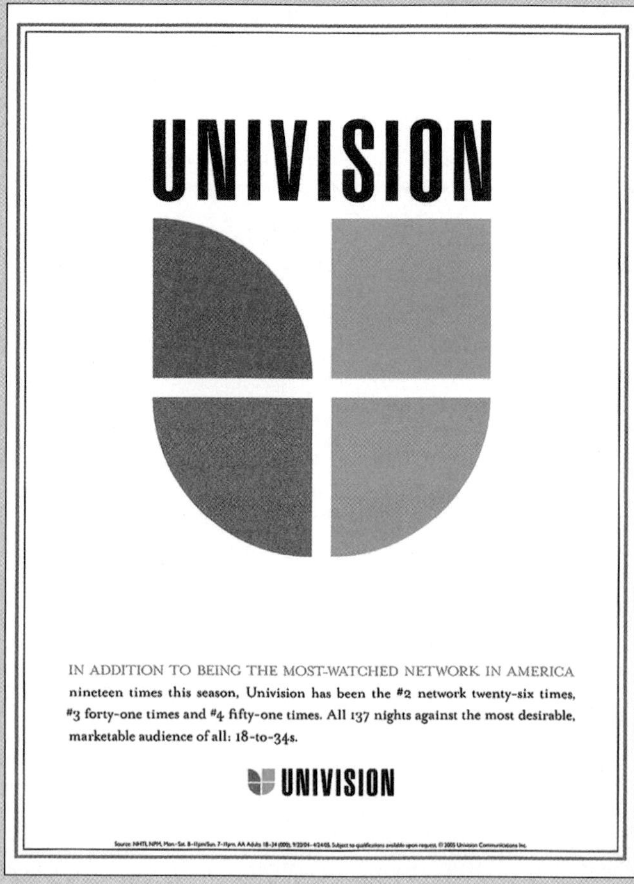

UNIVISION
IN ADDITION TO BEING THE MOST-WATCHED NETWORK IN AMERICA
nineteen times this season, Univision has been the #2 network twenty-six times, #3 forty-one times and #4 fifty-one times. All 137 nights against the most desirable, marketable audience of all: 18-to-34s.
UNIVISION

They also know that it is important to develop programs that attract Hispanic viewers because the programs appeal to them—not just because they are broadcast in Spanish. A large number of Hispanics born in the United States watch both Spanish- and English-language TV, which means that the networks must convince them to turn to Spanish-language programming. Both Univision and Telemundo are expanding their news, sports, and variety programming, offering non-novella drama series, and developing reality shows. Both networks are also targeting the late-night time slot popular among young adults. Of course, they face competition from English-language programs that appeal to the interests of young Hispanics but also have crossover appeal to the general population. An interesting battle is shaping up to determine who will be numero uno in reaching the fast-growing Hispanic market.

Sources: John Consoli, "Hispanic Expansion," *Adweek,* May 30, 2005, pp. SR28–29; Brooks Barnes and Miriam Jordan, "'Big Four' TV Networks Get a Wake-Up Call—in Spanish," *The Wall Street Journal,* May 2, 2005, pp. B1, 6; Jeffery D. Zbar, "Networks Give New Voice to Hispanic Households," *Advertising Age,* May 31, 2004, p. S-10.

Availability of time can also be a problem as more advertisers turn to network advertising to reach mass markets. Traditionally, most prime-time commercial spots, particularly on the popular shows, are sold during the **up-front market,** a buying period that occurs before the TV season begins. Advertisers hoping to use prime-time network advertising must plan their media schedules and often purchase TV time as much as a year in advance. Demands from large clients who are heavy TV advertisers force the biggest agencies to participate in the up-front market. However, TV time is also purchased during the **scatter market** that runs through the TV season. Some key incentives for buying up front, such as cancellation options and lower prices, are becoming more available in the quarterly scatter market. Network TV can also be purchased on a regional basis, so an advertiser's message can be aired in certain sections of the country with one media purchase.

Spot and Local Advertising

Spot advertising refers to commercials shown on local TV stations, with time negotiated and purchased directly from the individual stations. All nonnetwork advertising done by a national advertiser is known as **national spot advertising;** airtime sold to local firms such as retailers, restaurants, banks, and auto dealers is known as **local advertising.** Local advertisers want media whose coverage is limited to the geographic markets in which they do business. This may be difficult to accomplish with TV, but many local businesses are large enough to make efficient use of TV advertising.

Spot advertising offers the national advertiser flexibility in adjusting to local market conditions. The advertiser can concentrate commercials in areas where market potential is greatest or where additional support is needed. This appeals to advertisers with uneven distribution or limited advertising budgets, as well as those interested in test marketing or introducing a product in limited market areas. National advertisers often use spot television advertising through local retailers or dealers as part of their cooperative advertising programs and to provide local dealer support.

A major problem for national advertisers is that spot advertising can be more difficult to acquire, since the time must be purchased from a number of local stations. Moreover, there are more variations in the pricing policies and discount structure of individual stations than of the networks. However, this problem has been reduced somewhat by the use of **station reps,** individuals who act as sales representatives for a number of local stations in dealings with national advertisers.

Spot ads are subject to more commercial clutter, since local stations can sell time on network-originated shows only during station breaks between programs, except when network advertisers have not purchased all the available time. Viewership generally declines during station breaks, as people may leave the room, zap to another channel, attend to other tasks, or stop watching TV.

While spot advertising is mostly confined to station breaks between programs on network-originated shows, local stations sell time on their own programs, which consist of news, movies, syndicated shows, or locally originated programs. Most cities have independent stations that spot advertisers use. Local advertisers find the independent stations attractive because they generally have lower rates than the major network affiliates.

The decision facing most national advertisers is how to combine network and spot advertising to make effective use of their TV advertising budget. Another factor that makes spot advertising attractive to national advertisers is the growth in syndication.

Syndication Advertisers may also reach TV viewers by advertising on **syndicated programs,** shows that are sold or distributed on a station-by-station, market-by-market basis. A syndicator seeks to sell its program to one station in every market. There are several types of syndicated programming. *Off-network syndication* refers to reruns of network shows that are bought by individual stations. Shows that are popular in off-network syndication include *Seinfeld, Everybody Loves Raymond,* and *Friends.* The FCC prime-time access rule forbids large-market network affiliates from carrying these shows from 7 to 8 P.M., but independent stations are not affected by this restriction. A show must have a minimum number of episodes before it is eligible for syndication, and there are limits on network involvement in the financing or production of syndicated shows.

Off-network syndication shows are very important to local stations because they provide quality programming with an established audience. The syndication market is also very important to the studios that produce programs and sell them to the networks. Most prime-time network shows initially lose money for the studios, since the licensing fee paid by the networks does not cover production costs. Over four years (the time it takes to produce the number of episodes needed to break into syndication), half-hour situation comedies often run up a deficit of millions, and losses on a one-hour drama show are even higher. However, the producers recoup their money when they sell the show to syndication.

First-run syndication refers to shows produced specifically for the syndication market. The first-run syndication market is made up of a variety of shows, including some that did not make it as network shows. Examples of popular first-run syndication shows include talk shows such as *Live with Regis & Kelly* and *The Jerry Springer Show,* entertainment shows such as *Inside Edition* and *Entertainment Tonight,* and dramas such as *VIP.*

Advertiser-supported or *barter syndication* is the practice of selling shows to stations in return for a portion of the commercial time in the show, rather than (or in addition to) cash. The commercial time from all stations carrying the show is packaged into national units and sold to national advertisers. The station sells the remaining time to local and spot advertisers. Both off-network and first-run syndicated programs are offered through barter syndication. Usually, more than half of the advertising time is presold, and the remainder is available for sale by the local advertiser. Barter syndication allows national advertisers to participate in the syndication market with the convenience of a network-type media buy, while local stations get free programming and can sell the remainder of the time to local or spot advertisers. Recently, the straight barter deal has given way to more barter/cash arrangements, where the station pays for a program at a reduced rate and accepts a number of preplaced bartered ads. Top-rated barter syndicated programs include *Wheel of Fortune, Jeopardy,* and *The Oprah Winfrey Show.*

Exhibit 11-5 The SNTA promotes the advantages of syndication

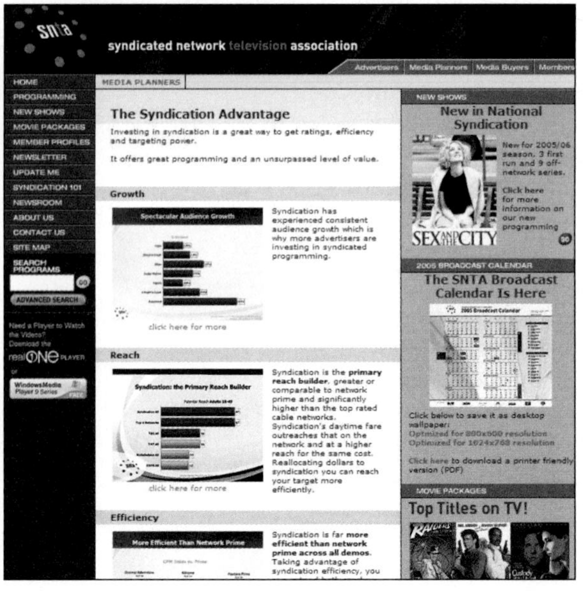

Syndication now accounts for more than a third of the national broadcast audience and has become a very big business, generating ad revenue comparable to any of the big-three networks. Syndicated shows have become more popular than network shows in certain dayparts, such as daytime, early prime time, and late fringe. In some markets, syndicated shows like *Wheel of Fortune* draw a larger audience than the network news.

Many national advertisers use syndicated shows to broaden their reach, save money, and target certain audiences. For example, off-network syndication shows such as *Friends, Seinfeld,* and *CSI* are popular with advertisers because they reach the highly sought after, and often difficult to reach, young-adult audience (age 18 to 34) and are about 15 to 20 percent lower on a cost-per-thousand basis than network shows.[21] Figure 11-3 shows the top 10 syndicated programs in 2004–2005. Syndication continues to gain in popularity, and more advertisers are making syndicated shows part of their television media schedules. Exhibit 11-5 shows a page from the website of the Syndicated Network Television Association (SNTA) promoting the advantages of syndication.

Rank	Program	Houseold Rating (%)
1	*Wheel of Fortune*	9.0
2	*Jeopardy!*	7.9
3	*The Oprah Winfrey Show*	7.6
4	*Everybody Loves Raymond*	6.9
5	*ESPN NFL Regular Season*	6.9
6	*Seinfeld*	5.9
7	*Friends*	5.6
8	*CSI: Crime Scene Investigation*	5.5
9	*Seinfeld* (weekend)	5.5
10	*ESPN NFL Regular Season 2*	5.4

Source: Nielsen Media Research.

Figure 11-3 Top 10 Regularly Scheduled Syndicated Programs 2004–2005 Season

Syndication has certain disadvantages. The audience for some syndicated shows is often older and more rural, and syndicators do not supply as much research information as the networks do. Syndication also creates more problems for media buyers, since a syndicated show may not be seen in a particular market or may be aired during an undesirable time period. Thus, media buyers have to look at each market and check airtimes and other factors to put together a syndication schedule.

Methods of Buying Time

In addition to deciding whether to use network versus spot advertising, advertisers must decide whether to sponsor an entire program, participate in a program, or use spot announcements between programs. Sponsorship of a program and participations are available on either a network or a local market basis, whereas spot announcements are available only from local stations.

Sponsorship

Under a **sponsorship** arrangement, an advertiser assumes responsibility for the production and usually the content of the program as well as the advertising that appears within it. In the early days of TV, most programs were produced and sponsored by corporations and were identified by their name, for example, *Texaco Star Theater* and *The Colgate Comedy Hour.* Today most shows are produced by either the networks or independent production companies that sell them to a network.

Some companies are still involved in the production business. For example, Procter & Gamble, which has been producing soap operas since 1950, entered into an agreement with Paramount Television Groups to develop shows for network TV and first-run syndication. Several major companies have been sponsoring special programs for many years, such as the Kraft Masterpiece Theater and Hallmark Hall of Fame dramatic series. In 1994, Hallmark acquired RHI Entertainment Inc., the company that produces its wholesome Hall of Fame productions as well as TV miniseries and movies. Sole sponsorship of programs is usually limited to specials and has been declining. However, some companies, including Ford, AT&T, General Electric, IBM, and DaimlerChrysler, do still use program sponsorships occasionally.

A company might choose to sponsor a program for several reasons. Sponsorship allows the firm to capitalize on the prestige of a high-quality program, enhancing the image of the company and its products. For example, the Ford Motor Company received a great deal of favorable publicity when it sponsored the commercial-free television debut of the Holocaust movie *Schindler's List.* Traditionally, commercial-free sponsorships have been rare, particularly on the major networks, as sponsoring an entire show can be very costly; it requires buying out all of the national time as well as the local minutes from network affiliates. However, recently a number of companies have paid for shows to run commercial free as part of a larger package involving placements of their products in the program. For example, the Ford Motor Company has sponsored commercial-free season premieres of the drama show *24* on Fox for several seasons in exchange for having its vehicles featured in the program. Cable network FX has often used commercial-free sponsorship deals in exchange for product placement guarantees for premieres of such shows as *Nip/Tuck* and *Rescue Me.*[22]

Companies also sponsor programs to gain more control over the shows carrying their commercials including the number, placement, and content of commercials. Commercials can be of any length as long as the total amount of commercial time does not exceed network or station regulations. Advertisers introducing new products or brands sometimes sponsor a program and run commercials that are several minutes long to launch them. For example, Ford used this strategy to introduce a new version of the Mustang by sponsoring a commercial-free episode of the drama show *American Dreams*. Ford bracketed the show with ads including a post-show five-minute short film.[23] While these factors make sponsorship attractive to some companies, the high costs of sole sponsorship limit this option to large firms. Most commercial time is purchased through other methods, such as participations.

Participations

Most advertisers either cannot afford the costs of sponsorship or want greater flexibility than sole sponsorship permits. Nearly 90 percent of network advertising time is sold as **participations,** with several advertisers buying commercial time or spots on a particular program. An advertiser can participate in a certain program once or several times on a regular or irregular basis. Participating advertisers have no financial responsibility for production of the program; this is assumed by the network or individual station that sells and controls the commercial time.

There are several advantages to participations. First, the advertiser has no long-term commitment to a program, and expenditures can be adjusted to buy whatever number of participation spots fits within the budget. This is particularly important to small advertisers with a limited budget. The second advantage is that the TV budget can be spread over a number of programs, thereby providing for greater reach in the media schedule.

The disadvantage of participations is that the advertiser has little control over the placement of ads, and there may also be problems with availability. Preference is given to advertisers willing to commit to numerous spots, and the firm trying to buy single spots in more than one program may find that time is unavailable in certain shows, especially during prime time.

Spot Announcements

As discussed previously, spot announcements are bought from the local stations and generally appear during time periods adjacent to network programs (hence the term **adjacencies**), rather than within them. Spot announcements are most often used by purely local advertisers but are also bought by companies with no network schedule (because of spotty or limited distribution) and by large advertisers that use both network and spot advertising.

Selecting Time Periods and Programs

Another consideration in buying TV time is selecting the right period and program for the advertiser's commercial messages. The cost of TV advertising time varies depending on the time of day and the particular program, since audience size varies as a function of these two factors. TV time periods are divided into **dayparts,** which are specific segments of a broadcast day.

The time segments that make up the programming day vary from station to station. However, a typical classification of dayparts for a weekday is shown in Figure 11-4. The various daypart segments attract different audiences in both size and nature, so advertising rates vary accordingly. Prime time draws the largest audiences, with 8:30 to 9 P.M. being the most watched half-hour time period and Sunday the most popular night for television. Since firms that advertise during prime time must pay premium rates, this daypart is dominated by the large national advertisers.

The various dayparts are important to advertisers since they attract different demographic groups. For example, daytime TV generally attracts women; early morning attracts women and children. The late-fringe (late-night) daypart period has become

Morning	7:00 A.M.–9:00 A.M., Monday through Friday
Daytime	9:00 A.M.–4:30 P.M., Monday through Friday
Early fringe	4:30 P.M.–7:30 P.M., Monday through Friday
Prime-time access	7:30 P.M.–8:00 P.M., Sunday through Saturday
Prime time	8:00 P.M.–11:00 P.M., Monday through Saturday, and 7:00 P.M.–11:00 P.M., Sunday
Late news	11:00–11:30 P.M., Monday through Friday
Late fringe	11:30–1:00 A.M., Monday through Friday

Figure 11-4 Common Television Dayparts

popular among advertisers trying to reach young adults who tune in to *The Late Show with David Letterman* on CBS and NBC's *The Tonight Show with Jay Leno.* Audience size and demographic composition also vary depending on the type of program.

Cable Television

The Growth of Cable

Perhaps the most significant development in the broadcast media has been the expansion of **cable television.** Cable, or CATV (community antenna television), which delivers TV signals through fiber or coaxial wire rather than the airways, was developed to provide reception to remote areas that couldn't receive broadcast signals. Cable then expanded to metropolitan areas and grew rapidly due to the improved reception and wider selection of stations it offered subscribers. Cable has experienced substantial growth during the past two decades. In 1975, only 13 percent of TV households had cable. By 2005, cable penetration reached 84 percent of the nation's 110 million households either through wired cable or through alternative delivery systems such as direct broadcast satellite (DBS).

Cable subscribers pay a monthly fee for which they receive an average of more than 60 channels, including the local network affiliates and independent stations, various cable networks, superstations, and local cable system channels. Cable networks and channels have a dual revenue stream; they are supported by both subscriber fees and ad revenue. Cable operators also offer programming that is not supported by commercial sponsorship and is available only to households willing to pay a fee beyond the monthly subscription charge. These premium channels include HBO, Showtime, and The Movie Channel.

Cable TV broadens the program options available to the viewer as well as the advertiser by offering specialty channels, including all-news, pop music, country music, sports, weather, educational, and cultural channels as well as children's programming. Figure 11-5 shows the most popular cable channels along with the types of programming they carry. Many cable systems also carry **superstations,** independent local stations that send their signals nationally via satellite to cable operators to make their programs available to subscribers. Programming on superstations such as TBS and WGN generally consists of sports, movies, and reruns of network shows. The superstations do carry national advertising and are a relatively inexpensive option for cable households across the country.

Cable has had a considerable influence on the nature of television as an advertising medium. First, the expanded viewing options have led to considerable audience fragmentation. Much of the growth in cable audiences has come at the expense of the three major networks. Cable channels now have more of the prime-time viewing audience than the major networks. Many cable stations have become very popular among consumers, leading advertisers to re-evaluate their media plans and the prices they are willing to pay for network and spot commercials on network affiliate stations. The networks, recognizing the growing popularity of cable, have become involved with the cable industry. ABC purchased ESPN, while NBC launched the Consumer News and Business Channel (CNBC) in 1989—and in 1996 entered in a joint venture with Microsoft to launch MSNBC, a 24-hour news channel.[24] In 2004, NBC joined with Vivendi Universal Entertainment to form NBC Universal, which owns and operates a motion picture company, television stations, and 10 different cable networks including CNBC, MSNBC, Bravo, USA Network, Sci Fi Channel, and mun2, which targets young Hispanics.

Figure 11-5 Major Cable Networks

Network	Type of Programming	Network	Type of Programming
ABC Family	Family/general/original	FX	Entertainment/original programs
A&E Network	Biographies/dramas/movies/documentaries	Galavision	Programming/entertainment for Hispanics
AMC	Movies/documentaries	GSN: The Network for Games	Game shows
Animal Planet	Wildlife and nature documentaries/adventure/children's entertainment	Golf Channel	Golf
BBC America	Drama/comedy/news/arts and lifestyle documentaries	Hallmark Channel	Original movies/miniseries
BET	Entertainment/information for African-Americans	HGTV	Decorating/gardening
BET Jazz: The Jazz Channel	Jazz music/documentaries/concerts	History Channel	Historical documentaries/movies
Black Family Channel	Variety of programming for African-Americans	Lifetime Television	News/information/women's interests
Bloomberg Television	Business and financial news	MSNBC	News/information
Bravo	Drama/movies/reality shows	MTV: Music Television	Music/videos/documentaries
Cartoon Network	Cartoons	mun2 Television	Bilingual programming for Hispanics/Latino youth culture
CMT: Country Music Television	Country music video/concert/specials	National Geographic Channel	Adventure/exploration/science/culture
CNBC	Financial and business news/interviews and discussions	Nickelodeon/Nick at Nite	Youth interest/cartoons/comedy/game shows
CNN	News/information	OLN	Sports/outdoors/nature
CNN en Espanol	News/information (Spanish language)	Oxygen	Movies/news/comedy/women's interests
CNN Headline News	News/information	SCI FI Channel	Science fiction
CNN fn	Financial and business news	Spike TV	Original programming/sports/entertainment for men
CNN Sports Illustrated	Sports	Superstation WGN	Movies/dramas/sports/sitcoms/reality-based programs
Comedy Central	Comedy programs/original	TBS	Entertainment/movies/sports
Court TV	Court/legal	TLC (Learning Channel)	Science/history/adventure/behavior
Discovery Channel	Family/health/technology/science	TNN: The National Network	Pop culture/movies/sports/drama
Discovery Health Channel	Health/medical	TNT	Movies/general entertainment/sports
E! Entertainment Television	Entertainment/celebrities/pop culture	Travel Channel	Travel information
ESPN	Sports/specials/events	TV Guide Channel	Television entertainment information
ESPN 2	Sports	USA Network	Entertainment/movies/sports
ESPN Sports Classics	Sports history/biographies	VH1	Music videos/movies/concerts/documentaries
ESPN Deportes	Sports (Spanish language)	Weather Channel	Weather
ESPNEWS	Sports news	WGN	Entertainment/sports/movies
Food Network	Food/cooking/entertainment		
FOX News Channel	News/information		
FOX Sports Net	Sports		

In addition to the networks, major cable operators also own cable networks. For example, Comcast, the largest cable operator, owns several networks including E! Entertainment Television, the Golf Channel, and the Outdoor Life Network (OLN). Comcast has been positioning OLN as a mainstream sports network to take on industry leader ESPN (see Exhibit 11-6). In 2005, OLN acquired the rights to broadcast National Hockey League games and is also expected to bid for rights to broadcast other professional sports including football and baseball.[25]

THE ONE TO WATCH
OLN is the place for action, adventure and drama. Over 64 million homes tune in for pulse-pounding, adrenaline-fueled entertainment. With best-in-class events like the NHL, The Tour de France, America's Cup and PBR, Field Sports' Finest and first-rate series, OLN continues to be the must-have network for thrillseekers.
OLN
©2005 Outdoor Life Network, LLC

Exhibit 11-6 OLN is becoming a major cable sports network

Advertising on Cable

Cable advertising revenues have increased steadily since the mid-1980s and exceeded $21 billion in 2005. Much of this growth has come from advertising on the national cable networks such as CNN, ESPN, USA, and MTV. However, many national advertisers have been shifting some of their advertising budgets to spot cable and purchasing through local operators as well as the national cable networks. Over the past four years, spot cable revenues have averaged 20 percent annual growth, reaching nearly $6 billion in 2005.

Like broadcast TV, cable time can be purchased on a national, regional, or local (spot) level. Many large marketers advertise on cable networks to reach large numbers of viewers across the country with a single media buy. Regional advertising on cable is available primarily through sports and news channels that cover a certain geographic area.

Many national advertisers are turning to spot advertising on local cable systems to reach specific geographic markets. Spot cable affords them more precision in reaching specific markets, and they can save money by using a number of small, targeted media purchases rather than making one network buy. The growth in spot cable advertising is also being facilitated by the use of **interconnects,** where a number of cable systems and networks in a geographic area are joined for advertising purposes. These interconnects increase the size of the audience an advertiser can reach with a spot cable buy. For example, the Comcast Spotlight interconnect in Chicago reaches more than 2.3 million cable TV households in the greater Chicago metropolitan area; the ADLINK Digital Interconnect delivers 3 million cable subscribers in Los Angeles and four surrounding counties. New York Interconnect reaches 3.3 million households in the largest market area in the country and offers advertisers targeting capabilities on 40 different networks (Exhibit 11-7). More sophisticated interconnect systems are developing that will pool large numbers of cable systems and allow spot advertisers to reach more viewers. These new systems will also allow local advertisers to make more selective cable buys, since they can purchase the entire interconnect or one of several zones within the system.

Exhibit 11-7 New York Interconnect promotes its targeting potential to advertisers

While spot cable is becoming very popular among national advertisers, it has some of the same problems as spot advertising on broadcast TV. The purchasing process is very complicated and time-consuming; media buyers must contact hundreds of cable systems to put together a media schedule consisting of spot cable buys. Local cable systems also do not provide advertisers with strong support or much information on demographics, lifestyle, or viewership patterns.

Advantages of Cable

Cable TV has experienced tremendous growth as an advertising medium because it has some important advantages. A primary one is selectivity. Cable subscribers tend to be younger, more affluent, and better educated than nonsubscribers and have greater purchasing power. Moreover, the specialized programming on the various cable networks reaches very specific target markets.

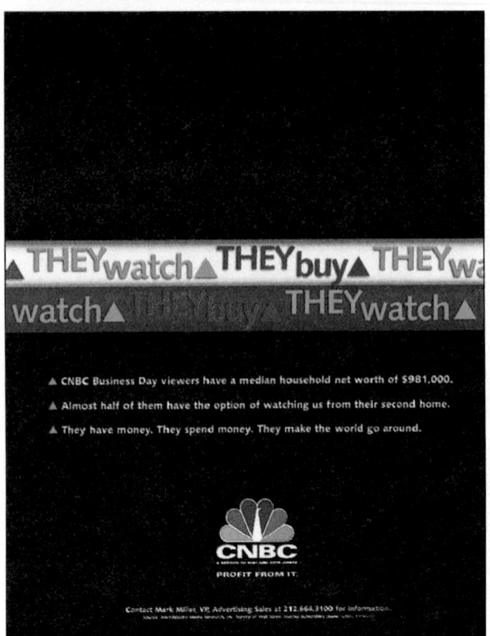

Exhibit 11-8 CNBC has become the leader in business news and has a very affluent viewing audience

Many advertisers have turned to cable because of the opportunities it offers for **narrowcasting,** or reaching very specialized markets. For example, MTV is used by advertisers in the United States and many other countries to reach teenagers and young adults. CNBC is now the worldwide leader in business news and reaches a highly educated and affluent audience (Exhibit 11-8). ESPN has become synonymous with sports and is very popular among advertisers who want to target men of all ages. As discussed in IMC Perspective 11-2, ESPN has become more than just a 24-hour sports network as it has changed the way sports are covered as well as consumed by TV viewers.

Advertisers are also interested in cable because of its low cost and flexibility. Advertising rates on cable programs are much lower than those for the shows on the major networks. Advertising time on network shows can cost two to three times as much on a cost-per-thousand basis in some time periods.[26] Spot advertising is also considerably cheaper on most cable stations, while local cable is the most affordable television advertising vehicle available. This makes TV a much more viable media option for smaller advertisers with limited budgets and those interested in targeting their commercials to a well-defined target audience. Also, cable advertisers generally do not have to make the large up-front commitments, which may be as much as a year in advance, the networks require.

The low costs of cable make it a very popular advertising medium among local advertisers. Car dealers, furniture stores, restaurants, and many other merchants are switching advertising spending from traditional media such as radio, newspapers, and even magazines to take advantage of the low rates of local cable channels. Local cable advertising is one of the fastest growing segments of the advertising market, and cable systems are increasing the percentage of revenue they earn from local advertising.

Limitations of Cable

While cable has become increasingly popular among national, regional, and local advertisers, it still has some drawbacks. One major problem is that cable is overshadowed by the major networks, as households with basic cable service still watch considerably more network and syndicated programming than cable shows. This stems from the fact that cable generally has less desirable programming than broadcast TV.

Another drawback of cable is audience fragmentation. Although cable's share of the TV viewing audience has increased significantly, the viewers are spread out among the large number of channels available to cable subscribers. The number of viewers who watch any one cable channel is generally quite low. Even MTV, ESPN, and CNN have prime-time ratings of only about 1 or 2. The large number of cable stations has fragmented audiences and made buying procedures more difficult, since numerous stations must be contacted to reach the majority of the cable audience in a market. There are also problems with the quality and availability of local ratings for cable stations as well as research on audience characteristics.

Cable also still lacks total penetration, especially in some major markets. As of 2005, overall cable penetration from both wired and alternative delivery systems such as satellite was 82 percent in the Los Angeles–designated market area (DMA), 77 percent in Houston, and 78 percent in the Dallas–Ft.Worth DMA. In some designated market areas, wired cable penetration is low as many households receive cable programming from alternative delivery systems that do not offer local advertising. For example, penetration of wired cable is under 60 percent in some major DMAs such as Los Angeles, Denver, and Dallas–Ft. Worth. Thus, local advertisers in these markets would not be able to reach a significant number of households by advertising on local cable networks.

IMC PERSPECTIVE 11-2

ESPN: Heaven for the Sports Fan

For many years, TV sports programming consisted primarily of football, baseball, and, to a lesser extent, basketball shown primarily on weekends on network television. Hard-core sports fans had to wait until the weekend to see major sporting events such as an NFL or college football game, and sports news coverage was limited to five-minute sportscasts on the 11 P.M. news on the local network affiliate. However, on September 7, 1979, a small cable network called ESPN began broadcasting from a trailer in a swampy industrial park in Bristol, Connecticut. The network was the idea of Bill Rasmussen, a former sportscaster whose original concept was for it to be a sports network for Connecticut but discovered that it would cost no more to offer the first cable network devoted entirely to sports programming on a national basis.

When ESPN was launched in 1979 the critics declared that "all the good sports are already on the three networks." They ridiculed the network for broadcasting such sports as stock car racing, which was described as "two hours of left turns." However, no one is laughing at ESPN today. It is one of the top cable networks, reaching 88 million homes in the United States, 10 million more than its closest competitor. Its signature show, *SportsCenter*—a one-hour sports news show that is aired numerous times throughout the day and night—is emblematic of the entire network and has helped position ESPN as the place for the ultimate sports fan, not just another cable channel showing sports. An award-winning advertising campaign consisting of humorous spots that purport to give viewers a behind-the-scenes look at *SportsCenter* has helped contribute to the popularity and image of the show and create a brand identity that has carried over to the entire network. Since the campaign was launched in 1995, nearly 250 promotional spots have been produced for the campaign.

ESPN (which originally was an acronym for Entertainment and Sports Program Network, but since 1984 has officially stood for nothing) is much more than the number-one cable network. It is a sports enterprise and brand that has become synonymous with sports in America as well as in many other countries. It has expanded beyond its stalwart network as the ESPN franchise now includes six other U.S. channels, a radio network, a popular website, *ESPN The Magazine,* and eight ESPN Zone restaurants. ESPN radio now has over 700 full-time affiliates and 255 more part-time, while *ESPN The Magazine,* which was launched in 1998, now has 1.75 million subscribers. ESPN.com is the most popular sports website receiving nearly 18 million unique visits per month and more than 2.3 million hits during peak hours. Research shows that an average of 94 million Americans consume ESPN media every week. The various businesses generate an estimated $3.3 billion in yearly revenues making ESPN one of the most lucrative assets in the portfolio of the Walt Disney Company, which acquired the company as part of a package deal for ABC/Capital Cities in 1995.

ESPN has clearly changed the way sports are covered as well as the consumption of sports. It has become the dominant vehicle by which America gets its sports highlights and news. And even though many of the major sports championship games are still shown on the major networks, ESPN attracts viewers by creating talk shows that sandwich the big events such as the NCAA basketball tournament, BCS college football bowl games, and the Super Bowl. In addition to being very popular among sports fans, the various ESPN properties have become very popular among advertisers as they are particularly good at delivering large numbers of young male sports fans, a group that is difficult to reach but highly coveted by marketers.

One of the reasons ESPN has been so successful is that management has recognized that the 25-year-old sports network needs to make some changes to sustain its growth and to continue as the preeminent sports network. In early 2002, ESPN, along with the ABC television network also owned by Disney, outbid NBC for the rights to televise National Basketball Association games. The $2.4 billion deal marked the first time a cable player has grabbed a major sports contract from the broadcast networks. In 2005, the network agreed to pay the National Football League $1.1 billion a year for the rights to *Monday Night Football* for eight years beginning in 2006. The popular Monday night games, which have become an integral part of American sports culture, had aired on its sister network ABC for 36 years.

ESPN has also become heavily involved with college sports as it airs more than 1,000 collegiate sporting events a year, including 21 men's and women's championships. ESPN's rights fees for college football and basketball games in particular have helped fund college athletic programs including many minor sports and women's sports. ESPN has also entered other new arenas including alternative sports such as the X Games and Great Outdoor Games as well as original programming, which includes variety shows, made-for-TV movies, reality shows, and game shows.

The first words ever spoken on ESPN by host Lee Leonard were, "If you're a fan, what you'll see in the next minutes, hours, and days to follow may convince you that you've gone to sports heaven." Twenty-five years later most sports fans do indeed feel they are in sports heaven when ESPN is airing on their TV sets.

Sources: Joe Flint and Stefan Fatsis, "ESPN Snatches NFL on Monday; NBC Scores, Too," *The Wall Street Journal,* April 19, 2005, pp. B1, 9; Joseph Guinto, "ESPN Is 25 Years Old, Sports Fans," *Southwest Airlines Spirit,* September 2004, pp. 97–104; Rudy Martzke and Reid Cherner, "Channeling How to View Sports," *USA TODAY,* August 17, 2004, pp. 1, 2C.

The Future of Cable Cable TV should continue to experience strong growth as its audience share increases and advertisers spend more money to reach cable viewers. However, the cable industry faces several challenges: increases in the number of channels, leading to fragmentation of the audience, changes in government regulations, and competition in the programming distribution business from other telecommunications companies and direct broadcast satellite services. Advances in technology such as digital video compression and fiber optics, coupled with massive investments in system upgrades, are making it possible for cable operators to offer more channels and thus subject existing cable channels to greater competition. Increases in the number of channels available lead to further fragmentation of the cable audience and make it more difficult for cable networks to charge the ad rates needed to finance original programming. Some of the growth in cable channels will come from **multiplexing,** or transmitting multiple channels from one network. Several major cable networks, including ESPN, VH1, and the Discovery Channel, own several channels.

The cable industry has also been affected by changes in government regulation. In the early 90s, concerns over poor service and high rates led to a revolt against the cable industry. As a result, Congress passed legislation in 1993 that rolled back the provisions of the Cable Television Act of 1984, allowed local governments to regulate basic cable rates, and forced cable operators to pay licensing fees for local broadcast programming they used to retransmit for free. The Telecommunications Act of 1996 allows local phone companies to offer cable service. However, as part of this act, federal regulation of the cable industry expired on April 1, 1999, and cable rates are now deregulated.[27]

One of the biggest threats facing the cable industry is competition from **direct broadcast satellite (DBS) services,** which use a system whereby TV and radio programs are sent directly from a satellite to homes equipped with a small dish. DBS companies such as DirecTV and EchoStar now have nearly 20 million subscribers, many of whom have come to them at the expense of cable companies. DBS companies have been aggressively marketing their service, superior picture quality, and greater channel choice as subscribers receive as many as 200 channels that include news, music, and sports in crisp, digital video and CD-quality sound. A major competitive restriction to DBS services was removed in late 1999 when the federal government passed legislation allowing satellite TV companies to carry local broadcast signals in most major markets.[28]

The future of cable as an advertising medium will ultimately depend on the size and quality of the audiences cable stations can reach with their programs. This in turn will depend on cable's ability to offer programs that attract viewers and subscribers. Cable's image as a stepchild in program development and acquisition has changed. Cable networks such as VH1, E!, TBS, ESPN, and others have been creating original films, documentaries, and other programs that draw significant ratings. Networks like A&E, the Discovery Channel, the National Geographic Channel, and the History Channel (Exhibit 11-9) provide outstanding cultural and educational programming.

Exhibit 11-9 The History Channel provides outstanding educational programming

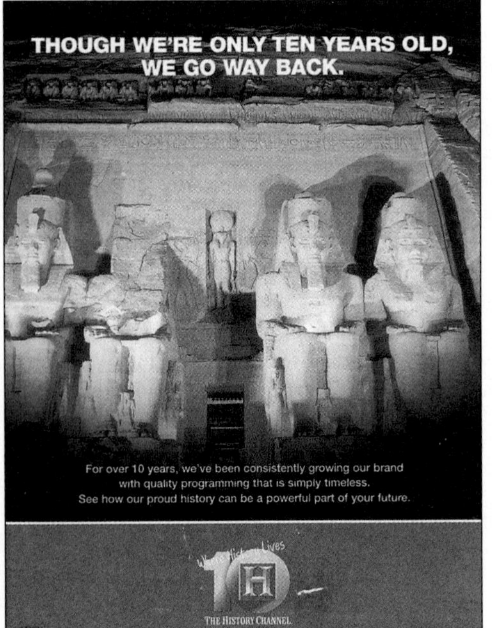

THOUGH WE'RE ONLY TEN YEARS OLD, WE GO WAY BACK.
For over 10 years, we've been consistently growing our brand with quality programming that is simply timeless.
See how our proud history can be a powerful part of your future.
THE HISTORY CHANNEL.

Cable TV will continue to be a popular source of sports programming and is very important to advertisers interested in reaching the male market. There are over 11 regional cable sports networks, and with companies such as Fox Sports, advertisers can buy multiple regions with one media buy. Cable networks are also paying large sums for the rights to sports programming. Deals by ESPN for Monday night coverage of National Football League and Major League Baseball games, along with its six-year deal to broadcast National Basketball Association games, have proved that cable networks can compete with the major networks in a sports bidding war.[29]

As cable penetration increases, its programming improves, and more advertisers discover its efficiency and ability to reach targeted market segments, cable's popularity as an advertising medium should continue to grow.

Many agencies have developed specialists to examine the use of cable in their clients' media schedules. Cable networks are also looking to international markets as a source of future growth. Both ESPN and MTV have expanded into South America, Europe, and Asia, while TV viewers throughout the world tune to CNN International for news.

Measuring the TV Audience

One of the most important considerations in TV advertising is the size and composition of the viewing audience. Audience measurement is critical to advertisers as well as to the networks and stations. Advertisers want to know the size and characteristics of the audience they are reaching when they purchase time on a particular program. And since the rates they pay are a function of audience size, advertisers want to be sure audience measurements are accurate.

Audience size and composition are also important to the network or station, since they determine the amount it can charge for commercial time. Shows are frequently canceled because they fail to attract enough viewers to make their commercial time attractive to potential advertisers. Determining audience size is not an exact science and has been the subject of considerable controversy through the years. In this section, we examine how audiences are measured and how advertisers use this information in planning their media schedules.

Audience Measures

The size and composition of television audiences are measured by ratings services. The sole source of network TV and local audience information is the Nielsen Media Research. For many years local audience information was also available from the Arbitron Co., but Arbitron exited the local TV ratings business at the end of 1993 due to steep financial losses.[30] Nielsen gathers viewership information from a sample of TV homes and then projects this information to the total viewing area. The techniques used to gather audience measurement information include diaries, electronic meters or recorders, and personal interviews. Nielsen provides various types of information that can be used to measure and evaluate a station's audience. These measures are important to media planners as they weigh the value of buying commercial time on a program.

Television Households The number of households in the market that own a TV is sometimes referred to as the *universe estimate (UE)*. Nielsen estimates that 110.2 million U.S. households owned at least one TV set as of August 2005. Since over 98 percent of U.S. households own a TV set, **television households** generally correspond to the number of households in a given market.[31]

Program Rating Probably the best known of all audience measurement figures is the **program rating,** the percentage of TV households in an area that are tuned to a specific program during a specific time period. The program rating is calculated by dividing the number of households tuned to a particular show by the total number of households in the area. For example, if 14 million households (HH) watched *The Apprentice,* the national rating would be 11.9, calculated as follows:

$$\text{Rating} = \frac{\text{HH tuned to show}}{\text{Total U.S. HH}} = \frac{14{,}000{,}000}{110{,}200{,}000} = 12.7$$

A **ratings point** represents 1 percent of all the television households in a particular area tuned to a specific program. On a national level, 1 ratings point represents 1,102,000 households. Thus, if a top-rated program like *The Apprentice* averages a rating of 12, it would reach 13.3 million households each week (12 × 1,102,000).

The program rating is the key number to the stations, since the amount of money they can charge for commercial time is based on it. Ratings points are very important to the networks as well as to individual stations. A 1 percent change in a program's ratings over the course of a viewing season can gain or lose millions of dollars in advertising revenue. Advertisers also follow ratings closely, since they are the key measure for audience size and commercial rates.

Households Using Television The percentage of homes in a given area where TV is being watched during a specific time period is called **households using television (HUT).** This figure, sometimes referred to as *sets in use,* is always expressed as a percentage. For example, if 70 million of the U.S. TV households have their sets turned on at 9 P.M. on a Thursday night, the HUT figure is 63.5 percent (70 million out of 110.2 million). Television usage varies widely depending on the time of day and season of the year.

Share of Audience Another important audience measurement figure is the **share of audience,** which is the percentage of households using TV in a specified time period that are tuned to a specific program. This figure considers variations in the number of sets in use and the total size of the potential audience, since it is based only on those households that have their sets turned on. Audience share is calculated by dividing the number of households (HH) tuned to a show by the number of households using television (HUT). Thus, if 70 million U.S. households had their sets turned on during the 9 P.M. time slot when *The Apprentice* is shown, the share of audience would be 20, calculated as follows:

$$\text{Share} = \frac{\text{HH tuned to show}}{\text{U.S. households using TV}} = \frac{14{,}000{,}000}{70{,}000{,}000} = 20$$

Audience share is always higher than the program rating unless all the households have their sets turned on (in which case they would be equal). Share figures are important since they reveal how well a program does with the available viewing audience. For example, late at night the size of the viewing audience drops substantially, so the best way to assess the popularity of a late-night program is to examine the share of the available audience it attracts relative to competing programs.

Ratings services also provide an audience statistic known as **total audience,** the total number of homes viewing any five-minute part of a telecast. This number can be broken down to provide audience composition figures that are based on the distribution of the audience into demographic categories.

Network Audience Information

Nielsen Television Index The source of national and network TV audience information is also Nielsen Media Research, which provides daily and weekly estimates of TV viewing and national sponsored network and major cable program audiences. For more than 50 years, Nielsen provided this information using a two-pronged system consisting of a national sample of metered households along with a separate sample of diary households. In the metered households, an electronic measurement device known as the **audimeter** (audience meter) was hooked up to the TV set to continuously measure the channels to which the set was tuned. Network viewing for the country (the famous Nielsen ratings) was based on the results provided by audimeters placed in a national sample of homes carefully selected to represent the population of U.S. households. The metered households were supported by a separate panel of households that recorded viewing information in diaries. Since the audimeter could measure only the channel to which the set was tuned, the diary panel was used to gather demographic data on the viewing audience.

For many years, the television and advertising industries expressed concern over the audimeter/diary system. The information from diaries was not available to the network and advertising analysts for several weeks, and studies indicated the method was overstating the size of some key demographic audiences. Cooperation rates among diary keepers declined, and often the person who kept a household's diary did not note what other family members watched when he or she wasn't home. The complex new video environment and explosion in viewing options also made it difficult for diary keepers to maintain accurate viewing records.

As a result of these problems, and in response to competitive pressure from an audience measurement company from England, AGB, in 1987 Nielsen made the people meter the sole basis of its national rating system and eliminated the use of the diary panel.

The People Meter The **people meter** is an electronic measuring device that incorporates the technology of the old-style audimeter in a system that records not only what is being watched but also by whom in 10,000 households. The actual device is a small box with eight buttons—six for the family and two for visitors—that can be placed on the top of the TV set (Exhibit 11-10). A remote control unit permits electronic entries from anywhere in the room. Each member of the sample household is assigned a button that indicates his or her presence as a viewer. The device is also equipped with a sonar sensor to remind viewers entering or leaving the room to log in or out on the meter.

The viewership information the people meter collects from the household is stored in the home system until it is retrieved by Nielsen's computers. Data collected include when the set is turned on, which channel is viewed, when the channel is changed, and when the set is off, in addition to who is viewing. The demographic characteristics of the viewers are also in the system, and viewership can be matched to these traits. Nielsen's operation center processes all this information each week for release to the TV and advertising industries. Nielsen uses a sample of metered households in 55 markets across the country to provide overnight viewing results.

Exhibit 11-10 Nielsen uses the people meter to measure national TV audiences

Local Audience Information

Information on local audiences is important to both local advertisers and firms making national spot buys. Nielsen Media Research's local market measurement service is called Nielsen Station Index (NSI), which measures viewing audiences in 210 local markets known as **designated market areas (DMAs).** DMAs are nonoverlapping areas used for planning, buying, and evaluating TV audiences and are generally a group of counties in which stations located in a metropolitan or central area achieve the largest audience share. RSI reports information on viewing by time periods and programs and includes audience size and estimates of viewing over a range of demographic categories for each DMA.

Nielsen measures viewing audiences in every television market at least four times a year. The major markets are covered six times a year. The ratings periods when all 210 DMAs are surveyed are known as **sweeps.** The networks and local stations use numbers gathered during the sweeps rating periods in selling TV time. Exhibit 11-11 shows how KFMB, the CBS affiliate in San Diego, promotes its dominance of the sweeps ratings for local prime time.

However, as discussed in IMC Perspective 11-3, many advertising professionals believe the audience estimates gathered during the sweeps are overestimated because of special programming and promotions that occur during these periods.

Developments in Audience Measurement

For years the advertising industry has been calling for changes in the way TV viewing audiences are measured, at both the national and local levels. Many people believe people meters are only the first step in improving the way audiences are measured. While the people meter is seen as an improvement over the diary method, it still requires cooperation on an ongoing basis from people in the metered homes. Viewers in the Nielsen households, including young children, must punch a preassigned number on the remote control device each time they start or stop watching. Media researchers argue that kids forget and adults tire of the task over the two years they are in the Nielsen sample. Nielsen has been trying to develop passive measurement systems that require less involvement by people in metered homes and can produce more accurate measures of the viewing audience. However, such a system does not appear to be forthcoming in the near future.

In 56 of the largest markets in the United States, viewing information is gathered from 400 to 500 households using audimeters that only measure the channel to which the TV set is tuned. This information is augmented at least four times a year with demographic data that are collected from separate samples of households which maintain a viewing diary for

Exhibit 11-11 KFMB promotes its dominance of the sweeps rating period for local news

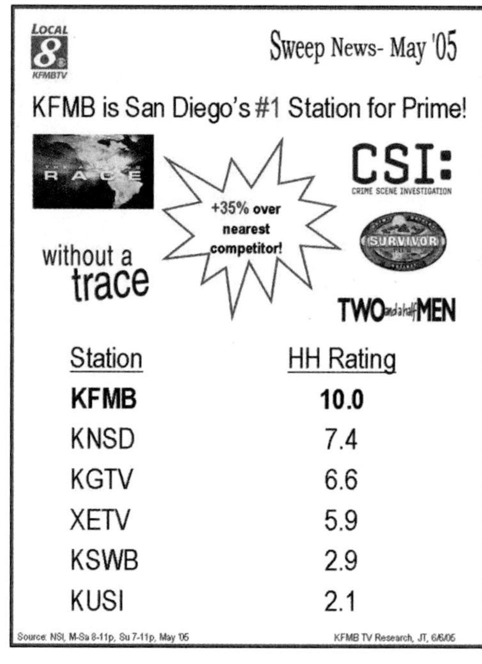

Station	HH Rating
KFMB	**10.0**
KNSD	7.4
KGTV	6.6
XETV	5.9
KSWB	2.9
KUSI	2.1

IMC PERSPECTIVE 11-3

Is It Time to Do Away with Sweeps Ratings?

The cornerstone of selling local television time is the sweeps ratings periods, which are held in February, May, November, and, to a lesser extent, August by Nielsen Media Research to determine what stations and shows are being watched in all 210 U.S. television markets. The term *sweeps* dates back to the 1950s, when Nielsen began mailing diaries to households and reporting the results, first with the East Coast markets before sweeping across the country. As TV networks gradually took control of programming, they needed better demographic numbers to calculate how much they could charge for commercials on specific shows. Local stations could not afford to measure TV viewing audiences year-round, as the networks do, so they settled on the four month-long sweeps ratings periods.

The numbers gathered during the sweeps periods are used as guideposts in the buying and selling of TV commercial time during the rest of the year and are extremely important to local stations. However, many people in the advertising industry are enraged over the tactics used by networks and their local affiliates to bolster their ratings during sweeps periods, such as special programming, contests, games, and other nontypical promotions. They argue that the extraordinary programming and promotion efforts inflate the ratings taken during these periods and that they are not indicative of audience sizes for the other 36 weeks of the year, when networks run their regular programming and promotions are not used to boost local viewing audiences. There is also concern over whether viewers fill out the diaries accurately. Nielsen Media Research maintains a toll-free helpline that people can call to ask questions about the diaries. One caller asked if she should log all the shows that were on one channel during the day, since that was the channel she left on for her pets. Another called to tell Nielsen she could not return the diary because her dog ate it (sound familiar?).

Advertisers and their agencies have become accustomed to the usual tactics used to beef up program schedules during the sweeps months, from blockbuster network programming to lurid sensationalism in local newscasts. Many local stations follow the accepted practice of producing and heavily promoting sex and scandal stories to lure viewers to their newscasts. For example, a Miami station ran an investigation into female college students who work as strippers to pay their tuition. Of much greater concern, however, is the blatant use of ratings grabbers such as big-prize sweepstakes, contests, and giveaways during sweeps periods. Nielsen Media Research has expressed concern over the number of unusual sweeps-period station promotions—most often giveaway contests on local newscasts. For example, a Houston station conducted a watch-and-win contest offering $2,000 each day to viewers of its 5 P.M., 6 P.M., and 10 P.M. newscasts. Nielsen's research has confirmed that giveaway promotions increase a station's audience share but that it generally drops back to precontest levels when the promotion ends.

Nielsen Media Research is working with the advertising industry to solve the sweeps problems. It provides red flags in its printed reports if stations use special promotions to bump up their ratings. However, the advertising industry argues that the only real solution to the problem is to increase the number of weeks Nielsen measures local audiences rather than relying on the artificially hyped numbers from sweeps periods. However, Nielsen argues that a continuous measurement system like that used for the network ratings would be very expensive and the TV and advertising industry would have to be willing to pay a higher price for local ratings information. Nielsen's director of communications notes, "In a perfect world, putting people meters in all the markets is what we'd want to do. But there's not enough advertising dollars in the smaller markets to make it worth their while."

Nielsen may also be getting some resistance from the local stations that have grown accustomed to getting higher ad rates year-round based on the inflated sweeps numbers. In the top 20 television markets, as much as half of a station's revenue comes from commercial time sold during the four or five hours of local newscasts aired each day, and a 30-second spot may sell for $2,500 to $3,000. Local stations are limited in the amount of airtime they can sell during network programs, so they concentrate on local newscasts to increase ad revenue. Ironically, however, some media researchers argue that sweeps don't always help boost a local station's ratings. They note that many viewers are loyal to local station news teams while others see through all of the sensational stories and promotional gimmicks.

Despite the many drawbacks of the system, many local stations continue to support sweeps for three main reasons: habit, fear, and money. However, nearly everyone in the advertising industry argues that some type of overhaul of the sweeps system is needed. The chair of the media research committee for the American Association of Advertising Agencies notes, "Sweeps are a travesty. Advertisers buy time on stations 365 days a year, yet we have no idea what ratings are for most of the year when there aren't those hyped, big-event programs." She speaks for many in the advertising industry when she concludes, "Sweeps should be done away with." It will be interesting to see if the television industry takes action to solve the sweeps problem or just continues to sweep it under the rug.

Sources: Michele Greppi, "Diary Helpline Staff Has Heard It All," *TelevisionWeek,* May 9, 2005, p. 6; Michael J. Weis, "Sweeps," *American Demographics,* May 2001, pp. 43–49; Allen Banks, "Close the Book on Sweeps," *Advertising Age,* March 15, 1999.

one week. Diary information is used to collect viewing information from sample homes in every one of the 210 local markets during the four sweeps periods.

Much of the concern over the Nielsen measurements involves the diary system used to measure viewing in local markets. This system requires that every 15 minutes viewers write down station call letters, channel numbers, programs, and who is watching. Many homes do not return completed diaries, and many of those that are returned are often not filled out correctly. Nielsen executives acknowledge the problems with its measurement system for local markets and is trying to correct them. The company is testing new diaries, sending out more of them, and working to improve the response rates.[32] Nielsen is also considering switching to a continuous measurement system for local markets rather than relying solely on the sweeps measurement system.[33] (See IMC Perspective 11-3.)

Recently a number of advertisers and ad agencies increased their criticism of Nielsen's local diary system, saying the handwritten method used to measure viewing audiences and gather demographic data in local audiences is antiquated. They argue that people meters are a far more accurate measurement system and should be used in local markets as well as on a national level. Nielsen has begun exploring the possibility of expanding the use of people meters to local markets. However, issues such as who will bear the cost of installing the people meters and how they would add to the cost of Nielsen's services are still major factors that have to be addressed. As of 2005 Nielsen was using local-people-meter (LPM) measurement in the six largest markets including New York, Chicago, Los Angeles, Philadelphia, Boston, and San Francisco.[34]

Nielsen has been battling with the networks, local TV stations, and ad agencies for years over the accuracy of its numbers. Many in the industry suspect that Nielsen is not moving fast enough to improve its audience measurement systems because it has a virtual monopoly in both the national and the local ratings business. They would like to see some competition.

The major networks, advertisers, and agencies have explored alternatives to Nielsen Media Research. One possible alternative to Nielsen is the *portable people meter (PPM)* system, which is being tested by Arbitron Inc.[35] The pager-size device detects an inaudible code embedded in the audio signal of a TV program, radio show, or Internet streaming audio. At the end of the day, users of the device drop it into a bay station, which then sends the ratings information to Arbitron's central database. Arbitron maintains that the PPM is superior to traditional set-top meters because it captures audience behavior year-round, it tracks media use outside the home, and it tracks all different types of media. The company began field tests of the system in Philadelphia in 2003 and began additional testing in Houston in 2005. Arbitron has skirted potential opposition to the system from Nielsen by giving its one-time rival the option to develop PPM technology if it goes into commercial production.

Many advertising professionals hope that a focus of new technology for measuring viewing audiences will be on developing rating systems for commercials, not just for programs. The Nielsen system measures the audiences for the programs surrounding the commercials rather than the commercials themselves. But with new technologies such as digital video recorders—as well as zipping, zapping, people leaving the room, and people being distracted from the TV during commercial breaks—there is a need to develop accurate ratings of more than just program audience viewing. Nielsen plans to make minute-by-minute audience data available for all national programming sources as of October 2006.[36] The service includes "flags" to indicate minutes of programming that contain commercials. However, critics have noted that minute-by-minute ratings are not the same as actual commercial ratings as many minutes in a show have a mix of programming and commercials, or commercials and promotions. Also, this data would not be able to account for viewers zapping between channels nor would it flag local commercials.[37]

Nielsen has announced that it can now monitor the digital video recorder behavior of all the U.S. TV households it monitors.[38] However, the impending arrival of convergence technology also means that people may soon routinely watch television shows on their computers, personal digital assistants, and other wireless devices such as cell phones, which will add to the problem of accurately measuring TV viewing.

For over 50 years consumers passively received TV programming and commercials. This is changing rapidly, however, as the major cable operators, telecommunications companies, and others bring various entertainment, information, and interactive services into homes via television. Researchers argue that the Nielsen system is being overwhelmed by the explosion in the number of TV sets, delivery systems, and program options available. These developments must be carefully monitored by advertisers and media planners as well as by people in the TV industry, as they can have a profound impact on audience size and composition and on the way advertisers use and pay for the use of TV as an advertising medium. Improvements in measurement technology are needed to accommodate these developments.

Media experts also argue that consideration must be given to measuring media involvement and determining when consumers are most tuned into television programs and open to receiving advertisements and other types of marketing messages.[39] Current audience measurement methods are often criticized for only reporting the sizes of viewing audiences and not distinguishing among them in terms of the intensity of their relationships with television programs. These limitations have prompted researchers to investigate the qualitative distinctions among viewers who may all be counted as "watching" a TV program but have very different levels of attention, attitudes, and even behaviors related to the show. Researchers Cristel Russell, Andrew Norman, and Susan Heckler have introduced the concept of audience *connectedness* to capture the fact that some television viewers build relationships, loyalty, and connections with certain TV shows, with the characters portrayed in these programs, and with fellow audience members.[40] These connected viewers are very different from viewers who are less involved with a program. They may be more attentive to advertising and product placements and more likely to engage in behaviors such as visiting a program's website or purchasing brands that are associated with the show.

Radio

Television has often been referred to as the ideal advertising medium, and to many people it personifies the glamour and excitement of the industry. Radio, on the other hand, has been called the Rodney Dangerfield of media because it gets no respect from many advertisers. Dominated by network programming and national advertisers before the growth of TV, radio has evolved into a primarily local advertising medium. Network advertising generally accounts for less than 5 percent of radio's revenue. Radio has also become a medium characterized by highly specialized programming appealing to very narrow segments of the population.

Exhibit 11-12 The Radio Advertising Bureau promotes the value of radio to advertisers

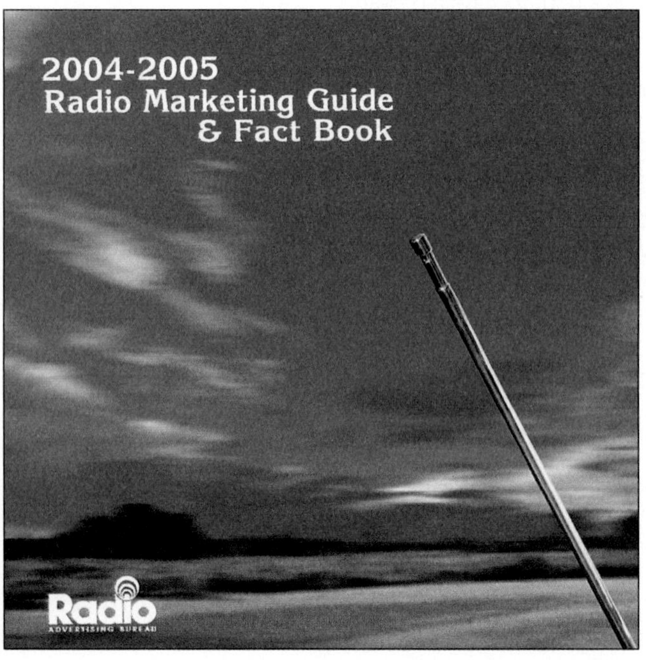

The importance of radio is best demonstrated by the numbers. There are more than 13,000 radio stations in this country, including 4,761 commercial AM stations and 6,213 commercial FM stations. There are over 576 million radios in use in the United States, an average of 5.6 per household. Radio reaches 74 percent of all Americans over the age of 12 each day and has grown into a ubiquitous background to many activities, among them reading, driving, running, working, and socializing. The average American listens to radio nearly 3 hours every weekday and 5 hours every weekend.[41] The pervasiveness of this medium has not gone unnoticed by advertisers; radio advertising revenue grew from $8.8 billion in 1990 to over $19 billion in 2005.

Radio plays an integral role in the lifestyle of consumers and has the power to reach and influence their purchase behavior. It has survived and flourished as an advertising medium because it has a number of advantages that make it an effective way for marketers to communicate with consumers. The radio industry promotes these advantages to advertisers to encourage use of the medium (Exhibit 11-12).

Advantages of Radio

Radio has many advantages over other media, including cost and efficiency, selectivity, flexibility, mental imagery, and integrated marketing opportunities.

Cost and Efficiency

One of the main strengths of radio as an advertising medium is its low cost. Radio commercials are very inexpensive to produce. They require only a script of the commercial to be read by the radio announcer or a copy of a prerecorded message that can be broadcast by the station. The cost for radio time is also low. A minute on network radio may cost only $5,000, which translates into a cost per thousand of only $3 to $4. Local advertising on radio stations costs about $6 per thousand households, compared to more than $20 for local TV advertising. The low relative costs of radio make it one of the most efficient of all advertising media, and the low absolute cost means the budget needed for an effective radio campaign is often lower than that for other media.

The low cost of radio means advertisers can build more reach and frequency into their media schedule within a certain budget. They can use different stations to broaden the reach of their messages and multiple spots to ensure adequate frequency. For example, a number of Internet start-ups have been heavy users of radio in their efforts to build brand awareness. Companies such as More.com, which sells drugstore items on the Internet, see radio as a fast and relatively inexpensive way to get their names known. Radio commercials can be produced more quickly than TV spots, and the companies can run them more often.[42] Many national advertisers also recognize the cost efficiency of radio and use it as part of their media strategy.

Selectivity

Another major advantage of radio is the high degree of audience selectivity available through the various program formats and geographic coverage of the numerous stations. Radio lets companies focus their advertising on specialized audiences such as certain demographic and lifestyle groups. Most areas have radio stations with formats such as adult contemporary, easy listening, classical music, country, news/talk shows, jazz, and all news, to name a few. Figure 11-6 shows the percentage of the radio listening audience captured by various radio formats for different age groups. For example, among 12- to 17-year-olds and 18- to 24-year olds, the most popular radio format is contemporary hits, while those between the ages of 45 and 64 prefer news/talk. Elusive consumers like teenagers, college students, and working adults can be reached more easily through radio than most other media.

Radio can reach consumers other media can't. Light television viewers spend considerably more time with radio than with TV and are generally an upscale market in terms of income and education level. Light readers of magazines and newspapers also spend more time listening to radio. Radio has become a popular way to reach specific non-English-speaking ethnic markets. Los Angeles, New York City, Dallas, and Miami have several radio stations that broadcast in Spanish and reach these areas' large Hispanic markets. As mass marketing gives way to market segmentation and regional marketing, radio will continue to grow in importance.

Flexibility

Radio is probably the most flexible of all the advertising media because it has a very short closing period, which means advertisers can change their message almost up to the time it goes on the air. Radio commercials can usually be produced and scheduled on very short notice. Radio advertisers can easily adjust their messages to local market conditions and marketing situations.

Mental Imagery

A potential advantage of radio that is often overlooked is that it encourages listeners to use their imagination when processing a commercial message. While the creative options of radio are limited, many advertisers take advantage of the absence of a visual element to let consumers create their own picture of what is happening in a radio message.

Radio may also reinforce television messages through a technique called **image transfer,** where the images of a TV commercial are implanted into a radio spot.[43] First the marketer establishes the video image of a TV commercial. Then it uses a similar,

Figure 11-6 Radio Format Audience Shares by Age Group

Format	12–17 Share (%)	Format	18–24 Share (%)
Contemporary hit radio (CHR, pop CHR, rhythmic CHR)	39.7	Contemporary hits radio (CHR, pop CHR, rhythmic CHR)	26.2
Urban (urban A/C, urban oldies, urban)	18.3	Urban (urban A/C, urban oldies, urban)	14.6
Alternative (AAA, alternative, new rock)	8.2	Adult contemporary (AC, hot A/C, modern A/C, soft A/C)	11.0
Adult contemporary (AC, hot A/C, modern A/C, soft A/C)	7.0	Rock ('70s, active rock, AOR, classic rock)	10.7
Hispanic (all varieties)	6.7	Hispanic (all varieties)	10.6
Rock ('70s, active rock, AOR, classic rock)	6.4	Alternative (AAA, alternative, new rock)	9.2
Country (classic country, country, new country)	6.0	Country (classic country, country, new country)	7.9
Oldies ('70s hits, '80s hits, classic hits, oldies, rhythmic oldies)	2.7	News/talk/information (all news, all sports, news/talk, all talk)	3.8
News/talk/information (all news, all sports, news/talk, all talk)	2.2	Oldies ('70s hits, '80s hits, classic hits, oldies, rhythmic oldies)	3.6
Religion (all varieties)	1.7	Religion (all varieties)	1.3
New AC/smooth jazz (jazz, NAC)	0.5	New AC/smooth jazz (jazz, NAC)	0.7
Classical	0.2	Classical	0.2
Adult standards (EZ listening, MOR, nostalgia, variety)	0.1	Adult standards (EZ listening, MOR, nostalgia, variety)	0.2
Remaining formats	0.1	Remaining formats	0.0

Format	25–34 Share (%)	Format	35–44 Share (%)
Contemporary hit radio (CHR, pop CHR, rhythmic CHR)	15.1	Adult contemporary (AC, hot A/C, modern A/C, soft A/C)	16.7
Adult contemporary (AC, hot A/C, modern A/C, soft A/C)	14.6	News/talk/information (all news, all sports, news/talk, all talk)	14.7
Hispanic (all varieties)	14.3	Rock ('70s, active rock, AOR, classic rock)	12.6
Urban (urban A/C, urban oldies, urban)	12.1	Urban (urban A/C, urban oldies, urban)	10.3
News/talk/information (all news, all sports, news/talk, all talk)	10.3	Hispanic (all varieties)	9.7
Rock ('70s, active rock, AOR, classic rock)	9.9	Country (classic country, country, new country)	8.9
Alternative (AAA, alternative, new rock)	8.0	Contemporary hit radio (CHR, pop CHR, rhythmic CHR)	8.5
Country (classic country, country, new country)	7.6	Oldies ('70s hits, '80s hits, classic hits, oldies, rhythmic oldies)	6.6
Oldies ('70s hits, '80s hits, classic hits, oldies, rhythmic oldies)	4.1	Alternative (AAA, alternative, new rock)	5.1
Religion (all varieties)	2.1	Religion (all varieties)	3.2
New AC/smooth jazz (jazz, NAC)	1.5	New AC/smooth jazz (jazz, NAC)	2.8
Classical	0.3	Classical	0.6
Adult standards (EZ listening, MOR, nostalgia, variety)	0.2	Adult standards (EZ listening, MOR, nostalgia, variety)	0.4
Remaining formats	0.0	Remaining formats	0.1

Figure 11-6 Continued

Format	45–54 Share (%)	Format	55–64 Share (%)
News/talk/information (all news, all sports, news/talk, all talk)	19.0	News/talk/information (all news, all sports, news/talk, all talk)	27.3
Adult contemporary (AC, hot A/C, modern A/C, soft A/C)	15.9	Adult contemporary (AC, hot A/C, modern A/C, soft A/C)	14.5
Oldies ('70s hits, '80s hits, classic hits, oldies, rhythmic oldies)	12.9	Oldies ('70s hits, '80s hits, classic hits, oldies, rhythmic oldies)	13.4
Country (classic country, country, new country)	9.7	Country (classic country, country, new country)	11.7
Rock ('70s, active rock, AOR, classic rock)	9.6	Hispanic (all varieties)	6.7
Urban (urban A/C, urban oldies, urban)	8.9	Urban (urban A/C, urban oldies, urban)	5.8
Hispanic (all varieties)	6.2	New AC/smooth jazz (jazz, NAC)	5.1
New AC/smooth jazz (jazz, NAC)	4.8	Religion (all varieties)	3.4
Contemporary hit radio (CHR, pop CHR, rhythmic CHR)	4.2	Rock ('70s, active rock, AOR, classic rock)	3.3
Religion (all varieties)	3.6	Classical	3.0
Alternative (AAA, alternative, new rock)	2.9	Adult standards (EZ listening, MOR, nostalgia, variety)	2.8
Classical	1.3	Contemporary hit radio (CHR, pop CHR, rhythmic CHR)	2.0
Adult standards (EZ listening, MOR, nostalgia, variety)	0.9	Alternative (AAA, alternative, new rock)	0.9
Remaining formats	0.3	Remaining formats	0.0

Source: Arbitron Format Trends Report, Spring 2004; 94 Continuous Measurement Markets; Monday–Sunday 6 A.M.–Midnight, Average Quarter Share for Demographic.

or even the same, audio portion (spoken words and/or jingle) as the basis for the radio counterpart. The idea is that when consumers hear the radio message, they will make the connection to the TV commercial, reinforcing its video images. Image transfer offers advertisers a way to make radio and TV ads work together synergistically. This promotional piece put out by the Radio Advertising Bureau shows how the image transfer process works (Exhibit 11-13).

Exhibit 11-13 The Radio Advertising Bureau promotes the concept of imagery transfer

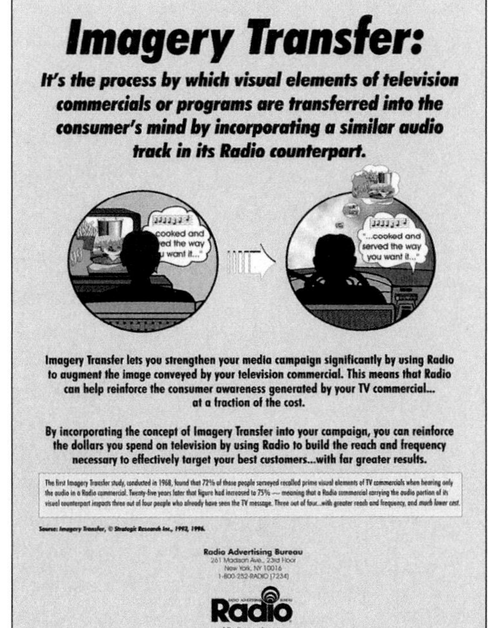

Integrated Marketing Opportunities Radio provides marketers with a variety of integrated marketing opportunities. It can be used in combination with other media including television, magazines, and newspapers to provide advertisers with synergistic effects in generating awareness and communicating their message. The radio industry recently sponsored a major research study to determine how radio works in combination with other media. The study found that the synergistic use of radio with television and newspapers had a positive impact on brand awareness and brand selection.[44] Exhibit 11-14 shows an ad run by the Radio Advertising Bureau promoting the synergy between radio and newspaper advertising.

Radio can also be used in conjunction with a variety of other IMC tools such as sales promotion, event marketing, and cause-related marketing. Radio stations are an integral part of many communities and the deejays and program hosts are often popular and influential figures. Advertisers often use radio stations and personalities to enhance their involvement with a local market and to gain influence with local retailers. Radio also works very effectively in conjunction with place-based/point-of-purchase promotions. Retailers often use on-site radio

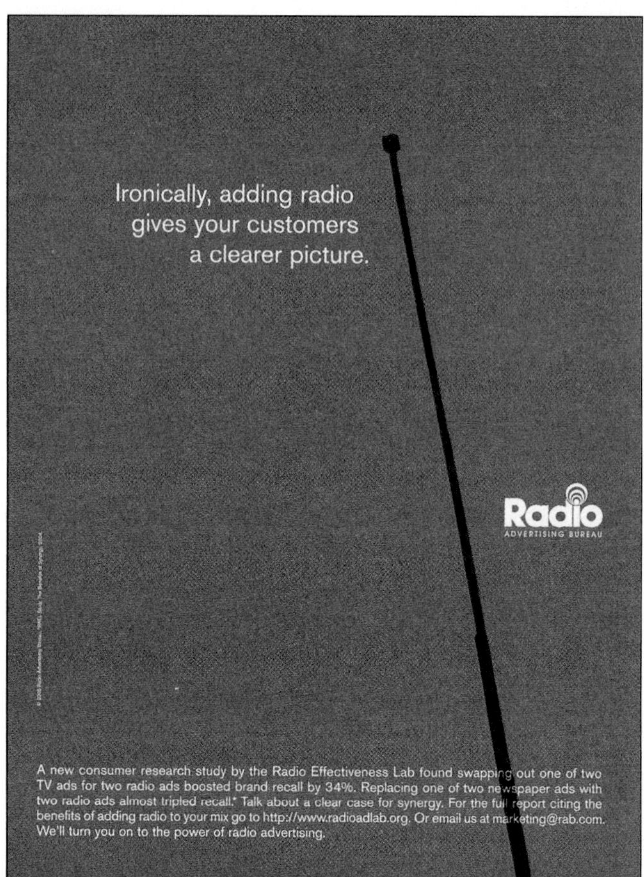

Ironically, adding radio gives your customers a clearer picture.
Radio
ADVERTISING BUREAU
A new consumer research study by the Radio Effectiveness Lab found swapping out one of two TV ads for two radio ads boosted brand recall by 34%. Replacing one of two newspaper ads with two radio ads almost tripled recall.* Talk about a clear case for synergy. For the full report citing the benefits of adding radio to your mix go to http://www.radioadlab.org. Or email us at marketing@rab.com. We'll turn you on to the power of radio advertising.

Exhibit 11-14 The radio industry promotes findings from a study showing the synergistic effects of radio

broadcasts combined with special sales or promotions to attract consumers to their stores and get them to make a purchase. Live radio broadcasts are also used in conjunction with event marketing. Marketers often sponsor live broadcast promotions at beaches, sporting events, and festivals, setting up product booths for sampling and giveaways.

Limitations of Radio

Several factors limit the effectiveness of radio as an advertising medium, among them creative limitations, fragmentation, chaotic buying procedures, limited research data, limited listener attention, and clutter. The media planner must consider them in determining the role the medium will play in the advertising program.

Creative Limitations A major drawback of radio as an advertising medium is the absence of a visual image. The radio advertiser cannot show the product, demonstrate it, or use any type of visual appeal or information. A radio commercial is, like a TV ad, a short-lived and fleeting message that is externally paced and does not allow the receiver to control the rate at which it is processed. Because of these creative limitations many companies tend to ignore radio, and agencies often assign junior people to the development of radio commercials.

Fragmentation Another problem with radio is the high level of audience fragmentation due to the large number of stations. The percentage of the market tuned to any particular station is usually very small. The top-rated radio station in many major metropolitan areas with a number of AM and FM stations may attract less than 10 percent of the total listening audience. Advertisers that want a broad reach in their radio advertising media schedule have to buy time on a number of stations to cover even a local market.

Chaotic Buying Procedures It should be readily apparent how chaotic the media planning and purchasing process can become for the advertiser that wants to use radio on a nationwide spot basis. Acquiring information and evaluating and contracting for time with even a fraction of the 10,500 commercial stations that operate across the country can be very difficult and time-consuming. This problem has diminished somewhat in recent years as the number of radio networks and of syndicated programs offering a package of several hundred stations increases.

Limited Research Data Audience research data on radio are often limited, particularly compared with TV, magazines, or newspapers. Most radio stations are small operations and lack the revenue to support detailed studies of their audiences. And most users of radio are local companies that cannot support research on radio listenership in their markets. Thus, media planners do not have as much audience information available to guide them in their purchase of radio time as they do with other media.

Limited Listener Attention Another problem that plagues radio is that it is difficult to retain listener attention to commercials. Radio programming, particularly music, is often the background to some other activity and may not receive the listeners' full attention. Thus they may miss all or some of the commercials. One environment where radio has a more captive audience is in cars. But getting listeners to pay attention to commercials can still be difficult. Most people preprogram their car radio and change stations during commercial breaks. A study by Avery Abernethy found large differences between exposure to radio programs versus advertising for listeners in cars. They were exposed to only half of the advertising broadcast and changed stations frequently to avoid commercials.[45] Another factor that is detracting from radio listening in motor vehicles is the rapid growth of cellular phones. A recent study found that half of commuters surveyed who own a cell phone reported listening to less radio than they did a year earlier.[46] Radio listening is also being impacted by the emergence of several digital-based technologies including satellite radio and MP3 players such as the tremendously popular iPod. IMC Perspective 11-4 discusses how these new technologies are affecting radio and how the industry is responding.

Clutter

Clutter is just as much a problem with radio as with other advertising media. Most radio stations carry an average of nearly 10 minutes of commercials every hour. During the popular morning and evening rush hours, the amount of commercial time may exceed 12 minutes. Also contributing to the clutter problem is the practice of some stations to offer "commercial-free" blocks of music to attract listeners. This practice results in more commercials being aired in a short time period and may also result in listeners switching to another station rather than listening through a long block of ads. Advertisers must create commercials that break through the clutter or use heavy repetition to make sure their messages reach consumers. In a study of radio listeners conducted by Edison Research, perceptions of increased ad clutter were cited by participants as a reason for spending less time listening to radio.[47]

A number of radio stations have begun to address the clutter problem by reducing the number of commercials. In 2005, Clear Channel Communications, which owns more than 1,200 radio stations across 300 markets in the United States, cut back on the number of minutes of commercials its stations run per hour to entice both listeners and advertisers. Other large companies that own radio stations including Viacom and Entercom Communications have also reduced the frequency of commercials as have some individual stations in many markets.[48]

Buying Radio Time

The purchase of radio time is similar to that of television, as advertisers can make either network, spot, or local buys. Since these options were reviewed in the section on buying TV time, they are discussed here only briefly.

Network Radio

Advertising time on radio can be purchased on a network basis using one of the national networks. There are currently three major national radio networks: Westwood One, ABC, and Premiere. There are also more than 100 regional radio networks across the country. Using networks minimizes the amount of negotiation and administrative work needed to get national or regional coverage, and the costs are lower than those for individual stations. However, the number of affiliated stations on the network roster and the types of audiences they reach can vary considerably, so the use of network radio reduces advertisers' flexibility in selecting stations.

An important trend in radio is the increasing number of radio networks and syndicated programs that offer advertisers a package of several hundred stations. For example, conservative Rush Limbaugh's radio show is syndicated nationally and is carried by more than 500 stations, reaching more than 11 million people weekly (Exhibit 11-15). Syndication reduces audience fragmentation and purchasing problems and increases radio's appeal to national advertisers.

Exhibit 11-15 Rush Limbaugh's talk radio show is syndicated nationally

Spot Radio

National advertisers can also use spot radio to purchase airtime on individual stations in various markets. The purchase of spot radio provides greater flexibility in selecting markets, individual stations, and airtime and adjusting the message for local market conditions. Spot radio accounts for about 20 percent of radio time sold.

Local Radio

By far the heaviest users of radio are local advertisers; nearly 79 percent of radio advertising time is purchased from individual stations by local companies. Auto dealers, retailers, restaurants, and financial institutions are

IMC PERSPECTIVE 11-4

Radio Faces a Digital Revolution

Commercial radio's obituary has been written many times over the past half century. The first time was in the 1950s when television became popular and became the primary form of entertainment in most households. The next threat came in the 1960s and '70s when eight-track tape and cassette players arrived on the scene, and then again in the late '80s and 1990s when music became available on compact discs. Over the past decade, radio has been threatened by the growing popularity of the Internet as many music fans now go online to listen to and download music. Despite all that has been done to make it obsolete, the radio industry still has not only survived these threats but actually grown as advertising revenues exceeded $20 billion for the first time in 2004. However, traditional radio is now facing several new digital-based technologies whose growing popularity makes them formidable competitors for consumers' time and ever-shrinking attention span.

The first major threat is satellite radio, which bounces signals off satellites stationed over the East and West Coasts and back down to receivers, which encode the signals digitally. The primary target for satellite radio is currently vehicle owners who purchase a receiver for about $100 and pay a monthly subscription fee of around $13 for virtually commercial-free digital radio that includes more than 100 channels of music, news, talk, sports, and children's programming. The leading satellite radio companies are industry leader XM Satellite Radio, which was launched in September 2001, and Sirius, which debuted 10 months later. The two satellite services now have more than 5 million monthly subscribers between them and are among the fastest growing technologies ever, having reached the same market penetration in four years that took cable television 13 years to achieve.

Some analysts predict that satellite radio could attract as many as 35 million subscribers by 2010 as both XM and Sirius are spending heavily to build their programming and to attract subscribers. Sirius paid $500 million to lure shock jock Howard Stern away from terrestrial radio by signing him to a five-year deal that began in 2006 while XM spent $650 million for an 11-year deal with Major League Baseball that allows the service to offer every locally broadcast game. Sirius already had signed deals for professional hockey, basketball, and football games while XM also carries various college sports and NASCAR. XM and Sirius have also been adding more locally tailored programming such as traffic and weather reports, which makes them more competitive against terrestrial stations in local markets.

In addition to satellite, terrestrial radio is also being significantly impacted by the growing popularity of MP3 players such as Apple's iPod. Apple Computer had sold more than 10 million iPods by 2005 with 4.6 million units being sold in the last quarter of 2004 alone. iPods and other digital music players let listeners carry thousands of songs with them in a device the size of a pack of cigarettes. Another technology that threatens radio is the growth of podcasting, which is a method of distributing audio content via the Internet. Podcasting enables independent producers to create their own radio shows and bypass the traditional entry barriers such as licenses, airwave frequencies, and transmission towers.

Radio listeners are tired of commercials, predictable playlists that are based on focus group research, government regulators, and fading signals. The growing popularity of satellite radio, iPods, and podcasting correlates with a decline in broadcast radio average quarter-hour (AQH) ratings, which measure the number of people tuned in during an average quarter-hour as a percentage of the population. Overall AQH ratings dropped 5.9 percent between 2000 and 2004 while declines among younger listeners were even more severe. Ratings among 12- to 17-year-olds decreased 8.5 percent, the decline among the 18- to 24-year-old group was 11 percent, and 25- to 34-year-olds dropped 8.2 percent.

The radio industry recognizes that it has to find a way to respond to the digital revolution that is impacting the industry. Media giant Clear Channel Communications, which owns more than a thousand stations, recently announced that it was reducing the number of commercials its stations would play and steering advertisers toward using 30-second rather than 60-second spots so listeners won't become bored. A number of stations are changing to the "Jack" format inspired by the iPod's shuffle option, which plays songs in the owner's library in random order. The format, which started in Canada and is spreading across the United States, involves expanding the playlist to more than 1,200 songs versus the traditional 300 to 400 titles and tripling the number of songs played on any given day. Station programmers also play two unlikely songs back-to-back to create jarring transitions known as "train wrecks." Major radio companies including Clear Channel, Viacom's Infinity Broadcasting, and Entercom Communications have also banded together to create an advertising campaign using the tagline "Radio—you hear it here first." The 30-second spots feature artists such as Ludacris, Avril Lavigne, and Ashanti talking up local radio and reminding listeners that they are exposed to breaking artists and emerging music formats via radio.

While radio is facing challenges from the digital revolution, the industry notes that terrestrial radio still reaches more than 94 percent of listeners 12 and older every week and is still a place where people go to hear new music and to learn about contests and promotions. As marketers continue to shift toward a more integrated approach, radio will continue to play an important role in their promotional programs. Many radio stations are responding to the challenges of new technologies and better serving the needs of local audiences. And unlike many of the new technologies, commercial radio has one big advantage—it is still free.

Sources: Sarah McBride, "Satellite Radio's New Local Content Riles Broadcasters," *The Wall Street Journal,* July 25, 2005, pp. B1, 2; Karia Peterson and Mark Saurer, "Radio Singing a New Tune," *San Diego Union Tribune,* April 13, 2005, pp. A1, 10; Heather Green, Tom Lowry, and Catherine Yang, "The New Radio Revolution," *BusinessWeek,* March 14, 2005, pp. 32–35; Sarah McBride, "Terrestrial-Radio Firms Get Serious," *The Wall Street Journal,* January 11, 2005, p. B4.

Figure 11-7 Dayparts for Radio

Morning drive time	6:00–10:00 A.M.
Daytime	10:00 A.M.–3:00 P.M.
Afternoon/evening drive time	3:00–7:00 P.M.
Nighttime	7:00 P.M.–12:00 A.M.
All night	12:00–6:00 A.M.

among the heaviest users of local radio advertising. But a number of radio advertisers are switching to local cable TV because the rates are comparable and there is the added advantage of TV's visual impact.

Time Classifications

As with television, the broadcast day for radio is divided into various time periods or dayparts, as shown in Figure 11-7. The size of the radio listening audience varies widely across the dayparts, and advertising rates follow accordingly. The largest radio audiences (and thus the highest rates) occur during the early morning and late afternoon drive times. Radio rates also vary according to the number of spots or type of audience plan purchased, the supply and demand of time available in the local market, and the ratings of the individual station. Rate information is available directly from the stations and is summarized in Standard Rate and Data Service's (SRDS's) Radio Advertising Source, which provides spot radio rates and data for both local stations and radio networks. Some stations issue rate cards like the one shown in Figure 11-8. But many stations do not adhere strictly to rate cards and the rates published in SRDS. Their rates are negotiable and depend on factors such as availability, time period, and number of spots purchased.

Figure 11-8 Sample Radio Rate Card

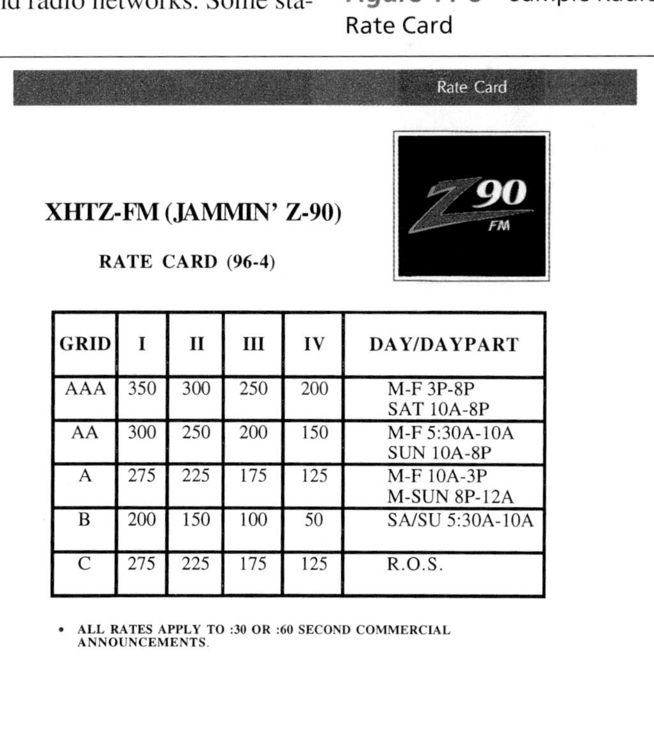

Rate Card

XHTZ-FM (JAMMIN' Z-90)

RATE CARD (96-4)

GRID	I	II	III	IV	DAY/DAYPART
AAA	350	300	250	200	M-F 3P-8P SAT 10A-8P
AA	300	250	200	150	M-F 5:30A-10A SUN 10A-8P
A	275	225	175	125	M-F 10A-3P M-SUN 8P-12A
B	200	150	100	50	SA/SU 5:30A-10A
C	275	225	175	125	R.O.S.

• ALL RATES APPLY TO :30 OR :60 SECOND COMMERCIAL ANNOUNCEMENTS.

XHTZ 90.3 FM • 1229 Third Avenue • Chula Vista, California 91911 • FAX (619) 426-3690 • (619) 585-9090

Audience Information

One problem with radio is the lack of audience information. Because there are so many radio stations and thus many small, fragmented audiences, the stations cannot support the expense of detailed audience measurement. Also, owing to the nature of radio as incidental or background entertainment, it is difficult to develop precise measures of who listens at various time periods and for how long. The major radio ratings services are owned by Arbitron, which provides audience information for local stations and network audiences.

Arbitron Arbitron covers 286 local radio markets with one to four ratings reports per year. Arbitron has a sample of representative listeners in each market maintain a diary of their radio listening for seven days. Audience estimates for the market are based on these diary records and reported by time period and selected

Figure 11-9 Partial Sample Page from Arbitron Radio Ratings Report

Target Audience, Persons 18–49								
	Monday–Friday 6–10 A.M.				Monday–Friday 10 A.M.–3 P.M.			
	AQH (00)	CUME (00)	AQH RTG	AQH SHR	AQH (00)	CUME (00)	AQH RTG	AQH SHR
KCBQ								
METRO	25	263	.2	.8	40	365	.3	1.3
TSA	25	263			40	365		
KCBQ-FM								
METRO	101	684	.7	3.1	117	768	.9	3.7
TSA	101	684			117	768		
KCEO								
METRO	11	110	.1	.3	8	81	.1	.3
TSA	11	110			8	81		
KFMB								
METRO	171	790	1.3	5.3	106	678	.8	3.3
TSA	171	790			106	678		

demographics in the Arbitron Radio Market Report, to which clients subscribe. Figure 11-9 provides a sample page from the Arbitron ratings report for people in the 18-to-49 age target audience across the various dayparts. The three basic estimates in the Arbitron report are

- Person estimates—the estimated number of people listening.
- Rating—the percentage of listeners in the survey area population.
- Share—the percentage of the total estimated listening audience.

These three estimates are further defined by using quarter-hour and cume figures. The **average quarter-hour (AQH) figure** expresses the average number of people estimated to have listened to a station for a minimum of five minutes during any quarter-hour in a time period. For example, station KCBQ has an average quarter-hour listenership of 2,500 during the weekday 6 to 10 A.M. daypart. This means that any weekday, for any 15-minute period during this time period, an average of 2,500 people between the ages of 18 and 49 are tuned to this station. This figure helps to determine the audience and cost of a spot schedule within a particular time period.

Cume stands for "cumulative audience," the estimated total number of different people who listened to a station for at least five minutes in a quarter-hour period within a reported daypart. In Figure 11-9, the cumulative audience of people 18 to 49 for station KCBQ during the weekday morning daypart is 26,300. Cume estimates the reach potential of a radio station.

The **average quarter-hour rating (AQH RTG)** expresses the estimated number of listeners as a percentage of the survey area population. The **average quarter-hour share (AQH SHR)** is the percentage of the total listening audience tuned to each station. It shows the share of listeners each station captures out of the total listening audience in the survey area. The average quarter-hour rating of station KCBQ during the weekday 6 to 10 A.M. daypart is 0.2, while the average quarter-hour share is 0.8.

Arbitron is conducting market trials of its portable people meter (PPM) device, which was discussed previously in the chapter, for use in measuring radio audiences. The radio industry and advertisers have always had concerns over the use of Arbitron's

Target Audience, Persons 18–49												
	Monday–Friday 3–7 P.M.				Monday–Friday 7 P.M.–Mid.				Weekend 10 A.M.–7 P.M.			
	AQH (00)	CUME (00)	AQH RTG	AQH SHR	AQH (00)	CUME (00)	AQH RTG	AQH SHR	AQH (00)	CUME (00)	AQH RTG	AQH SHR
KCBQ												
METRO	36	340	.3	1.4	6	138		.5	51	356	.4	2.4
TSA	36	340			6	138			51	356		
KCBQ-FM												
METRO	83	736	.6	3.2	23	354	.2	2.1	67	616	.5	3.2
TSA	83	736			23	354			67	616		
KCEO												
METRO	10	95	.1	.4		8			1	8		
TSA	10	95				8			1	8		
KFMB												
METRO	141	1092	1.0	5.4	87	827	.6	7.9	92	567	.7	4.4
TSA	141	1092			87	827			92	567		

diary method. Many view the new PPM technology as a more valid audience measurement system.[49] Arbitron continues to test the PPM and hopes to launch the system on a market-by-market basis beginning in 2006. A number of major radio companies are pressuring the company to implement the PPM system because they believe that better measurements will demonstrate that more people listen to radio, and this will, in turn, encourage advertisers to buy more commercial time.[50]

Arbitron also recently began measuring listenership to webcasts. Arbitron Webcast Ratings is an audience measurement service that measures Internet audio and video tuning across all webcasting sources. However, this service is still in a pilot testing phase.[51] Arbitron's research has found that 30 percent of online users have listened to Internet radio stations and the number continues to grow. This will make the measurement of radio listening over the Internet a very important area in the future.

RADAR Another rating service that is now owned by Arbitron is RADAR (National Radio Network Ratings), which is supported by radio networks, media services companies, and advertisers. RADAR measurements are based on information collected throughout the year by means of diary interviews from a probability sample of 85,000 respondents age 12 and older who live in telephone households. Respondents are instructed to record all radio listening as well as the day of the week, time of day, and location for a one-week period. Demographic information is also collected in the diaries.

RADAR reports are issued four times a year and provide network audience measures, along with estimates of audience and various segments. The audience estimates are time-period measurements for the various dayparts. RADAR also provides estimates of network audiences for all commercials and commercials within various programs.

As with TV, media planners must use the audience measurement information to evaluate the value of various radio stations in reaching the advertiser's target audience and their relative cost. The media buyer responsible for the purchase of radio time works with information on target audience coverage, rates, time schedules, and availability to optimize the advertiser's radio media budget.

Summary

Television and radio, or the broadcast media, are the most pervasive media in most consumers' daily lives and offer advertisers the opportunity to reach vast audiences. Both broadcast media are time- rather than space-oriented and organized similarly in that they use a system of affiliated stations belonging to a network, as well as individual stations, to broadcast their programs and commercial messages. Advertising on radio or TV can be done on national or regional network programs or purchased in spots from local stations.

TV has grown faster than any other advertising medium in history and has become the leading medium for national advertisers. No other medium offers its creative capabilities; the combination of sight, sound, and movement gives the advertiser a vast number of options for presenting a commercial message with high impact. Television also offers advertisers mass coverage at a low relative cost. Variations in programming and audience composition, along with the growth of cable, are helping TV offer more audience selectivity to advertisers. While television is often viewed as the ultimate advertising medium, it has several limitations, including the high cost of producing and airing commercials, a lack of selectivity relative to other media, the fleeting nature of the message, and the problem of commercial clutter. The latter two problems have been compounded in recent years by the trend toward shorter commercials.

Information regarding the size and composition of national and local TV audiences is provided by Nielsen Media Research. The amount of money networks or stations can charge for commercial time on their programs is based on its audience measurement figures. This information is also important to media planners, as it is used to determine the combination of shows needed to attain specific levels of reach and frequency with the advertiser's target market.

Future trends in television include the continued growth of cable, competition to local cable operators from direct broadcast satellite systems, and a resulting increase in channels available to television households. Changes are also likely to occur in the measurement of viewing audiences—for example, continuous measurement of audiences.

The role of radio as an entertainment and advertising medium has changed with the rapid growth of television. Radio has evolved into a primarily local advertising medium that offers highly specialized programming appealing to narrow segments of the market. Radio offers advertisers the opportunity to build high reach and frequency into their media schedules and to reach selective audiences at a very efficient cost. It also offers opportunities for integrated marketing programs such as place-based promotions and event sponsorships.

The major drawback of radio is its creative limitations owing to the absence of a visual image. The short and fleeting nature of the radio commercial, the highly fragmented nature of the radio audience, and clutter are also problems.

As with TV, the rate structure for radio advertising time varies with the size of the audience delivered. The primary sources of audience information are Arbitron for local radio and its RADAR studies for network audiences.

Key Terms

zipping, 341
zapping, 341
television network, 344
affiliates, 344
up-front market, 347
scatter market, 347
spot advertising, 347
national spot advertising, 347
local advertising, 347
station reps, 347
syndicated programs, 348
sponsorship, 349
participations, 350
adjacencies, 350
dayparts, 350
cable television, 351
superstations, 351
interconnects, 353
narrowcasting, 354
multiplexing, 356
direct broadcast satellite (DBS) services, 356
television households, 357
program rating, 357
ratings point, 357
households using television (HUT), 358
share of audience, 358
total audience, 358
audimeter, 358
people meter, 359
designated market areas (DMAs), 359
sweeps, 359
image transfer, 363
average quarter-hour (AQH) figure, 370
cume, 370
average quarter-hour rating (AQH RTG), 370
average quarter-hour share (AQH SHR), 370

Discussion Questions

1. Discuss the significant changes that have occurred in the television industry over the past 40 years and how they have affected the ways marketers use TV as an advertising medium.

2. Discuss the advantages and limitations of television as an advertising medium and how these factors affect its use by both major national advertisers as well as smaller local companies.

3. Explain what is meant by zipping and zapping and how they affect television viewing behavior. What are some of the ways advertisers can deal with the zapping problem?

4. IMC Perspective 11-1 discusses how digital video recorders (DVRs) and video on demand (VOD) are becoming more prevalent in U.S. homes. Discuss how these products/services are impacting the way people watch television. What are the implications for TV's traditional business model?

5. What are the various options available to advertisers for advertising time on television? How does the use of these options differ for national versus local advertisers?

6. Discuss how the growth of Spanish-language television networks in the United States such as Univision and Telemundo affects the media strategy of marketers targeting the Hispanic market.

7. What are the various forms of syndicated programs available to advertisers? Why might marketers advertise on syndicated programs rather than network shows?

8. Discuss the advantages and limitations of advertising on cable television networks. Why are cable networks such as ESPN so popular among advertisers?

9. Evaluate the use of sweeps rating periods as a method for measuring local television viewing audiences. Do you think sweeps ratings provide reliable and valid estimates of local television viewing audiences? How might they be improved?

10. Discuss the advantages and disadvantages of advertising on radio. Discuss how radio advertising can be used by national versus local advertisers.

11. Discuss how various new digital technologies are impacting radio listening. What are some of the ways the radio industry is responding to these challenges?

12. Discuss how the concept of image transfer can be used in radio advertising. Find an example of a radio campaign that is using this concept and evaluate it.

Evaluation of Print Media

12

Chapter Objectives

1. To examine the structure of the magazine and newspaper industries and the role of each medium in the advertising program.
2. To analyze the advantages and limitations of magazines and newspapers as advertising media.
3. To examine the various types of magazines and newspapers and the value of each as an advertising medium.
4. To discuss how advertising space is purchased in magazines and newspapers, how readership is measured, and how rates are determined.
5. To consider future developments in magazines and newspapers and how these trends will influence their use as advertising media.

Celebrity Magazines Are Hot

The American public has always been fascinated by celebrities. However, in recent years the interest in celebrities has become an obsession, and magazines that focus on the rich and famous, and sometimes even the infamous, are exploding in popularity. The number of magazines devoted to providing news, information, gossip, and, most important, pictures of celebrities such as Jessica Simpson, Tom Cruise, Brad Pitt, Britney Spears, Angelina Jolie, and other stars is growing as is their circulation. Magazines such as *US Weekly, In Touch, Star, OK!,* and *Life & Style Weekly* are attracting more readers as well as advertising pages, which translates into more revenue for their publishers.

A number of factors are fueling the growth in the popularity of star-obsessed magazines. Robert Thompson, a professor of popular culture and television at Syracuse University, notes that because our society has no aristocracy, Americans have always been obsessed with celebrity. However, until recently, there were few outlets which served the public's desire for celebrity news and gossip. Television exposure for celebrities was limited to late-night talk shows and an occasional network show such as *The Barbara Walters Special.* Only a few magazines, such as *People,* chronicled the lives of celebrities, as the stars were mostly covered in tabloids such as *The National Enquirer* or *Star.* Although the tabloids were fun to read, many people only scanned them in the supermarket checkout lines and were embarrassed if they were caught actually reading them. However, the growth of cable television and syndication gave rise to numerous programs that focus on celebrities, including *Access Hollywood, Entertainment Tonight, Extra!,* and *Inside Edition.*

Magazine industry experts note the growth in the number of celebrity-focused magazines began in 2000 when *US* was transformed from a monthly publication to a weekly. It took a few years for *US Weekly* to connect with its sharply defined target audience of women, but the magazine has found its way to a younger and wealthier audience. Paid circulation was up almost 24 percent in 2005 reaching 1.7 million, and studies by Mediamark Research show that *US Weekly*'s female readers have a median income of $83,365, which is higher than readers of such magazines as *Vanity Fair* and *In Style.* These numbers have attracted the attention of advertisers such as Mercedes-Benz and have led to a 15 percent increase in ad pages in 2005 for *US Weekly.*

A number of other celebrity-focused magazines have been introduced in the past few years. *In Touch* was launched in 2002 by Bauer Publishing USA and is one of the fastest growing magazines in the celebrity category as its paid circulation increased by nearly 50 percent in 2005 to 1.1 million. Bauer also recently introduced *Life & Style Weekly,* which features the latest Hollywood beauty, fashion, and lifestyle trends merged with celebrity and shopping news. American Media has spent several years overhauling *Star Magazine,* transforming it from a supermarket tabloid focusing on the weird to a celebrity magazine with a glossy format. The new *Star* has seen its circulation increase by almost 21 percent to 1.4 million readers. In the summer of 2005, *OK!*, a celebrity-drenched weekly magazine from the United Kingdom, hit the newsstands with an American version. In addition to the pictures of celebrities captured by the paparazzi, *OK!* pays celebrities large sums of money for exclusive access to their homes, weddings, and newborn babies. Even *TV Guide* is getting into the act with a new larger, full-color format and more stories about TV shows and stars.

While celebrity magazines have always been popular with a core audience of women in their 20s and 30s, the new breed of publications is also attracting younger readers as more teenage girls are reading them. A 2005 report by Simmons Research found that 23 percent of teen girls surveyed said they had read *US Weekly* in the last six months compared with only 6 percent in 2000, and 16 percent said they had read *Star* compared to 9 percent five years ago. With more teen girls reading entertainment weeklies, traditional teen magazines such as *CosmoGirl, Teen Vogue,* and *Teen People* are losing teen readers. Even *Seventeen,* which has long been a staple among teens, has seen its readership among teen girls decline from 71 percent in 2000 to 60 percent in 2005 and is shifting its focus to try to reach the college market.

Although celebrity magazines continue to gain in popularity, industry experts question whether the economics of the business can sustain the growth and competition. Unlike other publications, which are supported by subscriptions, celebrity magazines live and die by their newsstand sales. The publications essentially pay rent to be displayed in racks at grocery stores and other locations and have to pay for the "pockets" even if they do not sell enough copies. Many of the newer publications, including *In Touch, Life & Style,* and *Celebrity Living,* are priced under \$2.00, which is part of their appeal. The lower prices of the entertainment weeklies are posing problems for higher priced magazines, which have to compete against them on the newsstands.

Many in the magazine industry wonder how long Americans' insatiable appetite for pictures, stories, and gossip about celebrities will continue. While there are plenty of low-level celebrities, there are only a few megastars—such as Jennifer Aniston, Brad Pitt, and Angelina Jolie—who can really move magazines. Industry experts note that there doesn't appear to be any end in sight, however, as the increased media focus on celebrities makes people want to know even more about them. And as long as society asks for more news and gossip about celebrities, the magazines will be there to make sure they get it.

Sources: Jennifer Davies, "Gluttons for Gossip," *San Diego Union Tribune,* September 3, 2005, pp. C1, 4; Martha Irvine, "Teens Seeking Out Celeb Publications," *San Diego Union Tribune,* August 16, 2005, p. C3; Jon Fine, "Magazine of the Year *US Weekly,*" *Advertising Age,* October 25, 2004, pp. S1, 6; Joe Hagan, "Soon! Exclusive Photos!," *The Wall Street Journal,* June 20, 2005, pp. B1, 4.

Magazines and newspapers have been advertising media for more than two centuries; for many years, they were the only major media available to advertisers. With the growth of the broadcast media, particularly television, reading habits declined. More consumers turned to TV viewing not only as their primary source of entertainment but also for news and information. But despite the competition from the broadcast media, newspapers and magazines have remained important media vehicles to both consumers and advertisers.

Thousands of magazines are published in the United States and throughout the world. They appeal to nearly every specific consumer interest and lifestyle, as well as to thousands of businesses and occupations. By becoming a highly specialized medium that reaches specific target audiences, the magazine industry has prospered. Newspapers are still the primary advertising medium in terms of both ad revenue and number of advertisers. Newspapers are particularly important as a local advertising medium for hundreds of thousands of retail businesses and are often used by large national advertisers as well.

Magazines and newspapers are an important part of our lives. For many consumers, newspapers are their primary source of product information. They would not think of going shopping without checking to see who is having a sale or clipping coupons from the weekly food section or Sunday inserts. Many people read a number of different magazines each week or month to become better informed or simply entertained. Individuals employed in various occupations rely on business magazines to keep them current about trends and developments in their industries as well as in business in general.

While most of us are very involved with the print media, it is important to keep in mind that few newspapers or magazines could survive without the support of advertising revenue. Consumer magazines generate an average of 54 percent of their revenues from advertising; business publications receive nearly 73 percent. Newspapers generate 70 percent of their total revenue from advertising. In many cities, the number of daily newspapers has declined because they could not attract enough advertising revenue to support their operations. The print media must be able to attract large numbers of readers or a very specialized audience to be of interest to advertisers.

The Role of Magazines and Newspapers

The role of magazines and newspapers in the advertiser's media plan differs from that of the broadcast media because they allow the presentation of detailed information that can be processed at the reader's own pace. The print media are not intrusive like radio and TV, and they generally require some effort on the part of the reader for the advertising message to have an impact. For this reason, newspapers and magazines are often referred to as *high-involvement media.*[1] Over 80 percent of U.S. households subscribe to or purchase magazines, while the average household buys six different magazines each year.[2]

Newspapers are received in nearly two-thirds of American households daily. Most magazines, however, reach a very selective audience. Like radio, they can be valuable in reaching specific types of consumers and market segments. While both magazines and newspapers are print media, the advantages and disadvantages of the two are quite different, as are the types of advertising each attracts. This chapter focuses on these two major forms of print media. It examines the specific advantages and limitations of each, along with factors that are important in determining when and how to use newspapers and magazines in the media plan.

Magazines

Over the past several decades, magazines have grown rapidly to serve the educational, informational, and entertainment needs of a wide range of readers in both the consumer and business markets. Magazines are the most specialized of all advertising media. While some magazines—such as *Reader's Digest, Time,* and *TV Guide*—are general mass-appeal publications, most are targeted to a very specific audience. There is a magazine designed to appeal to nearly every type of consumer in terms of demographics, lifestyle, activities, interests, or fascination. Numerous magazines are targeted toward specific businesses and industries as well as toward individuals engaged in various professions (Exhibit 12-1).

The wide variety makes magazines an appealing medium to a vast number of advertisers. Although TV accounts for the largest dollar amount of advertising expenditures among national advertisers, more companies advertise in magazines than in any other medium. Users of magazines range from large consumer-product companies such as Procter & Gamble and General Motors, which spend over $500 million a year on magazine advertising, to a small company advertising scuba equipment in *Skin Diver* magazine.

Classifications of Magazines

To gain some perspective on the various types of magazines available and the advertisers that use them, consider the way magazines are generally classified. Standard

Exhibit 12-1 Magazines targeted to a specific industry or profession

Rate and Data Service (SRDS), the primary reference source on periodicals for media planners, divides magazines into three broad categories based on the audience to which they are directed: consumer, farm, and business publications. Each category is then further classified according to the magazine's editorial content and audience appeal.

Consumer Magazines Consumer magazines are bought by the general public for information and/or entertainment. SRDS divides 2,700 domestic consumer magazines into 75 classifications, among them general editorial, sports, travel, and women's. Another way of classifying consumer magazines is by distribution: They can be sold through subscription or circulation, store distribution, or both. *Time* and *Newsweek* are sold both through subscription and in stores; *Woman's World* is sold only through stores. *People* magazine was originally sold only through stores but then added subscription sales as it gained in popularity. Figure 12-1 shows the top 10 magazines in terms of subscriptions and single-copy sales, respectively. Magazines can also be classified by frequency; weekly, monthly, and bimonthly are the most common.

Consumer magazines represent the major portion of the magazine industry, accounting for nearly two-thirds of all advertising dollars spent in magazines. Consumer magazines are best suited to marketers interested in reaching general consumers of products and services as well as to companies trying to reach a specific target market. The most frequently advertised categories in consumer magazines are automotive, direct response, toiletries and cosmetics, computers, office equipment and stationery, and business and consumer services. Marketers of tobacco products spend most of their media budget in magazines, since they are prohibited from advertising in the broadcast media.

While large national advertisers tend to dominate consumer magazine advertising in terms of expenditures, the more than 2,700 consumer magazines are also important to smaller companies selling products that appeal to specialized markets. Special-interest magazines assemble consumers with similar lifestyles or interests and offer marketers an efficient way to reach these people with little wasted coverage or circulation. For example, a manufacturer of ski or snowboarding equipment such as Nordica, Rossignol, or Salomon might find *Powder* the best vehicle for advertising to skiers or snowboarders.

Figure 12-1 Top Magazines by Subscriptions and Single-Copy Sales

By Subscriptions		By Single-Copy Sales	
1. *AARP The Magazine**	22,558,000	1. *Cosmopolitan*	1,992,446
2. *AARP Bulletin**	22,042,940	2. *Woman's World*	1,508,188
3. *Reader's Digest*	9,659,940	3. *People*	1,485,038
4. *TV Guide*	8,758,689	4. *First for Women*	1,248,375
5. *Better Homes and Gardens*	7,414,303	5. *O, The Oprah Magazine*	1,106,712
6. *National Geographic*	5,273,053	6. *In Touch Weekly*	1,090,088
7. *Time*	3,893,374	7. *US Weekly*	989,011
8. *Good Housekeeping*	3,851,498	8. *National Enquirer*	947,820
9. *Ladies' Home Journal*	3,837,910	9. *Glamour*	892,520
10. *AAA Westways**	3,675,663	10. *Star*	879,356

Note: Figures are averages for first six months of 2005 based on Audit Bureau of Circulation statements.
*High proportion of title's circulation attributed to membership benefits.
Source; Magazine Publishers of America, fact sheet, www.magazine.org.

Not only are these specialty magazines of value to firms interested in reaching a specific market segment, but their editorial content often creates a very favorable advertising environment for relevant products and services. For example, avid skiers and snowboarders cannot wait for the first snowfall after reading the season's first issues of *Snowboarding* or *Powder* magazine and may be quite receptive to the ads they carry for skiing and snowboarding products and destination ski resorts (Exhibit 12-2).

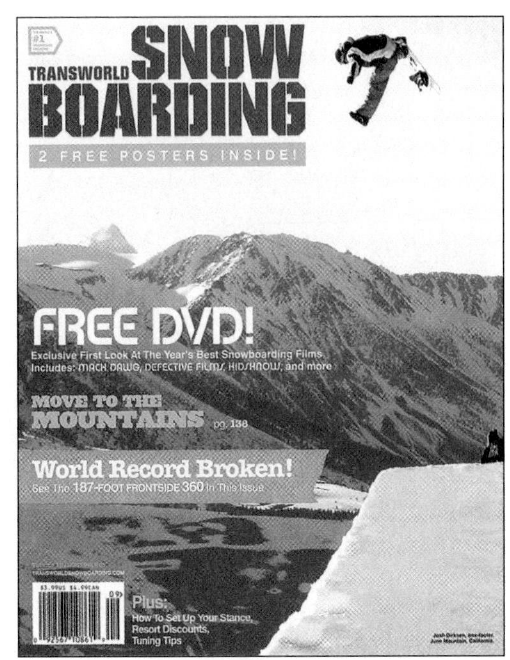

Exhibit 12-2 *Snowboarding* magazine is an excellent medium for reaching the serious snowboarder

Farm Publications The second major SRDS category consists of all the magazines directed to farmers and their families. About 300 publications are tailored to nearly every possible type of farming or agricultural interest. SRDS breaks farm publications into 9 classifications, ranging from general-interest magazines aimed at all types of farmers (e.g., *Farm Journal, Successful Farming, Progressive Farmer*) to those in specialized agricultural areas such as poultry (*Gobbles*), hog farming (*National Hog Farmer*), or cattle raising (*Beef*—see Exhibit 12-3). A number of farm publications are directed at farmers in specific states or regions, such as *Nebraska Farmer* or *Montana Farmer Stockman*. Farm publications are not classified with business publications because historically farms were not perceived as businesses.

Business Publications Business publications are those magazines or trade journals published for specific businesses, industries, or occupations. Standard Rate and Data Service breaks down over 9,300 U.S. magazines and trade journals into more than 220 market classifications. The major classifications include:

1. Magazines directed at specific professional groups, such as *National Law Review* for lawyers and *Architectural Forum* for architects.
2. Industrial magazines directed at businesspeople in various manufacturing and production industries—for example, *Iron and Steelmaker, Chemical Week,* and *Industrial Engineering.*
3. Trade magazines targeted to wholesalers, dealers, distributors, and retailers, among them *Progressive Grocer, Drug Store News, Women's Wear Daily,* and *Restaurant Business.*
4. General business magazines aimed at executives in all areas of business, such as *Forbes, Fortune,* and *BusinessWeek.* (General business publications are also included in SRDS's consumer publications edition.)
5. Health care publications targeted to various areas including dental, medical and surgical, nursing, biotechnological sciences, and hospital administration.

The numerous business publications reach specific types of professional people with particular interests and give them important information relevant to their industry, occupation, and/or careers. Business publications are important to advertisers because they provide an efficient way of reaching the specific types of individuals who constitute their target market. Much marketing occurs at the trade and business-to-business level, where one company sells its products or services directly to another.

Exhibit 12-3 *Beef* magazine is read by many cattle ranchers

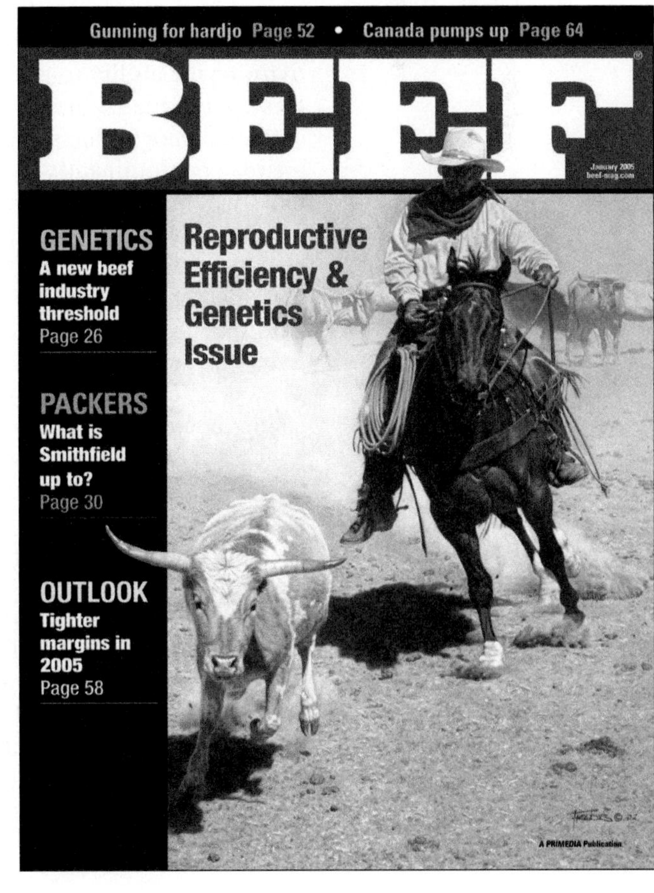

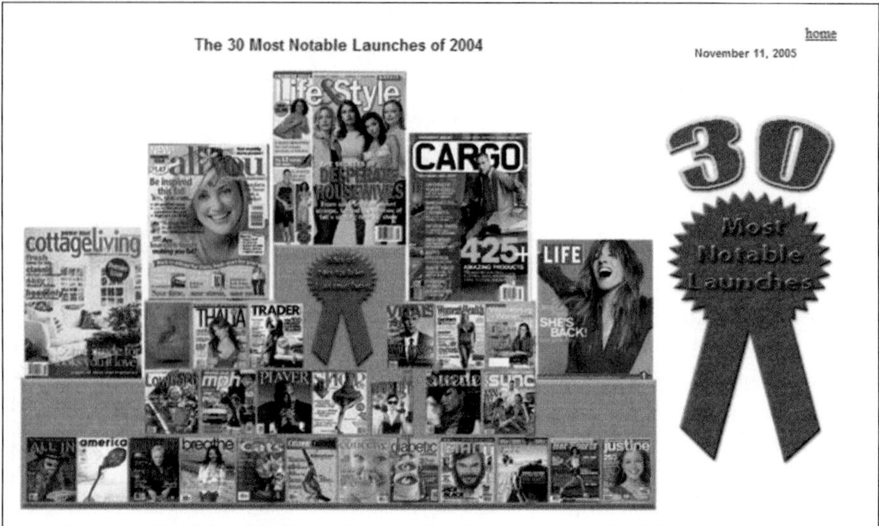

Exhibit 12-4 Magazine expert Samir Husni's 30 most notable magazine launches

Advantages of Magazines

Magazines have a number of characteristics that make them attractive as an advertising medium. Strengths of magazines include their selectivity, excellent reproduction quality, creative flexibility, permanence, prestige, readers' high receptivity and involvement, and services they offer to advertisers.

Selectivity

One of the main advantages of using magazines as an advertising medium is their **selectivity,** or ability to reach a specific target audience. Magazines are the most selective of all media except direct mail. Most magazines are published for special-interest groups. The thousands of magazines published in the United States reach all types of consumers and businesses and allow advertisers to target their advertising to segments of the population who buy their products. For example, *PC World* is targeted toward computer buffs, *Spin* reaches those with an avid interest in music, and *Ebony* focuses on the upscale African-American market. Many new magazines are introduced each year targeting new interests and trends. According to Dr. Samir Husni, who has been tracking magazine launches since 1985, an average of 75 new publications are launched each month.[3] New consumer magazines are continually being introduced to meet the changing needs, interests, and passions of the public in areas such as sports/recreation, entertainment/celebrity, travel, fashion/apparel, and beauty/grooming. New business publications are also frequently launched to respond to developments in business and industry. Exhibit 12-4 shows the 30 most notable magazine launches chosen by Dr. Husni for 2004.

In addition to providing selectivity based on interests, magazines can provide advertisers with high demographic and geographic selectivity. *Demographic selectivity,* or the ability to reach specific demographic groups, is available in two ways. First, most magazines are, as a result of editorial content, aimed at fairly well defined demographic segments. *Ladies' Home Journal, Ms., Self,* and *Cosmopolitan* are read predominantly by women; *Esquire, Playboy,* and *Sports Illustrated* are read mostly by men. Older consumers can be reached through publications like *Modern Maturity.* IMC Perspective 12-1 discusses how publishers have been introducing new magazines targeted at young males in an effort to reach this elusive, but important, market segment.

A second way magazines offer demographic selectivity is through special editions. Even magazines that appeal to broader audiences, such as *Reader's Digest, Time,* or *Newsweek,* can provide a high degree of demographic selectivity through their special demographic editions. Most of the top consumer magazines publish different editions targeted at different demographic markets.

Geographic selectivity lets an advertiser focus ads in certain cities or regions. One way to achieve geographic selectivity is by using a magazine that is targeted toward a particular area. Magazines devoted to regional interests include *Yankee* (New England), *Southern Living* (South), *Sunset* (West), and *Texas Monthly* (guess where?), among many others. One of the more successful media developments of recent years has been the growth of city magazines in most major American cities. *Los Angeles Magazine, Philadelphia,* and *Boston,* to name a few, provide residents of these areas with articles concerning lifestyle, events, and the like, in these cities and their surrounding metropolitan areas (Exhibit 12-5). City and regional magazines make it possible for advertisers to focus on specific local markets that may be of interest to them. These publications also have a readership profile that appeals to marketers of upscale brands: high income, college educated, loyal, and influential in their communities.

IMC PERSPECTIVE 12-1

Magazines Seek the Most Elusive Readers of All—Young Males

Teenagers are one of the fastest-growing market segments in America. There are more than 31 million teenagers in the United States, and according to Teenage Research Unlimited (TRU), a market research firm that specializes in teens, they spend more than $170 billion a year. While their numbers and purchasing power make them a very attractive segment for marketers, teens are very difficult to reach—particularly through magazines. Teenagers spend a lot more time listening to radio, watching TV, and surfing the Internet than reading magazines. And while teenagers in general are an elusive segment for advertisers, young males are a particularly difficult audience to capture.

According to TRU, 80 percent of girls between the ages of 12 and 19 read a magazine for pleasure every week compared to only 65 percent of boys. Teen magazines such as *Seventeen, Teen People, Teen Vogue,* and *CosmoGirl*—all target girls. Only *Teen People* manages to pull in a sizable male audience, as male teens account for around 20 percent of its readers. Conventional wisdom in the magazine industry says that teenage males are too antsy to cozy up with a magazine for any length of time. And when they do, they tend to read publications such as *Sports Illustrated, ESPN The Magazine,* or niche titles catering to specific interests such as extreme sports or video gaming. Publishers also note that teen guys are so worried about being teased by friends for needing advice on things such as muscle building or snagging girls that they balk at picking up magazines that deal with these topics. And today, no matter how racy the content, it's difficult for a magazine to compete with the raw subject matter available on the Internet and many cable TV channels.

Few magazines have been successful in reaching the elusive teenage male segment on a large scale, although publishers have tried to find the right formula to do so. For example, Rodale Inc. created a spin-off of its *Men's Health* magazine for teen guys called *MH-18.* The new magazine's content was similar to the girl's magazine *Seventeen* as it included boyish lifestyle fare: workout plans, girl-kissing tips, and ways to boost grades. When *MH-18* was launched, the editor acknowledged that it was a risky venture as he was not sure how teen guys would respond to the new magazine. It did not take long for him to get an answer as *MH-18* lasted only one year before being shuttered by the publisher.

Whereas *MH-18* was unsuccessful with a fairly tame editorial mix, another publisher, TransWorld Media, took a different approach with *Stance,* which was launched in 2000. *Stance* took its cover shot and content cues from "laddie" magazines such as *Gear, Maxim, Stuff,* and *FHM* by focusing on a combination of the things teenage boys want to look at: girls, action sports, video games, cars, music, and more girls. The magazine steered clear of grooming articles and girl-getting pointers and focused more on cool stuff to buy, for example, computers and video game players, and exotic things to do, such as snowboarding in Austria. *Stance* was initially very successful in attracting readers as well as a variety of advertisers. However, in April 2003, TransWorld Media, which is owned by Time Inc., discontinued publication of *Stance* and decided to focus on its other publications, including magazines for surfers, snowboarders, BMXers, and motocross. TransWorld's magazines such as *Skateboarding, Surf, Motocross,* and *ride bmx* have been very popular with advertisers who want to reach young people as well as be associated with cutting-edge extreme sports.

Magazine publishers will continue to look for the right formula to reach young males, and marketers will keep a close watch on new magazines that try to connect with them. Advertisers would love to see magazines succeed in attracting teenage boys so they can better target this elusive market segment. Publishers have already proven that they can attract teenage girls. Now if they can only get the guys to pick up a magazine!

Sources: Jon Fine, "Sales Plummet for Once-Hot Teen Titles," *Advertising Age,* September 27, 2004, pp. 4, 82; "Rodale Names Steve Murphy New CEO," *Advertising Age,* January 14, 2002, p. 7; Erin White, "Teen Mags for Guys Not Dolls," *The Wall Street Journal,* August 10, 2000, pp. B1, 4.

Exhibit 12-5 City magazines offer advertisers high geographic selectivity

Another way to achieve geographic selectivity in magazines is through purchasing ad space in specific geographic editions of national or regional magazines. A number of publications divide their circulation into groupings based on regions or major metropolitan areas and offer advertisers the option of concentrating their ads in these editions. A magazine may break the United States into geographic areas and offer regional editions for each, and/or offer advertisers their choice of editions directed to specific states or metropolitan areas. Many magazines allow advertisers to combine regional or metropolitan editions to best match the geographic market of interest to them.

SRDS lists more than 350 consumer magazines offering geographic and/or demographic editions. Regional advertisers can purchase space in editions that reach only areas where they have distribution, yet still enjoy the prestige of advertising in a major national magazine. National advertisers can use the geographic editions to focus their advertising on areas with the greatest potential or those needing more promotional support. They can also use regional editions to test-market products or alternative promotional campaigns in various regions of the country.

Ads in regional editions can also list the names of retailers or distributors in various markets, thus encouraging greater local support from the trade. The trend toward regional marketing is increasing the importance of having regional media available to marketers. The availability of regional and demographic editions can also reduce the cost per thousand for reaching desired audiences. Exhibit 12-6 shows a page from the online media kit for *Time* magazine listing the various editions available to advertisers.

Exhibit 12-6 *Time* offers a variety of editions to advertisers

TIME
Know why.
TIMEMEDIAKIT.COM

ABOUT TIME
CALENDAR
EDITORIAL
EDITIONS & RATES
National Edition
Demographic Editions
Geographic Editions
Multi-Editions
AUDIENCE
EVENTS & MARKETING PROGRAMS
SPECS
CONTACT US

HOME

Editions & Rates

There are more than 400 ways to buy advertising in TIME US. These include national edition, demographic editions, regional editions, 50 states and D.C. and 50+ spot markets.

Globally, TIME has five editions: TIME US, TIME Asia, TIME Canada, TIME EMEA (Europe, Middle East and Africa) and TIME South Pacific. Critical to TIME's global leadership in journalism are our 28 worldwide News Bureaus, more than any other newsmagazine.

Reproduction Quality

One of the most valued attributes of magazine advertising is the reproduction quality of the ads. Magazines are generally printed on high-quality paper stock and use printing processes that provide excellent reproduction in black and white or color. Since magazines are a visual medium where illustrations are often a dominant part of an ad, this is a very important property. The reproduction quality of most magazines is far superior to that offered by the other major print medium of newspapers, particularly when color is needed. The use of color has become a virtual necessity in most product categories, and more than two-thirds of all magazine ads now use color.

Creative Flexibility In addition to their excellent reproduction capabilities, magazines also offer advertisers a great deal of flexibility in terms of the type, size, and placement of the advertising material. Some magazines offer (often at extra charge) a variety of special options that can enhance the creative appeal of the ad and increase attention and readership. Examples include gatefolds, bleed pages, inserts, and creative space buys.

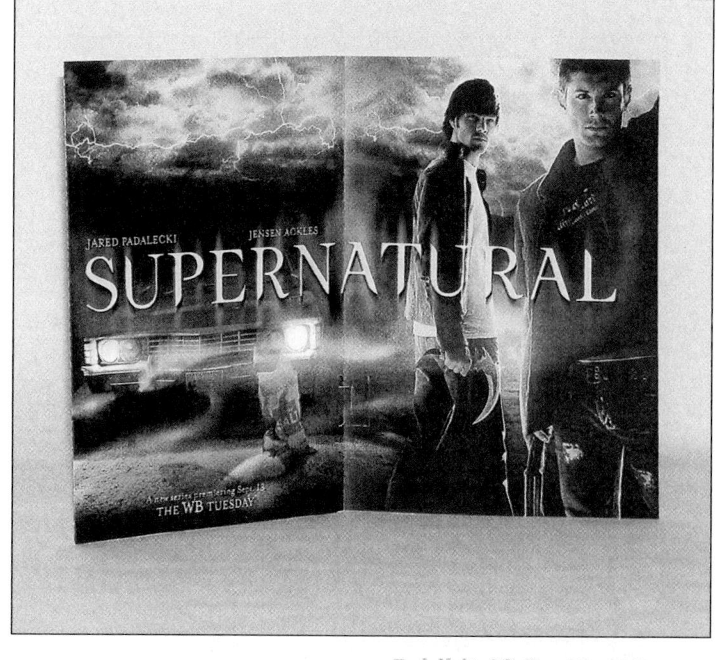

Exhibit 12-7 The WB Network used a creative insert to promote its new drama show "Supernatural"

Gatefolds enable an advertiser to make a striking presentation by using a third page that folds out and gives the ad an extra-large spread. Gatefolds are often found at the inside cover of large consumer magazines or on some inside pages. Advertisers use gatefolds to make a very strong impression, especially on special occasions such as the introduction of a new product or brand. For example, automobile advertisers often use gatefolds to introduce new versions of their cars each model year. Not all magazines offer gatefolds, however, and they must be reserved well in advance and are sold at a premium.

Bleed pages are those where the advertisement extends all the way to the end of the page, with no margin of white space around the ad. Bleeds give the ad an impression of being larger and make a more dramatic impact. Many magazines charge an extra 10 to 20 percent for bleeds.

In addition to gatefolds and bleed pages, creative options available through magazines include unusual page sizes and shapes. Some advertisers have grabbed readers' attention by developing three-dimensional pop-up ads that jump off the page. Various other *inserts* are used in many magazines. These include return cards, recipe booklets, coupons, records, and even product samples. Cosmetic companies use scratch-and-sniff inserts to introduce new fragrances, and some companies use them to promote deodorants, laundry detergents, or other products whose scent is important. Inserts are also used in conjunction with direct-response ads and as part of sales promotion strategies.

Scented ads, pop-ups, singing ads, heavy card stock, stickers, and CD-ROMs are among the types of inserts used by advertisers in magazines. Advertisers have been increasing their use of special inserts to break through the clutter in magazines and to capture readers' attention. For example, to introduce Aquafina sparkling water, PepsiCo had replicas of the bottle constructed partly out of bubble wrap inserted into copies of *People* magazine. The WB Network also used a very creative insert to promote its new drama show *Supernatural.* The insert appeared in *US Weekly* and *Rolling Stone.* As the insert is opened, a high-quality sound chip is triggered. The illustration of a 1967 Impala comes to life as the headlights illuminate and begin to flicker. And, as a haunting Dave Matthews tune sets the mood, the lead character's dialogue brings their supernatural story to life (Exhibit 12-7). Many magazine publishers are willing to work with advertisers who want to use creative inserts because they are eager to show that magazines can compete with new media as a way to showcase products. While the inserts pose challenges to production staff and printers, these costs along with any extra postage fees are generally passed onto the advertisers. The total cost of manufacturing inserts varies depending on the complexity, weight, assembly requirements, and other factors. Some of the very elaborate inserts can cost advertisers as much as several million dollars.[4]

There has been some backlash against various types of *printaculars.* Critics argue that they alter the appearance and feel of a magazine and the reader's relationship to it. Advertisers do not want to run regular ads that have to compete against heavy inserts, pop-ups, talking ads, or other distractions. Some advertisers and agencies are even asking publishers to notify them when they plan to run any spectacular inserts so that they can decide whether to pull their regular ads from the issue.[5]

USE #437
WD-40
Painter takes artistic license with WD-40®. *Van Fabel, an art teacher in North Carolina, says a shot of WD-40 and a little elbow grease are all he needs to clean his palette. It's great at removing crayon and scuff marks from walls and floors, too. Just spray, wait and wipe.*
WD-40. THERE'S ALWAYS ANOTHER USE.

USE #973
WD-40
Some fish story. *Several letters from avid fishermen across the country praise the benefits of WD-40®. And not just for cleaning their rods and reels and protecting fish hooks from rust and corrosion. They swear it actually attracts fish when sprayed on lures.*
WD-40. THERE'S ALWAYS ANOTHER USE.

USE #519
WD-40
Cycling fanatic finally loses his grip. *After struggling to remove his old handlebar grips, Gene Upshaw of Seattle found that a squirt of WD-40® was all he needed. It's great for cleaning and lubricating chains and protecting metal parts from corrosion, too.*
WD-40. THERE'S ALWAYS ANOTHER USE.

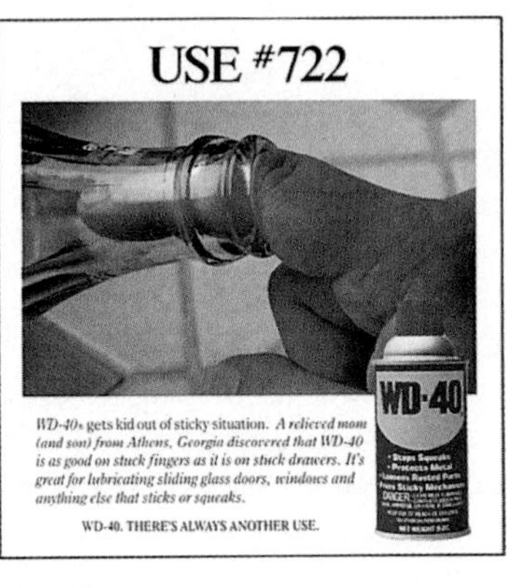

USE #722
WD-40
WD-40® gets kid out of sticky situation. *A relieved mom (and son) from Athens, Georgia discovered that WD-40 is as good on stuck fingers as it is on stuck drawers. It's great for lubricating sliding glass doors, windows and anything else that sticks or squeaks.*
WD-40. THERE'S ALWAYS ANOTHER USE.

Exhibit 12-8 WD-40 uses quarter-page ads to get greater impact from its media budget

Creative space buys are another option of magazines. Some magazines let advertisers purchase space units in certain combinations to increase the impact of their media budget. For example, WD-40, an all-purpose lubrication product, uses half- or quarter-page ads on consecutive pages of several magazines, mentioning a different use for the product on each page, as shown in Exhibit 12-8. This strategy gives the company greater impact for its media dollars and is helpful in promoting the product's variety of uses.

Permanence Another distinctive advantage offered by magazines is their long life span. TV and radio are characterized by fleeting messages that have a very short life span; newspapers are generally discarded soon after being read. Magazines, however, are generally read over several days and are often kept for reference. They are retained in the home longer than any other medium and are generally referred to on several occasions. A study of magazine audiences found that readers devote nearly an hour over a period of two or three days to reading an average magazine.[6] Studies have also found that nearly 75 percent of consumers retain magazines for future reference.[7] One benefit of the longer life of magazines is that reading occurs at a less hurried pace and there is more opportunity to examine ads in considerable detail. This means ads can use longer and more detailed copy, which can be very important for high-involvement and complex products or services. The permanence of magazines also means readers can be exposed to ads on multiple occasions and can pass magazines along to other readers.

Prestige Another positive feature of magazine advertising is the prestige the product or service may gain from advertising in publications with a favorable image. Companies whose products rely heavily on perceived quality, reputation, and/or image often buy space in prestigious publications with high-quality editorial content whose consumers have a high level of interest in the advertising pages. For example, *Esquire* and *GQ* cover men's fashions in a very favorable environment, and a clothing manufacturer may advertise its products in these magazines to enhance the prestige of its lines. *Architectural Digest* provides an impressive editorial environment that includes high-quality photography and artwork. The magazine's upscale readers are likely to have a favorable image of the publication that may transfer to the products advertised on its pages. *Good Housekeeping* provides a unique consumer's refund or replacement policy for products that bear the limited warranty seal or advertise in the magazine. This can increase a consumer's confidence in a particular brand and reduce the amount of perceived risk associated with a purchase.

While most media planners recognize that the environment created by a publication is important, it can be difficult to determine the image a magazine provides. Subjective estimates based on media planners' experience are often used to assess a magazine's prestige, as are objective measures such as reader opinion surveys.[8]

Consumer Receptivity and Involvement With the exception of newspapers, consumers are more receptive to advertising in magazines than in any other medium. Magazines are generally purchased because the information they contain interests the reader, and ads provide additional information that may be of value in making a purchase decision. The Study of Media Involvement conducted for the Magazine Publishers of America (MPA) found that magazines are the medium turned to most by consumers for knowledge, information, and usable ideas (see Figure 12-2). The study found that magazines are consumers' primary source of information for a variety of products and services, including automobiles, beauty and grooming, clothing and fashion, financial planning, and personal and business travel.[9] The magazine industry recently implemented a major campaign using the theme "Read On" that promotes one of the key strengths of magazines as advertising medium—their enduring power to engage readers, which makes them more receptive to ads.[10] Exhibit 12-9 shows an ad from the "Read On" campaign that is discussed in IMC Perspective 12-2.

In addition to their relevance, magazine ads are likely to be received favorably by consumers because, unlike broadcast ads, they are nonintrusive and can easily be ignored. Studies show that the majority of magazine readers welcome ads; only a small percentage have negative attitudes toward magazine advertising.[11] Some magazines, such as bridal or fashion publications, are purchased as much for their advertising as for their editorial content. MPA-sponsored studies have shown that magazine readers are more likely to attend to and recall ads than are TV viewers.

Figure 12-2 Magazines Are the Premier Source of Consumer Knowledge

The Study of Media Involvement, conducted by Beta Research, an independent research firm, reports that magazines are the medium turned to most by consumers for knowledge, information, and usable ideas. In fact, 95 percent of U.S. adults cite magazines as their premier source of insight and ideas. This is also true when consumers seek information about specific topics affecting their lives—ranging from automobiles to fashion to personal finance.

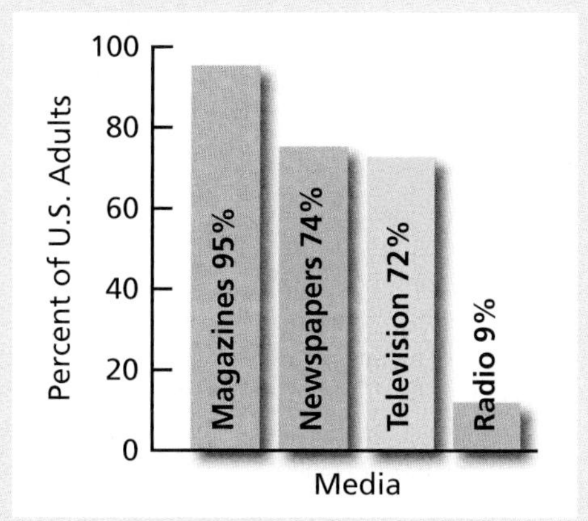

Note: Based on net of 12 measured product categories, multiple responses.

Area of Interest	Percent of Adults Referring to: Magazines	TV	Newspapers	Radio
Automobiles	39%	21%	29%	1%
Beauty and grooming	63	20	5	0
Clothing and fashion	58	18	15	0
Computers: hardware and software	54	14	11	0
Food	50	19	22	1
Fitness and exercise	49	36	6	1
Financial planning	45	11	31	2
Home repair/decorating	69	13	11	0
Sports: equipment/performance	49	24	7	1
Travel: personal and business	42	16	29	2

IMC PERSPECTIVE 12-2

Promoting the Value of Magazines to Advertisers

Media experts recognize that one of the major advantages of advertising in magazines is the ability of the medium to engage readers and hold their attention. Numerous studies have shown that consumers become involved with magazines when they read them and are also more likely to find ads acceptable, enjoyable, and even a valuable part of a publication. Intrusive media such as television and radio are struggling with the problems of their medium, such as consumer inattention and trying to avoid advertising messages. And as advertisers try harder to get their commercials seen and heard, consumers will search for more ways to tune them out. However, magazine readers recognize that they control the rate and duration of their exposure to both editorial content and advertisements, and thereby view ads as less disruptive to their media consumption experience.

While magazine publishers have always promoted these inherent advantages of magazines as an advertising medium, they recently decided it is time to go on the offensive and promote them more extensively. In early 2005, the magazine industry unveiled an advertising campaign touting one of the key strengths of magazines: the enduring power to engage readers. The $40 million three-year campaign, whose tagline is "Read On" and features both print and online components, was developed by Fallon New York and supported by the Magazine Marketing Coalition, a group representing magazine publishers and allied industries that work closely with magazines.

The campaign targets the marketing and advertising community including advertisers and the media decision makers. The communication strategy for the campaign grew out of an assessment of the advertising industry's view of the medium's strengths and weaknesses in the changing consumer landscape. The strategy was also supported by insights gained from a Northwestern University Reader Experience Study commissioned by the Magazine Publishers of America that defines consumer experiences when they read a magazine and quantifies how those experiences drive readership and impact. Nina Link, president and CEO of the MPA, notes: "The campaign plays on the idea that in an increasingly complicated world, with even more media disruptions and an impersonal digital landscape, consumers continue to choose magazines. It demonstrates the enduring power of magazines to captivate readers."

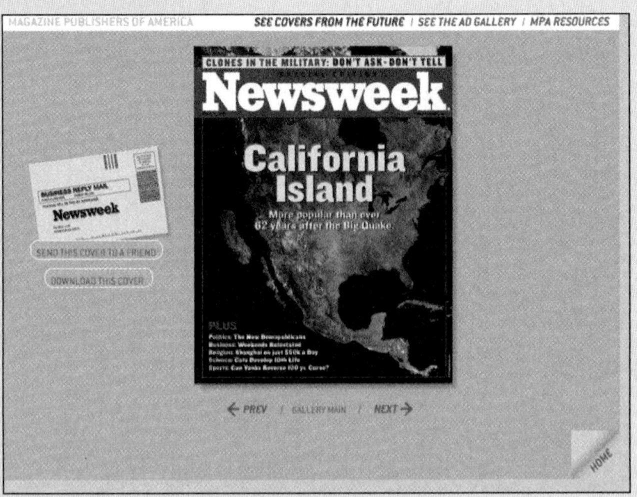

There are two key creative components to the Read On campaign. The core campaign consists of shots depicting people reading magazines in futuristic settings. One of the ads shows a man sitting on a park bench reading a magazine while a robot picks up litter in the background. Another shows a woman relaxing and reading a magazine in a futuristic-shaped bathtub. The copy in the ads provides glimpses of what life will be like in the future but also notes how magazines will continue to play an important role in our lives. The campaign tagline, "Read On," reinforces the message that people will always look for the personal connection magazines represent. The ads in the core campaign have been run in advertising and trade media press (*Advertising Age, Adweek Magazines, Media Magazine,* and *Creativity*), on trade media websites, in national newspapers such as *The New York Times* and *The Wall Street Journal,* and in MPA-member magazines.

The second creative component features magazine covers several decades into the future. For example, a faux futuristic cover of *Newsweek* features an aerial shot of the United States with California as an island off the West Coast. The cover caption reads: "California Island—More popular than ever 62 years after the Big Quake." Another shows a cover of *BusinessWeek* that features the cover story "Product Placement While You Sleep: Is It Ethical?" The concept behind the covers is to take advertisers by surprise while setting up the context of the future. Inside covers play off the faux covers with copy such as "No matter how things change or how complicated the world becomes, magazines will never go out of style. Read On." The futuristic covers were wrapped around complimentary copies of more than 40 weekly and monthly magazines. As part of the campaign Fallon also created a Read On website (www.magazine.org/readon), which features the advertising campaign and the futuristic covers and information about the power of magazine advertising.

The goal of the Read On campaign is to catapult magazines to a place where they are universally recognized for their value and their ability to contribute to the integrated marketing communication programs of marketers. The magazine industry wants marketers to recognize that in an age of interruption and advertising avoidance, consumers will continue to invite magazines into their lives and to value and trust magazine advertising.

Sources: "Magazine Industry Launches Campaign to Promote Enduring Power of Magazines to Engage Readers; Advertising Also Includes Futuristic Cover Wraps and Dedicated Website," *Business Wire,* February 28, 2005, p. 1; Erwin Ephron, "The Uninvited," *Mediaweek,* January 10, 2005, p. 16; Jon Fine, "Publishers Finally Unite to Rally behind 'Engagement,'" *Advertising Age,* November 1, 2004, p. 3.

Services A final advantage of magazines is the special services some publications offer advertisers. Some magazines have merchandising staffs that call on trade intermediaries like retailers to let them know a product is being advertised in their publication and to encourage them to display or promote the item. Another service offered by magazines (usually the larger ones) is research studies that they conduct on consumers. These studies may deal with general consumer trends, changing purchase patterns, and media usage or may be relevant to a specific product or industry.

An important service offered by some magazines is **split runs,** where two or more versions of an ad are printed in alternate copies of a particular issue of a magazine. This service is used to conduct a split-run test, which allows the advertiser to determine which ad generates the most responses or inquiries, providing some evidence as to their effectiveness. Technological developments have also made it possible for magazines to offer advertisers the opportunity to deliver personalized messages to tightly targeted audiences through selective binding and ink-jet imaging. **Selective binding** is a computerized production process that allows the creation of hundreds of copies of a magazine in one continuous sequence. Selective binding enables magazines to target and address specific groups within a magazine's circulation base. The magazine publishers can then send different editorial or advertising messages to various groups of subscribers within the same issue of a publication. **Ink-jet imaging** reproduces a message by projecting ink onto paper rather than using mechanical plates. This process makes it possible to personalize an advertising message. Many publishers believe selective binding and ink-jet imaging will let advertisers target their messages more finely and let magazines compete more effectively with direct mail and other direct-marketing vehicles. Exhibit 12-10 shows how *Newsweek* promotes the capabilities of ink-jet imaging for targeting advertising messages.

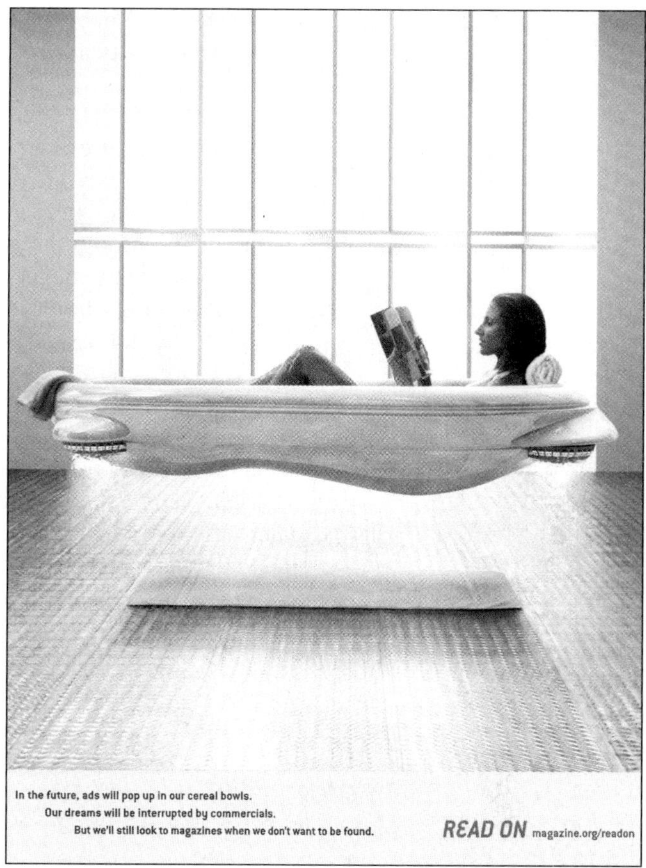

In the future, ads will pop up in our cereal bowls.
Our dreams will be interrupted by commercials.
But we'll still look to magazines when we don't want to be found.
READ ON magazine.org/readon

Exhibit 12-9 The "Read On" campaign promotes a key strength of magazines—their ability to engage readers

Disadvantages of Magazines

Although the advantages offered by magazines are considerable, they have certain drawbacks too. These include the costs of advertising, their limited reach and frequency, the long lead time required in placing an ad, and the problem of clutter and heavy advertising competition.

Costs The costs of advertising in magazines vary according to the size of the audience they reach and their selectivity. Advertising in large mass-circulation magazines like *TV Guide, Time,* or *Reader's Digest* can be very expensive. For example, a full-page, four-color ad in *Time* magazine's national edition (circulation 4.4 million) cost $234,000 in 2005. Popular positions such as the back cover cost over $500,000. By contrast, a full-page, four-color ad in *Tennis* (circulation 710,000) cost $52,500.

Like any medium, magazines must be considered not only from an absolute cost perspective but also in terms of relative costs. Most magazines emphasize their effectiveness in reaching specific target audiences at a low cost per thousand. Also, an increasing number of magazines are offering demographic and geographic editions, which helps lower their costs. Media planners generally focus on the relative costs of a publication in reaching their target audience. However, they may recommend a magazine with a high cost per thousand because of its ability to reach a small, specialized market segment. Of course, advertisers with limited

Exhibit 12-10 *Newsweek* promotes the value of ink-jet imaging

budgets will be interested in the absolute costs of space in a magazine and the costs of producing quality ads for these publications.

Limited Reach and Frequency Magazines are generally not as effective as other media in offering reach and frequency. While nearly 90 percent of adults in the United States read one or more consumer magazines each month, the percentage of adults reading any individual publication tends to be much smaller, so magazines have a thin penetration of households. For example, *Reader's Digest* has the third-highest circulation of any magazine, at 10.1 million, but this represents only 9 percent of the 110 million households in the United States.

As shown in Figure 12-3, only 33 magazines had a paid circulation over 2 million in 2005. Thus, advertisers seeking broad reach must make media buys in a number of magazines, which means more negotiations and transactions. For a broad-reach strategy, magazines are used in conjunction with other media. Since most magazines are monthly or at best weekly publications, the opportunity for building frequency through the use of the same publication is limited. Using multiple ads in the same issue of a publication is an inefficient way to build frequency. Most advertisers try to achieve frequency by adding other magazines with similar audiences to the media schedule.

Figure 12-3 Top 50 Magazines in Average Paid Circulation

Rank	Publication	Total Paid Circulation	Rank	Publication	Total Paid Circulation
1	*AARP The Magazine**	22,559,956	26	*Glamour*	2,340,958
2	*AARP Bulletin**	22,042,940	27	*Smithsonian*	2,049,062
3	*Reader's Digest*	10,128,943	28	*Parents*	2,047,279
4	*TV Guide*	9,073,543	29	*Seventeen*	2,037,457
5	*Better Homes and Gardens*	7,634,170	30	*Game Informer Magazine*	2,036,751
6	*National Geographic*	5,431,117	31	*Home & Away**	2,028,855
7	*Good Housekeeping*	4,606,800	32	*U.S. News & World Report*	2,021,485
8	*Family Circle*	4,298,117	33	*Parenting*	2,018,995
9	*Ladies' Home Journal*	4,131,243	34	*Real Simple*	1,947,004
10	*Time*	4,050,589	35	*Money*	1,942,531
11	*Woman's Day*	4,015,392	36	*AAA Living*	1,939,989
12	*People*	3,779,640	37	*Martha Stewart Living*	1,928,627
13	*AAA Westways**	3,675,663	38	*ESPN The Magazine*	1,858,079
14	*Sports Illustrated*	3,339,229	39	*Entertainment Weekly*	1,852,376
15	*Prevention*	3,331,686	40	*In Style*	1,793,902
16	*Newsweek*	3,200,413	41	*Men's Health*	1,773,612
17	*Playboy*	3,114,998	42	*Family Fun*	1,762,318
18	*Cosmopolitan*	2,932,554	43	*Cooking Light*	1,746,201
19	*Southern Living*	2,754,937	44	*Endless Vacation**	1,712,564
20	*Guideposts*	2,652,174	45	*Country Living*	1,706,017
21	*O, The Oprah Magazine*	2,622,718	46	*US Weekly*	1,674,267
22	*American Legion Magazine**	2,531,867	47	*Shape*	1,659,845
23	*Maxim*	2,531,681	48	*Woman's World*	1,602,619
24	*Via Magazine*	2,435,904	49	*Golf Digest*	1,564,885
25	*Redbook*	2,396,636	50	*VFW Magazine*	1,561,257

Note: Figures are averages for first six months of 2005 based on Audit Bureau of Circulation statements.
*High proportion of title's circulation attributed to membership benefits.
Source: Magazine Publishers of America, fact sheet, www.magazine.org.

Long Lead Time Another drawback of magazines is the long lead time needed to place an ad. Most major publications have a 30- to 60-day lead time, which means space must be purchased and the ad must be prepared well in advance of the actual publication date. No changes in the art or copy of the ad can be made after the closing date. This long lead time means magazine ads cannot be as timely as other media, such as radio or newspapers, in responding to current events or changing market conditions.

Exhibit 12-11
HealthExpressions is an online magazine published by Procter & Gamble

Clutter and Competition While the problem of advertising clutter is generally discussed in reference to the broadcast media, magazines also have this drawback. The clutter problem for magazines is something of a paradox: The more successful a magazine becomes, the more advertising pages it attracts, and this leads to greater clutter. In fact, magazines generally gauge their success in terms of the number of advertising pages they sell.

Magazine publishers do attempt to control the clutter problem by maintaining a reasonable balance of editorial pages to advertising. According to the Magazine Publishers of America, the average consumer magazine contains 48 percent advertising and 52 percent editorial.[12] However, many magazines contain ads on more than half of their pages. This clutter makes it difficult for an advertiser to gain readers' attention and draw them into the ad. Thus, many print ads use strong visual images, catchy headlines, or some of the creative techniques discussed earlier to grab the interest of magazine readers. Some advertisers create their own custom magazines to sidestep the advertising clutter problem as well as to have control over editorial content. A number of companies have also been publishing their own magazines to build relationships with their customers. For example, Farmer's Insurance sends its customers a magazine called *The Friendly Review* that contains useful articles on a variety of topics. Custom-published magazines have also become very popular among tobacco companies, such as Philip Morris, which direct-mail them to their customer base.[13] Some companies have begun offering online versions of their custom magazines. For example, Procter & Gamble began publishing *HomeMadeSimple* several years ago and recently expanded the concept to health care with another online magazine called *HealthExpressions,* which contains articles and information on health, wellness, healthy recipes, and other areas. The online magazine also provides information and special offers for various P&G health-related brands such as Crest, Prilosec, Always, and others (Exhibit 12-11). Kraft Foods also publishes an online magazine called *Kraft Food & Family* and the success of the online version led the company to begin offering a print version, which is sent to more than 3 million consumers.[14]

Clutter is not as serious an issue for the print media as for radio or TV, since consumers tend to be more receptive and tolerant of print advertising. They can also control their exposure to a magazine ad simply by turning the page.

Magazine Circulation and Readership

Two of the most important considerations in deciding whether to use a magazine in the advertising media plan are the size and characteristics of the audience it reaches. Media buyers evaluate magazines on the basis of their ability to deliver the advertiser's message to as many people as possible in the target audience. To do this, they must consider the circulation of the publication as well as its total readership and match these figures against the audience they are attempting to reach.

Circulation Circulation figures represent the number of individuals who receive a publication through either subscription or store purchase. The number of copies distributed to these original subscribers or purchasers is known as *primary circulation* and is the basis for the magazine's rate structure. Circulation fluctuates from issue to issue, particularly for magazines that rely heavily on retail or newsstand sales. Many publications base their rates on *guaranteed circulation* and give advertisers a rebate if the number of delivered magazines falls below the guarantee. To minimize rebating, most guaranteed circulation figures are conservative; that is, they are set safely below the average actual delivered circulation. Advertisers are not charged for any excess circulation.

Many publishers became unhappy with the guaranteed circulation concept, since it requires them to provide refunds if guarantees are not met but results in a bonus for advertisers when circulation exceeds the guarantee. Thus, many publications have gone to a circulation rate base system. Rates are based on a set average circulation that is nearly always below the actual circulation delivered by a given issue but carries no guarantee. However, circulation is unlikely to fall below the rate base, since this would reflect negatively on the publication and make it difficult to attract advertisers at prevailing rates.

Circulation Verification Given that circulation figures are the basis for a magazine's advertising rates and one of the primary considerations in selecting a publication, the credibility of circulation figures is important. Most major publications are audited by one of the circulation verification services. Consumer magazines and farm publications are audited by the Audit Bureau of Circulations (ABC), which was organized in 1914 and is sponsored by advertisers, agencies, and publishers. ABC collects and evaluates information regarding the subscriptions and sales of magazines and newspapers to verify their circulation figures. Only publications with 70 percent or more paid circulation are eligible for verification audits by ABC. In 2002 the ABC approved new guidelines for counting magazine circulation and sales. The changes did away with the long-standing "50 percent rule," in which copies that sold for less than half of the basic price of a magazine could not be counted as paid circulation. Under the new rules copies sold at any price may be counted, but the magazine must disclose sales and prices in its circulation statements.[15] More than 2,000 business publications are audited by the Business Publications Audit (BPA) of Circulation. Many of these are published on a **controlled-circulation basis,** meaning copies are sent (usually free) to individuals the publisher believes can influence the company's purchases.

Circulation verification services provide media planners with reliable figures regarding the size and distribution of a magazine's circulation that help them evaluate its worth as a media vehicle. The ABC statement also provides other important information. It shows how a magazine is distributed by state and size, as well as percentage of the circulation sold at less than full value and percentage arrears (how many subscriptions are being given away). Many advertisers believe that subscribers who pay for a magazine are more likely to read it than are those who get it at a discount or for free.

Circulation verification has come under very close scrutiny over the past two years as circulation scandals emerged at several high-profile magazines and newspapers. *PC Magazine,* for example, was discovered to have misclassified 320,000 subscriptions as "paid," which resulted in the publication overestimating its rate base by as much as 21 percent.[16] Disclosure regarding overstatements of circulation contributed to the demise of *YM* magazine, which ceased publication at the end of 2004. Problems have also been found in the newsstand sales reported by other magazines, which have led advertisers to more closely scrutinize the circulation numbers used by magazines.[17]

Media buyers are generally skeptical about publications whose circulation figures are not audited by one of the verification services, and some companies will not advertise in unaudited publications. Circulation data, along with the auditing source, are available from Standard Rate and Data Service or from the publication itself. Exhibit 12-12 shows a sample magazine publisher's statement, which is subject to audit by Audit Bureau of Circulations.

Readership and Total Audience Advertisers are often interested in the number of people a publication reaches as a result of secondary, or pass-along, readership. **Pass-along readership** can occur when the primary subscriber or purchaser gives a magazine to another person or when the publication is read in doctors' waiting rooms or beauty salons, on airplanes, and so forth.

MAGAZINE
PUBLISHER'S STATEMENT
Subject to Audit

Audit Bureau of Circulations
900 N. Meacham Road Schaumburg, IL 60173-4968
P: 847.605.0909 • F: 847.605.0483
URL: www.accessabc.com

Prototype Magazine

For the six months ended June 30, 2002

Field Served: Health Industry.

Established:	1990	ABC Member since:	1992
Frequency:	10 times/year	ABC Member Number:	04-0000-0

Published by XYZ Publications, Inc.
123 Any Lane • Anytown, IL 60000
P: 000.000.0000 • F: 000.000.000 • URL: www.prototype.com

AVERAGE CIRCULATION

1 **Total Average Paid Circulation:** 805,237

		% of Total	
Subscriptions:	657,209	81.6	
Association, See Par. 9(c) - Non-deductible	100,000	12.4	
Total Subscriptions:	757,209		
Single Copy Sales:	48,028	6.0	
Total Paid	805,237	100.0	
Paid Advertising Rate Base:			800,000
% Above/Below Rate Base (+/–)			0.7

PRICES

2A **AVERAGE PRICE**

Represents the price of individual subscriptions sold during the 12 month period ending December 31, 2001

Average subscription price:	Net	Gross
Per Copy	$1.58	$2.10 (optional)
Annualized	$15.80	$21.00 (optional)
Single copy cover price		$3.95
Publisher's suggested 1 year price		$24.95

2B **SUPPLEMENTAL ANALYSIS OF PRICE**

Gross individual subscriptions sold in the six month period ended June 30, 2002 at below 35% of average net price.

1 yr. $4.50, See Par. 9(d) 38,000
Total . . . . 38,000 (8.9% of total new and renewal subscriptions for the six-month period)

ANALYSIS OF TOTAL NEW AND RENEWAL SUBSCRIPTIONS

3 Total gross individual subscriptions (new and renewal) sold in the six month period ended June 30, 2002

A. DURATION		%
(a) One to six months (1 to 5 issues)	21,527	5.0
(b) Seven to eleven months (6 to 9 issues)	6,695	1.6
(c) Twelve months (10 issues)	270,530	63.3
(d) Thirteen to twenty-four months	71,149	16.7
(e) Twenty-five months and more	57,099	13.4
Total Subscriptions Sold in Period	427,000	100.0

B. USE OF PREMIUMS		
(a) Ordered without premium	427,000	100.0
(b) Ordered with material reprinted from this publication	None	
(c) Ordered with other premiums	None	
Total Subscriptions Sold in Period	427,000	100.0

C. CHANNELS		%
(a) Ordered by mail and/or direct request (may include direct mail, renewal mail, insert cards, television, direct mail agents, Internet and e-mail, etc.)	273,399	64.0
(b) Ordered through salespeople		
1. Catalog agencies and individual agents - includes institutional and library subscriptions	4,597	1.1
2. Publisher's own and independent salespeople - includes sales through both direct personal contact and telemarketing efforts for consumer, trade and public place subscriptions	116,853	27.4
3. Members of schools, churches, fraternal and similar organizations - includes fund raising programs directed to individuals	12,161	2.8
(c) Association members, See Par. 9(c)	20,000	4.7
Total Subscriptions Sold in Period	427,000	100.0

This publication also has Web Site Activity audited by ABC

www. ABC Interactive *June 1 - 30, 2002* Latest Data Available

	Total	Daily	Mon. to Fri.	Sat. & Sun.
Page Impressions	292,550	8,948	40,741	6,540
Unique Users	4,723,001	157,434	178,245	100,201

7/26/2002

ANALYSIS OF AVERAGE CIRCULATION

4A **PAID BY ISSUE**

Issue	Subscriptions	Single Copy Sales	Total Paid
Jan.	759,381	46,228	805,609
Feb.	758,848	46,601	805,449
Mar.	756,100	48,436	804,536
Apr.	753,899	51,602	805,501
May/June	757,818	47,273	805,091

4B **SUPPLEMENTAL ANALYSIS OF AVERAGE PAID CIRCULATION**

The following averages, as reported below, are included in Par. 1 and annotated here per applicable rules. See Par. 9 for full explanation.

Subscriptions:
Club/Membership (1), See Par. 9(f) 90,000
Public Place/Sponsored Sales (1), See Par. 9(g) 100,000

(1) This average exceeds 10% of average subscription circulation as reported in Par. 1.

AVERAGE CIRCULATION of Regional Metro and Demographic Editions

5

Edition & Number of Issues	Paid
South (5)	130,000
Northeast (5)	170,000

POST EXPIRATION COPIES

6 (a) Average number of copies served on subscriptions not more than three months after expiration. 3,750 0.4%

GEOGRAPHIC DATA for the April, 2002 Issue

7A **ANALYSIS BY ABCD COUNTY SIZE**

Paid circulation of this issue was 0.0% greater than the total average paid circulation.

County Size	% of Households	Paid Circulation	% of Total Circulation	Index (% of Circulation/ % of Households)
A	40	364,174	46.8	117
B	30	240,133	30.8	103
C	15	103,535	13.3	89
D	15	70,598	9.1	61

County Size Group Definitions by the A.C. Nielsen Company- Data for the conterminous 48 states.

Page 2 of 4 - Prototype Magazine (04-0000-0)

Exhibit 12-12 Example of an Audit Bureau of Circulations publisher's statement

Advertisers generally attach greater value to the primary in-home reader than the pass-along reader or out-of-home reader, as the former generally spends more time with the publication, picks it up more often, and receives greater satisfaction from it. Thus, this reader is more likely to be attentive and responsive to ads. However, the value of pass-along readers should not be discounted. They can greatly expand a magazine's readership. *People* magazine commissioned a media research study to determine that its out-of-home audience spends as much time reading the publication as do its primary in-home readers.

You can calculate the **total audience,** or **readership,** of a magazine by multiplying the readers per copy (the total number of primary and pass-along readers) by the circulation of an average issue. For example, a magazine that has a circulation of 1 million and 3.5 readers per copy has a total audience of 3.5 million. However, rate structures are generally based on the more verifiable primary circulation figures, and many media planners devalue pass-along readers by as much as 50 percent. Total readership estimates are reported by major syndicated magazine research services (discussed next), but media buyers view these numbers with suspicion.

Audience Information and Research for Magazines

A very valuable source for information on magazines is the Standard Rate and Data Service (SRDS), whose print and online service provides complete planning information on domestic and international consumer magazines as well as business and health care trade publications. The SRDS proprietary database contains standardized ad rates, circulation figures, dates, general requirements, contact information, and links to online media kits, websites, and audit statements that provide additional information on readership and positioning. Exhibit 12-13 shows an example of the type of information that is available about magazines from SRDS.

While circulation and total audience size are important in selecting a media vehicle, the media planner is also interested in the match between the magazine's readers and the advertiser's target audience. Information on readers is available from several

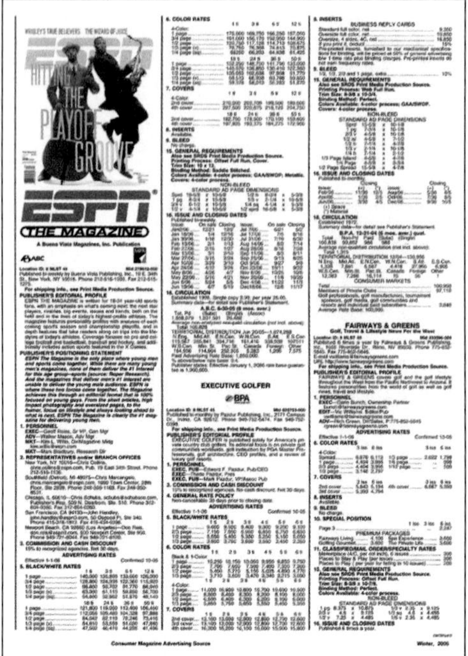
ESPN THE MAGAZINE

A Buena Vista Magazines, Inc. Publication

6. COLOR RATES

7. COVERS

8. INSERTS

9. BLEED

15. GENERAL REQUIREMENTS

16. ISSUE AND CLOSING DATES

18. CIRCULATION

EXECUTIVE GOLFER

FAIRWAYS & GREENS

Golf, Travel & Lifestyle News For the West

Consumer Magazine Advertising Source

Exhibit 12-13 Information about magazines is available from SRDS

sources, including the publication's own research and syndicated studies. Most magazines provide media planners with reports detailing readers' demographics, financial profile, lifestyle, and product usage characteristics. The larger the publication, the more detailed and comprehensive the information it usually can supply about its readers.

Syndicated research studies are also available. For consumer magazines, primary sources of information are Simmons Market Research Bureau's *Study of Media and Markets* and the studies of Mediamark Research Inc. (MRI). These studies provide a broad range of information on the audiences of major national and regional magazines, including demographics, lifestyle characteristics, and product purchase and usage data. Most large ad agencies and media buying services also conduct ongoing research on the media habits of consumers. All this information helps determine the value of various magazines in reaching particular types of product users.

Audience information is generally more limited for business publications than for consumer magazines. The widely dispersed readership and nature of business publication readers make audience research more difficult. Media planners generally rely on information provided by the publication or by sources such as Business Publication Audits, which provide the titles of individuals who receive the publication and the type of industry in which they work. This information can be of value in understanding the audiences reached by various business magazines.

Purchasing Magazine Advertising Space

Cost Elements

Magazine rates are primarily a function of circulation. Other variables include the size of the ad, its position in the publication, the particular editions (geographic, demographic) chosen, any special mechanical or production requirements, and the number and frequency of insertions.

Advertising space is generally sold on the basis of space units such as full page, half page, and quarter page, although some publications quote rates on the basis of column inches. The larger the ad, the greater the cost. However, many advertisers use full-page ads since they result in more attention and readership. Studies have found that full-page ads generated 30 percent more readership than half-page ads.[18]

Ads can be produced or run using black and white, black and white plus one color, or four colors. The more color used in the ad, the greater the expense because of the increased printing costs. On average, a four-color ad costs 30 percent more than a black-and-white ad. Advertisers generally prefer color ads because they have greater visual impact and are superior for attracting and holding attention.[19] Roper Starch Worldwide analyzed the effect of various factors on the readership of magazine ads. The "noted" scores (the percentage of readers who remember seeing the ad in a publication they read) are anywhere from 6 to 59 percent higher for a four-color full-page ad than for a black-and-white ad, depending on the product category. "Read-most" scores (the percentage who say they read more than half of the copy of an ad) are also higher for four-color versus black-and-white ads, by about 25 percent on average.[20] Other studies have examined the impact of size and color and found that a four-color spread (two facing pages) outperforms a one-page color ad by 30 percent and a black-and-white spread by 35 percent in terms of ad recall.[21] Ads requiring special mechanical production such as bleed pages or inserts may also cost extra.

Rates for magazine ad space can also vary according to the number of times an ad runs and the amount of money spent during a specific period. The more often an advertiser contracts to run an ad, the lower are the space charges. Volume discounts are based on the total space purchased within a contract year, measured in dollars. Advertisers can also save money by purchasing advertising in magazine combinations, or networks.

Magazine networks offer the advertiser the opportunity to buy space in a group of publications as a package deal. The publisher usually has a variety of magazines that reach audiences with similar characteristics. Networks can also be publishers of a group of magazines with diversified audiences or independent networks that sell space in groups of magazines published by different companies. For example, the News Network sells space in a group of news-oriented publications such as *Time, Newsweek,* and *U.S. News & World Report.* The Ivy League Magazine Network is a consortium of alumni magazines of Ivy League schools and one non-Ivy, Stanford University. Advertisers can purchase ad space and reach the well-educated, affluent alumni of all eight schools with one media purchase through the network (Exhibit 12-14).

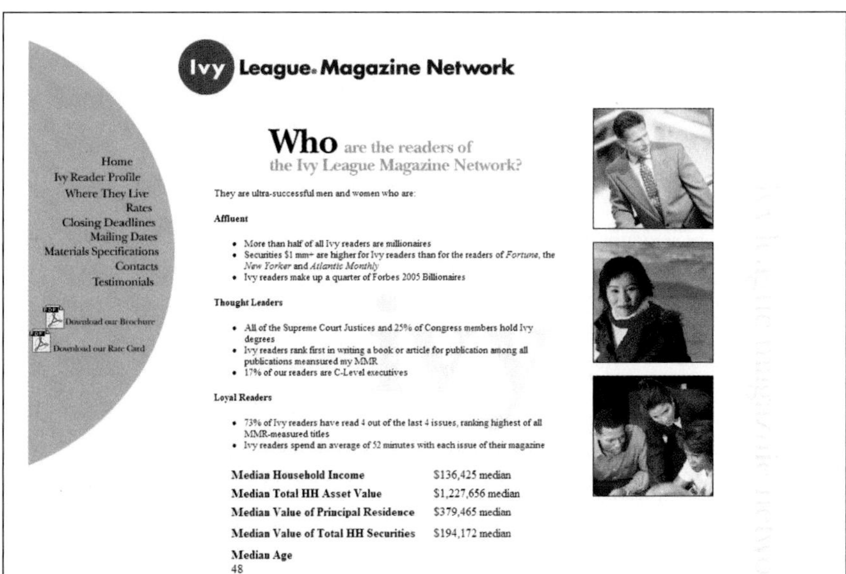

Exhibit 12-14 Advertisers can reach alumni of Ivy League schools through the Ivy League Network

The Future for Magazines

Like other major advertising media, magazines are strongly impacted by the economy and the increases and decreases in ad spending that occur with changes in economic situations. The past several years have been very difficult for the magazine industry; many publications experienced reductions in revenue as advertisers cut back on spending due to the recession.[22] Many publications saw their number of advertising pages decline and found it difficult to raise their rates to offset the reduction in ad pages. And while advertising revenue has been decreasing, publishers' other major revenue stream, circulation, has also been declining. Magazines such as *Rosie, YM, Working Woman,* and *Industry Standard* could not survive these reductions in revenue and ceased publication.[23]

A number of other magazines have experienced significant drops in circulation and have to make changes to survive. *TV Guide,* which was an iconic magazine for two generations of Americans, has seen its circulation drop from more than 12 million in 1998 to a guaranteed circulation of just over 3.2 million in 2005. The magazine struggled to remain relevant in an era where more people get TV listings from their newspapers or through on-screen programming guides from their cable and satellite providers. The magazine changed to a larger, full-color format with fewer listings and more stories about TV shows and stars.[24]

While the health of the economy has a major impact on the magazine industry, there are a number of other important issues facing the industry. The costs of paper and ink continue to rise, and the industry has had to weather several significant increases in postal rates in recent years, which have had a major impact on their cost structure.[25] Magazines are also facing strong competition from other media such as television, the Internet, and direct mail. IMC Perspective 12-3 discusses how many magazines are facing pressure from advertisers to offer them the opportunity for more creative ways to promote their products, some of which threaten the traditional church-and-state divide between editorial versus advertising. Publishers are looking at a number of ways to improve their position—including stronger editorial platforms, better circulation management, cross-magazine and media deals, database marketing, technological advances, and electronic delivery methods—to make advertising in magazines more appealing to marketers.

Stronger Editorial Platforms

Magazines with strong editorial platforms that appeal to the interests, lifestyles, and changing demographics of consumers as well as business and market trends in the new millennium are in the best position to attract readers and advertisers. For example, fashion magazines targeted to both men and women have been experiencing strong growth in circulation and advertising revenue as there is strong interest in their editorial content (as well as the ads), and they deliver

IMC PERSPECTIVE 12-3

Magazines Face Pressure to Blend Advertising with Content

As it becomes increasingly difficult to reach consumers with traditional advertising messages, many marketers have been turning to alternative ways to promote their products and services. Product placement is very common in movies and TV shows and brands have seeped into video games, websites, and even the plots of novels. And now marketers are attempting to mix ad messages and content in magazines in various ways such as running ads next to magazine stories about the same type of product or service, getting products mentioned in stories, creating contests linked to magazines, and running ads that look like magazine layouts. The marketers argue that they are trying to break through the clutter and come up with more creative media solutions as they are doing in other media. However, critics argue that they are threatening one of the most important assets of a magazine—its relationship with readers.

The church-and-state divide of editorial versus advertising has always been important; magazine and newspaper publishers regard the separation as essential to their independence and credibility. For years the American Society of Magazine Editors (ASME) has maintained guidelines for upholding that separation. ASME guidelines state that ad pages should not be related to editorial material in a manner that implies editorial endorsement, "including advertising that features the same celebrity or product image as the cover image." The guidelines also state that no ad or promotional contest may be promoted on the cover or in the table of contents, including cover stickers and other inserts; ad pages should look distinctly different than editorial pages, and if they don't, they must be "clearly and conspicuously identified as a message paid for by advertisers." Although the ASME has no formal means to enforce its guidelines, it does preside over the annual National Magazine awards, which are highly valued in the magazine industry. A magazine that violates the guidelines risks being declared ineligible for the awards or expelled from the society.

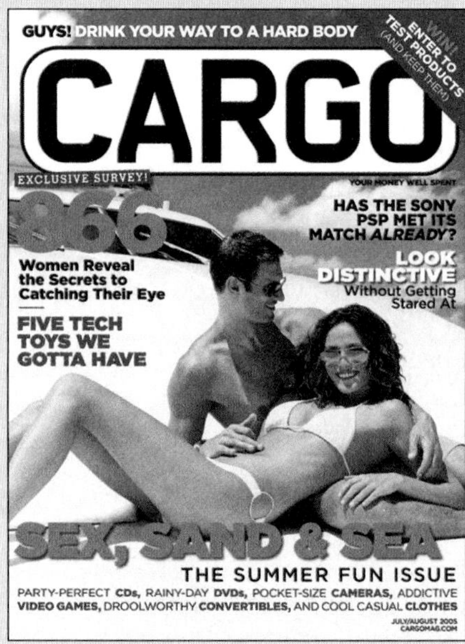

Some industry experts point out that these are very limited sanctions and there is really very little the ASME can do to prevent breaches of its guidelines. However, the magazine industry recognizes that it is important to adhere to them to maintain the integrity of their publications. Readers often view their magazines as authoritative and as a source of valuable information, and editorial content can strongly influence perceptions, opinions, and behavior. One of the advantages of magazines as an advertising medium is their relationship with readers and their opportunity to reach them at a time of intense focus and receptivity. Richard Beckman, chief marketing officer of Condé Nast Publications, notes, "No other media can offer that connectivity to the degree that print does. When that church-and-state line gets blurred, the long-term prognosis for those that do it is not good."

Although magazine publishers recognize that they must maintain the separation, they are increasingly pressured by some marketers to break down or breach the advertising-editorial divide. Marketers argue that they need more creative media solutions and have to be able to prove that magazine advertising can increase brand recognition or help boost sales. They are becoming accustomed to branded entertainment deals with other media such as television and the Internet and want to have similar options with magazines. They note that the lines between advertising and editorial are already blurred in areas such as custom publishing, where marketers can completely control the editorial content, and the emerging category of new "shopping" magazines or mag-a-logs such as *Lucky, Cargo,* and *Shop Etc.,* which have been launched by major publishers such as Condé Nast and Hearst. These publications contain a very high number of advertising pages, and the editorial content gives readers information on what products are in style as well as how much they cost, where to find them, and even phone numbers for merchandise orders.

The pressure on magazines to respond to the demands of marketers to allow a mix of advertising with content is getting greater, particularly since some publications are facing decline in circulation and advertising pages. Magazines are facing strong competition from other media, and if advertisers cannot do what they want in print, they may look to alternative media such as the Internet or video games where they have more opportunities to integrate their brands and messages into content. Industry executives note that we now live in a marketing-driven world where commercialization of the landscape now encompasses stadiums, arenas, and even public spaces such as national parks. They argue that magazines will have to adapt to remain competitive. However, others note that marketers are taking on their biggest challenge yet as they attempt to infiltrate the editorial content of magazines: the church-and-state division lies at the heart of what magazines sell to their readers, as well as the advertisers themselves.

Source: Scott Donaton, "Line between Editorial, Sales Still Needs Vigorous Defense," *Advertising Age,* December 13, 2004, p. 16; Brian Steinberg and James Bandler, "Blurring the Line?" *The Wall Street Journal,* August 9, 2004, pp. B1, 3; Jon Fine, "Mags &Vine," *Advertising Age,* April 12, 2004, pp. 1, 65, 66.

a very desirable, upscale audience to advertisers. Luxury brands including cars, clothing, jewelry, and consumer electronics have been increasing spending in women's publications such as *InStyle, Vogue,* and *Allure* as well as men's magazines such as *GQ* and *Esquire.* Publications such as *Maxim, FHM,* and *Stuff* have also been very successful at targeting a group described as "adultescents," 18- to 34-year-old males who cling to the trappings of youth culture.[26]

Circulation Management

One of the major challenges facing magazine publishers is trying to increase or even maintain their circulation bases. Circulation is the second major source of revenue for most publications, and publishers must carefully manage the costs of attracting and maintaining additional readers or subscribers. The cost of acquiring subscriptions has increased dramatically over the past decade. At the same time, there has been a decline in the prices consumers pay for subscriptions. In 1995, the average magazine subscription rate was $29.42. In 2004, it was $25.93. Thus, publishers have to pay more to maintain their rate bases (the circulation level guaranteed to advertisers), but they make less money on each subscription sold.

Publishers are also facing a drop in sweepstakes-generated circulation as a result of the controversy that developed over consumer confidence in the sweepstakes-related subscription offers. Agents such as Publishers Clearing House and American Family Enterprises have been going through changes, both self-imposed and externally dictated, that have greatly reduced the number of subscriptions they generate for publishers.[27] To compensate for losses from sweepstakes agents, publishers are looking to other methods of generating subscribers, such as making subscriptions available through websites, offering free trial copies online, conducting special promotions, or using other agents such as school-related subscription services.[28]

Many magazines are also focusing more attention on managing their circulation bases. For many years, magazines focused on increasing their circulation under the assumption that higher circulation meant higher advertising rates. However, publishers are now realizing that the cost of attracting and maintaining the last 10 to 15 percent of their circulation base is often greater than the additional revenue generated, since these subscribers require numerous direct-mail solicitations, premium offers, or discount subscriptions.

A number of magazines have reduced their circulation base in recent years. Many publishers believe they can pass on price increases more easily to their core readers or subscribers and offer advertisers a more loyal and focused audience. Many advertisers welcome the improvement in circulation management. They would rather reach a few hundred thousand fewer subscribers than pay for inefficient circulation and be hit with advertising rate increases each year. Many magazines are also using the monies saved on the circulation side to improve the editorial content of their publications, which should attract more readers—and advertisers.

Cross-Magazine and Media Deals

Another important development involves the way ad space is sold; there will be more cross- or multimagazine and cross-media ad packages. **Multimagazine deals** involve two or more publishers offering their magazines to an advertiser as one package. For example, *Newsweek* offers cross-magazine deals with several other publishers, including Meredith and Time & Media. Many magazines are also making **cross-media advertising** deals that include several different media opportunities from a single company or a partnership of media providers. For example, with the merger of America Online (AOL) and Time Warner, the new company offers advertisers the opportunity for cross-media deals whereby they can advertise in magazines owned by the media conglomerate, such as *Time, Sports Illustrated, People,* and *Fortune;* on its TV stations, such as CNN, TNT, TBS, and the WB Network; and through AOL and other websites.[29]

Database Marketing

Many advertisers are increasingly turning to magazines as a cost-efficient way of reaching specialized audiences. As marketers continue to move toward greater market segmentation, market niche strategies, and regional marketing, they are making greater use of magazines because of their high selectivity and ability to avoid wasted coverage or circulation. Magazines are using advances in technology and

Exhibit 12-15 Magazines such as *Mother Jones* are now available online

database marketing to divide their audiences on the basis of demographics, psychographics, or regions and to deliver more personalized advertising messages. Database marketing lets advertisers personalize their advertising by merging their own databases with those of a magazine. By selectively accessing information from a magazine's database, advertisers can choose from an array of information on consumers, such as product usage or purchase intention data. Marketers will increasingly advertise in magazines that are targeted specifically to narrow groups of subscribers.

Advances in Technology

Publishers are also developing new technologies that will enhance the creative opportunities available to magazine advertisers. Advertisers use a variety of techniques in print ads to capture readers' attention, including sound, scents, moving images, and pop-up ads. Current technologies are being refined and made more cost effective, and a number of new technologies are being incorporated into print ads. These include anaglyphic images (three-dimensional materials that are viewed with colored glasses); lenticular (color) images printed on finely corrugated plastic that seem to move when tilted; and pressure- or heat-sensitive inks that change color on contact. These technologies give advertisers ways to break through the advertising clutter. However, these new print technologies can be very costly. Moreover, many advertisers and agencies are concerned that ads that use these new technologies may do so at the expense of other ads in the magazine, so they may pressure publishers to control their use. Some creative people have also expressed concern that these new technologies are gimmicks being substituted for creative advertising ideas.[30]

Online Delivery Methods

Many magazines are keeping pace with the digital revolution and the continuing consumer interest in technology by making their publications available online. There are more than 600 magazines with online versions, and many more are becoming available each month. Online versions of magazines such as *Mother Jones* offer the many advantages of the Internet to publishers and subscribers (Exhibit 12-15). They also provide advertisers with the opportunity for sponsorships as well as banner ads and promotions on the online versions of the magazines. However, it remains to be seen whether people will want their magazines delivered online or prefer to read them in more traditional form. As the presence of magazines online grows, the industry will also have to address important issues regarding audience measurement and how to determine consumers' exposure to and interactions with online advertising. Advertising on the Internet is discussed in Chapter 15.

Newspapers

Newspapers, the second major form of print media, are the largest of all advertising media in terms of total dollar volume. In 2005, an estimated $44 billion was spent on newspaper advertising, or about 18 percent of the total advertising expenditures in the United States. Newspapers are an especially important advertising medium to local advertisers, particularly retailers. However, newspapers are also valuable to national advertisers. Many of the advertising dollars spent by local retailers are actually provided by national advertisers through cooperative advertising programs (discussed in Chapter 16). Newspapers vary in terms of their characteristics and their role as an advertising medium.

Types of Newspapers

The traditional role of newspapers has been to deliver prompt, detailed coverage of news as well as to supply other information and features that appeal to readers. The vast majority of newspapers are daily publications serving a local community. However, weekly, national, and special-audience newspapers have special characteristics that can be valuable to advertisers.

Daily Newspapers Daily newspapers, which are published each weekday, are found in cities and larger towns across the country. Many areas have more than one daily paper. Daily newspapers are read by nearly 54 percent of adults each weekday and by 63 percent on Sundays.[31] They provide detailed coverage of news, events, and issues concerning the local area as well as business, sports, and other relevant information and entertainment. Daily newspapers can further be classified as morning, evening, or Sunday publications. In 2004, there were 1,457 daily newspapers in the United States; of these, 47 percent were evening papers and 53 percent morning. There were also 917 Sunday newspapers, most of which were published by daily newspapers.

Weekly Newspapers Most weekly newspapers originate in small towns or suburbs where the volume of news and advertising cannot support a daily newspaper. These papers focus primarily on news, sports, and events relevant to the local area and usually ignore national and world news, sports, and financial and business news. There are 6,700 weekly newspapers published in the United States, and they have an average circulation of close to 7,500. Weeklies appeal primarily to local advertisers because of their geographic focus and lower absolute cost. Most national advertisers avoid weekly newspapers because of their duplicate circulation with daily or Sunday papers in the large metropolitan areas and problems in contracting for and placing ads in these publications. However, the contracting and scheduling problems associated with these papers have been reduced by the emergence of syndicates that publish them in a number of areas and sell ad space in all of their local newspapers through one office.

National Newspapers Newspapers in the United States with national circulation include *USA Today, The Wall Street Journal,* and *The Christian Science Monitor.* All three are daily publications and have editorial content with a nationwide appeal. *USA Today,* which positions itself as "the nation's newspaper," has the largest circulation of any newspaper in the country, at 2.3 million copies a day. *The Wall Street Journal* sells over 1.8 million copies a day and is an excellent means of reaching businesspeople. National newspapers appeal primarily to large national advertisers and to regional advertisers that use specific geographic editions of these publications. For example, *The Wall Street Journal* has three geographic editions covering 18 regions in which ads can be placed, while *USA Today* offers advertisers the opportunity to run ads in its national edition or any of 25 regionals.

In 1999, the *New York Times* was classified as a national newspaper rather than a regional publication by Competitive Media Reporting, which has developed a new policy on how it defines national newspapers.[32] This policy states that a paper must publish at least five times a week and have no more than 67 percent of its distribution in any one area. More than 33 percent of its display advertising must come from national advertising categories, and more than 50 percent of its advertising must come from national advertisers. Designation as a national newspaper is important to major newspapers in attracting national advertisers.[33] Exhibit 12-16 shows how *The New York Times* promotes its national and local reach.

Exhibit 12-16 *The New York Times* promotes its classification as a national newspaper

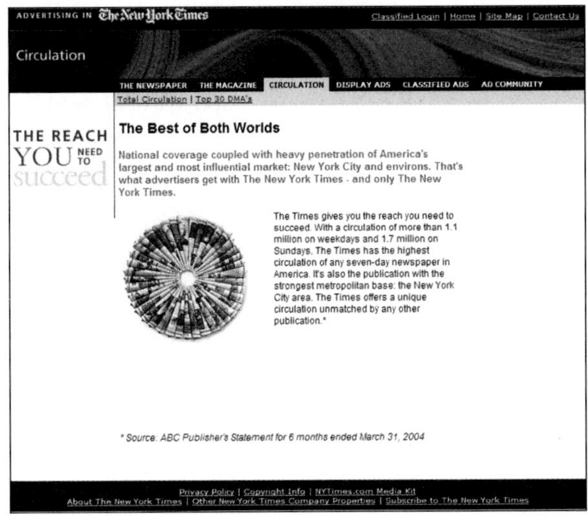

Special-Audience Newspapers A variety of papers offer specialized editorial content and are published for particular groups, including labor unions, professional organizations, industries, and hobbyists. Many people working in advertising read *Advertising Age,* while those in the marketing area read *Marketing News.* Specialized newspapers are also published in areas with large foreign-language-speaking ethnic groups, among them Polish, Chinese, Hispanics, Vietnamese, and Filipinos. In the United States, there are newspapers printed in more than 40 languages.

See what *The Daily Aztec* says about the campus Master Plan.

opinion page 13

Jeff Schemmel has a message for San Diego State students.

sports page 23

SAN DIEGO STATE UNIVERSITY

THE DAILY AZTEC

INDEPENDENT STUDENT NEWSPAPER

Wednesday, August 24, 2005

VOLUME 91 ISSUE 01

www.thedailyaztec.com

Tomorrow's weather: Mostly sunny; High: 74° F Low: 67° F

Friday's weather: Mostly cloudy; High: 77° F Low: 66° F

Today's surf: 2-3 ft., Waist high; Fair Conditions

San Diego AMERICA'S FINEST CITY

on $20 and a tank of gas.....

SAM HODGSON AND CONSUELA HEADRICK

CITY EDITOR, OPINION EDITOR

What does a starving student do for a good time in this town? For years, fraternity parties, cheap burritos and the prospect of getting laid has kept San Diego State students confined to the College Area for most of their freshman year. Why venture into the unknown when you've got good things within walking distance? Well, although the real world can be a scary place, the SDSU area can get old – fast.

In a typical school year, an SDSU student spends thousands of dollars on tuition, housing, rising book prices, transportation, food and the occasional health care expense. With bank accounts depleted and credit cards maxed out, many students find out the hard way that they live in one of the most expensive cities in the country. Without including personal expenses, the average student living on campus spends about $15,000 during the nine-month school year, according to SDSU's Office of Admissions Web site. Whether your parents are picking up the tab or you're already knee deep in debt, $15,000 is a lot of money. Whichever way you cut it, many students are left with little to no disposable income after taking care of the essentials.

see SAN DIEGO on page 19

Welcome

life is a highway.

Exhibit 12-17 College newspapers such as *The Daily Aztec* are an excellent way to reach students

Newspapers targeted at various religious groups compose another large class of special-interest papers. For example, more than 140 Catholic newspapers are published across the United States. Another type of special-audience newspaper is one most of you probably read regularly during the school year, the college newspaper. More than 1,300 colleges and universities publish newspapers that offer advertisers an excellent medium for reaching college students (Exhibit 12-17).

Newspaper Supplements Although not a category of newspapers per se, many papers include magazine-type supplements, primarily in their Sunday editions. Sunday supplements have been part of most newspapers for many years and come in various forms. One type is the syndicated Sunday magazine, such as *Parade* or *USA Weekend,* distributed in hundreds of papers throughout the country. *Parade* has a circulation of over 35 million; *USA Weekend* is carried by more than 600 newspapers with a combined circulation of over 22 million. These publications are similar to national magazines and carry both national and regional advertising.

Some large newspapers publish local Sunday supplements distributed by the parent paper. These supplements contain stories of more local interest, and both local and national advertisers buy ad space. *The New York Times Sunday Magazine* is the best-known local supplement. The *Washington Post, San Francisco Examiner,* and *Los Angeles Times* have their own Sunday magazines.

In some areas, papers have begun carrying regional supplements as well as specialized weekday supplements that cover specific topics such as food, sports, or entertainment. Supplements are valuable to advertisers that want to use the newspaper yet get four-color reproduction quality in their ads.

Types of Newspaper Advertising

The ads appearing in newspapers can also be divided into different categories. The major types of newspaper advertising are display and classified. Other special types of ads and preprinted inserts also appear in newspapers.

Display Advertising **Display advertising** is found throughout the newspaper and generally uses illustrations, headlines, white space, and other visual devices in addition to the copy text. Display ads account for approximately 70 percent of the advertising revenue of the average newspaper. The two types of display advertising in newspapers are local and national (general).

Local advertising refers to ads placed by local organizations, businesses, and individuals who want to communicate with consumers in the market area served by the newspaper. Supermarkets and department stores are among the leading local display advertisers, along with numerous other retailers and service operations such as banks and travel agents. Local advertising is sometimes referred to as retail advertising because retailers account for 85 percent of local display ads.

National or *general advertising* refers to newspaper display advertising done by marketers of branded products or services that are sold on a national or regional level. These ads are designed to create and maintain demand for a company's product or service and to complement the efforts of local retailers that stock and promote the advertiser's products. Major retail chains, automakers, and airlines are heavy users of newspaper advertising.

Classified Advertising **Classified advertising** also provides newspapers with a substantial amount of revenue. These ads are arranged under subheads according to the product, service, or offering being advertised. Employment, real estate, and automotive are the three major categories of classified advertising. While most classified ads are just text set in small type, some newspapers also accept classified display advertising. These ads are run in the classified section of the paper but use illustrations, larger type sizes, white space, borders, and even color to stand out.

Exhibit 12-18 Newspaper inserts are used to reach target markets

Special Ads and Inserts

Special advertisements in newspapers include a variety of government and financial reports and notices and public notices of changes in business and personal relationships. Other types of advertising in newspapers include political or special-interest ads promoting a particular candidate, issue, or cause. **Preprinted inserts** are another type of advertising distributed through newspapers. These ads do not appear in the paper itself; they are printed by the advertiser and then taken to the newspaper to be inserted before delivery. Many retailers use inserts such as circulars, catalogs, or brochures in specific circulation zones to reach shoppers in their particular trade areas. Exhibit 12-18 shows how the *San Diego Union-Tribune* promotes its insert distribution service to advertisers.

Advantages of Newspapers

Newspapers have a number of characteristics that make them popular among both local and national advertisers. These include their extensive penetration of local markets, flexibility, geographic selectivity, reader involvement, and special services.

Extensive Penetration

One of the primary advantages of newspapers is the high degree of market coverage, or penetration, they offer an advertiser. In most areas, 50 percent or more of households read a daily newspaper, and the reach figure may exceed 70 percent among households with higher incomes and education levels. Most areas are served by one or two daily newspapers, and often the same company owns both, publishing a morning and an evening edition. By making one space buy, the advertiser can achieve a high level of overall reach in a particular market.

The extensive penetration of newspapers makes them a truly mass medium and provides advertisers with an excellent opportunity for reaching all segments of the population with their message. Also, since many newspapers are published and read daily, the advertiser can build a high level of frequency into the media schedule.

Exhibit 12-19 Bridgestone Golf used a newspaper ad for a timely salute to professional golfer Stuart Appleby

Flexibility

Another advantage of newspapers is the flexibility they offer advertisers. First, they are flexible in terms of requirements for producing and running the ads. Newspaper ads can be written, laid out, and prepared in a matter of hours. For most dailies, the closing time by which the ad must be received is usually only 24 hours before publication (although closing dates for special ads, such as those using color, and Sunday supplements are longer). The short production time and closing dates make newspapers an excellent medium for responding to current events or presenting timely information to consumers. For example, Bridgestone Golf ran a newspaper ad congratulating professional golfer Stuart Appleby on his third victory at the Mercedes Championships a few days after the tournament. Appleby is a member of the Bridgestone Golf team and the newspaper ad was a very timely way to acknowledge his accomplishment and promote his use of Bridgestone golf clubs and balls (Exhibit 12-19).

A second dimension of newspapers' flexibility stems from the creative options they make available to advertisers. Newspaper ads can be produced and run in various sizes, shapes, and formats; they can use color or special inserts to gain the interest of readers. Ads can be run in Sunday magazines or other supplements, and a variety of scheduling options are possible, depending on the advertiser's purpose.

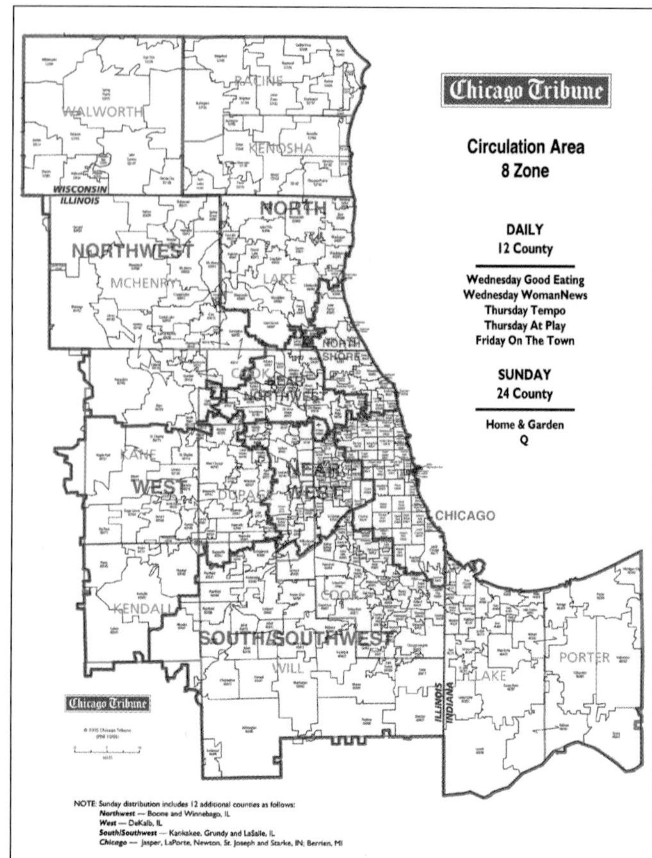

Exhibit 12-20 The *Chicago Tribune* offers advertisers combinations of different circulation area zones

MEDIA SNAPSHOT — SAN DIEGO MARKETBOOK

daily paper

THE SAN DIEGO UNION-TRIBUNE DAILY READERSHIP: 860,950

MAIN NEWS
The San Diego Union-Tribune is read by more San Diegans than any other newspaper — that's 860,950 consumers daily.

LOCAL NEWS
Six targeted editions cover the county completely, from the North Coastal cities to the South Bay and all points in between.

SPORTS
Award-winning coverage and nationally-ranked professional sports teams make the Sports section a prime pick.

SPORTS EXTRA — MONDAY
Recaps of the weekend's big games, results, trades, news and more. An in-depth vehicle to reach San Diego sports lovers.

BUSINESS
From the work week to Wall Street, Business covers national, regional and local news, plus stock and financial information.

BUSINESS / PERSONAL TECHNOLOGY — MONDAY
Local business news-makers, hot technology, computer tidbits and the latest in mergers.

QUEST — WEDNESDAY
Science and technology get front-page space in this special edition of Currents for readers of all ages and interests.

RELIGION & ETHICS — FRIDAY
Movie listings and reviews are always found in Currents, but every Friday the cover story focuses on religion and ethics.

FAMILY — SATURDAY
San Diego families find advice and resources in this Saturday edition devoted to family activities and problem-solving.

CLASSIFIEDS
Where the locals go to buy, sell, trade, find a date or a roommate. Daily and special sections cover all your needs.

FOOD — WEDNESDAY
Those who love to eat and cook turn to Food weekly for recipes, coupons and the newest trends in food and restaurants.

NIGHT & DAY — THURSDAY
This popular entertainment tab covers the latest in arts, dining and leisure. Reach 860,950 San Diegans looking for excitement.

CHANGE OF ADDRESS — SATURDAY
This full-color advertorial section is designed for San Diego's new-home builders to showcase their homes and communities.

WHEELS — SATURDAY
Your road to hot prospects. With four Saturday ads reach 55 percent of San Diegans who plan to buy or lease a new or used vehicle in the next 12 months.

Source: August 2002 - July 2003 San Diego Scarborough Report; The San Diego Union-Tribune ABC Audit for 12 months ending December 31, 2002

Exhibit 12-21 Ads can be run in various sections of most newspapers

Geographic Selectivity Newspapers generally offer advertisers more geographic or territorial selectivity than any other medium except direct mail. Advertisers can vary their coverage by choosing a paper—or combination of papers—that reaches the areas with the greatest sales potential. National advertisers take advantage of the geographic selectivity of newspapers to concentrate their advertising in specific areas they can't reach with other media or to take advantage of strong sales potential in a particular area. For example, BMW, Mercedes, and Volvo use heavy newspaper media schedules in California and New York/New Jersey to capitalize on the high sales potential for luxury import cars in these markets.

A number of companies, including General Motors, Ford, and Campbell, use newspapers in their regional marketing strategies. Newspaper advertising lets them feature products on a market-by-market basis, respond and adapt campaigns to local market conditions, and tie into more retailer promotions, fostering more support from the trade.

Local advertisers like retailers are interested in geographic selectivity or flexibility within a specific market or trade area. Their media goal is to concentrate their advertising on the areas where most of their customers are. Many newspapers now offer advertisers various geographic areas or zones for this purpose. For example, the *Chicago Tribune* offers advertisers a number of different circulation area zones as shown in Exhibit 12-20.

Reader Involvement and Acceptance Another important feature of newspapers is consumers' level of acceptance and involvement with papers and the ads they contain. The typical daily newspaper reader spends time each day reading the weekday newspaper and even more time reading the Sunday paper. Most consumers rely heavily on newspapers not only for news, information, and entertainment but also for assistance with consumption decisions.

Many consumers actually purchase a newspaper *because* of the advertising it contains. Consumers use retail ads to determine product prices and availability and to see who is having a sale. One aspect of newspapers that is helpful to advertisers is readers' knowledge about particular sections of the paper. Most of us know that ads for automotive products and sporting goods are generally found in the sports section, while ads for financial services are found in the business section. The weekly food section in many newspapers is popular for recipe and menu ideas as well as for the grocery store ads and coupons offered by many stores and companies. Exhibit 12-21 shows how the *San Diego Union-Tribune* promotes various sections of the paper to potential advertisers.

The value of newspaper advertising as a source of information has been shown in several studies. One study found that consumers look forward to ads in newspapers more than in other media. In another study, 80 percent of consumers said newspaper ads were most helpful to them in doing their weekly shopping. Newspaper advertising has also been rated the most believable form of advertising in numerous studies.

SAN DIEGO MARKET CLOSE-UP — SAN DIEGO MARKETBOOK

san diegans on the go

WHERE THEY GO AND HOW THEY GET THERE

With more than 80 of the best restaurants, bars, nightclubs, boutiques, art galleries and theaters, the historic Gaslamp District is San Diego's party central.

At the San Diego Convention Center, fiscal year 2003 was a record-breaking year in all categories. Economic impact soared to an unprecedented $996.1 million. 404,600 out-of-town delegates came with an overall attendance of 810,780 people, the highest in seven years.

Three theaters in one, the Old Globe produces at least a dozen plays each year, and is never dark. The complex's centerpiece, the Old Globe Theatre, was designed in the spirit of Shakespeare's original playhouse.

RECREATIONAL ACTIVITIES

ACTIVITY	PARTICIPANTS	PERCENT OF DMA
Gardening	1,021,525	47.0%
Swimming	811,875	37.4%
Arts & Crafts	640,905	29.5%
Jogging/running	610,665	28.1%
Free weights/circuit training	542,775	25.0%
Photography	539,300	24.8%
Bicycling	524,335	24.1%
Bowling	472,665	21.7%
Camping	466,055	21.4%
Team Sports	445,645	20.5%

Source: August 2002 - July 2003 San Diego Scarborough Report

The San Diego Padres, including Trevor Hoffman, play at the new PETCO Park in downtown's East Village.

SPORTING EVENT	ATTENDEES	PERCENT OF DMA
San Diego Padres Baseball	616,070	28.3%
San Diego Chargers Football	242,780	11.2%
San Diego State Aztec Football	112,330	5.2%
San Diego Gulls Hockey	101,675	4.7%
San Diego Sockers	37,285	1.7%

Source: August 2002 - July 2003 San Diego Scarborough Report

Running back LaDainian Tomlinson will carry a big load for the 2004 San Diego Chargers.

Exhibit 12-22 Newspaper publishers are often an excellent source for information on local markets

Services Offered

The special services newspapers offer can be valuable to advertisers. For example, many newspapers offer merchandising services and programs to manufacturers that make the trade aware of ads being run for the company's product and help convince local retailers they should stock, display, and promote the item.

Many newspapers are also excellent sources of local market information through their knowledge of market conditions and research like readership studies and consumer surveys. For example, the publisher of the *San Diego Union-Tribune,* the major daily newspaper in San Diego, provides information on the local market through reports such as the "San Diego Market Close-Up" (Exhibit 12-22).

Newspapers can also assist small companies through free copywriting and art services. Small advertisers without an agency or advertising department often rely on the newspaper to help them write and produce their ads.

Limitations of Newspapers

While newspapers have many advantages, like all media they also have disadvantages that media planners must consider. The limitations of newspapers include their reproduction problems, short life span, lack of selectivity, and clutter.

Poor Reproduction

One of the greatest limitations of newspapers as an advertising medium is their poor reproduction quality. The coarse paper stock used for newspapers, the absence of color, and the lack of time papers have available to achieve high-quality reproduction limit the quality of most newspaper ads. Newspapers have improved their reproduction quality in recent years, and color reproduction has become more available. Also, advertisers desiring high-quality color in newspaper ads can turn to such alternatives as freestanding inserts or Sunday supplements. However, these are more costly and may not be desirable to many advertisers. As a general rule, if the visual appearance of the product is important, the advertiser will not rely on newspaper ads. Ads for food products and fashions generally use magazines to capitalize on their superior reproduction quality and color.

Short Life Span

Unlike magazines, which may be retained around the house for several weeks, a daily newspaper is generally kept less than a day. So an ad is unlikely to have any impact beyond the day of publication, and repeat exposure is very unlikely.

Figure 12-4 U.S. Daily Newspaper Pages or Sections Usually Read

Section Readership	Percent of Weekly Audience					
	Adults	Men	Women	White	African-American	Spanish/Hispanic*
Business/finance	58%	63%	53%	60%	49%	49%
Classified	54	56	52	54	58	55
Comics	58	59	58	59	53	54
Entertainment (movies, theater, etc.)	66	61	70	66	63	64
Food/cooking	55	48	63	57	49	47
Local news section	83	81	85	84	78	75
Main news	88	87	88	88	82	82
Sports	60	73	46	60	58	57
TV/radio listings	52	51	52	53	49	44

*Defined as "of Spanish or Hispanic origin or descent."
Source: Newspaper Association of America, "Facts about Newspapers 2004," www.naa.org.

Compounding this problem are the short amount of time many consumers spend with the newspaper and the possibility they may not even open certain sections of the paper. Media planners can offset these problems somewhat by using high frequency in the newspaper schedule and advertising in a section where consumers who are in the market for a particular product or service are likely to look. Figure 12-4 shows readership figures for various sections of newspapers by gender and ethnic background.

Lack of Selectivity While newspapers can offer advertisers geographic selectivity, they are not a selective medium in terms of demographics or lifestyle characteristics. Most newspapers reach broad and very diverse groups of consumers, which makes it difficult for marketers to focus on narrowly defined market segments. For example, manufacturers of fishing rods and reels will find newspapers very inefficient because of the wasted circulation that results from reaching all the newspaper readers who don't fish. Thus, they are more likely to use special-interest magazines such as *Field & Stream* or *Fishing World.* Any newspaper ads for their products will be done through cooperative plans whereby retailers share the costs or spread them over a number of sporting goods featured in the ad.

Exhibit 12-23 Island ads are a way to break through the clutter in newspaper advertising

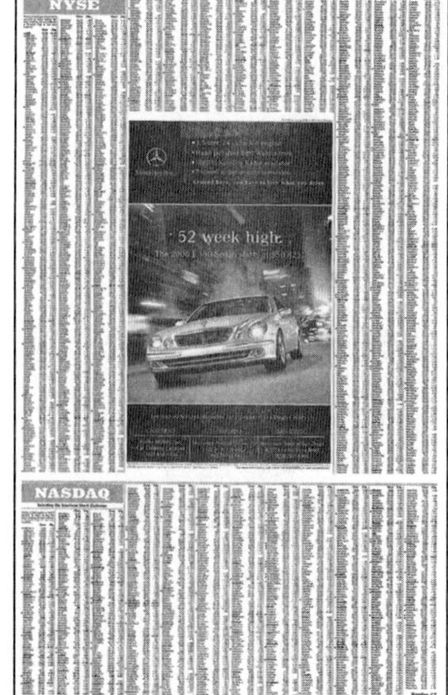

Clutter Newspapers, like most other advertising media, suffer from clutter. Because 64 percent of the average daily newspaper in the United States is devoted to advertising, the advertiser's message must compete with numerous other ads for consumers' attention and interest. Moreover, the creative options in newspapers are limited by the fact that most ads are black and white. Thus, it can be difficult for a newspaper advertiser to break through the clutter without using costly measures such as large space buys or color. Some advertisers use creative techniques like *island ads*—ads surrounded by editorial material. Island ads are found in the middle of the stock market quotes on the financial pages of many newspapers. This type of media placement can be a very effective way to reach upscale customers for various products and services such as luxury automobiles. Exhibit 12-23 shows an island ad for the Mercedes Benz E350 that uses a clever stock price–related headline.

The Newspaper Audience

As with any medium, the media planner must understand the nature and size of the audience reached by a newspaper in considering its value in the media plan. Since newspapers as a class of media do an excellent job of penetrating their market, the typical daily newspaper gives advertisers the opportunity to reach most of the households in a market. But, while local advertisers aim to cover a particular market or trade area, national advertisers want to reach broad regions or even the entire country. They must purchase space in a number of papers to achieve the desired level of coverage.

The basic sources of information concerning the audience size of newspapers come from the circulation figures available through rate cards, publishers' statements, or Standard Rate and Data Service's *Newspaper Advertising Source.* Circulation figures for many newspapers are verified by the Audit Bureau of Circulation, which was discussed earlier. Advertisers that use a number of papers in their media plan generally find SRDS the most convenient source.

Newspaper circulation figures are generally broken down into three categories: the city zone, the retail trading zone, and all other areas. The **city zone** is a market area composed of the city where the paper is published and contiguous areas similar in character to the city. The **retail trading zone** is the market outside the city zone whose residents regularly trade with merchants within the city zone. The "all other" category covers all circulation not included in the city or retail trade zone.

Sometimes circulation figures are provided only for the primary market, which is the city and retail trade zones combined, and the other area. Both local and national advertisers consider the circulation patterns across the various categories in evaluating and selecting newspapers.

National advertisers often buy newspaper space on the basis of the size of the market area they cover. For example, General Motors might decide to purchase advertising in the top 10 markets, the top 50 markets, the top 100 markets, and so on. A national advertiser gets different levels of market coverage depending on the number of market areas purchased.

Audience Information

Circulation figures provide the media planner with the basic data for assessing the value of newspapers and their ability to cover various market areas. However, the media planner also wants to match the characteristics of a newspaper's readers with those of the advertiser's target audience. Data on newspaper audience size and characteristics are available from studies conducted by the papers as well as from commercial research services. As for magazines, a very valuable source for information on newspapers is the SRDS, whose print and online service provides complete planning information on daily papers, newspaper groups, ethnic newspapers, college newspapers, comics, and newspaper-distributed magazines. The SRDS *Newspaper Advertising Source* data contain standardized ad rates, circulation figures, dates, general requirements, contact information, and other valuable information for media.

Companies such as Simmons Market Research Bureau and Mediamark Research Inc. provide syndicated research studies on lifestyles, media behavior, and product/brand preferences that include information on newspapers. These studies can be valuable for comparing newspapers with other media vehicles.

Many newspapers commission their own audience studies to provide current and potential advertisers with information on readership and characteristics of readers such as demographics, shopping habits, and lifestyles. These studies are often designed to promote the effectiveness of the newspaper in reaching various types of consumers. Since they are sponsored by the paper itself, many advertisers are skeptical of their results. Careful attention must be given to the research methods used and conclusions drawn by these studies.

Purchasing Newspaper Space

Advertisers are faced with a number of options and pricing structures when purchasing newspaper space. The cost of advertising space depends not only on the newspaper's circulation but also on factors such as premium charges for color or special sections as well as discounts available. The purchase process and the rates paid for newspaper space differ for general and local advertisers.

General versus Local Rates

Newspapers have different rate structures for general or national advertisers and local or retail advertisers. **General advertising rates** apply to display advertisers outside the newspaper's designated market area (DMA) and to any classification deemed by the publisher to be "general" in nature.

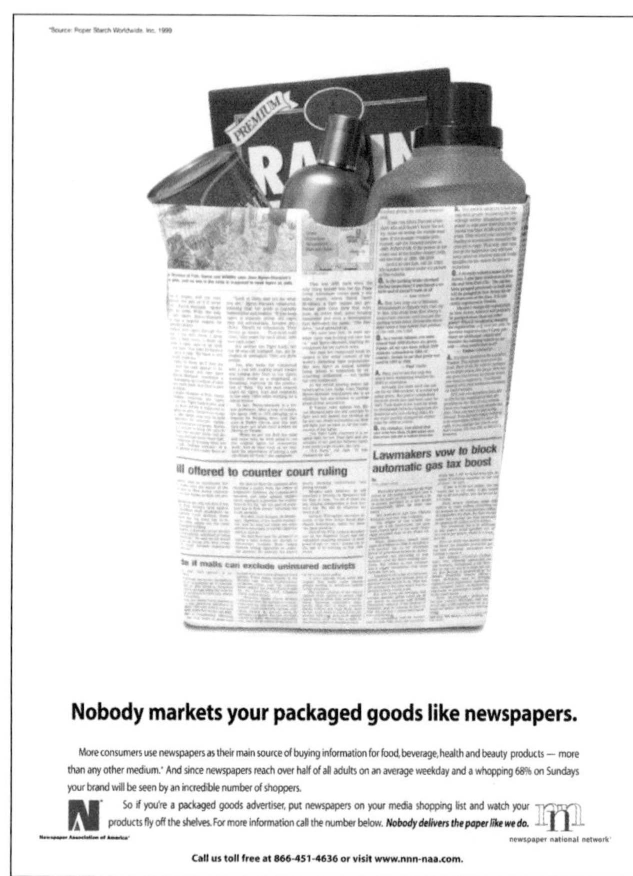

Lawmakers vow to block automatic gas tax boost
Nobody markets your packaged goods like newspapers.
More consumers use newspapers as their main source of buying information for food, beverage, health and beauty products — more than any other medium.* And since newspapers reach over half of all adults on an average weekday and a whopping 68% on Sundays your brand will be seen by an incredible number of shoppers.
So if you're a packaged goods advertiser, put newspapers on your media shopping list and watch your products fly off the shelves. For more information call the number below. Nobody delivers the paper like we do.
Newspaper Association of America
newspaper national network
Call us toll free at 866-451-4636 or visit www.nnn-naa.com.

Exhibit 12-24 The Newspaper National Network encourages national advertisers to run their ads in newspapers

This includes ads run by national advertisers such as automotive, tobacco, packaged-goods, and pharmaceutical companies. **Retail** or **local advertising rates** apply to advertisers that conduct business or sell goods or services within the DMA. The rates paid by general advertisers are, on average, 75 percent higher than those paid by local advertisers. Newspaper publishers claim the rate differential is justified for several reasons. First, they argue it costs more to handle general advertising since ad agencies get a 15 percent commission and commissions must also be paid to the independent sales reps who solicit nonlocal advertising. Second, they note that general advertising is less dependable than local advertising; general advertisers usually don't use newspapers on a continual basis like local advertisers do. Finally, newspaper publishers contend that demand for general advertising is inelastic—it will not increase if rates are lowered or decrease if rates are raised. This means there is no incentive to lower the national advertisers' rates.

National advertisers do not view these arguments as valid justification for the rate differential. They argue that the costs are not greater for handling national advertising than for local business and that many national advertisers use newspapers on a regular basis. Since they use an agency to prepare their ads, national advertisers are less likely to request special services. The large and costly staff maintained by many newspapers to assist in the design and preparation of advertising is used mostly by local advertisers.

The differential rate structure for national versus local advertising has been the source of considerable controversy. Some newspapers are making efforts to narrow the rate differential, as is the Newspaper Association of America (NAA). In 1993, the NAA created the Newspaper National Network (NNN) to target national advertisers in six low-use categories: automotive, cosmetics and toiletries, food, household products, liquor and beverages, and drugs and remedies.[34] The network's goal is to attract more advertising dollars from national advertisers in these categories by promoting the strategic use of newspapers and facilitating the purchase of newspaper space with their one order/one bill model. Exhibit 12-24 shows an ad encouraging national advertisers to place their ads in newspapers through the NNN.

Many marketers sidestep the national advertiser label and the higher rates by channeling their newspaper ads through special category plans, cooperative advertising deals with retailers, and local dealers and distributors that pay local rates. However, the rate differential does keep many national advertisers from making newspapers a larger part of their media mix.

Newspaper Rates

Traditionally, newspaper space for national advertisers has been sold by the agate line. The problem is that newspapers use columns of varying width. Some have six columns per page, while others have eight or nine, which affects the size, shape, and costs of an ad. This results in a complicated production and buying process for national advertisers purchasing space in a number of newspapers.

To address this problem and make newspapers more comparable to other media that sell space and time in standard units, the newspaper industry switched to **standard advertising units (SAUs)** in 1984. All newspapers under this system use column widths $2^{1}/_{16}$ inches wide, with tabloid-size papers five columns wide and standard or broadcast papers six columns. The column inch is the unit of measurement to create the 57 standard units or format sizes shown in Figure 12-5.

A national advertiser can prepare one ad in a particular SAU, and it will fit every newspaper in the country that accepts SAUs. Rates are quoted on that basis. Since over

1,400 (about 90 percent) of daily newspapers use the SAU system, the purchase and production process has been simplified tremendously for national advertisers.

Newspaper rates for local advertisers continue to be based on the column inch, which is 1 inch deep by 1 column wide. Advertising rates for local advertisers are quoted per column inch, and media planners calculate total space costs by multiplying the ad's number of column inches by the cost per inch.

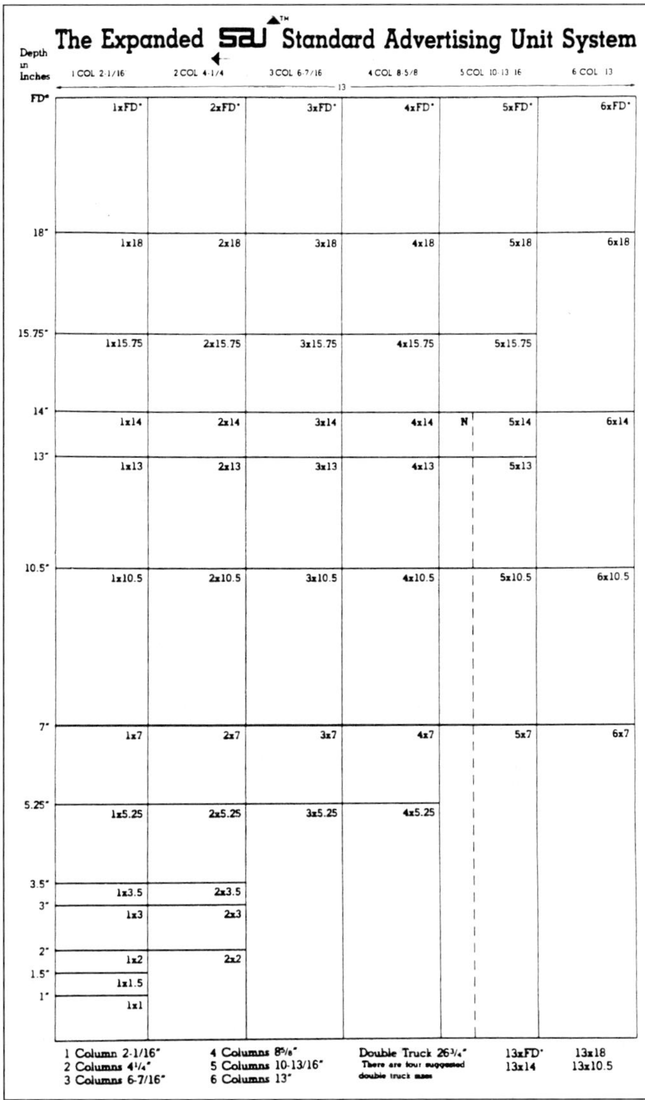

Figure 12-5 The Standard Advertising Unit System

Rate Structures

While the column inch and SAU are used to determine basic newspaper advertising rates, the media planner must consider other options and factors. Many newspapers charge **flat rates,** which means they offer no discount for quantity or repeated space buys. Others have an **open-rate structure,** which means various discounts are available. These discounts are generally based on frequency or bulk purchases of space and depend on the number of column inches purchased in a year.

Newspaper space rates also vary with an advertiser's special requests, such as preferred position or color. The basic rates quoted by a newspaper are **run of paper (ROP),** which means the paper can place the ad on any page or in any position it desires. While most newspapers try to place an ad in a requested position, the advertiser can ensure a specific section and/or position on a page by paying a higher **preferred position rate.** Color advertising is also available in many newspapers on an ROP basis or through preprinted inserts or Sunday supplements.

Advertisers can also buy newspaper space based on **combination rates,** where they get a discount for using several newspapers as a group. Typically, a combination rate occurs when a publisher owns both a morning and an evening newspaper in a market and offers a reduced single rate for running the same ad in both newspapers, generally within a 24-hour period. Combination discounts are also available when the advertiser buys space in several newspapers owned by the publisher in a number of markets or in multiple newspapers affiliated in a syndicate or newspaper group. Exhibit 12-25 shows an ad promoting the three newspapers published by the *Miami Herald* in the south Florida market.

The Future for Newspapers

Newspapers remain the largest advertising medium in terms of total advertising volume. Newspapers' largest advertising category is retail, and consolidation among department stores and grocery chains is likely to lead to a slight decline in ad volume. National advertising in newspapers is growing as major advertisers such as Procter & Gamble, Kraft, Nestlé, and General Motors use the medium more. However, newspapers have fallen behind TV and magazines as a medium for national advertisers; they accounted for only 4.7 percent of the estimated $165 billion spent by national advertisers in 2004.

Newspapers' major strength lies in their role as a medium that can be used effectively by local advertisers on a continual basis. It is unlikely that newspapers' importance to local advertisers will change in the near future. However, there are a number of problems and issues newspapers must address to maintain their strong position as a dominant local advertising medium and to gain more national advertising. These include competition from other advertising media, maintaining and managing circulation, cross-media opportunities, and declining readership.

It takes 3 newspapers to reach the #1 retail market in the U.S.
The Herald BROWARD
el Nuevo
The Miami Herald
Afghan plane seized in air
We publish them all.
The Miami/Ft. Lauderdale DMA leads the nation in retail spending per household.
And there's no better way to reach this big-spending market than by advertising in The Miami Herald, El Nuevo Herald (the nation's #1 Spanish-language daily) and The Herald in Broward County.
Together, these three newspapers have the highest reach in South Florida.
The Miami Herald
www.herald.com
el Nuevo Herald
www.elherald.com
The Herald
www.herald.com
For more information call Ric Banciella, National Marketing Manager, at (305) 376-2694 or (800) HERALD5, ext. 2694, e-mail: rbanciella@herald.com
Or, visit our websites at www.herald.com or www.elherald.com
Source: Demographics USA, 1999 Market Statistics; Scarborough Multi-Media Study, 1999

Exhibit 12-25

Marketers can advertise in the three newspapers published by the *Miami Herald*

Competition from Other Media The newspaper industry's battle to increase its share of national advertising volume has been difficult. In addition to the problems of reproduction quality and rate differentials, newspapers face competition from other media for both national and local advertisers' budgets. The newspaper industry is particularly concerned about the *bypass,* or loss of advertisers to direct marketing and telemarketing.

To deal with this problem, many newspapers will have to gear up to compete as direct marketers. Many papers are already building databases by collecting information from readers that potential advertisers can use to target specific groups or for direct marketing. Newspapers already have a distribution system that can reach nearly every household in a market every day. It is likely that many newspapers will find ways to make their extensive databases and distribution systems available to marketers that want to target consumers with direct-marketing efforts. By supplementing newspaper advertising with direct mail, marketers can be encouraged to invest more of their advertising dollars with newspaper publishers.

The intermedia battle that newspapers find themselves involved in is no longer limited to national advertising. Many companies are investigating the Internet as a marketing tool and a place to invest advertising dollars that might otherwise go to newspapers. Local radio and TV stations (particularly cable stations), as well as the expanding number of Yellow Pages publishers, are aggressively pursuing local advertisers. Newspapers will have to fight harder to retain those advertisers.

Newspapers are also facing new competition from various online sites for classified and employment advertising, which have long been important major profit centers. Classified advertising revenue for U.S. newspapers has declined steadily since 2000, while help-wanted advertising revenue in 2005 was only half of what it was in 2001. Newspapers must now compete against online employment sites such as Monster.com and Job.com for job listings. Websites such as eBay and Craigslist have become very popular ways for selling a variety of merchandise that traditionally was sold through classified ads in local newspapers. Craigslist, which began as a type of counterculture message board for young people in the San Francisco area, has now expanded to most major cities and has become popular among people under 30. The online site includes sections for selling merchandise, apartment rentals, services, personals, and job listings.

Some newspapers are recognizing that it is very difficult to compete against online sites for classified ads and are responding by offering free classified ads for merchandise under certain price points as a way to grow readership.[35] For example, in 2005, the *Miami Herald* began offering free classified ads for merchandise valued at $500 or less while the *San Diego Union-Tribune* began offering free classified ads in both the traditional paper and online version for merchandise valued under $5,000 (Exhibit 12-26).

Newspapers are doing a number of other things to respond to the challenges from other media. Many papers have expanded their marketing capabilities and are making efforts to develop and sustain relationships with their advertisers. Some have created sophisticated databases and direct-mail capabilities, which they offer as value-added services. Others are increasing their marketing research departments, preparing comprehensive market studies for major customers, and, in some cases, serving as media advisors and marketing partners.

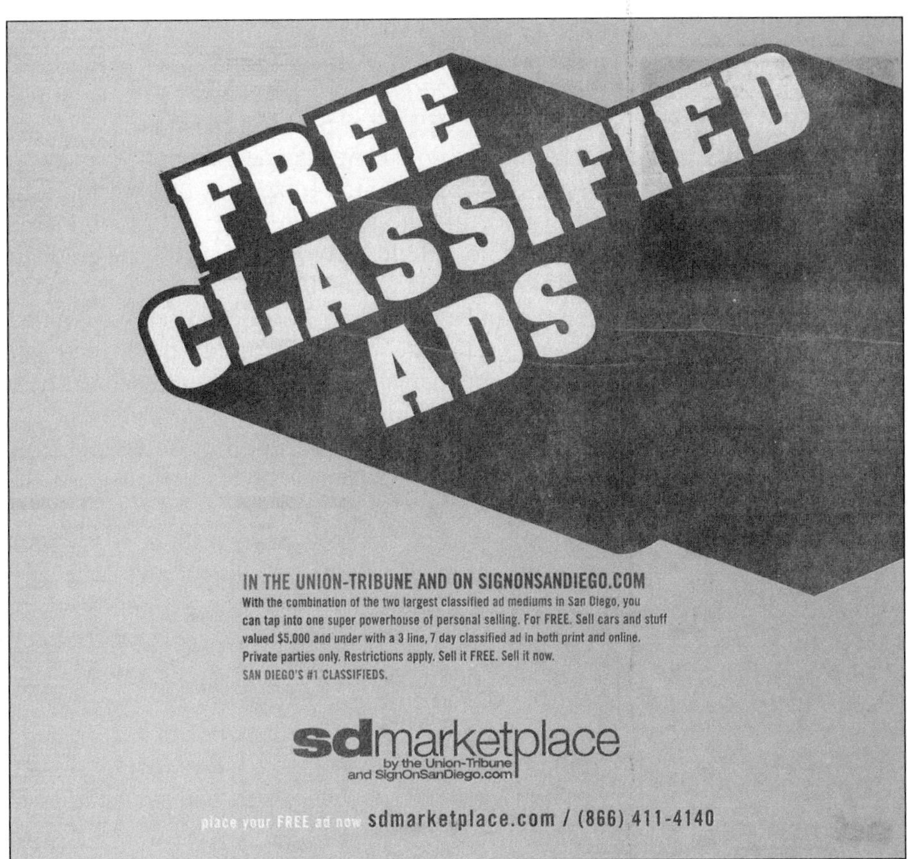

Exhibit 12-26 Some newspapers offer free classified ads as a way to attract and retain readers

Circulation

The newspaper industry has been struggling for years to reverse declining circulation.[36] IMC Perspective 12-4 discusses some of the reasons many of the major newspapers in the United States have been experiencing a decline in circulation and how they are finding ways to respond to the problem, such as by emphasizing readership measures and developing online versions of their papers. Like magazines, many newspapers are taking a closer look at their circulation and analyzing whether the cost of getting additional circulation is justified by the advertising revenue it generates. Many papers are raising newsstand and home delivery rates, and circulation revenue is accounting for more of their total revenue.

Several major metropolitan newspapers have found that advertisers use newspapers to reach consumers within specific geographic areas and do not want to pay for readers in outlying areas. Thus, some papers are eliminating what has been called "ego circulation" and focusing more on regional editions in their immediate trade area.

Cross-Media Buys

Another area where newspapers may be following the lead of magazines is cross-newspaper and media buys. Newspapers within, as well as across, various regions are banding together to offer national advertisers a package of newspapers so they won't have to purchase space in individual papers. A number of newspaper networks are being formed to help newspapers compete for more of the media expenditures of national advertisers.

Cross-media buys involving newspapers with other media vehicles are also likely to become more prevalent. For example, *Newsweek* has been involved in cross-media deals with the *Washington Post,* its parent company, while large companies that own newspapers, magazines, and broadcast media are also offering cross-media packages to advertisers (Exhibit 12-27).

Attracting and Retaining Readers

The growth of newspapers as an advertising medium may be limited by the reduced popularity of the medium itself. Newspaper readership has been on a steady decline for the past two decades. The percentage

NEWSWEEK POST COMBINATION

TAP INTO THE POWER OF THE WASHINGTON POST COMPANY

TRIPLE EXPOSURE

Here's an opportunity to harness the power, prestige and credibility of the world's premiere global news-gathering organization, The Washington Post Company.

Three publications from the Washington Post Company—Newsweek, the Washington Post Magazine and the Washington Post National Weekly—have joined forces to create a unique marketing opportunity. It's the most effective way to reach key decision makers and opinion leaders in Washington and all across America.

SPECIAL DISCOUNT

Based on your ad commitment in Newsweek, corporate and policy advertisers receive a special discount rate to also run in the Washington Post Magazine and the Washington Post National Weekly Edition.

NEWSWEEK

Provocative, insightful and innovative but still irreverent, feisty and fun, Newsweek has reinvented the spirit of the news magazine.

>> Prestigious magazine renowned and respected the world over

>> Award-winning, news-making reporting on politics, social issues, business, technology, health, medicine, the arts and more

>> Delivers a fresh perspective to 19 million+ affluent, sophisticated readers†

>> Newsweek is #1 in coverage among the newsweeklies and business books in reaching opinion leaders who influence legislative/government policy issues.*

>> Among regular news magazine readers (3 out of 4 issues), Newsweek delivers more opinion leaders than Time or U.S. News in these important leadership groups: federal government, executive branch, congressional branch, associations, law and science.*

*Sources: †Fall 1998 MRI; *1998–99 Opinion Leaders Study by Erdos & Morgan*

THE WASHINGTON POST MAGAZINE

The Washington Post's tradition of journalistic excellence is carried to another level by its Sunday Magazine.

>> One of the best-read components of the Sunday Post

>> High-impact cover stories that consistently attract Washington's opinion leaders

>> Recently launched 11 new features, including "What Works," a unique, positive editorial environment focusing on government, innovation and the public sector

>> Exceptional readership and reach—reaches over 80% of leaders involved in defense, communication, transportation, energy, environmental and health-care issues**

***Washington Leadership Study by Q & A Research and Strategy, 1995*

THE WASHINGTON POST NATIONAL WEEKLY EDITION

The Washington Post National Weekly edition was created in 1983 to extend the Post's world-class coverage of politics, government, the economy and international affairs.

>> Distributed nationally by mail subscription and at selected newsstands and bookstores

>> Reaches America's "grass-roots" influentials, readers who influence Washington, D.C., legislators

>> Delivers upscale readers who are active in the community and in the marketplace

For more information, contact your Newsweek sales representative or Bill Youngberg, Sales Development Director, 312-565-3516.

Newsweek

Exhibit 12-27 *Newsweek* and the *Washington Post* offer advertisers a cross-media opportunity

of the adult population reading a newspaper on the average weekday has declined from 78 percent in 1970 to 54 percent in 2005. The percentage of U.S. households receiving a daily newspaper has declined from 77 percent in 1980 to 60 percent. The decline in newspaper readership can be attributed to several factors, including the fast-paced, time-poor lifestyle of the modern dual-income household and the continued growth, popularity, and viewing options of TV.

A number of newspapers have been redesigned to be more interesting and easier and faster to read. Changes include the increased use of color and graphics as well as expanded coverage of sports and entertainment. Some papers have begun providing short summaries of articles in each section of the paper so readers can skim them and decide what they want to read.

Of particular concern to publishers is the decline in newspaper readership among important market segments such as women and young adults. Surveys show that the percentage of women who read a newspaper on a typical day declined from 67 percent in 1981 to 54 percent in 2004.[37] Newspapers and advertisers are concerned because women are far more likely than men to make buying decisions. Many newspapers are introducing new women's sections and revising old ones to make them more appealing to modern women. This means including articles on such issues as health, parenting, and careers—for example, how women with children and jobs manage their time.

Newspapers are also concerned about where their future readers will come from, since many young people are heavy TV viewers and also are spending more and more time surfing the Internet. However, a recent study found that newspaper readership is high among teens, and many papers are making special efforts to attract teenagers in hopes they will become and remain regular readers. The newspaper industry is also taking steps to maintain readership among young people. For example, the Newspaper Association of America (NAA) developed an advertising campaign using the theme "It all starts with newspapers" that encourages young people to read the newspaper every day.[38] The ads ask parents to "encourage your child to read a newspaper every day" and feature celebrities such as musician Jon Bon Jovi, basketball star Grant Hill, and actress Meryl Streep promoting newspapers as literacy tools. Exhibit 12-28 shows one of the ads from that campaign, featuring Jackie Chan, the popular action-movie star, reading *The Tuxedo Times.* The ad was run to coincide with the release of Chan's action-comedy film *The Tuxedo.*

Exhibit 12-28 This ad is part of a campaign encouraging young people to read newspapers

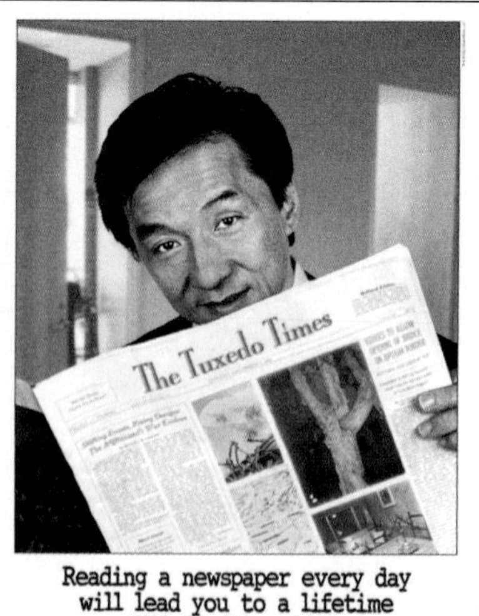

The newspaper industry faces a major challenge. To increase circulation and readership and continue to attract advertising revenue, it must make newspapers more interesting to readers by targeting specific groups and expanding services to encourage advertisers to continue using newspapers. The newspaper industry launched a comprehensive program to address some of these issues. Called the Newspaper Readership Initiative, this program seeks to reverse the decline in newspaper readership and circulation and make newspapers a part of every advertiser's media plan.[39]

The growth of the Internet and online services is another factor that may erode newspaper readership. As penetration of the Internet into households increases, newspapers and magazines are among the most threatened of the major media. A survey conducted for *Advertising Age* found that consumers with home Internet access are less likely to use magazines or newspapers as a primary information source when shopping for a car, financial services, travel, or fashion. The study also found that consumers from teens to seniors are comfortable with the idea of using the Internet in the future to read books, magazines, and newspapers.[40]

IMC PERSPECTIVE 12-4

Tough Times for Newspapers

The last few years have been difficult for the newspaper industry. A number of the major metropolitan newspapers have been struggling to regain their footing following the recession that hit the advertising industry over the past four years. However, they are facing a number of obstacles in their efforts to rebound including competition from other media, declining circulation, and image problems. More people are getting their news from the Internet, their local TV station, or one of the many 24-hour news channels such as CNN, MSNBC, Headline News, or Fox News. The circulation of many newspapers has been declining, which impacts the rate they can charge for advertising, and traditional newspapers are finding it increasingly difficult to get consumers to pay full price for their product.

The Newspaper Association of America conducted an analysis of figures provided by the Audit Bureau of Circulation (ABC) for the first part of 2005 and found that the average daily circulation of the newspapers dropped 1.9 percent to 47.4 million, while overall Sunday circulation fell 2.5 percent to just over 51 million. A number of major newspapers have experienced declines in circulation or seen their circulation figures remain flat. ABC figures showed that average daily circulation declined for 39 of the top 50 newspapers. Circulation for major dailies such as the *Los Angeles Times, Chicago Tribune, Rocky Mountain News,* and *San Diego Union-Tribune* fell by more than 6 percent. Circulation figures for the largest newspapers including *USA Today* and *The Wall Street Journal* have remained flat while *The New York Times* has lost circulation in its hometown even while it has made gains nationally.

Newspaper executives attribute the circulation decline to a number of factors. They note that the Federal Trade Commission's do-not-call legislation significantly blunted their telemarketing programs, which have been an important way of soliciting new subscribers. Newspapers have also become more strict in accurately counting their circulation in the wake of a circulation scandal that rocked the industry in 2004 when four major newspapers including the Tribune Company's Long Island *Newsday* and Spanish-language *Hoy, The Chicago Sun Times,* and the *Dallas Morning News* admitted they had been overstating their circulation. The publishers had to compensate the advertisers who paid to reach a larger audience than the papers actually delivered. The Tribune Company alone had to set aside $90 million for anticipated settlements with advertisers.

The declines in circulation will ultimately pose a problem for newspapers as they may lose their pricing power over advertisers, who will demand that papers lower their rates because they are reaching fewer people. National advertising, which has been the fastest-growing segment of newspaper advertising, is particularly vulnerable as papers will find it more difficult to command premium rates from large advertisers. Some argue that the decline in circulation may be very difficult to reverse given the lifestyle changes occurring among readers and the alternative ways they can get their news.

Newspaper companies are responding to the problems facing their industry. Many are trying to case their decline in circulation in a softer light by emphasizing "readership" measures. Readership tries to gauge the quality of readers by measuring how long readers have subscribed to a newspaper, how many minutes a day they spend reading it, and the various sections they read. A number of papers are converting to a readership model rather than pure circulation numbers and working to educate advertisers about the quality of their circulation.

Many newspapers are also responding by offering a variety of new products including niche publications as well as their own websites. Most dailies now offer online versions of their newspapers and thus are capturing readers who prefer to get their news from websites. One study estimated that having a website increased a newspaper's audience footprint by up to 35 percent. Visitors to newspaper websites are younger, better educated, and more likely to make a purchase than general Internet users. Many papers are using this information to promote their online editions to advertisers.

Sources: Jon Fine, "Newspapers' Free-Fall: Paid Circ Continues to Shrink," *Advertising Age,* May 9, 2005, pp. 4, 78; Joseph T. Hallinan, "Newspapers Now Push 'Readership,'" *The Wall Street Journal,* April 18, 2005, p. B4; James Bandler and Brian Steinberg, "Newspaper-Circulation Inquiry Sparks Anxiety for Advertisers," *The Wall Street Journal,* October 14, 2004, p. B8.

Exhibit 12-29
SignOnSanDiego.com is a very successful online newspaper

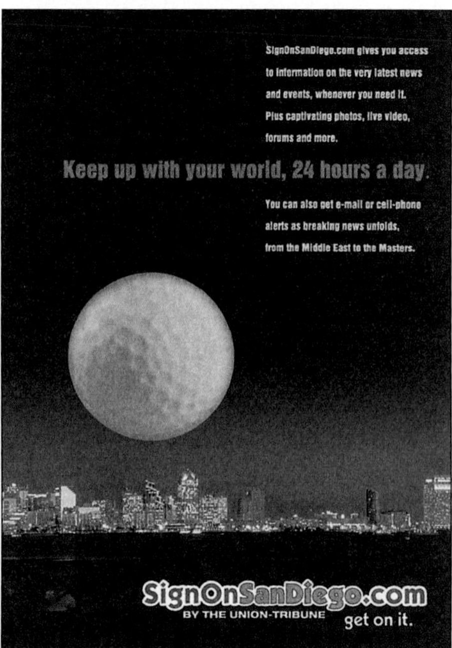

Newspaper publishers are addressing this threat by making their papers available online. Nearly every major newspaper has established a website, and many publishers now make their papers available online. The number of U.S. newspapers available online increased from less than 100 in 1995 to more than 1,500 in 2005. Many papers are also developing innovative programs for advertisers to attract their online advertising dollars. Networks are forming to help local newspapers go online and to facilitate the sale and purchase of banner ads and sponsorships. Exhibit 12-29 shows an ad promoting SignOnSanDiego.com, the online newspaper published by the *San Diego Union-Tribune* newspaper.

Summary

Magazines and newspapers, the two major forms of print media, play an important role in the media plans and strategy of many advertisers. Magazines are a very selective medium and are very valuable for reaching specific types of customers and market segments. The three broad categories of magazines are consumer, farm, and business publications. Each of these categories can be further classified according to the publication's editorial content and audience appeal.

In addition to their selectivity, the advantages of magazines include their excellent reproduction quality, creative flexibility, long life, prestige, and readers' high receptivity to magazine advertising, as well as the services they offer to advertisers. Disadvantages of magazines include their high cost, limited reach and frequency, long lead time, and the advertising clutter in most publications.

Advertising space rates in magazines vary according to a number of factors, among them the size of the ad, position in the publication, particular editions purchased, use of color, and number and frequency of insertions. Rates for magazines are compared on the basis of the cost per thousand, although other factors such as the editorial content of the publication and its ability to reach specific target audiences must also be considered.

Newspapers represent the largest advertising medium in terms of total volume, receiving nearly a fourth of all advertising dollars. Newspapers are a very important medium to local advertisers, especially retailers. They are also used by national advertisers, although the differential rate structure for national versus local advertisers is a source of controversy. Newspapers are a broad-based medium that reaches a large percentage of households in a particular area. Newspapers' other advantages include flexibility, geographic selectivity, reader involvement, and special services. Drawbacks of newspapers include their lack of high-quality ad reproduction, short life span, lack of audience selectivity, and clutter.

Trends toward market segmentation and regional marketing are prompting many advertisers to make more use of newspapers and magazines. However, both magazines and newspapers face increasing competition from such other media as radio, cable TV, direct marketing, and the Internet. Both magazines and newspapers are working to improve the quality of their circulation bases, offer database marketing services, and initiate cross-media deals. Rising costs and declining readership are problems for many magazines and newspapers. Both magazines and newspapers are making their publications available online, but problems with audience measurement and interactions with ads are important issues that must be resolved.

Key Terms

selectivity, 380
gatefolds, 383
bleed pages, 383
split runs, 387
selective binding, 387
ink-jet imaging, 387
controlled-circulation basis, 390
pass-along readership, 390
total audience/readership, 391
magazine networks, 392
multimagazine deals, 395
cross-media advertising, 395
display advertising, 398
classified advertising, 398
preprinted inserts, 399
city zone, 403
retail trading zone, 403
general advertising rates, 403
retail advertising rates, 404
standard advertising units (SAUs), 404
flat rates, 405
open-rate structure, 405
run of paper (ROP), 405
preferred position rate, 405
combination rates, 405

Discussion Questions

1. The opening vignette to the chapter discusses the growing popularity of celebrity magazines. Discuss some of the reasons why celebrity magazines have become so popular. What types of companies might choose to advertise in these publications?

2. Discuss the role of magazines as part of an advertiser's media strategy. What are the advantages and limitations of magazines?

3. What is meant by selectivity with regard to the purchase of advertising media? Discuss the various ways magazines offer selectivity to advertisers.

4. Choose a specific target market that an advertiser might want to reach. Discuss how magazines and/or newspapers can be used to reach this particular market segment in a cost-effective manner.

5. Why are young males such a difficult market to reach through magazines? What types of magazines might be effective in reaching the young male market?

6. The magazine industry promotes magazines as having advantages over other media in terms of consumer receptivity and involvement. Why might consumers be more receptive to and involved with advertising in magazines versus other media?

7. If you were purchasing print advertising space for a manufacturer of golf clubs such as Callaway or TaylorMade, what factors would you consider? Would your selection of magazines be limited to golf publications? Why or why not?

8. Discuss the role of newspapers as part of an advertiser's media strategy. What are the advantages and limitations of newspapers?

9. What is an island ad? What types of companies might consider using island ads in newspapers?

10. What are the major challenges facing the newspaper industry and the use of newspapers as an advertising medium? How can newspapers respond to these challenges?

Support Media

13

Chapter Objectives

1. To recognize the various traditional and nontraditional support media available to the marketer in developing an IMC program.

2. To develop an understanding of the advantages and disadvantages of support media.

3. To examine the role of support media in the IMC program.

4. To know how audiences for support media are measured.

Product Placements—The New Substitute for Television Commercials?

We almost feel guilty about telling you this for fear that you might never be able to watch a movie the same way again. But we will anyway, because we probably aren't telling you anything you don't already know: Movies have become

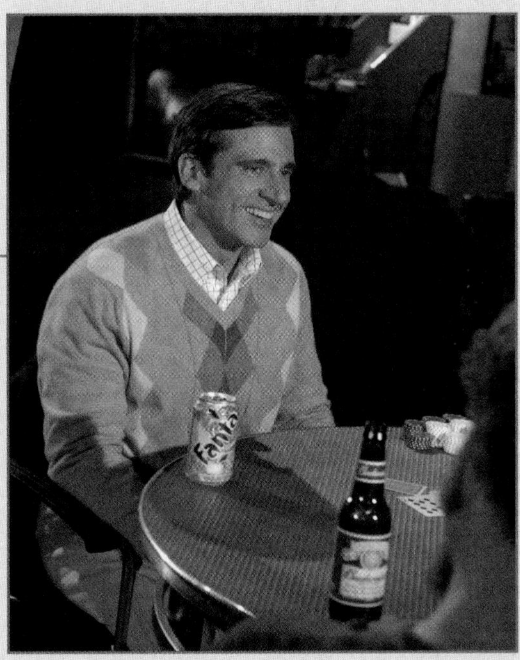

the new mantra for marketing products. The next time you watch a movie, pay attention to the number of product placements (plugs) that appear in it. Everything from Starbucks coffee to Taco Bell nachos, Apple computers, and BMWs appear either in the background or very prominently (sometimes too prominently!) throughout the movie. And it's not just in the movies. Product placements appear regularly in TV shows and books and have made their way to Broadway plays and magazine articles. California's governor Schwarzenegger has been accused of using product placements in his political advertisements. Everyone seems to want to get onboard.

But why product placements? And why now? Product placements are nothing new, having been around as long as there have been soap operas on TV and maybe as early as the 1930s. Products also appeared in movies as well, as many producers believe that they added a sense of realism to the scenes (as opposed to brand X, which would detract from viewers' attention). But the frequency of their use pales in comparison to what is going on now. Blame a lot of it on advertisers' fears that viewers are no longer watching commercials. With the advent of DVRs, it is easy to skip commercials, and advertisers are afraid their ads will be among those not seen. But with product placements woven into the scenes, or even the plots, exposure is inevitable for anyone paying attention. The same is true for reading a book ("She was sitting in the corner of Starbucks, sipping on a latte"), in a comic book, video game, or rap song (McDonald's tried this one!).

Consider this. Spending on product placements in 2005 was expected to top $4.25 billion—a 23 percent increase over 2004. Placements have occurred on the top-rated TV show *Desperate Housewives* (Buick, KB Homes), in books like *The Bulgari Connection* (Bulgari) and *Surf Girls* (Roxy), in video games and comic books (BMW), and in the Neil Simon Broadway play *Sweet Charity* (Grand Centenario: the Tequila). So many movies have employed this medium that, in some, the placements are becoming the driver of the plot. Anheuser-Busch considered *Wedding Crashers* an opportunity for "one big Budweiser commercial," and the website PerfectMatch.com was written into the script as a major plot element in *Must Love Dogs*. There are many, many more examples to discuss.

But do the placements work? Examples of the success of Reese's Pieces (in *E.T.*) and RayBan sunglasses (*Top Gun*) have been known for quite some time—before placements saturated the media. But what about now? Adidas is just one of the many companies that think they are still effective. The company responded to a request by filmmaker Buena Vista by adapting a 1959 training sneaker to the script of *The Life Aquatic.* Since the movie aired, Adidas has received hundreds of requests by phone and e-mail from stores and consumers wanting to purchase the product. Homemade knockoffs have appeared for sale on eBay. Others like tai chi Onistuka Tigers shoes (*Kill Bill, Vol.1*) and Lexus and Audi (*Minority Report* and *I, Robot*) also experienced high demand for products that were specifically made for the movies but didn't actually exist.

But there are also those who think product placements may have reached their limits. Jim Edwards, writing in *Brandweek,* is one who thinks there may be a "bubble." Edwards notes that the incredible growth in the use of placements and the sheer number of placements (in the second quarter of 2005, the top 10 placed brands appeared 6,077 times in prime-time TV, and the top 10 shows allowing placements had 11,579 "shout-outs") will soon lead to oversaturation and loss of effectiveness. He also notes that there really aren't any bona fide measures of effectiveness—a troublesome factor for many of the current and potential users. Others agree on the issue of oversaturation. When Sony Pictures forged an alliance with Major League Baseball to place *Spider-Man 2* logos on the bases in 15 major league ballparks, baseball fans had had enough, expressing outrage at the proposition. Apparently, it worked, as the deal was called off. Will others follow suit, or will the bubble never burst?

Sources: Jim Edwards, "The Tracker: Will Product Placement Get Its Own Dot-Comeuppance?" *Insidebrandedentertainment.com,* August 3, 2005, pp. 1–3; Marc Graser, "Movie Placement Creates Demand for Nonexistent Shoe," Adage.com, January 31, 2005, pp. 1–3; T. L. Stanley, "*Must Love Dogs* Becomes Product Placement Bonanza," Adage.com, July 18, 2005, pp. 1–3; Gregory Cancelada, "A-B Hails New Movie as One Big Budweiser Commercial," *St. Louis Post Dispatch* (STLtoday.com), June 28, 2005, pp. 1–2; Marc Graser, "Product-Placement Spending Poised to Hit $4.25 Billion in '05," *Advertising Age,* April 4, 2005, p. 16; Rich Thomaselli, "First Baseball Field Product Placement Sparks Controversy," Adage.com, May 6, 2004, pp.1–2.

The tremendous growth in the number of product placements is just one of the trends (albeit a major one) that is altering the media landscape. Given the increasing concern with consumers' abilities to avoid advertising, advertisers have turned to other ways to get their messages in front of prospective buyers. The result of this is increased attention to getting exposure, which, in turn, has led to significant changes in the media industry. Over the past few years there has been significant growth in the use of support media—both traditional and new media forms. In many ways, the consumers' efforts to avoid commercial exposure may have had an opposite effect, as it seems ads now appear in many places not previously home to such messages.

Ads have appeared on manhole covers, inside rest-room stalls, on lettuce wrappers in grocery stores, on hubcaps, on cell phones, and even on beepers. In this chapter, we review a number of support media, some that are new to the marketplace and others that have been around a while. We discuss the relative advantages and disadvantages, how they are used, cost information, and audience measurement of each. We refer to them as **support media** because the media described in the previous chapters dominate the media strategies of large advertisers, particularly national advertisers. Support media are used to reach those people in the target market the primary media may not have effectively reached and to reinforce, or support, their messages. It is important to remember that some of these media are not used only for support, but for some companies may be the primary or sole medium used.

You may be surprised at how many different ways there are to deliver the message and how often you are exposed to them. Let's begin by examining the scope of the support media industry and some of the many alternatives available to marketers.

The Scope of the Support Media Industry

Support media are referred to by several titles, among them **alternative media, nonmeasured media,** and **nontraditional media.** These terms describe a vast variety of channels used to deliver communications and to promote products and services. In this chapter we will discuss many of these media (though, as you might imagine, it would be impossible for us to discuss them all).

Many advertisers, as well as the top 100 advertising agencies, have increased their use of support media, and as new alternatives are developed, this use will continue to grow. Given the rapid emergence of a variety of new media, we will further divide support media into *traditional* and *nontraditional* support media categories. There is no particular necessity for this further distinction other than to demonstrate that many of the various forms of support media have been around for quite some time, while others have surfaced only recently. Let us examine some of these in more detail.

Traditional Support Media

Out-of-home advertising media encompass many advertising forms (see Figure 13-1). As can be seen, the Outdoor Advertising Association of America, Inc. (OAAA) categorizes these media as outdoor—including billboards, street furniture, alternative media, and transit—as well as specific forms of radio. As shown in Figure 13-2, billboards and street furniture together constitute 76 percent of the outdoor billings. Given the similarity of these forms, we will discuss them together while addressing transit and alternative media subsequently.

Outdoor Advertising

Outdoor advertising has probably existed since the days of cave dwellers. Both the Egyptians and the Greeks used it as early as 5,000 years ago. Outdoor is certainly one of the more pervasive communication forms, particularly if you live in an urban or suburban area.

Even though outdoor accounts for only about 2.3 percent of all advertising expenditures and the number of billboards has decreased, the medium has grown steadily in terms of dollars billed. In 1982, approximately $888 million was spent in this area; in

Figure 13-1 Out-of-Home Media: A Diverse Cross-Section of Formats Comprise Outdoor Advertising Today

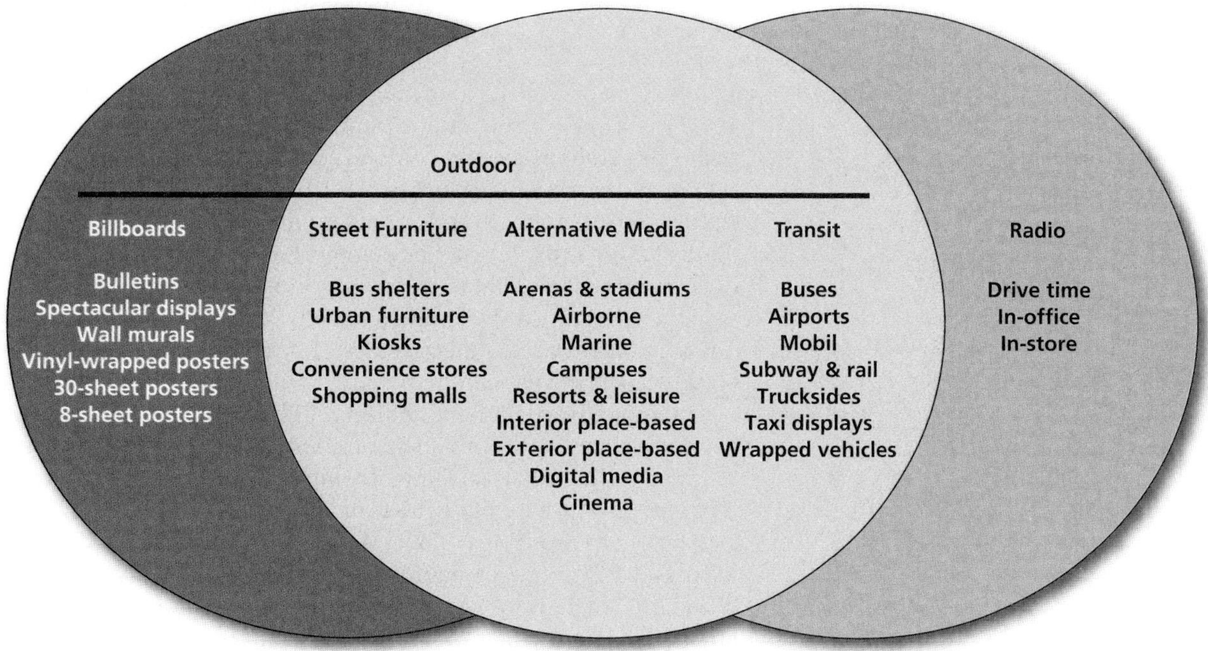

Source: OAAA.

Figure 13-2 Four Major Product Categories of Outdoor

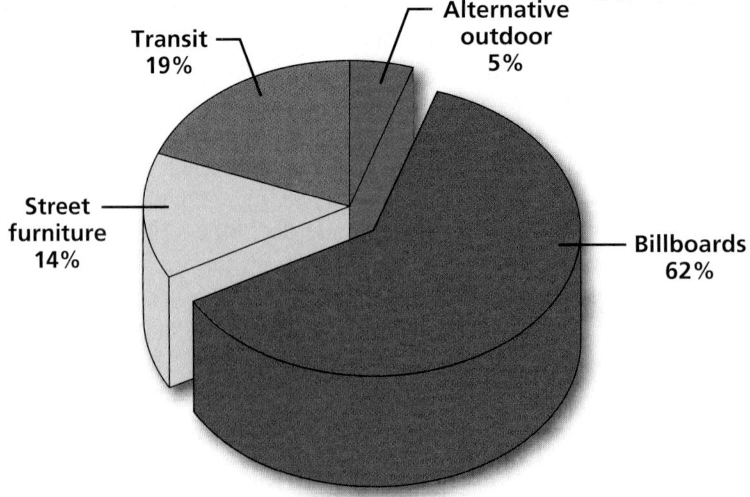

Source: OAAA.

2005, expenditures reached $5.8 billion.[1] As the medium was once dominated by tobacco advertisers (25 percent of its $1.5 billion revenue came from cigarette advertising in 1991), there were concerns in the industry when an agreement was reached with 46 states in November 1998 to ban all cigarette ads. Increased expenditures from automotive, retail, and financial companies and from new advertisers such as the dot-coms have more than made up for the losses. Companies like McDonald's, American Express, P&G, and AT&T are some of the top spenders in this medium. As shown in Figure 13-3, outdoor continues to be used by a broad client base, a demonstration of its continued acceptance in the industry. The increase in the number of women in the work force has led to more advertising of products targeted to this segment, and the increases in the number of vehicles on the road and the number of miles driven have led to increased expenditures by gas companies, food and lodging providers, and other media.

A major reason for the continued success of outdoor is its ability to remain innovative through technology. As Exhibit 13-1 shows, billboards are no longer limited to standard sizes and two dimensions; 3-D forms and extensions are now used to attract attention. Digital outdoor media have also contributed to the success. Digital messages on billboards, transit signs, and in lobbies have allowed more advertisers to participate as messages can be changed quickly and often. In addition, it allows outdoor advertising to appear in places previously unavailable, and in a timely fashion. For example, Yahoo! used a billboard in Times Square featuring an interactive videogame that passersby could access using their cell phones to relaunch their site (Exhibit 13-2). You probably have been exposed to either signboards or electronic billboards at sports stadiums, in supermarkets, in the campus bookstore and dining halls, in shopping malls, on the freeways, or on the sides of buildings, from neon signs on skyscrapers in New York City to Mail Pouch Tobacco signs painted on the sides of barns in the Midwest. This is truly a pervasive medium.

Figure 13-3 Top 10 Outdoor Advertising Categories

1. Local services and amusements
2. Media and advertising
3. Public transportation, hotels, and resorts
4. Retail
5. Insurance and real estate
6. Financial
7. Automotive dealers and services
8. Restaurant
9. Automotive, auto access, and equipment
10. Telecommunications

Source: OAAA.

Outdoor advertising, particularly billboards, does have its critics. Ever since Lady Bird Johnson tried to rid the interstate highways of billboard advertising during her husband's presidency with the Highway Beautification Act of 1965, there has been controversy regarding its use. As previously noted, legislation has passed in 46 states banning the advertising of cigarettes on billboards. In addition, a number of cities and states have considered extending the ban to alcoholic beverages. Consumers themselves seem to have mixed emotions about the medium. In a Maritz AmeriPoll asking consumers about their opinions of bill-

Exhibit 13-1 Outdoor advertising goes beyond two dimensions

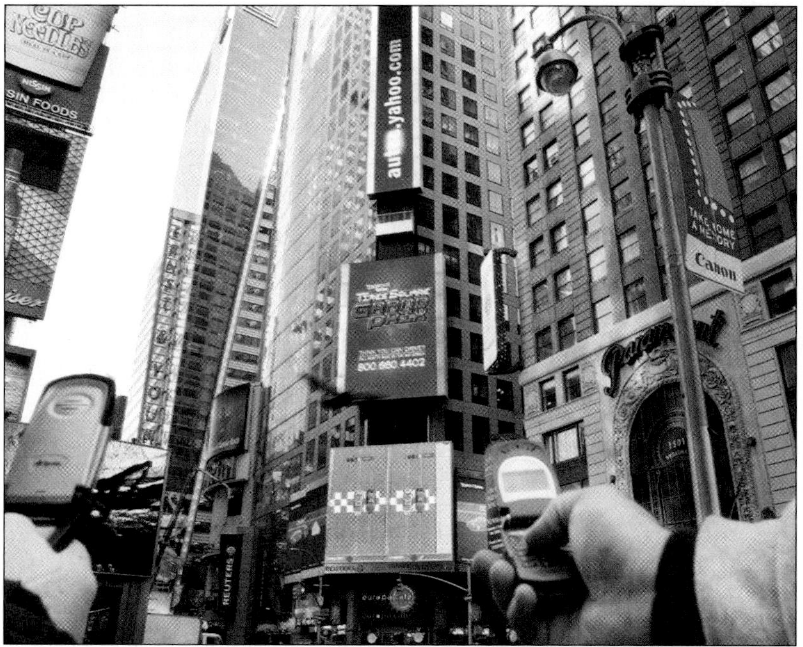

Exhibit 13-2 Yahoo!'s interactive billboard in Times Square

boards, 62 percent of the respondents said they thought billboards should not be banned, while 52 percent said they should be strictly regulated. When asked if billboards were entertaining, 80 percent of those surveyed said no, and when asked if billboards could be beautiful, only 27 percent said yes.[2]

At the same time, a number of research studies and case histories have proven outdoor to be effective.

Alternative Out-of-Home Media

Several other forms of outdoor advertising are also available including aerial advertising, place-based, mobile boards, and more. The OAAA classifies these as alternative media. Let's examine a few of these.

Exhibit 13-3 A variety of companies use blimps as an advertising medium

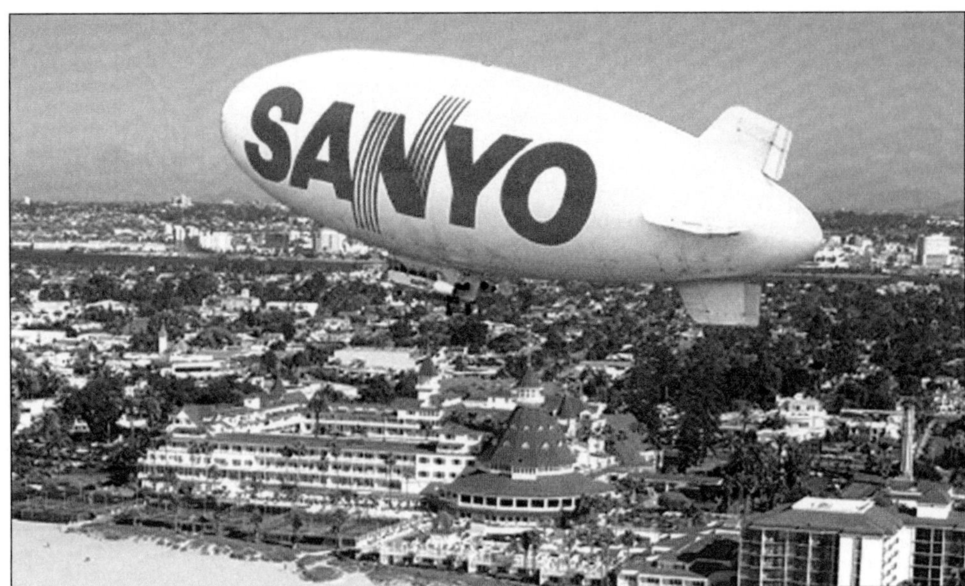

Aerial Advertising

Airplanes pulling banners, skywriting (in letters as high as 1,200 feet), and blimps all constitute another form of outdoor advertising available to the marketer: **aerial advertising.** Generally these media are not expensive in absolute terms and can be useful for reaching specific target markets. For example, Coppertone has often used skywriting over beach areas to promote its tanning lotions, beer companies (among others) commonly employ aerial advertising at sporting events, and local advertisers promote special events, sales, and the like. Exhibit 13-3 shows one of the many products, services, and/or events that have used this medium. Perhaps one of the more interesting examples of aerial advertising is that shown in Exhibit 13-4. Pizza

Figure 13-4 In-Store Media Options

Company/Program	Medium
ActMedia	
Act Now	Co-op couponing/sampling
Aisle Vision	Ad posters inserted in stores' directory signs
Carts	Ad placed on frame inside/outside shopping cart
Impact	Customized in-store promotion events
Instant Coupon Machine	Coupon dispensers mounted in shelf channels
Act Radio	Live format in-store radio network
Shelf Take-One	Two-sided take-one offers in plastic see-through cartridges placed at shelf
Shelf Talk	Plastic frames on shelf near product
Catalina Marketing	
Checkout Prizes	Print awards and certificates and offers of in-store sweepstakes
Checkout Coupon	Scanner-driven coupon program that generates coupons at checkout
Checkout Message	Targeted ad messages delivered at checkout
Save Now	Instant electronic discounts
Loyalty Card Services	Offer consumer loyalty programs
In-Store Advertising	Integrated and standalone in-store advertising and sampling programs
Stratmar Systems	Audits, mystery shoppers, cut-ins

Hut paid about $1 million to have a 30-foot version of its new logo on an unmanned Russian Proton rocket. The logo was visible for only a few seconds, but Pizza Hut felt the exposure was well worth the investment. (The company also put pizza on the Space Shuttle for those assembling the orbiting space platform.)

Exhibit 13-4 Pizza Hut takes aerial advertising to new heights

Mobile Billboards Another outdoor medium is **mobile billboards.** Some companies paint Volkswagen Beetles with ads called Beetleboards; others paint trucks and vans. Still others put ads on small billboards, mount them on trailers, and drive around and/or park in the geographic areas being targeted (Exhibit 13-5). Costs depend on the area and the mobile board company's fees, though even small and large organizations have found the medium affordable. One company in California found that its five mobile cars account for 25 percent of its earnings, and a study conducted jointly by 3M and the American Trucking Association estimated that one truck traveling about 60,000 miles a year would create about 10 million viewer impressions of the ad placed on it.[3] In a study employing tracking methodology, the Traffic Audit Bureau (TAB) estimated that three trucks with a Seiko watch ad on them were seen by an average of 121,755 people per day in the Chicago area.[4] America Online, Lexus, Wolfgang Puck, and numerous dot-com companies are some of the advertisers that have used this medium.

In-Store Media

Advertisers use **in-store media** such as in-store ads, aisle displays, store leaflets, shopping cart signage, and in-store TV to reach shoppers at the place where they buy. A recent study by MEC Sensor and BMRB International revealed that one-third of shoppers say in-store ads influence them to make a purchase decision, 44 percent say they notice such ads, and 75 percent of those who noticed the ads said they are likely to purchase the advertised brand.[5] Figure 13-4 lists a few of the many in-store media options.

Much of the attraction of point-of-purchase media is based on figures from the Point of Purchase Advertising Institute (POPAI) that states that approximately two-thirds of consumers' purchase decisions are made in the store; some impulse categories demonstrate an 80 percent rate.[6] Many advertisers are spending more of their dollars where decisions are made now that they can reach consumers at the point of purchase, providing additional product information while reducing their own efforts.

Miscellaneous Outdoor Media

As shown in Figure 13-5, there are numerous outdoor media available, adding to the pervasiveness of this medium. The next time you are out, take a few moments to observe how many different forms of outdoor advertising you are exposed to.

Exhibit 13-5 An interesting and unusual example of a mobile billboard

Trucks often serve as mobile billboards

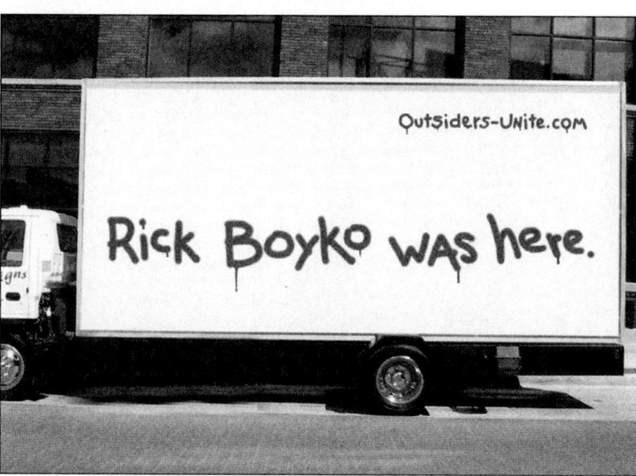

Figure 13-5 Out-of-Home Advertising Faces/Vehicles

Traditional Outdoor	Nontraditional Outdoor		
Billboards	Alternative	Street Furniture	Transit
Bulletins 143,230 faces	**Arenas and stadiums** 77 facilities	**Bus shelters** 37,205 displays	**Buses** 370,216 faces
30-sheet posters 201,750 faces	**Interior place-based** 34,000 displays	**Convenience stores** 10,000 displays	**Airports** 200+
8-sheet posters 106,020 faces	**Airborne** **Marine**	**Shopping malls** 10,138 displays	**Subway & rail** 13,000 displays
Spectacular displays **Wall murals** **Vinyl-wrapped posters**	**Resorts and leisure** **Exterior place-based** **Digital media**	**Urban furniture** **Kiosks**	**Trucksides** **Taxi displays** **Wrapped vehicles**

Source: OAAA.

Transit Advertising

Another form of out-of-home advertising is **transit advertising.** Transit is targeted at the millions of people who are exposed to commercial transportation facilities, including buses, taxis, commuter trains, trolleys, airplanes, and subways.

Transit advertising has been around for a long time, but recent years have seen a renewed interest in this medium. Due in part to the increased number of women in the work force (they can be reached on their way to work more easily than at home), audience segmentation, and the rising cost of TV advertising, yearly transit ad spending increased from $43 million in 1972 to over $1.1 billion in 2004.[7] Much of this spending has come from companies such as *The Wall Street Journal,* McDonald's, Sprint, Saab, and others, which like transit's lower costs, frequency of exposures, flexibility, and point of sale presence. Other retailers, movie studios, and business-to-business companies have also increased expenditures in this area (Exhibit 13-6).

Types of Transit Advertising

There are actually three forms of transit advertising: (1) inside cards, (2) outside posters, and (3) station, platform, or terminal posters.

Inside Cards If you have ever ridden a commuter bus, you have probably noticed the **inside cards** placed above the seats and luggage area advertising restaurants, TV or radio stations, or a myriad of other products and services. An innovation is the elec-

Exhibit 13-6 The FBI uses outdoor to recruit

tronic message boards that carry current advertising information. Companies in New York and Atlanta are installing flat-panel TV screens in transit vehicles which deliver news, restaurant information, and video ads. The ability to change the message and the visibility provide the advertiser with a more attention-getting medium.

Transit cards can be controversial. For example, in the New York subway system, many of the ads for chewing gum, soup, and Smokey the Bear have given way to public service announcements about AIDS, unwanted pregnancies, rape, and infant mortality. While subway riders may agree that such issues are important, many of them complain that the ads are depressing and intrusive.

Exhibit 13-7 Electronic outside posters often appear on taxicabs

Outside Posters Advertisers use various forms of outdoor transit posters to promote products and services. These **outside posters** may appear on the sides, backs, and/or roofs of buses, taxis, trains, and subway and trolley cars.

The increasing sophistication of this medium is demonstrated by a technology, developed by Vert, Inc., that transforms ads on top of taxicabs into real-time animated electronic billboards. A Web server that communicates with a global positioning satellite (GPS) is built into the taxi-top screen. The GPS determines the taxi's location and sends it to the local server, which then delivers the relevant ads for a particular area. A taxi traveling through a Hispanic community can have a message in Spanish, stock quotes could appear in the financial district, and so on. The ads appear in color in a format similar to banner ads, at 10 times the brightness of a TV screen. (See Exhibit 13-7.)

Station, Platform, and Terminal Posters Floor displays, island showcases, electronic signs, and other forms of advertising that appear in train or subway stations, airline terminals, and the like are all forms of transit advertising. As Exhibit 13-8 shows, **terminal posters** can be very attractive and attention-getting. Bus shelters often provide the advertiser with expanded coverage where other outdoor boards may be restricted. Electronic signs on subway platforms have become a common sight.

Exhibit 13-8 Terminal posters can be used to attract attention

Advantages and Disadvantages of Outdoor Advertising

Outdoor advertising offers a number of advantages:

1. *Wide coverage of local markets.* With proper placement, a broad base of exposure is possible in local markets, with both day and night presence. A 100 GRP **showing** (the percentage of duplicated audience exposed to an outdoor poster daily) could yield exposure to an equivalent of 100 percent of the marketplace daily, or 3,000 GRPs over a month. This level of coverage is likely to yield high levels of reach.

2. *Frequency.* Because purchase cycles are typically for 30-day

Figure 13-6 Relative Costs of Media

Average CPM for Adults 18+*			
Outdoor	Men	Women	Adults
30-sheet posters 350 weekly GRP level	$3.32	$4.02	$1.71
Rotary bulletins	5.61	6.80	3.07
Radio			
:30 Network	10.85	9.05	
:30 Spot	11.95	11.55	
Magazines			
4-color page			
Newsweeklies	11.76	—	
Women's fashion	—	11.91	
Television			
:30 Early AM network	19.15	12.05	
:30 Primetime network	29.95	23.20	
:30 Early news network	14.25	11.15	
:30 Late fringe network	29.75	25.65	
:30 Primetime cable	10.85	10.55	
Newspapers			
One-third page black and white	25.65	24.25	

*Based on the top 100 markets in the United States.
Source: SQAD (Winter 2005), Media Dynamics, Inc.

periods, consumers are usually exposed a number of times, resulting in high levels of frequency.

3. *Geographic flexibility.* Outdoor can be placed along highways, near stores, or on mobile billboards, almost anywhere that laws permit. For local advertisers, outdoor can reach people in specific geographic and/or demographic areas. Local, regional, or even national markets may be covered.

4. *Creativity.* As shown in Exhibit 13-1, outdoor ads can be very creative. Large print, colors, and other elements attract attention.

5. *Ability to create awareness.* Because of its impact (and the need for a simple message), outdoor can lead to a high level of awareness.

6. *Efficiency.* Outdoor usually has a very competitive CPM when compared to other media. The average CPM of outdoor is approximately one-half of radio and far less than that of TV, magazines, and newspapers (Figure 13-6). Transit is one of the least expensive media in both relative and absolute costs.

7. *Effectiveness.* Outdoor advertising can be effective, as demonstrated in Figure 13-7. In a study reported by BBDO advertising, 35 percent of consumers surveyed said they had called a phone number they saw on an out-of-home ad.[8] A study reported by Mukesh Bhargava and Naveen Donthu showed that outdoor advertising can have a significant effect on sales, particularly when combined with a promotion.[9]

8. *Production capabilities.* Modern technologies have reduced production times for outdoor advertising to allow for rapid turnaround time.

9. *Timeliness.* Many outdoor ads appear in or near shopping areas or on or in the vehicles taking customers there, thus resulting in timely exposures.

At the same time, however, there are limitations to outdoor, many of them related to its advantages:

1. *Waste coverage.* While it is possible to reach very specific audiences, in many cases the purchase of outdoor results in a high degree of waste coverage. It is not likely that everyone driving past a billboard is part of the target market.

2. *Limited message capabilities.* Because of the speed with which most people pass by outdoor ads, exposure time is short, so messages are limited to a few words and/or an illustration. Lengthy appeals are not likely to be effective. Some transit forms are not conducive to creative messages.

3. *Wearout.* Because of the high frequency of exposures, outdoor may lead to a quick wearout. People are likely to get tired of seeing the same ad every day.

4. *Cost.* Because of the decreasing signage available and the higher cost associated with inflatables, outdoor advertising can be expensive in both an absolute and a relative sense.

5. *Measurement problems.* One of the more difficult problems of outdoor advertising lies in the accuracy of measuring reach, frequency, and other effects. (As you will see in the measurement discussion, this problem is currently being addressed, though it has not been resolved.)

Figure 13-7 Outdoor Continues to Demonstrate Effectiveness

Brand	Medium Used	Results
ESPN	Bulletins, transit, street furniture	11 percent ratings increase
Levis jeans for women	Posters, bulletins, transit	200 percent ad awareness increase; 1,200 percent brand identification increase
Starbucks frapuccino	Bulletins, street furniture, transit, aerial	11 percent sales increase
Wake Forest University MBA	Posters, bulletins	54 percent average rise in inquiries

6. *Image problems.* Outdoor advertising has suffered some image problems as well as some disregard among consumers.

In sum, outdoor advertising has both advantages and disadvantages for marketers. Some of these problems can be avoided with other forms of out-of-home advertising.

Advantages and Disadvantages of Transit Advertising

In addition to sharing some of the advantages and disadvantages of other outdoor media, transit has a few more specific to this medium. Advantages of using transit advertising include the following:

1. *Exposure.* Long length of exposure to an ad is one major advantage of indoor transit forms. The average ride on mass transit is 45 minutes, allowing for plenty of exposure time. As with airline tickets, the audience is essentially a captive one, with nowhere else to go and nothing much to do. As a result, riders are likely to read the ads—more than once. A second form of exposure transit advertising provides is the absolute number of people exposed. About 9 million people ride mass transit every week, and over 9.4 billion rides were taken in 2004, providing a substantial number of potential viewers.[10]

2. *Frequency.* Because our daily routines are standard, those who ride buses, subways, and the like are exposed to the ads repeatedly. If you rode the same subway to work and back every day, in one month you would have the opportunity to see the ad 20 to 40 times. The locations of station and shelter signs also afford high frequency of exposure.

Some disadvantages are also associated with transit:

1. *Reach.* While an advantage of transit advertising is the ability to provide exposure to a large number of people, this audience may have certain lifestyles and/or behavioral characteristics that are not true of the target market as a whole. For example, in rural or suburban areas, mass transit is limited or nonexistent, so the medium is not very effective for reaching these people.

2. *Mood of the audience.* Sitting or standing on a crowded subway may not be conducive to reading advertising, let alone experiencing the mood the advertiser would like to create. Controversial ad messages may contribute to this less than positive feeling. Likewise, hurrying through an airport may create anxieties that limit the effectiveness of the ads placed there.

Measurement in Out-of-Home Media

A number of sources of audience measurement and other information are available:

- Competitive Media Reports (formerly BAR/LNA) provides information on expenditures on outdoor media by major advertisers.
- Simmons Market Research Bureau conducts research annually for the Institute of Outdoor Advertising, providing demographic data, exposures, and the like. Mediamark Research Inc. (MRI) provides similar data.

• The Point of Purchase Advertising Institute is a trade organization of point-of-purchase advertisers collecting statistical and other market information on POP advertising.

• The Outdoor Advertising Association of America (OAAA) is the primary trade association of the industry. It assists members with research, creative ideas, and more effective use of the medium and has a website at www.oaa.org.

• The Traffic Audit Bureau (TAB) is the auditing arm of the transit industry. TAB conducts traffic counts on which the published rates are based.

• Scarborough publishes local market studies providing demographic data, product usage, and outdoor media usage.

• The American Public Transportation Association (APTA) provides ridership statistics, studies, and other transit usage information.

Promotional Products Marketing

According to the Promotional Products Association International (PPA), **promotional products marketing** is "the advertising or promotional medium or method that uses promotional products, such as ad specialties, premiums, business gifts, awards, prizes, or commemoratives." Promotional products marketing is the more up-to-date name for what used to be called specialty advertising. **Specialty advertising** has now been provided with a new definition:

> A medium of advertising, sales promotion, and motivational communication employing imprinted, useful, or decorative products called advertising specialties, a subset of promotional products.
>
> Unlike premiums, with which they are sometimes confused (called advertising specialties), these articles are always distributed free—recipients don't have to earn the specialty by making a purchase or contribution.[11]

As you can see from these descriptions, specialty advertising is often considered both an advertising and a sales promotion medium. In our discussion, we treat it as a supportive advertising medium in the IMC program.

There are more than 15,000 *advertising specialty* items, including ballpoint pens, coffee mugs, key rings, calendars, T-shirts, and matchbooks. Unconventional specialties such as plant holders, wall plaques, and gloves with the advertiser's name printed on them are also used to promote a company or its product; so are glassware, trophies, awards, and vinyl products. In fact, advertisers spend over $17.3 billion per year on specialty advertising items (Figure 13-8).[12]

If you stop reading for a moment and look around your desk (or bed or beach blanket), you'll probably find some specialty advertising item nearby. It may be the pen you are using, a matchbook, or even a book cover with the campus bookstore name on it. Specialty items are used for many promotional purposes: to thank a customer for patronage, keep the name of the company in front of consumers, introduce new products, or reinforce the name of an existing company, product, or service (Figure 13-9). Advertising specialties are often used to support other forms of product promotions.

Advantages and Disadvantages of Promotional Products Marketing

Like any other advertising medium, promotional products marketing offers the marketer both advantages and disadvantages. Advantages include the following:

1. *Selectivity.* Because specialty advertising items are generally distributed directly to target customers, the medium offers a high degree of selectivity. The communication is distributed to the desired recipient, reducing waste coverage.

2. *Flexibility.* As the variety of specialty items in Figure 13-8 demonstrates, this medium offers a high degree of flexibility. A message as simple as a logo or as long as is necessary can be distributed through a number of means. Both small and large com-

Figure 13-8 Promotional Products Sales by Product Category

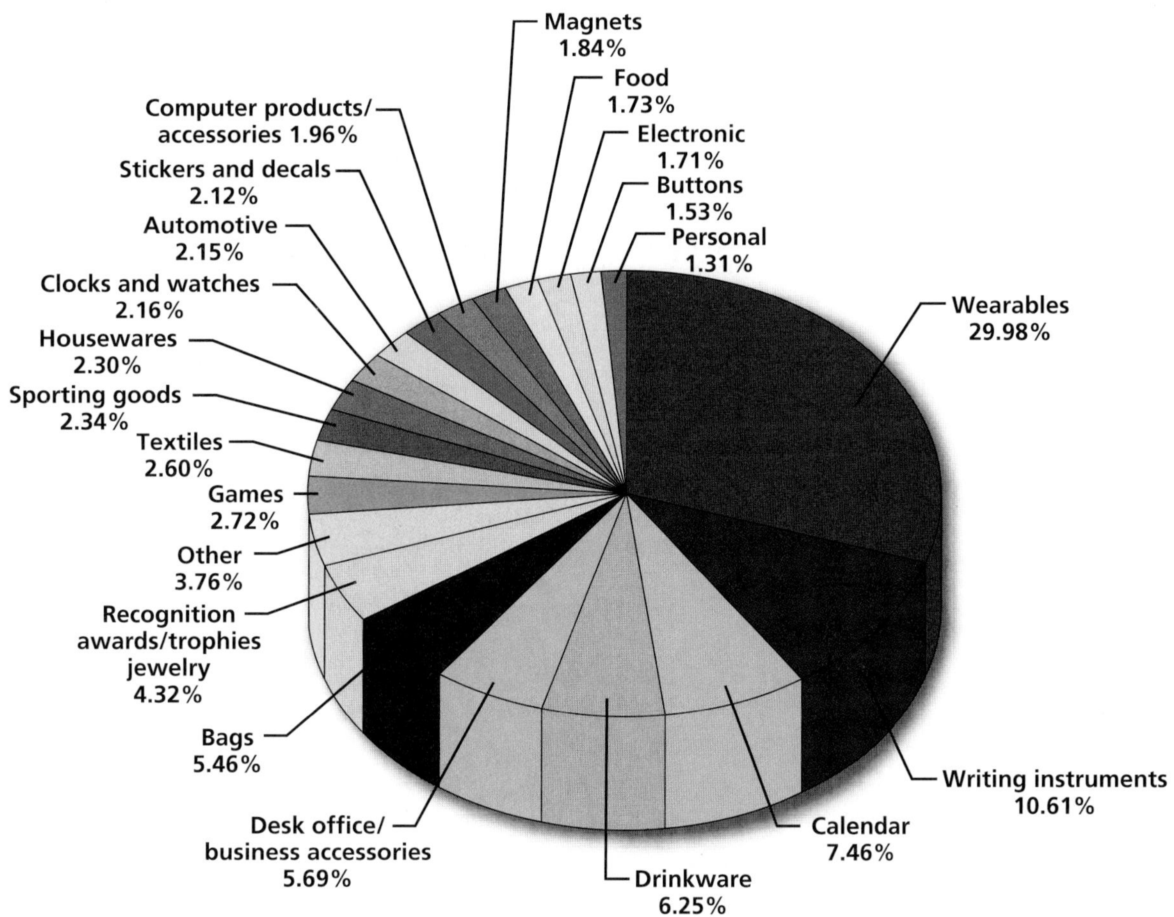

Source: http://www.ppa.org/ProductsResources/Research/SalesVolumeEstimates/

panies can employ this medium for a variety of objectives limited only by their own creativity.

3. *Frequency.* Most forms of specialty advertising are designed for retention. Key chains, calendars, and pens remain with the potential customer for a long time, providing repeat exposures to the advertising message at no additional cost.

4. *Cost.* Some specialty items are rather expensive (for example, leather goods), but most are affordable to almost any size organization. While they are costly on a CPM basis when compared with other media, the high number of repeat exposures drives down the relative cost per exposure of this advertising medium.

5. *Goodwill.* Promotional products are perhaps the only medium that generates goodwill in the receiver. Because people like to receive gifts and many of the products are functional (key chains, calendars, etc.), consumers are grateful to receive them. The products also lead to a favorable impression of the advertiser.

6. *High recall.* Specialties lead to high recall of both the advertisers' name and message.

7. *Supplementing other media.* A major advantage of promotional products marketing is its ability to supplement other media. Because of its low cost and repeat exposures, the simplest message can reinforce the appeal or information provided through other forms.

Promotional products have also been used to support trade shows, motivate dealers, recognize employees, and promote consumer and sales force contests.

Figure 13-9 Specialty Items Are Used for a Variety of Purposes

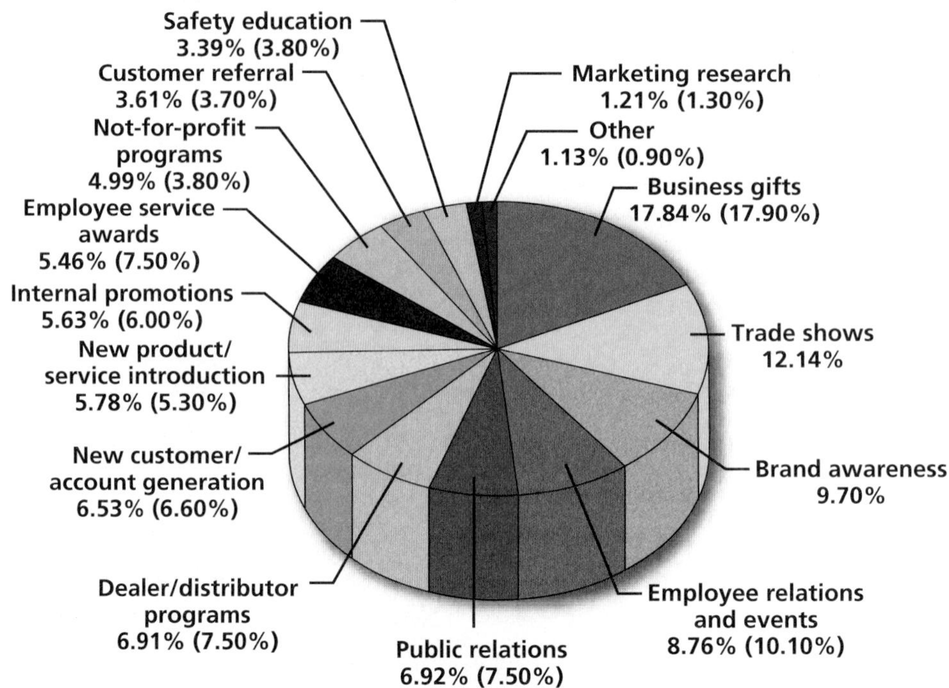

Source: http://www.ppa.org/ProductsResources/Research/SalesVolumeEstimates/
Note: Numbers in ( ) indicate 2003 figures.

Disadvantages of promotional products marketing include the following:

1. *Image.* While most forms of specialty advertising are received as friendly reminders of the store or company name, the firm must be careful choosing the specialty item. The company image may be cheapened by a chintzy or poorly designed advertising form.

2. *Saturation.* With so many organizations now using this advertising medium, the marketplace may become saturated. While you can always use another ballpoint pen or book of matches, the value to the receiver declines if replacement is too easy, and the likelihood that you will retain the item or even notice the message is reduced. The more unusual the specialty, the more value it is likely to have to the receiver.

3. *Lead time.* The lead time required to put together a promotional products message is significantly longer than that for most other media.

Even with its disadvantages, promotional products marketing can be an effective medium.

Measurement in Promotional Products Marketing

Owing to the nature of the industry, specialty advertising has no established ongoing audience measurement system. Research has been conducted in an attempt to determine the impact of this medium, however, including the following more recent reports.

In a 2004 study of 536 travelers through DFW Airport, the results showed the following:

- 71 percent report having received a promotional product in the last 12 months.
- 33.7 percent still had the item on them.
- 76 percent recalled the advertiser's name.
- 52 percent conducted business with the advertiser after receiving the promotional item.
- 52.1 percent had improved impressions of the company.
- 73 percent of those using the promotion used it once a week, 45.2 percent once a day.
- 55 percent kept it more than one year.[13]

A second study conducted by Georgia Southern University showed that 71.6 percent of attendees at a trade show remembered the name of the company that gave them the specialty; 65.5 percent thought it was useful; and 76.3 percent had a favorable attitude toward the company as a result.[14]

The Promotional Products Association International (www.ppai.org) is the trade organization of the field. The PPAI helps marketers develop and use specialty advertising forms. It also provides promotional and public relations support for specialty advertising and disseminates statistical and educational information.

Yellow Pages Advertising

When we think of advertising media, many of us overlook one of the most popular forms in existence—the **Yellow Pages.** While most of us use the Yellow Pages frequently, we tend to forget they are advertising. More than 250 publishers produce more than 7,000 Yellow Pages throughout the United States, generating $15.5 billion in advertising expenditures.[15]

More than 90 percent of the industry's ad revenues are accounted for by six big operators: Verizon, SBC, Bell South, Dex Media, RH Donnelley, and Yellowbook.[16] Local advertisers constitute the bulk of the ads in these directories (about 88 percent), though national advertisers such as U-Haul, Sears, and General Motors use them as well.[17]

Interestingly, there are several forms of Yellow Pages. (Because AT&T never copyrighted the term, any publisher can use it.) They include the following:

- *Specialized directories.* Directories are targeted at select markets such as Hispanics, blacks, Asians, and women. Also included in this category are toll-free directories, Christian directories, and many others.
- *Internet Yellow Pages.* The acquisition of yellowpages.com by SBC and Bell South combined with superpages.com led to 1.5 billion references in 2004 (compared to 16 billion in the paper Yellow Pages).[18] Continued growth is expected in this area.
- *Other services.* Some Yellow Pages directories offer coupons and freestanding inserts. In Orange County, California, telephone subscribers received samples of Golden Grahams and Cinnamon Toast Crunch cereals when their Yellow Pages were delivered.

The Yellow Pages are often referred to as a **directional medium** because the ads do not create awareness or demand for products or services; rather, once consumers have decided to buy, the Yellow Pages point them in the direction where their purchases can be made.[19] The Yellow Pages are thus considered the final link in the buying cycle, as shown in Exhibit 13-9. As shown in Figure 13-10, the Yellow Pages can extend the reach of other IMC media.

Exhibit 13-9 The Yellow Pages are the final link in the buying cycle

Advantages and Disadvantages of Yellow Pages

The Yellow Pages offer the following advantages to advertisers:

1. *Wide availability.* A variety of directories are published. According to the

Figure 13-10 How Yellow Pages Extend the Reach of Other Media

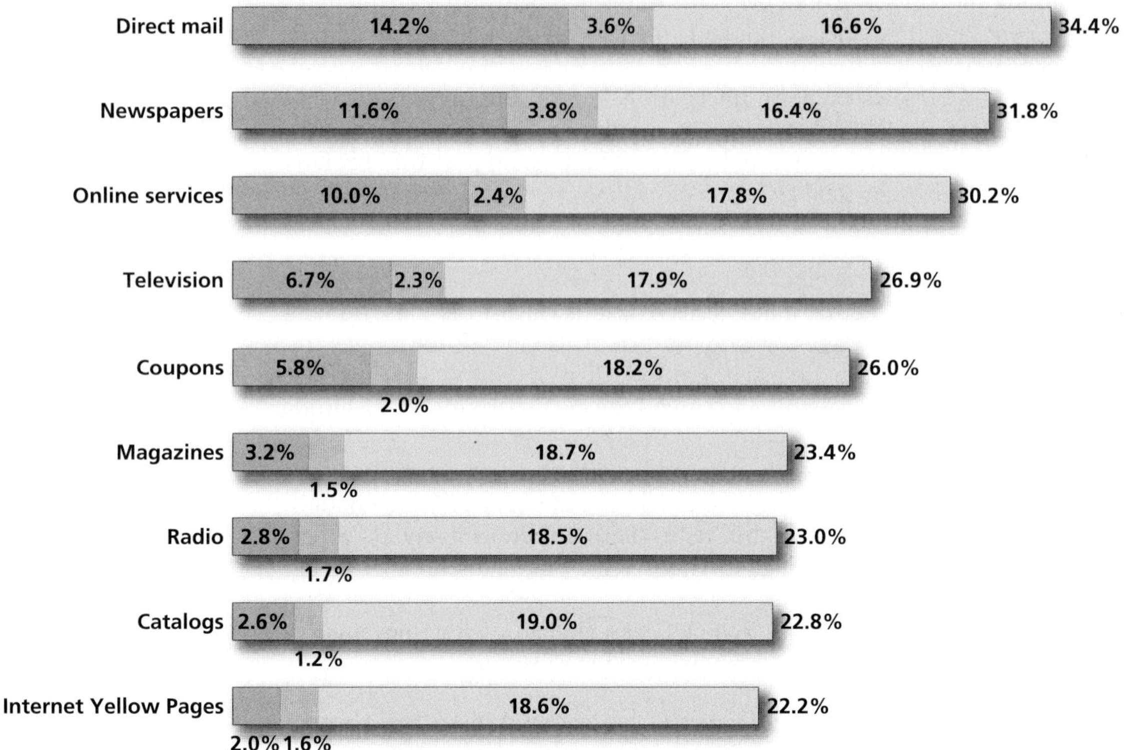

Note: Percent estimates represent a median percent based on media usage across 155 products and service categories among those consumers involved in a purchase decision. For a list of the product and service categories investigated, please contact YPA at (908-286-2380).
Source: 2005 Media Impact Study conducted by TNS.

Yellow Pages Publishers Association, consumers refer to the Yellow Pages more than 16.3 billion times yearly.[20]

2. *Action orientation.* Consumers use the Yellow Pages when they are considering, or have decided to take, action.

3. *Costs.* Ad space and production costs are relatively low compared to other media.

4. *Frequency.* Because of their longevity (Yellow Pages are published yearly), consumers return to the directories time and again.

5. *Nonintrusiveness.* Because consumers choose to use the Yellow Pages, they are not considered an intrusion. Studies show that most consumers rate the Yellow Pages very favorably.[21] Among users, 79 percent agree that the Yellow Pages are an important source of information, and 76 percent report that the books are helpful for learning about new products.

Disadvantages of the Yellow Pages include the following:

1. *Market fragmentation.* Since Yellow Pages are essentially local media, they tend to be very localized. Add to this the increasing number of specialized directories, and the net result is a very specific offering.

2. *Timeliness.* Because print Yellow Pages are printed only once a year, they become outdated. Companies may relocate, go out of business, or change phone numbers in the period between editions. (This problem is greatly reduced with the Internet pages.)

3. *Lack of creativity.* While the Yellow Pages are somewhat flexible, their creative aspects are limited, though the use of four-color processes is increasing.

4. *Lead times.* Printing schedules require that ads be placed a long time before the publications appear. It is impossible to get an ad in after the deadline, and advertisers need to wait a long time before the next edition.

5. *Clutter.* A study by Avery Abernethy indicated that the Yellow Pages (like other media) experience problems with clutter. (Though the Yellow Pages trade organization offers research evidence to contradict this conclusion.)[22]

6. *Size requirements.* Response to Yellow Pages ads is directly tied to the size of the ad. A study by Abernethy and Laband indicates that for large directories a minimum of one-half page may be required just to get noticed.[23]

As noted, many of these disadvantages will be reduced or eliminated with the Internet.

Audience Measurement in the Yellow Pages

Two forms of audience measurement are employed in the Yellow Pages industry. As with other print media, *circulation* is counted as the number of either individuals or households possessing a particular directory. But Yellow Pages advertisers have resisted the use of circulation figures for evaluating audience size, arguing that this number represents only *potential* exposures to an ad. Given that households may possess more than one directory, advertisers argued for a figure based on *usage.* The National Yellow Pages Monitor (NYPM) now provides Yellow Pages directory ratings and usage behavior by market. Using a diary method similar to that used for broadcast media, this ratings method allows advertisers to determine both the absolute and relative costs of advertising in different directories. Statistical Research Inc. (SRI) conducts national studies to measure Yellow Pages usage. Simmons and MRI provide demographic and usage information.

The trade association for the Yellow Pages, the Yellow Pages Integrated Media Association (www.yellowpagesima.org and www.yppa.org), provides industry information, rates, educational materials, and assistance to advertisers and potential advertisers. The YPPA also disseminates educational and statistical information.

Other Traditional Support Media

There are numerous other traditional ways to promote products. Some are reviewed here.

Advertising in Movie Theaters

Another method of delivering the message that is increasing quickly (to the dismay of many) is the use of movie theaters to promote products and/or services. Commercials shown before the film and previews, with both local and national sponsorships, are now regularly shown in movie theaters. In addition, ads in theater lobbies, at kiosks, and on popcorn tubs and drink cups are used. For example, PepsiCo has frequently advertised their brands in movie theaters. At least one study has estimated that more than one-half of all theaters show ads before the films. The growth rate has increased steadily since the 1980s, resulting in a $438 million industry by 2004—$82 million more than in 2003.[24]

Consumer reaction to ads in movie theaters is mixed. A number of studies have shown that most people think these ads are annoying or very annoying. Bills have been introduced in the Connecticut state legislature and the New York City council in response to public reaction against the commercials, and the Loews theater chain recently announced that its movie listings will announce the true start time of their movies for those who want to skip the advertising.[25]

Adam Snyder, writing in *Brandweek* magazine, believes that pushing movies is acceptable but beyond that consumers are likely to react negatively.[26] Nevertheless, Blake Thomas, marketing vice president for MGM/UA Home Entertainment, claims, "We could conceivably sell as much air time as we want, since advertisers cannot resist the temptation of reaching tens of millions of viewers."[27] In addition, a research study commissioned by one in-theater advertising broker showed that the ads were three times as likely to be remembered as TV ads.[28]

Advantages of Movie Theater Advertising

Movies provide a number of advantages to advertisers, including the following:

1. *Exposure.* The number of people attending movies is substantial: over 1.53 billion tickets were sold in 2004.[29] Ticket sales are over $9.0 billion per year.
2. *Mood.* If viewers like the movie, the mood can carry over to the product advertised.
3. *Cost.* The cost of advertising in a theater varies from one setting to the next. However, it is low in terms of both absolute and relative costs per exposure.
4. *Recall.* Research indicates that the next day about 83 percent of viewers can recall the ads they saw in a movie theater. This compares with a 20 percent recall rate for television.[30]
5. *Clutter.* Lack of clutter is another advantage offered by advertising in movie theaters. Most theaters limit the number of ads.
6. *Proximity.* Since many theaters are located in or adjacent to shopping malls, potential customers are "right next door." (Of moviegoers, 73 percent combine the activity with dining out, 69% percent with shopping.)
7. *Segmentation.* A key advantage of movie advertising is the ability to target specific demographic segments. The profile of the moviegoer is above-average in education and affluence. The movie titles and ratings enable advertisements to reach specific groups.

Disadvantages of Movie Theater Advertising

Some of the disadvantages associated with movie theaters as advertising media follow:

1. *Irritation.* Perhaps the major disadvantage is that many people do not wish to see advertising in these media. A number of studies suggest these ads may create a high degree of annoyance.[31] This dissatisfaction may carry over to the product itself, to the movies, or to the theaters. Mike Stimler, president of the specialty video label Water Bearer Films, says, "People boo in movie theaters when they see product advertising."[32] Anne-Marie Marcus, vice president of sales for Screen Vision, contends that the furor has died down, though the T. J. Maxx retail chain says it is unlikely to use this form of advertising again.[33]
2. *Cost.* While the cost of advertising in local theaters has been cited as an advantage because of the low rates charged, ads exposed nationally are often as much as 20 percent higher than an equal exposure on television. CPMs also tend to be higher than in other media.

While only two disadvantages of theater advertising have been mentioned, the first is a strong one. Many people who have paid to see a movie perceive advertising as an intrusion. In a study by Michael Belch and Don Sciglimpaglia, many moviegoers stated that not only would they not buy the product advertised, but they would consider boycotting it. So advertisers should be cautious in their use of this medium. If they want to use movies, they might consider an alternative—placing products in the movies.

In-Flight Advertising

Another rapidly growing medium is **in-flight advertising.** As the number of flying passengers increases, so too does the attractiveness of this medium. In-flight advertising includes four forms:

- *In-flight magazines.* Free magazines (like the one shown in Exhibit 13-10) published by the airlines are offered on almost every plane in the air. United Airlines distributes over 1 million of its *Hemispheres* magazines each month and estimates potential exposures at 1.9 million.[34]

- *In-flight videos.* In-flight videos have been common on international flights for some time and are now being used on domestic flights. Commercials were not originally included in these videos. While not all airlines offer in-flight commercials, companies like Japan Air Lines, Delta, American, and Alitalia are participating. American's *CBS Eye on American* is broadcast in English and Spanish.
- *In-flight radio.* XM satellite radio is now available on some airlines as is CNN news.
- *In-flight catalogs.* Almost all domestic airlines (as well as Amtrak) now offer in-flight shopping catalogs, reaching 88 percent of the domestic airline market.[35] The Sky Mall catalog (Exhibit 13-11) reaches over 1.8 million travelers per day and includes products from a variety of companies including Frontgate, Magellans, Casio, Bose, and Hammacher Schlemmer. Sky Mall also offers in-flight commercials.

Flight attendants promoting Saab's new SUV or signing up customers for Bank of America Visa cards, ads on seat backs and napkins, and companies placing such products as pretzels and cookies are other forms of advertising that are now taking place in-flight.

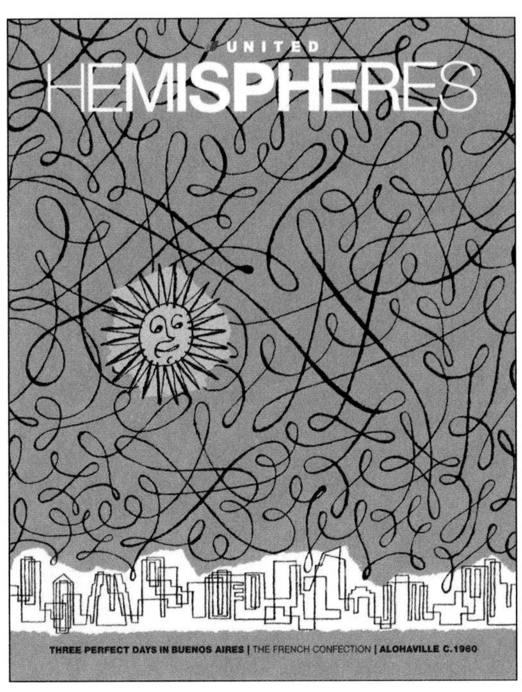

Exhibit 13-10 Hemispheres reaches the airline traveler

Advantages and Disadvantages of In-Flight Advertising

Advantages of in-flight advertising include the following:

1. *A desirable audience.* The median traveler is 43 years old and has a household income over $114,000. Both business and tourist travelers tend to be upscale, an attractive audience to companies targeting these groups. Thirteen percent of these passengers hold top management positions in their firms. *Hemispheres* reaches over 56 percent of business professionals and estimates that almost 93 percent of the magazine's readership are college educated (Figure 13-11).[36]
2. *A captive audience.* As noted in the discussion about ticket covers, the audience in an airplane cannot leave the room. Particularly on long flights, many passengers are willing (and even happy) to have in-flight magazines to read, news to listen to, and even commercials to watch.
3. *Cost.* The cost of in-flight commercials is lower than that of business print media. A four-color ad in *Hemispheres* costs approximately $48,320. A four-color spread in *Forbes* and *Fortune* would cost double that amount.
4. *Segmentation capabilities.* In-flight allows the advertiser to reach specific demographic groups, as well as travelers to a specific destination. For example, both business and pleasure travelers flying domestic or international can be targeted.

Disadvantages of in-flight advertising include the following:

1. *Irritation.* Many consumers are not pleased with the idea of ads in general and believe they are already too intrusive. In-flight commercials are just one more place, they think, where advertisers are intruding.
2. *Limited availability.* Many airlines limit the amount of time they allow for in-flight commercials.
3. *Lack of attention.* Many passengers may decide to tune out the ads, not purchase the headsets required to get the volume, or simply ignore the commercials.
4. *Wearout.* Given projections for significant increases in the number of in-flight ads being shown, airline passengers may soon be inundated by these commercials.

Exhibit 13-11 Sky Mall reaches travelers through print catalogs and commercials

Figure 13-11 In-Flight Media Reach a Desirable Target Audience

	US Adults	Hemispheres	
	Comp%	Comp	Index
Demographics			
Men	48.0%	64.0%	133
Women	52.0%	36.0%	6
Married	56.6%	69.9%	123
Single	43.4%	30.1%	69
Age			
18–49 Years	62.2%	71.6%	115
25–54 Years	58.1%	75.7%	130
35–49 Years	30.8%	41.1%	133
35–54 Years	39.6%	50.4%	127
Education			
College Educated	51.8%	92.9%	179
Graduated College or Further	24.8%	74.2%	300
Post-Graduate Degree	8.3%	28.7%	346
Employment			
Full Time Employment	53.2%	72.7%	137
Professional/Managerial	22.5%	56.4%	250
Top Management	4.0%	12.9%	325
Home Ownership			
Owns a Home	71.6%	80.1%	112
Value of Owned Home: $200,000+	28.3%	61.2%	216
Value of Owned Home: $500,000+	5.9%	22.3%	379
Affluence			
HHI $75,000+	30.9%	74.7%	242
HHI $100,000+	17.8%	60.5%	341
HHI $150,000+	6.8%	23.8%	350
IEI $75,000+	7.0%	44.1%	626
IEI $100,000+	3.4%	26.6%	774
IEI $150,000+	1.2%	8.6%	691

Nontraditional Support Media

Branded Entertainment

Perhaps the major change that has occurred in the area of integrated marketing communications over the past few years is the enormous growth associated with **branded entertainment.** Branded entertainment is a form of advertising that blends marketing and entertainment through television, film, music talent, and technology. Essentially, the goal is to use entertainment media to gain consumers' attention and exposure to products and/or brands. In a study conducted by the Association of National Advertisers, 63 percent of the advertising executives surveyed said that their companies currently use some form of branded entertainment, with another 11 percent stating that although they do not use this medium, they plan to do so within the next year.[37]

Let's take a look at the ways companies use branded entertainment.

Product Placements While **product placements** account for only a small portion of major advertisers' budgets, the use of this medium has increased tremendously in recent years (46.4 percent from 2003 to 2004, and a projected growth of 22.7 percent in 2005), to where it now constitutes a $4.3 billion industry (Figure 13-12).[38] Industry analysts expect this trend to continue as placements move from traditional media to alternative media, as personal video recorder growth sales continue (allowing for increased avoidance of commercials), and as consumers' lifestyles change.

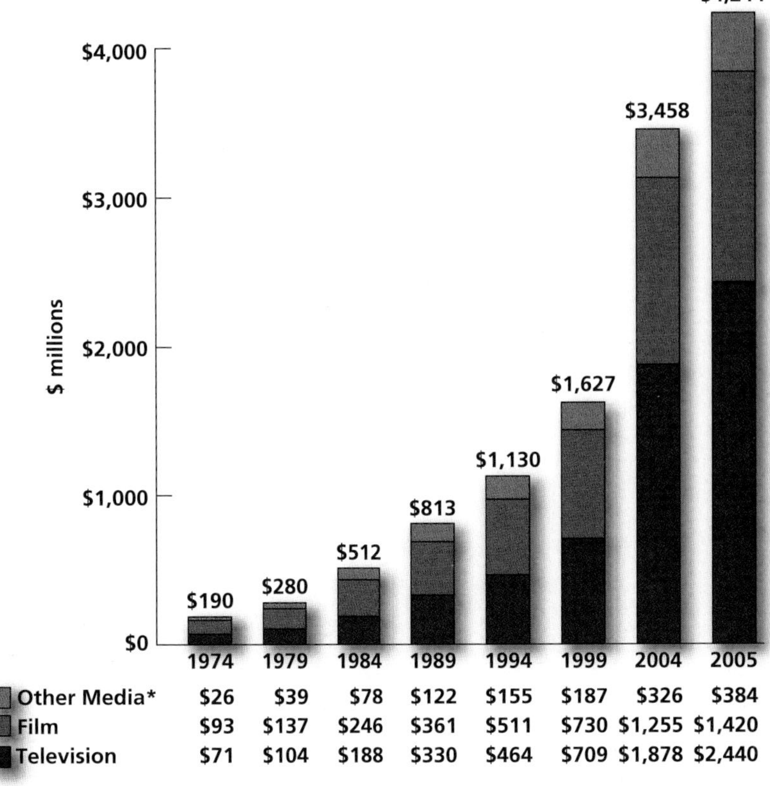

*Magazines, newspapers, videogames, Internet, recorded music, books, radio

Source: Adapted from *PQ Media,* February 2006.

Figure 13-12 Expenditures on Product Placements Continue to Increase

Interestingly, product placements are not a new phenomenon as placements are known to have existed as early as the 1930s and were commonly employed via soap operas in the 1950s. However, it was not until the turn of the century that the number of placements skyrocketed. Today, product placements are used to gain exposure by numerous companies large and small (Exhibit 13-12) and are a very important part of the IMC strategy for companies like BMW, Apple Computers, PepsiCo, and Anheuser Busch (just to name a few). Much of the logic behind product placement is that since the placement is embedded in the script or program setting, it cannot be avoided, thereby increasing exposure. Given the lack of intrusiveness of the placement, consumers may not have the same negative reactions to it as they may to a commercial. Further, research has demonstrated that association with a program or movie—or particularly with a celebrity—will enhance the image of the product and, in some instances, lead to increased sales.[39,40]

Given the intense growth in the number of product placements, some marketers are concerned that placements may be becoming too common. In the second quarter of 2005, the 10 most frequently seen brands on TV appeared 6,077 times, while the top 10 shows with placements had 11,579 placements.[41] It is very rare to watch a movie or TV show without being exposed to one or more placements. Given the obvious attempt to gain exposure in many of these, placements may be becoming more obvious; consumers may perceive them more like ads and, as a result, they may have less impact on the viewer.[42] Some industry watchdogs have called for more regulation of placements, contending that they blur the lines between advertising and programming and therefore may be deceptive. However, in 2005 the FTC ruled against requiring placement disclosures on TV shows.

As of this time, however, product placements continue to increase both in number and in dollar amounts. In addition, placements are appearing in media and situations never before imagined (see the lead-in to this chapter).

Exhibit 13-12 Apple Computers makes frequent use of product placements

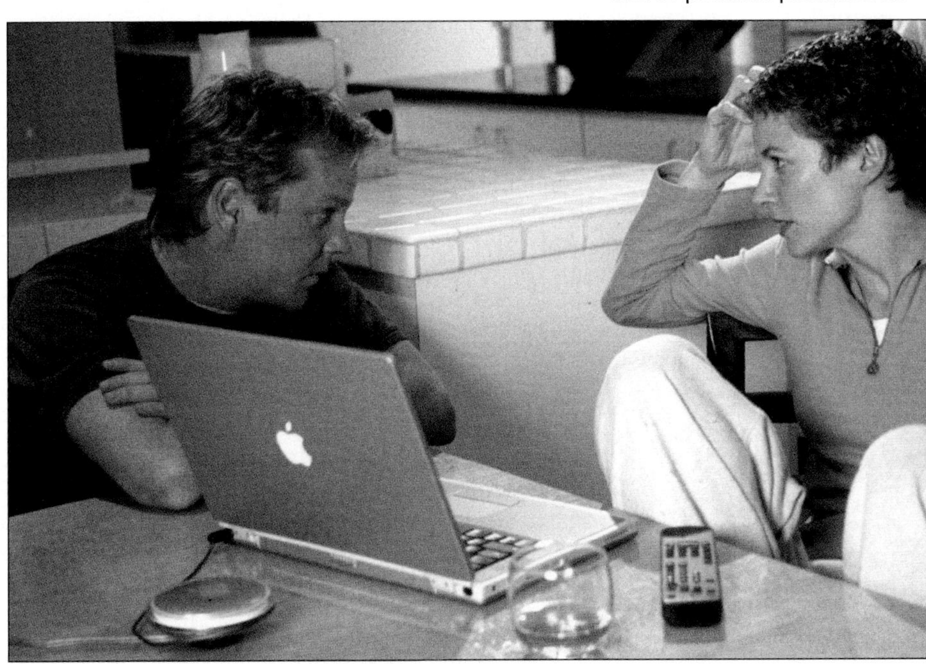

Source: *L.A. Times,* January 19, 2005, p. A1. Danny Field ABC Photo.

Product Integration A more involved form of product placements actually leads to the placement being integrated throughout the program content and/or script. In **product integrations** the product is woven throughout the program (*American Idol*) or becomes the program itself (*The Apprentice*). (See IMC Perspective 13-1.) Like product placements, product integrations are on the increase as the networks continue to search for new program content, and the proliferation of cable media channels affords marketers with numerous integration opportunities. Each of the major networks, as well as the WB, expects the trend to continue in the near future; in fact, CBS is considering charging separate integration fees.[43]

Advertainment The creation of video and/or music content by an advertiser in an attempt to entertain viewers while advertising their products is known as advertainment. For example, Coca-Cola developed a long-form advertainment to reach TiVo viewers. The program included 25 minutes of interviews, music videos, behind-the-scenes footage, and live performances with recording artists Sting, Mary J. Blige, Ashanti, and Leona Ness. Coca-Cola ads were tagged so that TiVo users could see them and then click on an icon to download the program. Unilever developed a mini-soap opera parody to promote its "I Can't Believe Its Not Butter" brand, and the manufacturers of Nestea, Angel Soft toilet paper, and numerous others have also created their own advertainment programs or sites.

Content Sponsorship Rather than developing their own content, some advertisers agree to sponsor specific programs, receiving product placements, integration, and promotions in return. For example, P&G has collaborated with the Discovery Health Channel on a *National Body Challenge* 12-week weight loss program. Kmart provided wardrobe for five shows on the WB Television Network, which the stars wore in various episodes, while Campbell Soup Company backed an essay contest with NBC's *American Dreams* program. Home Depot and PepsiCo are among numerous others pursuing this strategy.

Ad-Supported Video on Demand (VOD) VODs are specialized content programs offered through cable TV networks that are developed by advertisers and provided to the cable operators for free. For example, General Motors produced a short feature on the history of the Corvette to be shown on CNN through Time Warner and Comcast's VOD channels, which currently reach more than 10 million viewers. Reebok has developed a VOD program to run in Philadelphia to show their advertisements and footage of interviews with Allen Iverson and hip-hop stars Jay-Z and 50 Cent; the San Diego Zoo provides a video tour to San Diego cable subscribers; and the NFL provides 10-minute game summaries. On some VODs advertisers can buy placements, commercials, and/or virtual signage or sponsor specific segments.

Others While other forms of branded entertainment continue to develop through wireless, mobile, and "branded locations," space does not allow us to discuss each in detail. Suffice it to say that the use of branded entertainment continues to increase and will continue to do so as more and more technological innovations provide opportunities.

Advantages of Branded Entertainment A number of advantages of branded entertainment have been suggested:

1. *Exposure.* In regard to product placements, a large number of people see movies each year (over 1.5 billion admissions per year). The average film is estimated to have a life span of three and one-half years (with 75 million exposures), and most moviegoers are very attentive audience members. When this is combined with the increasing home video rental market and network and cable TV (for example, HBO, Showtime, the Movie Channel), the potential exposure for a product placed in a movie or on television is enormous. And this form of exposure is not subject to zapping, at least not in the theater.

   High exposure numbers are also offered for TV placements, based on the ratings and the possibility to direct the ad to a defined target market.

2. *Frequency.* Depending on how the product is used in the movie (or program), there may be ample opportunity for repeated exposures (many, for those who like to watch a program or movie more than once). For example, if you are a regular watcher of the

IMC PERSPECTIVE 13-1

Selling through Product Integration Becomes the New TV Show Success Story

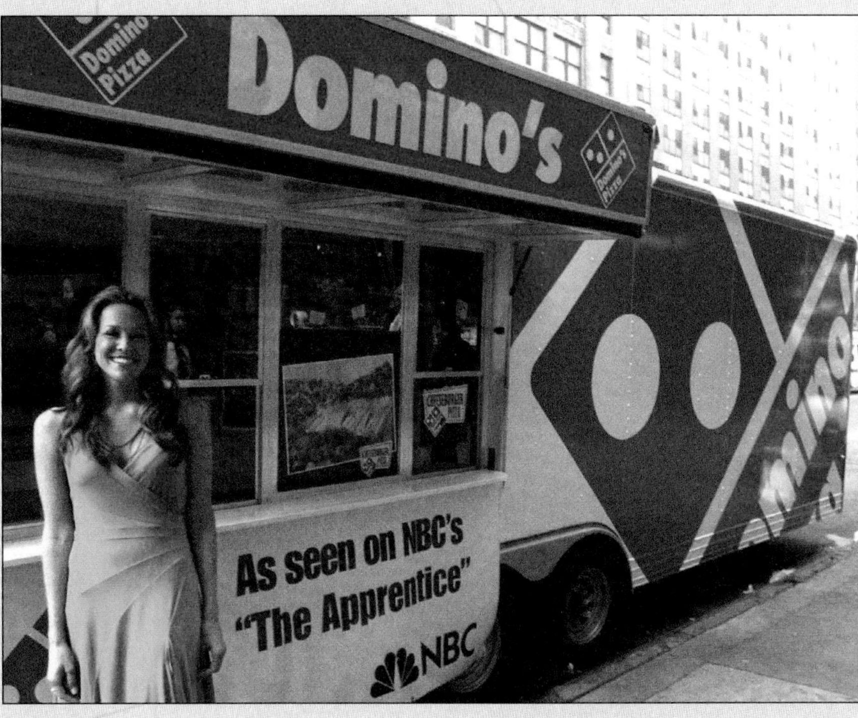

The market concern (or maybe panic?) with the ability of TV viewers to avoid commercials has led to a search to find new ways to deliver messages about products and services. One of the most popular of the new media with advertisers is product placement, in which products appear in a TV program, either in the background or in use. Based on the logic that if something is good, more of it must be better, product placements have now been extended not only to appear in TV shows, but to become the TV shows themselves. Like reality TV, some believe that these product integrations are the future for TV—at least in the short run.

Perhaps the most well-known integration TV show is *The Apprentice.* The popular program, starring real estate mogul Donald Trump and produced by Mark Burnett, is a reality-type show in which teams compete against each other with individuals eliminated each week until only one is left—essentially, a *Survivor* show where the competition is based on business acumen. The winner receives a job in Trump's organization. In the first season, the contestants competed by designing marketing plans on projects like selling lemonade and operating rickshaws. But as the ratings increased, so did the interest by large companies, who saw the show as an opportunity to get their products in front of the public in an innovative fashion—and for a lot longer than a 30-second commercial. Mattel, Procter and Gamble's Crest, Levi Strauss & Company, Pepsi's Edge, Burger King, The Home Depot, Dove Soap, and Mars' M-Azing candy bar are just some of the products and brands that became stars in the show, for a placement fee of somewhere between $2 million and $5 million.

In ABC's *Extreme Makeover: Home Edition,* down-and-out everyday people have a new house built or remodeled in seven days. Each week the builders shop at Sears for products for the remodel, fitting it with Kenmore appliances and other top-of-the-line items. Also participating are Ford (which provides vehicles for the family and the heavy-duty trucks that transport the materials) and Pella (which provides windows), among others.

Banana Republic has also entered the integration game with a reality series called *Project Runway,* a one-hour series hosted by model Heidi Klum in which contestants compete for a job as a "big fashion designer" for Banana Republic. The goal is to improve the store's brand image. L'Oreal provides the beauty care products used in the show. *Queer Eye for the Straight Guy,* another product-integrated program, redresses and restyles men with, of course, brand name designer products. Even *The Oprah Winfrey Show* has episodes built around integration, such as the "Great Pontiac Giveaway" in which all 276 audience members were given new Pontiac G-6 autos. The program also included footage of Oprah helping on the product's assembly line and praising the car's features.

Where will it end? Will TV programming become just one more way to sell products? So far, the sponsors are impressed. Virtually all of the companies participating in *The Apprentice* are pleased with the results, claiming increases in everything from brand awareness to website hits to actual sales increases. The Pontiac giveaway on *Oprah* was considered an unprecedented success in terms of receiving an enormous amount of public relations and has been leveraged into even more marketing events.

But how long can this go on? Won't America tire of this blatant and obvious attempt to sell products disguised as TV programming? Some of those involved in marketing and TV think so. Calling such programming "high-end infomercials" and "advertisements disguised as TV shows," MSNBC contributor Andy Dehnart says the sponsors are not always winners. Dehnart notes that on certain episodes of *The Apprentice* the product integrations have not helped, and have maybe even hurt the company's image. For example, in some episodes the companies have been blamed for the contestant's failures, products and/or campaigns were poorly designed or never implemented, and, in at least one case, a competitor stole the idea developed on the program. Others have criticized the programs as deceptive because the viewers are not informed that companies have paid for the product integrations. The consumers themselves may also be weighing in, as ratings for *The Apprentice* have significantly declined. But why take it so seriously? It's only a TV show, right?

Sources: David Kiley, "Extreme Makeover: A Product Placement Dream," *BusinessWeek Online,* April 7, 2005, pp. 1–2; Claire Atkinson, "Banana Republic Sponsors New Reality TV Show," AdAge.com, May 24, 2004, pp. 1–2; Meg James, "Products Are Stars in New Ad Strategy," *Los Angeles Times,* December 2, 2004, pp. C1, C10; Andy Dehnart, "*Apprentice* Sponsors Are the Real Losers," msnbc.msn.com, April 8, 2005, pp. 1–4.

programs containing placements and/or integrations, you will be exposed to the products placed therein a number of times.

3. *Support for other media.* Branded entertainment supports other promotional tools. A trend in the movie industry is to have the client that is placing the product cross-promote the product and movie tie-in in multiple media venues as well as through the Internet and sales promotions. As noted, the tie-ins reinforce and are reinforced by ads and commercials.

4. *Source association.* In Chapter 6 we discussed the advantages of source identification. When consumers see their favorite TV celebrities or movie stars using certain brands, the association may lead to a favorable product image or even to sales. In one study of 524 eight- to fourteen-year-olds, 75 percent stated that they notice when brands are placed on their favorite shows, and 72 percent said that seeing a favorite character using a brand makes them want to purchase that brand.[44] Another study among adults showed that one-third of viewers said they try a product after seeing it on a TV show or movie.[45] Reebok, for example, may benefit from its association with Allen Iverson or 50 Cent.

5. *Cost.* While the cost of branded entertainment may range from free samples to $2 million, the latter is an extreme. The CPM for this form of advertising can be very low, owing to the high volume of exposures it generates.

6. *Recall.* A number of firms have measured the impact of product placements on next-day recall. Results ranged from Johnson's Baby Shampoo registering 20 percent to Kellogg's Corn Flakes registering 67 percent. Average recall is approximately 38 percent. Again, these scores are better than those reported for TV viewing. A study provided by Pola Gupta and Kenneth Lord showed that prominently displayed placements led to strong recall.[46]

7. *Bypassing regulations.* In the United States as well as many foreign countries, some products are not permitted to advertise on television or to specific market segments. Product placements and integrations have allowed the cigarette and liquor industries to have their products exposed, circumventing these restrictions. Recently there have been attempts to control the bypassing of regulations. The Marin Institute, an alcohol industry watchdog group, has filed suit against Budweiser for their tie-ins to the movie *The Wedding Crasher,* arguing that the movie encourages underage drinking. Spirits manufacturers Diageo, Bacardi USA, and Brown-Forman have also been named in lawsuits for similar reasons.[47]

8. *Acceptance.* A study by Pola Gupta and Stephen Gould indicated that viewers are accepting of product placements and in general evaluate them positively, though some products (alcohol, guns, cigarettes) are perceived as less acceptable.[48] Other studies report similar results, with one showing that as many as 80 percent of consumers say they have a positive attitude toward placements.[49] In a study conducted with tweens, 43 percent said they found placements to be funny, 39 percent found them to be informative, and 35 percent found them entertaining and interesting.[50]

9. *Targeting.* Content sponsorships and VOD may effectively reach potential customers with a strong interest in the subject matter (i.e., fashion, football).

Disadvantages of Product Placements

Some disadvantages are also associated with product placements:

1. *High absolute cost.* While the CPM may be very low for various forms of branded entertainment, the absolute costs may be very high, pricing some advertisers out of the market. The increased demand for branded entertainment, coupled with the rising emphasis by the studios for cross-promotions, drives costs up considerably. A study conducted by the National Association of Advertisers in 2005 indicated that 79 percent of advertisers believe that the costs of branded entertainment deals were too high.[51] One of the pioneers of branded entertainment—BMW—has ceased using this form of promotion citing the rising costs.

2. *Time of exposure.* While the way some products are exposed to the audience has an impact, there is no guarantee viewers will notice the product. Some product placements are more conspicuous than others. When the product is not featured prominently, the advertiser runs the risk of not being seen (although, of course, the same risk is present in all forms of media advertising).

CAREER PROFILE

Nancie Vann

Vice-President and Sales Manager of The Adcentive Group

Never in my wildest imagination while growing up in Detroit, Michigan did I think I would end up in the position I am in today. My path after graduation from Michigan State University with a B.S. in speech and hearing sciences took many twists and turns and each one helped me find my home at The Adcentive Group.

After graduation, I began working as a special education teacher in the Detroit area working with severely disabled children. While working I got my graduate degree from the University of Michigan in counseling and guidance. Shortly thereafter, I married and moved to Mexico City, Mexico and was unable to work there legally because of the type of papers with which I came into the country. Over the next 10 years, I did some private speech therapy, became fluent in Spanish, and had three children. In 1978, I moved with my family to San Diego. Once my children were in school, I knew I had to find something to do to keep my mind and body active and challenged.

About a year after our move a friend introduced me to another friend who had just moved to San Diego to retire. When we started talking about the business he was retiring from, I learned about the amazing world of promotional products advertising. He and I would talk for hours about the field and I became fascinated by this unique form of advertising. My father had been a partner of one of the largest mass media agencies in Detroit, but this was a whole new arena for me. After a few months, my new friend decided that San Diego was ripe for a locally based agency and made the decision to go back into the business. He made me an offer to start the company with him, while still having time for my family and having fun working with clients on creative projects. How could I possibly say no?

And so our journey began. I knew very little about the sales process, the market, or the ins and outs of the industry, but I had a true professional to learn from. My new partner had run some of General Motors most successful premium and recognition programs and was very eager to share his knowledge with me. When I asked if I could go out on a sales call with him just to see how it was done, he told me, "No. I don't want you to turn in to a mini-me. You need to be yourself." I had so much to learn and was quite concerned about how I was going to manage with no real sales experience. He gave me a crash course in product information and told me he would always be there to brainstorm with me. He was true to his word. I remember not knowing who to call on to see if they needed my services. Deciding that I loved to travel, I started going through the phone book and tried to make appointments with travel agents. At least I felt I could speak their language! At one of my first appointments, the owner of a company told me about an upcoming trip to China he was planning for a large group and asked if I could get personalized fortune cookies for him to distribute. I had no idea if I could or could not, but told him I would check with my sources and get back to him. With my heart pounding I left his office and went on my quest. Sure enough, I could get what he wanted and called him immediately to let him know it could be taken care of. I felt so exhilarated and proud and knew this new "occupation" was going to be fun.

> "If there is a problem that arises, come up with a solution and let the client know what is happening."

Before long, we moved out of the bonus room office and into real office space. We hired two new account executives to sell, and two full-time people on the support side. Every hour of every day proved to be different, creative, challenging, and exciting. No two clients ever seemed to need or want the same thing. I was providing my clients with an opportunity to get directly into their target market's space. Whether it was items for the desktop that carried a logo or a product that was used in the home or worn by a person, I could come up with ideas. The more I sold, the more confident I became. I quickly learned not to take rejection personally and made myself a creative resource to all my clients. The more I could understand the client's businesses and what their needs were, the more valuable I would become to them. We work so hard to get a client that it's imperative we do everything we can to keep them as a client. Through the years I learned that communication is the key to having good relationships. Whether you have good news or bad news about a project you are working on, it is a must to communicate with the client in a timely manner. If there is a problem that arises, come up with a solution and let the client know what is happening. This has served me well.

After The Adcentive Group celebrated its 12th year and we had 10 account executives I added the role of sales manager to my daily tasks. My own client list had grown to well over 150 companies for whom I was providing imprinted items that were used for internal and external promotions, trade shows, recognition programs, sales incentives, grand openings, and a myriad of other purposes. With the hiring of new account executives, I felt it was important to make myself available to go out on sales calls with them if they so desired. Some took me up on the offer, others did not. Trying to be as accessible as possible is something I have always strived to do.

The love I have for my job is something I enjoy sharing with others, whether they are people in the business, clients, or students. Most people are not aware of the power of promotional products advertising. Today, in 2006, it is a $17 billion-dollar-a-year industry and continues to grow every year. Twenty-six years ago, when I began, the industry was doing about $6 million a year. To think that I have been a part of that growth is very exciting. The Adcentive Group now has 17 account executives and this girl from Michigan has been blessed to have had the opportunity to get in to a profession that she loves and didn't even realize existed until 26 years ago.

3. *Limited appeal.* The appeal that can be made in some of these media forms is limited. There is no potential for discussing product benefits or providing detailed information. Rather, appeals are limited to source association, use, and enjoyment. The endorsement of the product is indirect, and the flexibility for product demonstration is subject to its use in the medium.

4. *Lack of control.* In many movies, the advertiser has no say over when and how often the product will be shown. Many companies have found that their placements in movies did not work as well as expected. Fabergé developed an entire Christmas campaign around its Brut cologne and its movie placement, only to find the movie was delayed until February. Others have had their placements cut from the script.

5. *Public reaction.* Many TV viewers and moviegoers are incensed at the idea of placing ads in programs or movies. These viewers want to maintain the barrier between program content and commercials. If the placement is too intrusive, they may develop negative attitudes toward the brand. The increased use of placements and integrations has led many consumers to be annoyed by what they consider to be crass commercialization. The FTC has explored options for limiting placements without consumer notification, though they have not sought increased regulation.

6. *Competition.* The appeal of branded entertainment has led to increased competition to get one's product placed, increasing demand and costs.

7. *Negative placements.* Some products may appear in movie scenes that are disliked by the audience or create a less than favorable mood. For example, in the movie *Missing,* a very good, loyal father takes comfort in a bottle of Coke, while a Pepsi machine appears in a stadium where torturing and murders take place—not a good placement for Pepsi.

8. *Clutter.* The rapid growth of branded entertainment tie-ins has led to an overwhelming number of placements and integrations as noted previously. Like other forms of advertising, too many placements and integrations will eventually lead to clutter and loss of effectiveness.

Measurement in Branded Entertainment

With the rapid growth in branded entertainment have come a number of research studies and companies attempting to monitor and measure the impact of this media form. At this time, there is no one accepted standard used by advertisers or industry members.[52] However, a number of high-profile companies now offer services in this area including those listed below.

- *Nielsen Media Research.* The TV ratings company currently tracks product placements on network television. The company has plans to track cable programs in the near future.
- *IAG Research.* IAG maintains a panel where an average of 5,000 daily viewers take an online quiz about the previous night's prime-time programs, the commercials, and product placements therein. The information is used to determine which ads work best; what shows, spots, and placements are being remembered; and viewers' attitudes toward the same.
- *Deutsch/iTVX.* The advertising agency and product integration valuation company have combined efforts to measure Results-Oriented-Integration. The method values the quality of each hundredth of a second of an integration, and then translates them into a Product Placement/Commercial Cost Ratio to value the integration by comparing it to the value of a commercial.
- *Brand Advisors.* The company attempts to value brand integration in feature films. A number of other companies have begun to offer various services including NextMedium, Delivery Agent, IEG, Image Impact, and others. As noted, however, none of these has received universal acceptance in the industry or among advertisers.

In addition to the studies reported earlier, research by Eva Steortz showed that viewers had an average recall for placements of 38 percent.[53] And Damon Darlin has provided evidence that an aura of glamour is added to products associated with celebrities.[54]

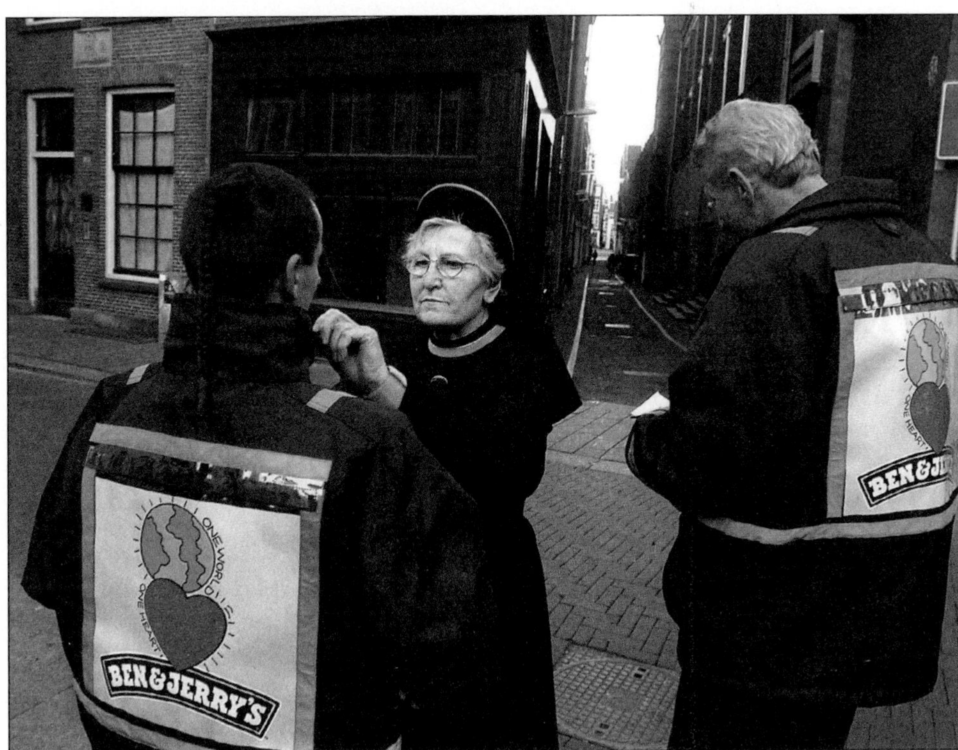

Exhibit 13-13 Ben & Jerry's take to the street to advertise

Guerilla Marketing In addition to branded entertainment another nontraditional way that advertisers are now attempting to reach consumers is referred to by a variety of names including guerilla marketing, stealth, street, buzz, ambush, or viral marketing. Whatever it is called, there seems to be no end in sight to where advertisers will attempt to reach you. While previously targeted primarily to college students and others of the same age group, these efforts have now been expanded to reach additional audiences as well (Exhibit 13-13).[55] In addition, larger portions of the communications budgets (while still small) are being allocated to this media form, and the size of the various projects is getting larger as well.[56] Commonly employed by brands such as AXE and Red Bull, these guerilla-type of campaigns are now being adopted by companies targeting broader audiences (such as Sony Ericsson), business-to-business customers (Johnson & Johnson's McNeil Consumer & Specialty Pharmaceuticals), and for social causes (Toyota Scion).[57] Thus, many marketers believe that these media have now become "mainstream." As IMC Perspective 13-2 shows, however, one might have to describe *mainstream* very broadly to characterize them as such.

Miscellaneous Other Media

As you can tell from IMC Perspective 13-2, the variety of options for placing ads appears endless. Obviously, we have reported on only a few of these. Chapter 15 will discuss a few more, specifically online vehicles. Before leaving this chapter, however, we would like to mention a few of the faster growing and more widely used options.

- *Videogame ads.* The number of videogamers, now an estimated 108 million, is expected to grow to more than 126 million by 2008, with advertising in this medium expected to reach $8.3 million.[58] Companies such as Orbitz and Chrysler have found videogame ads to be successful, as have Nike, Coca-Cola, Nokia, Levi Strauss & Company, and others. A videogame advertising network was launched in 2005.
- *Parking lot ads.* An out-of-home medium showing increased growth is that of parking lot signage. From signs on cart docks to painting the walls of indoor parking

IMC PERSPECTIVE 13-2

Is Nothing Sacred? Advertisers Seek New Media to Get Their Messages Out

There are those who might argue that advertisers have gone too far in their efforts to get their messages out. In their continuing search for exposure, no place and no thing is too sacred for an advertisement. Likewise, in the quest to be on the receiving end of the revenue stream, everyone seems to want to offer an advertising medium. Consider the following, which is just a sampling of where ads now appear.

- *Forehead for rent.* In Omaha, Nebraska, a 20-year-old Web designer named Andrew Fischer auctioned off the use of his forehead as advertising space on eBay. Fischer received $37,375 for allowing a company to place a bright red temporary tattoo on his head. The company—a snoring remedy company—believes it easily received its money's worth, as Fischer and his forehead appeared on ABC's *Good Morning America,* Fox TV's *Fox and Friends,* and numerous other media, including this textbook.
- *Body for rent.* If you can rent a forehead, why not the rest of your body? Courtney Van Dunk, a 21-year-old business major from New Jersey, auctioned her bikini-clad body as advertising space: tatoos on the abdomen for beach ads, and other body parts for other venues such as the mall, sporting events, or other public places. Van Dunk received an offer from a New Jersey wine retailer for $11,300 a month, and had calls from as far away as Zambia.
- *More skin.* It must be the craze! Bodybillboardz.com recently listed 21 different persons willing to offer up body locations where advertisers could place an ad. At least one listing offered up an arm and a forehead for $1,500 a month. Porn or nudity is not encouraged (unless the advertiser offers more money!).
- *Celebrity hair.* While NBA stars argue over who has the best-looking hairdo—cornrows, color, flattop, pigtails, and shaved heads are all in contention—the winner in the entrepreneurial category may very well be Richard Hamilton. Hamilton, a guard for the Detroit Pistons, recently sported a haircut reflecting the tread on Goodyear's Assurance Triple Tred tire. Hamilton's stylist braided his hair in the same pattern that appeared on the tire, while Goodyear paid for the exposure. The amount paid for the space was not revealed, though Goodyear did throw in a few tires for good measure. Maybe this is the start of a new "tre(n)d"?
- *Urinal voice messages.* Just to demonstrate how far it has gone in the not-on-the-body category, Country Music Television (CMT) recently announced that it would place ads in urinals in bars, concert venues, colleges, and radio stations to promote the CMT *Outlaws* concert. The ads are planned to appear on the drain filter cover with an antiglare viewing display, prerecorded audio message, and flashing lights. When activated, a woman's voice says, "Don't miss *Outlaws* on CMT. You seem to miss everything else!" The devices are designed to last for 10,000 flushes. Nintendo considered this medium instrumental in one of its most successful game launches: "Conker's Bad Fur Day."

No, we are not kidding!

Sources: Whitelaw Reid, "Dos & Don'ts," *San Diego Union Tribune,* February 14, 2005, pp. C1, 10; Lee Drutman, "All the World's an Ad," *The Providence Journal,* promo.com, May 16, 2005, p.1; "N.J. College Student Auctions Body on eBay," boston.com, May 19, 2005, p.1; "CMT Drops Voice Messages in Urinals," Primemediabusiness.com, October 20, 2004, p. 1; Patricia Odell, "Alternative Marketing: Skin for Sale," *PROMO XTRA,* primediabusiness.com, February 22, 2005, p. 1.

garages, more companies are finding this medium attractive—particularly for point-of-purchase items. The ads reach a variety of demographics, depending on where they are placed. PepsiCo is just one of a number of companies employing this medium.

Exhibit 13-14 Ads often appear in the strangest places

- *Bathroom ads.* Besides the medium described in IMC Perspective 13-2, other forms of bathroom advertising are catching on. Traditional mini-boards, urinal screens, and electrically charged vinyl posters are just a few of the ways such companies as Sony, AXE, Volkswagen, and others have placed their ads.

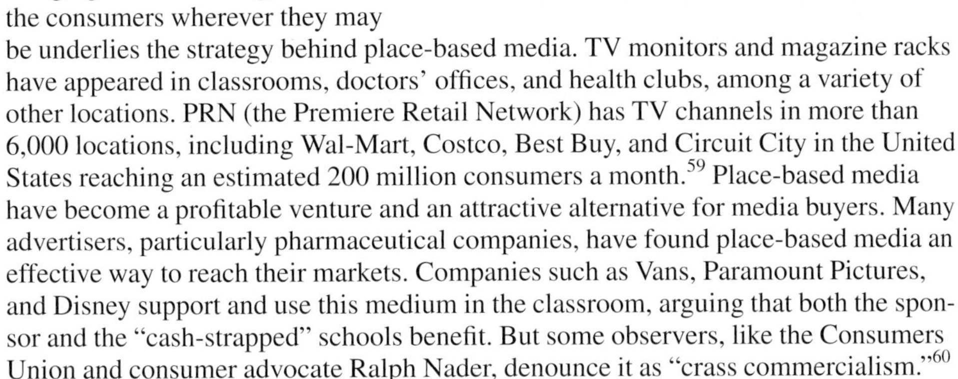

- *Place-based media.* The idea of bringing the advertising medium to the consumers wherever they may be underlies the strategy behind place-based media. TV monitors and magazine racks have appeared in classrooms, doctors' offices, and health clubs, among a variety of other locations. PRN (the Premiere Retail Network) has TV channels in more than 6,000 locations, including Wal-Mart, Costco, Best Buy, and Circuit City in the United States reaching an estimated 200 million consumers a month.[59] Place-based media have become a profitable venture and an attractive alternative for media buyers. Many advertisers, particularly pharmaceutical companies, have found place-based media an effective way to reach their markets. Companies such as Vans, Paramount Pictures, and Disney support and use this medium in the classroom, arguing that both the sponsor and the "cash-strapped" schools benefit. But some observers, like the Consumers Union and consumer advocate Ralph Nader, denounce it as "crass commercialism."[60]

- *Others.* Just a few other examples of the use of support media: Coca-Cola installed 1,000 feet of light boxes in the Atlanta subway to show motion picture ads for Dasani; Motorola is advertising on pagers; Muzak, a provider of background music, has teamed with Tyme ATMs to broadcast ads at bank ATM sites; ads now appear on luggage conveyors at some airports, on hubcaps, in elevators, on fruit, and on gasoline pumps (visual and talking). There are many other examples, as is well demonstrated in Exhibit 13-14 (at least he earned something from the fight!).

Advantages and Disadvantages of Miscellaneous Alternative Media

Advantages of alternative media include the following:

- *Awareness and attention.* Perhaps the major advantage of these tactics is their ability to attract attention. Given their novelty and the nontraditional locations in which they appear, they are likely to create awareness and gain attention.
- *Cost efficiencies.* Because of the nontraditional nature of alternative media, many advertisers are using media not previously used for advertising, or that, in general, do not require high expenditures. As such, the absolute and relative costs are not yet that high.
- *Targeting.* Depending on the tactic used, the campaign can be very targeted. It can be exposed only to a specific event, location, age, or interest group.

Disadvantages of alternative media include the following:

- *Irritation.* Unless the advertiser is careful, advertising placed in the wrong medium may have a negative impact, resulting in irritation, negative attitudes toward the advertiser, or even opportunities for the competitor. When Microsoft logos were painted on sidewalks, the city and consumers were not impressed and Microsoft was fined. One of their competitors gained significant public relations benefits when the company announced it would be happy to remove the paintings.

- *Wearout.* For now, many of these campaigns are novel and unique and are attracting consumer interest. As the number of efforts increases, however, there is the potential to lose the uniqueness associated with them.

Summary

This chapter introduced you to the vast number of support media available to marketers. These media, also referred to as nontraditional or alternative media, are just a few of the many ways advertisers attempt to reach their target markets. We have barely scratched the surface here. Support media include out-of-home advertising (outdoor, in-store, and transit), promotional products, and in-flight advertising, among many others. The fastest growing area is that of branded entertainment including product placements, product integrations, and others.

Support media offer a variety of advantages. Cost, ability to reach the target market, and flexibility are just a few of those cited in this chapter. In addition, many of the media discussed here have effectively demonstrated the power of their specific medium to get results.

But each of these support media has disadvantages. Perhaps the major weakness with most is the lack of audience measurement and verification. Unlike many of the media discussed earlier in this text, most nontraditional media do not provide audience measurement figures. So the advertiser is forced to make decisions without hard data or based on information provided by the media.

As the number and variety of support media continue to grow, it is likely the major weaknesses will be overcome. When that occurs, these media may no longer be considered nontraditional or alternative.

Key Terms

support media, 414
alternative media, 415
nonmeasured media, 415
nontraditional media, 415
out-of-home advertising, 415
aerial advertising, 418
mobile billboards, 419
in-store media, 419
transit advertising, 420
inside cards, 420
outside posters, 421
terminal posters, 421
showing, 421
promotional products marketing, 424
specialty advertising, 424
Yellow Pages, 427
directional medium, 427
in-flight advertising, 430
branded entertainment, 432
product placements, 432
product integrations, 434

Discussion Questions

1. Over the past few years there has been enormous growth in the use of product placements. Explain some of the reasons for this growth. Do you think this growth will likely continue into the future? Why or why not?

2. What is going to happen to the Yellow Pages directories? The Yellow Pages, which have been in existence for quite some time, seem to be at a crossroads for their future. As consumers become more and more comfortable with the Internet, there are indications that customers are using this medium to provide the services the traditional hard-copy books have provided. Do you think the traditional Yellow Pages directories will eventually go away? What should the Yellow Pages be doing to ensure their survival?

3. Discuss some of the various forms of branded entertainment. Why has branded entertainment promotion become so popular? Discuss some of the advantages and disadvantages with various branded entertainment forms.

4. While most traditional forms of advertising and promotion have been experiencing a decline in expenditures, outdoor has been an exception. Ad spending in outdoor has actually seen a gain over the past few years. Explain why you think this has occurred, and discuss some of the factors leading to this growth.

5. Discuss some of the various means of measuring effectiveness in branded entertainment, and their advantages and disadvantages. Given the emphasis by marketers on ROI, discuss how these measures fit in with this attempt to determine return on investment.

6. Transit advertising takes a variety of forms, and many advertisers may be reluctant to use these media. Discuss some of the various forms of transit advertising and their relative advantages and disadvantages. Give examples of which products and/or services might effectively utilize this medium.

7. Describe what is meant by "guerilla marketing." Give examples of products and/or services that you know have employed this strategy. Then describe some of the characteristics of companies that might most benefit from stealth marketing.

8. There seems to be a growing interest among marketers to engage in the use of product placements. These marketers are attracted by the success experienced by prior product placements. Give examples of product placements that you have seen. Then discuss what factors impact the success or lack of success of product placements.

9. Advertising in movie theaters is on the increase. A variety of reasons as to why this medium may be effective are offered in the chapter. Discuss the reasons why movie theater advertising may be advantageous. Then discuss some of the reasons why it might not be as successful as planned.

10. As advertisers engage in stealth marketing tactics, many companies are taking action to prohibit such activities. Ethical issues are raised on both sides—one side claiming free speech, while the other argues that such activities are unfair to paying advertisers, sponsors, and the like. Discuss the positions of each side. Which do you favor?

Direct Marketing

14

Chapter Objectives

1. To recognize the area of direct marketing as a communications tool.
2. To know the strategies and tactics involved in direct marketing.
3. To demonstrate the use of direct-marketing media.
4. To determine the scope and effectiveness of direct marketing.

From Balding Cures and "Sweatin' to the Oldies" to LandRover and Disney: The Infomercial Turns 20

The infomercial recently celebrated its 20th birthday, and it is fair to say that the medium and the industry have seen some interesting transformations along the way. When President Reagan signed the Cable Communications Policy Act deregulating television in 1984, the networks and cable channels started selling unsold inventory in large blocks to the highest bidder. Usually, these time slots were in the very late hours or early mornings when there is low viewership. It was a win-win situation for the networks, which were getting rid of unsold time, and for the advertisers, who could purchase the time for very low prices. Companies started purchasing 30-minute blocks and more to create advertisements in a program-like format that typically lasted 30 minutes to an hour, producing the birth of the infomercial.

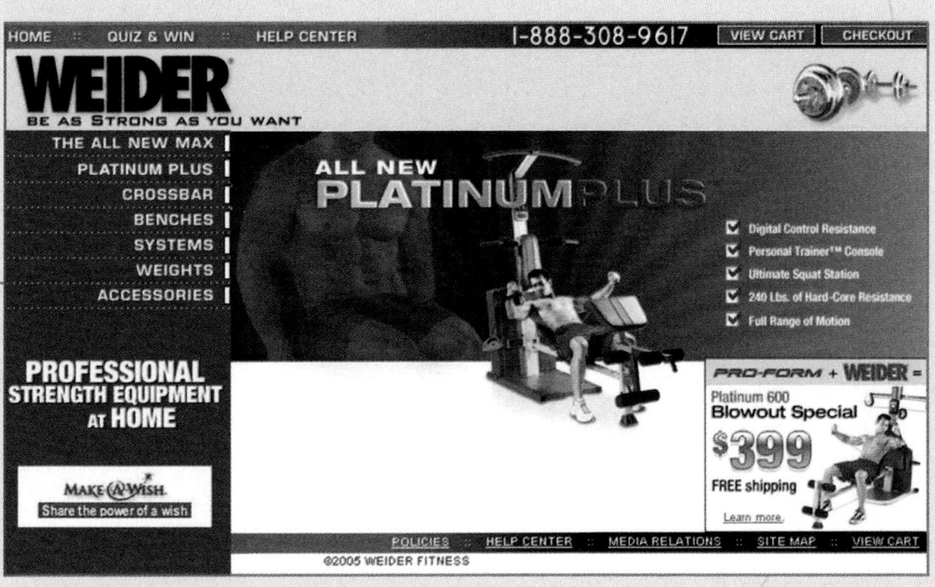

Along with HerbaLife's 90-minute infomercial, many of the early buyers were real estate companies, manufacturers of skin care products and baldness cures, and self-help companies. Many of the ads were hard to distinguish from regular TV programming. In 1987, Soloflex introduced one of the most successful infomercials. The exercise company's infomercial led marketers to recognize that upscale products could successfully employ this advertising form, and this changed the infomercial world forever.

By the 1990s, infomercials were featuring household products, impotence cures, and waxes that would let you light your car on fire without damaging it. Dionne Warwick's Psychic Friends infomercial was extremely successful, though Ross Perot's use of the medium in his presidential campaign fared less well. But the 1990s also saw an acceptance of the infomercial form and increased usage by many Fortune 100 companies, such as Volvo, Apple, Time Life, and Nissan, which had the impact of driving up demand and costs for the services provided as well as the media time. In the early days, a company could get a one-hour infomercial produced for as little as $15,000, and could buy an hour on the Discovery channel for $50. Today, production costs average about $350,000 and can be as high as $1 million if a celebrity is used. A small market media buy is in the $20,000 range, with a one-week national rollout costing about $1 million a week.

Today, the infomercial business has become an industry itself. Media billings are in the $1 billion range. In 2004, 2,036 infomercials aired, 714 of which were new. Fortune 1,000 firms now account for 20 percent of all infomercials in the United States, and it is not unusual to see celebrities such as Cindy Crawford (Meaningful Beauty skin care) or Britney Spears (Proactiv Solution skin care products) in the ads. A number of products such as the George Foreman grill and the Ronco rotisserie oven have generated over $1 billion through this medium. Bowflex, one of the most successful infomercials ever, enjoys about the same brand awareness as Nike.

But not everything is rosy in infomercial land. Besides the fact that media rates are now about 500 percent higher than they were in the 1980s and that respectable companies have adopted the infomercial to promote their products, an image problem still exists. Junk products are still commonly offered, and more than one company using the medium has been investigated by the Federal Trade Commission (FTC) for deceptive advertising. In fall 2004, the FTC banned Kevin Trudeau, a highly successful infomercial user for more than a decade, from "appearing in, producing, or disseminating future infomercials that advertise any type of product, service, or program to the public." The ban was part of a $2 million settlement; Trudeau also had to pay $500,000 in cash, and turn over one of his homes and his $180,000 Mercedes-Benz for deceptively advertising Coral Calcium Supreme as a cancer cure. Miss Cleo's psychic reading service faced similar charges, as did others over the years. Between the charges of deception and the prevalence of weight loss and spray-on hair products, the infomercial industry has struggled to gain respectability.

Where will the infomercial be on its 40th birthday? Probably still here, but as a different-looking product. But then, don't all 40-year-olds look different than they did when they were 20?

Sources: Thomas Mucha, "Stronger Sales in Just 28 Minutes," *Business 2.0,* June 2005, pp. 56–60; Frank Ahrens, "FTC Pulls Plug on Infomercial Giant," *Washington Post,* September 8, 2004, p. E1; Timothy Hawthorne, "Media Zone: 20 Years of the Bests and Worst," *Response Magazine,* November 1, 2004 (Responsemagazine.com), pp. 1–3.

The discussion of the evolution of the infomercial in this chapter's lead-in demonstrates one of the means of effectively utilizing direct marketing. It is important to realize that the infomercial is only one of the tools used by direct marketers and that the industry offers numerous methods for reaching one's target market. This chapter will discuss these direct media.

Direct Marketing

While many companies rely on a variety of promotional mix elements to move their products and services through intermediaries, an increasing number are going directly to the consumer. These companies believe that while promotional mix tools such as advertising, sales promotion, support media, and personal selling are effective in creating brand image, conveying information, and/or creating awareness, going direct can generate an immediate behavioral response. Direct marketing is a valuable tool in the integrated communications program, though it usually seeks somewhat different objectives.

In this chapter, we discuss direct marketing and its role as a communications tool. Direct marketing is one of the fastest-growing forms of promotion in terms of dollar expenditures, and for many marketers it is rapidly becoming the medium of choice for reaching consumers. Stan Rapp and Thomas Collins, in their book *Maximarketing,* propose that direct marketing be the driving force behind the overall marketing program.[1] Others have agreed. Rapp and Collins present a nine-step model that includes creating a database, reaching prospects, developing the sale, and developing the relationship. We begin by defining direct marketing and then examine direct-marketing media and their use in the overall communications strategy. The section concludes with a basis for evaluating the direct-marketing program and a discussion of the advantages and disadvantages of this marketing tool.

Defining Direct Marketing

As noted in Chapter 1, **direct marketing** is a system of marketing by which organizations communicate directly with target customers to generate a response or transaction. This response may take the form of an inquiry, a purchase, or even a vote. In his *Dictionary of Marketing Terms,* Peter Bennett defines direct marketing as

> the total of activities by which the seller, in effecting the exchange of goods and services with the buyer, directs efforts to a target audience using one or more media (direct selling, direct mail, telemarketing, direct-action advertising, catalogue selling, cable TV selling, etc.) for the purpose of soliciting a response by phone, mail, or personal visit from a prospect or customer.[2]

First we must distinguish between direct marketing and direct-marketing media. As you can see in Figure 14-1, direct marketing is an aspect of total marketing—that is, it involves marketing research, segmentation, evaluation, and the like, just as our planning model in Chapter 1 did. Direct marketing uses a set of **direct-response media,** including direct mail, telemarketing, interactive TV, print, the Internet, and other media. These media are the tools by which direct marketers implement the communications process.

The purchases of products and services through direct-response advertising currently exceed $2 trillion and are projected to reach $2.8 trillion by the year 2006.[3,4] Firms that use this marketing method range from major retailers such as the Gap, Restoration Hardware, and Victoria's Secret to publishing companies to computer retailers to financial services. Business-to-business and industrial marketers have also significantly increased their direct-marketing efforts, with an estimated $1.4 trillion in sales forecast by 2007.[5]

The Growth of Direct Marketing

Direct marketing has been around since the invention of the printing press in the 15th century. Ben Franklin was a very successful direct marketer in the early 1700s, and Warren Sears and Montgomery Ward were using this medium in the 1880s.

The major impetus behind the growth of direct marketing may have been the development and expansion of the U.S. Postal Service, which made catalogs available to both urban and rural dwellers. Catalogs revolutionized America's buying habits; consumers could now shop without ever leaving their homes.

But catalogs alone do not account for the rapid growth of direct marketing. A number of factors in American society have led to the increased attractiveness of this medium for both buyer and seller:

- *Consumer credit cards.* There are now more than 1 billion credit cards—bank, oil company, retail, and so on—in circulation in the United States. This makes it feasible for consumers to purchase both low- and high-ticket items through direct-response channels and assures sellers that they will be paid. It is estimated that over $2.5 trillion was charged on credit cards in the year 2004.[6] Of course, not all of this was through direct marketing, but a high percentage of direct purchases do use this method of payment, and companies such as American Express, Diners Club, MasterCard, and Visa are among the heaviest direct advertisers.
- *Direct-marketing syndicates.* Companies specializing in list development, statement inserts, catalogs, and sweepstakes have opened many new opportunities to marketers. The number of these companies continues to expand, creating even more new users.
- *The changing structure of American society and the market.* One of the major factors contributing to the success of direct marketing is that so many Americans are now "money-rich and time-poor."[7] The rapid increase in dual-income families has meant more income. (It is estimated that by 2008 women will make up about 48 percent of the labor force.)[8] At the same time, the increased popularity of physical fitness, do-it-yourself crafts and repairs, and home entertainment has reduced the time available for shopping and has increased the attractiveness of direct purchases.
- *Technological advances.* The rapid technological advancement of the electronic media and of computers has made it easier for consumers to shop and for marketers to be successful in reaching the desired target markets. Well over 110 million television

Figure 14-1 DM Advertising Expenditures by Medium and Market (Millions of Dollars)

	2003	2004	2005	2006	2007	Compound Annual Growth 03-07
Magazine	**$9,798**	**$10,383**	**$10,995**	**$11,628**	**$12,308**	**5.87%**
B-to-B	$5,231	$5,587	$5,888	$6,216	$6,566	5.85%
Consumer	$4,567	$4,816	$5,107	$5,413	$5,743	5.89%
Direct Mail	**$48,643**	**$51,359**	**$54,034**	**$56,724**	**$59,590**	**5.21%**
B-to-B	$19,477	$20,858	$22,074	$23,250	$24,487	5.89%
Consumer	$29,166	$30,501	$31,959	$33,474	$35,103	4.74%
Newspaper	**$18,502**	**$19,467**	**$20,373**	**$21,442**	**$22,496**	**5.01%**
B-to-B	$7,628	$8,122	$8,525	$8,986	$9,442	5.48%
Consumer	$10,874	$11,346	$11,848	$12,456	$13,055	4.67%
Other	**$16,146**	**$17,234**	**$18,479**	**$19,509**	**$20,578**	**6.25%**
B-to-B	$7,497	$8,106	$8,715	$9,208	$9,713	6.69%
Consumer	$8,648	$9,128	$9,765	$10,301	$10,865	5.87%
Radio	**$7,678**	**$8,229**	**$8,742**	**$9,277**	**$9,798**	**6.29%**
B-to-B	$4,096	$4,413	$4,687	$4,972	$5,243	6.36%
Consumer	$3,581	$3,816	$4,055	$4,306	$4,555	6.20%
Telephone	**$79,711**	**$84,335**	**$89,297**	**$94,230**	**$99,651**	**5.74%**
B-to-B	$51,567	$54,869	$58,134	$61,320	$64,768	5.86%
Consumer	$28,144	$28,486	$31,163	$32,911	$34,882	5.51%
Television	**$24,302**	**$25,880**	**$27,523**	**$29,196**	**$30,956**	**6.24%**
B-to-B	$11,887	$12,725	$13,522	$14,332	$15,184	6.31%
Consumer	$12,415	$13,155	$14,001	$14,864	$15,771	6.17%
Total	**$204,778**	**$216,888**	**$229,444**	**$242,007**	**$255,376**	**5.68%**
B-to-B	$107,384	$114,660	$121,546	$128,284	$135,402	5.97%
Consumer	$97,396	$102,228	$107,897	$113,724	$119,974	5.35%

Source: The DMA's Economic Impact.

homes receive home shopping programs, and home channel purchases, which were projected to reach $15.6 billion by 2006, will likely far exceed that amount.[9]

• *Miscellaneous factors.* A number of other factors have contributed to the increased effectiveness of direct marketing, including changing values, more sophisticated marketing techniques, and the industry's improved image. These factors will also ensure the success of direct marketing in the future. The variety of companies employing direct marketing demonstrates its potential.

While some organizations rely on direct marketing solely to generate a behavioral response, for many others direct marketing is an integral part of the IMC program. They use direct marketing to achieve other than sales goals and integrate it with other program elements. We first examine the role of direct marketing in the IMC program and then consider its more *traditional* role.

The Role of Direct Marketing in the IMC Program

Long the stepchild of the promotional mix, direct marketing has now become an important component in the integrated marketing programs of many organizations. In fact, direct-marketing activities support and are supported by other elements of the promotional mix.

Combining Direct Marketing with Advertising

Obviously, direct marketing is in itself a form of advertising. Whether through mail, print, or TV, the direct-response offer is an ad. It usually contains a toll-free or 900 number or a form that requests mailing information. Sometimes the ad supports the direct-selling effort. For example, Victoria's Secret runs image ads and commercials to support its store and catalog sales. Both Marlboro and Benson & Hedges advertise their cigarettes, achieving a carryover effect of their image to their direct-response merchandise catalogs. Direct-response ads or infomercials are also referred to in retail outlet displays. Sometimes an advertisement will be sent through direct mail (Exhibit 14-1).

Combining Direct Marketing with Public Relations

As you will see later in this text, public relations activities often employ direct-response techniques. Private companies may use telemarketing activities to solicit funds for charities or co-sponsor charities that use these and other direct-response techniques to solicit funds. Likewise, corporations and/or organizations engaging in public relations activities may include toll-free numbers or website URLs in their ads or promotional materials. After hurricane Katrina devastated Louisiana and Mississippi in 2005, the Direct Marketing Organization urged its 5,200 corporate and affiliate members to assist victims of the disaster. Home shopping channel QVC pledged to raise $3 million for a relief fund.[10] Direct mail has also been shown to be effective in recruiting job candidates.[11]

Combining Direct Marketing with Personal Selling

Telemarketing and direct selling are two methods of personal selling (others will be discussed in Chapter 18). Nonprofit organizations like charities often use telemarketing to solicit funds. As you will see, for-profit companies are also using telemarketing with much greater frequency to screen and qualify prospects (which reduces selling costs) and to generate leads. Direct-mail pieces are often used to invite prospective customers to visit auto showrooms to test-drive new cars; the salesperson then assumes responsibility for the selling effort. The GM and BMW examples cited earlier in this text demonstrate effective use of this approach.

Exhibit 14-1 Elfa uses direct mail to advertise

Exhibit 14-2 Costco sends promotional offers through the mail

Combining Direct Marketing with Sales Promotions How many times have you received a direct-mail piece notifying you of a sales promotion or event or inviting you to participate in a contest or sweepstakes? Ski shops regularly mail announcements of special end-of-season sales. Airlines send out mailers or e-mails announcing promotional airfares. Nordstom and other retail outlets call their existing customers to notify them of special sales promotions. Each of these is an example of a company using direct-marketing tools to inform customers of sales promotions (Exhibit 14-2). In turn, the sales promotion event may support the direct-marketing effort. Databases are often built from the names and addresses acquired from a promotion, and direct mail and/or telemarketing calls follow.

Exhibit 14-3 San Diego encourages visits through direct mail

WWW.SANDIEGO.ORG
THERE'S NO SUBSTITUTE FOR
SAN DIEGO
For a vacation destination which *Holiday Magazine* described as "the only area in the United States with perfect weather," featuring relaxing resort accommodations, a diverse array of acclaimed artistic and cultural offerings, fine dining, and world-renowned attractions, there is no substitute for San Diego.

Combining Direct Marketing with Support Media Adding a promotional product to a direct mailer has proved to increase response rates. One company included a promotional product in half of its 10,000 mailers and not in the other half. The former generated 65 percent more orders. 3M used a promotional product as an incentive for people responding to a direct-mail offer. The incentive generated a 23 percent response rate versus only 9 percent for the regular mailer.

To successfully implement direct-marketing programs, companies must make a number of decisions. As in other marketing programs, they must determine (1) what the program's objectives will be, (2) which markets to target (through the use of a list or marketing database), (3) what direct-marketing strategies will be employed, and (4) how to evaluate the effectiveness of the program.

Direct-Marketing Objectives

The direct marketer usually seeks a direct response. The objectives of the program are normally behaviors—for example, test drives, votes, contributions, and/or sales. A typical objective is defined through a set response, perhaps a 2 to 3 percent response rate.

Not all direct marketing seeks a behavioral response, however. Many organizations use direct marketing to build an image, maintain customer satisfaction, and inform and/or educate customers in an attempt to lead to future actions. Exhibit 14-3 shows how the city of San Diego uses direct mail to encourage tourism.

Developing a Database

As we have discussed throughout this text, market segmentation and targeting are critical components of any promotional program. Direct-marketing programs employ these principles even more than others, since the success of a direct-marketing program is in large part tied to the ability to do *one-to-one marketing.* To segment and target their markets, direct marketers use a **database,** a listing of customers and/or potential customers. Research by the U.S. Postal Service showed that 65 percent of the companies surveyed rely on their internal databases for marketing purposes.[12] This database is a tool for **database marketing**—the use of specific information about individual customers and/or prospects to implement more effective and efficient marketing communications.[13]

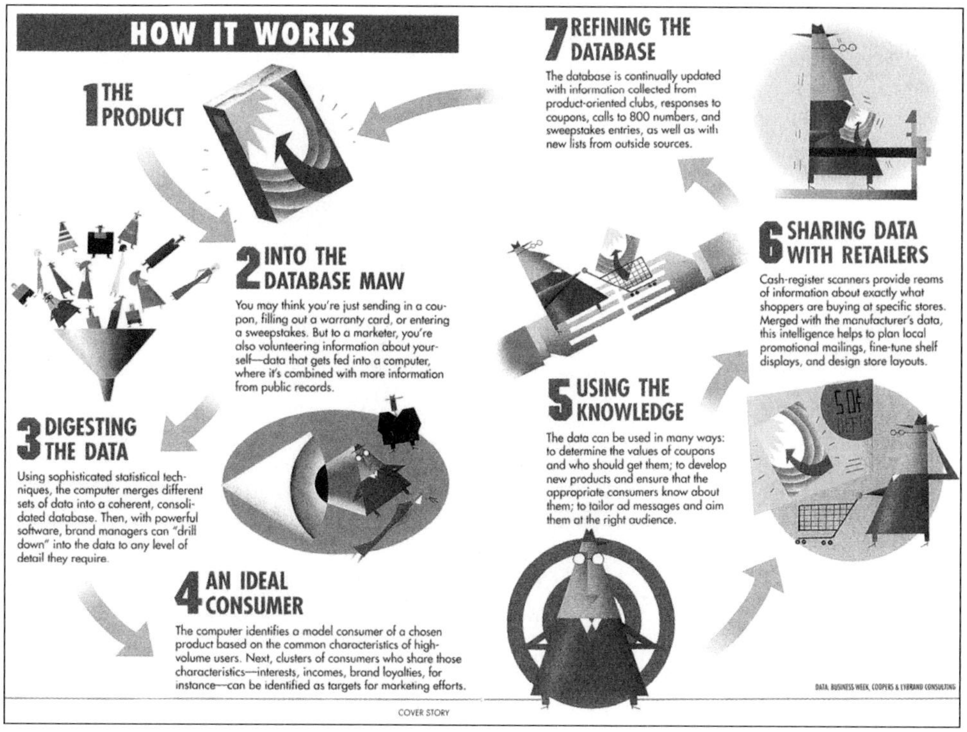

Figure 14-2 demonstrates how database marketing works. As you can see, the database marketing effort must be an integral part of the overall IMC program. At the very least, this list contains names, addresses, and Zip codes; more sophisticated databases include information on demographics and psychographics, purchase transactions and payments, personal facts, neighborhood data, and even credit histories (see Figure 14-3). This database serves as the foundation from which the direct-marketing programs evolve. Databases are used to perform the following functions:[14]

Figure 14-2 How Database Marketing Works

- *Improving the selection of market segments.* Some consumers are more likely to be potential purchasers, users, voters, and so on than others. By analyzing the

Consumer Database	Business-to-Business Database
Name	Name of company/contact/decision maker(s)
Address/Zip code	Title of contact
Telephone number	Telephone number
Length of residence	Source of order/inquiry or referral
Age	Credit history
Gender	Industrial classification
Marital status	Size of business
Family data (number of children, etc.)	Revenues
Education	Number of employees
Income	Time in business
Occupation	Headquarters location
Transaction history	Multiple locations
Promotion history	Purchase history
Inquiring history	Promotion history
Unique identifier	Inquiry history
	Unique identifier

Figure 14-3 Contents for a Comprehensive Database

Exhibit 14-4 Hertz seeks permission to use receivers' names

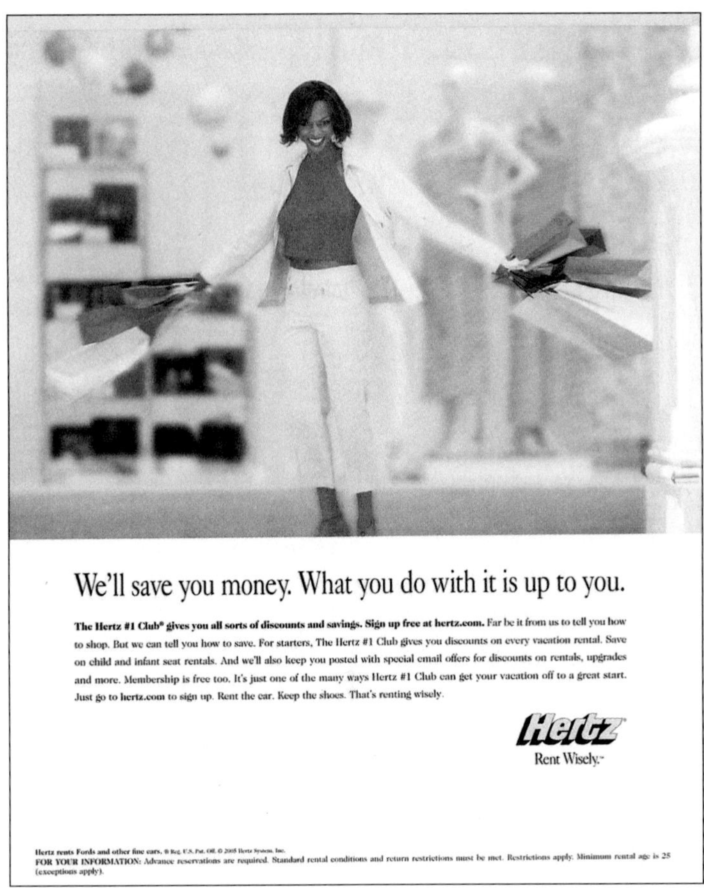

We'll save you money. What you do with it is up to you.
The Hertz #1 Club® gives you all sorts of discounts and savings. Sign up free at hertz.com. Far be it from us to tell you how to shop. But we can tell you how to save. For starters, The Hertz #1 Club gives you discounts on every vacation rental. Save on child and infant seat rentals. And we'll also keep you posted with special email offers for discounts on rentals, upgrades and more. Membership is free too. It's just one of the many ways Hertz #1 Club can get your vacation off to a great start. Just go to hertz.com to sign up. Rent the car. Keep the shoes. That's renting wisely.
Hertz
Rent Wisely.™
Hertz rents Fords and other fine cars. ® Reg. U.S. Pat. Off. © 2005 Hertz System, Inc.
FOR YOUR INFORMATION: Advance reservations are required. Standard rental conditions and return restrictions must be met. Restrictions apply. Minimum rental age is 25 (exceptions apply).

characteristics of the database, a marketer can target a greater potential audience. For example, catalog companies have become very specialized. Companies such as Lands' End, Lilly's Kids, and Johnson & Murphy have culled their lists and become much more efficient, targeting only those who are most likely to purchase their products.

- *Stimulate repeat purchases.* Once a purchase has been made, the customer's name and other information are entered into the database. These people are proven direct-marketing users who offer high potential for repurchase. Magazines, for example, routinely send out renewal letters and/or call subscribers before the expiration date. Blockbuster Entertainment helps its video-rental customers select movies, locate additional Blockbuster stores, and review their membership. Companies from window cleaners to carpet cleaners to car dealers build a base of customers and contact them when they are "due" to repurchase.

- *Cross-sell.* Customers who demonstrate a specific interest also constitute strong potential for other products of the same nature. For example, the National Geographic Society has successfully sold globes, maps, videos, travel magazines, and an assortment of other products to subscribers who obviously have an interest in geography and/or travel. Likewise, Victoria's Secret has expanded its clothing lines primarily through sales to existing customers, and Kraft–GF has successfully cross-sold products in its varied food line. Upon responding to the direct-mail piece sent by Hertz (Exhibit 14-4), you are asked for your permission for Hertz to provide your name to its parent company, Ford, and others, and to allow Hertz to send you information on other products and services. Notice how many cross-selling offers are contained in the Blockbuster piece in Exhibit 14-5.

- *Customer relationship management.* Customer relationship management (CRM), which is described in more detail in Chapter 16, requires that the marketer develop and maintain a significant amount of information about its clients. The aim of CRM is to establish a relationship with one's customers through affinities, personalized communications, and product/service offerings. For CRM to work effectively, a database is required. While CRM relies on technology specifically designed for managing customer relationships, there are overlapping characteristics of CRM and database marketing. Suffice it to say at this point that many of the techniques employed in database marketing are necessary to develop an effective CRM program.

Numerous other companies have established comprehensive databases on existing and potential customers both in the United States and internationally. IMC Perspective 14-1 provides additional examples, both good and bad. Database marketing has become so ubiquitous that many people are concerned about invasion of privacy. Direct marketers are concerned as well. The Direct Marketing Association (DMA), the trade association for direct marketers, has asked its members to adhere to ethical rules of conduct in their marketing efforts. It points out that if the industry does not police itself, the government will.

Exhibit 14-5 Blockbuster uses mailers to cross-promote

Sources of Database Information There are many sources of information for direct-marketing databases:

- *The U.S. Census Bureau.* Census data provide information on almost every household in the United States. Data include household size, demographics, income, and other information.
- *The U.S. Postal Service.* Postal Zip codes and the extended four-digit code provide information on both household and business locations.
- *List services.* Many providers of lists are available. The accuracy and timeliness of the lists vary.
- *Standard Rate and Data Service.* SRDS provides information regarding both consumer and business lists. Published in two volumes, *Direct Mail List Rates and Data* contains over 50,000 list selections in hundreds of classifications.
- *Simmons Market Research Bureau.* SMRB conducts an annual study of customers who buy at home via mail, telephone, or Internet. MRI provides these data as well (see Figure 14-4). It compiles information on total orders placed, types of products purchased, demographics, and purchase satisfaction, among others.
- *Direct Marketing Association.* The direct marketers' trade organization promotes direct marketing and provides statistical information on direct-marketing use. The DMA's *Fact Book of Direct Marketing* contains information regarding use, attitudes toward direct marketing, rules and regulations, and so forth.

Consumer-goods manufacturers, banks, credit bureaus, retailers, charitable organizations, and other business operations also sell lists and other selected information. Companies can build their own databases through completed warranty cards, surveys, and so on.

Determining the Effectiveness of the Database While many companies maintain a database, many do not use them effectively. Collecting names and information is not enough; the list must be kept current, purged of old and/or inactive customers, and updated frequently. The more information about customers that can be contained in the database, the more effective it will be. The Postal Service recommends an **RFM scoring method** for this purpose.[15] *RFM* stands for the recency, frequency, and monetary transactions between the company and the customer.

Figure 14-4 SMRB Provides Information on Consumers Who Ordered Merchandise by Mail, Phone, or Internet

	Total U.S. (000)	Total Buyers: Mail or Phone or Internet (000)	% Any Product	Total Buyers: Mail or Phone (000)	% Any Product
All	211,845	88,246	41.66	60,037	28.34
Men	101,655	37,997	37.38	24,549	24.15
Women	110,190	50,250	45.60	35,488	32.21
Age 18–24	27,492	8,569	31.17	4,888	17.78
Age 25–34	39,096	16,953	43.36	9,410	24.07
Age 35–44	44,333	20,526	46.30	13,563	30.59
Age 45–54	40,026	19,689	49.19	13,634	34.06
Age 55–64	26,743	12,008	44.90	9,219	34.47
Age 65+	34,155	10,501	30.75	9,323	27.29
Graduated college	51,908	29,626	57.07	18,867	36.35
Attended college	57,213	26,058	45.55	17,209	30.08
Graduated high school	67,355	22,617	33.58	16,376	24.31
Did not graduate high school	35,327	6,817	19.30	5,277	14.94
Professional	22,111	14,452	65.36	9,052	40.94
Manager/administrative	20,682	12,648	61.15	7,875	38.08
Technical/clerical/sales	38,455	18,982	49.36	12,110	31.49
Precisions/craft/repair	14,379	4,743	32.99	2,838	19.74
Other employed	39,596	13,309	33.61	9,388	23.71
Single (never married)	51,782	17,671	34.13	10,898	21.05
Respondent's marital status: married	119,963	59,965	47.49	38,708	32.27
Divorced/separated/widowed	40,100	13,610	33.94	10,431	26.01
Northeast census	40,543	19,758	48.73	13,840	34.14
South	76,644	28,269	36.88	19,262	25.13
North central	47,979	20,872	43.50	14,879	31.01
West	46,680	19,347	41.45	12,055	25.82
Household income: $0–$4,999	4,044	752	18.59	567	14.01
Household income: $5,000–$9,999	8,926	1,154	12.93	955	10.70
Household income: $10,000–$14,999	10,695	1,890	17.67	1,461	13.66
Household income: $15,000–$19,999	11,381	2,475	21.75	1,873	16.45
Household income: $20,000–$24,999	12,101	2,824	23.34	2,361	19.51
Household income: $25,000–$29,999	12,013	3,349	27.88	2,632	21.91
Household income: $30,000–$34,999	12,198	3,459	28.36	2,634	21.60
Household income: $35,000–$39,999	11,281	4,038	35.80	2,820	25.00
Household income: $40,000–$44,999	11,092	3,994	36.01	2,860	25.79
Household income: $45,000–$49,999	10,050	4,128	41.07	2,892	28.78
Household income: $50,000–$59,999	18,915	8,609	45.52	5,914	31.26
Household income: $60,000–$74,999	24,052	12,134	50.45	7,658	31.84
Household income: $75,000–$99,999	27,650	16,294	58.93	10,436	37.74
Household income: $100,000–$149,999	23,358	14,162	60.63	9,110	39.00
Household income: $150,000+ (plus)	14,089	8,984	63.77	5,864	41.62
No. of people in houseold: 1 person	29,319	9,959	33.97	7,572	25.83
No. of people in houseold: 2 people	69,030	29,570	42.84	20,825	30.17
No. of people in houseold: 3 or 4 people	80,800	36,373	45.02	23,456	29.03
No. of people in houseold: 5 or more people	32,696	12,343	37.75	8,184	25.03
No children in household	122,752	50,164	40.87	35,204	28.68
Children under 2 years old	17,104	6,696	39.15	4,199	24.55
2–5 years	31,352	13,311	42.45	8,643	27.57
6–11 years	41,500	17,269	41.61	11,379	27.42
12–17 years	42,792	18,168	42.46	11,838	27.66
Own or rent home: own	153,606	70,797	46.09	48,907	31.84
Own or rent home: rent	55,634	16,547	29.74	10,633	19.11

Source: MediaMark, 2005.

IMC PERSPECTIVE 14-1

The Database: One of Marketing's Most Powerful Tools?

Have you ever begun to purchase something from Radio Shack or an Apple store when they insist on getting your Zip code before they complete the transaction? Do you have a customer card with your local supermarket that entitles you to receive discounts when you shop there? Well, you may or may not know it, but every time you make a purchase at one of these places they are collecting data on you. Don't worry though, the data collection is designed to make your shopping experience even more enjoyable, and most companies just collect the data but don't use it. So why collect it, you ask? Well, for some companies, the database offers an insight into their customers that can be used for one-to-one marketing, in which product offerings, promotions, and the like are tailored to your specific needs and wants. Consider the following examples:

- *Wyndham Hotels.* Wyndham Hotels asks hotel guests to register through their Wyndham by Request program online. When they do, they are asked a series of questions requesting information such as their preferences as to room type, smoking or nonsmoking, what they would like for their complimentary snack and drink upon check-in, and more. The St. Regis hotel chain has a similar system, even asking the guest to specify which brand of bottled water he or she prefers in the room. Other essential information, such as credit card number for bill payment, is also requested. Check-in and check-out are almost automatic; the guest need not go to the front desk and complete a lengthy registration and/or check-out process. Once in the room, the guest is greeted with his or her preferred food and drink.
- *Rental car companies.* Avis, Hertz, National, and other rental car companies maintain a database on their customers, so that when they pick up their rentals they can go directly to the car without waiting in line. All the pertinent information in regard to car type, payment arrangements, and so forth are already known, making the rental process much quicker and more enjoyable.
- *Red Lobster.* The Red Lobster's Overboard Club has grown to a database of over 800,000 loyal customers. Collecting data from surveys and the website, the restaurant chain gathers information on customers' favorite talk show hosts, menu preferences, and whether or not they usually split the check. From this information, the company sends out e-mails tailored to their dining choices, buying patterns, and geography. They also promote events such as wine lovers' cruises or provide information about the customer's favorite foods. By asking questions such as the driving time to the nearest Red Lobster, the company can determine where to place new stores. Customers love the interaction, as is evidenced by the 50 to 60 percent growth rate in the database each year.
- *PNC Bank.* Financial institutions were early adopters of database marketing and continue to be the leaders in innovative uses of the information acquired. Pittsburgh's PNC Bank and the BMO Bank of Montreal are two prime examples. PNC uses its database to improve customer relations by informing customers of services that they might want to use, solving their service problems, and more. Once the service issues have been resolved, cross-selling efforts may take place. The program, referred to as Service Sells, has resulted in more than $100 million in new business in the first year it was started. BMO's database scores their customers based on five dimensions: profitability, future potential, risk, bank relationships, and attitudinal and psychographic data. The system then sends out specific offers to each layer and provides the information to the bank managers as well. Every time a customer walks into a branch, the manager already knows the customer's potential. The results indicate a 10 to 15 percent increase in market share and a 20 percent increase in new customer accounts.

While these success stories represent just a few of many companies that have learned the benefits of database marketing, not everyone has quite figured it out. Many companies have a wealth of data on their customers, but seldom or ever use it. Others have used it, but not very effectively; for example (we will keep the names anonymous):

- *Credit card company A.* One credit card company attempted to use its database to sell flight insurance to air travelers. The company built a model predicting who was most likely to respond to an offer. The offer was successful, but required that the customer fly. Most of those responding, however, were infrequent flyers, leading to little revenue generation.
- *Telephone company B.* Based on an extensive analysis of its database, the company was able to predict which customers were most likely to abandon their phone service for a competitor. The model worked as predicted; unfortunately, the customers identified had already left.
- *Catalog company C.* A database model was built to predict the potential of customers to purchase products from an electronics catalog. Once built, the catalog was mailed and, as predicted, led to a higher than normal level of response. Unfortunately, it also resulted in a higher than normal number of product returns (29 percent)!

So the next time someone collects data on you, don't fret. It will probably be to your benefit—if it is ever used at all.

Sources: Mila D'Antonio, "Red Lobster Goes Overboard for Its Customers," *1 to 1 Magazine,* January/February 2005, p. 13; Mila D'Antonio, "BMO Invests in a New Paradigm," *1 to 1 Magazine,* January/February 2005, p. 14; Karen Henrie, "PNC Invests in Sales and Service," *1 to 1 Magazine,* January/February 2005, p. 15; Ray Schultz, "Live from NCDM: Tales of Database Buffoonery," *Direct Magazine,* December 7, 2004, pp. 1–2; Jonah Bloom, "Ignoring One of Marketing's Most Powerful Tools," *AdAge.com,* November 8, 2004, pp. 1–2.

More specifically, data need to be entered each time there is a transaction so the company can track how recently purchases have been made, how often they are made, and what amounts of money are being spent. In addition, tracking which products and/or services are used increases the ability to conduct the activities previously mentioned. By analyzing the database on a regular basis, the company or organization can identify trends and buying patterns that will help it establish a better relationship with its customers by more effectively meeting their needs.

Direct-Marketing Strategies and Media

As with all other communications programs discussed in this text, marketers must decide the message to be conveyed, the size of the budget, and so on. Perhaps the major difference between direct-marketing programs and other promotional mix programs regards the use of media.

As shown in Figure 14-1, direct marketing employs a number of media, including direct mail, telemarketing, direct-response broadcasting, the Internet, and print. Each medium is used to perform specific functions, although they all generally follow a one- or two-step approach.

In the **one-step approach,** the medium is used directly to obtain an order. You've probably seen TV commercials for products like wrench sets, workout equipment, or magazine subscriptions in which the viewer is urged to phone a toll-free number to place an order immediately. Usually these ads accept credit cards or cash on delivery and give an address. Their goal is to generate an immediate sale when the ad is shown.

The **two-step approach** may involve the use of more than one medium. The first effort is designed to screen, or qualify, potential buyers. The second effort generates the response. For example, many companies use telemarketing to screen on the basis of interest, and then follow up to interested parties with more information designed to achieve an order or use personal selling to close the sale.

Direct Mail

Direct mail is often called "junk mail"—the unsolicited mail you receive. More advertising dollars continue to be spent in direct mail than in almost any other advertising medium—an estimated $52.2 billion in 2004.[16] Direct mail is not restricted to small companies seeking our business. Respected large companies such as General Electric, American Express, and Citicorp have increased their expenditures in this area, as have many others. Over 54 percent of companies state that they have increased their use of this medium in 2004 to 2005.[17]

Many advertisers shied away from direct mail in the past, fearful of the image it might create or harboring the belief that direct mail was useful only for low-cost products. But this is no longer the case. For example, Porsche Cars North America, Inc., uses direct mail to target high-income, upscale consumers who are most likely to purchase its expensive sports cars (Exhibit 14-6). In one example, Porsche developed a direct-mail piece that was sent to a precisely defined target market: physicians in specialties with the highest income levels. This list was screened to match the demographics of Porsche buyers and narrowed further to specific geographic areas. The direct-mail piece was an X ray of a Porsche 911 Carrera 4 written in the language of the medical audience. This creative campaign generated one of the highest response rates of any mailing Porsche has done in recent years.[18] The materials shown in Exhibit 14-7 are just some of the ones sent by Mercedes to market its new R-Class. Mercedes had achieved great success with a similar strategy when it introduced its SUV.

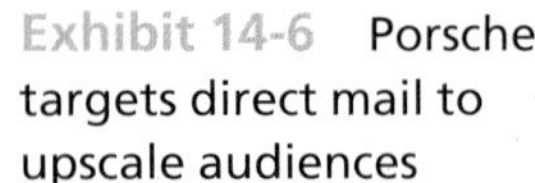
Exhibit 14-6 Porsche targets direct mail to upscale audiences

Keys to the success of direct mail are the **mailing list,** which constitutes the database from which names are generated, and the ability to segment markets. Lists have become more current and more selective, eliminating waste coverage. Segmentation on the basis of geography (usually through Zip codes), demographics, and lifestyles has led to increased effectiveness. The most commonly used lists are of individuals who have already purchased direct-mail products.

The importance of the list has led to a business of its own. It has been estimated that there are over 38 billion names on lists, and many companies have found it profitable to sell the names of purchasers of their products and/or services to list firms. Companies like A. B. Zeller Experian and VNU Business Media (Exhibit 14-8) provide such lists on a national level, and in most metropolitan areas there are firms providing the same service locally.

While direct mail continues to be a favorite medium of many advertisers, and projections are that the market will continue to grow, this medium has been seriously threatened by the Internet. The lower cost of e-mail and the convenience of the Internet have raised concerns among traditional direct-mail marketers. Interestingly, the Internet is both a threat and an opportunity, as Internet companies have increased their expenditures in direct mail to drive potential customers to their sites. For example, AOL frequently mails disks with free time to induce trial of its Internet service. Nevertheless, the direct-mail business has experienced lower response rates from customers than in the past and has seen many advertisers shift dollars from this medium to the Net. Many companies, particularly in the business-to-business market, have shifted from print to online catalogs, and legal problems have also hurt the industry.

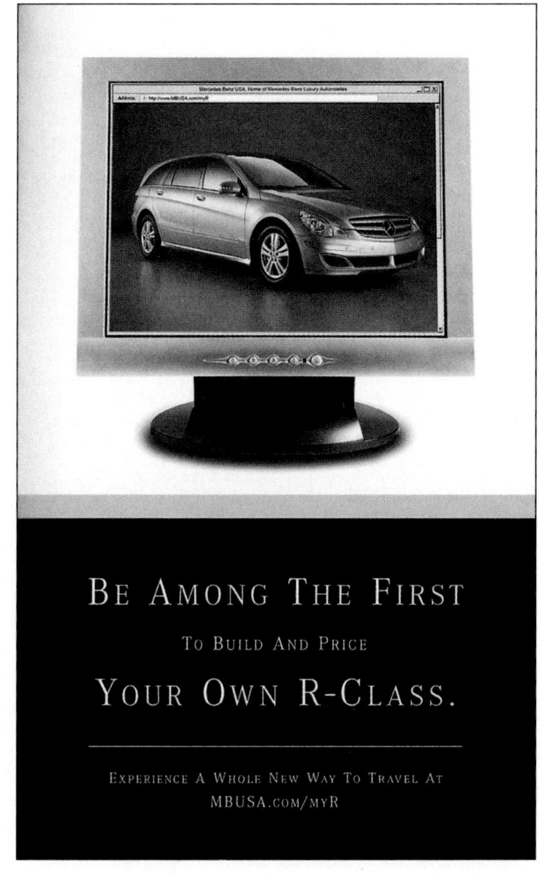

BE AMONG THE FIRST
TO BUILD AND PRICE
YOUR OWN R-CLASS.
EXPERIENCE A WHOLE NEW WAY TO TRAVEL AT
MBUSA.COM/MYR

Exhibit 14-7 Mercedes used direct mail to introduce its new R-Class

Catalogs Major participants in the direct-marketing business include catalog companies. The number of catalogs mailed and the number of catalog shoppers have increased significantly since 1984, with sales continuing to grow. Catalog sales are expected to reach $19.2 billion by 2007.[19]

Many companies use catalogs in conjunction with their more traditional sales and promotional strategies. For example, companies like Pottery Barn, Nordstrom, and Illuminations sell directly through catalogs but also use them to inform consumers of product offerings available in the stores. Some companies (for example, Fingerhut and Oriental Trading Company) rely solely on catalog sales. Others that started out exclusively as catalog companies have branched into retail outlets, among them The Sharper Image, Eddie Bauer, Banana Republic, and Illuminations (Exhibit 14-9). Land's End is now owned by Sears. The products being offered through this medium have reached new heights as well. The 2005 Neiman Marcus Christmas catalog featured:

- A full-sized replica of an Indy race car with simulator for $65,000 to $75,000.
- A super-sized train set with 20 miles of track for $200,000.
- A $3.5 million flying car.
- A personal photo booth for $20,000.

Exhibit 14-8 VNU provides lists for purchase

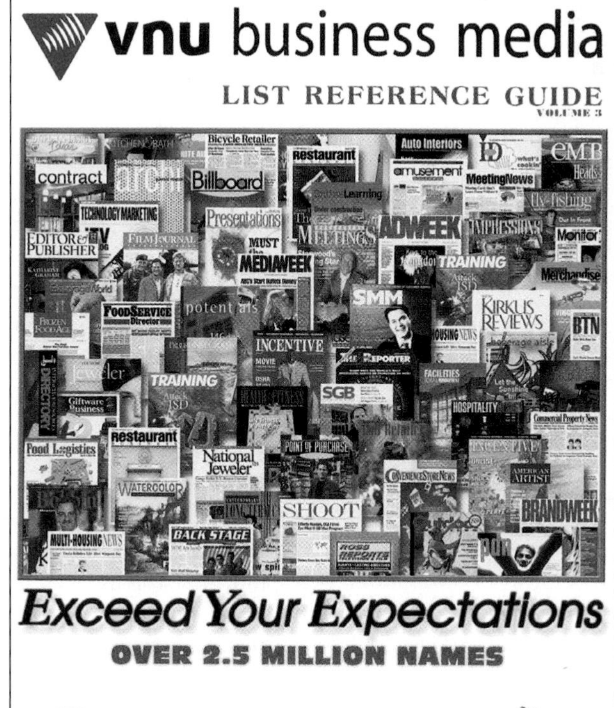

In addition to the traditional hard copies, catalogs are now available on the Internet for both consumer and business-to-business customers. In some instances in the consumer market the catalog merchandise is available in retail stores as well. In others, the catalog and retail divisions are treated as separate entities. For example, if you purchase through the Eddie Bauer catalog, you can exchange

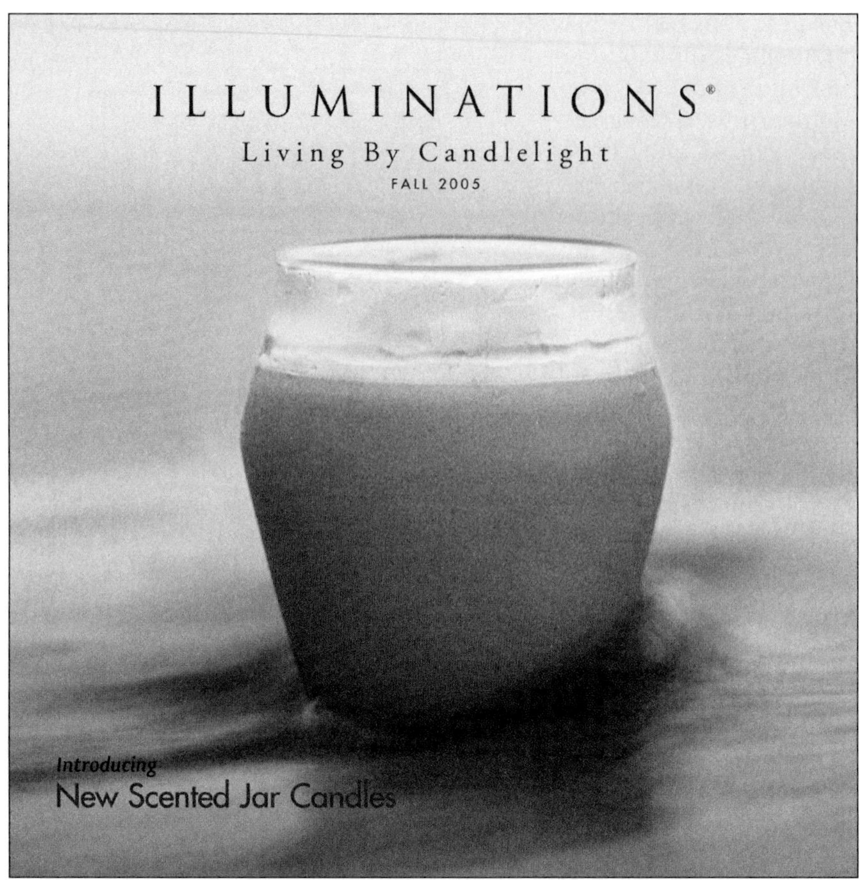

ILLUMINATIONS®
Living By Candlelight
FALL 2005
Introducing
New Scented Jar Candles

Exhibit 14-9 Illuminations is one of many successful catalog companies

or return the merchandise to the retail stores. Victoria's Secret products must be returned to the catalog department. At the Gap, the catalog is used to supplement the inventory in stock, and phone orders for different sizes and so on can be made from the store and shipped for free.

Broadcast Media The success of direct marketing in the broadcast industry has been truly remarkable; as far back as 1996 over 77 percent of the U.S. population reported that they had viewed a direct-response appeal on TV.[20] Direct-response TV is estimated to have generated more than $167 billion in sales in 2004.[21]

Two broadcast media are available to direct marketers: television and radio. While radio was used quite extensively in the 1950s, its use and effectiveness have dwindled substantially in recent years, now accounting for less than one-half of the sales generated by TV.[22] Thus, the majority of direct-marketing broadcast advertising now occurs on TV, which receives the bulk of our attention here. It should be pointed out, however, that the two-step approach is still very common on the radio, particularly with local companies.

Direct marketing in the broadcast industry involves both direct-response advertising and support advertising. In **direct-response advertising,** the product or service is offered and a sales response is solicited, through either the one- or two-step approach previously discussed. Examples include ads for magazine subscriptions, exercise equipment, and tips on football or basketball betting. Toll-free phone numbers are included so that the receiver can immediately call to order. **Support advertising** is designed to do exactly that—support other forms of advertising. Ads for Publishers Clearing House or *Reader's Digest* or other companies telling you to look in your mailbox for a sweepstakes entry are examples of support advertising.

Direct-response TV encompasses a number of media, including direct-response TV spots like those just mentioned, infomercials, and home shopping shows (teleshopping). And as noted in Chapter 10, Internet TV has recently been introduced.

TV Spots Referred to in the direct-marketing industry as *short-form programs,* these spots include direct-response commercials commonly seen on television for products such as magazines, encyclopedias, household products, and more. Figure 14-5 demonstrates the variety of these spots.

Infomercials The lower cost of commercials on cable and satellite channels has led advertisers to a new form of advertising. An **infomercial** is a long commercial that ranges from 30 to 60 minutes. Many infomercials are produced by the advertisers and are designed to be viewed as regular TV shows. Today's infomercials use both one- and two-step approaches. Programs such as "Liquid Luster," "Amazing Discoveries," and "Stainerator" (the so-called miracle-product shows) were the most common form of infomercial in the 1980s. While this form of show is still popular, the infomercial industry has been adopted by many large, mainstream marketers, as noted in the lead-in to this chapter (see Exhibits 14-10 and 14-11).

As to their effectiveness, studies indicate that infomercials are watched and sell products. The demographics of the infomercial shopper reflect a single female, 18 to 34, earn-

Rank	Product Name	Marketing Company	Price	S&H
1	Relacore	Carter-Reed Co.	$0.00	$0.00
2	CortiSlim	Window Rock Enterprises	$0.00	$0.00
3	Estrin D	Covaxil Laboratories Inc.	$0.00	$0.00
4	Ab Lounge	Fitness Quest Inc.	$14.95	$0.00
5	Freedom Tower Silver Dollar	National Collector's Mint	$19.95	$5.00
6	Bowflex Xtreme	The Nautilus Group	$0.00	$0.00
7	Micro Touch Trimmer	Ideavillage	$14.99	$5.99
8	Songbird	Songbird Hearing Inc.	$138.00	$8.95
9	Free Money To Pay Bills	Information USA	$37.95	$7.00
10	Propolene	Obesity Research Institute	$29.95	$9.95
11	Comb 'n Cut	Wahl Clipper Company	$39.00	$9.95
12	Bell & Howell Alarm System	Emson Corp.	$19.95	$6.95
13	Smoke Away	Emerson Direct	$0.00	$0.00
14	First Alert Alarm	TELEBrands	$9.99	$6.95
15	PowerSwing	Sportcraft Ltd.	$0.00	$0.00
16	Laser Straight	Ideavillage	$19.99	$7.99
17	Girls Gone Wild	Mantra Entertainment	$9.99	$4.99
18	Focus Factor	Vital Basics Inc.	$0.00	$5.00
19	Sonic Earz	Emson Corp.	$19.95	$6.95
20	Disney's Greatest	Time-Life Music	$26.99	$5.99

Source: *Response,* November 2004, p. 16.

Figure 14-5 Short-Form Programs

ing $50,000 to $99,900 per year.[23] This advertising medium is indeed effective with a broad demographic base, not significantly different from the infomercial nonshopper in age, education, income, or gender. Retail stores are benefiting from infomercials as well, as brand awareness leads to increased in-store purchases. For example, a $500,000 print campaign combined with an infomercial for the George Foreman grill led to more sales at retail stores than through Direct TV.[24]

The popularity of the infomercial has led companies to expand into the more frequently watched daytime TV market and the creation of infomercial networks. GM's OnStar system has offered a daytime version of the infomercial it refers to as a "documercial," and two new infomercial networks called ExpoTV and TV101 have been launched.[25,26]

However, some people are not sold on the idea of ads disguised as programs. For example, infomercials disguised as "ultrahip" TV shows have been targeted at teenagers, raising fears that kids under the age of 13 will be susceptible to their lure. Consumer complaints are on the rise, and the FTC has already levied fines for deceptive endorsements against infomercial sponsors. Four consumer groups (the Consumer Federation of America, Center for the Study of Commercialism, Center for Media Education, and Telecommunications Research and Action Center) have asked the FCC to require all infomercials to display a symbol that indicates a "paid ad" or "sponsored by" so that viewers won't confuse them with regular programming.

Exhibit 14-10 A variety of companies use infomercials to sell their products

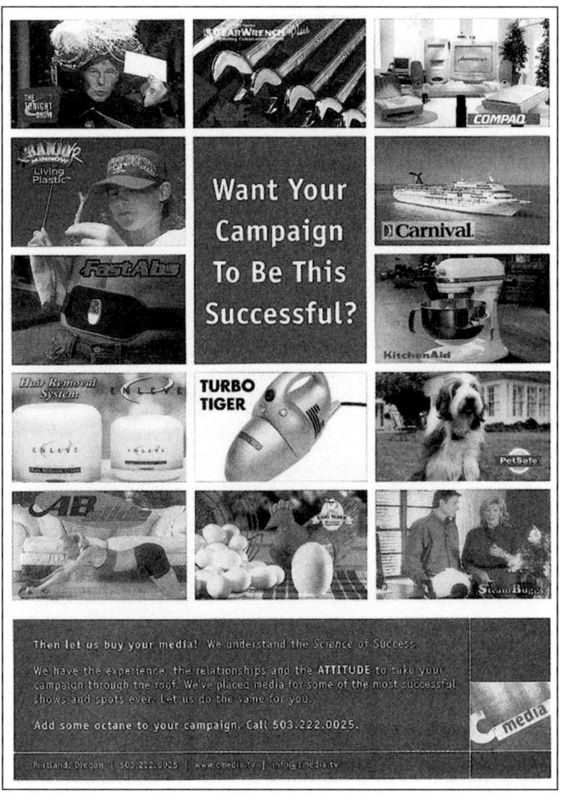

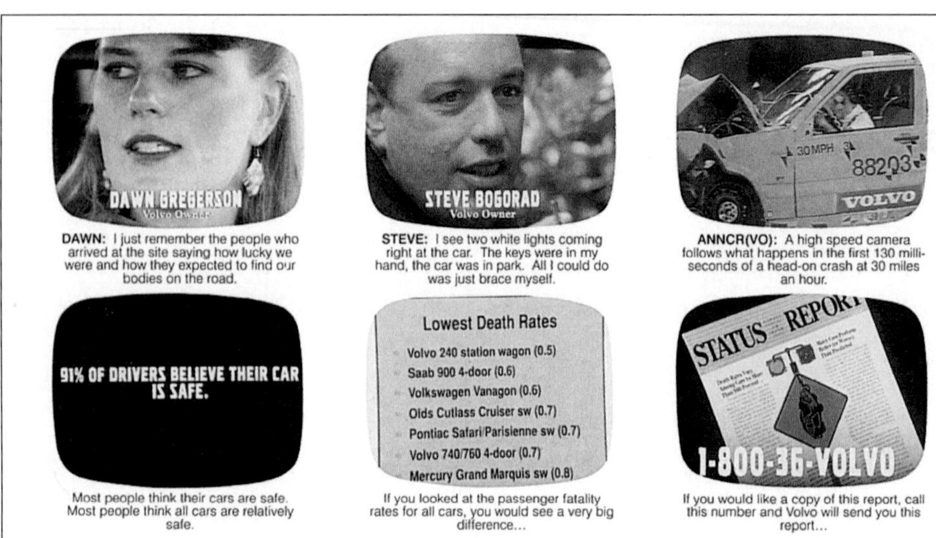

Exhibit 14-11 Volvo uses an infomercial to attract buyers

Homeshopping The development of toll-free telephone numbers, combined with the widespread use of credit cards, has led to a dramatic increase in the number of people who shop via their TV sets through home shopping channels. Jewelry, kitchenware, fitness products, insurance, household products, and a variety of items are now promoted (and sold) this way. The major shopping channel in the United States (QVC) accounted for over $5.69 billion worth of sales in 2004, a 16 percent increase over the previous year.[27] HSN's revenue increased 7 percent to $2.38 billion.[28] The success of home shopping networks has led to a proliferation of shopping channels including Shop@homeTV, Shop NBC, and the Jewelry Channel to name just a few. QVC is pursuing international markets (including the United Kingdom, Canada, and Latin America) to follow up on its successes in Germany and Japan. As the demographics of shopping channel buyers continue to move upscale (over 25 percent of households earn over $100,000 per year), the products offered on these channels continue to move upscale as well. Shop@home considers itself a "TV boutique" given the more expensive line that it carries.

Print Media Magazines and newspapers are difficult media to use for direct marketing. Because these ads have to compete with the clutter of other ads and because the space is relatively expensive, response rates and profits may be lower than in other media. Exhibit 14-12 shows a direct ad that appeared in a magazine. You can find many more in specific interest areas like financial newspapers or sports, sex, or hobby magazines.

Exhibit 14-12 A direct-response print ad

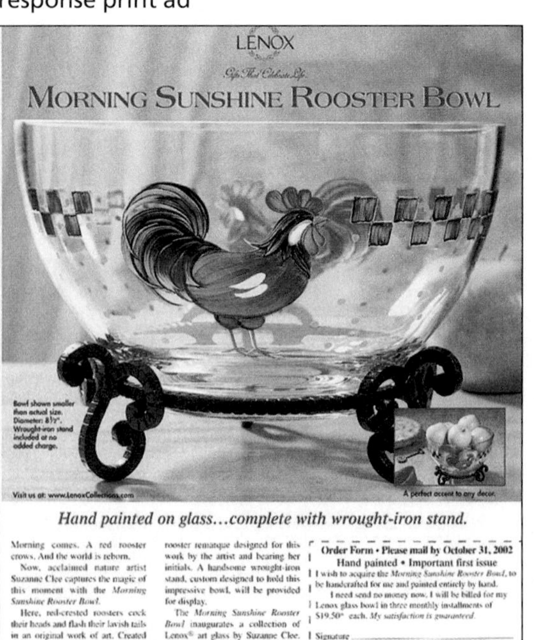

Telemarketing If you have a telephone, you probably do not have to be told about **telemarketing,** or sales by telephone. Both profit and charitable organizations have employed this medium effectively in both one- and two-step approaches. Combined telemarketing sales (consumer and business-to-business) totaled over $654 billion in 2004—down from $661 billion in 2001.[29,30] Telemarketing is still a very big industry. Consider these facts:

- Over 6.3 million people are now employed in the telemarketing industry.[31]
- There are over 165,000 call centers in the United States.[32]
- Marketers spend an estimated $76.2 billion a year on outbound telemarketing calls.[33]

Along with business to consumers and nonprofits, business-to-business marketers like Adobe Systems, Kaiser Permanente, and Hewlett-Packard are just a few of the many companies that use this direct-marketing medium effectively. B-to-b sales are expected to reach $588 billion by 2006.[34]

As telemarketing continues to expand in scope, a new dimension referred to as **audiotex** or **telemedia** has evolved. Tom Eisenhart defines telemedia as the "use of telephone and voice information services (900, 800, and 976 numbers) to market, advertise, promote, entertain, and inform."[35] Many telemedia programs are interactive. While many people still think of 900 and 976 numbers as rip-offs or "sex, lies, and phone lines," over 7,000 programs are carried on 900

Figure 14-6 The Use of 800, 900, and 976 Numbers in Marketing

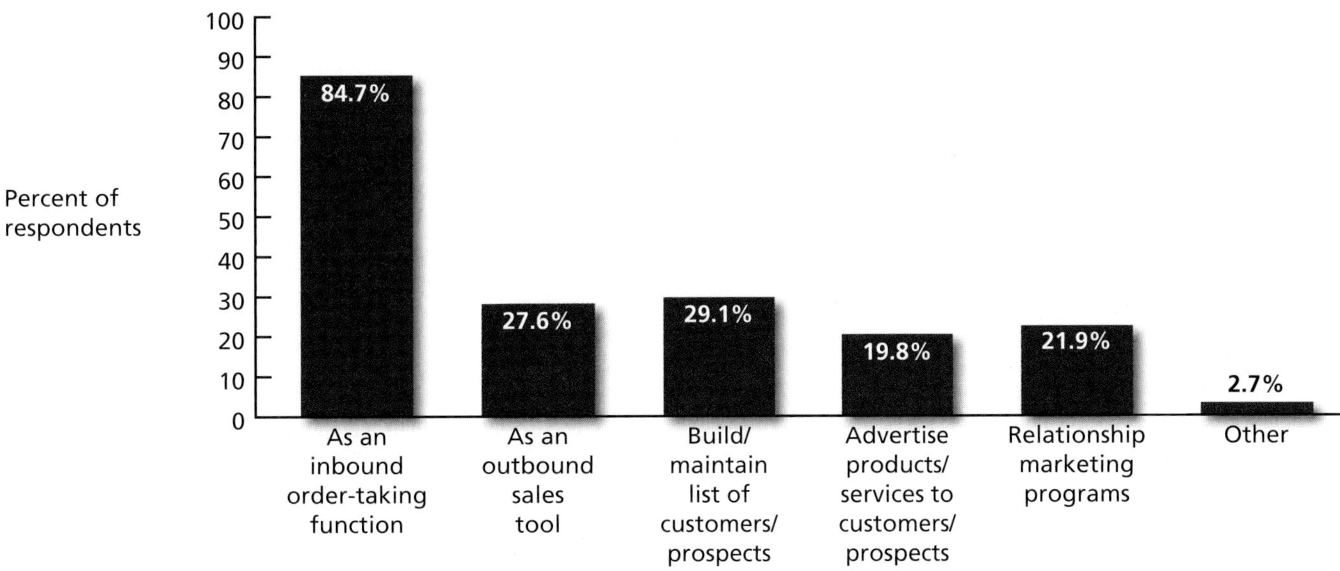

numbers alone, including entertainment, health care, banking and finance companies, and government services. Figure 14-6 shows more specifically how 800, 976, and 900 numbers are used as marketing tools.

Problems associated with telemarketing include its potential for fraud and deception and its potential for annoyance. (Doesn't it seem as if every time you sit down to dinner you receive a phone call from someone trying to sell you something or asking for a donation?) These developments have led to the development of a Do Not Call list (see Ethical Perspective 14-1).

Those in the telemarketing and telemedia industry have responded to public criticisms. Dial-a-Porn and its ilk hold a diminishing share of 800, 900, and 976 offerings.

Electronic Teleshopping

Unlike infomercials and home shopping channels, which have relied on broadcast or cable TV, **electronic teleshopping** is an online shopping and information retrieval service accessed through personal computers. While we will discuss e-commerce in detail in the next chapter, it is important to reiterate that Internet shopping is a direct-response medium that traditional direct marketers are adding to their businesses as well. For example, QVC, the home shopping channel, has started iQVC, an Internet home shopping channel that complements its cable TV channel and adds incremental sales (the cable channel drives customers to the website). The company was one of the first "Web department stores" to turn a profit. More information on e-commerce and direct mail via the Internet will be provided in Chapter 15.

Direct Selling

An additional element of the direct-marketing program is **direct selling,** the direct, personal presentation, demonstration, and sales of products and services to consumers in their homes. Avon, Cutco, Mary Kay, Inc., and Tupperware are some of the best-known direct-selling companies in the United States and are now extending these programs overseas (Exhibit 14-13). Close to 13.3 million people engage in direct selling throughout the United States and 47 million worldwide; 99 percent of them are independent contractors (not employees of the firm they represent). These 13.3 million generate over $29 billion in sales.[36]

The three forms of direct selling are

1. *Repetitive person-to-person selling.* The salesperson visits the buyer's home, job site, or other location to sell frequently purchased products or services (for example, Amway). Mary Kay gave away its 100,000th Cadillac—the company's symbol of sales success—in 2005.
2. *Nonrepetitive person-to-person selling.* The salesperson visits the buyer's home, job site, or other location to sell infrequently purchased products or services (for example, *Encyclopaedia Britannica*).

ETHICAL PERSPECTIVE 14-1

The Do Not Call List: Not Everyone Wins

If you have noticed that you can now sit down to dinner without the phone ringing with someone trying to sell you something, you can thank the Federal Trade Commission (FTC). Responding to a multitude of consumer complaints, the FTC instituted the Do Not Call list in October 2003. Since that time it has become "the most popular service offered to the public by the federal government in quite some time," according to Eileen Harrington, the FTC's associate director for marketing practices. By its second anniversary in 2005, the registry had reached 100 million numbers.

The registry is a database that consumers can access through a website to sign up their phone number to make it off-limits to telemarketers. The registration is good for five years. If a telemarketer calls a number on the list and the recipient complains, the caller is subject to a fine. For companies that make a lot of calls (even by error), the fines could run into millions of dollars. The popularity of the service has led to a do not call registry for cell phones, and a similar list for e-mails is currently under consideration. Estimates are that the number of telemarketing calls has been reduced by 50 percent as a result of the Do Not Call list. Consumers are elated by the service.

But not everyone is so happy. Two major marketing trade groups, the Direct Marketing Association (DMA) and the American Teleservices Association, challenged the action in court as a violation of free speech. Some companies, including those that have conducted business with the customer within the past 18 months, are exempt, as are politicians (naturally!) and charities. The organizations argued that institution of the list would result in the loss of more than 2 million jobs and would reduce revenues generated from the calls by 50 percent. The organizations also argued that the FTC could have found other ways to regulate the annoying calls without barring all telemarketing calls.

Others are unhappy as well. Not all telemarketers are attempting to sell you insurance, aluminum siding, or financial services, they say. Local merchants, doctors, lawyers, and others who have not had an established relationship with the recipient over the past 18 months are also banned from calling for the purposes of acquiring clients. The magazine industry, which generates as much as 39 percent of new subscriptions through telemarketing, has been hit hard. Those who stand to lose their jobs as a result of the decline in calling are not too happy about the call list either.

The legality of the Do Not Call list was challenged all the way to the U.S. Supreme Court, where it was upheld in October 2004. While violations have been rare, two timeshare sellers and their telemarketer were forced to pay the FTC $500,000 to settle charges that they violated the Do Not Call rule by calling thousands of people whose numbers were on the list. They did not pay the registry access fees for some of the area codes they called. In addition, the companies were banned from engaging in future telemarketing calls to registered numbers or for making calls to an area code without paying registry access fees first.

Sources: Patricia Odell, "Do-Not-Call Registry Reaches 100 Million Numbers," *promomagazine.com,* August 31, 2005, p. 1; "FTC Settles with Do Not Call Violators," *Computer and Internet Lawyer,* May 2005, pp. 24–26; Ira Teinowitz, "Do Not Call Law Upheld as Constitutional," *adage.com,* February 17, 2004, pp. 1–2; Paul Sweeney, "Telemarketing Curbs Not a Boon to All," *Financial Executive,* March/April 2004, pp. 37–39.

3. *Party plans.* The salesperson offers products or services to groups of people through home or office parties and demonstrations (for example, Tupperware and PartyLite Gifts).

While a number of products and services are sold through direct selling, home and family care products (32 percent) and personal care products (29.4 percent) are the most popular. The "typical" direct-selling representative is female (79.9 percent), married (76 percent), and between 35 and 44 years of age (Figure 14-7). For most of the representatives, direct selling is not a full-time job but an opportunity to earn additional income and a way to get the product at a discount for themselves. Over half of those employed in this industry spend fewer than 10 hours a week selling, and 85.1 percent spend less than 30 hours a week.

Evaluating the Effectiveness of Direct Marketing

Because they generate a direct response, measuring the effectiveness of direct-marketing programs is not difficult. Using the **cost per order (CPO),** advertisers can evaluate the relative effectiveness of an ad in only a few minutes based on the number of calls generated. By running the same ad on different stations, a direct marketer can determine the relative effectiveness of the medium itself. For example, if the advertiser targets a $5 return per order and a broadcast commercial (production and print) costs $2,500, the ad is considered effective if it generates 500 orders. Similar measures have been developed for print and direct-mail ads.

For direct-marketing programs that do not have an objective of generating a behavioral response, traditional measures of effectiveness can be applied. (We discuss these measures in Chapter 19.)

Advantages and Disadvantages of Direct Marketing

Many of the advantages of direct marketing have already been presented. A review of these and some additions follow:

1. *Selective reach.* Direct marketing lets the advertiser reach a large number of people and reduces or eliminates waste coverage. Intensive coverage may be obtained through broadcast advertising or through the mail. While not everyone drives on highways where there are billboards or pays attention to TV commercials, virtually everyone receives mail. A good list allows for minimal waste, as only those consumers with the highest potential are targeted. For example, a political candidate can direct a message at a very select group of people (those living in a certain Zip code or members of the Sierra Club, say); a book club can target recent purchasers of Avid readers.

2. *Segmentation capabilities.* Marketers can purchase lists of recent product purchasers, car buyers, bank-card holders, and so on. These lists may allow segmentation on the basis of geographic area, occupation, demographics, and job title, to mention a few. Combining this information with the geocoding capabilities of Prizm or VALS (discussed in Chapter 2), marketers can develop effective segmentation strategies.

Exhibit 14-13 Cutco uses direct selling successfully in marketing their knives

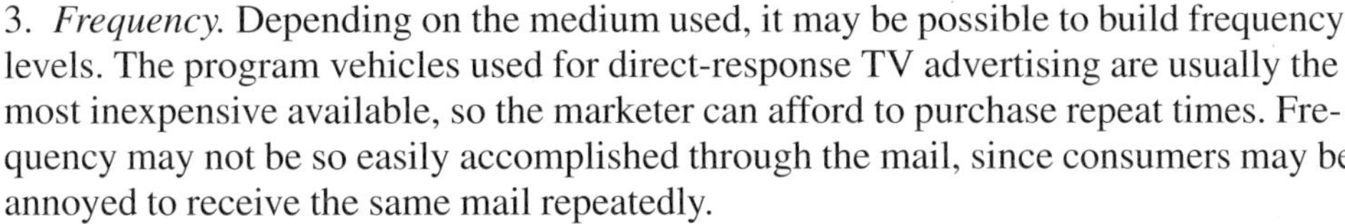

3. *Frequency.* Depending on the medium used, it may be possible to build frequency levels. The program vehicles used for direct-response TV advertising are usually the most inexpensive available, so the marketer can afford to purchase repeat times. Frequency may not be so easily accomplished through the mail, since consumers may be annoyed to receive the same mail repeatedly.

4. *Flexibility.* Direct marketing can take on a variety of creative forms. For example, the Discovery Network sent 17-inch TV sets to media buyers through the mail. The only message accompanying the TV sets was one on the cord that said "Plug me in" and another on a videotape that read "Play me." Upon doing so, the recipient was greeted with a seven-minute promotional video. Direct-mail pieces also allow for detailed copy that provides a great deal of information. The targeted mailing of videotapes containing product information has increased dramatically, as companies have found this a very effective way to provide potential buyers with product information.

Figure 14-7 Direct Sales Force Demographics

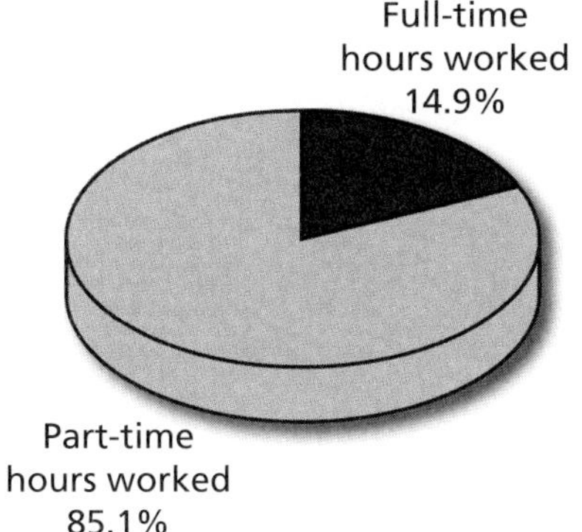

Demographics of Direct Salespeople	
Independent contractors	99.8%
Married	76
Female	79.9
Age: 35–54	54
Less than 30 hours per week	85.1

Source: From DSA's 2005 Salesforce Survey, DSA.org.

5. *Timing.* While many media require long-range planning and have long closing dates, direct-response advertising can be much more timely. Direct mail, for example, can be put together very quickly and distributed to the target population. TV programs typically used for direct-response advertising are older, less sought programs that are likely to appear on the station's list of available spots. Another common strategy is to purchase available time at the last possible moment to get the best price.

6. *Personalization.* No other advertising medium can personalize the message as well as direct media. Parents with children at different age levels can be approached, with their child's name included in the appeal. Car owners are mailed letters congratulating them on their new purchase and offering accessories. Computer purchasers are sent software solicitations. Graduating college students receive very personalized information that recognizes their specific needs and offers solutions (such as credit cards).

7. *Costs.* While the CPM for direct mail may be very high on an absolute and a relative basis, its ability to specifically target the audience and eliminate waste coverage reduces the actual CPM. The ads used on TV are often among the lowest-priced available. As you will see, direct mail via the Internet is extremely inexpensive.

A second factor contributing to the cost effectiveness of direct-response advertising is the cost per customer purchasing. Because of the low cost of media, each sale generated is very inexpensive.

8. *Measures of effectiveness.* No other medium can measure the effectiveness of its advertising efforts as well as direct response. Feedback is often immediate and always accurate.

Disadvantages of direct marketing include the following:

1. *Image factors.* As we noted earlier, the mail segment of this industry is often referred to as junk mail. Many people believe unsolicited mail promotes junk products, and others dislike being solicited. Even some senders of direct mail, including Motorola, GM, and Air Products & Chemicals, say they throw out most of the junk mail they receive. This problem is particularly relevant given the increased volume of mail being sent. (One study estimates the typical American receives 14 pieces of junk mail per week.)[37] Another predicts that by 2007 consumers will receive over 3,900 junk e-mails per year.[38] In 2004, more than 205.7 billion pieces of mail were sent in the United States, over 99 billion of which was advertising related.[39]

Likewise, direct-response ads on TV are often low-budget ads for lower-priced products, which contributes to the image that something less than the best products are marketed in this way. (Some of this image is being overcome by the home shopping channels, which promote some very expensive products.) Telemarketing is found to be irritating to many consumers, as is "spam" or Internet junk mail. Other factors have also created image problems for the direct-marketing industry.

2. *Accuracy.* One of the advantages cited for direct mail and telemarketing was targeting potential customers specifically. But the effectiveness of these methods depends on the accuracy of the lists used. People move, change occupations, and so on, and if the lists are not kept current, selectivity will decrease. Computerization has greatly improved the currency of lists and reduced the incidence of bad names; however, the ability to generate lists is becoming a problem. The cost of generating a lead can range from a few dollars to as much as hundreds depending on its quality.

3. *Content support.* In our discussion of media strategy objectives in Chapter 10, we said the ability of magazines to create mood contributes to the overall effectiveness of the ads they carry. In direct-response advertising, mood creation is limited to the surrounding program and/or editorial content. Direct mail and online services are unlikely to create a desirable mood.

4. *Rising costs.* As postal rates increase, direct-mail profits are immediately and directly impacted. The same is true for print costs, which drives up the costs of mailers and catalogs. The low cost of e-mail has led many companies to switch to this medium.

Summary

This chapter introduced you to the rapidly growing field of direct marketing, which involves a variety of methods and media beyond direct mail and telemarketing. The versatility of direct marketing offers many different types of companies and organizations a powerful promotional and selling tool.

Direct marketing continues to outpace other advertising and promotional areas in growth; many of the Fortune 500 companies now use sophisticated direct-marketing strategies. Database marketing has become a critical component of many marketing programs.

Advantages of direct marketing include its selective reach, segmentation, frequency, flexibility, and timing. Personalized and custom messages, low costs, and the ability to measure program effectiveness are also advantages of direct-marketing programs.

At the same time, a number of disadvantages are associated with the use of direct marketing. Image problems, the proliferating sale and use of databases (some of them based on inaccurate lists), lack of content support, and the intrusive nature of the medium make some marketers hesitant to use direct-marketing tools. However, self-policing of the industry and involvement by large, sophisticated companies have led to significant improvements. As a result, the use of direct marketing will continue to increase.

Key Terms

direct marketing, 447
direct-response media, 447
database, 451
database marketing, 451
RFM scoring method, 453
one-step approach, 456
two-step approach, 456
mailing list, 456
direct-response advertising, 458
support advertising, 458
infomercial, 458
telemarketing, 460
audiotex, 460
telemedia, 460
electronic teleshopping, 461
direct selling, 461
cost per order (CPO), 462

Discussion Questions

1. Explain how companies use database marketing. Name some of the companies that may have your information in their database. Explain how this information is used to reach you.

2. What is the difference between the one- and two-step approaches to direct marketing? Give examples of companies that pursue both methods.

3. As the Internet continues to grow in popularity, some marketers predict that the print catalogs will cease to exist, replaced by Internet catalogs. Others disagree. Explain some of the reasons why this situation may or may not occur.

4. Describe the various forms of direct-response advertising. Discuss some of the reasons for the success of direct-response advertising.

5. The chapter details some of the pros and cons of the "do not call" list. Discuss these in detail. Do you think that direct marketing will be seriously impacted by this and other proposed "do not" lists?

6. Many marketers thought that the Internet would hurt the direct-mail catalog industry. In fact, this has not been the case. Explain some of the similar characteristics of catalog shopping and shopping on the Internet. Then explain why you think the mail catalog business has not been hurt.

7. What is the difference between direct marketing and direct selling? Describe the various forms of direct selling and some of the characteristics of the industry that make it unique.

8. What are the characteristics of the infomercial watcher? In viewing this profile, does it surprise you? Explain why or why not.

9. Explain why companies like KitchenAid, Soloflex, and others have been successful in adopting direct-marketing techniques. Describe the conditions that contribute to the successful implementation of direct-marketing programs.

10. Identify some of the factors that have contributed to the growth of direct marketing. Do you see these factors being as relevant today? Discuss why or why not, and the impact they will have on direct marketing in the future.

The Internet and Interactive Media

15

Chapter Objectives

1. To understand the role of the Internet and interactive media in an IMC program.
2. To know the advantages and disadvantages of the Internet and interactive media.
3. To examine the role of additional online media.
4. To understand how to evaluate the effectiveness of communications through the Internet.

The Internet: Does It Mean the Death of Television Advertising?

In August 2005, an article appeared in backchannelmedia.com titled "Advertising Is Dead: Long Live Advertising." The article noted that advertising spending in the United States that year would reach more than $279 billion, up 5.7 percent, setting a new record for expenditures. The article went on to say that while the Internet accounted for only a small percentage of this amount, within five years the advertising landscape would be very different; for example, TV advertising would no longer exist as it does today. Interestingly, this was not the only article that made a dire prediction for the future of mass-media advertising. Critics contend that although we have heard all of this before, this time we may have more reason to worry.

A number of studies have examined the changing media habits of consumers. Most of these have concluded pretty much the same thing—consumers, particularly young consumers—are spending more time online and less time with traditional media. Consider some of the results of the studies that follow.

A study by eMarketer indicates that 73.4 percent of all teens ages 12 to 17 access the Internet, as do 39.4 percent of those ages 3 to 11. The study concludes that for these age groups, there is virtually no distinction between online and offline media. In other words, both online and offline are media options, and that is about it. Another study reports that being online continues to cause a reduction in the number of hours children spend watching television (the first time a reduction occurred was in 1998). Internet users spend 28 percent less time watching TV than nonusers, though they still spend more time watching TV than being online. The same reduction is now occurring in time spent with print media, the study concludes. Yet another study concludes that when people 18 to 24 must choose between two media, the majority (50.5 percent) would choose the Internet, and only 28.5 percent would choose TV.

But that study is of young people. Surely adults would be more inclined to stay with more traditional media. Given the same choice of only two media, the age groups 25 to 34 and 35 to 54 also chose the Internet by margins of about 43 percent to 37 percent. In addition, the number of adults who use the Internet as their main source of news has grown over 35 percent from 2000 to 2004—at the direct expense of television and newspapers. It gets worse. In the latter survey, 97 percent of respondents thought that online services were equal or better than magazines for finding information about products or music, 83 percent said reading a news story online was better than reading it in the newspaper, and 67 percent said that watching a news clip online is the same or better than watching it on TV.

Finally, in a study where consumers were deprived of the use of the Internet, the median time consumers said they could "exist" without the Web was five days. Over half said they could not survive over two weeks because such daily activities as booking travel, communicating with friends, and checking the news were too severely impaired. Many consumers expressed that they suffered severe withdrawal symptoms, such as feelings of loss and deprivation.

What all of this means for advertisers, at least according to the doomsayers, is that advertising as we know it is dead—or at least on life support. But, of course, not everyone agrees. The results are misleading, some analysts say, or at least, leave out some very important details. For example, one of the studies indicates that while consumers use the Net to gather information, 86 percent said they are most likely to watch TV for entertainment and 65 percent said it was a way for them to relax. Among entertainment options, the Internet ranked fifth. Television advertisers also note that many Internet users are online only for brief periods of two to three minutes—often during commercial breaks on TV. Over half are multitasking, that is, using TV and the Internet at the same time. Both teens and adults, they say, spend more time watching TV than being online, and neither group appears ready to give up their TV sets just yet. The group also cites data from Mediamark Research, Inc., and Multimedia Scan which show that adults who go online most frequently also watch *more* shows and read *more* newspapers than their less-wired counterparts. As noted by Jeffrey Cole, director of the UCLA Center for Communication Policy, "TV is still the best game in town . . . I don't think you'll see one-third of media budgets going to interactive. But you don't hear as much about people making fun of the Internet anymore."

So, is TV advertising dead? While many TV advocates say they heard this story even before the dot-com bust, most know that the studies necessitate change. Television, like other traditional media, will have to adapt. Some believe that TV will adopt an Internet-like model, with user-initiated commercials. Some market tests indicate that consumers have already agreed to "opt-in" to watch infomercials, and other studies indicate that the number of viewers skipping or not watching TV commercials has not significantly declined over the past few years. If you keep it interesting they will come, they say. Only time will tell.

Sources: Wendy Davis, "Carat Heavy Web Users Don't Make Other Media Losers," mediapost.com, March 16, 2005, pp. 1–2; "Advertising Is Dead; Long Live Advertising," backchannelmedia.com, August 1, 2005, pp. 1–2; Jack Neff, "Internet Erosion of TV Viewing Habits Deepens," AdAge.com, February 9, 2004, pp. 1–2; Kate Kaye, "Internet Users Would Rather Give Up TV Than Web," *Media Daily News,* September 22, 2004, pp. 1–2; Mickey Alam Khan, "Study: Internet Preferred Method for Getting News," *DM News,* September 22, 2004, pp. 1–2; "Yahoo! And OMD Reveal Study Depicting Life without the Internet," September 22, 2004, tmcnet.com, p.1.

As you can see from the lead-in to this chapter, the Internet has certainly had a major impact on the media landscape and the way that marketers communicate with their existing and potential customers. In many ways, the impact of the Internet has been much different than originally expected—which, in part, accounts for the initial growth of expenditures in this medium, followed by a short bust, then enormous growth again. While the Net has not become the "end all and be all" that some expected, it has spawned a number of new forms of communication, has led marketers to reconsider their use of traditional media, and has impacted the marketing world in a way not seen since the advent of television.

This chapter will examine the role of the Internet as well as other interactive media. In this chapter we will examine the history of the Internet, its role in an IMC program, and some of the advantages and disadvantages associated with this medium. We will also discuss the various new media options that have resulted from the Internet and their roles in an IMC program. The chapter will conclude with a discussion of the measurement of these media.

A Brief History of the Internet

A history of the Internet (the Net), of course, is brief, as this medium has not existed for very long. However, given the Internet's incredibly rapid adoption and the dynamic influence it has had on society, it is important to provide some insight as to how it has developed, particularly over the past decade, when Web advertising began.

The **Internet** started on September 2, 1969, through the connection of two computers: one at UCLA and the other at Stanford University. Initially called ARPANET (Advanced Research Project Agency), the network was developed by the U.S. Department of Defense as a failsafe way to connect vital research agencies across the United States. After an initial attempt failed, a connection was made, and it was the beginning of what changed the world forever. From that initial connection, observed by about 15 people, the network has grown to consist of over 1 billion users worldwide. In 2005, the total number of Web pages exceeded 600 billion—more than 100 for each person on earth.[1]

What has changed the Internet the most is the development of the **World Wide Web (WWW),** the business component of the Net. Virtually unknown in 1993, no other medium other than black-and-white television has been adopted as rapidly as the Internet. By 2001, over 50 percent of U.S. homes were wired to the Internet. That compares to nine years for 50 percent of U.S. homes to purchase a radio, 10 for the VCR, 17 for personal computers, 39 for cable TV, and 70 for the telephone.[2] Today an estimated 68 percent of households in North America are connected.[3]

The first advertisements on the Web were introduced on HotWired in 1994 for brands including Zima, Club Med, and AT&T in the form of banner ads. The growth of the Web and Web-based advertising expenditures continued until 2000, at which point there was a "bust," when advertising expenditures dropped by 25 percent from 2000 to 2002.[4] Much of the bust is attributed to a lack of understanding of how to use the Web as a marketing tool, as the number of consumers using the Internet rose rapidly during this same period. Many of the companies who initially advertised on this medium (such as Pets.com, Boo.com, Toysmart.com) no longer exist.

As advertisers saw the adoption of the Net continue to grow and recognized its potential, other companies replaced those that had left. These included Fortune 100 companies, many of whom, including P&G, AT&T, and McDonald's, were among the top advertisers in traditional media. VisaUSA, for example, has seen its online budget increase steadily each year since 2001, as the company continues to test emerging platforms.[5] By 2005, advertising on the Internet exceeded $10 billion, with projections of the amount reaching $22.3 billion by 2009.[6] Spending on Internet advertising grew by 33 percent from 2003 to 2004—more than triple that of other traditional media (see Figure 15-1).

Why the Rapid Adoption of the Internet?

The almost unprecedented growth of the Internet—the "digital revolution"—has led a number of academicians and practitioners to offer reasons for why this occurred. Reasons include consumers' desire for information as well as for control over the information they receive. In addition, the speed and convenience of acquiring this information as well as conducting e-commerce through personal computers is very attractive to the money-rich but time-poor consumers who were described as contributing to the success of direct marketing in the previous chapter.

Figure 15-1 U.S. Online Ad Spending Growth, 2001 to 2009 (as a Percent Increase/Decrease vs. Prior Year)

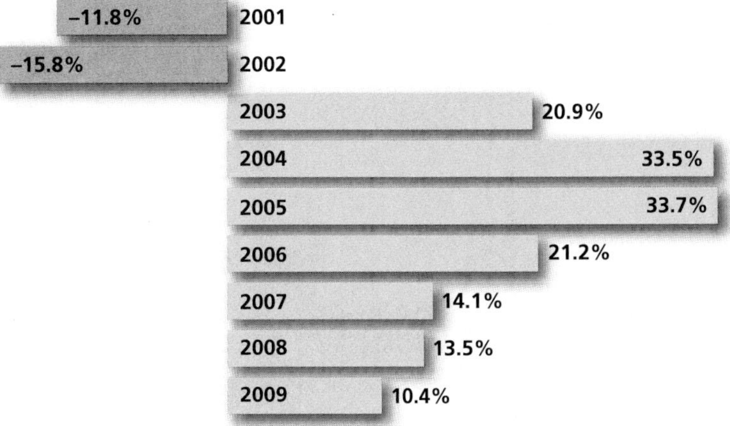

In addition to consumers' desire for control, the ability to target customers effectively through the Net is attractive to marketers. The increased attention for accountability on the part of businesses led to a view of the Internet as a medium that would provide more direct feedback on the value of marketing expenditures. As was true of direct marketing, companies liked the fact that, unlike traditional media, it was often easier to account for the ROI of their expenditures. In fact, in its earliest stages, a number of marketing companies perceived the Internet as a direct-response medium. While a large component of the Web is still that of e-commerce, today's marketers now employ the medium for numerous other communications and marketing objectives (as we will discuss shortly). Other factors that have contributed to increased attention on the Internet include the increase in high-speed Internet connections which has led Americans to spend more time online, and has increased use of visual advertising, technologies that allow for tracking consumers, and advertisers' growing confidence in the medium.[7]

Today's World Wide Web has evolved into a different medium than anyone could have expected 10 years ago. Unlike other media, which are essentially unidirectional and responsible for the content provided and products and services offered for sale, the Internet is interactive, allowing for a two-way flow. Consumers not only control when and which messages and content they are exposed to, but now provide their own content, offer their own goods, and services for sale and provide feedback on the same as provided by others. Consider that eBay has as many as 50 million auctions taking place at any one time, and more than $11 billion worth of vehicles were sold in this medium in 2004.[8]

Web Objectives

When major corporations first began to conduct business on the Internet, they put up websites primarily for information purposes. Companies like K-Mart and Maytag had sites that were really not much more than online catalogs, while those of other companies were designed for information purposes only. The role of the website quickly changed, however, as sites are now designed to accomplish a number of objectives and have become much more creative, by promoting brand images, positioning, and offering promotions, product information, and products and services for sale. With the introduction of Java in 1995, it became possible to create fancier graphics, audio, and animation online. This resulted in marketers' utilizing the Internet in an entirely new way, moving beyond the purely informational role. As you will see, the objective of disseminating information and selling products remains, but additional communications and sales objectives are also being pursued.

Developing and Maintaining a Website

Before we discuss marketers' Web objectives in detail, it is important that you understand the role of the **website**—the place where providers make information available to

Exhibit 15-1 Factors that lead to an effective website

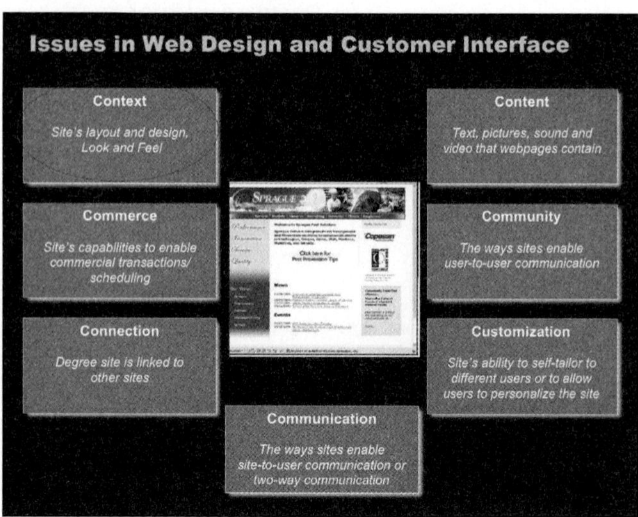

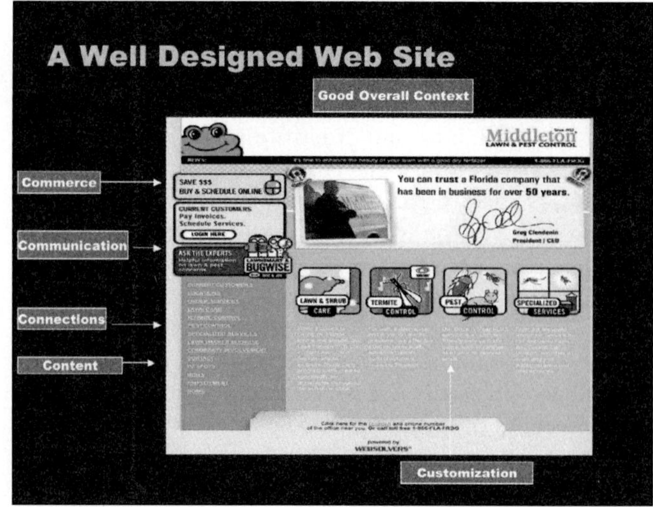

users of the Internet. Developing and maintaining a successful website requires significant time and effort. To attract visitors to the site and have them return to it requires a combination of creativity, effective marketing, and continual updating of the site. In addition, the site must be integrated with other media in regard to objectives, appearance, and other factors.

Exhibit 15-2 HUGGIES homepage

Exhibit 15-1 demonstrates the factors that contribute to an effective website. Making a site work and having one work successfully are not the same thing, however, and whether a site is effective is determined by what it is that management hopes to achieve through the site. As already noted, some sites are offered for informational purposes only (this tends to be more common in the business-to-business market than in the consumer market), while others approach the market much more aggressively. For example, Kimberly-Clark Corporation, the manufacturer of HUGGIES brand of diapers, Pull-Ups training pants, and Little Swimmers swim pants, has been extremely successful in its Internet marketing efforts. The HUGGIES homepage (Exhibit 15-2) goes well beyond providing information. The site has additional objectives, such as developing a long-term relationship with parents, establishing a brand image for the products, and supporting sales. The HUGGIES Baby Network provides expectant mothers with encouragement and ideas as to how to maintain a happy and healthy pregnancy. By clicking onto this part of the site, the expectant mother is provided with informative articles, experts' opinions, weekly newsletters, and the opportunity to personalize the site to her personal needs. The site also provides information to be used once the baby has been born. Tips on how to create a nursery, games to play with the baby, and more information from experts are just part of this section of the site. The site is designed to develop one-on-one relationships by offering very useful informaton, as well as product samples and more to anyone who sends in his or her name, address, and e-mail address. Thousands of people have responded to the offer, providing Kimberly-Clark with an enormous database the company can use for future marketing efforts. Also included are links to editorial partners such as American Baby.com, Parenting.com, and other content providers, as well as special offers, sweepstakes, and additional information about HUGGIES products. Finally, to support sales, the site directs customers to the nearest retail store that sells HUGGIES brands.

As the HUGGIES example demonstrates, a website can be an effective tool for the marketer. Depending on the nature of one's business and one's marketing objectives for the Internet, a website can range from a very simple source of information about the company and its products to a powerful tool for developing a brand image, sampling, and even generating sales. Figure 15-2 shows *Adweek* magazine's first Website Hot List, which lists the many different factors that make a website effective. The figure also lists some of the objectives sought by those marketing on the Internet.

IMC Perspective 15-1 demonstrates the U.S. Army's effective use of their website as an integral component of their IMC program.

Figure 15-2 The Website Hot List

Adweek magazine's Best Performers of 2005 based on key audience metrics and being a favorite of the online community

Weather.com	Delivers a mass audience; proficient in targeting campaigns based on geography, lifestyles, etc.
Forbes.com	One of the best for translation of print to Web; editorial depth
Myspace.com	Web phenomenon for 18–25 demo; 27 million registered voters spend average 1 hour 42 minutes on site
Nick.com	Combines best of online and TV
BusinessWeekOnline	Redesign led to double-digit gains in unique audience and other audience metrics
MSNBC.com	High marks for free video content; highly innovative
AskMen.com	Sizeable male audience impressive to advertisers; smart use of search
IMDb	12 million unique visitors per month spend 15 minutes on site
AOLMusic.com	Destination using TV-like programming and other attractions
HGTV.com	As good as the cable channel; 40% increase in time spent on site

Source: *Adweek,* September 2005.

IMC PERSPECTIVE 15-1

The U.S. Army Makes GoArmy.com the Hub of Its IMC Program

During the early to mid-1990s, the U.S. Army had little trouble attracting enough young people to enlist for military service. The collapse of the Soviet Union had all but ended the Cold War, and military warfare was becoming more high-tech, which meant that fewer soldiers were needed. Thus, the Army was downsized by 40 percent, making it easy to reach modest recruitment goals. Recruitment advertising used the "Be All That You Can Be" tagline and relied primarily on expensive television commercials to deliver the self-actualization message. The ads also emphasized how joining the Army provided opportunities for career training, college scholarships, and other financial incentives.

While its recruitment marketing strategy worked well in the early to mid-'90s, by the latter part of the decade the Army found itself losing the battle to recruit America's youth. The military recruiting environment had changed as the booming economy of the '90s created many other opportunities for high school graduates. The Army's financial package was not enough to attract qualified recruits, and many high school graduates were not willing to endure the demands of basic training. All of these factors resulted in the Army missing its recruiting goals three out of five years during the late '90s despite spending more money on recruitment advertising than any branch of the military.

In early 2000, Secretary of the Army Louis Caldera announced that "we are totally changing the way we do Army advertising. We have to adopt the kinds of practices that the best marketing companies use to attract today's youth." His new marketing strategy called for a new integrated marketing communications program with less reliance on broad-reach television ads and greater use of the Internet, "e-recruiting," and one-to-one communication. In June 2000, Caldera announced the hiring of Leo Burnett USA, Chicago, as its new agency, replacing Young & Rubicam, which had created Army ads since 1987.

Leo Burnett developed a new "big idea" that became the basis for the integrated marketing campaign—"An Army of One." The creative strategy behind the theme is that soldiers are the Army's most important resource and each individual can and does make a difference; that his or her contributions are important to the success of the whole team. The "An Army of One" campaign sends a message that a soldier is not nameless or faceless but is part of a unified group of individuals who together create the strength of the U.S. Army.

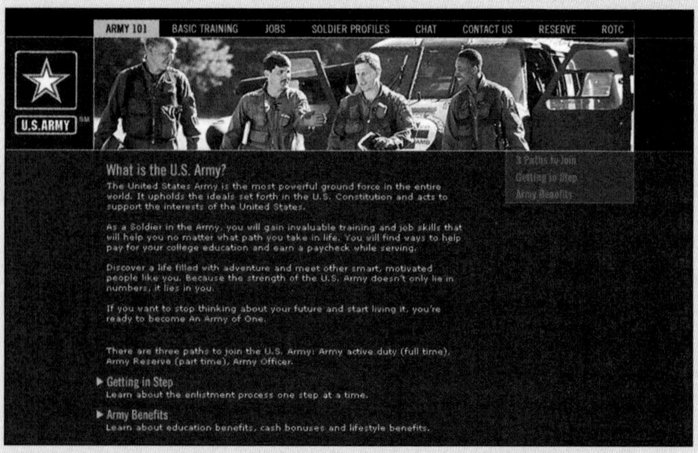

A major goal of the "An Army of One" campaign is to provide young adults with an accurate look into what it means to be a soldier in today's Army. Because more than 90 percent of the Army's target audience of 18- to 24-year-olds is online at least once a week, Leo Burnett decided that it would make the Army website (www.goarmy.com) the hub of the IMC program. The site provides great detail about what it is like to be in the Army. Once a potential recruit is on the site, he or she is provided with detailed and interesting information. The site is also used to capture potential leads as the site has a contact section where visitors can request more information, have questions answered, chat with or locate a recruiter, and learn more about how to join the Army.

Initially, a key component of the IMC campaign was called Basic Training, which used a reality-based television format made popular by the hit show *Survivor.* The unscripted TV spots featured brief profiles of six actual army recruits as they progressed through basic training, giving viewers a glimpse of their personal experiences and opinions as they transform from civilians into soldiers. The ads also encouraged prospective recruits to visit the Army website to experience a complete, in-depth multimedia "webisode" presentation including commentary from the recruits. The site now has a section called "Soldier Life" where potential recruits can learn more about what it is like to become a soldier, to be a soldier, and what their prospects are for the future. Video clips are available under each section of the site so prospects can learn more about life in today's Army. Prospects can overcome fears about basic training, increase their understanding of available career opportunities, and be introduced to soldiers similar to themselves. The site also features a chat room that is hosted by online recruiters where potential recruits can anonymously ask questions about the Army. On average, 750 people chat each day; of those, about 10 percent ultimately enlist.

Another popular feature of the GoArmy.com website is the games section. A professor at West Point noticed his students' obsession with computer games and initiated a plan to develop a game as a recruiting tool. The game, America's Army: Operations, was developed by a team of students at the Naval Postgraduate School, who spent a year training at 20 bases to ensure that it was realistic. When America's Army: Operations debuted on July 4, 2002, the demand overloaded the Army's servers. Since then, the game has been modified several times and has attracted nearly 6 million registered players and an average of 1.6 million hours of play daily, making it consistently one of the top online action games. The game can be downloaded from the website and is also available on a CD-ROM format from Army recruiters.

The U.S. Army provides potential recruits with valuable information through the GoArmy.com website on the Internet

The GoArmy.com website has become one of the most important parts of the Army's IMC program. Television, print, radio, and online banner ads on other sites such as MTV.com and Real.com are used to drive traffic to the Army website, and once there, visitors provide Army recruiters with hundreds of thousands of leads that they can contact and pursue on a one-on-one basis. The website has won several awards including a prestigious Cannes Cyber Lion and has become a focal point for the Army's recruitment efforts.

Sources: Bill Siuru, "Virtual Soldiering," *ComputerEdge,* September 23, 2005, pp. 14, 16; Mark Mazzetti, "Army Fights to Sell Itself to the Parents of America," *Los Angeles Times,* August 22, 2005, pp. A1, 11; Thomas Mucha, "Operation Sign 'Em Up," *Business 2.0,* April 2003; Michael Mc Carthy, "Army Enlists Net to Be All It Can Be," *USA TODAY,* April 19, 2000, p. 10B.

Communications Objectives

Unlike other media discussed thus far in the text, the Internet is actually a hybrid of media. In part, it is a communications medium, allowing companies to create awareness, provide information, and influence attitudes, as well as pursue other communications objectives. But for some it is also a direct-response medium, allowing the user to both purchase and sell products through e-commerce. Thus, we will discuss two sets of objectives pursued by companies that use the Internet. Let's first look at some of the communications objectives these companies want to achieve.

Create Awareness

Advertising on the Web can be useful in creating awareness of an organization as well as its specific product and service offerings. For small companies with limited budgets, the Web offers the opportunity to create awareness well beyond what might be achieved through traditional media. For example, a company in Los Angeles that distributed paper to business-to-business firms in the local market now conducts 80 percent of its business internationally as a result of posting its website. While a valuable tool for creating awareness—particularly for smaller companies that may have limited advertising budgets—the Internet is not likely to be the most effective of the IMC elements for achieving this objective. Mass-media advertising may be more useful for this purpose, given its larger reach and lower cost per exposure (as the TV people will be glad to remind you!).

Generate Interest

A visit to AOLMusic.com will quickly demonstrate how a site can be used to generate interest. The site provides music news, video shows, information on exclusive releases, news, fashion, and other content that is of interest to viewers. In addition, visitors can purchase concert tickets, download music, and more. Snapple.com also demonstrates how companies attempt to use the Web to generate interest in their sites as well as in their products and services. Snapple, in its attempt to attract visitors and hold their interest, has created a fun site with many places to visit while learning about Snapple products (see Exhibit 15-3). An information center, games, product information, sales items, and even an opportunity to personalize the site are all available. The objectives of these sites are simple: Create interest that will bring visitors back to learn more about the products—and, of course, to sell stuff.

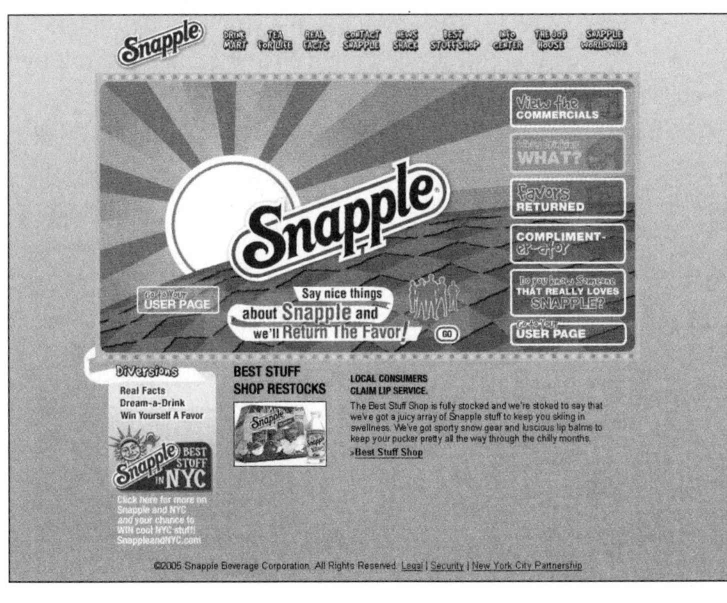

Exhibit 15-3 Snapple offers a number of reasons to visit its website

Disseminate Information

One of the primary objectives for using the Web is to provide in-depth information about a company's products and services. In business-to-business markets, having a website has become a necessity, as more and more buyers expect that a company will have a site providing them with detailed information about its offerings. In the government sector, contracts are often put out to bid on the Internet. Information regarding requirements, specifications, submission dates, and so on, is disseminated more quickly, to more potential candidates,

Exhibit 15-4 An example of an information-oriented website

and at a much lower cost via the Net than it is through other media. For many consumer companies, their websites serve as a means of communicating more information about their products and services. Weather.com is an excellent example of an information-oriented website (Exhibit 15-4).

Create an Image Many websites are designed to reflect the image a company wants to portray. For example, check out the consumer site at www.akademiks.com (Exhibit 15-5) or the business-to-business site at www.qualcomm.com (Exhibit 15-6). Both of these are excellent examples of websites used for image building. Interestingly, one of the difficulties traditional marketers have experienced is that of creating a brand image on the Internet. While some of these companies have been successful, others have not fared as well and have come to realize that branding and image-creating strategies must be specifically adapted to this medium.

Create a Strong Brand The Internet—as part of an integrated marketing communications program—can be a useful tool for branding. Unfortunately, many companies have not yet figured out how to successfully brand through the Internet. A review of the literature over the past decade will lead to a number of articles discussing this very topic and the difficulties in achieving this objective. While space does not permit an in-depth review, let's discuss just a few of the many reasons why companies attempting to create branding through the Internet may not be achieving their goals.

Branding Is a Complicated Process While creating a strong brand is not easy in any communications effort, some marketers believe that it may be even more difficult to do on the Internet. As noted by Karen Benezra, editor of *Brandweek* magazine, many companies—dot-coms as well as traditional—have spent millions of dollars trying to brand by advertising on the Internet, with only lukewarm success. One reason behind this problem, Benezra notes, is the lack of a clear understanding of the role the Web should assume in the branding process. New or less well-known brands may have to assume different strategies than those used by more established brands such as Volvo, BMW, or The Gap. Another reason is that many marketers mistakenly believe that simply creating awareness or attention will lead to a strong brand. While these elements are certainly necessary, they are not likely to be sufficient. Finally, notes Benezra, it takes a long time to establish a brand relationship with a customer, and the Internet hasn't been around long enough to prove its branding capabilities.[9]

Exhibit 15-5 A website used for image building

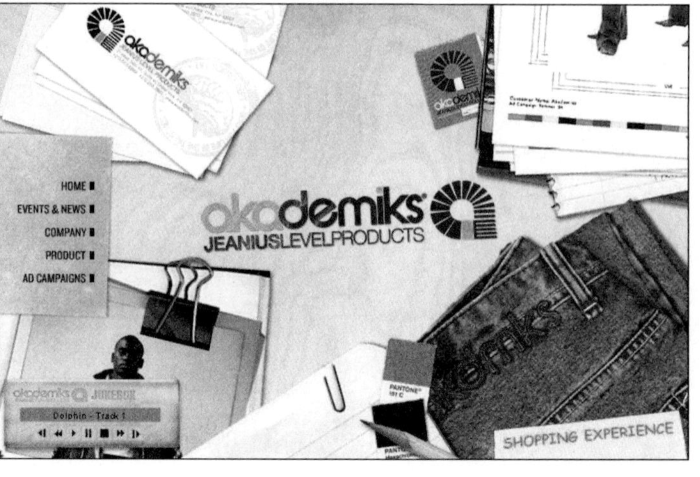

Branding and Direct Response May Be Counterobjectives Noting the similarities between the Internet and other direct-response media such as catalogs or interactive TV, some marketers think that the Internet is best suited to be a direct-response medium. They contend that direct marketing requires a very targeted effort, searching for high-probability buyers. Branding, on the other hand, is much less targeted and reaches out to numerous audiences. According to Erwin Ephron of *Advertising Age,* the Internet is somewhere in-between, and trying to achieve both objectives at the same time has led to unsuccessful branding efforts.[10]

The Costs Are Too High Successful branding does not take place overnight. Unfortunately, many marketers aren't willing, or feel that they can't afford, to wait. Such marketers may view the Internet as a quick fix that will allow them to establish their brands instantly. When they discover that the Internet is not able to provide instant identity, they may quickly return to their focus on ROI or the bottom line. Cutting advertising and brand identity efforts on the Internet will immediately reflect cost savings and a return to business as normal.[11]

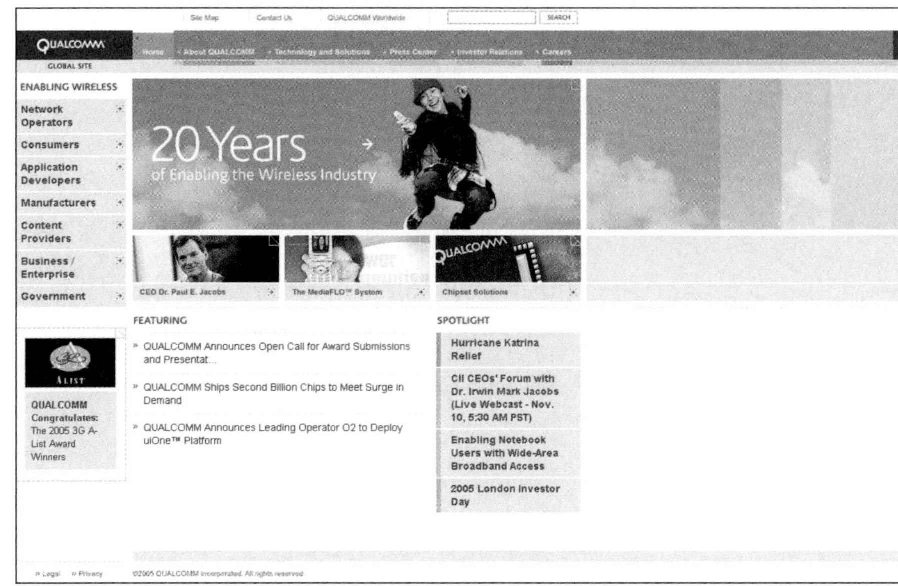

Exhibit 15-6 A website used for image building in the business-to-business market

The preceding are just a few of many reasons that can be offered as to why branding on the Internet has been less successful than many hoped. We believe that the Internet, as part of an integrated marketing communications program, can be used for branding purposes, as well as for other objectives.

Stimulate Trial

Many marketers have found the Internet to be an effective medium for stimulating trial of their products or services. Some websites offer electronic coupons in an attempt to stimulate trial of their products. Others offer samples, promotions, and sweepstakes designed to encourage trial. Music sites, like iTunes.com, allow for a "sampling" of songs before you purchase, while some business-to-business sites allow you to test their software online.

E-Commerce

The Internet also offers the opportunity to sell directly to customers in both the consumer market and the business-to-business market. This direct selling of goods and services has been labeled **e-commerce.** Sales through e-commerce were expected to reach $142.5 billion in the United States in 2005, with the profile of the online shopper reflecting that of the nation as a whole.[12,13] Many of the sites already mentioned in this chapter have a sales component—as either a primary or secondary goal.

Many companies maintain their existing "brick and mortar" stores while also selling through the Internet. Consumer-targeted companies like Eddie Bauer, The Gap, and Barnes and Noble are a few examples. Walmart.com, the online sales channel for Wal-Mart, recorded over 500 million visitors and $1.17 billion in sales in 2005. The company expects a 40 percent increase in visitors in 2006.[14] Circuit City allows customers to order online and pick up merchandise at the store. Others including Amazon.com and eBay.com maintain Internet sites only (Exhibit 15-7).

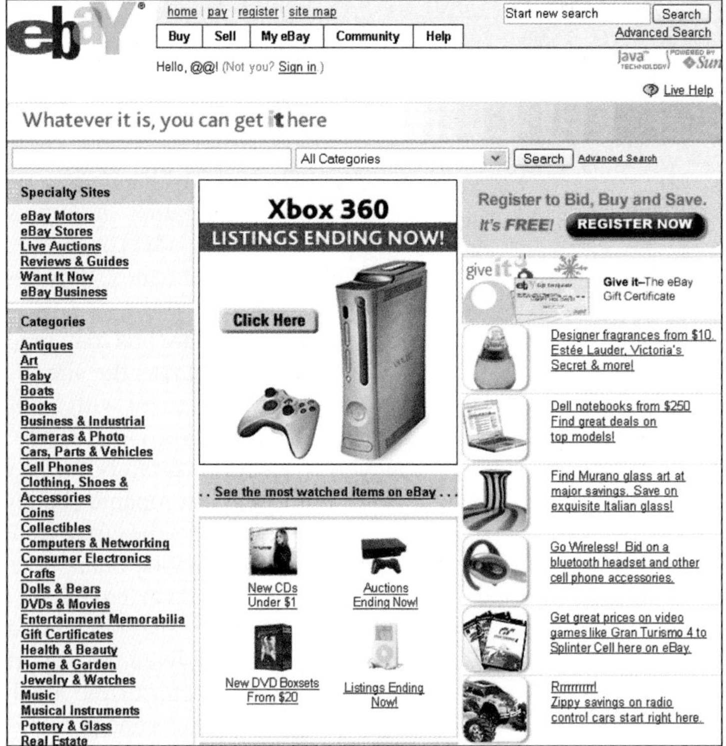

Exhibit 15-7 e-bay is one of the most popular e-commerce sites

We will discuss more about e-commerce and strategies employed in this area a little later in the chapter. Before we do, let's have a look at how the Internet can be used as part of an IMC program.

The Internet and Integrated Marketing Communications

Up to this point, we have mentioned the need for using the Internet as part of an IMC program. In this section, we discuss how the Web can be used with other program elements.

Advertising on the Internet

Like broadcast or print, the Internet is an advertising medium. Companies and organizations working to promote their products and services must consider this medium as they would television, magazines, outdoor, and so on. Advertising on the Internet employs a variety of forms, including banners, sponsorships, pop-ups and pop-unders, interstitials, push technologies, links, paid searches, behavior targeting, contextual ads, and rich media.

Banners

The most common form of advertising on the Web is **banner ads.** Interestingly, the size of banner ads has remained unchanged since the first AT&T ad. Banner ads may be used for creating awareness or recognition, entering viewers into contests and sweepstakes, or direct-marketing objectives. Banner ads may take on a variety of forms, as shown in Exhibit 15-8, as well as a number of names such as *side panels, skyscrapers,* or *verticals.* Initially banner ads constituted the vast majority of advertising on the Net, but studies indicating their questionable effectiveness have led to a decline in usage. Reports on click-through rates vary, but most studies indicate a less than 1 percent response rate.[15] At the same time, at least one study employing eye tracking methodology supports the likelihood of low click-through rates, but provides strong evidence that banner ads may be very effective in creating recall and brand building. The study also revealed a strong dislike for flashing banner ads, indicating that viewers almost immediately dismiss them.[16] In addition, a Ponemon Institute study conducted in 2004 showed that 66 percent of respondents said they would find relevant banner ads less annoying while 52 percent indicated they would even be likely to respond to a relevant banner ad.[17]

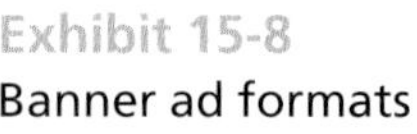
Exhibit 15-8
Banner ad formats

Sponsorships

Another common form of advertising is **sponsorships.** There are two types of sponsorships. *Regular sponsorships* occur when a company pays to sponsor a section of a site, for example, *A House Beautiful* magazine or *Cosmopolitan* magazine sponsorship on iVillage.com, or a corporate sponsorship of a page on Forbes.com. A more involved agreement is the **content sponsorship,** in which the sponsor not only provides dollars in return for name association but participates in providing the content itself. In some cases, the site is responsible for providing content and having it approved by the sponsor; in other instances, the sponsor may contribute all or part of the content.

Pop-Ups/Pop-Unders

When you access the Internet, you no doubt have seen a window or a creature of some sort appear on your screen in an attempt to get your attention. These advertisements are known as **pop-ups,** and they often appear when you access certain sites. Pop-ups are usually larger than banner ads but smaller than a full screen.

Pop-unders are ads that appear underneath the Web page and become visible only when the user leaves the site. For example, if you have ever visited a travel website, you probably were hit with a pop-under ad for Orbitz, one of the heaviest users of this form of Web advertising. Go to the *Los Angeles Times* website and when you leave, you will almost certainly see an example of this form of advertising.

While some companies believe that pop-ups and pop-unders are effective forms of advertising, others disagree. Consumer complaints have led Google.com, iVillage.com, and Earthlink, among others, to no longer accept these advertising forms. A study conducted by TNS revealed that 93 percent of respondents found pop-up ads annoying or very annoying.[18] The frequency and effectiveness of pop-ups and pop-unders have been greatly reduced given the opportunity for Intenet users to purchase pop-up screeners, which will screen out the ads before they appear on your screen. Some marketers believe that pop-ups and pop-unders are in the decline stage of their life cycle.

Interstitials **Interstitials** are ads that appear on your screen while you are waiting for a site's content to download. Although some advertisers believe that interstitials are irritating and more of a nuisance than a benefit, a study conducted by Grey Advertising found that only 15 percent of those surveyed felt that the ads were irritating and that 47 percent liked the ads. Perhaps more important, while ad recall of banner ads was approximately 51 percent, recall of interstitials was much higher, at 76 percent.[19] Acura introduced its Integra Type R model using an interstitial; Coca-Cola, TriStar, and Macy's have also employed this advertising form. Unfortunately for advertisers who may want to employ this medium, however, interstitials can also be blocked by pop-up blockers.

Push Technologies **Push technologies,** or **webcasting** technologies, allow companies to "push" a message to consumers rather than waiting for them to find it. Push technologies dispatch Web pages and news updates and may have sound and video geared to specific audiences or individuals. For example, a manager whose job responsibilities involve corporate finance might log on to his or her computer and find that new stories have automatically been placed there covering the economy, stock updates, or a summary of a speech by the Federal Reserve chairperson. Companies provide screen savers that automatically "hook" the viewer to their sites for sports, news, weather reports, and/or other information that the viewer has specified. Users can use **personalization**—that is, they can personalize their sites to request the kinds of specific information they are most interested in viewing. For example, if you are into college sports, you can have updates sent to you through sites providing college sports information. The service is paid for by advertisers who flash their messages on the screen.

Links While considered by some as not a type of advertising, **links** serve many of the same purposes as are served by the types discussed above. For example, a visitor to one site may click on a link that provides additional information and/or related materials at another site. At the bottom of the homepage at women.com are a number of links to magazines, including *Cosmopolitan* and *Good Housekeeping* among others. Clicking on one of these takes you to the magazine's site where usually a pop-up for a subscription to the magazine appears.

Paid Search By far the fastest growing form of advertising on the Internet is that of **paid search,** or search engine advertising, in which advertisers pay only when a consumer clicks on their ad or link from a search engine page. In an effort to more specifically target customers that may be interested in their offerings, advertisers buy ads on search engine sites such as Google, Yahoo!, or MSN so that when the visitor to the site keys in a specific search word or phrase, an advertisement targeted to that category appears. Advertisers bid for the placement; those who pay the most get the best locations (Exhibit 15-9). For example, typing in the word *automobile* could lead to a Ford ad (or commercial), or the words *surf camp* could lead to "surf trips for everyone," "trips to Costa Rica and Mexico," or more.[20] While the concept of paid search ads was considered prior to the dot-com bust and initiated by

Exhibit 15-9 Yahoo! promotes its paid search program

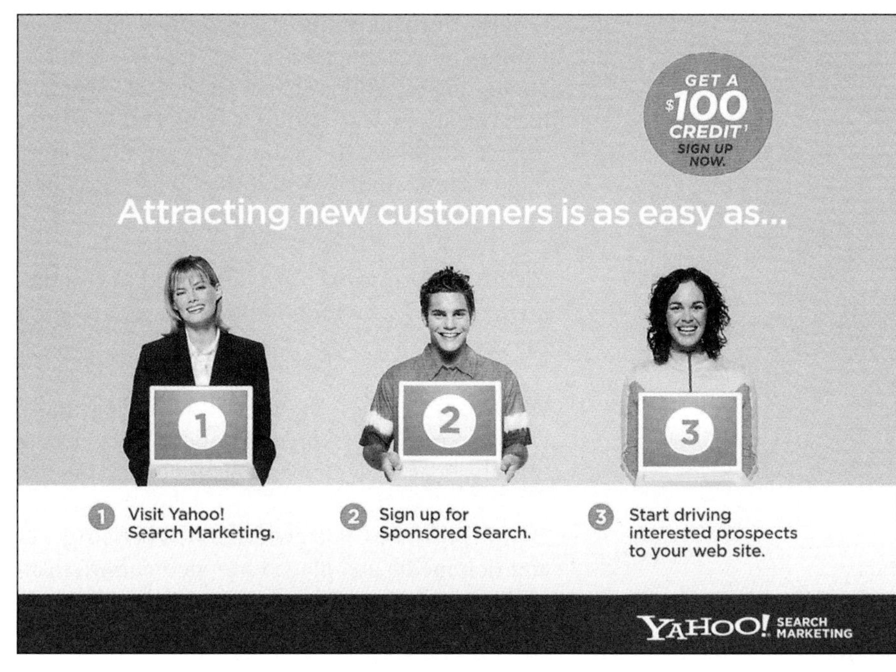

Overture in 2001, it did not really take hold until Google started offering the service (Overture was later purchased by Yahoo!). Proponents of sponsored search contend that it allows companies to specifically target those interested in their products and/or services, and add that even small companies can compete equitably since they only pay when a user clicks on their ad. Opponents of the form accuse paid search of being crassly commercial, or even deceptive, as consumers may not know that the information that appears has been paid for. In 2002, the consumer group Commercial Alert brought suit against paid search advertising. However, the Federal Trade Commission later upheld its legality.

Behavioral Targeting Another Internet advertising concept that has only recently gained acceptance is **behavioral targeting.** Behavioral targeting is based on advertisers' targeting consumers according to their website-surfing behaviors. By compiling clickstream data and Internet protocol (IP) information, segments of potential buyers can be identified and ads directed specifically to them. For example, by tracking an individual's visits to a number of automobile websites, an ad for cars or a dealership could be served to that individual. A frequent visitor to employment classifieds might be a promising target for an employment service firm, and so on.

Contextual Ads Advertisers who target their ads based on the content of the Web page are using **contextual advertising.** Whereas behavioral advertising tracks surfing behaviors, contextual ads are determined by the content on the web page. For example, an advertiser may place an airline ad on a travel site, or a golf club ad on a golf site, or even in or near a story about golf on another site. In September 2005, Yahoo! announced that it would provide a service to automatically place advertisers' messages near relevant content sites, including blogs—a service also offered by Google, though Google has had difficulty implementing the service.[21]

Rich Media The increased penetration of broadband into households has increased the attention given to streaming video. **Rich media,** as defined by the *Wikipedia,* are "a broad range of interactive digital media that exhibit dynamic motion, taking advantage of enhanced sensory features such as video, audio and animation."[22] Others state that rich media include all content that is created in flash.[23] The successful adoption of music videos, sports clips, news, and more has led advertisers to create a variety of forms of streaming video advertising content. Maybelline, Jeep, and Sony are just a few of the companies employing rich media, and—as you can imagine—movie producers such as Disney have been among the first to embrace the technology.

Types of rich media include the following.

Online Commercials The equivalent of traditional television commercials, online commercials are appearing on the Net. Some companies have created their own Web commercials, while others run the same spots they show on TV. A number of companies (recall the Carl's Junior Paris Hilton example of Chapter 6) have been successful in blending the two media, showing the commercial on TV and then directing interested viewers to the Web if they wish to see it again or to view longer versions. Many others now use the same strategy.

Video on Demand As described in Chapter 13, video clips of various entertainment activities (which include ads or are sponsored) are also available through the Internet.

Webisodes Short featured films such as those created by Skyy Vodka and BMW, as well as American Express's Superman episodes featuring Jerry Seinfield, are examples of webisodes, in which companies create their own content to advertise their products.

Other Forms of Rich Media Advertising Interactive banner ads, expandable ads, and rich media ads placed in video games, instant messaging, podcasts, and video ads within blogs are additional ways that rich media are currently employed. By the time this book is published, there will no doubt be even more not mentioned here!

Additional Internet Advertising Forms

As the Internet evolves, more and more ways to deliver advertising messages appear. Unfortunately, we do not have the space to discuss all of these in this text; however, three of these media warrant attention here: podcasting, RSS, and blogs.

Podcasting **Podcasting** is a medium that uses the Internet to distribute radiolike files for downloading into iPods and other MP3 players. As the market for iPods and MP3 players grows (it reached 22 million in 2005), the attractiveness of this medium does as well.[24] Radio stations, including Clear Channel Communications and National Public Radio, and television programs, such as *60 Minutes,* now podcast. The Podcast.net directory listed more than 4,000 different podcasters in 2005.[25] Traditional advertisers have adopted the medium, while others have found it useful as well (Exhibit 15-10). For example, Durex, a condom manufacturer, has purchased product placements in podcasts—in part to reach young listeners with risque marketing messages while skirting FCC decency rules.[26]

Exhibit 15-10 Podcasts are becoming popular with a number of advertisers

RSS **Really Simple Syndication (RSS)** is a specification that uses XML to organize and format Web-based content in a standard way. Content owners create an RSS feed, which usually consists of titles and brief descriptions of about 10 articles elsewhere on the site. The difference between Web content and an RSS feed is that the latter can send out notifications whenever new material is available.[27] Because the alerts can be customized to the viewers' preferences, advertisers have found it useful for disseminating information to those who may be most interested. For example, the *Washington Post* allows for advertising in its RSS feeds, and companies like American Express, Continental Airlines, and Verizon have all run ads through RSS feeds.

Blogs As discussed in Ethical Perspective 15-1, a **blog** (or weblog) is a Web-based publication consisting primarily of periodic articles, normally presented in reverse chronological order. As noted, blogs may reflect the writings of an individual, a community, a political organization, or a corporation, and they offer advertisers a new way to reach their target audiences. While some marketers are excited about the potential of blogs to reach large audiences at a small cost, others are more skeptical, noting numerous potential problems with their use. Ethical Perspective 15-1 discusses some of the pros and cons associated with the use of blogs. Given the fact that blogs have been around for only a short period of time, questions regarding the advantages and disadvantages of their use by marketers remain unanswered at this time.

Sales Promotion on the Internet

Companies have found the Internet to be a very effective medium for disseminating sales promotions. As noted earlier, HUGGIES ties in the use of sales promotions with its website as do numerous others. Other examples include Twentieth Television's use of a $7 million campaign and sweepstakes to promote their TV show *The Bernie Mac Show.* Nielsen Media Research has offered participants a chance to win $50,000 in cash, a new car, or a trip around the world for participating in a panel to provide them with insight about the future of the Internet. Yahoo! has started its own *Apprentice*-like online reality show, and Yahoo! and MTV have teamed up to start an online reality show about long-distance dating in which three couples compete for a two-week European vacation. MTV will follow each couple as they stay in touch and communicate

ETHICAL PERSPECTIVE 15-1

Blogs: A Great Marketing Opportunity—To Cheat?

As blogs continue to attract viewers—the top 50 blog sites draw an estimated 20 percent of Internet users, and 30 percent of users say they have visited a blog—marketers are rushing to take advantage of this new medium. A group of marketers, research professionals, and public relations specialists who attended a Search Engine Strategies Conference held in New York concluded that blogs will soon be "an indispensable marketing tool." Many of their colleagues seem to agree, as companies already are using blogs to replace focus groups for research, to develop better customer relations programs, to promote new brands, to conduct public relations activities, and more. Procter & Gamble uses a blog to appeal to young females 7 to 14 to sell their Secret Sparkle Body Spray. GM's vice chairman Bob Lutz has a blog, as do high-ranking managers at Boeing, Sun Microsystems, and Hewlett-Packard, among others. VH1, TBS, and several PBS stations have promoted their programs on BlogAds—the leading blog advertising network. Besides the fact that blogs can now reach millions of potential customers, the cost of advertising on a blog is very inexpensive relative to other traditional media or even to advertising on the Internet sites or portals, making the medium quite attractive to companies.

While many marketers have embraced this opportunity to communicate with their customers (and potential customers) and to garner objective feedback from bloggers, others have seen a different side of the blog. Some marketers believe that the blogosphere is a dangerous place to be. Noting that true blogs allow consumers to write what they please, including being critical of products and/or brands, they envision a situation where a company could be advertising in a space where negative things are being said about them. To avoid this, some corporate blogs do not allow others to post. (Then, is it really a blog? some ask.) Pundits argue that a blog that doesn't allow for free speech is a sham. Others are more critical. Sharon Morgen, writing on webpronews.com, reports on a company that markets itself as an Internet company but that hires people with expertise in a specific area to involve themselves into a blogging community. The employees hang out in the blog until they are known and trusted, and then begin to chat excitedly about a new product they purportedly just bought. This form of stealth marketing (or sleaze marketing as Morgen calls it) is deceptive and manipulative, playing on the trust of others. In another questionable practice, a number of research companies offer a service to clients to monitor blogs, eavesdropping on what is being said about their product(s) and then reporting back to them—without informing the bloggers about their efforts. Given that the most common topics written about on blogs are such personal issues as family, friends, and hobbies, one has to question the ethics of such research. Marketers, on the other hand, drool over insights to be gained from the frank and intimate discussions that may not occur if participants know they are being monitored.

Even some well-known companies have attempted to take possible unfair advantage of the potential of blogs. Dr Pepper once recruited a group of young bloggers to write about its Raging Cow milk drink. When it was discovered, the effort drew widespread condemnation from bloggers who ridiculed it as greedy corporate exploitation. Mazda also received its fair share of criticism for creating a fake blog with viral videos created by a fictional 22-year-old blogger. And then there was the fake blog talking about a Lincoln-shaped french fry established by McDonald's just before their Super Bowl campaign. The farce was quickly discovered, resulting in a considerable amount of bad public relations for McDonald's. Maybe they should have tried Washington? Who knows how many others there have been, or still are out there. Some believe that there are more companies pretending to be bloggers than we know of. The blogosphere offers marketers a golden opportunity. Unfortunately, for some, it is a golden opportunity to cheat!

Sources: Christine Larson, "Blogging Bosses," *U.S. News & World Report,* July 25, 2005, pp. 2–5; Shankar Gupta, "TV Networks Tout Shows on Blogs," mediapost.com, September 16, 2005, pp. 1–2; George O'Malley, "Will Blogs Become the Ultimate Marketing Tool?" mediapost.com, March 2, 2005, pp. 1–2; Jack Neff, "P&G Markets Children's Deodorant with Blogs and iPods," adage.com, April 28, 2005, pp. 1–2; Brian Morrissey, "Blogs Growing into the Ultimate Focus Group," *Adweek,* June 20, 2005, p. 12; Sharon Drew Morgen, "Blogs: A New Communication Tool or a Marketing Avenue?" webpronews.com, March 24, 2004, pp. 1–3.

using only Yahoo! communication devices, including Yahoo Mail, Yahoo Mobile, Yahoo Messenger with Voice, and the new Yahoo 360 community service with blogging and photo sharing tools (see Exhibit 15-11).[28]

Exhibit 15-11 Sales promotions are common on websites

Personal Selling on the Internet

The Internet has been both a benefit and a detriment to many of those involved in personal selling—particularly those in the business-to-business market. For some, the Internet has been a threat that might take away job opportunities. Companies have found that they can remain effective, or even increase effectiveness, by building a strong Web presence. The high-cost and poor-reach disadvantages of personal selling are allowing these companies to reduce new hires and even cut back on their existing sales forces.

On the positive side, websites have been used quite effectively to enhance and support the selling effort. As noted earlier, the Web has become a primary source of information for millions of customers in the consumer and business-to-business markets. Visitors to websites can gain volumes of information about a company's products and services. In return, the visitors become a valuable resource for leads that both internal and external salespersons can follow up, and they become part of a prospect database. Not only can potential customers learn about the company's offerings, but the selling organization can serve and qualify prospects more cost-effectively.

The Web can also be used to stimulate trial. For many companies, personal salespersons can reach only a fraction of the potential customer base. Through trial demonstrations or samples offered online, customers can determine if the offering satisfies their needs and, if so, request a personal sales call. In such cases both parties benefit from time and cost savings.

Some companies have used the Internet to improve their one-on-one relationships with customers. By providing more information in a more timely and efficient manner, a company enables customers to learn more about what it has to offer. This increases the opportunity for cross-selling and customer retention. A good example of this is the Caterpillar website, which is designed for easy access to information in order to help serve the needs of its customers (Exhibit 15-12).

In a well-designed IMC program, the Internet and personal selling are designed to be complementary tools, working together to increase sales. It appears that more and more companies are coming to this realization.

Exhibit 15-12 Caterpillar's website is designed to provide easy access to information

Exhibit 15-13 Chrysler uses its website for public relations purposes

Public Relations on the Internet

The Internet is a useful medium for conducting public relations activities. Many sites devote a portion of their content to public relations activities, including the provision of information about the company, its philanthropic activities, annual reports, and more.

Companies, nonprofit organizations, and political parties have become quite adept at using the Internet for public relations purposes. An excellent example of the use of public relations on the Internet is provided by Chrysler (Exhibit 15-13). The site provides up-to-date news stories and other forms of content, photo images, and cross-references to other sites or media as well as press kits and a calendar of upcoming events. It also provides information about Chrysler automobiles and the corporation itself and allows for customer feedback and registration for updates. In addition, Daimler-Chrysler's homepage contains many of the articles written about the corporation, including awards won and philanthropic efforts achieved such as its concern for the environment and their $1.1 million support for Hurricane Katrina victims.

Other examples of the effective use of public relations activities on the Internet are also available, as you will see in the chapter on public relations. The Web is a useful medium for conducting public relations activities, and its use for this function is on the increase.

At the same time, many philanthropic and nonprofit organizations have found the Internet to be a useful way to generate funds. Several companies have developed sites to perform the functions that are required in traditional fund-raising programs. For example, Ben & Jerry's uses its website to promote its products and image as well as showcasing the causes it supports and champions such as global warming, peace, and social and environmental issues (see Exhibit 15-14). Charitable organizations have also formed sites to handle public relations activities, provide information regarding the causes the charity supports, collect contributions, and so on. In an example of integrating the Internet with public relations and television, companies have found the Internet to be extremely useful for providing information in times of a crisis, and for gathering feedback about their products and services and about themselves (particularly through blogs and RSS feeds).

Direct Marketing on the Internet

Our discussion of direct marketing and the Internet will approach the topic from two perspectives: the use of direct-marketing tools for communications objectives (as discussed in Chapter 14) and e-commerce. As we stated previously, many direct-marketing tools like direct mail, infomercials, and the like, have been adapted to the Internet, as you will see. At the same time, e-commerce—selling directly to the consumer via the Internet—has become an industry all its own.

Exhibit 15-14 Ben & Jerry's supports global causes through its website

Direct Mail Direct mail on the Internet **(e-mail)** is essentially an electronic version of regular mail. Like regular mail it is highly targeted, relies heavily on lists, and attempts to reach consumers with specific needs through targeted messages. The Direct Marketing Association estimates that e-mail volume may reach as much as $2.7 trillion by 2007.[29] A study by Jupiter Research in 2005 indicated that as many as 71 percent of advertisers said that they had employed this method in the previous year, with another 12 percent indicating they were likely to do so in the near future.[30] As we discussed earlier on the subject of personalization, consumers can opt to have specific types of e-mail sent to them and other types not sent. For example, if you permit, the *New York Times* will e-mail you information about specific promotions, articles that will appear, books on sale, and other items that you might purchase.

Sometimes users may also receive less-targeted and unwanted e-mails. The electronic equivalent of junk mail, these messages are referred to as **SPAM.** Because of the high volumes of SPAM and the fact that many consumers consider it a nuisance, the U.S. government has passed laws regulating its use. In addition, antispam software like that created to screen pop-ups viruses has been developed.

Catalog-oriented companies such as RoadRunner Sports have also increased their use of electronic media. Within one year of introducing their online catalog, the highly successful direct mail company now sells approximately 50 percent of its products online. Another highly successful direct marketer, Lands' End, also has seen its business grow after going online (Exhibit 15-15). Interestingly, unlike many other e-mail marketers, the company does not use SPAM. It sends messages only to those who have agreed to receive them—an indication that junk mailing may not be necessary to be successful.[31] The company has also aired television commercials to promote the ease and efficiency of using its online catalog and has sent customers in its existing database direct-mail pieces. In turn, many e-marketing companies now send out print catalogs to promote their sites.

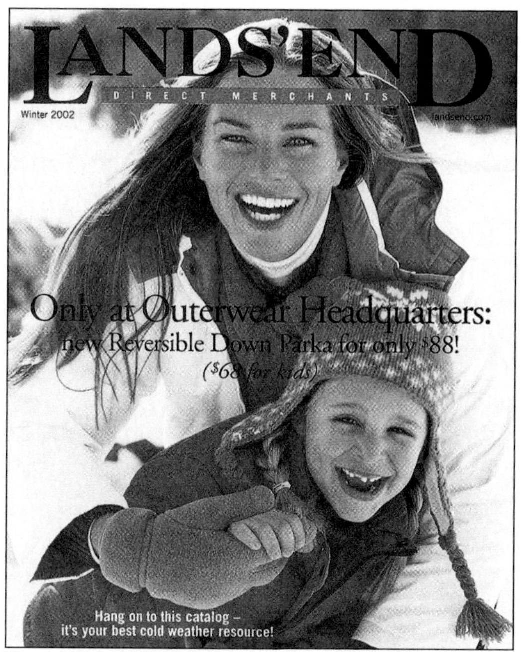

Exhibit 15-15 Lands' End is an effective Internet user

While many consumers don't like SPAM or other forms of e-mail, studies have shown the effectiveness of e-mails, and, as we have noted, all indications are that the end of this form of marketing is not in sight.

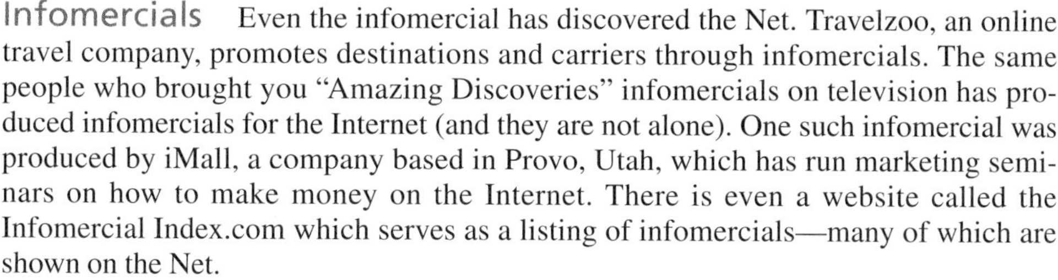

Infomercials Even the infomercial has discovered the Net. Travelzoo, an online travel company, promotes destinations and carriers through infomercials. The same people who brought you "Amazing Discoveries" infomercials on television has produced infomercials for the Internet (and they are not alone). One such infomercial was produced by iMall, a company based in Provo, Utah, which has run marketing seminars on how to make money on the Internet. There is even a website called the Infomercial Index.com which serves as a listing of infomercials—many of which are shown on the Net.

E-Commerce E-commerce, or direct sales on the Internet, has truly taken off. Online spending for the fourth quarter was expected to reach $142.5 billion by 2005, with strong growth predicted over the next few years. In addition, as many as 69 percent of respondents state that they research products online but make their purchases through traditional outlets.[32]

While more and more consumers may buy products online, consumer sales amount to only about one-fifth of those of business-to-business marketers. Business-to-business sales exceeded $6 trillion in 2004.[33] Many business-to-business companies such as Applied Industrial Technologies, National SemiConductor, and Xerox have also found success in the world of e-commerce.

Home-Shopping Channels In the direct-marketing chapter, we mentioned that QVC has taken its home-shopping TV channel to the Internet in the form of iQVC. HSN also has an Internet shopping channel, as does buy.com. Amazon and eBay, while they are not purely home-shopping channels, nevertheless, sell a lot of products online.

Measuring Effectiveness of the Internet

Companies measuring the effectiveness of the Internet employ a variety of methods, most of which can be done electronically. As you will see, a number of companies provide Internet measures as part of a package; that is, they provide audience measurement information (demographics, psychographics, etc.) as "up-front' information, as well as some of the effectiveness measures described below. First, we will discuss

Figure 15-3 Measures of Internet Effectiveness

Clicks
Post-click conversions
Cost per conversion
Unique reach of delivered ads
Average frequency
Frequency to conversion ratios
Advertising exposure time
Ad interaction rate
View-through rate
Share of voice
Web page eye tracking
Offline sales lift
Cross-media econometric models

Source: 2005 DoubleClick, Inc.

some of the measures used to determine the effectiveness of a website. Then, we will discuss some of the companies providing these measures.

Audience Measures and Measures of Effectiveness

When the Internet industry first developed its own measures of effectiveness, problems with these measures led to a slower rate of adoption by traditional media buyers. In an attempt to respond to criticism of the audience metrics employed, as well as to standardize some of the measures used to gauge effectiveness of the Internet, the Interactive Advertising Bureau (IAB)—the largest and most influential trade group—formed a task force in November 2004, consisting of major global corporations involved in advertising and research. The task force was created to examine and create standardized measures to measure advertising impact that could be used to assess the impact of ads and to eliminate confusion. The three key points of the new recommendations are detailed in a 20-page report available from the IAB.net. Industry experts believe that adoption of these guidelines, along with objective auditing, would make the Internet a more attractive medium for many of those who advertise in traditional media. The guidelines have the support of major online publishers, as well as the nearly 40 major proprietary online ad-server technologies and major associations worldwide.[34]

Measures of Effectiveness

Internet-Specific Measures One of the perceived advantages of the Internet is a company's ability to measure commercial effectiveness, due in part to its ability to measure activity in real time. Figure 15-3 shows many of the measures that are currently used by companies. These measures include those specific to the Internet and interactive industry, as well as more traditional measures such as ad recall, brand awareness, and purchase intentions. (For a detailed explanation of each of these terms, visit www. IAB.net.)

Cross-Media Optimization Studies (XMOS) One of the more extensive attempts to measure the effectiveness of integrating interactive and traditional media are cross-media optimization studies. As noted by the IAB, the objective of the XMOS studies is the following:

> [To] help marketers and their agencies answer the question "What is the optimal mix of advertising vehicles across different media, in terms of frequency, reach and budget allocation for a given campaign to achieve its marketing goals?" . . . The XMOS studies simultaneously measure online and offline advertising in the same campaign to determine the optimal weight and mix of each medium.[35]

What makes the XMOS studies important is that they provide insight into (1) the relative contributions of each medium in the mix, (2) the combined contribution of multiple media, (3) optimal media budget allocations, and (4) actional media mix strategies. Colgate-Palmolive, ING Investment Management, and Universal Studios have participated in the most recent round of studies, while McDonald's, Kimberly-Clark's Kleenex, and Unilever's Dove participated in earlier ones. Figure 15-4 details the results of the most recent XMOS findings.

Traditional Measures In addition to the Internet-specific and cross-media studies, companies employ a number of traditional marketing and communications measures. Some of these include the following.

- *Recall and retention.* A number of companies use traditional measures of recall and retention to test their Internet ads. These same measures have been used to pretest online commercials as well.

Figure 15-4 Results of XMOS Studies

Company and Product	Objective	Methodology	Results
Ford F-150 pickup truck	To increase sales	Use English/Spanish TV, outdoor, print, direct mail, radio, Internet, experimental design, behavioral tracking	49% exposure to online ads; 6% sales increase directly attributable to online; website visitors twice as likely to buy as nonvisitors
ING Investment Management funds	Brand familiarity; purchase consideration	Use TV, magazines, online, survey design, continuous tracking	Use of three media together more effective than any one or two alone
Universal Studios movies	Release of *ET: The Extra Terrestrial* on DVD; to generate purchase interest among 25–49 market	Survey design, continuous tracking	Use of TV and rich media more effective than banner ad or TV alone
Unilever Dove Nutrium soap products	To increase awareness, image, purchase intent	Use TV, print, interactive, ratings information, media cost	Combining interactive led to increase in awareness, branding, purchase, purchase intent

• *Surveys.* Survey research, conducted both online and through traditional methods, is employed to determine everything from site usage to attitudes toward a site.

• *Sales.* For the e-commerce marketers, a prime indicator of effectiveness is the volume of sales generated. Adding information regarding demographics, user behaviors, and so on, can increase the effectiveness of this measure.

• *Tracking.* Some companies now offer more traditional tracking measures. For example, Dynamic Logic provides information such as brand awareness, ad recall, message association, and purchase intent.

The aforementioned measures reveal that the Internet has its own set of criteria for measuring effectiveness and is also borrowing from traditional measures; for example, brand recall has become a major area of focus. The Association of Advertising Agencies and the Association of National Advertisers uses a system called Advertising Digital Identification (Ad-Id). Ad-Id assigns advertising across all media a specific media code to facilitate cross-media buys. The goal of the coalition is to develop cross-media standards employing reach/frequency comparisons that include the Internet. Many of the companies that provide research information in traditional media (Nielsen, Ipsos-ASI) are now extending their reach into the Internet world. Others (Insights.com, Forrester) have developed measures specifically for online users. Academics are also beginning to publish articles related to measuring effectiveness on the Internet. Studies on consumers' attitudes toward a site, response variations in e-mail surveys, and similarities between brick-and-mortar retailing and e-commerce are just a few of the many articles being published in academic journals to advance the measurement of Internet use.

Unfortunately, not all of the methods used to measure Internet activity and effectiveness are accurate. We discuss some of these problems later in this chapter, when considering disadvantages of the Internet.

Sources of Measurement Data

The number of sources available that provide information about the Internet is enormous. Below we provide a partial list just to give you some indication of the types of information available. Most of the companies listed are the largest and/or most cited sources, and the list is by no means intended to be exhaustive.

• *Arbitron.* Arbitron provides demographic, media usage, and lifestyle data on users of the Internet as well as other interactive media.

• *MRI and SMRB.* Both of these companies (discussed in Chapter 10) provide information regarding viewership profiles for the Internet and other interactive media. Nielsen Media Research offers similar data.

• *Audit Bureau of Circulations.* This print agency has developed a product called WebFacts to certify Web counts.

• *Interactive Advertising Bureau (IAB).* A trade organization of the Internet, IAB provides information on statistics, usage, and strategies regarding the Internet.

• *eMarketer.* This company publishes comparative data from various research sources and explains the different methods used to arrive at the projections. It also publishes its own projections.

• *Nielsen Net Ratings.* Nielsen provides audience information and analyses based on click-by-click Internet behavior through a meter installed on users' computers at home and work.

• *Jupiter MediaMetrics, Inc.* Previously separate companies, Jupiter, PC Meter, and MediaMetrics have joined to provide statistics and website information, including data on users, projections, trends, and so on.

Advantages and Disadvantages of the Internet

A number of advantages of the Internet can be cited:

1. *Target marketing.* A major advantage of the Web is the ability to target very specific groups of individuals with a minimum of waste coverage. For those in the business-to-business market, the Internet resembles a combination trade magazine and trade show, as only those most interested in the products and/or services a site has to offer will visit the site (others have little or no reason to do so). In the consumer market, through personalization and other targeting techniques, sites are becoming more tailored to meet one's needs and wants.

2. *Message tailoring.* As a result of precise targeting, messages can be designed to appeal to the specific needs and wants of the target audience. The interactive capabilities of the Net make it possible to carry on one-to-one marketing with increased success in both the business and the consumer markets.

3. *Interactive capabilities.* Because the Internet is interactive, it provides strong potential for increasing customer involvement and satisfaction and almost immediate feedback for buyers and sellers.

4. *Information access.* Perhaps the greatest advantage of the Internet is its availability as an information source. Internet users can find a plethora of information about almost any topic of their choosing merely by conducting a search. Once they have visited a particular site, users can garner a wealth of information regarding product specifications, costs, purchase information, and so on. Links will direct them to even more information if it is desired.

5. *Sales potential.* The numbers provided previously in this chapter demonstrate the incredible sales numbers being generated in both the business-to-business and the consumer segments. Forecasts are for continued growth in the future. In addition, the number of persons who shop online and then purchase offline has continued to increase.

6. *Creativity.* Creatively designed sites can enhance a company's image, lead to repeat visits, and positively position the company or organization in the consumer's mind. Visit some of the sites mentioned earlier to see what we mean.

7. *Exposure.* For many smaller companies, with limited budgets, the World Wide Web enables them to gain exposure to potential customers that heretofore would have been impossible. For a fraction of the investment that would be required using traditional media, companies can gain national and even international exposure in a timely manner.

8. *Speed.* For those requesting information on a company, its products, and/or its service offerings, the Internet is the quickest means of acquiring this information.

9. *Complement to IMC.* The Net both complements and is complemented by other IMC media. As such, it serves as a vital link in the integrative process. In a recent

study conducted by eMarketer, business managers perceive the ability for the Internet to enhance and complement other media to be its major advantage.[36]

While it is a potentially effective medium, the Internet also has its disadvantages, including the following:

1. *Measurement problems.* One of the greatest disadvantages of the Internet is the lack of reliability of the research numbers generated. A quick review of forecasts, audience profiles, and other statistics offered by research providers will demonstrate a great deal of variance—leading to a serious lack of validity and reliability. One company mentioned earlier, eMarketer, has attempted to reconcile such differences and explain the reasoning for the discrepancies (differences in methodologies employed), but the problem still exists. The recent actions taken by the IAB to standardize metrics will help in reducing some of this problem. But due to difficulties involved in both measuring and forecasting in this medium, it remains necessary to proceed with caution when using these numbers.

2. *Annoyance.* At times, downloading information from the Net takes a long time. Having to install additional software, experiencing difficulty in navigation, and encountering other pet peeves have led many consumers to permanently leave sites.[37]

3. *Clutter.* As the number of ads proliferates, the likelihood of one's ad being noticed drops accordingly. The result is that some ads may not get noticed, and some consumers may become irritated by the clutter. Some studies already show that banner ads have lost effectiveness for this very reason.

4. *Potential for deception.* The Center for Media Education has referred to the Web as "a web of deceit" in regard to advertisers' attempts to target children with subtle advertising messages. The Center, among others, has asked the government to regulate the Internet. In addition, data collection without consumers' knowledge and permission, hacking, and credit card theft are among the problems confronting Internet users.

5. *Privacy.* Like their direct-marketing counterparts, Internet marketers must be careful not to impinge upon the privacy of users. The IAB has issued a policy on privacy to which it asks companies to adhere (see www.iab.net).

6. *Poor reach.* While the Internet numbers are growing by leaps and bounds, its reach still lags behind that of television. As a result, Internet companies have turned to traditional media to achieve their reach and awareness goals.

8. *Irritation.* Numerous studies have reported on the irritating aspects of some Web tactics. These studies have shown consumers' discontent with clutter, e-mail SPAM, and pop-ups and pop-unders. These irritating aspects can deter visitors from coming to and or returning to the sites.

Overall, the Internet offers marketers some very definite advantages over traditional media. At the same time, disadvantages and limitations render this medium as less than a one-stop solution. However, as part of an IMC program, the Internet is a very valuable tool.

Additional Interactive Media

While the Internet has captured most of the attention of marketers, additional interactive media are also available and can be used as a contributor to an IMC program. Video on demand, interactive CD-ROMs, kiosks, and interactive phones have been used by marketers to provide information to their audiences. Agency executives note that the most important capability of these media was their ability to be linked with traditional marketing projects.

One of the more attention-getting and promising of the new interactive media is interactive TV. **Interactive TV,** or iTV, allows the viewer of a television program to interact with the progam and the ads. Many marketers, including Hewlett-Packard and Microsoft, are betting that future computer users will access the Internet through their television sets. Multitasking allows television viewers to watch an event—for

Exhibit 15-16 ABC's Enhanced TV allows viewers to interact with their TVs in numerous ways

example, a football game—and to pull up information on players, history of the matchups between the teams, and other statistics without ever leaving the couch or the game. ABC's Enhanced TV, which provides coverage of various sports, entertainment and reality programs, and awards shows including *Monday Night Football,* the *Academy Awards, Super Millionaire,* and *Extreme Makeover: Home Edition,* allows viewers to play games, vote in polls, answer trivia questions, compete to win prizes, and get background information while watching TV (see Exhibit 15-16). Mercedes-Benz used iTV to launch its 2006 M. Class through the Dish Network. Viewers were able to use their remote control to view an expanded 90-second version of the commercial shown on traditional TV, to order brochures, and to view separate video ads. Reebok, Subaru, and Chrysler, among others, are expanding their iTV efforts. For the first time ever, Dish Network subscribers in 12 states can wager on horse races from their living rooms.

Wink-enhanced advertisements allow advertisers to communicate directly with Wink subscribers during a traditional 30- or 60-second spot. By clicking on an icon, advertisers can pose questions, offer samples, solicit contest entries, or even make a sale. For example, one Wink-enabled Ford ad appearing on OpenTV asked viewers if they would like to receive a Ford Outfitters catalog (Exhibit 15-17). If they were interested, they were asked to select a model (Excursion, Expedition, or Explorer) and then to specify their interest in a two-door, four-door, or sport Track edition. Direct-mail pieces were then sent to respondents. GlaxoSmithKline ran a similar ad allowing viewers to request information about its migraine medicine Imitrex. The company's six-month response goal was achieved in one week.[38] The Discovery Channel and The Learning Channel have also employed this medium.

Many marketers believe that the rapid adoption of iTV is just around the corner. Others regard it as a very large corner, given that the promise of iTV has not yet been fulfilled though the technology has been around for quite some time. One study indicated that only 50 percent of Americans have heard of interactive TV, with only 11 percent familiar or somewhat familiar with the medium. Only 15 percent stated that they were interested in playing games on TV—marketed as a key benefit to the iTV offerings.[39] In Europe, iTV has been more rapidly adopted than in the United States. On Rupert Murdoch's BSkyB satellite service in the United Kingdom, viewers can make home-shopping purchases, play games, and even change camera angles during soccer matches. Apparently these options are more attractive to the European market than to the current U.S. viewer.

Exhibit 15-17 A Wink-enabled Ford ad

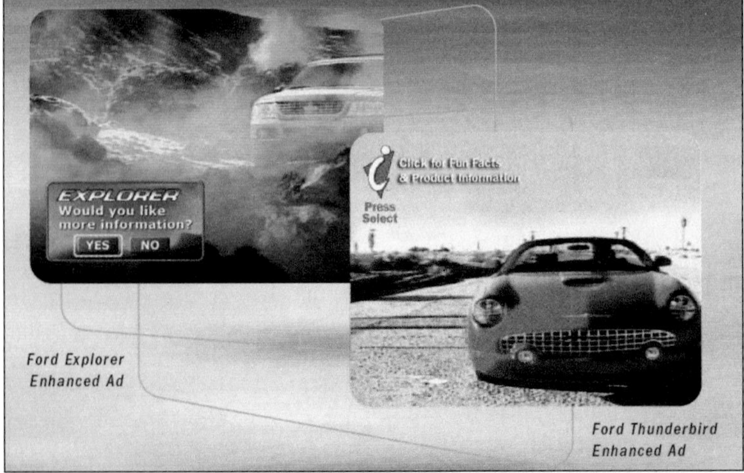

Nevertheless, some companies have demonstrated successful interactive campaigns, and as more consumers purchase broadband access, the marketing potential of the medium is likely to increase. As for now, it may just be that when viewers are watching TV, they just want to watch TV. We will wait to see.

Wireless

A rapidly growing interactive medium capturing the attention of marketers is **wireless** communication. While still in its early stages, some companies are already sending advertisements, coupons, and direct-response offers through cell phones and personal digital assistants (PDAs). Burger King sent out extended versions of its 2006 Super Bowl commercial to Sprint cellphone users.[40] The shows *Lost, CSI,* and

CAREER PROFILE

Lisa Minjares

Creative Director, New Media, KFMB Stations, San Diego

My career in art began at a very young age—when I was 4-years-old to be exact! I won my first art contest at my preschool with a very elaborate 3-dimensional piece. It was Humpty Dumpty (the top of an egg carton) who sat on his wall (a cardboard box) dressed in some very fancy clothes that I created from scraps of fabric that my mom had lying around the house. As I grew up and continued in school, art became a very big part of my life—it was my way of saying "hello," "happy birthday," and "I'm sorry."

My graphic design skills began to develop in elementary school during penmanship lessons. I would throw away sheet after sheet of paper because my handwriting wasn't (at least in my mind) perfect; and when the teacher gleefully told me that I had graduated from a pencil to a pen, I cried! I could erase pencil, but not the pen. During middle school and high school, I would write and rewrite notes if the layout wasn't perfect—and that obsessive behavior continued throughout college!

After three years at a junior college, I eventually transferred in to the art department at San Diego State University where I spent two years and graduated with a BA in art with an emphasis in graphic design. While in school, I worked as a graphic designer for the City of Chula Vista and interned for a local TV station. After graduating, I accepted my first position as a graphic designer for a small design studio. I was the only applicant for the position with an online resume, which caught the studio's attention. My online resume was the only website I had created, but my new employer saw potential and my career as an interactive designer was born!

Over a year after working at my first job and creating a few websites for the studio's clients, I was hired by an interactive multimedia company, where I was thrown into the fire. I began working on extremely involved projects with very intense deadlines. This is the job where I earned my stripes and gained invaluable experience. I averaged 14-hour workdays, six to seven days a week; and although my title was "graphic designer," I was also programmer, project manager, and salesperson for each of the projects that I worked on. The company's poor structure worked to my benefit in the long run, because I was forced to learn all facets of a project from beginning to end. I wouldn't be where I am today without the experience I gained at this company.

> "I talked with the art director and, although there weren't any positions available, I insisted on coming in to show him my portfolio."

After yet another late night and exhausting deadline, I finally decided that I wanted to put the experience I had gained at my current job to good use at a new company. I interned at a local TV station when I was in college and developed a love of the industry. In a "moment of clarity" while I was driving home, I decided that I wanted to pursue a job with our local CBS Affiliate, KFMB Channel 8. They had the strongest graphics package on air, but a terrible website—although, in all fairness, they were one of the only TV stations in town that even had a website—I called the next day.

I assumed that they weren't hiring, and they weren't. I talked with the art director and, although there weren't any positions available, I insisted on coming in to show him my portfolio. A week after my phone call, I sat down with the art director and went through my body of work. He mentioned that they were looking for a freelancer to redesign the company website and felt as if I would be able to tackle the project. I jumped at the opportunity—it was my foot in the door.

After finishing the KFMB website (www.kfmb.com), I was approached with an opportunity for a full-time position with KFMB. They were planning to develop their online presence and needed someone to help. After a few interviews with different managers within the company, I was hired. It was all about being in the right place at the right time.

I've learned so much in the past six years with KFMB. I work with extremely competent managers in other departments and I had the opportunity to hire and develop an amazing team. The only downside to my evolving career is that I now spend a lot of time managing and very little time designing. I try to reserve time to design whenever I can, but it is difficult. As the creative director, I am involved with projects from beginning to end; and in between balancing a budget and dealing with personnel issues, I still remain an integral part of the creative process.

I now work as a creative director and manage an amazing team of eight people. The team consists of a project manager, two designers, two programmers, and three content managers. As a team, we are responsible for designing, managing, and maintaining the KFMB family of websites: www.kfmb.com (KFMB-TV), www.760kfmb.com (KFMB-AM), and www.sandiegojack.com (KFMB-FM). In addition to managing the website creative and content, I manage the budget for all Internet-related expenses as well as our email marketing campaigns and daily newsletters. The entire new media team works very closely with most of the individual departments in the company to create what we believe are the most effective television and radio station websites in the San Diego market. All facets of the websites are created, programmed, and managed in-house, allowing us much more creative freedom than our competitors. I feel fortunate to have been able to find a position that is so rewarding.

Exhibit 15-18 Cellphone users in Asia can use their phones in a number of ways

Laguna Beach are available through Apple iPod.[41] SmartVideo Technologies of Atlanta has launched a free music video channel for cell phone users. In exchange for the free content, viewers will be required to watch 15-second commercials between videos as well as ad overlays.[42] By 2010, an estimated 2 percent of advertisers' online budgets will be spent online.[43]

Adoption of wireless technology in Asia has outpaced that in the United States as it is common for Asian cell phone users to send e-mails, buy music, and surf the Web, all the while being exposed to banner ads, banded contests, and coupons (over a $100 million sent in Japan in 2004) (Exhibit 15-18).[44] At this time, it is illegal in the United States to send unsolicited promotions through cell phones, though consumers can opt in to receive some promotions.[45] Given that technologies diffuse rapidly and the success of advertisers in integrating wireless into their IMC programs, U.S. companies have already begun to gear up for increasing their use of this medium.

Summary

This chapter introduced you to the Internet and interactive media. It explained some of the objectives for these media and how they can be used in an IMC program.

The discussion of the Internet focused on understanding the history and growth of the Internet, the objectives sought when using the Internet, and Internet communications strategies. In addition, we discussed the role of the Internet in an IMC program, explaining how all the IMC program elements can be used with the Internet.

The chapter discussed a number of new online tools including paid search, behavioral targeting, contextual ads, rich media, blogs, RSS, and podcasting. We noted advantages of the Internet—including targeting markets, using interactive capabilities, and building relationships. In addition, we reviewed disadvantages—including high costs, unreliable measurements and statistics, and relatively low reach (compared to that of traditional media). We also provided sources of Internet measurement data.

The Internet has been the most rapidly adopted medium of our time. It holds great potential for both business-to-business and consumer marketers. However, contrary to popular belief, the Internet is not a stand-alone medium. Its role in an integrated marketing communications program strengthens the overall program as well as the effectiveness of the Internet itself.

Interactive media have not yet fulfilled their promise. While still in its infancy, the medium has not received the level of acceptance and use expected. Test market indications are that the medium still needs improvements—particularly in content—before reaching mass acceptance. Wireless communication is starting to experience growth.

Key Terms

Internet, 469
World Wide Web (WWW), 469
website, 470
e-commerce, 475
banner ads, 476
sponsorships, 476
content sponsorship, 476
pop-ups, 476
pop-unders, 476
interstitials, 477
push technologies, 477
webcasting, 477
personalization, 477
links, 477
paid search, 477
behavioral targeting, 478
contextual advertising, 478
rich media, 478
podcasting, 479
RSS, 479
blogs, 479
SPAM, 483
interactive TV (iTV), 487
wireless, 488

Discussion Questions

1. IMC Perspective 15-1 discusses the U.S. Army's use of the Internet as the hub of its IMC strategy. Numerous other companies have adopted this strategy, including many of the 2006 Super Bowl advertisers. Discuss this strategy using communications objectives as the basis for your discussion.

2. Discuss the various objectives that may be sought when using the Internet in an IMC strategy. Provide examples of companies that are pursuing each of these objectives.

3. The chapter discusses a variety of new Internet advertising forms including Podcasting, RSS, and blogs. Explain what each of these are. What are some of the potential advantages and disadvantages associated with the use of each?

4. Exhibit 15-1 demonstrates the factors that are essential to an effective website. Discuss each of these factors, and provide examples of websites that demonstrate them in practice.

5. One of the most difficult objectives to achieve on the Internet is that of creating a strong brand image. Discuss the factors that contribute to the development of a strong brand image. What factors make it difficult to achieve this objective? Cite examples of companies that have effectively achieved this objective.

6. One of the problems slowing the rate of adoption of the Internet as an advertising medium is the fact that this medium has been slow to adopt traditional advertising metrics. Discuss why this has been the case, and what must be done to overcome this problem.

7. Interactive television has not been adopted by consumers as rapidly as was expected. Give some reasons for this slower than expected adoption rate, and what iTV must do to overcome these problems.

8. What is meant by wireless? Provide examples of companies that currently are employing this communications medium. For what type of companies might wireless best be suited?

9. The IAB recently provided guidelines for metrics for use by those in the Internet industry. Explain what these guidelines entailed and why they are important.

10. Provide examples of companies with which you are familiar that have successfully integrated the Internet into their communications programs. Explain the role of the Internet in these IMC programs.

Sales Promotion

16

Chapter Objectives

1. To understand the role of sales promotion in a company's integrated marketing communications program and to examine why it is increasingly important.
2. To examine the various objectives of sales promotion programs.
3. To examine the types of consumer- and trade-oriented sales promotion tools and the factors to consider in using them.
4. To understand how sales promotion is coordinated with advertising.
5. To consider potential problems and abuse by companies in their use of sales promotion.

Mountain Dew and Other Brands Use Extreme Sports to Connect with Gen Y

For several decades marketers have used involvement with sports as a way to promote their products and services. Many companies use sponsorships and promotional deals with major sports such as professional football, soccer, basketball, baseball, golf, tennis, and NASCAR to help them market their

brands. Events and tie-ins to these sports have proven to be an effective way to reach baby boomers and generation Xers. However, marketers recognize that involvement with traditional sports is becoming less effective as a way to connect with the younger generation of consumers. Gen Y, the 60-million-strong age cohort born between 1981 and 1995, is more interested in extreme sports such as skateboarding than they are in baseball, basketball, or soccer. And whereas many marketers have found it difficult to break into the action sports scene and be seen as credible, PepsiCo's Mountain Dew is one mainstream brand that has found success in this arena.

Extreme sports, or what are sometimes known as alternative sports, took off in the 1990s when teen enthusiasts transformed casual activities such as mountain biking, skateboarding, snowboarding, BMX biking, and in-line skating into highly technical, creative, and often dangerous sports. As these sports became increasingly risky and creative, they began to attract spectators. The cable sports network ESPN began aggressively promoting circuits and tournaments to showcase and subsequently professionalize these new sports, which culminated in the Extreme Games in 1994, a type of nontraditional Olympics. Mountain Dew was one of the founding sponsors of the Extreme Games, which later became the X Games, and signed partnerships with action sports athletes even before the organized competitions began.

Mountain Dew has continued its involvement with extreme sports over the past 10 years by supporting competitions, competitors, and the fans, and it has become a well-respected member of the action sports community. In 2005, the brand raised its involvement with action sports to a new level when it launched Dew Action Sports Tour (DAST), a five-event series that is co-owned by NBC Sports and Clear Channel Entertainment. Mountain Dew marketers had good reason for starting the tour: DAST's senior director of marketing Ethan Green notes that research shows there are more U.S. youth participating in action sports than there are playing Little League Baseball. Green also notes that teens and tweens are attracted to action sports because of the individuality factor, which is very important to them. Extreme sports are about a nonconforming lifestyle, from clothes to music, and young people respond to brands that make an authentic connection and become part of the action sports community.

From a marketing perspective, the key to the Dew Action Sports Tour is the promotional opportunities associated with the various events. At each tour site, Mountain Dew's agency constructs the House of Dew, which reflects the action sports lifestyle. Sponsored skaters hang out at the house to interact with fans, who can also hit the Napster lounge and download tunes from their favorite athlete's play lists, go into the PlayStation2 room and play video games, or visit the tattoo parlor for a temporary air-brushed design. And they can also go to the product sampling kitchen where they can try some Mountain Dew as well as various other products.

Mountain Dew also develops a number of off-site promotions to support DAST. For example, one promotion was exclusive to Wal-Mart and involved more than 25 million 14-ounce collectible cans featuring DAST athletes such as skateboarders Shaun White and Paul Rodriguez. PepsiCo also developed an under-the-cap promotion offer tied to DAST where winners of the Go Pro! contest could attend a World Series game or a DASTDew event, or qualify for caps, T-shirts, and key chains. Fans would enter the code found under the cap at websites including Dewgopro.com or Pepsigopro.com, or text to a Yahoo Mobile account.

A number of other brands have recognized Mountain Dew's street credibility with young people and have signed up as sponsors of DAST including Panasonic, shoe maker Vans, Toyota, Gillette Right Guard, and Sony PlayStation. These brands activate events at the various tour stops, run contests and sweepstakes that tie into the tour, and develop account-specific retail promotions. Right Guard deodorant has developed special TV spots featuring the athletes it sponsors, which run in a two-hour loop on Wal-Mart's in-store television network. Vans distributes free admission tickets to events to its retail partners and also brings athletes such as skateboarder Bucky Lasek into Vans retail stores for autograph signings in tour stop markets. In-store promotions give consumers a chance to win a pair of Bucky Lasek 2 shoes.

Toyota is also using DAST as a way back into action sports after exiting as a sponsor of the Gravity Games in 2001. The centerpiece of its on-site event promotion is a Tacoma pickup truck customized by motocross bike and helmet maker Troy Lee. The truck is displayed at tour stops and given away as the grand prize of an online sweepstakes along with other daily prizes such as Yamaha dirt bikes, DVDs, skateboards, and gift cards from Target. Toyota collects leads from spectators who ask for information about its vehicles as well as text messages about other on-site events, athlete interaction opportunities, and chances for prizes while they are at DAST.

Marketers targeting teens and tweens recognize that Gen Y presents them with an opportunity they haven't seen since the baby boom hit. However, marketing to this cohort requires different approaches than those used to attract either their parents or Gen X. Many marketers think that Gen Y responds best when marketers bring their message to places they congregate, particularly when done without the air of heavy commercialism. Companies hoping to win their hearts and wallets are recognizing that the best way to reach Gen Y is to think extreme.

Sources: Ryan White, "Next Big Thing for Action Sports," *Knight-Ridder Tribune Business News,* August 14, 2005, p. 1; Tim Parry, "Winning Gen-Xtreme," *Promo,* July 2005, pp. 20–23.

The opening vignette shows how marketers can use a variety of sales promotion tools to market their products. PepsiCo leverages Mountain Dew's association with extreme sports into events that are very popular among its target audience of young people and also integrates a number of other promotional tools into the Dew Action Sports Tour including sampling programs, contests and sweepstakes, and promotions with retailers. Marketers recognize that advertising alone is not always enough to move their products off store shelves and into the hands of consumers. They are using a variety of sales promotion methods targeted at both consumers and the wholesalers and retailers that distribute their products to stimulate demand. Most companies' IMC programs include consumer and trade promotions that are coordinated with their advertising, direct marketing, publicity/publications, and online/Web-related marketing as well as their personal selling efforts.

This chapter focuses on the role of sales promotion in a firm's IMC program. We examine how marketers use both consumer- and trade-oriented promotions to influence the purchase behavior of consumers as well as wholesalers and retailers. We explore the objectives of sales promotion programs and the various types of sales promotion tools that can be used at both the consumer and trade level. We also consider how sales promotion can be integrated with other elements of the promotional mix and look at problems that can arise when marketers become overly dependent on consumer and trade promotions, especially the latter.

The Scope and Role of Sales Promotion

Sales promotion has been defined as "a direct inducement that offers an extra value or incentive for the product to the sales force, distributors, or the ultimate consumer with the primary objective of creating an immediate sale."[1] Keep in mind several important aspects of sales promotion as you read this chapter.

First, sales promotion involves some type of inducement that provides an *extra incentive* to buy. This incentive is usually the key element in a promotional program; it may be a coupon or price reduction, the opportunity to enter a contest or sweepstakes, a money-back refund or rebate, or an extra amount of a product. The incentive may also be a free sample of the product, given in hopes of generating a future purchase or a premium such as the free movie DVD mail-in offer used by Kellogg's Corn Flakes (Exhibit 16-1). Most sales promotion offers attempt to add some value to the product or service. While advertising appeals to the mind and emotions to give the consumer a reason to buy, sales promotion appeals more to the pocketbook and provides an incentive for purchasing a brand.

Sales promotion can also provide an inducement to marketing intermediaries such as wholesalers and retailers. A trade allowance or discount gives retailers a financial incentive to stock and promote a manufacturer's products. A trade contest directed toward wholesalers or retail personnel gives them extra incentive to perform certain tasks or meet sales goals.

A second point is that sales promotion is essentially an *acceleration tool,* designed to speed up the selling process and maximize sales volume.[2] By providing an extra incentive, sales promotion techniques can motivate consumers to purchase a larger quantity of a brand or shorten the purchase cycle of the trade or consumers by encouraging them to take more immediate action.

Companies also use limited-time offers such as price-off deals to retailers or a coupon with an expiration date to accelerate the purchase process.[3] Sales promotion attempts to maximize sales volume by motivating customers who have not responded to advertising. The ideal sales promotion program generates sales that would not be achieved by other means. However, as we shall see later, many sales promotion offers end up being used by current users of a brand rather than attracting new users.

A final point regarding sales promotion activities is that they can be *targeted to different parties* in the marketing channel. As shown in Figure 16-1, sales promotion can be broken into two major categories: consumer-oriented and trade-oriented promotions. Activities involved in **consumer-oriented sales promotion** include sampling, couponing, premiums, contests and sweepstakes, refunds and rebates, bonus packs, price-offs, frequency programs, and event marketing. These promotions are directed at consumers, the end purchasers of goods and services, and are designed to induce them to purchase the marketer's brand.

As discussed in Chapter 2, consumer-oriented promotions are part of a promotional pull strategy; they work along with advertising to encourage consumers to purchase a particular brand and thus create demand for it. Consumer promotions are also used by retailers to encourage consumers to

Exhibit 16-1 A premium offer is used to provide extra incentive to purchase Kellogg's Corn Flakes

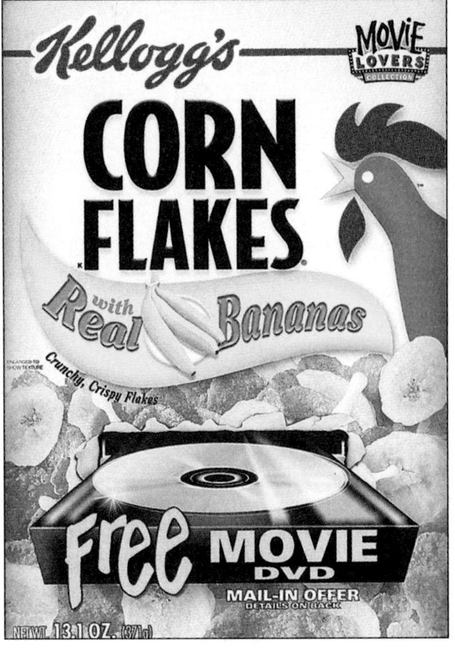

Figure 16-1 Types of Sales Promotion Activities

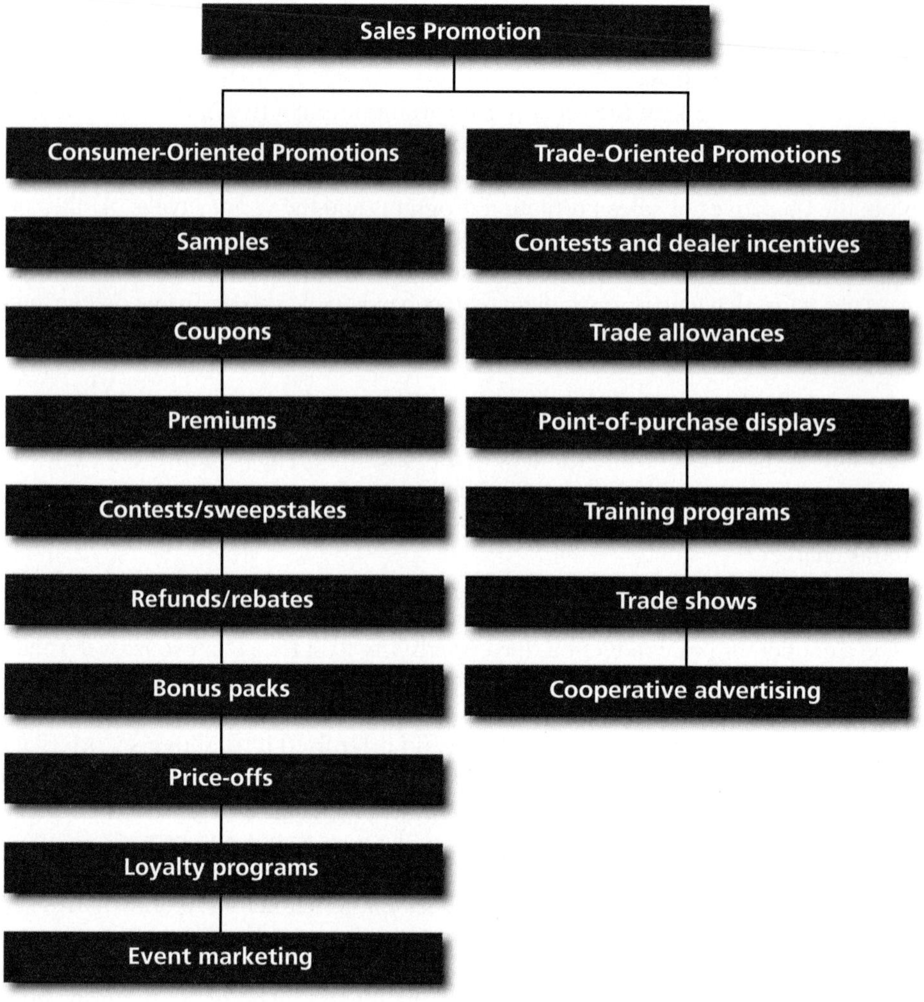

shop in their particular stores. Many grocery stores use their own coupons or sponsor contests and other promotions to increase store patronage.

Trade-oriented sales promotion includes dealer contests and incentives, trade allowances, point-of-purchase displays, sales training programs, trade shows, cooperative advertising, and other programs designed to motivate distributors and retailers to carry a product and make an extra effort to push it to their customers. Many marketing programs include both trade- and consumer-oriented promotions, since motivating both groups maximizes the effectiveness of the promotional program.

The Growth of Sales Promotion

While sales promotion has been part of the marketing process for a long time, its role and importance in a company's integrated marketing communications program have increased dramatically over the past decade. Consumer sales promotion–related spending increased from $56 billion in 1991 to nearly $343 billion in 2005.[4] Marketers also spend an estimated $150 billion each year on promotions targeted at retailers and wholesalers. Consumer packaged goods firms continue to be the core users of sales promotion programs and tools. However, sales promotion activity is also increasing in other categories, including health care, computer hardware and software, consumer electronics, and service industries.

Not only has the total amount of money spent on sales promotion increased, but the percentage of marketers' budgets allocated to promotion has grown as well. For many years advertising was the major component in the promotional mix of most consumer-product companies. Until the 1980s, nearly half of marketers' promotional dollars was spent on advertising campaigns designed to create or reinforce brand awareness and build long-term loyalty. However by the mid- to late 80s, a fundamental change had occurred in the way most consumer-product companies were marketing their products. The proportion of the marketing budget allocated to sales promotion rose sharply, while the amount spent on media advertising declined. The increase in spending on sales promotion at the expense of media advertising continued throughout the decade of the 90s and into the new millennium. Currently, estimates are that marketers spend between 60 and 75 percent of their promotional budgets on sales promotion, with the remainder being allocated to media advertising.[5]

Allocation of marketing budgets among consumer promotions, trade promotions, and media advertising varies by industry and company. For example, trade promotion accounts for nearly 50 percent of the budget for consumer packaged-goods companies, with 27 percent going to consumer promotion and 24 percent to media advertising.[6] Moreover, a significant amount of the monies that marketers allocate to media advertising is spent on ads that deliver promotional messages regarding contests, games, sweepstakes, and rebate offers.[7] Surveys have shown that marketers devote about 17 percent of their ad budgets to promotional messages.[8] Promotional messages are also used to help attract attention to image-building ads. For example, the ad shown in Exhibit 16-2 delivers a message informing consumers of the Chevy Avalanche Outdoor Adventure Sweepstakes.

Exhibit 16-2 Advertisements are often used to deliver messages about promotions such as sweepstakes

Reasons for the Increase in Sales Promotion

The reallocation of the marketing budget concerned many marketers who still viewed media advertising as the primary tool for brand building and saw sales promotion programs as little more than gimmicks that contributed little to brand equity. However, most have recognized that consumers may love certain brands but often want an extra incentive to buy them. Marketers also know they must partner effectively with trade accounts, and this often means providing them with an additional incentive to stock and promote their brands and participate in various promotional programs.

A major reason for the increase in spending on sales promotion is that the promotion industry has matured over the past several decades. Increased sophistication and a more strategic role and focus have elevated the discipline and its role in the IMC program of many companies.[9] In the past, sales promotion specialists would be brought in after key strategic branding decisions were made. Promotional agencies were viewed primarily as tacticians whose role was to develop a promotional program such as a contest or sweepstakes or a coupon or sampling program that could create a short-term increase in sales. However, many companies are now making promotional specialists part of their strategic brand-building team, a move that puts sales promotion on par with media advertising. Promotional agencies have expanded their integrated marketing capabilities as well as their expertise in branding and helping their clients build relationships with their customers. For example, Exhibit 16-3 shows an ad for DVC Worldwide, one of the leading promotion agencies, that touts the agency's expertise in strategy and brand building.

There are also a number of other factors that have led to the increase in the importance of sales promotion and the shift in marketing dollars from media advertising to consumer and trade promotions. Among them are the growing power of retailers, declining brand loyalty, increased promotional sensitivity, brand proliferation, fragmentation of the consumer market, the short-term focus of many marketers, increased accountability, competition, and clutter.

Exhibit 16-3 DVC Worldwide touts its expertise in branding

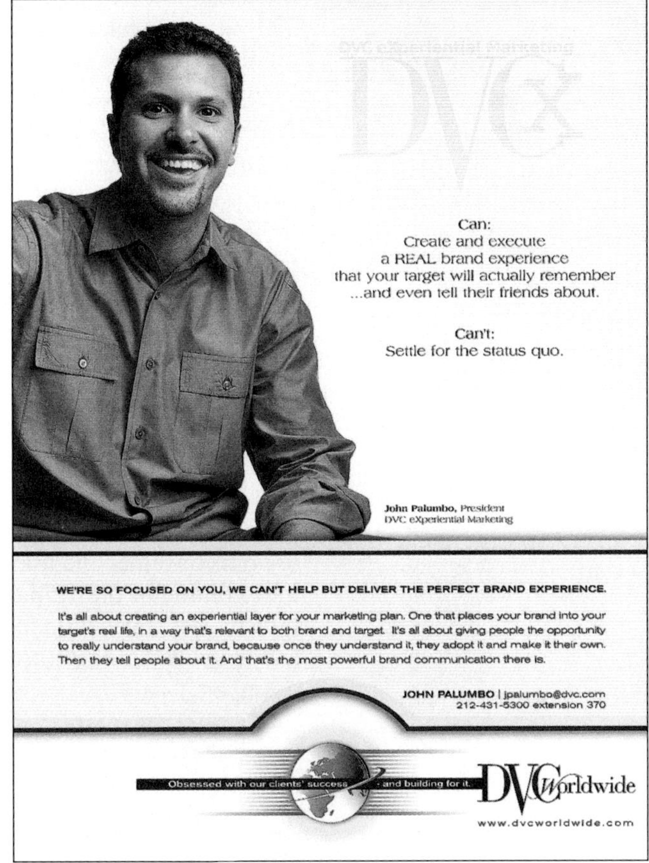

The Growing Power of Retailers

One reason for the increase in sales promotion is the power shift in the marketplace from manufacturers to retailers. For many years, manufacturers of national brands had the power and influence; retailers were just passive distributors of their products. Consumer-product manufacturers created consumer demand for their brands by using heavy advertising and some consumer-oriented promotions, such as samples, coupons, and premiums, and exerted pressure on retailers to carry the products. Retailers did very little research and sales analysis; they relied on manufacturers for information regarding the sales performance of individual brands.

In recent years, however, several developments have helped to transfer power from the manufacturers to the retailers. With the advent of optical checkout scanners and sophisticated in-store computer systems, retailers gained access to data concerning how quickly products turn over, which sales promotions are working, and which products make money.[10] Retailers use this information to analyze sales of manufacturers' products and then demand discounts and other promotional support from manufacturers of lagging brands. Companies that fail to comply with retailers' demands for more trade support often have their shelf space reduced or even their product dropped.

Another factor that has increased the power of retailers is the consolidation of the grocery store industry, which has resulted in larger chains with greater buying power and clout. These large chains have become accustomed to trade promotions and can pressure manufacturers to provide deals, discounts, and allowances. Consolidation has also given large retailers more money for advancing already strong private label initiatives, and sales promotion is the next step in the marketing evolution of private label brands. Private label brands in various packaged-good categories such as foods, drugs, and health and beauty care products are giving national brands more competition for retail shelf space and increasing their own marketing, including the use of traditional sales promotion tools. Well-marketed private label products are forcing national brand leaders, as well as second-tier brands, to develop more innovative promotional programs and to be more price-competitive.[11]

One of the most significant developments among retailers is the tremendous growth of Wal-Mart, which has become the largest company in the world as well as the most powerful retailer.[12] IMC Perspective 16-1 discusses how Wal-Mart's size and power impact the sale promotion programs of the companies that supply the retailing giant.

Declining Brand Loyalty

Another major reason for the increase in sales promotion is that consumers have become less brand loyal and are purchasing more on the basis of price, value, and convenience. Some consumers are always willing to buy their preferred brand at full price without any type of promotional offer. However, many consumers are loyal coupon users and/or are conditioned to look for deals when they shop. They may switch back and forth among a set of brands they view as essentially equal. These brands are all perceived as being satisfactory and interchangeable, and consumers purchase whatever brand is on special or for which they have a coupon.

Increased Promotional Sensitivity

Marketers are making greater use of sales promotion in their marketing programs because consumers respond favorably to the incentives it provides. A major research project completed by Promotion Decisions, Inc., tracked the purchase behavior of over 33,000 consumers and their response to both consumer and trade promotions. The results showed that 42 percent of the total unit volume of the 12 packaged-good products analyzed was purchased with some type of incentive while 58 percent was purchased at full price. Coupons were particularly popular among consumers, as 24 percent of the sales volume involved the use of a coupon.[13]

An obvious reason for consumers' increased sensitivity to sales promotion offers is that they save money. Another reason is that many purchase decisions are made at the point of purchase by consumers who are increasingly time-sensitive and facing too many choices. Some studies have found that up to 70 percent of purchase decisions are made in the store, where people are very likely to respond to promotional

IMC PERSPECTIVE 16-1

Dealing with the Power of Wal-Mart

In late January 2005, Procter & Gamble announced that it was purchasing the Gillette Co. for $54 billion. P&G had long coveted Gillette whose razor business, as well as other strong brands such as Oral-B and Duracell, is a natural extension of P&G's stable of global consumer products, which range from Tide laundry detergent to Crest toothpaste and Pantene shampoo. However, a number of industry analysts suggested that a major factor behind Procter & Gamble's decision to buy Gillette was concern about retailing giant Wal-Mart. Over the past 15 years, Wal-Mart has increasingly dominated its relationships with manufacturers by flexing its market muscle, demanding lower prices, and seizing pricing power by selling its own private-label products. Some experts believe that P&G's acquisition of Gillette is designed to take back some power from Wal-Mart and other large retailers as it expands the number of strong brands in the company's portfolio.

Procter & Gamble, as well as many other marketers, is greatly concerned by Wal-Mart's increasing power and for good reason, as the Bentonville, Arkansas–based company is not just the world's largest retailer—it is the world's largest company. Wal-Mart had sales of nearly $300 billion in 2005 and a recent study by research firm Retail Forward predicts that its sales will reach $500 billion by 2010. The company does more business each year than Target, Sears, Kmart, JCPenney, Safeway, and Kroger combined. It operates more than 3,500 stores in the United States alone including nearly 500 Supercenters, which average nearly $80 million in annual revenue. In its category of general merchandise and groceries, Wal-Mart has no real rivals, and its clout is hard to overstate. Wal-Mart's share of consumer staples such as toothpaste, hair care products, and paper towels is currently about 30 percent and could reach 50 percent by the end of the decade. The retailer is also Hollywood's biggest outlet, accounting for 15 to 20 percent of all sales of CDs, videos, and DVDs. Wal-Mart controls a large and rapidly increasing share of the business done by every major U.S. consumer-products company including 28 percent of the total sales for Dial, 24 percent of Del Monte Foods, 23 percent of Clorox, and so on down the line. A contract with Wal-Mart is critical to even the largest consumer-goods company. For example, if Dial lost its Wal-Mart account, it would have to double its sales to its next nine customers just to stay even.

Wal-Mart uses its power to bring the lowest possible prices to its customers. "Everyday Low Prices" is more than just an advertising slogan; it is the fundamental tenet of the company. Over the years, Wal-Mart has relentlessly rung tens of billions of dollars in cost efficiencies out of the retail supply chain and has passed most of the savings along to consumers in the form of low prices. Wal-Mart has a clear policy for suppliers: On basic products that don't change, the price Wal-Mart will pay, and will charge its customers, must drop year after year.

Wal-Mart's power to squeeze price concessions from them is a mixed blessing for the 21,000 companies that supply the retailer. For well-run companies with strong brands, Wal-Mart can be one of its most profitable customers. It is known for continuous improvement in its ability to handle, move, and track merchandise, which improves operational efficiencies. Unlike many retailers, the company does not charge slotting fees for access to its shelves and is very willing to share sales and market research data with manufacturers. In return, however, Wal-Mart dictates delivery schedules and inventory levels and also influences product specifications. The retailer often forces its suppliers to redesign everything from packaging to their computer systems and often tells them what their profit margins will be for items sold in its stores.

Wal-Mart has also been known to use its power to influence the way marketers use sales promotions. Like many large retailers, Wal-Mart often asks for account-specific promotions that are designed for and offered only through its stores. The retailer also can use its power to influence whether a supplier can even use a promotion. A former vice president at Nabisco recalled how the company planned to offer a 25-cent newspaper coupon for a large bag of Lifesavers in advance of Halloween. However, Wal-Mart told Nabisco to add up what it would spend on the promotion for the newspaper ads, the coupons, and handling, and just to take that amount off of the price instead. While such mandates result in lower prices for shoppers, they are not always good for the manufacturer who is interested in drawing attention to its brands.

Edward Fox, head of Southern Methodist University's Center for Retailing Excellence, notes that "Wal-Mart is more powerful than any retailer has ever been. It is, in fact, so big and so furtively powerful as to have become an entirely different order of corporate being." Wal-Mart might also well be America's most admired and most hated company. The more size and power that "the Beast of Bentonville" amasses, the greater the backlash it generates among competing retailers, organized labor, community activists, and vendors. Many companies know that the best way to deal with Wal-Mart's clout is to have strong brands and to develop innovative products that consumers need but cannot be bid out to private-label manufacturers. A study by the management consulting firm Bain & Company found that in many product categories consumers are often more loyal to strong brands than they are to Wal-Mart.

While market leaders such as Procter & Gamble have the power to stand up to Wal-Mart, many companies have no choice but to continue to cut their costs to keep up with Wal-Mart's demands for lower prices. As one management consultant notes, the second worst thing a manufacturer can do is sign a contract with Wal-Mart. The worst? Not sign one.

Sources: Lorrie Grant," Wal-Mart Sets Sights on Target While Keeping Core Customers," *USA Today,* August 5, 2005, pp. B1, 2; Andy Serwer, "Bruised in Bentonville," *Fortune,* April 18, 2005, pp. 84–89; Constance L. Hays and Eric Dash, "What's Behind the Procter Deal? Wal-Mart," *The New York Times,* January 29, 2005, p. C1; Charles Fishman, "The Wal-Mart You Don't Know," *Fast Company,* December 2003, pp. 68–80.

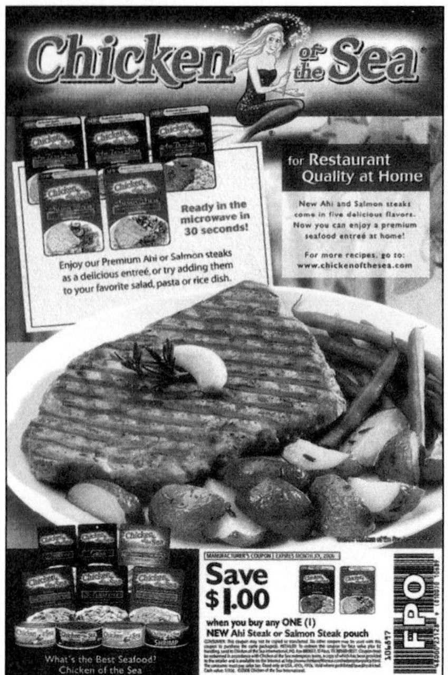

Exhibit 16-4 Sales promotion tools such as coupons are often used to encourage trial of a new brand

deals.[14] Buying a brand that is on special or being displayed can simplify the decision-making process and solve the problem of overchoice. Professor Leigh McAlister has described this process:

> As consumers go down the supermarket aisle they spend 3 to 10 seconds in each product category. They often don't know the regular price of the chosen product. However, they do have a sense of whether or not that product is on promotion. As they go down the aisle, they are trying to pensively fill their baskets with good products without tiresome calculations. They see a "good deal" and it goes in the cart.[15]

Brand Proliferation A major aspect of many firms' marketing strategies over the past decade has been the development of new products. Consumer-product companies are launching nearly 30,000 new products each year, according to the research firm Marketing Intelligence Service (compared with only 2,689 in 1980).[16] The market has become saturated with new brands, which often lack any significant advantages that can be used as the basis of an advertising campaign. Thus, companies increasingly depend on sales promotion to encourage consumers to try these brands. In Chapter 4, we saw how sales promotion techniques can be used as part of the shaping process to lead the consumer from initial trial to repeat purchase at full price. Marketers are relying more on samples, coupons, rebates, premiums, and other innovative promotional tools to achieve trial usage of their new brands and encourage repeat purchase (Exhibit 16-4).

Promotions are also important in getting retailers to allocate some of their precious shelf space to new brands. The competition for shelf space for new products in stores is enormous. Supermarkets carry an average of 30,000 products (compared with 13,067 in 1982). Retailers favor new brands with strong sales promotion support that will bring in more customers and boost their sales and profits. Many retailers require special discounts or allowances from manufacturers just to handle a new product. These slotting fees or allowances, which are discussed later in the chapter, can make it expensive for a manufacturer to introduce a new product.

Fragmentation of the Consumer Market As the consumer market becomes more fragmented and traditional mass-media–based advertising less effective, marketers are turning to more segmented, highly targeted approaches. Many companies are tailoring their promotional efforts to specific regional markets. Sales promotion tools have become one of the primary vehicles for doing this, through programs tied into local flavor, themes, or events. For example, fast-food restaurants and take-out pizza chains such as Domino's spent a high percentage of their marketing budget on local tie-ins and promotions designed to build traffic and generate sales from their trade areas.

Marketers are also shifting more of their promotional efforts to direct marketing, which often includes some form of sales promotion incentive. Many marketers use information they get from premium offers, trackable coupons, rebates, and sweepstakes to build databases for future direct-marketing efforts. As marketers continue to shift from media advertising to direct marketing, promotional offers will probably be used even more to help build databases. The technology is already in place to enable marketers to communicate individually with target consumers and transform mass promotional tools into ways of doing one-to-one marketing.[17]

Short-Term Focus Many businesspeople believe the increase in sales promotion is motivated by marketing plans and reward systems geared to short-term performance and the immediate generation of sales volume. Some think the packaged-goods brand management system has contributed to marketers' increased dependence on sales promotion. Brand managers use sales promotions routinely, not only to introduce new products or defend against the competition but also to meet quarterly or yearly sales and market share goals. The sales force, too, may have short-term quotas or goals to meet and may also receive requests from retailers and wholesalers for promotions. Thus, reps may pressure marketing or brand managers to use promotions to help them move the products into the retailers' stores.

Many managers view consumer and trade promotions as the most dependable way to generate short-term sales, particularly when they are price-related. The reliance on sales promotion is particularly high in mature and slow-growth markets, where it is difficult to stimulate consumer demand through advertising. This has led to concern that managers have become too dependent on the quick sales fix that can result from a promotion and that the brand franchise may be eroded by too many deals.

Increased Accountability In addition to pressuring their marketing or brand managers and sales force to produce short-term results, many companies are demanding to know what they are getting for their promotional expenditures. Results from sales promotion programs are generally easier to measure than those from advertising. Many companies are demanding measurable, accountable ways to relate promotional expenditures to sales and profitability. For example, some companies use computerized sales information from checkout scanners in determining compensation for marketing personnel. Part of the pay managers receive depends on the sales a promotion generates relative to its costs.[18]

Managers who are being held accountable to produce results often use price discounts or coupons, since they produce a quick and easily measured jump in sales. It takes longer for an ad campaign to show some impact and the effects are more difficult to measure. Marketers are also feeling pressure from the trade as powerful retailers demand sales performance from their brands. Real-time data available from computerized checkout scanners make it possible for retailers to monitor promotions and track the results they generate on a daily basis.

Competition Another factor that led to the increase in sales promotion is manufacturers' reliance on trade and consumer promotions to gain or maintain competitive advantage. The markets for many products are mature and stagnant, and it is increasingly difficult to boost sales through advertising. Exciting, breakthrough creative ideas are difficult to come by, and consumers' attention to mass-media advertising continues to decline. Rather than allocating large amounts of money to run dull ads, many marketers have turned to sales promotion.

Many companies are tailoring their trade promotions to key retail accounts and developing strategic alliances with retailers that include both trade and consumer promotional programs. A major development in recent years is **account-specific marketing** (also referred to as *co-marketing*), whereby a manufacturer collaborates with an individual retailer to create a customized promotion that accomplishes mutual objectives. For example, Coppertone's promotion agency created an account-specific promotion for "Spot the Dog Scavenger Hunt" that was based on the iconic Little Miss Coppertone losing her dog in a Wal-Mart store (Exhibit 16-5). The in-store scavenger hunt involved having consumers find clues throughout the store, fill in a game piece, and receive a prize. The game piece promoted Coppertone's rub-free adult and children's spray and included a $2 Wal-Mart–specific rebate coupon. The promotion resulted in a 6 percent increase in Coppertone sales during the promotion.

Exhibit 16-5 Coppertone developed an account-specific promotion for Wal-Mart

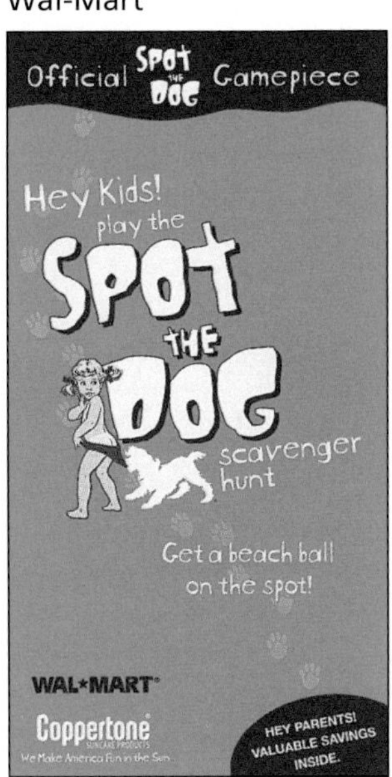

Estimates are that marketers will soon be spending more than half of their promotion budgets on account-specific marketing. A number of companies are developing promotional programs for major retail accounts such as supermarket chains, mass merchandisers, and convenience stores.[19]

Retailers may use a promotional deal with one company as leverage to seek an equal or better deal with its competitors. Consumer and trade promotions are easily matched by competitors, and many marketers find themselves in a promotional trap where they must continue using promotions or be at a competitive disadvantage. (We discuss this problem in more detail later in the chapter.)

Clutter A promotional offer in an ad can break through the clutter that is prevalent in most media today. A premium offer may help attract consumers' attention to an ad, as will a contest or sweepstakes. Some studies have shown that readership scores are higher for print ads with coupons than for ads without them.[20] However, more recent studies by Starch INRA Hooper suggest that magazine ads with coupons do not generate higher readership.[21] A recent study found that promotional messages are very prevalent in both magazine and newspaper ads, particularly the latter. Sweepstakes, games, and contests were prevalent in magazine ads, while coupons and sales offers were used the most in newspaper advertising.[22]

Concerns about the Increased Role of Sales Promotion

Many factors have contributed to the increased use of sales promotion by consumer-product manufacturers. Marketing and advertising executives are concerned about how this shift in the allocation of the promotional budget affects brand equity. As noted in Chapter 2, *brand equity,* or consumer franchise, is an intangible asset of added value or goodwill that results from consumers' favorable image, impressions of differentiation, and/or strength of attachment to a brand.

Some critics argue that sales promotion increases come at the expense of brand equity and every dollar that goes into promotion rather than advertising devalues the brand.[23] They say trade promotions in particular contribute to the destruction of brand franchises and equity as they encourage consumers to purchase primarily on the basis of price.

Proponents of advertising argue that marketers must maintain strong franchises if they want to differentiate their brands and charge a premium price for them. They say advertising is still the most effective way to build the long-term franchise of a brand: It informs consumers of a brand's features and benefits, creates an image, and helps build and maintain brand loyalty. However, many marketers are not investing in their brands as they take monies away from media advertising to fund short-term promotions.

Marketing experts generally agree that advertising plays an important role in building and maintaining a brand's image and position, which are core components of its equity. Many are concerned that if the trend toward spending more on sales promotion at the expense of media advertising continues, brands may lose the equity that advertising helped create and be forced to compete primarily on the basis of price. Many of these concerns are justified, but not all sales promotion activities detract from the value of a brand. It is important to distinguish between consumer franchise-building and nonfranchise-building promotions.

Consumer Franchise-Building versus Nonfranchise-Building Promotions

Sales promotion activities that communicate distinctive brand attributes and contribute to the development and reinforcement of brand identity are **consumer franchise-building (CFB) promotions.**[24] Consumer sales promotion efforts cannot make consumers loyal to a brand that is of little value or does not provide them with a specific benefit. But they can make consumers aware of a brand and, by communicating its specific features and benefits, contribute to the development of a favorable brand image. Consumer franchise-building promotions are designed to build long-term brand preference and help the company achieve the ultimate goal of full-price purchases that do not depend on a promotional offer.

For years, franchise or image building was viewed as the exclusive realm of advertising, and sales promotion was used only to generate short-term sales increases. But now marketers are recognizing the image-building potential of sales promotion and paying attention to its CFB value. Surveys have found that nearly 90 percent of senior marketing executives believe consumer promotions can help build brand equity while nearly 60 percent think trade promotions can contribute.[25] Marketers recognize that the value of sales promotion extends well beyond quick-fix tactics such as price-off deals. Most sales promotion agencies recognize the importance of developing consumer and trade promotions that can help build brand equity. For example, Exhibit 16-6 shows an ad for Ryan Partnership that stresses how the agency develops trade promotions that help build brand equity.

Companies can use sales promotion techniques in a number of ways to contribute to franchise building. Rather than using a one-time offer, many companies are developing frequency programs that encourage repeat purchases and long-term patronage.

Many credit cards have loyalty programs where consumers earn bonus points every time they use their card to charge a purchase. These points can then be redeemed for various items. Most airlines and many hotel chains offer frequent-flyer or guest programs to encourage repeat patronage. Many retail stores have also begun using frequency programs to build loyalty and encourage repeat purchases.[26]

Exhibit 16-6 This promotion agency ad stresses the importance of using trade promotions to build brand equity

Nonfranchise-building (non-FB) promotions are designed to accelerate the purchase decision process and generate an immediate increase in sales. These activities do not communicate information about a brand's unique features or the benefits of using it, so they do not contribute to the building of brand identity and image. Price-off deals, bonus packs, and rebates or refunds are examples of non-FB sales promotion techniques. Trade promotions receive the most criticism for being nonfranchise building—for good reason. First, many of the promotional discounts and allowances given to the trade are never passed on to consumers. Most trade promotions that are forwarded through the channels reach consumers in the form of lower prices or special deals and lead them to buy on the basis of price rather than brand equity.

Many specialists in the promotional area stress the need for marketers to use sales promotion tools to build a franchise and create long-term continuity in their promotional programs. Whereas non-FB promotions merely borrow customers from other brands, well-planned CFB activities can convert consumers to loyal customers. Short-term non-FB promotions have their place in a firm's promotional mix, particularly when competitive developments call for them. But their limitations must be recognized when a long-term marketing strategy for a brand is developed.

Consumer-Oriented Sales Promotion

As discussed in IMC Perspective 16-2, marketers have been using various types of sales promotion for more than a hundred years and have found a variety of ways to give consumers an extra incentive to purchase their products and services. In this section, we examine the various sales promotion tools and techniques marketers can use to influence consumers. We study the consumer-oriented promotions shown in Figure 16-1 and discuss their advantages and limitations. First, we consider some objectives marketers have for sales promotion programs targeted to the consumer market.

Objectives of Consumer-Oriented Sales Promotion

As the use of sales promotion techniques continues to increase, companies must consider what they hope to accomplish through their consumer promotions and how they interact with other promotional activities such as advertising, direct marketing, and personal selling. When marketers implement sales promotion programs without considering their long-term cumulative effect on the brand's image and position in the marketplace, they often do little more than create short-term spikes in the sales curve.

Not all sales promotion activities are designed to achieve the same objectives. As with any promotional mix element, marketers must plan consumer promotions by conducting a situation analysis and determining sales promotion's specific role in the integrated marketing communications program. They must decide what the promotion is designed to accomplish and to whom it should be targeted. Setting clearly defined

IMC PERSPECTIVE 16-2

Sales Promotion Has an Interesting History as Well

Advertising has a long and fascinating history and has had a major impact, both good and bad, on our culture. Advertising has entertained, moved, and motivated consumers for more than a century, and many of the images created by advertisers have become cultural icons—Ronald McDonald, the Marlboro Man, Tony the Tiger, and the Energizer Bunny, to name just a few. Much has been written about the history of advertising and how it reflects society and its whole range of activities. However, sales promotion also has a very rich and interesting history: Marketers have developed and used a variety of techniques over the past century to give consumers an extra incentive to use their products and services. Many of the sales promotion offers that motivate consumers today and have become part of their everyday lives have been around for nearly a century or more.

The oldest, most widely used, and most effective sales promotion tool is the cents-off coupon. Coupons have been around since 1895 when the C. W. Post Co. first began using the penny-off coupon to help sell its new Grape Nuts cereal brand. Procter & Gamble began using coupons in 1920, and its first ones were metal coins that were good for discounts or buy-one-get-one-free deals. Those were soon replaced by cheaper, more convenient paper versions, which have been around ever since. Another classic promotional tool is the premium offer, which dates back to 1912 when Cracker Jack began offering "a prize in every box." Ovaltine developed one of the first interactive premiums in 1930, when it gave away decoder rings that were needed to decode secret messages broadcast in *Little Orphan Annie* radio shows in the 30s. The promotion was brought back 20 years later as television became the new mass medium and the rings were used to decode messages in *Texas Rangers* TV shows. Perhaps no company has used premium offers as effectively as McDonald's, which launched its Happy Meals in 1979 and has been using them ever since. Happy Meals account for a significant portion of McDonald's sales and have made the company the world's largest toy manufacturer.

Marketers also have a long history of taking their promotional programs to the customer. Procter & Gamble was one of the first companies to use event marketing on a large scale when the company's public relations counsel launched a National Soap Sculpture contest for Ivory soap in 1925. Early contests featured huge works by professional sculptors using 500- to 1,000-pound blocks of soap. By 1934, the contest featured nearly 4,000 sculptures and attracted more than 28,000 spectators to Rockefeller Center in New York City. At one point the contest drew a high of 8,000 entries for national judging and thousands locally. P&G stopped the contest from 1942 to 1947 as soap became rationed, but resumed it in 1948. By the time the company ended the contest in 1961, it had generated tens of millions of bars of incremental sales and helped make Ivory soap the cornerstone of P&G's empire.

The first Oscar Mayer Wienermobile hit the streets in 1936, when the nephew of the company's founder had the idea of introducing a 13-foot-long hot dog on wheels. Soon it was seen driving the streets of Chicago, promoting Oscar Mayer "German Style Wieners." Seven updates and 66 years later, there is now a fleet of eight Wienermobiles that cruise the highways of America and other countries playing 21 versions of the famous Wiener Jingle and helping to promote the brand. Pepsi is another company that took a promotional program on the road, with its launch of the famous Pepsi Challenge in 1975, which was one of the most successful promotions ever used to attract users of a competing brand. Pepsi took on its archrival and industry leader Coca-Cola in a hard-hitting promotion that challenged consumers to taste the two brands in blind taste tests. Pepsi ran the challenge promotion for nearly a decade and relaunched it again in 2000 as it began cruising for a new generation.

Contests and sweepstakes also have an interesting history. Pillsbury launched its first Bake-Off Contest in 1949, when the company's advertising agency created the contest to celebrate the company's 80th birthday and invited homemakers to share their treasured recipes. The response was so great that Pillsbury decided to hold the contest again in subsequent years, and the Bake-Off has become an institution as well as the nation's most prestigious cooking competition. Many of the winning recipes in each year's competition have become part of the repertoire of home cooks and have led to innovative new products from Pillsbury.

McDonald's has taken another institution, the world-famous Monopoly board game, and turned it into a long-running and immensely popular contest. The first McDonald's Monopoly game contest was in 1987, and its collect-and-win format and big prizes generated tremendous interest and excitement and was very effective at generating repeat business. McDonald's began running the game annually in 1991, tweaking it each year by adding new partners and prizes and making the game more complex with new iterations such as the Pick Your Prize twist. However, in 2001 the game had the most surprising twist of all: The FBI used it to collect evidence against an embezzlement ring that had been stealing high-value game pieces throughout the years. While McDonald's stopped using games and sweepstakes for several years, the company brought back the popular Monopoly game in 2003.

Another promotional program of historical significance is the American Airlines AAdvantage frequent-flier program, which was launched in 1981. The program created a new currency and has set the gold standard for loyalty marketing as it now has nearly 44 million members. American also has a steady stream of partners that offer AAdvantage miles as an incentive to encourage consumers to purchase their products and services. Loyalty programs have also become very prevalent in many other industries such as hospitality, rental cars, and retailing.

Many of the marketers discussed here are promotional pioneers, as they have found creative ways to provide consumers with an extra incentive to purchase their brands. The success of these promotions has had a major impact on consumers throughout the years and also has resulted in similar programs being developed by competitors. Such promotions show that advertising is not the only IMC tool with a rich and interesting history.

Sources: Rod Taylor, "99 and 44/100% Art," *Promo,* February 2004, pp. 81, 82; "A Look at 16 Campaigns That Helped Redefine Promotion Marketing," *Promo,* March 2002, pp. 58–70; www.bakeoff.com/history.

objectives and measurable goals for their sales promotion programs forces managers to think beyond the short-term sales fix (although this can be one goal).

While the basic goal of most consumer-oriented sales promotion programs is to induce purchase of a brand, the marketer may have a number of different objectives for both new and established brands—for example, obtaining trial and repurchase, increasing consumption of an established brand, defending current customers, targeting a specific market segment, or enhancing advertising and marketing efforts.

Obtaining Trial and Repurchase

One of the most important uses of sales promotion techniques is to encourage consumers to try a new product or service. While thousands of new products are introduced to the market every year, as many as 90 percent of them fail within the first year. Many of these failures are due to the fact that the new product or brand lacks the promotional support needed either to encourage initial trial by enough consumers or to induce enough of those trying the brand to repurchase it. Many new brands are merely new versions of an existing product without unique benefits, so advertising alone cannot induce trial. Sales promotion tools have become an important part of new brand introduction strategies; the level of initial trial can be increased through techniques such as sampling, couponing, and refund offers.

The success of a new brand depends not only on getting initial trial but also on inducing a reasonable percentage of people who try the brand to repurchase it and establish ongoing purchase patterns. Promotional incentives such as coupons or refund offers are often included with a sample to encourage repeat purchase after trial. For example, when Lever Brothers introduced its Lever 2000 brand of bar soap, it distributed millions of free samples along with a 75-cent coupon. The samples allowed consumers to try the new soap, while the coupon provided an incentive to purchase it.

Increasing Consumption of an Established Brand

Many marketing managers are responsible for established brands competing in mature markets, against established competitors, where consumer purchase patterns are often well set. Awareness of an established brand is generally high as a result of cumulative advertising effects, and many consumers have probably tried the brand. These factors can create a challenging situation for the brand manager. Sales promotion can generate some new interest in an established brand to help increase sales or defend market share against competitors.

Marketers attempt to increase sales for an established brand in several ways, and sales promotion can play an important role in each. One way to increase product consumption is by identifying new uses for the brand. Sales promotion tools like recipe books or calendars that show various ways of using the product often can accomplish this. One of the best examples of a brand that has found new uses is Arm & Hammer baking soda. Exhibit 16-7 shows a clever freestanding insert (FSI) that promotes the brand's new fridge-freezer pack, which absorbs more odors in refrigerators and freezers.

Another strategy for increasing sales of an established brand is to use promotions that attract nonusers of the product category or users of a competing brand. Attracting

Exhibit 16-7 Arm & Hammer used this FSI to promote a specific use for the product

Challenge the call.
Throw the flag and take the Miller Taste Challenge. You have a choice.
Miller
Good call.

Exhibit 16-8 Miller Lite's Taste Challenge was a very successful promotion for attracting users of competing brands

nonusers of the product category can be very difficult, as consumers may not see a need for the product. Sales promotions can appeal to nonusers by providing them with an extra incentive to try the product, but a more common strategy for increasing sales of an established brand is to attract consumers who use a competing brand. This can be done by giving them an incentive to switch, such as a coupon, premium offer, bonus pack, or price deal. Marketers can also get users of a competitor to try their brand through sampling or other types of promotional programs.

One of the most successful promotions ever used to attract users of a competing brand was the Pepsi Challenge. In this campaign, Pepsi took on its archrival, industry leader Coca-Cola, in a hard-hitting comparative promotion that challenged consumers to taste the two brands in blind taste tests. The Pepsi Challenge promotion included national and local advertising, couponing, and trade support as part of a fully integrated promotional program. The campaign was used from 1975 to the early 80s and was instrumental in helping Pepsi move ahead of Coke to become the market share leader in supermarket sales. In response Coke launched a variety of counterattacks, including the controversial decision to change its formula and launch New Coke in 1986.

The Miller Brewing Company also used a Taste Challenge promotion recently to help regain market share for its flagship brand, Miller Lite, which had lost its category leadership to Bud Light. A key component of this integrated campaign was an interactive, on-premise promotion in bars, restaurants, and night clubs where consumers were given the opportunity to compare the taste of Miller Lite against Bud Light. Mobile computer tablets were used to track responses to the comparisons and national TV commercials were run showing the outcome of several of the blind taste tests. An additional phase of the promotion featured a "Make the Call for More" in which Miller Lite promotion specialists dressed as football referees approached consumers who were drinking competitive brands and challenged them to a football-themed Taste Challenge that showed why Miller Lite offers more (Exhibit 16-8). Over 400,000 consumers were engaged with the Taste Challenge promotion during 2004 and the promotion helped increase sales and market share by an average of 13 percent in markets where the challenge was conducted and over 11 percent overall.[27]

Defending Current Customers With more new brands entering the market every day and competitors attempting to take away their customers through aggressive advertising and sales promotion efforts, many companies are turning to sales promotion programs to hold present customers and defend their market share. A company can use sales promotion techniques in several ways to retain its current customer base. One way is to load them with the product, taking them out of the market for a certain time. Special price promotions, coupons, or bonus packs can encourage consumers to stock up on the brand. This not only keeps them using the company's brand but also reduces the likelihood they will switch brands in response to a competitor's promotion.

Targeting a Specific Market Segment Most companies focus their marketing efforts on specific market segments and are always looking for ways to reach their target audiences. Many marketers are finding that sales promotion tools such as contests and sweepstakes, events, coupons, and samplings are very effective ways to reach specific geographic, demographic, psychographic, and ethnic markets. Sales promotion programs can also be targeted to specific user-status groups such as nonusers or light versus heavy users.

In addition, promotions programs can be developed to coincide with peak sales periods for certain products and services. For example, candy companies such as Mars and Hershey often develop sales promotions that are run right before Halloween while clothing and school supply companies targeting children and teens run promotions in late summer when most of the back-to-school shopping occurs.

Enhancing Integrated Marketing Communications and Building Brand Equity A final objective for consumer-oriented promotions is to enhance or support the integrated marketing communications effort for a brand or company. While building and/or maintaining brand equity was traditionally viewed as something that was done through media advertising, it has also become an important goal for marketers as they develop their sales promotion programs. Companies are asking their promotion agencies to think strategically and develop promotional programs that can do more than simply generate short-term sales. They want promotions that require consumers to become more involved with their brands and offer a way of presenting the brand essence in an engaging way. Many marketers are recognizing that a well-designed and executed promotion can be a very effective way to engage consumers and to differentiate their brands. Sales promotion techniques such as contests or sweepstakes and premium offers are often used to draw attention to an advertising campaign, to increase involvement with the message and product or service, and to help build relationships with consumers.

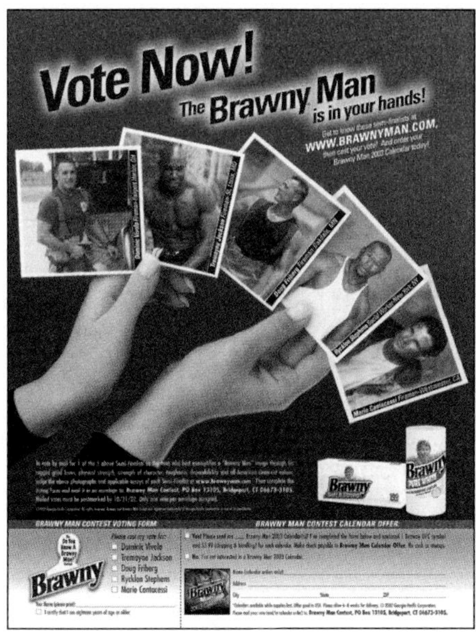

Exhibit 16-9 Brawny used a contest to increase consumer involvement and interest in the brand

A number of marketers are recognizing the value of contests to create interest and excitement in their brands that can get consumers to become more involved with them. For example, when the Georgia-Pacific Corporation acquired the Brawny paper towel brand a few years ago, the company used a contest to help rebuild the struggling brand. The goals of the contest were to build brand equity by leveraging the Brawny man icon as well as to gain insight into the modern woman's opinions as to what makes a man brawny. Georgia-Pacific's promotional agency developed the "Do you know a Brawny Man?" promotion, which included a contest asking women to send in a photo and a 150-word description explaining why their guy is as rugged as the product. More than 40,000 entries were downloaded from the Brawnyman.com website and over 4,000 women wrote the company to nominate someone to be the new Brawny man. Five finalists were selected and consumers were able to vote online and through the mail to select a winner whose picture appeared on the package for a few weeks (Exhibit 16-9). Information gathered from the entrants was used by the Brawny marketing team to develop a new Brawny Man image to replace the smiling lumberjack who was long overdue for a makeover. As the brand manager for Brawny paper towels noted, "For the winner, the contest provides 15 minutes of fame. For the consumer, it provides a better opportunity to relate to the brand than just seeing it as they walk down the aisle."[28]

Consumer-Oriented Sales Promotion Techniques

Sampling

Marketers use various sales promotion techniques to meet the objectives just discussed. Figure 16-2 shows the extent to which these consumer promotions are used by packaged-goods companies.

Sampling involves a variety of procedures whereby consumers are given some quantity of a product for no charge to induce trial. Sampling is generally considered the most effective way to generate trial, although it is also the most expensive. As a sales promotion technique, sampling is often used to introduce a new product or brand to the market. However, as Figure 16-2 shows, sampling is also used for established products as well. Some companies do not use sampling for established products, reasoning that samples may not induce satisfied users of a competing brand to switch and may just go to the firm's current customers, who would buy the product anyway. This may not be true when significant changes (new and improved) are made in a brand.

Manufacturers of packaged-goods products such as food, health care items, cosmetics, and toiletries are heavy users of sampling since their products meet the three criteria for an effective sampling program:

1. The products are of relatively low unit value, so samples do not cost too much.
2. The products are divisible, which means they can be broken into small sample sizes that are adequate for demonstrating the brand's features and benefits to the user.
3. The purchase cycle is relatively short, so the consumer will consider an immediate purchase or will not forget about the brand before the next purchase occasion.

Figure 16-2 Types of Consumer Promotions Used by Packaged-Goods Manufacturers

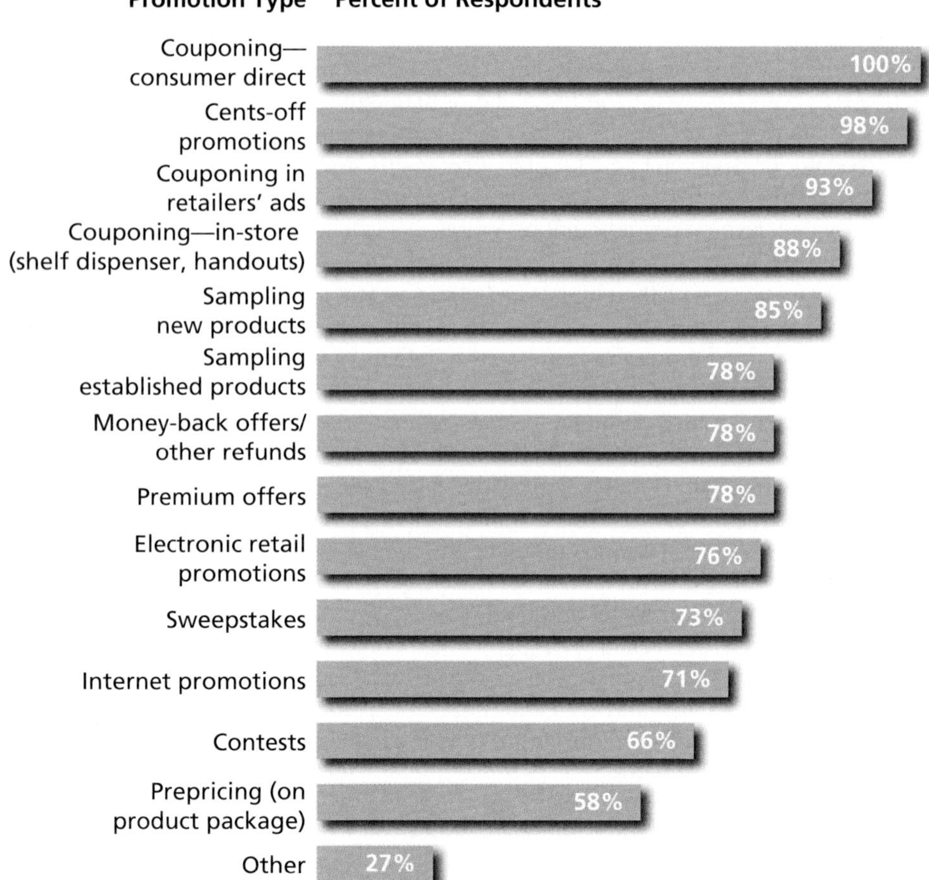

Benefits and Limitations of Sampling Samples are an excellent way to induce trial as they provide consumers with a risk-free way to try new products. A major study conducted by the Promotion Marketing Association found that the vast majority of consumers receiving a sample either use it right away or save it to use sometime later.[29] Sampling generates much higher trial rates than advertising or other sales promotion techniques.

Getting people to try a product leads to a second benefit of sampling: Consumers experience the brand directly, gaining a greater appreciation for its benefits. This can be particularly important when a product's features and benefits are difficult to describe through advertising. Many foods, beverages, and cosmetics have subtle features that are most appreciated when experienced directly. Nearly 70 percent of the respondents in the PMA survey indicated they have purchased a product they did not normally use after trying a free sample. The study also found that samples are even more likely to lead to purchase when they are accompanied by a coupon.

While samples are an effective way to induce trial, the brand must have some unique or superior benefits for a sampling program to be worthwhile. Otherwise, the sampled consumers revert back to other brands and do not become repeat purchasers. The costs of a sampling program can be recovered only if it gets a number of consumers to become regular users of the brand at full retail price.

Another possible limitation to sampling is that the benefits of some products are difficult to gauge immediately, and the learning period required to appreciate the brand may require supplying the consumer with larger amounts of the brand than are affordable. An example would be an expensive skin cream that is promoted as preventing or reducing wrinkles but has to be used for an extended period before any effects are seen.

Sampling Methods One basic decision the sales promotion or brand manager must make is how the sample will be distributed. The sampling method chosen is important not only in terms of costs but also because it influences the type of consumer who receives the sample. The best sampling method gets the product to the best prospects for trial and subsequent repurchase. Some basic distribution methods include door-to-door, direct-mail, in-store, and on-package approaches.

Door-to-door sampling, in which the product is delivered directly to the prospect's residence, is used when it is important to control where the sample is delivered. This distribution method is very expensive because of labor costs, but it can be cost-effective if the marketer has information that helps define the target market and/or if the prospects are located in a well-defined geographic area. Some companies have samples delivered directly to consumers' homes by including them with newspapers. Sunday papers have become an increasingly attractive way of mass distributing samples. However, there are also a number of newspapers that can now distribute a sample into a subscriber segment as small as 250 households with little increase in costs to marketers. Many newspapers distribute samples through polybags, which are plastic bags that serve as covers for the paper and deliver a promotional message along with the sample (Exhibit 16-10).

Exhibit 16-10 Polybags are used by many newspapers to distribute samples

Sampling through the mail is common for small, lightweight, nonperishable products. A major advantage of this method is that the marketer has control over where and when the product will be distributed and can target the sample to specific market areas. Many marketers are using information from geodemographic target marketing programs such as Claritas's Prizm to better target their sample mailings. The main drawbacks to mail sampling are postal restrictions and increasing postal rates.

In-store sampling is increasingly popular, especially for food products. The marketer hires temporary demonstrators who set up a table or booth, prepare small samples of the product, and pass them out to shoppers. The in-store sampling approach can be very effective for food products, since consumers get to taste the item and the demonstrator can give them more information about the product while it is being sampled. Demonstrators may also give consumers a cents-off coupon for the sampled item to encourage immediate trial purchase. While this sampling method can be very effective, it can also be expensive and requires a great deal of planning, as well as the cooperation of retailers.

On-package sampling, where a sample of a product is attached to another item, is another common sampling method (see Exhibit 16-11). This procedure can be very cost-effective, particularly for multiproduct firms that attach a sample of a new product to an existing brand's package. A drawback is that since the sample is distributed only to consumers who purchase the item to which it is attached, the sample will not reach nonusers of the carrier brand. Marketers can expand this sampling method by attaching the sample to multiple carrier brands and including samples with products not made by their company.

Event sampling has become one of the fastest-growing and most popular ways of distributing samples. Many marketers are using sampling programs that are part of integrated marketing programs that feature events, media tie-ins, and other activities that provide consumers with a total sense of a brand rather than just a few tastes of a food or beverage or a trial size of a packaged-goods product. Event sampling can take place in stores as well as at a variety of other venues such as concerts, sporting events, and other places.

Exhibit 16-11 Armor All uses on-package samples for related products

Other Methods of Sampling

The four sampling methods just discussed are the most common, but several other methods are also used. Marketers may insert packets in magazines or newspapers (particularly Sunday supplements). Some tobacco and cereal companies send samples to consumers who call toll-free numbers to request them or mail in sample request forms. As discussed in Chapter 14, these sampling methods are becoming popular because they can help marketers build a database for direct marketing.

Many companies also use specialized sample distribution service companies. These firms help the company identify consumers who are nonusers of a product or users of a competing brand and develop appropriate procedures for distributing a sample to them. Many college students receive sample packs at the beginning of the semester

Exhibit 16-12 Consumers can request samples from websites such as StartSampling.com

that contain trial sizes of such products as mouthwash, toothpaste, headache remedies, and deodorant.

The Internet is yet another way companies are making it possible for consumers to sample their products, and it is adding a whole new level of targeting to the mix by giving consumers the opportunity to choose the samples they want. Several companies offer websites where consumers can register to receive free samples for products that interest them including StartSampling, Eversave, and MyTownOffers. Exhibit 16-12 shows the home page from the website of StartSampling.com promoting the samples and offers it makes available to consumers. The service asks consumers qualifying questions on product usage that can be used by marketers to target their samples and other promotional offers more effectively.

Couponing

The oldest, most widely used, and most effective sales promotion tool is the cents-off coupon. Coupons have been around since 1895, when the C. W. Post Co. started using the penny-off coupon to sell its new Grape-Nuts cereal. In recent years, coupons have become increasingly popular with consumers, which may explain their explosive growth among manufacturers and retailers that use them as sales promotion incentives. As Figure 16-2 showed, coupons are the most popular sales promotion technique as they are used by nearly all the packaged-goods firms.

Coupon distribution rose dramatically over the past 30 years. The number of coupons distributed by consumer packaged-goods (CPG) marketers increased from 16 billion in 1968 to a peak of 310 billion in 1994. However, for the next seven years, coupon distribution declined steadily and dropped to 239 billion in 2001. Over the past several years, coupon distribution has rebounded reaching 258 billion in 2003, and distribution patterns indicate that this growth will continue. According to NCH Promotional Services, a company that tracks coupon distribution and redemption patterns, 75 percent of consumers in the United States use coupons and nearly 21 percent say they always use them when they shop. The average face value of coupons distributed increased from 21 cents in 1981 to \$1.03 in 2004. The average face value of the 3.6 billion coupons that were redeemed in 2004 was 82 cents.[30]

Adding additional fuel to the coupon explosion of the past several decades has been the vast number of coupons distributed through retailers that are not even included in these figures. In most markets, a number of grocery stores make manufacturers' coupons even more attractive to consumers by doubling the face value.

Advantages and Limitations of Coupons

Coupons have a number of advantages that make them popular sales promotion tools for both new and established products. First, coupons make it possible to offer a price reduction only to those consumers who are price-sensitive. Such consumers generally purchase *because* of coupons, while those who are not as concerned about price buy the brand at full value. Coupons also make it possible to reduce the retail price of a product without relying on retailers for cooperation, which can often be a problem. Coupons are generally regarded as second only to sampling as a promotional technique for generating trial. Since a coupon lowers the price of a product, it reduces the consumer's perceived risk associated with trial of a new brand. Coupons can encourage repurchase after initial trial. Many new products include a cents-off coupon inside the package to encourage repeat purchase.

Coupons can also be useful promotional devices for established products. They can encourage nonusers to try a brand, encourage repeat purchase among current users, and get users to try a new, improved version of a brand. Coupons may also help coax users of a product to trade up to more expensive brands. The product category where coupons are used most is disposable diapers, followed by cereal, detergent, and deodorant. Some of the product categories where coupons are used the least are carbonated beverages, candy, and gum.

But there are a number of problems with coupons. First, it can be difficult to estimate how many consumers will use a coupon and when. Response to a coupon is rarely immediate; it typically takes anywhere from two to six months to redeem one. A study of coupon redemption patterns by Inman and McAlister found that many coupons are redeemed just before the expiration date rather than in the period following the initial coupon drop.[31] Many marketers are attempting to expedite redemption by shortening the time period before expiration. The average length of time from issue date to expiration date for coupons in 2003 was 2.9 months for grocery products. However, coupons remain less effective than sampling for inducing initial product trial in a short period.

A problem associated with using coupons to attract new users to an established brand is that it is difficult to prevent the coupons from being used by consumers who already use the brand. Rather than attracting new users, coupons can end up reducing the company's profit margins among consumers who would probably purchase the product anyway.

Other problems with coupons include low redemption rates and high costs. Couponing program expenses include the face value of the coupon redeemed plus costs for production, distribution, and handling of the coupons. Figure 16-3 shows the calculations used to determine the costs of a couponing program using an FSI (free-standing insert) in the Sunday newspaper and a coupon with a face value of $1.00. As can be seen from these figures, the cost of a couponing program can be very high. Former Procter & Gamble chairman Durk Jager, who led efforts to rein in the company's use of coupons in the late 90s, has argued that they are extremely inefficient. He contends that it may cost as much as $50 to move a case of goods with coupons that may generate only $10 to $12 in gross profit.[32] Marketers should track coupon costs very carefully to ensure their use is economically feasible.

Another problem with coupon promotions is misredemption, or the cashing of a coupon without purchase of the brand. Coupon misredemption or fraud occurs in a number of ways, including:

- Redemption of coupons by consumers for a product or size not specified on the coupon.
- Redemption of coupons by salesclerks in exchange for cash.
- Gathering and redemption of coupons by store managers or owners without the accompanying sale of the product.
- Gathering or printing of coupons by criminals who sell them to unethical merchants, who, in turn, redeem them.
- Web-source coupon fraud, whereby phony coupons are produced and distributed online.

Coupon fraud and misredemption cost manufacturers an estimated $500 million a year in the United States alone. However, with the surge in Internet-related coupon fraud in recent years, this number is considered low.[33] Many manufacturers hold firm in their policy to not pay retailers for questionable amounts or suspicious types of coupon submissions. However, some companies are less aggressive, and this affects their profit margins. Marketers must allow a certain percentage for misredemption when estimating the costs of a couponing program. Ways to identify and control coupon misredemption, such as improved coding, are being developed, but it still remains a problem. Many retailers are tightening their policies regarding Internet coupons. For example, Wal-Mart will not

Figure 16-3 Calculating Couponing Costs

Cost per Coupon Redeemed: An Illustration	
1. Distribution cost 55,000,000 circulation × $6.25/M	$343,750
2. Redemptions at 1.5%	825,000
3. Redemption cost 825,000 redemptions × $1.00 face value	$825,000
4. Retailer handling cost and processor fees 825,000 redemptions × $.10	$82,500
5. Creative costs	$1,500
6. Total program cost Items 1 + 3 + 4 + 5	$1,252,750
Cost per coupon redeemed Cost divided by redemption	$1.52
7. Actual product sold on redemption (misredemption estimated at 20%) 825,000 × 80%	660,000
8. Cost per product moved Program cost divided by amount of product sold	$1.90

accept Internet coupons unless they have a valid expiration date, remit address, and bar code.

Coupon Distribution

Coupons can be disseminated to consumers by a number of means, including freestanding inserts in Sunday newspapers, direct mail, newspapers (either in individual ads or as a group of coupons in a cooperative format), magazines, and packages. Distribution through newspaper *freestanding inserts* is by far the most popular method for delivering coupons to consumers, accounting for 87 percent of all coupons distributed. This growth has come at the expense of vehicles such as manufacturers' ads in newspapers (newspaper ROP), newspaper co-op ads, and magazines.

There are a number of reasons why FSIs are the most popular way of delivering coupons, including their high-quality four-color graphics, competitive distribution costs, national same-day circulation, market selectivity, and the fact that they can be competition-free due to category exclusivity (by FSI company). Prices for a full-page FSI are currently about $6 to $7 per thousand, which makes FSI promotions very efficient and affordable. Because of their consumer popularity and predictable distribution, coupons distributed in FSIs are also a strong selling point with the retail trade.

The increased distribution of coupons through FSIs has, however, led to a clutter problem. Consumers are being bombarded with too many coupons, and although each FSI publisher offers product exclusivity in its insert, this advantage may be negated when there are three inserts in a Sunday paper. Redemption rates of FSI coupons have declined from 4 percent to only 1 percent and even lower for some products (Figure 16-4). These problems are leading many marketers to look at ways of delivering coupons that will result in less clutter and higher redemption rates, such as direct mail.

Direct mail accounts for about 2 percent of all coupons distributed. Most are sent by local retailers or through co-op mailings where a packet of coupons for many different products is sent to a household. These couponing programs include Metromail's Red Letter Day, Advo System's Super Coups, and Cox Target Media's Valpak. IMC Perspective 16-3 discusses how Cox Target Media recently redesigned the familiar Valpak blue envelope that delivers billions of coupons each year and created an advertising campaign to improve the image of the direct-mail piece.

Figure 16-4 Coupon Redemption Rates by Media Type

Media	Grocery Products	Health and Beauty Products
FSI	1.0%	1.1%
Newspaper	1.0	0.3
Magazine	1.1	0.4
Direct mail	3.7	4.2
Regular in-pack	5.2	3.6
Regular on-pack	7.5	20.8
In-pack cross-ruff	1.8	1.4
On-pack cross-ruff	4.8	6.8
Instant on-pack	20.0	41.1
Instant on-pack cross-ruff	4.7	23.9
Handout electronically dispensed	6.4	4.3
On-shelf distributed	7.3	8.3
All other handouts in store	3.2	5.2
All other handouts away from store	5.6	1.4
Internet	3.1	2.7

Source: NCH Marketing Services, 2004 Trend Report.

IMC PERSPECTIVE 16-3

Getting Consumers to Love the Valpak Blue Envelope

She loves talking to her friends
(saved 10% on long distance)
comfortable clothes
(saved $2 on a sweater)
relaxing at home
(saved $50 on home furnishings)
and the blue envelope.
There's something in it for you®.
Discover great savings like these inside the envelope and online at www.valpak.com.
To advertise, call 800-355-9642, today.

Cox Target Media provides direct-marketing services and solutions to advertisers who want to reach specific target audiences. Its first branded product, the Valpak blue envelope, has been mailed to consumers for over 35 years and is currently distributed to more than 50 million homes and businesses throughout the United States, Canada, Puerto Rico, and the United Kingdom. Every year, 500 Valpak mailings deliver over 20 billion coupons and advertising offers to consumers in highly recognizable light blue envelopes. Valpak is sold through a network of over 200 independent franchisees and has a varied reputation that depends on the quality of the local business owner and content mix. As a direct-mail product, Valpak relies on consumers to open the envelope and examine the contents to spur increased redemptions of the coupons and other promotional offers for its clients' products.

In 2001, Cox Target Media conducted extensive research to determine the overall awareness, growth potential, and consumer perception of the blue envelope. The research showed that Valpak's blue envelope was perceived as a locally mailed product and that its dated design, which had not changed in 15 years, was a turn-off to image-conscious national advertisers. Cox wanted to attract new advertisers as users of its service and leverage relationships with its existing clients, and it recognized that these problems had to be addressed. In 2002 Cox redesigned the blue envelope and launched an extensive advertising campaign to reposition Valpak with the consumer. The new design includes an updated Valpak logo as well as a Valpak.com logo to send shoppers online, splashy graphics and reenergized blue colors to refresh the envelope, and lively color photos that change with the seasons.

Cox also created the Valpak "Loves" advertising campaign with the goal of upscaling the Valpak image in the mind of consumers and potential advertisers. The campaign was designed to connect the contents of the blue envelope with the activities and objects that are already central to the end-users' lives. Television commercials and complementary print ads were created featuring consumers who closely profile the demographics of people who already take advantage of the coupons and other savings offers found within Valpak. They are everyday, yet upscale, people who enjoy everyday pleasures like improving their homes or engaging in a family outing. The ads also highlight the categories of content and savings that Cox's research indicated consumers want to find inside the blue envelope. The tagline used in all of the commercials and print ads is "There's something in it for you," which reinforces the benefits consumers receive from the offers contained in the Valpak envelope.

The TV commercials created for the campaign run on national spot television in 92 Nielsen Designated Market Area territories. Valpak franchise owners were also invited to supplement the national spot placement by purchasing additional time on local stations. For the national print campaign, Valpak ads are run in a selection of women's aspirational magazines including *Martha Stewart Living* and *O: The Oprah Magazine* as well as service publications such as *Woman's Day, Redbook,* and *Good Housekeeping.*

The "Loves" campaign has been successful in improving both consumer and advertiser perceptions of the quality associated with the Valpak brand and the contents of the blue envelope. Valpak has always been perceived as the best, as well as the best known, of all the cooperative direct-mail marketing vehicles. The repositioning campaign has helped Cox attract a number of high-profile, national advertisers as promotional partners, including Burger King and CBS. For example, CBS has partnered with Valpak for several years to promote the network's prime-time television lineup through mailings and on the Valpak.com website, which is the company's Internet extension. It has also been successful in getting consumers to think twice before tossing out the ubiquitous blue envelopes that appear in their mailboxes. They know there truly is "something in it" for them.

Source: Melissa Fisher, vice president of marketing and communication, Cox Target Media; "CBS Tunes in Primetime Viewer with Valpak," *Business Wire,* September 12, 2005, p. 1.

Direct-mail couponing has several advantages. First, the mailing can be sent to a broad audience or targeted to specific geographic or demographic markets such as teenagers, senior citizens, Hispanics, and other market segments. Firms that mail their own coupons can be quite selective about recipients. Another important advantage of direct-mail couponing is a redemption rate of nearly 3 percent, much higher than for FSIs. Direct-mail couponing can also be combined with a sample, which makes it a very effective way to gain the attention of consumers.

The major disadvantage of direct-mail coupon delivery is the expense relative to other distribution methods. The cost per thousand for distributing coupons through co-op mailings ranges from $10 to $15, and more targeted promotions can cost $20 to $25 or even more. Also, the higher redemption rate of mail-delivered coupons may result from the fact that many recipients are already users of the brand who take advantage of the coupons sent directly to them.

The use of *newspapers* and *magazines* as couponing vehicles has declined dramatically since the introduction of FSIs as only 1 percent of coupons are distributed via newspapers. The advantages of newspapers as a couponing vehicle include market selectivity, shorter lead times with timing to the day, cooperative advertising opportunities that can lead to cost efficiencies, and promotional tie-ins with retailers. Other advantages of newspaper-delivered coupons are the broad exposure and consumer receptivity. Many consumers actively search the newspaper for coupons, especially on Sundays or "food day" (when grocery stores advertise their specials). This enhances the likelihood of the consumer at least noticing the coupon. Problems with newspapers as couponing vehicles include higher distribution costs, poor reproduction quality, clutter, and declining readership of newspapers; all contribute to low redemption rates.

The use of magazines as a couponing vehicle has also declined steadily since the introduction of FSIs. Magazines now account for only about 2 percent of the total number of coupons distributed each year. Distribution of coupons through magazines can take advantage of the selectivity of the publication to reach specific target audiences, along with enhanced production capabilities and extended copy life in the home. However, the cost of distributing coupons through magazines is very high and redemption rates are low (just under 1 percent).

Placing coupons either *inside* or on the *outside* of the *package* is a distribution method that accounts for about 2 percent of the coupons distributed. The in/on-package coupon has virtually no distribution costs and a much higher redemption rate than other couponing methods, averaging between 4 and nearly 20 percent. An in/on-pack coupon that is redeemable for the next purchase of the same brand is known as a **bounce-back coupon.** This type of coupon gives consumers an inducement to repurchase the brand.

Bounce-back coupons are often used with product samples to encourage the consumer to purchase the product after sampling. They may be included in or on the package during the early phases of a brand's life cycle to encourage repeat purchase, or they may be a defensive maneuver for a mature brand that is facing competitive pressure and wants to retain its current users. The main limitation of bounce-back coupons is that they go only to purchasers of the brand and thus do not attract nonusers. A bounce-back coupon placed on the package for Kellogg Company's Eggo brand waffles is shown in Exhibit 16-13.

Exhibit 16-13 Kellogg Company uses an on-package coupon to encourage repurchase

Another type of in/on-pack coupon is the **cross-ruff coupon,** which is redeemable on the purchase of a different product, usually one made by the same company but occasionally through a tie-in with another manufacturer. Cross-ruff coupons have a redemption rate of 4 to 7 percent and can be effective in encouraging consumers to try other products or brands. Companies with wide product lines, such as cereal manufacturers, often use these coupons.

Yet another type of package coupon is the **instant coupon,** which is attached to the outside of the package so the consumer can rip it off and redeem it immediately at the time of purchase. Instant coupons have the highest redemption levels of all types of coupons, averaging around 20 percent for grocery products and jumping to over 40 percent for health and beauty items. However, the redemption level is much lower for instant cross-ruff coupons, as it averages around 5 percent. Instant coupons give consumers an immediate point-of-purchase incentive, and can be selectively placed in terms of promotion timing and market region. Some companies prefer instant coupons to price-off deals because the latter require more cooperation from retailers and can be more expensive, since every package must be reduced in price.

Another distribution method that has experienced strong growth over the past 10 years or so is **in-store couponing,** which includes all co-op couponing programs distributed in a retail store environment. This medium now accounts for around 6 percent of total coupon distribution. Coupons are distributed to consumers in stores in several ways, including tear-off pads, handouts in the store (sometimes as part of a sampling demonstration), on-shelf dispensers, and electronic dispensers.

Exhibit 16-14 Catalina Marketing promotes its Simply Smart Marketing program

Most of the coupons distributed in stores are through ActMedia's Instant Coupon Machine. This coupon dispenser is mounted on the shelf in front of the product being promoted. It has blinking red lights to draw consumers' attention to the savings opportunity. These in-store coupons have several advantages: They can reach consumers when they are ready to make a purchase, increase brand awareness on the shelf, generate impulse buying, and encourage product trial. They also provide category exclusivity. In-store couponing removes the need for consumers to clip coupons from FSIs or print ads and then remember to bring them to the store. Redemption rates for coupons distributed by the Instant Coupon Machine average about 6 to 8 percent.

Another popular way to distribute in-store coupons is through electronic devices such as kiosks or at the checkout counter. Some electronically dispensed coupons, such as Catalina Marketing Corp.'s Checkout Coupon, are tied to scanner data at each grocery store checkout. When the specified product, such as a competitive brand, is purchased, the consumer receives a coupon at the checkout for the company's brand. Companies also use this system to link purchases of products that are related. For example, a consumer who purchases a caffeine-free cola might be issued a coupon for a decaffeinated coffee. Checkout coupons are part of the Simply Smart Marketing program offered by Catalina Marketing (Exhibit 16-14).

Major advantages of electronically dispensed checkout coupons are that they are cost-effective and can be targeted to specific categories of consumers, such as users of competitive or complementary products. Since 65 to 85 percent of a manufacturer's coupons are used by current customers, marketers want to target their coupons to users of competitive brands. Redemption rates for electronically dispensed coupons, average around 4 to 6 percent.

Couponing Trends Marketers are increasing their use of coupons once again after cutting back in recent years. The average U.S. household is still barraged with nearly 3,000 coupons per year. However, the consumer redemption of coupons is declining as the attractiveness of coupon offers has changed. For example, marketers have significantly reduced the durational period, with expiration dates of three months or less becoming prevalent, and moved to greater use of multiple-item purchase requirements. Consumers now redeem fewer than 2 percent of the hundreds of billions of coupons distributed each year. Concerns over the cost and effectiveness of coupons have led many marketers to cut back on their use. Critics argue that coupons cost too much to print, distribute, and process and that they do not benefit enough consumers. Former Procter & Gamble CEO Durk Jager echoed the sentiment of many consumer-product companies when he said, "Who can argue for a practice that fails 98 percent of the time?"[34]

Despite the growing sentiment among major marketers that coupons are inefficient and costly, very few companies, including Procter & Gamble, are likely to abandon them entirely.[35] Although most coupons never get used, consumers use some of them and have come to expect them. More than 80 percent of consumers use coupons and nearly one-quarter say they use them every time they shop. With so many consumers

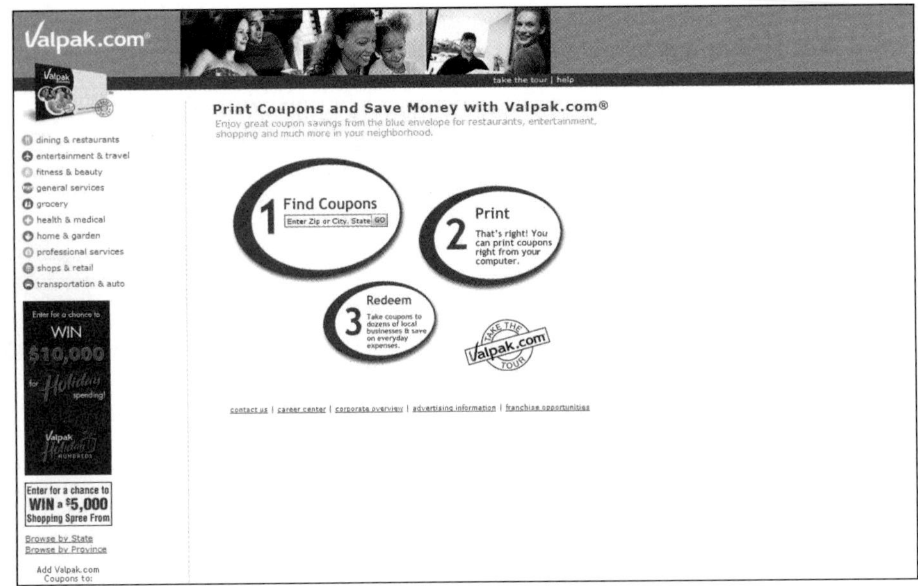

Exhibit 16-15 Coupons are now available online

eager for coupons, marketers will continue to accommodate them. However, companies as well as the coupon industry are looking for ways to improve on their use.

Marketers are continually searching for more effective couponing techniques. General Mills, Kellogg Company, and Post Cereals replaced brand-specific coupons with universal coupons good for any of their cereal brands. For example, to make its couponing spending more efficient, Post began using universal coupons worth $1.50 off two boxes (matching the average cereal-coupon discount of 75 cents) and cut coupon distribution in half.

Some marketers are broadening their use of account-specific direct-mail couponing, in which coupons are co-branded with individual retailers but can be used by consumers at any retail store. Procter & Gamble began using account-specific couponing with Tide detergent and has broadened the program to include mailings for a number of other brands.[36]

Some marketers and retailers are looking to the Internet as a medium for distributing coupons. Several companies now offer online couponing services. Catalina Marketing started Valupage.com as a way for marketers to reach consumers at home with promotions traditionally offered in-store, including coupons. Consumers can log on to the website, type in their Zip code, and choose from a list of participating grocery stores in their area and download manufacturer- and retailer-sponsored coupons. A number of retailers, particularly supermarkets, are also using the Internet to distribute coupons to encourage consumers to shop at their stores. Cox Target Media also offers consumers the opportunity to access coupons online, through Valpak.com. The website makes the same coupons and offers available to consumers that come in the Valpak direct-mail envelope (Exhibit 16-15).

Premiums

Premiums are a sales promotion device used by many marketers. A **premium** is an offer of an item of merchandise or service either free or at a low price that is an extra incentive for purchasers. Many marketers are eliminating toys and gimmicks in favor of value-added premiums that reflect the quality of the product and are consistent with its image and positioning in the market. Marketers spend over $4 billion a year on value-added premium incentives targeted at the consumer market. The two basic types of offers are the free premium and the self-liquidating premium.

Free Premiums

Free premiums are usually small gifts or merchandise included in the product package or sent to consumers who mail in a request along with a proof of purchase. In/on-package free premiums include toys, balls, trading cards, or other items included in cereal packages, as well as samples of one product included with another.

Surveys have shown that in/on-package premiums are consumers' favorite type of promotion.[37]

Package-carried premiums have high impulse value and can provide an extra incentive to buy the product. However, several problems are associated with their use. First, there is the cost factor, which results from the premium itself as well as from extra packaging that may be needed. Finding desirable premiums at reasonable costs can be difficult, particularly for adult markets, and using a poor premium may do more harm than good.

Exhibit 16-16 McDonald's Happy Meals use toys to help attract children

Another problem with these premiums is possible restrictions from regulatory agencies such as the Federal Trade Commission and the Food and Drug Administration or from industry codes regarding the type of premium used. The National Association of Broadcasters has strict guidelines regarding the advertising of premium offers to children. There is concern that premium offers will entice children to request a brand to get the promoted item and then never consume the product. The networks' policy on children's advertising is that a premium offer cannot exceed 15 seconds of a 30-second spot, and the emphasis must be on the product, not the premium.

Since most free mail-in premium offers require the consumer to send in more than one proof of purchase, they encourage repeat purchase and reward brand loyalty. But a major drawback of mail-in premiums is that they do not offer immediate reinforcement or reward to the purchaser, so they may not provide enough incentive to purchase the brand. Few consumers take advantage of mail-in premium offers; the average redemption rate is only 2 to 4 percent.[38]

Free premiums have become very popular in the restaurant industry, particularly among fast-food chains such as McDonald's and Burger King, which use premium offers in their kids' meals to attract children. McDonald's has become the world's largest toymaker on a unit basis, commissioning about 750 million toys per year for its Happy Meals (Exhibit 16-16). Many of the premium offers used by the fast-food giants have cross-promotional tie-ins with popular movies and can be very effective at generating incremental sales. McDonald's 10-year marketing partnership with Walt Disney Company, which gave the company exclusive rights to promotional tie-ins with Disney movies, ended in 2006. It is likely that McDonald's will negotiate movie tie-in deals on a case-by-case basis with a number of studios, including DreamWorks Animation SKG and Pixar Animation Studios, as well as Disney. McDonald's uses movie tie-ins as the basis for many of its Happy Meal promotions.[39]

Exhibit 16-17 American Airlines promotes the value of AAdvantage miles as a purchase incentive

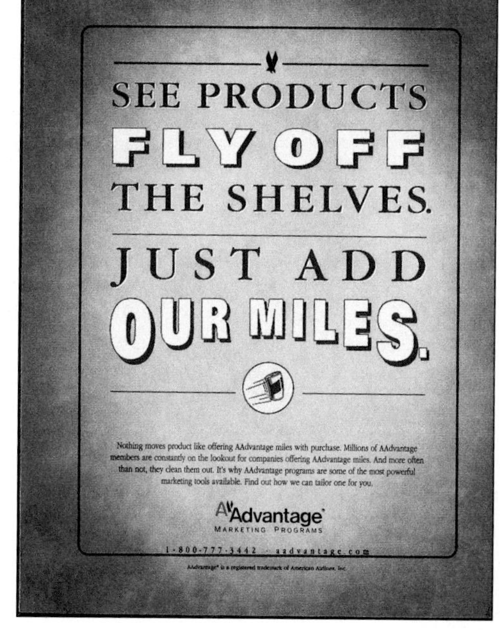

One of the fastest-growing types of incentive offers being used by marketers is airline miles, which have literally become a promotional currency. U.S. airlines make more than an estimated $2 billion each year selling miles to other marketers. Consumers are now choosing credit-card services, phone services, hotels, and many other products and services on the basis of mileage premiums for major frequent-flyer programs such as American Airlines' AAdvantage program or United Airlines' Mileage Plus program. Exhibit 16-17 shows a trade ad run by American Airlines promoting the value of AAdvantage miles as a promotional incentive that companies can offer their customers to help generate sales.

Self-Liquidating Premiums

Self-liquidating premiums require the consumer to pay some or all of the cost of the premium plus handling and mailing costs. The marketer usually purchases items used as self-liquidating premiums in large quantities and offers them to consumers at lower-than-retail prices. The goal is not to make a profit on the premium item but rather just to cover costs and offer a value to the consumer.

In addition to cost savings, self-liquidating premiums offer several advantages to marketers. Offering values to consumers through the premium products can create interest in the brand and goodwill that enhances the brand's image. These premiums can also encourage trade support and gain in-store displays for the brand and the premium offer. Self-liquidating premiums are often tied directly to the advertising campaign, so they extend the advertising message and contribute to consumer franchise building for a brand. For example, Philip Morris offers Western wear, outdoor items, and other types of Marlboro gear through its Marlboro Country catalog, which reinforces the cigarette brand's positioning theme.

Self-liquidating premium offers have the same basic limitation as mail-in premiums: a very low redemption rate. Fewer than 10 percent of U.S. households have ever sent for a premium, and fewer than 1 percent of self-liquidating offers are actually redeemed.[40] Low redemption rates can leave the marketer with a large supply of items with a logo or some other brand identification that makes them hard to dispose of. Thus, it is important to test consumers' reaction to a premium incentive and determine whether they perceive the offer as a value. Another option is to use premiums with no brand identification, but that detracts from their consumer franchise-building value.

Contests and Sweepstakes

Contests and sweepstakes are an increasingly popular consumer-oriented promotion. Marketers spent nearly $2 billion on these promotions in 2004. These promotions seem to have an appeal and glamour that such tools as cents-off coupons lack. Contests and sweepstakes are exciting because, as one expert has noted, many consumers have a "pot of gold at the end of the rainbow mentality" and think they can win the big prizes being offered.[41] The lure of sweepstakes and promotions has also been influenced by the "instant-millionaire syndrome" that has derived from huge cash prizes given by many state lotteries in recent years. Marketers are attracted to contests and sweepstakes as a way of generating attention and interest among a large number of consumers.

There are differences between contests and sweepstakes. A **contest** is a promotion where consumers compete for prizes or money on the basis of skills or ability. The company determines winners by judging the entries or ascertaining which entry comes closest to some predetermined criteria (e.g., picking the winning teams and total number of points in the Super Bowl or NCAA basketball tournament). Contests usually provide a purchase incentive by requiring a proof of purchase to enter or an entry form that is available from a dealer or advertisement. Some contests require consumers to read an ad or package or visit a store display to gather information needed to enter. Marketers must be careful not to make their contests too difficult to enter, as doing so might discourage participation among key prospects in the target audience.

A **sweepstakes** is a promotion where winners are determined purely by chance; it cannot require a proof of purchase as a condition for entry. Entrants need only submit their names for the prize drawing. While there is often an official entry form, handwritten entries must also be permitted. One form of sweepstakes is a **game,** which also has a chance element or odds of winning. Scratch-off cards with instant winners are a popular promotional tool. Some games occur over a longer period and require more involvement by consumers. Promotions where consumers must collect game pieces are popular among retailers and fast-food chains as a way to build store traffic and repeat purchases.

Because they are easier to enter, sweepstakes attract more entries than contests. They are also easier and less expensive to administer, since every entry does not have to be checked or judged. Choosing the winning entry in a sweepstakes requires only the random selection of a winner from the pool of entries or generation of a number to match those held by sweepstakes entrants. Experts note that the costs of mounting a sweepstakes are also very predictable. Companies can buy insurance to indemnify them and protect against the expense of awarding a big prize. In general, sweepstakes present marketers with a fixed cost, which is a major advantage when budgeting for a promotion.

Contests and sweepstakes can involve consumers with a brand by making the promotion product relevant or by connecting the prizes to the lifestyle, needs, or interests of the target audience. For example, Gillette often uses contests and sweepstakes that involve sports and offer prizes such as trips to major championship sporting events.

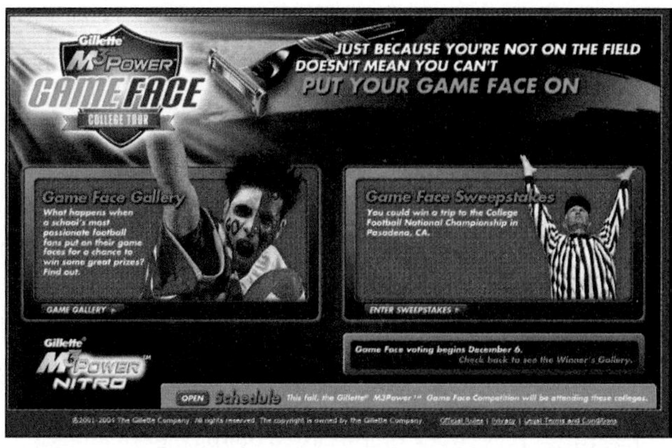

Exhibit 16-18 Gillette's M3 Power Game Face Sweepstakes ties in well to the product and the interest of the target audience

Exhibit 16-18 shows a creative promotion for the Gillette M3 Power razor, which targeted college football fans. The Game Face Sweepstakes was part of Gillette's Game Face College tour, which set up a tent at 24 selected college football games around the country. Fans could have their face shaved and/or painted or could come with their face already painted to show what they believed an M3 Power "Game Face" would look like. Pictures were taken of the faces, and sports fans could visit a website to vote for the best Game Face as well as enter the sweepstakes for a chance to win a trip to the College National Football championship game.

Many companies are developing contests, sweepstakes, and games that are interactive and delivered by cell phones and/or the Internet.[42] For example, PepsiCo has run several under-the-cap sweepstakes offering 100 million free Apple iTune downloads. Winning codes were randomly seeded under the caps of various brands such as Pepsi Cola and Sierra Mist. Winners could enter the code on the iTunes.com Music Store website and download a 99-cent song from the vast catalog. Some companies are now developing games that take advantage of the growth in use of cell phones and text messaging. There are now 165 mobile phone subscribers in the United States, 90 percent of whom can both send and receive text. As we discussed in Chapter 1, Frito-Lay used a text messaging and Internet-based promotion to launch its Doritos Black Pepper Jack brand. Chevrolet also used text messaging to drive entries to a sweepstakes offering a chance to win a 2005 Chevy Cobalt. Consumers could text the brand name to special operators as a way of entering the sweepstakes.[43]

Problems with Contests and Sweepstakes While the use of contests and sweepstakes continues to increase, there are some problems associated with these types of promotions. Many sweepstakes and/or contest promotions do little to contribute to consumer franchise building for a product or service and may even detract from it. The sweepstakes or contest often becomes the dominant focus rather than the brand, and little is accomplished other than giving away substantial amounts of money and/or prizes. Many promotional experts question the effectiveness of contests and sweepstakes. Some companies have cut back or even stopped using them because of concern over their effectiveness and fears that consumers might become dependent on them.[44] The sweepstakes industry also received a considerable amount of negative publicity recently. Lawsuits were filed by a number of states against American Family Publishing (AFP) for misleading consumers regarding their odds of winning large cash prizes in AFP's annual magazine subscription solicitation sweepstakes.[45]

Numerous legal considerations affect the design and administration of contests and sweepstakes.[46] These promotions are regulated by several federal agencies, and each of the 50 states has its own rules. The regulation of contests and sweepstakes has helped clean up the abuses that plagued the industry in the late 1960s and has improved consumers' perceptions of these promotions. But companies must still be careful in designing a contest or sweepstakes and awarding prizes. Most firms use consultants that specialize in the design and administration of contests and sweepstakes to avoid any legal problems, but they may still run into problems with promotions, as discussed in IMC Perspective 16-4.

A final problem with contests and sweepstakes is participation by professionals or hobbyists who submit many entries but have no intention of purchasing the product or service. Because most states make it illegal to require a purchase as a qualification for a sweepstakes entry, consumers can enter as many times as they wish. Professional players sometimes enter one sweepstakes several times, depending on the nature of the prizes and the number of entries the promotion attracts. Newsletters and websites are even available that inform them of all the contests and sweepstakes being held, the entry dates, estimated probabilities of winning for various numbers of entries, how to enter, and solutions to any puzzles or other information that might be needed. The presence of these professional entrants not only defeats the purpose of the promotion but also may discourage entries from consumers who think their chances of winning are limited.

IMC PERSPECTIVE 16-4

Marketers and Consumers Learn the Perils of Promotions

Contests, sweepstakes, and premium offers are often used by marketers to give consumers an extra incentive to purchase their products. However, when these promotions don't go as planned, they can embarrass a company or even create legal problems. A number of high-profile companies known for their marketing excellence have experienced problems with promotions over the years. These botched promotions were embarrassing for the companies and resulted in the loss of goodwill as well as money.

Kraft was one of the first to learn how expensive it can be when a promotion goes awry. In 1989, a printing error resulted in the printing of too many winning game pieces for a match-and-win game promotion. Kraft canceled the promotion but still had to spend nearly $4 million to compensate the winners—versus the $36,000 budgeted for prizes. The snafu gave birth to the "Kraft clause," a disclaimer stating that a marketer reserves the right to cancel a promotion if there are problems and hold a random drawing if there are more winners than prizes.

A few years later, PepsiCo had a major problem when a bottle-cap promotion offering a grand prize of 1 million pesos (about $36,000) went wrong in the Philippines. Due to a computer glitch, the winning number appeared on more than 500,000 bottle caps, which would have made the company liable for more than $18 billion in prize money. When the error was discovered, Pepsi announced that there was a problem and quickly offered to pay $19 for each winning cap, which ended up costing the company nearly $10 million. The furor caused by the botched promotion prompted anti-Pepsi rallies, death threats against Pepsi executives, and attacks on Pepsi trucks and bottling plants.

Harrah's Entertainment, Inc. recently made a major couponing error that ended up costing the company nearly $6 million. A mailing sent to its Total Rewards cardholders in its loyalty program included a coupon that members could redeem at Harrah's Joliet Casino near Chicago. Only a small number of the coupons were supposed to be worth $525 each, however, a printing error resulted in 11,000 coupons worth $525 being sent out. The coupons were barcoded but most of the codes did not match the $525 printed on the coupon's face value and casino staff initially refused to honor the coupons when the bar codes did not match the face value. However, the Illinois gaming board ordered Harrah's to honor all of the coupons and most were eventually redeemed.

McDonald's also ran into a major problem with a promotion when winning game pieces were embezzled from its popular Monopoly game promotion. McDonald's ran its first Monopoly game promotion in 1987 and began running it annually in 1991. However, in August 2001 the Federal Bureau of Investigation arrested eight people for embezzling winning game pieces from the Monopoly game as well as the company's "Who Wants to Be a Millionaire" sweepstakes in order to divert nearly $24 million worth of prizes to co-conspirators.

The conspiracy is believed to have begun as early as 1995, and the FBI investigation, which was conducted with McDonald's cooperation, lasted two years before the arrests were made. Fifty-one people were indicted in the case, nearly all of whom either pleaded guilty or were convicted following trial. Among those pleading guilty was the director of security for McDonald's promotional agency, Simon Marketing, who stole the winning tickets and conspired with the others to distribute them to a network of recruiters who solicited individuals to falsely claim they were legitimate game winners.

Following the arrests McDonald's immediately fired Simon Marketing, as did several other of the agency's clients, including Kraft Foods and Philip Morris Co. To win back consumer confidence, McDonald's ran a five-day instant giveaway promotion in which consumers could win 55 cash prizes ranging from $1,000 to $1 million. The company also created an independent task force comprised of antifraud and game security experts to review procedures for future promotions. McDonald's began running the Monopoly promotion again in 2003, and it has again become very popular among consumers. Most industry experts maintain that McDonald's was a rare victim in an industry conducted honestly and legitimately and policed by many private and public watchdogs.

Marketers are not the only ones who encounter problems with promotions as consumers who win contests and sweepstakes often learn that there may be unexpected tax consequences because the prizes are treated as income by the Internal Revenue Service. For example, in 2004, 276 audience members on *The Oprah Winfrey Show* each won a Pontiac G6 automobile valued at $28,500. Winners could decline the prize, accept the car and pay the taxes, or immediately sell the car and get the difference in cash and pay taxes on that amount. A winner of a recent American Airlines "We know why you fly" contest faced even greater tax liability as the grand prize was 12 round-trip restricted coach tickets for two to anywhere in the world the airline flies. The contest's official rules explained that winners must pay federal and state income taxes, where applicable, on American's approximated retail value of the 24 tickets, which the airline valued at $2,200 per ticket or $52,800. The New York resident who won the contest was facing taxes on the tickets that could amount to nearly $19,000 and so declined the prize.

While marketers continue to use contests, sweepstakes, and games, they are taking precautions to safeguard them in an attempt to avoid the problems these companies encountered. Consumers who enter these promotions might also be well-advised to read the fine print to understand the tax liability associated with the prize and make sure they can really afford to win.

Sources: Kate McArthur, "Guilty Verdict for Four in McDonald's Sweepstakes Scandal," AdAge.com, September 3, 2002; Kate McArthur, "McSwindle," *Advertising Age,* August 27, 2002, pp. 1, 22; Betsy Spethmann, "The Perils of Promotion," *Promo,* November 1996, pp. 22, 134; Melanie Trottman and Ron Lieber, "Contest Winner Declines 'Free' Airline Tickets," *The Wall Street Journal,* July 6, 2005; Betsy Spethmann, "Harrah's Coupon Error To Cost $2.8 Billion," *promomagazine.com,* November 23, 2005.

Refunds and Rebates

Refunds (also known as *rebates*) are offers by the manufacturer to return a portion of the product purchase price, usually after the consumer supplies some proof of purchase. Consumers are generally very responsive to rebate offers, particularly as the size of the savings increases. Rebates are used by makers of all types of products, ranging from packaged goods to major appliances, cars, and computer software. Exhibit 16-19 shows an ad promoting a rebate on Intuit's popular tax and financial software products, TurboTax and Quicken.

Exhibit 16-19 Intuit uses a rebate offer in a free copy of Quicken to purchasers of TurboTax

Packaged-goods marketers often use refund offers to induce trial of a new product or encourage users of another brand to switch. Consumers may perceive the savings offered through a cash refund as an immediate value that lowers the cost of the item, even though those savings are realized only if the consumer redeems the refund or rebate offer. Redemption rates for refund offers typically range from 1 to 3 percent for print and point-of-purchase offers and 5 percent for in/on-package offers.

Refund offers can also encourage repeat purchase. Many offers require consumers to send in multiple proofs of purchase. The size of the refund offer may even increase as the number of purchases gets larger. Some packaged-goods companies are switching away from cash refund offers to coupons or cash/coupon combinations. Using coupons in the refund offer enhances the likelihood of repeat purchase of the brand.

Evaluating Refunds and Rebates

Rebates can help create new users and encourage brand switching or repeat purchase behavior, or they can be a way to offer a temporary price reduction. This offer can influence purchase even if the consumer fails to realize the savings, so the marketer can reduce price for much less than if it used a direct price-off deal.

Some problems are associated with refunds and rebates. Many consumers are not motivated by a refund offer because of the delay and the effort required to obtain the savings. They do not want to be bothered saving cash register receipts and proofs of purchase, filling out forms, and mailing in the offer.[47] A study of consumer perceptions found a negative relationship between the use of rebates and the perceived difficulties associated with the redemption process.[48] The study also found that consumers perceive manufacturers as offering rebates to sell products that are not faring well. Nonusers of rebates were particularly likely to perceive the redemption process as too complicated and to suspect manufacturers' motives. This implies that companies using rebates must simplify the redemption process and use other promotional elements such as advertising to retain consumer confidence in the brand.

When small refunds are being offered, marketers may find other promotional incentives such as coupons or bonus packs more effective. They must be careful not to overuse rebate offers and confuse consumers about the real price and value of a product or service. Also, consumers can become dependent on rebates and delay their purchases or purchase only brands for which a rebate is available. Many retailers have become disenchanted with rebates and the burden and expense of administering them.[49]

Exhibit 16-20 Bonus packs provide more value for consumers

Bonus Packs

Bonus packs offer the consumer an extra amount of a product at the regular price by providing larger containers or extra units (Exhibit 16-20). Bonus packs result in a lower cost per unit for the consumer and provide extra value as well as more product for the money. There are several advantages to bonus pack promotions. First, they give marketers a direct way to provide extra value without having to get involved with complicated coupons or refund offers. The additional value of a bonus pack is generally obvious to the consumer and can have a strong impact on the purchase decision at the time of purchase.

Bonus packs can also be an effective defensive maneuver against a competitor's promotion or introduction of a new brand. By loading current users with large amounts of its product, a marketer can often remove these consumers from the market and make them less susceptible to a competitor's promotional efforts. Bonus packs may result in larger purchase orders and favorable display space in the store if relationships with retailers are good. They do, however, usually require additional shelf space without providing any extra profit margins for the retailer, so the marketer can encounter problems with bonus packs if trade relationships are not good. Another problem is that bonus packs may appeal primarily to current users who probably would have purchased the brand anyway or to promotion-sensitive consumers who may not become loyal to the brand.

Price-Off Deals

Another consumer-oriented promotion technique is the direct **price-off deal,** which reduces the price of the brand. Price-off reductions are typically offered right on the package through specially marked price packs, as shown in Exhibit 16-21. Typically, price-offs range from 10 to 25 percent off the regular price, with the reduction coming out of the manufacturer's profit margin, not the retailer's. Keeping the retailer's margin during a price-off promotion maintains its support and cooperation.

Marketers use price-off promotions for several reasons. First, since price-offs are controlled by the manufacturer, it can make sure the promotional discount reaches the consumer rather than being kept by the trade. Like bonus packs, price-off deals usually present a readily apparent value to shoppers, especially when they have a reference price point for the brand and thus recognize the value of the discount.[50] So price-offs can be a strong influence at the point of purchase when price comparisons are being made. Price-off promotions can also encourage consumers to purchase larger quantities, preempting competitors' promotions and leading to greater trade support.

Price-off promotions may not be favorably received by retailers, since they can create pricing and inventory problems. Most retailers will not accept packages with a specific price shown, so the familiar *X* amount off the regular price must be used. Also, like bonus packs, price-off deals appeal primarily to regular users instead of attracting nonusers. Finally, the Federal Trade Commission has regulations regarding the conditions that price-off labels must meet and the frequency and timing of their use.

Exhibit 16-21 Examples of price-off packages

Loyalty Programs

One of the fastest-growing areas of sales promotion is the use of **loyalty programs** (also referred to as *continuity* or *frequency programs*). American Airlines was one of the first major companies to use loyalty programs when it introduced its AAdvantage frequent-flyer program in 1981. Since then frequency programs have become commonplace in a number of product and service categories, particularly travel and hospitality, as well as among retailers. Virtually every airline, car rental company, and hotel chain has some type of frequency program. American Airlines has nearly 44 million members in its AAdvantage program, while Marriott International has enlisted more than 18 million business travelers into its Rewards program.

Many packaged-goods companies are also developing loyalty programs. Pillsbury, Nestlé, Kraft, and others have recently introduced continuity programs that offer consumers the opportunity to accumulate points for continuing to purchase their brands; the points can be redeemed for gifts and prizes. For example, Kellogg launched a frequency program called "Eet and Ern" that targets younger consumers. The program allows them to find a 10-character code on the inside of specially marked packages of Kellogg products, enter the code at the EetandErn.com website, and receive a downloadable reward. They can also participate in other special promotions including contests, sweepstakes, special offers, games, and other activities. The frequency program has been very effective and has won awards for its loyalty impact.[51]

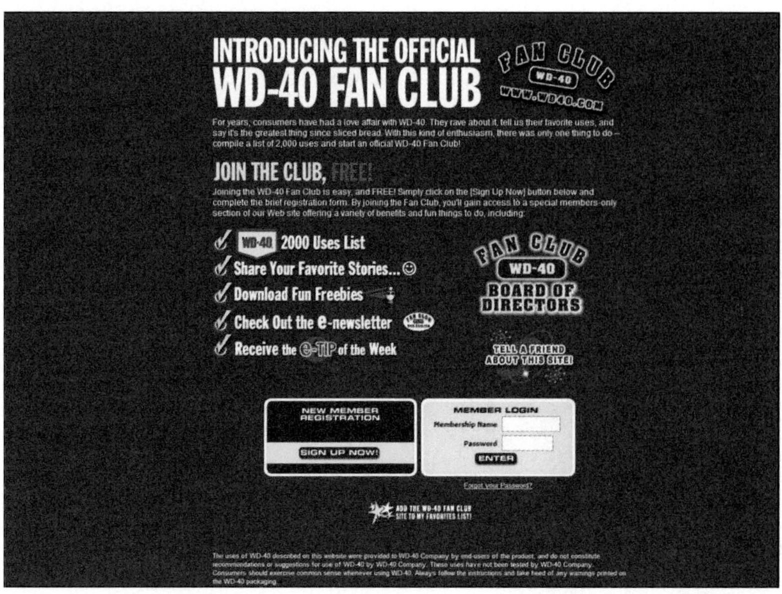

Exhibit 16-22 The WD-40 Fan Club is a popular customer loyalty program

Loyalty programs have become particularly popular among grocery stores.[52] Nearly 7,000 supermarkets now have loyalty programs that offer members discounts, a chance to accumulate points that can be redeemed for rewards, newsletters, and other special services. Loyalty programs are also used by a variety of other retailers, including department stores, home centers, bookstores, and even local bagel shops.

There are a number of reasons why loyalty programs have become so popular. Marketers view these programs as a way of encouraging consumers to use their products or services on a continual basis and as a way of developing strong customer loyalty. Many companies are also realizing the importance of customer retention and understand that the key to retaining and growing market share is building relationships with loyal customers. Frequency programs also provide marketers with the opportunity to develop databases containing valuable information on their customers that can be used to better understand their needs, interests, and characteristics as well as to identify and track a company's most valuable customers. These databases can also be used to target specific programs and offers to customers to increase the amount they purchase and/or to build stronger relationships with them. For example, the WD-40 Fan Club is a loyalty program for the brand which provides members with product information, usage tips, newsletters, downloads of games, and other benefits (Exhibit 16-22). The fan club has nearly 70,000 members who educate each other about creative ways to use the solvent and serve as advocates for the brand.[53]

As frequency programs become more common, marketers will be challenged to find ways to use them as a means of differentiating their product, service, business, or retail store. It has been argued that many of the loyalty programs developed by marketers are really short-term promotions that overreward regular users and do little to develop long-term loyalty.[54] A recent study by a loyalty marketing firm found that 66 percent of consumers say that discounts are the main reason they participate in loyalty programs. This study also found that many consumers drop out of loyalty programs because of the length of time it takes to accumulate reward points.[55] Marketers must find ways to make their loyalty programs more than just discount or frequent-buyer programs. This will require the careful management of databases to identify and track valuable customers and their purchase history and the strategic use of targeted loyalty promotions.

Event Marketing

Another type of consumer-oriented promotion that has become very popular in recent years is the use of event marketing. It is important to make a distinction between *event marketing* and *event sponsorships,* as the two terms are often used interchangeably yet they refer to different activities. **Event marketing** is a type of promotion where a company or brand is linked to an event or where a themed activity is developed for the purpose of creating experiences for consumers and promoting a product or service. Marketers often do event marketing by associating their product with some popular activity such as a sporting event, concert, fair, or festival. However, marketers also create their own events to use for promotional purposes. For example, the opening

CROWD BUILDING TAKES CREATIVITY
Planners rank advance attendance methods by importance
1 Other (Internet, e-mail, phone, cross-promotion with partner venues)
2 Direct Mail
3 Guerilla marketing
4 In-store promotion
5 Local radio
6 Locally distributed FSI
7 Local TV

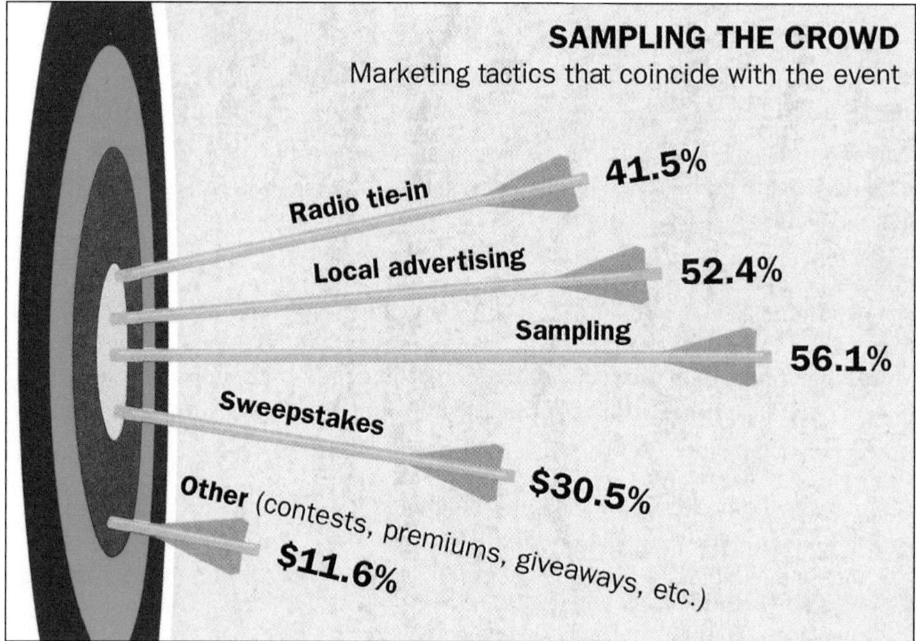

Exhibit 16-23 A variety of activities are used both to promote events and as part of the events

vignette to this chapter discussed how PepsiCo created the Dew Action Sports Tour and holds events in various cities.

An **event sponsorship** is an integrated marketing communications activity where a company develops actual sponsorship relations with a particular event and provides financial support in return for the right to display a brand name, logo, or advertising message and be identified as a supporter of the event. Event marketing often takes place as part of a company's sponsorship of activities such as concerts, the arts, social causes, and sporting events. Decisions and objectives for event sponsorships are often part of an organization's public relations activities and are discussed in the next chapter.

Event marketing has become a very popular part of the integrated marketing communications programs of many companies as they view them as excellent promotional opportunities and a way to associate their brands with certain lifestyles, interests, and activities.[56] Events can be an effective way to connect with consumers in an environment where they are comfortable with receiving a promotional message. Moreover, consumers often expect companies to be part of events and welcome their participation as they make the events more entertaining, interesting, and exciting. Marketers can use events to distribute samples as well as information about their products and services or to actually let consumers experience their brands. As illustrated in Exhibit 16-23, event planners use a variety of techniques to drive attendance to their events as well as a number of marketing tactics that coincide with the event.

Summary of Consumer-Oriented Promotions and Marketer Objectives

The discussion of the various sales promotion techniques shows that marketers use these tools to accomplish a variety of objectives. As noted at the beginning of the chapter, sales promotion techniques provide consumers with an *extra incentive* or *reward* for engaging in a certain form of behavior such as purchasing a brand. For some types of sales promotion tools the incentive the consumer receives is immediate, while for others the reward is delayed and is not realized immediately. Marketers often evaluate sales promotion tools in terms of their ability to accomplish specific objectives and consider whether the impact of the promotion will be immediate or delayed. Figure 16-5 outlines which sales promotion tools can be used to accomplish various

Figure 16-5 Consumer-Oriented Sales Promotion Tools for Various Marketing Objectives

Consumer Reward Incentive	Marketing Objective: Induce trial	Customer retention/loading	Support IMC program/ build brand equity
Immediate	• Sampling • Instant coupons • In-store coupons • In-store rebates	• Price-off deals • Bonus packs • In- and on-package free premiums • Loyalty programs	• Events • In- and on-package free premiums
Delayed	• Media- and mail-delivered coupons • Mail-in refunds and rebates • Free mail-in premiums • Scanner- and Internet-delivered coupons	• In- and on-package coupons • Mail-in refunds and rebates • Loyalty programs	• Self-liquidating premiums • Free mail-in premiums • Contests and sweepstakes • Loyalty programs

objectives of marketers and identifies whether the extra incentive or reward is immediate or delayed.[57]

It should be noted that in Figure 16-5 some of the sales promotion techniques are listed more than once because they can be used to accomplish more than one objective. For example, loyalty programs can be used to retain customers by providing both immediate and delayed rewards. Shoppers who belong to loyalty programs sponsored by supermarkets and receive discounts every time they make a purchase are receiving immediate rewards that are designed to retain them as customers. Some loyalty promotions such as frequency programs used by airlines, car rental companies, and hotels offer delayed rewards by requiring that users accumulate points to reach a certain level or status before the points can be redeemed. Loyalty programs can also be used by marketers to help build brand equity. For example, when an airline or car rental company sends its frequent users upgrade certificates, the practice helps build relationships with these customers and thus contributes to brand equity.

While marketers use consumer-oriented sales promotions to provide current and/or potential customers with an extra incentive, they also use these promotions as part of their marketing program to leverage trade support. Retailers are more likely to stock a brand, purchase extra quantities, or provide additional support such as end-aisle displays when they know a manufacturer is running a promotion during a designated period. The development of promotional programs targeted toward the trade is a very important part of the marketing process and is discussed in the next section.

Trade-Oriented Sales Promotion

Objectives of Trade-Oriented Sales Promotion

Like consumer-oriented promotions, sales promotion programs targeted to the trade should be based on well-defined objectives and measurable goals and a consideration of what the marketer wants to accomplish. Typical objectives for promotions targeted to marketing intermediaries such as wholesalers and retailers include obtaining distribution and support for new products, maintaining support for established brands, encouraging retailers to display established brands, and building retail inventories.

Obtain Distribution for New Products

Trade promotions are often used to encourage retailers to give shelf space to new products. Manufacturers recognize that only a limited amount of shelf space is available in supermarkets, drugstores, and other major retail outlets. Thus, they provide retailers with financial incentives to stock new products. For example, Lever Brothers used heavy sampling and high-value coupons in the successful introduction of Lever 2000 bar soap. However, in addition to these consumer promotions, the company used discounts to the trade to encourage retailers to stock and promote the new brand.

While trade discounts or other special price deals are used to encourage retailers and wholesalers to stock a new brand, marketers may use other types of promotions to get them to push the brand. Merchandising allowances can get retailers to display a new product in high-traffic areas of stores, while incentive programs or contests can encourage wholesale or retail store personnel to push a new brand.

Maintain Trade Support for Established Brands

Trade promotions are often designed to maintain distribution and trade support for established brands. Brands that are in the mature phase of their product life cycle are vulnerable to losing wholesale and/or retail distribution, particularly if they are not differentiated or face competition from new products. Trade deals induce wholesalers and retailers to continue to carry weaker products because the discounts increase their profit margins. Brands with a smaller market share often rely heavily on trade promotions, since they lack the funds required to differentiate themselves from competitors through media advertising.

Even if a brand has a strong market position, trade promotions may be used as part of an overall marketing strategy. For example, Heinz has relied heavily on trade promotions to hold its market share position for many of its brands. Many consumer packaged-goods companies count on trade promotions to maintain retail distribution and support.

Encourage Retailers to Display Established Brands

Another objective of trade-oriented promotions is to encourage retailers to display and promote an established brand. Marketers recognize that many purchase decisions are made in the store and promotional displays are an excellent way of generating sales. An important goal is to obtain retail store displays of a product away from its regular shelf location. A typical supermarket has approximately 50 display areas at the ends of aisles, near checkout counters, and elsewhere. Marketers want to have their products displayed in these areas to increase the probability shoppers will come into contact with them. Even a single display can increase a brand's sales significantly during a promotion.

Exhibit 16-24 This brochure shows retailers the various promotions Chicken of the Sea planned to use for its various products

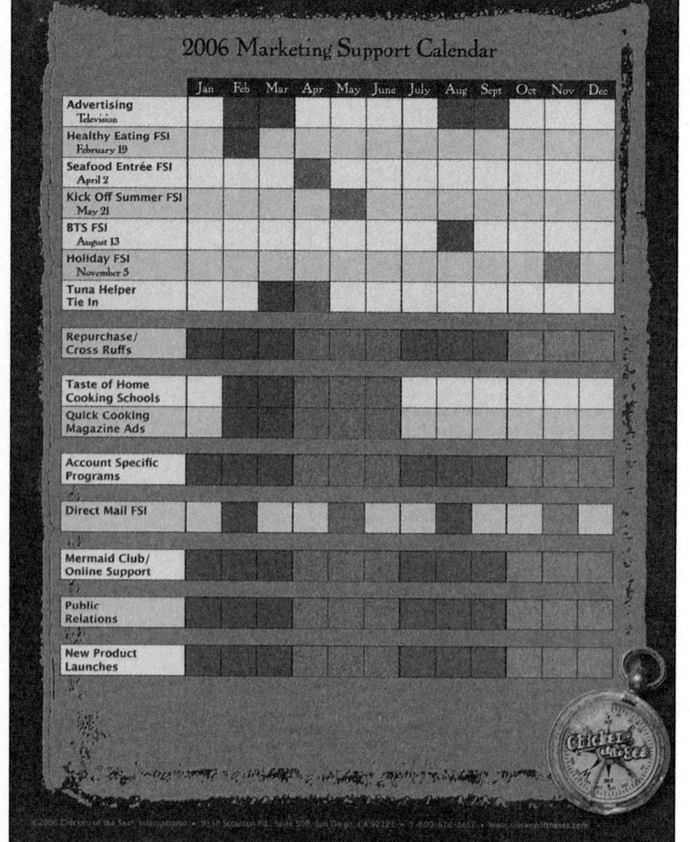

Manufacturers often use multifaceted promotional programs to encourage retailers to promote their products at the retail level. For example, Exhibit 16-24 shows a marketing support calendar that Chicken of the Sea International provided to retailers showing the various promotions the company planned to use during the year for its Chicken of the Sea brands. The company uses a variety of IMC tools including media advertising, public relations, online support of its Mermaid Club loyalty program, and a number of sales promotion tools. These include FSI distribution via direct mail as well as newspapers, account-specific promotions, repurchase/cross ruff coupons, and event marketing through the Taste of Home Cooking schools, which visit 125 cities nationwide.

Build Retail Inventories

Manufacturers often use trade promotions to build the inventory levels of retailers or other channel members. There are several reasons manufacturers want to load retailers with their products. First, wholesalers and retailers are more likely to push a product when they have high inventory levels rather than storing it in their warehouses or back rooms. Building channel members' inventories also ensures they will not run out of stock and thus miss sales opportunities.

Some manufacturers of seasonal products offer large promotional discounts so that retailers will stock up on their products before the peak selling season begins. This enables the manufacturer to smooth out seasonal fluctuations in its production schedule and passes on some of the inventory carrying costs to retailers or wholesalers. When retailers stock up on a product before the peak selling season, they often run special promotions and offer discounts to consumers to reduce excess inventories.

Exhibit 16-25 This contest sponsored by Chicken of the Sea was targeted toward food-service distributors

Types of Trade-Oriented Promotions

Manufacturers use a variety of trade promotion tools as inducements for wholesalers and retailers. Next we examine some of the most often used types of trade promotions and some factors marketers must consider in using them. These promotions include contests and incentives, trade allowances, displays and point-of-purchase materials, sales training programs, trade shows, and co-op advertising.

Contests and Incentives

Manufacturers may develop contests or special incentive programs to stimulate greater selling effort and support from reseller management or sales personnel. Contests or incentive programs can be directed toward managers who work for a wholesaler or distributor as well as toward store or department managers at the retail level. Manufacturers often sponsor contests for resellers and use prizes such as trips or valuable merchandise as rewards for meeting sales quotas or other goals. Exhibit 16-25 shows a contest Chicken of the Sea sponsored for food-service distributors who call on restaurants.

Contests or special incentives are often targeted at the sales personnel of the wholesalers, distributors/dealers, or retailers. These salespeople are an important link in the distribution chain because they are likely to be very familiar with the market, more frequently in touch with the customer (whether it be another reseller or the ultimate consumer), and more numerous than the manufacturer's own sales organization. Manufacturers often devise incentives or contests for these sales personnel. These programs may involve cash payments made directly to the retailer's or wholesaler's sales staff to encourage them to promote and sell a manufacturer's product. These payments are known as **push money** (pm) or *spiffs*. For example, an appliance manufacturer may pay a $25 spiff to retail sales personnel for selling a certain model or size. In sales contests, salespeople can win trips or valuable merchandise for meeting certain goals established by the manufacturer. As shown in Figure 16-6, these incentives may be tied to product sales, new account placements, or merchandising efforts.

While contests and incentive programs can generate reseller support, they can also be a source of conflict between retail sales personnel and management. Some retailers want to maintain control over the selling activities of their sales staffs. They don't want their salespeople devoting an undue amount of effort to trying to win a contest or receive incentives offered by the manufacturer. Nor do they want their people becoming too aggressive in pushing products that serve their own interests instead of the product or model that is best for the customer.

Many retailers refuse to let their employees participate in manufacturer-sponsored contests or to accept incentive payments. Retailers that do allow them often have strict guidelines and require management approval of the program.

Trade Allowances

Probably the most common trade promotion is some form of **trade allowance,** a discount or deal offered to retailers or wholesalers to encourage them to stock, promote, or display the manufacturer's products. Types of allowances offered to retailers include buying allowances, promotional or display allowances, and slotting allowances.

Figure 16-6 Three Forms of Promotion Targeted to Reseller Salespeople

- Product or Program Sales

  Awards are tied to the selling of a product, for example:

  Selling a specified number of cases

  Selling a specified number of units

  Selling a specified number of promotional programs

- New Account Placements

  Awards are tied to:

  The number of new accounts opened

  The number of new accounts ordering a minimum number of cases or units

  Promotional programs placed in new accounts

- Merchandising Efforts

  Awards are tied to:

  Establishing promotional programs (such as theme programs)

  Placing display racks, counter displays, and the like

Buying Allowances A buying allowance is a deal or discount offered to resellers in the form of a price reduction on merchandise ordered during a fixed period. These discounts are often in the form of an **off-invoice allowance,** which means a certain per-case amount or percentage is deducted from the invoice. A buying allowance can also take the form of *free goods;* the reseller gets extra cases with the purchase of specific amounts (for example, 1 free case with every 10 cases purchased).

Buying allowances are used for several reasons. They are easy to implement and are well accepted, and sometimes expected, by the trade. They are also an effective way to encourage resellers to buy the manufacturer's product, since they will want to take advantage of the discounts being offered during the allowance period. Manufacturers offer trade discounts expecting wholesalers and retailers to pass the price reduction through to consumers, resulting in greater sales. However, as discussed shortly, this is often not the case.

Exhibit 16-26 Chicken of the Sea encourages retailers to use in-store displays of its products

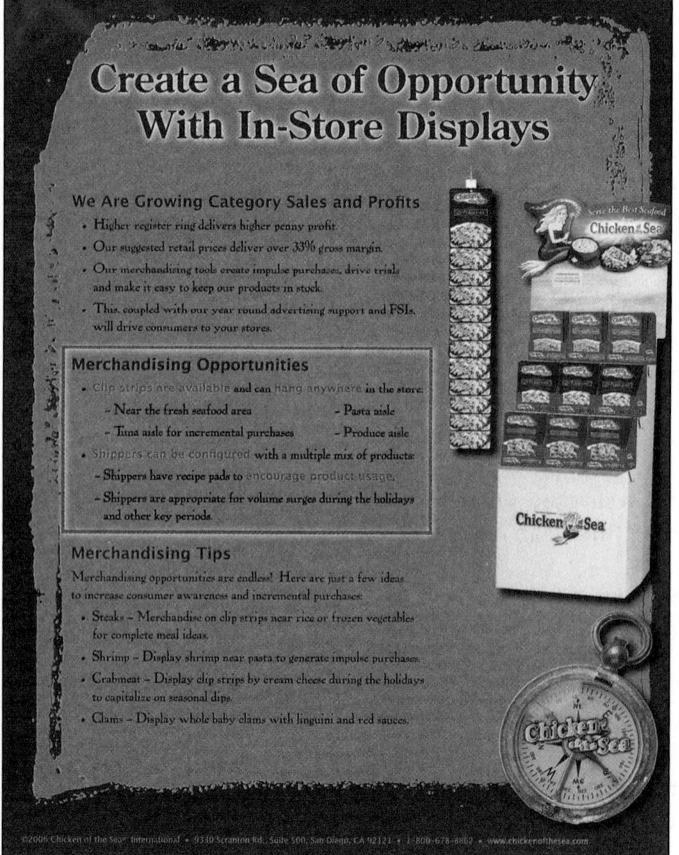

Promotional Allowances Manufacturers often give retailers allowances or discounts for performing certain promotional or merchandising activities in support of their brands. These merchandising allowances can be given for providing special displays away from the product's regular shelf position, running in-store promotional programs, or including the product in an ad. The manufacturer generally has guidelines or a contract specifying the activity to be performed to qualify for the promotional allowance. The allowance is usually a fixed amount per case or a percentage deduction from the list price for merchandise ordered during the promotional period.

Exhibit 16-26 shows a trade promotional piece used by Chicken of the Sea International to inform retailers of the merchandising opportunities available for its products and to encourage them to use in-store displays. An important goal of the company's trade marketing efforts is to get retailers to set up more displays of its products in various areas of their stores where related products are sold.

Slotting Allowances In recent years, retailers have been demanding a special allowance for agreeing to handle a new product. **Slotting allowances,** also called *stocking allowances, introductory allowances,* or *street money,* are fees retailers charge for providing a slot or position to accommodate the new product. Retailers justify these fees by pointing out the costs associated with taking on so many new products each year, such as redesigning store shelves, entering the product into their computers, finding warehouse space, and briefing store employees on the new product.[58] They also note they are assuming some risk, since so many new product introductions fail.

Slotting fees can range from a few hundred dollars per store to $50,000 or more for an entire retail chain. Manufacturers that want to get their products on the shelves nationally can face several million dollars in slotting fees. Many marketers believe slotting allowances are a form of blackmail or bribery and say some 70 percent of these fees go directly to retailers' bottom lines.

Retailers can continue charging slotting fees because of their power and the limited availability of shelf space in supermarkets relative to the large numbers of products introduced each year. Some retailers have even been demanding **failure fees** if a new product does not hit a minimum sales level within a certain time. The fee is charged to cover the costs associated with stocking, maintaining inventories, and then pulling the product.[59] Large manufacturers with popular brands are less likely to pay slotting fees than smaller companies that lack leverage in negotiating with retailers.

In late 1999, the Senate Committee on Small Business began taking action against the practice of using slotting fees in the grocery, drugstore, and computer software industries because of the fees' negative impact on small business.[60] The committee recommended that the Federal Trade Commission and Small Business Administration take steps to limit the use of slotting fees because they are anticompetitive. A study by Paul Bloom, Gregory Gundlach, and Joseph Cannon examined the views of manufacturers, wholesalers, and grocery retailers regarding the use of slotting fees. Their findings suggest that slotting fees shift the risk of new product introductions from retailers to manufacturers and help apportion the supply and demand of new products. They also found that slotting fees lead to higher retail prices, are applied in a discriminatory fashion, and place small marketers at a disadvantage.[61]

Problems with Trade Allowances Many companies are concerned about the abuse of trade allowances by wholesalers, retailers, and distributors. Marketers give retailers these trade allowances so that the savings will be passed through to consumers in the form of lower prices, but companies such as Procter & Gamble claim that only 30 percent of trade promotion discounts actually reach consumers because 35 percent is lost in inefficiencies and another 35 percent is pocketed by retailers and wholesalers. Moreover, many marketers believe that the trade is taking advantage of their promotional deals and misusing promotional funds.

For example, many retailers and wholesalers engage in a practice known as **forward buying,** where they stock up on a product at the lower deal or off-invoice price and resell it to consumers after the marketer's promotional period ends. Another common practice is **diverting,** where a retailer or wholesaler takes advantage of the promotional deal and then sells some of the product purchased at the low price to a store outside its area or to a middleperson who resells it to other stores.

Forward buying and diverting are widespread practices. Industry studies show that nearly 40 percent of wholesalers' and retailers' profits come from these activities. In addition to not passing discounts on to consumers, forward buying and diverting create other problems for manufacturers. They lead to huge swings in demand that cause production scheduling problems and leave manufacturers and retailers always building toward or drawing down from a promotional surge. Marketers also worry that the system leads to frequent price specials, so consumers learn to make purchases on the basis of what's on sale rather than developing any loyalty to their brands.

The problems created by retailers' abuse led Procter & Gamble, one of the country's most powerful consumer-product marketers, to try using **everyday low pricing (EDLP),** which lowers the list price of over 60 percent of its product line by 10 to 25 percent while cutting promotional allowances to the trade. The price cuts leave the overall cost of the product to retailers about the same as it would have been with the various trade allowance discounts.[62]

P&G argued that EDLP eliminates problems such as deal buying, leads to regular low prices at the retail level, and helps build brand loyalty among consumers. Yet the EDLP strategy caused great controversy in the trade, which depends heavily on promotions to attract consumers. Some retailers took P&G products off the shelf; others cut their ads and displays of the company's brands. Retailers prefer to operate on a *high/low strategy* of frequent price specials and argue that EDLP puts them at a disadvantage against the warehouse stores and mass merchandisers that already use everyday low pricing. They also say that some products, such as those that are bought on impulse, thrive on promotions and don't lend themselves to EDLP. Retailers rely on promotions like end-of-aisle displays and price discounts to create excitement and generate incremental sales and profits from products like soft drinks, cookies, and candy.[63]

Critics of EDLP also note that while the strategy may work well for market leaders whose brands enjoy high loyalty, it is not effective for marketers trying to build market share or prop up lagging products. Moreover, many consumers are still motivated more by promotional deals and specials than by advertising claims from retailers promoting everyday low prices.

Displays and Point-of-Purchase Materials

The next time you are in a store, take a moment to examine the various promotional materials used to display and sell products. Point-of-purchase (POP) displays are an important promotional tool because they can help a manufacturer obtain more effective in-store merchandising of products. Companies in the United States spend more than $15 billion a year on point-of-purchase materials, including end-of-aisle displays, banners, posters, shelf cards, motion pieces, and stand-up racks, among others. Point-of-purchase displays are very important to marketers since many consumers make their purchase decisions in the store. In fact, some studies estimate that nearly two-thirds of a consumer's buying decisions are made in a retail store. Thus, it is very important for marketers to get the attention of consumers, as well as to communicate a sales or promotional message, through POP displays.

A recent measurement study from Point-of-Purchase Advertising International (an industry trade association) and the Advertising Research Foundation estimates that the cost-per-thousand-impressions figure for POPs is $6 to $8 for supermarket displays.[64] The CPM figure is based on findings that a grocery store display makes an average of 2,300 to 8,000 impressions per week, depending on store size and volume. Although this study has shown that POP displays are very effective at reaching consumers, difficulties in getting retail stores to comply with requests for displays often make it difficult for marketers to use them.[65] Moreover, many retailers are decreasing the amount of signage and displays they will accept as well as the messages they can communicate. Also, as account-specific promotions become more popular, some retailers are requiring customized POP materials. For example, 7-Eleven has taken over the responsibility for the production of all POP materials from vendors—who must still pay for them. The goal is to give 7-Eleven complete control over its in-store environment.

Despite these challenges, marketers recognize that point-of-purchase displays are an important part of their promotional programs. Many continue to develop innovative methods to display their products efficiently, make them stand out in the retail environment, and communicate a sales message to consumers. It should be noted that the importance of creative POP displays is not limited to grocery or convenience stores. Point-of-purchase displays are also important to companies that distribute their products through other types of retail outlets, such as home improvement, consumer electronic, and sporting goods stores. For example, Exhibit 16-27 shows an award-winning POP display for Wilson Sporting Goods Co. that was designed to keep the company's high-end baseball gloves off the shelves and separate from other gloves. The gloves needed a product-specific display that would promote them as the "Official Glove of Major League Baseball" and also maximize space while merchandising more product.

Many manufacturers help retailers use shelf space more efficiently through **planograms,** which are configurations of products that occupy a shelf section in a store. Some manufacturers are developing computer-based programs that allow retailers to input information from their scanner data and determine the best shelf layouts by experimenting with product movement, space utilization, profit yields, and other factors.[66]

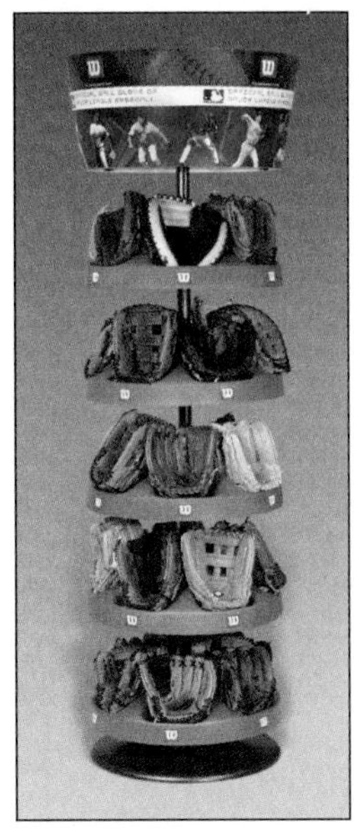

Exhibit 16-27 This award-winning point-of-purchase display plays an important role in the merchandising of Wilson baseball gloves

Sales Training Programs Another form of manufacturer-sponsored promotional assistance is sales training programs for reseller personnel. Many products sold at the retail level require knowledgeable salespeople who can provide consumers with information about the features, benefits, and advantages of various brands and models. Cosmetics, appliances, computers, consumer electronics, and sporting equipment are examples of products for which consumers often rely on well-informed retail sales personnel for assistance.

Manufacturers provide sales training assistance to retail salespeople in a number of ways. They may conduct classes or training sessions that retail personnel can attend to increase their knowledge of a product or a product line. These training sessions present information and ideas on how to sell the manufacturer's product and may also include motivational components. Sales training classes for retail personnel are often sponsored by companies selling high-ticket items or complex products such as personal computers, cars, or ski equipment.

Another way manufacturers provide sales training assistance to retail employees is through their own sales force. Sales reps educate retail personnel about their product line and provide selling tips and other relevant information. The reps can provide ongoing sales training as they come into contact with retail sales staff on a regular basis and can update them on changes in the product line, market developments, competitive information, and the like.

Manufacturers also give resellers detailed sales manuals, product brochures, reference manuals, and other material. Many companies provide videocassettes for retail sales personnel that include product information, product-use demonstrations, and ideas on how to sell their product. These selling aids can often be used to provide information to customers as well.

Trade Shows Another important promotional activity targeted to resellers is the **trade show,** a forum where manufacturers can display their products to current as well as prospective buyers. According to the Trade Show Bureau, nearly 100 million people attend the 5,000 trade shows each year in the United States and Canada, and the number of exhibiting companies exceeds 1.3 million. In many industries, trade shows are a major opportunity to display one's product lines and interact with customers. They are often attended by important management personnel from large retail chains as well as by distributors and other reseller representatives.

A number of promotional functions can be performed at trade shows, including demonstrating products, identifying new prospects, gathering customer and competitive information, and even writing orders for a product. Trade shows are particularly valuable for introducing new products, because resellers are often looking for new merchandise to stock. Shows can also be a source of valuable leads to follow up on through sales calls or direct marketing. The social aspect of trade shows is also important. Many companies use them to entertain key customers and to develop and maintain relationships with the trade. A recent academic study demonstrated that trade shows generate product awareness and interest and can have a measurable economic return.[67] For example, the International-Dairy-Deli-Bakery Association's annual seminar and expo is the leading trade show for manufacturers of dairy, deli, and bakery products. Companies competing in these industries attend the conference to show their new products, make new contacts, and learn about new ideas. Exhibit 16-28 shows the booth used by the California Milk Advisory Board at a recent IDDBA expo.

Cooperative Advertising The final form of trade-oriented promotion we examine is **cooperative advertising,** where the cost of advertising is shared by more than one party. There are three types of cooperative advertising. Although the first two are not trade-oriented promotion, we should recognize their objectives and purpose.

Exhibit 16-28 Trade shows are important for reaching retailers in many industries

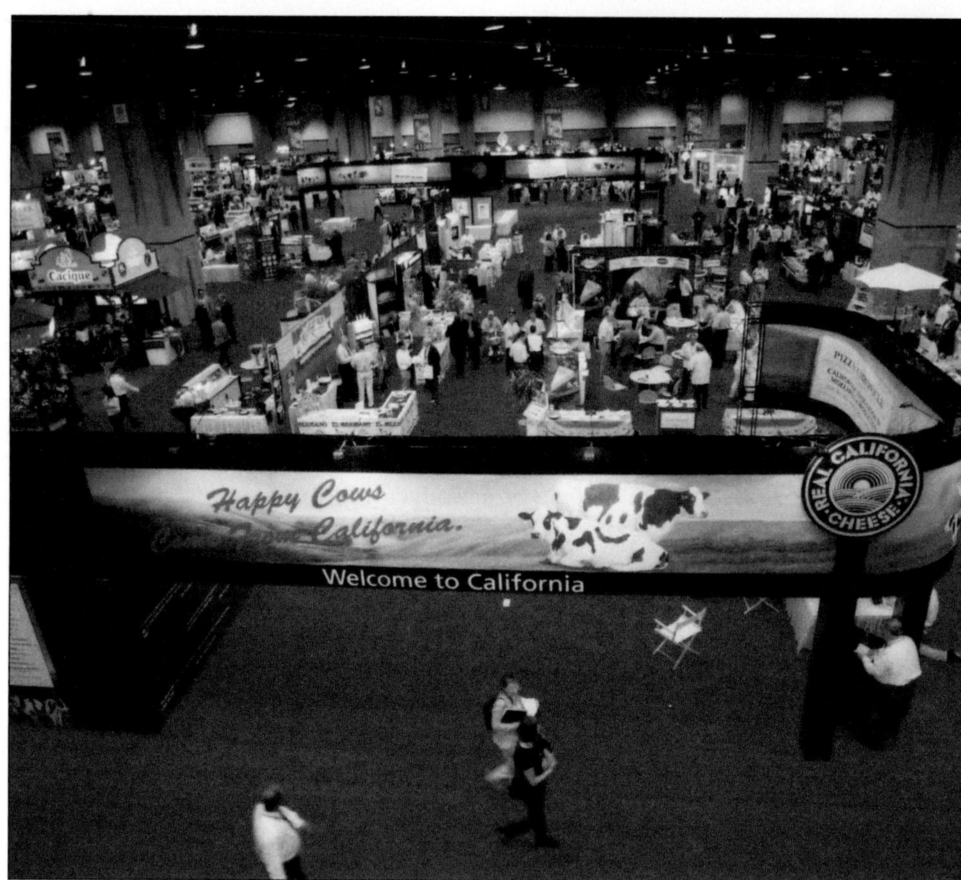

Horizontal cooperative advertising is advertising sponsored in common by a group of retailers or other organizations providing products or services to the market. For example, automobile dealers who are located near one another in an auto park or along the same street often allocate some of their ad budgets to a cooperative advertising fund. Ads are run promoting the location of the dealerships and encouraging car buyers to take advantage of their close proximity when shopping for a new automobile.

Ingredient-sponsored cooperative advertising is supported by raw materials manufacturers; its objective is to help establish end products that include the company's materials and/or ingredients. Companies that often use this type of advertising include Du Pont, which promotes the use of its materials such as Teflon, Thinsulate, and Kevlar in a variety of consumer and industrial products, and NutraSweet, whose artificial sweetener is an ingredient in many food products and beverages. Perhaps the best-known, and most successful, example of this type of cooperative advertising is the "Intel Inside" program, sponsored by Intel Corporation, which the company has been using since 1991.[68] Under this program, computer manufacturers get back 5 percent of what they pay Intel for microprocessors in return for showing the "Intel Inside" logo in their advertising as well as on their PCs. The monies received from Intel must be applied to ads paid for jointly by the PC maker and Intel. Nearly 90 percent of the PC print ads run in the United States carry the "Intel Inside" logo, and the program has helped Intel grow its share of the microprocessor market from 56 percent in 1990 to nearly 80 percent in 2005 (Exhibit 16-29).

The most common form of cooperative advertising is the trade-oriented form, **vertical cooperative advertising,** in which a manufacturer pays for a portion of the advertising a retailer runs to promote the manufacturer's product and its availability in the retailer's place of business. Manufacturers generally share the cost of advertising run by the retailer on a percentage basis (usually 50/50) up to a certain limit.

The amount of cooperative advertising the manufacturer pays for is usually based on a percentage of dollar purchases. If a retailer purchases $100,000 of product from a manufacturer, it may receive 3 percent, or $3,000, in cooperative advertising money. Large retail chains often combine their co-op budgets across all of their stores, which gives them a larger sum to work with and more media options.

intel inside
pentium
EXTREME
EDITION

Exhibit 16-29 The "Intel Inside" cooperative advertising program has been extremely successful

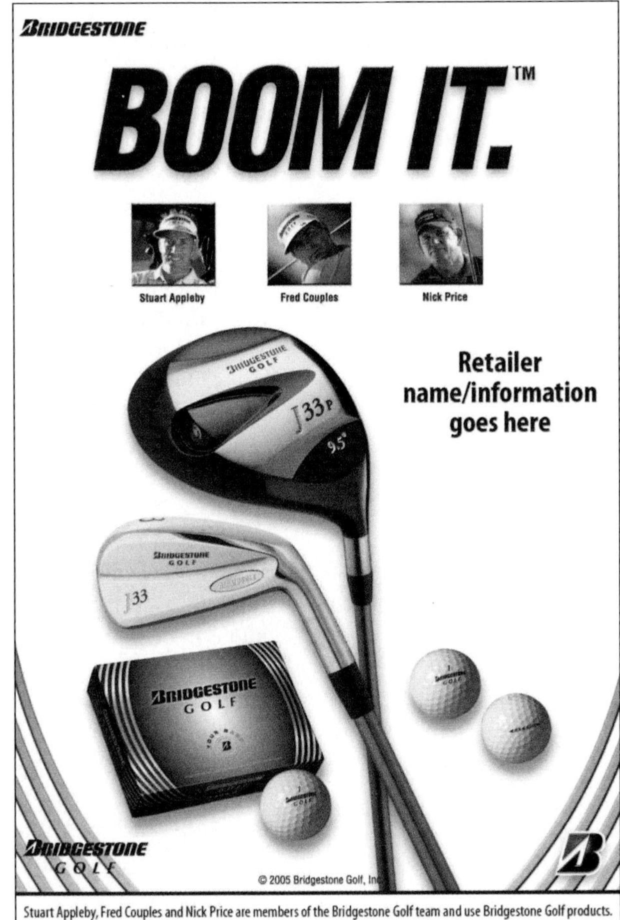
BRIDGESTONE
BOOM IT.™
Stuart Appleby
Fred Couples
Nick Price
Retailer name/information goes here
BRIDGESTONE GOLF
© 2005 Bridgestone Golf, Inc.
Stuart Appleby, Fred Couples and Nick Price are members of the Bridgestone Golf team and use Bridgestone Golf products. They may or may not utilize all products shown here.

Exhibit 16-30 This Bridgestone Golf ad is an example of vertical cooperative advertising

Cooperative advertising can take on several forms. Retailers may advertise a manufacturer's product in, say, a newspaper ad featuring a number of different products, and the individual manufacturers reimburse the retailer for their portion of the ad. Or the ad may be prepared by the manufacturer and placed in the local media by the retailer. Exhibit 16-30 shows a cooperative ad format for Bridgestone Golf that retailers in various market areas can use by simply inserting their store name and location.

Once a cooperative ad is run, the retailer requests reimbursement from the manufacturer for its percentage of the media costs. Manufacturers usually have specific requirements the ad must meet to qualify for co-op reimbursement, such as size, use of trademarks, content, and format. Verification that the ad was run is also required, in the form of a tearsheet (print) or an affidavit from the radio or TV station (broadcast) and an invoice.

As with other types of trade promotions, manufacturers have been increasing their cooperative advertising expenditures in recent years. Some companies have been moving money out of national advertising into cooperative advertising because they believe they can have greater impact with ad campaigns in local markets. There is also a trend toward more cooperative advertising pro\grams initiated by retailers, which approach manufacturers with catalogs, promotional events they are planning, or advertising programs they have developed in conjunction with local media and ask them to pay a percentage of the cost. Manufacturers often go along with these requests, particularly when the retailer is large and powerful.[69]

Coordinating Sales Promotion and Advertising

Those involved in the promotional process must recognize that sales promotion techniques usually work best in conjunction with advertising and that the effectiveness of an ad campaign can be enhanced by consumer-oriented sales promotion efforts. Rather than separate activities competing for a firm's promotional budget, advertising and sales promotion should be viewed as complementary tools. When properly planned and executed to work together, advertising and sales promotion can have a *synergistic effect* much greater than that of either promotional mix element alone.

Proper coordination of advertising and sales promotion is essential for the firm to take advantage of the opportunities offered by each tool and get the most out of its promotional budget. Successful integration of advertising and sales promotion requires decisions concerning not only the allocation of the budget to each area but also the coordination of the ad and sales promotion themes, the timing of the various promotional activities, and the target audience reached.

Budget Allocation

While many companies are spending more money on sales promotion than on media advertising, it is difficult to say just what percentage of a firm's overall promotional budget should be allocated to advertising versus consumer- and trade-oriented promotions. This allocation depends on a number of factors, including the specific promotional objectives of the campaign, the market and competitive situation, and the brand's stage in its life cycle.

Consider, for example, how allocation of the promotional budget may vary according to a brand's stage in the product life cycle. In the introductory stage, a large amount of the budget may be allocated to sales promotion techniques such as sampling and couponing to induce trial. In the growth stage, however, promotional dollars may be used primarily for advertising to stress brand differences and keep the brand name in consumers' minds.

When a brand moves to the maturity stage, advertising is primarily a reminder to keep consumers aware of the brand. Consumer-oriented sales promotions such as coupons, price-offs, premiums, and bonus packs may be needed periodically to maintain consumer loyalty, attract new users, and protect against competition. Trade-oriented promotions are needed to maintain shelf space and accommodate retailers' demands for better margins as well as encourage them to promote the brand. A study on the synergistic effects of advertising and promotion examined a brand in the mature phase of its life cycle and found that 80 percent of its sales at this stage were due to sales promotions. When a brand enters the decline stage of the product life cycle, most of the promotional support will probably be removed and expenditures on sales promotion are unlikely.

Coordination of Ad and Promotion Themes

To integrate the advertising and sales promotion programs successfully, the theme of consumer promotions should be tied in with the advertising and positioning theme wherever possible. Sales promotion tools should attempt to communicate a brand's unique attributes or benefits and to reinforce the sales message or campaign theme. In this way, the sales promotion effort contributes to the consumer franchise-building effort for the brand.

At the same time, media advertising should be used to draw attention to a sales promotion program such as a contest, sweepstakes, or event or to a special promotion offer such as a price reduction or rebate program. An example of this is the ad shown in Exhibit 16-31 for WD-40, which promotes the Search for 2000 Uses Sweepstakes. Note how both the magazine ad and the sweepstakes promotion integrate the variety-of-uses positioning theme used for WD-40.

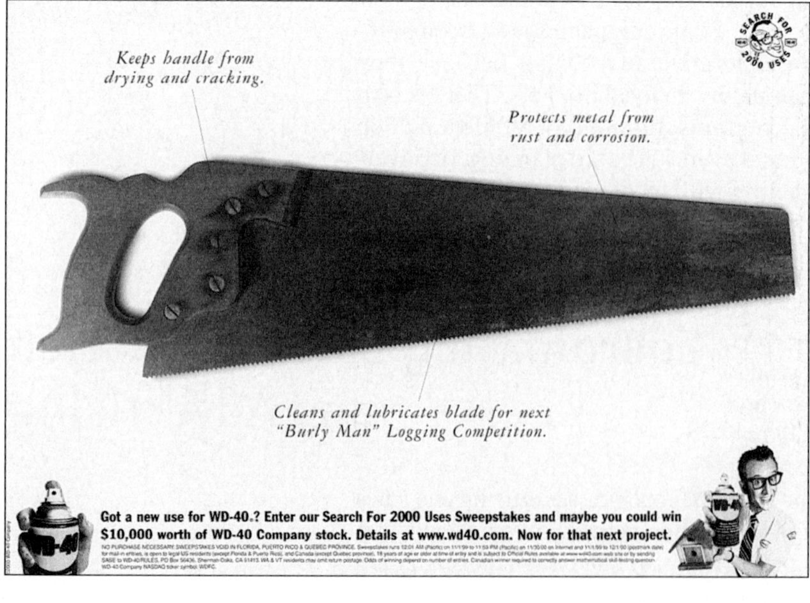

Search for 2000 Uses
Keeps handle from drying and cracking.
Protects metal from rust and corrosion.
Cleans and lubricates blade for next "Burly Man" Logging Competition.
Got a new use for WD-40.? Enter our Search For 2000 Uses Sweepstakes and maybe you could win $10,000 worth of WD-40 Company stock. Details at www.wd40.com. Now for that next project.

Exhibit 16-31 This WD-40 ad promotes the 2000 Uses Sweepstakes and is consistent with the positioning theme used for the brand

Media Support and Timing

Media support for a sales promotion program is critical and should be coordinated with the media program for the ad campaign. Media advertising is often needed to deliver such sales promotion materials as coupons, sweepstakes, contest entry forms, premium offers, and even samples. It is also needed to inform consumers of a promotional offer as well as to create awareness, interest, and favorable attitudes toward the brand.

By using advertising in conjunction with a sales promotion program, marketers can make consumers aware of the brand and its benefits and increase their responsiveness to the promotion. Consumers are more likely to redeem a coupon or respond to a price-off deal for a brand they are familiar with than one they know nothing about. Moreover, product trial created through sales promotion techniques such as sampling or high-value couponing is more likely to result in long-term use of the brand when accompanied by advertising.[70]

Using a promotion without prior or concurrent advertising can limit its effectiveness and risk damaging the brand's image. If consumers perceive the brand as being promotion dependent or of lesser quality, they are not likely to develop favorable attitudes and long-term loyalty. Conversely, the effectiveness of an ad can be enhanced by a coupon, a premium offer, or an opportunity to enter a sweepstakes or contest.

An example of the effective coordination of advertising and sales promotion is the introductory campaign developed for Lever 2000 bar soap. Unilever used high-value coupons, sent samples to half of U.S. households, and offered discounts to retailers as part of its introductory marketing blitz. These sales promotion efforts were accompanied by heavy advertising in print and TV with the tagline "Presenting some of the 2000 body parts you can clean with Lever 2000" (Exhibit 16-32).

Exhibit 16-32 Creative advertising was coordinated with sales promotion in the successful introduction of Lever 2000 soap

Sales promotion was important in inducing trial for Lever 2000 and continued after introduction in the form of couponing. But it was the strong positioning created through effective advertising that converted consumers to regular users. Repeat sales of the brand were at about 40 percent even after heavy discounting ended. Just six months after its introduction, Lever 2000 became the number-two deodorant soap in dollar volume.[71]

To coordinate their advertising and sales promotion programs more effectively, many companies are getting their sales promotion agencies more involved in the advertising and promotional planning process. Rather than hiring agencies to develop individual, nonfranchise-building types of promotions with short-term goals and tactics, many firms are having their sales promotion and advertising agencies work together to develop integrated promotional strategies and programs. Figure 16-7 shows how the role of sales promotion agencies is changing.

Figure 16-7 The Shifting Role of the Promotion Agency

Traditional	New and Improved
1. Primarily used to develop short-term tactics or concepts.	1. Used to develop long- and short-term promotional strategies as well as tactics.
2. Hired/compensated on a project-by-project basis.	2. Contracted on annual retainer, following formal agency reviews.
3. Many promotion agencies used a mix—each one hired for best task and/or specialty.	3. One or two exclusive promotion agencies for each division or brand group.
4. One or two contact people from agency.	4. Full team or core group on the account.
5. Promotion agency never equal to ad agency—doesn't work up front in annual planning process.	5. Promotion agency works on equal basis with ad agency—sits at planning table up front.
6. Not directly accountable for results.	6. Very much accountable—goes through a rigorous evaluation process.

Sales Promotion Abuse

The increasing use of sales promotion in marketing programs is more than a passing fad. It is a fundamental change in strategic decisions about how companies market their products and services. The value of this increased emphasis on sales promotion has been questioned by several writers, particularly with regard to the lack of adequate planning and management of sales promotion programs.[72]

Are marketers becoming too dependent on this element of the marketing program? Consumer and trade promotions can be a very effective tool for generating short-term increases in sales, and many brand managers would rather use a promotion to produce immediate sales than invest in advertising and build the brand's image over an extended time. As the director of sales promotion services at one large ad agency noted: "There's a great temptation for quick sales fixes through promotions. It's a lot easier to offer the consumer an immediate price savings than to differentiate your product from a competitor's."[73]

Overuse of sales promotion can be detrimental to a brand in several ways. A brand that is constantly promoted may lose perceived value. Consumers often end up purchasing a brand because it is on sale, they get a premium, or they have a coupon, rather than basing their decision on a favorable attitude they have developed. When the extra promotional incentive is not available, they switch to another brand. A study by Priya Raghubir and Kim Corfman examined whether price promotions affect pretrial evaluations of a brand.[74] They found that offering a price promotion is more likely to lower a brand's evaluation when the brand has not been promoted previously compared to when it has been frequently promoted; that price promotions are used as a source of information about a brand to a greater extent when the evaluator is not an expert but does have some product or industry knowledge; and that promotions are more likely to result in negative evaluations when they are uncommon in the industry. The findings from this study suggest that marketers must be careful in the use of price promotions as they may inhibit trial of a brand in certain situations.

Alan Sawyer and Peter Dickson have used the concept of *attribution theory* to examine how sales promotion may affect consumer attitude formation.[75] According to this theory, people acquire attitudes by observing their own behavior and considering why they acted in a certain manner. Consumers who consistently purchase a brand because of a coupon or price-off deal may attribute their behavior to the external promotional incentive rather than to a favorable attitude toward the brand. By contrast, when no external incentive is available, consumers are more likely to attribute their purchase behavior to favorable underlying feelings about the brand.

Another potential problem with consumer-oriented promotions is that a **sales promotion trap** or spiral can result when several competitors use promotions extensively.[76] Often a firm begins using sales promotions to differentiate its product or service from the competition. If the promotion is successful and leads to a differential advantage (or even appears to do so), competitors may quickly copy it. When all the competitors are using sales promotions, this not only lowers profit margins for each firm but also makes it difficult for any one firm to hop off the promotional bandwagon.[77] This dilemma is shown in Figure 16-8.

Figure 16-8 The Sales Promotion Trap

	Our Firm	
All Other Firms	**Cut back promotions**	**Maintain promotions**
Cut back promotions	Higher profits for all	Market share goes to our firm
Maintain promotions	Market share goes to all other firms	Market share stays constant; profits stay low

IMC PERSPECTIVE 16-5

Employee Pricing Helps the Big Three Move Cars—But at What Price?

For the past several years, General Motors (GM), along with other major automobile companies, has relied heavily on various types of incentives or discounts to help sell vehicles. In 2004, GM gave an estimated $17 billion in incentives to its customers. In 2005, the company decided that it wanted to move to a more "brand-value focus" strategy and price its vehicles closer to what they actually sell for in the showroom. To implement new pricing strategy, GM decided to introduce value pricing for 2006, whereby it would lower the sticker prices of its vehicles rather than inflate them to make room for incentives. However, before introducing value pricing, Steve Hill, GM's director of retail planning, recognized that the company had to reduce the inventory of 2005 vehicles that remained in stock across the company's eight divisions.

As Hill contemplated his options in early May 2005, he considered a program that GM had implemented a year earlier whereby GM had allowed executives to offer employee pricing to customers outside the company. Hill had offered the employee price to a couple of college buddies to get them into GM vehicles and wondered how the idea would work on a broader scale. He discussed the idea with company vice presidents, who joined him in pitching the program to the GM dealer council. The dealers were enthusiastic about the idea and on June 1 GM kicked off its "Employee Discount for Everyone" campaign across all eight of its divisions.

Under the program, GM offered consumers the same discount available to its own employees. To advertise the program, GM used actual employees in a series of ads touting its employee-pricing plan. In the ads, the employees were shown in front of various models, such as the GMC Yukon Denali, talking about their pride in GM and saying, "The company is doing something that we've never done before." The final frame featured an employee saying, "You pay what we pay. Not a cent more." The employee-pricing discount program was extremely successful; GM sales soared 41 percent in June to their highest monthly total in 19 years.

Initially, the other two U.S. automakers, Ford and Chrysler, did not match GM's employee pricing and experienced lackluster sales during June. However, when GM announced in early July that it was continuing the program, both companies joined the battle. Ford began advertising its "Ford Family Plan" program while Chrysler initiated a $75 million advertising campaign to tout its "Employee Pricing Plus" program. Chrysler even brought back former chairman and CEO Lee Iacocca to be the pitchman in its ads along with his old tagline "If you can find a better car, buy it." Iacocca, who led Chrysler Corporation's comeback from near bankruptcy in the early '80s, appeared in ads promoting the program along with other celebrities such as actor Jason Alexander and rap singer Snoop Dogg.

In July, the big three automakers sold a record 1.8 million units, and in early August, GM's competitors turned the tables on the company when Ford announced that it was extending its program to some key 2006 models while Chrysler said it would continue employee pricing indefinitely on 2005 models. Nevertheless, August sales for GM dropped sharply while Ford and Chrysler showed only small gains compared to August 2004 as customers who were interested in the discounts had apparently already made a purchase, and inventories thinned down leaving fewer bargains to lure new customers. In early September, GM announced that it was ending its employee-pricing program at the end of that month and would begin to transition to its new "Total Value Promise" pricing program. Under this program, the sticker prices of 2006 GM models are closer to what the prices would have been *after* various incentives are included.

Analysts' evaluations of the employee-pricing programs used by the Big 3 automakers were mixed. Some called it a brilliant marketing move as it helped them sell the most vehicles in any month in the history of the industry and to reduce a backlog of inventory. The employee-pricing programs were also seen as an effective way to break through the clutter of incentives and promotions. However, some industry analysts expressed concern that the employee-pricing discounts were really just another name for incentives and would further heighten consumers' expectations for discounts on domestic vehicles. They note that the Big 3 auto manufacturers have to reduce their dependence on incentives, which can devalue what consumers think their vehicles are really worth, and focus more on building brand equity. There is also concern that one of the automakers might initiate another round of incentives leaving the other competitors no choice but to match them.

Source: Lee Hawkins Jr. "GM Tells Dealers It Will End Employee-Pricing Plan Sept. 30," *Advertising Age,* September 9, 2005, p. 8; Barbara Lipert, "The Odd Couple," *Adweek,* August 15, 2005, p. 23; Jim Mateja, "Auto Sales' Jump Starter," *Chicago Tribune,* August 14, 2005, p. 3; Bradley Johnson, " 'Discount' Ploy Could Bite Detroit," *Advertising Age,* July 11, 2005, pp. 1, 33.

A number of industries have fallen into this promotional trap. In the cosmetics industry, gift-with-purchase and purchase-with-purchase promotional offers were developed as a tactic for getting buyers to sample new products. But they have become a common, and costly, way of doing business.[78] In many areas of the country, supermarkets have gotten into the trap of doubling or even tripling manufacturers' coupons, which cuts into their already small profit margins. Fast-food chains have also fallen into the trap with promotions featuring popular menu items for 99 cents.

The sales promotion war spread to yet another industry a few years ago when Dell began using promotional offers to help stimulate sluggish demand for personal computers. Consumers buying Dell computers were automatically entered into a Trip-a-Day Giveaway promotion in which the winner would win a trip worth up to $50,000. Competitors quickly matched Dell's promotion: Compaq and Hewlett-Packard developed their own sweepstakes and began using rebates. Gateway offered free printers and scanners with certain PC purchases, and Apple offered no-payment financing. The promotions cut into the already narrow profit margins of the various competitors in the PC industry and made it difficult for any one company to develop a promotion-based competitive advantage.[79] IMC Perspective 16-5 discusses the promotional battle that took place in the U.S. automobile industry in the summer of 2005 as General Motors, Ford, and Chrysler all offered employee-discount pricing programs to help clear out inventory.

Marketers must consider both the short-term impact of a promotion and its long-term effect on the brand. The ease with which competitors can develop a retaliatory promotion and the likelihood of their doing so should also be considered. Marketers must be careful not to damage the brand franchise with sales promotions or to get the firm involved in a promotional war that erodes the brand's profit margins and threatens its long-term existence. Marketers are often tempted to resort to sales promotions to deal with declining sales and other problems when they should examine such other aspects of the marketing program as channel relations, price, packaging, product quality, or advertising.

After reading this chapter you can see that there are a number of factors that marketers must consider in developing and implementing effective sales promotion programs as they involve much more than just offering consumers an extra economic incentive to purchase a product. Priya Raghub, Jeffrey Inman, and Hans Grande suggest that there are three aspects to consumer promotions including economic, informative, and affective effects.[80] They note that in addition to economic effects, marketers must consider the information and signals a promotional offer conveys to the consumer as well as the affective influences. These include the consumer feelings and emotions aroused by exposure to a promotion or associated with purchasing the brand or company that is offering a deal. By considering all of these effects, managers can design and communicate consumer promotions more efficiently as well as more effectively.

Summary

For many years, advertising was the major promotional mix element for most consumer-product companies. Over the past two decades, however, marketers have been allocating more of their promotional dollars to sales promotion. There has been a steady increase in the use of sales promotion techniques to influence consumers' purchase behavior. The growing power of retailers, erosion of brand loyalty, increase in consumers' sensitivity to promotions, increase in new product introductions, fragmentation of the consumer market, short-term focus of marketing and brand managers, and increase in advertising clutter are some of the reasons for this increase.

Sales promotions can be characterized as either franchise building or nonfranchise building. The former contribute to the long-term development and reinforcement of brand identity and image; the latter are designed to accelerate the purchase process and generate immediate increases in sales.

Sales promotion techniques can be classified as either trade- or consumer-oriented. A number of consumer-oriented sales promotion techniques were examined in this chapter, including sampling, couponing, premiums, contests and sweepstakes, rebates and refunds, bonus packs, price-off deals, loyalty programs, and event marketing. The characteristics of these promotional tools were examined, along with their advantages and limitations. Various trade-oriented promotions were also examined, including trade contests and incentives, trade allowances, displays and point-of-purchase materials, sales training programs, trade shows, and cooperative advertising.

Advertising and sales promotion should be viewed not as separate activities but rather as complementary tools. When planned and executed properly, advertising and sales promotion can produce a synergistic effect that is greater than the response generated from either promotional mix element alone. To accomplish this, marketers must coordinate budgets, advertising and promotional themes, media scheduling and timing, and target audiences.

Sales promotion abuse can result when marketers become too dependent on the use of sales promotion techniques and sacrifice long-term brand position and image for short-term sales increases. Many industries experience sales promotion traps when a number of competitors use promotions extensively and it becomes difficult for any single firm to cut back on promotion without risking a loss in sales. Overuse of sales promotion tools can lower profit margins and threaten the image and even the viability of a brand.

Key Terms

sales promotion, 495
consumer-oriented sales promotion, 495
trade-oriented sales promotion, 496
account-specific marketing, 501
consumer franchise-building (CFB) promotions, 502
nonfranchise-building (non-FB) promotions, 503
sampling, 507
bounce-back coupon, 514
cross-ruff coupon, 514
instant coupon, 514
in-store couponing, 515
premium, 516
self-liquidating premiums, 517
contest, 518
sweepstakes, 518
game, 518
refund, 521
bonus packs, 522
price-off deal, 522
loyalty programs, 522
event marketing, 523
event sponsorship, 524
push money, 527
trade allowance, 527
off-invoice allowance, 528
slotting allowance, 529
failure fees, 529
forward buying, 529
diverting, 529
everyday low pricing (EDLP), 529
planograms, 531
trade show, 531
cooperative advertising, 531
horizontal cooperative advertising, 532
ingredient-sponsored cooperative advertising, 532
vertical cooperative advertising, 532
sales promotion trap, 536

Discussion Questions

1. The opening vignette to the chapter discusses how companies such as PepsiCo, Toyota and others are using sponsorship of action sports events to reach Gen Y consumers. Discuss the various ways marketers can integrate various sales promotion tools into their sponsorship of these events.

2. Discuss how sales promotion can be used as an acceleration tool that can speed up the selling and/or purchasing process and help increase sales volume.

3. Discuss the various factors that have led to companies shifting more of their marketing budgets to sales promotion. Discuss the pros and cons of marketers spending more of their IMC budgets on sales promotion.

4. Discuss how the size and power of major retailers such as Wal-Mart are impacting the marketing programs of consumer products companies. What options, if any, do these companies have in dealing with the demands of these powerful retailers?

5. Discuss how sales promotion programs can be integrated with a company's online strategy and how the Internet can be used as part of a company's sales promotion efforts.

6. In recent years many marketers have questioned the economic feasibility of couponing programs. Discuss the various reasons marketers are questioning the value of coupons. Evaluate the arguments for and against the use of coupons.

7. Discuss what marketers can do to avoid some of the promotional problems discussed in IMC Perspective 16-4. Do you think the problems that companies such as McDonald's experienced with their Monopoly game could have been avoided?

8. What is meant by trade-oriented sales promotion? Discuss the various types of trade promotions and reasons marketers use them.

9. A recent report by a rebate fulfillment service showed that the average redemption rate for a $50 rebate on a product that costs $200 is only 35 percent. Why do you think redemption rates for rebates are so low? How might these low redemption rates affect a marketer's decision regarding the use of rebates as a promotional tool?

10. Describe the various forms of cooperative advertising and the reasons they are used by marketers.

11. What is meant by a sale promotion trap or spiral? Evaluate the promotional war that was begun by General Motors when the company began using its "Employee Discount for Everyone" in the summer of 2005. What were the options for other automobile companies in deciding whether to match GM's discount pricing promotion?

Public Relations, Publicity, and Corporate Advertising

17

Chapter Objectives

1. To recognize the roles of public relations, publicity, and corporate advertising in the promotional mix.
2. To know the difference between public relations and publicity and demonstrate the advantages and disadvantages of each.
3. To understand the reasons for corporate advertising and its advantages and disadvantages.
4. To know the methods for measuring the effects of public relations, publicity, and corporate advertising.

Did Janet Jackson's Wardrobe Malfunction Help GoDaddy.com's Success?

A few years back, when Janet Jackson's "wardrobe malfunctioned" (Justin Timberlake ripped off her top and exposed her breast) during a halftime show for Super Bowl XXXVIII, the event became the focus of media attention for weeks on end. But not only the media got involved; so too did the public (hundreds, maybe thousands, of phone calls decrying it as a bad publicity stunt). The FCC investigated the incident, Congress held hearings, CBS was widely criticized—as was Viacom, the owner of CBS—and MTV, which produced the halftime show. While both Jackson and Timberlake apologized, many believe that the negative publicity hurt sales of Jackson's next CD. Whether or not it did, there definitely was an impact on advertisers and producers for Super Bowl XXXIX, who were warned to be extremely cautious in planning for the next year's event. There would be ramifications for noncompliance. As a result, the halftime performance and advertising on Super Bowl XXXIX was, shall we say, "toned down."

But not everyone reacted the same way to the wardrobe malfunction. There were many who thought that the negative responses were an overreaction: By giving the incident so much attention, the public was making a mountain out of a molehill, while giving Jackson and Timberlake just what they wanted—free publicity. Nevertheless, the NFL and the Fox Network, which was airing the next Super Bowl, were extremely cautious. They required the halftime show and the commercials to be approved prior to airtime. Mark Dollins, PepsiCo's vice president of public relations, commented that in reviewing his spots, Fox and the NFL definitely did their "due diligence" (though he declined to elaborate), while Lou D'Ermiilio, head of public relations for Fox Sports Networks, noted more specifically, "I will tell you that this is the fifth Super Bowl I've worked from a network PR perspective, but it's the first that I will have a pre-thought strategy about dealing with editorial and commercial content."

Enter GoDaddy.com, the online domain and Internet services company from Scottsdale, Arizona. Bob Parsons, founder of GoDaddy.com, and the AdStore, a New York–based advertising agency, apparently saw an opportunity in all of the attention following the Jackson and Timberlake incident. They decided to place their own commercial on Super Bowl XXXIX which would make fun of the increasing broadcast censorship, while gaining awareness for GoDaddy. After reviewing approximately 75 potential scripts, the GoDaddy.com and AdStore team seized upon the idea of a Senate hearing in which a woman wearing a GoDaddy.com T-shirt tells a panel of fuddy-duddies just what GoDaddy.com offers—and assures them that her shirt won't fall off during the commercial. According to Paul Capelli, the AdStore's CEO and head of creative, the idea of poking fun at broadcast censorship was quite topical, and it "had the potential to be drop-dead funny."

But how could Parsons and Capelli get the commercial past the censors? GoDaddy.com had committed millions of dollars to the airing of the commercial, which cost an estimated $1 million to produce, purchasing two spots at over $2 million dollars each. But the storyboard would have to be presented to Fox for approval well ahead of airtime. The network approved the storyboard on December 3, 2004, but "upon further review" reversed the decision and later in December informed AdStore that the "content of the commercial" was "inappropriate for air on Fox." After threat of a lawsuit, the network again reversed its decision and agreed to show the commercial if there was no excessive "décolletage," "revealing cleavage," and no reference to a "wardrobe malfunction." They insisted on approving the final cut of the commercial, along with some other restrictions. After more back and forth discussion, and another rejection, the commercial was approved to air, for both time spots. After it aired in the first half of the game, someone at Fox and the NFL decided it was inappropriate, and the second airing was pulled—replaced by a promo for *The Simpsons!*

So much for GoDaddy.com's attempt to garner publicity, right? Wrong. After the game, one of Fox's websites, Fox Funhouse, featured the actress in the commercial as one of their candidates for "Fox of the Week." And, as has become the norm for Super Bowl ads, there was plenty of exposure on other news networks, talk shows, radio programs, newspaper articles, and websites. Numerous interviews with Bob Parsons also followed, resulting in even more free exposure. Did getting only one showing of its commercial thwart GoDaddy's objectives? Not exactly. According to A. C. Nielsen, the commercial received the highest recall rating of all of the ads shown on the game; site visits the next day increased fivefold to 1.1 million; and eventually more than 2.6 million viewers watched the ad. Sales skyrocketed from $102 million in 2004 to over a projected $200 million in 2005. By September 2005, GoDaddy.com was the number-one shared hosting provider in the United States.

If Janet Jackson's objective was to gain free publicity, it worked. But not in the way she intended. For GoDaddy.com, things may have gone just as planned.

Sources: John Draper, "Shock Value," *Entrepreneur,* August 2005, p. 69; Tim Arnold, "Who's Your Daddy?" *Adweek,* February 21, 2005, pp. 15–16; Keith O'Brien, *PRweek,* January 24, 2005, p. 4; Deanna Zammit, "GoDaddy Severs Ties to Ad Store," *Adweek,* March 28, 2005, p. 7.

The lead-in to this chapter clearly demonstrates the power of publicity—both positive and negative. As you will see in this chapter, publicity is often out of the control of the marketer, but increasingly the management of publicity is being adopted as a marketing strategy. While attempts to generate positive publicity are nothing new, as these efforts increase, they signify changes in the public relations functions of companies and organizations. Although the importance and role of public relations in the IMC program may be argued, one thing is clear: The role of public relations in the communications program has changed. While some people may disagree as to the importance and power of this program element, few, if any, would contend that it is business as usual.

Publicity, public relations, and corporate advertising all have promotional program elements that may be of great benefit to marketers. They are integral parts of the overall promotional effort that must be managed and coordinated with the other elements of the promotional mix. However, these three tools do not always have the specific objectives of product and service promotion, nor do they always involve the same methods you have become accustomed to as you have read this text. Typically, these activities are designed more to change attitudes toward an organization or issue than to promote specific products or affect behaviors directly (though you will see that this role is changing in some organizations). This chapter explores the roles of public relations, publicity, and corporate advertising, the advantages and disadvantages of each, and the process by which they are employed.

Public Relations

What is public relations? How does it differ from other elements of marketing discussed thus far? Perhaps a good starting point is to define what the term *public relations* has traditionally meant and then to introduce its new role.

The Traditional Definition of PR

A variety of books define **public relations (PR),** but perhaps the most comprehensive definition is that offered by the *Public Relations News* (the weekly newsletter of the industry):

> [T]he management function which evaluates public attitudes, identifies the policies and procedures of an organization with the public interest, and executes a program of action (and communication) to earn public understanding and acceptance.[1]

Public relations is indeed a management function. The term *management* should be used in its broadest sense; it is not limited to business management but extends to other types of organizations, including nonprofit institutions.

In this definition, public relations requires a series of stages, including:

1. The determination and evaluation of public attitudes.
2. The identification of policies and procedures of an organization with a public interest.
3. The development and execution of a communications program designed to bring about public understanding and acceptance.

This process does not occur all at once. An effective public relations program continues over months or even years.

Finally, this definition reveals that public relations involves much more than activities designed to sell a product or service. The PR program may involve some of the promotional program elements previously discussed but use them in a different way. For example, companies may send press releases to announce new products or changes in the organization, companies may organize special events to create goodwill in the community, and companies may use advertising to state the firm's position on a controversial issue.

The New Role of PR

An increasing number of marketing-oriented companies have established new responsibilities for public relations. PR takes on a much broader (and more marketing-oriented) perspective, designed to promote the organization as well as its products and/or services.

The way that companies and organizations use public relations might best be viewed as a continuum. On one end of the continuum is the use of PR from a traditional perspective. In this perspective, public relations is viewed as a nonmarketing function whose primary responsibility is to maintain mutually beneficial relationships between the organization and its publics. In this case, customers or potential customers are only part of numerous publics—employees, investors, neighbors, special-interest groups, and so on. Marketing and public relations are separate departments; if external agencies are used, they are separate agencies. At the other end of the continuum, public relations is considered primarily a marketing communications function. All noncustomer relationships are perceived as necessary only in a marketing context.[2] In these organizations, public relations reports to marketing. At the same time, for many companies the PR function is moving more and more toward a new role, which is much closer to a marketing function than a traditional one.

In the new role of public relations, managers envision both strong marketing and strong PR departments. Rather than each department operating independently, the two work closely together, blending their talents to provide the best overall image of the firm and its product or service offerings. In a recent poll conducted among members of the Public Relations Society of America (PRSA) and subscribers to *PR News,* 76 percent of respondents stated that they regularly work with the marketing department; 78 percent thought that the marketing department had a positive perception of the PR department, and an equal number indicated the same perception about marketing. While the degree of coordination differed by activity, the study clearly reflects coordination and cooperation.[3]

Some have argued for an even stronger involvement of PR. In their book titled *The Fall of Advertising and the Rise of PR,* Al Ries and his daughter Laura argue that while advertising is still the most dominant medium used by marketers, declining advertising effectiveness means that this communications tool is no longer effective for introducing and building new brands. The only way to build a brand now, they contend, is through public relations.[4] While this thesis obviously led to book burnings in advertising agencies around the world, what made matters worse is that authors Al Ries and his daughter Laura Ries are well-known and respected marketers! Al Ries (along with a former coauthor, Jack Trout) is best known for first introducing the concept of positioning. As you would expect, however, not a lot of marketers necessarily agree with this position.

Writing in *Advertising Age,* William N. Curry notes that organizations must use caution in establishing this relationship because PR and marketing are not the same thing, and when one department becomes dominant, the balance required to operate at maximum efficiency is lost.[5] He says losing sight of the objectives and functions of public relations in an attempt to achieve marketing goals may be detrimental in the long run. Others take an even stronger view that if public relations and marketing distinctions continue to blur, the independence of the PR function will be lost, and it will become much less effective.[6] In fact, as noted by Cutlip, Center, and Broom, marketing and public relations are complementary functions, "with each making unique but complementary contributions to building and maintaining the many relationships essential for organizational survival and growth. To ignore one is to risk failure in the other."[7] This position is consistent with our perception that public relations is an important part of the IMC process, contributing in its own way but also in a way consistent with marketing goals.

Integrating PR into the Promotional Mix

Given the broader responsibilities of public relations, the issue is how to integrate it into the promotional mix. Philip Kotler and William Mindak suggest a number of alternative organizational designs: Either marketing or public relations can be the dominant function; both can be equal but separate functions; or the two can perform the same roles.[8] Although each of these designs has its merits, in this text we regard public relations as an IMC program element. This means that its broad role must include traditional responsibilities.

Whether public relations takes on a traditional role or a more marketing-oriented one, PR activities are still tied to specific communications objectives. Assessing public attitudes and creating a favorable corporate image are no less important than promoting products or services directly.

Marketing Public Relations Functions

Thomas L. Harris has referred to public relations activities designed to support marketing objectives as **marketing public relations (MPR)** functions.[9] Marketing objectives that may be aided by public relations activities include raising awareness, informing and educating, gaining understanding, building trust, giving consumers a reason to buy, and motivating consumer acceptance. MPR adds value to the integrated marketing program in a number of ways:

- *Building marketplace excitement before media advertising breaks.* The announcement of a new product, for example, is an opportunity for the marketer to obtain publicity and to dramatize the product, thereby increasing the effectiveness of ads. When Apple introduced its iPod, a great deal of anticipation was created through public relations prior to the availability of the product. When iPod later introduced the video iPod, the announcement received even more extensive press coverage, including a five-minute segment on the *Today Show* discussing the new product's features and capabilities, and was the subject of numerous reports in the press.
- *Improving ROI.* By reducing overall marketing costs, while at the same time delivering meaningful marketing outcomes, MPRs help improve ROI.
- *Creating advertising news where there is no product news.* Ads themselves can be the focus of publicity. There seems to be as much hype about the ads on the Super

Bowl as there is for the game itself. The lead-in to this chapter clearly demonstrates the usefulness of this hype.

- *Introducing a product with little or no advertising.* This strategy has been implemented successfully by a number of companies, including Hewlett-Packard, Segway, Ty, and Crayola. Gillette uses PR as the lead medium in every new product launch.[10]
- *Providing a value-added customer service.* Butterball established a hotline where people can call in to receive personal advice on how to prepare their turkeys. The company handled 25,000 calls during the first holiday season. Many companies provide such services on their Internet sites. Chicken of the Sea provides recipes to visitors of its site (which, of course, suggest using Chicken of the Sea tuna).
- *Building brand-to-customer bonds.* The Pillsbury Bake-Off has led to strong brand loyalty among Pillsbury customers, who compete by submitting baked goods. The winner now receives a $1 million prize!
- *Influencing the influentials.* That is, providing information to opinion leaders.
- *Defending products at risk and giving consumers a reason to buy.* By taking constructive actions to defend or promote a company's products, PR can actually give consumers a reason to buy the products. Energizer's national education campaign that urged consumers to change the batteries in their fire alarms when they reset their clocks in the fall resulted in a strong corporate citizen image and increased sales of batteries. General Mills's "Box Tops for Education" program has led to millions of dollars being given to K-12 schools.

Figure 17-1 lists additional successful implementations of MPRs.

Figure 17-1 Examples of MPR in Practice

Orkin Pest Control	Combining public relations and sales efforts, the pest control company created the Gold Medal Integrated Pest Management Partner Awards to recognize customers who have followed Orkin recommendations on how to prevent future pest problems. The program aids in customer retention, while at the same time gains trade press attention that assists the sales department in cross selling and gaining new accounts.
Syngenta Professional Products	Syngenta offers products that help grow lawns and flowers, primarily marketing to flower growers and golf course operators. Positioning its spokespeople as experts, the company conducts seminars and lectures on environmental issues, product safety, and other factors of importance to their customer base. Held three to four times a year, Syngenta invites buyers to attend lectures given by experts in these areas, to keep them knowledgeable about their industry. Attendees place great value on being selected, providing Syngenta with a database of buyers, goodwill, and a step up on its competitors. (See Exhibit 17-1.)
Meriwest Credit Union	Previously named the IBM Pacific Employees Credit Union, Meriwest expanded its membership base to those outside of IBM. The company had to develop a new positioning and increase marketing and PR activities. Using the annual report as a sales tool to help corporate human resource directors to understand the benefits the credit union offers and working with the salespeople to get involved in community events, the company generates goodwill in the community while gaining new prospects.
Mitsubishi	After watching its sales continue to slide since 2003 in an incredibly competitive market, Mitsubishi used stronger marketing and PR to turn around the slide with the introduction of its 2006 line. Focusing on improving the brand image and the morale of dealers and employees, the new campaign focused more attention on Japanese culture. However, the main benefit may have been the publicity generated by the sales promotion offering free gas for one year (in a market where gasoline prices were soaring) with the purchase of any 2006 Mitsubishi model. The promotion was extremely successful in generating buzz and in getting potential customers into the showrooms, and was under consideration to be extended through the 2006 year.
Hall & Oates	Although they had already sold over 60 million albums, the legendary rockers were now attempting to cross over from rock to R&B. The group's management team felt that they needed additional publicity to establish a new image. By securing positive reviews from *People* magazine and *USA Today,* the team was able to leverage them into appearances on BET and the *Tavis Smiley Show.* Media coverage increased significantly with follow-up appearances on *American Idol* and *Jimmy Kimmel Live.* Sales after the media blitz increased 103 percent and continued to remain strong.

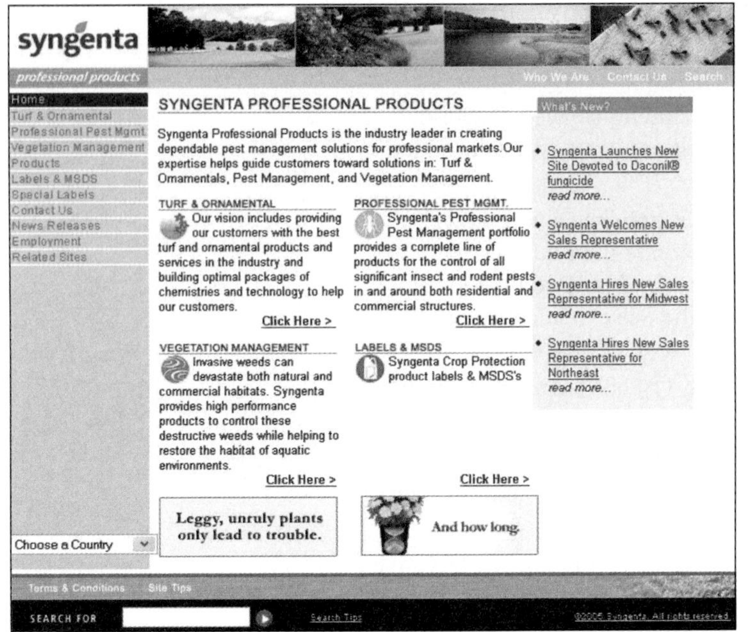

Exhibit 17-1 Syngenta provides information to customers

Harris notes that there are a number of advantages of using MPR:[11]

- It is a cost-effective way to reach the market.
- It is a highly targeted way to conduct public relations.
- It benefits from the endorsement of independent and objective third parties who have no association with the product.
- It achieves credibility.
- It supports advertising programs by making messages more credible.
- It breaks through the clutter.
- It circumvents consumer resistance to sales efforts.

In addition to these advantages, Mark Weiner adds a few more:[12]

- There can be improved media involvement among consumers.
- It can create influence among opinion leaders and trendsetters.
- It can improve ROI.

Harris also notes some disadvantages, including the following:

- There is a lack of control over the media.
- It is difficult to tie in slogans and other advertising devices.
- Media time and space are not guaranteed.
- There are no standard effectiveness measures.

One of the major threats of using an MPR structure, as expressed by Harris, is that public relations functions may become subservient to marketing efforts—a concern expressed by many opponents of MPR. However, if employed properly and used in conjunction with other traditional public relations practices as well as IMC elements, MPR can continue to be used effectively. Weiner also notes that the key to the successful use of MPRs is integration with IMC, though such a task may prove to be difficult to accomplish.

The Process of Public Relations

The actual process of conducting public relations and integrating it into the promotional mix involves a series of both traditional and marketing-oriented tasks.

Determining and Evaluating Public Attitudes

You have learned that public relations is concerned with people's attitudes toward the firm or specific issues beyond those directed at a product or service. The first question you may ask is why. Why is the firm so concerned with the public's attitudes?

One reason is that these attitudes may affect sales of the firm's products. A number of companies have experienced sales declines as a result of consumer boycotts. Procter & Gamble, Coors, Nike, and Bumble Bee Seafoods are just a few companies that responded to organized pressures. A string of SUV accidents led to major problems for 102-year-old Bridgestone/Firestone. In response to the problem, Firestone replaced nearly 900,000 tires and implemented a communications program to counter the negative publicity, a program including television commercials, personal visits to dealers, and print advertising such as that shown in Exhibit 17-2. As a result of the campaign, Firestone lost none of its 10,000 independent tire dealers and two years later was on the road to recovery.

Second, no one wants to be perceived as a bad citizen. Corporations exist in communities, and their employees generally both work and live there. Negative attitudes carry over to employee morale and may result in a less-than-optimal working environment internally and in the community.

Due to their concerns about public perceptions, many privately held corporations, publicly held companies, utilities, and media survey public attitudes. The reasons for conducting this research are many, but include the following:

1. *It provides input into the planning process.* Once the firm has determined public attitudes, they become the starting point in the development of programs designed to maintain favorable positions or change unfavorable ones.

2. *It serves as an early warning system.* Once a problem exists, it may require substantial time and money to correct. By conducting research, the firm may be able to identify potential problems and handle them effectively before they become serious issues.

3. *It secures support internally.* If research shows a problem or potential problem exists, it will be much easier for the public relations arm to gain the support it needs to address this problem.

4. *It increases the effectiveness of the communication.* The better it understands a problem, the better the firm can design communications to deal with it.[13]

Making It Right.

You have our word on that.

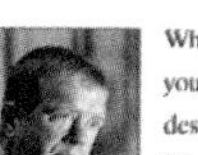

When you buy tires, you're not just buying rubber and steel... you want the confidence that your tires will get you to your destination—safely. Your safety is our primary concern. We want you to have confidence in the way Firestone tires are made and the way they perform. We'll do whatever it takes, however long it takes, to gain your trust.

We call this our *"Making It Right"* plan. With your satisfaction as our goal, Firestone is expanding warranties and making important enhancements in manufacturing and quality control. In the role of watchdogs, a new team of top technical and quality control managers has been assembled to continuously analyze tire and safety data. They'll act to uncover issues ***before*** they become problems. We believe in our tires. We want to prove to you that you can believe in them as well. ***We'll make it right. It's that simple.***

John Lampe,
CEO, Firestone

Exhibit 17-2 Firestone responds to negative publicity

Establishing a PR Plan

For some companies, their PR programs involve little more than press releases, press kits for trade shows, and new product announcements. Further, these tools are often not designed into a formal public relations effort but rather are used only as needed. In other words, no structured program for conducting PR is evident. As we noted earlier, the public relations process is an ongoing one, requiring formalized policies and procedures for dealing with problems and opportunities. Just as you would not develop an advertising and/or promotions program without a plan, you should not institute public relations efforts haphazardly. Moreover, the PR plan needs to be integrated into the overall marketing communications program. Figure 17-2 provides some questions marketers should ask to determine whether their PR plan is workable.

Cutlip, Center, and Broom suggest a four-step process for developing a public relations plan: (1) define public relations problems, (2) plan and program, (3) take action and communicate, and (4) evaluate the program.[14] The questions in Figure 17-2 and the four-step planning process tie in with the promotional planning process stressed throughout this text.

Figure 17-2 Ten Questions for Evaluating Public Relations Plans

1. Does the plan reflect a thorough understanding of the company's business situation?
2. Has the PR program made good use of research and background sources?
3. Does the plan include full analysis of recent editorial coverage?
4. Do the PR people fully understand the product's strengths and weaknesses?
5. Does the PR program describe several cogent, relevant conclusions from the research?
6. Are the program objectives specific and measurable?
7. Does the program clearly describe what the PR activity will be and how it will benefit the company?
8. Does the program describe how its results will be measured?
9. Do the research, objectives, activities, and evaluations tie together?
10. Has the PR department communicated with marketing throughout the development of the program?

Developing and Executing the PR Program

Because of the broad role that public relations may be asked to play, the PR program may need to extend beyond promotion. A broader definition of the target market, additional communications objectives, and different messages and delivery systems may be employed. Let us examine this process.

Determining Relevant Target Audiences

The targets of public relations efforts may vary, with different objectives for each. Some may be directly involved in selling the product; others may affect the firm in a different way (e.g., they may be aimed at stockholders or legislators). These audiences may be internal or external to the firm.

Internal audiences may include the employees, stockholders, and investors of the firm as well as members of the local community, suppliers, and current customers. As noted in Figure 17-1, Mitsubishi's public relations programs were designed, in part, to improve morale among employees and dealers. Why are community members and customers of the firm considered internal rather than external? According to John Marston, it's because these groups are already connected with the organization in some way, and the firm normally communicates with them in the ordinary routine of work.[15] **External audiences** are those people who are not closely connected with the organization (e.g., the public at large).

It may be necessary to communicate with these groups on an ongoing basis for a variety of reasons, ranging from ensuring goodwill to introducing new policies, procedures, or even products. A few examples may help.

Employees of the Firm Maintaining morale and showcasing the results of employees' efforts are often prime objectives of the public relations program. Organizational newsletters, notices on bulletin boards, awards ceremonies and events, direct mail, and annual reports are some of the methods used to communicate with these groups. Exhibit 17-3 shows one such internal communication used by the Business School at San Diego State University.

Exhibit 17-3 An example of a newsletter used for internal communication

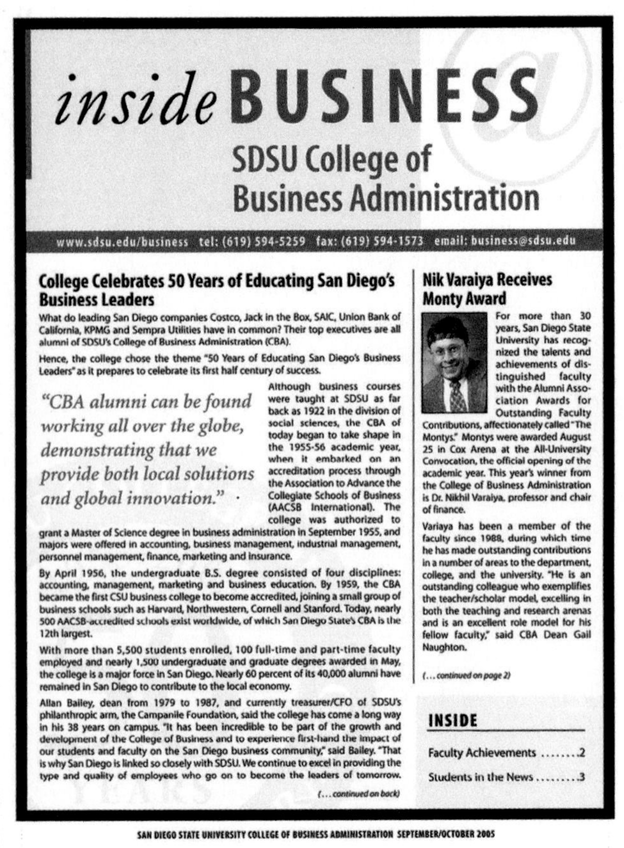

inside **BUSINESS**

SDSU College of Business Administration

www.sdsu.edu/business tel: (619) 594-5259 fax: (619) 594-1573 email: business@sdsu.edu

College Celebrates 50 Years of Educating San Diego's Business Leaders

What do leading San Diego companies Costco, Jack in the Box, SAIC, Union Bank of California, KPMG and Sempra Utilities have in common? Their top executives are all alumni of SDSU's College of Business Administration (CBA).

Hence, the college chose the theme "50 Years of Educating San Diego's Business Leaders" as it prepares to celebrate its first half century of success.

"CBA alumni can be found working all over the globe, demonstrating that we provide both local solutions and global innovation."

Although business courses were taught at SDSU as far back as 1922 in the division of social sciences, the CBA of today began to take shape in the 1955-56 academic year, when it embarked on an accreditation process through the Association to Advance the Collegiate Schools of Business (AACSB International). The college was authorized to grant a Master of Science degree in business administration in September 1955, and majors were offered in accounting, business management, industrial management, personnel management, finance, marketing and insurance.

By April 1956, the undergraduate B.S. degree consisted of four disciplines: accounting, management, marketing and business education. By 1959, the CBA became the first CSU business college to become accredited, joining a small group of business schools such as Harvard, Northwestern, Cornell and Stanford. Today, nearly 500 AACSB-accredited schools exist worldwide, of which San Diego State's CBA is the 12th largest.

With more than 5,500 students enrolled, 100 full-time and part-time faculty employed and nearly 1,500 undergraduate and graduate degrees awarded in May, the college is a major force in San Diego. Nearly 60 percent of its 40,000 alumni have remained in San Diego to contribute to the local economy.

Allan Bailey, dean from 1979 to 1987, and currently treasurer/CFO of SDSU's philanthropic arm, the Campanile Foundation, said the college has come a long way in his 38 years on campus. "It has been incredible to be part of the growth and development of the College of Business and to experience first-hand the impact of our students and faculty on the San Diego business community," said Bailey. "That is why San Diego is linked so closely with SDSU. We continue to excel in providing the type and quality of employees who go on to become the leaders of tomorrow.

(...continued on back)

Nik Varaiya Receives Monty Award

For more than 30 years, San Diego State University has recognized the talents and achievements of distinguished faculty with the Alumni Association Awards for Outstanding Faculty Contributions, affectionately called "The Montys." Montys were awarded August 25 in Cox Arena at the All-University Convocation, the official opening of the academic year. This year's winner from the College of Business Administration is Dr. Nikhil Varaiya, professor and chair of finance.

Variaya has been a member of the faculty since 1988, during which time he has made outstanding contributions in a number of areas to the department, college, and the university. "He is an outstanding colleague who exemplifies the teacher/scholar model, excelling in both the teaching and research arenas and is an excellent role model for his fellow faculty," said CBA Dean Gail Naughton.

(...continued on page 2)

INSIDE

SAN DIEGO STATE UNIVERSITY COLLEGE OF BUSINESS ADMINISTRATION SEPTEMBER/OCTOBER 2005

Personal methods of communicating may be as formal as an established grievance committee or as informal as an office Christmas party. Other social events, such as corporate bowling teams or picnics, are also used to create goodwill.

Stockholders and Investors You may think an annual report like the one in Exhibit 17-4 provides stockholders and investors only with financial information regarding the firm. While this is one purpose, annual reports are also a communications channel for informing this audience about why the firm is or is not doing well, outlining future plans, and providing other information that goes beyond numbers.

For example, McDonald's has successfully used annual reports to fend off potential PR problems. One year the report described McDonald's recycling efforts to alleviate consumers' concerns about waste; another report included a 12-page spread on food and nutrition. In a recent McDonald's annual report, a clearly enunciated goal for 2005 was to "continue the focus on the well-being of customers" by "providing education and information about our foods, and encouraging physical activity."[16] Other companies use similar strategies, employing shareholders' meetings, video presentations, and other forms of direct mail. General Motors' annual public interest report is sent to shareholders and community members to detail the company's high standards of corporate responsibility. GM also produces a sustainability report to update interested parties on its progress. Companies have used these approaches to generate additional investments, to bring more of their stocks "back home" (i.e., become more locally controlled and managed), and to produce funding to solve specific problems, as well as to promote goodwill.

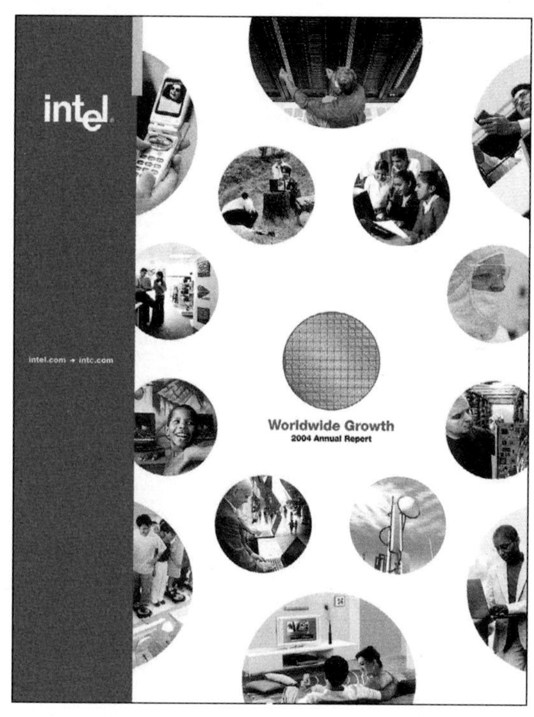

Exhibit 17-4 Annual reports serve a variety of purposes

Community Members People who live and work in the community where a firm is located or doing business are often the target of public relations efforts. Such efforts may involve ads informing the community of activities that the organization is engaged in, for example, reducing air pollution, cleaning up water supplies, or preserving wetlands. (The community can be defined very broadly.) As you can see in Exhibit 17-5, a number of oil companies are involved in this form of public relations, by demonstrating to people that the organization is a good citizen with their welfare in mind.

Suppliers and Customers An organization wishes to maintain *goodwill* with its suppliers as well as its consuming public. If consumers think a company is not socially conscious, they may take their loyalties elsewhere. Suppliers may be inclined to do the same.

Sometimes sponsoring a public relations effort results in direct evidence of success. For example, the "Just say no" to drugs campaign was a boon to companies manufacturing drug testing kits, hospitals offering drug rehabilitation programs, and TV news programs' ratings.[17] Indirect indications of the success of PR efforts may include more customer loyalty, less antagonism, or greater cooperation between the firm and its suppliers or consumers.

Public relations efforts are often targeted to more than one group, and are a direct result of concerns initiated in the marketplace. As noted earlier, along with potential consumers, trade association members, human resource directors, buyers, and suppliers often constitute the target audience for PR efforts.

Relevant audiences may also include people not directly involved with the firm. The press, educators, civic and business groups, governments, and the financial community can be external audiences.

Exhibit 17-5 BP demonstrates concern for the public

It's time to go on a low-carbon diet.

Natural Gas By shifting the balance of the energy fuel mix from coal to natural gas, the cleanest burning fossil fuel, the U.S. could reduce carbon dioxide emissions in new power generation by up to 50%. Today, natural gas accounts for about 40% of BP's global production.

Hydrogen BP is the largest partner in the Department of Energy's hydrogen program, working with automakers to test hydrogen-powered cars. Though several decades away, we've already launched the program's first pilot refueling sites to better learn how we can supply hydrogen in the future.

Solar BP is teaming with The Home Depot® at more than 200 stores in California, New Jersey and Long Island, making it easier for homeowners to lower or eliminate monthly utility bills, while producing 100% emission-free electricity. Today, BP is one of the largest providers of solar energy in the world.

bp

beyond petroleum®

bp.com

The Media Perhaps one of the most critical external publics is the media, which determine what you will read in your newspapers or see on TV, and how this news will be presented. Because of the media's power, they should be informed of the firm's actions. Companies issue press releases and communicate through conferences, interviews, and special events. The media are generally receptive to such information as long as it is handled professionally; reporters are always interested in good stories.

In turn, the media are also concerned about how the community perceives them. Exhibit 17-6 is a public relations piece distributed by a San Diego TV station that describes a variety of ways the station benefits the community.

Educators A number of organizations provide educators with information regarding their activities. The Direct Marketing Association, the Promotional Products Association, and the Yellow Pages Association (YPA), among others, keep educators informed in an attempt to

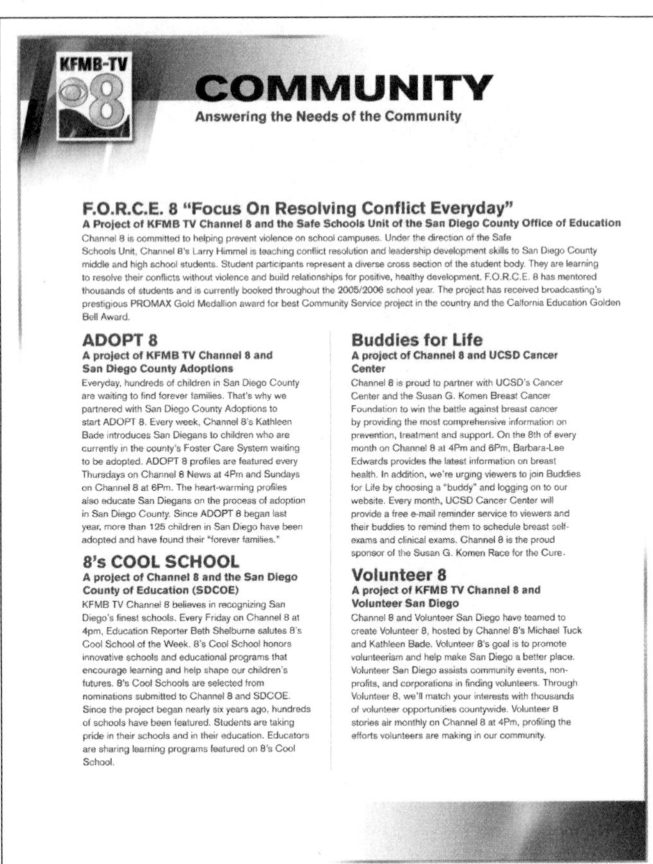

KFMB-TV 8
COMMUNITY
Answering the Needs of the Community
F.O.R.C.E. 8 "Focus On Resolving Conflict Everyday"
A Project of KFMB TV Channel 8 and the Safe Schools Unit of the San Diego County Office of Education
Channel 8 is committed to helping prevent violence on school campuses. Under the direction of the Safe Schools Unit, Channel 8's Larry Himmel is teaching conflict resolution and leadership development skills to San Diego County middle and high school students. Student participants represent a diverse cross section of the student body. They are learning to resolve their conflicts without violence and build relationships for positive, healthy development. F.O.R.C.E. 8 has mentored thousands of students and is currently booked throughout the 2005/2006 school year. The project has received broadcasting's prestigious PROMAX Gold Medallion award for best Community Service project in the country and the Calfornia Education Golden Bell Award.
ADOPT 8
A project of KFMB TV Channel 8 and San Diego County Adoptions
Everyday, hundreds of children in San Diego County are waiting to find forever families. That's why we partnered with San Diego County Adoptions to start ADOPT 8. Every week, Channel 8's Kathleen Bade introduces San Diegans to children who are currently in the county's Foster Care System waiting to be adopted. ADOPT 8 profiles are featured every Thursdays on Channel 8 News at 4Pm and Sundays on Channel 8 at 6Pm. The heart-warming profiles also educate San Diegans on the process of adoption in San Diego County. Since ADOPT 8 began last year, more than 125 children in San Diego have been adopted and have found their "forever families."
8's COOL SCHOOL
A project of Channel 8 and the San Diego County of Education (SDCOE)
KFMB TV Channel 8 believes in recognizing San Diego's finest schools. Every Friday on Channel 8 at 4pm, Education Reporter Beth Shelburne salutes 8's Cool School of the Week. 8's Cool School honors innovative schools and educational programs that encourage learning and help shape our children's futures. 8's Cool Schools are selected from nominations submitted to Channel 8 and SDCOE. Since the project began nearly six years ago, hundreds of schools have been featured. Students are taking pride in their schools and in their education. Educators are sharing learning programs featured on 8's Cool School.
Buddies for Life
A project of Channel 8 and UCSD Cancer Center
Channel 8 is proud to partner with UCSD's Cancer Center and the Susan G. Komen Breast Cancer Foundation to win the battle against breast cancer by providing the most comprehensive information on prevention, treatment and support. On the 8th of every month on Channel 8 at 4Pm and 6Pm, Barbara-Lee Edwards provides the latest information on breast health. In addition, we're urging viewers to join Buddies for Life by choosing a "buddy" and logging on to our website. Every month, UCSD Cancer Center will provide a free e-mail reminder service to viewers and their buddies to remind them to schedule breast self-exams and clinical exams. Channel 8 is the proud sponsor of the Susan G. Komen Race for the Cure.
Volunteer 8
A project of KFMB TV Channel 8 and Volunteer San Diego
Channel 8 and Volunteer San Diego have teamed to create Volunteer 8, hosted by Channel 8's Michael Tuck and Kathleen Bade. Volunteer 8's goal is to promote volunteerism and help make San Diego a better place. Volunteer San Diego assists community events, non-profits, and corporations in finding volunteers. Through Volunteer 8, we'll match your interests with thousands of volunteer opportunities countywide. Volunteer 8 stories air monthly on Channel 8 at 4Pm, profiling the efforts volunteers are making in our community.

Exhibit 17-6 The media show community involvement

generate goodwill as well as exposure for their causes. These groups and major corporations provide information regarding innovations, state-of-the-art research, and other items of interest (Exhibit 17-7). The YPA provides materials including case examples and lecture notes specifically designed for educators.

Educators are a target audience because, like the media, they control the flow of information to certain parties—in this case, people like you. *BusinessWeek, Fortune,* and *Fast Company* magazines attempt to have professors use their magazines in their classes, as does *The Wall Street Journal, The New York Times,* and *Advertising Age,* among others. In addition to selling more magazines, such usage also lends credibility to the mediums.

Civic and Business Organizations The local Jaycees, Kiwanis, and other nonprofit civic organizations also serve as gatekeepers of information. Companies' financial contributions to these groups, speeches at organization functions, and sponsorships are all designed to create goodwill. Corporate executives' service on the boards of nonprofit organizations also generates positive public relations.

Governments Public relations often attempts to influence government bodies directly at both local and national levels. Successful lobbying may mean immediate success for a product, while regulations detrimental to the firm may cost it millions. Imagine for a moment what FDA approval of a product can mean for sales, or what could happen to the beer and wine industries if TV advertising were banned. The pharmaceutical industry lobbied hard for permission to advertise prescription drugs directly to the consumer. Within the first five years of approval, an estimated 65 million consumers approached their doctors to inquire about the drugs as a result.[18] In turn, environmentalists, trade unions, and other groups with specific agendas will attempt to influence government legislation in their behalf.

Exhibit 17-7 The Yellow Pages provide information about the medium

Besides funding significant lobbies to have their positions heard, companies, organizations, and industries often take their positions to the public directly. For example, one of the primary agendas of the George W. Bush administration was Social Security reform. Exhibit 17-8 shows that the AARP wanted to inform the public of their position regarding the proposed changes.

In other instances, once the government has passed significant legislation, groups may undertake educational efforts to inform the public. For example, in November 2005, a number of senior citizens became eligible for Medicare drug care benefits. However, those not enrolled in the program by May 2006 would be required to pay higher premiums to receive the benefits. The U.S. Department of Health and Human Services initiated a three-year, $300 million IMC campaign to educate seniors about the sign-up deadline, benefits, and requirements for participation in the program. Much of the campaign was run by the public relations firm Ketchum, Inc.[19]

Financial Groups In addition to current shareholders, potential shareholders and investors may be relevant target markets for PR efforts. Financial advisors, lending institutions, and others must be kept abreast of new developments as well as of financial information, since they offer the potential for new sources of funding. Press releases and corporate reports play an important role in providing information to these publics.

Implementing the PR Program

Once the research has been conducted and the target audiences identified, the public relations program must be developed and delivered to the receivers. A number of PR tools are available for this purpose, including press releases, press conferences, exclusives, interviews, and community involvement.

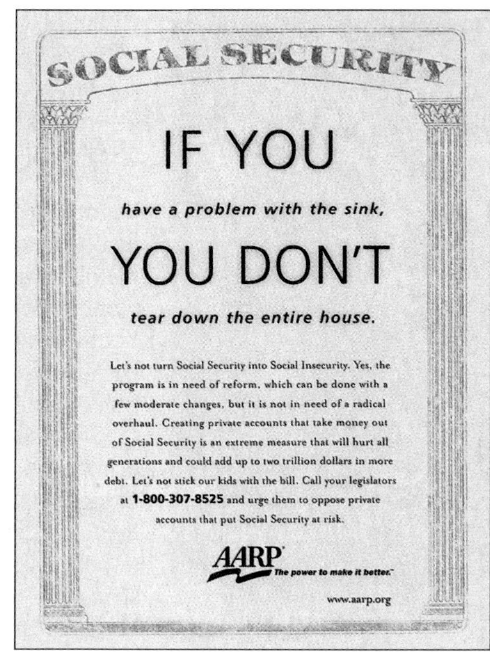

Exhibit 17-8 The AARP provides its position on Social Security reform

The Press Release

One of the most important publics is the press. To be used by the press, information must be factual, true, and of interest to the medium as well as to its audience. The source of the **press release** can do certain things to improve the likelihood that the "news" will be disseminated, such as ensuring that it reaches the right target audience, making it interesting, and making it easy to pass along.

The information in a press release won't be used unless it is of interest to the readers of the medium it is sent to. For example, financial institutions may issue press releases to business trade media and to the editor of the business section of a general-interest newspaper. Information on the release of a new rock album is of more interest to radio disk jockeys than to TV newscasters; sports news also has its interested audiences as do those in the beer industry (see Exhibit 17-9).

Press Conferences

We are all familiar with **press conferences** held by political figures. Although used less often by organizations and corporations, this form of delivery can be very effective. The topic must be of major interest to a specific group before it is likely to gain coverage. Usually major accomplishments (such as the awarding of the next Super Bowl or Olympics location), major breakthroughs (such as medical cures), emergencies, or catastrophes warrant a national press conference. On a local level, community events, local developments, and the like may receive coverage. Companies often call press conferences when they have significant news to announce, such as the introduction of a new product or advertising campaign. Sports teams use this tool to attract fan attention and interest when a new star is signed. TV3, a Malaysian broadcast system, held an international press conference to announce its introduction of an interactive TV service. Reebok held a press conference and issued a press release to announce it had signed rock star Shakira to an endorsement agreement. The Grammy Award–winning artist would be featured in Reebok's advertising campaign, and Reebok would sponsor her tour. Print ads, billboards, in-store displays, and consumer promotions were also included as part of the IMC package (Exhibit 17-10).

Exhibit 17-9 Sample press release

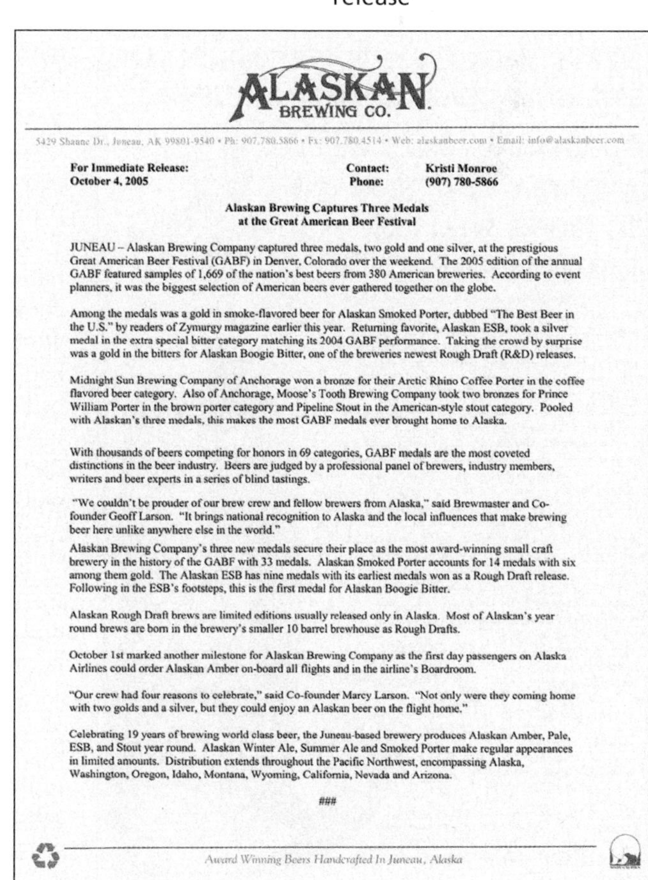

ALASKAN BREWING CO.

5429 Shaune Dr., Juneau, AK 99801-9540 • Ph: 907.780.5866 • Fx: 907.780.4514 • Web: alaskanbeer.com • Email: info@alaskanbeer.com

For Immediate Release:
October 4, 2005

Contact: **Kristi Monroe**
Phone: **(907) 780-5866**

Alaskan Brewing Captures Three Medals at the Great American Beer Festival

JUNEAU – Alaskan Brewing Company captured three medals, two gold and one silver, at the prestigious Great American Beer Festival (GABF) in Denver, Colorado over the weekend. The 2005 edition of the annual GABF featured samples of 1,669 of the nation's best beers from 380 American breweries. According to event planners, it was the biggest selection of American beers ever gathered together on the globe.

Among the medals was a gold in smoke-flavored beer for Alaskan Smoked Porter, dubbed "The Best Beer in the U.S." by readers of Zymurgy magazine earlier this year. Returning favorite, Alaskan ESB, took a silver medal in the extra special bitter category matching its 2004 GABF performance. Taking the crowd by surprise was a gold in the bitters for Alaskan Boogie Bitter, one of the breweries newest Rough Draft (R&D) releases.

Midnight Sun Brewing Company of Anchorage won a bronze for their Arctic Rhino Coffee Porter in the coffee flavored beer category. Also of Anchorage, Moose's Tooth Brewing Company took two bronzes for Prince William Porter in the brown porter category and Pipeline Stout in the American-style stout category. Pooled with Alaskan's three medals, this makes the most GABF medals ever brought home to Alaska.

With thousands of beers competing for honors in 69 categories, GABF medals are the most coveted distinctions in the beer industry. Beers are judged by a professional panel of brewers, industry members, writers and beer experts in a series of blind tastings.

"We couldn't be prouder of our brew crew and fellow brewers from Alaska," said Brewmaster and Co-founder Geoff Larson. "It brings national recognition to Alaska and the local influences that make brewing beer here unlike anywhere else in the world."

Alaskan Brewing Company's three new medals secure their place as the most award-winning small craft brewery in the history of the GABF with 33 medals. Alaskan Smoked Porter accounts for 14 medals with six among them gold. The Alaskan ESB has nine medals with its earliest medals won as a Rough Draft release. Following in the ESB's footsteps, this is the first medal for Alaskan Boogie Bitter.

Alaskan Rough Draft brews are limited editions usually released only in Alaska. Most of Alaskan's year round brews are born in the brewery's smaller 10 barrel brewhouse as Rough Drafts.

October 1st marked another milestone for Alaskan Brewing Company as the first day passengers on Alaska Airlines could order Alaskan Amber on-board all flights and in the airline's Boardroom.

"Our crew had four reasons to celebrate," said Co-founder Marcy Larson. "Not only were they coming home with two golds and a silver, but they could enjoy an Alaskan beer on the flight home."

Celebrating 19 years of brewing world class beer, the Juneau-based brewery produces Alaskan Amber, Pale, ESB, and Stout year round. Alaskan Winter Ale, Summer Ale and Smoked Porter make regular appearances in limited amounts. Distribution extends throughout the Pacific Northwest, encompassing Alaska, Washington, Oregon, Idaho, Montana, Wyoming, California, Nevada and Arizona.

###

Award Winning Beers Handcrafted In Juneau, Alaska

Exclusives

Although most public relations efforts seek a variety of channels for distribution, an alternative strategy is to offer one particular medium exclusive rights to the story if that medium reaches a substantial number of people in the target audience. Offering an **exclusive** may enhance the likelihood of acceptance. As you watch television over the next few weeks, watch for the various networks' and local stations' exclusives. Notice how the media actually use these exclusives to promote themselves.

Interviews

When you watch TV or read magazines, pay close attention to the personal interviews. Usually someone will raise specific questions, and a spokesperson provided by the firm will answer them. For example, Microsoft's president, Steve Ballmer, appeared in a number of personal interviews to present the company's position in a legal case brought against it by the U.S. government. Dan Brown, the

Exhibit 17-10 Reebok announces sponsorship of Shakira

author of *The Da Vinci Code* and *Angels and Demons* was interviewed on a number of networks after signing a contract to write additional books. Monica Lewinsky's first TV interview with Barbara Walters of ABC was a major coup for the network, as the ratings were among the highest ever recorded. (The interview just happened to take place during "sweeps"!)

Community Involvement Many corporations enhance their public image through involvement in the local community. This involvement may take many forms, including membership in local organizations like the Kiwanis or Jaycees and contributions to or participation in community events. For example, after hurricanes Katrina and Rita hit the Southeast, U.S. companies donated hundreds of millions of dollars in aid. Chevron, the BP Foundation, Home Depot, and Johnson & Johnson, among others, contributed $1 million or more to disaster agencies. The UnitedHealth Group gave $10 million in cash to relief groups, and Anheuser-Busch and its wholesalers shipped over a million cans of drinking water to the stricken area.[20] The Oreck Corporation provided assistance in a number of ways. Headquartered in New Orleans, with production facilities in Mississippi, the family owned corporation brought in temporary housing, food, and medical services to help employees, guaranteed continued employment, established a relief fund, and sponsored the program shown in Exhibit 17-11. WNBC-TV in New York produced a live hourlong program in conjunction with UNICEF to seek aid for tsunami victims after the December 26, 2004, disaster. Numerous other companies came to the aid of earthquake victims in Pakistan and flood victims in Central America when disasters hit there in late 2005. Most of these efforts, while appreciated, go largely unheralded by the public.

The Internet As mentioned briefly in Chapter 15, the Internet has become a means by which companies and organizations can disseminate public relations information. Just as in the print media, companies have used the Web to establish media relations and government, investor, and community relationships; to deal with crises; and even to conduct cause marketing. Companies have used their websites to address issues, as well as to provide information about products and services, archive press releases, link to other articles and sites, and provide lists of activities and events. In August 2005, a state jury in Angleton, Texas, awarded $24.4 million in actual damages and $229 million in punitive damages to Carol Ernst, whose late husband Robert died in his sleep in 2001 after taking Vioxx, Merck's painkiller drug. Merck's response to the verdict was posted on its website along with other information about its product, refund and prescription information, and information for wholesalers and retailers.

Exhibit 17-11 Oreck attempts to help out hurricane victims

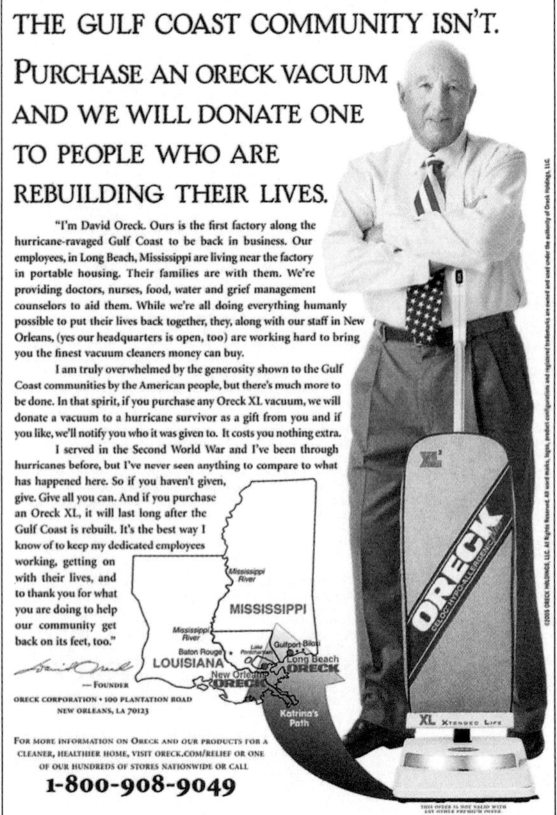

WE'RE BACK ON OUR FEET AGAIN BUT THE GULF COAST COMMUNITY ISN'T.
PURCHASE AN ORECK VACUUM AND WE WILL DONATE ONE TO PEOPLE WHO ARE REBUILDING THEIR LIVES.
"I'm David Oreck. Ours is the first factory along the hurricane-ravaged Gulf Coast to be back in business. Our employees, in Long Beach, Mississippi are living near the factory in portable housing. Their families are with them. We're providing doctors, nurses, food, water and grief management counselors to aid them. While we're all doing everything humanly possible to put their lives back together, they, along with our staff in New Orleans, (yes our headquarters is open, too) are working hard to bring you the finest vacuum cleaners money can buy.
I am truly overwhelmed by the generosity shown to the Gulf Coast communities by the American people, but there's much more to be done. In that spirit, if you purchase any Oreck XL vacuum, we will donate a vacuum to a hurricane survivor as a gift from you and if you like, we'll notify you who it was given to. It costs you nothing extra.
I served in the Second World War and I've been through hurricanes before, but I've never seen anything to compare to what has happened here. So if you haven't given, give. Give all you can. And if you purchase an Oreck XL, it will last long after the Gulf Coast is rebuilt. It's the best way I know of to keep my dedicated employees working, getting on with their lives, and to thank you for what you are doing to help our community get back on its feet, too."
— FOUNDER
ORECK CORPORATION • 100 PLANTATION ROAD
NEW ORLEANS, LA 70123
MISSISSIPPI
Mississippi River
LOUISIANA
Baton Rouge
New Orleans
Long Beach
Gulfport
ORECK
Katrina's Path
XL XTENDED LIFE
FOR MORE INFORMATION ON ORECK AND OUR PRODUCTS FOR A CLEANER, HEALTHIER HOME, VISIT ORECK.COM/RELIEF OR ONE OF OUR HUNDREDS OF STORES NATIONWIDE OR CALL
1-800-908-9049

A few years ago, poultry processor Pilgrim's Pride issued a nationwide recall of 27.4 million pounds of its Wampler brand cooked sandwich meat—the largest meat recall in U.S. history—after warnings of possible contamination from listeria. While they had not been linked directly to the illness, the company wanted to be sure that its products were not responsible. To assist in providing information to consumers, Pilgrim's Pride called a press conference, issued press releases, and provided information on its website (see Exhibit 17-12).[21] Other Internet tools, including e-mails and e-mail newsletters, have also been used effectively.

Shel Holtz notes that while there are many similarities between public relations activities conducted in traditional media and those conducted on the Internet, three main elements account for the differences between the two:

1. The Internet allows information to be presented quickly.
2. The Internet offers the opportunity to build internal links that provide the media with instant access to additional sources of information on the issue. And to get what they need.
3. The Internet offers the ability to provide much more substantial information. Print and broadcast materials are confined by

time and space limitations, while the Internet can literally provide volumes of information at a fingertip—or click of a mouse.[22]

Other methods of distributing information include photo kits, bylined articles (signed by the firm), speeches, and trade shows. Of course, the specific mode of distribution is determined by the nature of the story and the interest of the media and its publics.

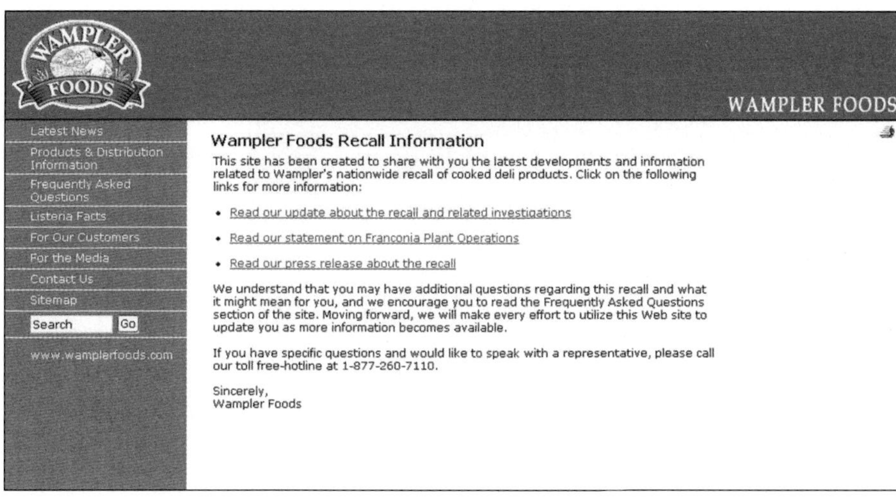

Exhibit 17-12 Pilgrim's Pride responds to negative publicity

Advantages and Disadvantages of PR

Like the other program elements, public relations has both advantages and disadvantages.

Advantages include the following:

1. *Credibility.* Because public relations communications are not perceived in the same light as advertising—that is, the public does not realize the organization either directly or indirectly paid for them—they tend to have more credibility. The fact that the media are not being compensated for providing the information may lead receivers to consider the news more truthful and credible. For example, an article in newspapers or magazines discussing the virtues of aspirin may be perceived as much more credible than an ad for a particular brand of aspirin.

Automotive awards presented in magazines such as *Motor Trend* have long been known to carry clout with potential car buyers. Now marketers have found that even coverage from lesser media means a lot as well. General Motors' Pontiac division played up an award given to Pontiac as "the best domestic sedan" by *MotorWeek* in a 30-minute program carried by about 300 public broadcasting stations. Likewise, Chrysler trumpeted the awards given to its Jeep Cherokee by *4-Wheel* and *Off Road* magazines.[23] It has become a common practice for car companies to promote their achievements.

News about a product may in itself serve as the subject of an ad. Exhibit 17-13 demonstrates how General Mills used favorable publicity from a variety of sources to promote the importance of whole grain in a healthy diet and promote the use of whole grain in its cereals. A number of companies including Marriott and Fidelity Insurance have also taken advantage in their ads of high customer satisfaction, product quality, and buying behavior analysis (see Exhibit 17-14).

2. *Cost.* In both absolute and relative terms, the cost of public relations is very low, especially when the possible effects are considered. While a firm can employ public relations agencies and spend millions of dollars on PR, for smaller companies this form of communication may be the most affordable alternative available.

Krispy Kreme, a donut shop, started in 1934 in Winston-Salem, N.C. Although the one store slowly grew into a 34-state chain over the years, it was really not a popular, well-known national brand. Then with a strong PR program and a subsequent IPO, Krispy Kreme took off. For a short period of time, when a new Krispy Kreme shop would open, the ensuing press coverage and free publicity almost eliminated the need for advertising. (Unfortunately for Krispy Kreme, publicity also led to the company's significant downturn in the industry as legal problems, declining sales, and other issues led to a more than 89 percent decline in the stocks value by February 2005, and rumors of bankruptcy by October of the same year.)[24]

Many public relations programs require little more than the time and expenses associated with putting the program together and getting it distributed, yet they still accomplish their objectives.

Exhibit 17-13 General Mills capitalizes on positive publicity

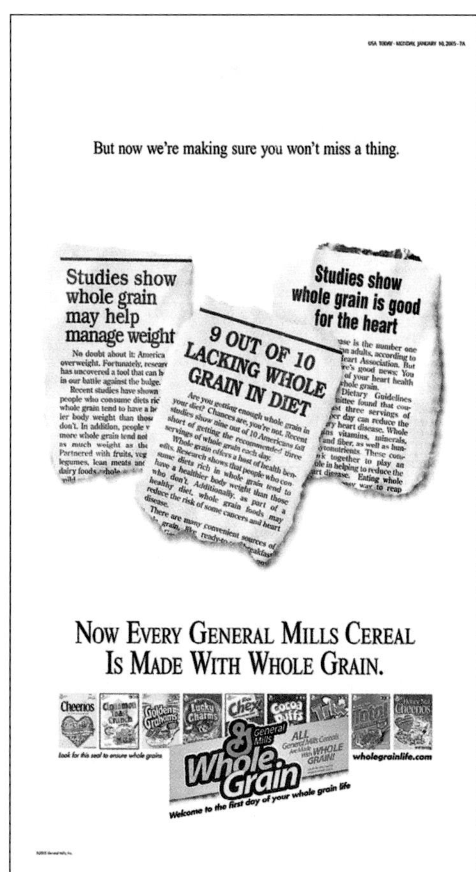

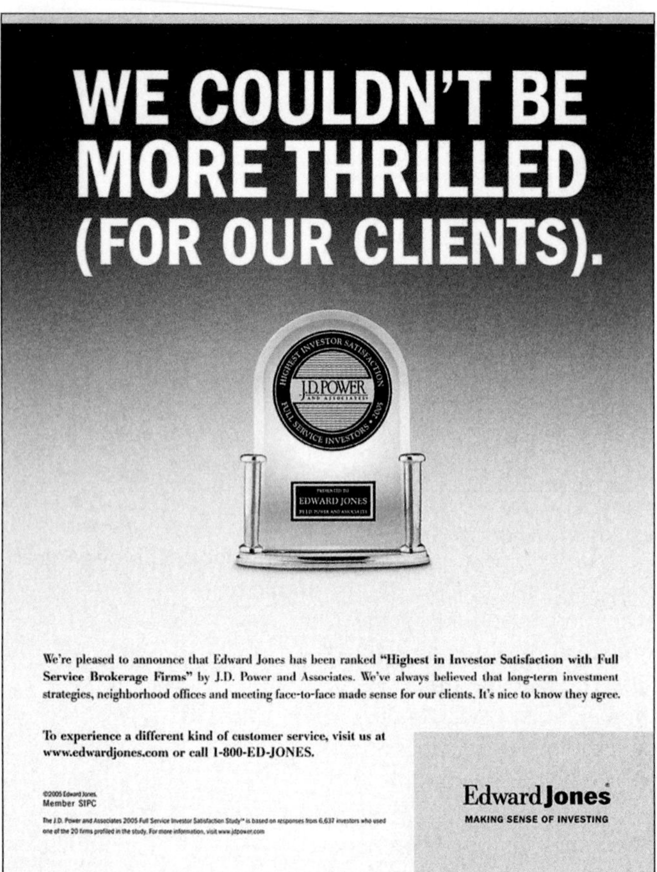

WE COULDN'T BE MORE THRILLED (FOR OUR CLIENTS).
J.D. POWER
EDWARD JONES
We're pleased to announce that Edward Jones has been ranked "Highest in Investor Satisfaction with Full Service Brokerage Firms" by J.D. Power and Associates. We've always believed that long-term investment strategies, neighborhood offices and meeting face-to-face made sense for our clients. It's nice to know they agree.
To experience a different kind of customer service, visit us at www.edwardjones.com or call 1-800-ED-JONES.
©2005 Edward Jones.
Member SIPC
The J.D. Power and Associates 2005 Full Service Investor Satisfaction Study℠ is based on responses from 6,637 investors who used one of the 20 firms profiled in the study. For more information, visit www.jdpower.com
Edward Jones
MAKING SENSE OF INVESTING

Exhibit 17-14 Edward Jones promotes its J.D. Power Award

3. *Avoidance of clutter.* Because they are typically perceived as news items, public relations messages are not subject to the clutter of ads. A story regarding a new product introduction or breakthrough is treated as a news item and is likely to receive attention. When Steven Jobs (the founder of Apple Computer) announced his return to Apple after being with another firm for years, the networks covered it, as did major newspapers and magazines. Some (including CNN) devoted two- to three-minute segments to the story.

4. *Lead generation.* Information about technological innovations, medical breakthroughs, and the like results almost immediately in a multitude of inquiries. These inquiries may give the firm some quality sales leads.

5. *Ability to reach specific groups.* Because some products appeal to only small market segments, it is not feasible to engage in advertising and/or promotions to reach them. If the firm does not have the financial capabilities to engage in promotional expenditures, the best way to communicate to these groups is through public relations.

6. *Image building.* Effective public relations helps to develop a positive image for the organization. A strong image is insurance against later misfortunes. For example, in 1982, seven people in the Chicago area died after taking Extra Strength Tylenol capsules that had been laced with cyanide (after they reached the store). Within one week of the poisonings, Tylenol's market share fell from 35 to only 6.5 percent. Strong public relations efforts combined with an already strong product and corporate image helped the product rebound (despite the opinions of many experts that it had no chance of recovering). A brand or firm with a lesser image would never have been able to come back. The ad in Exhibit 17-15 demonstrates the power of a strong image. The Firestone tire recall cited earlier is another example. Because of a strong image established over 102 years of doing business, Firestone was able to weather the storm and recover from the incident.

Perhaps the major disadvantage of public relations is the potential for not completing the communications process. While public relations messages can break through the clutter of commercials, the receiver may not make the connection to the source. Many firms' PR efforts are never associated with their sponsors in the public mind.

Public relations may also misfire through mismanagement and a lack of coordination with the marketing department. When marketing and PR departments operate independently, there is a danger of inconsistent communications, redundancies in efforts, and so on.

The key to effective public relations is to establish a good program, worthy of public interest, and to manage it properly. To determine if this program is working, the firm must measure the effectiveness of the PR effort.

Measuring the Effectiveness of PR

As with the other promotional program elements, it is important to evaluate the effectiveness of the public relations efforts. In addition to determining the contribution of this program element to attaining communications objectives, the evaluation offers other advantages:

1. It tells management what has been achieved through public relations activities.
2. It provides management with a way to measure public relations achievements quantitatively.
3. It gives management a way to judge the quality of public relations achievements and activities.

WHY A STRONG BRAND IMAGE GIVES YOU AN ALMOST UNFAIR ADVANTAGE.

[In a world of parity products and services, nothing can tilt things more dramatically in your favor than powerful brand and corporate advertising.]

A brand or corporate image is not something that can be seen, touched, tasted, defined, or measured. Intangible and abstract, it exists solely as an idea in the mind. Yet it is often a company's most precious asset.

When in the 1980s, corporations laid out billions for the companies that owned brands like Kraft, Jell-O, Del Monte, Maxwell House and Nabisco, it wasn't the products themselves they were after, but the enduring power of warm images, feelings, and impressions associated with the brand names. In fact, when the dust finally settles, it will become clear that the megamergers, takeovers, and leveraged buyouts of that decade were primarily about the acquisition of brands.

Yet despite their enormous value, brands are not immune to neglect, and in the face of a tough economy and strong competition, companies are often tempted to sacrifice brand and corporate advertising for short-term promotion. While such strategies can yield immediate results, over time they can weaken and tarnish the brand.

AD/PROMOTION RATIO & MARKET POSITION
Ad/Promo Ratio
31% Followers
35% Marginal Leaders
42% Dominators
Market Position

Studies conducted on the PIMS (Profit Impact on Market Strategy) data base prove that companies that put more money behind (their) image advertising are more likely to be market dominators, ranking first in a category and having sales volume one-and-a-half times greater than the nearest competitor. Moreover, the larger the ratio of brand advertising to promotion, the greater the return on investment (ROI).

AD/PROMOTION RATIO & ROI
Return On Investment
18% Promo 76% Ads 24%
27% Promo 56% Ads 44%
31% Promo < 50% Ads > 50%
Ad/Promotion Ratio

When only a quarter of a company's advertising/promotion budget is spent on brand advertising, the ROI is 18%. When the ratio is increased to 50/50, the return can be over 70% higher.

Backing your brand in good times and bad–keeping that image in front of people–can mean higher profits as well as leadership.

PROTECTING AND NURTURING A brand is one of advertising's most important jobs. And that means choosing the media for your message with care. For more and more companies, the best environment is The Wall Street Journal. The Journal has always operated on the principle that there is a direct link between the quality of our editorial and the quality of the advertising we attract. Witness the impressive list of corporations appearing in any Journal issue.

In The Myers Marketing & Research survey of The Worldwide Marketing Leadership Panel, The Journal was awarded top honors in five separate categories, including editorial quality and reader involvement–more evidence of The Journal's unmatched stature and prestige.

If you're looking for a publication that can add value to your brand, there's no better brand than ours: The Wall Street Journal.

THE WALL STREET JOURNAL.
THE WORLD'S BUSINESS DAILY. IT WORKS.

Exhibit 17-15 This *Wall Street Journal* ad stresses the value of a strong brand and/or corporate image

As outlined in Figure 17-3, a number of criteria may be used to measure the effects of PR programs. Additional means for accomplishing this evaluation process include the following:

- *Personal observation and reaction.* Personal observation and evaluation by one's superiors should occur at all levels of the organization.
- *Matching objectives and results.* Specific objectives designed to attain the overall communications objectives should be related to actions, activities, or media coverage. For example, placing a feature story in a specific number of media is an objective, quantitative, and measurable goal.[25]
- *The team approach.* Harold Mendelsohn suggests that one way to achieve attitude and behavior modification through public information campaigns is the **team approach,** whereby evaluators are actually involved in the campaign.[26] By using research principles and working together, the team develops—and accomplishes—goals.

Figure 17-3 Criteria for Measuring the Effectiveness of PR

A system for measuring the effectiveness of the public relations program has been developed by Lotus HAL. The criteria used in the evaluation process follow:

- Total number of impressions over time
- Total number of impressions on the target audience
- Total number of impressions on specific target audiences
- Percentage of positive articles over time
- Percentage of negative articles over time
- Ratio of positive to negative articles
- Percentage of positive/negative articles by subject
- Percentage of positive/negative articles by publication or reporter
- Percentage of positive/negative articles by target audience

- *Management by objectives.* Executives and their managers act together to identify goals to be attained and the responsibilities of the managers. These goals are then used as a standard to measure accomplishments.
- *Public opinion and surveys.* Research in the form of public opinion surveys may be used to gather data to evaluate program goal attainment.
- *Audits.* Both internal and external audits may be used. **Internal audits** involve evaluations by superiors or peers within the firm to determine the performance of the employee (or his or her programs). **External audits** are conducted by consultants, the client (in the case of a PR agency), or other parties outside the organization.

Mark Weiner, in discussing measures of effectiveness of MPRs, also suggests using the following methods:[27]

- *Media content analysis.* Systematically and objectively identifying the characteristics of messages that appear in the media, analyzing the content to determine trends and perceptions relevant to the product or brand.
- *Survey research.* Quantitatively assessing consumers' attitudes toward the product or brand.
- *Marketing-mix modeling.* Drawing data from multiple sources and integrating them to provide insight into the process.

A number of other bases for evaluation can be used. Walter Lindenmann says three levels of measures are involved: (1) the basic, which measures the actual PR activities undertaken; (2) the intermediate, which measures audience reception and understanding of the message; and (3) the advanced, which measures the perceptual and behavioral changes that result.[28]

Some organizations may use a combination of measures, depending on their specific needs. For example, Hewlett-Packard uses impression counts, awareness and preference studies, in-house assessments, press clippings counts, and tracking studies.[29]

In summary, the role of public relations in the promotional mix is changing. As PR has become more marketing oriented, the criteria by which the programs are evaluated have also changed. At the same time, nonmarketing activities will continue to be part of the public relations department and part of the basis for evaluation.

Publicity

Publicity refers to the generation of news about a person, product, or service that appears in broadcast or print media. To many marketers, publicity and public relations are synonymous. In fact, publicity is really a subset of the public relations effort.

But there are several major differences. First, publicity is typically a *short-term* strategy, while public relations is a concerted program extending over a period of time. Second, public relations is designed to provide positive information about the firm and is usually controlled by the firm or its agent. Publicity, on the other hand, is not always positive and is not always under the control of, or paid for by, the organization. Both positive and negative publicity often originates from sources other than the firm.

In most organizations, publicity is controlled and disseminated by the public relations department. In this section, we discuss the role publicity plays in the promotional program and some of the ways marketers use and react to these communications.

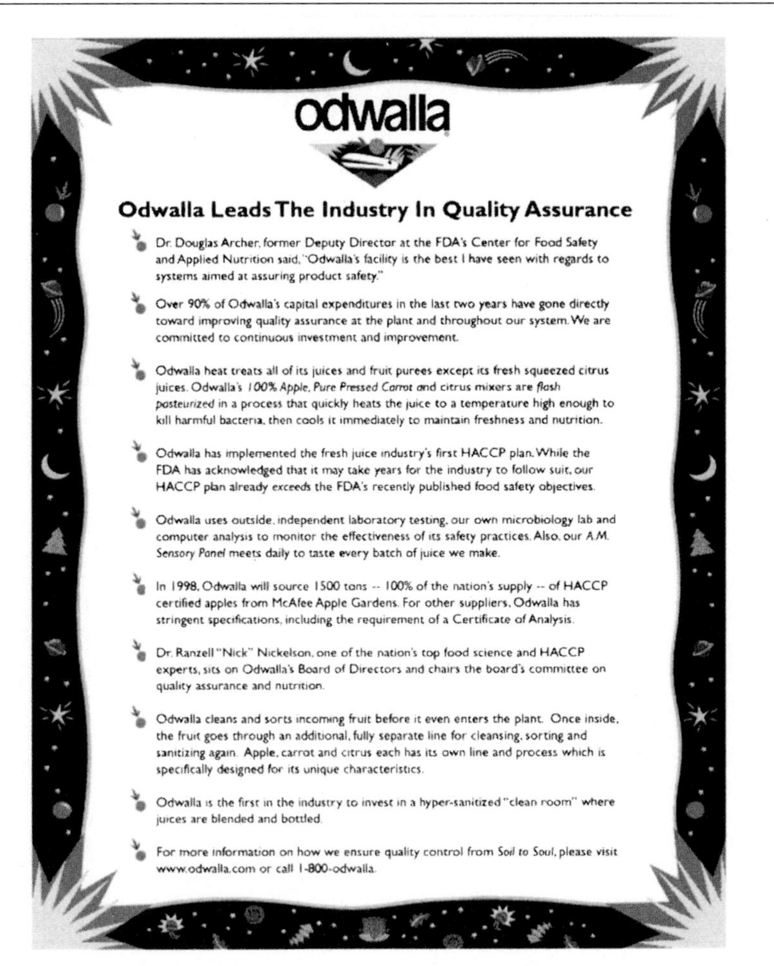

Exhibit 17-16 Odwalla assures customers of its quality

The Power of Publicity

One of the factors that most sets off publicity from the other program elements is the sheer power this form of communication can generate. Unfortunately for marketers, this power is not always realized in the way they would like it to be. Publicity can make or break a product or even a company.

Earlier we discussed the substantial drop in Tylenol sales after extensive media coverage of the tampering with its products while on store shelves. The Johnson & Johnson marketing efforts (including a strong public relations emphasis) designed to aid recovery were a model in proficiency that will be studied by students of marketing in both the classroom and the boardroom for many years. By January 1983, almost 100 percent of the original brand share had been regained. Similarly, when Odwalla's brand was threatened by negative publicity resulting from contaminated juice, the company immediately recalled the product, increased safety measures, and paid medical bills for those who had become ill. It also established a website and toll-free telephone numbers to make information easily available to concerned customers (see Exhibit 17-16). The company has regained 100 percent of its market share as a result of these efforts. Unfortunately, a marketer cannot always capitalize on positive publicity or control the effects of negative publicity so effectively.

Why is publicity so much more powerful than advertising or sales promotion—or even other forms of public relations? First, publicity is highly credible. Unlike advertising and sales promotions, publicity is not usually perceived as being sponsored by the company (in negative instances, it never is). So consumers perceive this information as more objective and place more confidence in it. In fact, *Consumer Reports,* the medium responsible for one of the examples previously cited, ran an ad campaign designed to promote its credibility by noting it does not accept advertising and therefore can be objective in its evaluations.

Publicity information may be perceived as endorsed by the medium in which it appears. For example, publicity regarding a breakthrough in the durability of golf balls will go far to promote them if it is reported by *Golf* magazine. *Car & Driver*'s award for car of the year reflects the magazine's perception of the quality of the auto selected.

Still another reason for publicity's power is its news value and the frequency of exposure it generates. When the publicity is positive, companies stand to benefit. When it is not, companies may suffer negative consequences such as lost sales, impacts on image, and even litigation. How to respond to these instances is the topic of IMC Perspective 17-1.

The bottom line is that publicity is news, and people like to pass on information that has news value. Publicity thus results in a significant amount of free, credible, word-of-mouth information regarding the firm and its products.

IMC PERSPECTIVE 17-1

Negative Publicity: Companies Assume Different Strategies to Deal with Crisis Management

There are many in the business world who believe that any publicity—including negative publicity—is good for the company. The authors of this text are not to be included in that group. We could cite numerous examples including Audi, Ford, Enron, and Tyco among others to support our position. If a company does not respond appropriately and in a timely fashion, it could result in serious losses (both in image and finance). Effective responses, on the other hand, may lead to gains in both of these areas. The issue is in how to respond.

Consider, for example, Wal-Mart. While the success and innovativeness of the retail giant has been lauded by many, the company also has its fair share of opponents—and we don't just mean competitors. While it was not much of an issue in the past, or in certain parts of the United States, when Wal-Mart wants to open up a new store now, an increasing number of communities say no. Cities in Vermont, California, and Vancouver, British Columbia, are just a few of the many who have fought to keep the retail giant out of their neighborhoods. Citing Wal-Mart's labor practices, seemingly uncompromising positions, and (in some cases) greed, the opponents tell them they are not welcome. The efforts to keep Wal-Mart out of communities have led to a strategic public relations effort. Fifty different groups have formed a coalition to distribute print ads, videos, and books; to develop a viral Internet campaign; to conduct press conferences; and to create a blog (WakeUpWalmart.com) in an attempt to change the practices of the largest corporation in the United States.

Wal-Mart, until recently, pretty much ignored their critics. But now that the coalition appears to be getting stronger and more effective (Wal-Mart was able to build only about 50 percent of the stores in the time frame it sought in California and has had to alter its architectural design in other cities), Wal-Mart has found it necessary to respond—and fight back—and they have, with a well-organized PR blitz of their own. In January 2005, the company launched its first ever corporate image campaign, "Wal-Mart is Working for Everyone," which included TV spots, and print and radio ads touting the positive aspects of the company and its work environment. The campaign cited the many good things Wal-Mart has done, for example, their "Acres for America" campaign, in which the company agrees to preserve one acre of land for each acre used for a Wal-Mart store. They have written or supported books in their favor such as *The United States of Wal-Mart,* and have hired both advertising and public relations agencies to get their position told (essentially, that Wal-Mart is good for America, and the very practices being criticized have led people to shop in their stores to get the very lowest prices and best values).

Wal-Mart is not the only company that has been forced to respond to negative publicity. Nike, Chiquita, and Krispy Kreme (among numerous others) have all had to respond to negative publicity (the former two for their labor practices, Krispy Kreme for giving away a free donut for every A on a student's report card). Like Wal-Mart, they have determined that the options of "laying low" or remaining silent did not work. Consumer activists are getting too strong.

Others have put a more positive spin on these companies' potential crises. For example, American International Group, Inc. (AIG), the subject of accounting scandals, angry regulators, and a dramatic showdown with their chairman and CEO, increased its advertising expenditures to promote its marketplace prowess (while ignoring the scandals). AIG immediately asked its CEO to step down, distancing the company from the CEO's alleged improprieties, while putting out positive messages to show the company was sound. AIG tracked public attitudes and conducted focus groups with internal and external audiences to monitor the impact of the scandal (there seemed to be little or no effect). After the Vioxx problem, Merck and Co. also engaged in corporate image advertising designed to show the company's good side by showing their fight against childhood diseases and offering discounts on its drugs to senior citizens. Morgan Stanley increased its image advertising expenditures, while insurance broker Marsh & McLennan Companies released its campaign, "The New Marsh: Making Changes to Restore Your Trust," after negative publicity created problems for the companies.

One of the more interesting examples of crisis management was that of Wendy's. In early 2005, the fast-food chain's image and sales were severely damaged when a woman in San Jose, California, claimed she found a severed finger in her beef chili at a Wendy's store. While the previously discussed cases were the result of internal decisions, this crisis was brought about by a fraudulent claim in which the woman making the claim was subsequently arrested. Nevertheless, through no fault of its own, Wendy's suffered losses of 2 percent among its 6,250 stores over 15 months, and 20 to 50 percent in the Bay Area. Wendy's decided to make a limited response, giving away free milkshakes in a promotion promoted as customer appreciation weekend in local newspapers and through direct-mail coupons in the Bay Area. The company considered no increases in advertising on a regional or national basis, and no other augmentations to the marketing plan, noted Dennis Lynch, the company's senior vice president for communications, though the market would be monitored and changes made if required. The company decided that "for us to make significant changes to our current marketing plan would send a clearly mixed signal," said Lynch, as Wendy's did nothing wrong and did not want to remind consumers of the issue. (Though Lynch did tell Fox News they would give no further interviews until the network stopped showing the severed finger!) The company was clearly between a rock and a hard place: promoting their innocence would keep bringing attention to the incident—and not the kind of attention they wanted. In the fall of 2005, the woman who filed the false claim pleaded guilty to fraud—hopefully ending the issue.

Crisis conditions are brought on by numerous causes. For every crisis, the experts have a different opinion as to how it should best be resolved. Two things are certain. Crises will continue to occur, and experts will continue to take different approaches to solving them.

Sources: Diane Brady, Michael Arndt, and Amy Barrett, "When Your Name Is Mud, Advertise," *BusinessWeek,* July 4, 2005, pp. 56–59; Mya Frazier, "Wal-Mart under Attack: But Should It Fight Back?" *Advertising Age,* April 18, 2005, p. 12; Stuart Elliott, "Wendy's Gets a Break, but Still Has Work Ahead of It," *The New York Times* (nytimes.com), April 29, 2005, p. 1.

The Control and Dissemination of Publicity

In some of the examples cited previously, the control of publicity was not in the hands of the company. In some instances it is the firm's own blunder which allows information to leak out. Companies such as Wal-Mart and Merck and Co. could do nothing to stop the media from releasing negative information about them. When publicity becomes news, it is reported by the media, sometimes despite efforts by the firm. In these instances, the organization needs to react to the potential threat created by the news. Unfortunately, simply ignoring the problem will not make it go away.

A good example of one company's efforts to respond to adverse publicity is shown in Exhibit 17-17. Tree Top's problems began when all the major news media reported that the chemical Alar, used by some growers to regulate the growth of apples, might cause cancer in children. Despite published statements by reliable scientific and medical authorities (including the surgeon general) that Alar does not cause cancer, a few special-interest groups were able to generate an extraordinary amount of adverse publicity, causing concern among consumers and purchasing agents. A few school districts took apples off their menus, and even applesauce and juice were implicated. Tree Top ran the ad shown in Exhibit 17-17 to state its position and alleviate consumers' fears. It also sent a direct mailing to nutritionists and day care operators. The campaign was successful in assuring consumers of the product's safety and rebuilding their confidence.

Exhibit 17-17 Tree Top responds to the threat of negative publicity

In other instances, however, publicity must be managed like any other promotional tool. For example, when Martha Stewart was convicted by the SEC (Securities and Exchange Commission) of insider trading, the negative publicity had severe consequences for her company. Sales dropped, stocks plummeted, and advertisers pulled their ads from her TV program. Many media observers all but buried her brand. However, while still in jail, Stewart cultivated a softer image than her past reputation as a harsh taskmaster, by befriending inmates and dispensing tips for better prison food. Upon her release, stock prices increased, many advertisers returned, and a Martha Stewart *Apprentice* TV show aired. Brand experts said the show of humility was key to Stewart's comeback.[30]

Publicity can also work for marketers. Kids' toys frequently achieve significant sales due to high levels of positive publicity and word-of-mouth advertising. Sales of Cabernet Savignon increased an average of 45 percent in the month after a CBS *60 Minutes* report indicating that daily moderate consumption of red wine can reduce the risk of heart disease, and green tea sales skyrocketed when the word spread that consumption of the product was effective in preventing cancer. There are many more examples of the positive impact publicity can have.

Marketers like to have as much control as possible over the time and place where information is released. One way to do this is with the **video news release (VNR),** a publicity piece produced by publicists so that stations can air it as a news story. The videos almost never mention that they are produced by the subject organization, and most news stations don't mention it either. Many pharmaceutical companies like Pfizer, Aventis, and AstraZeneca have used VNRs, as have GNC, Mercedes, Neiman Marcus, and others. The use of VNRs without disclosing the source has led some consumer advocates to protest such actions, as is discussed in Ethical Perspective 17-1.

In their efforts to manage publicity and public relations, marketers are continuously learning more about these activities. Courses are offered, websites are devoted to the topic, and books written on how to manage publicity. These books cover how to make a presentation, whom to contact, how to issue a press release, and what to know about each medium addressed, including TV, radio, newspapers, magazines, the Internet,

ETHICAL PERSPECTIVE 17-1

Video News Releases: Promoting the News or Deceptive Advertising?

The Video News Release (VNR) has been a tool of public relations for decades. Causes, corporations, political candidates, even national tourism boards have used freely dispensed "news stories" to get their messages on the air. The stories are produced, copied onto video, and distributed to television stations free of charge. Television stations welcome the VNRs, particularly if they are well done, topical, and might hold interest for their viewers. Usually, the video bears the label of the sponsor of the VNR, for example, the name of the company or organization responsible for its production and distribution. To many, including consumer watchdog organizations, the television media, and even some in the public relations industry, the VNR walked a thin line between news and advertising. Nevertheless, the VNR continued to be used, and, in fact, usage increased even as skeptics and opponents quietly sat by and watched.

Recently, however, the VNR—or should we say the producers of VNRs—have come under attack from a variety of sources, and the criticism has not been quiet. It started with a series of VNRs produced by the Bush administration promoting a new Medicare program in early 2004—an election year. In the VNRs a public relations professional posed as a journalist and painted the Bush position on Medicare in a very favorable light. The "news releases" aired on 40 television stations in 33 markets. Because the public relations professional was not identified as such, and the sponsorship of the VNR was so poorly identified, Democrats cried foul, calling the VNRs "covert advertising," "fake news," and other not so nice things. They raised enough noise to lead the government watchdog General Accounting Office (GAO) to open an inquiry into the incident.

But the Medicare VNRs were not the only time that the promotion of Bush's political agenda used this tactic. Another program, this time touting an educational program, called "No Child Left Behind," also employed the distribution of video news releases to local and national newscasts. This series used Armstrong Williams, a broadcast commentator as the "journalist." The fact that Williams was paid $250,000 for his participation went undisclosed. Again the Democrats complained, and again the GAO investigated. The GAO's report released October 2005 concluded that the dissemination of the VNRs violated prohibitions on funding a "covert propaganda campaign."In December 2005 a Superior Court judge in California ruled that Governor Schwarzenegger's administrations use of fake VNRs to promote his proposals violated the law. The judge ordered the administration to immediately stop production and distribution of the video news releases.

In the wake of the Williams investigation, additional agencies began to inquire about the ethics of VNRs. The Federal Communications Commission (FCC) issued a directive that broadcasters must clearly disclose the nature, source, and sponsorship of a video news release. In the same week, the Senate also placed restrictions on government-issued VNRs. The Radio Television News Directors Association developed formal guidelines requiring better identification of the source, and the Public Relations Society of America (PRSA) weighed in with their position—a 32-page document filed with the FCC. Each of the groups indicated their support for full disclosure.

But not everyone is happy about the new disclosure requirements. Many nonprofits and major marketers also use VNRs to get their stories told. Those employed in the $150 million per year VNR production industry are not so pleased either, concerned that their business could be hurt or even destroyed. They argued, along with the PRSA, that most VNRs are clearly labeled when they are delivered to broadcast organizations, and that the examples cited above were the result of "procedural breakdowns," not a problem pervading the industry. Further, they say, most VNRs are distributed free to the stations, they are not paid to air them, and the station managers can use their own discretion as to whether they are fake advertisements or misleading statements to the public. They contend that the most likely to be hurt are the smaller stations and their audiences, as they rely on the VNRs to keep their own news production costs down; if they could not use the freebies, it would result in significant cost increases. Besides, the use of VNRs is an age-old strategy, and one should not throw out all of the apples because one is bad.

Nevertheless, the PRSA agreed with the FCC that the need for full disclosure outweighed the potential risks associated with increased restrictions. The existing federal laws and regulations coupled with self-enforcement and ethical standards will ensure that disclosure takes place in the future, they said. Larry Moskowitz, president, CEO, and chairman of Medialink, the biggest producer of VNRs, agreed. He called the FCC action "nothing new," stating that "there would be some dust . . . but at the end of the day the industry would evolve." And everyone will be better off, right? Not according to Wayne Friedman, who criticized the FCC directive in an editorial appearing in MediaPosts' *TVWATCH*. Friedman believes labeling has gone too far because people need to judge for themselves how much information they need. But won't it be easier if that information is disclosed?

Sources: Dan Morain, "Gov's Fake News Videos Ruled Illegal," *Los Angeles Times*, December 2, 2005, p. B6; Wayne Friedman, "GAO: Payments For 'Fake' TV Newscasts Are Illegal," *Media Post Publications*, mediapost.com, October 3, 2005, pp. 1–2; Ira Tenowitz and Matthew Creamer, "Fake News Videos Unmasked in FCC Crackdown," *Advertising Age*, April 18, 2005, p. 3; Wayne Friedman, "How Much Labeling Do We Need on U.S. Television Programming?" MediaPosts' *TVWATCH*, March 22, 2005, p. 1; Cedric Bess, "FCC Mulls Expanding Regulation for Prepackaged News, PR Calls for Vigorous Application of Existing Industry-Wide Disclosure Standards," PRSA.org, June 24, 2005, pp. 1–2.

and direct-response advertising. They discuss such alternative media as news conferences, seminars, events, and personal letters, as well as insights on how to deal with government and other legislative bodies. Because this information is too extensive to include as a single chapter in this text, we suggest you peruse one of the many books available on this subject for additional insights.

Advantages and Disadvantages of Publicity

Publicity offers the advantages of credibility, news value, significant word-of-mouth communications, and a perception of being endorsed by the media. Beyond the potential impact of negative publicity, two major problems arise from the use of publicity: timing and accuracy.

Timing Timing of the publicity is not always completely under the control of the marketer. Unless the press thinks the information has very high news value, the timing of the press release is entirely up to the media—if it gets released at all. Thus, the information may be released earlier than desired or too late to make an impact.

Accuracy A major way to get publicity is the press release. Unfortunately, the information sometimes gets lost in translation, that is, it is not always reported the way the provider wishes it to be. As a result, inaccurate information, omissions, or other errors may result. Sometimes when you see a publicity piece that was written from a press release, you wonder if the two are even about the same topic.

Measuring the Effectiveness of Publicity

The methods for measuring the effects of publicity are essentially the same as those discussed earlier under the broader topic of public relations. Rather than reiterate them here, we thought it would be more interesting to show you an actual example. Figure 17-4 is a model developed by Ketchum Public Relations for tracking the effects of publicity. (I guess we just provided Ketchum with some free publicity.)

Corporate Advertising

One of the more controversial forms of advertising is **corporate advertising.** Actually an extension of the public relations function, corporate advertising does not promote any one specific product or service. Rather, it is designed to promote the firm overall, by enhancing its image, assuming a position on a social issue or cause, or seeking direct involvement in something. Why is corporate advertising controversial? A number of reasons are offered:

1. *Consumers are not interested in this form of advertising.* A Gallup and Robinson study reported in *Advertising Age* found consumers were 35 percent less interested in corporate ads than in product-oriented advertising.[31] This may be because consumers do not understand the reasons behind such ads. Of course, much of this confusion results from ads that are not very good from a communications standpoint.
2. *It's a costly form of self-indulgence.* Firms have been accused of engaging in corporate image advertising only to satisfy the egos of top management. This argument stems from the fact that corporate ads are not easy to write. The message to be communicated is not as precise and specific as one designed to position a product, so the top managers often dictate the content of the ad, and the copy reflects their ideas and images of the corporation.
3. *The firm must be in trouble.* Some critics believe the only time firms engage in corporate advertising is when they are in trouble—either in a financial sense or in the public eye—and are advertising to attempt to remedy the problem. There are a number of forms of corporate advertising, each with its own objectives. These critics argue that these objectives have become important only because the firm has not been managed properly.
4. *Corporate advertising is a waste of money.* Given that the ads do not directly appeal to anyone, are not understood, and do not promote anything specific, critics say the monies could be better spent in other areas. Again, much of this argument has its foundation in the fact that corporate image ads are often intangible. They typically do not ask directly

Figure 17-4 The Ketchum Effectiveness Yardstick (KEY)—A Strategic Approach to the Measurement of Public Relations Results

At Ketchum, we believe strongly that it is possible to measure public relations effectiveness. We also believe strongly that measuring public relations results can be done in a timely and cost-efficient manner.

Our strategic approach to public relations measurement involves a two-step process:

1. Setting in advance very specific and clearly defined public relations goals and objectives, and,
2. Pinpointing those levels of measurement that are crucial to the organization in determining to what extent those specific public relations goals and objectives have been met.

In the model, there are three levels for measuring PR effectiveness:

- *Level #1*—the Basic level for measuring public relations OUTPUTS. This measures the amount of exposure an organization receives in the media, the total number of placements, the total number of impressions, and/or the likelihood of having reached specific target audience groups. Research tools often used when conducting Level #1 measurement include content analysis or publicity tracking studies, secondary analysis, segmentation analysis, and basic public opinion polls.
- *Level #2*—the Intermediate level for measuring public relations OUTGROWTHS. Outgrowths measure whether or not target audience groups actually received the messages directed at them, paid attention to them, understood the messages, and retained those messages in any shape or form. Research tools often used when conducting Level #2 measurement include focus groups; in-depth interviews; telephone, mail, face-to-face, or mall intercept surveys; testing techniques; and recall studies.
- *Level #3*—the Advanced level for measuring public relations OUTCOMES. This measures opinion, attitude, and/or behavior change to determine if there has been a shift in views and/or how people act when it comes to an organization, its products, or its services. Research tools often used when conducting Level #3 measurement include before-and-after studies, experimental and quasi-experimental research, ethnographic studies, communications audits, and multivariate analyses of data.
- The different levels of measuring public relations impact can be plotted on a yardstick in a hierarchical fashion. Here is a graphic displaying the KETCHUM EFFECTIVENESS YARDSTICK (KEY), which summarizes from left to right these levels of public relations measurement:

Level #1	Level #2	Level #3
Basic—Measuring OUTPUTS	Intermediate—Measuring OUTGROWTHS	Advanced—Measuring OUTCOMES
Media placements Impressions Targeted Audiences	Receptivity Awareness Comprehension Retention	Opinion change Attitude change Behavior change

More detailed information about Ketchum's strategic approach to measuring public relations effectiveness may be obtained by contacting Graham Hueber, Vice President and Director of Research at Ketchum.

for a purchase; they do not ask for investors. Rather, they present a position or try to create an image. Because they are not specific, many critics believe their purpose is lost on the audience and these ads are not a wise investment of the firm's resources.

Despite these criticisms and others, corporate advertising has increased in use. It has been estimated that more than 7 percent of all advertising dollars spent are for corporate advertising, meaning billions of dollars are spent on this form of communication.[32] Tyco spent an estimated $10 million in an attempt to improve its image after the indictment and conviction of its CEO.[33]

While corporate advertising has generally been regarded as the domain of companies such as USX, General Dynamics, TRW, and Union Carbide (that is, companies that do not primarily sell directly to the consumer market), this is no longer the case. Beatrice Foods, BASF, and Procter & Gamble are just a few consumer-product companies running corporate image ads, and numerous others have also increased expenditures in this area.

Since the term *corporate advertising* tends to be used as a catchall for any type of advertising run for the direct benefit of the corporation rather than its products or services, much advertising falls into this category. For purposes of this text (and to attempt to bring some perspective to the term), we use it to describe any type of advertising designed to promote the organization itself rather than its products or services.

Objectives of Corporate Advertising

Corporate advertising may be designed with two goals in mind: (1) creating a positive image for the firm and (2) communicating the organization's views on social, business, and environmental issues. More specific applications include:

- Boosting employee morale and smoothing labor relations.
- Helping newly deregulated industries ease consumer uncertainty and answer investor questions.
- Helping diversified companies establish an identity for the parent firm rather than relying solely on brand names.[34]

As these objectives indicate, corporate advertising is targeted at both internal and external audiences and involves the promotion of the organization as well as its ideas.

Types of Corporate Advertising

Marketers seek attainment of corporate advertising's objectives by implementing image, advocacy, or cause-related advertising. Each form is designed to achieve specific goals.

Image Advertising

One form of corporate advertising is devoted to promoting the organization's overall image. **Image advertising** may accomplish a number of objectives, including creating goodwill both internally and externally, creating a position for the company, and generating resources, both human and financial. A number of methods are used:

1. *General image or positioning ads.* As shown in Exhibit 17-18, ads are often designed to create an image of the firm in the public mind. The exhibit shows how Tyco is attempting to create an image of itself as a market leader and health care expert, not a *toy* company. A number of companies have created new names—for example, Accenture, Verizon, and Allianz—in an attempt to create a new image.

Other companies and organizations have used image advertising to attempt to change an existing image. After the Merck and Co. lawsuits over Vioxx, the pharmaceutical companies spent heavily on image advertising. In the first six months of 2005 the companies collectively spent over $191 million on nondrug ads, a 32 percent increase from the prior year.[35] The American Medical Association (AMA), responding to its less-than-positive image among many Americans who perceive doctors negatively, ran a series of ads portraying doctors in a more sensitive light. It spent more than $1.75 million to highlight the caring, sharing, and sensitive side of AMA members.[36] In 2002, Philip Morris Company, Inc., shareholders voted to change the company's name to Altria Group, Inc. Altria is derived from the Latin word meaning to "reach higher." Philip Morris CEO, Geoffrey Bible, said that the name was being changed to reflect the fact that the company is no longer just a cigarette company and that the new name better reflects its diversity. Others contend the move was an attempt to disassociate itself from the negative image of cigarettes.

2. *Sponsorships.* A firm often runs corporate image advertising on TV programs or specials. For example, the Hallmark or IBM specials and documentaries on network TV and ExxonMobil's support of program sponsorships on public TV and other educational programs are designed to promote the corporation as a good citizen. By associating itself with high-quality or educational programming, ExxonMobil hopes for a carryover effect that benefits its own image.

Exhibit 17-18 Tyco uses image advertising to avoid confusion

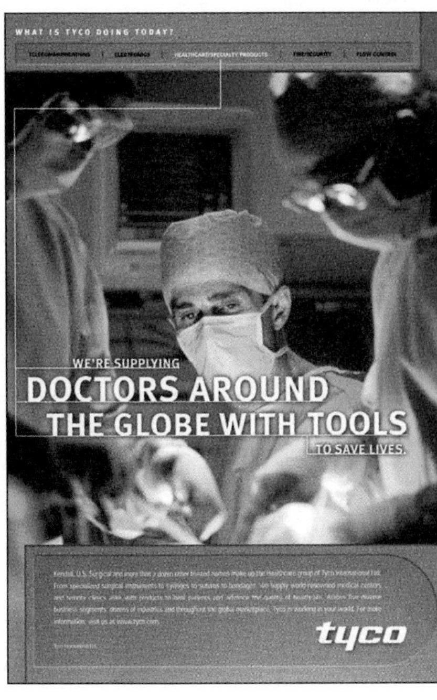

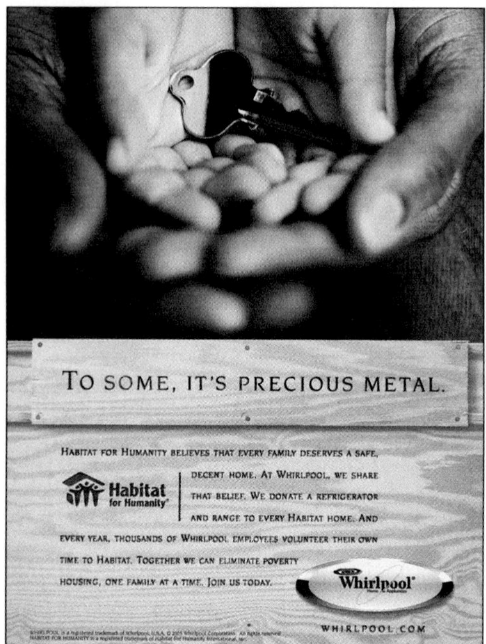

To some, it's precious metal.
Habitat for Humanity believes that every family deserves a safe, decent home. At Whirlpool, we share that belief. We donate a refrigerator and range to every Habitat home. And every year, thousands of Whirlpool employees volunteer their own time to Habitat. Together we can eliminate poverty housing, one family at a time. Join us today.
Habitat for Humanity
Whirlpool
whirlpool.com

Exhibit 17-19 Whirlpool supports the fight to eliminate poverty housing

Other examples of sponsorships include those run by Outback Steak House (LUPUS), Providian Financial (children and youth), McDonald's (UNICEF), and GM (Make-A-Wish). Exhibit 17-19 shows Whirlpool's sponsorship of the Habitat for Humanity and its efforts to fight poverty housing. Visa considers sponsorships an important part of its integrated marketing communications. It has sponsored the Olympics, the U.S. decathlon team, U.S. basketball's dream team, the U.S. Gymnastics Federation, the U.S. Open Tennis Championships, and Major League Baseball's All-Star game. According to John Bennett, senior vice president for international marketing communications, the sponsorships are designed to fulfill specific business objectives while providing support for the recipients.[37] Figure 17-5 shows a few of the companies that decided an Olympic sponsorship would be good for them.

3. *Recruiting.* The Grant Thornton ad presented in Exhibit 17-20 is a good example of corporate image advertising designed to attract new employees. If you have a passion for accounting and want to work with others who share that passion, you might be interested in the Grant Thornton accounting firm.

The Sunday employment section of most major metropolitan newspapers is an excellent place to see this form of corporate image advertising at work. Notice the ads in these papers and consider the images the firms are presenting.

4. *Generating financial support.* Some corporate advertising is designed to generate investments in the corporation. By creating a more favorable image, the firm makes itself attractive to potential stock purchasers and investors. More investments mean more working capital, more monies for research and development, and so on. In this instance, corporate image advertising is almost attempting to make a sale; the product is the firm.

While there is no concrete evidence that corporate image advertising leads directly to increased investment, at least one study shows a correlation between the price of stock and the amount of corporate advertising done.[38] Firms that spend more on corporate advertising also tend to have higher-priced stocks (though a direct relationship is very difficult to substantiate).

Figure 17-5 U.S. Olympic Sponsors and Partners

- Coca-Cola
- Budweiser
- GM
- John Hancock
- McDonald's
- Samsung
- The Home Depot
- Visa
- AT&T
- GE
- Kodak
- Johnson & Johnson
- Panasonic
- Bank of America
- Omega
- Kellogg's

Exhibit 17-20 Corporate image advertising designed to attract employees

There is a select group of individuals in this world who have a passion for the business of accounting. Yes, that's right, accounting. And that group happens to be the accountants at Grant Thornton.
Recently, J.D. Power and Associates ranked Grant Thornton "Highest Performance Among Audit Firms Serving Companies with up to $1 Billion in Annual Revenue" in a U.S. study that looked at understanding client operations and industry, responding to requests and questions, and trustworthiness.
With Grant Thornton you get easy access to partners that's been the hallmark of Grant Thornton in the U.S. for 80 years. And you get the benefit of Grant Thornton International member firms in 110 countries that fast-growth companies look for in today's global markets. Why not give our CEO, Ed Nusbaum, a call at 312.602.8003 or contact our partners at www.GrantThornton.com?
Find out how it feels to work with people who love what they do!

Kim Nunley
Office Managing Partner

This thing called *image* is not unidimensional. Many factors affect it. Figure 17-6 shows the results of a survey conducted by *Fortune* magazine on the most admired corporations in the United States. The most admired firms did not gain their positions merely by publicity and word of mouth (nor, we guess, did the least admired).

A positive corporate image cannot be created just from a few advertisements. Quality of products and services, innovation, sound financial practices, good corporate citizenship, and wise marketing are just a few of the factors that contribute to overall image. In addition,

Figure 17-6 *Fortune's* List of America's Most Admired Companies (2005)

Rank	Company	Industry Rank
1	Kinder Morgan Energy Partners	1
2	FedEx	1
3	Apple Computer	1
4	Starbucks	1
5	Alcoa	1
6	Nike	1
7	Fortune Brands	1
8	Pactiv	1
9	American Express	1
10	Procter & Gamble	1

Figure 17-7 *Business Ethics'* List of Top Corporate Citizens

Rank (2005)	Company
1	Intel
2	South Mountain Company
3	New Leaf Paper
4	Weaver Street Cooperative
Rank (2004)	**Company**
1	Gap, Inc.
2	Chroma Technology Corp.
3	Dell, Inc.
4	Clif Bar, Inc.
5	King Arthur Flour

Source: www.business-ethics.com/100best.htm.

the type of product marketed and emotional appeal also contribute. The *Fortune* survey cited above demonstrates that profits and stock performances have little to do with reputation and that once a reputation is acquired, it has lasting power. A study conducted by Harris Interactive and the Reputation Institute shows that companies are ranked differently on key corporate attributes including emotional appeal, social responsibility, workplace environment, and vision and leadership (among 16 other factors).[39] Figure 17-7 shows some of the results of *Business Ethics* magazine's analysis of the 100 best corporate citizens for 2002.

Event Sponsorships As we noted in the last section, corporate sponsorships of charities and causes has become a popular form of public relations. While some companies sponsor specific events or causes with primarily traditional public relations objectives in mind, a separate and more marketing-oriented use of sponsorships is also on the increase. Such **event sponsorships** take on a variety of forms, as shown in Figure 17-8. Anything from golf apparel and equipment to concerts, stadiums, and college football bowl games are now candidates for corporate sponsorship. Like any other relationship, however, risks must be assumed by both sides in such agreements. For example, many companies who have had their names placed on stadiums—TWA Dome (St. Louis), PSINet (Baltimore), Fruit of the Loom (Miami)—have gone bankrupt, while others have had their images tarnished—Enron, Edison Electric—which is not good for the cities. A risk taken by a company in naming a stadium is the cost of hundreds of millions of dollars, which can cause stockholders and consumers concern over the value of such an investment.

Figure 17-8 Annual Sponsorship Spending in 1996–2004

	1996	1997	1998	1999	2002	2004
Sports	$3,540	$3,840	$4,556	$5,100	$6,430	$7,690
Entertainment tours/attractions	566	650	680	756	865	1,060
Festivals, fairs, events	512	558	612	685	834	792
Causes	485	535	544	630	828	991
Arts	323	354	408	460	610	612
Total	$5,426	$5,937	$6,800	$7,631	$9,567	$11,140

Source: Adapted from *Cause Marketing Forum*, 2005.

Companies spent more than $166 billion on event sponsorships in 2004, with sports receiving the majority of event sponsorship monies.[40] Among the most popular sporting events for sponsorship are auto racing, golf and tennis tournaments, and track events. Professional sports leagues and teams as well as Olympic teams and competitions also receive large amounts of sponsorship money. Bicycle racing, beach volleyball, skiing, and various water sports are also attracting corporate sponsorship. Traditionally, tobacco, beer, and car companies have been among the largest sports event sponsors. Now a number of other companies have become involved in event sponsorships, including beverage companies, airlines, telecommunications and financial services companies, and high-tech firms.

Many marketers are attracted to event sponsorship because it gets their company and product names in front of consumers. By choosing the right events for sponsorship, companies can get visibility among their target market. For example, RJR Nabisco was heavily involved in sponsoring auto racing under its Winston and Camel cigarette brands. The company's market research showed that racing fans fit the demographic profile of users of these brands, and consumers would purchase a product that sponsored their favorite sport.[41] For tobacco companies, which are prohibited from advertising on radio and TV, event sponsorship was also a way to have their brand names seen on TV. President Clinton issued an executive order in 1996 that would have prohibited any form of advertising of tobacco sponsorships at sporting events after 1998. The tobacco companies appealed this order in the courts on the grounds that to prohibit advertising a legal product violates free speech.[42] In 2000, the Supreme Court struck down the law, although a settlement did place further restrictions on such sponsorships.[43] A number of international sports have also considered such bans.[44]

Nevertheless, in 2003, RJR Nabisco pulled its sponsorships and the NASCAR Winston Cup Series was taken over by telecommunications giant Nextel. The NASCAR Nextel Cup remains an attractive event to numerous companies, despite the increasing costs of sponsorship (Exhibit 17-21). Many companies are attracted to event sponsorships because effective IMC programs can be built around them, and promotional tie-ins can be made to local, regional, national, and even international markets. Companies are finding event sponsorships an excellent platform from which to build equity and gain affinity with target audiences as well as a good public relations tool.

Most companies focus their marketing efforts on specific market segments and are always looking for ways to reach these target audiences. Many marketers are finding that sales promotion tools such as event sponsorships, contests and sweepstakes, and sampling are very effective ways to reach specific geographic, demographic, psychographic, and ethnic markets.

Event sponsorship has become a good sales promotion tool for reaching specific target markets. Golf tournaments are a popular event for sponsorship by marketers of luxury automobiles and other upscale products and services. For example, the PGA tour partnering sponsors include Buick, Celebrex, Cialis, FedEx, Forbes, and MNBA America, among numerous others. The golf audience is affluent and highly educated, and marketers believe that golfers care passionately about the game, leading them to form emotional attachments to brands they associate with the sport. And, as you can see, a variety of companies believe there is a marketing advantage to be gained from this relationship.

Exhibit 17-21 NASCAR is an attractive sponsorship for many companies

A major issue that continues to face the event sponsorship industry is incomplete research. As marketers continue to become more interested in ROI, they will want more evidence that event sponsorship is effective and is a good return on their investment. At least one study, however, has shown that becoming an "official product" of a professional sports team can be profitable for both the team and the sponsor. The study of 53 companies showed that sponsors gained an average of $257 million in stock value in the first trading week after announcing a sponsorship deal with the NBA, NFL, NHL, PGA, or Major League Baseball. Sponsorships with MLB or the NFL led to no changes in value, while the PGA sponsors gained 3 percent, NBA sponsors gained 1.9 percent, and NHL sponsors gained 1.8 percent. Companies with smaller brand shares were likely to gain the most, as were those with products that were relevant to the sport and showed a relevant connection.[45]

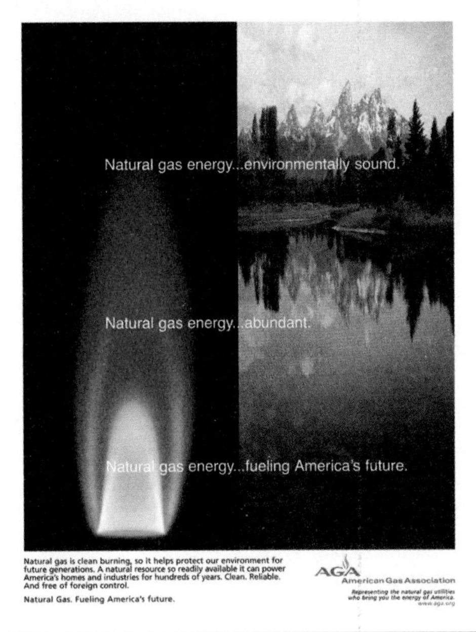

Exhibit 17-22 An example of an advocacy ad

Exhibit 17-23 Issue ads are on the increase

Advocacy Advertising A third major form of corporate advertising addresses social, business, or environmental issues. Such **advocacy advertising** is concerned with propagating ideas and elucidating controversial social issues of public importance in a manner that supports the interests of the sponsor.[46]

While still portraying an image for the company or organization, advocacy advertising does so indirectly, by adopting a position on a particular issue rather than promoting the organization itself. An example of advocacy advertising by the American Gas Association is shown in Exhibit 17-22. Advocacy advertising has increased in use over the past few years and has also met with increased criticism. The ads may be sponsored by a firm or by a trade association and are designed to tell readers how the firm operates or explain management's position on a particular issue. Sometimes the advertising is a response to negative publicity or to the firm's inability to place an important message through its regular public relations channels. At other times, the firm just wants to get certain ideas accepted or to have society understand its concerns.

Another form of advocacy advertising, **issue ads** are increasingly appearing in the media. While considered a form of advocacy advertising, issue ads may have no affiliation with a corporate or trade sponsor but may be sponsored by an organization to bring attention to what they consider to be an important issue (Exhibit 17-23). For example, after failed negotiations between The Humane Society of the United States and grocery store chain Trader Joe's, the animal welfare organization placed the above ad. The response from Trader Joe's customers was enormous. And the company publicly announced that it would convert all of its brand eggs to cage free within three months (Exhibit 17-23).

Advocacy advertising has been criticized by a number of sources (including consumer advocate Ralph Nader). But as you can see in Exhibit 17-24, this form of communication has been around for a long time. AT&T engaged in issues-oriented advertising way back in 1908 and has continued to employ this form of communication throughout the 21st century. Critics

Exhibit 17-24 AT&T has used advocacy ads for years

Figure 17-9 A Few of the Many Corporations Involved in Cause Marketing

Cause	Corporations Involved
Children's Miracle Network	Wal-Mart, Kroger Co., Delta Airlines, Coca Cola, and 24 others
Keep America Beautiful	AT&T Wireless, PepsiCo, Georgia-Pacific Corp., Lysol Brand Products
NeighborWorks	Washington Mutual, Wells Fargo, Citigroup
KaBOOM	Home Depot, Target, Sprint, Stanley Tools, Ben & Jerry's

Source: *Promo Magazine*, 2005.

contend that companies with large advertising budgets purchase too much ad space and time and that advocacy ads may be misleading, but the checks and balances of regular product advertising also operate in this area.

For example, an ad run by the seven regional Bell operating companies that addressed the threat of Japanese technologies in the telecommunications industry was perceived by some members of Congress (the group the ads were designed to influence) as Japan bashing and offensive. When the ad backfired, the campaign was immediately halted and the agency that developed it was fired.[47] The ultimate judge, of course, is always the reader.

Cause-Related Advertising

An increasingly popular method of image building is **cause-related marketing,** in which companies link with charities or nonprofit organizations as contributing sponsors. The company benefits from favorable publicity, while the charity receives much-needed funds. Spending on cause-related marketing has increased more than 300 percent since 1990, reaching an estimated $1 billion in the United States and $25 billion worldwide.[48] Figure 17-9 shows some of the many causes and their sponsors—and obviously, this is just a small sampling. Proponents of cause marketing say that association with a cause may differentiate one brand or store from another, increase consumer acceptance of price increases, generate favorable publicity, and even win over skeptical officials who may have an impact on the company.[49] Cause-marketing relationships can take a variety of forms. Making outright donations to a nonprofit cause, having companies volunteer for the cause, donating materials or supplies, running public service announcements, or even providing event refreshments are some of the ways companies get involved. Exhibit 17-25 shows an innovative campaign sponsored by the Arizona Department of Health Services and developed by Phoenix-based agency Moses Anshell. The campaign was targeted to teenage girls, their sex partners, and their parents in an attempt to reduce the rate of teenage pregnancies in Arizona, which has the second highest rate in the country. Besides the strong creative message, the campaign was unique given its heavy use of nontraditional media including cell phone text messaging, e-mail messaging, and the Internet, along with television, radio, posters, and billboards.

Exhibit 17-25 This ad was part of a campaign that included nontraditional advertising forms

While companies receive public relations benefits from their association with causes, with 80 percent of consumers saying they have a more positive impression of companies that support a cause, they sometimes receive financial rewards as well.[50] Visa's "Reading Is Fundamental" campaign led to a 17 percent increase in sales; BMW saw sales increase when it sponsored a program to eradicate breast cancer; and Wendy's International in Denver saw sales increase by more than 33 percent when a portion of purchases was contributed to Denver's Mercy Medical Center.[51]

At the same time, not all cause marketing is a guarantee of success. Cause marketing requires more than just associating with a social issue, and it takes time and effort. Companies have gotten into trouble by misleading consumers about their relationships, and others have wasted money by supporting a cause that offered little synergism. One survey showed that more than 300 companies associated themselves with breast cancer concerns, but most became lost in sponsorship clutter. Others have simply picked the wrong cause—finding that their customers and potential customers either have little interest in or don't support the cause. In some cases, cause marketing is considered nothing more than shock advertising. Finally, the results of cause-marketing efforts can sometimes be hard to quantify.

Advantages and Disadvantages of Corporate Advertising

A number of reasons for the increased popularity of corporate advertising become evident when you examine the advantages of this form of communication:

1. *It is an excellent vehicle for positioning the firm.* Firms, like products, need to establish an image or position in the marketplace. Corporate image ads are one way to accomplish this objective. A well-positioned product is much more likely to achieve success than is one with a vague or no image. The same holds true of the firm. Stop and think for a moment about the image that comes to mind when you hear the name IBM, Apple, Johnson & Johnson, or Procter & Gamble.

   Now what comes to mind when you hear Unisys, USX, or Navistar? How many consumer brands can you name that fall under ConAgra's corporate umbrella? (Banquet, Wesson, Butterball, and many others.) While we are not saying these latter companies are not successful—because they certainly are—we are suggesting their corporate identities (or positions) are not as well entrenched as the identities of those first cited. Companies with strong positive corporate images have an advantage over competitors that may be enhanced when they promote the company overall.

2. *It takes advantage of the benefits derived from public relations.* As the PR efforts of firms have increased, the attention paid to these events by the media has lessened (not because they are of any less value, but because there are more events to cover). The net result is that when a company engages in a public relations effort, there is no guarantee it will receive press coverage and publicity. Corporate image advertising gets the message out, and though consumers may not perceive it as positively as information from an objective source, the fact remains that it can communicate what has been done.

3. *It reaches a select target market.* Corporate image advertising should not be targeted to the general public. It is often targeted to investors and managers of other firms rather than to the general public. It doesn't matter if the general public does not appreciate this form of communication, as long as the target market does. In this respect, this form of advertising may be accomplishing its objectives.

Some of the disadvantages of corporate advertising were alluded to earlier in the chapter. To these criticisms, we can add the following:

1. *Questionable effectiveness.* There is no strong evidence to support the belief that corporate advertising works. Many doubt the data cited earlier that demonstrated a correlation between stock prices and corporate image advertising. A study by Bozell & Jacobs Advertising of 16,000 ads concluded that corporate advertising contributed to only 4 percent of the variability in the company's stock price, compared with a 55 percent effect attributable to financial factors.[52] A second study also casts doubts on earlier studies that concluded that corporate advertising worked.[53]

2. *Constitutionality and/or ethics.* Some critics contend that since larger firms have more money, they can control public opinion unfairly. This point was resolved in the courts in favor of the advertisers. Nevertheless, many consumers still see such advertising as unfair and immediately take a negative view of the sponsor.

A number of valid points have been offered for and against corporate advertising. Two things are certain: (1) No one knows who is right, and (2) the use of this communications form continues to increase.

Measuring the Effectiveness of Corporate Advertising

As you can tell from our discussion of the controversy surrounding corporate advertising, there need to be methods for evaluating whether or not such advertising is effective:

• *Attitude surveys.* One way to determine the effectiveness of corporate advertising is to conduct attitude surveys to gain insights into both the public's and investors' reactions to ads. A study conducted by Janas Sinclair and Tracy Irani on advocacy advertising in the biotechnology industry employed a survey research methodology to demonstrate that public accountability was a good predictor of corporate trustworthiness, and this and attitude toward the advertiser would predict consumers' attitude toward the ad, biotechnology, and purchase intentions.[54] The Phase II study conducted by market research firm Yankelovich, Skelly & White is one of the best-known applications of this measurement method.[55] The firm measured recall and attitude toward corporate advertisers and found that corporate advertising is more efficient in building recall for a company name than is product advertising alone. Frequent corporate advertisers rated better on virtually all attitude measures than those with low corporate ad budgets.

• *Studies relating corporate advertising and stock prices.* The Bozell & Jacobs study cited earlier is one of many that have examined the effect of various elements of corporate advertising (position in the magazine, source effects, etc.) on stock prices. These studies have yielded conflicting conclusions, indicating that while the model for such measures seems logical, methodological problems may account for at least some of the discrepancies.

• *Focus group research.* Focus groups have been used to find out what investors want to see in ads and how they react after the ads are developed. As with product-oriented advertising, this method has limitations, although it does allow for some effective measurements.

While the effectiveness of corporate advertising has been measured by some of the methods used to measure product-specific advertising, research in this area has not kept pace with that of the consumer market. (One study reported that only 35 of the Fortune 500 companies ever attempted to measure the performance of their annual reports.[56]) The most commonly offered reason for this lack of effort is that corporate ads are often the responsibility of those in the highest management positions in the firm, and these parties do not wish to be held accountable. It is interesting that those who should be most concerned with accountability are the most likely to shun this responsibility!

Summary

This chapter examined the role of the promotional elements of public relations, publicity, and corporate advertising. We noted that these areas are all significant to the marketing and communications effort and are usually considered differently from the other promotional elements. The reasons for this special treatment stem from the facts that (1) they are typically not designed to promote a specific product or service, and (2) in many instances it is harder for the consumer to make the connection between the communication and its intent.

Public relations was shown to be useful in its traditional responsibilities as well as in a more marketing-oriented role. In many firms, PR is a separate department operating independently of marketing; in others, it is considered a support system. Many large firms have an external public relations agency, just as they have an outside ad agency.

In the case of publicity, another factor enters the equation: lack of control over the communication the public will receive. In public relations and corporate advertising, the organization remains the source and retains much more control. Publicity often takes more of a reactive than a proactive approach, yet it may be more instrumental (or detrimental) to the success of a product or organization than all other forms of promotion combined.

While not all publicity can be managed, the marketer must nevertheless recognize its potential impact. Press releases and the management of information are just two of the factors under the company's control. Proper reaction and a strategy to deal with uncontrollable events are also responsibilities.

Corporate advertising was described as controversial, largely because the source of the message is top management, so the rules for other advertising and promoting forms are often not applied. This element of communication definitely has its place in the promotional mix. But to be effective, it must be used with each of the other elements, with specific communications objectives in mind.

Finally, we noted that measures of evaluation and control are required for each of these program elements, just as they are for all others in the promotional mix. We presented some methods for taking such measurements and some evidence showing why it is important to use them. As long as the elements of public relations, publicity, and corporate advertising are considered integral components of the overall communications strategy, they must respect the same rules as the other promotional mix elements to ensure success.

Key Terms

public relations (PR), 543
marketing public relations (MPR), 544
internal audiences, 548
external audiences, 548
press release, 551
press conference, 551
exclusive, 551
team approach, 555
internal audits, 556
external audits, 556
publicity, 556
video news release (VNR), 559
corporate advertising, 561
image advertising, 563
event sponsorship, 565
advocacy advertising, 567
issue ads, 567
cause-related marketing, 568

Discussion Questions

1. The use of MPRs has irked traditional public relations people. Discuss why MPRs may be controversial. Explain the reasons why MPRs should and should not be used.

2. The chapter discusses the increasing use of advocacy advertising and issue advertising. Explain what these advertising forms are, and why there has been such an increase in their use by profit and nonprofit organizations.

3. Many accuse companies like GoDaddy.com of exploitation of the media. They contend that events like Janet Jackson's wardrobe malfunction and the NFL's refusal to show GoDaddy's commercials are designed strategies to gain publicity. Discuss whether you feel these are designed strategies and whether they are likely to be effective. Cite other examples of such efforts.

4. There is a saying that "any publicity is good publicity." Discuss what you think about this statement.

5. The growth of video news releases (VNRs) has increased significantly. The Bush administration and Governor Schwarzenegger of California have both employed this strategy. Describe what a VNR is, and discuss some of the ethical issues surrounding their use. Should VNRs have to carry a message noting that they are VNRs?

6. Some marketers and PR people believe that public relations should replace advertising as the primary means of introducing new products. Explain arguments in favor of and opposed to this position. What do you conclude?

Personal Selling

18

Chapter Objectives

1. To understand the role of personal selling in the integrated marketing communications program.
2. To know the advantages and disadvantages of personal selling as a promotional program element.
3. To understand how personal selling is combined with other elements in an IMC program.
4. To know ways to determine the effectiveness of the personal selling effort.

Does More Sophisticated Marketing in the Pharmaceutical Industry Mean the End of Detailing?

For just about as long as anyone can remember, the big pharmaceutical companies have hired attractive people as personal sales representatives. These reps have been trained well, and rewarded accordingly, with some of the highest paying salaries of any sales jobs. According to industry spokespeople, however, their reps do not sell, they detail—that is, they explain and inform physicians about their drugs in an attempt to persuade them to prescribe them. And they have done well, averaging an estimated $1.9 million in sales per year. But the pharmaceutical industry is changing, and some are beginning to question the cost-effectiveness of the detailers and whether they should continue to play as big a role as they have in the past.

side effects
x
(a kathleen slattery-moschkau film)
Katherine Heigl
Lucian McAfee
Dorian DeMichele
Dave Durbin
Temeceka Harris
Mo Productions
(Why not?)
Produced by Holly Mosher & Kathleen Slattery-Moschkau
Editor & Associate Producer Dan Kattman
Director of Photography Carl Whitney
Script Supervisor Steve Moschkau
A very special thanks to Harry
Written & Directed by Kathleen Slattery-Moschkau

A number of changes in the way pharmaceutical companies now market their drugs have contributed to the reevaluation. First, the drug manufacturers can now advertise to consumers directly. New Zealand is the only other country to permit this practice. Since 1998, when the FDA first allowed advertising directly targeted to consumers, the advertising budgets of the large companies have increased to the point where more than $4 billion per year is spent on direct-to-consumer communications, including advertising on television, on the Internet, and through direct marketing. Some of the monies previously targeting doctors through trade journals, conferences, and promotional products have been reassigned to consumer media, though most of the monies have resulted from increased budgets. Proponents argue that direct-to-consumer advertising helps make patients aware of medical conditions they may not have known about and gives them more information for discussing their condition with their doctor. Critics counter that such promotion encourages consumers to request or even insist upon the drugs from their physicians.

Because of the increased advertising, the public outcry against the pharmaceutical industry's practices has been deafening, leading the industry to adopt guidelines that focus more attention on educating doctors than on driving volume through marketing. The guidelines placed restrictions on some of the advertising practices, leading some companies to look for other ways to promote their products and, claim the critics, to get around the guidelines. One method quickly adopted was that of public relations (PR). Getting experts and executives quoted in magazines, giving appearances on talk shows, and other PR methods have increased. Promotions on the Internet also rose by 36 percent, with much of the money spent on "e-detailing." Also increasing were the number of contractual discounts offered to hospitals and medical facilities if they agreed to limit what they say about the drugs, and not "counter detail," that is, provide information to counter the claims made by the drug companies, which often leads to the adoption of competitors or generics.

But what about the detailers? Are their jobs in jeopardy? Well, yes and no. Some of the larger companies such as Wyeth (4,714 reps) and Sanofi-Aventis (4,817 reps) are taking a critical look at the size and effectiveness of their sales forces. Wyeth announced a sales force reduction of 750 detailers in 2005, filling their positions with e-detailing staff and part-time salespeople. GlaxoSmithKline froze its sales force, Pfizer announced minor reductions in its staff of 11,000 reps, and AstraZeneca axed 500 positions. But not every company is making cuts. Sanofi-aventis has plans to grow its sales force by 10 percent, and others are afraid to make cuts for fear of losing sales to competitors.

So while changes are taking place in the industry, as reflected by significant increases in promotional budgets and the use of the Internet, some things remain the same. For one, the cozy relationship that exists between doctors and the detailers still exists. The practice of wining, dining, and giving free trips continues, to the chagrin of both those inside and outside the industry. Many of those familiar with the industry consider some of these marketing practices unethical, if not illegal. The negative feelings society has for these marketing practices may have intensified in September 2005 with the release of the movie *Side Effects.* The movie provides insights (including both fiction and fact) into the inner workings of the industry as revealed by an ex-detailer. And it won't be pretty: The industry is not impressed.

In the meantime, despite all the changes, it is almost business as usual for the detailers. The 3 Fs—food, flattery, and friendship—are still the mantra of the day.

Sources: Rich Tomaselli, "Big Pharma Finds Way into Doctors' Pockets," *Advertising Age,* September 19, 2005, pp. 4, 52; Sarah Rubenstein, "How Lilly Influences What Prescribers Say about Cymbalta," *The Wall Street Journal,* August 5, 2005, p. B1; "Wyeth to Replace Reps with Part-Timers, E-Detailing," *Medical Marketing and Media,* July 2005, p. 8; Rich Thomaselli, "PR Seems to Be the Rx to Get around DTC Rules," *Advertising Age,* September 26, 2005, p. 6; "Survey: Devil in the Detail," *The Economist,* June 18, 2005, p. 9.

The Scope of Personal Selling

While the pharmaceutical industry may not be typical of other industries employing a sales force, it is typical in the way that changes are taking place that cause marketers to reconsider the role of personal selling in the marketing program. The changing marketplace has had a significant impact on how personal selling activities are conducted and how successful firms will compete in the future. In Chapter 1, we stated that while we recognize the importance of personal selling and the role it plays in the overall marketing and promotions effort, it is not emphasized in this text. Personal selling is typically under the control of the sales manager, not the advertising and promotions department. A study conducted by *Sales & Marketing Management* showed that in 46 percent of the companies surveyed, sales and marketing are totally separate departments.[1] But personal selling does make a valuable contribution to the promotions program. In addition, IMC tools are used in conjunction with personal selling, and the sales force itself may become a target of the communications program (as will be seen later in this chapter). To develop a promotional plan effectively, a firm must integrate the roles and responsibilities of its sales force into the communications program. Strong cooperation between the departments is also necessary.

This chapter focuses on the role personal selling assumes in the IMC program, the advantages and disadvantages of this program element, and the basis for evaluating its contributions to attaining communications objectives. In addition, we explore how personal selling is combined with other program elements, both to support them and to receive support from them.

Personal selling involves selling through a person-to-person communications process. The emphasis placed on personal selling varies from firm to firm depending on a variety of factors, including the nature of the product or service being marketed, size of the organization, and type of industry. Personal selling often plays the dominant role in industrial firms, while in other firms, such as makers of low-priced consumer nondurable goods, its role is minimized. In many industries, these roles are changing to a more balanced use of promotional program elements. In an integrated marketing communications program, personal selling is a partner with, not a substitute for, the other promotional mix elements.

The Role of Personal Selling in the IMC Program

Manufacturers may promote their products *directly* to consumers through advertising and promotions and/or direct-marketing efforts or *indirectly* through resellers and salespeople. (A sales force may call on customers directly—for example, in the insurance industry or real estate. But this chapter focuses on the personal selling function as it exists in most large corporations or smaller companies—that is, as a link to resellers or dealers in business-to-business transactions.) Depending on the role defined by the organization, the responsibilities and specific tasks of salespeople may differ, but ultimately these tasks are designed to help attain communications and marketing objectives.

Personal selling differs from the other forms of communication presented thus far in that messages flow from a sender (or group of senders) to a receiver (or group of receivers) directly (usually face to face). This *direct* and *interpersonal communication* lets the sender immediately receive and evaluate feedback from the receiver. This communications process, known as **dyadic communication** (between two people or groups), allows for more specific tailoring of the message and more personal communications than do many of the other media discussed. The message can be changed to address the receiver's specific needs and wants.

In some situations, this ability to focus on specific problems is mandatory; a standard communication would not suffice. Consider an industrial buying situation in which the salesperson is an engineer. To promote the company's products and/or services, the salesperson must understand the client's specific needs. This may mean understanding the tensile strength of materials or being able to read blueprints or plans to understand the requirements. Or say a salesperson represents a computer graphics firm. Part of his or her responsibility for making a sale may involve the design of a software program to solve a problem unique to this customer. Mass communications cannot accomplish these tasks. Personal selling plays a critical role not just in industrial settings but in the consumer market as well.

The great entrepreneur Marshall Field said, "The distance between the salesperson and the potential buyer is the most important three feet in business."[2] Personal selling is important in selling to consumers and resellers. Consumer-product companies must secure distribution, motivate resellers to stock and promote the product, and so on.

Why is personal selling so important? Let's examine its role with respect to other promotional program elements.

Determining the Role of Personal Selling

The first questions a manager needs to ask when preparing the promotional program are what the specific responsibilities of personal selling will be and what role it will assume relative to the other promotional mix elements. To determine its role, management should be guided by four questions:

1. What specific information must be exchanged between the firm and potential customers?
2. What are the alternative ways to carry out these communications objectives?
3. How effective is each alternative in carrying out the needed exchange?
4. How cost effective is each alternative?[3]

- *Determining the information to be exchanged.* In keeping with the objectives established by the communications models in Chapter 5, the salesperson may have a variety of messages to communicate, such as creating awareness of the product or service offering, demonstrating product benefits for evaluation, initiating trial, and/or closing the sale. It may also be necessary to answer questions, counter misconceptions, and discover potentially unmet needs.

- *Examining promotional mix alternatives.* In previous chapters, we discussed the roles of advertising and sales promotion, direct marketing, and public relations/publicity. Each of these program elements offers specific advantages and disadvantages, and each needs to be considered when the promotional mix is developed. Personal selling is an alternative that offers distinct advantages in some situations but is less appropriate in others, as evidenced in Figure 18-1.
- *Evaluating the relative effectiveness of alternatives.* The effectiveness of each program element must be evaluated based on the target market and the objectives sought. Personal selling is effective in many situations, but other program elements may be more attractive in other cases. For example, advertising may do a better job of repeating messages or reaching a large number of people with one distinct, consistent message.
- *Determining cost-effectiveness.* One of the major disadvantages of personal selling is the cost involved. (Cahners Research estimates the average cost per sales call could reach $379 by 2006[4] (see Figure 18-2).) While the cost of a personal sales call may not be prohibitive in industrial settings where a single purchase can be worth millions of dollars, the same cost may be unfeasible in a consumer market. Other media may be able to communicate the required message at a much lower cost.

The Nature of Personal Selling

To integrate the personal selling effort into the overall promotional program, we must understand the nature of this tool. Let us look at how personal selling has evolved over the years and then examine some of its characteristics.

The personal selling task encompasses a variety of responsibilities (some of which we discuss in the next section). Like other aspects of the promotional mix, these responsibilities are constantly changing. As noted by Thomas Wotruba, the personal selling area is constantly evolving as the marketing environment itself evolves.[5] Wotruba identifies five distinct stages of personal selling evolution, shown in Figure 18-3.

Figure 18-1 When the Sales Force Is a Major Part of the IMC Mix

Product or Service	Channels
Complex products requiring customer application assistance (computers, pollution control system, steam turbines) Major purchase decisions, such as food items purchased by supermarket chains Features and performance of the product requiring personal demonstration and trial by the customer (private aircraft)	Channel system relatively short and direct to end-users Product and service training and assistance needed by channel intermediaries Personal selling needed to push product through channel Channel intermediaries available to perform personal selling function for supplier with limited resources and experience (brokers or manufacturer's agents)
Price	**Advertising**
Final price is negotiated between buyer and seller (appliances, cars, real estate) Selling price or quality purchased enables an adequate margin to support selling expenses (traditional department store compared to discount house)	Advertising media do not provide effective link with market targets Information needed by buyer cannot be provided entirely through advertising and sales promotion (life insurance) Number and dispersion of customers will not enable acceptable advertising economies

1. **Provider stage.** Selling activities are limited to accepting orders for the supplier's available offering and conveying it to the buyer.
2. **Persuader stage.** Selling involves an attempt to persuade market members to buy the supplier's offerings.
3. **Prospector stage.** Activities include seeking out selected buyers who are perceived to have a need for the offering as well as the resources and authority to buy it.
4. **Problem-solver stage.** Selling involves obtaining the participation of buyers to identify their problems, which can be translated into needs, and then presenting a selection from the supplier's offerings that corresponds with those needs and can solve those problems.
5. **Procreator stage.** Selling defines the buyer's problems or needs and their solutions through active buyer-seller collaboration and then creates a market offering uniquely tailored to the customer.

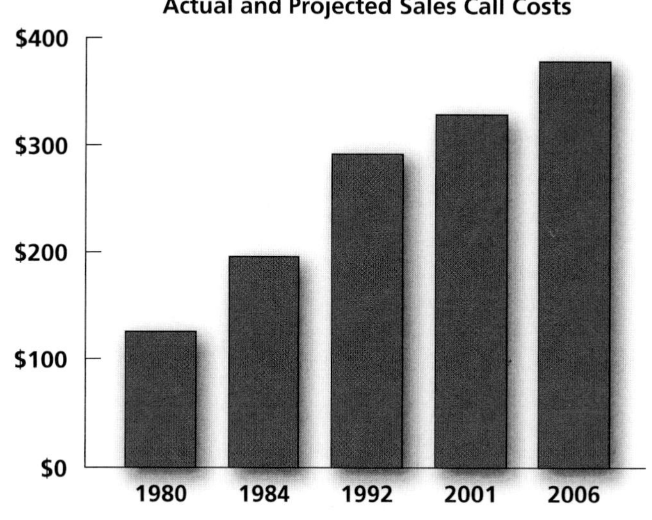

Figure 18-2 Actual and Projected Sales Call Costs

According to Wotruba, firms evolving through these five stages have to assume different market orientations, as well as different organizational designs, staffing, and compensation programs. The different stages require different promotional strategies, each integrated with personal selling to achieve the maximum communications effect.

The New Role of Personal Selling As previously noted, the business world is going through a very rapid transition as (1) individuals and corporations gain more knowledge and economic power, (2) value is replacing efficiency, and (3) industry

Figure 18-3 The Stages in the Evolution of Selling

	Characteristics of Stages			
Stages and Description	Customer Needs	Type of Market	Nature and Intensity of Competition	Examples
1. *Provider:* accepts orders and delivers to buyer.	Assumed to exist; not a concern	Sellers'	None	Route salespeople/drivers; some retail salesclerks
2. *Persuader:* attempts to convince anyone to buy available offerings.	Created, awakened	Buyers'	Undifferentiated; slight intensity	Telemarketers for photo studio; many new car dealers
3. *Prospector:* seeks out prospects with need for available offering and resources to buy.	Considered but inferred	Segmented	Differentiated; growing	Car insurance salespeople calling on new car buyers; office supplies sellers calling on small businesses
4. *Problem solver:* matches available offerings to solve customer-stated problems.	Diagnosed, with attention to customer input	Participative	Responsive and counteractive with increasing resources	Communication systems salespeople for a telephone company; architectural services sellers calling on building contractors
5. *Procreator:* creates a unique offering to match the buyer's needs as mutually specified, involving any or all aspects of the seller's total marketing mix.	Mutually defined; matched with tailored offering	Coactive	Focused; growing in breadth of market and service offerings	Materials handling equipment salespeople who design and sell a system to fit a buyer's manufacturing facility

boundaries are changing—for example, competitors are joining forces to achieve more buying power.[6] As a result, the role of the sales force will also significantly change, according to Kevin Hoffberg and Kevin Corcoran. Along with retaining their traditional roles, described by Wotruba, salespeople will have to acquire new roles to remain effective. That is, in addition to being information providers, influencers through proximity (i.e., through personal contact), and demonstrators, salespeople will engage in:

- *Surveying*—educating themselves more about their customers' businesses and regularly assessing these businesses and their customers to achieve a position of knowledgeable authority.
- *Mapmaking*—outlining both an account strategy and a solutions strategy (for the customer). This means laying out a plan, discussing it with the customer, and revising it as changes require.
- *Guiding*—bringing incremental value to the customer by identifying problems and opportunities, offering alternative options and solutions, and providing solutions with tangible value.
- *Fire starting*—engaging customers and driving them to commit to a solution.[7]

This new role, say Hoffberg and Corcoran, will create added value and develop a relationship between buyer and seller. IMC Perspective 18-1 demonstrates the fact that even the way that companies attempt to motivate their salespeople is changing.

Relationship Marketing

As noted, personal selling is evolving from a focus on persuasive techniques used to sell a product or service to a much more marketing-oriented *partnership* with the customer. This new role requires much broader thinking and expertise on the part of the seller and a more extensive use of the various promotional tools. The modern salesperson is attempting to establish a long-term, symbiotic relationship with clients, working with them as a solutions provider.

Relationship marketing is defined as "an organization's effort to develop a long-term, cost-effective link with individual customers for mutual benefit."[8] Rather than focusing on a short-term sale, the sales rep tries to establish a long-term bond. And rather than just selling, the sales department works with marketing to use techniques like database marketing, message differentiation to different target markets, and tracking of promotional effects to improve the relationship. For example, customer relationship management (CRM) tools have been used by a number of companies. These companies, including Gateway, Honeywell, America Online, among others, make extensive uses of their databases on purchase behavior and frequency and duration of customer interactions to estimate profitability at the individual account level. A number of companies now offer software to assist in implementing CRM programs, including Seibel Systems, Salesforce.com, SAP, and PeopleSoft (Exhibit 18-1). AT&T builds databases of customers with similar profiles, flagging those with the most potential for up-selling. As noted by Copulsky and Wolf, such marketing uses a more personalized form of communication that crosses the previous boundaries between personal selling and the other promotional tools. Relationship building also requires trust, as noted by Pepper and Rodgers; if the customer does not trust the salesperson, there is no relationship and the sale will focus only on price. In a long-term relationship, the buyer and seller collaborate within the context of previous and future transactions.[9] Figure 18-4 shows some of the factors considered important in maintaining customers.

Exhibit 18-1 SAP designs software to assist customer relationship management (CRM)

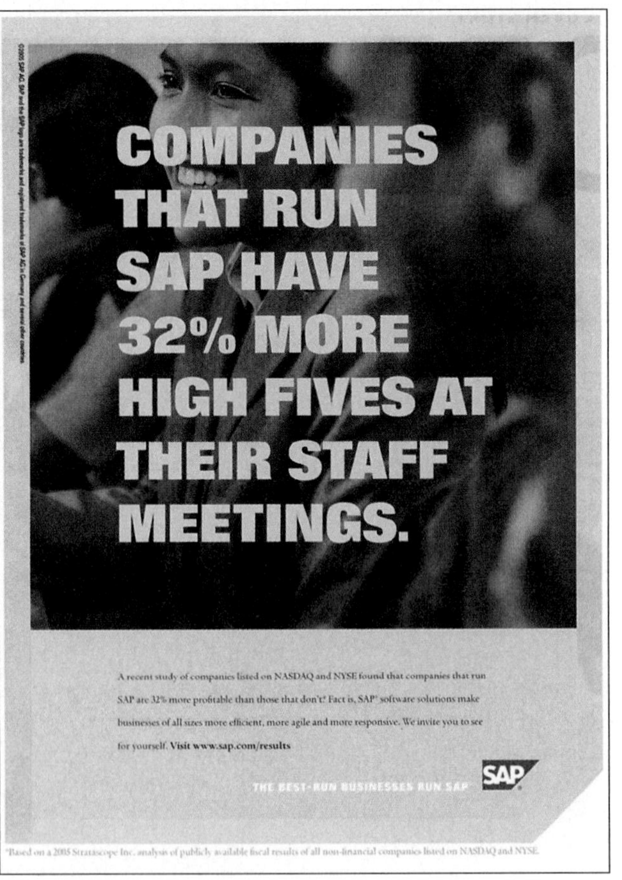

IMC PERSPECTIVE 18-1

Motivating the Sales Force—No Longer a Requirement?

For years, companies have struggled to determine ways to motivate their sales forces. The prevailing attitude was pretty much that regardless of how good one's advertising, public relations, and other IMC programs are, for many companies, it is the sales force that is called on to close the deal—particularly those in the business-to-business market. As you might imagine, there is always a need for good salespeople, and companies do whatever they can to attract and retain them and to motivate them to continue to do good work—regardless of the industry.

As the business environment changes, so too do the needs and wants of the sales force. In the past, when the salesman was the breadwinner, money as incentive worked well. By providing the sales force with the opportunity to earn more money by working harder, motivation was easily achieved. But now, times have changed. Dual-worker families, more emphasis on lifestyles, and more opportunities are just some of the factors that result in more diversified salespeople and that explain why money by itself doesn't motivate like it used to. Now there is growing sentiment among some companies that many of these motivation attempts are of little or no value because good salespeople may not even need to be motivated.

Let's first take a look at some of the ways companies have attempted to use incentives other than money to motivate their sales forces:

- *Gallup Organization.* The research and consulting organization has its own version of the Academy Awards. Each time an employee votes for another, a "drop" is created in the employee's "bucket," symbolizing the capacity for positive emotions. Each quarter (or, in some locations, each month), the persona achievements are recognized through campuswide meetings. Once a year, top achievers from across the country are invited to Gallup's own version of the Oscars—a high-class ceremony to award them. Recipients may receive a plaque or even the coveted "Love Cup," a trophy modeled after the one given to the winner of the Kentucky Derby.
- *MTM Recognition.* The Oklahoma City–based company recognizes its top employees with a custom-made ring. The rings bear the corporate logo, the award year, and the recipient's name, along with a diamond that symbolizes each achievement, whether it is for years of service, attaining a sales goal, or other. The rings not only symbolize outstanding performances internally, but convey to the prospective customer that they are "talking to a professional, at the top of their game," notes vice president Alan Axley.
- *Toshiba America Medical Systems.* The company instituted an annual "Extreme Performers" incentive program in which the top 30 performers and their spouses receive an incentive trip and subsequent recognition at the annual company meeting. Both individuals and teams at all levels within the organization are eligible.
- *Jupiter Media Metrix.* As the competition for Internet research services intensified between Jupiter and its number-one rival Forrester Research, Forrester hung a sign in its headquarters' office telling employees to "Beat Jupiter." In response, Jupiter initiated a motivation device of its own: displaying leather boxing gloves in the lobby showcase of its New York offices. Each quarter, the sales rep who "scores the biggest knockout" against rival Forrester gets to autograph the gloves.

Other companies have their own incentives, ranging from money awards to trips to trophies. The companies believe that the recognitions are well worth their expense, contributing to a more positive corporate culture, creating a feeling of success and attachment to the organization, and even improving sales. For example, Toshiba's awards led to 20 to 25 percent sales increases each year since the program's implementation. As noted by Renee Evenson writing in *The Amercian Salesman* magazine, "By showing the sales team you really do care by communicating, acknowledging, recognizing and encouraging them, they will be motivated to strive to be their best in everything."

But Evenson also notes the dangers in offering sales rewards and compensations; in particular, these recognitions should not become the salesperson's primary incentive for doing well. Others take an even more critical view. Willliam H. Murphy of the University of Wisconsin, in a study of 827 salespeople, notes that most of the literature regarding the motivation of salespeople presumes a correlation between motivation and effort; however, other consequences that are not always positive may come from increasing motivation. Murphy found that affective commitment and relationship to the supervisor may be more effective than status aspirations and competitiveness in reducing behaviors problematic to the organization. Other analysts have found that reward schemes may not be as motivating as a corporate culture of recognition and informal praise—a position agreed upon by numerous marketers who stress that positive reinforcement, praise, and a positive outlook are often more motivating than monetary awards.

Michelle Marchetti, writing in *Sales and Marketing Management,* notes that the use of sales incentives could actually do more harm than good. David Cichelli, a management consultant, agrees, citing sales managers who believe that using too many incentives could result in a "coin-operated sales force," in which salespeople "wouldn't function unless you put a coin in." In some companies, for example, sales reps may withhold orders until the incentives are offered. Cichelli also reports on sales reps who ignored contests as they became overloaded with them.

So what is the sales manager to do? Some companies believe that incentives work, while others don't. Both sides can cite evidence to support their positions. While they may disagree on the overall value of motivation programs, they do agree on one thing—the sales rep must be motivated. What they disagree on is exactly how that motivation should be encouraged, and at what level. The guiding principle perhaps should be "everything in moderation."

Sources: Renee Evenson, "Managing an All-Star Sales Team," *The American Salesman,* October 2005, pp. 21–27; Julia Chang, "Going for the GOLD," *Sales and Marketing Management,* October 2005, pp. 40–44; William H. Murphy, "In Pursuit of Short-Term Goals: Anticipating the Unintended Consequences of Using Special Incentives to Motivate the Sales Force," *Journal of Business Research,* November 2004, Vol. 57, p. 1265; "Rewards Fail to Motivate Staff," *Incentive Business,* April 2005, p. 5; Michele Marchetti, "Why Sales Contests Don't Work," *Sales and Marketing Management,* January 2004, p. 19.

Adoption of a CRM approach will require sales managers to develop nontraditional sales strategies, according to some observers. Ingram and colleagues note that companies will need to move to a more strategic, less tactical approach, using emerging technologies to support this effort. Bob Donath agrees, noting that traditional communications performance standards—the number of qualified and converted leads generated from a medium—will be less important. Donath notes that a company's reliance on websites and banner ads, as well as ads in print publications, will need to be more strategic, direct marketing will assume a greater role, and the use of more sophisticated CRM programs will be required to be successful.

The Costs of Personal Selling In some industries, personal selling constitutes a substantial portion of the communications effort and may account for most of the promotional budget. This is true because (1) much attention is devoted to this function due to its advantages over other communication methods and (2) it is an expensive form of communication. The average cost per sales call varies by industry, though on average it has increased at the rate of $9.60 per year since 1980, when the average was only $126.00.

When the cost per sales call is compared with the cost per message delivered through other media, these figures seem outrageous. We saw in earlier chapters that these costs could be as low as 3 cents. But taking these numbers at face value may lead to unfair comparisons. In evaluating the costs of personal selling, we must consider the nature of the call, the objectives sought, and whether other program elements could deliver the message as effectively. It may be that the higher costs cannot be avoided.

The costs of personal selling are even higher when you consider that one sales call is not likely to be enough to close a deal. This is particularly true in building and construction; while it may take (on the average) only 3.34 sales calls to close a deal in the building and construction industry, the same close in electronics and computer manufacturing may require 6.5 visits.[10] The industry average is 5.12. As you can see through simple multiplication, the cost per sale is now even more intimidating (though in industrial markets the returns may easily warrant the expense).

Figure 18-4 Factors That Are Very Important in Keeping a Customer, by Company Type

Product Quality and Customer Service Are the Very Important Factors in Keeping a Customer

Very Important	Consumer Only	B-to-B Only	Both	All Respondents
Perceived price to value proposition	71%	71%	60%	67%
Customer service	71	69	75	73
Product quality	78	79	71	75
Product uniqueness	48	36	35	40
Depth of product line	31	44	34	35
Loyalty/reward program	13	11	12	12

Source: The DMA 2005 Customer Prospecting and Retention Report.

Figure 18-5 Types of Sales Jobs

Order Taking

Once the initial sale has taken place, the creative seller may be replaced (not physically!) by an order taker, whose role is much more casual. It may simply involve a straight rebuy—that is, the order does not change much. (A bottled-water delivery person is an example.) When a slight change is considered, the order taker may be involved in a modified rebuy, which may require some creative selling (for example, a salesperson calling on a wholesale food company may have a list of products to sell). If a major purchase decision is required, however, the role of making the sale may again be turned over to the creative seller. Order takers are often classified as *inside* order takers, who work inside the sales office and receive orders by phone, mail, or the Internet, and *field* order takers, who travel to customers to get their orders.

Creative Selling

Creative selling jobs may require the most skill and preparation. In addition to prospecting, the salesperson must assess the situation, determine the needs to be met, present the capabilities for satisfying these needs, and get an order. The salesperson is often the "point person" who has established the initial contact on behalf of the firm and who is primarily responsible for completing the exchange. He or she is, in fact, the order getter. Sales personnel may focus on current customers, encouraging more sales and cross selling, and/or they may seek new customers.

Missionary Sales Reps

The missionary representative is essentially a support role. While performing many of the tasks assumed in creative selling, the missionary rep may not actually take the order. He or she introduces new products, new promotions, and/or new programs, with the actual order to be taken by the company's order taker or by a distributor representing the company's goods. The missionary sales rep may have additional account service responsibilities including customer relationship management. Missionary reps are most often employed in industries where the manufacturer uses a middleperson to distribute the product (for example, food products or pharmaceuticals).

Overall, personal selling is an expensive way to communicate. Yet it does usually involve more than just communicating, and the returns (more direct sales) may be greater than those from the other program elements.

Personal Selling Responsibilities

Sales & Marketing Management uses three categories to classify salespeople: **order taking, creative selling,** and **missionary sales**[11] (see Figure 18-5). Of course, not all firms treat each of these responsibilities the same, nor are their salespeople limited to only these tasks (Exhibit 18-2). Personal selling has evolved to include responsibilities beyond these. Job requirements may include (1) locating prospective customers, (2) determining customers' needs and wants that are not being satisfied, (3) recommending a way to satisfy these needs and/or wants, (4) demonstrating the capabilities of the firm and its products for providing this satisfaction, (5) closing the sale and taking the order, and (6) following up and servicing the account. Let's discuss these job classifications and some of the responsibilities assigned to each:

Exhibit 18-2 Salespeople may assume multiple responsibilities

1. *Locating prospective customers.* The process of locating new customers (often referred to as **prospecting**) involves the search for and qualification of prospective customers. Salespeople must follow up on **leads** (those who may become customers) and **prospects** (those who need the product or service). They must also determine whether these prospects are **qualified prospects**—that is, able to make the buying decision and pay for the product. Exhibit 18-3 shows a page from the website for Salesgenie.com, an online tool that helps salespeople generate leads and find new prospects through access to a wide range of business and consumer databases. Leads360 offers a system to distribute, analyze, and track prospects, as well as assisting in planning, implementation, and maintenance of sales force strategies. The system gathers all leads, and then with automated scripts and questionnaires the leads are qualified by phone, fax, or Internet. The

system then arranges each lead by "grade" and priority status and directs it to the appropriate salesperson. Dell and Cisco, among others, use a Web-based system.

2. *Determining customers' needs and wants.* At this stage, the salesperson gathers more information on the prospect and decides the best way to approach him or her. The rep must determine what the customer needs or wants and make certain the person being approached is capable of making the purchase decision. In some instances the salesperson may have to assist the customer in determining what he or she needs.

3. *Recommending a way to satisfy the customers' needs and wants.* Here the salesperson recommends a possible solution to the problem and/or needs of the potential customer. This may entail providing information the prospect had not considered or identifying alternative solutions that might work. As noted earlier, the salesperson acts as a systems provider.

4. *Demonstrating the capabilities of the firm and its products.* At this stage, the salesperson demonstrates the capabilities of the firm and shows the prospect why that firm is the obvious choice. As you might expect, corporate image (created through advertising and other promotional tools) is important to the salesperson.

5. *Closing the sale.* The key ingredient in any sales presentation is the **close**—getting the prospect's commitment. For many salespeople, this is the most difficult task. Many reps are adept at prospecting, identifying customer needs, and making presentations, but they are reluctant to ask for the sale. Most managers work with their sales forces to close the sale and help reluctant or uncertain buyers make a decision.

6. *Following up and servicing the account.* The responsibilities of the sales force do not end once the sale has been made. It is much easier to keep existing customers than to attract new ones. Maintaining customer loyalty, generating repeat sales, and getting the opportunity to **cross sell**—that is, sell additional products and services to the same customer—are some of the advantages of keeping customers satisfied through follow-up activities. In a relationship marketing versus selling orientation, follow-up is necessary and expected.

A primary advantage a salesperson offers is the opportunity to assess the situation firsthand and adapt the sales message accordingly (a *direct feedback* network). No other promotional element provides this opportunity. The successful salesperson constantly analyzes the situation, reads the feedback provided by the receiver, and shapes the message to specifically meet the customer's needs.

While you might expect this to be an easy task, it isn't always the case. Sometimes buyers will not or cannot express their needs accurately. Other times, the salesperson must become a problem solver for the client. More and more, salespeople are being asked to assist in the buyers' decision-making process. The more salespeople can become involved in planning and decision making, the more confidence the buyer places in them, and the more bonding the relationship becomes.

Exhibit 18-3
Salesgenie.com offers salespeople expertise on how to qualify leads

Sometimes the true motivation for purchasing is not the one the customer gives. You might expect buyers to base their decisions on rational, objective factors, but this is not always the case. Even in industrial markets (where product specifications may be critical) or reseller markets (where product movements and/or profits are important), many purchase decisions are made on what might be called nonrational criteria (not irrational, but involving factors beyond cost or other product benefits). Since it is generally believed these purchase situations involve less emotion and more rational thinking than many consumer purchases, this is an important insight.

Consider the marketer's dilemma. If a firm provides advertising and promotions that speak only to the rational purchase motives, it may not be able to make the sale. On the other hand, how could an advertiser possibly know all the emotional or nonrational criteria influencing the deci-

Figure 18-6 Ten Traits of Effective Salespeople

A *Sales & Marketing Management* survey of 209 salespeople representing 189 companies in 37 industries determined that the following traits characterize top sales performers:

1. *Ego strength:* a healthy self-esteem that allows one to bounce back from rejection.
2. A *sense of urgency:* wanting to get it done now.
3. *Ego drive:* a combination of competitiveness and self-esteem.
4. *Assertiveness:* the ability to be firm, lead the sales process, and get one's point across confidently.
5. *Willingness to take risk:* willing to innovate and take a chance.
6. *Sociable:* outgoing, friendly, talkative, and interested in others.
7. *Abstract reasoning:* ability to understand concepts and ideas.
8. *Skepticism:* a slight lack of trust and suspicion of others.
9. *Creativity:* the ability to think differently.
10. *Empathy:* the ability to place oneself in someone else's shoes.

sion, let alone integrate this information into its messages? The personal sales effort may be the only way to uncover the many motivations for purchasing and address them.

When you review this list of responsibilities, it becomes clear that the salesperson of today is no mere huckster. Figure 18-6 provides a list of the 10 traits that are common to successful salespeople (the list is consistent with other studies conducted), while Figure 18-7 shows the results of one company's survey of buyers' likes and dislikes regarding the sales force.

The importance of personal selling in the integrated marketing communications program should now be clear. This program element provides opportunities that no other form of message delivery does. But while the tasks performed by salespeople offer some distinct advantages to the marketing program, they may also constitute disadvantages, as you will now see.

Advantages and Disadvantages of Personal Selling

The nature of personal selling positions this promotional tool uniquely among those available to marketers. Its advantages include the following:

1. *Allowing for two-way interaction.* The ability to interact with the receiver allows the sender to determine the impact of the message. Problems in comprehension or objections can be resolved and in-depth discussions of certain selling points can be provided immediately. In mass communications this direct feedback is not available and such information cannot be obtained immediately (if at all).

2. *Tailoring of the message.* Because of the direct interaction, messages can be tailored to the receiver. This more precise message content lets the sender address the consumer's specific concerns, problems, and needs. The sales rep can also determine when to move on to the next selling point, ask for the sale, or close the deal.

3. *Lack of distraction.* In many personal selling situations, a one-to-one presentation is conducted. The likelihood of distractions is minimized and the buyer is generally paying close attention to the sales message. Even when the presentation is made by a group of salespeople or more than one decision maker is present, the setting is less distracting than those in which nonpersonal mass media are used.

4. *Involvement in the decision process.* Through consultative selling and relationship marketing, the seller becomes more of a partner in the buying decision process, acting in conjunction with the buyer to solve problems. This leads the buyer to rely more on the salesperson and his or her products and services. An added benefit may be increasing the involvement of the organization's own employees.

5. *Source of research information.* In a well-integrated marketing/sales department the sales force can be the "eyes and ears" of the firm. Sales reps can collect information on competitors' products and services, promotions, pricing, and so on, firsthand. In addition, they can learn about the buying needs and wants of customers and potential customers.

Figure 18-7 Buyers' Likes and Dislikes about Salespeople

Traits Buyers Consider Most Helpful In Salespeople*	Traits Buyers Consider Most Objectionable In Salespeople*
1. *Knowledgeable.* They want salespeople who know products and policies thoroughly. They value technical support most highly.	1. *Unprepared.* Buyers hate salespeople who waste time by calling without clear purposes, especially on a busy day.
2. *Empathy.* They want salespeople who are interested in them. They want salespeople who listen and learn about them, their problems, and their goals.	2. *Uninformed.* They are vociferous about dealing with salespeople who don't know their products or lines and can't answer simple questions.
3. *Well organized.* They want salespeople who come prepared and do not waste their time. They strongly prefer salespeople who have written objectives.	3. *Aggressive.* They are turned off by "pushy" salespeople who argue and who "care more about their commission than the customer."
4. *Promptness.* They expect quick replies to requests for information, especially when a problem rears its ugly head.	4. *Undependability.* They cite salespeople who do not return calls promptly and who are never there when needed.
5. *Follow-through.* They look for salespeople who will follow through without continuous badgering. This spells personal reliability.	5. *Poor follow-through.* They are disgusted with calling salespeople several times to get information the salespeople promised.
6. *Solutions.* They want salespeople to present innovative solutions to problems. They seek responsiveness and creativity.	6. *Presumptuousness.* Many are offended by salespeople asking for competitors' quotes.
7. *Punctuality.* They expect salespeople to keep appointments promptly and to let them know if they will be late. They will excuse tardiness occasionally, but not frequently.	7. *"Walk-ins."* They list people who call without appointments, with no specific purposes. They also feel invaded by many telemarketers.
8. *Hard work.* They appreciate salespeople who work hard. They are impressed by salespeople who put in long and hard hours.	8. *"Gabbers."* They dislike compulsive talkers who go on and on and don't listen. They describe the "Gift of Gab" as boring. They are tired of hearing the "latest jokes."
9. *Energetic.* They are impressed by a positive attitude, enthusiasm, affability, consistency, and flexibility.	9. *Problem avoiders.* They dislike salespeople who go to pieces in a crisis, those with no clout, and those who are afraid of their principals.
10. *Honesty.* They want specifics instead of generalities. They look for personal integrity.	10. *Lack of personal respect.* They resent salespeople who go to other people in the company without their knowledge.

*In order of greatest number of times mentioned.

As you can see, the advantages of personal selling focus primarily on the dyadic communications process, the ability to alter the message, and the opportunity for direct feedback. Sometimes, however, these potential advantages are not always realized. In fact, they may become disadvantages.

Disadvantages associated with personal selling include the following:

1. *Inconsistent messages.* Earlier we stated that the ability to adapt the message to the receiver is a distinct advantage of personal selling. But the lack of a standardized message can become a disadvantage. The message to be communicated is generally designed by the marketing staff with a particular communications objective in mind. Once this message has been determined, it is communicated to all receivers. But the salesperson may alter this message in ways the marketer did not intend. Thus, the marketing staff is at the mercy of the sales force with respect to what exactly is communicated. (Sales communications aids can offset this problem to some degree, as you will see later in this chapter.)

2. *Sales force/management conflict.* Unfortunately, there are situations in even the best companies when one wonders if the sales staff and marketing staff know they work for the same company and for the same goals. Because of failure to communicate, corporate politics, and myriad other reasons, the sales force and marketing may

not be working as a team. The marketing staff may not understand the problems faced by the sales staff, or the salespeople may not understand why marketing people do things the way they do. The result is that the sales force may not use materials provided from marketing, marketing may not be responsive to the field's assessment of customer needs, and so forth. The bottom line is that the communications process is not as effective as it could be due to faulty internal communications and/or conflicts.

3. *High cost.* We discussed earlier the high cost of personal selling. As the cost per sales call continues to climb, the marketer may find mass communications a more cost-effective alternative.

4. *Poor reach.* Personal selling cannot reach as many members of the target audience as other elements. Even if money were no object (not a very likely scenario!), the sales force has only so many hours and so many people it can reach in a given time. Further, the frequency with which these accounts are reached is also low.

5. *Potential ethical problems.* Because the manager does not have complete control over the messages the salespeople communicate and because income and advancement are often directly tied to sales, sometimes sales reps bend the rules. They may say and do things they know are not entirely ethical or in the best interest of the firm in order to get a sale. Other, perhaps more serious, problems can also occur. For example, many organizations are concerned about salespersons committing bribery. In a study reported in *Sales & Marketing Management,* 25 percent of managers and/or sales reps reported that they sometimes or often have felt pressured by a client to give the client something worth more than $100 in exchange for their business. Even more scary is that almost 89 percent said that they had offered such gifts in exchange for business.[12] The potential for this problem has led to a renewed emphasis on ethics in the marketplace and has caused as many as 20 percent of companies to use surveillance measures to ensure that their representatives are not engaging in illegal activities.[13]

Combining Personal Selling with Other Promotional Tools

Like the other program elements, personal selling is usually one component of the integrated marketing communications program. Rarely, if ever, is it used alone. Rather, this promotional tool both supports and is supported by other program elements.

Combining Personal Selling and Advertising

With specific market situations and communications objectives, the advantages of advertising make it more effective in the early stages of the response hierarchy (for example, in creating awareness and interest), whereas personal selling is more likely to be used in the later stages (for example, stimulating trial and getting the order). Thus, each may be more or less appropriate depending on the objectives sought. These elements can be combined in the promotional mix to compensate for each other's weaknesses and complement each other.

Consider a new product introduction. Given an adequate budget, the initial objective might be to reach as many people in the target market as quickly and cost effectively as possible. Since the primary objective is awareness and a simple message will suffice, advertising will likely be the most appropriate medium.

Now suppose specific benefits must be communicated that are not very obvious or easy to comprehend, and a product demonstration would be useful. Or consider a situation in which the objective is to ask for the sale and/or to establish a relationship. Here personal selling is a more appropriate tool than advertising. In common marketing situations like these, you can see how well advertising and personal selling work together to attain the objectives sought.

A number of studies bear out this complementary relationship. A study by Theodore Levitt showed that sales reps from well-known companies are better received than those from companies that do not spend advertising dollars to create awareness.[14] (Once they are in the door, however, the buyer expects the salesperson to perform better than those from lesser-known companies.) If a salesperson from a lesser-known company can get in to see the buyer, he or she is as likely to make the

Which would you rather have?
A company that's simple to do business with or a company that makes business simple?
Why choose?
intel inside pentium III
At Gateway, we believe that customizing technology is a lot more than a simple sales pitch. It's a powerful way to help your business succeed. All you have to do is contact us either by phone, Internet, or through our Gateway Business Solution℠ centers, which offer face-to-face service and the chance to test-drive the latest technology, like the Gateway GP-Series PCs featuring Intel® Pentium® III processors. Then we'll get to know your business, your needs and your budget. Innovative lease options, and client care and enhanced service plans let us craft a technology bundle that truly fits your needs and respects your budget. Call, click or come into your nearest Gateway Country® location. It's the simplest way to get business technology to work for you.
GP-Series Professional Desktop
GP7-450
Intel® Pentium® III Processor 450MHz with 512K Cache
64MB SDRAM (expandable to 384MB)
6.8GB Ultra ATA Hard Drive
EV700 17" Color Monitor (15.9" viewable)
16MB AGP Graphics
17X min/40X max CD-ROM Drive
10/100 Ethernet Network Card
Iomega® Internal ZIP™ Drive
Business Audio & Speakers
Microsoft® Windows® 95 or Windows 98
MS® Office 2000 Small Business Software
$1299 or $45/mo.
36 mos. business lease¹

Connect with us.
Complete your solution by choosing from thousands of business hardware accessories and software at gateway.com
CALL 1-800-216-3360
CLICK www.gateway.com
OR COME IN TO A GATEWAY BUSINESS SOLUTIONS℠ CENTER Gateway Country®

Exhibit 18-4 Gateway's IMC campaign informs customers that Gateway is in the business-to-business market

sale. But in risky situations, the well-advertised company rep has the advantage. Gateway used a $50 million IMC campaign (Exhibit 18-4) using advertising, direct marketing, sales promotion, and the Internet to create awareness that Gateway is interested in companies' business (Gateway has been perceived by many as being a consumer PC). The campaign was designed to position the company as a solutions provider and to assist and enhance the sales force's efforts.

In other studies, John Morrill found that selling costs were 2 to 28 percent lower if the buyer had received an advertising message before the salesperson's arrival.[15] McGraw-Hill Corp., in a review of 54 studies, concluded the combination of advertising and personal selling is important since "less than 10 percent of industrial decision makers had been called upon by a salesperson from a specific company about a specific product in the previous two months."[16]

The studies suggest that combining advertising and personal selling is likely to improve reach, reduce costs, and increase the probability of a sale (assuming the advertising is effective, a concern reflected in Exhibit 18-5). Unfortunately, many salespeople do not understand the role that advertising plays and the contribution it can make to supporting their sales efforts. Some view the impact advertising makes with skepticism and/or believe that the monies would be better spent on commissions, price reductions, and so on. Ted Pollock, writing in *The American Salesman,* discusses the fact that advertising contributes to the sales process, and he enumerates 12 ways salespersons can use advertising to help them sell more (Figure 18-8).

Combining Personal Selling and Public Relations

The job descriptions presented earlier demonstrate that personal selling involves much more than just selling products and/or services. The personal selling agent is often the firm's best source of public relations. In their day-to-day duties, salespeople represent the firm and its products. Their personalities, servicing of the account, cooperation, and empathy not only influence sales potential but also reflect on the organizations they represent.

The salesperson may also be used directly in a PR role. Many firms encourage sales reps to participate in community activities like the Jaycees and Little League. Sometimes sales reps, in conjunction with the company, sacrifice time from their daily duties to help people in need. For example, after hurricanes Katrina, Rita, and Wilma devastated the Southeast in 2005, many companies offered their support in a variety of ways (as noted in Chapter 17). These efforts also involved many sales forces. Insurance companies set up shop to help victims file claims, while others were granted time off to aid in the reconstruction efforts or to use their expertise to assist in any way they could. These, as well as other public relations activities, result in goodwill toward both the company and its products while at the same time benefiting society.

Exhibit 18-5 Advertising and personal selling should be designed to work together

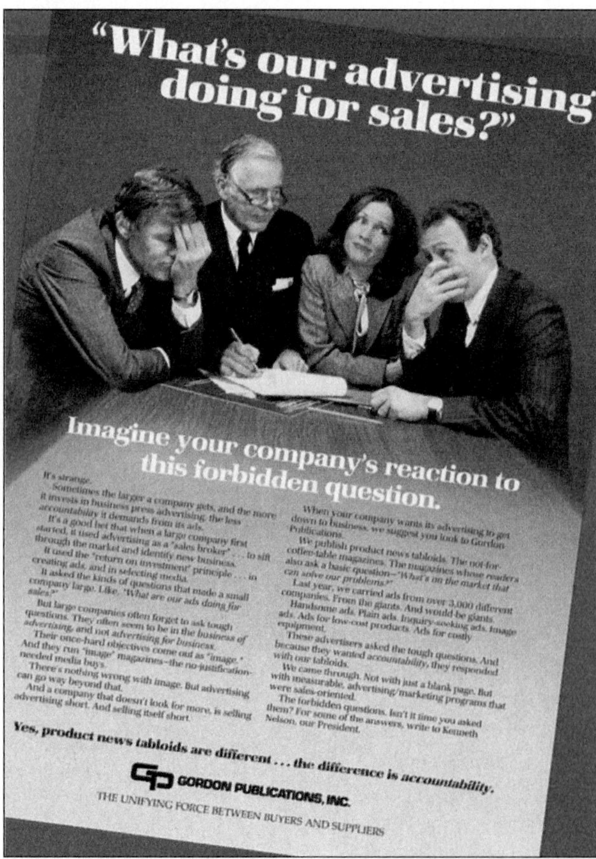

"What's our advertising doing for sales?"
Imagine your company's reaction to this forbidden question.
Yes, product news tabloids are different... the difference is accountability.
GORDON PUBLICATIONS, INC.
THE UNIFYING FORCE BETWEEN BUYERS AND SUPPLIERS

Combining Personal Selling and Direct Marketing

Companies have found that integrating direct marketing, specifically telemarketing, into their field sales operations makes their sales efforts more effective. The cost of a sales call and the cost associated with closing the sale are already very high and on the increase. Many marketers have reduced these costs by combining telemarketing and sales efforts (a typical telesales call costs about 11 cents for each $1 in revenue

Figure 18-8 Twelve Ways to Use Advertising to Sell More

1. *Save sales force time.* Sending a reprint of an advertisement ahead of time familiarizes the potential client with the product or service.
2. *Save lengthy explanations.* Sometimes ads can explain much of what the product does and even what it doesn't do, saving time as the salesperson only has to explain what is not already conveyed.
3. *Visual aids.* Ads can add impact to the presentation, reinforcing selling points.
4. *Ego boosters.* Telling prospects that an ad will appear in the media often makes the buyer feel she is important, and that she has inside information. Seeing the ad reinforces this.
5. *Personal refreshers.* Reviewing ad copy will often add insights to the salesperson, or remind him of key points that can be useful in a presentation.
6. *Clues to prospects' interests.* Sometimes prospects call in reference to an ad. By reviewing the ad, the salesperson can gain insights into the benefits the potential customer may be most interested in.
7. *Prove a point.* The printed word adds credibility to salespersons' verbal claims. One medium reinforces the other.
8. *Nudge indecisive prospects.* For indecisive prospects, a review of the ad campaign can often be the closer. If the ad is to include dealers' names, an additional benefit is offered, as the dealer may now directly benefit.
9. *Create preference.* Consistent advertising helps to build brand preference. Keeping customers and prospects aware of advertising creates favorable impressions of the company, the product or service, and the salesperson.
10. *Provide follow-ups.* Sending a reprint of an ad after the sales presentation serves as a good reminder, and can be used to focus attention on key benefits offered in the ad and in the presentation. It also demonstrates concern on the part of the salesperson.
11. *Fight lower-priced competitors.* Ads can be used to show support and ward off low-priced competitors. The salesperson can explain how the ad will help support the customer's own sales efforts and not have to get into price wars.
12. *Getting the customer into the act.* Asking the customer about the ads and getting his inputs helps cement relationships and provides valuable feedback to one's own organization. Often customers have ideas that may never have been thought of.

Source: Adapted from Ted Pollock, "12 Ways to Use Your Advertising to Sell More," *American Salesman.*

generated).[17] A number of companies now offer consulting services to help organizations in the sales process including assisting in the development and implementation of direct-marketing methods, as shown in Exhibit 18-6.

The telemarketing department is used to screen leads and—after qualifying potential buyers on the basis of interest, credit ratings, and the like—pass them on to the sales force. The net result is a higher percentage of sales closings, less wasted time by the sales force, and a lower average cost per sale. For example, IBM teamed up with Zacson Corp. to open an integrated teleservices center for its northern California territory. The group handles inquiries, lead generation, and qualification; develops promotional campaigns; distributes PR materials; and does problem solving for IBM clients. The new relationship reduced IBM's customer contact costs by 97 percent, lowered sales visit costs from $500 to $15, and exceeded customer expectations 78 percent of the time.[18]

As shown in Figure 18-9, there has been a rapid growth in the use of the telemarketing/sales combination for other firms as well. They have determined the phone can be used effectively for service and follow-up functions as well as for growth-related activities. Supplementing personal selling efforts with phone calls frees the sales force to spend more time selling.

In addition to selling and supporting the sales efforts, the telemarketing staff provides a public relations dimension. Communicating with buyers more often creates goodwill, improving customer satisfaction and loyalty.

In addition to telemarketing, other forms of direct marketing have been combined successfully with personal selling. Direct mail and e-mail are commonly used methods for supporting sales. For example, many companies send out lead cards to screen prospective customers. The salesperson follows up on those who express

Exhibit 18-6 Research and consulting companies offer businesses direct-marketing services

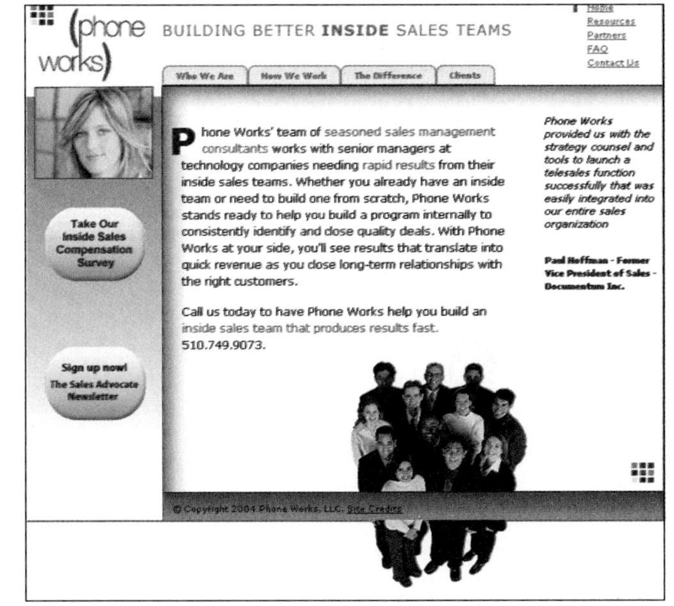

Figure 18-9 The Growth of Telemarketing as a Sales Function: Reasons for Growth (in percent)

	Telephone Sales and Service*	Field Sales*
Total growth related	58.0%	61.8%
Overall business growth or expansion	44.7	43.1
Adding product lines	10.2	8.0
Adding territories	3.1	10.7
Total system related	20.8	7.5
Added centralized telemarketing department	11.5	1.8
Added/changed computer system	6.2	4.4
Centralized sales and marketing	3.1	1.3
Customer demand	10.5	10.2
Cost efficiencies	1.4	0
Other	2.0	2.2
Can't tell/no response	9.8	18.2

*Figures add to more than 100 percent due to multiple mentions.

a genuine interest, saving valuable time and increasing the potential for a sale. Other uses include database building and mining. Exhibit 18-7 shows an example of a highly used software program available to assist marketers in creating and managing a database.

Combining Personal Selling and Sales Promotion

The program elements of sales promotion and personal selling also support each other. For example, many of the sales promotions targeted to resellers are presented by the sales force, who will ultimately be responsible for removing or replacing them as well.

Exhibit 18-7 Oracle is one of the more popular database management tools

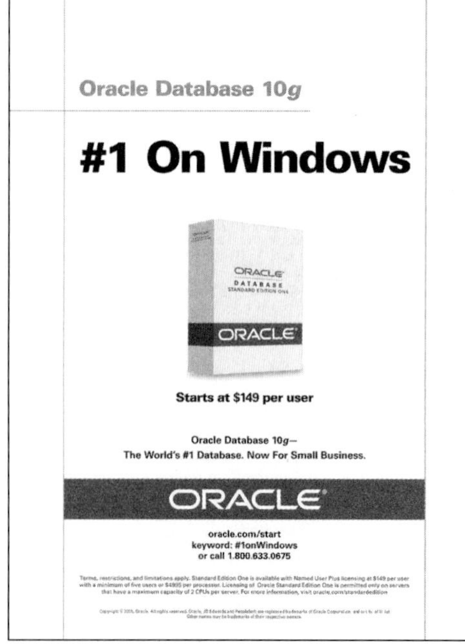

While trade sales promotions are designed to support the reseller and are often targeted to the ultimate consumer, many other promotional tools are designed to assist the sales staff. Flip charts, leave-behinds, and specialty ads may be designed to assist salespeople in their presentations, serve as reminders, or just create goodwill. The number of materials available may range from just a few to hundreds, depending on the company. (If you ever get the chance, look into the trunk of a consumer-product salesperson's car. You will find everything from pens to calendars to flip charts to samples to lost baseball mitts—all but the last of which are used in the selling effort.) Other forms of sales promotions like contests and sweepstakes are also used, as noted earlier.

Likewise, many sales promotions are targeted at the sales force itself. Incentives such as free trips, cash bonuses, or gifts are often used to stimulate sales efforts. And, as we saw with resellers, contests and sweepstakes may also be used.

Combining Personal Selling with the Internet

In the Internet chapter, we discussed the increasing use of the Internet as a support to personal selling. As noted, the Internet has been used to provide product information, generate leads, screen prospects, and build and market from databases. While many marketing managers were originally concerned about the Internet taking business away from channel members and direct sales, most have found that it has been more of an advantage than a disadvantage to their selling efforts. Many managers think that the Web will be used to fulfill the more mundane tasks of order fulfillment and providing information. This, in turn, will allow the sales force to be more effective in closing orders, doing close selling, and focusing more attention on high-value and/or new customers. Future salespeople will do what is more profitable for the future—that is, sell and develop relationships, not take orders.

A rapidly growing use of the Internet is that of conducting online meetings in which the sales force and/or clients and potential clients participate. Some companies have found that they can save both time and money by conducting their sales meetings online rather than at a central location. More involved presentations—often referred to as "webinars"—may include a variety of purposes, from conducting job training for employees to making presentations and providing in-depth product information to existing and potential customers. (See Exhibit 18-8.)

Exhibit 18-8 The Internet is used to conduct online meetings

It is important that the elements of the promotional program work together, as each has its specific advantages and disadvantages. While personal selling is valuable in accomplishing certain objectives and supporting other promotional tools, it must be supported by the other elements. In an effective marketing organization personal selling and other communications tools work hand in hand to promote the marketing effort. Before leaving this section, IMC Perspective 18-2 provides an excellent example of how Red Bull's success can be directly attributed to the successful integration of marketing and sales.

Evaluating the Personal Selling Effort

Like all other elements of the promotional mix, personal selling must be evaluated on the basis of its contribution to the overall promotional effort. The costs of personal selling are often high, but the returns may be just as high.

Because the sales force is under the supervision of the sales manager, evaluations are typically based on sales criteria. Sales may be analyzed by total sales volume, territories, product line, customer type, or sales rep.[19] Steve Deist and Rick Johnson suggest that an evaluation of the sales force should focus on "doing the right things, not just doing things right."[20] They propose a number of criteria that should be used in the sales force evaluation as shown in Figure 18-10. They also note that the process is critical to the success of the salesperson and that the review should be an opportunity to create enthusiasm, not a session for reprimand or criticism. Other sales-related

- Review of all target accounts.
- Review of all cross-functional selling activities or the lack of them.
- Review of specific territory objectives including sales to plan and gross profit to plan, and assigned account objectives.
- Knowledge of products, customers, and customer organizations.
- Ability to apply this market knowledge.
- Development of a favorable attitude as it pertains to that knowledge and those applied skills.
- Required course corrections.

Source: Steve Deist and Rick Johnson, "Developing an Effective Sales Force," *Industrial Distribution,* April 2005, pp. 75–79.

Figure 18-10 Factors to Be Considered in the Sales Review Process

IMC PERSPECTIVE 18-2

Red Bull: How the Combination of a Successful IMC Program and Sales Resulted in the World's Number-One Cult Drink

Red Bull doesn't do well in taste tests. It also doesn't try to hide its ingredients—they are posted right on the can, and they are not patented. Nevertheless, Red Bull is the leading energy drink in more than 100 countries worldwide, capturing as much as 70 to 90 percent of the market share, despite the efforts of over 100 competitors including brands from Coca-Cola and Anheuser-Busch. What makes the success of the product even more interesting is that when Red Bull first introduced its product in 1997, there was no such thing as an energy drink category. By 2001, estimates are that the market was somewhere between $140 million and $200 million. By 2004, Red Bull sold approximately $1.6 billion worldwide.

Red Bull has been variously described as "an international cult drink," "a kinky concoction," and "the new sex drink," all of which suit the company just fine. It is exactly the mystique attributed to the drink that helps create the "buzz" that makes it sell. Many marketers believe that it is Red Bull's alternative image that accounts for much of its success. Even the company's marketing department likes to maintain the illusions while claiming the product is a "nonmarketed brand."

But while the mystique part of Red Bull may be true, the "nonmarketed" claims may not necessarily be so. As noted by the *Economist,* it takes a lot of marketing money to sustain this image. The magazine notes that Red Bull's founder, Dietrich Mateschitz from Austria, "spent three years developing the drink's image, its packaging and its low-key, grassroots marketing strategy."

Gerhard Gschwandtner, writing for SellingPower.com, attributes most of the drink's success to Mateschitz—Austria's only billionaire. He notes that Mateschitz generates brilliant sales and marketing ideas, executes them well, and has a natural talent for selling. It was his sales capabilities, according to Gschwandtner, that allowed him to get the product through the conservative bureaucracy of Austria (after 3 years of scientific tests), to maintain financing, and to convince a soft drink bottler to produce the cans for the drink.

Mateschitz, besides being an excellent salesperson, is a prolific marketer as well. Rather than spending millions of dollars for traditional advertising, he relied heavily on "buzz" marketing, hiring college students to cruise around college campuses to distribute samples at parties, to drive Minis with a big Red Bull can strapped to the top, and to walk along beaches with a can strapped to their backs, handing out free samples. He originated numerous publicity stunts, throwing pre-event parties at which there were plenty of beautiful women, Red Bull, and, of course, people. It was he who called Arnold Schwarzenegger with an idea to create an annual award for the world's best stuntmen and stuntwomen. When Schwarzenegger declined his offer, Mateschitz created the award anyway, and the first Taurus World Stunt Award show was held in Los Angeles a year later. Schwarzenegger was given his own honorary award. And by donating the proceeds to stunt performers in need earned Mateschitz a great deal of free publicity.

But much of the success of Red Bull can also be attributed to the effectiveness of the company's IMC program. *Advertising Age* estimates that Red Bull puts about 35 percent of its revenues back into advertising, although advertising is not the only IMC component the company successfully employs. At the product launch in Europe, students were persuaded to drive around in Volkswagen Beetles or Minis with a Red Bull can strapped on the top and to stop whereever someone might need a boost, including construction sites, gyms, office buildings, and bars. They were also encouraged to conduct Red Bull parties using wild and unusual themes. A marketing director from Procter & Gamble was hired to oversee strategic planning for the brand in North America (he later was named one of *Brandweek*'s Marketers of the Year). Anything to create buzz.

At present, Red Bull's marketing efforts still employ grassroots efforts but have expanded to include more traditional media as well, such as sponsoring the Red Bull Musical Academy in Berlin. What seems to make Red Bull successful, however, is the nontraditional approach to the product messages—essentially attempting to do the opposite of what everyone else does, and creating buzz. The first order of business in any market is to determine four or five accounts in a particular market area that sustain the image—underage discos, surf shops, and so on—rather than attempting to gain widespread distribution. Spokespeople (deejays, alternative sports stars, etc.) are recruited to spread the word and to be seen using the product. Sponsorship of alternative sports like the Red Bull Streets of San Francisco (a street luge event), Red Bull Rampage (a free-ride mountain bike competition), Pororoca (a surfing competition on the Amazon in Brazil), and the Red Bull X-fighters motocross event in Madrid, Spain, is also extremely effective, as has been the use of "education teams"—hip locals who drive around in a Red Bull auto handing out samples and promoting the brand. Fueling rumors about the product's ingredients ("You can get drunk and stay wide awake;" "It's the poor man's cocaine") have led to even more buzz and free publicity.

The more mainstream media are also used, though on a market-by-market basis rather than through mass media. And even these traditional efforts may take on a less traditional form. For example, the advertising campaign ("Red Bull gives you wings") uses animated television and radio spots featuring the devil trying the product and sprouting wings. The company also sponsors a number of more traditional events ranging from soapbox derbies to Formula 1 racing cars, as well as extensive public relations programs to reach youth.

Now that Mateschitz and Red Bull have created a new beverage category, can they hold on to it? Success attracts competitors; many who have the potential to provide more marketing clout than Red Bull, including Coca-Cola, Pepsi, and Anheuser-Busch, have all introduced their own energy drinks, though none have yet successfully penetrated the market. However, Mateschitz is not oblivious to the competition. He and his marketing team are continually developing more wacky ideas to maintain Red Bull's alternative and mystical image, and his IMC program continues to expand. Mateschitz is an extremely good salesperson and an equally good marketer.

Sources: Gerhard Gschwandtner, "The Powerful Sales Strategy behind Red Bull," SellingPower.com, October 24, 2005, pp. 1–8; Lucio Guerrero, "Red Bull Challenger Hopes to Become the Bomba; Austrian Firm Makes Chicago Battleground in Energy-Drink War," *Chicago Sun-Times,* August 12, 2004, p. 14; "Selling Energy," *Economist,* May 11, 2002, p. 62; Kenneth Hein, "Red Bull Charging Ahead," *Brandweek,* October 15, 2001, pp. 38–42; Hillary Chula, "Grabbing Bull by Tail," *Advertising Age,* June 11, 2001, pp. 4–6; David Noonan, "Red Bull's Good Buzz," *Newsweek,* May 14, 2001, p. 39.

criteria such as new account openings and personal traits are also sometimes considered and may be increasing in importance (Figure 18-11).

In a recent study of high-performing sales organizations, five characteristics were identified as being critical for differentiating effective versus noneffective performances. These characteristics include

1. The strength of the field manager.
2. A clear link between company culture and values to sales strategies.
3. Rigorous management processes that drive performance.
4. Consistent training that leads to consistent execution.
5. The courage to change.

From a promotional perspective, sales performance is important, as are the contributions of individuals in generating these sales. On the other hand, the promotions manager must evaluate the performance of personal selling as one program element contributing to the overall promotional program. So he or she needs to use different criteria in determining its effectiveness.

Criteria for Evaluating Personal Selling

A number of criteria may be used to evaluate the contribution of the personal selling effort to the promotional program. They include the following:

- *Provision of marketing intelligence*—the ability of the sales force to feed back information regarding competitive programs, customer reactions, market trends, and other factors that may be important in the development of the promotional program.
- *Follow-up activities*—the use and dissemination of promotional brochures and correspondences with new and existing customers, providing feedback on the effectiveness of various promotional programs.
- *Program implementations*—the number of promotional programs implemented; the number of shelf and/or counter displays used, and so forth; the implementation and assessment of cooperative advertising programs.
- *Attainment of communications objectives*—the number of accounts to whom presentations were made (awareness, evaluation), the number of trial offers accepted, and the like.

Combining these criteria with those used by the sales department, the promotions manager should be able to accurately assess the effectiveness of the personal selling program. Making these evaluations requires a great deal of cooperation between the departments.

Figure 18-11 Criteria Used to Evaluate Sales Forces

Quantitative Measures	
Sales Results	Sales Efforts
Orders	***Sales Calls***
Number of orders obtained	Number made on current customers
Average order size (units or dollars)	Number made on potential new accounts
Batting average (orders ÷ sales calls)	Average time spent per call
Number of orders canceled by customers	Number of sales presentations
Sales Volume	Selling time versus nonselling time
Dollar sales volume	Call frequency ratio per customer type
Unit sales volume	***Selling Expenses***
By customer type	Average per sales call
By product category	As percentage of sales volume
Translated into market share	As percentage of sales quota
Percentage of sales quota achieved	By customer type
Margins	By product category
Gross margin	Direct-selling expense ratios
Net profit	Indirect-selling expense ratios
By customer type	***Customer Service***
By product category	Number of service calls
Customer Accounts	Displays set up
Number of new accounts	Delivery cost per unit sold
Number of lost accounts	Months of inventory held, by customer type
Percentage of accounts sold	Number of customer complaints
Number of overdue accounts	Percentage of goods returned
Dollar amount of accounts receivable	
Collections made of accounts receivable	

Qualitative Measures	
Sales Results	Sales Efforts
Selling Skills	***Sales-Related Activities***
Knowing the company and its policies	Territory management: sales call preparation, scheduling, routing, and time utilization
Knowing competitors' products and sales strategies	Marketing intelligence: new product ideas, competitive activities, new customer preferences
Use of marketing and technical backup teams	Follow-ups: use of promotional brochures and correspondence with current and potential accounts
Understanding of selling techniques	Customer relations
Customer feedback (positive and negative)	Report preparation and timely submission
Product knowledge	Personal characteristics
Customer knowledge	Cooperation, human relations, enthusiasm, motivation, judgment, care of company property, appearance, self-improvement efforts, patience, punctuality, initiative, resourcefulness, health, sales management potential, ethical and moral behavior
Execution of selling techniques	
Quality of sales presentations	
Communication skills	

Summary

This chapter discussed the nature of personal selling and the role this program element plays in the promotional mix. The role of personal selling in the IMC program varies depending on the nature of the industry, competition, and market conditions. In many industries (for example, industrial markets) the personal selling component may receive the most attention, while in others (for example, consumer nondurables) it plays a minor role. However, managers in most industries believe the importance of this program element will continue to increase over the next few years.

Personal selling offers the marketer the opportunity for a dyadic communications process (a two-way exchange of information). The salesperson can instantly assess the situation and the effects of the communication and adapt the message if necessary.

While this exchange lets the sales rep tailor the message specifically to the needs and wants of the receiver, its disadvantage is a nonstandardized message, since the final message communicated is under the salesperson's control. In an attempt to develop a standard communication, marketers provide their reps with flip charts, leave-behinds, and other promotional pieces.

Evaluation of the personal selling effort is usually under the control of the sales department, since sales is the most commonly used criterion. The promotions manager must assess the contribution of personal selling with nonsales-oriented criteria as well, integrating this element into the overall IMC program.

Key Terms

personal selling, 575
dyadic communication, 575
provider stage, 577
persuader stage, 577
prospector stage, 577
problem-solver stage, 577
procreator stage, 577
relationship marketing, 578
order taking, 581
creative selling, 581
missionary sales, 581
prospecting, 581
leads, 581
prospects, 581
qualified prospects, 581
close, 582
cross sell, 582

Discussion Questions

1. The lead-in to this chapter discusses changes taking place in the pharmaceutical industry in regard to how drugs can be marketed. There are some who are concerned that the pharmaceutical industry may be engaging in unethical marketing practices. Describe how the marketing of drugs has changed and discuss whether or not you feel the industry is engaging in potentially unethical practices.

2. Describe what is meant by relationship marketing. Explain the reasons why it is so important for companies to engage in this practice.

3. There are many who believe that allowing pharmaceutical companies to advertise and promote their products directly to consumers should not be allowed. Others counter by noting that using the push strategy of marketing to doctors leads to the same results, as doctors will then push the product onto the patient. Discuss both sides of this issue.

4. The text discusses the *Sales & Marketing Management* survey that identifies traits that define effective salespeople. Discuss these traits and explain why you think they are so important.

5. Figure 18-5 describes three types of sales positions. Discuss each of these. Describe some of the industries in which each might play a more important role.

6. Companies often attempt to motivate salespersons in various ways, including offering them monetary incentives. Following up on this, give some examples of how integrating other program elements might also be effective in motivating the sales force.

7. Explain what is meant by "the new role of personal selling." How does this new role differ from what personal selling has involved in the past?

8. Explain why the high costs of personal selling might be warranted. Give a specific example of a situation where this is the case.

9. Explain why the combination of personal selling and advertising may provide benefits that exceed just personal selling alone.

10. Describe some of the criteria used to evaluate qualitative aspects of the effectiveness of the salesperson. How might these be used to support the IMC program?

Measuring the Effectiveness of the Promotional Program

19

Chapter Objectives

1. To understand reasons for measuring promotional program effectiveness.
2. To know the various measures used in assessing promotional program effectiveness.
3. To evaluate alternative methods for measuring promotional program effectiveness.
4. To understand the requirements of proper effectiveness research.

From Econometrics to Plotting Love on a Graph, Marketers Continue Their Search to Measure Communications Effectiveness

No doubt, for as long as there have been marketing communications, people have tried to determine how effective their messages are. Academics have been enamored with the challenge for decades, while practitioners are under increasing pressure to show that their monies are being well spent. The old adage that you can't measure the effectiveness of advertising is no longer acceptable. Add to this the number of new media options that have come on the scene and the need to know the relative contribution that each makes, and you can feel the pressure for accountability rise. Although measures of effectiveness seem to come and go—one company used pictures of people with different facial expressions to attempt to gauge reactions to ads, but that didn't last long—some have endured forever. It seems everyone has a need to know if their communications are working, and, as we know, necessity is the mother of invention!

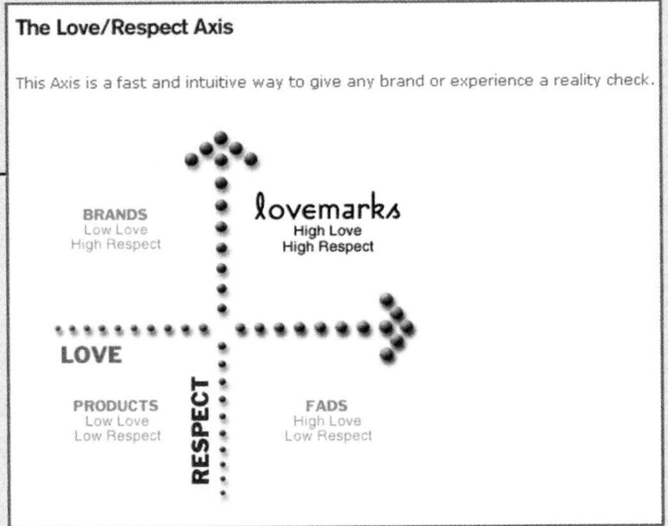

Here are some of the latest measures used to measure effectiveness—some new, some old.

- *The Love/Respect Axis.* While businesspeople don't typically use the term *love* when discussing the relationship they want consumers to have with their brand, Kevin Roberts, CEO of the giant global advertising agency Saatchi & Saatchi, thinks they should. Roberts, along with the British company QIQ International, Ltd., has developed a tool to quantify the emotional power of a brand. Whereas marketers are used to advertising a brand's performance, trust, and/or reputation, they are less likely to have measured the product's mystery, sensuality, and intimacy. But Roberts thinks they should and has been convincing others to do so. He encourages companies to visit his website (www.lovemarks.com) to see how their brand scores on these dimensions. Then what? Consider the example of Procter & Gamble's Tide. In the late 1990s, the brand was at risk of becoming a commodity as its advertising focused on the product's cleaning power. James Stengel, global marketing officer for P&G, knew that the appeal wasn't working and infused some emotion into the campaign by showing mothers caring for their babies while at the same time showing empathy for their busy lifestyles. The combined appeals led to as much as a 25 percent sales increase in some markets. When research showed that General Mills' Cheerios cereal was considered to be not emotional enough, the company replaced the picture of the bowl on the package with a drawing of a heart and repositioned its advertising to stress emotional rather than functional attributes. Cheerios is now the number-one cereal brand in the country.

- *Eyetools.* The use of eye tracking to measure the effectiveness of ads has been around since the 1970s and has fallen in and out of favor over the years. But now, eye tracking is back, albeit in a very different way. In the '70s, the eye-tracking methodology involved the use of cumbersome headgear and goggles, and generated enormous sets of data that were time consuming to analyze. Now results are presented in a single diagram with heat maps to indicate where the eyes focus. The new Eyetools technology automates the analysis and is very inexpensive. The laboratory setting of older eye-tracking methods was not appealing to many advertisers or their agencies. But Eyetools tests are conducted in an environment that looks very much like one's home or office, thereby adding a great deal of realism. Companies such as IBM, American Express, and Cisco are just some of the clients who have used the technology for eye tracking e-mail marketing messages to see what companies see and what they ignore. What have they learned? Well for one, they found that the majority of viewers see less than one half of the copy, and the word "free" is usually skipped.
- *RFID (radio frequency identification).* Born in the research lab at MIT's Media Lab, RFID uses a microchip, an antenna, and radio waves to identify people or objects. While most attempts to measure the effectiveness of print ads in magazines use written surveys, telephone interviews, and/or face-to-face interviews with respondents, RFID automates the whole process. MediaMark Research and TagSense, Inc., a technology development company, are conducting studies in controlled environments to place sensors in magazines and tag the readers to see what they read, as well as how much time they spend looking at an advertisement. The companies draw an analogy between the chips and where bar codes were 10 years ago—that is, useful, but not realizing their potential.
- *MindShare and OMD Metrics.* MindShare is a media buying company owned by WPP Group, one of the world's largest advertising agencies. MindShare has increased the number of employees that work on econometric models from 20 to 150 over the past five years. OMD, owned by the Omnicom Group, has expanded its staff of econometricians from 6 to 45 over the past three years. These companies, among others, hope that econometrics (a very complex statistical methodology) will be the answer to measuring ad effectiveness. What econometrics does is to attempt to model the relationship between different sets of events, such as the effect on sales of different factors including the weather, price cuts, and, of course, advertising. Although not everyone in the advertising business—especially creative types—like the idea of their work being analyzed by mathematical models, econometrics has its share of believers. *The Economist* magazine believes it can measure the impact of the money the company spends on brand marketing on sales of the magazine, while the British supermarket chain Sainsbury claims that an econometric modeling of their TV campaign featuring celebrity chef Jamie Oliver led to the success of the campaign and the renewal of his contract.

While the increased emphasis on accountability has led these and many other more traditional methods to gain popularity and use, not everyone is sold on their value. Many in the advertising industry—old and young, alike—still believe that the effects of advertising cannot be measured, and apparently are not willing to try, regardless of the advances in technology being made. At an advertising symposium conducted in Cannes, France, in the summer of 2005, Sir Martin Sorrell, the CEO of the WPP Group, was touting the creativity of advertising as well as the use of econometrics and scientific analyses to measure its impact. Sharing the stage with Sir Martin was Chuck Porter, the chairperson of Miami advertising agency Crispin,

Porter & Bogusky. In response to the remarks of Sir Martin, Porter said, "I don't understand what we are talking about." Apparently the many people in the audience who cheered Porter's comments didn't either. Maybe they didn't pass their econometrics tests!

Sources: Aaron O. Patrick, "Econometrics Buzzes Ad World as a Way of Measuring Results; Method Claims to Identify Campaigns That Lift Sales; Sir Martin's 'Holy Grail,'" *The Wall Street Journal,* August 16, 2005, p. B-8; Phillip J. Britt, "RFID Positioned to Aid Measurement of Traditional Print: Pilots Offer New Possibilities," *EContent,* July/August 2005, p. 12; Mathew Creamer, "Eye-Tracking Technology Draws New Interest," adage.com, July 4, 2005, pp. 1–3; Linda Tischler, "How Do I Love Thee?" *Fast Company,* July 2004, pp. 64–65.

As noted throughout this text, the increased emphasis on accountability is forcing many companies to evaluate, or re-evaluate, their IMC plans. Both clients and agencies are continually striving to determine whether their communications are working and how well they are working relative to other options. Unfortunately, there seems to be little agreement on the best measures to use. Almost everyone agrees that research is required, but they disagree on how it should be conducted and how the results should be used. At the same time, as can be seen by the lead-in to this chapter, companies and organizations continue to work together in an attempt to provide answers to these questions, and to develop new ways to measure communications effectiveness.

Measuring the effectiveness of the promotional program is a critical element in the promotional planning process. Research allows the marketing manager to evaluate the performance of specific program elements and provides input into the next period's situation analysis. It is a necessary ingredient to a continuing planning process, yet it is often not carried out.

In this chapter, we discuss some reasons firms should measure the effectiveness of their IMC programs, as well as why many decide not to. We also examine how, when, and where such measurements can be conducted. Most of our attention is devoted to measuring the effects of advertising because much more time and effort have been expended developing evaluation measures in advertising than in the other promotional areas. We will, however, discuss measurement in other areas of the IMC program as well. (In some of these areas, the measures are more directly observable—for example, direct marketing and personal selling.) You'll recall that we addressed the methods used to evaluate many of the other promotional elements in previous chapters.

It is important to understand that in this chapter we are concerned with research that is conducted in an evaluative role—that is, to measure the effectiveness of advertising and promotion and/or to assess various strategies before implementing them. This is not to be confused with research discussed earlier in the text to help develop the promotional program, although the two can (and should) be used together. While evaluative research may occur at various times throughout the promotional process (including the development stage), it is conducted specifically to assess the effects of various strategies. We begin our discussion with the reasons effectiveness should be measured as well as some of the reasons firms do not do so.

Arguments for and Against Measuring Effectiveness

Almost any time one engages in a project or activity, whether for work or fun, some measure of performance occurs. In sports you may compare your golf score against par or your time on a ski course to other skiers' performance. In business, employees are generally given objectives to accomplish, and their job evaluations are based on their ability to achieve these objectives. Advertising and promotion should not be an exception. It is important to determine how well the communications program is working and to measure this performance against some standards.

Reasons to Measure Effectiveness

Assessing the effectiveness of ads both before they are implemented and after the final versions have been completed and fielded offers a number of advantages:

1. *Avoiding costly mistakes.* The top three advertisers in the United States spent over $11 billion in advertising and promotion in 2005. The top 10 spent a total of over $30 billion. This is a lot of money to be throwing around without some understanding of how well it is being spent. If the program is not achieving its objectives, the marketing manager needs to know so he or she can stop spending (wasting) money on it.

Just as important as the out-of-pocket costs is the opportunity loss due to poor communications. If the advertising and promotions program is not accomplishing its objectives, not only is the money spent lost but so too is the potential gain that could result from an effective program. Thus, measuring the effects of advertising does not just save money. It also helps the firm maximize its investment. For example, one mass merchant discovered that promoting Tide detergent generated more cross-selling opportunities than did promotions of nonpremium brands like Purex (Exhibit 19-1). At the same time, promotions of motor oil had no cross-selling impact.[1]

2. *Evaluating alternative strategies.* Typically a firm has a number of strategies under consideration. For example, there may be some question as to the degree to which each medium should be used or whether one message is more effective than another. Or the decision may be between two promotional program elements. We have noted previously that many marketers are shifting dollars from traditional to nontraditional media. Heineken recently announced that they would no longer advertise on TV in the United Kingdom, moving their ad dollars to increased sales promotions and sponsorhips.[2] The question is, should research be spent on sponsorships or on advertising or in what combination? One retailer found that advertising do-it-yourself products on the radio was effective in rural areas but not in urban locales.[3] Research may be designed to help the manager determine which strategy is most likely to be effective. Companies often test alternate versions of their advertising in different cities to determine which ad communicates most effectively. They may also explore different forms of couponing.

3. *Increasing the efficiency of advertising in general.* You may have heard the expression "can't see the forest for the trees." Sometimes advertisers get so close to the project they lose sight of what they are seeking, and because they know what they are trying to say, they expect their audience will also understand. They may use technical jargon that not everyone is familiar with. Or the creative department may get too creative or too sophisticated and lose the meaning that needs to be communicated. How many times have you seen an ad and asked yourself what it was trying to say, or how often have you seen an ad that you really like, but you can't remember the brand name? Conducting research helps companies develop more efficient and effective

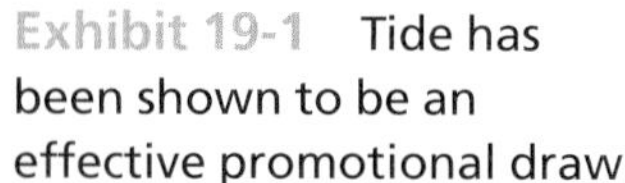

Exhibit 19-1 Tide has been shown to be an effective promotional draw

communications. An increasing number of clients are demanding accountability for their promotional programs and putting more pressure on the agencies to produce. As IMC Perspective 19-1 demonstrates, effective research can be used for both of these purposes.

4. *Determining if objectives are achieved.* In a well-designed IMC plan, specific objectives are established. If objectives are attained, new ones need to be established in the next planning period. An assessment of how program elements led to the attainment of the goals should take place, and/or reasons for less-than-desired achievements must be determined. As noted by Spike Cramphorn, research should address whether the advertising delivers the stated objectives and how appropriate the measures used to make this assessment are.[4]

Reasons Not to Measure Effectiveness

While it seems obvious that it makes sense to measure effectiveness, the fact remains that in too many instances this is not done. Two recent studies provide additional insight into this area (Figure 19-1). As can be seen, whereas advertisers know that it is important to measure effectiveness, with as many as 90 percent considering it a priority, many do not do so, or if they do, they are not confident of the results. On the positive side, 60 percent of these managers say they will increase their expenditures in this area in the next year.

Companies give a number of reasons for not measuring the effectiveness of advertising and promotions strategies:

1. *Cost.* Perhaps the most commonly cited reason for not testing (particularly among smaller firms) is the expense. In one of the surveys reported in Figure 19-1, it was noted that while some companies spend as much as 25 percent of their revenue on marketing and advertising, 70 percent of them spend less than 2 percent on measuring effectiveness.[5] Good research can be expensive, in terms of both time and money. Many managers decide that time is critical and they must implement the program while the opportunity is available. Many believe the monies spent on research could be better spent on improved production of the ad, additional media buys, and the like.

While the first argument may have some merit, the second does not. Imagine what would happen if a poor campaign were developed or the incentive program did not motivate the target audience. Not only would you be spending money without the desired effects, but the effort could do more harm than good. Spending more money to buy media does not remedy a poor message or substitute for an improper promotional mix. For example, one of the nation's leading brewers watched its test-market sales for a new brand of beer fall short of expectations. The problem, it thought, was an insufficient media buy. The solution, it decided, was to buy all the TV time available

Figure 19-1 Marketers' Views toward Measuring Effectiveness*

Issue	Percent Agreeing
It is important to define, measure, and take concrete steps in the area of advertising accountability.	61.5%
I am satisfied with our ability to take these steps.	19.5
I am confident that I understand the effects that an advertising or marketing campaign would have on sales.	27.0
I am able to forecast the impact on sales of a 10% cut in marketing spending.	37.0
Our company has a formal marketing performance measurement system (MPM).	16.8
MPM is a key priority for today's technology companies.	90.0
I am dissatisfied with the ability to demonstrate our marketing programs' business impact and value.	80.0

*Study one = Chief Marketing Officer Council survey of 320 global technology marketers.
Study two = Association of National Advertisers' survey of advertisers conducted jointly with Forrester Research and Marketing Management Analytics.
Sources: Stuart Elliott, "How Effective Is This Ad, in Real Numbers? Beats Me," nytimes.com, July 20, 2005, pp. 1–2; Robyn Greenspan, "Marketers Missing Measurements," clickz.com, June 4, 2004, pp. 1–2.

IMC PERSPECTIVE 19-1

The Ogilvy Awards—2005

One of the most prestigious awards an advertiser can receive is the David Ogilvy Award. The award is given by the Advertising Research Foundation (ARF) in honor of researcher-turned-adman David Ogilvy, whose own work always stressed the role of research in developing, evaluating, and improving advertising. To win an Ogilvy Award, the candidate must demonstrate how research was used in developing a program and also must show marketing success. Awards are given in three areas: (1) services, (2) durables, and (3) packaged goods. Then an overall grand-prize winner is announced. Judges come from academia, advertising agencies, companies, and research firms. This year's winners included the following.

• *Grand Winner—Lexus.* For all of our lives two categories of automobiles have been available for sale: new cars and used cars. However, as both the quality of automobiles and the number of leased vehicles have increased, Lexus found that many of the cars that were being turned in from these leases were very well taken care of and had few defects. Lexus marketers believed that to group them into the "used" category would be to understate their value. So Lexus created a "third category" of automobiles: Certified Pre-Owned (CPO), which had tighter qualifications to qualify, including lower miles and a manufacturer's warranty. Unfortunately, the CPO concept initiated very little interest, and Lexus marketers knew just another advertising campaign would not be sufficient. That's when the company embarked on a number of research studies to determine how to create interest in the CPO concept.

The research showed that the buyers who came into the showroom looking for a pre-owned vehicle were in more of a new-car-buyer state of mind—looking for the brand but not price—and that the CPO message was being missed almost entirely. The result was that upon visiting a Lexus dealership, potential buyers were uninformed and uninterested in the CPO concept. Based on this finding and research that showed that 75 percent of car buyers use the Internet as their first source of information about cars, Lexus decided to place more emphasis on the third category of automobiles—CPO—with the Internet as the core medium for its new campaign. Partnering with eight auto sites including Autobytel.com and Edmunds.com, Lexus introduced the third category on these sites and provided in-depth information about the vehicles, including prices and comparative data.

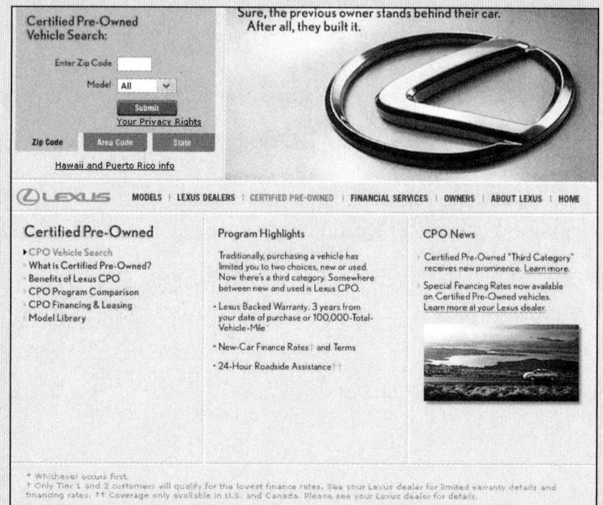

The results were impressive. A new car category was created and then adopted by other automobile manufacturers. Buying consideration increased by 58 percent, familiarity by 64 percent, leads by 222 percent, Lexus CPO.com visits by 40 percent, and—the bottom line—Lexus had the best sales year in its history.

• *Service Category Winner—UBS.* UBS is the largest bank in Switzerland, and the sixth largest financial institution in the world. Unfortunately, not too many people knew that, so the company set out to create a differentiated branding image for itself. Working with research and branding teams, UBS and its partners set out to determine the feasibility of a single global brand, and the potential relevance of the brand to target consumers and business investors. Qualitative research was designed to determine customer motivation for choosing a financial institution. Linkage research quantified the motivations; then validation research quantified the appeal, uniqueness, credibility, and importance of each brand element. When the final executions were developed, they were tested using standard copy-testing methodologies.

The "You and Us" campaign was launched in 2004. The results show that the campaign led to increased awareness and interest in the bank, and, after only one year, *BusinessWeek* ranked UBS as one of the world's top global brands. Only five financial service companies have achieved this prestigious positioning.

• *Shared: Package Goods—Chef Boyardee.* Using IRI scanner research, Chef Boyardee realized that their share of the children's market was seriously eroding, being taken over by other competing brands of convenience foods. Additional research revealed additional decline in brand relevance among parents and a loss of importance to kids. Though the parents were loyal to the brand, kids were more interested in competitive products. The company conducted qualitative research. After having kids eat the product, researchers probed for insights. What they found was that kids loved the brand for its taste and its fun character, which pleased parents because they believed they were both giving the kids what they wanted and feeding them a nutritional product. These insights led to the development of the campaign message "Rolling Can" reflecting the fact that Chef Boyardee was irresistible.

The second phase of the research was designed to test media effectiveness by targeting the message to children or their parents. The results showed a 3 percent gain when the ad was placed in kids' media but produced no change at all when targeted to their parents. Two additional rounds of research were conducted to determine the effectiveness of the irresistibility message. The "Rolling Can" appeals were evaluated based on the message communicated, the ease of delivering the communication, and brand imagery.

The results were so unusually positive that the company skipped its usual development of animatics, going directly to finished product. The commercials were tested on kids and parents using Ipsos-ASI's Next TV copy testing, where they surpassed norms for the product category. For moms and dads, related recall scores were almost twice the norms (46 percent to 26 percent), brand link (81 percent versus the norm of 61 percent, a 50 percent increase in purchase motivation), and two box purchase intentions increased (50 percent versus 34 percent) in the control group. For kids, the very important score of "intent to ask mom" was 76 percent versus 65 percent in the control group. Once the ad campaign was implemented, tracking showed that among kids, prompted recall was 81 percent (versus the norm of 68 percent), and the branding link was .77. Scanner volume showed a 4 percent increase (after 36 months of decline), and additional tracking showed that repurchase intent increased by 8 percent in the first quarter the commercials ran versus no growth for competitive products in the category. Not only did research save the brand, but it resulted in the highest ROI ever recorded by Chef Boyardee.

While there are numerous other Ogilvy Awards winners including Chevrolet, Jaguar, Procter & Gamble, and Con Agra Foods, space permits mentioning just a few. These few examples, nevertheless, clearly demonstrate the power of research in the development and evaluation of advertising campaigns.

Source: "2005 ARF David Ogilvy Awards: The Stories behind the Winners," Advertising Research Foundation, 2005.

that matched its target audience. After two months sales had not improved, and the product was abandoned in the test market. Analysis showed the problem was not in the media but rather in the message, which communicated no reason to buy. Research would have identified the problem, and millions of dollars and a brand might have been saved. The moral: Spending research monies to gain increased exposure to the wrong message is not a sound management decision.

2. *Research problems.* A second reason cited for not measuring effectiveness is that it is difficult to isolate the effects of promotional elements. Each variable in the marketing mix affects the success of a product or service. Because it is often difficult to measure the contribution of each marketing element directly, some managers become frustrated and decide not to test at all. They say, "If I can't determine the specific effects, why spend the money?"

This argument also suffers from weak logic. While we agree that it is not always possible to determine the dollar amount of sales contributed by promotions, research can provide useful results. As demonstrated by the introduction and examples in IMC Perspective 19-1, communications effectiveness can be measured and may carry over to sales or other behaviors.

3. *Disagreement on what to test.* The objectives sought in the promotional program may differ by industry, by stage of the product life cycle, or even for different people within the firm, and, as shown in the lead-in to this chapter there are numerous ways to measure these. The sales manager may want to see the impact of promotions on sales, top management may wish to know the impact on corporate image, and those involved in the creative process may wish to assess recall and/or recognition of the ad. Lack of agreement on what to test often results in no testing.

Again, there is little rationale for this position. With the proper design, many or even all of the above might be measured. Since every promotional element is designed to accomplish its own objectives, research can be used to measure its effectiveness in doing so.

4. *The objections of creative.* It has been argued by many (and denied by others) that the creative department does not want its work to be tested and many agencies are reluctant to submit their work for testing. This is sometimes true. Ad agencies' creative departments argue that tests are not true measures of the creativity and effectiveness of ads; applying measures stifles their creativity; and the more creative the ad, the more likely it is to be successful. They want permission to be creative without the limiting guidelines marketing may impose. The Chiat/Day ad shown in Exhibit 19-2 reflects how many people in the advertising business feel about this subject. The comment made by Chuck Porter and

Exhibit 19-2 Chiat/Day expresses its opinion of recall tests

To advertisers interested in 'day after recall,' we submit a case history:

On January 24th, Apple Computer will introduce Macintosh. And you'll see why 1984 won't be like "1984."
On January 22, 1984, one commercial for Apple Computer ran on network television.
With all due respect to Burke, we didn't bother to test it.
Unlike a lot of advertising agencies, we prefer a different form of measurement:
When the product mentioned in the commercial, Apple's new Macintosh," was unveiled on January 24, over 200,000 people lined up to see it in person.
Within 6 hours, they bought $3,500,000 worth of Macintosh computers. And left cash deposits for $1,000,000 more.
ABC, CBS, NBC and CNN featured the commercial in network news segments.
Dan Rather covered it at night. Bryant Gumbel covered it at dawn.
The BBC ran it in England.
Associated Press put it on the wire.
27 TV stations in major U.S. markets ran it on local news programs.
Steven Spielberg called.
As did The New York Times, The Wall Street Journal, The Washington Post, the Philadelphia Inquirer, USA Today, the Boston Globe, the Los Angeles Times, the San Francisco Chronicle and, of course, the San Jose Mercury News.
Not to mention Time, Newsweek, Fortune, Forbes, Business Week and, of course, Advertising Age.
Apple is now producing one Macintosh every 27 seconds. And selling one every 20 seconds.
Not bad for one 60-second spot on the Super Bowl.
Chiat/Day
Los Angeles, San Francisco, New York

apparently supported by others ("I don't understand what we are talking about"—see the lead-in to this chapter) also seems to support this view.

At the same time, the marketing manager is ultimately responsible for the success of the product or brand. Given the substantial sums being allocated to advertising and promotion, it is the manager's right, and responsibility, to know how well a specific program—or a specific ad—will perform in the market. Interestingly, in a study examining the 200 most awarded commercials over a 2-year span, it was shown that 86 percent were deemed effective in achieving their goals, versus only 33 percent for other ads—proving that creative ads are effective.[6]

5. *Time.* A final reason given for not testing is a lack of time. Managers believe they already have too much to do and just can't get around to testing, and they don't want to wait to get the message out because they might miss the window of opportunity.

Planning might be the solution to the first problem. Although many managers are overworked and time poor, research is just too important to skip.

The second argument can also be overcome with proper planning. While timeliness is critical, getting the wrong message out is of little or no value and may even be harmful. There will be occasions where market opportunities require choosing between testing and immediate implementation. But even then some testing may help avoid mistakes or improve effectiveness. For example, after the terrorist attacks on September 11, 2001, Motorola developed an ad designed to portray the quality of its mobile phones by showing an FDNY firefighter using one. While the ad may have had good intentions, many people thought it was an attempt to capitalize on a tragedy. As a result, much negative publicity was generated. The problem could have been avoided had Motorola pretested consumers' responses to the ad. In most instances, proper planning and scheduling will allow time for research.

Conducting Research to Measure Advertising Effectiveness

What to Test

We now examine how to measure the effects of communications. This section considers what elements to evaluate, as well as where and how such evaluations should occur.

In Chapter 5, we discussed the components of the communications model (source, message, media, receiver) and the importance of each in the promotional program. Marketers need to determine how each is affecting the communications process. Other decisions made in the promotional planning process must also be evaluated.

Source Factors

An important question is whether the spokesperson being used is effective and how the target market will respond to him or her. For example, Tiger Woods has proved to be a successful salesperson for Nike and Buick. Or a product spokesperson may be an excellent source initially but, owing to a variety of reasons, may lose impact over time. For example, Britney Spears had been an effective spokesperson for Pepsi, particularly with the teen market. The question was whether she would be able to retain this relationship as she got older. Apparently Pepsi thought not, as her contract was not renewed. In other instances, changes in the source's attractiveness or likeability or other external factors may lead to changes in source effectiveness. Pepsi pulled a TV sport featuring rapper Ludacris after Fox TV's Bill O'Reilly attacked the violent lyrics in Ludacris's songs.[7] Ads featuring model Kate Moss and basketball star Kobe Bryant were also pulled by their sponsors after the stars received negative publicity.

Message Variables

Both the message and the means by which it is communicated are bases for evaluation. For example, in the beer example discussed earlier, the message never provided a reason for consumers to try the new product. In other instances, the message may not be strong enough to pull readers into the ad by attracting their attention or clear enough to help them evaluate the product. Sometimes the message is memorable but doesn't achieve the other goals set by management. One study showed that 7 of the 25 products that scored highest on interest and memorability in Video Storyboard Tests' ad test had flat or declining sales.[8] A number of factors regarding the message and its delivery may have an impact on its effectiveness, including the headline, illustrations, text, and layout. A recent study examined what effect sexually themed print ads would have on viewers. Among the numerous results was that men favor sex appeals more than women and that recall of the brands was lower for sexual ads than for nonsexual ones. Whereas men responded that sexual ads have "high stopping power" for them, their lower brand recall seems to indicate that they are paying more attention to other aspects of the ad than the marketers would prefer.[9]

Many ads are never seen by the public because of the message they convey. For example, an ad in which Susan Anton ate a slice of Pizza Hut pizza was considered too erotic for the company's small-town image. Likewise, an ad created for General Electric in which Uncle Sam got slapped in the face (to demonstrate our growing trade imbalance) was killed by the company's chair.[10]

Media Strategies

Media decisions need to be evaluated. Research may be designed to determine which media class (for example, broadcast versus print), subclass (newspaper versus magazines), or specific vehicles (which newspapers or magazines) generate the most effective results. The location within a particular medium (front page versus back page) and size of ad or length of commercial also merit examination. For example, research has demonstrated that readers pay more attention to larger ads.[11] A variety of methods have been employed to measure the effectiveness of advertising on the Internet. Similarly, direct-response advertisers on TV have found that some programs are more effective than others. One successful direct marketer found that old TV shows yield more responses than first runs:

> The fifth rerun of "Leave It to Beaver" will generate much more response than will the first run of a prime-time television program. Who cares if you miss something you have seen four times before? But you do care when it's the first time you've seen it.[12]

Another factor is the **vehicle option source effect,** "the differential impact that the advertising exposure will have on the same audience member if the exposure occurs in one media option rather than another." People perceive ads differently depending on their context.[13]

Another factor to consider in media decisions involves scheduling. The evaluation of flighting versus pulsing or continuous schedules is important, particularly given the increasing costs of media time. As discussed in Chapter 10, there is evidence to support the fact that continuity may lead to a more effective media schedule than does flighting. Likewise, there may be opportunities associated with increasing advertising weights in periods of downward sales cycles or recessions. The manager experimenting with these alternative schedules and/or budget outlays should attempt to measure their differential impact.[14]

Finally, as more and more companies and organizations move toward an integrated media mix, it becomes increasingly important to attempt to determine the individual contributions of various media as well as their synergistic effect. As you will see later in this chapter, progress is being made in this regard, but making such a determination is not a simple task.

Budgeting Decisions

A number of studies have examined the effects of budget size on advertising effectiveness and the effects of various ad expenditures on sales. Many companies have also attempted to determine whether increasing their ad budget directly increases sales. This relationship is often hard to determine, perhaps because using sales as an indicator of effectiveness ignores the impact of other marketing mix elements. More definitive conclusions may be possible if other dependent variables, such as the communications objectives stated earlier, are used. IMC Perspective 19-2 discusses the value of placing an ad on the Super Bowl.

When to Test

Virtually all test measures can be classified according to when they are conducted. **Pretests** are measures taken before the campaign is implemented; **posttests** occur after the ad or commercial has been in the field. A variety of pretests and posttests are

IMC PERSPECTIVE 19-2

Is Putting an Ad on the Super Bowl a Wise Investment?

America's biggest event from a sports fan's standpoint is probably the Super Bowl—the National Football League's championship football game that matches the winner of the American Conference against the winner of the National Conference. Now in its 40th year, the event has become a big part of American culture. From an advertiser's perspective, the Super Bowl is certainly *the* event of the year. With the cost of a commercial now exceeding $2 million and an estimated worldwide TV audience of close to 90 million people, it is, without a doubt, the place for advertisers to demonstrate their capabilities. And the advertisers have taken the challenge, turning the Super Bowl into a creative competition off the field just as the game is on the field. Companies that have never advertised before, companies that have already participated in this contest, and the agencies' creative teams plan for this event as hard as the football teams do (maybe even more, because they know well ahead of time that they will be in the big game!).

As the cost of advertising during the Super Bowl continues to increase, many companies have begun to question the viability of spending approximately $80,000 per second for airtime. As you would imagine, the discussions in the boardrooms and the agencies get pretty intense, with the focus on one question: Is it worth it? Advocates cite the success of such past advertisers as Apple, Monster.com, and GoDaddy.com. Opponents bring up the failures—and they have a lot more examples to draw from. What it all comes down to is whether or not the advertisement is effective. This is where the problem starts, as it seems that there are as many ways to make this determination as there are advertisements to show.

Consider just a few. Brand Keys, a branding consultancy firm from New York City, computes a return on equity (ROI) formula that quantifies consumer loyalty gains and losses from Super Bowl spots. Surveying 1,100 consumers who plan to watch the game, Brand Keys attempts to gauge fans' likely responses to seeing specific brands' commercials before, on, or after the game. The formula predicts fans' increased awareness of the ads, esteem of the brand's image, and increased likelihood to purchase the brand. In Super Bowl XXXIX, Brand Keys predicted that the likely winners would gain a 10 to 15 percent return on equity, while the (likely) losers would lose as much as 3 to 6 percent. But this was just a prediction.

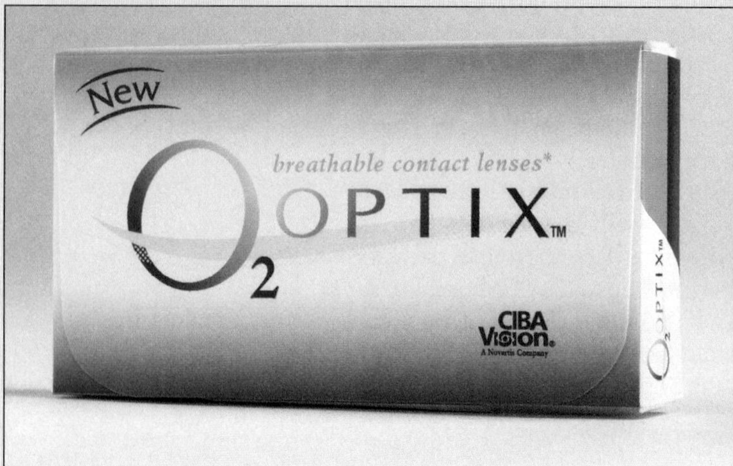

However, an online survey conducted by Insight Express on 500 consumers who were likely to watch the game found that while 54 percent of Americans planned to watch the big game, 50 percent said they planned to watch specifically for the commercials, and 58 percent said they pay closer attention to the ads during the Super Bowl than they do to those they see every day. The findings are consistent with over a decade of Super Bowl ad research conducted by Bruzzone Research Company, which shows that viewers' recall of Super Bowl advertising a week later is better than recall of other prime-time advertising—even if the ad was shown only once. But, says president Don Bruzzone, to be effective the ad needs to be creative, as the highest rated ads are eight times more likely to be remembered than those judged least creative, with recall ranging from 12 to 79 percent.

But viewer recall is only one measure of an ad's effectiveness. As indicated by the Brand Keys research, other factors must be taken into consideration. But when you consider other factors that come with the Super Bowl spots, the positive outcomes are reinforced. For example, advertisers receive considerable free publicity before and after the game on TV, radio, and in newspapers. The Super Bowl may be the only place left where consumers actually watch for the ads and talk about them rather than avoid them. And, as noted by Mike Hess, director of global research and consumer insights for Omnicom Group's OMD, "It is well known in experimental psychology that if you discuss something after seeing it . . . it helps reinforce the memory"—an added value for ROI, he says. Hess believes that the most expensive advertising available on TV may also be the most effective.

Interestingly, two of the companies cited in the Brand Keys survey as likely losers were Novartis Ciba Vision, which would likely lose 4 percent return on equity, and Go Daddy.com, which would lose 6 percent. Jeff Cohen, Novartis's vice president for lens and lens care marketing and a first-time Super Bowl advertiser, said that his company's commercial led to a 20 percent increase in consumer awareness of the brand. In addition, when the accompanying public relations coverage was included, it was by far the most effective way the company could have advertised their new product. And, as seen previously in this text (Chapter 17), GoDaddy.com didn't do too badly either. Does this mean Brand Keys is wrong? Maybe; maybe not. It may just be a question of what and how we measure advertising's effectiveness.

So who is going to win the battle of the Super Bowl advertising effectiveness studies? On one side you have a strong team demonstrating the effectiveness of the ads. On the other side you also have a strong team pointing out flaws in the game plan. But perhaps the biggest problem is that—unlike the football game itself—everyone isn't playing by the same rules. Imagine if we tried to play a football game like that! No one would ever agree who won there either.

Sources: Jack Neff, "Is a Super Bowl Ad Worth $80,000 a Second?" adage.com, January 31, 2005, pp. 1–3; "Super Bowl Ads Don't Float All Brands: Survey," Promomagazine.com, January 27, 2005, p. 1.

Pretests		
Laboratory Methods		
Consumer juries	Theater tests	Readability tests
Portfolio tests	Rough tests	Comprehension and reaction tests
Physiological measures	Concept tests	
Field Methods		
Dummy advertising vehicles	On-air tests	
Posttests		
Field Methods		
Recall tests	Single-source systems	Recognition tests
Association measures	Inquiry tests	Tracking studies

Figure 19-2 Classification of Testing Methods

available to the marketer, each with its own methodology designed to measure some aspect of the advertising program. Figure 19-2 classifies these testing methods.

Pretesting Pretests may occur at a number of points, from as early on as idea generation to rough execution to testing the final version before implementing it. More than one type of pretest may be used. For example, concept testing (which is discussed later in this chapter) may take place at the earliest development of the ad or commercial, when little more than an idea, basic concept, or positioning statement is under consideration. Ogilvy Award winner Jaguar used pretests to determine various aspects of its new campaign, such as stopping power of the ads and communications effectiveness. In other instances, layouts of the ad campaign that include headlines, some body copy, and rough illustrations are used. For TV commercials, storyboards and animatics may be tested. In these tests specific shortcomings may be identified, and changes made to enhance certain executional elements. As noted by Cramphorn, the best reason to pretest is to identify winners, to enhance good ads, and to eliminate bad ones. He notes that it is important to know the probable effect the ad will have before committing to its use.[15]

The methodologies employed to conduct pretests vary. In focus groups, participants freely discuss the meanings they get from the ads, consider the relative advantages of alternatives, and even suggest improvements or additional themes. In addition to or instead of the focus groups, consumers are asked to evaluate the ad on a series of rating scales. (Different agencies use different measures.) In-home interviews, mall intercept, or laboratory methods may be used to gather the data.

The advantage of pretesting at this stage is that feedback is relatively inexpensive. Any problems with the concept or the way it is to be delivered are identified before large amounts of money are spent in development. Sometimes more than one version of the ad is evaluated to determine which is most likely to be effective.

A study of 4,637 on-air commercials designed to build normative intelligence conducted by MSW Group (formerly McCollum Spielman Worldwide) found that only 19 percent were considered outstanding or really good. Nearly twice as many (34 percent) were failures. On the other hand, of those spots that were pretested before the final form was aired, the share of good to outstanding rose to 37 percent, while the failure rate fell to 9 percent.[16] A study of online pretesting of message creativity showed that 80 percent of the campaigns initially presented for consideration in the Interactive Advertising Bureau's XMOS studies had to be totally redeveloped.[17] This is certainly a testimonial to the value of pretesting.

The disadvantage is that mock-ups, storyboards, or animatics may not communicate nearly as effectively as the final product. The mood-enhancing and/or emotional aspects of the message are very difficult to communicate in this format. Another disadvantage is time delays. Many marketers believe being first in the market offers them a distinct advantage over competitors, so they forgo research to save time and ensure this position.

Exhibit 19-3 Research affirmed the value of a NASCAR sponsorship for Lowe's

Posttesting Posttesting is also common among both advertisers and ad agencies (with the exception of testing commercials for wearout). Posttesting is designed to (1) determine if the campaign is accomplishing the objectives sought and (2) serve as input into the next period's situation analysis. An excellent example of using research to guide future advertising strategies is reflected in an experiment conducted by Lowe's, the nation's second-largest home improvement retailer. In a study designed to test 36 different versions of covers for its catalogs (which are sent to between 30 and 40 million homes per year), the company determined that by putting more products on the covers, using real pictures rather than cartoons, and reducing the size of the catalog, the catalogs were more effective. Other tests varying the number of TV spots, newspaper ads, and sports sponsorships led to increases in advertising spending and affirmation of the company's sponsorship of NASCAR auto racing (Exhibit 19-3).[18] A variety of posttest measures are available, most of which involve survey research methods.

Where to Test

In addition to when to test, decisions must be made as to *where.* These tests may take place in either laboratory or field settings.

Laboratory Tests In **laboratory tests,** people are brought to a particular location where they are shown ads and/or commercials. The testers either ask questions about them or measure participants' responses by other methods—for example, pupil dilation, eye tracking, or galvanic skin response.

The major advantage of the lab setting is the *control* it affords the researcher. Changes in copy, illustration, formats, colors, and the like can be manipulated inexpensively and the differential impact of each assessed. This makes it much easier for the researcher to isolate the contribution of each factor.

The major disadvantage is the lack of *realism.* Perhaps the greatest effect of this lack of realism is a **testing bias.** When people are brought into a lab (even if it has been designed to look like a living room), they may scrutinize the ads much more closely than they would at home. A second problem with this lack of realism is that it cannot duplicate the natural viewing situation, complete with the distractions or comforts of home. Looking at ads in a lab setting may not be the same as viewing at home on the couch, with the spouse, kids, dog, cat, and parakeet chirping in the background. (A bit later you will see that some testing techniques have made progress in correcting this deficiency. No, they did not bring in the dogs and the parakeets.) Overall, however, the control offered by this method probably outweighs the disadvantages, which accounts for the frequent use of lab methods.

Field Tests **Field tests** are tests of the ad or commercial under natural viewing situations, complete with the realism of noise, distractions, and the comforts of home. Field tests take into account the effects of repetition, program content, and even the presence of competitive messages.

The major disadvantage of field tests is the lack of control. It may be impossible to isolate causes of viewers' evaluations. If atypical events occur during the test, they may bias the results. Competitors may attempt to sabotage the research. And field tests usually take more time and money to conduct, so the results are not available to be acted on quickly. Thus, realism is gained at the expense of other important factors. It is up to the researcher to determine which trade-offs to make.

How to Test

Our discussion of what should be tested, when, and where was general and designed to establish a basic understanding of the overall process as well as some key terms. In this section, we discuss more specifically some of the methods commonly used at each

1. Provide measurements that are relevant to the objectives of the advertising.
2. Require agreement about how the results will be used in advance of each specific test.
3. Provide multiple measurements (because single measurements are not adequate to assess ad performance).
4. Be based on a model of human response to communications—the reception of a stimulus, the comprehension of the stimulus, and the response to the stimulus.
5. Allow for consideration of whether the advertising stimulus should be exposed more than once.
6. Require that the more finished a piece of copy is, the more soundly it can be evaluated and require, as a minimum, that alternative executions be tested in the same degree of finish.
7. Provide controls to avoid the biasing effects of the exposure context.
8. Take into account basic considerations of sample definition.
9. Demonstrate reliability and validity.

Figure 19-3 Positioning Advertising Copy Testing (PACT)

stage. First, however, it is important to establish some criteria by which to judge ads and commercials.

Conducting evaluative research is not easy. Twenty-one of the largest U.S. ad agencies have endorsed a set of principles aimed at "improving the research used in preparing and testing ads, providing a better creative product for clients, and controlling the cost of TV commercials."[19] This set of nine principles, called **PACT (Positioning Advertising Copy Testing),** defines *copy testing* as research "which is undertaken when a decision is to be made about whether advertising should run in the marketplace. Whether this stage utilizes a single test or a combination of tests, its purpose is to aid in the judgment of specific advertising executions."[20] The nine principles of good copy testing are shown in Figure 19-3.

As you can see, advertisers and their clients are concerned about developing *appropriate* testing methods. Adherence to these principles may not make for perfect testing, but it goes a long way toward improving the state of the art and alleviates at least one of the testing problems cited earlier.

The Testing Process

Testing may occur at various points throughout the development of an ad or a campaign: (1) concept generation research; (2) rough, prefinished art, copy, and/or commercial testing; (3) finished art or commercial pretesting; and (4) market testing of ads or commercials (posttesting).

Concept Generation and Testing

Figure 19-4 describes the process involved in advertising **concept testing,** which is conducted very early in the campaign development process in order to explore the

Objective:	Explores consumers' responses to various ad concepts as expressed in words, pictures, or symbols.
Method:	Alternative concepts are exposed to consumers who match the characteristics of the target audience. Reactions and evaluations of each are sought through a variety of methods, including focus groups, direct questioning, and survey completion. Sample sizes vary depending on the number of concepts to be presented and the consensus of responses.
Output:	Qualitative and/or quantitative data evaluating and comparing alternative concepts.

Figure 19-4 Concept Testing

Figure 19-5 Weaknesses Associated with Focus Group Research

- The results are not quantifiable.
- Sample sizes are too small to generalize to larger populations.
- Group influences may bias participants' responses.
- One or two members of the group may steer the conversation or dominate the discussion.
- Consumers become instant "experts."
- Members may not represent the target market. (Are focus group participants a certain type of person?)
- Results may be taken to be more representative and/or definitive than they really are.

targeted consumer's response to a potential ad or campaign or have the consumer evaluate advertising alternatives. Positioning statements, copy, headlines, and/or illustrations may all be under scrutiny. The material to be evaluated may be just a headline or a rough sketch of the ad. The colors used, typeface, package designs, and even point-of-purchase materials may be evaluated.

One of the more commonly used methods for concept testing is focus groups, which usually consist of 8 to 10 people in the target market for the product. Companies have tested everything from product concepts to advertising concepts using focus groups. For most companies, the focus group is the first step in the research process. The number of focus groups used varies depending on group consensus, strength of response, and/or the degree to which participants like or dislike the concepts. Some companies use 50 or more groups to develop a campaign, although fewer than 10 are usually needed to test a concept sufficiently.

While focus groups continue to be a favorite of marketers, they are often overused. The methodology is attractive in that results are easily obtained, directly observable, and immediate. A variety of issues can be examined, and consumers are free to go into depth in areas they consider important. Also, focus groups don't require quantitative analysis. Unfortunately, many managers are uncertain about research methods that require statistics; and focus groups, being qualitative in nature, don't demand much skill in interpretation. Weaknesses with focus groups are shown in Figure 19-5. Clearly, there are appropriate and inappropriate circumstances for employing this methodology.

Another way to gather consumers' opinions of concepts is mall intercepts, where consumers in shopping malls are approached and asked to evaluate rough ads and/or copy. Rather than participating in a group discussion, individuals assess the ads via questionnaires, rating scales, and/or rankings. New technologies allow for concept testing over the Internet, where advertisers can show concepts simultaneously to consumers throughout the United States, garnering feedback and analyzing the results almost instantaneously. Internet methods are becoming increasingly popular given the cost savings and time efficiences associated with these research methods (Figure 19-6).

Rough Art, Copy, and Commercial Testing

Because of the high cost associated with the production of an ad or commercial (many network commercials cost hundreds of thousands of dollars to produce), advertisers are increasingly spending more monies testing a rendering of the final ad at early stages. Slides of the artwork posted on a screen or animatic and photomatic roughs may be used to test at this stage. (See Figure 19-7 for an explanation of terminology.) Because such tests can be conducted for about $5,000 to $7,000, research at this stage is becoming ever more popular.

But cost is only one factor. The test is of little value if it does not provide relevant, accurate information. Rough tests must indicate how the finished commercial would perform. Some studies have demonstrated that these testing methods are reliable and the results typically correlate well with the finished ad.[21]

Figure 19-6 Testing via the Internet Is Gaining in Popularity

iTest assessments	iTest Product Line					
	iTest Identity (corporate identity, trade names, and trademarks)	**iTest Ad** (TV, radio, print, and Flash email advertising)	**iTest Package** (package designs)	**iTest Product** (product designs)	**iTest Message** (PR and positioning messages)	**iTest Collateral** (promotion and merchandising material)
Quantitative Measures:						
Pre/post brand awareness change	•	•	•	•	•	•
On-shelf visibility			•			
Pick-up power			•			
Correct brand recall	•	•	•	•	•	•
Likability	•	•	•	•	•	•
Persuasion		•	•		•	•
Information completeness			•			•
Brand appropriateness	•	•	•	•	•	•
Brand associations	•	•	•	•	•	•
Competitor associations	•		•	•	•	
Purchase consideration	•	•	•	•		•
Inclination to take desired action					•	
Communication diagnostics	•	•	•	•	•	•
Demographic drivers	•	•	•	•		•
Qualitative Understanding:						
Follow-up phone interviews for expanded understanding of issues and responses	Optional	Optional	Optional	Optional	Optional	Optional

Figure 19-7 Rough Testing Terminology

A *rough* commercial is an unfinished execution that may fall into three broad categories:

Animatic Rough	*Photomatic Rough*	*Live-Action Rough*
Succession of drawings/cartoons	Succession of photographs	Live motion
Rendered artwork	Real people/scenery	Stand-in/nonunion talent
Still frames	Still frames	Nonunion crew
Simulated movement: Panning/zooming of frame/ rapid sequence	Simulated movements: Panning/zooming of frame/ rapid sequence	Limited props/minimal opticals
		Location settings

A Finished Commercial Uses:

Live motion/animation

Highly paid union talent

Full union crew

Exotic props/studio sets/special effects

Most of the tests conducted at the rough stage involve lab settings, although some on-air field tests are also available. Popular tests include comprehension and reaction tests and consumer juries. Again, the Internet allows field settings to be employed at this stage.

1. *Comprehension and reaction tests.* One key concern for the advertiser is whether the ad or commercial conveys the meaning intended. The second concern is the reaction the ad generates. Obviously, the advertiser does not want an ad that evokes a negative reaction or offends someone. **Comprehension and reaction tests** are designed to assess these responses (which makes you wonder why some ads are ever brought to the marketplace).

Tests of comprehension and reaction employ no one standard procedure. Personal interviews, group interviews, and focus groups have all been used for this purpose, and sample sizes vary according to the needs of the client; they typically range from 50 to 200 respondents.

2. *Consumer juries.* This method uses consumers representative of the target market to evaluate the probable success of an ad. **Consumer juries** may be asked to rate a selection of layouts or copy versions presented in pasteups on separate sheets. The objectives sought and methods employed in consumer juries are shown in Figure 19-8.[22] Sample questions asked of jurists are shown in Figure 19-9.

Figure 19-8 Consumer Juries

Objective:	Potential viewers (consumers) are asked to evaluate ads and give their reactions to and evaluation of them. When two or more ads are tested, viewers are usually asked to rate or rank order the ads according to their preferences.
Method:	Respondents are asked to view ads and rate them according to either (1) the order of merit method or (2) the paired comparison method. In the former, the respondent is asked to view the ads and then rank them from one to *n* according to their perceived merit. In the latter, ads are compared only two at a time. Each ad is compared to every other ad in the group, and the winner is listed. The best ad is that which wins the most times. Consumer juries typically employ 50 to 100 participants.
Output:	An overall reaction to each ad under construction as well as a rank ordering of the ads based on the viewers' perceptions.

1. Which of these ads would you most likely read if you saw it in a magazine?
2. Which of these headlines would interest you the most in reading the ad further?
3. Which ad convinces you most of the quality or superiority of the product?
4. Which layout do you think would be most effective in causing you to buy?
5. Which ad did you like best?
6. Which ad did you find most interesting?

Figure 19-9 Questions Asked in a Consumer Jury Test

While the jury method offers the advantages of control and cost effectiveness, serious flaws in the methodology limit its usefulness:

- *The consumer may become a self-appointed expert.* One of the benefits sought from the jury method is the objectivity and involvement in the product or service that the targeted consumer can bring to the evaluation process. Sometimes, however, knowing they are being asked to critique ads, participants try to become more *expert* in their evaluations, paying more attention and being more critical than usual. The result may be a less than objective evaluation or an evaluation on elements other than those intended.
- *The number of ads that can be evaluated is limited.* Whether *order of merit* or *paired comparison* methods are used, the ranking procedure becomes tedious as the number of alternatives increases. Consider the ranking of 10 ads. While the top two and the bottom two may very well reveal differences, those ranked in the middle may not yield much useful information.

  In the paired comparison method, the number of evaluations required is calculated by the formula

  $$\frac{n(n-1)}{2}$$

  If six alternatives are considered, 15 evaluations must be made. As the number of ads increases, the task becomes even more unmanageable.
- *A halo effect is possible.* Sometimes participants rate an ad good on all characteristics because they like a few and overlook specific weaknesses. This tendency, called the **halo effect,** distorts the ratings and defeats the ability to control for specific components. (Of course, the reverse may also occur—rating an ad bad overall due to only a few bad attributes.)
- *Preferences for specific types of advertising may overshadow objectivity.* Ads that involve emotions or pictures may receive higher ratings or rankings than those employing copy, facts, and/or rational criteria. Even though the latter are often more effective in the marketplace, they may be judged less favorably by jurists who prefer emotional appeals.

Some of the problems noted here can be remedied by the use of ratings scales instead of rankings. But ratings are not always valid either. Thus, while consumer juries have been used for years, questions of bias have led researchers to doubt their validity. As a result, a variety of other methods (discussed later in this chapter) are more commonly employed.

Pretesting of Finished Ads

Pretesting finished ads is one of the more commonly employed studies among marketing researchers and their agencies. At this stage, a finished advertisement or commercial is used; since it has not been presented to the market, changes can still be made.

Many researchers believe testing the ad in final form provides better information. Several test procedures are available for print and broadcast ads, including both laboratory and field methodologies.

Print methods include portfolio tests, analyses of readability, and dummy advertising vehicles. Broadcast tests include theater tests and on-air tests. Both print and broadcast may use physiological measures.

Pretesting Finished Print Messages

A number of methods for pretesting finished print ads are available. One is *Gallup & Robinson's Impact System,* described in Figure 19-10. The most common of these methods are portfolio tests, readability tests, and dummy advertising vehicles.

Portfolio Tests **Portfolio tests** are a laboratory methodology designed to expose a group of respondents to a portfolio consisting of both control and test ads. Respondents are then asked what information they recall from the ads. The assumption is that the ads that yield the *highest recall* are the most effective.

While portfolio tests offer the opportunity to compare alternative ads directly, a number of weaknesses limit their applicability:

1. Factors other than advertising creativity and/or presentation may affect recall. Interest in the product or product category, the fact that respondents know they are participating in a test, or interviewer instructions (among others) may account for more differences than the ad itself.
2. Recall may not be the best test. Some researchers argue that for certain types of products (those of low involvement) ability to recognize the ad when shown may be a better measure than recall.

One way to determine the validity of the portfolio method is to correlate its results with readership scores once the ad is placed in the field. Whether such validity tests are being conducted or not is not readily known, although the portfolio method remains popular in the industry.

Readability Tests The communications efficiency of the copy in a print ad can be tested without reader interviews. This test uses the **Flesch formula,** named after its developer, Rudolph Flesch, to assess readability of the copy by determining the average number of syllables per 100 words. Human interest appeal of the material, length of sentences, and familiarity with certain words are also considered and correlated with the educational background of target audiences. Test results are compared to previously established norms for various target audiences. The test suggests that copy is best comprehended when sentences are short, words are concrete and familiar, and personal references are drawn.

This method eliminates many of the interviewee biases associated with other tests and avoids gross errors in understanding. The norms offer an attractive standard for comparison.

Disadvantages are also inherent, however. The copy may become too mechanical, and direct input from the receiver is not available. Without this input, contributing elements like creativity cannot be addressed. To be effective, this test should be used only in conjunction with other pretesting methods.

Dummy Advertising Vehicles In an improvement on the portfolio test, ads are placed in "dummy" magazines developed by an agency or research firm. The magazines contain regular editorial features of interest to the reader, as well as the test ads,

Figure 19-10 Gallup & Robinson's Impact System

Objective:	Evaluation of print advertising in magazines or newspapers. Can also be used to pretest rough advertising executions.
Method:	Interviewers contact potential respondents door to door or by telephone and screen for qualification.
Output:	Scores include recall, idea communication, persuasion, brand rating, and ad liking. Diagnostics in regard to ad reactions and brand attributes are also reported.

Objective:	To assist advertisers in copy testing of print advertisements to determine (1) main idea communication, (2) likes and dislikes, (3) believability, (4) ad attribute ratings, (5) overall likeability, and (6) brand attribute ratings.
Method:	Tests are conducted in current issues of newsstand magazines such as *People, Better Homes & Gardens,* and *Newsweek.* The recall measure consists of 150 responses. Diagnostic measures range from 105 to 150 responses. Highly targeted audiences are available through a version known as the Targeted Print Test.
Output:	Standard scores and specific diagnostics.

Figure 19-11 Ipsos-ASI's Next*Print

and are distributed to a *random sample* of homes in predetermined geographic areas. Readers are told the magazine publisher is interested in evaluations of editorial content and asked to read the magazines as they normally would. Then they are interviewed on their reactions to both editorial content and ads. Recall, readership, and interest-generating capabilities of the ad are assessed.

The advantage of this method is that it provides a more natural setting than the portfolio test. Readership occurs in the participant's own home, the test more closely approximates a natural reading situation, and the reader may go back to the magazine, as people typically do.

But the dummy magazine shares the other disadvantages associated with portfolio tests. The testing effect is not eliminated, and product interest may still bias the results. Thus, while this test offers some advantages over the portfolio method, it is not a guaranteed measure of the advertising's impact.

While all the previously described measures are available, the most popular form of pretesting of print ads now involves a series of measures. Companies like Millward-Brown and Ipsos-ASI offer copy testing services that have improved upon many of the shortcomings cited above. The tests can be used for rough and/or finished ads and are most commonly conducted in the respondents' homes. For example, Millward-Brown's link copy test includes measures of emotional responses to ads, assessing metrics such as enjoyment, engagement, likes, and dislikes to address overall emtional response. Ipsos-ASI's Next*Print methodology also offers multiple measures, as shown in Figure 19-11.

Pretesting Finished Broadcast Ads

A variety of methods for pretesting broadcast ads are available. The most popular are theater tests, on-air tests, and physiological measures.

Theater Tests In the past, one of the most popular laboratory methods for pretesting finished commercials was **theater testing.** In theater tests participants are invited by telephone, mall intercepts, and/or tickets in the mail to view pilots of proposed TV programs. In some instances, the show is actually being tested, but more commonly a standard program is used so audience responses can be compared with normative responses established by previous viewers. Sample sizes range from 250 to 600 participants.

On entering the theater, viewers are told a drawing will be held for gifts and are asked to complete a product preference questionnaire asking which products they would prefer if they win. This form also requests demographic data. Participants may be seated in specific locations in the theater to allow observation by age, sex, and so on. They view the program and commercials, and a form asking for evaluations is distributed. Participants are then asked to complete a second form for a drawing so that changes in product preference can be noted. In addition to product/brand preference, the form may request other information:

1. Interest in and reaction to the commercial.
2. Overall reaction to the commercial as measured by an adjective checklist.
3. Recall of various aspects of the commercial.
4. Interest in the brand under consideration.
5. Continuous (frame-by-frame) reactions throughout the commercial.

The methods of theater testing operations vary, though all measure brand preference changes. For example, many of the services now use videotaped programs with the commercials embedded for viewing in one's home or office rather than in a theater. Others establish viewing rooms in malls and/or hotel conference rooms. Some do not take all the measures listed here; others ask the consumers to turn dials or push buttons on a keypad to provide the continual responses. An example of one methodology is shown in Figure 19-12.

Those opposed to theater tests cite a number of disadvantages. First, they say the environment is too artificial. The lab setting is bad enough, but asking respondents to turn dials or, as one service does, wiring people for physiological responses takes them too far from a natural viewing situation. Second, the contrived measure of brand preference change seems too phony to believe. Critics contend that participants will see through it and make changes just because they think they are supposed to. Finally, the group effect of having others present and overtly exhibiting their reactions may influence viewers who did not have any reactions themselves.

Proponents argue that theater tests offer distinct advantages. In addition to control, the established norms (averages of commercials' performances) indicate how one's commercial will fare against others in the same product class that were already tested. Further, advocates say the brand preference measure is supported by actual sales results.

Despite the limitations of theater testing, most major consumer-product companies have used it to evaluate their commercials. This method may have shortcomings, but it allows them to identify strong or weak commercials and to compare them to other ads.

On-Air Tests Some of the firms conducting theater tests also insert the commercials into actual TV programs in certain test markets. Typically, the commercials are in finished form, although the testing of ads earlier in the developmental process is becoming more common. This is referred to as an **on-air test** and often includes single-source ad research (discussed later in this chapter). Information Resources, Ipsos-ASI, MSW Group, and Nielsen are well-known providers of on-air tests.

On-air testing techniques offer all the advantages of field methodologies, as well as all the disadvantages. Further, there are negative aspects to the specific measures taken through the on-air systems. One concern is associated with **day-after recall scores,** the primary measure used in these tests. Lyman Ostlund notes that measurement errors may result from the natural environment—the position of the ad in the series of commercials shown, the adjacent program content, and/or the number of commercials shown.[23] While the testing services believe their methods overcome many of these criticisms, each still uses recall as one of the primary measures of effectiveness. Since recall tests best reflect the degree of attention and interest in an ad, claims that the tests predict the ad's impact on sales may be going too far. (In 28 studies reviewed by Jack Haskins, only 2 demonstrated that factual recall could be related to sales.)[24] Joel Dubow's research indicates that recall is a necessary but not sufficient measure, while research by Jones and Blair was even more demonstrative, noting that "it is unwise to look to recall for an accurate assessment of a commercial's sales effect."[25]

On the plus side, most of the testing services have offered evidence of both validity and reliability for on-air pretesting of commercials. Both Ipsos-ASI and MSW Group claim their pretest and posttest results yield the same recall scores 9 out of 10 times—a strong indication of reliability and a good predictor of the effect the ad is likely to have when shown to the population as a whole.

Figure 19-12 The AD*VANTAGE/ACT Theater Methodology

Advertising Control for Television (ACT), a lab procedure of The MSW Group, uses about 400 respondents representing four cities. It measures initial brand preference by asking participants which brands they most recently purchased. Respondents are then divided into groups of 25 to view a 30-minute program with seven commercials inserted in the middle. Four are test commercials; the other three are control commercials with established viewing norms. After viewing the program, respondents are given a recall test of the commercials. After the recall test, a second 30-minute program is shown, with each test commercial shown again. The second measure of brand preference is taken at this time, with persuasion measured by the percentage of viewers who switched preferences from their most recently purchased brand to one shown in the test commercials.

In summary, on-air pretesting of finished or rough commercials offers some distinct advantages over lab methods and some indications of the ad's likely success. Whether the measures used are as strong an indication as the providers say still remains in question.

Physiological Measures A less common method of pretesting finished commercials involves a laboratory setting in which physiological responses are measured. These measures indicate the receiver's *involuntary* response to the ad, theoretically eliminating biases associated with the voluntary measures reviewed to this point. (Involuntary responses are those over which the individual has no control, such as heartbeat and reflexes.) Physiological measures used to test both print and broadcast ads include pupil dilation, galvanic skin response, eye tracking, and brain waves:

1. *Pupil dilation.* Research in **pupillometrics** is designed to measure dilation and constriction of the pupils of the eyes in response to stimuli. Dilation is associated with action; constriction involves the body's conservation of energy.

Advertisers have used pupillometrics to evaluate product and package design as well as to test ads. Pupil dilation suggests a stronger interest in (or preference for) an ad or implies arousal or attention-getting capabilities. Other attempts to determine the affective (liking or disliking) responses created by ads have met with less success.

Because of high costs and some methodological problems, the use of pupillometrics has waned over the past decade. But it can be useful in evaluating certain aspects of advertising.

2. *Galvanic skin response.* Also known as **electrodermal response,** GSR measures the skin's resistance or conductance to a small amount of current passed between two electrodes. Response to a stimulus activates sweat glands, which in turn increases the conductance of the electrical current. Thus, GSR/EDR activity might reflect a reaction to advertising. In their review of the research in this area, Paul Watson and Robert Gatchel concluded that GSR/EDR (1) is sensitive to affective stimuli, (2) may present a picture of attention, (3) may be useful to measure long-term advertising recall, and (4) is useful in measuring ad effectiveness.[26] In interviews with practitioners and reviews of case studies, Priscilla LaBarbera and Joel Tucciarone also concluded that GSR is an effective measure and is useful for measuring affect, or liking, for ads.[27] While a number of companies have offered skin response measures, this research methodology is not commonly used now, and LaBarbera and Tucciarone believe that it is underused, given its potential.

3. *Eye tracking.* A methodology that is more commonly employed is **eye tracking** (Figure 19-13), in which viewers are asked to view an ad while a sensor aims a beam of infrared light at the eye. The beam follows the movement of the eye and shows the exact spot on which the viewer is focusing. The continuous reading of responses demonstrates which elements of the ad are attracting attention, how long the viewer is focusing on them, and the sequence in which they are being viewed.

Eye tracking can identify strengths and weaknesses in an ad. For example, attractive models or background action may distract the viewer's attention away from the brand or product being advertised. The advertiser can remedy this distraction before fielding the ad. In other instances, colors or illustrations may attract attention and create viewer interest in the ad.

Eye tracking has increasingly been used to measure the effectiveness of websites and online ads, and, as noted earlier, e-mails.

Figure 19-13 Eye Movement Research

Objective:	Tracks viewers' eye movements to determine what viewers read or view in print ads and where their attention is focused in TV commercials, websites, or billboards.
Method:	Fiber optics, digital data processing, and advanced electronics are used to follow eye movements of viewers and/or readers as they process an ad.
Output:	Relationship among what readers see, recall, and comprehend. Scan movement paths on print ads, billboards, commercials, print materials, and websites. (Can also be used to evaluate package designs.)

4. *Brain waves.* **Electroencephalographic (EEG) measures** can be taken from the skull to determine electrical frequencies in the brain. These electrical impulses are used in two areas of research, alpha waves and hemispheric lateralization:

- **Alpha activity** refers to the degree of brain activation. People are in an alpha state when they are inactive, resting, or sleeping. The theory is that a person in an alpha state is less likely to be processing information (recall correlates negatively with alpha levels) and that attention and processing require moving from this state. By measuring a subject's alpha level while viewing a commercial, researchers can assess the degree to which attention and processing are likely to occur.
- **Hemispheric lateralization** distinguishes between alpha activity in the left and right sides of the brain. It has been hypothesized that the right side of the brain processes visual stimuli and the left processes verbal stimuli. The right hemisphere is thought to respond more to emotional stimuli, while the left responds to logic. The right determines recognition, while the left is responsible for recall.[28] If these hypotheses are correct, advertisers could design ads to increase learning and memory by creating stimuli to appeal to each hemisphere. However, some researchers believe the brain does not function laterally and an ad cannot be designed to appeal to one side or the other.

While EEG research has engaged the attention of academic researchers, it has been much less successful in attracting the interest of practitioners.

Market Testing of Ads

The fact that the ad and/or campaign has been implemented does not mean there is no longer a need for testing. The pretests were conducted on smaller samples and may in some instances have questionable merit, so the marketer must find out how the ad is doing in the field. In this section, we discuss methods for posttesting an ad. Some of the tests are similar to the pretests discussed in the previous section and are provided by the same companies.

Exhibit 19-4 Reader response cards are popular in business-to-business markets

TARGET MARKETING

Receive the information you need to market smarter instantly!
Go to: **www.targetonline.com** and click on free information.

Or...Fill out this card and either FAX your request today: 215-238-5388 or mail.

Free Subscription

Do you wish to receive (continue to receive) a FREE subscription to TARGET MARKETING? ☐ YES ☐ NO

Signature ____________ Date ______

Name (please print) ____________ Title ______

Company Name ____________

Address ____________

City/State/Zip ____________

Telephone ____________ FAX ____________

Email Address: ____________

1. TYPE OF BUSINESS AT THIS LOCATION: (Check One)
- 04 ☐ Catalogers, Mail Order Companies
- 05 ☐ Retailers, Wholesaler/Distributor
- 06 ☐ On-line Merchant
- 03 ☐ Financial Services: Banks, Insurance, Credit Cards, Investment
- 21 ☐ Fund Raisers: Non-Profit Groups, Charities
- 33 ☐ High Technology: Internet Services, Computers, Software, Telecommunications, Office Equipment
- 12 ☐ Manufacturers, Package Goods and Other Business-to-Business Marketers
- 31 ☐ Non Financial Services Marketers: Associations, Clubs, Educational, Government Agencies, Health Care, Membership Organizations, Personnel Services, Real Estate, Utilities, Communications, Tourism and Travel
- 13 ☐ Publishers: Magazines, Books, Newsletters, Newspapers, Book & Record Clubs On-line publications
- 01 ☐ Advertising/DM Agencies, Freelance Creative and Consultants
- 09 ☐ Mailing List Professionals: Brokers, Compilers, Owners
- 20 ☐ Other: (Please Specify) ____________

2. JOB FUNCTION: (Check One)
- 10 ☐ Corporate and General Management (Excluding Sales, Marketing and Advertising Management)
- 02 ☐ Marketing, List and Sales Management
- 01 ☐ Advertising Promotion and Public Relations Management
- 08 ☐ Operational, Technical and Telemarketing Management
- 06 ☐ Circulation Management
- 11 ☐ Other: (Please Specify) ____________

3. MY FIRM'S MARKETING ACTIVITY: (Check All That Apply)
- 1 ☐ Catalog
- 2 ☐ Direct Mail
- 09 ☐ Internet
- 3 ☐ Telemarketing
- 10 ☐ Alternate Media
- 5 ☐ Consumer
- 6 ☐ Business-to-Business
- 7 ☐ International
- 8 ☐ None of the Above

4. IN THE PERFORMANCE OF YOUR JOB, CHECK THE ONE THAT BEST DESCRIBES YOUR PURCHASING AUTHORITY: (Check One)
- 1 ☐ Authorize/Approve Purchase
- 2 ☐ Recommend/ Specify Purchase
- 3 ☐ No Purchasing Authority

Free Information

Circle the free info number for the products and services that interest you

001	002	003	004	005	006	007	008	009	010	011	012
013	014	015	016	017	018	019	020	021	022	023	024
025	026	027	028	029	030	031	032	033	034	035	036
037	038	039	040	041	042	043	044	045	046	047	048
049	050	051	052	053	054	055	056	057	058	059	060
061	062	063	064	065	066	067	068	069	070	071	072
073	074	075	076	077	078	079	080	081	082	083	084
085	086	087	088	089	090	091	092	093	094	095	096
097	098	099	100	101	102	103	104	105	106	107	108
109	110	111	112	113	114	115	116	117	118	119	120
121	122	123	124	125	126	127	128	129	130	131	132
133	134	135	136	137	138	139	140	141	142	143	144
145	146	147	148	149	150	151	152	153	154	155	156
157	158	159	160	161	162	163	164	165	166	167	168
169	170	171	172	173	174	175	176	177	178	179	180

For Information on Product/Service Categories

To request information on any of the following areas of interest, check the appropriate free information number:

- 501 ☐ Agencies/Consultants/Creative Services
- 502 ☐ Alternate Media/Delivery
- 503 ☐ Broadcast Media/Services
- 504 ☐ Call Center Equipment
- 505 ☐ Credit/Collection Services
- 506 ☐ Database Management Systems/ Services/Software
- 507 ☐ Delivery Services
- 529 ☐ E-mail Marketing
- 508 ☐ Envelopes/Order Forms/Labels
- 509 ☐ Fulfillment Services/Operations
- 510 ☐ Int'l Call Centers
- 511 ☐ Int'l Delivery Services
- 512 ☐ Int'l DM Agencies
- 525 ☐ International DM Services
- 530 ☐ Internet Services
- 513 ☐ Lettershop Services
- 514 ☐ Lists-Business-to-Business
- 515 ☐ Lists-Consumer
- 528 ☐ Lists-E-mail
- 516 ☐ Lists-International
- 517 ☐ List Services
- 518 ☐ Mailing Equipment/Services
- 520 ☐ Paper
- 521 ☐ Premiums/Promotional Products
- 522 ☐ Prepress Equipment/Services
- 523 ☐ Printers
- 527 ☐ Printing Systems/Equipment
- 524 ☐ Telemarketing Services

RS0110

Posttests of Print Ads

A variety of print posttests are available, including inquiry tests, recognition tests, and recall tests.

Inquiry Tests Used in both consumer and business-to-business market testing, **inquiry tests** are designed to measure advertising effectiveness on the basis of inquiries generated from ads appearing in various print media, often referred to as "bingo cards." The inquiry may take the form of the number of coupons returned, phone calls generated, or direct inquiries through reader cards. Exhibit 19-4 shows an example of a reader response card, and studies have shown that this form (though on the decline) is still the more commonly employed method of determining response to trade ads. If you called in a response to an ad in a local medium recently, perhaps you were asked how you found out about the company or product or where you saw the ad. This is a very simple measure of the ad's or medium's effectiveness.

Objective:	Determining recognition of print ads and comparing them to other ads of the same variety or in the same magazine.
Method:	Samples are drawn from 20 to 30 urban areas reflecting the geographic circulation of the magazine. Personal interviewers screen readers for qualifications and determine exposure and readership. Samples include a minimum of 200 males and females, as well as specific audiences where required. Participants are asked to go through the magazines, looking at the ads, and provide specific responses.
Output:	*Starch Ad Readership Reports* generate three recognition scores: • Noted score—the percentage of readers who remember seeing the ad. • Seen-associated score—the percentage of readers who recall seeing or reading any part of the ad identifying the product or brand. • Read-most score—the percentage of readers who report reading at least half of the copy portion of the ad.

Figure 19-14 The *Starch Ad Readership Report*

More complex methods of measuring effectiveness through inquiries may involve (1) running the ad in successive issues of the same medium, (2) running **split-run tests,** in which variations of the ad appear in different copies of the same newspaper or magazine, and/or (3) running the same ad in different media. Each of these methods yields information on different aspects of the strategy. The first measures the *cumulative* effects of the campaign; the second examines specific elements of the ad or variations on it. The final method measures the effectiveness of the medium rather than the ad itself.

While inquiry tests may yield useful information, weaknesses in this methodology limit its effectiveness. For example, inquiries may not be a true measure of the attention-getting or information-providing aspects of the ad. The reader may be attracted to an ad, read it, and even store the information but not be motivated to inquire at that particular time. Time constraints, lack of a need for the product or service at the time the ad is run, and other factors may limit the number of inquiries. But receiving a small number of inquiries doesn't mean the ad was not effective; attention, attitude change, awareness, and recall of copy points may all have been achieved. At the other extreme, a person with a particular need for the product may respond to any ad for it, regardless of specific qualities of the ad.

Major advantages of inquiry tests are that they are inexpensive to implement and they provide some feedback with respect to the general effectiveness of the ad or medium used. But they are usually not very effective for comparing different versions or specific creative aspects of an ad.

Recognition Tests Perhaps the most common posttest of print ads is the **recognition method,** most closely associated with Roper ASW. The *Starch Ad Readership Report* lets the advertiser assess the impact of an ad in a single issue of a magazine, over time, and/or across different magazines (see Exhibit 19-5). Starch measures over 25,000 ads in more than 400 issues representing more than 100 consumer, farm, and business magazines and newspapers per year and provides a number of measures of the ad's effectiveness. An example of a Starch-scored ad is shown in Figure 19-14.

Starch claims that (1) the pulling power of various aspects of the ad can be assessed through the control offered, (2) the effectiveness of competitors' ads can be compared through the norms provided, (3) alternative ad executions can be tested, and (4) readership scores are a useful indication of consumers' *involvement* in the ad or campaign. (The theory is that a reader must read and become involved in the ad before the ad can communicate. To the degree that this readership can be shown, it is a direct indication of effectiveness.)

Of these claims, perhaps the most valid is the ability to judge specific aspects of the ad. Many researchers have criticized other aspects of the

Exhibit 19-5 The Starch method of testing is widely employed

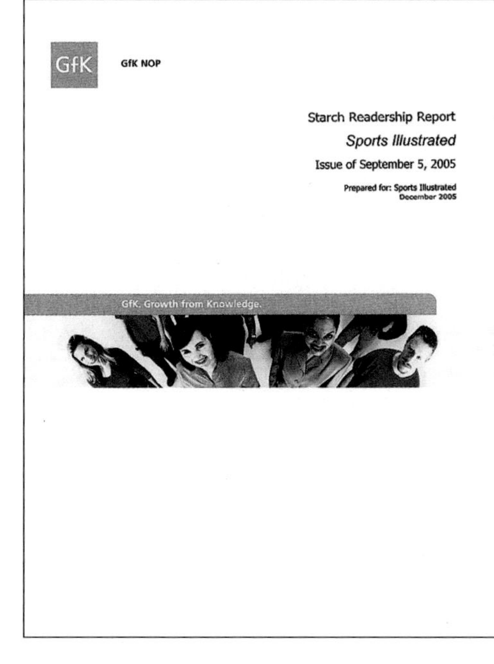

Starch recognition method (as well as other recognition measures) on the basis of problems of false claiming, interviewer sensitivities, and unreliable scores:

1. *False claiming.* Research shows that in recognition tests, respondents may claim to have seen an ad when they did not. False claims may be a result of having seen similar ads elsewhere, expecting that such an ad would appear in the medium, or wanting to please the questioner. Interest in the product category also increases reporting of ad readership. Whether this false claiming is deliberate or not, it leads to an overreporting of effectiveness. On the flip side, factors such as interview fatigue may lead to an underreporting bias—that is, respondents not reporting an ad they did see.

2. *Interviewer sensitivities.* Any time research involves interviewers, there is a potential for bias. Respondents may want to impress the interviewer or fear looking unknowledgeable if they continually claim not to recognize an ad. There may also be variances associated with interviewer instructions, recordings, and so on, regardless of the amount of training and sophistication involved.

3. *Reliability of recognition scores.* Starch admits that the reliability and validity of its readership scores increase with the number of insertions tested, which essentially means that to test just one ad on a single exposure may not produce valid or reliable results.

In sum, despite critics, the Starch readership studies continue to dominate the posttesting of print ads. The value provided by norms and the fact that multiple exposures can improve reliability and validity may underlie the decisions to employ this methodology.

Recall Tests There are several tests to measure recall of print ads. Perhaps the best known of these are the Ipsos-ASI Next*Print test and the Gallup & Robinson Magazine Impact Research Service (MIRS) (described in Figure 19-15). These **recall tests** are similar to those discussed in the section on pretesting broadcast ads in that they attempt to measure recall of specific ads.

In addition to having the same interviewer problems as recognition tests, recall tests have other disadvantages. The reader's degree of involvement with the product and/or the distinctiveness of the appeals and visuals may lead to higher-than-accurate recall scores, although in general the method may lead to lower levels of recall than actually exist (an error the advertiser would be happy with). Critics contend the test is not strong enough to reflect recall accurately, so many ads may score as less effective than they really are, and advertisers may abandon or modify them needlessly.

On the plus side, it is thought that recall tests can assess the ad's impact on memory. Proponents of recall tests say the major concern is not the results themselves but how they are interpreted. In one very interesting study of the effects of brand name suggestiveness on recall, Kevin Keller, Susan Heckler, and Michael Houston found that suggestive brand names (those that convey relevant attribute or benefit information about

Figure 19-15 Gallup & Robinson Magazine Impact Research Service (MIRS)

Objective: Tracking recall of advertising (and client's ads) appearing in magazines to assess performance and effectiveness.

Method: Test magazines are placed in participants' homes and respondents are asked to read the magazine that day. A telephone interview is conducted the second day to assess recall of ads, recall of copy points, and consumers' impressions of the ads. Sample size is 150 people.

Output: Three measurement scores are provided:

- Proven name registration—the percentage of respondents who can accurately recall the ad.
- Idea communication—the number of sales points the respondents can recall.
- Favorable buying attitude—the extent of favorable purchase reaction to the brand or corporation.

the product) facilitate the initial recall of the brand's benefits but inhibit recall of subsequently advertised claims. These results would seem to indicate that a suggestive brand name could facilitate initial positioning of the brand but make it more difficult to introduce new attributes at a later time. The authors suggest that these results might be useful in explaining why Jack in the Box has had trouble developing a more adult image and why Old Spice and Oldsmobile (now no longer in business) have had difficulty appealing to younger audiences.[29]

A very extensive longitudinal study was conducted by the Netherlands Institute of Public Opinion (NIPO) to assess the relationship between recall and recognition. The results indicated that the average correlation between recall and recognition in both newspapers and magazines was very high ($r = .96$ and .95, respectively). The study concluded that recall actually stems from recognition, in that 99 percent of 3,632 cases of recall also had recorded recognition. In addition, likable and interesting ads doubled the recall scores and increased the recall share of recognition. Creative advertising was much more effective for creating perceptions and recall than was the size of the ad.[30]

Posttests of Broadcast Commercials

A variety of methods exist for posttesting broadcast commercials. The most common provide a combination of day-after recall tests, persuasion measures, and diagnostics. Test marketing and tracking studies, including single-source methods, are also employed.

Day-After Recall Tests The most popular method of posttesting employed in the broadcasting industry for decades was the *Burke Day-After Recall test.* While a number of companies offered day-after recall methodologies, the "Burke test" for all intents and purposes became the generic name attached to these tests. While popular, day-after recall tests also had problems, including limited samples, high costs, and security issues (ads shown in test markets could be seen by competitors). In addition, the following disadvantages with recall tests were also suggested:

1. DAR tests may favor unemotional appeals because respondents are asked to verbalize the message. Thinking messages may be easier to recall than emotional communications, so recall scores for emotional ads may be lower.[31] A number of other studies have also indicated that emotional ads may be processed differently from thinking ones; some ad agencies, for example, Leo Burnett and BBDO Worldwide, have gone so far as to develop their own methods of determining emotional response to ads.[32]
2. Program content may influence recall. The programs in which the ad appears may lead to different recall scores for the same brand. The net result is a potential inaccuracy in the recall score and in the norms used to establish comparisons.[33]
3. A prerecruited sample (Gallup & Robinson) may pay increased attention to the program and the ads contained therein because the respondents know they will be tested the next day. This effect would lead to a higher level of recall than really exists.

The major advantage of day-after recall tests is that they are field tests. The natural setting is supposed to provide a more realistic response profile. These tests are also popular because they provide norms that give advertisers a standard for comparing how well their ads are performing. In addition to recall, a number of different measures of the commercial's effectiveness are now offered, including persuasive measures and diagnostics. (The Burke test itself no longer exists.)

Persuasive Measures As noted earlier in our discussion of pretesting broadcast commercials, a measure of a commercial's persuasive effectiveness is gathered by asking consumers to choose a brand that they would want to win in a drawing and then—after exposure to the ad—ask the question again. In theater settings this is accomplished by announcing a series of prize drawings, with viewers indicating which of the brands they would choose if they won. In field settings, it is accomplished by taking a brand preference measure when the video is delivered and then again the next day. Some of the services offer additional persuasion measures, including purchase-intent and frequency-of-purchase criteria.

Figure 19-16 Ipsos-ASI's Next*TV

Objectives:	To assist advertisers in copy testing of their commercials through multiple measures to determine (1) the potential of the commercial for impacting sales, (2) how the ad contributes to brand equity, (3) how well it is in line with existing advertising strategies and objectives, and (4) how to optimize effectiveness.
Method:	Consumers are recruited to evaluate a TV program, with ads embedded into the program as they would be on local prime-time television. Consumers view the program on a videotape in their homes to simulate actual field conditions. (The option to use local cable television programs with commercial inserts is also provided.)
Output:	Related recall (day-after recall) scores; persuasion scores, including brand preference shifts, purchase intent and frequency, brand equity differentiation, and relevance and communication; and reaction diagnostics to determine what viewers take away from the ad and how creative elements contribute to or distract from advertising effectiveness.

Diagnostics In addition to measuring recall and persuasion, copy testing firms also provide diagnostic measures. These measures are designed to garner viewers' evaluations of the ads, as well as how clearly the creative idea is understood and how well the proposition is communicated. Rational and emotional reactions to the ads are also examined. A number of companies offer diagnostic measures, including Diagnostic Research, Inc., Gallup & Robinson, and Millward Brown.

Comprehensive Measures While each of the measures just described provides specific input into the effectiveness of a commercial, many advertisers are interested in more than just one specific input. Thus, some companies provide comprehensive approaches in which each of the three measures just described can be obtained through one testing program. Figure 19-16 describes one such comprehensive program, Ipsos-ASI's Next*TV test (Exhibit 19-6).

Test Marketing Many companies conduct tests designed to measure their advertising effects in specific test markets before releasing them nationally. The markets chosen are representative of the target market. For example, a company may test its ads in Portland, Oregon; San Antonio, Texas; or Buffalo, New York, if the demographic and socioeconomic profiles of these cities match the product's market. A variety of factors may be tested, including reactions to the ads (for example, alternative copy points), the effects of various budget sizes, or special offers. The ads run in finished form in the media where they might normally appear, and effectiveness is measured after the ads run.

Exhibit 19-6 Ipsos-ASI offers a comprehensive testing measure

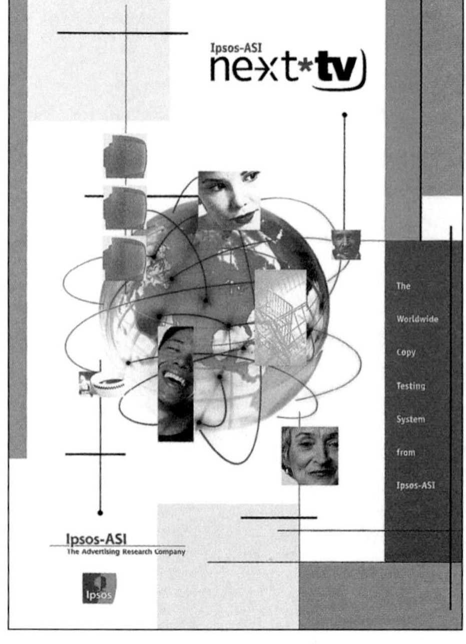

The advantage of test marketing of ads is realism. Regular viewing environments are used and the testing effects are minimized. A high degree of control can be attained if the test is designed successfully. For example, an extensive test market study was designed and conducted by Seagram and Time, Inc., over three years to measure the effects of advertising frequency on consumers' buying habits. This study demonstrated just how much could be learned from research conducted in a field setting but with some experimental controls. It also showed that proper research can provide strong insights into the impact of ad campaigns. (Many advertising researchers consider this study one of the most conclusive ever conducted in the attempt to demonstrate the effects of advertising on sales.)

The Seagram study also reveals some of the disadvantages associated with test market measures, not the least of which are cost and time. Few firms have the luxury to spend three years and hundreds of thousands of dollars on such a test. In addition, there is always the fear that competitors may discover and intervene in the research process.

A number of companies, including Procter & Gamble and Toyota, have test marketed interactive commercials. Reckitt—the world's largest manufacturer of household cleaning products—and Whirlpool have joined efforts to test *i*TV ads. Customers were offered three different enticements to interact with the campaign: (1) register to win a Whirlpool dishwasher, (2) register for free samples of Finish Dishwater Freshener, or (3) order money-off coupons for Finish Dishwater Tablets. After eight months of testing, Reckitt reported that the target goal of 35,000 responses was exceeded.[34] Sears and Ford have both tested the impact of ads placed on Gemstar—*TV Guide*'s interactive program guide—while Chrysler has experimented with online gaming to generate leads and stimulate buzz.[35]

Test marketing can provide substantial insight into the effectiveness of advertising if care is taken to minimize the negative aspects of such tests.

Single-Source Tracking Studies Since the 1980s the focus of many research efforts has been on single-source tracking methods. **Single-source tracking methods** track the behaviors of consumers from the television set to the supermarket checkout counter. Participants in a designated area who have cable TV and agree to participate in the studies are given a card (similar to a credit card) that identifies their household and gives the research company their demographics. The households are split into matched groups; one group receives an ad while the other does not, or alternate ads are sent to each. Their purchases are recorded from the bar codes of the products bought. Commercial exposures are then correlated with purchase behaviors.

Earlier we mentioned the use of single-source ad research in pretesting commercials. One study demonstrated that the single-source method can also be used effectively to posttest ads, allowing for a variety of dependent measures and tracking the effects of increased ad budgets and different versions of ad copy—and even ad effects on sales.[36]

A 10-year study conducted by Information Resources' BehaviorScan service demonstrated long-term effects of advertising on sales. The study examined copy, media schedules, ad budgets, and the impact of trade promotions on sales in 10 markets throughout the United States and concluded that advertising can produce sales growth as long as two years after a campaign ends.[37] (The study also concluded that results of copy recall and persuasion tests were unlikely to predict sales reliably.) A number of single-source methods have been used, among them BehaviorScan (Information Resources) and MarketSource. The A. C. Nielsen company's Scantrack is another commonly employed single-source tracking system.

Many advertisers believe these single-source measures will change the way research is conducted due to the advantages of control and the ability to measure directly the ads' effects on sales. A number of major corporations and ad agencies are now employing this method, including companies and their agencies in the automotive, entertainment, financial services, packaged goods, and pharmaceutical industries among others. After using scanner data to review the advertising/sales relationship for 78 brands, John Jones concluded that single-source data are beginning to fulfill their promise now that more measurements are available.[38]

While single-source testing is a valuable tool, it still has some problems. One researcher says, "Scanner data focus on short-term sales effects, and as a result capture only 10 to 30 percent of what advertising does."[39] Others complain that the data are too complicated to deal with, as an overabundance of information is available. Still another disadvantage is the high cost of collecting single-source data. While the complexity of single-source data resulted in a slow adoption rate, this method of tracking advertising effectiveness became widely adopted in the 1990s by the research companies mentioned earlier (Gallup & Robinson, Millward-Brown, and Ipsos-ASI).

Tracking Print/Broadcast Ads One of the more useful and adaptable forms of posttesting involves tracking the effects of the ad campaign by taking measurements at regular intervals. **Tracking studies** have been used to measure the effects of advertising on awareness, recall, interest, and attitudes toward the ad and/or brand as well as purchase intentions. (Ad tracking may be applied to both print and broadcast ads but is

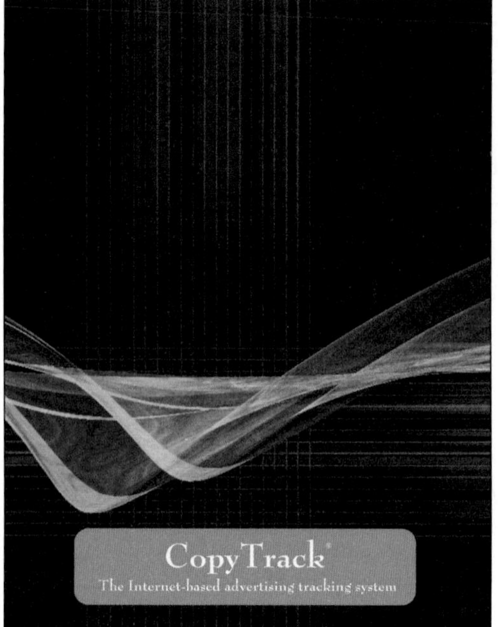

Exhibit 19-7 Tracking studies provide useful measures

Figure 19-17 Factors to Measure in Tracking Studies

Market share	Unit sales
Penetration rates	ROMI (return on marketing investment)
Operating ratios	Budget factors
Gross margin percentage	Cost per customer acquisition
Net profit percentage	
Response rates	

Source: Tiffany Hancock, "Did It Work? Tracking Tips for Marketing Campaigns," *Rural Telecommunications,* May/June 2004, pp. 32–36.

much more common with the latter.) Personal interviews, phone surveys, mall intercepts, and even mail surveys have been used. Sample sizes typically range from 250 to 500 cases per period (usually quarterly or semiannually). Tracking studies yield perhaps the most valuable information available to the marketing manager for assessing current programs and planning for the future. (See Exhibit 19-7.)

The major advantage of tracking studies is that they can be tailored to each specific campaign and/or situation. A standard set of questions can track effects of the campaign over time. The effects of various media can also be determined, although with much less effectiveness. Tracking studies have also been used to measure the differential impact of different budget sizes, the effects of flighting, brand or corporate image, and recall of specific copy points. Figure 19-17 summarizes some of the factors suggested by Tiffany Hancock that might be measured using tracking studies. Hancock notes that tracking studies can be used to measure the impact of various IMC media, not just advertising. As you will see later in the chapter, however, it is often difficult to quantify some of the measures suggested. Finally, when designed properly, as shown in Figure 19-18, tracking studies offer a high degree of reliability and validity.[40]

Figure 19-18 Factors That Make or Break Tracking Studies

1. Properly defined objectives
2. Alignment with sales objectives
3. Properly designed measures (e.g., adequate sample size, maximum control over interviewing process, adequate time between tracking periods)
4. Consistency through replication of the sampling plan
5. Random samples
6. Continuous interviewing (that is, not seasonal)
7. Evaluate measures related to behavior (attitudes meet this criterion; recall of ads does not)
8. Critical evaluative questions asked early to eliminate bias
9. Measurement of competitors' performance
10. Skepticism about questions that ask where the advertising was seen or heard (TV always wins)
11. Building of news value into the study
12. "Moving averages" used to spot long-term trends and avoid seasonality
13. Data reported in terms of relationships rather than as isolated facts
14. Integration of key marketplace events with tracking results (e.g., advertising expenditures of self and competitors, promotional activities associated with price changes in ad campaigns, introductions of new brands, government announcements, changes in economic conditions)

Some of the problems of recall and recognition measures are inherent in tracking studies, since many other factors may affect both brand and advertising recall. Despite these limitations, however, tracking studies are a very effective way to assess the effects of advertising campaigns.

In summary, you can see that each of the testing methods considered in this chapter has its strengths and its limitations. You may wonder: Can we actually test advertising effectiveness? What can be done to ensure a valid, reliable test? The next section of this chapter suggests some answers.

Establishing a Program for Measuring Advertising Effects

There is no surefire way to test advertising effectiveness. However, in response to pressures to determine the contribution of ads to the overall marketing effort, steps are being taken to improve this measurement task. Let's begin by reviewing the major problems with some existing methods and then examine possible improvements.

Problems with Current Research Methods

When current testing methods are compared to the criteria established by PACT (see Figure 19-3), it is clear that some of the principles important to good copy testing can be accomplished readily, whereas others require substantially more effort. For example, principle 6 (providing equivalent test ads) should require a minimum of effort. The researcher can easily control the state of completion of the test communications. Also fairly easy are principles 1 and 2 (providing measurements relative to the objectives sought and determining *a priori* how the results will be used).

We have seen throughout this text that each promotional medium, the message, and the budget all consider the marketing and communications objectives sought. The integrated marketing communications planning model establishes the roles of these elements. So by the time one gets to the measurement phase, the criteria by which these programs will be evaluated should simply fall into place.

Slightly more difficult are principles 3, 5, and 8, although again these factors are largely in the control of the researcher. Principle 3 (providing multiple measurements) may require little more than budgeting to make sure more than one test is conducted. At the most, it may require considering two similar measures to ensure reliability. Likewise, principle 5 (exposing the test ad more than once) can be accomplished with a proper research design. Finally, principle 8 (sample definition) requires little more than sound research methodology; any test should use the target audience to assess an ad's effectiveness. You would not use a sample of nondrinkers to evaluate new liquor commercials.

The most difficult factors to control—and the principles that may best differentiate between good and bad testing procedures—are PACT requirements 4, 7, and 9. Fortunately, however, addressing each of these contributes to the attainment of the others.

The best starting point is principle 4, which states the research should be guided by a model of human response to communications that encompasses reception, comprehension, and behavioral response. It is the best starting point, in our opinion, because it is the principle least addressed by practicing researchers. If you recall, Chapter 5 proposed a number of models that could fulfill this principle's requirements. Yet even though these models have existed for quite some time, few if any common research methods attempt to integrate them into their methodologies. Most current methods do little more than provide recall scores, despite the fact many researchers have shown that recall is a poor measure of effectiveness. Models that do claim to measure such factors as attitude change or brand preference change are often fraught with problems that severely limit their reliability. An effective measure must include some relationship to the communications process.

It might seem at first glance that principle 7 (providing a nonbiasing exposure) would be easy to accomplish. But lab measures, while offering control, are artificial and vulnerable to testing effects. And field measures, while more realistic, often lose control. The Seagram and Time study may have the best of both worlds, but it is too large a task for most firms to undertake. Some of the improvements associated with the single-source systems help to solve this problem. In addition, properly designed ad tracking studies provide truer measures of the impact of the communication. As technology develops and more attention is paid to this principle, we expect to see improvements in methodologies soon.

Last but not least is principle 9, the concern for reliability and validity. Most of the measures discussed are lacking in at least one of these criteria, yet these are two of the most critical distinctions between good and bad research. If a study is properly designed, and by that we mean it addresses principles 1 through 8, it should be both reliable and valid.

Essentials of Effective Testing

Simply put, good tests of advertising effectiveness must address the nine principles established by PACT. One of the easiest ways to accomplish this is by following the decision sequence model in formulating promotional plans.

- *Establish communications objectives.* We have stated that except for a few instances (most specifically direct-response advertising), it is nearly impossible to show the direct impact of advertising on sales. So the marketing objectives established for the promotional program are not usually good measures of communication effectiveness. For example, it is very difficult (or too expensive) to demonstrate the effect of an ad on brand share or on sales. On the other hand, attainment of communications objectives can be measured and leads to the accomplishment of marketing objectives.
- *Use a consumer response model.* Early in this text we reviewed hierarchy of effects models and cognitive response models, which provide an understanding of the effects of communications and lend themselves to achieving communications goals.
- *Use both pretests and posttests.* From a cost standpoint—both actual cost outlays and opportunity costs—pretesting makes sense. It may mean the difference between success or failure of the campaign or the product. But it should work in conjunction with posttests, which avoid the limitations of pretests, use much larger samples, and take place in more natural settings. Posttesting may be required to determine the true effectiveness of the ad or campaign.
- *Use multiple measures.* Many attempts to measure the effectiveness of advertising focus on one major dependent variable—perhaps sales, recall, or recognition. As noted earlier in this chapter, advertising may have a variety of effects on the consumer, some of which can be measured through traditional methods, others that require updated thinking (recall the discussion on physiological responses). For a true assessment of advertising effectiveness, a number of measures may be required. The Ogilvy Award winners mentioned earlier all employed multiple measures to track the effects on communications objectives.
- *Understand and implement proper research.* It is critical to understand research methodology. What constitutes a good design? Is it valid and reliable? Does it measure what we need it to? There is no shortcut to this criterion, and there is no way to avoid it if you truly want to measure the effects of advertising.

A major study sponsored by the Advertising Research Foundation (ARF), involving interviews with 12,000 to 15,000 people, addressed some of these issues.[41] While we do not have the space to analyze this study here, note that the research was designed to evaluate measures of copy tests, compare copy testing procedures, and examine some of the PACT principles. Information on this study has been published in a number of academic and trade journals and by the ARF.

Measuring the Effectiveness of Other Program Elements

Throughout this text, we have discussed how and when promotional program elements should be used, the advantages and disadvantages of each, and so on. In many chapters we have discussed measures of effectiveness used to evaluate these programs. In the final section of this chapter, we add a few measures that were not discussed earlier.

Measuring the Effectiveness of Sales Promotions

Sales promotions are not limited to retailers and resellers of products. Sports marketers have found them a very effective way to attract crowds and have been able to

Figure 19-19 Measuring the Effects of FSIs

A study by Promotion Decisions Inc. examined the actual purchase data of users and nonusers of 27 coupon promotions in its National Shopper Lab (75,000 households) over a period of 18 months. The findings:

- FSI coupons generated significant trial by new and lapsed users of a product (53%).
- Repeat purchase rates were 11.8% higher among coupon redeemers than nonredeemers.
- 64.2% of repeat volume among coupon redeemers was without a coupon.
- There was no significant difference in share of volume between buyers who used coupons and those who did not.
- Coupons returned between 71% and 79% of their cost within 12 weeks.
- Full-page ads provided higher redemption rates, incremental volume, redemption by new users, and a higher number of repeat buyers than half-page ads.
- Consumers who used coupons were brand loyal.

measure their relative effectiveness by the number of fans attending games. Major League Baseball teams have seen their attendance increase for those games in which promotions are offered.

A number of organizations measure sales promotions. One firm, MarketSource, provides marketers with a basis for measuring the effectiveness of their sampling programs. While too involved to discuss in detail here, the program calculates a breakeven rate by dividing the sampling investment by the profit for the user. If the conversions exceed the breakeven rate, the sampling program is successful.[42] Promotion Decisions Inc. examines the impact of freestanding inserts (FSIs) (Figure 19-19).

Other measures of sales promotions are also available. Schnucks (St. Louis), Smitty's Super Valu (Phoenix), and Vons (Los Angeles) have all used pretests with effects measured through scanner data. Others have employed this methodology to examine brand and store switching, alternative promotions, price discounts, and merchandising techniques.[43] Other advertisers use awareness tracking studies and count the number of inquiries, coupon redemptions, and sweepstakes entries. They also track sales during promotional and nonpromotional periods while holding other factors constant.

One recent technological development designed to track the effectiveness of sales promotions at the point of sale is offered by Shopper Trak. Shopper Trak places sensors in the store that track whether a person is coming or going, calculate the shopper's height (to differentiate between adults and children), and gauge traffic patterns. The system helps retailers evaluate the effectiveness of promotions or displays located throughout the store.[44]

Elizabeth Gardener and Minakshi Trivedi offer a communications framework to allow managers to evaluate sales promotion strategies over a given set of specific criteria. Borrowing from advertising applications, and using four communications goals—attention, comprehension (understanding), persuasion, and purchase—the researchers show the impact of four promotional tools and everyday low pricing (EDLP) on each goal (Figure 19-20). In addition, the impact of everyday low pricing, Procter & Gamble's strategy for discontinuing the use of sales promotions, is also discussed in the article.[45]

Figure 19-20 Conceptual Framework Analysis

		Communication Factors			
		Attention/ Impression	Communication/ Understanding	Persuasion	Purchase
Sales Promotions	FSI coupons	√√	√√√	√√	√√
	On-shelf coupons	√√√	√√√	√√√	√√√
	On-pack promotions	√	√	√√	√
	Bonus packs	√√√	√√	√√	√√
	EDLP	√	√√	√√	√

Note: Promotional tendency to fulfill factor: √√√ = strong; √√ = moderate; √ = weak.

Measuring the Effectiveness of Nontraditional Media

In Chapter 13, we noted that one of the disadvantages of employing nontraditional media is that it is usually difficult to measure the effectiveness of the programs. But some progress has been made, as shown in these examples:

- *The effects of shopping cart signage.* Earlier we discussed sales increases that occurred when shopping cart signage was used. We have also noted throughout this chapter that while increasing sales is a critical goal, many other factors may contribute to or detract from this measure. (It should be noted that these results are provided by the companies that sell these promotional media.) At least one study has examined the effectiveness of shopping cart signage on data besides sales.[46] This study used personal interviews in grocery stores to measure awareness of, attention to, and influence of this medium. Interestingly, it suggests shopping carts are much less effective than the sign companies claim.
- *The effectiveness of ski resort–based media.* In Chapter 13, we discussed advertising on ski chair lifts and other areas to attempt to reach selective demographic groups. Now the Traffic Audit Bureau (TAB) is tracking the effectiveness of this form of advertising to give advertisers more reliable criteria on which to base purchase decisions. The TAB data verify ad placements, while the media vendors have employed Simmons Market Research Bureau and Nielsen Media Research to collect ad impressions and advertising recall information.[47] These measures are combined with sales tracking data to evaluate the medium's effectiveness.
- *The effects of in-store radio and television.* In the fall of 2005, Interactive Market Systems (IMS) introduced software that would enable clients to measure the effectiveness of in-store radio. The company planned to introduce similar software designed to measure in-store television advertising effectiveness in 2006.[48]
- *The effectiveness of other media.* A number of companies provide effectiveness measures to determine the impact of package designs, POP displays, trade show exhibits, and the like. Nielsen Entertainment and Massive, Inc., now offer a service to measure videogame advertising effectiveness.[49] While it is not possible to list them all here, suffice it to say that if one wants to measure the impact of various IMC elements, the resources are available.

Measuring the Effectiveness of Sponsorships

In earlier chapters we discussed the growth in sponsorships and the reasons why organizations have increased their investments in this area. Along with the increased expenditures have come a number of methods for measuring the impact of sponsorships. Essentially, measures of sponsorship effectiveness can be categorized as exposure-based methods or tracking measures:[50]

- *Exposure methods.* Exposure methods can be classified as those that monitor the quantity and nature of the media coverage obtained for the sponsored event and those that estimate direct and indirect audiences. While commonly employed by corporations, scholars have heavily criticized these measures. For example, Pham argues that media coverage is not the objective of sponsorships and should not be considered as a measure of effectiveness. He argues that the measures provide no indication of perceptions, attitude change, or behavioral change and should therefore not be considered as measures of effectiveness.[51]
- *Tracking measures.* These measures are designed to evaluate the awareness, familiarity, and preferences engendered by sponsorship based on surveys. A number of empirical studies have measured recall of sponsors' ads, awareness of and attitudes toward the sponsors and their products, and image effect including brand and corporate images.

A number of companies now measure the effectiveness of sports sponsorships. For example, Joyce Julius & Associates of Ann Arbor, Michigan, assigns a monetary value to the amount of exposure the sponsor receives during the event. It reviews broadcasts

Product	Market	Sales During Event (Dollar or Volume)	Percent Change from Average Sales
Snacks	Louisville	$119,841	+52%
	Salt Lake City	$135,500	+47
	Indianapolis	$347,940	+105
Soap	Atlanta	950 cases	+375
	Minneapolis	880 cases	+867
	Cleveland	972 cases	+238
	Portland, OR	580 cases	+580
	St. Louis	1,616 cases	+1,454
Salad dressing	Atlanta	NA	+175
	Salt Lake City	NA	+143

Figure 19-21 Sales Impact of Concert Sponsorships (average four to six weeks)

and adds up the number of seconds a sponsor's product name or logo can be seen clearly (for example, on signs or shirts). A total of 30 seconds is considered the equivalent of a 30-second commercial. (Such measures are of questionable validity.)

Performance Research in Newport, Rhode Island, measures impact on brand awareness and image shifts. PS Productions, a Chicago-based research organization, provides clients with a measure of event sponsorships based on increased sales. PS calculates sales goals based on the cost of the event and the value of extras like donated media, customized displays, ads for key retailers, and tickets given away. An event is a success if it brings in at least that amount in additional sales (Figure 19-21).

While each of these measures has its advantages and disadvantages, we suggest using several in assessing the impact of sponsorships. In addition to those mentioned here, the eight-step process suggested in Figure 19-22 could be used to guide these evaluations.

Measuring the Effectiveness of Other IMC Program Elements

Many of the organizations mentioned in this chapter offer research services to measure the effectiveness of specific promotional program elements. As we noted at the outset of this chapter, the increased use of integrated marketing communications programs has led to more interest in determining the synergistic effects of all program elements.

1. Narrowly define objectives with specifics.
2. Establish solid strategies against which programming will be benchmarked and measure your programming and effectiveness against the benchmark.
3. Set measurable and realistic goals; make sure everything you do supports them.
4. Enhance, rather than just change, other marketing variables.
5. Don't pull Marketing Plan 101 off the shelf. Programming should be crafted to reflect the particulars of your company's constituencies and target audiences.
6. Define the scope of your involvement. Will it involve multiple areas within the company? Who internally and externally comprises the team?
7. Think "long term." It takes time to build brand equity. Also, think of leveraging your sponsorship through programming for as long as possible, before and after the event.
8. Build evaluation and a related budget into your overall sponsoring program. Include items such as pre- and post-event attitude surveys, media analysis, and sales results.

Figure 19-22 Eight Steps to Measuring Event Sponsorship

A review of the Ogilvy Award winners from 1993 to date demonstrates the increased integration of additional media (as opposed to specifically the best advertising campaign) and the value of measuring their contribution to the program's success. Also departing from the specific focus on advertising are the awards given by the London-based *Institute of Practitioners,* which in 2002 opened the competition for the first time to nontraditional media as well as public relations, sales promotions, and other entries.[52]

As noted throughout the chapter, a number of studies have been implemented to determine the combined effects of two or more media as well as their synergistic impact. The number of studies being designed to specifically measure synergistic effects continues to increase—most of which demonstrate a higher effectiveness when multiple media are employed. For example, after receiving negative publicity from a number of sources in 2004, Wal-Mart increased its public relations activities and its advertising designed to enhance its corporate image. By early 2005, Wal-Mart was able to show significant improvement in its image, which the company directly attributes to the combined use of the two program elements.[53]

Other companies are applying traditional advertising effectiveness measures offered by companies such as Millward Brown and Nielsen Media Research to their online advertising to assess their overall communications effects.[54] One very effective approach to measuring the impact of the IMC program is that provided by the marketing communications research company Integration. Based on the belief that integrated marketing communications improves both the efficiency and the effectiveness of a campaign, integration contends that most traditional measurement techniques focus only on the former of these (see Figure 19-23). Noting the increased demand for marketing managers to prioritize the media vehicles used to promote their brands, Integration developed Market ContactAudit to measure both the efficiency and the effectiveness of media used to establish contacts with consumers. By measuring consumers' understanding, evaluation, and perceptions of the contacts and their association with the brand, the Market ContactAudit allows marketers to assess the overall effectiveness as well as the relative contribution of individual IMC elements.[55]

Before we close, we would like to cite one final example of the impact of a combination of media. This case is particularly interesting because it demonstrates that companies do not have to be as large as Microsoft, spend millions of dollars on communications, or employ large research agencies to measure effectiveness.

Heart-wear, a small jewelry manufacturer with almost no advertising budget, relies to a large degree on word of mouth and its Internet site as the primary means of creating awareness and interest in the brand. By tracking visitors to its site, Heart-wear was able to determine the impact of having its product appear in various publications, thus getting an indication of the value of publicity. In February, Heart-wear page requests ranged from a low of 5 to as high as 726 per day, with an average of 199 (see Figure 19-24). In March, the average number dropped. Then the jewelry was shown in various magazines—not as an ad but with someone wearing the product or just with a small print name mention. As can be seen, the appearances in *Teen People, YM,* and

Figure 19-23 Measuring Effectiveness Not Only Efficiency

The most important issue for IMC planning is identifying the most appropriate contact mix, i.e., which contacts to prioritize.

Questions: Are we . . .

Being Effective: 1. Doing the right things?

Being Efficient: 2. Doing things right?

Current techniques meaure only efficiency

-Reach, frequency, GRPs (media surveys)

-Weight of market activity (stochastic)

MCA by integration measures effectiveness and efficiency

-Influence of contacts

-Consumer brand experience

Figure 19-24 Heart-wear.com Hits

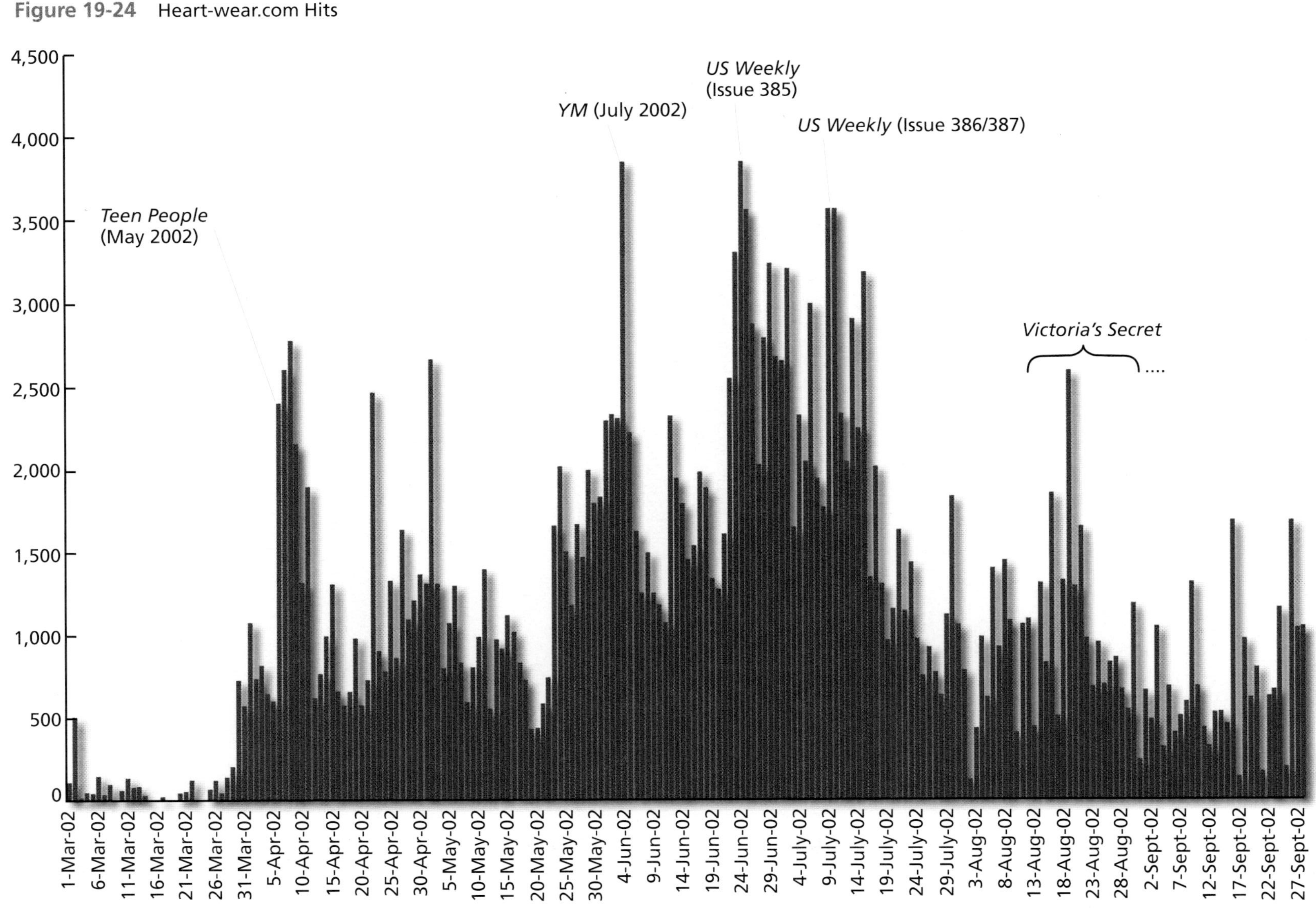

US Weekly significantly increased the number of hits to almost 4,000 each time the jewelry appeared. The actual exposures were minimal but still led to significant increases in visits, with lower numbers associated with no exposure periods. The August and September spikes were associated with appearances in Victoria's Secret catalog mailings, with each increase correlated with the mailing period. Sales figures also correlated highly with the site visits.

The Heart-wear example is just one more indication of the value of measuring the effectiveness of the impact of various IMC elements. Perhaps just as important, it indicates that the excuse of not measuring due to costs has little or no merit.

All the advertising effectiveness measures discussed here have their inherent strengths and weaknesses. They offer the advertiser some information that may be useful in evaluating the effectiveness of promotional efforts. While not all promotional efforts can be evaluated effectively, progress is being made.

Summary

This chapter introduced you to issues involved in measuring the effects of advertising and promotions. These issues include reasons for testing, reasons companies do not test, and the review and evaluation of various research methodologies. We arrived at a number of conclusions: (1) Advertising research to measure effectiveness is important to the promotional program, (2) not enough companies test their ads, and (3) problems exist with current research methodologies. In addition, we reviewed the criteria for sound research and suggested some ways to accomplish effective studies.

All marketing managers want to know how well their promotional programs are working. This information is critical to planning for the next period, since program adjustments and/or maintenance are based on evaluation of current strategies. Problems often result when the measures taken to determine such effects are inaccurate or improperly used.

This chapter demonstrated that testing must meet a number of criteria (defined by PACT) to be successful. These evaluations should occur both before and after the campaigns are implemented.

A variety of research methods were discussed, many provided by syndicated research firms such as Ipsos-ASI, MSW, Arbitron, and A. C. Nielsen. Many companies have developed their own testing systems. There has been an increase in testing through the Internet.

Single-source research data were discussed. These single-source systems offer strong potential for improving the effectiveness of ad measures in the future, since commercial exposures and reactions may be correlated to actual purchase behaviors.

It is important to recognize that different measures of effectiveness may lead to different results. Depending on the criteria used, one measure may show that an ad or promotion is effective while another states that it is not. This is why clearly defined objectives and the use of multiple measures are critical to determining the true effects of an IMC program.

Key Terms

vehicle option source effect, 603
pretests, 603
posttests, 603
laboratory tests, 606
testing bias, 606
field tests, 606
PACT (Positioning Advertising Copy Testing), 607
concept testing, 607
comprehension and reaction tests, 610
consumer juries, 610
halo effect, 611
portfolio tests, 612
Flesch formula, 612
theater testing, 613
on-air test, 614
day-after recall scores, 614
pupillometrics, 615
electrodermal response, 615
eye tracking, 615
electroencephalographic (EEG) measures, 616
alpha activity, 616
hemispheric lateralization, 616
inquiry tests, 616
split-run tests, 617
recognition method, 617
recall tests, 618
single-source tracking methods, 621
tracking studies, 621

Discussion Questions

1. The lead-in to this chapter discusses a number of ways that companies attempt to measure the effectiveness of advertising. Discuss the methods presented in the lead-in. What are some of the advantages and disadvantages associated with each?

2. Most of this chapter focuses attention on the measurement of traditional forms of advertising. How are companies measuring nontraditional advertising forms?

3. The chapter notes that while companies may spend a substantial portion of their revenues on advertising, over 70 percent spend less than 2 percent of their budgets on measuring advertising effectiveness. Explain why this is the case. Do you agree or disagree with this strategy?

4. Explain why it is so difficult to measure the effectiveness of an IMC program that uses multiple program elements.

5. Advertising rates on Super Bowl XL were well over $2 million per spot. For some companies this may be a wise investment, while for others it may be less valuable. Discuss the types of companies for which it may or may not be a wise investment and provide reasons why.

6. Discuss some of the reasons why some companies decide not to measure the effectiveness of their promotional programs. Explain why this may or may not be a good strategy.

7. Discuss the differences between pretesting and posttesting. Give examples of each.

8. What is the difference between a lab test and a field test? When should each be employed?

9. Give examples of the various types of rough testing methodologies. Describe why a company might wish to test at this phase of the process. When might it wish to test only completed ads?

10. Major changes have taken place in the way that theater tests are conducted. Describe some of these changes and the changes in measures that have also occurred in this testing method.

International Advertising and Promotion

20

Chapter Objectives

1. To examine the importance of international marketing and the role of international advertising and promotion.
2. To review the various factors in the international environment and how they influence advertising and promotion decisions.
3. To consider the pros and cons of global versus localized marketing and advertising.
4. To examine the various decision areas of international advertising.
5. To understand the role of other promotional mix elements in the international integrated marketing communications program.

Marketers Head to China

For many years marketers could only dream of selling their products to China's 1.3 billion consumers. However, with the end of the Cultural Revolution in 1979 and its massive modernization drive over the past three decades, China has become one of the

fastest-growing consumer markets in the world. Advertising, once banned as a capitalist scourge, is now encouraged by the Chinese government, which views it as a catalyst that can accelerate China's economic development. The country's leaders believe that advertising helps stimulate the national economy by encouraging consumption as well as helping to educate its consumers and business leaders about developments in the rest of the world.

Underlying the growth of advertising in China is the tremendous economic growth of the country, particularly in the urban areas that are home to more than a third of the country's population. There is also a new spirit of consumption, as reform in China has brought about dramatic increases in the purchasing power and size of the middle class. During the 1980s, demand for products such as radios, cameras, motorcycles, black-and-white TVs, and electric fans boomed. During the '90s, products such as refrigerators, microwave ovens, color TVs, washing machines, home stereos, and air conditioners became popular. However, over the past five years the average annual disposable income of urban Chinese has risen from $713 to nearly $1,200, and demand is increasing for many other products including personal computers, mobile phones, clothing, and fast food.

The newly emerging middle class in China is very brand conscious, and demand for popular Western products as well as goods from Japan and Korea is increasing because they mean one thing to Chinese consumers: status. Chinese consumers are now buying Dell computers; Samsung, LG, and Motorola phones; Whirlpool appliances; Procter & Gamble toiletries and cosmetics; and Nike shoes and apparel. They are meeting at Starbucks, which has opened more than 100 stores in China and plans hundreds more, as well as at fast-food chains such as Kentucky Fried Chicken, Pizza Hut, McDonald's, and Taco Bell. The rise of an affluent class is also creating a red-hot market for luxury brands such as Armani, Dior, BMW, and Mercedes.

While imported products are extremely popular among consumers, Chinese companies are fighting back by developing strong brands in many product categories. Traditionally, Chinese companies competed on the basis of price, but many are trying to move away from the low end of the market by developing higher-end products with more brand equity. A number of Chinese companies are striving to improve their brand images including the Haier Group, a $10 billion maker of refrigerators, washing machines, and other appliances; TCL, which makes TVs and mobile phones; and Tsingtao, China's leading brand of beer. Li Ning is a fast-growing maker of athletic shoes and apparel, which is sponsoring up-and-coming young Chinese athletes to grow its brand recognition. Lenovo Group, the leading computer company in China, changed its name from Legend and in 2005 acquired IBM's personal computer business. The company also became the first Chinese company to be an official top Olympic sponsor when it signed as a sponsor for the 2008 games to be held in Beijing.

One company that has been extremely successful in marketing its products in China is Nike, which is regarded as the coolest brand among young consumers in the country. In 2004, Nike surpassed Li Ning as the top athletic shoe brand, even though its shoes sell for $100 or more a pair—twice that of other brands. The first phase of Nike's IMC strategy for China actually began in 1995 and involved building brand awareness and recognition. This was done by outfitting top Chinese athletes and sponsoring all of the teams in China's new professional basketball league. The director of sports marketing for Nike in China also recognized that it was important for the company to become involved with sports at a grassroots level. He donated equipment to Shanghai high schools, paid them to open their basketball courts to the public after hours, organized three-on-three tournaments, and founded the city's first high school basketball league, which has since spread to 17 other cities. Nike made American culture a major selling point by developing TV ads that challenged the group-oriented ethos of Chinese society. The ads focused on the more individualistic American style of basketball, complete with a theme song blending traditional Chinese music and American hip-hop. The ads were timed to coincide with basketball tournaments around the country; teaser clips were also shown on the Internet.

Another important part of Nike's strategy was to partner with the National Basketball Association (NBA), which had begun televising games in China, and to bring such players as Michael Jordan and others to the country for visits and clinics. Nike also contracted with China's most famous living person, NBA star Yao Ming of the Houston Rockets, from 1999 until 2003 when he defected to Reebok for an estimated $100 million. However, the company has already signed China's next likely NBA star, seven-foot Yi Jianlian, who is 18 and currently plays for the Guandong Tigers.

Nike has extended its sponsorships to other sports as well. When hurdler Liu Xiang became the country's first Olympic medalist in a short-distance speed event by winning a gold medal in the 110-meter hurdles at the 2004 Olympics in Athens, Nike immediately launched a TV ad in China to celebrate his victory. The spot showed him destroying the field as a set of questions that challenged stereotypes of Chinese athletes were superimposed on the screen: Asians lack muscle? Asians lack the will to win? The commercial ended by showing Xiang raising his arms in victory above the trademark Nike swoosh on this shoulder as the words "Stereotypes are made to be broken" were shown on the screen.

A number of other companies are also taking advantage of the growing interest in sports and fitness, particularly among China's urban professionals who are turning to leisure-time sports to stay fit as they work longer hours and face more stress. For example, Bally now operates 18 fitness clubs in major Chinese cities and plans to expand to more than 1,000 in the next few years. The company recently worked with the government-owned Beijing TV station to co-produce a television series featuring club members and how exercise changed their lives.

Multinational companies recognize that the enormous size of the Chinese market, along with its strong economic development and growth, makes it imperative for them to be there. China has grown into the Coca-Cola Co.'s sixth largest global market and Coke expects it to become its third largest market in five years. Per capita consumption of Coke products in China stands at just 10 units a year versus 400 units in the United States. Thus, it is obvious why Coca-Cola, along with many other companies, sees China as the key to their future growth.

Sources: Qiu Haixu, "In China, Sports Take Flight," *The Wall Street Journal,* August 11, 2005, pp. B1, 3; Dexter Roberts, "China's Power Brands," *BusinessWeek,* November 8, 2004, pp. 77–84; Matthew Forney, "How Nike Figured Out China," *Time Bonus Section,* November 2004, pp. A7–14.

The primary focus of this book so far has been on integrated marketing communications programs for products and services sold in the U.S. market. Many American companies have traditionally devoted most of their marketing efforts to the domestic market, since they often lack the resources, skills, or incentives to go abroad. This is changing rapidly, however, as U.S. corporations recognize the opportunities that foreign markets offer for new sources of sales and profits as well as the need to market their products internationally. Many companies are striving to develop global brands that can be advertised and promoted the world over.

In this chapter, we look at international advertising and promotion and the various issues marketers must consider in communicating with consumers around the globe. We examine the environment of international marketing and how companies often must adapt their promotional programs to conditions in each country. We review the debate over whether a company should use a global marketing and advertising approach or tailor it specifically for various countries.

We also examine how firms organize for international advertising, select agencies, and consider various decision areas such as research, creative strategy, and media selection. While the focus of this chapter is on international advertising, we also consider other promotional mix elements in international marketing, including sales promotion, personal selling, publicity/public relations, and the Internet. Let's begin by discussing some of the reasons international marketing has become so important to companies.

The Importance of International Markets

One of the major developments in the business world during the decade of the 90s was the globalization of markets. The emergence of a largely borderless world has created a new reality for all types of companies. Today, world trade is driven by global competition among global companies for global consumers.[1] With the development of faster communication, transportation, and financial transactions, time and distance are no longer barriers to global marketing. Products and services developed in one country quickly find their way to other countries where they are finding enthusiastic acceptance. Consumers around the world wear Nike shoes and Calvin Klein jeans, eat at McDonald's, shave with Gillette razors, use Dell computers, listen to music on Apple iPods, drink Coca-Cola and Pepsi Cola soft drinks and Starbucks coffee, talk on cellular phones made by Nokia and Motorola, and drive cars made by global automakers such as Ford, Honda, and Nissan.[2]

Companies are focusing on international markets for a number of reasons. Many companies in the United States and Western Europe recognize that their domestic markets offer them limited opportunities for expansion because of slow population growth, saturated markets, intense competition, and/or an unfavorable marketing environment. For example, U.S. tobacco companies face declining domestic consumption as a result of restrictions on their marketing and advertising efforts and the growing antismoking sentiment in this country. Companies such as R. J. Reynolds and Philip Morris are turning to markets outside the United States such as Asia and South America, where higher percentages of people smoke, nonsmokers are far more tolerant of the habit, opposition is less organized, and consumers are less litigious.[3] Many U.S.-based brewers, among them Anheuser-Busch and Coors, are looking to international markets to sustain growth as beer sales in the United States decline and regulatory pressures increase. However, these brewers are facing strong competition from foreign companies that are also targeting international markets. For example, in 2002 the Miller Brewing Co. was purchased by South African Breweries, whose largest markets are in Asia and Africa. The acquisition gives SAB access to the U.S. beer market while expanding opportunities for Miller brands in global markets.[4]

Many companies must focus on foreign markets to survive. Most European nations are relatively small in size and without foreign markets would not have the economies of scale to compete against larger U.S. and Japanese companies. For example, Swiss-based Nestlé and Netherlands-based Unilever are two of the world's largest consumer-product companies because they have learned how to market their brands to consumers in countries around the world. Two of the world's major marketers of cellular telephones are from Scandinavian countries. Nokia is based in Finland and Ericsson is located in Sweden. Australia's tourist industry is a major part of its economy and relies heavily on visitors from other countries. Tourism Australia, the federal government agency responsible for the country's international and domestic tourism marketing, recently launched a global campaign called "Australian Invitation," which is designed to attract visitors by showcasing the diversity of experiences available across Australia in a range of geographical and environmental settings. The integrated campaign includes television, print, outdoor, and online advertising, as well as trade and point-of-sales ads and direct marketing.[5] Exhibit 20-1 shows one of the print ads from the campaign.

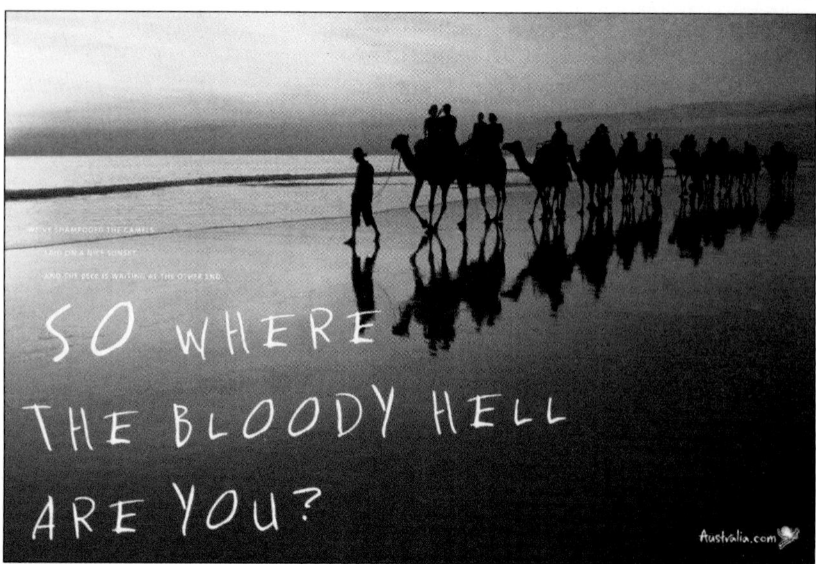

SO WHERE THE BLOODY HELL ARE YOU?
Australia.com

Exhibit 20-1 Tourism Australia promotes the country as a tourist destination

Companies are also pursuing international markets because of the opportunities they offer for growth and profits. The dramatic economic, social, and political changes around the world in recent years have opened markets in Eastern Europe and China. China's joining of the World Trade Organization in 2001 has provided foreign competitors with access to 1.3 billion potential Chinese consumers, and Western marketers are eager to sell them a variety of products and services.[6] The growing markets of the Far East, Latin America, and other parts of the world present tremendous opportunities to marketers of consumer products and services as well as business-to-business marketers.

Many companies in the United States as well as in other countries have long recognized the importance and potential profitability of international markets. General Electric, Ford, General Motors, Nissan, Nestlé, and Procter & Gamble have made the world their market and generate much of their sales and profits from abroad. Gillette sells more than 800 products in more than 200 countries. Colgate-Palmolive generates almost 80 percent of its nearly $11 billion in sales from outside the United States and Canada.[7] Starbucks sells lattes around the world as its name and image connect with consumers in Europe and Asia as well as North America. The company has coffee shops in 35 countries and operates nearly 4,000 international outlets from Beijing to Sydney to London. Starbucks' projected growth plan includes establishing 30,000 stores worldwide, with at least 15,000 locations outside the United States.[8] Coca-Cola, Pepsi, Nike, KFC, Dell, McDonald's, and many other U.S. companies and brands are known all over the world.

Many U.S.-based companies have formed joint ventures or strategic alliances with foreign companies to market their products internationally. For example, General Mills and Swiss-based Nestlé entered into a joint venture to create Cereal Partners Worldwide (CPW), taking advantage of General Mills' popular product line and Nestlé's powerful distribution channels in Europe, Asia, Latin America, and Africa. CPW is now the world's second-largest cereal company, operating in 75 international markets, and it generated nearly $700 million in sales in 2005.[9] Nestlé also has entered into joint ventures with Coca-Cola to have the beverage giant distribute its instant coffee and tea throughout the world. Häagen-Dazs entered into a joint venture in Japan with Suntory Ltd., and its premium ice cream, frozen yogurt, and other brands are now sold throughout Asia.

International markets are important to small and mid-size companies as well as the large multinational corporations. Many of these firms can compete more effectively in foreign markets, where they may face less competition or appeal to specific market segments or where products have not yet reached the maturity stage of their life cycle. For example, the WD-40 Co. has saturated the U.S. market with its lubricant product and now gets much of its sales growth from markets in Europe, Asia, Latin America, and Australia (Exhibit 20-2).

Exhibit 20-2 The WD-40 Co. gets much of its sales growth from foreign markets such as Latin America

Another reason it is increasingly important for U.S. companies to adopt an international marketing orientation is that imports are taking a larger and larger share of the domestic market for many products. The United States has been running a continuing **balance-of-trade deficit;** the monetary value of our imports exceeds that of our exports. American companies are realizing that we are shifting from being an isolated, self-sufficient, national economy to being part of an interdependent *global economy.* This means U.S. corporations must defend against foreign inroads into the domestic market as well as learn how to market their products and services to other countries.

While many U.S. companies are becoming more aggressive in their pursuit of international markets, they face stiff competition from large multinational corporations from other countries. Some of the world's most formidable marketers are European companies such as Unilever, Nestlé, Siemens, Philips, and Renault, as well as the various Japanese car and electronic manufacturers and packaged-goods companies such as Suntory, Shiseido, and Kao.

The Role of International Advertising and Promotion

Advertising and promotion are important parts of the marketing program of firms competing in the global marketplace. An estimated $276 billion was spent on advertising in the United States in 2005, with much of this money being spent by multinational companies headquartered outside this country.[10] Advertising expenditures outside the United States have increased by nearly 60 percent since 1990, reaching an estimated $294 million in 2005, as global marketers based in the United States, as well as European and Asian countries, increase their worldwide advertising.[11] Figure 20-1 shows the top 10 companies in terms of advertising spending outside the United States.

Figure 20-1 Top 10 Companies by Advertising Spending outside the United States, 2004

			Ad Spending (Millions US Dollars)		
Rank	Advertiser	Headquarters	Outside the U.S.	U.S.	Worldwide
1.	Procter & Gamble Co.	Cincinnati, Ohio	$4,350	$3,572	$7,922
2.	Unilever	London/Rotterdam	2,859	603	3,462
3.	L'Oreal	Paris, France	1,878	768	2,646
4.	Toyota Motor Corp.	Toyota City, Japan	1,510	1,098	2,608
5.	Nestlé	Vevey, Switzerland	1,401	498	1,899
6.	Ford Motor Co.	Dearborn, Michigan	1,155	1,643	2,798
7.	Coca-Cola Co.	Atlanta, Georgia	1,128	379	1,507
8.	General Motors	Detroit, Michigan	1,120	2,798	3,918
9.	Volkswagen	Wolfsburg, Germany	1,037	418	1,455
10.	PSA Peugeot Citroen	Paris, France	1,032	0	1,032

Source: Top 100 Global Marketers, *Advertising Age,* November 14, 2005, p. 4.

In addition, estimates are that another $500 billion is spent on sales promotion efforts targeted at consumers, retailers, and wholesalers around the world. The United States is still the world's major advertising market, accounting for nearly half of the estimated $570 billion in worldwide ad expenditures. Nearly 90 percent of the money spent on advertising products and services around the world is concentrated in the United States and Canada along with the industrialized countries of Western Europe and the Pacific Rim, including Japan, South Korea, and Australia. However, advertising spending is increasing rapidly in China and in several Latin American countries, such as Mexico and Brazil.[12]

More and more companies recognize that an effective promotional program is important for companies competing in foreign markets. As one international marketing scholar notes:

> Promotion is the most visible as well as the most culture bound of the firm's marketing functions. Marketing includes the whole collection of activities the firm performs in relating to its market, but in other functions the firm relates to the market in a quieter, more passive way. With the promotional function, however, the firm is standing up and speaking out, wanting to be seen and heard.[13]

Many companies have run into difficulties developing and implementing advertising and promotion programs for international markets. Companies that promote their products or services abroad face an unfamiliar marketing environment and customers with different sets of values, customs, consumption patterns, and habits, as well as differing purchase motives and abilities. Languages vary from country to country and even within a country, such as India or Switzerland. Media options are quite limited in many countries, owing to lack of availability or limited effectiveness. These factors demand different creative and media strategies as well as changes in other elements of the advertising and promotional program for foreign markets.

The International Environment

Just as with domestic marketing, companies engaging in international marketing must carefully analyze the major environmental factors of each market in which they compete, including economic, demographic, cultural, and political/legal variables. Figure 20-2 shows some of the factors marketers must consider in each category when analyzing the environment of each country or market. These factors are important in evaluating the potential of each country as well as designing and implementing a marketing and promotional program.

The Economic Environment

A country's economic conditions indicate its present and future potential for consuming, since products and services can be sold only to countries where there is enough income to buy them. This is generally not a problem in developed countries such as the United States, Canada, Japan, and most of Western Europe, where consumers generally have higher incomes and standards of living. Thus, they can and want to purchase a variety of products and services. Developed countries have the **economic infrastructure** in terms of the communications, transportation, financial, and distribution networks needed to conduct business in these markets effectively. By contrast, many developing countries lack purchasing power and have limited communications networks available to firms that want to promote their products or services to these markets.

For most companies, industrialized nations represent the greatest marketing and advertising opportunities. But most of these countries have stable population bases, and their markets for many products and services are already saturated. Many marketers are turning their attention to parts of the world whose economies and consumer markets are growing. In the early to mid-1990s many marketers began turning their attention to the "four Tigers" of Asia—South Korea, Singapore, Hong Kong, and Taiwan—which were among the fastest-growing markets in the world.[14] These markets experienced a severe recession when the Asian economic crisis hit in the late '90s and carried into the new millennium. Markets in Asia, as well as in Europe and South

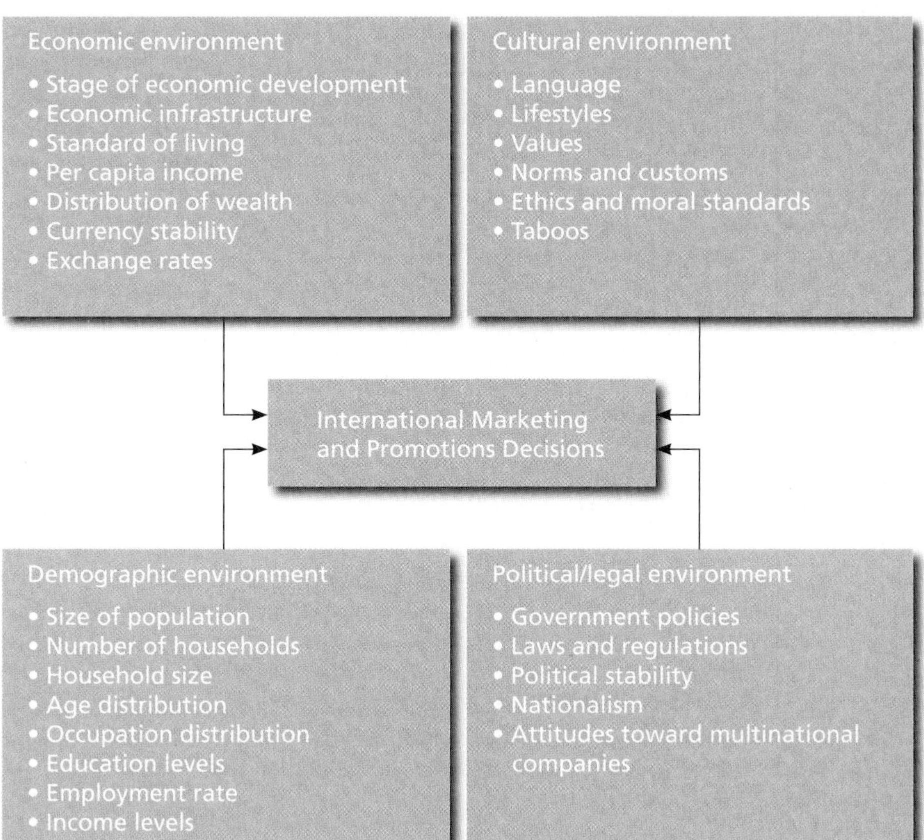

Economic environment
• Stage of economic development
• Economic infrastructure
• Standard of living
• Per capita income
• Distribution of wealth
• Currency stability
• Exchange rates
Cultural environment
• Language
• Lifestyles
• Values
• Norms and customs
• Ethics and moral standards
• Taboos
International Marketing and Promotions Decisions
Demographic environment
• Size of population
• Number of households
• Household size
• Age distribution
• Occupation distribution
• Education levels
• Employment rate
• Income levels
Political/legal environment
• Government policies
• Laws and regulations
• Political stability
• Nationalism
• Attitudes toward multinational companies

Figure 20-2 Forces in the International Marketing Environment

America, were stagnant for a number of years, which led to reductions in advertising spending in most countries. However, these markets are experiencing strong economic growth as are countries such as Russia, Brazil, Chile, China, and India, which is resulting in greater consumer spending as well as increases in advertising.[15]

China and India in particular are two countries that are transforming the global economy. The two countries together account for a third of the world's population, and they both have had economic growth rates ranging from 6 to 10 percent over the past several years, which is much greater than other countries in the world. Each country has the fundamentals to sustain the high growth rates including young populations, high savings, and a growing number of consumers who have the ability to purchase, as well as the need for, many products.[16]

Marketers of products such as mobile phones, TVs, personal computers, cars, as well as luxury items such as jewelry and designer clothing are focusing more attention on consumers in India and China.[17] The growing middle class in these countries is also creating growth opportunities for marketers of consumer packaged-goods products. Procter & Gamble, Unilever, Nestlé, PepsiCo, and Coca-Cola are focusing a great deal of attention and spending more on advertising to reach these consumers. China has become the third-largest advertising market in the world trailing only the United States and Japan.[18] Many multinational companies are also turning their attention to third-world countries where consumer markets are slowly emerging. Global Perspective 20-1 discusses the opportunities that these markets present as well as the challenges of marketing to them.

The Demographic Environment

Major demographic differences exist among countries as well as within them. Marketers must consider income levels and distribution, age and occupation distributions of the population, household size, education, and employment rates. In some countries, literacy rates are also a factor; people who cannot read will not respond well to print ads. Demographic data can provide insight into the living standards and lifestyles in a particular country to help companies plan ad campaigns.

GLOBAL PERSPECTIVE 20-1

Marketing to 4 Billion of the World's Poorest Consumers

Most multinational companies generate the majority of their sales and profits by selling products and services to consumers and businesses in highly developed countries. When they do venture into developing nations such as India or China, they have traditionally focused on urban areas where incomes are higher and communication, transportation, and distribution systems are available to implement their marketing programs. However, many multinational marketers have begun turning their attention to the 4 billion consumers who live in the remote, rural communities of developing countries. These people are yearning for a better way of life and are eager to become consumers for a variety of products.

While this emergent trend has been given various labels such as B2-4B (business-to-4-billion) selling, selling to the "bottom of the pyramid," or selling to premarkets, a number of companies are recognizing that they can turn a profit while having a positive effect on people not normally considered potential consumers. However, they also realize that it is a tremendous challenge to market to these consumers. Many of the world's poor live in severe poverty, subsisting on less than $1,500 a year, and are illiterate or nearly so. They often live in tiny villages in remote areas that are completely beyond the reach of mass media and common distribution channels. Their access to and ability to use products are determined by the available infrastructure—water, roads, electricity—or lack thereof. Clearly marketers have to package, price, and distribute their products differently as well as find innovative ways to communicate with these consumers.

So how do global marketers such as Procter & Gamble and Unilever sell soap to consumers who use mud to bathe, or how do they market toothpaste to someone who uses wood from a tree to clean his teeth? These companies often start by examining the daily lives of the consumers, including their needs, aspirations, and habits, to better understand what they may want as consumers. In many cases, advertising agencies are following or often leading their clients into these rural areas. For example, the Interpublic Group's Lowe Lintas & Partners set up "Linterland," an extension of its integrated marketing communications department, to help clients such as Unilever market to hard-to-reach consumers in Indonesia. Lowe's director of IMC estimates that about 64 percent of Indonesia's population (about 135 million people) lives in rural areas but can afford relatively inexpensive consumer goods such as soft drinks, shampoo, and toothpaste. The director of Linterland Indonesia notes that conventional media are not capable of reaching these rural consumers, and so a different form of marketing communications—one that relies on events, road shows, and sampling—is needed to reach them.

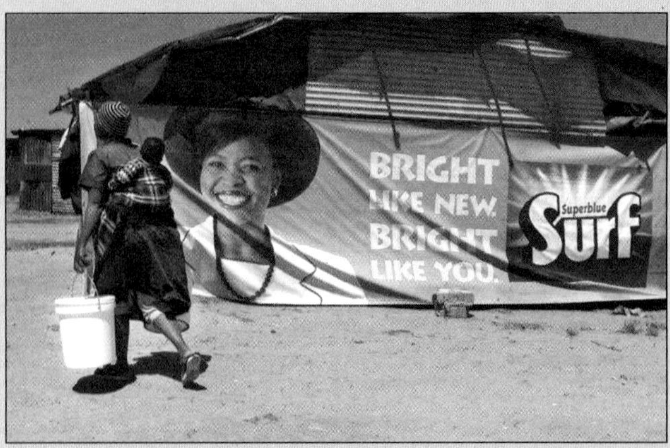

Other ad agencies have set up similar operations to reach the vast rural populations in other Asian countries. For example, in India, 75 percent of the population (700 million people) is spread out in 600,000 villages that are virtually untouched by mass media, and they speak more than 360 dialects. WPP Group's Ogilvy and Mather launched its own special unit, Ogilvy Outreach, consisting of 35 teams in four offices that coordinate rural marketing activities across 14 states, using a network of 15,000 field-workers. Ogilvy Outreach has resorted to unusual practices such as painting cows' horns, branding water sources, organizing folk performances, and relying on schoolteachers, village heads, and local health workers to relay marketing messages for clients such as Hinustan Lever, Castrol, or Amara Raja batteries.

Word of mouth is the supreme marketing tool for reaching consumers in these markets, followed by education and product demonstrations. Marketers also have to adapt their products for these markets by making them available in single-use sachets that cost the equivalent of pennies rather than dollars and can be easily distributed and sold through the small kiosks found in rural villages.

While packaged-goods marketers have sold products such as soap, toothpaste, and shampoo to the villagers for years, other companies are now trying to sell them bigger items. For example, Philips Electronics created an inexpensive product line, including a wind-up radio and back-to-basics television set, which is demonstrated in village market stalls and sold in tiny one-stop shops that sell everything from medicine to food to cement. In Kaler, a small town of 300 families in northeastern Punjab, Hyundai Motor Co. was able to reach the marketer's dream—the village headman, an opinion leader whose advice is sought on marriages, crops, and, increasingly, on which TV set or car to buy.

Many developing countries are becoming more stable and open to trade and direct foreign investment, while education levels are also improving. The World Bank has reported that the economic growth rate for developing countries is about twice that of developed nations and is expected to reach nearly 4 percent. While investment in these markets still requires a long-term perspective, many companies are recognizing that the billions of consumers in the third world are eager to become consumers and represent a rich opportunity.

Sources: Dana James, "B2-4B Spells Profits," *Marketing News,* November 5, 2001, pp. 1, 11–14; Pete Engardio, "A New World Economy," *BusinessWeek,* August 22 and 29, 2005, pp. 52–58; Cris Prystay, "Companies Market to India's Have—Littles," *The Wall Street Journal,* June 5, 2003, pp. B1, 12.

Demographic information can reveal the market potential of various foreign markets. India's population topped 1 billion in 2005. Only China, with 1.3 billion people, has a larger population. Latin America remains one of the world's largest potential markets, although the meager income of most consumers in the region is still a problem. Brazil, the largest consumer market in South America, now has a population of 200 million and is a growing market for many products and services. More than 50 percent of the Latin American market is younger than age 26, and 30 percent is under 15. Moreover, children are the fastest-growing segment of that market. These numbers have caught the attention of international advertisers such as Mattel, Hasbro, Burger King, and others.[19] Indonesia also has a very young population, with more people under the age of 16 than the United States, and they are very receptive to Western ways and products.

The Cultural Environment

Another important aspect of the international marketing environment is the culture of each country. Cultural variables marketers must consider include language, customs, tastes, attitudes, lifestyles, values, and ethical/moral standards. Nearly every country exhibits cultural traits that influence not just the needs and wants of consumers but how they go about satisfying them.

Marketers must be sensitive not only in determining what products and services they can sell foreign cultures but also in communicating with them. Advertising is often the most effective way to communicate with potential buyers and create markets in other countries. But it can also be one of the most difficult aspects of the international marketing program because of problems in developing messages that will be understood in various countries.

International advertisers often have problems with language. The advertiser must know not only the native tongue of the country but also its nuances, idioms, and subtleties. International marketers must be aware of the connotations of words and symbols used in their messages and understand how advertising copy and slogans are translated. Marketers often encounter problems in translating their advertising messages and brand names into various languages. The Heineken ad in Exhibit 20-3 is one example. Although this ad worked well in the United States and other English-speaking countries, the line "you don't have to make a great fuss" could not be translated in a meaningful way into many other languages.

Advertisers can encounter problems with the connotative meaning of signs and symbols used in their messages. For example, the thumbs-up sign, which signifies affirmation to most Americans, has offensive meaning in some countries such as Russia and Poland if the palm of the hand is visible but is acceptable if the back of the hand is shown. There can also be problems associated with the symbolic meanings of colors. In Japan, as in many Asian countries, white is a color for mourning rather than black, and purple is associated with death in many Latin American countries. An American ad campaign using various shades of green was a disaster in Malaysia, where the color symbolizes death and disease.

Exhibit 20-3 This Heineken ad did not translate well into some languages

Brewers don't have to be good talkers.
Heineken
When you make a great beer, you don't have to make a great fuss.

Problems arising from language diversity and differences in signs and symbols can usually be best solved with the help of local expertise. Marketers should consult local employees or use an ad agency knowledgeable in the local language that can help verify that the advertiser is saying what it wants to say. Many companies turn to agencies that specialize in translating advertising slogans and copy into foreign languages.[20]

Tastes, traditions, and customs are also an important part of cultural considerations. The customs of a society affect what products and services it will buy and how they must be marketed. In France, cosmetics are used heavily by men as well as women, and advertising to the male market is common. There are also cultural differences in the grooming and hygiene habits of consumers in various countries. For example, though many U.S. consumers use products like deodorant and shampoo daily, consumers in many other Western countries are not as fanatical about personal hygiene, so consumption of products such as deodorants and mouthwash is much lower than in the United States.

Exhibit 20-4 New Balance shoes have become very popular in France

Another aspect of culture that is very important for international marketers to understand is values. **Cultural values** are beliefs and goals shared by members of a society regarding ideal end states of life and modes of conduct. Society shapes consumers' basic values, which affect their behavior and determine how they respond to various situations. For example, cultural values in the United States place a major emphasis on individual activity and initiative, while many Asian societies stress cooperation and conformity to the group. Values and beliefs of a society can also affect its members' attitudes and receptivity toward foreign products and services.[21] Values such as *ethnocentrism,* which refers to the tendency for individuals to view their own group or society as the center of the universe, or nationalism often affect the way consumers in various countries respond to foreign brands or even advertising messages.[22] For many years, consumers in many European countries were reluctant to buy American brands and there was even a backlash against American imagery. In fact, many U.S. companies doing business in Europe were careful not to flaunt their American roots.

One European country, in particular, where American-made products were not well received for many years is France. The French have always been very protective of their culture; for example, they have quotas for French-language shows on TV and music on the radio. As historian Richard Pells notes: "France, like the U.S., has traditionally seen itself as a country with a mission and a country whose culture and civilization is worthy of being exported around the world."[23] However, in recent years many American brands have become popular in France, particularly among younger consumers. For example, the French subsidiary of New Balance, the Boston-based athletic-shoe company, experienced strong sales growth in France when its 576 model shoe became *de rigueur* among the fashion elite (Exhibit 20-4). In recent years, U.S. brands have become popular in many other European countries as well as in Asia. Marketers attribute the rising popularity of many U.S.-made products to the worldwide distribution of American music, films, and TV shows; the growth of the Internet; and the increase in travel to the United States. These factors have made consumers in foreign countries more familiar with American culture, values, and lifestyle.[24]

Japan is one of the more difficult markets for many American advertisers to understand because of its unique values and customs.[25] For example, the Japanese have a very strong commitment to the group; social interdependence and collectivism are as important to them as individualism is to most Americans. Ads stressing individuality and nonconformity have traditionally not done well in Japan, but westernized values have become more prevalent in Japanese advertising in recent years.[26] However, the Japanese dislike ads that confront or disparage the competition and tend to prefer soft rather than hard sells.[27] A recent study found that Japanese and American magazine ads tend to portray teenage girls in different ways and that the differences correspond to each country's central concepts of self and society. In many American ads teens are associated with images of independence, rebelliousness, determination, and even defiance that are consistent with the American value of individuality. In contrast, Japanese ads tend to portray a happy, playful, childlike, girlish image that is consistent with the Japanese culture's sense of self, which is more dependent on others.[28] Another recent study examined gender-role portrayals in Japanese magazine advertising and found that some of the previously used hard-line stereotyping of both men and women has softened considerably since the 1980s. Men are not associated as much with stereotypical male traits, while women are shown in more positive ways. The researchers suggest that this may reflect the westernization of the depictions of men and women in Japan.[29]

As advertisers turn their attention to China, more consideration is also being given to understanding the cultural system and values of the world's most populous country. Chinese values are centered around Confucianism, which stresses loyalty and interpersonal relationships. Chinese culture also emphasizes passive acceptance of fate by seeking harmony with nature; inner experiences of meaning and feeling; stability and harmony; close family ties; and tradition.[30] A recent study of advertising appeals used in China found that advertising reflects these traditional Chinese cultural values. Chinese advertisers tend to base their advertising strategies on creating liking for a product through image and emotional appeals rather than information-laden ads. However, the study also found subtle changes in appeals to cultural values used by advertisers, particularly for ads targeting younger consumers. Youth and modernity appeals were found to be prevalent, reflecting the westernization, as well as the modernization, trend in China.[31] Marketing is just beginning to emerge in China, and advertising is a relatively new social phenomenon, so it will be important for marketers to develop a better understanding of Chinese cultural values and their implication for communications strategy.[32]

Nike recently ran into a problem over a commercial that aired in China showing NBA basketball star LeBron James winning a battle with a Chinese dragon and a kung fu master. The commercial was banned by government regulators who stated that it created indignant feelings among Chinese television viewers because it showed an American sports icon defeating the dragon, a symbol of Chinese culture, and the martial arts master, a symbol of national pride. A statement posted on the website of China's State Administration for Radio, Film, and Television stated that the ad violated the regulation that "all advertisements must uphold national dignity and interest, and respect the motherland's culture." Nike's China marketing director said that it was not the company's intention to show disrespect to the Chinese culture, explaining that the ad was meant to inspire youth to overcome internal fear and obstacles in order to improve themselves. Toyota Motor Co. of Japan also had to retract and issue an apology for an ad that ran in magazines and newspapers in China depicting stone lions, a traditional sign of Chinese power, saluting and bowing to a Prado Land Cruiser sport utility vehicle.[33]

Religion is another aspect of culture that affects norms, values, and behaviors. For example, in many Arab countries, advertisers must be aware of various taboos resulting from conservative applications of the Islamic religion. Alcohol and pork cannot be advertised. Human nudity is forbidden, as are pictures of anything sacred, such as images of a cross or photographs of Mecca. The faces of women may not be shown in photos, so cosmetics use drawings of women's faces in ads.[34] In conservative Islamic countries, many religious authorities are opposed to advertising on the grounds that it promotes Western icons and culture and the associated non-Islamic consumerism.[35] Procter & Gamble recently took on tradition in Egypt by underwriting a new groundbreaking TV talk show on feminine hygiene called "Frankly Speaking" that tackles some of the most sensitive issues facing women in an Islamic country. The program has the support of the Egyptian government, which has launched its own health education drive. P&G does not promote its products during the show, but the program does contain numerous commercials for its Always brand, which has 85 percent of the disposable sanitary pad market in the country.[36]

The Political/Legal Environment

The political and legal environment in a country is one of the most important factors influencing the advertising and promotional programs of international marketers. Regulations differ owing to economic and national sovereignty considerations, nationalistic and cultural factors, and the goal of protecting consumers not only from false or misleading advertising but, in some cases, from advertising in general. It is difficult to generalize about advertising regulation at the international level, since some countries are increasing government control of advertising while others are decreasing it. Government regulations and restrictions can affect various aspects of a company's advertising program, including:

- The types of products that may be advertised.
- The content or creative approach that may be used.
- The media that all advertisers (or different classes of advertisers) are permitted to employ.
- The amount of advertising a single advertiser may use in total or in a specific medium.
- The use of foreign languages in ads.

- The use of advertising material prepared outside the country.
- The use of local versus international advertising agencies.
- The specific taxes that may be levied against advertising.[37]

A number of countries ban or restrict the advertising of various products. Cigarette advertising is banned in some or all media in numerous countries besides the United States, including Argentina, Canada, France, Italy, Norway, Sweden, and Switzerland. The Australian government limits tobacco advertising to point of purchase. The ban also excludes tobacco companies from sponsoring sporting events. In Malaysia, a government ban on cigarette-related advertising and sponsorship was initiated in 2003 in an effort to curb the rising number of smokers in the country.[38] In China, tobacco and liquor advertising are banned except in hotels for foreigners.

Recently the tobacco industry has been reducing its advertising efforts in markets around the world, including Asia and Eastern Europe, where they have enjoyed much more regulatory freedom. Three of the largest tobacco companies are leading an effort to implement self-imposed restrictions and requirements for their advertising.[39] For example, the tobacco industry agreed to stop all television advertising in Mexico at the end of 2002 as part of a raft of new self-regulatory measures.[40] Many of these restrictions are already being forced on the companies in North America, Western Europe, and North Asia, where governments take a tough stance on tobacco advertising. However, regulations in many other countries, such as Indonesia and the Philippines, are minimal. The industry's self-regulatory efforts are seen as a move to head off a campaign by the World Health Organization for a worldwide ban on all tobacco advertising.

In Europe there has been a longstanding ban on advertising for prescription-drug products, which is designed to keep government-subsidized health care costs under control. The European Union has argued that advertising increases the marketing budgets of drug companies and results in higher prices. The ban prevents prescription-drug companies from mentioning their products even on their websites or in brochures, although some relaxation of these restrictions is being considered by the European Commission for drugs used to treat AIDS, diabetes, and respiratory ailments.[41]

While international marketers are accustomed to restrictions on the advertising of cigarettes, liquor, and pharmaceuticals, they are often surprised by restrictions on other products or services. For example, margarine cannot be advertised in France, nor can restaurant chains. For many years, the French government restricted travel advertising because it encourages the French to spend their francs outside the country.[42]

Many countries restrict the media advertisers can use. In 1999, the European Commission threw out an appeal against Greece's national ban on toy advertising on daytime television. Thus, advertisers can advertise toys on TV only during the evening hours.[43] Some of the most stringent advertising regulations in the world are found in Scandinavian countries. Commercial TV advertising did not begin in Sweden until 1992, and both Sweden and Denmark limit the amount of time available for commercials. Advertising aimed at young children has not been legal in Sweden since commercial television was introduced in the country a decade ago. The Swedish government believes that young people are not able to differentiate between advertising and programming and are not capable of understanding the selling intent of commercials.[44] Saudi Arabia opened its national TV system to commercial advertising in 1986, but advertising is not permitted on the state-run radio system. Advertising in magazines and newspapers in the country is subject to government and religious restrictions.[45]

Many governments have rules and regulations that affect the advertising message. For example, comparative advertising is legal and widely used in the United States and Canada but is illegal in some countries such as Korea and Belgium. In Europe, the European Commission has developed a directive to standardize the basic form and content of comparative advertising and develop a uniform policy.[46] Currently, comparative advertising is legal in many European countries, illegal in some, and legal and rarely used in others such as Great Britain. Many Asian and South American countries have also begun to accept comparative ads. However, Brazil's self-regulatory advertising codes are so strict that few advertisers have been able to create a comparative message that has been approved.[47] Many countries restrict the types of claims advertisers can make, the words they can use, and the way products can be represented in ads. In Greece, specific claims for a product, such as "20 percent fewer calories," are not permitted in an advertising message.[48] Copyright and other legal restrictions make it difficult to maintain the same name from market to market. For example, Diet Coke is known as Coca-Cola Light in Germany, France, and many other countries because of legal restrictions prohibiting the word *diet* (Exhibit 20-5).

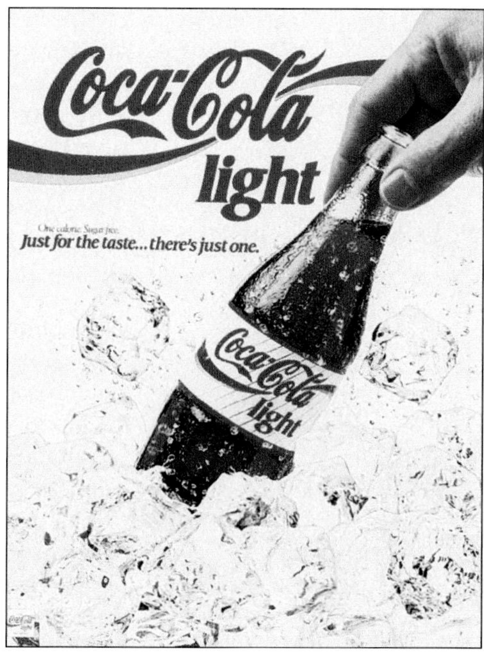

Exhibit 20-5 Diet Coke must use a different name in some countries

China has also begun cracking down on advertising claims as consumer groups slowly become a more powerful force in the country. For years, government regulation of advertising was less stringent than in developed markets and many companies were very aggressive with their advertising claims. However, government officials have begun enforcing a 1995 law that stipulates that statistical claims and quotations "should be true and accurate with sources clearly indicated." In 2005, the Chinese government launched a crackdown on false and illegal ads with a focus on cosmetic, beauty, health, and pharmaceutical products.[49]

Government restrictions can influence the use of foreign languages in advertising as well as the production of the ad. Most countries permit the use of foreign languages in print ads and direct mail. However, some do not allow foreign-language commercials on TV or radio or in cinema ads, and some restrict foreign-language ads to media targeted to foreigners in their country.[50] Some countries also restrict the use of foreign-produced ads and foreign talent. For example, with few exceptions, such as travel advertising, all commercials aired on Malaysian television must be made in Malaysia. However, the Asian country is considering changing its rules to allow foreign commercials to air on the new legalized satellite signals into the country.[51]

These restrictions are motivated primarily by economic considerations. Many countries require local production of at least a portion of commercials to build local film industries and create more jobs for local producers of print and audiovisual materials. Nationalistic and cultural factors also contribute to these restrictions, along with a desire to prevent large foreign ad agencies from dominating the advertising business in a country and thus hampering its development. Restrictions affecting the advertising industry took a new twist recently in China when the government began strictly enforcing regulations governing licenses it requires of magazine publishers. Since the new enforcement took effect on January 1, 2000, Western publishers have been required to use a direct translation of the often-obscure name that appears on their license or use no English name at all. Thus, magazines such as *Cosmopolitan, Esquire,* and *Woman's Day* are not able to use their popular names.[52]

In some countries, steps are being taken to ease some of the legal restrictions and other barriers facing international advertisers. For example, the Maastricht Treaty was designed to create a single European market and remove many of the barriers to trade among the 12 member nations of the European Community. One of the goals of this plan was a single advertising law throughout the EC, but when the treaty was ratified in November 1993, many of the advertising directives were not agreed upon—so many advertising regulations are still decided by each country. A directive was passed by the European Commission banning all tobacco advertising, which most of the 15 European Union countries are now implementing. The European Commission may also take steps to restrict alcohol advertising and marketing. Sweden has been leading a Pan-European effort to ban TV advertising targeted at children under the age of 12 that has been gaining support from other members of the European Union.[53] However, marketers, ad agencies, media, and trade associations in several European countries including the United Kingdom and France have begun pushing for self-regulation that would include efforts to help children understand and interpret advertising effectively rather than banning efforts to reach them.[54] An area that is receiving a great deal of attention in Europe, as well as in the United States, is the marketing and advertising of food products that are considered to contribute to childhood obesity. In 2005, the

European Health Commission called upon advertisers of a variety of food products to set their own regulations to curb the advertising of so-called junk food to the 450 million consumers in the European Union. The commission has also recommended that these companies do not advertise directly to children and has even threatened to ban advertising icons such as Ronald McDonald and Tony the Tiger.[55]

Global versus Localized Advertising

The discussion of differences in the marketing environments of various countries suggests that each market is different and requires a distinct marketing and advertising program. However, in recent years a great deal of attention has focused on the concept of **global marketing,** where a company uses a common marketing plan for all countries in which it operates, thus selling the product in essentially the same way everywhere in the world. **Global advertising** falls under the umbrella of global marketing as a way to implement this strategy by using the same basic advertising approach in all markets.

The debate over standardization versus localization of marketing and advertising programs began years ago.[56] But the idea of global marketing was popularized by Professor Theodore Levitt, who says the worldwide marketplace has become homogenized and consumers' basic needs, wants, and expectations transcend geographic, national, and cultural boundaries.[57] One writer described Levitt's position on global marketing as follows:

> Levitt's vision of total worldwide standardization is global marketing at the extreme. He argues that, thanks to cheap air travel and new telecommunications technology, consumers the world over are thinking—and shopping—increasingly alike. According to Levitt, the New Republic of Technology homogenizes world tastes, wants, and possibilities into global marketing proportions, which allows for world standardized products.[58]

Not everyone agrees with Levitt's global marketing theory, particularly with respect to advertising. Many argue that products and advertising messages must be designed or at least adapted to meet the differing needs of consumers in different countries.[59] We will consider the arguments for and against global marketing and advertising, as well as situations where it is most appropriate.

Advantages of Global Marketing and Advertising

A global marketing strategy and advertising program offer certain advantages to a company, including the following:

- Economies of scale in production and distribution.
- Lower marketing and advertising costs as a result of reductions in planning and control.
- Lower advertising production costs.
- Abilities to exploit good ideas on a worldwide basis and introduce products quickly into various world markets.
- A consistent international brand and/or company image.
- Simplification of coordination and control of marketing and promotional programs.

Advocates of global marketing and advertising contend that standardized products are possible in all countries if marketers emphasize quality, reliability, and low prices. They say people everywhere want to buy the same products and live the same way. Product standardization results in lower design and production costs as well as greater marketing efficiency, which translates into lower prices for consumers. Product standardization and global marketing also enable companies to roll out products faster into world markets, which is becoming increasingly important as product life cycles become shorter and competition increases.

A number of companies, including IBM, DeBeers, Merrill Lynch, British Airways, and American Express, have successfully used the global advertising approach. Gillette has used the "Best a Man Can Get" as its global advertising theme for over a decade and has launched a number of new razor products including the Sensor, Mach3, and Mach3 Turbo using a global approach.[60] Gillette uses the same advertising theme in each country and maintains websites with similar content and layout, with only language differences. Exhibit 20-6 shows Gillette's German website for the M3 Power razor. In 2006, Gillette introduced its revolutionary six-bladed Fusion shaver with a nearly $1 billion global campaign featuring British soccer star David Beckham.[61]

Exhibit 20-6 Gillette uses a global approach to market its razors in various countries, such as Germany

Problems with Global Advertising

Opponents of the standardized global approach argue that very few products lend themselves to global advertising.[62] Differences in culture, market, and economic development; consumer needs and usage patterns; media availabilities; and legal restrictions make it extremely difficult to develop an effective universal approach to marketing and advertising. Advertising may be particularly difficult to standardize because of cultural differences in circumstances, language, traditions, values, beliefs, lifestyle, music, and so on. Moreover, some experts argue that cultures around the world are becoming more diverse, not less so. Thus, advertising's job of informing and persuading consumers and moving them toward using a particular brand can be done only within a given culture.

Consumer usage patterns and perceptions of a product may vary from one country to another, so advertisers must adjust their marketing and advertising approaches to different problems they may face in different markets. For example, when Nestlé introduced its Nescafé instant coffee brand, the company faced at least five different situations in various parts of the world:

1. In the United States, the idea of instant coffee had great penetration but Nescafé had the minor share.
2. In continental Europe, Nescafé had the major share of the market, but the idea of instant coffee was in the early stages.
3. In the tea-drinking countries, such as the United Kingdom and Japan, tea drinkers had to be converted not just to coffee but to instant coffee.
4. In Latin America, the preferred coffee was a heavy one that could not be duplicated with an instant version.
5. In Scandinavia, Nestlé had to deal with the ingrained custom of keeping a pot of coffee on the stove from early morning until late at night.

Nestlé had to use different advertising strategies for each market; a global campaign would not have been able to address the varying situations adequately. Exhibit 20-7 shows Nescafé ads used in Japan and Norway. Nestlé encountered yet another challenge when it entered the Israeli market in 1995. *Nescafé* was the generic word for instant coffee as Israelis assumed that it was an abbreviation of the Hebrew word *namess* (dissolving). Israeli consumers were also not very demanding with respect to the quality of their coffee and considered the low-quality powdered coffee, or *nescafé,* produced by a local company, suitable fare. To overcome the generic connotation of Nescafé, all of the advertising

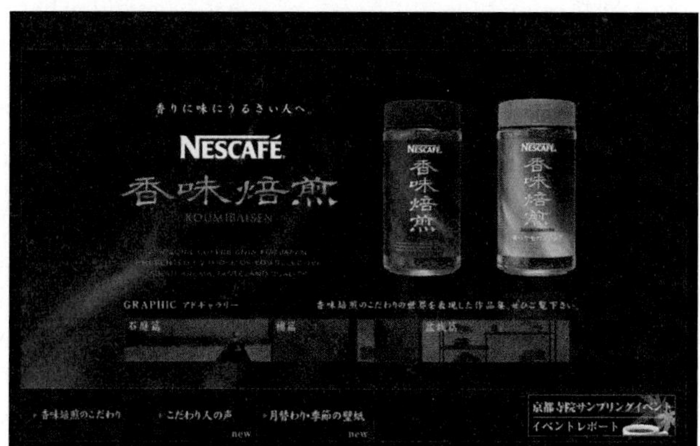

Exhibit 20-7 (A) Nescafé instant coffee ad used in Japan. (B) Nescafé Gull instant coffee ad used in Norway

presented the Nescafé Classic brand as "Nescafé of Nestlé" and portrayed it as the coffee choice of people all around the world (Exhibit 20-8). The company also relied on taste testing at the points of sale so consumers could experience Nescafé Classic's superior quality. Within one year Nestlé had 30 percent of the instant coffee market in Israel.[63]

Exhibit 20-8 Nestlé had to reshape Israel's definition of instant coffee

Many experts believe that marketing a standardized product the same way all over the world can turn off consumers, alienate employees, and blind a company to diversities in customer needs. For example, when McDonald's expanded to Puerto Rico, it alienated consumers by using American TV ads dubbed in Spanish and then using Hispanic ads that were brought in from New York, which subsequent research showed looked too Mexican.[64]

Multinational companies can also encounter problems when they use global advertising as local managers in countries or regions often resent the home office standardizing the advertising function and mandating the type of advertising used in their markets. Sir Martin Sorrell, Chairman of the United Kingdom–based WPP Group, argues that there are limits to global advertising and that the one-size-fits-all pendulum has gone too far. He urges his executives to focus on consumer needs in the countries they serve and advocates the use of country managers to build contacts and adapt campaigns to local markets.[65]

Some major companies are moving away from a completely standardized approach. For example, the Colgate-Palmolive Co. has used global advertising for many of its brands, including the Colgate, Palmolive, Fab, and Ajax product lines, and continues to endorse the use of global appeals. Under its current marketing strategy, however, advertising is often modified for a specific country or region, particularly where local creativity can improve the advertising over the global standard. An example of this approach is the advertising used for Colgate toothpaste in Russian (see Exhibit 20-9). The globe/smile image is used as the visual in nearly every country where Colgate is marketed, but the copy varies.

Exhibit 20-9 Advertising for Colgate toothpaste uses a consistent visual image, but the copy may vary for different markets

Some marketing experts claim much of the attention to the advantages of global advertising stems from large ad agencies trying to increase business by encouraging clients to use one agency to handle their marketing communications worldwide.[66] Many large multinational companies are indeed consolidating their business with one or a few agencies who have offices around the world and offer international advertising capabilities. However, the consolidations are often driven by the client's increasing emphasis on global markets.[67]

When Is Globalization Appropriate?

While globalization of advertising is viewed by many in the advertising industry as a difficult task, some progress has been made in learning what products and services are best suited to worldwide appeals:[68]

1. Brands or messages that can be adapted for a visual appeal, avoiding the problems of trying to translate words into dozens of languages.
2. Brands that are promoted with image campaigns that play to universal needs, values, and emotions.
3. High-tech products and new products coming to the world for the first time, not steeped in the cultural heritage of the country.
4. Products with nationalistic flavor if the country has a reputation in the field.

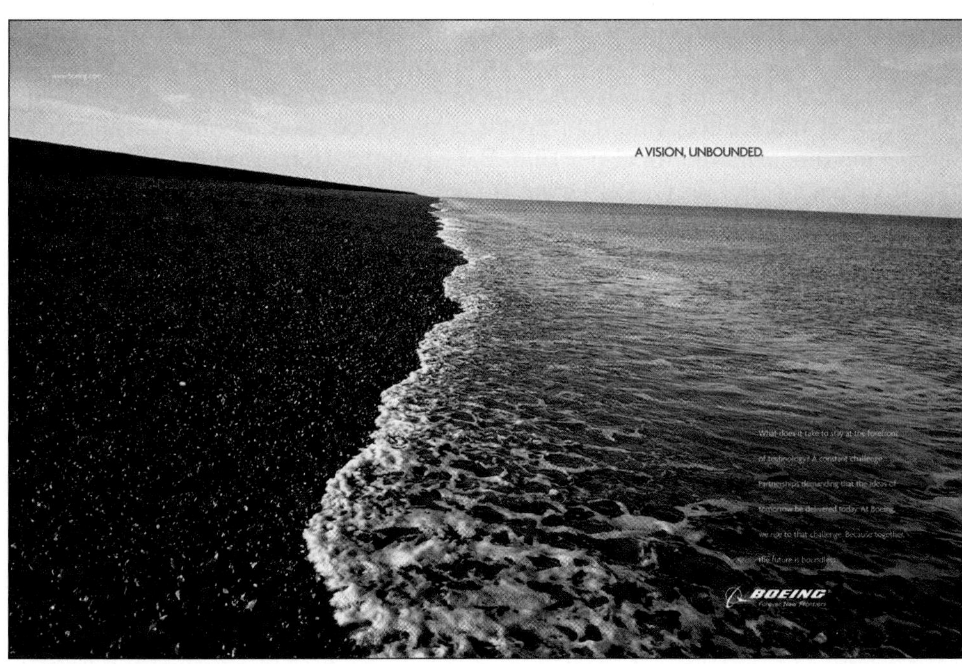

Exhibit 20-10 Visual appeals work well in global advertising, such as that used by the Boeing company

5. Products that appeal to a market segment with universally similar tastes, interests, needs, and values.

Many companies and brands rely heavily on visual appeals that are easily adapted for use in global advertising campaigns. For example, Boeing launched its first global image campaign in 2000 as part of its effort to be known as more than an airplane manufacturer. While Boeing is the world's leading manufacturer of commercial jets, a series of acquisitions has transformed the company into a major force in markets for military aircraft, rockets, satellites, and broadband communications. Boeing is setting the stage for its future with a global image and branding campaign that uses the tagline "Boeing Forever New Frontiers." The corporate campaign features TV spots as well as print ads, such as the one shown in Exhibit 20-10, that symbolize optimism and future orientation.

Products such as jewelry, liquor, cosmetics, and cigarettes can be promoted using image advertising, the second category. Marlboro uses its cowboy/western imagery around the world, and many cosmetic companies use similar image campaigns in different countries.

Levitt, like many advertisers, believes that joy, sentiment, excitement, and many other emotions are universal. Thus, it is common for global advertising campaigns to use emotional and image appeals. One advertising executive said:

> What it all boils down to is that we are all human. We share the gift of emotional response. We feel things. And we feel them in remarkably similar ways. We speak different languages, we observe different customs, but we are wired to each other and to an ultimate power source that transcends us in a way that makes us subject to a common emotional spectrum.[69]

Companies whose products appeal to universal needs, values, and emotions are also recognizing that they can advertise their brands with global campaigns. For example, Calvin Klein, one of the leading fashion and design companies and a brand name recognized around the world, has used global campaigns for its clothing and fragrance brands. Mazda used its first-ever global campaign in 2005 to launch the new MX-5 Miata sports car (formerly known as the Miata). The "Be the Car" campaign targets male drivers in various countries with ads that focus on the more aggressive body styling of the MX5-Miata and appeal to the oneness between the car and driver.[70]

High-tech products such as mobile phones, personal computers, DVD players, plasma and LCD television sets, videogames, and MP3 players are products in the third category. Marketers of business-to-business products and services such as Hewlett-Packard, IBM, and Citigroup have also used global campaigns for their companies and product lines.

Products in the fourth category are those whose national reputation for quality can be the basis for a global advertising campaign. Examples include Swiss watches, French wine, and German beer or automobiles. Many U.S. companies are taking advantage of the cachet American products have acquired among consumers in Europe and other international markets. For example, Jeep promotes itself as "the American legend" in Europe and Japan. Brown-Forman has been using an American theme for its Jack Daniel's and Southern Comfort liquor brands since it began selling them in foreign markets more than two decades ago.

In the final category for which globalization is appropriate are products and services that can be sold to common market segments around the world, such as those identified by Salah Hassan and Lea Katsansis.[71] One such segment is the world's elite—people who, by reason of their economically privileged position, can pursue a lifestyle that includes fine jewelry, expensive clothing, quality automobiles, and the like. Marketers of high-quality products such as Bally leather goods, Cartier jewelry, Godiva chocolates, and Louis Vuitton luggage can use global advertising to appeal to the elite market segment around the world. Well-known international brands competing in the luxury goods marketplace often present a singular image of prestige and style to the entire world.

An example of a marketer of luxury products that uses global advertising is Swiss watchmaker TAG Heuer, who targets upscale consumers, many of whom are world travelers. Thus, the company feels that it is important to have a consistent advertising message and image in each country. Creative elements of TAG Heuer ads such as the layout, logo, pictures of the product, slogan, and tagline remain clear, consistent, and visually recognizable at first glance all over the world. The only element of the ad that changes from country to country is the celebrity ambassador who appears in the ad. For example, actor Brad Pitt is used in TAG Heuer ads in Europe and Asia as is race car driver Kimi Raiknonen. In India, the ambassadors include A-list Bollywood actors and actresses such as Sushmita Sen, and in the United States the ambassadors include Tiger Woods and Uma Thurman (Exhibit 20-11).

Another segment of global consumers who have similar needs and interests and seek similar features and benefits from products and services is teenagers. There are more than 200 million teens in Europe, Latin America, and the Pacific Rim countries of Asia whose lifestyles are converging with those of the 40 million teens in the United States and Canada to create a vast, free-spending global market.[72] Teens now have intense exposure to television, magazines, movies, music, travel, and global advertising from companies such as Levi Strauss, Benetton, Nike, Coca-Cola, Pepsi, and many others. MTV is now seen in 136 countries.

Exhibit 20-11 TAG Heuer uses a global campaign featuring different celebrity ambassadors for various countries

Global Products, Local Messages

While the pros and cons of global marketing and advertising continue to be debated, many companies are taking an in-between approach by standardizing their products and basic marketing strategy but localizing their advertising messages. This approach recognizes similar desires, goals, needs, and uses for products and services but tailors advertising to the local cultures and conditions in each market. Some agencies call this approach "Think globally, act locally" while others describe it as "global vision with a local touch."

Although some marketers use global ads with little or no modification, most companies adapt their messages to respond to differences in language, market conditions, and other factors. Many global marketers use a strategy called **pattern advertising;** their ads follow a basic approach, but themes, copy, and sometimes even visual elements are adapted to differences in local markets. For example, Unilever's Dove soap uses the same basic advertising and positioning theme globally, but models from Australia, France, Germany, and Italy are used to appeal to women in those countries.

Another company that uses pattern advertising is the TaylorMade golf company, recognized globally as having the leading brand of drivers. However, the brand positioning is different in various countries such as the United States and the United Kingdom. In the United States, TaylorMade is a premium brand founded on innovation while in the United Kingdom it is still somewhat of a value brand, resulting from discounting in the retail environment. Exhibit 20-12 shows ads used by TaylorMade in 2005 when the British Open Golf Tournament was held at St. Andrews in Scotland, which is considered to be the birthplace of golf. While the ads are similar, the focus in the American ad is on a connection to the game at the highest level, and the ad is used as a simple "Thank you for the game" tribute to St. Andrews. In the United Kingdom, where TaylorMade still needs product validation from association with major golf championships, the focus in the ad was on the historic dominance of events such as the British Open through recent wins and continuing to be the most used driver at major tournaments worldwide.

Another way global marketers adapt their campaigns to local markets is by producing a variety of ads with a similar theme and format and allowing managers in various countries or regions to select those messages they believe will work best in their markets. Some companies are also giving local managers more autonomy in adapting global campaign themes to local markets. For example, Coca-Cola recently developed a new model for its global advertising and brand communication model: Rather than authorizing the heads of individual markets to run their own advertising, various regions of the world are consolidated into a series of hubs or clusters.

Exhibit 20-12

TaylorMade uses pattern advertising with different messages to promote its ads in the United States and United Kingdom

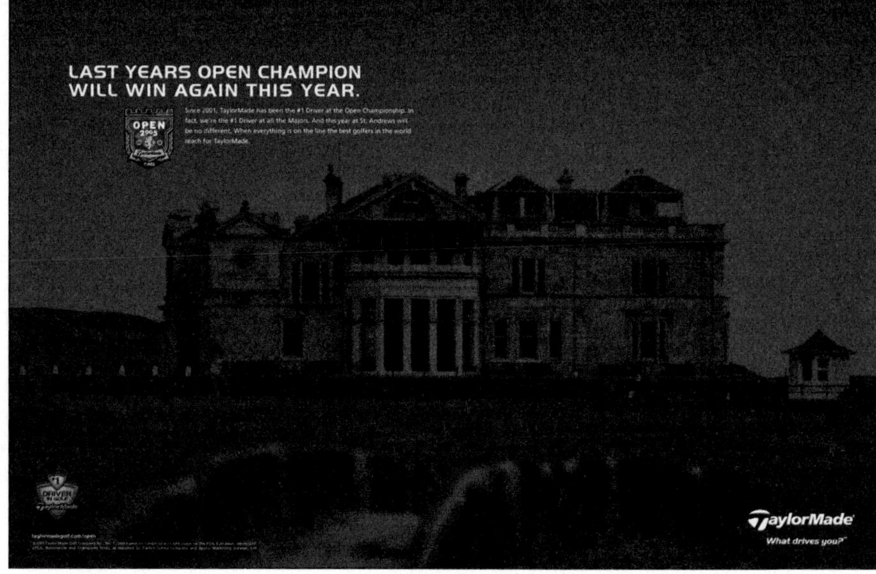

Although the company provides local marketing support for each cluster, a global team oversees creative work that can be used in various markets, thus allowing for fewer creative executions. Coca-Cola's chief creative officer notes that the new structure "allows us to feel more like global brands with local relevance."[73]

Although many marketers are striving to develop global brands, research suggests most are doing so by using a localized approach. A study of international advertising strategies of successful U.S. multinational corporations found that only 9 percent used totally standardized global advertising for all foreign markets, while 37 percent used all localized advertising. The remaining 54 percent used a combination strategy, standardizing portions of their advertising but adapting it for local markets.[74] Marketers said a major risk of the global approach was a lack of communication owing to cultural differences. Another study found that most U.S. consumer durable goods manufacturers used a localized advertising approach—but most used some standardized messages.[75]

A more recent study of international advertising decision makers found that "think globally, act locally" still appears to be the dominant strategy of international advertisers, but with a slight revision: "Think globally, act regionally."[76] Most of the respondents in this survey said their companies' worldwide headquarters play a dominant role in determining their international advertising messages so they are consistent worldwide. However, there is a trend toward giving regional offices the autonomy to adapt the global theme for their local markets. A number of U.S. companies have had to move away from global campaigns recently to deal with the problem of the anti-American sentiment that has developed in many countries. Global Perspective 20-2 discusses the reasons why attitudes toward the United States have become more negative and how the business community is responding to this problem.

Most managers believe it is important to adapt components of their advertising messages—such as the language, models, scenic backgrounds, message content, and symbols—to reflect the culture and frame of reference of consumers in various countries. Many companies are making these tactical adjustments to their advertising messages while still pursuing global strategies that will help them project a consistent global image and turn their products and services into global brands.

Decision Areas in International Advertising

Companies developing advertising and promotional programs for international markets must make certain organizational and functional decisions similar to those for domestic markets. These decisions include organization style, agency selection, advertising research, creative strategy and execution, and media strategy and selection.

Organizing for International Advertising

One of the first decisions a company must make when it decides to market its products to other countries is how to organize the international advertising and promotion function. This decision is likely to depend on how the company is organized overall for international marketing and business. Three basic options are centralization at the home office or headquarters, decentralization of decision making to local foreign markets, or a combination of the two.

Centralization

Many companies prefer to *centralize* the international advertising and promotion function so that all decisions about agency selection, research, creative strategy and campaign development, media strategy, and budgeting are made at the firm's home office.

Complete centralization is likely when market and media conditions are similar from one country to another, when the company has only one or a few international agencies handling all of its advertising, when the company can use standardized advertising, or when it desires a consistent image worldwide. Centralization may also be best when a company's international business is small and it operates through foreign distributors or licensees who do not become involved in the marketing and promotional process.

GLOBAL PERSPECTIVE 20-2

U.S. Brands Deal with Anti-American Sentiment

The past several years has seen an alarming rise in anti-American sentiment around the globe. Resentment toward the United States has been caused by several factors including the war in Iraq and the government's go-it-alone attitude in recent years, which has shaped the country's position and policies on various political, economic, and environmental issues. Although much of the anti-Americanism is targeted toward the U.S. government, businesspeople are concerned that the growing hostility is spilling over into negative attitudes toward American people and brands. A recent study by the Council of Foreign Relations found that the image of U.S. brands is indeed being battered along with the country's image.

The rise in anti-American sentiment is causing a great deal of concern in the U.S. business community as many believe that it is only a matter of time until the negative attitudes begin to affect behavior. In 2004, a private-sector task force called Business for Diplomatic Action (BDA) was founded by Keith Reinhard, the chairman of the DDB Worldwide agency, and Thomas Miller, a former executive with the NOP World research firm. The mission statement of the BDA is: "To sensitize American companies and individuals to the rise of anti-Americanism in the world and to enlist the U.S. business community in specific actions aimed at addressing the issue and reducing the problem."

The BDA notes that while much of the anti-American sentiment is related to perceptions of U.S. foreign policy, research also points to other deeply rooted causes. One of these is the effects of globalization as people in other countries think that the global business expansion of American companies has been exploitive and they can never be part of or enjoy the benefits of it. They feel that American companies have not truly engaged or partnered with them in a meaningful way and believe that they are left out of the globalization movement. Other root causes are the perceptions that Americans are insensitive and lack humility as a people. Many find that American culture has become too all pervasive such that the values promoted by American companies and brands threaten their local and national cultural values.

The negative sentiment toward America is changing the way U.S. companies promote themselves and their brands abroad.

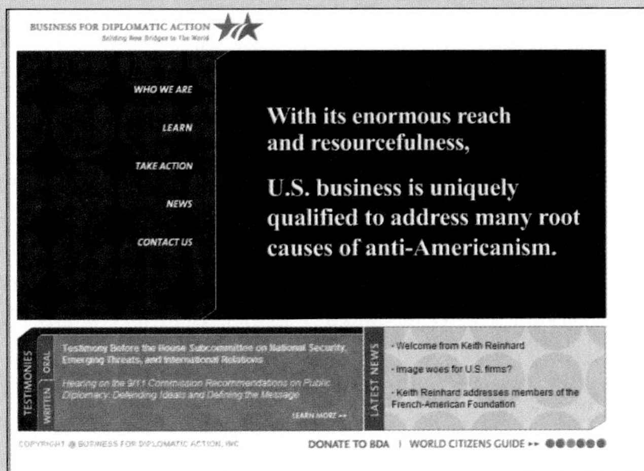

Gone are the days when U.S. brands boasted about their national heritage, and many are working hard to give their products more of a local appeal. They are attempting to weave their products into the local culture by hiring local managers and adapting everything from product content to packaging to marketing communications to local markets. For example, Nike features soccer stars and other local athletes in its ads for various European, Asian, and Latin American countries. PepsiCo uses British soccer star David Beckham in its commercials in the United Kingdom. PepsiCo has also nurtured a homegrown image in India by using local celebrities in ads as well as by sponsoring the hugely popular sport of cricket.

Although many companies are adapting their marketing programs to local markets and remaining low-key about their country of origin, American brands continue to do very well around the world. U.S. labels have dominated the annual *BusinessWeek*/Interbrand ranking of the most valuable global brands for a number of years. In the 2005 ranking, 53 U.S. brands were among the top 100, including 8 of the top 10 spots. A number of top-ranked brands such as Coca-Cola, Microsoft, and McDonald's have risen above the noise of political dissent and are experiencing stronger growth overseas than at home. Many companies still believe that consumers in other countries remain fascinated with American lifestyles and that promoting an American image gives their brands a certain cachet that makes them popular, particularly among younger generations.

Some marketing experts argue that in today's world of globalization, consumers are only vaguely aware of the country of origin for many of the brands that they buy. The experts believe that even when the consumers can identify the national origin of a multinational brand, they are more inclined to think of it as a global product rather than one associated with a particular country. Harvard Business School professor John Quelch notes that only a small percentage of consumers around the world will not buy global brands and questions whether the average consumer in the world is going to let his or her view of American foreign policy affect his or her brand choice behavior.

While many American brands are still doing well around the globe, the Business for Diplomatic Action task force is concerned that purchasing behavior may soon follow the anti-American attitude and is taking steps to address the problem. The group has already published a quarter of a million copies of the *World Citizens Guide,* a publication underwritten by PepsiCo and UPS for U.S. students overseas. The BDA is also working with companies, governments, and media organizations to change attitudes toward America. The U.S. government has recognized the need to change world opinion and in 2005 awarded contracts worth a total of $300 million to ad agencies to conduct media campaigns to garner support for U.S. government policies and objectives in foreign countries.

Sources: Ira Teinowtiz, "Brands Feel Pain of U.S. Image Woes," *Advertising Age,* May 23, 2005, pp. 1, 150; Peter Gumbel, "Branding America," *Time,* March 13, 2005, pp. A13–14; Gerry Khermouch and Diane Brady, "Brands in an Age of Anti-Americanism," *BusinessWeek,* August 4, 2003, pp. 69–71.

Many companies prefer the centralized organizational structure to protect their foreign investments and keep control of the marketing effort and corporate and/or brand image. Centralization can save money, since it reduces the need for staff and administration at the local subsidiary level. As the trend toward globalized marketing and advertising strategies continues, more companies are likely to move more toward centralization of the advertising function to maintain a unified world brand image rather than presenting a different image in each market. Some foreign managers may actually prefer centralized decision making, as it removes them from the burden of advertising and promotional decisions and saves them from defending local decisions to the home office.

However, many marketing and advertising managers in foreign markets oppose centralized control. They say the structure is too rigid and makes it difficult to adapt the advertising and promotional program to local needs and market conditions. Parker Pen encountered such resistance when it attempted to implement a global advertising strategy in the mid-1980s.

Decentralization

Under a *decentralized* organizational structure, marketing and advertising managers in each market have the authority to make their own advertising and promotional decisions. Local managers can select ad agencies, develop budgets, conduct research, approve creative themes and executions, and select advertising media. Companies using a decentralized approach put a great deal of faith in the judgment and decision-making ability of personnel in local markets. This approach is often used when companies believe local managers know the marketing situation in their countries the best. They may also be more effective and motivated when given responsibility for the advertising and promotional program in their markets. Decentralization also works well in small or unique markets where headquarters' involvement is not worthwhile or advertising must be tailored to the local market.

International fragrance marketer Chanel, Inc., uses a decentralized strategy. Chanel found that many of its fragrance concepts do not work well globally and decided to localize advertising. For example, the U.S. office has the option of using ads created by the House of Chanel in Paris or developing its own campaigns for the U.S. market. Chanel executives in the United States think that the French concept of prestige is not the same as Americans' and the artsy ads created in France do not work well in this country.[77]

Combination

While there is an increasing trend toward centralizing the international advertising function, many companies combine the two approaches. The home office, or headquarters, has the most control over advertising policy, guidelines, and operations in all markets. The international advertising manager works closely with local or regional marketing managers and personnel from the international agency (or agencies) and sets advertising and promotional objectives, has budgetary authority, approves all creative themes and executions, and approves media selection decisions, especially when they are made on a regional basis or overlap with other markets.

Advertising managers in regional or local offices submit advertising plans and budgets for their markets, which are reviewed by the international advertising manager. Local managers play a major role in working with the agency to adapt appeals to their particular markets and select media.

The combination approach allows for consistency in a company's international advertising yet permits local input and adaptation of the promotion program. Most consumer-product companies find that local adaptation of advertising is necessary for foreign markets or regions, but they want to maintain control of the overall worldwide image they project. Kodak, for example, provides central strategy and support to local offices and acts as consultant to them. Although each country is autonomous, the main office controls the quality of advertising and advertising policy. Media buying is done on a local level, but the main office becomes involved in special media opportunities and overall strategy for events such as Olympic sponsorship and regionalized campaigns. Levi's created a centralized vice president of global marketing position to oversee the company's marketing in over 60 countries but still provides a great deal of autonomy to regional marketing directors.

Agency Selection

One of the most important decisions for a firm engaged in international marketing is the choice of an advertising agency. The company has three basic alternatives in selecting an agency to handle its international advertising. First, it can choose a major agency with both domestic and overseas offices. Many large agencies have offices all over the world and have become truly international operations. Some Western agencies have opened offices in Eastern Europe and Russia to create ads for the multinational companies participating in the free-market economies that are developing in these countries. Many agencies are moving their offices from Hong Kong to Shanghai to be closer to the world's largest consumer market, on the mainland of China.[78]

Many American companies prefer to use a U.S.-based agency with foreign offices; this gives them greater control and convenience and also facilitates coordination of overseas advertising. Companies often use the same agency to handle international and domestic advertising. As discussed in Chapter 3, the flurry of mergers and acquisitions in the ad agency business in recent years, both in the United States and in other countries, has created large global agencies that can meet the international needs of global marketers. A number of multinational companies have consolidated their advertising with one large agency. The consolidation trend began in 1994 when IBM dismissed 40 agencies around the world and awarded its entire account to Ogilvy & Mather Worldwide.[79] A year later, Colgate-Palmolive consolidated all of its global advertising with New York–based Young & Rubicam. The move, which followed the worldwide restructuring of Colgate's manufacturing and distribution system, marked the first time a large multibrand advertiser put all of its billings with one agency.[80]

There are a number of reasons why global marketers consolidate their advertising with one agency. Many companies recognize they must develop a consistent global image for the company and/or its brands and speak with one coordinated marketing voice around the world. For example, IBM officials felt the company had been projecting too many images when its advertising was divided among so many agencies. The consolidation enabled IBM to present a single brand identity throughout the world while taking advantage of one of the world's best-known brand names (Exhibit 20-13). In 2005 IBM sold its personal computer business to the Lenovo Group, the largest manufacturer and marketer of computer systems in China. However, Lenovo retained Ogilvy & Mather to handle its global advertising and to build brands such as the ThinkPad notebooks, the Tablet, and ThinkCentre desktops. Lenovo is drawing off the strong brand heritage of the IBM PC products and using the same agency to maintain a consistent image for the brands.[81]

Exhibit 20-13 IBM uses the Ogilvy & Mather agency to handle all of its global advertising

Companies are also consolidating their global advertising in an effort to increase efficiency and gain greater leverage over their agencies. Colgate notes that a major reason for its agency consolidation is to achieve greater cost efficiency. The company has moved into 25 new countries in recent years and increased its advertising and promotional spending in many markets around the globe. Consolidation has generated savings that can be invested in additional advertising. Consolidation also gives advertisers greater leverage over their agencies. When a major client puts all of its advertising with one agency, that company often becomes the agency's most important account. And, as one IBM executive notes, "You become a magnet for talent and attention."[82]

Advertising executives also noted that a major reason for all of the account consolidation is that agencies now have the ability to communicate and manage globally. Fax machines, e-mail, and airline connections make it much easier to manage accounts around the globe. Of course, placing an entire global advertising account with one agency can be risky. If the agency fails to deliver an effective campaign, the client has no backup agency to make a fast rebound and the search for a new agency can be very time-consuming. Clients who consolidate also face the problem of selling the idea to regional offices, which often previously enjoyed their own local agency relationship. However, it appears that more and more companies are willing to take these risks and rely on one agency to handle their advertising around the world.

A second alternative for the international marketer is to choose an agency that, rather than having its own foreign offices or branches, is affiliated with agencies in other countries or belongs to a network of foreign agencies. A domestic agency may acquire an interest in several foreign agencies or become part of an organization of international agencies. The agency can then sell itself as an international agency offering multinational coverage and contacts. Many of the large agency holding companies such as the WPP Group, Publicis Groupe, Omincom, and the Interpublic Group own agencies throughout the world that can handle their clients' advertising in various countries. For example, the Korean consumer electronics giant Samsung recently awarded its global brand advertising account to the WPP Group, which is based in London. While Berlin Cameron/Red Cell New York is the lead creative agency, other WPP agencies such as J. Walter Thompson work on the account along with media companies such as MindShare and Group M.[83]

The advantage of this arrangement is that the client can use a domestic-based agency yet still have access to foreign agencies with detailed knowledge of market conditions, media, and so on in each local market. There may be problems with this approach, however. The local agency may have trouble coordinating and controlling independent agencies, and the quality of work may vary among network members. Companies considering this option must ask the local agency about its ability to control the activities of its affiliates and the quality of their work in specific areas such as creative and media.

The third alternative for the international marketer is to select a local agency for each national market in which it sells its products or services. Since local agencies often have the best understanding of the marketing and advertising environment in their country or region, they may be able to develop the most effective advertising.

Some companies like local agencies because they may provide the best talent in each market. In many countries, smaller agencies may, because of their independence, be more willing to take risks and develop the most effective, creative ads. Choosing local agencies also increases the involvement and morale of foreign subsidiary managers by giving them responsibility for managing the promotion function in their markets. Some companies have the subsidiary choose a local agency, since it is often in the best position to evaluate the agency and will work closely with it.

Criteria for Agency Selection

The selection of an agency to handle a company's international advertising depends on how the firm is organized for international marketing and the type of assistance it needs to meet its goals and objectives in foreign markets. Figure 20-3 lists some criteria a company might use in selecting an agency. In a study conducted among marketing directors of European companies, creative capability was ranked the most important factor in selecting an advertising agency network, followed by understanding of the market, understanding of marketing goals, and

Figure 20-3 Criteria for Selecting an Agency to Handle International Advertising

- Ability of agency to cover relevant markets
- Quality of agency work
- Market research, public relations, and other services offered by agency
- Relative roles of company advertising department and agency
- Level of communication and control desired by company
- Ability of agency to coordinate international campaign
- Size of company's international business
- Company's desire for local versus international image
- Company organizational structure for international business and marketing (centralized versus decentralized)
- Company's level of involvement with international operations

CAREER PROFILE

Joanne Redmond, Advertising Manager

IBM Global Services

Travel. Excitement. Glamour. These are terms commonly associated with the world of advertising. Fatigue. Last minute deadlines. A scramble to get the work out the door in time. These are less known words to describe the profession. Which group best describes life in advertising? Both.

My career in marketing began nearly 20 years ago when I entered the real world, Kent State University bachelor's degree tightly in hand, as an English-language teacher. After my first year in the public schools, a flux of Japanese families moved to my community, and I was referred to one as a language tutor. Once I had one family signed up for English lessons, I soon had them all. I left my teaching job and began my first business venture, an entrepreneur working with Japanese expatriates. I decided my skills were better suited for the business world (how is anyone in their early twenties supposed to decide what they want to do for the rest of their life?) and began pursuing an MBA at the University of Akron while continuing to work with international families. During this time, I studied the Japanese language with vigor. When I couldn't find a good book to study, I wrote one, called *Beginner's Japanese.* Its fifth edition will be released by Hippocrene Books in 2006.

After earning my MBA and publishing my first book, I wondered, "Where could a person with teaching skills, writing ability, and an entrepreneurial flair find a career that would utilize all of these diverse talents?" The answer: Marketing. Teaching and marketing go hand in hand. As an instructor, you have to know your students and understand what makes them tick. You also have valuable information you want to communicate to them, and you need to do it in a way that's compelling and motivating. Marketing is the same—you must know your target audience, be well versed in their pain points, and position your product/information/service in a way that spurs them to action.

"The world of advertising is not for the faint of heart."

Soon after earning my MBA, I was hired by an international plastics supplier, A. Schulman. A year into the job, I observed the firm lacked a cohesive marketing communications strategy—each product line had its own logo, brand image, advertising, and collateral. I made a proposal to the president of the company recommending we integrate all marketing communications activities under one umbrella. The president agreed this was a good idea, and a new department was born. While I enjoyed working for A. Schulman, and learned a great deal about the world of advertising and marketing, I eventually longed to work for a company where campaigns could be executed on a larger scale, where I could use my Japanese language skills, and where I could work for one of the most recognized brands in the world. I set my eyes on New York City.

In 1999, IBM hired me to work in the marketing communications department of their largest, fastest growing division, Global Services. Many of the challenges I encountered in my previous firm were similar: different business units communicating their services to the marketplace in a not-so-cohesive fashion. My team worked to develop a more unified approach to our client base. One great aspect of working for IBM is that you can have a variety of different jobs over the course of your career. After working for the IBM Global Services worldwide team in marketing and advertising for a few years, I became the marketing communications manager for Asia Pacific, where I helped oversee the advertising, events, Internet activities, and collateral for the region. In my current role of advertising manager for IBM Global Services, I help develop the strategy and execution of our division's campaigns. Working in advertising requires multiple hats. I have to liaise between IBM's marketing management and our advertising agency, Ogilvy & Mather; attend focus groups to ensure our messaging and copy resonate with our target; participate in photoshoots; and put out fires from time to time.

The current campaign I'm working on strives to expand the IBM brand to be recognized as not just a world-leading technology firm, but also a company that provides business consulting services. The campaign, highlighting "The OTHER IBM," contains television, print, online, and outdoor advertising in the United States, Europe, and Asia. Results to date show that clients are beginning to view IBM as a leading provider of both business and information technology solutions.

The world of advertising is not for the faint of heart. But if you enjoy the thrill of seeing your work on the back of a passerby's newspaper or on a billboard above Times Square, work well under pressure and fluctuating deadlines, and don't mind hectic hours, you'll find a world that is satisfying and rewarding.

ability to produce integrated communications. Size of the agency and agency reputation were cited as important criteria by less than 2 percent of the respondents.[84] Another recent study found that most clients choose an agency based on its creative reputation and the creative presentation it had made. However, a large number of clients felt their agencies lacked international expertise and account coordination ability.[85]

Some companies choose a combination of the three alternatives just discussed because their involvement in each market differs, as do the advertising environment and situation in each country. Several experts in international marketing and advertising advocate the use of international agencies by international companies, particularly those firms moving toward global marketing and striving for a consistent corporate or brand image around the world. The trend toward mergers and acquisitions and the formation of mega-agencies with global marketing and advertising capabilities suggests the international agency approach will become the preferred arrangement among large companies.

Advertising Research

Research plays the same important role in the development of international advertising and promotion programs that it does domestically—helping managers make better, more informed decisions. However, many companies do not conduct advertising research in international markets. Probably the main reason for this is the high cost of conducting research in foreign markets, coupled with the limited budgets many firms have for international advertising and promotion. When international markets represent a small percentage of overall sales, investments in research are difficult to justify. Rather than quality marketing information, generalizations based on casual observations of foreign markets have guided the promotional process.

As companies increase their investment in international marketing, they are recognizing the importance of conducting marketing and advertising research to better understand the characteristics and subtleties of consumers in foreign markets. There are a number of areas where research on foreign markets can help firms make better advertising decisions:

- Information on demographic characteristics of markets.
- Information on cultural differences such as norms, lifestyles, and values.
- Information on consumers' product usage, brand attitudes, and media preferences.
- Information on media usage and audience size.
- Copy testing to determine reactions to different types of advertising appeals and executions.
- Research on the effectiveness of advertising and promotional programs in foreign markets.

Exhibit 20-14 The *World Fact Book* is a valuable source of information on different countries

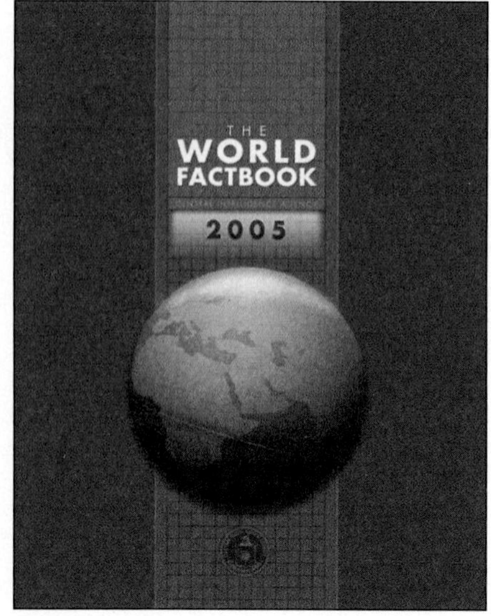

A great deal of information on international markets is available through secondary sources. One of the most valuable sources of information for companies based in this country is the U.S. Department of Commerce, which works closely with American companies to help them sell their products overseas through its International Trade Administration (ITA) division. The ITA publishes a series of *Overseas Business Reports* that provide valuable information on most major world markets, including economic and marketing data as well as laws and regulations. Information on markets is sometimes available from other countries' government agencies, embassies, or consulates. The ITA also publishes *Export America,* which is a monthly magazine that provides valuable information on foreign markets and issues related to global business. The Central Intelligence Agency (CIA) publishes the *World Fact Book,* which contains information on more than 250 countries in eight categories, including geography, population, economy, government, communications, transportation, military, and transnational issues (Exhibit 20-14). The information includes data on telephones, radios, television sets, and communication-satellite use for nearly every country in the world and is usually updated annually. Circulation figures for the world's newspapers are also published every year.

The *United Nations Statistical Yearbook,* which is published annually, provides demographic and economic data on more than 200 countries. Yearbooks and other reports are also available for regions such as Latin America, Europe, and Asia. Other international organizations that can provide valuable information on world markets include the International Monetary Fund and regional organizations like the Japanese External Trade Organization and the European Union. The World Bank's annual *World Development Reports* has many national statistics including per capita incomes, literacy rates, imports, exports, and a variety of other information.

Information on product and brand attitudes, usage patterns, and media habits is generally more difficult to find, particularly in developing countries. However, more information is becoming available. A. C. Nielsen Worldwide Consumer Panel Services provides marketers with key consumer insights for 18 countries around the world. The company tracks consumer purchases in nearly 125,000 households using scanning technology or, in some markets, more traditional purchase diaries. Information from the panels is useful for understanding purchase behavior and shopping patterns for different segments of the population across various retail outlets. NCH Nù World Marketing Limited now collects information on coupon distribution and redemption patterns in the United States and a number of European countries. Data on media usage in European countries have increased tremendously over the past decade. However, information on TV audiences is still lacking in many countries.

Much of the information advertisers need must be gathered from research generated by the company and/or ad agency. Consumer needs and wants, purchase motives, and usage patterns often vary from one country to another, and research is needed to understand these differences. Some companies and their agencies conduct psychographic research in foreign markets to determine activities, interests, and opinions as well as product usage patterns.

Advertisers should also research consumers' reactions to the advertising appeal and execution style they plan to use in foreign markets. One agency researcher recommends testing the basic premise and/or selling idea to be used in a global campaign first to be sure it is relevant to the target audiences in the markets where it will appear.[86]

Creative Decisions

Another decision facing the international advertiser is determining the appropriate advertising messages for each market. Creative strategy development for international advertising is basically similar in process and procedure to that for domestic advertising. Advertising and communications objectives should be based on the marketing strategy and market conditions in foreign markets. Major selling ideas must be developed and specific appeals and execution styles chosen.

An important factor in the development of creative strategy is the issue of global versus localized advertising. If the standardized approach is taken, the creative team must develop advertising that will transcend cultural differences and communicate effectively in every country. For example, Tropicana uses a global advertising campaign for its pure premium orange juice. Its ads, though tailored a bit for each market, stress the superior, nearly fresh-squeezed taste of its juice over local brands that are often reconstituted from concentrates.

When companies follow a **localized advertising strategy,** the creative team must determine what type of selling idea, ad appeal, and execution style will work in each market. A product may have to be positioned differently in each market depending on consumers' usage patterns and habits. For example, General Foods found that in France, people drink very little orange juice and almost none at breakfast. Thus, when the company decided to market its Tang instant breakfast drink in France, the agency developed ads positioning the brand as a refreshment for any time of day rather than as a substitute for orange juice (the approach used in the United States).

Marketers must also figure out what type of advertising appeal or execution style will be most effective in each market. Emotional appeals such as humor may work well in one country but not in another because of differences in cultural backgrounds and consumer perceptions of what is or is not funny. While humorous appeals are popular in

Exhibit 20-15 Coca-Cola has adapted its advertising to catch the attention of consumers in Thailand

the United States and Britain, they are not used often in Germany, where consumers do not respond favorably to them. German advertising typically uses rational appeals that are text-heavy and contain arguments for a product's superiority.[87] France, Italy, and Brazil are more receptive to sexual appeals and nudity in advertising than are most other societies. The French government recently stepped up its efforts to convince advertisers and their ad agencies to tone down the use of sexual imagery and violence in their advertising.[88] France's Truth in Advertising Commission, which is the main self-regulatory body, has issued new standards regarding the presentation of human beings in advertising.

Countries such as Japan, Brazil, and Thailand appreciate creativity: Humorous and irreverent ads are often needed to catch the attention of consumers. In Thailand, which has become the creative nerve center of Asian advertising, the unusual blend of culture, religion, politics, and language influences the advertising. Thailand's *sabi-sabai* ("take it easy") attitude is partly a product of the country's Buddhist religion, which teaches disciples to forgive and look on the sunny side of life, as well as the country's heritage as a peaceful kingdom. Thailand has a very high literacy rate but few people read as a leisure activity, which results in most ads being visual in nature rather than be based upon language.[89] Many marketers have found that ads that are more humorous, irreverent, or adventurous break through the clutter and attract the attention of Thai consumers. For example, Coca-Cola recently developed a series of high-energy kung fu action spots featuring PiBig, a zany big brother character who overcomes evil forces for a can of Coke (Exhibit 20-15).

In China, marketers must deal with a very decentralized market with distinct differences in culture, language, food preferences, and lifestyles among the various regions and 2,000 cities. In general, the Chinese place a high emphasis on group and family values. Advertisers must be careful when using humor and sexual appeal, particularly for national campaigns, as language and values vary greatly from province to province. Human interest stories are used as the basis for ads in southern China but less so in cities such as Beijing and Shanghai where residents prefer more information-based ads.[90]

Media Selection

One of the most challenging areas for international marketers is media strategy and selection. Companies generally find major differences in the media available outside their home markets, and media conditions may vary considerably from one country to another. In less developed countries such as Vietnam, Kenya, and Egypt, most consumers do not have contact with a marketer's advertising and promotion efforts until they enter a store. Packaging and other point-of-purchase elements, rather than media advertising, will have the greatest impact on purchase decisions. On the other hand, advertising bombards consumers in the more affluent countries of Europe, the Pacific Rim, and North America through a variety of print and broadcast as well as interactive media. Media planners face a number of problems in attempting to communicate advertising and promotional messages to consumers in various countries. First, the types of media available are different in different countries. Many homes in developing countries do not have TV sets. For example, in many South and Central African nations (such as Uganda, Tanzania, Kenya, and Zimbabwe), radio is the dominant medium and access to TV sets is very limited. For many years, access to television was limited in countries such as Vietnam, and outdoor advertising was the best way to reach consumers along with point-of-purchase material. However, the number of households with televisions is growing rapidly in less developed countries such as India, China, and Vietnam as are other media such as the Internet.

The amount of time people spend watching television also varies from one country to the next. In the United States, the average person spends nearly 4.5 hours watching television. However, in Europe average daily viewing averages 3.5 hours and ranges from a low of 2.4 hours in Switzerland to a high of 3.9 hours in Greece.

Many European countries have hundreds of channels available to cable households or homes with satellite connections. However, cable and satellite penetration is lower than in the United States as many homes rely primarily on national broadcast channels.[91]

In some countries, TV advertising is not accepted or the amount of commercial time is severely limited. For example, in Germany advertising is not permitted after 8 P.M. on government-owned channels and is prohibited on Sundays and holidays. However, the restrictions do not apply to Germany's privately owned television stations, which can devote up to 20 percent of their airtime to commercials. In the Netherlands, TV spots are limited to 5 percent of airtime and must be booked up to a year in advance. Programs also do not have fixed time slots for ads, making it impossible to plan commercial buys around desired programs. In some countries, the limited number of channels and demand for commercial time result in extremely high levels of advertising clutter.

The number of TV sets is increasing tremendously in India, but there is still controversy over TV advertising. Commercials are restricted to only 10 percent of programming time and must appear at the beginning or end of a program.[92] Australia lifted a ban on cable TV advertising in 1997. However, some cable channels won't accept any advertising, and Australian consumers will not tolerate as much advertising on cable channels as on free TV networks.[93]

The characteristics of media differ from country to country in terms of coverage, cost, quality of reproduction, restrictions, and the like. In some countries, media rates are negotiable or may fluctuate owing to unstable currencies, economic conditions, or government regulations. For example, in China TV stations charge a local rate for Chinese advertisers, a foreign rate, and a joint venture rate.[94] Although its 900 million TV viewers make China the world's largest television market, the medium is strictly controlled by the Communist Party. State-owned China Central Television (CCTV) controls the national networks. Politics frequently intrude into program selection and scheduling: A show might be delayed for several months to coincide with a key political event, or programs from foreign countries may be pulled off the air.[95]

Another problem international advertisers face is obtaining reliable media information such as circulation figures, audience profiles, and costs. Many countries that had only state-owned TV channels are now experiencing a rapid growth in commercial channels, which is providing more market segmentation opportunities. However, reliable audience measurement data are not available, and media buyers often rely on their instincts when purchasing TV time. A number of research companies are developing audience measurement systems for countries in Eastern Europe, Russia, and China. In China, A. C. Nielsen began using PeopleMeters in urban areas such as Shanghai and the southern city of Guangzhou. Television research also is available from China Sofres Media (CSM), a joint venture formed by the French company Sofres and the state-owned China Viewers Survey & Consulting Centre. CSM has become the leading TV-ratings provider in China but has ratings panels in only 15 of the country's 32 provinces. Major cities and the more affluent provinces are well-covered, but viewership of many local channels in other provinces is not measured. Thus, advertising agencies and media companies often estimate viewing audiences by benchmarking cities and provinces at a similar level of economic development.[96] International advertising and television trade groups are also working to develop standardized measurement principles for global TV advertising.[97]

The goal of international advertisers is to select media vehicles that reach their target audience most effectively and efficiently. Media selection is often localized even for a centrally planned, globalized campaign. Local agencies or media buyers generally have more knowledge of local media and better opportunities to negotiate rates, and subsidiary operations can maintain control and adapt to media conditions and options in their market. Media planners have two options: using national or local media or using international media.

Local Media Many advertisers choose the local media of a country to reach its consumers. Print is the most used medium worldwide, since TV commercial time and

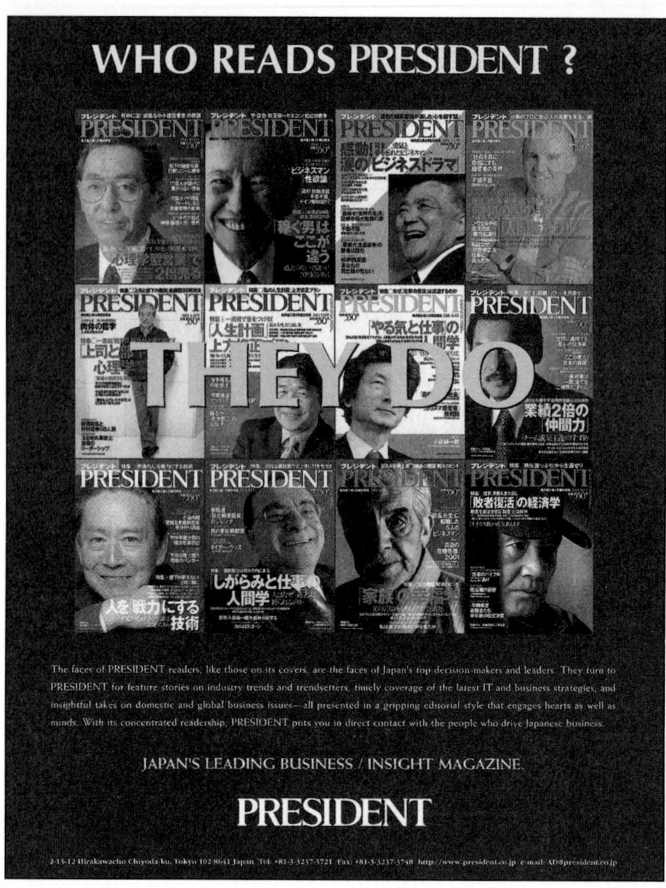

Exhibit 20-16 *President* magazine targets top Japanese executives

the number of homes with TV sets are limited in many countries. Many countries have magazines that are circulated nationwide as well as national or regional newspapers that carry advertising directed to a national audience. Most countries also have magazines that appeal to special interests or activities, allowing for targeting in media selection. For example, Exhibit 20-16 shows an ad promoting *President,* which is a magazine that reaches top executives in Japan.

Although restrictions and regulations have limited the development of TV as a dominant advertising medium in many countries, it is a primary medium for obtaining nationwide coverage in most developed countries and offers tremendous creative opportunities. Restrictions on television may be lessening in some countries, and time availability may increase. For example, the number of TV stations and television advertising in Italy have exploded in the past decade since government restrictions against private broadcasting were lifted. Advertising groups are using economic, legal, and political pressure to get more television commercial time from reluctant European governments. The increase in TV channels through direct broadcasting by satellite to many European households (discussed later in this section) is hastening this process.

In addition to print and television, local media available to advertisers include radio, direct mail, billboards, cinema, and transit advertising. These media give international advertisers great flexibility and the opportunity to reach specific market segments and local markets within a country. Most international advertisers rely heavily on national and local media in their media plans for foreign markets.

International Media

The other way for the international advertiser to reach audiences in various countries is through international media that have multimarket coverage. The primary focus of international media has traditionally been magazines and newspapers. A number of U.S.-based consumer-oriented publications have international editions, including *Time, Newsweek, Reader's Digest,* and *National Geographic* as well as the newspaper *USA Today. Cosmopolitan* publishes 29 international editions that reach over 30 million readers in various countries (Exhibit 20-17). U.S.-based business publications with foreign editions include *BusinessWeek, Fortune, Harvard Business Review,* and *The Wall Street Journal.*

International publications offer advertisers a way to reach large audiences on a regional or worldwide basis. Readers of these publications are usually upscale, high-income individuals who are desirable target markets for many products and services. There are, however, several problems with these international media that can limit their attractiveness to many advertisers. Their reach in any one foreign country may be low, particularly for specific segments of a market. Also, while they deliver desirable audiences to companies selling business or upscale consumer products and services, they do not cover the mass consumer markets or specialized market segments very well. Other U.S.-based publications in foreign markets do offer advertisers ways to reach specific market segments.

While print remains the dominant medium for international advertising, many companies are turning their attention to international commercial TV. Packaged-goods companies in particular, such as Gillette, McDonald's, Pepsi, and Coca-Cola, view TV advertising as the best way to reach mass markets and effectively communicate their advertising messages. Satellite technology has helped spread the growth of TV in other countries and made global television networks a reality. Global Perspective 20-3 discusses how MTV has become one of the largest global television networks in the world by localizing its content for various countries and regions.

A major development affecting broadcasting in Europe, Asia, and Latin America is **direct broadcast by satellite (DBS)** to homes and communities equipped with small, low-cost receiving dishes. A number of satellite networks operate in these regions and beam entertainment programming across several countries. For example, media baron Rupert Murdoch owns News Corporation satellite networks, which deliver TV programs to five continents, all but dominating Britain, Italy, and major portions of the Middle East.[98] News Corporation has a controlling interest in British Sky Broadcasting (BSkyB), which beams more than 300 channels to 7 million subscribers, or about 30 percent of Britain's 25 million TV homes. In 1993, News Corporation purchased Satellite Television Asian Region (STAR TV), which is now the world's largest satellite network, stretching from the Middle East and India to South Korea (Exhibit 20-18). It broadcasts 40 services in eight languages and reaches more than 300 million viewers throughout 53 Asian countries. In India and China alone, it produces over 16,000 hours of original programming each year.[99] In 1996, Star entered into a partnership with two Hong Kong companies to launch the Phoenix Satellite Television Co. Along with airing reruns of popular American shows, the Mandarin-language Phoenix Chinese Channel offers a mix of locally produced sports, news, and talk shows. Phoenix has greater reach in China than any other foreign channel, particularly among upscale, educated viewers in urban areas such as Beijing, Shanghai, and Guangzhou. The favorable demographics make the channel popular among blue-chip advertisers.[100]

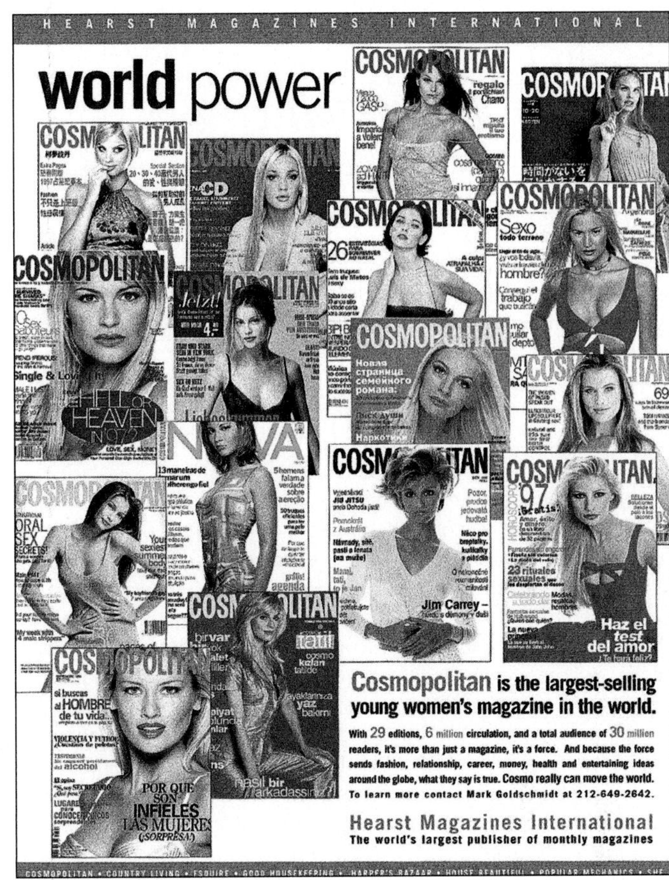

Exhibit 20-17
Cosmopolitan reaches women around the world with 29 international editions

The main incentive to the growth of these satellite networks has been the severely limited program choices and advertising opportunities on government-controlled stations in many countries. However, many European and Asian governments are moving to preserve cultural values and protect advertising revenues from going to foreign-based networks. In India, for example, advertising revenue has been shifting to ISkyB, a subsidiary of STAR TV, from Doordarshan, the state-run television network.[101] The Indian government is considering legislation that would regulate foreign satellite channels and advertisers and favor Doordarshan. India's minister for information and broadcasting says foreign satellite channels are a threat to India's cultural fabric and should be curbed. He cites offensive program content and the amount of nudity on foreign channels as reasons why the Indian government needs to regulate satellite channels. In China, most people are officially barred from receiving foreign satellite broadcasts, but millions do anyway from unauthorized cable operators or through their satellite dishes. In 1999, the government did begin enforcing the ban, particularly in Beijing, but the Phoenix channel remains popular among Chinese viewers who want more options than China's state-run television.[102] China remains a politically sensitive TV market. In 2002, the government issued a rule stating that foreign channels must sell and transmit signals only through the state-run company China International Television Corporation. In 2005, the Chinese government blocked plans by News Corporation to operate a prime-time television channel in China.[103]

Exhibit 20-18 STAR TV reaches more than 100 million homes across Asia

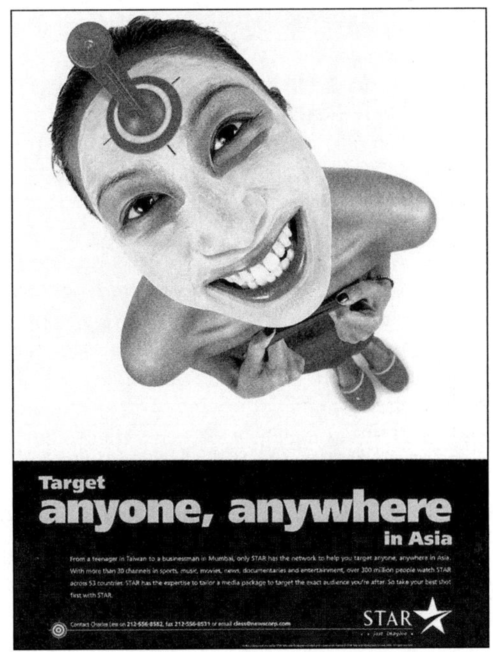

Advances in satellite and communications technology, the expansion of multinational companies with global marketing perspectives, and the development of global ad agencies mean advertisers' use of television as a global medium is likely to increase.

GLOBAL PERSPECTIVE 20-3

MTV Goes Global—But with a Local Touch

MTV (Music Television) Network was launched in the United States in 1981 as a joint venture between American Express and Warner Communications. Almost from the outset, the pioneering 24-hour music video cable channel put young viewers in a trance, influencing how they looked, talked, and shopped. The outfit that all but invented the rock video has become perhaps the biggest force in the music world. It is also the premier platform for marketers trying to woo young consumers in the United States as well as numerous other countries around the world. Every second of every day nearly 2 million people watch their MTV—and 60 percent of them tune in from outside the United States.

In 1986, Viacom International purchased MTV, and it is now part of the company's MTV Networks division, which operates 72 international channels, including versions of Nickelodeon and VH1, that reach 321 million homes in Europe, Asia, Latin America, Canada, and Australia. Music is a common language that travels, and MTV has a formula that entrances young people around the globe. However, while MTV is a global brand, only a small part of its programming, like its annual Video Music Awards, crosses cultural boundaries. MTV recognized that it had to build local channels and now airs more than two dozen different feeds around the world, all tailored for their respective markets. MTV Network International president Bill Roedy notes that one country's MTV looks very little like another's: "MTV India is very colorful, self-effacing, full of humor, a lot of street culture. China's is about family values, nurturing, a lot of love songs. In Indonesia, with our largest Islamic population, there's a call to prayer five times a day on the channel. Brazil is very sexy. Italy is stylish, elegant, with food shows, because of the love of food there. Japan's very techie, a lot of wireless product."

MTV's five largest international markets are Britain, Germany, Italy, Japan, and Brazil. In 1995, MTV changed its strategy and broke Europe into regional feeds. It now has five feeds on the Continent: one for the United Kingdom and Ireland; another for Germany, Austria, and Switzerland; one for Scandinavia; a broader broadcast for Belgium, Greece, France, and Israel; and one just for Italy alone. Viacom is also pushing MTV ever deeper into markets in Asia. Its first Chinese channel was launched in 1995, and since then it has boosted distribution dramatically with a mix of cable, direct-satellite, and broadcast TV. From its base in Singapore, MTV Asia operates separate Mandarin feeds for China and Taiwan, English and local channels across Southeast Asia, and a Korean outlet for South Korea. However, except for Japan, Asia has been a very difficult region for MTV to crack.

One Asian country where MTV is focusing a great deal of attention is India, which is home to more than 1 billion people and has a middle class that is expanding rapidly. India's economy is experiencing strong growth along with expenditures on advertising as consumers are getting their first credit cards and buying mobile phones, computers, motor scooters, and, of course, TV sets. MTV has gradually overtaken the local Indian music channel called [V], which is owned by News Corporation, to become the top-rated music channel in India. MTV has been successful in India because it tailored its content to fit the local market. It quickly realized that it could not blast its Western programming at Indian teenagers who do not like rock or rap music. Global pop

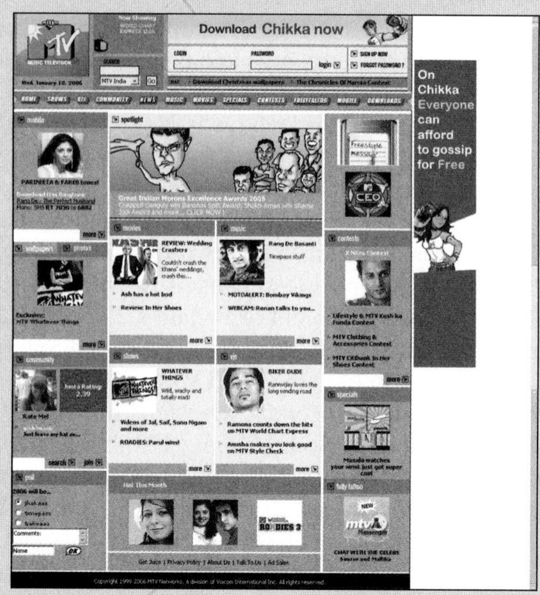

music has given way to the songs of "Bollywood," the name given to the vibrant and rapidly expanding movie and music scene in India. MTV India produces homegrown shows hosted by local veejays who speak Hinglish, a kind of hip, city-bred blend of Hindi and English. It has also come up with hit shows including *MTV Bakra,* which is an Indian-style *Candid Camera* where the host plays gags on unsuspecting people. MTV has also tapped into young people's passions for cricket and fashion.

India is still a very challenging market for MTV as the country's TV industry is very fragmented across all genres, and there are too many channels chasing too few advertising dollars. Since most families own only one TV set, they tend to watch television together, which means that MTV India has to compete with news, sports, and entertainment channels. MTV faces strong competition from Star TV, which delivers nine cable channels to India, and Sony Entertainment Television, which owns two Indian channels and distributes six others. MTV has responded to the competition by inviting advertisers to help it develop new programs. For example, when Unilever wanted to launch its Axe deodorant brand with the theme of long-lasting freshness, MTV staged what it called the world's longest dance party (55 hours) in a suburb of Delhi that was attended by 15,000 people.

Currently about 25 million homes in India can watch MTV. However, there is considerable room to grow given that there are 100 million TV households in the country and more than half of India's population is under the age of 25. MTV International is taking a long-term perspective in India, as well as in other countries, as it recognizes that it has a very powerful global brand—particularly when it is localized.

Sources: Marc Gunther, "MTV's Passage to India," *Fortune,* August 2, 2004, pp. 117–125; Anne-Marie Crawford, "MTV: Out of Its Teens," *Adage Global,* May 2001, pp. 25–26; Brett Pulley and Andrew Tanzer, "Sumner's Gemstone," *Forbes,* February 21, 2000, pp. 106–111.

The Roles of Other Promotional Mix Elements in International Marketing

This chapter has focused on advertising, since it is usually the primary element in the promotional mix of the international marketer. However, as in domestic marketing, promotional programs for foreign markets generally include such other elements as sales promotion, personal selling, public relations, and websites on the Internet. The roles of these other promotional mix elements vary depending on the firm's marketing and promotional strategy in foreign markets.

Sales promotion and public relations can support and enhance advertising efforts; the latter may also be used to create or maintain favorable images for companies in foreign markets. For some firms, personal selling may be the most important promotional element and advertising may play a support role. This final section considers the roles of some of these other promotional mix elements in the international marketing program.

Sales Promotion

Sales promotion activity in international markets is growing due in part to the transfer of promotion concepts and techniques from country to country and in part to the proliferation of media. The growth also stems from the liberalization of trade, the rise of global brands, the spread of cable and satellite TV, and the deregulation and/or privatization of media. Sales promotion and direct-response agencies have been becoming more common, particularly in Europe and more recently in South American, Asian, and Middle Eastern countries. In many less developed countries, spending on sales promotion often exceeds media spending on TV, radio, and print ads.[104]

As we saw in Chapter 16, sales promotion is one of the fastest-growing areas of marketing in the United States. Companies increasingly rely on consumer- and trade-oriented sales promotion to help sell their products in foreign markets as well. Many of the promotional tools that are effective in the United States, such as free samples, premiums, event sponsorships, contests, coupons, and trade promotions, are also used in foreign markets. For example, Häagen-Dazs estimates it gave out more than 5 million free tastings of its ice cream as part of its successful strategy for entering the European market. Since taste is the major benefit of this premium product, sampling was an appropriate sales promotion tool for entering foreign markets. The WD-40 Company uses samples in the United States as well as foreign markets to educate consumers about the versatility of the product and encourage trial. The sample shown in Exhibit 20-19, which uses the front headline "One Can. One Thousand Uses," was translated into 20 different languages. This makes it possible for the distributors in different countries to use a sampling tool in their local languages.

Exhibit 20-19 WD-40 uses product samples in various countries to encourage trial

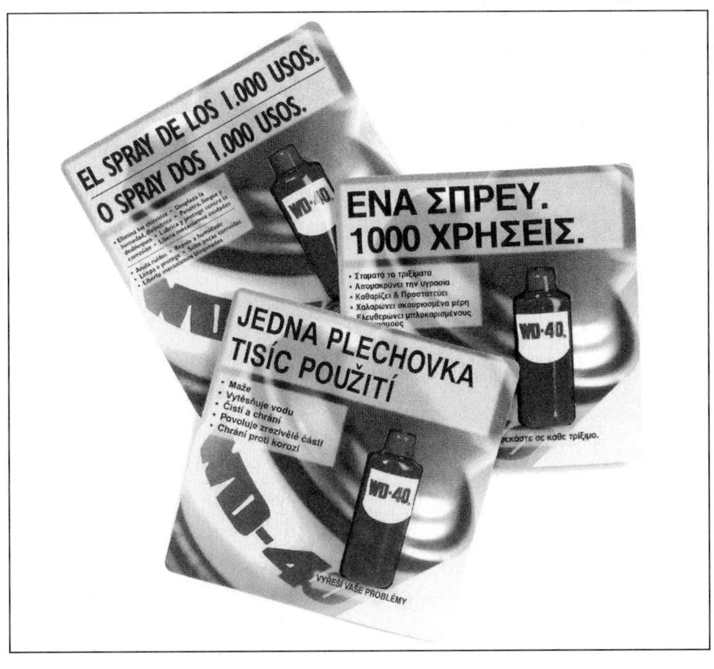

A type of promotion that has become very popular in foreign markets is event sponsorship. Many companies sponsor sporting events, concerts, and other activities in foreign countries to promote their products and enhance corporate image. Sponsorship of sporting events has become a cornerstone of the Coca-Cola Company's promotional efforts. The company is now the largest corporate sports sponsor in the world, spending nearly $1 billion a year on global sports sponsorships. Its programs pervade several different levels, from grassroots sponsorship of youth sports programs to global sponsorship of major sporting events such as the Olympic Games and World Cup soccer. A number of other multinational companies are also involved with sponsorship of sporting events in foreign markets. MasterCard, Canon, and Gillette sponsor Asian soccer teams and tournaments, while Nike sponsors the Brazilian national soccer team. Visa was an official sponsor of the Rugby World Cup in Australia, which is one of the world's most popular sporting events, attracting more than 3 billion viewers in over 200 countries. Visa used the sponsorship to deliver benefits to member banks, merchants, and cardholders. As part of its sponsorship, Visa provided 10,000 tickets worldwide for cardholders to win when Visa cards were used as part of merchant and company promotions.

Sponsorship of concert tours by popular performers has also become an important part of many companies' global marketing programs. For example, E Trade Financial sponsored the North American leg of the Rolling Stones world tour in 2002–2003, which took the legendary rock group to China and India for the first time.

Unlike advertising, which can be done on a global basis, sales promotions must be adapted to local markets. Kamran Kashani and John Quelch noted several important differences among countries that marketers must consider in developing a sales promotion program.[105] They include the stage of economic development, market maturity, consumer perceptions of promotional tools, trade structure, and legal restrictions and regulations:

- *Economic development.* In highly developed countries such as the United States, Canada, Japan, and Western European nations, marketers can choose from a wide range of promotional tools. But in developing countries they must be careful not to use promotional tools such as in- or on-package premiums that would increase the price of the product beyond the reach of most consumers. Free samples and demonstrations are widely used, effective promotional tools in developing countries. But coupons, which are so popular with consumers in the United States, are rarely used because of problems with distribution and resistance from retailers. In the United States and Britain, most coupons are distributed through newspapers (including FSIs) or magazines. Low literacy rates in some countries make print media an ineffective coupon distribution method, so coupons are delivered door to door, handed out in stores, or placed in or on packages. Figure 20-4 shows the total number of coupons distributed and redeemed in various countries in 2003.
- *Market maturity.* Marketers must also consider the stage of market development for their product or service in various countries when they design sales promotions. To introduce a product to a country, consumer-oriented promotional tools such as sampling, high-value coupons, and cross-promotions with established products and brands are often effective. The competitive dynamics of a foreign market are also often a function of its stage of development. More competition is likely in well-developed mature mar-

Figure 20-4 Number of Coupons Distributed and Redeemed in Various Countries, 2003

Number of Coupons Distributed and Redeemed in Various Countries (2003)

Country	Coupons distributed	Coupons redeemed
U.S.	258 billion	3.6 billion
U.K.	5.9 billion	.52 billion
Canada	2.6 billion	.097 billion
Italy	.682 billion	.091 billion
Spain	.450 billion	.038 billion

Source: NCH Marketing Services 2004 Trend Report.

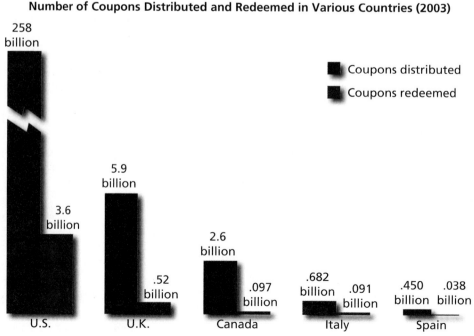

kets, which will influence the types of sales promotion tools used. For example, there may be competitive pressure to use trade allowances to maintain distribution or consumer promotions that will maintain customer loyalty, such as bonus packs, price-off deals, or coupons.

- *Consumer perceptions.* An important consideration in the design of sales promotion programs is how they are perceived by consumers as well as the trade. Consumer perceptions of various sales promotion tools vary from market to market. For example, Japanese women are less likely to take advantage of contests, coupons, or other promotions than are women in the United States.[106] Premium offers in particular must be adapted to the tastes of consumers in various markets. A recent study by Huff and Alden examined consumers' opinions toward the use of coupons and sweepstakes in three Asian countries: Taiwan, Malaysia, and Thailand. The study found differences among the three countries with consumers in Taiwan having more negative attitudes and lower levels of use of both sweepstakes and coupons than consumers in Malaysia and Thailand.[107]
- *Trade structure.* In areas with highly concentrated retailing systems, such as northern Europe, the trade situation is becoming much like the United States and Canada as pressure grows for more price-oriented trade and in-store promotions. In southern Europe, the retail industry is highly fragmented and there is less trade pressure for promotions. The willingness and ability of channel members to accommodate sales promotion programs must also be considered. Retailers in many countries do not want to take time to process coupons, post promotional displays, or deal with premiums or packaging that require special handling or storage. In countries like Japan or India, where retailing structures are highly fragmented, stores are too small for point-of-purchase displays or in-store sampling.
- *Regulations.* An important factor affecting the use of sales promotions in foreign countries is the presence of legal restrictions and regulations. Laws affecting sales promotions are generally more restrictive in other countries than in the United States. Some countries ban contests, games, or lotteries, while others restrict the size or amount of a sample, premium, or prize. For example, fair-trade regulations in Japan limit the maximum value of premiums to 10 percent of the retail price; in France the limit is 5 percent. Canada prohibits games of pure chance unless a skill element is used to determine the winner. In Japan the amount of a prize offer is limited to a certain percentage of the product tied to the promotion.[108] In some countries, a free premium must be related to the nature of the product purchased. Many countries have strict rules when it comes to premium offers for children, and some ban them altogether.

Variations in rules and regulations mean marketers must often develop separate consumer sales promotion programs for each country. Many companies have found it difficult to do any promotions throughout Europe because sales promotion rules differ so from one country to another. While the treaty on European Union may result in a more standardized legal environment in Europe, laws regarding sales promotion are still likely to vary. This is why many companies use local agencies or international sales promotion companies to develop sales promotion programs for foreign markets.

Management of Sales Promotion in Foreign Markets

Although sales promotion programs of multinational companies have traditionally been managed locally, this is changing somewhat as marketers create global brands. Many global marketers recognize the importance of giving local managers the autonomy to design and execute their own sales promotion programs. However, the ways local promotions influence and contribute to global brand equity must also be considered.

Kashani and Quelch developed a framework for analyzing the role of centralized (headquarters) versus local management in sales promotion decisions based on various stages of globalization (Figure 20-5). This model suggests headquarters' influence will be greatest for global brands and least for local brands. Since global brands require uniformity in marketing communications, the promotional program should be determined at the headquarters level. Decisions regarding overall promotional strategy—including international communications objectives, positioning, allocation of the communications budget to sales promotion versus advertising, and weight of consumer versus trade promotions—are made at the headquarters level.[109]

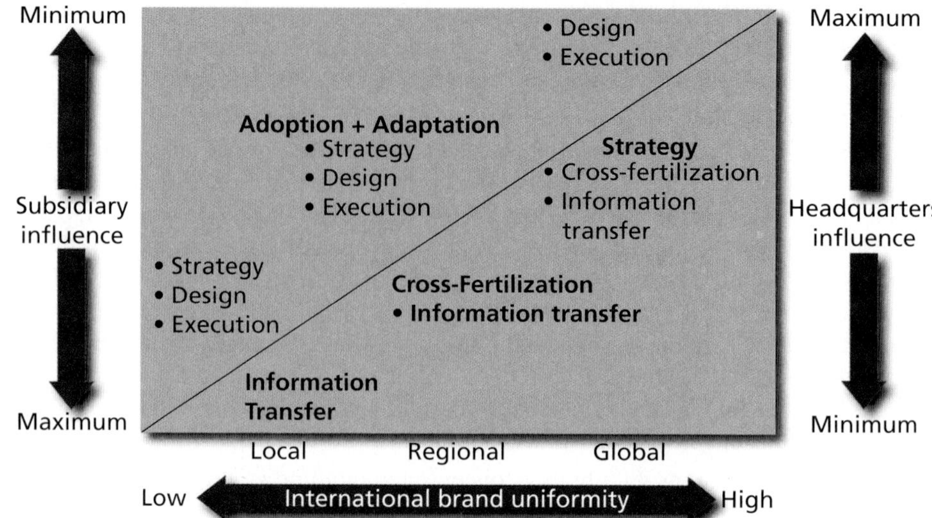

Figure 20-5 Central versus local roles in international sales promotion

While the promotional strategy for global brands is determined by global product managers at headquarters, implementation of the programs should be left to local management. It is important to make the promotional strategy broad enough to allow for differences in diverse local markets. Headquarters is also responsible for encouraging the cross-fertilization of ideas and practices among local managers and facilitating the transfer of information. Some companies are now using promotional agencies that have offices around the globe and can coordinate programs in various markets. Exhibit 20-20 shows an ad for DVC Worldwide touting the agency's integrated marketing communications capabilities in local as well as global markets.

Regional brands usually do not require the same level of standardization as global brands, and the promotional strategy can be developed by regional offices and carried out at the local level. However, regional promotions should avoid contradictory brand communications and promotional activities that might upset local activities in nearby markets. The role of national-level brand managers is adoption and adaptation. They determine what promotional ideas to adopt from the region and adapt them to local conditions.

For local brands, decisions regarding promotional strategy, program design, and execution are left to local managers. Of course, local managers may benefit from information about the promotions used in other local markets.

Exhibit 20-20
Promotional agencies such as DVC Worldwide have offices in cities around the world

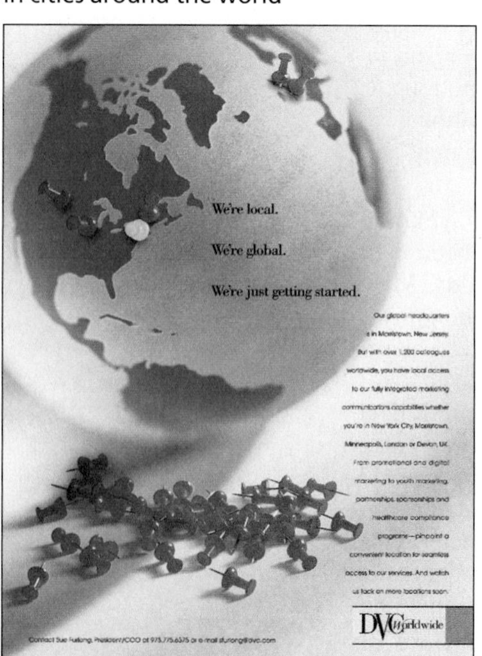

Personal Selling

As a company's most direct contact with its customers in foreign markets, personal selling is an important part of the marketing and promotional process. Companies selling industrial and high-tech products generally rely heavily on personal selling as the primary method for communicating with their customers, internationally as well as domestically. Consumer-product firms may also use personal selling to call on distributors, wholesalers, or major retailing operations in foreign markets. Due to low wages in many developing countries, some companies hire large sales staffs to perform missionary activities and support selling and advertising efforts. For example, Citibank launched its credit cards in many Asian countries using a multifaceted marketing program that included advertising, direct mail, and personal selling. The company found personal selling a very focused and cost-effective way to reach prospective credit-card applicants in countries such as India, Malaysia, and Thailand. Citibank captured 40 percent of Thailand's credit-card market, relying primarily on a sales force of 600 part-timers who were paid a fee for each applicant approved.[110]

A number of differences in the business environments and cultures of the United States and other countries impact the personal selling process.[111] First of all, U.S.-based salespeople generally encounter a longer sales cycle in foreign markets than they do domestically, a situation that may be due to several factors such as cultural differences, business practices, and more tenuous economic conditions. In countries such as Italy and Spain, as well as in Latin America, salespeople must spend more time on the social aspects of selling, and this can prolong the sales cycle. There is a tendency toward more conservative business practices in countries such as Germany, where the business culture is older and very ingrained. Germans are more risk-averse and thorough in evaluating business deals. They require strong reassurance and will conduct extensive reviews and ask for multiple references before closing a deal.[112] In the Middle East, price negotiations are common, and buyers often want to feel they extracted some concessions from sellers. Unstable economic conditions in many countries in the Middle East and Latin America can also complicate the selling process, as currency devaluations are common and financing is a major issue that must be addressed.

Because it involves personal contact and communication, personal selling is generally even more culture bound than advertising. So most companies use sales reps from the host country and adapt personal selling activities and sales programs to each market. Management of the sales force is usually decentralized to the local subsidiaries, although the international marketer sets the general sales policy and advises foreign managers on the role personal selling should play in their market, the development of the sales program, and various aspects of sales management.

Public Relations

Many companies involved in international marketing are recognizing the importance of using public relations to support and enhance their marketing and advertising efforts.[113] Public relations activities are needed to deal with local governments, media, trade associations, and the general public, any of which may feel threatened by the presence of a foreign multinational. The job of PR agencies in foreign markets is not only to help the company sell its products or services but also to present the firm as a good corporate citizen concerned about the future of the country.

Companies generally need a favorable image to be successful in foreign markets. Those perceived negatively may face pressure from the media, local governments, or other relevant publics, or even boycotts by consumers. Often, public relations is needed to deal with specific problems a company faces in international markets. For example, NutraSweet had problems getting its low-calorie sweetener into some markets because of strong sugar lobbies in Australia, Canada, and Europe. These lobbies encouraged the foreign press to pick up some unfavorable news about the product from the U.S. media. The company retained Burson-Marsteller, the second-largest PR company in the world, to help design factual ads about the product and to conduct other PR activities to counter the problems and get the facts out about NutraSweet.

Coca-Cola had to deal with a severe public relations crisis in Europe after several hundred Belgians, many of them schoolchildren, became ill after drinking Coke products in the summer of 1999. Several countries banned all Coca-Cola products, while others issued health warnings until the problem, which was traced to bad carbon dioxide in a bottling plant, was resolved. Facing a public relations crisis of global dimensions, Coca-Cola retained the European advertising and PR firm Publicis, which had experience in handling crisis management situations for European companies such as Nestlé, Perrier, and Heineken. Publicis worked closely with executives at Coke's Atlanta headquarters to develop communication strategies and handle contacts with the media. When the ban on Coca-Cola products was lifted in Belgium, Coke and Publicis hired several hundred thousand people to deliver vouchers and coupons for one free family-size bottle of Coke to each of the country's 4.4 million homes. The program was backed by newspaper advertising. In France an existing commercial made by Coke's U.S. agency and adapted for France with the catchline "Today more than ever, we thank you for your loyalty" was aired. In Poland newspaper ads were run guaranteeing the integrity of locally produced Coke products.

Coca-Cola is the world's most valuable brand, and its strong brand equity helped carry the company through the crisis. However, in the process the Coca-Cola Company learned that even the most powerful brand in the world is not immune from a crisis.

Recently the Coca-Cola Company, as well as PepsiCo, has had to deal with problems in India where their sales plummeted following accusations by a local environmental group that the level of pesticide residues in their products was too high.[114] Global Perspective 20-4 discusses the problems this controversy has created for the beverage giants as well as the public relations problems other U.S. companies have been facing in various countries.

The Internet

Worldwide Growth of the Internet

The Internet is coming of age as a global marketing medium and is becoming an important IMC tool for companies around the world, both large and small. Marketers are using the Internet to promote their companies, build their brands, and engage in e-commerce transactions in their own countries as well as across borders. As more homes and offices become connected to the Internet, its importance as an integrated marketing communications tool and way of transacting business will increase tremendously for companies selling consumer products and services as well as business-to-business marketers.

During its formative years the Internet was largely a North American phenomenon. By the end of the '90s, nearly 54 percent of all online users were in North America and English was the language used on three-fourths of all websites and nearly all e-commerce sites, even though it is the primary language of only 8 percent of the world's population. However, this is changing rapidly. As of 2005, there were nearly 1 billion Internet users around the world with the largest number of users residing in Asia followed by Europe and North America. The United States is the country with the largest number of people online, with an estimated 203 million users, followed by China with 103 million and Japan with 78 million. Internet penetration is very high in Scandinavian countries such as Sweden and Finland as well as in Asian countries such as Taiwan and South Korea.[115] Most multinational companies are developing websites in a variety of languages as Internet penetration increases and more consumers in various countries go online for information and entertainment.

While the use of the Internet around the globe continues to grow, there is still tremendous variation in consumer usage as well as the level of marketing activity occurring online. In the Asia Pacific region, Internet use is higher in the urban areas of mainland China as well as in Hong Kong. Singapore and Thailand have considerable numbers of upscale users and several domestic service providers. By contrast, in India personal computer penetration is still less than 10 percent, and less than half of the estimated 1 million households with PCs have Internet access. The number of people online is increasing rapidly in Latin America; Internet penetration averages around 13 percent for the entire region but is 20 percent in Argentina and 36 percent in Chile. The region is becoming one of the fastest-growing e-commerce markets in the world. However, factors such as unreliable delivery services, low usage of credit cards, security concerns, and customs duties are likely to be daunting obstacles to the growth of e-commerce in the region.[116]

Exhibit 20-21 TaylorMade Golf developed a website specifically for Japan

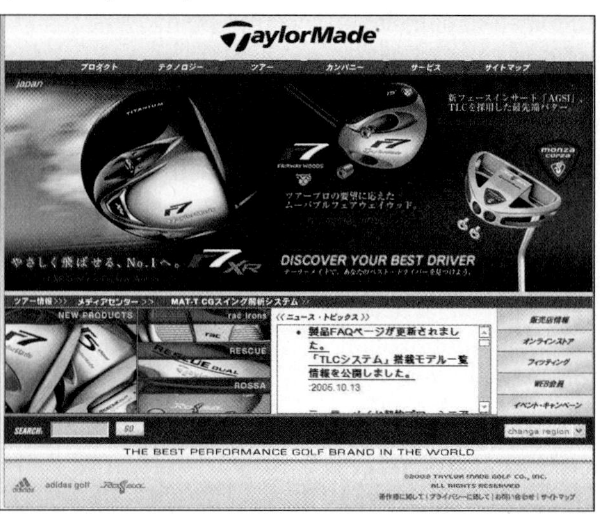

Use of the Internet in International Marketing

The use of the Internet as an IMC tool by companies in various countries is increasing as more marketers learn how to develop and maintain websites and improvements in the systems and technologies needed to support these sites occur. Many multinational companies are developing websites in a number of different languages and making them an important part of their integrated marketing communications programs. Marketers are also using mass-media advertising to drive consumers to their websites and provide them with detailed information about their products and services, encourage them to participate in online promotions, or allow them to make purchases. Exhibit 20-21 shows a page from the website used by the TaylorMade Golf Comany in Japan. A number of global business-to-business marketers such as Dell Computer, IBM, Xerox, and Hewlett-Packard are using websites to provide customers with information and conduct business with them.

GLOBAL PERSPECTIVE 20-4

U.S. Companies Deal with Public Relations Problems Abroad

One of the challenges facing multinational companies operating in foreign markets is that various groups such as consumers, government, the media, and other relevant groups may feel threatened by their presence. Resentment and concern over their presence in a country can make public relations problems and crisis situations even more difficult for large multinational companies, as Coca-Cola Company, PepsiCo, McDonald's, and others have learned over the past few years.

Beverage giants Coca-Cola and PepsiCo, which together have 95 percent of the soft-drink sales in India, have been slugging it out in India's rapidly emerging soft-drink market for years. The Indian market is valued at more than $2.5 billion and is one of the most important emerging markets in the world for both companies. However, over the past several years, the two companies have found themselves battling governmental agencies, as well as consumer activist and environmental groups, rather than each other.

The problem began in 2003 when a local environmental group, the New Delhi–based Center for Science and Environment, issued a report claiming that samples of Pepsi and Coke contained levels of pesticides and insecticides far above the levels determined to be safe by the European Union, which has set some of the world's most stringent standards. Executives from both companies, however, repeatedly argued that the water used in their drinks met not only local standards but also those used in Europe and the United States. The Indian government then tested the companies' soft drinks and issued an announcement that the level of pesticide residue conformed to local quality standards. Despite this, opposition lawmakers pushed the government to institute a public inquiry into the allegations, and numerous state governments began doing their own tests on Coke and Pepsi products.

The problems for Coca-Cola in particular became worse when Amit Srivastava, an Indian consumer activist, along with several other nongovernmental organizations accused the company of a number of other egregious offenses in India including selling drinks laced with pesticides. Srivastava and other activists vowed to continue their anti-Coke campaign until the company closes three controversial bottling plants and meets a number of other demands. The allegations have taken their toll on Coca-Cola sales in India, and the former president of the company's Asian division referred to India as "a work in progress," noting that the company has continued to feel the effects of the pesticide scare.

McDonald's has also had to deal with a public relations crisis in a foreign country. In the late '90s, McDonald's began receiving negative publicity as a by-product of an ongoing anti-American protest by angry French farmers. The farmers' movement had been triggered by a World Trade Organization ruling ordering Europe to accept hormone-fed beef produced in the United States. The farmers were also protesting sanctions the U.S. government imposed on a host of imported French foods, including Roquefort cheese, truffles, and Dijon mustard. The farmers' protests included dumping tons of animal manure and rotting vegetables at McDonald's restaurants all over France, acts which have attracted mass-media attention in the country. Additional protests against McDonald's were led by Jose Bove, a French citizen who has been described as a professional militant and is known for headline-grabbing acts of civil disobedience.

Initially McDonald's took a low-key approach to the protests and attacks, declining to press charges for vandalism against its restaurants and placing posters in its restaurants explaining how McDonald's is a major partner of the French agricultural sector. Later, McDonald's France began countering the negative publicity by launching a "Made in France" corporate advertising campaign in 60 regional daily newspapers across the country. The ads informed consumers that while its brand may be American, the products served in France's nearly 800 McDonald's outlets were French in origin. The ads underscored McDonald's policy of buying French products and its role in France's agricultural sector, while thanking consumers who have remained loyal. In response to the farmers' concerns, McDonald's also began substituting locally produced specialties targeted by the U.S. sanctions, such as duck breast and Roquefort cheese, for traditional ingredients in the company's Big Mac and cheeseburger menu items.

McDonald's France executives told their countrymen that it is essentially a French company staffed by industrious employees and to stop using it as a symbol in a fight against U.S. trade sanctions. The company also pointed to its efforts to ensure that supplies of its product are obtained locally in France and are of high quality. It appears that the McDonald's public relations efforts have succeeded as sales in France have been increasing and its French operation has been the fastest-growing in Europe. However, recently McDonald's had to deal with yet another public relations problem related to concerns over the nutritional value of its food. The latest controversy erupted in response to a report showing child obesity in France had doubled to 16 percent in 10 years.

Concerns over the problem of childhood obesity have spread to other European countries, and McDonald's is not the only company that must deal with the nutritional issue as food companies such as Kraft Foods, Kellogg Company, and PepsiCo are also being criticized. In 2005, the European Union called on the food industry to regulate so-called junk food advertising aimed at consumers across the continent and has threatened to ban advertising icons such as Ronald McDonald and Tony the Tiger. Multinational companies are finding that public relations problems have indeed become global.

Sources: Steve Stecklow, "How a Global Web of Activists Gives Coke Problems in India," *The Wall Street Journal,* June 27, 2005, pp. A1, 6; Stephanie Thompson, "Europe Slams Icons as Food Fights Back," *Advertising Age,* January 31, 2005, pp. 1, 38; Marian Burros, "McDonald's France Says Slow Down on the Fast Food," *The New York Times,* October 30, 2002, p. C7; David Woodruff, "Just Say No: Jose Bove Has Made a Career as a Professional Agitator; His Latest Target: Globalization," *The Wall Street Journal,* October 1, 2001, p. A1; Larry Speer, "McDonald's Self Defense Is Its French Connection," *Advertising Age,* September 13, 1999, p. 26.

As the digital revolution continues, marketers will be making greater use of the Internet in their global as well as local IMC programs. However, they will also face some challenges with respect to the way they approach global marketing and branding. As more consumers worldwide have access to the same information and same brands via the World Wide Web, many marketers will have to rethink their strategies of producing the same product under different names and tailoring promotions to local markets. It is predicted that marketers will use more global brands and promotional campaigns to take advantage of the worldwide exposure that will be available through the Internet.

Summary

Many U.S. companies are recognizing not only the opportunities but also the necessity of marketing their products and services internationally because of saturated markets and intense competition from both domestic and foreign competitors. Advertising and promotion are important parts of the international marketing program of a multinational corporation. Advertising is generally the most cost-effective way to communicate with buyers and create a market in other countries.

International marketers must carefully analyze the major environmental forces in each market where they compete, including economic, demographic, cultural, and political/ legal factors. These factors are important not only in assessing the potential of each country as a market but also in designing and implementing advertising and promotional programs.

In recent years, much attention has focused on global marketing, where a standard marketing program is used in all markets. Part of global marketing is global advertising, where the same basic advertising approach is used in all markets. Opponents of the global (standardized) approach argue that differences in culture, market and economic conditions, and consumer needs and wants make a universal approach to marketing and advertising impractical. Many companies use an in-between approach, standardizing their basic marketing strategy but localizing advertising messages to fit each market.

There are a number of important decision areas in the development of advertising and promotional programs for international markets. These include organization, agency selection, advertising research, creative strategy and execution, and media strategy and selection.

Sales promotion, personal selling, public relations, and Internet websites are also part of the promotional mix of international marketers. Sales promotion programs usually must be adapted to local markets. Factors to consider include stage of market development, market maturity, consumer perceptions of promotional tools, trade structure, and legal restrictions and regulations. Personal selling is the most important element of some companies' international marketing programs, since it is their main form of contact with foreign customers. PR programs are also important to help international marketers develop and maintain favorable relationships with governments, media, and consumers in foreign countries. The use of the Internet as a marketing tool varies by region. In some countries, there are few Internet users and few local companies with websites. But as the number of consumers online grows, so too does the number of large international marketers using the Internet to support their ad campaigns.

Key Terms

balance-of-trade deficit, 637
economic infrastructure, 638
cultural values, 642
global marketing, 646
global advertising, 646
pattern advertising, 651
localized advertising strategy, 659
direct broadcast by satellite (DBS), 663

Discussion Questions

1. The opening vignette to the chapter discusses how multinational companies are expanding into China. Discuss some of the reasons why China has become such an important market for these companies. What challenges do marketers face in developing integrated marketing communication programs for the Chinese market?

2. Why are international markets so important to U.S. companies such as Starbucks, McDonald's, and Coca-Cola, as well as to European companies such as Nestlé, Unilever, and Nokia? Discuss the role of advertising and other forms of promotion in these companies' international marketing programs.

3. Discuss the importance of the economic environment in a country in evaluating its market potential. How do the economic conditions and factors impact the type of integrated marketing communications program a company can use in a country?

4. Global Perspective 20-1 discusses how many multinational companies have begun focusing more attention on the 4 billion consumers who live in the remote, rural communities of developing countries. Discuss the challenges companies face in marketing their products to the world's poorest consumers. How do they have to adapt their integrated marketing communication programs in selling to these consumers?

5. What are some of the cultural variables that marketers must consider in developing advertising and promotional programs in a foreign market? Choose one of these cultural variables and discuss how it has created a problem or challenge for a company in developing an advertising and promotional program in a specific country.

6. Discuss the arguments for and against the use of global marketing and advertising. What types of products and services are best suited for global advertising?

7. Global Perspective 20-2 discusses the growing anti-American sentiment that has emerged in a number of countries around the world. What are some of the reasons that the United States has such a negative image in many countries? Discuss some of the ways the U.S. government as well as corporations can address the anti-American attitudes of many consumers in foreign countries.

8. What is meant by a global market segment? Provide an example of a company that has identified a global market segment and advertises its product or service the same way around the world to this market.

9. Discuss the problems and challenges international marketers face in developing media strategies for foreign markets.

10. Global Perspective 20-4 discusses the public relations problem Coca-Cola and PepsiCo have been facing in India resulting from accusations regarding the level of pesticide residue in their products. What are some of the ways these companies might deal with the PR problem they are facing in India?

Regulation of Advertising and Promotion

21

Chapter Objectives

1. To examine how advertising is regulated, including the role and function of various regulatory agencies.
2. To examine self-regulation of advertising and evaluate its effectiveness.
3. To consider how advertising is regulated by federal and state government agencies, including the Federal Trade Commission.
4. To examine rules and regulations that affect sales promotion, direct marketing, and marketing on the Internet.

Direct-to-Consumer Drug Advertising Comes Under Attack

For years, pharmaceutical companies marketed most of their prescription drugs directly to physicians, either through their sales force or by advertising in medical journals. However, in 1997, the Food and Drug Administration (FDA) issued new guidelines to make it easier for pharmaceutical companies to advertise prescription drugs on television as well as in print media. Consumers still must have the explicit permission of a physician to buy a prescription medication so drug companies still have the challenge of motivating consumers to see their doctor while touting their brand as a remedy to the problem. However, with the change in guidelines, direct-to-consumer (DTC) drug advertising has exploded, and pharmaceutical companies are some of the largest consumer advertisers.

Direct-to-consumer drug advertising spending soared from $859 million in 1997 to over $4 billion in 2005. Brand-name prescription drugs such as Lipitor, Zoloft, Celebrex, Viagra, and Levitra have become as well-known to consumers as brands of soft drinks. It is hard to make it through a television show today without seeing a drug commercial hawking prescription drugs for a variety of medical problems and conditions including allergies, heartburn, arthritis, depression, and impotence. Drug companies use celebrities and athletes to pitch their products just as frequently and effectively as other marketers. Pfizer used former vice president Bob Dole, who is also a war hero, as an advertising spokesperson when it launched Viagra in 1998 to help overcome the stigma surrounding erectile dysfunction and to encourage men to speak with their physician and their partner about the problem. However, the marketing for the brand has evolved from using a respected politician as a spokesman to using sports heroes, NASCAR sponsorships, and ads promoting a mischievous lifestyle.

The pharmaceutical companies argue that the increased spending on drug advertising has helped educate consumers about their options and has caused people, who might not do so otherwise, to see doctors about medications. However, a number of physicians, consumers, and health care groups have expressed concern over the increase in drug advertising for several reasons. A major concern is the accuracy of the ads and whether they inform consumers of all the risks associated with taking a drug. Consumer groups asked the Food and Drug Administration to enforce the "fair balance" provision, an FDA regulation governing broadcast commercials that requires drug ads to give both the benefits and the risks of taking a medication.

The FDA is charged with the responsibility of ensuring that drug advertising is fair, balanced, and truthful. However, the number of ads submitted annually for FDA scrutiny, including TV spots, magazine ads, Internet sites, and even pamphlets used by sales representatives has jumped nearly 35 percent over the past eight years from just over 25,000 to more than 35,000. The number of citation letters issue by the FDA to drug companies for ads that might be false, misleading, or otherwise out of compliance has been steadily declining.

The pharmaceutical companies say that the drop in citations shows that their advertisements are cleaner than before and that they are much more knowledgeable about the FDA guidelines than they were in 1997. However, the FDA's director of the Division of Drug Marketing, Advertising, and Communication notes that with its limited resources the division cannot investigate all of the ads, so it focuses on ads deemed most critical: those that appear on television, make unusual claims, or raise a major public health issue.

Many watchdog organizations such as the Public Citizen's Heath Research Group believe that the drug companies' advertising and marketing pitches are not more honest or balanced than in the past. They also argue that the FDA citations are little more than slaps on the wrist to the powerful drug companies and that it has to be given the authority to levy stiff fines against companies that repeatedly violate its guidelines. Consumer advocates have also argued for stricter regulations on drug ads noting that while advertisers must include statements about negative side effects or toxicity, the images of people with allergies romping happily outside or of someone who has chronic heartburn downing a pepperoni pizza are what people remember—not the cautionary voiceover. Both doctors and critics are also concerned that the ads lead patients to insist on specific drugs when other drugs or lifestyle changes might be better for them

The FDA has recently been under attack from several sectors that have linked drug safety and DTC advertising. In 2004, Congressman Henry Waxman, who has been very critical of DTC advertising, issued a report claiming that lax enforcement of existing laws by the FDA allowed "false and misleading" advertisements to keep running for six months or more before they were pulled. Concerns over DTC drug advertising escalated in the fall of 2004 when Merck and Co. had to pull its popular antiarthritis medication Vioxx from the market after it was determined that the drug increased patients' risk of heart attack. Soon thereafter, the FDA asked Pfizer to cease all marketing for its arthritis medication, Celebrex, and a few months later to pull Bextra, a sibling product, from the market. The FDA also issued a warning that a number of well-known and well-advertised painkillers can cause heart damage.

Critics have called for a moratorium on the advertising of new drugs following their approval until the product is in the marketplace long enough for the FDA to have confidence that it is as safe as it was throught to be when first approved. The FDA may be moving in this direction: In 2005, the FDA approved several new drugs with the condition that the pharmaceutical company not advertise the drug directly to consumers or in medical journals for one year. The FDA has also increased the number of letters it has sent to drug makers warning them that they are violating promotional regulations. Consumers also appear to be cooling to the deluge of drug ads targeted at them. In 1999, more than half of the respondents to an FDA consumer survey said that they liked seeing the drug ads, but three years later the number was less than a third, and 60 percent indicated that the ads do not provide enough information about the risks of a drug.

The pharmaceutical industry is recognizing that it needs to address the problems with DTC advertising. In August 2005, the Pharmaceutical Research and Manufacturers of America (PhRMA), the industry's trade organization, released its Guiding Principles on Direct to Consumer Advertisements about Prescriptions Medications. The voluntary guidelines call for better presentation of risk information and for drug companies to spend an appropriate amount of time to educate health care professionals about a new drug. They should also clarify the risks and benefits. However, critics argue that the PhRMA has come up with its own standards to preempt stricter guidelines that the FDA might impose. In late 2005, the FDA began holding public hearings on the issue of DTC drug advertising, and it is likely that more stringent guidelines will be forthcoming.

Sources: Rich Thomaselli, "FDA to Hold New DTC Advertising Hearings," AdAge.com, October 5, 2005; Rich Thomaselli, "Pharmaceutical Industry Issues DTC Ad Guidelines," AdAge.com, August 2, 2005; Betsy Querna, "The Big Pill Pitch," *U.S. News & World Report,* June 6, 2005, pp. 52–53; Rich Thomaselli, "FDA Ruling Threatens DTC Dollars," *Advertising Age,* April 11, 2005, pp. 1, 93; Christine Bittar, "Creating an Rx Monster," *Brandweek,* July 29, 2002, pp. 22–29.

Suppose you are the advertising manager for a consumer-product company and have just reviewed a new commercial your agency created. You are very excited about the ad. It presents new claims about your brand's superiority that should help differentiate it from the competition. However, before you approve the commercial you need answers. Are the claims verifiable? Did researchers use proper procedures to collect and analyze the data and present the findings? Do research results support the claims? Were the right people used in the study? Could any conditions have biased the results?

Before approving the commercial, you have it reviewed by your company's legal department and by your agency's attorneys. If both reviews are acceptable, you send the ad to the major networks, which have their censors examine it. They may ask for more information or send the ad back for modification. (No commercial can run without approval from a network's Standards and Practices Department.)

Even after approval and airing, your commercial is still subject to scrutiny from such state and federal regulatory agencies as the state attorney general's office and the Federal Trade Commission. Individual consumers or competitors who find the ad misleading or have other concerns may file a complaint with the National Advertising Division of the Council of Better Business Bureaus. Finally, disparaged competitors may sue if they believe your ad distorts the facts and misleads consumers. If you lose the litigation, your company may have to retract the claims and pay the competitor damages, sometimes running into millions of dollars.

After considering all these regulatory issues, you must ask yourself if the new ad can meet all these challenges and is worth the risk. Maybe you ought to continue with the old approach that made no specific claims and simply said your brand was great.

Regulatory concerns can play a major role in the advertising decision-making process. Advertisers operate in a complex environment of local, state, and federal rules and regulations. Additionally, a number of advertising and business-sponsored associations, consumer groups and organizations, and the media attempt to promote honest, truthful, and tasteful advertising through their own self-regulatory programs and guidelines. The legal and regulatory aspects of advertising are very complex. Many parties are concerned about the nature and content of advertising and its potential to offend, exploit, mislead, and/or deceive consumers.

Advertising has also become increasingly important in product liability litigation involving products that are associated with consumer injuries. In many of these cases the courts have been willing to consider the impact of advertising on behavior of consumers that leads to injury-causing situations. Thus advertisers must avoid certain practices and proactively engage in others to ensure that their ads are comprehended correctly and do not misrepresent their products or services.[1]

Numerous guidelines, rules, regulations, and laws constrain and restrict advertising. These regulations primarily influence individual advertisers, but they can also affect advertising for an entire industry. For example, cigarette advertising was banned from the broadcast media in 1970, and many groups are pushing for a total ban on the advertising of tobacco products.[2] Legislation now being considered would further restrict the advertising of alcoholic beverages, including beer and wine.[3] Advertising is controlled by internal self-regulation and by external state and federal regulatory agencies such as the Federal Trade Commission (FTC), the Federal Communications Commission (FCC), the Food and Drug Administration (FDA), and the U.S. Postal Service. And recently state attorneys general have become more active in advertising regulation. While only government agencies (federal, state, and local) have the force of law, most advertisers also abide by the guidelines and decisions of internal regulatory bodies. In fact, internal regulation from such groups as the media and the National Advertising Review Board probably has more influence on advertisers' day-to-day operations and decision making than government rules and regulations.

Decision makers on both the client and agency side must be knowledgeable about these regulatory groups, including the intent of their efforts, how they operate, and how they influence and affect advertising and other promotional mix elements. In this chapter, we examine the major sources of advertising regulation, including efforts by the industry at voluntary self-regulation and external regulation by government agencies. We also examine regulations involving sales promotion, direct marketing, and marketing on the Internet.

Self-Regulation

For many years, the advertising industry has practiced and promoted voluntary **self-regulation.** Most advertisers, their agencies, and the media recognize the importance of maintaining consumer trust and confidence. Advertisers also see self-regulation as a way to limit government interference, which, they believe, results in more stringent and troublesome regulations. Self-regulation and control of advertising emanate from all segments of the advertising industry, including individual advertisers and their agencies, business and advertising associations, and the media.

Self-Regulation by Advertisers and Agencies

Self-regulation begins with the interaction of client and agency when creative ideas are generated and submitted for consideration. Most companies have specific guidelines, standards, and policies to which their ads must adhere. Recognizing that their ads reflect on the company, advertisers carefully scrutinize all messages to ensure they are consistent with the image the firm wishes to project. Companies also review their ads to be sure any claims made are reasonable and verifiable and do not mislead or deceive consumers. Ads are usually examined by corporate attorneys to avoid potential legal problems and their accompanying time, expense, negative publicity, and embarrassment.

Internal control and regulation also come from advertising agencies. Most have standards regarding the type of advertising they either want or are willing to produce, and they try to avoid ads that might be offensive or misleading. Most agencies will ask their clients to provide verification or support for claims the clients might want to make in their advertising and will make sure that adequate documentation or substantiation is available. However, agencies will also take formal steps to protect themselves from legal and ethical perils through agency-client contracts. For example, many liability issues are handled in these contracts. Agencies generally use information provided by clients for advertising claims, and in standard contracts the agency is protected from suits involving the accuracy of those claims. Contracts will also absolve the agency of responsibility if something goes wrong with the advertised product and consumers suffer damages or injury or other product liability claims arise.[4] However, agencies have been held legally responsible for fraudulent or deceptive claims and in some cases have been fined when their clients were found guilty of engaging in deceptive advertising.[5] Many agencies have a creative review board or panel composed of experienced personnel who examine ads for content and execution as well as for their potential to be perceived as offensive, misleading, and/or deceptive. Most agencies also employ or retain lawyers who review the ads for potential legal problems. Exhibit 21-1 shows an ad for a legal firm specializing in advertising law and intellectual property.

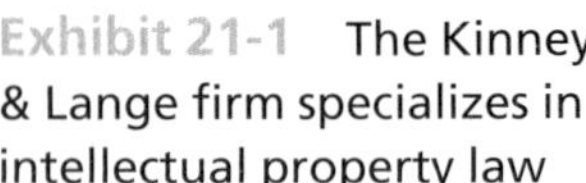

Exhibit 21-1 The Kinney & Lange firm specializes in intellectual property law

Without protection, great ideas can't grow.
KINNEY & LANGE
INTELLECTUAL PROPERTY ATTORNEYS

Self-Regulation by Trade Associations

Like advertisers and their agencies, many industries have also developed self-regulatory programs. This is particularly true in industries whose advertising is prone to controversy, such as liquor and alcoholic beverages, drugs, and various products marketed to children. Many trade and industry associations develop their own advertising guidelines or codes that member companies are expected to abide by.

The Wine Institute, the U.S. Brewers Association, and the Distilled Spirits Council of the United States all have guidelines that member companies are supposed to follow in advertising alcoholic beverages.[6] No specific law prohibits the advertising of hard liquor on radio or television. However, such advertising was effectively banned for over five decades as a result of a code provision by the National Association of Broadcasters and by agreement of liquor manufacturers and their self-governing body, the Distilled Spirits Council (DISCUS). However, in November 1996, DISCUS amended its code of good practice and overturned its self-imposed ban on broadcast advertising.[7] IMC Perspective 21-1 discusses the reasons why the council decided to overturn the ban, as well as the controversy that has resulted from its decision. Other industry trade associations with advertising codes and guidelines include the Toy Industry Association, the Motion Picture Association of America, and the Pharmaceutical Research and Manufacturers of America whose guidelines for prescription drug advertising were discussed in the opening vignette to the chapter.

Many professions also maintain advertising guidelines through local, state, and national organizations. For years professional associations like the American Medical Association (AMA) and the American Bar Association (ABA) restricted advertising by their members on the basis that such promotional activities lowered members' professional status and led to unethical and fraudulent claims. However, such restrictive codes have been attacked by both government regulatory agencies and consumer groups. They argue that the public has a right to be informed about a professional's services, qualifications, and background and that advertising will improve professional services as consumers become better informed and are better able to shop around.[8]

In 1977, the Supreme Court held that state bar associations' restrictions on advertising are unconstitutional and that attorneys have First Amendment freedom of speech rights to advertise.[9] Many professional associations subsequently removed their restrictions, and advertising by lawyers and other professionals is now common (Exhibit 21-2).[10] In 1982, the Supreme Court upheld an FTC order permitting advertising by dentists and physicians.[11]

Research shows that consumers generally favor increased use of professional advertising. However, professionals continue to have reservations. They worry that advertising has a negative impact on their image, credibility, and dignity and see benefits to consumers as unlikely.[12] Still, advertising by professionals is increasing, particularly among newcomers to medicine, dentistry, and law. Associations such as the AMA and the ABA developed guidelines for members' advertising to help maintain standards and guard against misleading, deceptive, or offensive ads.

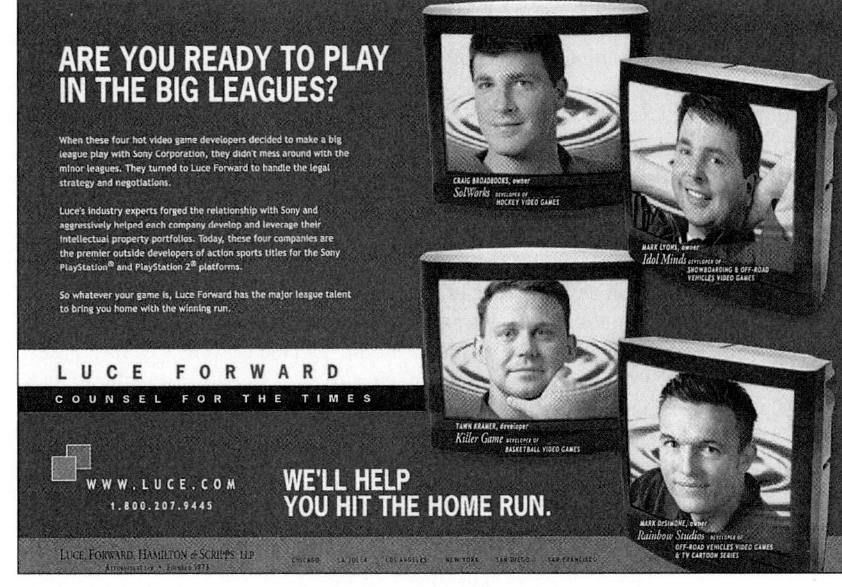

Exhibit 21-2 Advertising by lawyers has become more common as the result of a 1977 Supreme Court ruling

The issue of professional advertising, particularly by attorneys, is still hotly debated. Some traditional law firms resist using advertising, particularly on TV, due to concern that it might hurt the profession's image. Many in the legal profession worry that ads soliciting personal injury victims only worsen the public's perception of attorneys. A sizable faction within the American Bar

IMC PERSPECTIVE 21-1

Hard Liquor Advertisers Continue to Break Down Barriers

For more than five decades, distilled spirits were not advertised on television or radio because of a self-imposed ban by members of the Distilled Spirits Council of the United States (DISCUS). Council members agreed in 1936 to avoid radio advertising and extended the ban to TV in 1948. But Seagram, the second-largest distiller in the world at the time, ended the U.S. spirits industry's long-standing ban on broadcast advertising in June 1996 by airing commercials for its Crown Royal Canadian Whiskey brand on an affiliate in Corpus Christi, Texas.

Seagram issued a statement that it was ending the liquor industry's decades-old practice of not advertising on TV because DISCUS's voluntary code of good practice placed spirits at a competitive disadvantage to beer and wine, which did not have any such restrictions. Seagram also argued that the ban had become outdated as radio and TV have become more targeted and they could pinpoint their advertising message to people of legal drinking age. A number of distillers, eager to turn around the long, slow decline in hard liquor sales, watched Seagram test the water with its TV ads before rolling out their own commercials. Some held discussions with TV stations but waited for a formal amendment to the DISCUS code of good practice before proceeding. The amendments came on November 7, 1996, when DISCUS members voted unanimously to overturn the self-imposed ban on broadcast ads. The DISCUS president noted that spirits makers wanted to break down the public perception that spirits are stronger or more dangerous than beer and wine and thus deserving of harsher social and political treatment.

After the DISCUS ban was lifted, the four major broadcast TV networks as well as major cable networks such as ESPN and MTV continued to refuse liquor ads prompting consumer and public interest groups to applaud their actions. In fact, analysts have argued that it was really the refusal by TV stations and networks to accept liquor advertising rather than the DISCUS code that had kept them off the air. However, the major networks cannot control the practices of affiliate stations they do not own and many of them began accepting liquor ads, as did local cable channels and independent broadcast stations. By the fall of 2001, DISCUS estimated that about 400 local stations and cable channels were permitting or considering spirit ads, although most restricted the ads to after 9 P.M.

In December 2001, NBC, which is owned by the General Electric Co., announced that it would become the first broadcast network to accept hard liquor advertising. NBC planned to limit the liquor ads to programs where at least 85 percent of viewers are 21 or older such as during late-night time slots. The network also adopted a set of guidelines under which the makers of distilled spirits could advertise in a way similar to beer and wine makers. Under the guidelines, liquor companies had to run four months of so-called social responsibility ads on subjects like designated drivers before general product promotion spots could air.

NBC was not joined by the three other major broadcast networks—ABC, CBS, and Fox—in its decision to accept liquor commercials. While executives from the other networks stated that they did not think it was the right thing to do, industry experts noted that they were also wary of alienating beer companies who spend more than $500 million each year advertising their products on network television. Although NBC's lead in accepting liquor ads did not generate support from the other networks, it did engender a considerable amount of controversy and criticism from members of Congress, federal regulators, the American Medical Association, and many public advocacy groups. Critics of NBC's decision expressed concern that airing liquor ads on TV would glamorize drinking and encourage children and teenagers to drink. Facing a widening backlash over its decision, in March 2002, NBC announced that it was dropping its plans to accept liquor advertising.

The national broadcast networks have continued their self-imposed ban, recognizing that they are held to a higher standard. However, the amount of liquor advertising on television continues to increase as more than 600 local broadcast stations accepted liquor advertising in 2005. Together, the cable and local broadcast stations carried more than $100 million worth of liquor advertising in 2004, and this number is expected to increase as major cable networks such as CNN now plan to accept liquor ads.

The liquor industry has also been able to break through several other promotional barriers more recently. A major breakthrough occurred when NASCAR lifted its long-standing ban on liquor sponsorships in 2005. For many years, NASCAR officials were skeptical about lifting the ban. However, liquor giants Diageo, Jim Beam Brands, and Brown-Forman started lobbying the racing league in the late '90s. They see NASCAR sponsorship as not only a good fit with their target audience but also a symbolic step into mainstream marketing of their brands. All of the ads connected to NASCAR must have a strong responsible drinking component. For example, Jack Daniel's, which is new to NASCAR sponsorship, created a spot featuring its NASCAR race car using the slogan "Pace yourself. Especially when you're drinking."

The increase in advertising and promotion appears to be having an impact as total U.S. liquor sales reached nearly $15 billion in 2004, a 12 percent increase from two years ago, while total cases sold were up by 7 percent. It is the first time case sales have been up more than 3 percent in two consecutive years since the 1980s. The industry expects the sales surge to continue as the number of consumers reaching the legal drinking age of 21 will surge over the next decade. Many liquor marketers are taking advantage of the new opportunities on TV. Diageo, which has 10 of the top 20 spirit brands in the United States and holds a 23 percent market share, spent an estimated $150 million in advertising in 2004, up 30 percent from a few years ago, with much of the increase coming in TV ads.

Restrictions on the advertising of hard liquor continue to loosen as DISCUS has made major inroads into putting liquor advertising more on par with advertising for beer and wine. However, consumer groups such as the Center for Science in the Public Interest and the American Medical Association are not giving up the fight. The AMA has an active campaign against NASCAR sponsorships as well as TV ads arguing that one of the fastest growing segments of the racing league's audience is 12- to 18-year-olds. AMA president Dr. J. Edward Hill notes, "Advertising liquor on the actual race cars that youth idolize sends the wrong message." However, right or wrong, advertising hard liquor is becoming a lot easier these days.

Sources: David Kiley, "A Green Flag for Booze," *BusinessWeek,* March 7, 2005, p. 95; James B. Arndorfer and Jon Fine, "Spirit Marketers Bingeing on Cable," *Advertising Age,* September 20, 2004, pp. 1, 55; Kate Fitzgerald, "Cable Wrestles with Liquor Ads," *Advertising Age,* June 10, 2002, p. S-16; Stuart Elliott, "Facing Outcry, NBC Ends Plan to Run Liquor Ads," *The New York Times,* March 21, 2002, p. C1; Joe Flint and Shelly Branch, "In Face of Widening Backlash, NBC Gives Up Plan to Run Liquor Ads," *The Wall Street Journal,* March 21, 2002, pp. B1, 3.

Association (ABA) blames the legal profession's image problem on sleazy ads. The ABA's Commission on Advertising held a series of public hearings on what, if any, restrictive measures to recommend to state ethics panels. Some states, such as Iowa and Florida, already restrict the content of attorney ads and the way they can be delivered. For example, Iowa lawyers are limited to "tombstone" print ads that merely list their name, location, and objective qualifications. And all ads require a disclaimer urging consumers not to base their attorney selection on an advertisement. Florida attorneys cannot use testimonials or endorsements, dramatizations, self-laudatory statements, illustrations, or photos.[13]

Many attorneys are incensed over efforts to restrict their rights to promote themselves because they use advertising to help build their practices. Several cases are currently being litigated, but ultimately the Supreme Court may have to decide just how far states can go in curtailing advertising.

Although industry associations are concerned with the impact and consequences of members' advertising, they have no legal way to enforce their guidelines. They can only rely on peer pressure from members or other nonbinding sanctions to get advertisers to comply.

Self-Regulation by Businesses

A number of self-regulatory mechanisms have been established by the business community in an effort to control advertising practices.[14] The largest and best known is the **Better Business Bureau (BBB),** which promotes fair advertising and selling practices across all industries. The BBB was established in 1916 to handle consumer complaints about local business practices and particularly advertising. Local BBBs are located in most large cities throughout the United States and supported entirely by dues of the more than 100,000 member firms.

Local BBBs receive and investigate complaints from consumers and other companies regarding the advertising and selling tactics of businesses in their area. Each local office has its own operating procedures for handling complaints; generally, the office contacts the violator and, if the complaint proves true, requests that the practice be stopped or changed. If the violator does not respond, negative publicity may be used against the firm or the case may be referred to appropriate government agencies for further action.

While BBBs provide effective control over advertising practices at the local level, the parent organization, the **Council of Better Business Bureaus,** plays a major role at the national level. The council assists new industries in developing advertising codes and standards, and it provides information about advertising regulations and legal rulings to advertisers, agencies, and the media. The council also plays an important self-regulatory role through its National Advertising Division (NAD) and Children's Advertising Review Unit (CARU). The NAD works closely with the **National Advertising Review Board** (NARB) to sustain truth, accuracy, and decency in national advertising.

The National Advertising Review Council and the NAD/NARB

In 1971 four associations—the American Advertising Federation (AAF), the American Association of Advertising Agencies (AAAA), the Association of National Advertisers (ANA), and the Council of Better Business Bureaus—joined forces to establish the **National Advertising Review Council (NARC).** The NARC's mission is to sustain high standards of truth, accuracy, and social responsibility in national advertising. The council has two operating arms, the National Advertising Division of the Council of Better Business Bureaus and the National Advertising Review Board. The NAD is the first level that investigates the truthfulness and accuracy of an ad. The NAD reviews only national advertisements, those disseminated on a nationwide or broadly regional basis. Product performance claims, superiority claims against competitive products, and all kinds of scientific and technical claims made in national advertising are the types of cases accepted by the NAD. When an advertiser or a challenger disagrees with the NAD's findings, the decision can be appealed to the NARB for additional review. The NAD/NARB has become the advertising industry's primary self-regulatory mechanism.

The NAD's advertising monitoring program is the source of many of the cases it reviews (Figure 21-1). It also reviews complaints from consumers and consumer groups, local BBBs, and competitors. For example, the NAD received a complaint from the Center for Science in the Public Interest, a consumer advocacy group, over an ad run by Campbell Soup for the company's V8 vegetable juice that suggested a link between the tomato-based product and a reduced risk of cancer. Though the NAD decided that Campbell provided competent and reliable evidence to support certain claims, it recommended that the company modify language stating "for prostate cancer, a lower risk is apparent when five or more servings (of tomato products) are consumed per week." Campbell agreed to change the wording of the ad.[15] During the 1970s and '80s, many of the complaints to the NAD came from consumers. However, with the increased use of comparative advertising, the majority of the complaints are now coming from marketers that are challenging competitors' comparisons with their brands.[16] For example, BMW filed a complaint with the NAD over a Volvo commercial claiming the Volvo 850 Turbo Sportswagon accelerates faster than a BMW 328I.[17] Procter & Gamble recently filed a challenge with the NAD over a TV commercial from Fort James Corp. that claimed Brawny paper towels were stronger than P&G's Bounty brand. The commercial in question was the popular "Grannies" spot that showed two grandmothers pushing over a refrigerator to make a mess that was more easily cleaned with Brawny paper towels than with Bounty.[18]

The NAD acts as the investigative arm of the NARC. After initiating or receiving a complaint, it determines the issue, collects and evaluates data, and makes the initial decision on whether the advertiser's claims are substantiated. The NAD may ask the advertiser to supply substantiation for the claim in question. If the information provided is considered adequate to support the claim, the case is deemed substantiated. In the Volvo case, the NAD ruled that the company did have test results to support its superior-acceleration claim and the case was considered substantiated. If the substanti-

Figure 21-1 Sources of NAD Cases and Decisions, 2004

Sources	Number	Percent	Decisions	Number	Percent
Competitor challenges	82	61%	Modified/discontinued	68	50%
NAD monitoring	43	32	Administratively closed	23	17
Local BBB challenges	2	1	Substantiated	15	11
Consumer challenges	8	6	Compliance	14	10
Total	135	100%	Referred to government	15	11
			Total	135	100%

ation is unsatisfactory, the NAD negotiates with the advertiser to modify or discontinue the advertising. For example, in the case involving Brawny and Bounty paper towels, the NAD found that several performance claims in the Brawny ads were substantiated. However, the NAD also found that the Brawny ads conveyed an overall-superiority claim that could not be supported, and it recommended that Fort James modify the spot or discontinue using it.

If the NAD and the advertiser fail to resolve the controversy, either can appeal to a five-person panel from the National Advertising Review Board. For example, Fort James Corp. chose to appeal the NAD decision regarding its overall-superiority claim for Brawny versus Bounty paper towels to the NARB rather than modify its ad. The NARB is composed of 85 advertising professionals and prominent public-interest/academia members. If the NARB panel agrees with the NAD and rules against the advertiser, the advertiser must discontinue the advertising. If the advertiser refuses to comply, the NARB refers the matter to the appropriate government agency and indicates the fact in its public record. NAD/NARB decisions are released to the press and also are published in its monthly publication, *NAD Case Reports.*

Although the NARB has no power to order an advertiser to modify or stop running an ad and no sanctions it can impose, advertisers who participate in an NAD investigation and NARB appeal rarely refuse to abide by the panel's decision. Most cases do not even make it to the NARB panel. For example, in 2004, of the 135 NAD investigations, 15 ad claims were substantiated, 15 were referred to the government, and 68 were modified or discontinued (Figure 21-1). Of the 68 cases where the advertising claims were modified or discontinued, in only 5 did the advertiser appeal to the NARB for resolution.[19]

The National Advertising Review Council is also involved in the self-regulation of children's advertising through the Children's Advertising Review Unit (CARU) of the Council of Better Business Bureaus. The NARC board sets policy for CARU's self-regulatory program, which is administered by the Council of Better Business Bureaus and funded directly by members of the children's advertising industry. The CARU's activities include the review and evaluation of child-directed advertising in all media, as well as online privacy issues that affect children. The CARU also provides a general advisory service for advertisers and agencies and has developed self-regulatory guidelines for children's advertising. CARU recognizes that the special nature and needs of a youthful audience require particular care and diligence on the part of advertisers. As such, CARU's Self-Regulatory Guidelines for Children's Advertising go beyond truthfulness and accuracy to address children's developing cognitive abilities.

In 2004, the NARC became involved in the self-regulation of electronic retailing when it initiated the Electronic Retailing Self-Regulation Program (ERSP). The program is sponsored by the Electronic Retailers Association (ERA), although it works independently of the ERA to create an unbiased self-regulatory system. The mission of the ERSP is to enhance consumer confidence in electronic retailing, to discourage advertising and marketing in the electronic retailing industry that contains unsubstantiated claims, and to demonstrate a commitment to meaningful and effective self-regulation (Exhibit 21-3). The majority of claims reviewed under the ERSP program are for direct-response TV ads including long- and short-form infomercials. Reviews apply to all aspects of a marketing campaign including radio and Internet marketing. SPAM e-mails along with website pop-up ads that lead to further e-commerce are in the ERSP's purview as well as advertising on TV shopping channels.[20]

Exhibit 21-3 The Electronic Retailing Self-Regulation Program is a new area of self-regulation by the NARC

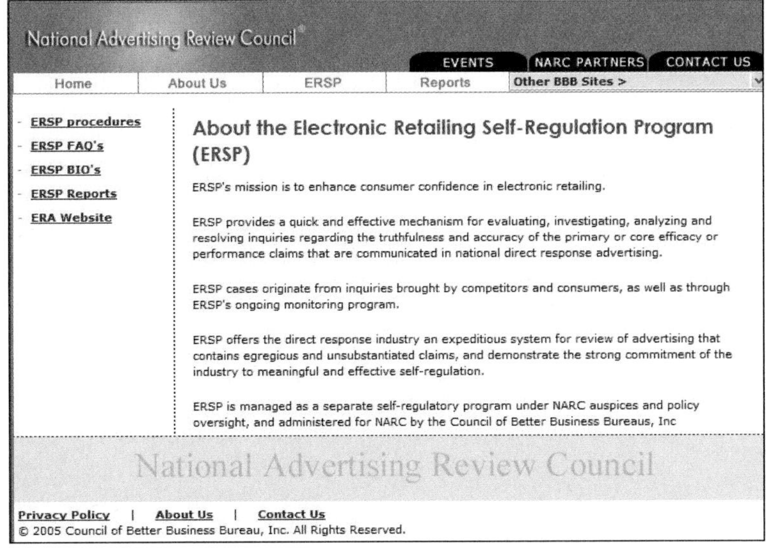

National Advertising Review Council
EVENTS
NARC PARTNERS
CONTACT US
Home
About Us
ERSP
Reports
Other BBB Sites >
ERSP procedures
ERSP FAQ's
ERSP BIO's
ERSP Reports
ERA Website
About the Electronic Retailing Self-Regulation Program (ERSP)
ERSP's mission is to enhance consumer confidence in electronic retailing.
ERSP provides a quick and effective mechanism for evaluating, investigating, analyzing and resolving inquiries regarding the truthfulness and accuracy of the primary or core efficacy or performance claims that are communicated in national direct response advertising.
ERSP cases originate from inquiries brought by competitors and consumers, as well as through ERSP's ongoing monitoring program.
ERSP offers the direct response industry an expeditious system for review of advertising that contains egregious and unsubstantiated claims, and demonstrate the strong commitment of the industry to meaningful and effective self-regulation.
ERSP is managed as a separate self-regulatory program under NARC auspices and policy oversight, and administered for NARC by the Council of Better Business Bureaus, Inc
National Advertising Review Council
Privacy Policy | About Us | Contact Us
© 2005 Council of Better Business Bureau, Inc. All Rights Reserved.

The National Advertising Review Council, working through the NAD/NARB and CARU, has become a valuable and effective self-regulatory body. Cases brought to it are handled at a fraction of the cost (and with much less publicity) than those brought to court and are expedited more

quickly than those reviewed by a government agency such as the FTC. The system also works because judgments are made by the advertiser's peers, and most companies feel compelled to comply. Firms may prefer self-regulation rather than government intervention in part because they can challenge competitors' unsubstantiated claims through groups like the NARB.[21]

Advertising Associations Various groups in the advertising industry also favor self-regulation. The two major national organizations, the American Association of Advertising Agencies and the American Advertising Federation, actively monitor and police industrywide advertising practices. The AAAA, which is the major trade association of the ad agency business in the United States, has established standards of practice and its own creative code. It also issues guidelines for specific types of advertising such as comparative messages (Figure 21-2). The AAF consists of advertisers, agencies, media, and numerous advertising clubs. The association has standards for truthful and responsible advertising, is involved in advertising legislation, and actively influences agencies to abide by its code and principles.

Self-Regulation by Media

The media are another important self-regulatory mechanism in the advertising industry. Most media maintain some form of advertising review process and, except for political ads, may reject any they regard as objectionable. Some media exclude advertising for an entire product class; others ban individual ads they think offensive or objectionable. For example, *Reader's Digest* does not accept advertising for tobacco or liquor products. A number of magazines in the United States and other countries

Figure 21-2 AAAA Policy Statement and Guidelines for Comparative Advertising

The Board of Directors of the American Association of Advertising Agencies recognizes that when used truthfully and fairly, comparative advertising provides the consumer with needed and useful information.

However, extreme caution should be exercised. The use of comparative advertising, by its very nature, can distort facts and, by implication, convey to the consumer information that misrepresents the truth.

Therefore, the Board believes that comparative advertising should follow certain guidelines:

1. The intent and connotation of the ad should be to inform and never to discredit or unfairly attack competitors, competing products, or services.
2. When a competitive product is named, it should be one that exists in the marketplace as significant competition.
3. The competition should be fairly and properly identified but never in a manner or tone of voice that degrades the competitive product or service.
4. The advertising should compare related or similar properties or ingredients of the product, dimension to dimension, feature to feature.
5. The identification should be for honest comparison purposes and not simply to upgrade by association.
6. If a competitive test is conducted, it should be done by an objective testing source, preferably an independent one, so that there will be no doubt as to the veracity of the test.
7. In all cases the test should be supportive of all claims made in the advertising that are based on the test.
8. The advertising should never use partial results or stress insignificant differences to cause the consumer to draw an improper conclusion.
9. The property being compared should be significant in terms of value or usefulness of the product to the consumer.
10. Comparatives delivered through the use of testimonials should not imply that the testimonial is more than one individual's thought unless that individual represents a sample of the majority viewpoint.

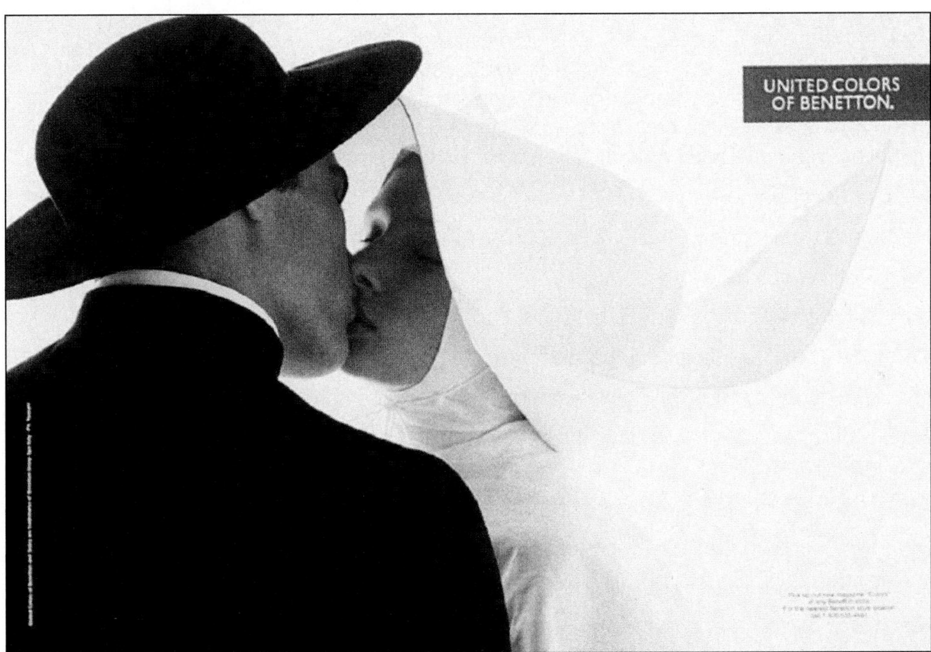

Exhibit 21-4 A number of magazines refused to run this Benetton ad

refused to run some of Benetton's shock ads on the grounds that their readers would find them offensive or disturbing (Exhibit 21-4).[22]

Newspapers and magazines have their own advertising requirements and restrictions, which often vary depending on the size and nature of the publication. Large, established publications, such as major newspapers or magazines, often have strict standards regarding the type of advertising they accept. Some magazines, such as *Parents* and *Good Housekeeping,* regularly test the products they advertise and offer a "seal of approval" and refunds if the products are later found to be defective. Such policies are designed to enhance the credibility of the publication and increase the reader's confidence in the products it advertises.

Advertising on television and radio has been regulated for years through codes developed by the industry trade association, the National Association of Broadcasters (NAB). Both the radio code (established in 1937) and the television code (1952) provided standards for broadcast advertising for many years. Both codes prohibited the advertising of certain products, such as hard liquor. They also affected the manner in which products could be advertised. However, in 1982, the NAB suspended all of its code provisions after the courts found that portions (dealing with time standards and required length of commercials in the TV code) were in restraint of trade. While the NAB codes are no longer in force, many individual broadcasters, such as the major TV networks, have incorporated major portions of the code provisions into their own standards.[23]

The four major television networks have the most stringent review process of any media. All four networks maintain standards and practices divisions, which carefully review all commercials submitted to the network or individual affiliate stations. Advertisers must submit for review all commercials intended for airing on the network or an affiliate.

A commercial may be submitted for review in the form of a script, storyboard, animatic, or finished commercial (when the advertiser believes there is little chance of objection). A very frustrating, and often expensive, scenario for both an agency and its client occurs when a commercial is approved at the storyboard stage but then is rejected after it is produced. Commercials are rejected for a variety of reasons, including violence, morbid humor, sex, politics, and religion. Network reviewers also consider whether the proposed commercial meets acceptable standards and is appropriate for certain audiences. For example, different standards are used for ads designated for prime-time versus late-night spots or for children's versus adults' programs (see Figure 21-3). Although most of these guidelines remain in effect, ABC and NBC loosened their rules on celebrity endorsements.[24]

Figure 21-3 A Sampling of the TV Networks' Guidelines for Children's Advertising

Each of the major TV networks has its own set of guidelines for children's advertising, although the basics are very similar. A few rules, such as the requirement of a static "island" shot at the end, are written in stone; others, however, can sometimes be negotiated. Many of the rules below apply specifically to toys. The networks also have special guidelines for kids' food commercials and for kids' commercials that offer premiums.

Must not overglamorize product

No exhortative language, such as "Ask Mom to buy . . ."

No realistic war settings

Generally no celebrity endorsements

Can't use "only" or "just" in regard to price

Show only two toys per child or maximum of six per commercial

Five-second "island" showing product against plain background at end of spot

Animation restricted to one-third of a commercial

Generally no comparative or superiority claims

No costumes or props not available with the toy

No child or toy can appear in animated segments

Three-second establishing shot of toy in relation to child

No shots under one second in length

Must show distance a toy can travel before stopping on its own

The four major networks receive nearly 50,000 commercials a year for review; nearly two-thirds are accepted, and only 3 percent are rejected. Most problems with the remaining 30 percent are resolved through negotiation, and the ads are revised and resubmitted.[25] Most commercials run after changes are made. For example, censors initially rejected a humorous "Got milk?" spot that showed children watching an elderly neighbor push a wheelbarrow. Suddenly, the man's arms rip off, presumably because he doesn't drink milk. The spot was eventually approved after it was modified so that the man appears unhurt after losing his limbs and there was no expression of pain (Exhibit 21-5).[26]

Network standards regarding acceptable advertising change constantly. The networks first allowed lingerie advertisers to use live models rather than mannequins in 1987. Advertising for contraceptives is now appearing on some stations. The networks also loosened long-standing restrictions on endorsements and competitive advertising claims.[27] Network standards will continue to change as society's values and attitudes toward certain issues and products change. Also, many advertising people believe these changes are a response to competition from independent and cable stations,

Exhibit 21-5 This humorous "Got milk?" commercial had to be modified slightly to satisfy network censors

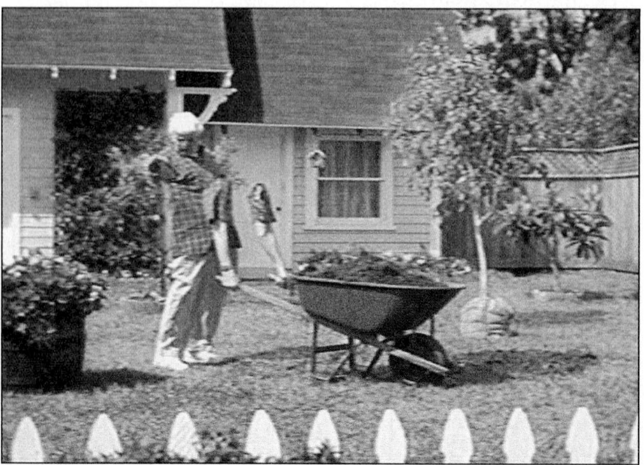

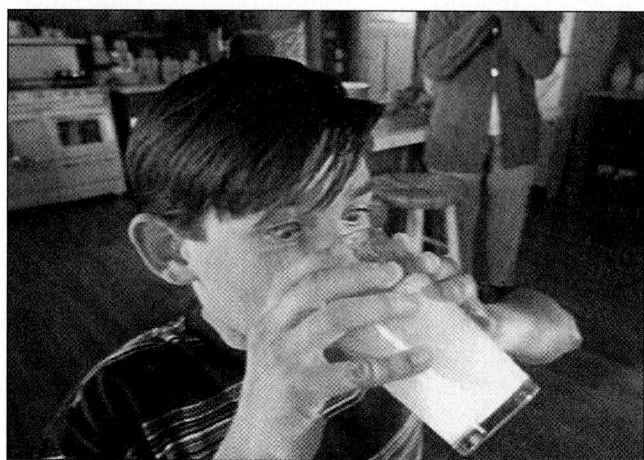

CAREER PROFILE

Bob Hansen

Consumer Reporter, NBC-TV San Diego

I actually began my career in advertising but ended up on a different side of the business working as a consumer reporter for a television station. After graduating from the University of California, San Diego, with a degree in communications/visual arts, I began working for an advertising agency. I started as a still photographer but eventually was asked to handle some accounts. It was while pitching a story idea to the *Los Angeles Times* that I decided I'd rather be working for a newspaper than bugging the editors to cover my client. It was then that I decided to return to school and I earned a master's degree in journalism from the University of Missouri.

My professional career started as a copy boy for the *Houston Chronicle*. I did everything from make coffee for the reporters to rip wire copy and hand them out to the newspaper editors. Before computers, the news was literally printed out on huge rolls of paper. We would cut them up by subject and distribute the stories to the appropriate parties. I also worked as a freelance photographer for the Associated Press. It was my first glimpse into real news. While I never planned on getting into television, my love of writing and pictures made it a logical next step. I decided to become a TV news reporter and began working as a one-man-band in Fort Myers, Florida, sometimes both shooting and reporting my own stories. I eventually became the weekend anchor for the NBC affiliate. I then moved to a station in Louisville, Kentucky, where I worked as a TV reporter and also did feature stories for National Public Radio out of Washington, D.C.

"The best way to work with news reporters is to understand their needs, their deadlines, and their audience."

For the past 15 years I have been specializing in consumer reporting. I work for KNSD-TV, the NBC owned station in San Diego, where I am known as "Consumer Bob." I have my own segment every weekday on the evening news, which talks about things that matter in people's lives as consumers. My consumer segment is different than general news because it has more of an immediate connection with the audience. The stories cover a wide range of issues and topics, such as warning viewers about the latest e-mail scam, providing tips for finding the perfect pair of jeans, taste-testing a new soft drink, or reporting on the latest high-tech product such as digital cameras. My consumer reports are designed to appeal to a large cross section of our station's viewers. I look for stories that are interesting and also that can easily be told in a two-minute news segment. Time and money are always considerations in doing a story as I do not have the luxury or the budget to spend weeks or even days on a story. In television news, you are always working under a deadline. Ninety percent of what you see on the air was shot that day. A public relations professional needs to know that so he or she will be brief and to the point when pitching a story to the media.

As a consumer reporter for a television station, you are everyone's best friend and everyone's enemy—often at the same time. Television news influences public opinion. The reputation of a company, a product, service, or sales campaign can be tarnished or enhanced by news coverage. That's why corporations spend millions of dollars trying to influence the news media, from radio and television stations to newspapers, magazines, and Internet websites. A 30-second commercial can cost thousands of dollars to run in a local market and hundreds of thousands on a network level. However, a news story on a particular company or product can last three times as long and does not cost the company a penny. Besides airing in San Diego, many of my stories end up on TV newscasts across the country. Today network-owned stations and their affiliates are constantly sharing video and news story ideas. Therefore a local story one day may get national exposure the next.

Public relations experts spend a great deal of time and effort trying to find ways to get news reporters to cover their company, brand, or event. I receive hundreds of story ideas each week. Companies and public relations firms send me e-mails, letters, faxes, and make calls trying to convince me to cover their product. It's my job to determine which story to cover and how to go about it. It's not a perfect science. I may do a story on organic dog food one day and get flooded with other dog-food-related ideas, but as good as they may be, I'll jump to a different subject the next day. That can be very frustrating for someone trying to get "air time" for their company. Getting a story on the air at any particular station is a mixture of timing, determination, and luck.

Not everyone is always happy with the stories I do on their companies or products. They get upset when I don't like the product or they may feel that my story did not portray them favorably. That's not my problem. A good reporter will be fair and objective and cannot be unduly influenced by outside pressure. Media coverage comes with some risk as you might be able to get the ear of a reporter, but you can't control what he or she says about your product. That is what makes publicity very different from advertising. The best way to work with news reporters is to understand their needs, their deadlines, and their audience. And it also helps to have an interesting story for them to tell.

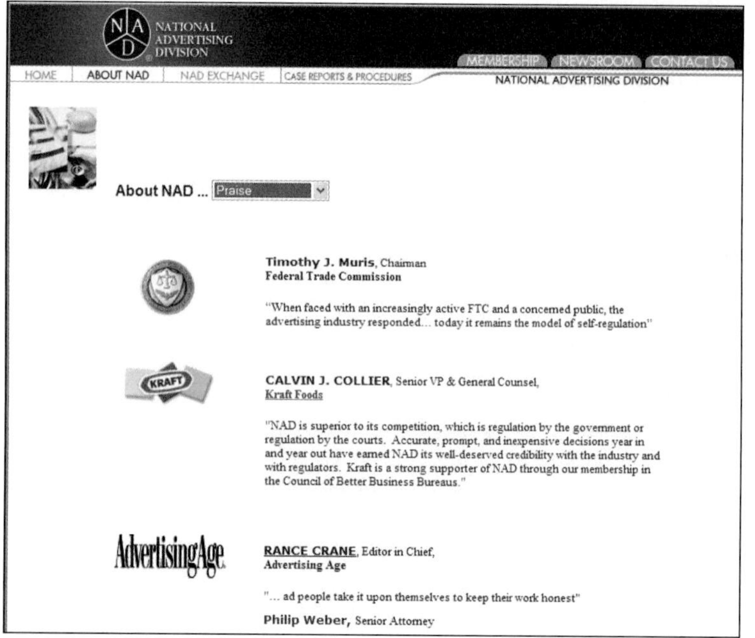

NAD
NATIONAL ADVERTISING DIVISION
MEMBERSHIP
NEWSROOM
CONTACT US
HOME
ABOUT NAD
NAD EXCHANGE
CASE REPORTS & PROCEDURES
NATIONAL ADVERTISING DIVISION
About NAD ... Praise
Timothy J. Muris, Chairman
Federal Trade Commission
"When faced with an increasingly active FTC and a concerned public, the advertising industry responded... today it remains the model of self-regulation"
KRAFT
CALVIN J. COLLIER, Senior VP & General Counsel,
Kraft Foods
"NAD is superior to its competition, which is regulation by the government or regulation by the courts. Accurate, prompt, and inexpensive decisions year in and year out have earned NAD its well-deserved credibility with the industry and with regulators. Kraft is a strong supporter of NAD through our membership in the Council of Better Business Bureaus."
AdvertisingAge
RANCE CRANE, Editor in Chief,
Advertising Age
"... ad people take it upon themselves to keep their work honest"
Philip Weber, Senior Attorney

Exhibit 21-6 Praise for the NAD is noted on its website

which tend to be much less stringent in their standards and practices. However, since television is probably the most carefully scrutinized and frequently criticized of all forms of advertising, the networks must be careful not to offend their viewers and detract from advertising's credibility.

Appraising Self-Regulation

The three major participants in the advertising process—advertisers, agencies, and the media—work individually and collectively to encourage truthful, ethical, and responsible advertising. The advertising industry views self-regulation as an effective mechanism for controlling advertising abuses and avoiding the use of offensive, misleading, or deceptive practices, and it prefers this form of regulation to government intervention. Self-regulation of advertising has been effective and in many instances probably led to the development of more stringent standards and practices than those imposed by or beyond the scope of legislation.

A senior vice president and general counsel at Kraft Foods, while praising the NAD, summarized the feelings of many advertisers toward self-regulation. In his testimonial he stated: "NAD is superior to its competition, which is regulation by the government or regulation by the courts. Accurate, prompt, and inexpensive decisions year in and year out have earned NAD its well-deserved credibility with the industry and with regulators." Former Federal Trade Commission chairman Timothy Murris has described the NAD as a "model of self-regulation" (Exhibit 21-6).

There are, however, limitations to self-regulation, and the process has been criticized in a number of areas. For example, the NAD may take six months to a year to resolve a complaint, during which time a company often stops using the commercial anyway. Budgeting and staffing constraints may limit the number of cases the NAD/NARB system investigates and the speed with which it resolves them.[28] And some critics believe that self-regulation is self-serving to the advertisers and advertising industry and lacks the power or authority to be a viable alternative to federal or state regulation.

Many do not believe advertising can or should be controlled solely by self-regulation. They argue that regulation by government agencies is necessary to ensure that consumers get accurate information and are not misled or deceived. Moreover, since advertisers do not have to comply with the decisions and recommendations of self-regulatory groups, it is sometimes necessary to turn to the federal and/or state government.

Federal Regulation of Advertising

Advertising is controlled and regulated through federal, state, and local laws and regulations enforced by various government agencies. The federal government is the most important source of external regulation since many advertising practices come under the jurisdiction of the **Federal Trade Commission.** In addition, depending on the advertiser's industry and product or service, other federal agencies such as the Federal Communications Commission, the Food and Drug Administration, the U.S. Postal Service, and the Bureau of Alcohol, Tobacco, and Firearms may have regulations that affect advertising. We will begin our discussion of federal regulation of advertising by considering the basic rights of marketers to advertise their products and services under the First Amendment.

Advertising and the First Amendment

Freedom of speech or expression, as defined by the First Amendment to the U.S. Constitution, is the most basic federal law governing advertising in the United States. For many years, freedom of speech protection did not include advertising and other forms of speech that promote a commercial transaction. However, the courts have extended First Amendment protection to **commercial speech,** which is speech that promotes a commercial transaction. There have been a number of landmark cases over the past three decades where the federal courts have issued rulings supporting the coverage of commercial speech by the First Amendment.

In a 1976 case, *Virginia State Board of Pharmacy* v. *Virginia Citizens Consumer Council,* the U.S. Supreme Court ruled that states cannot prohibit pharmacists from advertising the prices of prescription drugs, because such advertising contains information that helps the consumer choose between products and because the free flow of information is indispensable.[29] As noted earlier, in 1977 the Supreme Court ruled that state bar associations' restrictions on advertising are unconstitutional and attorneys have a First Amendment right to advertise their services and prices.[30] In another landmark case in 1980, *Central Hudson Gas & Electric Corp.* v. *New York Public Service Commission,* the Supreme Court ruled that commercial speech was entitled to First Amendment protection in some cases. However, the Court ruled that the U.S. Constitution affords less protection to commercial speech than to other constitutionally guaranteed forms of expression. In this case the Court established a four-part test, known as the **Central Hudson Test,** for determining restrictions on commercial speech.[31] In a more recent case, the Supreme Court's 1996 decision in *44 Liquormart, Inc.* v. *Rhode Island* struck down two state statutes designed to support the state's interest in temperance. The first prohibited the advertising of alcoholic beverage prices in Rhode Island except on signs within a store, while the second prohibited the publication or broadcast of alcohol price ads. The Court ruled that the Rhode Island statutes were unlawful because they restricted the constitutional guarantee of freedom of speech, and the decision signaled strong protection for advertisers under the First Amendment.[32]

In the cases regarding advertising, the U.S. Supreme Court has ruled that freedom of expression must be balanced against competing interests. For example, the courts have upheld bans on the advertising of products that are considered harmful, such as tobacco. The Court has also ruled that only truthful commercial speech is protected, not advertising or other forms of promotion that are false, misleading, or deceptive.

In a recent and important case involving Nike, the California Supreme Court issued a ruling that is likely to impact the way companies engage in public debate regarding issues that affect them. Nike was sued for false advertising under California consumer protection laws for allegedly making misleading statements regarding labor practices and working conditions in its foreign factories. Nike argued that statements the company made to defend itself against the charges should be considered political speech, which is protected by the First Amendment, rather than commercial speech, which is subject to advertising regulations. However, the California high court ruled that statements made by the company to defend itself against the allegations were commercial in nature and thus subject to the state's consumer protection regulations. Nike appealed the case to the U.S. Supreme Court, which sent it back to California for trial to determine if the company's statements were deceptive and misleading. However, as discussed in IMC Perspective 21-2, Nike settled the case rather than risking a long and costly court battle. While the ruling in this case only applies to California, it is important as the courts ruled that speech in the form of press releases or public statements by company representatives can be considered commercial and subject to consumer protection laws.[33]

The job of regulating advertising at the federal level and determining whether advertising is truthful or deceptive is a major focus of the Federal Trade Commission. We now turn our attention to federal regulation of advertising and the FTC.

Background on Federal Regulation of Advertising

Federal regulation of advertising originated in 1914 with the passage of the **Federal Trade Commission Act** (FTC Act), which created the FTC, the agency that is today the most active in, and has primary responsibility for, controlling and regulating advertising. The FTC Act was originally intended to help enforce antitrust laws, such as the Sherman and Clayton acts, by helping to restrain unfair methods of competition.

IMC PERSPECTIVE 21-2

Nike Fights a First Amendment Battle over Public Statements

The United States Constitution places a high value on the freedom of speech, and the U.S. Supreme Court has developed a system of law that is highly protective of this right. However, not all categories of speech receive the same protection as noncommercial speech (political and religious), which is regarded as high value whereas commercial speech is low value. While the courts have ruled that advertising and other forms of commercial speech are protected, they are subject to consumer protection laws, which require companies to prove the accuracy of their claims and statements. On the other hand, statements a company makes through its public relations (PR) effort have always been considered protected political speech and have not been scrutinized for their accuracy or veracity. However, a ruling by the California Supreme Court in a case involving Nike is changing the way companies look at the statements they make through press releases and other PR activities.

The Nike case arose after the company took steps to defend itself against stories that began surfacing in the media in 1996, alleging abusive working conditions and labor practices at the overseas factories that produce its shoes. In 1997, Nike hired Andrew Young, the former United Nations ambassador, to evaluate factories in Asia that make its shoes. Young issued a favorable report, and Nike issued press releases about his findings. The company also wrote letters to colleges such as the University of North Carolina where activists had been urging the schools to boycott Nike products and cancel contracts with athletic departments to outfit its sports team. Nike also ran ads in the school newspaper, the *Daily Tar Heel,* highlighting its good corporate citizenship and emphasizing its code of conduct requiring factory contractors to adhere to humane labor practices.

In 1998, San Francisco activist Marc Kasky sued Nike for false advertising under California consumer protection laws alleging that Nike's statements misled the public about working conditions in its factories. In response, Nike argued that its statements concerned labor practices, not products, and therefore should be considered protected political speech. Two lower courts in California agreed with Nike. However, in April 2003, the California Supreme Court reversed the lower courts' decisions and ruled that Nike's PR campaign should be considered commercial speech, even though it did not talk specifically about its shoes. The court ruled that corporations know that issues such as labor conditions and policies contribute to the public's perception of a company and consumers' willingness to buy its products. The court reasoned that "because the messages were directed by a commercial speaker to a commercial audience, and because they made representations of fact about the speaker's own business operations for the purpose of promoting sales of its products, we conclude that these messages are commercial speech for purposes of applying state laws barring false and misleading commercial messages." The justices did not decide whether Nike really did abuse workers or mislead consumers, leaving these questions for a trial court to decide later.

At issue here in the case is how to distinguish between political and commercial speech. The U.S. Supreme Court has held that political speech, even when inaccurate, is protected by the First Amendment. However, this is not true for advertising and other forms of commercial speech that are used to sell a product or service. Nike argued that the public relations activities used to defend its labor practices and working conditions are not the same as advertising and cannot be considered commercial in nature. However, the California Supreme Court ruled in a 4 to 3 decision that if Nike could misrepresent the conditions under which its shoes are made through its public relations efforts without any punishment, then any company could use the First Amendment to make false statements about its products or practices with the intent of increasing sales.

The dissenting state court justices argued that it was improper and unconstitutional to restrict Nike's ability to engage in the important worldwide debate regarding the use of foreign labor to manufacture goods sold in the United States. One dissent emphasized that Nike's campaign had not been made through product labels, inserts, packaging, or commercial advertising intended to reach only the company's actual or potential customers, but rather via press releases, letters to newspapers, and letters to university presidents and athletic directors. As such, Nike's statements, regardless of whether they were true or false, should have been treated as noncommercial speech entitled to the full breadth of protection under the First Amendment. Another justice dissented on the grounds that "Nike's speech is more like noncommercial speech than commercial speech because its commercial elements are inextricably intertwined with its noncommercial element." Thus, Nike's statements warrant full First Amendment protection.

Following the California Supreme Court's decision, Nike petitioned the case to the U.S. Supreme Court, hoping for a classification of its public relations statements as commercial or noncommercial speech. However, after hearing oral arguments, reviewing 34 briefs, and stating that the case represents novel First Amendment questions, the high court dismissed the case for lack of jurisdiction and sent it back to California for trial. Rather than risking a costly and protracted trial, Nike decided to bring the five years of litigation to an end and settled with Kasky for $1.5 million. Under the settlement, Nike agreed to pay the $1.5 million over three years to the Fair Labor Association.

The California Supreme Court decision in the *Kasky* v. *Nike* case now stands as legally authoritative, and companies doing business in the state now run the risk of attracting a lawsuit if their PR campaigns touch upon their products or operations. The case was closely watched by corporations throughout the country as the outcome alters the definition of commercial speech and leads to new restrictions on claims that companies can make about their policies, practices, and behavior. Treating press releases, letters, and other public statements defending a company's actions as equivalent to advertising could also result in companies being less willing to speak out on important public issues and have a profound impact on their public relations activities. Some are also concerned that the commercial versus noncommercial distinction, or lack thereof, made in this case might have far-reaching and unintended consequences in other areas as well. Some legal experts have noted that press releases that mention the names of competitors or the names of individuals might also be open to attack on grounds of right of publicity and trademark dilution.

Sources: Ben Lau and Peter Bowal, "Just Say It, If You Dare," *Journal of the Academy of Marketing Science* 33, no. 2 (Spring 2005), pp. 242–243; Mary Baty, "Silencing Corporate Speakers: The California Supreme Court's Broad New Definition of Commercial Speech Goes Unchecked," *Journal of Corporation Law* 30, no. 1 (Fall 2004), pp. 141–165; Stanley Holmes, "Free Speech or False Advertising?" *BusinessWeek,* April 28, 2003, pp. 69–70.

The main focus of the first five-member commission was to protect competitors from one another; the issue of false or misleading advertising was not even mentioned. In 1922, the Supreme Court upheld an FTC interpretation that false advertising was an unfair method of competition, but in the 1931 case *FTC* v. *Raladam Co.,* the Court ruled the commission could not prohibit false advertising unless there was evidence of injury to a competitor.[34] This ruling limited the power of the FTC to protect consumers from false or deceptive advertising and led to a consumer movement that resulted in an important amendment to the FTC Act.

In 1938, Congress passed the **Wheeler-Lea Amendment.** It amended section 5 of the FTC Act to read: "Unfair methods of competition in commerce and unfair or deceptive acts or practices in commerce are hereby declared to be unlawful." The amendment empowered the FTC to act if there was evidence of injury to the public; proof of injury to a competitor was not necessary. The Wheeler-Lea Amendment also gave the FTC the power to issue cease-and-desist orders and levy fines on violators. It extended the FTC's jurisdiction over false advertising of foods, drugs, cosmetics, and therapeutic devices. And it gave the FTC access to the injunctive power of the federal courts, initially only for food and drug products but expanded in 1972 to include all products in the event of a threat to the public's health and safety.

In addition to the FTC, numerous other federal agencies are responsible for, or involved in, advertising regulation. The authority of these agencies is limited, however, to a particular product area or service, and they often rely on the FTC to assist in handling false or deceptive advertising cases.

The Federal Trade Commission

The FTC is responsible for protecting both consumers and businesses from anticompetitive behavior and unfair and deceptive practices. The major divisions of the FTC include the bureaus of competition, economics, and consumer protection. The Bureau of Competition seeks to prevent business practices that restrain competition and is responsible for enforcing antitrust laws. The Bureau of Economics helps the FTC evaluate the impact of its actions and provides economic analysis and support to antitrust and consumer protection investigations and rule makings. It also analyzes the impact of government regulation on competition and consumers. The Bureau of Consumer Protection's mandate is to protect consumers against unfair, deceptive, or fraudulent practices. This bureau also investigates and litigates cases involving acts or practices alleged to be deceptive or unfair to consumers. The Division of Advertising Practices of the Bureau of Competition protects consumers from deceptive and unsubstantiated advertising and enforces the provisions of the FTC Act that forbid misrepresentation, unfairness, and deception in general advertising at the national and regional level (Exhibit 21-7). The Division of Marketing Practices of the Bureau of Competition engages in activities that are related to various marketing and warranty practices such as fraudulent telemarketing schemes, 900-number programs, and disclosures relating to franchise and business opportunities.

The FTC has had the power to regulate advertising since passage of the Wheeler-Lea Amendment. However, not until the early 1970s—following criticism of the commission in a book by "Nader's Raiders" and a special report by the American Bar Association citing its lack of action against deceptive promotional practices—did the FTC become active in regulating advertising.[35] The authority of the FTC was increased considerably throughout the 1970s. The Magnuson-Moss Act of 1975, an important piece of legislation, dramatically broadened the FTC's powers and substantially increased its budget. The first section of the act dealt with consumers' rights regarding product warranties; it

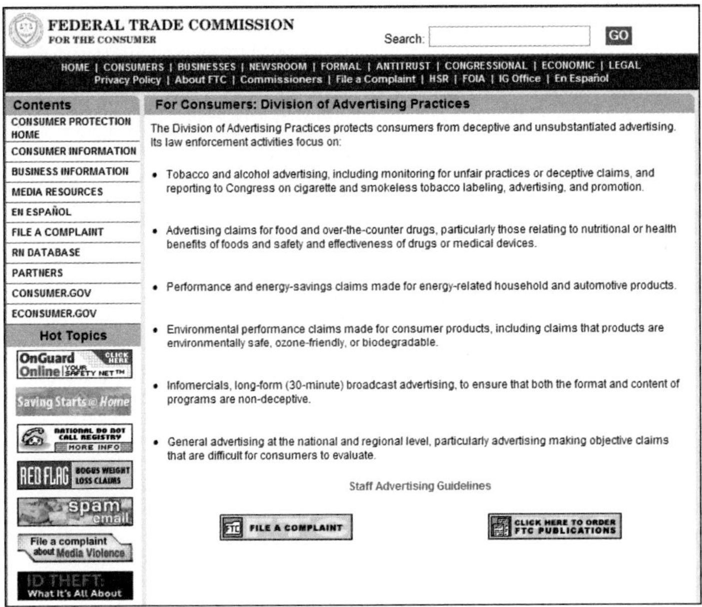

Exhibit 21-7 The Division of Advertising Practices protects consumers from deceptive and unsubstantiated advertising claims

allowed the commission to require restitution for deceptively written warranties where the consumer lost more than $5. The second section, the FTC Improvements Act, empowered the FTC to establish **trade regulation rules (TRRs),** industrywide rules that define unfair practices before they occur.

During the 1970s, the FTC made enforcement of laws regarding false and misleading advertising a top priority. Several new programs were instituted, budgets were increased, and the commission became a very powerful regulatory agency. However, many of these programs, as well as the expanded powers of the FTC to develop regulations on the basis of "unfairness," became controversial. At the root of this controversy is the fundamental issue of what constitutes unfair advertising.

The Concept of Unfairness

Under section 5 of the FTC Act, the Federal Trade Commission has a mandate to act against unfair or deceptive advertising practices. However, this statute does not define the terms *unfair* and *deceptive,* and the FTC has been criticized for not doing so itself. While the FTC has taken steps to clarify the meaning of *deception,* people have been concerned for years about the vagueness of the term *unfair.*

Controversy over the FTC's authority to regulate unfair advertising practices began in 1978, when the agency relied on this mandate to formulate its controversial "kid vid" rule restricting advertising to children.[36] This interpretation caused widespread concern in the business community that the term *unfair* could be used to encompass anything FTC commissioners might find objectionable. For example, in a 1980 policy statement the FTC noted that "the precise concept of consumer unfairness is one whose precise meaning is not immediately obvious." Consequently, in 1980 Congress responded by suspending the children's advertising rule and banning the FTC from using unfairness as a legal basis for advertising rulemaking.

The FTC responded to these criticisms in December 1980 by sending Congress a statement containing an interpretation of unfairness. According to FTC policy, the basis for determining **unfairness** is that a trade practice (1) causes substantial physical or economic injury to consumers, (2) could not reasonably be avoided by consumers, and (3) must not be outweighed by countervailing benefits to consumers or competition. The agency also stated that a violation of public policy (such as of other government statutes) could, by itself, constitute an unfair practice or could be used to prove substantial consumer injury. Practices considered unfair are claims made without prior substantiation, claims that might exploit such vulnerable groups as children and the elderly, and instances where consumers cannot make a valid choice because the advertiser omits important information about the product or competing products mentioned in the ad.[37]

The FTC's statement was intended to clarify its interpretation of unfairness and reduce ambiguity over what might constitute unfair practices. However, efforts by the FTC to develop industrywide trade regulation rules that would define unfair practices and have the force and effect of law were limited by Congress in 1980 with the passage of the FTC Improvements Act. Amidst calls to end the stalemate over the FTC's regulation of unfair advertising by having the agency work with Congress to define its advertising authority, in 1994 Congress and the advertising industry agreed on a definition of unfair advertising that is very similar to the FTC's 1980 policy statement discussed earlier. However, the new agreement requires that before the FTC can initiate any industrywide rule, it has to have reason to believe that the unfair or deceptive acts or practices are prevalent.[38]

The FTC does have specific regulatory authority in cases involving deceptive, misleading, or untruthful advertising. The vast majority of advertising cases that the FTC handles concern deception and advertising fraud, which usually involve knowledge of a false claim.

Deceptive Advertising

In most economies, advertising provides consumers with information they can use to make consumption decisions. However, if this information is untrue or misleads the consumer, advertising is not fulfilling its basic function. But what constitutes an untruthful or deceptive ad? Deceptive advertising can take a number of forms, ranging from intentionally false or misleading claims to ads that, although true, leave some consumers with a false or misleading impression.

The issue of deception, including its definition and measurement, receives considerable attention from the FTC and other regulatory agencies. One of the problems regulatory agencies deal with in determining deception is distinguishing between false or misleading messages and those that, rather than relying on verifiable or substantiated objective information about a product, make subjective claims or statements, a practice known as puffery. **Puffery** has been legally defined as "advertising or other sales presentations which praise the item to be sold with subjective opinions, superlatives, or exaggerations, vaguely and generally, stating no specific facts."[39] The use of puffery in advertising is common. For example, Bayer aspirin calls itself the "wonder drug that works wonders," Nestlé claims "Nestlé makes the very best chocolate," Snapple advertises that its beverages are "made from the best stuff on Earth," and BMW uses the tagline "The Ultimate Driving Machine." Superlatives such as *greatest, best,* and *finest* are puffs that are often used.

Puffery has generally been viewed as a form of poetic license or allowable exaggeration. The FTC takes the position that because consumers expect exaggeration or inflated claims in advertising, they recognize puffery and don't believe it. But some studies show that consumers may believe puffery and perceive such claims as true.[40] One study found that consumers could not distinguish between a verifiable fact-based claim and puffery and were just as likely to believe both types of claims.[41] Ivan Preston argues that puffery has a detrimental effect on consumers' purchase decisions by burdening them with untrue beliefs and refers to it as "soft-core deception" that should be illegal.[42]

Advertisers' battle to retain the right to use puffery was supported in the latest revision of the Uniform Commercial Code in 1996. The revision switches the burden of proof to consumers from advertisers in cases pertaining to whether certain claims were meant to be taken as promises. The revision states that the buyer must prove that an affirmation of fact (as opposed to puffery) was made, that the buyer was aware of the advertisement, and that the affirmation of fact became part of the agreement with the seller.[43]

The use of puffery as a defense for advertising claims is periodically challenged in court. IMC Perspective 21-3 discusses a recent legal battle involving Pizza Hut and Papa John's in which the U.S. Supreme Court issued a decision in support of the use of puffery as the basis for a comparative advertising claim.

Since unfair and deceptive acts or practices have never been precisely defined, the FTC is continually developing and refining a working definition in its attempts to regulate advertising. The traditional standard used to determine deception was whether a claim had the "tendency or capacity to deceive." However, this standard was criticized for being vague and all-encompassing.

In 1983, the FTC, under Chair James Miller III, put forth a new working definition of **deception:** "The commission will find deception if there is a misrepresentation, omission, or practice that is likely to mislead the consumer acting reasonably in the circumstances to the consumer's detriment."[44] There are three essential elements to this definition of deception.[45] The first element is that the representation, omission, or practice must be *likely to mislead* the consumer. The FTC defines *misrepresentation* as an express or implied statement contrary to fact, whereas a *misleading omission* occurs when qualifying information necessary to prevent a practice, claim, representation, or reasonable belief from being misleading is not disclosed.

The second element is that the act or practice must be considered from the perspective of *the reasonable consumer.* In determining reasonableness, the FTC considers the group to which the advertising is targeted and whether their interpretation of or reaction to the message is reasonable in light of the circumstances. The standard is flexible and allows the FTC to consider factors such as the age, education level, intellectual capacity, and frame of mind of the particular group to which the message or practice is targeted. For example, advertisements targeted to a particular group, such as children or the elderly, are evaluated with respect to their effect on a reasonable member of that group.

IMC PERSPECTIVE 21-3

The Pizza Wars Legal Battle Upholds the Use of Puffery

The use of unsubstantiated superlatives such as *good, better,* and *best* have long been a staple of American advertising. The Federal Trade Commission views the use of these terms, as well as other forms of marketing bravado, as puffery and takes the position that consumers would not expect these claims to be documented or take them seriously. However, a recent legal battle between Pizza Hut and Papa John's over the latter's use of puffery nearly resulted in a redefining of the limits of advertising claims that would have opened a large can of worms for the entire industry.

In 1997, Papa John's began running ads comparing its product to market leader Pizza Hut and using the tagline "Better ingredients. Better pizza." The battle heated up in 1998 when Papa John's ran a series of ads designed to show just why it believed that better ingredients do indeed make a better pizza. One spot featured Papa John's brash founder, John Schnatter, claiming consumers preferred his chain's tomato sauce because Papa John's uses fresh tomatoes picked from the vine while Pizza Hut uses "remanufactured paste." Another spot explained that Papa John's dough is made with clear filtered water and yeast given several days to work its magic while the "biggest chain" (Pizza Hut) uses whatever comes out of the tap to make frozen dough or dough made the same day.

Pizza Hut responded with what it called a "corrective ad" on the dough issue and, after getting no sympathy from the National Advertising Division of the Council of Better Business Bureaus, filed a lawsuit against Papa John's in 1998 claiming that much of its advertising was false and misleading. The suit was heard in November 1999 and after weeks of testimony in federal court, which included dough experts and sauce demonstrations, a jury sided with Pizza Hut, ruling that Papa John's "Better ingredients. Better pizza" slogan was false and misleading because the chain had failed to prove its sauce and dough were superior. The judge in the case upheld the jury's decision and ruled that the slogan was acceptable puffery until Papa John's began running ads touting its tomato sauce and pizza dough as superior. He held that the slogan then became tainted to the extent that its continued use should be stopped. The judge admonished both sides for the dubious nature of their advertising, but ordered Papa John's to pay Pizza Hut $468,000 in damages and also issued an injunction against the entire "Better ingredients. Better pizza" integrated marketing blitz, including use of the slogan on store signage, pizza boxes, car toppers, menus, napkins, and hats as well as in advertisements.

In January 2000, Papa John's appealed the decision, arguing that the judge had misinterpreted the law as use of the "Better ingredients. Better pizza" slogan was legally acceptable puffery. The court of appeals handed down a complicated ruling that sided with Papa John's on the puffery issue and lifted the injunction. The appellate judges ruled that Papa John's ads were misleading but argued that Pizza Hut had not provided enough evidence that the misrepresentation was "material" and had a negative effect on consumers' purchase behavior. Pizza Hut was outraged by the ruling, arguing that as "evidence" it had produced three different consumer surveys at the original trial, all of which indicated that consumers were wrongly influenced by the Papa John's campaign. However, all three surveys were ignored by the courts on technicalities.

Pizza Hut continued to believe that if the judges thought the advertising was misleading, and their ruling said they did, they should have punished Papa John's. So, in December 2000, Pizza Hut's lawyers decided to appeal the case to the U.S. Supreme Court on the basis that the appeals judges had required an unusually high standard of evidence to prove that consumers had been misled by Papa John's. An attorney for Pizza Hut who argued the case before the Supreme Court stated, "There is no social value in false advertising, and the concept that you turn a blind eye to false advertising simply because of the inability to prove very precise purchasing decisions strikes me as a standard of proof that is extremely high and completely unwarranted." However, in March 2001, the Supreme Court handed down its two-word decision: "Petition denied." The court of appeals ruling favoring Papa John's was allowed to stand.

Despite being disappointed at losing the case, Pizza Hut's general counsel was philosophical about the ruling, noting that it trapped Papa John's in a curious catch-22: If Pizza Hut won, it could describe Papa John's advertising as false; but if Papa John's won, it would be only because it had successfully argued that its advertising was mere puffery—not to be believed—which is exactly what happened. Papa John's expressed satisfaction with the case and indicated that it was glad the matter was over—and for good reason. The company's financial reports indicated that it had spent at least $7 million to cover the legal costs of the case. Experts noted that it is reasonable to assume that Pizza Hut incurred similar costs.

The advertising industry was also relieved that the Supreme Court had ruled in favor of Papa John's. The case had put many executives on edge, as a ruling against the puffery defense could have prompted other challenges and a redrawing of the blurry line separating so-called puffery and outright false advertising. With this ruling, advertisers are still free to use words such as *good, better,* and *best* and let consumers determine what they really mean.

While Papa John's legal battle with Pizza Hut may be over, the company recently picked a food fight outside of the courtroom with yet another competitor—Domino's Pizza, the country's second largest pizza chain. In 2005, Domino's paid more than $2 million for a promotional package with the NBC hit reality show *The Apprentice,* which included ad time and integrating its brand into the show's plot line. Papa John's tried to outwit Domino's, as well as *Apprentice* star Donald Trump and NBC, by running local ads around the country touting a meatball pizza—a product similar to the Domino's pizza featured during the show. Unable to buy ad time on the national broadcast from NBC, Papa John's purchased ad time during the show in 64 local markets, and ran a 30-second spot that showed chairman John Schnatter in a boardroom setting asking consumers to tell the competition "they were fired" as he introduced Papa John's new Spicy Meatball pizza.

Papa John's president called its decision to promote its meatball pizza in local ads during the show a coincidence, noting that the plans had been in the works for months. Domino's played down the incident; a spokeswoman for the company stated, "It's flattering that they would spend their money on a show that was all about us."

Sources: Jim Edwards, "Sour Dough: Pizza Hut v. Papa John's," *Brandweek,* May 21, 2001, pp. 26–30; Davan Maharaj and Greg Johnson, "Battle over Pizza Puffery Could Reshape Ad Landscape," *Los Angeles Times,* April 2, 2000, pp. C1, 4; Michael Fumento, "Free-a-the Papa!" *Forbes,* February 21, 2000, p. 53; Louise Kramer, "Jury Finds Papa John's Ads Misled," *Advertising Age,* November 22, 1999, p. 46; Suzanne Vranica, "Pizza Maker's Ad Aims to Top Rival," *The Wall Street Journal,* April 4, 2005, p. B6.

The third key element to the FTC's definition of deception is *materiality.* According to the FTC a "material" misrepresentation or practice is one that is likely to affect a consumer's choice or conduct with regard to a product or service. What this means is that the information, claim, or practice in question is important to consumers and, if acted upon, would be likely to influence their purchase decisions. In some cases the information or claims made in an ad may be false or misleading but would not be regarded as material since reasonable consumers would not make a purchase decision on the basis of this information.

Miller's goal was to help the commission determine which cases were worth pursuing and which were trivial. Miller argued that for an ad to be considered worthy of FTC challenge, it should be seen by a substantial number of consumers, it should lead to significant injury, and the problem should be one that market forces are not likely to remedy. However, the revised definition may put a greater burden on the FTC to prove that deception occurred and that the deception influenced the consumers' decision-making process in a detrimental way.

Determining what constitutes deception is still a gray area. Two of the factors the FTC considers in evaluating an ad for deception are (1) whether there are significant omissions of important information and (2) whether advertisers can substantiate the claims made for the product or service. The FTC has developed several programs to address these issues.

Affirmative Disclosure

An ad can be literally true yet leave the consumer with a false or misleading impression if the claim is true only under certain conditions or circumstances or if there are limitations to what the product can or cannot do. Thus, under its **affirmative disclosure** requirement, the FTC may require advertisers to include certain types of information in their ads so that consumers will be aware of all the consequences, conditions, and limitations associated with the use of a product or service. The goal of affirmative disclosure is to give consumers sufficient information to make an informed decision. An ad may be required to define the testing situation, conditions, or criteria used in making a claim. For example, fuel mileage claims in car ads are based on Environmental Protection Agency (EPA) ratings since they offer a uniform standard for making comparisons. Cigarette ads must contain a warning about the health risks associated with smoking.

An example of an affirmative disclosure ruling is the FTC's case against Campbell Soup for making deceptive and unsubstantiated claims. Campbell's ads, run as part of its "Soup is good food" campaign, linked the low-fat and -cholesterol content of its soup with a reduced risk of heart disease. However, the advertising failed to disclose that the soups are high in sodium, which may increase the risk of heart disease. In a consent agreement accepted in 1991, Campbell agreed that, for any soup containing more than 500 milligrams of sodium in an 8-ounce serving, it will disclose the sodium content in any advertising that directly or by implication mentions heart disease in connection with the soup. Campbell also agreed it would not imply a connection between soup and a reduction in heart disease in future advertising.[46]

Another area where the Federal Trade Commission is seeking more specificity from advertisers is in regard to country of origin claims. The FTC has been working with marketers and trade associations to develop a better definition of what the "Made in the USA" label means. The 50-year-old definition used until recently required full manufacturing in the United States, using U.S. labor and parts, with only raw materials from overseas.[47] Many companies argue that in an increasingly global economy, it is becoming very difficult to have 100 percent U.S. content and remain price-competitive. However, the FTC argues that advertising or labeling a product as "Made in the USA" can provide a company with a competitive advantage. For many products some consumers do respond to the claim, as they trust the quality of domestic-made products and/or feel patriotic when they buy American. For example, athletic-shoe maker New Balance is a company that promotes its commitment to domestic manufacturing and the fact that a percentage of its products are made in the United States (Exhibit 21-8).

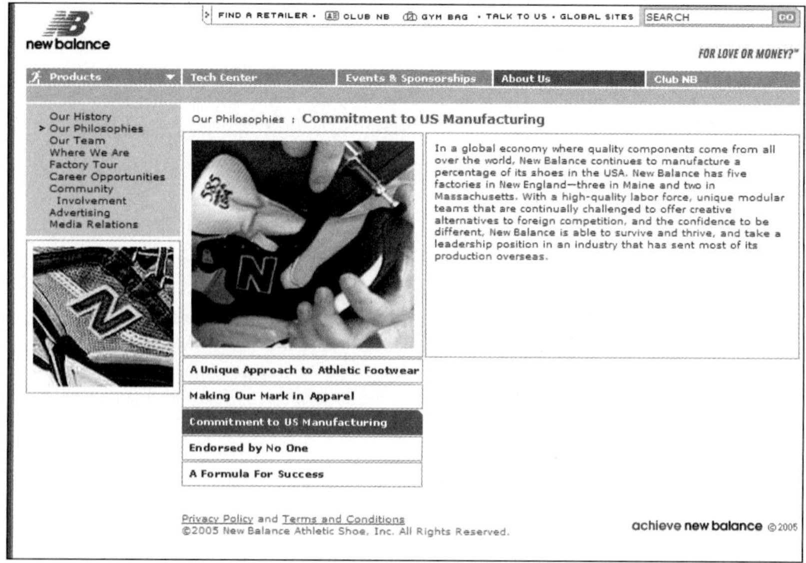

Exhibit 21-8 New Balance promotes its commitment to U.S. manufacturing

In December 1998, the FTC issued new guidelines for American-made products. The guidelines spell out what it means by "all or virtually all" in mandating how much U.S. content a product must have to wear a "Made in USA" label or be advertised as such. According to the new FTC guidelines, all significant parts and processing that go into the product must be of U.S. origin and the product should have no or very little foreign content. Companies do not have to receive the approval of the FTC before making a "Made in USA" claim. However, the commission does have the authority to take action against false and unsubstantiated "Made in USA" claims just as it does with other advertising claims.[48]

Advertising Substantiation

A major area of concern to regulatory agencies is whether advertisers can support or substantiate their claims. For many years, there were no formal requirements concerning substantiation of advertising claims. Many companies made claims without any documentation or support such as laboratory tests and clinical studies. In 1971, the FTC's **advertising substantiation** program required advertisers to have supporting documentation for their claims and to prove the claims are truthful.[49] Broadened in 1972, this program now requires advertisers to substantiate their claims before an ad appears. Substantiation is required for all express or implied claims involving safety, performance, efficacy, quality, or comparative price.

The FTC's substantiation program has had a major effect on the advertising industry, because it shifted the burden of proof from the commission to the advertiser. Before the substantiation program, the FTC had to prove that an advertiser's claims were unfair or deceptive.

Ad substantiation seeks to provide a basis for believing advertising claims so consumers can make rational and informed decisions and companies are deterred from making claims they cannot adequately support. The FTC takes the perspective that it is illegal and unfair to consumers for a firm to make a claim for a product without having a "reasonable basis" for the claim. In their decision to require advertising substantiation, the commissioners made the following statement:

> Given the imbalance of knowledge and resources between a business enterprise and each of its customers, economically it is more rational and imposes far less cost on society, to require a manufacturer to confirm his affirmative product claims rather than impose a burden on each individual consumer to test, investigate, or experiment for himself. The manufacturer has the ability, the know-how, the equipment, the time and resources to undertake such information, by testing or otherwise, . . . the consumer usually does not.[50]

Many advertisers respond negatively to the FTC's advertising substantiation program. They argue it is too expensive to document all their claims and most consumers either won't understand or aren't interested in the technical data. Some advertisers threaten to avoid the substantiation issue by using puffery claims, which do not require substantiation.

Generally, advertisers making claims covered by the substantiation program must have available prior substantiation of all claims. However, in 1984, the FTC issued a new policy statement that suggested after-the-fact substantiation might be acceptable in some cases and it would solicit documentation of claims only from advertisers that are under investigation for deceptive practices.

In a number of cases, the FTC has ordered advertisers to cease making inadequately substantiated claims. In 1993, the FTC took on the weight-loss industry when it filed a complaint charging that none of five large, well-known diet program marketers had sufficient evidence to back up claims that their customers achieved their weight-loss goals or maintained the loss (Exhibit 21-9). Three of the companies agreed to publicize the fact that most weight loss is temporary and to disclose how long their customers kept off the weight they lost. The agreement required the companies to substantiate their weight-loss claims with scientific data and to document claims that their customers keep off the weight by monitoring a group of them for two years.[51]

Nearly 10 years later, the FTC held a workshop to once again explore the problem of misleading weight-loss promotional pitches. The FTC used the 2002 workshop as a forum to suggest that the media should play a more active role in screening ads for diet products and programs. Professor Herbert Rotfeld has evaluated the FTC's efforts to deal with the problem of deceptive advertising in the weight-loss industry and concludes that its efforts to curb the deceptions have largely failed and that new strategies are needed. He believes the media can supplement the commission's efforts but should not be forced into the de facto role of regulators.[52]

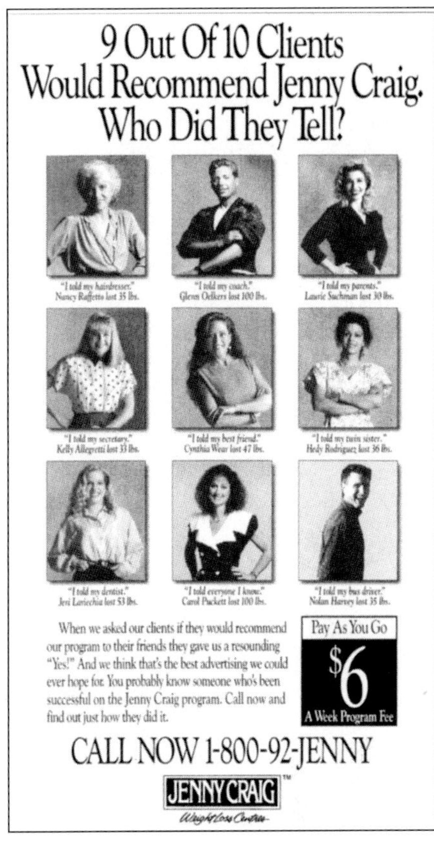

Exhibit 21-9 Weight-loss program marketers are now required to substantiate their claims as a result of an FTC ruling

Recently the FTC has stepped up its action against false and unsubstantiated claims in ads and infomercials. A few years ago, the commission fined the Home Shopping Network $1.1 million for making unsubstantiated advertising claims for two weight-loss products, an acne treatment, and a dietary supplement for menopause and premenstrual syndrome. Under the settlement Home Shopping is enjoined from making product claims about curing and treating diseases without "reliable scientific evidence."

The FTC's Handling of Deceptive Advertising Cases

Consent and Cease-and-Desist Orders Allegations of unfair or deceptive advertising come to the FTC's attention from a variety of sources, including competitors, consumers, other government agencies, or the commission's own monitoring and investigations. Once the FTC decides a complaint is justified and warrants further action, it notifies the offender, who then has 30 days to respond. The advertiser can agree to negotiate a settlement with the FTC by signing a **consent order,** which is an agreement to stop the practice or advertising in question. This agreement is for settlement purposes only and does not constitute an admission of guilt by the advertiser. Most FTC inquiries are settled by consent orders because they save the advertiser the cost and possible adverse publicity that might result if the case went further.

If the advertiser chooses not to sign the consent decree and contests the complaint, a hearing can be requested before an administrative law judge employed by the FTC but not under its influence. The judge's decision may be appealed to the full five-member commission by either side. The commission either affirms or modifies the order or dismisses the case. If the complaint has been upheld by the administrative law judge and the commission, the advertiser can appeal the case to the federal courts.

The appeal process may take some time, during which the FTC may want to stop the advertiser from engaging in the deceptive practice. The Wheeler-Lea Amendment empowers the FTC to issue a **cease-and-desist order,** which requires that the advertiser stop the specified advertising claim within 30 days and prohibits the advertiser from engaging in the objectionable practice until after the hearing is held. Violation of a cease-and-desist order is punishable by a fine of up to $10,000 a day. Figure 21-4 summarizes the FTC complaint procedure.

Figure 21-4 FTC Complaint Procedure

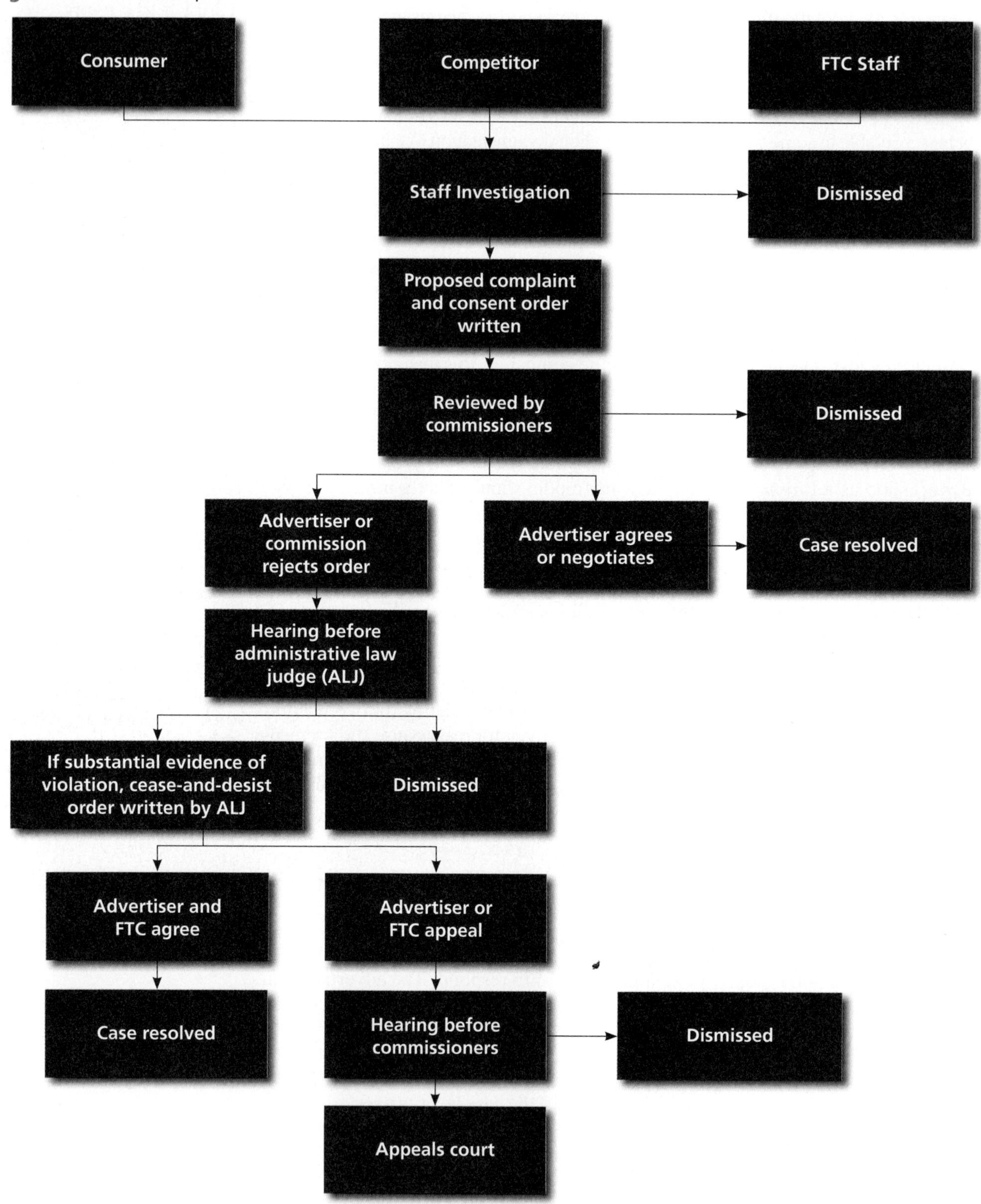

Corrective Advertising By using consent and cease-and-desist orders, the FTC can usually stop a particular advertising practice it believes is unfair or deceptive. However, even if an advertiser ceases using a deceptive ad, consumers may still remember some or all of the claim. To address the problem of residual effects, in the 1970s, the FTC developed a program known as **corrective advertising.** An advertiser found guilty of deceptive advertising can be required to run additional advertising designed to remedy the deception or misinformation contained in previous ads.

Figure 21-5 Examples of Corrective Advertising Messages

Profile Bread	Ocean Spray	STP
"Hi, [celebrity's name] for Profile Bread. Like all mothers, I'm concerned about nutrition and balanced meals. So, I'd like to clear up any misunderstanding you may have about Profile Bread from its advertising or even its name. "Does Profile have fewer calories than any other breads? No. Profile has about the same per ounce as other breads. To be exact, Profile has seven fewer calories per slice. That's because Profile is sliced thinner. But eating Profile will not cause you to lose weight. A reduction of seven calories is insignificant. It's total calories and balanced nutrition that count. And Profile can help you achieve a balanced meal because it provides protein and B vitamins as well as other nutrients. "How does my family feel about Profile? Well, my husband likes Profile toast, the children love Profile sandwiches, and I prefer Profile to any other bread. So you see, at our house, delicious taste makes Profile a family affair." (To be run in 25 percent of brand's advertising, for one year.)	"If you've wondered what some of our earlier advertising meant when we said Ocean Spray Cranberry Juice Cocktail has more food energy than orange juice or tomato juice, let us make it clear: we didn't mean vitamins and minerals. Food energy means calories. Nothing more. "Food energy is important at breakfast since many of us may not get enough calories, or food energy, to get off to a good start. Ocean Spray Cranberry Juice Cocktail helps because it contains more food energy than most other breakfast drinks. "And Ocean Spray Cranberry Juice Cocktail gives you and your family Vitamin C plus a great wake-up taste. It's . . . the other breakfast drink." (To be run in one of every four ads for one year.)	As a result of an investigation by the Federal Trade Commission into certain allegedly inaccurate past advertisements for STP's oil additive, STP Corporation has agreed to a $700,000 settlement. With regard to that settlement, STP is making the following statement: "It is the policy of STP to support its advertising with objective information and test data. In 1974 and 1975 an independent laboratory ran tests of the company's oil additive which led to claims of reduced oil consumption. However, these tests cannot be relied on to support the oil consumption reduction claim made by STP. "The FTC has taken the position that, in making the claim, the company violated the terms of a consent order. When STP learned that the test did not support the claim, it stopped advertising containing that claim. New tests have been undertaken to determine the extent to which the oil additive affects oil consumption. Agreement to this settlement does not constitute an admission by STP that the law has been violated. Rather, STP has agreed to resolve the dispute with the FTC to avoid protracted and prohibitively expensive litigation."

The impetus for corrective advertising was another case involving Campbell Soup, which placed marbles in the bottom of a bowl of vegetable soup to force the solid ingredients to the surface, creating a false impression that the soup contained more vegetables than it really did. (Campbell Soup argued that if the marbles were not used, all the ingredients would settle to the bottom, leaving an impression of fewer ingredients than actually existed!) While Campbell Soup agreed to stop the practice, a group of law students calling themselves SOUP (Students Opposed to Unfair Practices) argued to the FTC that this would not remedy false impressions created by prior advertising and contended Campbell Soup should be required to run advertising to rectify the problem.[53]

Although the FTC did not order corrective advertising in the Campbell case, it has done so in many cases since then. Profile Bread ran an ad stating each slice contained fewer calories than other brands, but the ad did not mention that slices of Profile bread were thinner than those of other brands. Ocean Spray cranberry juice was found guilty of deceptive advertising because it claimed to have more "food energy" than orange or tomato juice but failed to note it was referring to the technical definition of food energy, which is calories. In each case, the advertisers were ordered to spend 25 percent of their annual media budgets to run corrective ads. The STP Corporation was required to run corrective advertising for claims regarding the ability of its oil additive to reduce oil consumption. Many of the corrective ads run in the STP case appeared in business publications to serve notice to other advertisers that the FTC was enforcing the corrective advertising program. The texts of the corrective messages required in each of these cases are shown in Figure 21-5.

Corrective advertising is probably the most controversial of all the FTC programs.[54] Advertisers argue that corrective advertising infringes on First Amendment rights of freedom of speech. In one of the most publicized corrective advertising cases ever, involving Listerine mouthwash, Warner-Lambert tested the FTC's legal power to order corrective messages.[55] For more than 50 years Warner-Lambert had advertised that gargling with Listerine helped prevent colds and sore throats or lessened their severity because it killed the germs that caused these illnesses. In 1975, the FTC ruled these claims could not be substantiated and ordered Warner-Lambert to stop making them. In addition, the FTC argued that corrective advertising was needed to rectify the erroneous beliefs that had been created by Warner-Lambert as a result of the large amount of advertising it had run for Listerine over the prior 50 years.

Warner-Lambert argued that the advertising was not misleading and, further, that the FTC did not have the power to order corrective advertising. Warner-Lambert appealed the FTC decision all the way to the Supreme Court, which rejected the argument that corrective advertising violates advertisers' First Amendment rights. The powers of the FTC in the areas of both claim substantiation and corrective advertising were upheld. Warner-Lambert was required to run $10 million worth of corrective ads over a 16-month period stating, "Listerine does not help prevent colds or sore throats or lessen their severity."

Since the Supreme Court ruling in the Listerine case, there have been several other situations where the FTC has ordered corrective advertising on the basis of the "Warner-Lambert test," which considers whether consumers are left with a latent impression that would continue to affect buying decisions and whether corrective ads are needed to remedy the situation.

In a more recent case involving Novartis Consumer Health Corp.'s Doan's Pills, the FTC sent a strong message to advertisers and agencies that it will require marketers to run corrective ads to remedy any misleading impressions that were created through unsubstantiated advertising claims.[56] In this case, Novartis was ordered to spend $8 million, or the equivalent of the average annual ad budget for Doan's Pills over an eight-year period, on corrective ads to remedy any impressions that might exist from previous advertising that the brand is more effective than other analgesics for relieving back pain. Novartis was ordered to include the statement "Although Doan's is an effective pain reliever, there is no evidence that Doan's is more effective than other pain relievers for back pain" on packaging and in ads until $8 million was spent on the campaign. Novartis appealed the FTC decision ordering corrective advertising. However, in August 2000, the U.S. Court of Appeals unanimously upheld the FTC's right to demand corrective advertising in this case. Also at issue in the appeal was the FTC's standard for determining whether a lingering false impression exists from deceptive advertising and whether the commission has to prove that the years of advertising created the false impression or could assume that years of advertising would have done so. The courts described the evidence of lingering effect the FTC had amassed as "thin and somewhat fragmentary," but upheld the commission's decision based on the record as a whole.[57]

The appeals court decision in this case has very important implications for the FTC as well as for advertisers. The ruling reaffirmed the commission's authority to order corrective advertising and gave it greater freedom to use the remedy, whereas a loss could have limited its authority to do so. The ruling also has repercussions for advertisers who expressed concern over the FTC's contention that "corrective advertising is not a drastic remedy" but is an appropriate method for restoring the status quo. Advertisers fear that this is a sign the FTC will be more willing to apply the remedy in future cases. However, FTC officials indicated that the ruling would not substantially change its request for corrective ads: This appears to be the case thus far.

Current Status of Federal Regulation by the FTC

By the end of the 1970s, the FTC had become a very powerful and active regulator of advertising. However, Congress was concerned about the FTC's broad interpretation of unfairness, which led to the restrictive legislation of the 1980 FTC Improvements Act. During the 1980s, the FTC became less active and cut back its regulatory efforts, due in large part to the Reagan administration's laissez-faire attitude toward the regulation of business in general. Some feared that the FTC had become too narrow in its regulation of national advertising, forcing companies and consumer groups to seek relief from other sources such as state and federal courts or through self-regulatory groups such as the NAD/NARB.[58]

In 1988–89, an 18-member panel chosen by the American Bar Association undertook a study of the FTC as a 20-year follow-up to the 1969 report used by President Richard Nixon to overhaul the commission. The panel's report expressed strong concern over the FTC's lack of sufficient resources and staff to regulate national advertising effectively and called for more funding.

After more than a decade of relative inactivity, the Federal Trade Commission has once again become active in the regulation of advertising. The commission has shown particular interest in cracking down on misleading advertising in areas such as health, nutrition, weight loss, and environmental claims as well as advertising directed to children and the elderly.[59] The FTC has also become more involved with potential fraud and deception through various other promotional methods such as telemarketing, 900 numbers, infomercials, and the Internet. In addition to monitoring deceptive claims made over the Internet, the FTC has become very involved in privacy issues and the collection of personal information on websites.

Robert Pitofsky, who served as FTC chairman during the Clinton administration, focused the commission's attention on developing new policies, particularly as the growth of the Internet created the need for laws and regulations regarding online privacy and ways of protecting children online. However, empirical evidence from a study conducted by Avery Abernethy and George Franke indicates that during this period when the FTC was most active and stringent in requiring advertising substantiation, the objective information contained in advertising actually decreased substantially. Abernethy and Franke suggest that it became more expensive for companies to provide factual information in their ads due to the regulatory burden placed on advertising. Thus, the overall information content of advertising fell, which suggests that increased government regulation can have unintended negative consequences.[60]

Under the Bush administration the FTC has focused its attention on the enforcement of existing regulations, particularly in areas such as telemarketing and Internet privacy.[61] The FTC also has focused on eliminating false e-mail advertising and has stepped up its enforcement against senders of deceptive or misleading claims via e-mail. The commission also scrutinized the use of testimonial ads more carefully, particularly with respect to the use of a "results not typical" disclosure in situations where the outcomes are more likely to vary substantially than be typical for most consumers.[62]

While the FTC is the major regulator of advertising for products sold in interstate commerce, several other federal agencies and departments also regulate advertising and promotion.

Additional Federal Regulatory Agencies

The Federal Communications Commission The FCC, founded in 1934 to regulate broadcast communication, has jurisdiction over the radio, television, telephone, and telegraph industries. The FCC has the authority to license broadcast stations as well as to remove a license or deny renewal to stations not operating in the public's interest. The FCC's authority over the airways gives it the power to control advertising content and to restrict what products and services can be advertised on radio and TV. The FCC can eliminate obscene and profane programs and/or messages and those it finds in poor taste. While the FCC can purge ads that are deceptive or misleading, it generally works closely with the FTC in the regulation of advertising. For example, the Federal Communications Commission and the FTC held a joint workshop and publicly accused long-distance phone marketers of deceiving consumers in their advertising. Officials of both commissions expressed concern over per-minute ads for long distance and so-called dial-around long-distance services. They also warned long-distance marketers that they would take action if steps were not taken to clean up their advertising.[63]

Many of the FCC's rules and regulations for TV and radio stations have been eliminated or modified. The FCC no longer limits the amount of television time that can be devoted to commercials. (But in 1991, the Children's Television Act went into effect. The act limits advertising during children's programming to 10.5 minutes an hour on weekends and 12 minutes an hour on weekdays.)

Under the Reagan administration, the controversial Fairness Doctrine, which required broadcasters to provide time for opposing viewpoints on important issues, was repealed on the grounds that it was counterproductive. It was argued that the Fairness Doctrine actually reduced discussion of important issues because a broadcaster might be afraid to take on a paid controversial message in case it might be required to provide equal free exposure for opposing viewpoints. It was under this doctrine that the FCC required stations to run commercials about the harmful effects of smoking before passage of the Public Health Cigarette Smoking Act of 1970, which banned broadcast advertising of cigarettes. Many stations still provide time for opposing viewpoints on controversial issues as part of their public service requirement, not necessarily directly related to fairness.

Several pieces of legislation passed in recent years involve the FCC and have an impact on advertising and promotion. The Cable Television Consumer Protection and Competition Act, passed in 1992, allows the FCC and local governments to regulate basic cable TV rates and forces cable operators to pay licensing fees for local broadcast programming they retransmit for free. One purpose of this bill is to improve the balance between cable rates and rapidly escalating advertising revenue. FCC rules affecting telemarketing will be discussed toward the end of this chapter.

In recent years the FCC has become very active in enforcing laws governing the airing of obscene, indecent, and profane material. For example, in 2004, the commission fined "shock jock" Howard Stern $495,000 for broadcasting indecent content and also levied fines against Clear Channel Communications, the nation's largest owner of radio stations, which carried his syndicated show.[64] Concern over Stern's constant battling with the FCC led to a decision by Clear Channel to drop his daily radio show.[65] Stern subsequently signed a five-year contract with Sirius Satellite radio, the subscription-based radio service, where his show is not subject to FCC regulations. The FCC also stepped up its enforcement of obscenity in the wake of the controversy following the baring of Janet Jackson's breast during the halftime show of the 2004 Super Bowl (Exhibit 21-10).[66] These incidents resulted in federal legislation dramatically increasing the amount both radio and television networks and stations can be fined for broadcast obscenity violations. In 2005, the FCC launched a new website explaining its broadcast obscenity, indecency, and profanity rules as well as complaint procedures and enforcement actions.

Exhibit 21-10 Janet Jackson's "wardrobe malfunction" during the 2004 Super Bowl halftime show led to greater enforcement of obscenity laws by the FCC

The FCC has also recently become involved in issues affecting the area of publicity and public relations. In 2005, the commission issued a missive insisting that broadcasters screen video news releases to ensure that they clearly disclose "the nature, source and sponsorship" of the material. The crackdown is designed to address a marketing practice whereby prepackaged promotional videos sent to TV stations by companies, organizations, and government agencies are represented as news stories.[67]

The Food and Drug Administration

Now under the jurisdiction of the Department of Health and Human Services, the FDA has authority over the labeling, packaging, branding, ingredient listing, and advertising of packaged foods and drug products. The FDA is authorized to require caution and warning labels on potentially hazardous products and also has limited authority over nutritional claims made in food advertising. This agency has the authority to set rules for promoting these products and the power to seize food and drugs on charges of false and misleading advertising.

Like the FTC, the Food and Drug Administration has become a very aggressive regulatory agency in recent years. The FDA has cracked down on a number of commonly used descriptive terms it believes are often abused in the labeling and advertising of food products—for example, *natural, light, no cholesterol,* and *fat free.* The FDA has also become tougher on nutritional claims implied by brand names that might send a misleading message to consumers. For example,

Exhibit 21-11 The Nutritional Labeling and Education Act requires that labels be easy for consumers to understand

Great Foods of America was not permitted to continue using the HeartBeat trademark under which it sold most of its foods. The FDA argued the trademark went too far in implying the foods have special advantages for the heart and overall health.

Many changes in food labeling are a result of the Nutritional Labeling and Education Act, which Congress passed in 1990. Under this law the FDA established legal definitions for a wide range of terms (such as *low fat, light,* and *reduced calories*) and required straightforward labels for all foods beginning in early 1994 (Exhibit 21-11). In its current form the act applies only to food labels, but it may soon affect food advertising as well. The FTC would be asked to ensure that food ads comply with the new FDA standards.

Another regulatory area where the FDA has been heavily involved is the advertising and promotion of tobacco products. In 1996, President Bill Clinton signed an executive order declaring that nicotine is an addictive drug and giving the FDA board jurisdiction to regulate cigarettes and smokeless tobacco. Many of the regulations resulting from this order were designed to keep teenagers from smoking.[68] However, the tobacco industry immediately appealed the order. While continuing to fight its legal battle with the federal government over the FDA regulations, the tobacco makers did agree to settle lawsuits brought by 46 states against the industry in late 1998 by signing the Master Settlement Agreement. This settlement was considered a better deal for the tobacco industry, as many of the onerous cigarette marketing restrictions contained in the original FDA proposal settlement were missing. The agreement allows large outdoor signs at retailers, whereas the original proposal banned all outdoor ads. The original deal banned all use of humans and cartoons in ads, while the current settlement bans only cartoons and even permits their use on cigarette packs. And while the original proposal eliminated sports sponsorships, the current agreement allows each company to continue one national sponsorship.[69]

An important provision of the Master Settlement Agreement was that the tobacco companies agreed not to target youth (those under the age of 18) in the advertising, promotion, and marketing of tobacco products either directly or indirectly. However, over the past several years there has been considerable debate over whether tobacco companies are complying with the agreement. Much of this debate centers on what is called the 15 percent rule, under which the tobacco companies voluntarily pledged not to advertise in magazines that have more than 15 percent of their readers under the age of 18. Some major tobacco companies such as Philip Morris have stopped advertising in magazines that have a substantial number of youth readers, such as *People, Sports Illustrated, Spin,* and *Rolling Stone.* However, other tobacco companies still advertise in these publications, and it appears that there remains a number of battles to fight in the war over the marketing and advertising of cigarettes.[70]

A number of consumer advocacy groups as well as health departments in many states run ads warning consumers against the dangers of smoking and tobacco-related diseases. For example, the American Legacy Foundation, which was established as part of the 1998 tobacco settlement and is dedicated to reducing tobacco use, has run a number of hard-hitting ads warning consumers of the risk of smoking (Exhibit 21-12).

Another area where the Food and Drug Administration is being asked to become more involved is the advertising of prescription drugs. Tremendous growth in direct-to-consumer drug advertising has occurred since the FDA issued new guidelines making it easier for pharmaceutical companies to advertise prescription drugs to consumers. However, as discussed in the opening vignette to the chapter, there is considerable concern over the amount and nature of direct-to-consumer prescription drug advertising, and the FDA is likely to develop more stringent guidelines and regulations to address these issues.

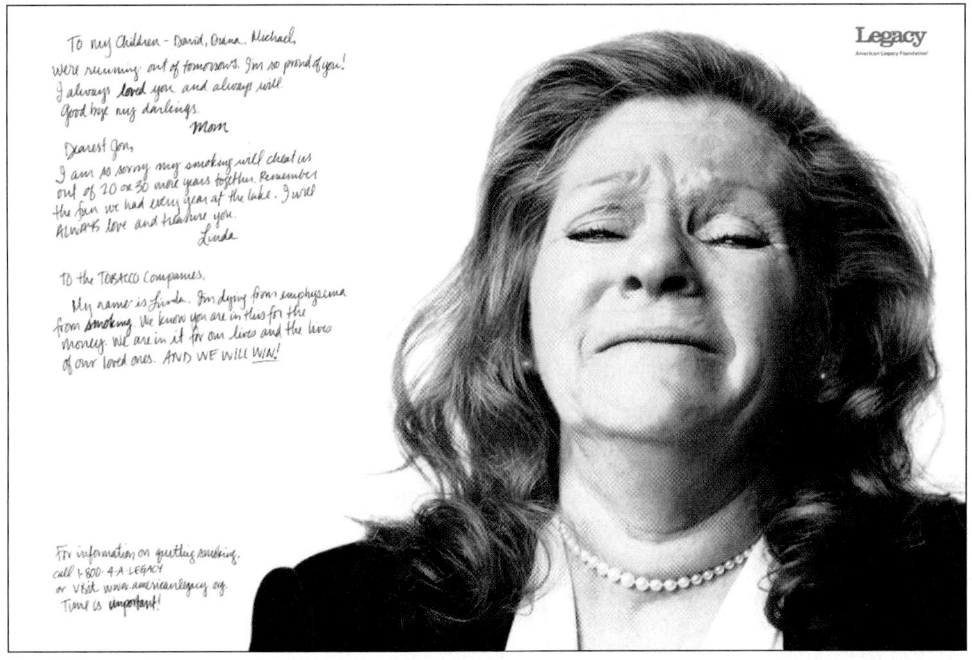

Exhibit 21-12 The American Legacy Foundation was established as part of the Tobacco Settlement Agreement and is dedicated to reducing tobacco use in the United States

The U.S. Postal Service Many marketers use the U.S. mail to deliver advertising and promotional messages. The U.S. Postal Service has control over advertising involving the use of the mail and ads that involve lotteries, obscenity, or fraud. The regulation against fraudulent use of the mail has been used to control deceptive advertising by numerous direct-response advertisers. These firms advertise on TV or radio or in magazines and newspapers and use the U.S. mail to receive orders and payment. Many have been prosecuted by the Post Office Department for use of the mail in conjunction with a fraudulent or deceptive offer.

Bureau of Alcohol, Tobacco, and Firearms The Bureau of Alcohol, Tobacco, and Firearms (BATF) is an agency within the Treasury Department that enforces laws, develops regulations, and is responsible for tax collection for the liquor industry. The BATF regulates and controls the advertising of alcoholic beverages. The agency determines what information can be provided in ads as well as what constitutes false and misleading advertising. It is also responsible for including warning labels on alcohol advertising and banning the use of active athletes in beer commercials. The BATF can impose strong sanctions for violators. The advertising of alcoholic beverages has become a very controversial issue, with many consumer and public-interest groups calling for a total ban on the advertising of beer, wine, and liquor.

The Lanham Act

While most advertisers rely on self-regulatory mechanisms and the FTC to deal with deceptive or misleading advertising by their competitors, many companies are filing lawsuits against competitors they believe are making false claims. One piece of federal legislation that has become increasingly important in this regard is the Lanham Act. This act was originally written in 1947 as the Lanham Trade-Mark Act to protect words, names, symbols, or other devices adopted to identify and distinguish a manufacturer's products. The **Lanham Act** was amended to encompass false advertising by prohibiting "any false description or representation including words or other symbols tending falsely to describe or represent the same." While the FTC Act did not give individual advertisers the opportunity to sue a competitor for deceptive advertising, civil suits are permitted under the Lanham Act.

More and more companies are using the Lanham Act to sue competitors for their advertising claims, particularly since comparative advertising has become so common. For example, a court ordered Ralston Purina to pay Alpo Petfoods $12 million for damages it caused by making false claims that its Purina Puppy Chow dog food could ameliorate and help prevent joint disease. The court ruled that the claim was based on faulty data and that the company continued the campaign after learning its research was in error. Alpo was awarded the money as compensation for lost revenue and for the costs of advertising it ran in response to the Puppy Chow campaign.[71]

Wilkinson Sword and its advertising agency were found guilty of false advertising and ordered to pay $953,000 in damages to the Gillette Co. Wilkinson had run TV and print ads claiming its Ultra Glide razor and blades produced shaves "six times smoother" than Gillette's Atra Plus blades. This case marked the first time an agency was held liable for damages in connection with false claims made in a client's advertising.[72] Although the agency was later found not liable, the case served as a sobering reminder to agencies that they can be drawn into litigation over advertising they create for their clients. To deal with this problem, many agencies insist on indemnification clauses in contracts with their clients.

Suing competitors for false claims was made even easier with passage of the Trademark Law Revision Act of 1988. According to this law, anyone is vulnerable to civil action who "misrepresents the nature, characteristics, qualities, or geographical origin of his or her or another person's goods, services, or commercial activities." This wording closed a loophole in the Lanham Act, which prohibited only false claims about one's own goods or services. While many disputes over comparative claims are never contested or are resolved through the NAD, more companies are turning to lawsuits for several reasons: the broad information discovery powers available under federal civil procedure rules, the speed with which a competitor can stop the offending ad through a preliminary injunction, and the possibility of collecting damages.[73] However, companies do not always win their lawsuits. Under the Lanham Act you are required to prove five elements to win a false advertising lawsuit containing a comparative claim.[74] You must prove that:

- False statements have been made about the advertiser's product or your product.
- The ads actually deceived or had the tendency to deceive a substantial segment of the audience.
- The deception was "material" or meaningful and is likely to influence purchasing decisions.
- The falsely advertised products or services are sold in interstate commerce.
- You have been or likely will be injured as a result of the false statements, by either loss of sales or loss of goodwill.

In recent years there has been a significant increase in the use of comparative advertising, and it has resulted in more and more companies' suing one another under the Lanham Act. In the mid-90s the Campbell Soup Co. advertised that its Prego brand of spaghetti sauce was thicker than Van Den Bergh Food's Ragu brand. Van Den Bergh sued to have Campbell's comparative ads for Prego halted but lost the case in district court as well as in appeals court. Campbell capitalized on its victory by creating an ad based on it. The ad tweaked Ragu by showing snippets of the comparison ads and then a shot of Prego with a breadstick standing up in the sauce (Exhibit 21-13). The tagline was, "Ragu took us to court. We made our case stand. Just like our breadstick." The two companies finally declared a truce in the spaghetti sauce wars in late 1999.[75]

Exhibit 21-13 Comparative claims involving the Prego and Ragu brands of spaghetti sauce resulted in a lawsuit

In 2002, Energizer Holdings filed a suit against Duracell, which is a division of the Gillette Company, over a commercial touting the endurance superiority of the Duracell Coppertop brand over "heavy-duty" competitors. While the ad claim was technically correct, it failed to note that all alkaline batteries outlast so-called heavy-duty batteries, which in industry parlance refers to inexpensive, old-fashioned zinc batteries. Energizer claimed that consumer confusion resulted from the advertisement because consumers thought the commercial was comparing Duracell Coppertop to Energizer alkaline batteries. Gillette agreed to modify the commercial by adding a disclaimer stating "excluding alkaline batteries." However, Energizer plans to pursue the lawsuit and is seeking damages for confusion resulting from the Duracell commercial.[76]

Marketers using comparative ads have to carefully consider whether their messages have the potential to mislead consumers or may overstate their brand's performance relative to that of competitors. A study by Michael J. Barone and his colleagues provides a framework for developing measures to assess the misleading effects that may arise from various types of comparative advertising.[77]

State Regulation

In addition to the various federal rules and regulations, advertisers must also concern themselves with numerous state and local controls. An important early development in state regulation of advertising was the adoption in 44 states of the *Printers Ink* model statutes as a basis for advertising regulation. These statutes were drawn up in 1911 by *Printers Ink,* for many years the major trade publication of the advertising industry. Many states have since modified the original statutes and adopted laws similar to those of the Federal Trade Commission Act for dealing with false and misleading advertising. For example, in California, the Business and Professional Code prohibits "unlawful, unfair, or fraudulent" business practices and "unfair, deceptive, untrue, or misleading advertising."

In addition to recognizing decisions by the federal courts regarding false or deceptive practices, many states have special controls and regulations governing the advertising of specific industries or practices. As the federal government became less involved in the regulation of national advertising during the 1980s, many state attorneys general (AGs) began to enforce state laws regarding false or deceptive advertising. For example, the attorneys general in New York and Texas initiated investigations of Kraft ads claiming the pasteurized cheese used in Cheez Whiz was real cheese.[78] The well-publicized "monster truck" deceptive advertising case involving Volvo and its advertising agency that occurred in the early 90s was initiated by the attorney general's office in the state of Texas.[79]

The **National Association of Attorneys General (NAAG)** moved against a number of national advertisers as a result of inactivity by the FTC during the Reagan administration. In 1987, the NAAG developed enforcement guidelines on airfare advertising that were adopted by more than 40 states. The NAAG has also been involved in other regulatory areas, including car-rental price advertising as well as advertising dealing with nutrition and health claims in food ads. The NAAG's foray into regulating national advertising raises the issue of whether the states working together can create and implement uniform national advertising standards that will, in effect, supersede federal authority. An American Bar Association panel concluded that the Federal Trade Commission is the proper regulator of national advertising and recommended the state AGs focus on practices that harm consumers within a single state.[80] This report also called for cooperation between the FTC and the state attorneys general.

Advertisers are concerned about the trend toward increased regulation of advertising at the state and local levels because it could mean that national advertising campaigns would have to be modified for every state or municipality. Yet the FTC takes the position that businesses that advertise and sell nationwide need a national advertising policy. While the FTC recognizes the need for greater cooperation with the states, the agency believes regulation of national advertising should be its responsibility.[81] Just in case, the advertising industry is still keeping a watchful eye on changes in advertising rules, regulations, and policies at the state and local levels.

Regulation of Other Promotional Areas

So far we've focused on the regulation of advertising. However, other elements of the promotional mix also come under the surveillance of federal, state, and local laws and various self-regulatory bodies. This section examines some of the rules, regulations, and guidelines that affect sales promotion, direct marketing, and marketing on the Internet.

Sales Promotion

Both consumer- and trade-oriented promotions are subject to various regulations. The Federal Trade Commission regulates many areas of sales promotion through the Marketing Practices Division of the Bureau of Consumer Protection. Many promotional practices are also policed by state attorneys general and local regulatory agencies. Various aspects of trade promotion, such as allowances, are regulated by the Robinson-Patman Act, which gives the FTC broad powers to control discriminatory pricing practices.

Contests and Sweepstakes As noted in Chapter 16, numerous legal considerations affect the design and administration of contests and sweepstakes, and these promotions are regulated by a number of federal and state agencies. There are two important considerations in developing contests (including games) and sweepstakes. First, marketers must be careful to ensure their contest or sweepstakes is not classified as a *lottery,* which is considered a form of gambling and violates the Federal Trade Commission Act and many state and local laws. A promotion is considered a lottery if a prize is offered, if winning a prize depends on chance and not skill, and if the participant is required to give up something of value in order to participate. The latter requirement is referred to as *consideration* and is the basis on which most contests, games, and sweepstakes avoid being considered lotteries. Generally, as long as consumers are not required to make a purchase to enter a contest or sweepstakes, consideration is not considered to be present and the promotion is not considered a lottery.

The second important requirement in the use of contests and sweepstakes is that the marketer provide full disclosure of the promotion. Regulations of the FTC, as well as many state and local governments, require marketers using contests, games, and sweepstakes to make certain all of the details are given clearly and to follow prescribed rules to ensure the fairness of the game.[82] Disclosure requirements include the exact number of prizes to be awarded and the odds of winning, the duration and termination dates of the promotion, and the availability of lists of winners of various prizes (Exhibit 21-14). The FTC also has specific rules governing the way games and contests are conducted, such as requirements that game pieces be randomly distributed, that a game not be terminated before the distribution of all game pieces, and that additional pieces not be added during the course of a game.

Recently a number of states have responded to what they believe is widespread fraud on the part of some contest and sweepstakes operators. In 1995, at least 13 states either passed or tightened prize notification laws, requiring fuller disclosure of rules, odds, and the retail value of prizes. And many of the states are following through with tougher enforcement of these laws. For example, Publishers Clearing House, known for its million-dollar giveaways, agreed to pay $490,000 to 14 states and to change some of its language, better defining terms like "finalist" and "tie breaker." It also began to disclose the odds of winning prizes. More recently the controversy resulting

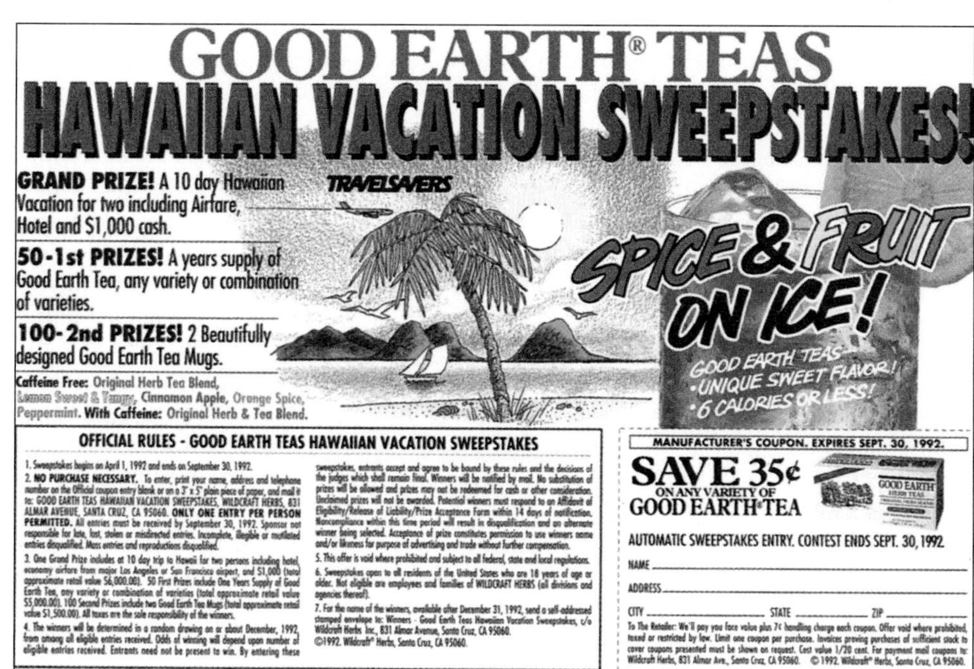

Exhibit 21-14 Marketers are required to provide consumers with full details of a contest or sweepstakes

from the lawsuits filed against American Family Publishing for misleading consumers regarding their odds of winning large cash prizes in its annual magazine subscription solicitation sweepstakes has led to investigations and stricter regulation of sweepstakes in a number of states.[83] For example, New York passed a law requiring the odds of winning a sweepstakes "must be conspicuously disclosed in the same type face, size and boldness and adjacent to the most prominent listing of the prizes on the front of the first page of the offer." The state law also prohibits statements that someone is a "winner" or that his or her name "has been selected" when no prize has been won. The law carries a fine of $1,000 per incident, which could be $1,000 per letter received by New York residents.[84] Some of the most ambitious legal actions are taking place in individual states, where prosecutors are taking sweepstakes and contest companies to court for misleading and deceptive practices.[85]

Premiums Another sales promotion area subject to various regulations is the use of premiums. A common problem associated with premiums is misrepresentation of their value. Marketers that make a premium offer should list its value as the price at which the merchandise is usually sold on its own. Marketers must also be careful in making premium offers to special audiences such as children. While premium offers for children are legal, their use is controversial; many critics argue that they encourage children to request a product for the premium rather than for its value. The Children's Advertising Review Unit has voluntary guidelines concerning the use of premium offers. These guidelines note that children have difficulty distinguishing a product from a premium. If product advertising contains a premium message, care should be taken that the child's attention is focused primarily on the product. The premium message should be clearly secondary. Conditions of a premium offer should be stated simply and clearly. "Mandatory" statements and disclosures should be stated in terms that can be understood by the child audience.[86] However, a recent study of children's advertising commissioned by CARU found the single most prevalent violation involved devoting virtually an entire commercial message to information about a premium. CARU guidelines state that advertising targeted to children must emphasize the product rather than the premium offer.[87]

Trade Allowances Marketers using various types of trade allowances must be careful not to violate any stipulations of the Robinson-Patman Act, which prohibits price discrimination. Certain sections of the Robinson-Patman Act prohibit a manufacturer from granting wholesalers and retailers various types of promotional allowances and/or payments unless they are made available to all customers on proportionally equal terms.[88] Another form of trade promotion regulated by the Robinson-Patman Act is vertical cooperative advertising. The FTC monitors cooperative advertising programs to ensure that co-op funds are made available to retailers on a proportionally equal basis and that the payments are not used as a disguised form of price discrimination.

As noted in Chapter 16, another trade promotion area where the FTC is becoming involved is the use of slotting fees or allowances paid to retailers for agreeing to handle a new product. In 1999, the Senate Committee on Small Business charged retailers in the grocery, drugstore, and computer software industries with illegally using slotting fees to lock out competitors and prevent consumers from having their choice of the best products. Packaged-goods marketers and retailers have argued that examining slotting fees alone is unfair since they are just part of a wide variety of inducements marketers use to secure the best shelf space. The FTC is investigating the use of slotting fees as anticompetitive weapons that make it difficult for small-size companies to secure retail shelf space.[89] In 2000, the FTC launched its first direct attack on slotting fees when it accused McCormick & Co., the leading spice maker, of offering discriminatory discounts on its products to several grocery chains. McCormick agreed to settle a complaint that the discounts were a way of paying some retailers disproportionately more in slotting fees than others. The FTC charged that the slotting fees were a way for McCormick to gain more shelf space at the expense of smaller rivals. The practice that was deemed illegal by the FTC is a standard way of doing business in the grocery trade as well as other industries, and some legal experts have argued that this case could impact the use of slotting fees in the future.[90]

Direct Marketing As we saw in Chapter 14, direct marketing is growing rapidly. Many consumers now purchase products directly from companies in response to TV and print advertising or direct selling. The Federal Trade Commission enforces laws related to direct marketing, including mail-order offers, the use of 900 telephone numbers, and direct-response TV advertising. The U.S. Postal Service enforces laws dealing with the use of the mail to deliver advertising and promotional messages or receive payments and orders for items advertised in print or broadcast media.

A number of laws govern the use of mail-order selling. The FTC and the Postal Service police direct-response advertising closely to ensure the ads are not deceptive or misleading and do not misrepresent the product or service being offered. Laws also forbid mailing unordered merchandise to consumers, and rules govern the use of "negative option" plans whereby a company proposes to send merchandise to consumers and expects payment unless the consumer sends a notice of rejection or cancellation.[91] FTC rules also encourage direct marketers to ship ordered merchandise promptly. Companies that cannot ship merchandise within the time period stated in the solicitation (or 30 days if no time is stated) must give buyers the option to cancel the order and receive a full refund.[92]

Another area of direct marketing facing increased regulation is telemarketing. With the passage of the Telephone Consumer Protection Act of 1991, marketers who use telephones to contact consumers must follow a complex set of rules developed by the Federal Communications Commission. These rules require telemarketers to maintain an in-house list of residential telephone subscribers who do not want to be called. Consumers who continue to receive unwanted calls can take the telemarketer to state court for damages of up to $500. The rules also ban telemarketing calls to homes before 8:00 A.M. and after 9:00 P.M., automatic dialer calls, and recorded messages to emergency phones, health care facilities, and numbers for which the call recipient may be charged. They also ban unsolicited junk fax ads and require that fax transmissions clearly indicate the sender's name and fax number.[93]

The Federal Trade Commission has also been actively involved with the regulation of advertising that encourages consumers to call telephone numbers with a 900 prefix, whereupon they are automatically billed for the call. While there are many legitimate uses for 900-number technology, it has also been heavily used for sleazy sex operations, contest scams, and other unscrupulous activities.[94] One area of particular concern to the FTC has been ads targeting children and encouraging them to call 900 numbers. In 1993, the FTC issued its 900-Number Rule for advertising directed at children. The rule restricts advertisers from targeting children under the age of 12 with ads containing 900 numbers unless they provide a bona fide educational service. The rule also requires that 900-number ads directed at those under the age of 18 must contain a "clear and conspicuous" disclosure statement that requires the caller to have parental/guardian permission to complete the call. The rule also obligates advertisers to disclose the cost of the call and give the caller the opportunity to hang up without incurring any costs.[95]

The FTC enacted the 900-Number Rule under the provision that it would be reviewed within four years to consider its costs and benefits.[96] This review was undertaken and the rule was retained and revised, although under a new name. The name was changed to the Pay-Per-Call Rule, and in 1998 the rule was revised to give the FTC the authority to broaden its scope and add new provisions. Among other things, the new provisions combat telephone bill cramming, which is the placing of unauthorized charges on consumers' phone bills.[97]

In 2003, Congress approved a Federal Trade Commission proposal for the formation of a National Do Not Call Registry allowing consumers to opt out of most commercial telemarketing.[98] Consumers can place their home phone numbers, as well as personal cell phone numbers, on the National Do Not Call Registry (Exhibit 21-15). Commercial telemarketers must pay a fee to access the registry and generally are prohibited from calling the listed numbers. Telemarketers have three months to comply once a number goes on the list, and a consumer's registration lasts five years. Political

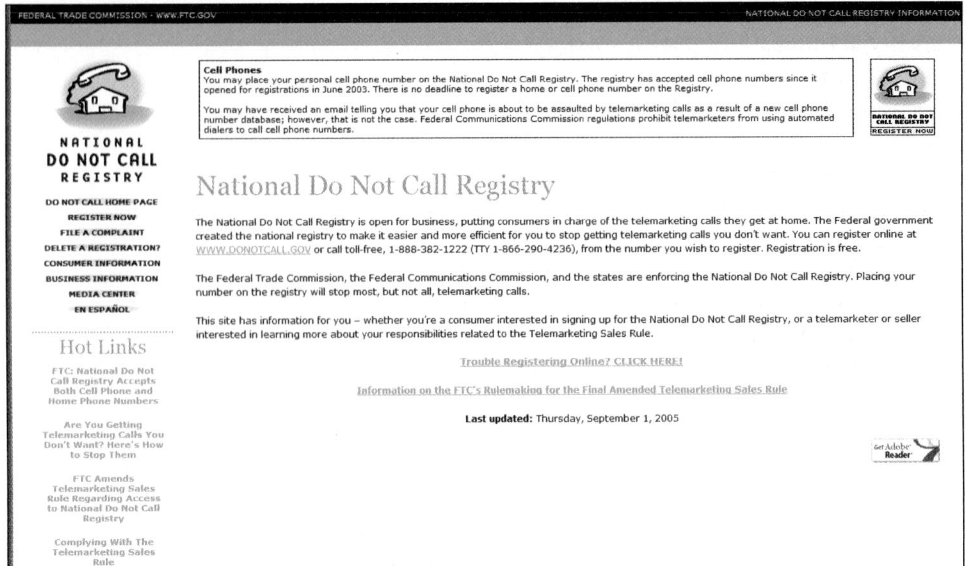

FEDERAL TRADE COMMISSION - WWW.FTC.GOV
NATIONAL DO NOT CALL REGISTRY INFORMATION
Cell Phones
You may place your personal cell phone number on the National Do Not Call Registry. The registry has accepted cell phone numbers since it opened for registrations in June 2003. There is no deadline to register a home or cell phone number on the Registry.
You may have received an email telling you that your cell phone is about to be assaulted by telemarketing calls as a result of a new cell phone number database; however, that is not the case. Federal Communications Commission regulations prohibit telemarketers from using automated dialers to call cell phone numbers.
NATIONAL DO NOT CALL REGISTRY
REGISTER NOW
NATIONAL DO NOT CALL REGISTRY
DO NOT CALL HOME PAGE
REGISTER NOW
FILE A COMPLAINT
DELETE A REGISTRATION?
CONSUMER INFORMATION
BUSINESS INFORMATION
MEDIA CENTER
EN ESPAÑOL
Hot Links
FTC: National Do Not Call Registry Accepts Both Cell Phone and Home Phone Numbers
Are You Getting Telemarketing Calls You Don't Want? Here's How to Stop Them
FTC Amends Telemarketing Sales Rule Regarding Access to National Do Not Call Registry
Complying With The Telemarketing Sales Rule
National Do Not Call Registry
The National Do Not Call Registry is open for business, putting consumers in charge of the telemarketing calls they get at home. The Federal government created the national registry to make it easier and more efficient for you to stop getting telemarketing calls you don't want. You can register online at WWW.DONOTCALL.GOV or call toll-free, 1-888-382-1222 (TTY 1-866-290-4236), from the number you wish to register. Registration is free.
The Federal Trade Commission, the Federal Communications Commission, and the states are enforcing the National Do Not Call Registry. Placing your number on the registry will stop most, but not all, telemarketing calls.
This site has information for you – whether you're a consumer interested in signing up for the National Do Not Call Registry, or a telemarketer or seller interested in learning more about your responsibilities related to the Telemarketing Sales Rule.
Trouble Registering Online? CLICK HERE!
Information on the FTC's Rulemaking for the Final Amended Telemarketing Sales Rule
Last updated: Thursday, September 1, 2005
Get Adobe Reader

Exhibit 21-15 The National Do Not Call Registry protects consumers from calls by telemarketers

and charitable solicitation calls are not affected by the regulation, and telemarketers can call consumers with whom they have an established relationship. Marketers face penalties of $11,000 per incident for calling someone on the list. The Federal Trade Commission, the Federal Communications Commission, and individual states are enforcing the National Do Not Call Registry, which contained nearly 90 million phone numbers as of 2005.

The National Do Not Call Registry affects the direct-marketing industry as it greatly reduces the number of households that telemarketers can call. As might be expected, the direct-marketing industry is strongly opposed to the registry, arguing that it violates their First Amendment rights and, further, that such a program is not needed. The Direct Marketing Association (DMA), which is the primary trade group for the direct-marketing industry, has argued that consumers already have a number of do-not-call options. They can ask to be excluded from an individual company's telemarketing list at the same time they can sign up with state lists or pay $5 to sign up on the voluntary national list maintained by the Direct Marketing Association. The DMA argues that the national registry will impose more bureaucracy on the direct-marketing industry and that the same goal can be achieved by the industry itself with better education and enforcement.

The Direct Marketers Association and the American Teleservices Association, which represent callers, challenged the legality of the registry on the grounds that it took away their rights to First Amendment–protected speech and that it was excessive and poorly drafted, with competitive marketers forced to abide by different rules. However, in February 2004, the U.S. Court of Appeals upheld the registry's validity, ruling that it is a valid commercial speech regulation. The appellate court said that because the registry doesn't affect political or charitable calls and because there is a danger of abusive telemarketing and invasion of consumer privacy from telemarketers, the government has a right to regulate its use. The two major trade associations have been reviewing the ruling and may yet appeal the case to the U.S. Supreme Court.[99]

Direct marketers have been adjusting their telemarketing strategies to deal with the restrictions imposed by the do-not-call registry. They are focusing more attention on generating leads through promotional efforts such as sweepstakes and direct-mail programs, prompting consumers to opt in and agree to receive calls from direct marketers.[100] Some industry experts as well as academics argue that the do-not-call registry may actually improve telemarketing practice and the general efficiency of the business because direct marketers must focus more attention on consumers who are receptive to receiving their telemarketing calls.[101]

The direct-marketing industry is also scrutinized by various self-regulatory groups, such as the Direct Marketing Association and the Direct Selling Association, that have specific guidelines and standards member firms are expected to adhere to and abide by.

Marketing on the Internet

The rapid growth of the Internet as a marketing tool has created a new area of concern for regulators. The same consumer protection laws that apply to commercial activities in other media apply to online as well. The Federal Trade Commission Act, which prohibits "unfair or deceptive acts or practices," encompasses Internet advertising, marketing, and sales. Claims made in Internet ads or on websites must be substantiated, especially when they concern health, safety, or performance, and disclosures are required to prevent ads from being misleading and to ensure that consumers receive material information about the terms of a transaction. There are several areas of particular concern with regard to marketing on the Internet. These include privacy issues, online marketing to children, and the use of spam or unsolicited e-mails for commercial purposes.

The major privacy issue regarding the Internet that has emerged involves undisclosed profiling whereby Web marketers can profile a user on the basis of name, address, demographics, and online/offline purchasing data. Marketers have suggested that profiling offers them an opportunity to target specific niches and reach consumers with custom-tailored messages. However, the FTC has stated that Internet sites that claim they don't collect information but permit advertisers to surreptitiously profile viewer sites are violating consumer protection laws and are open to a charge of deception.[102] In 1999, DoubleClick, the company that is the leader in selling and managing online advertising as well as tracking Web users, set off a controversy by connecting consumers' names, addresses, and other personal information with information it collects about where consumers go on the Internet. The controversy resulted in the company being investigated by the Federal Trade Commission and lawsuits being filed in some states.[103]

In response to the profiling controversy, companies that collect Internet usage data and information joined together under the banner of the Network Advertising Initiative (NAI) to develop a self-regulatory code.[104] The NAI has developed a set of privacy principles in conjunction with the Federal Trade Commission that provides consumers with explanations of Internet advertising practices and how the practices affect both consumers and the Internet itself. The NAI has also launched a website (www.networkadvertising.org) that provides consumers with information about online advertising practices and gives them the choice to opt out of targeted advertising delivered by NAI member companies (Exhibit 21-16). Another industry-driven initiative is the Platform for Privacy Preferences (P3P), which is a new technology that lets consumers screen out websites via operating system software. This technology gives consumers greater control over the collection of information by allowing them to specify their privacy preferences electronically and screen out websites that do not meet these preferences. The privacy debate is likely to escalate, and it is expected that legislation will be introduced to force companies to seek consumers' approval before sharing personal information captured from their websites.

While these proposals are aimed at protecting the privacy rights of adults, one of the biggest concerns is over restricting marketers whose activities or websites are targeted at children. These concerns over online marketing to children led to the passage of the **Children's Online Privacy Protection Act** of 1998 (**COPPA**), which the FTC began enforcing in April 2000.[105] This act places tight restrictions on collecting information from children via the Internet and requires that websites directed at children and young teens have a privacy policy posted on their home page and areas of the site where information is collected. The law also requires websites aimed at children under age 13 to obtain parental permission to collect most types of personal information and to monitor chat rooms and bulletin boards to make sure children do not disclose personal information there. When the law was enacted in 2000, it was left to the FTC to determine how to obtain the required permission, and the FTC temporarily allowed websites to let parents simply return an e-mail to approve certain information. Since then no other solution to the permission issue has surfaced, and the FTC is proposing to make the solution permanent.[106]

Concerns over consumer privacy have become a major issue among the government and various regulatory agencies such as the FTC.[107] The federal

Exhibit 21-16 The Network Advertising Initiative website provides consumers with information about online advertising practices

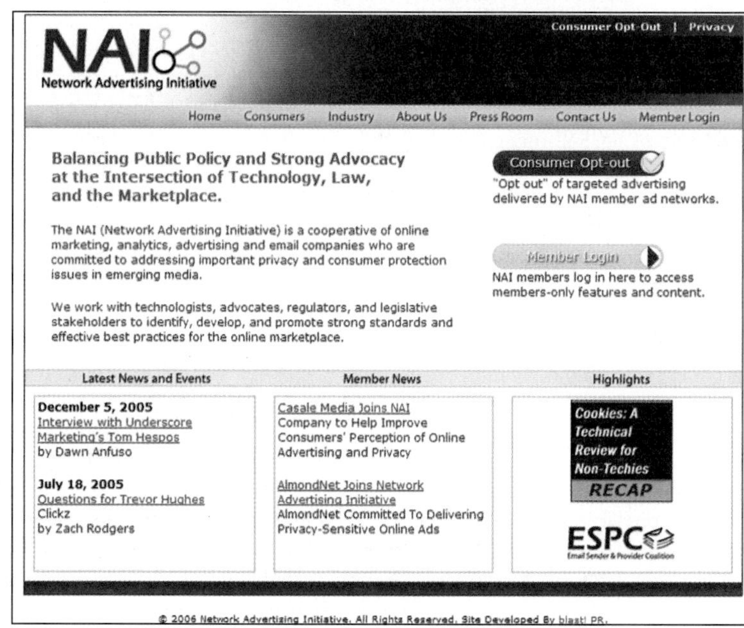

government is currently considering a number of privacy-related laws, many of which would have an impact on marketing and advertising over the Internet. The proposed laws include the Online Privacy Protection Act, which requires the FTC to prescribe regulations to protect the privacy of individuals not covered by COPPA and to provide greater individual control over the collection and use of information.[108]

Another Internet-related area receiving regulatory attention is **spamming,** which is the sending of unsolicited multiple commercial electronic messages. Spamming has become a major problem; studies show that the typical Internet user spends the equivalent of 10 working days a year dealing with incoming spam.[109] Spam also costs businesses billions of dollars every year in terms of lost worker productivity and network maintenance. Moreover, most of these messages are fraudulent or deceptive in one or more respects.

A number of states have enacted antispamming legislation, and a comprehensive federal antispam bill, the Controlling the Assault of Non-Solicited Pornography and Marketing Act of 2003 (CAN-SPAM Act), went into effect on January 1, 2004. The act's general requirements for commercial e-mails include the following requirements:

- A prohibition against false or misleading transmission information.
- Conspicuous notice of the right to opt-out and a functioning Internet-based mechanism that a recipient may use to request to not receive future commercial e-mail messages from the sender.
- Clear and conspicuous identification that the message is an advertisement.
- A valid physical postal address for the sender.

Violations of the CAN-SPAM law include both civil and criminal penalties including a fine of $250 (calculated on a per e-mail basis) up to a maximum of $2 million. While the CAN-SPAM Act carries severe penalties for violators, thus far it has done little to stop unsolicited e-mail messages. Spammers have been able to stay one step ahead of law enforcement officials by operating offshore and by constantly moving the Internet hosting source.[110]

Summary

Regulation and control of advertising stem from internal regulation or self-regulation as well as from external control by federal, state, and local regulatory agencies. For many years the advertising industry has promoted the use of voluntary self-regulation to regulate advertising and limit government interference with and control over advertising. Self-regulation of advertising emanates from all segments of the advertising industry, including advertisers and their agencies, business and advertising associations, and the media.

The NAD/NARB, the primary self-regulatory mechanism for national advertising, has been very effective in achieving its goal of voluntary regulation of advertising. Various media also have their own advertising guidelines. The major television networks maintain the most stringent review process and restrictions.

Traditionally, the federal government has been the most important source of external regulation, with the Federal Trade Commission serving as the major watchdog of advertising in the United States. The FTC protects both consumers and businesses from unfair and deceptive practices and anticompetitive behavior. The FTC became very active in the regulation of advertising during the 1970s when it began several new programs and policies, including affirmative disclosure, advertising substantiation, and corrective advertising. Since 1980 the FTC has not been allowed to implement industrywide rules that would define unfair advertising practices. However, the advertising industry and Congress are nearing agreement on a definition of unfairness, and this power may be restored to the FTC.

In 1983, the FTC developed a new working definition of deceptive advertising. Recently the FTC has become more active in policing false and deceptive advertising. Under the Lanham Act, many companies are taking the initiative by suing competitors that make false claims. Many states, as well as the National Association of Attorneys General, are also active in exercising their jurisdiction over false and misleading advertising.

A number of laws also govern the use of other promotional mix elements, such as sales promotion and direct marketing. The Federal Trade Commission regulates many areas of sales promotion as well as direct marketing. Various consumer-oriented sales promotion tools such as contests, games, sweepstakes, and premiums are subject to regulation. Recently many states have become very active in the regulation of contests and sweepstakes. Trade promotion practices, such as the use of promotional allowances and vertical cooperative advertising, are regulated by the Federal Trade Commission under the Robinson-Patman Act. The FTC also enforces laws in a variety of areas that relate to direct marketing and mail-order selling, while the FCC has rules governing telemarketing companies.

The rapid growth of the Internet as a marketing tool has created a new area of concern for regulators. The same consumer protection laws that apply to commercial activities in other media apply online as well. Major areas of concern with regard to advertising and marketing on the Internet are privacy, online marketing to children, and spamming or the sending of unsolicited commercial e-mail messages. Concerns over online marketing to children have led to the passage of the Children's Online Privacy Protection Act, which the FTC began enforcing in early 2000. The federal government passed the CAN-SPAM Act, which went into effect on January 1, 2004. This legislation sets stringent requirements for commercial e-mail messages.

Key Terms

self-regulation, 678
Better Business Bureau (BBB), 681
Council of Better Business Bureaus, 681
National Advertising Review Board (NARB), 681
National Advertising Review Council (NARC), 682
Federal Trade Commission (FTC), 688
commercial speech, 689
Central Hudson Test, 689
Federal Trade Commission Act, 689
Wheeler-Lea Amendment, 691
trade regulation rules (TRRs), 692
unfairness, 692
puffery, 693
deception, 693
affirmative disclosure, 695
advertising substantiation, 696
consent order, 697
cease-and-desist order, 697
corrective advertising, 698
Lanham Act, 704
National Association of Attorneys General (NAAG), 706
Children's Online Privacy Protection Act (COPPA), 711
spamming, 712

Discussion Questions

1. The opening vignette to the chapter discusses the debate over the direct-to-consumer advertising of prescription drugs. Do you agree with the decision by the Food and Drug Administration to issue new guidelines making it easier for pharmaceutical companies to advertise their products directly to consumers? Can the problems that have arisen be handled effectively by voluntary guidelines?

2. Discuss the role the media play in the self-regulation of advertising. Do you view self-regulation as an effective way of protecting consumers from offensive or misleading advertising?

3. IMC Perspective 21-1 discusses the debate over hard liquor companies advertising on television. Do you agree with the DISCUS argument that hard liquor companies are at a competitive disadvantage against beer and wine marketers if they cannot advertise on television? Evaluate the decision by NASCAR to drop its long-standing ban on sponsorships by hard liquor companies.

4. IMC Perspective 21-2 discusses the decision by the California Supreme Court in the *Nike* v. *Kasky* case to view statements about a company's labor policies or operations in advertising or press releases as commercial, rather than political, in nature and thus not subject to First Amendment protection. Do you agree or disagree with this ruling? Discuss how this ruling might impact various forms of integrated marketing communications used by Nike and other companies in California.

5. IMC Perspective 21-3 discusses the legal battle between Pizza Hut and Papa John's over the latter's use of the tagline "Better ingredients. Better pizza." Which company do you side with in this controversy and why?

6. Find several examples of advertising claims or slogans that are based on puffery rather than substantiated claims. Discuss whether you feel these advertising claims can be defended on the basis of puffery.

7. Discuss the Lanham Act and how it affects advertising. What elements are necessary to win a false advertising claim under the Lanham Act?

8. Discuss how the do-not-call registry developed by the Federal Trade Commission is impacting the direct marketing industry. What arguments might direct marketers make in their efforts to have this program rescinded?

9. Discuss how areas such as sales promotion and direct marketing are impacted by laws and regulations. Do you think it is as important to regulate these areas as media advertising?

10. What are the various areas of concern with regard to marketing on the Internet? Discuss the various steps being taken by regulators to address these concerns.

Evaluating the Social, Ethical, and Economic Aspects of Advertising and Promotion

22

Chapter Objectives

1. To consider various perspectives concerning the social, ethical, and economic aspects of advertising and promotion.
2. To evaluate the social criticisms of advertising.
3. To examine the economic role of advertising and its effects on consumer choice, competition, and product costs and prices.

Dove Challenges the Stereotypical Norms of Beauty

Most women firmly believe that the media and advertising set an unrealistic standard of beauty that they cannot achieve. More than two-thirds of the women in a recent worldwide study expressed this viewpoint. Only 13 percent of the women indicated that they are very satisfied with their body weight and shape, only 2 percent of the women around the world considered themselves beautiful, and more than half of the women said their bodies disgust them. Inspired by these findings, Unilever's Dove, the global beauty brand, recently launched an integrated marketing campaign that is intended to challenge the stereotypical view of beauty, celebrate diversity, and make women feel beautiful every day. The Dove Campaign for Real Beauty is a global effort that is intended to serve as a starting point for societal change and act as a catalyst for widening the definition and discussion of beauty.

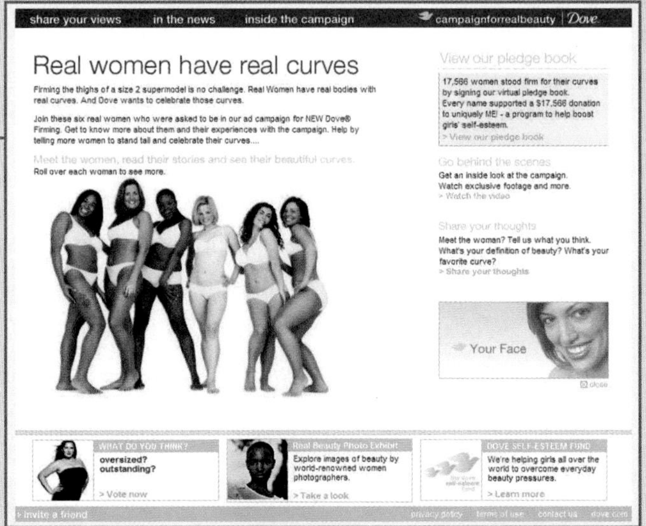

Unilever launched the Dove Campaign for Real Beauty in September 2004 with a much-talked-about ad campaign featuring real women whose appearances are outside the stereotypical norms of beauty. The ads asked viewers to judge the women's looks (Oversized? Outstanding? or Wrinkled? Wonderful?) and invited them to cast their votes and join in a discussion of beauty issues on a special website (campaignforrealbeauty.com). As part of the launch for the campaign, Dove invited women to rediscover the beauty in their own hair. Television ads were run challenging society's narrow vision that "one size fits all" hair is for everyone. A diverse group of women celebrated the individuality of their own beautiful hair as they shed the stereotypical long, blonde-haired image.

In June 2005, Dove kicked off the second phase of the Campaign for Real Beauty with advertising featuring six "real women" with real bodies and real curves. These "real women" are not professional models and vary in shape and size. They come from all walks of life and include two students, a kindergarten teacher, a manicurist, an administrative assistant, and a café barista. The images of the real women, which were shot by leading fashion photographer Rankin, show the women posing proudly and confidently in their underwear. The photos were not altered or retouched as is often done when shooting images of models. The new phase of the campaign was designed to address the issue of body image and to encourage women to "Stand Firm to Celebrate Their Curves." The second phase of the campaign was designed to support the new line of Dove firming products with messages encouraging women to challenge beauty stereotypes. One of the ads shows an image of one woman along with two simple lines of copy: "New Dove Firming. As tested on real curves." The copy for another ad reads, "Let's face it, firming the thighs of a size 2 supermodel is no challenge."

Unilever has developed an extensive integrated marketing communications program to support the Campaign for Real Beauty. The campaign appeals to women through national and local television and magazine advertising as well as interactive billboards, transit station signage, and bus ads. The website allows women to engage in ongoing dialogue about beauty by posting to discussion boards, to hear other women's perspectives on beauty, and to download research studies about beauty. Women can also cast their votes on issues and questions raised in the advertising campaign. Since the site was launched, more than a million votes have been tabulated globally and more are counted every day. The campaign is also supported by customized retail promotions and partnerships that help generate awareness and discussion in local markets.

The IMC program for the campaign includes grassroots marketing as well as the use of cause-related marketing. To launch the campaign, Dove partnered with the American Women in Radio and Television to bring together thought leaders in the media and beauty arena. These influential women engaged in a panel discussion to debate the definition of real beauty. To further discussion of the campaign at a grassroots level, Dove sponsors local market panel events. The company also uses cause-related marketing by establishing the Dove Self-Esteem Fund to raise awareness of the link between beauty and body-related self-esteem. The new initiative continues an ongoing effort by Dove to fund programs that raise self-esteem in girls and young women. The Dove Self-Esteem Fund also works through the Unilever Foundation to sponsor *uniquely ME!,* a partnership program with the Girl Scouts of the USA that helps build self-confidence in girls 8 to 14.

Dove's Campaign for Real Beauty has touched a cultural hot button, which set off a flurry of media coverage that includes articles in a number of national magazines and newspapers and culminating with models from the ads appearing on the cover of *People* magazine. A number of prominent experts have praised the Campaign for Real Beauty including noted feminist Gloria Steinem and psychologist Dr. Joyce Brothers, who notes that "Dove helps show that we may have come a long way when we no longer have to try to look exactly like every other woman who has been declared by some fashion magazine or film czar to be the epitome of beauty." Psychologist Mary Pipher, who has written the best-selling book *Reviving Ophelia,* which deals with teens' and adolescent girls' sense of self, notes that "any change in the culture of advertising that allows for a broader definition of beauty and encourages women to be accepting and comfortable with their natural appearance is a step in the right direction."

Other marketers have introduced marketing and advertising campaigns that are portraying women in a more realistic way and telling them they do not have to look like the supermodels shown in most ads. For example, retailer Bath & Body Works launched a line of shampoos and lotions under the licensed brand name "American Girl realbeauty Inside and Out." Nike also launched a campaign that celebrates women's big butts, thunder thighs, and tomboy knees. The campaign includes a website, Nikewomen.com, which features short films of women discussing topics such as their bodies and working out.

Some critics note that there is somewhat of a contradiction in the message of the "real beauty" campaigns as they still suggest that you need to use the marketer's products to be beautiful. However, many feel that these ads send a message that many parents have tried to teach their daughters for years: Be happy with who you are.

Sources: Rich Thomaselli, "Beauty's New, ER, Face," *Advertising Age,* August 15, 2005, pp. 1, 21; Dr. Joyce Brothers, "Beauty Is No Longer Exclusive Domain of Magazines and Films," *Advertising Age,* August 1, 2005, p. 14; Theresa Howard, "Ad Campaigns Tell Women to Celebrate Who They Are," *USA TODAY,* July 8, 2005, p. 5B; "Real Women Bare Their Real Curves," press release, Edelman/Unilever, June 23, 2005.

> If I were to name the deadliest subversive force within capitalism, the single greatest source of its waning morality—I would without hesitation name advertising. How else should one identify a force that debases language, drains thought, and undoes dignity?[1]

The primary focus of this text has been on the role of advertising and other promotional variables as marketing activities used to convey information to, and influence the behavior of, consumers. We have been concerned with examining the advertising and promotion function in the context of a business and marketing environment and from a perspective that assumes these activities are appropriate. However, as you can see in this quote from economist Robert Heilbroner, not everyone shares this viewpoint. Advertising and promotion are the most visible of all business activities and are prone to scrutiny by those who are concerned about the methods marketers use to sell their products and services.

Proponents of advertising argue that it is the lifeblood of business—it provides consumers with information about products and services and encourages them to improve their standard of living. They say advertising produces jobs and helps new firms enter the marketplace. Companies employ people who make the products and provide the services that advertising sells. Free market economic systems are based on competition, which revolves around information, and nothing delivers information better and at less cost than advertising.

Not everyone, however, is sold on the value of advertising. Critics argue that most advertising is more propaganda than information; it creates needs and faults consumers never knew they had. Ads suggest that children won't succeed without a computer, that our bodies should be leaner, our faces younger, and our houses cleaner. They point to the sultry, scantily clad bodies used in ads to sell everything from perfume to beer to power tools and argue that advertising promotes materialism, insecurity, and greed.

One of the reasons advertising and other forms of integrated marketing communications are becoming increasingly criticized is because they are so prevalent. Not only are there more magazine, newspaper, outdoor, TV, and radio ads than ever, but more and more public space is becoming commercialized. Advertising professor David Helm notes: "Between the stickered bananas and the ads over the urinals and the ones on the floor of the supermarkets, we're exposed to 3,000 commercial messages a day. That's one every 15 seconds, assuming we sleep for 8 hours, and I'd guess right now there's someone figuring out how to get us while our eyes are closed."[2]

As marketers intensify their efforts to get the attention of consumers, resentment against their integrated marketing communications efforts is likely to increase. Concern is growing that there will be a consumer backlash as integrated marketing efforts move to new heights and marketers become increasingly aggressive. Diane Cook, a former advertising executive who founded the AdCenter at Virginia Commonwealth, says: "The growing practice of placing ads and logos everywhere seems a desperate last attempt to make branding work according to the old rules. As telemarketing, advertising, promotions and the rest continue at a frenzied pace, the value of the messages decrease. The system seems headed for a large implosion."[3] Ethical Perspective 22-1 discusses how new-age marketers are creating and delivering ads and other types of messages that are being woven into our everyday lives by making them part of popular culture and the backlash against these practices.

Because of its high visibility and pervasiveness, along with its persuasive character, advertising has been the subject of a great deal of controversy and criticism. Numerous books are critical of not only advertising's methods and techniques but also its social consequences. Various parties—including scholars, economists, politicians, sociologists, government agencies, social critics, special-interest groups, and consumers—have attacked advertising and other forms of marketing communications for a variety of reasons, including their excessiveness, the way they influence society, the methods they use, their exploitation of consumers, and their effect on our economic system.

Advertising is a very powerful force, and this text would not be complete without a look at the criticisms regarding its social and economic effects as well as some defenses against these charges. We consider the various criticisms of advertising and promotion from an ethical and societal perspective and then appraise the economic effects of advertising.

Concerns Grow over Use of Advertainment

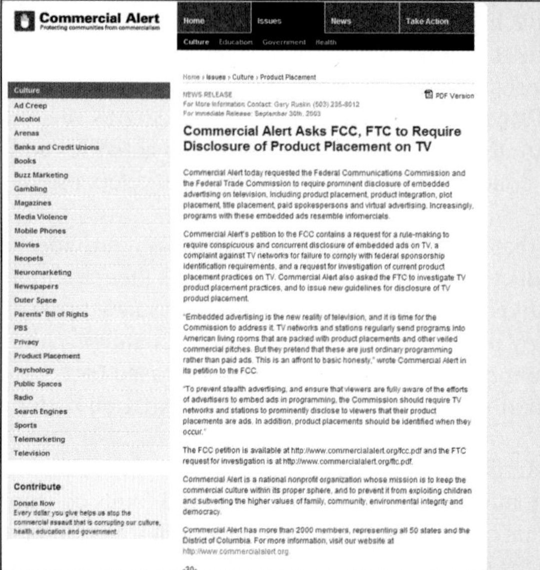

Commercial Alert
Protecting communities from commercialism

Home | Issues | News | Take Action
Culture | Education | Government | Health

Culture
Ad Creep
Alcohol
Arenas
Banks and Credit Unions
Books
Buzz Marketing
Gambling
Magazines
Media Violence
Mobile Phones
Movies
Neopets
Neuromarketing
Newspapers
Outer Space
Parents' Bill of Rights
PBS
Privacy
Product Placement
Psychology
Public Spaces
Radio
Search Engines
Sports
Telemarketing
Television

Contribute

Donate Now
Every dollar you give helps us stop the commercial assault that is corrupting our culture, health, education and government.

Home › Issues › Culture › Product Placement

NEWS RELEASE
PDF Version
For More Information Contact: Gary Ruskin (503) 235-8012
For Immediate Release: September 30th, 2003

Commercial Alert Asks FCC, FTC to Require Disclosure of Product Placement on TV

Commercial Alert today requested the Federal Communications Commission and the Federal Trade Commission to require prominent disclosure of embedded advertising on television, including product placement, product integration, plot placement, title placement, paid spokespersons and virtual advertising. Increasingly, programs with these embedded ads resemble infomercials.

Commercial Alert's petition to the FCC contains a request for a rule-making to require conspicuous and concurrent disclosure of embedded ads on TV, a complaint against TV networks for failure to comply with federal sponsorship identification requirements, and a request for investigation of current product placement practices on TV. Commercial Alert also asked the FTC to investigate TV product placement practices, and to issue new guidelines for disclosure of TV product placement.

"Embedded advertising is the new reality of television, and it is time for the Commission to address it. TV networks and stations regularly send programs into American living rooms that are packed with product placements and other veiled commercial pitches. But they pretend that these are just ordinary programming rather than paid ads. This is an affront to basic honesty," wrote Commercial Alert in its petition to the FCC.

"To prevent stealth advertising, and ensure that viewers are fully aware of the efforts of advertisers to embed ads in programming, the Commission should require TV networks and stations to prominently disclose to viewers that their product placements are ads. In addition, product placements should be identified when they occur."

The FCC petition is available at http://www.commercialalert.org/fcc.pdf and the FTC request for investigation is at http://www.commercialalert.org/ftc.pdf.

Commercial Alert is a national nonprofit organization whose mission is to keep the commercial culture within its proper sphere, and to prevent it from exploiting children and subverting the higher values of family, community, environmental integrity and democracy.

Commercial Alert has more than 2000 members, representing all 50 states and the District of Columbia. For more information, visit our website at http://www.commercialalert.org.

-30-

In 1957, social critic Vance Packard wrote his classic best-seller *The Hidden Persuaders,* in which he purported to reveal all of the secret techniques used by advertisers to dig deeply into the psyches of consumers and manipulate them. When interviewed 40 years later, Packard was still fuming over what he saw coming out of Madison Avenue. Packard was angry not because advertisers had sharpened their brainwashing skills; rather, he was puzzled by modern-day advertising because it seemed to be unrelated to selling anything at all. He noticed that a change had taken place in the way marketers advertise their products, as there is now an obsession with images and feelings and a lack of concrete claims about a product and why anyone should buy it.

Packard was indeed correct in his observation that advertising has changed. However, what he failed to notice was that marketers have actually become less dependent on the traditional forms of mass-media advertising that he thought could be used to manipulate consumers. In the modern-day world of marketing, the debate is less over the ads that consumers see and hear and more about the persuasive messages they receive unknowingly. In recent years marketers have recognized that consumers are tired of the myriad of advertisements and other forms of promotion they are exposed to every day and are becoming very cynical about the sales pitches. To get around this problem, many companies are obliterating the line between marketing communications and entertainment by creating and delivering ads and other messages that appear to be part of popular culture. New-age marketers are redefining the notion of what advertising and other forms of marketing communications are and how they can be used. "Stealth messages" are being woven into our everyday lives, and as consumers we are often unaware of their persuasive intent.

Product placements have been around for years, and branded products are now commonplace in many movies and TV shows. However, the concept of paying to have a product or service promoted covertly has moved into other arenas, often without consumer awareness. Celebrities such as Lauren Bacall, Kathleen Turner, and Rob Lowe have appeared on talk shows and praised prescription drugs without revealing that the drug companies were paying them or making donations to their favorite charities in return for the endorsement. Producers of reality shows, soap operas, and sitcoms and even authors of best-selling books take money to build plots around certain brands of products such as makeup or jewelry. And of course marketers are hiring trendsetters to generate "buzz" for their products on college campuses and in trendy bars and nightclubs as well as other places. Many of the people who recommend products to us are actually pitchpersons in disguise who are being paid to deliver subtle promotional messages.

Critics of these stealth marketing techniques say they are tinkering with our minds. The executive director of the Center for Digital Democracy has called the phenomenon the "brand washing of America." Many advertising industry executives are worried that it could all too easily backfire, making consumers even more wary. Keith Reinhard, former chairman of DDB Worldwide, has spoken out against the covert techniques, noting, "I'm against any form of deception. In the end, its bad business." Consumer advocate Ralph Nader has accused marketers of creating "prime-time infomercials" with no line between entertainment and ads. He notes, "What these people on Madison Avenue don't understand is, consumers will reach a saturation point. They'll reach a point where they just tip over and go, 'Yuck.'"

While many marketers realize that they may be alienating consumers with all of these stealth techniques, they argue that they really have no choice. That's because the old approach of relying on 30-second TV spots and other forms of mass-media advertising is becoming less effective. They note that digital video recorders such as TiVo will soon become as common as VCRs and give TV viewers the ability to banish commercials. Some media experts argue that commercial-supported free TV is an endangered species and marketers have to find new ways to reach consumers with their messages. Thus, like it or not, consumers are probably going to see more and more unexpected, and undercover, messages.

Many advertising experts argue that "branded content" is the wave of the future, and there is a growing clamor to reinvent advertising and other forms of marketing communications to be something more akin to entertainment. However, advertising and marketing watchdog groups such as Commercial Alert note that the memories of the movies and TV shows Hollywood is making today are being corrupted by commercialization that has mushroomed beyond mere product placement to include script doctoring and related sins. Gary Ruskin, executive director of Commercial Alert, argues that artistic concerns take a back seat when advertising is integrated into films and TV shows. He has also expressed concern over the effect "advertainment" will have on children who cannot identify or properly process the barrage of advertising messages directed at them, particularly when they are embedded in movies and TV shows.

Ruskin has argued that sponsorship identification has been a core part of American broadcast law and that consumers have a right to know by whom they are being persuaded. Recently the Federal Trade Commission and Federal Communications Commission reviewed the practice of product placements in response to a complaint by Commercial Alert. The agencies are considering requiring the TV networks to disclose that they or their producers have been paid to integrate commercial interests into programming.

Many argue that the Brave New World of advertainment and branded content will be exciting and cool. However, critics argue that people would like to have some places in their lives where they are free from ads and efforts to sell them something. Unfortunately, these places are becoming more difficult to find.

Sources: Daniel Eisenberg, "It's an Ad, Ad, Ad, World," *Time,* September 2, 2002, pp. 38–41; Jennifer Davies, "Where Do Films Start, Ads Stop?" *San Diego Union Tribune,* August 8, 2002, pp. C1, 3; Jim Edwards, "Regulators Take Another Look At Product Placement," *Brandweek,* October 10, 2005, p. 1; Claire Atkinson, "FTC and FCC Nearing Product-Placement Decisions," adage.com, October 29, 2004.

Advertising and Promotion Ethics

In the previous chapter, we examined the regulatory environment in which advertising and promotion operate. While many laws and regulations determine what advertisers can and cannot do, not every issue is covered by a rule. Marketers must often make decisions regarding appropriate and responsible actions on the basis of ethical considerations rather than on what is legal or within industry guidelines. **Ethics** are moral principles and values that govern the actions and decisions of an individual or group.[4]

A particular action may be within the law and still not be ethical. A good example of this involves target marketing. No laws restrict tobacco companies from targeting advertising and promotion for new brands to African-Americans. However, given the high levels of lung cancer and smoking-related illnesses among the black population, many people would consider this an unethical business practice.

Throughout this text we have presented a number of ethical perspectives to show how various aspects of advertising and promotion often involve ethical considerations. Ethical issues must be considered in integrated marketing communications decisions. And advertising and promotion are areas where a lapse in ethical standards or judgment can result in actions that are highly visible and often very damaging to a company.

The role of advertising in society is controversial and has sometimes resulted in attempts to restrict or ban advertising and other forms of promotion to certain groups or for certain products. College students are one such group. The level of alcohol consumption and binge drinking by college students has become a serious problem. Alcohol-related problems have proliferated on college campuses in recent years and have resulted in many negative consequences, including death.[5] Several studies have shown that there has been a significant increase in binge drinking among college students and have advocated a ban on alcohol-related advertising and promotion.[6] Many colleges and universities have imposed restrictions on the marketing of alcoholic beverages to their students. These restrictions include banning sponsorships or support of athletic, musical, cultural, or social events by alcoholic-beverage companies and limiting college newspaper advertising to price and product information ads.

A great deal of attention is being focused on the issue of whether alcoholic-beverage companies target not only college students but underage drinkers as well. As noted in Chapter 21, the actions of beer, wine, and liquor marketers are being closely scrutinized in the wake of the distilled-spirits industry's decisions to reverse its long-standing ban on television and radio advertising. Many people believe the industry's push to join beer and wine advertisers on television is testing the public's attitudes and may lead to support for more government restrictions and regulations on alcohol advertising.[7]

A study by the Center on Alcohol Marketing and Youth at Georgetown University concluded that underage drinkers are increasingly being targeted by magazine ads for beer and hard liquor.[8] According to the study, magazines that have a significant number of readers under the age of 21, such as *Spin, Vibe, Allure, Maxim,* and *Sports Illustrated,* accounted for nearly one-third of all alcohol advertising in magazines. The study concluded that despite the Federal Trade Commission's recommendation that the alcohol industry avoid marketing to youth audiences, the advertising practices of the beer and liquor companies fail to follow the commission's guidelines. The study called on the FTC to conduct a new and more rigorous review of the advertising practices of the alcoholic beverage companies.[9]

Recently the magazine industry has responded to this issue as some publications such as *ESPN The Magazine, Rolling Stone, Vibe,* and *Spin* have begun offering special print runs designed to reach only subscribers who are at least 21 years old. To create their 21-plus editions, the publishers take the names and addresses of their subscribers and run them against up to three outside databases, including that of the credit rating agency Equifax. Although the screening process is an extra cost for the magazines, the publishers note that it is a way to help insulate hard liquor and beer advertisers from accusations that they are targeting minors. Companies

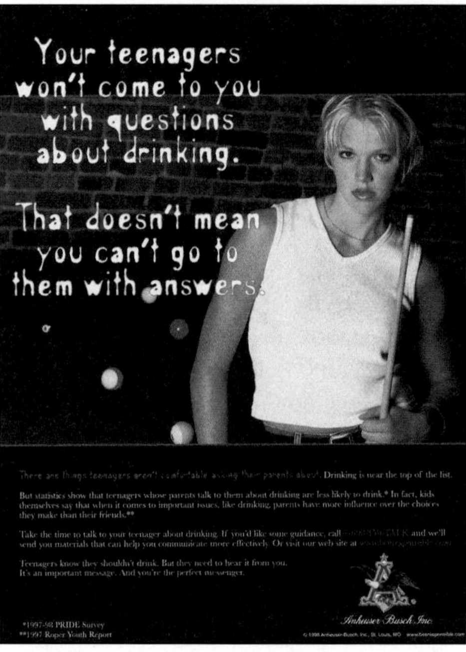

Exhibit 22-1 This ad is part of a campaign by Anheuser-Busch to encourage parents to talk to their teenagers about the risks of underage drinking

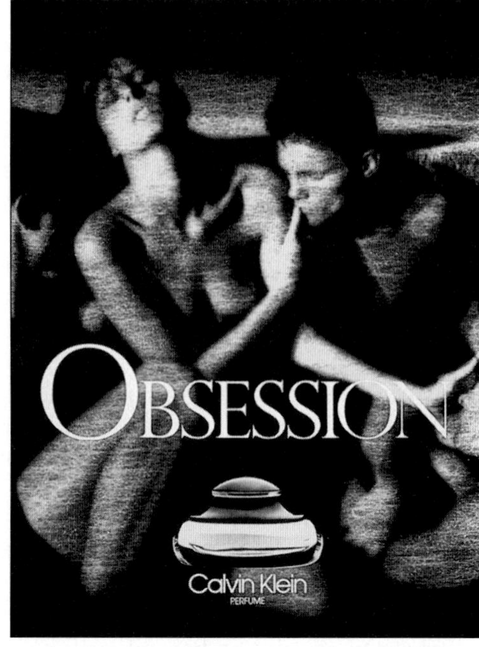

Exhibit 22-2 Ads by Calvin Klein have been the target of criticism by women's groups and others

and brands that have used the 21-plus editions include Heineken, Boston Beer's Samuel Adams, Diageo PLC, and Absolut vodka.[10]

Companies marketing alcoholic beverages such as beer and liquor recognize the need to reduce alcohol abuse and drunken driving, particularly among young people. Many of these companies have developed programs and ads designed to address this problem. For example, Anheuser-Busch has been running a campaign that uses ads such as the one shown in Exhibit 22-1 to encourage parents to talk to their kids about the risks of underage drinking. The company has also teamed up with parents, teachers, community organizations, law enforcement officials, and others to ensure progress in the fight against alcohol abuse.

Criticism often focuses on the actions of specific advertisers. Groups like the National Organization for Women and Women Against Pornography have been critical of advertisers such as Calvin Klein for promoting sexual permissiveness and objectifying women in their ads (Exhibit 22-2). The company was heavily criticized and even boycotted over the controversial "kiddie porn" ads it ran a few years ago featuring intimate snapshots of teenagers in provocative states of undress.[11]

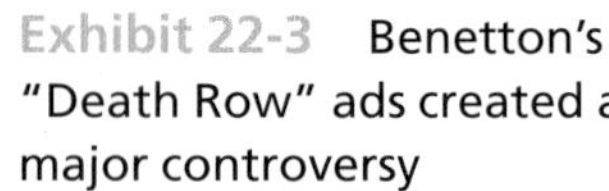
Exhibit 22-3 Benetton's "Death Row" ads created a major controversy

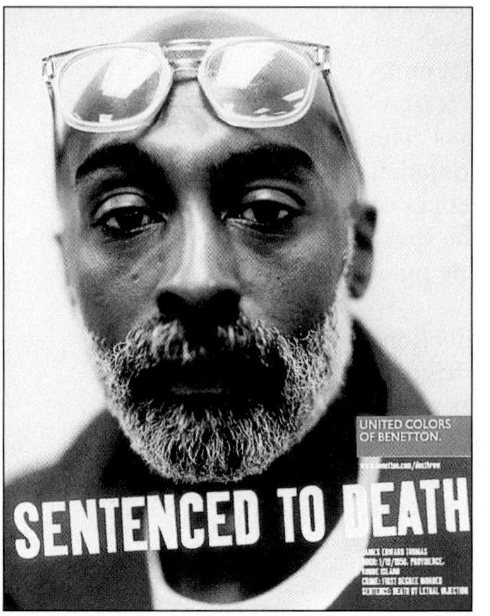

Another company that has received a great deal of criticism for its advertising over the years is Benetton. For nearly two decades the Italian-based clothing company ran numerous "shock" ads containing controversial images such as a black woman nursing a white baby, an AIDS patient and his family moments before his death, and a priest kissing a nun (see Exhibit 21-4). Oliviero Toscani, Benetton's former creative director who developed most of these ads, noted that the controversial images were designed to raise public awareness of social issues and position the company as a cutting-edge, socially conscious marketer.[12] The company's most controversial ads, at least in the United States, were those used in its "Death Row" campaign that ran in 2000. The campaign, aimed at drawing attention to the use of capital punishment in the United States, featured ads showing piercing portraits of death-row inmates (Exhibit 22-3).

The campaign created a storm of controversy; the state of Missouri sued Toscani and Benetton for misrepresenting themselves while interviewing four death-row inmates featured in the campaign. Protests from the families of the inmates' victims and threatened boycotts from enraged consumers resulted in Sears Roebuck and Co. dropping the Benetton line. A year later the lawsuit was settled when Benetton agreed to write letters of apology to the four Missouri families whose relatives were murdered by the inmates featured in the ads and to make a donation to the Missouri Crime Victims Compensation Fund.[13]

As you read this chapter, remember that the various perspectives presented reflect judgments of people with different backgrounds, values, and interests. You may see nothing wrong with the ads for cigarettes or beer or sexually suggestive ads. Other students, however, may oppose these actions on moral and ethical grounds. While we attempt to present the arguments on both sides of these controversial issues, you will have to draw your own conclusions as to who is right or wrong.

Social and Ethical Criticisms of Advertising

Much of the controversy over advertising stems from the ways many companies use it as a selling tool and from its impact on society's tastes, values, and lifestyles. Specific techniques used by advertisers are criticized as deceptive or untruthful, offensive or in bad taste, and exploitative of certain groups, such as children. We discuss each of these criticisms, along with advertisers' responses. We then turn our attention to criticisms concerning the influence of advertising on values and lifestyles, as well as charges that it perpetuates stereotyping and that advertisers exert control over the media.

Advertising as Untruthful or Deceptive

One of the major complaints against advertising is that many ads are misleading or untruthful and deceive consumers. A number of studies have shown a general mistrust of advertising among consumers.[14] A study by Banwari Mittal found that consumers felt that less than one-quarter of TV commercials are honest and believable.[15] Sharon Shavitt, Pamela Lowery, and James Haefner conducted a major national survey of more than 1,000 adult consumers to determine the general public's current attitudes toward and confidence in advertising. They found that Americans generally do not trust advertising, although they tend to feel more confidence in advertising claims when focused on their actual purchase decisions.[16]

A more recent study conducted by Forrester Research found that consumers mistrust ads for most types of products and rely on word of mouth from friends and family as the most trusted source of information. Brand websites were rated the second most trusted source of information with 8 percent of consumers reporting that they completely trust brand websites versus only 1 to 2 percent for most other media. The study found that consumers ignore most ads because the number and intrusiveness of them is too high and their relevance is too low.[17]

Attempts by industry and government to regulate and control deceptive advertising were discussed in Chapter 21. We noted that advertisers should have a reasonable basis for making a claim about product performance and may be required to provide evidence to support their claims. However, deception can occur more subtly as a result of how consumers perceive the ad and its impact on their beliefs.[18] The difficulty of determining just what constitutes deception, along with the fact that advertisers have the right to use puffery and make subjective claims about their products, tends to complicate the issue. But a concern of many critics is the extent to which advertisers are *deliberately* untruthful or misleading.

Sometimes advertisers have made overtly false or misleading claims or failed to award prizes promoted in a contest or sweepstakes. However, these cases usually involve smaller companies and a tiny portion of the hundreds of billions of dollars spent on advertising and promotion each year. Most advertisers do not design their messages with the intention to mislead or deceive consumers or run sweepstakes with no intention of awarding prizes. Not only are such practices unethical, but the culprits would damage their reputation and risk prosecution by regulatory groups or government agencies. National advertisers in particular invest large sums of money to develop loyalty to, and enhance the image of, their brands. These companies are not likely to risk hard-won consumer trust and confidence by intentionally deceiving consumers.

Figure 22-1 Advertising Principles of the American Advertising Federation

1. *Truth.* Advertising shall reveal the truth, and shall reveal significant facts, the omission of which would mislead the public.
2. *Substantiation.* Advertising claims shall be substantiated by evidence in possession of the advertiser and the advertising agency prior to making such claims.
3. *Comparisons.* Advertising shall refrain from making false, misleading, or unsubstantiated statements or claims about a competitor or his products or service.
4. *Bait advertising.* Advertising shall not offer products or services for sale unless such offer constitutes a bona fide effort to sell the advertised products or services and is not a device to switch consumers to other goods or services, usually higher priced.
5. *Guarantees and warranties.* Advertising of guarantees and warranties shall be explicit, with sufficient information to apprise consumers of their principal terms and limitations or, when space or time restrictions preclude such disclosures, the advertisement shall clearly reveal where the full text of the guarantee or warranty can be examined before purchase.
6. *Price claims.* Advertising shall avoid price claims that are false or misleading, or savings claims that do not offer provable savings.
7. *Testimonials.* Advertising containing testimonials shall be limited to those of competent witnesses who are reflecting a real and honest opinion or experience.
8. *Taste and decency.* Advertising shall be free of statements, illustrations, or implications that are offensive to good taste or public decency.

The problem of untruthful or fraudulent advertising and promotion exists more at the local level and in specific areas such as mail order, telemarketing, and other forms of direct marketing. Yet there have been many cases where large companies were accused of misleading consumers with their ads or promotions. Some companies test the limits of industry and government rules and regulations to make claims that will give their brands an advantage in highly competitive markets.

While many critics of advertising would probably agree that most advertisers are not out to deceive consumers deliberately, they are still concerned that consumers may not be receiving enough information to make an informed choice. They say advertisers usually present only information that is favorable to their position and do not always tell consumers the whole truth about a product or service.

Many believe advertising should be primarily informative in nature and should not be permitted to use puffery or embellished messages. Others argue that advertisers have the right to present the most favorable case for their products and services and should not be restricted to just objective, verifiable information.[19] They note that consumers can protect themselves from being persuaded against their will and that the various industry and government regulations suffice to keep advertisers from misleading consumers. Figure 22-1 shows the advertising principles of the American Advertising Federation, which many advertisers use as a guideline in preparing and evaluating their ads.

Advertising as Offensive or in Bad Taste

Another common criticism of advertising, particularly by consumers, is that ads are offensive, tasteless, irritating, boring, obnoxious, and so on. In the study by Shavitt and her colleagues, about half of the respondents reported feeling offended by advertising at least sometimes. A number of other studies have found that consumers feel most advertising insults their intelligence and that many ads are in poor taste.[20]

Sources of Distaste Consumers can be offended or irritated by advertising in a number of ways. Some object when certain products or services such as contraceptives or personal hygiene products are advertised at all. Most media did not accept ads for condoms until the AIDS crisis forced them to reconsider their restrictions. The major TV networks gave their affiliates permission to accept condom advertising in 1987, but the first condom ad did not appear on network TV until 1991, when Fox broadcast a spot.

In 1994, the U.S. Department of Health's Centers for Disease Control and Prevention (CDC) began a new HIV prevention campaign that includes radio and TV commercials urging sexually active people to use latex condoms. The commercials prompted strong protests from conservative and religious groups, which argue that the government should stress abstinence in preventing the spread of AIDS among young people. NBC and ABC agreed to broadcast all the commercials, while CBS said it would air certain spots.[21]

Advertising for condoms has now been appearing on TV for the past 15 years, but only in late-night time slots or on cable networks. However, in 2005, the broadcast networks agreed to accept commercials for condoms during prime time by agreeing to run heath-oriented ads for the Trojan brand.[22] The tone of the Trojan advertising is informational and provides facts and figures designed to raise viewers' consciousness and awareness about the potential consequences of unprotected sex among those who are sexually active (Exhibit 22-4).

1 out of 4 people with HIV
don't tell their partners

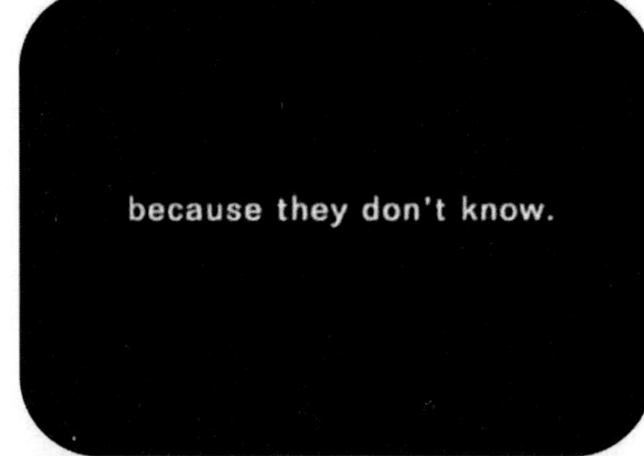

because they don't know.

Use a condom every time.

Exhibit 22-4 Many of the broadcast networks now accept ads for condoms during prime time

A study of prime-time TV commercials found a strong product class effect with respect to the types of ads consumers perceived as distasteful or irritating. The most irritating commercials were for feminine hygiene products; ads for women's undergarments and hemorrhoid products were close behind.[23] Another study found that consumers are more likely to dislike ads for products they do not use and for brands they would not buy.[24] Ads for personal products have become more common on television and in print, and the public is more accepting of them.[25] However, advertisers must still be careful of how these products are presented and the language and terminology used. There are still many rules, regulations, and taboos advertisers must deal with to have their TV commercials approved by the networks.[26]

Another way advertising can offend consumers is by the type of appeal or the manner of presentation. For example, many people object to appeals that exploit consumer anxieties. Fear appeal ads, especially for products such as deodorants, mouthwash, and dandruff shampoos, are criticized for attempting to create anxiety and using a fear of social rejection to sell these products. Some ads for home computers were also criticized for attempting to make parents think that if their young children couldn't use a computer, they would fail in school.

Sexual Appeals

The advertising appeals that have received the most criticism for being in poor taste are those using sexual appeals and/or nudity. These techniques are often used to gain consumers' attention and may not even be appropriate to the product being advertised. Even if the sexual appeal relates to the product, people may be offended by it. Many people object to both nudity in advertising and sexually suggestive ads.

A common criticism of sexual appeals is that they can demean women (or men) by depicting them as sex objects. Ads for cosmetics and lingerie are among the most criticized for their portrayal of women as sex objects. Some ads have even been criticized for being implicitly suggestive. For example, some women's groups criticized the Airwalk ad shown in Exhibit 22-5, arguing that it showed a submissive and sexually available woman. A critic argued that the ad contained a number of symbolic cues that are sexually suggestive and combine to reinforce an image of the woman's sexual submission to the man.[27]

Critics have been particularly concerned about the use of sexual appeals in the advertising of products such as cigarettes, liquor, and beer. Sexual appeals and risqué images have long been used in advertising for alcoholic beverages. In the early 90s an advertising campaign for Old Milwaukee beer featuring the "Swedish Bikini Team," a group of Scandinavian-looking women wearing blue bikinis who appeared out of

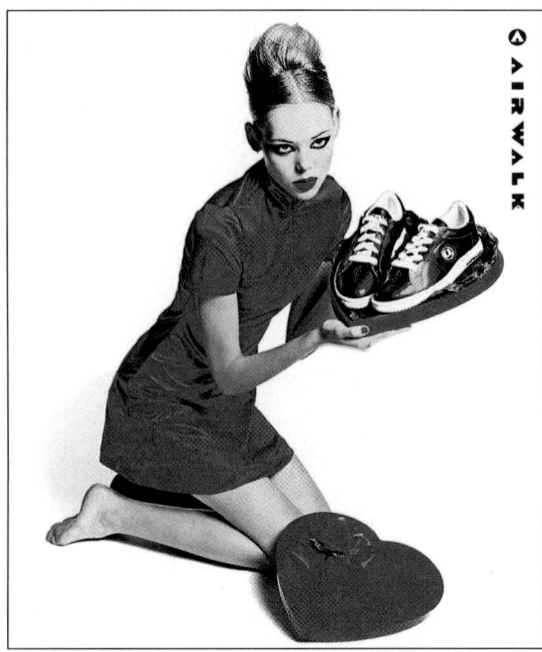

Exhibit 22-5 This Airwalk ad was criticized for being suggestive and symbolizing sexual submission

nowhere in front of groups of beer-drinking men, ignited a major controversy. A number of consumer groups were very critical of the ads, and female employees even sued the Stroh Brewing Co., arguing that the ads contributed to an atmosphere that was conducive to sexual harassment in the workplace.[28]

Recently Skyy Spirits has used provocative, sexually oriented ads to promote its popular namesake vodka brand. Some of its ads, which use stylized images placing the brand's distinctive blue bottle in suggestive situations, have been criticized by some conservative groups (Exhibit 22-6). However, a company spokesperson has responded to the criticisms by noting, "Style is a maker of interpretation and like with all art we appreciate all points of view."[29]

Attitudes toward the use of sex in advertising is a polarizing issue as opinions regarding its use vary depending upon the individual's values and religious orientation, as well as across various demographic groups including age, education, and gender. A recent study found major differences between men and women in their attitudes toward sex in advertising.[30] As you can see in Figure 22-2, while almost half of men said they liked sexual ads, only 8 percent of women felt the same way. Most men (63 percent) indicated that sexual ads have high stopping power and get their attention, but fewer women thought the same (28 percent). Also, most women (58 percent) said there is too much sex in advertising versus only 29 percent of the men. Women were also much more likely than men to say that sexual ads promote a deterioration of moral and social values and that they are demeaning of the models used in them.

Liquor companies are often criticized not only for their advertising but for some of their other promotional methods as well. For example, in 2002 the Boston Beer Co., which markets the popular Samuel Adams Boston Lager brand, was criticized for its involvement with a "Sex for Sam" radio promotion that encouraged people to have sex in various public places to win a trip to the company's brewery. The promotion was run in conjunction with a talk-radio station whose shock jocks provided listeners with detailed reports of couples' sexual activity. The controversy resulted in a boycott of the company's products in some bars in Boston, where the company is headquartered. Although the company denied that it was aware of the exact nature of the radio promotion, the chairman of Boston Beer issued a public apology for his company's participation.[31]

Exhibit 22-6 Ads are often criticized for being sexually suggestive

Shock Advertising

With the increasing clutter in the advertising environment, advertisers continue to use sexual appeals and other techniques that offend many people but catch the attention of consumers and may even generate publicity for their companies. In recent years, there has been an increase in what is often referred to as **shock advertising,** in which marketers use nudity, sexual suggestiveness, or other startling images to get consumers' attention. As discussed earlier in the chapter, shock advertising is nothing new; companies such as Benetton and Calvin Klein have been using this tactic in their ads since the 1980s. However, a number of other marketers have been criticized for using shock techniques in their ads as well as in other promotional materials.[32] For example, clothing retailer Abercrombie & Fitch has been criticized numerous times for the content and images used in its quarterly catalogs, which have included sex tips from porn star Jenna Jameson, a spoof interview with

Figure 22-2 Attitudes toward Sex in Advertising: Men versus Women

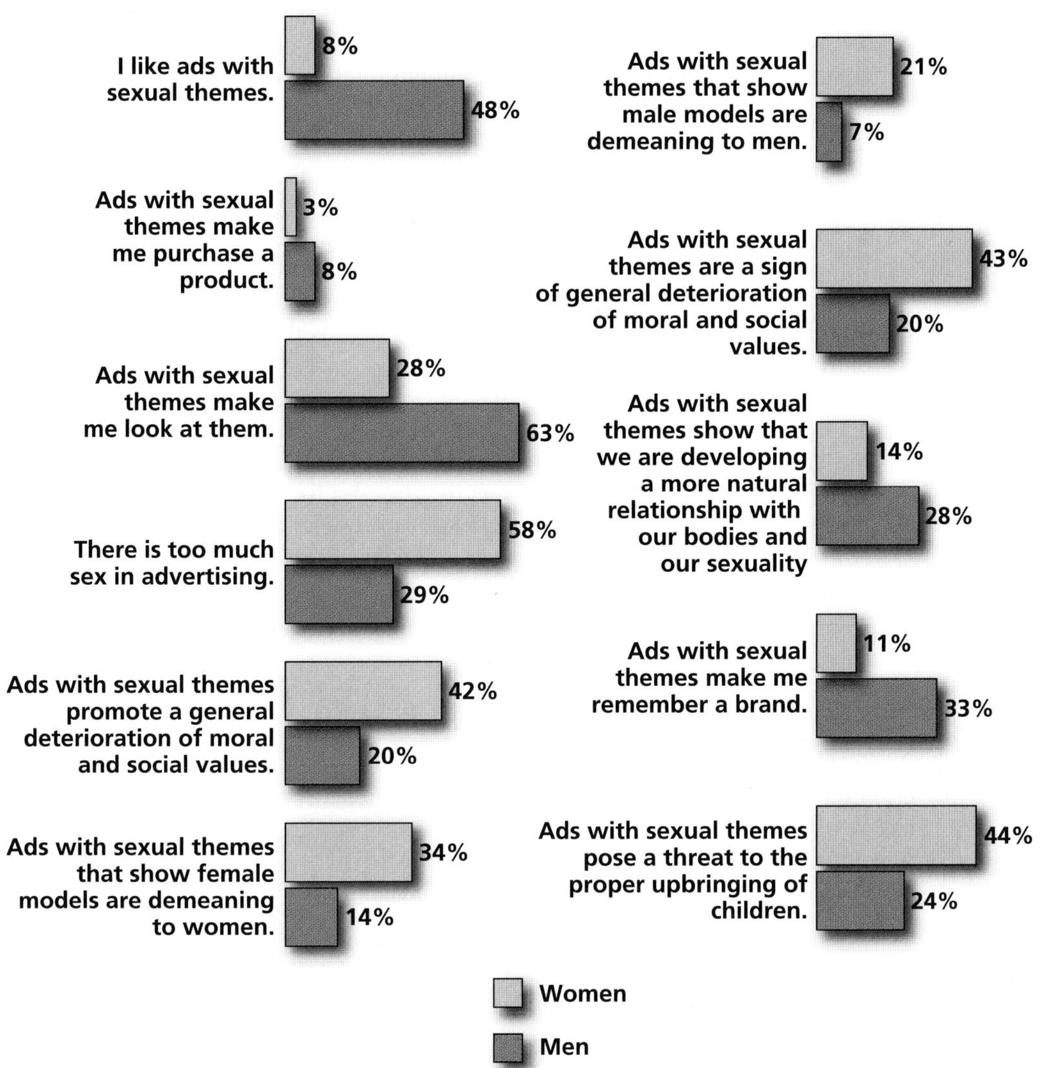

a shopping mall Santa portrayed as a pedophile, and nude photos. A few years ago the retailer promoted its Christmas catalog with an advertisement across the plastic covering stating, "Two-hundred and eighty pages of sex and Xmas fun" (Exhibit 22-7).[33] A few years ago officials in four states threatened or pursued legal action against the company, which responded by implementing a policy of carding would-be buyers of the catalog to ensure they are at least 18 years old. Abercrombie & Fitch has recently changed its business strategy and moved away from the sultry and sexy advertising, a marketing tool used to create a chic and cool image for the brand but often intimidated the teens who shop in its stores. While the Abercrombie & Fitch brand still has a sexy ethos, the company has eliminated the racy catalogs and ads that offended many parents.[34]

Another company known for its whimsical, and sometimes controversial, ads is Bijan. The fragrance marketer's ads attracted a great deal of attention a few years ago when it decided to forgo the tall, thin, glamorous supermodels typically used in fragrance ads and use very large, naked women instead. The company's founder, Beverly Hills fashion maven Bijan, defended the ads by stating that they were his homage to artists such as Rubens, who used full-figured models (Exhibit 22-8).

Exhibit 22-7 Abercrombie & Fitch's catalogs have been criticized over the use of sex and nudity

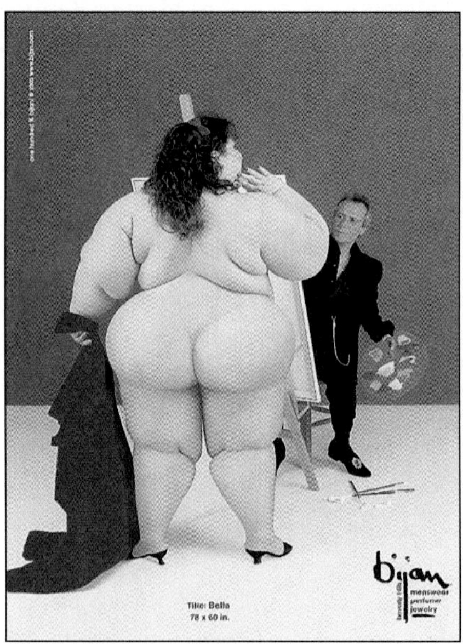

Exhibit 22-8 Bijan often uses whimsical and controversial ads

Many advertising experts argue that what underlies the increase in the use of shock advertising is the pressure on marketers and their agencies to do whatever it takes to get their ads noticed. However, critics argue that the more advertisers use the tactic, the more shocking the ads have to be to get attention. How far advertisers can go with these appeals will probably depend on the public's reaction. When consumers think the advertisers have gone too far, they are likely to pressure the advertisers to change their ads and the media to stop accepting them.

While marketers and ad agencies often acknowledge that their ads push the limits with regard to taste, they also complain about a double standard that exists for advertising versus editorial television program content. The creative director for Abercrombie & Fitch's agency argues that there is a double standard and hypocrisy in the shock advertising debate: "When advertising uses sex, everybody complains—when editorial does it, nobody cares."[35] Advertisers and agency creative directors argue that even the most suggestive commercials are bland compared with the content of many television programs. Ethical Perspective 22-2 discusses the process by which the standards and practices departments of the four major networks review the thousands of commercials they receive each year and try to resolve issues regarding their tastefulness.

Advertising and Children

One of the most controversial topics advertisers must deal with is the issue of advertising to children. TV is a vehicle through which advertisers can reach children easily. Current estimates are that children spend an average of 5 hours a day using media including television, videogames, and Internet websites. They watch nearly 22 hours of TV a week, and the typical child is exposed to more than 40,000 commercials a year.[36] Approximately 80 percent of all advertising targeted to children falls within four product categories: toys, cereals, candy, and fast-food restaurants.[37] Advertisers spend more than $12 billion a year to reach children as they are an important target market, in terms of both their direct purchases and their influence on family purchase decisions. Studies show that television is an important source of information for children about products.[38] Concern has also been expressed about marketers' use of other promotional vehicles and techniques such as radio ads, point-of-purchase displays, premiums in packages, and the use of commercial characters as the basis for TV shows.

Critics argue that children, particularly young ones, are especially vulnerable to advertising because they lack the experience and knowledge to understand and evaluate critically the purpose of persuasive advertising appeals. Research has shown that preschool children cannot differentiate between commercials and programs, do not perceive the selling intent of commercials, and cannot distinguish between reality and fantasy.[39] Research has also shown that children need more than a skeptical attitude toward advertising; they must understand how advertising works in order to use their cognitive defenses against it effectively.[40] Because of children's limited ability to interpret the selling intent of a message or identify a commercial, critics charge that advertising to them is inherently unfair and deceptive and should be banned or severely restricted.

At the other extreme are those who argue that advertising is a part of life and children must learn to deal with it in the **consumer socialization process** of acquiring the skills needed to function in the marketplace.[41] They say existing restrictions are adequate for controlling children's advertising. A study by Tamara Mangleburg and Terry Bristol provided support for the socialization argument. They found that adolescents developed skeptical attitudes toward advertising that were learned through interactions with socialization agents such as parents, peers, and television. They also found that marketplace knowledge plays an important role in adolescents' skepticism toward advertising. Greater knowledge of the marketplace appears to give teens a basis by which to evaluate ads and makes them more likely to recognize the persuasion techniques used by advertisers.[42]

ETHICAL PERSPECTIVE 22-2

Networks and Advertisers Battle over Tasteful Advertising

Before any commercial airs on network television, it is reviewed by the standards and practices departments of the major networks. There are approximately 30 censors working for the four major broadcast networks who dictate to advertising agencies and their clients what they can and cannot show on national television. The censors review ads often as early as in the storyboard stage and comment on about half of the ads they see, most often with questions about accuracy. However, along with ensuring that product claims are accurate, the censors also concern themselves with the tastefulness of the ads they review. Ads containing sex, violence, adult language, morbid humor, unsafe or antisocial behavior, and controversial political reviews receive very careful scrutiny.

The network clearance departments argue that advertisers and agencies welcome their feedback and that the system is not an adversarial one. However, frustrated marketers and ad agencies often argue that the clearance process is arbitrary and unfair, with an abundance of double standards and unwritten rules. For example, Rich Silverstein, co-chairman of Goodby Silverstein & Partners in San Francisco, notes,"The networks don't play fair about blood, guts and sex. Judgments about the ads depend on who is judging that day. And their standards are a moving target." His agency has been involved in squabbles with the networks over commercials for clients such as E*Trade and the California Milk Advisory Board. The agency has pushed the envelope with censors several times with humorous ads created for the long-running "Got milk?" campaign. For example, one of the spots in the campaign showed a frustrated priest kicking a vending machine when it failed to dispense a carton of milk. Censors cried foul—not because it portrayed the priest in an unflattering light but because it is a misdemeanor to vandalize a vending machine and ads cannot depict criminal actions.

Another issue that is often raised with the networks is whether they have a double standard, holding commercials to a higher standard than they do their own programs. For example, during the 2005 Super Bowl, the Fox Network ran a commercial for GoDaddy.com, a company that manages and sells Internet domain names, during the first quarter of the game but refused to run it again during the fourth quarter after the National Football League became upset over the ad. The spot was set in a mock congressional hearing and featured a woman dressed in a very skimpy camisole that suffered a near "wardrobe malfunction." The commercial was intended as a satirical jab at the famous Janet Jackson "wardrobe malfunction" that occurred during the halftime show of the 2004 Super Bowl and the government's ensuing moves to more tightly regulate TV and radio content. The managing partner of the Ad Store, the agency that created the spot, questioned the network's double standard. He noted that the Fox Network broadcasts and promotes Paris Hilton's and Nicole Richie's overexposed body parts in the reality show *The Simple Life,* and its programming also includes a number of other racy shows.

Those who work in the standards and practices departments for the networks do not agree with their critics, arguing that they give agencies ample leeway to communicate their advertising messages. A CBS clearance editor states, "We do not act as censors. We work in a constructive way with advertisers to make sure that we, as carriers of the public trust, present things in the best possible light to viewers." Roland McFarland, who runs the standards and practices department at Fox, argues that his department tries to assist both agencies and television viewers: "We help agencies tailor and craft their ads for the broad-spectrum audience. We are part of the creative process. We know what plays with our audience and what will have more impact."

Advertisers also become frustrated by the lack of consistency in the decisions across the major networks, as commercials accepted by reviewers at one network are not always accepted by other networks. For example, while Fox is known for its irreverent programming, the network has a reputation as "family friendly" and is considered more cautious and conservative than the Big Three. However, the networks argue that inconsistency among standards and practices departments is uncommon and that if one network has problems with a commercial, the others usually will as well.

Advertisers that feel they have been treated unfairly by a network can appeal the decision to the network's sales department, which has the authority to overrule the censors. However, because clearance editors tend to stay in their jobs for years and have long memories, agencies and clients are leery of this option. Thus, they prefer to negotiate with the clearance editors and often will make changes and modifications in their ads to satisfy the editors' concerns. In some cases, the networks are persuaded to allow an ad to run to gauge the public's reactions. Ads often run subject to viewer complaint—if the network receives negative reactions from viewers, the ad is pulled.

In some cases advertisers give up trying to please the networks and instead seek approval from the network affiliates, which have their own standards and practices departments and usually are easier to please than the network censors. Advertisers also will take their ads to independent broadcasters as well as cable stations, which may be even less stringent in their reviews. The advertising recession that has plagued the industry in recent years has resulted in a decline in demand for TV commercial time, particularly on syndicated programs and cable. Thus it is often easier to get ads accepted on their programs than by the major networks.

The clearance editors at the networks review 50 to 150 commercials a day, sometimes examining revisions of a spot three and four times. While they acknowledge that the process is subjective, they argue that they do their best to serve the sometimes competing interests of advertisers, the viewing audience, and the network affiliates. They argue that they have to please a large number of viewers with very different values and opinions as to what is tasteful and responsible advertising. While they do not feel they are censors, they do think of themselves as protectors of social values.

Sources: Joan Voight and Wendy Melillo, "Rough Cut," *Adweek,* March 11, 2002, pp. 27–29; Joan Voight and Wendy Melillo, "To See or Not to See?" *Adweek,* March 11, 2002, p. 30; Tim Arnold, "Inside GoDaddy.com's Super Bowl Fight with Fox," adweek.com, February 21, 2005.

This issue received a great deal of attention in 1979 when the Federal Trade Commission held hearings on proposed changes in regulations regarding advertising to children. An FTC staff report recommended banning all TV advertising for any product directed to or seen by audiences composed largely of children under age eight because they are too young to understand the selling intent of advertising.[43]

The FTC proposal was debated intensely. The advertising industry and a number of companies argued strongly against it, based on factors including advertisers' right of free speech under the First Amendment to communicate with those consumers who make up their primary target audience.[44] They also said parents should be involved in helping children interpret advertising and can refuse to purchase products they believe are undesirable for their children.

The FTC proposal was defeated, and changes in the political environment resulted in less emphasis on government regulation of advertising. But parent and consumer groups like the Center for Science in the Public Interest are still putting pressure on advertisers regarding what they see as inappropriate or misleading ads for children. One activist group, Action for Children's Television (ACT), was disbanded in 1992, but first it was instrumental in getting Congress to approve the Children's Television Act in October 1990. The act limits the amount of commercial time in children's programming to 10.5 minutes per hour on weekends and 12 minutes on weekdays.[45]

In 1996, broadcasters, children's advocates, and the federal government reached an agreement requiring TV stations to air three hours of children's educational shows a week.[46] Many believe advertisers will play a major role in implementing the new initiative by providing financial backing for the educational shows—which have long had trouble luring sponsors.[47]

Children are also protected from the potential influences of commercials by network censors and industry self-regulatory groups such as the Council of Better Business Bureaus' Children's Advertising Review Unit (CARU). CARU has strict self-regulatory guidelines regarding the type of appeals, product presentation and claims, disclosures and disclaimers, the use of premiums, safety, and techniques such as special effects and animation. The CARU guidelines for advertising addressed to children under 12 are presented in Figure 22-3.

As we saw in Chapter 21, the major networks also have strict guidelines for ads targeted to children. For example, in network TV ads, only 10 seconds can be devoted to animation and special effects; the final 5 seconds are reserved for displaying all the toys shown in the ad and disclosing whether they are sold separately and whether accessories such as batteries are included. Networks also require 3 seconds of every 30-second cereal ad to portray a balanced breakfast, usually by showing a picture of toast, orange juice, and milk.[48]

Concerns over advertising and other forms of promotion directed at children diminished somewhat during the late '90s and the early part of the new decade. However, the issue has once again begun receiving a considerable amount of attention as various groups are calling for restrictions on advertising targeted to children. In 2004, the American Psychological Association (APA), the nation's largest organization of psychologists, issued a report criticizing the increasing commercialization of childhood and calling for new curbs on marketing aimed at children.[49] The APA report faulted marketers for taking advantage of an ever-fragmenting media landscape of cable channels and websites to target children. The report noted that marketing activities focused on America's youth has reached unprecedented levels and called for restrictions on advertising in TV programming that appeals primarily to children under the age of eight and a total ban on advertising in programs aimed at very young children in this group. The report also found that the Internet is a particularly effective, and thus potentially harmful, means of sending advertising messages to children as websites blur, if not ignores the boundaries between commercial and noncommercial content. Marketing and advertising trade groups have been critical of the report and continue to defend their right to advertise on the basis that parents of younger children, rather than the children themselves, make purchase decisions.[50]

In addition to concerns over the increasing amount of advertising targeted to children, there are a number of other issues that consumer groups and regulatory agencies

Seven basic principles underlie these guidelines for advertising directed to children:

1. Advertisers should always take into account the level of knowledge, sophistication, and maturity of the audience to which their message is primarily directed. Younger children have a limited capability for evaluating the credibility of information they receive. They also may lack the ability to understand the nature of the personal information they disclose on the Internet. Advertisers, therefore, have a special responsibility to protect children from their own susceptibilities.
2. Realizing that children are imaginative and that make-believe play constitutes an important part of the growing-up process, advertisers should exercise care not to exploit unfairly the imaginative quality of children. Unreasonable expectations of product quality or performance should not be stimulated either directly or indirectly by advertising.
3. Products and content inappropriate for children should not be advertised or promoted directly to children.
4. Recognizing that advertising may play an important part in educating the child, advertisers should communicate information in a truthful and accurate manner and in language understandable to young children with full recognition that the child may learn practices from advertising which can affect his or her health and well-being.
5. Advertisers are urged to capitalize on the potential of advertising to influence behavior by developing advertising that, wherever possible, addresses itself to positive and beneficial social behavior, such as friendship, kindness, honesty, justice, generosity, and respect for others.
6. Care should be taken to incorporate minority and other groups in advertisements in order to present positive and pro-social roles and role models wherever possible. Social stereotyping and appeals to prejudice should be avoided.
7. Although many influences affect a child's personal and social development, it remains the prime responsibility of the parents to provide guidance for children. Advertisers should contribute to this parent–child relationship in a constructive manner.

These Principles embody the philosophy upon which CARU's mandate is based. The Principles, and not the Guidelines themselves, determine the scope of our review. The Guidelines effectively anticipate and address many of the areas requiring scrutiny in child-directed advertising, but they are illustrative rather than limiting. Where no specific Guideline addresses the issues of concern to CARU, it is these broader Principles that CARU applies in evaluating advertising directed to the uniquely impressionable and vulnerable child audience.

Figure 22-3 Children's Advertising Review Unit Principles

have raised with respect to young people, These include an increase in the number of ads encouraging children to call 900 numbers, the increase in the number of toy-based programs on TV, and general concerns over the content of children's programming, particularly with regard to violence.

The marketing of violent entertainment to minors and the advertising practices and rating systems of the film, music, and electronic game industries are also being monitored very carefully. The issue of what young consumers are watching, listening to, and playing and how much violence that entertainment contains became an area of great concern following the shootings at Columbine High School as well as several other schools. In 2001 legislation was proposed that would have given the FTC authority to take action against companies that violated their own industry's voluntary policies governing the marketing of violent products to minors. However, the bill was suspended following FTC reports that the companies had made improvements.[51]

As discussed in the previous chapter, there is also growing concern over how marketers are using the Internet to communicate with and sell to children. Another issue that has received a great deal of attention recently is the role of advertising and other marketing practices in contributing to the obesity problem among children as well as adults. Ethical Perspective 22-3 discusses this controversy and the attacks being made against the food industry.

ETHICAL PERSPECTIVE 22-3

Food Marketers Come Under Attack

Obesity is, by far, the leading health problem in the United States. A report in the *Journal of the American Medical Association* found that 31 percent of Americans are obese, up from 23 percent a decade ago, and nearly two-thirds are overweight. America's battle with the bulge also begins at a very young age as 13 percent of children age 6 to 11 and 14 percent of kids 14 to 19 are overweight, triple the number 20 years ago. Much more than vanity is at stake here as obesity increases the risks of heart disease, cancer, diabetes, and high blood pressure among other ailments. It also accounts for nearly 300,000 deaths a year, ranking second only to cancer.

Health experts point to a number of factors that are responsible for the alarming rise in obesity including an environment that encourages overeating, the eating of unhealthy foods, and a lack of physical activity. Another factor that is increasingly being cited as a major reason for the obesity epidemic is the marketing and advertising practices of the food industry. High-calorie, artery-clogging foods are cheap and plentiful, and serving sizes have ballooned in recent years. Fast-food restaurants have been promoting their value menus and offering "super sizes" of menu items such as hamburgers, french fries, and soda. Convenience stores including 7-Eleven and AM-PM offer 32-ounce sizes of Big Gulps and Slurpees as well as sodas and other beverages that are high in sugar. Also coming under attack are the high levels of advertising and promotion used to promote food products.

The food industry spends an estimated $42 billion a year on advertising and promotion with $20 billion spent for media advertising and $22 billion on consumer and trade promotions. While the experts acknowledge that the food industry's advertising and promotion are not solely to blame for the fattening of Americans, they argue that the ads do encourage people to eat more than they should. Consumer and health groups are particularly concerned about the rising obesity problem in children and argue that it is directly related to the amount of advertising they are exposed to every day. According to a report by the Kaiser Family Foundation, children spend 5.5 hours using media each day and are exposed to 40,000 ads a year on television alone. Much of this advertising promotes foods that are high in calories and sugar such as candy, soda, and snack products.

Another area of concern is that fast-food products are becoming more prevalent in the nation's schools. Many school districts have awarded contracts to fast-food franchisees who sell more products and make more money for the schools because the price markup on fast foods is higher than on federally subsidized school meals. A large number of school districts also make money by selling "pouring rights" to soft drink companies such as Coca-Cola or PepsiCo. These contracts give the companies exclusive rights to sell their products in school cafeterias or in vending machines, and the school districts make more money if the students drink more.

Food companies are recognizing that they are under attack and are taking steps to address the concerns by developing more healthy products and by changing their advertising and promotion practices. In early 2005, Kraft Foods pledged to stop advertising popular snack-food items including Kool-Aid, Chips Ahoy!, and Oreo cookies, and its fat-laden Oscar Mayer Lunchables to children under 12. A year earlier, Kraft stopped in-school marketing and began its Health & Wellness Advisory Council to revamp its marketing guidelines. Coca-Cola has also recently updated its guidelines to eliminate advertising and sampling to kids under 12, and its promotions and ads do not show kids under 12 consuming Coke products unless they are with an adult. In August 2005, Coca-Cola, PepsiCo, and other beverage marketers announced a set of voluntary restrictions to limit sales of their drinks in schools.

While a number of food marketers have been taking steps to appease consumers and advocacy groups, many believe that the industry has not gone far enough. In early 2005, the Center for Science in the Public Interest (CSPI) released a set of far-reaching food marketing guidelines, which specify acceptable nutritional content, portion size, packing design, and logo use. The guidelines also seek to control advertising and other forms of marketing communication in TV shows, videogames, websites, and books as well as the use of premiums, in-store displays, and other sale promotion tools.

The food industry, as well as the advertising and marketing community, are concerned by the attacks by the CSPI and other consumer advocacy groups on the food industry. Industry executives do not think they should take the blame for the fattening of America and point to the need for more personal and parental responsibility, nutritional education, dietary balance and moderation, and physical activity. They are also concerned that the ultimate goal of government regulators and consumer health advocates is putting an end to the marketing and even sale of unhealthy foods. Some have been critical of Kraft's decision to stop advertising various snack products as a tacit acknowledgment of guilt in fueling the obesity problem and one that implicates them as well. A number of major food marketers including General Mills, Kellogg Co., and Kraft along with the trade group Grocery Manufacturers of America and various advertising industry trade associations have formed the Alliance for American Advertising to formally take on the critics and defend food marketers. It appears that the food fight is just beginning.

Sources: Betsy McKay, "Soda Marketers Will Cut Back Sales to Schools," *The Wall Street Journal,* August 17, 2005, pp. B1, 3; Bob Liodice, "Beware of the Food Nanny," *Advertising Age,* January 24, 2005, p. 26; Stephanie Thompson, "Food Fight Breaks Out," *Advertising Age,* January 17, 2005, pp. 1, 25; Betsy Spethmann, "Tipping the Scale," *Promo,* February 25, 2004, pp. 24–29.

Advertising to children will remain a controversial topic. Some groups feel that the government is responsible for protecting children from the potentially harmful effects of advertising and other forms of promotion, while others argue that parents are ultimately responsible for doing so. Various consumer groups have also urged the media, particularly television broadcasters, as well as marketers to assume responsibility for the programs and advertising and promotional messages they offer to children.[52] A study comparing the attitudes of business executives and consumers regarding children's advertising found that marketers of products targeted to children believe advertising to them provides useful information on new products and does not disrupt the parent–child relationship. However, the general public did not have such a favorable opinion. Older consumers and those from households with children had particularly negative attitudes toward children's advertising.[53] A survey of 12,500 young people up to 18 years of age was conducted for *Advertising Age* regarding their attitudes toward advertising and various media. The study found that two-thirds of those surveyed believed the main goal of advertising is to make them buy things while only 11 percent felt that its objective is to provide information.[54]

It is important to many companies to communicate directly with children. However, only by being sensitive to the naiveté of children as consumers will they be able to do so freely and avoid potential conflict with those who believe children should be protected from advertising and other forms of promotion.

Social and Cultural Consequences

Concern is often expressed over the impact of advertising on society, particularly on values and lifestyles. While a number of factors influence the cultural values, lifestyles, and behavior of a society, the overwhelming amount of advertising and its prevalence in the mass media lead many critics to argue that advertising plays a major role in influencing and transmitting social values. In his book *Advertising and Social Change,* Ronald Berman says:

> The institutions of family, religion, and education have grown noticeably weaker over each of the past three generations. The world itself seems to have grown more complex. In the absence of traditional authority, advertising has become a kind of social guide. It depicts us in all the myriad situations possible to a life of free choice. It provides ideas about style, morality, behavior.[55]

Mike Hughes, president and creative director of the Martin Agency, notes that advertising has a major impact on society: "Ads help establish what is cool in society; their messages contribute to the public dialogue. Gap ads show white, black and Hispanic kids dancing together. Hilfiger ads showed it's cool for people to get along. Ikea showed a gay couple." He argues that advertising agencies have a social and ethical responsibility to consider the impact of the advertising messages they create for their clients.[56]

While there is general agreement that advertising is an important social influence agent, opinions as to the value of its contribution are often negative. Advertising is criticized for encouraging materialism, manipulating consumers to buy things they do not really need, perpetuating stereotypes, and controlling the media.

Advertising Encourages Materialism

Many critics claim advertising has an adverse effect on consumer values by encouraging **materialism,** a preoccupation with material things rather than intellectual or spiritual concerns. The United States is undoubtedly the most materialistic society in the world, which many critics attribute to advertising that

- Seeks to create needs rather than merely showing how a product or service fulfills them.
- Surrounds consumers with images of the good life and suggests the acquisition of material possessions leads to contentment and happiness and adds to the joy of living.
- Suggests material possessions are symbols of status, success, and accomplishment and/or will lead to greater social acceptance, popularity, sex appeal, and so on.

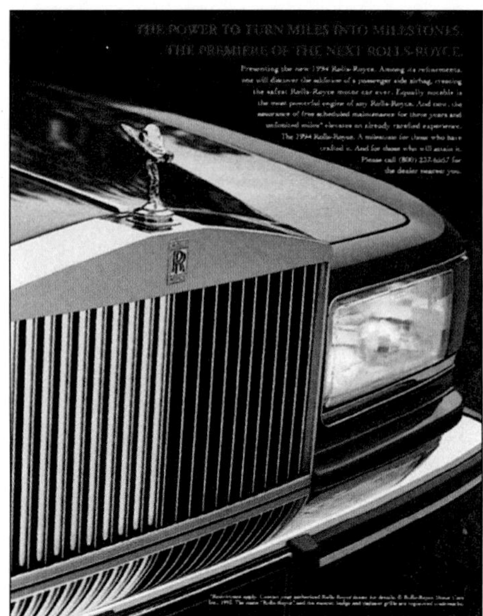

Exhibit 22-9 Rolls-Royce appeals to consumers' materialism

Critics argue that advertising for expensive products such as automobiles is an example of how advertising can promote materialistic values (Exhibit 22-9).

This criticism of advertising assumes that materialism is undesirable and is sought at the expense of other goals. But many believe materialism is an acceptable part of the **Protestant ethic,** which stresses hard work and individual effort and initiative and views the accumulation of material possessions as evidence of success. Others argue that the acquisition of material possessions has positive economic impact by encouraging consumers to keep consuming after their basic needs are met. Many Americans believe economic growth is essential and materialism is both a necessity and an inevitable part of this progress.

Economist John Kenneth Galbraith, often a vocal critic of advertising, describes the role advertising plays in industrialized economies by encouraging consumption:

> Advertising and its related arts thus help develop the kind of man the goals of the industrial system require—one that reliably spends his income and works reliably because he is always in need of more. In the absence of the massive and artful persuasion that accompanies the management of demand, increasing abundance might well have reduced the interest of people in acquiring more goods. Being not pressed by the need for these things, they would have spent less reliably to get more. The consequence—a lower and less reliable propensity to consume—would have been awkward for the industrial system.[57]

It has also been argued that an emphasis on material possessions does not rule out interest in intellectual, spiritual, or cultural values. Defenders of advertising say consumers can be more interested in higher-order goals when basic needs have been met. Raymond Bauer and Stephen Greyser point out that consumers may purchase material things in the pursuit of nonmaterial goals.[58] For example, a person may buy an expensive stereo system to enjoy music rather than simply to impress someone or acquire a material possession.

Even if we assume materialism is undesirable, there is still the question of whether advertising is responsible for creating and encouraging it. While many critics argue that advertising is a major contributing force to materialistic values, others say advertising merely reflects the values of society rather than shaping them.[59] They argue that consumers' values are defined by the society in which they live and are the results of extensive, long-term socialization or acculturation.

Exhibit 22-10 The advertising industry argues that advertising reflects society

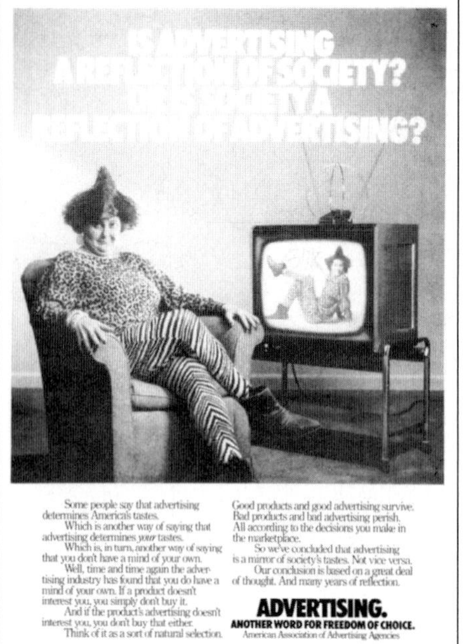

The argument that advertising is responsible for creating a materialistic and hedonistic society is addressed by Stephen Fox in his book *The Mirror Makers: A History of American Advertising and Its Creators.* Fox concludes advertising has become a prime scapegoat for our times and merely reflects society. Regarding the effect of advertising on cultural values, he says:

> To blame advertising now for those most basic tendencies in American history is to miss the point. It is too obvious, too easy, a matter of killing the messenger instead of dealing with the bad news. The people who have created modern advertising are not hidden persuaders pushing our buttons in the service of some malevolent purpose. They are just producing an especially visible manifestation, good and bad, of the American way of life.[60]

The ad shown in Exhibit 22-10 was developed by the American Association of Advertising Agencies and suggests that advertising is a reflection of society's tastes and values, not vice versa. The ad was part of a campaign that addressed criticisms of advertising.

Advertising does contribute to our materialism by portraying products and services as symbols of status, success, and achievement and by encouraging consumption. As Richard Pollay says, "While it may be true that advertising reflects cultural values, it does so on a very selective basis, echoing and reinforcing certain attitudes, behaviors, and values far more frequently than others."[61]

Individuals from a variety of backgrounds are concerned over the values they see driving our society. They believe that materialism, greed, and selfishness increasingly dominate American life and that advertising is a major reason for these undesirable values. The extent to which advertising is responsible for materialism and the desirability of such values are deep philosophical issues that will continue to be part of the debate over the societal value and consequences of advertising.

Advertising Makes People Buy Things They Don't Need

A common criticism of advertising is that it manipulates consumers into buying things they do not need. Many critics say advertising should just provide information useful in making purchase decisions and should not persuade. They view information advertising (which reports price, performance, and other objective criteria) as desirable but persuasive advertising (which plays on consumers' emotions, anxieties, and psychological needs and desires such as status, self-esteem, and attractiveness) as unacceptable. Persuasive advertising is criticized for fostering discontent among consumers and encouraging them to purchase products and services to solve deeper problems. Critics say advertising exploits consumers and persuades them to buy things they don't need.

Defenders of advertising offer a number of rebuttals to these criticisms. First, they point out that a substantial amount of advertising is essentially informational in nature.[62] Also, it is difficult to separate desirable informational advertising from undesirable persuasive advertising. Shelby Hunt, in examining the *information-persuasion dichotomy,* points out that even advertising that most observers would categorize as very informative is often very persuasive.[63] He says, "If advertising critics really believe that persuasive advertising should not be permitted, they are actually proposing that no advertising be allowed, since the purpose of all advertising is to persuade."[64]

Defenders of advertising also take issue with the argument that it should be limited to dealing with basic functional needs. In our society, most lower-level needs recognized in Maslow's hierarchy, such as the need for food, clothing, and shelter, are satisfied for most people. It is natural to move from basic needs to higher-order ones such as self-esteem and status or self-actualization. Consumers are free to choose the degree to which they attempt to satisfy their desires, and wise advertisers associate their products and services with the satisfaction of higher-order needs.

Proponents of advertising offer two other defenses against the charge that advertising makes people buy things they do not really need. First, this criticism attributes too much power to advertising and assumes consumers have no ability to defend themselves against it. Second, it ignores the fact that consumers have the freedom to make their own choices when confronted with persuasive advertising. While they readily admit the persuasive intent of their business, advertisers are quick to note it is extremely difficult to make consumers purchase a product they do not want or for which they do not see a personal benefit. If advertising were as powerful as the critics claim, we would not see products with multi-million-dollar advertising budgets failing in the marketplace. The reality is that consumers do have a choice and they are not being forced to buy. Consumers ignore ads for products and services they do not really need or that fail to interest them (see Exhibit 22-11).

Exhibit 22-11 The AAAA responds to the claim that advertising makes consumers buy things they do not need

DESPITE WHAT SOME PEOPLE THINK, ADVERTISING CAN'T MAKE YOU BUY SOMETHING YOU DON'T NEED.
Some people would have you believe that you are putty in the hands of every advertiser in the country.
They think that when advertising is put under your nose, your mind turns to oatmeal.
It's mass hypnosis. Subliminal seduction. Brain washing. Mind control. It's advertising.
And you are a pushover for it.
It explains why your kitchen cupboard is full of food you never eat.
Why your garage is full of cars you never drive.
Why your house is full of books you don't read, TV's you don't watch, beds you don't use, and clothes you don't wear.
You don't have a choice. You are forced to buy.
That's why this message is a cleverly disguised advertisement to get you to buy land in the tropics.
Got you again, didn't we? Send in your money.
ADVERTISING
ANOTHER WORD FOR FREEDOM OF CHOICE.
American Association of Advertising Agencies

Advertising and Stereotyping

Advertising is often accused of creating and perpetuating stereotypes through its portrayal of women, ethnic minorities, and other groups.

Women The portrayal of women in advertising is an issue that has received a great deal of attention through the years.[65] Advertising has received much criticism for stereotyping women and failing to recognize the changing role of women in our society. Critics have argued that advertising often depicts women as preoccupied with beauty, household duties, and motherhood or shows them as decorative objects or sexually provocative figures. The various research studies conducted through the years show a consistent picture of gender stereotyping that has varied little over time. Portrayals of adult women in American television and print advertising have emphasized passivity, deference, lack of intelligence and credibility, and punishment for high levels of efforts. In contrast, men have been portrayed as constructive, powerful, autonomous, and achieving.[66]

Research on gender stereotyping in advertising targeted to children has found a pattern of results similar to that reported for adults. A recent study found sex-role stereotyping in television advertising targeted at children in the United States as well as in Australia.[67] Boys are generally shown as being more knowledgeable, active, aggressive, and instrumental than girls. Nonverbal behaviors involving dominance and control are associated more with boys than girls. Advertising directed toward children has also been shown to feature more boys than girls, to position boys in more dominant, active roles, and to use male voiceovers more frequently than female ones.[68] A recent study examining race and gender stereotyping of children's advertising on the Turner Cartoon Network found that the primary target for most of the commercials was active, white boys. Girls were portrayed in traditional roles and shown performing limited passive, indoor activities, while boys were shown in the outdoor world engaging in more exciting and active things.[69]

Feminist groups such as the National Organization for Women (NOW) and the Sexual Assault Prevention and Awareness Center argue that advertising that portrays women as sex objects contributes to violence against women. These groups often protest to advertisers and their agencies about ads they find insulting to women and have even called for boycotts against offending advertisers. NOW has also been critical of advertisers for the way they portray women in advertising for clothing, cosmetics, and other products. The organization feels that many of these ads contribute to the epidemic of eating disorders and smoking among women and girls who hope such means will help them control their weight.[70]

Exhibit 22-12 Many advertisers now portray women in powerful roles

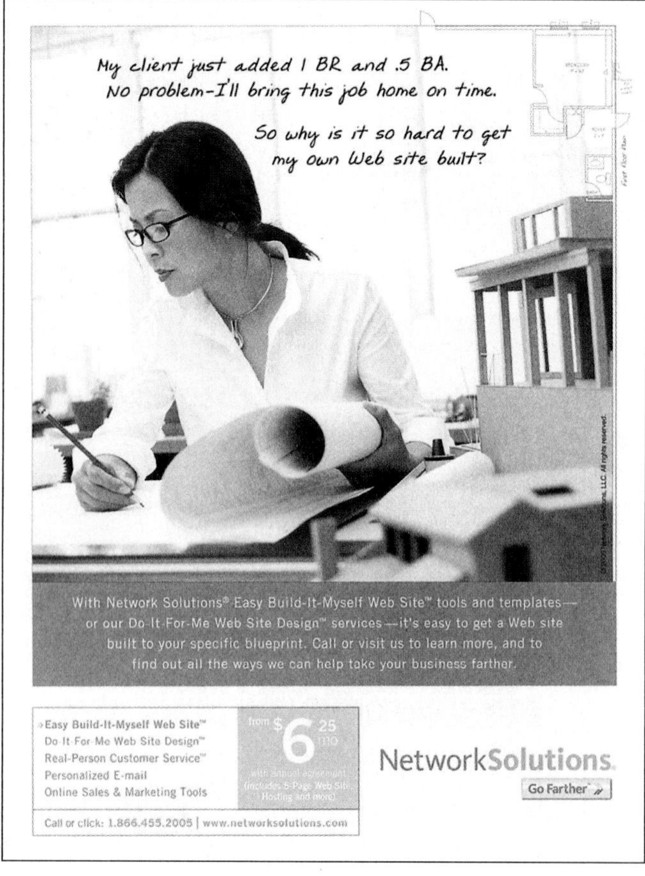

While sexism and stereotyping still exist, advertising's portrayal of women is improving in many areas. Many advertisers have begun to recognize the importance of portraying women realistically. The increase in the number of working women has resulted not only in women having more influence in family decision making but also in more single-female households, which mean more independent purchasers.

Researchers Steven Kates and Glenda Shaw-Garlock argue that the transformed social positioning of women in North American society is perhaps the most important social development of this century.[71] They note that as women have crossed the boundary from the domestic sphere to the professional arena, expectations and representations of women have changed as well. For example, a number of magazines, such as *MS* and *Working Woman,* now incorporate and appeal to the sociocultural shifts in women's lives. Many advertisers are now depicting women in a diversity of roles that reflect their changing place in society. In many ads, the stereotypic character traits attributed to women have shifted from weak and dependent to strong and autonomous. The ad for Network Solutions shown in Exhibit 22-12 is an example of how advertisers are changing the way they portray women in their ads. One reason for the changes in the way women are portrayed in advertising is the

CAREER PROFILE

Patti A. Wakeling

Senior Marketing Manager, Dove Masterbrand

My career path into marketing was not nearly as direct as that of most of my colleagues. My original goal was to be involved in the medical field and to help provide the necessary information healthcare professionals require to care for their patients. That led me in the direction of becoming a medical/clinical information specialist. I graduated from Western Michigan University with a degree in pre-medical science and then went on to get a Masters of Science in Library Science from Case Western Reserve University specializing in the medical field. An important element in my career decisions was to make sure that I explored jobs at the top institutions in the field. That led me to Texas, where I spent the first seven years of my career as a clinical information services librarian at the Texas Medical Center Library and UTHSC Brisco Library. My first industry job was with Boehringer Ingelheim Pharmaceuticals, where I worked as medical market research/corporate information specialist.

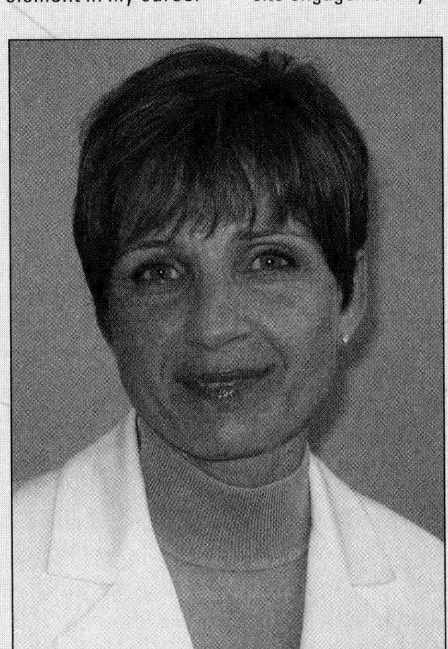

After spending eight years working in healthcare-related institutions, I felt it was necessary to expand my background. I moved to the consumer packaged goods industry, taking a position with Richardson-Vicks division of Procter & Gamble, where I was a market information specialist with responsibility for supporting the company's business scientific and technical research. My tenure at Richardson-Vicks was invigorating, but short, as Procter & Gamble made a decision to move Richardson-Vicks to Cincinnati, Ohio. This taught me another important career lesson, make sure you network with other corporations in your area and apply for positions that you are passionate about.

My next position was as a senior business information specialist at the Pepsi-Cola Company. I was responsible for managing and marketing the operations, services, and personnel of PepsiCo's business information center to support the company's worldwide competitive, marketing, and business information needs. I initiated the development of a competitive intelligence program for strategic planning as well as a knowledge management market research database. Another career lesson that I learned was be aware of what's required to reach your goals. After seven years at Pepsi-Cola I realized that to make my next career move would require a Masters in Business Administration, which I earned by going to graduate school full-time in the evening.

> "Working on [Dove's] Campaign for Real Beauty has been an incredible experience . . ."

I took a new position with Computer Sciences Corporation as a senior business researcher and market analyst, which exposed me to different types of industries and projects. I had the opportunity to co-develop an integrated, technology enabled customer relationship management (CRM) system for CSC, which provided the company with the tools and technology to acquire, retain, and grow relationships with high-profit customers.

I left CSC in 2000 to join Unilever as a senior relationship marketing insight manager. At Unilever, I had a boss who was willing to take a chance on me because I had drive and passion. My first position was in a "think-tank" group that allowed exploration of futuristic ideas. I was responsible for all market research and consumer targeting for a new innovative $10 million corporate relationship marketing program. This program defined, targeted, and tracked our most valuable consumers and provided strategic recommendations to optimize the program based on consumer research.

My next promotion was to senior relationship marketing manager for Unilever's Dove brand, where I was responsible for managing the $19 million Dove relationship marketing program and turning it into a profitable program in just one year. We focused on understanding the consumer and leveraging best practices that had been developed in other relationship marketing programs. The RM program participants doubled their incremental revenue per household for Dove products and improved their website engagement by 400 percent. This was accomplished by designing and implementing a new relationship marketing strategy for the brand.

I am currently in the most-rewarding position I've ever held, senior marketing manager for the Dove Masterbrand in the United States, overseeing the strategy, planning, and execution of the Dove Campaign for Real Beauty. I manage all direct, interactive, consumer promotion, relationship marketing, public relations, media, and channel planning for Dove Masterbrand. Working on the Campaign for Real Beauty has been an incredible experience as the campaign has helped change society's definition of beauty and has had a significant impact on women and girls of all ages. I believe in the Campaign's philosophy and mission and live them every day. It also provides me the opportunity to give back to women and the next generation, which is very important to me.

The Campaign was launched in 2004, following a major global study that found today's narrow definition of beauty is having a profound affect on the self-esteem of women and young girls. The Dove mission is to challenge beauty stereotypes and invite women to join in a discussion about beauty. We are now moving into the third phase of the Campaign, in which we hope to educate young girls and raise their self-esteem to make them feel more beautiful and confident every day so they reach their full potential. It is our goal to truly make a difference in the lives of more than a million young people globally by the end of 2008, and I am very proud to be a part of such an impactful program. Listening to women and young girls express support for the Campaign and for what Dove is doing makes my job very rewarding.

My career path has been an interesting journey driven by my desire to help others and to make a difference. Each position has taught me something different and added to my knowledge of business marketing and marketing research. My advice to students would be to be passionate about your job. If you're not, it is difficult to develop new and exciting ideas and to make a difference. Find a mentor in your company. My supervisor at Unilever has been an amazing mentor and has pushed me to think differently. Be flexible. You will need to adapt your skills to changes in the marketplace and within your own company. All companies undergo restructuring and you may end up changing jobs many times. Volunteer for special projects, even if it means extra work. This will give you exposure to new, influential people, who may be able to open doors for you. Develop a passion for being challenged and making a difference. This will provide you the most rewarding experiences in your career. Become proficient in influencing people, flexing your communication style, and identifying influencers in your organization that you can tap into for support. Finally, believe in yourself and what you want to achieve.

emergence of females in key agency roles. Women advertising executives are likely to be more sensitive to the portrayal of their own gender and to strengthen the role of women beyond stereotypical housewives or a position of subservience to men.[72]

Exhibit 22-13 Ikea broke new ground with this ad showing an interracial couple shopping for furniture

Blacks and Hispanics African-Americans and Hispanics have also been the target of stereotyping in advertising. For many years, advertisers virtually ignored all nonwhite ethnic groups as identifiable subcultures and viable markets. Ads were rarely targeted to these ethnic groups, and the use of blacks and Hispanics as spokespeople, communicators, models, or actors in ads was very limited.[73]

Several studies in the late 1980s and early 90s examined the incidence of minorities in advertising. A study conducted in 1987 found that 11 percent of the people appearing in commercials were African-Americans.[74] Another study conducted two years later found that African-Americans appeared in 26 percent of all ads on network TV that used live models but Hispanics appeared in only 6 percent of the commercials with live models. The researchers also found that TV ads in which blacks appeared were overwhelmingly integrated and the blacks were likely to have played either minor or background roles in the majority of the ads.[75] A study conducted in 1995 found that 17 percent of prime-time network TV ads featured African-Americans as dominant characters and the majority of commercials featured them in minor roles.[76]

Although research suggests that the number of African-Americans shown as dominant characters has not increased dramatically, many advertisers are changing blacks' social and role status in advertising. For example, blacks are increasingly being shown in executive positions in many ads. FedEx said that a commercial featuring a black female executive beating out her white male adversaries in a conference call showdown over a high-stakes business deal was one of its most successful ads in years.[77]

Exhibit 22-14 Many marketers are creating ads specifically for the African-American market

Nothing should get in the way of being close.

Ads are increasingly likely to be racially integrated. Recently some advertisers have begun breaking the taboo against suggesting interracial attraction. For example, furniture retailer Ikea ran a TV commercial showing an interracial couple shopping for a "daddy chair" and discussing their plans to conceive[78] (Exhibit 22-13). Advertisers are also finding that advertising developed specifically for the African-American market, such as the Head & Shoulders ad shown in Exhibit 22-14, is an effective way of reaching this ethnic market. A study by Corliss L. Green found that ads targeting African-Americans through racially targeted media, especially with race-based products, benefit from featuring African-American models with a dominant presence in the ad.[79]

Another minority group that has received attention recently from those researching advertising and stereotyping is Asian-Americans, whose affluence, high education, work ethic, and growth rate has made this group a popular target market. A study of prime-time TV commercials found that Asian male and female models are overrepresented in terms of their proportion of the U.S. population (3.6 percent), appearing in 8.4 percent of the commercials. However, Asian models were more likely than members of other minority groups to appear in background roles, and Asian women were rarely depicted in major roles. The study also found that portrayals of Asian-Americans put more emphasis on the work ethic and less on other aspects of their lives.[80]

There is little question that advertising has been guilty of stereotyping women and ethnic groups in the past and, in some cases, still does so. But as the role of women changes, advertisers are changing their portrayals to remain accurate and appeal to their target audience. Advertisers are also trying to increase the incidence of minority groups in ads while avoiding stereotypes and negative role portrayals. They are being careful to avoid ethnic stereotyping and striving to develop advertising that has specific appeals to various ethnic groups.

Other Groups While the focus here has been on women and ethnic minorities, some other groups feel they are victims of stereotyping by advertisers. Many groups in our society are battling against stereotyping and discrimination, and companies must consider whether their ads might offend them. It is increasingly difficult not to offend some segment of the public. Creative personnel in agencies are feeling restricted as their ideas are squelched out of concern that they might offend someone or be misinterpreted.[81] However, advertisers must be sensitive to the portrayal of specific types of people in their ads, for both ethical and commercial reasons.

One area where significant changes have taken place recently is in advertising targeted to gay consumers. In 1995 Ikea broke new ground with a TV commercial featuring a gay couple shopping for furniture. For years beer companies targeted this market by placing ads in local gay media to support or sponsor AIDS awareness, Gay Pride festivals, and the Gay Games. However, a number of beer companies, including Anheuser-Busch and Miller Brewing Co., now run gay-specific, brand-specific ads in national gay publications.[82]

A number of other companies, including IBM and United Airlines, also now run ads with gay themes, although they generally confine them to magazines and newspapers targeting the gay market. While a TV commercial or print ad with a gay reference occasionally runs in the mainstream media, it usually is so subtle or ambiguous that many heterosexuals do not perceive it as a gay message. However, in 2000 the Gay Financial Network, an online company (gfn.com) with a gay-friendly financial news and information website, became the first gay-oriented company to advertise in major U.S. business news and entertainment publications.[83] The gfn.com ads take a gentle swipe at homophobia in the business world (Exhibit 22-15).

More advertisers are turning to gay themes in their mainstream commercials, though often subtly. However, few run these ads on network television; they limit them to spot TV and local stations in more gay-friendly cities such as New York, Los Angeles, and San Francisco. The Miller Brewing Co. did take a bold step recently by airing a gay-themed commercial on network television. The ad was for Miller Lite beer and showed a gay couple holding hands in a straight bar to the dismay of two women who are interested in them.[84]

Exhibit 22-15 The Gay Financial Network broke barriers by becoming the first gay-oriented company to advertise in the mainstream media

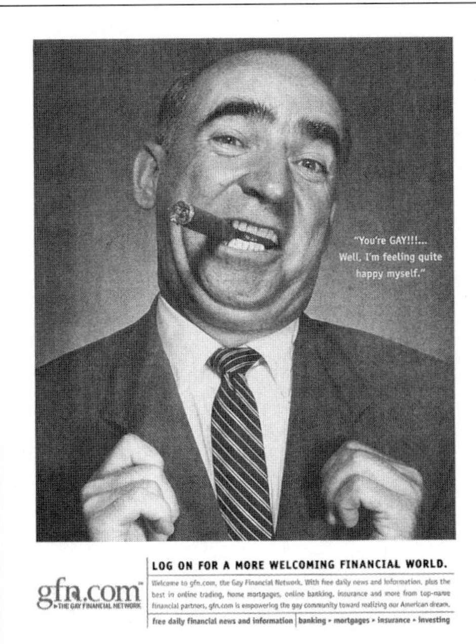

Advertising and the Media

The fact that advertising plays such an important role in financing the media has led to concern that advertisers may influence or even control the media. It is well documented that *economic censorship* occurs, whereby the media avoid certain topics or even present biased news coverage, in acquiescence to advertiser demands.[85] In fact, Professors Lawrence Soley and Robert Craig say, "The assertion that advertisers attempt to influence what the public sees, hears, and reads in the mass media is perhaps the most damning of all criticisms of advertising, but this criticism isn't acknowledged in most advertising textbooks."[86] We will address this important issue in this book by considering arguments on both sides.

Arguments Supporting Advertiser Control Advertising is the primary source of revenue for nearly all the news and entertainment media in the United States. Some critics charge that the media's dependence on advertisers' support makes them susceptible to various forms of influence, including exerting control over the editorial content of magazines and newspapers; biasing editorial opinions to favor the position of an advertiser; limiting coverage of a controversial story that might reflect negatively on a company; and influencing the program content of television.

Newspapers and magazines receive nearly 70 percent of their revenue from advertising; commercial TV and radio derive virtually all their income from advertisers. Small, financially insecure newspapers, magazines, or broadcast stations are the most susceptible to pressure from advertisers, particularly companies that account for a large amount of the media outlet's advertising revenue. A local newspaper may be reluctant to print an unfavorable story about a car dealer or supermarket chain on whose advertising it depends. For example, a few years ago more than 40 car dealers canceled their ads in the *San Jose Mercury News* when the paper printed an article titled "A Car Buyer's Guide to Sanity." The dealers objected to the tone of the article, which they felt implied consumers should consider car dealers unethical adversaries in the negotiation process.[87] A survey of 147 daily newspapers found that more than 90 percent of editors have been pressured by advertisers and more than one-third of them said advertisers had succeeded in influencing news at their papers.[88]

While larger, more financially stable media should be less susceptible to an advertiser's influence, they may still be reluctant to carry stories detrimental to companies that purchase large amounts of advertising time or space.[89] For example, since cigarette commercials were taken off radio and TV in 1970, tobacco companies have allocated most of their budgets to the print media. The tobacco industry outspends all other national advertisers in newspapers, and cigarettes constitute the second-largest category of magazine advertising (behind transportation). This has led to charges that magazines and newspapers avoid articles on the hazards of smoking to protect this important source of ad revenue.[90] One study found that magazines relying on cigarette advertising are far less likely than others to publish stories about the health hazards associated with smoking.[91]

Individual TV stations and even the major networks also can be influenced by advertisers. Programming decisions are made largely on the basis of what shows will attract the most viewers and thus be most desirable to advertisers. Critics say this often results in lower-quality television as educational, cultural, and informative programming is usually sacrificed for shows that get high ratings and appeal to the mass markets. It is well recognized that advertisers often avoid TV shows that deal with controversial issues. Most advertisers also have contract stipulations allowing them to cancel a media buy if, after prescreening a show, they are uncomfortable with its content or feel sponsorship of it may reflect poorly on their company.

Advertisers have also been accused of pressuring the networks to change their programming. Many advertisers have withdrawn commercials from programs that contain too much sex or violence, often in response to threatened boycotts of their products by consumers if they advertise on these shows. For example, groups such as the American Family Association have been fighting sex and violence in TV programs by calling for boycotts. A number of companies, including Procter & Gamble, Mars Inc., and Kraft Foods, pulled their advertising from certain talk shows, like those of Jerry Springer, because of some of their incendiary topics.[92]

Arguments against Advertiser Control The commercial media's dependence on advertising means advertisers can exert influence on their character, content, and coverage of certain issues. However, media executives offer several reasons why advertisers do not exert undue influence over the media.

First, they point out it is in the best interest of the media not to be influenced too much by advertisers. To retain public confidence, they must report the news fairly and accurately without showing bias or attempting to avoid controversial issues. Media executives point to the vast array of topics they cover and the investigative reporting they often do as evidence of their objectivity. They want to build a large audience for their publications or stations so that they can charge more for advertising space and time.

Media executives also note that an advertiser needs the media more than they need any individual advertiser, particularly when the medium has a large audience or does a good job of reaching a specific market segment. Many publications and stations have a very broad base of advertising support and can afford to lose an advertiser that attempts to exert too much influence. This is particularly true for the larger, more established, financially secure media. For example, a consumer-product company would find it difficult to reach its target audience without network TV and could not afford to boycott a network if it disagreed with a station's editorial policy or program content. Even the local advertiser in a small community may be dependent on the local newspaper, since it may be the most cost-effective media option available.

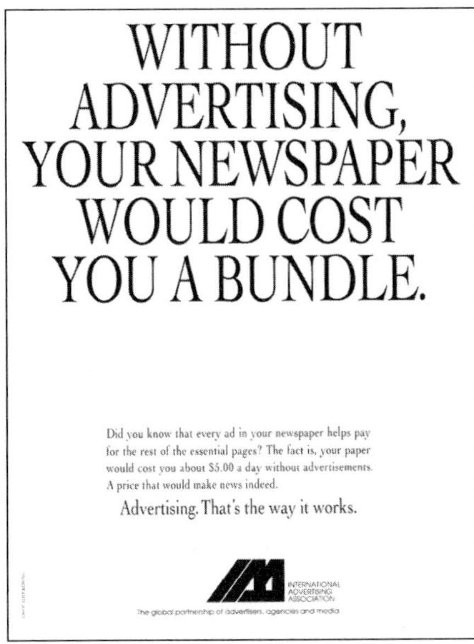

Exhibit 22-16 This ad points out how advertising lowers the cost of newspapers for consumers

Most magazine and newspaper publishers insist they do not allow advertiser pressure to influence their editorial content. They argue that they have long regarded the formal separation of their news and business departments as essential to their independence and credibility. This separation is often referred to as "The Wall" and is often spoken of with a mixture of reverence and trepidation.[93] Many magazines and newspapers have traditionally discouraged employees on the publishing side—including advertising, circulation, and other business departments—from interacting with those on the editorial side, who write and edit the articles. This is done by separating editorial and advertising offices, barring the sales force from reading articles before they are printed, and prohibiting editorial employees from participating in advertising sales calls.

Most magazines and newspapers are very concerned over maintaining the concept of The Wall and ensuring that decisions on the writing, editing, and publishing of stories are made on journalistic merit rather than on whether they will attract or repel advertisers. However, the new economics of the publishing industry is making it difficult to maintain the separation: Competition from cable TV, direct mail, and the Internet is increasing, and newspaper and magazine readership continues to decline. There have been several well-publicized situations in recent years where major magazines and newspapers were found to have given favorable editorial consideration to an advertiser.[94] Ethical Perspective 22-4 discusses how the media face challenges from companies who pull their advertising from publications when they find their editorial coverage objectionable or threaten to do so.

The media in the United States are basically supported by advertising; this means we can enjoy them for free or for a fraction of what they would cost without advertising.[95] The alternative to an advertiser-supported media system is support by users through higher subscription costs for the print media and a fee or pay-per-view system with TV. The ad in Exhibit 22-16, part of a campaign by the International Advertising Association, explains how advertising lowers the cost of print media for consumers. Another alternative is government-supported media like those in many other countries, but this runs counter to most people's desire for freedom of the press. Although not perfect, our system of advertising-supported media provides the best option for receiving information and entertainment.

Summarizing Social Effects

We have examined a number of issues and have attempted to analyze the arguments for and against them. Many people have reservations about the impact of advertising and promotion on society. The numerous rules, regulations, policies, and guidelines marketers comply with do not cover every advertising and promotional situation. Moreover, what one individual views as distasteful or unethical may be acceptable to another.

Negative opinions regarding advertising and other forms of promotion have been around almost as long as the field itself, and it is unlikely they will ever disappear. However, the industry must address the various concerns about the effects of advertising and other forms of promotion on society. Advertising is a very powerful institution, but it will remain so only as long as consumers have faith in the ads they see and hear every day. Many of the problems discussed here can be avoided if individual decision makers make ethics an important element of the IMC planning process.

The primary focus of this discussion of social effects has been on the way advertising is used (or abused) in the marketing of products and services. It is important to note that advertising and other IMC tools, such as direct marketing and public relations, are also used to promote worthy causes and to deal with problems facing society

ETHICAL PERSPECTIVE 22-4

Media Face Challenges in Maintaining "The Wall"

Advertising is the primary source of revenue for nearly all media companies. Because advertising pays the bills, newspapers and magazine publishers, as well as TV and radio networks and their station executives, must keep their advertisers happy. Some have called this a "task not unlike feeding crocodiles" as the inherent danger is that advertisers might use their economic influence to act as unofficial censors of the media and discourage them from publishing or broadcasting certain material.

It is well recognized that advertisers often avoid controversial issues, such as abortion or homosexuality. Most advertisers have contract stipulations allowing them to cancel a media purchase if, after prescreening a show, they are uncomfortable with its content or feel it may reflect poorly on their company. Television is not the only medium that must deal with the threats of advertiser defection or attempts to influence its content. Advertisers can also influence the editorial content of magazines and newspapers by pressuring them to run only positive stories about their products and services. For example, in 2005, several companies including energy giant BP and financial services company Morgan Stanley instituted "ad pull" policies for print publications whereby their ads will be pulled from any editions containing objectionable editorial coverage.

Most magazine and newspaper publishers insist they do not allow advertiser pressure to influence their editorial content. They argue that they have long regarded the formal separation of their news and business departments as essential to their independence and credibility. This separation is often referred to as "The Wall" and is often spoken of with a mixture of reverence and trepidation. Many magazines and newspapers have traditionally discouraged employees on the publishing side, including advertising, circulation, and other business departments, from interacting with those on the editorial side who write and edit the articles. This can be done by separating editorial and advertising offices, barring the sales force from reading articles before they are printed, and prohibiting editorial employees from participating in advertising sales calls. For many years, the *Chicago Tribune* went so far as to program the elevators that went to the advertising and other business departments to bypass the fourth floor where the editorial staff worked.

Journalists agree that giving favorable editorial consideration to a company simply because it advertises in the publication would be unethical. Yet critics argue that this does sometimes occur. As one print executive notes, "It's a generally known principle, sort of subconsciously, that if you have a big advertiser you are not going to do something that's critical of them in your editorial coverage." For example, a few years ago a controversy arose in business publishing when *Fortune* magazine published an article accusing its fierce rival, *Forbes*, of "turning downbeat stories into upbeat stories in order to keep advertisers happy—even at the risk of misleading their own readers." *Forbes* issued a statement saying, "The *Forbes* advertising department has no input into the *Forbes* editorial process." However, the magazine did acknowledge that its publisher sees all stories before they go to print, and "if he does not like what he sees, he complains to a top editor. Very occasionally, these queries lead to changes in these stories."

There is also concern that the newspaper industry may be lowering The Wall in their search for new ways to increase readership and revenue as competition from TV, specialty magazines, and the Internet increases and newspaper readership continues to decline. At many newspapers, editors and executives routinely meet to discuss readership, advertising, the creation of sections, and a wide range of other issues. This concerns many journalists, as well as consumer advocates, who note that it is important that newspaper reporting not be influenced by concerns over flattering or offending advertisers.

One newspaper that is maintaining its Wall and does not appear to be concerned about offending even its largest advertisers is the *Los Angeles Times.* In April 2005, General Motors canceled all of its advertising in the paper after a series of articles that were unflattering of the automaker. GM, which is the nation's second biggest advertiser and spends an estimated $21 million in the *Los Angeles Times* each year, claimed that "factual errors and misrepresentations" in various articles led it to withdraw its advertising in the paper. The paper had run several articles critical of some General Motors' vehicles, such as the Hummer and Pontiac G6, and also suggested that some senior GM executives should be dismissed because of the company's recent sales and profit woes. GM's advertising boycott of the *Los Angeles Times* lasted four months and was finally ended after executives from the two sides met to resolve their differences.

Magazines and newspapers are still very much concerned over maintaining the concept of The Wall and ensuring that decisions on the writing, editing, and publishing of stories are made on journalistic merit rather than on whether they will attract or repel advertisers. Some executives defend the advertisers, noting that they have the right to spend their money the way they want to, which may include avoiding advertising in media that are critical of them. However, media experts argue that if companies use their advertising budgets as weapons to attempt to control newsrooms, they threaten the bond between the media and their audiences, which is the very thing that gives media its value to advertisers.

Sources: Nat Ives, "GM Ends 'L.A. Times' Boycott, Resumes Advertising," www. Adage.com, August 2, 2005; Rance Crain, "Ad Groups, Where's the Outrage over Morgan Stanley and BP?" *Advertising Age,* June 6, 2005, p. 26; Jon Fine and Jean Halliday, "GM Shoots the Messenger as Woes Mount," www.Adage .com, April 11, 2005; David Shaw, "An Uneasy Alliance of News and Ads," *Los Angeles Times,* March 29, 1998, pp. A1, 28.

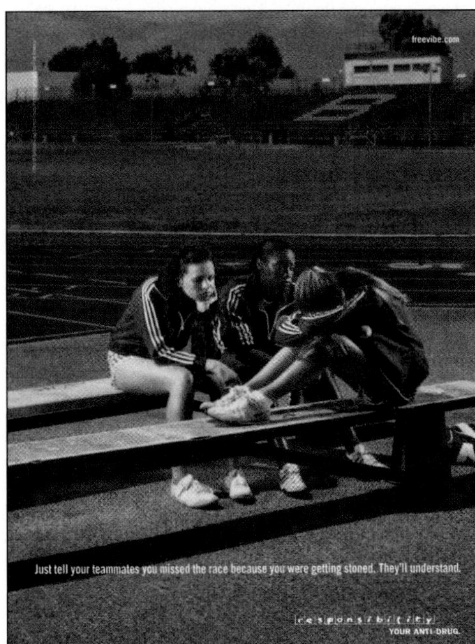

Exhibit 22-17 The ONDCP uses advertising to fight the war on drugs

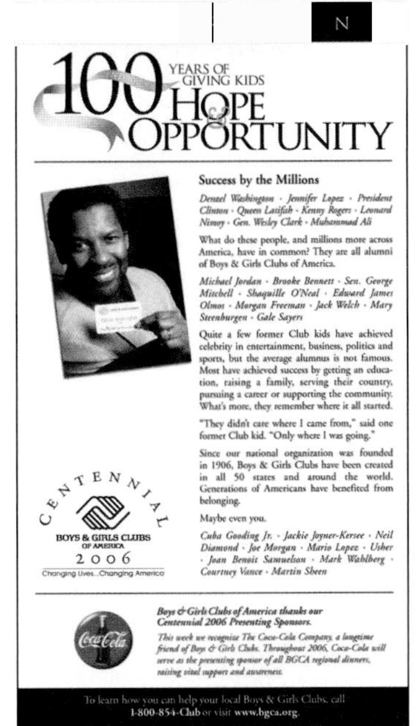

Exhibit 22-18 This ad campaign for the Boys & Girls Clubs is an example of the pro bono work often done by advertising agencies for nonprofit organizations

(drunk driving, drug abuse, and the AIDS crisis, among others). For example, the Partnership for a Drug Free America and now the U.S. government are using advertising to help fight the war against drugs in the United States. Exhibit 22-17 shows an ad from the media campaign sponsored by the U.S. Office of National Drug Control Policy (ONDCP), the government agency created to deal with the problem of illicit drug use. Campaigns for nonprofit organizations and worthy causes are often developed pro bono by advertising agencies, and free advertising time and space are donated by the media.

Exhibit 22-18 shows an ad from a very successful public service campaign for the Boys & Girls Clubs of America featuring actor Denzel Washington. The campaign is designed to establish an image to distinguish the Boys & Girls Clubs from other public service groups and to encourage adults to organize clubs.[96]

Economic Effects of Advertising

Advertising plays an important role in a free-market system like ours by making consumers aware of products and services and providing them with information for decision making. Advertising's economic role goes beyond this basic function, however. It is a powerful force that can affect the functioning of our entire economic system (Exhibit 22-19).

Advertising can encourage consumption and foster economic growth. It not only informs customers of available goods and services but also facilitates entry into markets for a firm or a new product or brand; leads to economies of scale in production, marketing, and distribution, which in turn lead to lower prices; and hastens the acceptance of new products and the rejection of inferior products.

Critics of advertising view it as a detrimental force that not only fails to perform its basic function of information provision adequately but also adds to the cost of products and services and discourages competition and market entry, leading to industrial concentration and higher prices for consumers.

In their analysis of advertising, economists generally take a macroeconomic perspective: They consider the economic impact of advertising on an entire industry or on the economy as a whole rather than its effect on an individual company or brand. Our examination of the economic impact of advertising focuses on these broader macro-level issues. We consider its effects on consumer choice, competition, and product costs and prices.

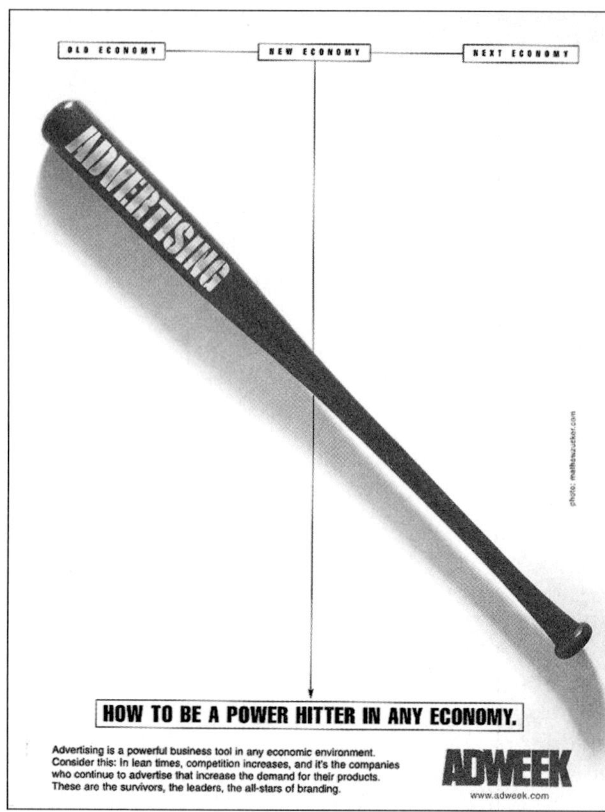

Exhibit 22-19 This ad promotes the economic value of advertising

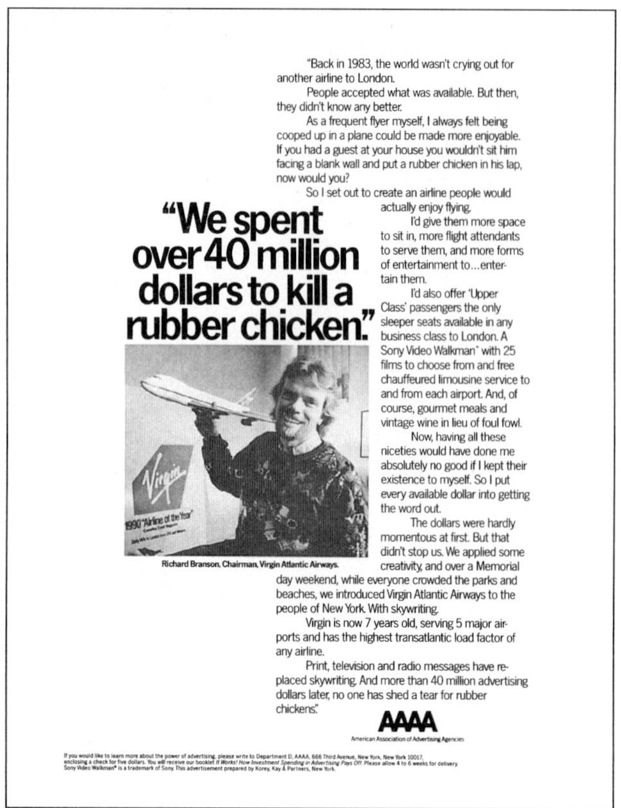

Exhibit 22-20 Virgin Atlantic Airways chair Richard Branson acknowledges the importance of advertising

Effects on Consumer Choice

Some critics say advertising hampers consumer choice, as large advertisers use their power to limit our options to a few well-advertised brands. Economists argue that advertising is used to achieve (1) **differentiation,** whereby the products or services of large advertisers are perceived as unique or better than competitors', and (2) brand loyalty, which enables large national advertisers to gain control of the market, usually at the expense of smaller brands.

Larger companies often end up charging a higher price and achieve a more dominant position in the market than smaller firms that cannot compete against them and their large advertising budgets. When this occurs, advertising not only restricts the choice alternatives to a few well-known, heavily advertised brands but also becomes a substitute for competition based on price or product improvements.

Heavily advertised brands dominate the market in certain product categories, such as soft drinks, beer, and cereals.[97] But advertising generally does not create brand monopolies and reduce the opportunities for new products to be introduced to consumers. In most product categories, a number of different brands are on the store shelves and thousands of new products are introduced every year. The opportunity to advertise gives companies the incentive to develop new brands and improve their existing ones. When a successful new product such as a personal computer is introduced, competitors quickly follow and use advertising to inform consumers about their brand and attempt to convince them it is superior to the original. Companies like Virgin Atlantic Airways recognize that advertising has been an important part of their success (Exhibit 22-20).

Effects on Competition

One of the most common criticisms economists have about advertising concerns its effects on competition. They argue that power in the hands of large firms with huge advertising budgets creates a **barrier to entry,** which makes it difficult for other firms to enter the market. This results in less competition and higher prices. Economists note that smaller firms already in the market find it difficult to compete against the large advertising budgets of the industry leaders and are often driven out of business. For example, in the U.S. beer industry, the number of national brewers has declined dramatically. In their battle for market share, industry giants Anheuser-Busch and Miller increased their ad budgets substantially and reaped market shares that total over 60 percent. Anheuser-Busch alone spent nearly $800 million on advertising in 2005. However, these companies are spending much less per barrel than smaller firms, making it very difficult for the latter to compete.

Large advertisers clearly enjoy certain competitive advantages. First, there are **economies of scale** in advertising, particularly with respect to factors such as media costs. Firms such as Procter & Gamble and PepsiCo, which spend over $2 billion a year on advertising and promotion, are able to make large media buys at a reduced rate and allocate them to their various products.

Large advertisers usually sell more of a product or service, which means they may have lower production costs and can allocate more monies to advertising, so they can afford the costly but more efficient media like network television. Their large advertising outlays also give them more opportunity to differentiate their products and develop brand loyalty. To the extent that these factors occur, smaller competitors are at a disadvantage and new competitors are deterred from entering the market.

While advertising may have an anticompetitive effect on a market, there is no clear evidence that advertising alone reduces competition, creates barriers to entry, and thus increases market concentration. Lester Telser noted that high levels of advertising are not always found in industries where firms have a large market share. He found an inverse relationship between intensity of product class advertising and stability of market share for the leading brands.[98] These findings run contrary to many economists' belief that industries controlled by a few firms have high advertising expenditures, resulting in stable brand shares for market leaders.

Defenders of advertising say it is unrealistic to attribute a firm's market dominance and barriers to entry solely to advertising. There are a number of other factors, such as price, product quality, distribution effectiveness, production efficiencies, and competitive strategies. For many years, products such as Coors beer and Hershey chocolate bars were dominant brands even though these companies spent little on advertising. Hershey did not advertise at all until 1970. For 66 years, the company relied on the quality of its products, its favorable reputation and image among consumers, and its extensive channels of distribution to market its brands. Industry leaders often tend to dominate markets because they have superior product quality and the best management and competitive strategies, not simply the biggest advertising budgets.[99]

While market entry against large, established competitors is difficult, companies with a quality product at a reasonable price often find a way to break in. Moreover, they usually find that advertising actually facilitates their market entry by making it possible to communicate the benefits and features of their new product or brand to consumers. For example, LG Electronics, which is a division of the South Korean conglomerate LG, began marketing products such as digital appliances, mobile phones, DVD players, and plasma TVs, in the United States in 2001 and has become a formidable competitor. LG now spends more than $100 million on advertising and other forms of marketing communication and has created a strong brand identity in the U.S. market[100] (Exhibit 22-21).

Exhibit 22-21 LG has advertised heavily to penetrate the U.S. consumer electronics market

Effects on Product Costs and Prices

A major area of debate among economists, advertisers, consumer advocates, and policymakers concerns the effects of advertising on product costs and prices. Critics argue that advertising increases the prices consumers pay for products and services. First, they say the large sums of money spent advertising a brand constitute an expense that must be covered and the consumer ends up paying for it through higher prices. This is a common criticism from consumer advocates. Several studies show that firms with higher relative prices advertise their products more intensely than do those with lower relative prices.[101] As discussed in the previous chapter, concern has been expressed that the tremendous increase in direct-to-consumer drug advertising by pharmaceutical companies in recent years is driving up the cost of prescription drugs. Critics argue that the millions of dollars spent on advertising and other forms of promotion are an expense that must be covered by charging higher prices.[102]

A second way advertising can result in higher prices is by increasing product differentiation and adding to the perceived value of the product in consumers' minds. Paul Farris and Mark Albion note that product differentiation occupies a central position in theories of advertising's economic effects.[103] The fundamental premise is that advertising increases the perceived differences between physically homogeneous products and enables advertised brands to command a premium price without an increase in quality.

Critics of advertising generally point to the differences in prices between national brands and private-label brands that are physically similar, such as aspirin or tea bags, as evidence of the added value created by advertising. They see consumers' willingness to pay more for heavily advertised national brands rather than purchasing the lower-priced, nonadvertised brand as wasteful and irrational. The prescription drug industry is again a very good example of this, as critics argue that the increase in advertising is encouraging consumers to request brand-name drugs and steering them away from lower-priced generics.[104] However, consumers do not always buy for rational, functional reasons. The emotional, psychological, and social benefits derived from purchasing a national brand are important to many people. Moreover, say Albion and Farris,

> Unfortunately there seems to be no single way to measure product differentiation, let alone determine how much is excessive or attributable to the effects of advertising . . . Both price insensitivity and brand loyalty could be created by a number of factors such as higher product quality, better packaging, favorable use experience and market position. They are probably related to each other but need not be the result of advertising.[105]

Exhibit 22-22 This ad refutes the argument that reducing advertising expenditures will lead to lower prices

Proponents of advertising offer several other counterarguments to the claim that advertising increases prices. They acknowledge that advertising costs are at least partly paid for by consumers. But advertising may help lower the overall cost of a product more than enough to offset them. For example, advertising may help firms achieve economies of scale in production and distribution by providing information to and stimulating demand among mass markets. These economies of scale help cut the cost of producing and marketing the product, which can lead to lower prices—if the advertiser chooses to pass the cost savings on to the consumer. The ad in Exhibit 22-22, from a campaign sponsored by the American Association of Advertising Agencies, emphasizes this point.

Advertising can also lower prices by making a market more competitive, which usually leads to greater price competition. A study by Lee Benham found that prices of eyeglasses were 25 to 30 percent higher in states that banned eyeglass advertising than in those that permitted it.[106] Robert Steiner analyzed the toy industry and concluded that advertising resulted in lower consumer prices. He argued that curtailment of TV advertising would drive up consumer prices for toys.[107] Finally, advertising is a means to market entry rather than a deterrent and helps stimulate product innovation, which makes markets more competitive and helps keep prices down.

Overall, it is difficult to reach any firm conclusions regarding the relationship between advertising and prices. After an extensive review of this area, Farris and Albion concluded, "The evidence connecting manufacturer advertising to prices is neither complete nor definitive . . . consequently, we cannot say whether advertising is a tool of market efficiency or market power without further research."[108]

Economist James Ferguson argues that advertising cannot increase the cost per unit of quality to consumers because if it did, consumers would not continue to respond positively to advertising.[109] He believes advertising lowers the costs of information about brand qualities, leads to increases in brand quality, and lowers the average price per unit of quality.

Summarizing Economic Effects

Albion and Farris suggest that economists' perspectives can be divided into two principal schools of thought that make different assumptions regarding the influence of advertising on the economy.[110] Figure 22-4 summarizes the main points of the "advertising equals market power" and "advertising equals information" perspectives.

Advertising Equals Market Power

The belief that advertising equals market power reflects traditional economic thinking and views advertising as a way to change consumers' tastes, lower their sensitivity to price, and build brand loyalty among buyers of advertised brands. This results in higher profits and market power for large advertisers, reduces competition in the market, and leads to higher prices and fewer choices for consumers. Proponents of this viewpoint generally have negative attitudes regarding the economic impact of advertising.

Advertising Equals Information

The belief that advertising equals information takes a more positive view of advertising's economic effects. This model sees advertising as providing consumers with useful information, increasing their price

Figure 22-4 Two Schools of Thought on Advertising's Role in the Economy

Advertising = Market Power		Advertising = Information
Advertising affects consumer preferences and tastes, changes product attributes, and differentiates the product from competitive offerings.	Advertising	Advertising informs consumers about product attributes but does not change the way they value those attributes.
Consumers become brand loyal and less price sensitive and perceive fewer substitutes for advertised brands.	Consumer buying behavior	Consumers become more price sensitive and buy best "value." Only the relationship between price and quality affects elasticity for a given product.
Potential entrants must overcome established brand loyalty and spend relatively more on advertising.	Barriers to entry	Advertising makes entry possible for new brands because it can communicate product attributes to consumers.
Firms are insulated from market competition and potential rivals; concentration increases, leaving firms with more discretionary power.	Industry structure and market power	Consumers can compare competitive offerings easily and competitive rivalry increases. Efficient firms remain, and as the inefficient leave, new entrants appear; the effect on concentration is ambiguous.
Firms can charge higher prices and are not as likely to compete on quality or price dimensions. Innovation may be reduced.	Market conduct	More informed consumers pressure firms to lower prices and improve quality; new entrants facilitate innovation.
High prices and excessive profits accrue to advertisers and give them even more incentive to advertise their products. Output is restricted compared with conditions of perfect competition.	Market performance	Industry prices decrease. The effect on profits due to increased competition and increased efficiency is ambiguous.

WHEN ADVERTISING DOES ITS JOB, MILLIONS OF PEOPLE KEEP THEIRS.

Good advertising doesn't just inform. It sells. It helps move product and keep businesses in business. Every time an ad arouses a consumer's interest enough to result in a purchase, it keeps a company going strong. And it helps secure the jobs of the people who work there.

Advertising. That's the way it works.

INTERNATIONAL ADVERTISING ASSOCIATION

The global partnership of advertisers, agencies and media

Exhibit 22-23 This ad is part of a global campaign by the International Advertising Association to educate consumers about the economic value of advertising

sensitivity (which moves them toward lower-priced products), and increasing competition in the market. Advertising is viewed as a way to communicate with consumers and tell them about a product and its major features and attributes. More informed and knowledgeable consumers pressure companies to provide high-quality products at lower prices. Efficient firms remain in the market, whereas inefficient firms leave as new entrants appear. Proponents of this model believe the economic effects of advertising are favorable and think it contributes to more efficient and competitive markets.

There is considerable evidence that advertising does provide the information consumers need to make purchase decisions. Avery Abernethy and George Franke performed a meta-analysis of studies examining the information content of advertising and found that more than 84 percent of 91,000 ads analyzed in these studies contain at least one information cue. The most commonly provided types of information included performance, availability, components, price, and quality, all of which are important to consumers in making an informed choice.[111]

It is unlikely the debate over the economic effects and value of advertising will be resolved soon. Many economists will continue to take a negative view of advertising and its effects on the functioning of the economy, while advertisers will continue to view it as an efficient way for companies to communicate with their customers and an essential component of our economic system. The International Advertising Association has been running a campaign for several years to convince consumers around the world of the economic value of advertising. Ads like the one shown in Exhibit 22-23 are used in countries such as China and Russia, where consumers are unfamiliar with the concept of advertising. The goal of the campaign is to get consumers in these countries to recognize the role advertising plays in contributing to their economic well-being.[112]

The advertising industry in the United States continually promotes the value of advertising. Major advertising associations, such as the American Association of Advertising Agencies (AAAA), the American Advertising Federation (AAF), along with trade associations for various media often run campaigns reminding the general public of advertising's contributions to the economy as well as to consumers' social well-being. However, sometimes the industry must also remind advertisers themselves of the value of advertising. Recently the American Advertising Federation, which is the advertising industry's primary trade organization, decided to take action to change the way advertising is viewed by companies.[113] The AAF decided that the best way to get marketers to recognize the value of advertising was to practice what it preaches, and thus an integrated marketing communications campaign was developed to redefine advertising in the eyes of corporate executives.

Exhibit 22-24 The AAF promotes the value of advertising in building strong brands

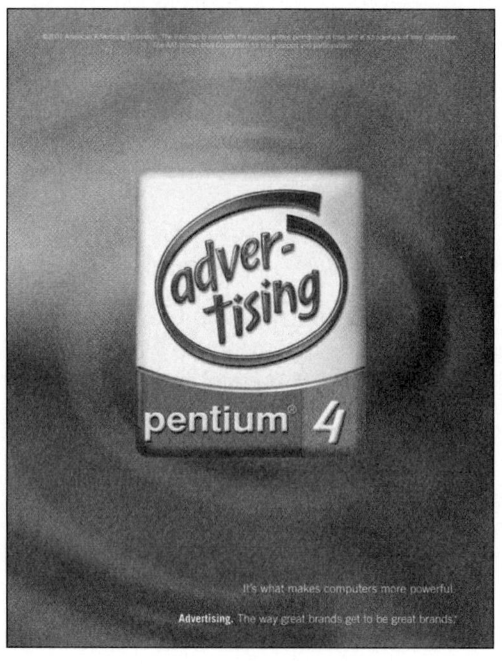

The campaign is targeted at corporate executives who are responsible for establishing and maintaining budget levels for advertising. The theme of the campaign is "Advertising. The way great brands get to be great brands," and it cautions corporate executives not to neglect their brand development. The Great Brands campaign promotes the economic power of advertising by featuring companies that are synonymous with quality advertising and for whom advertising has played a critical role in building brand equity. Exhibit 22-24 shows one of the ads from the campaign featuring Intel, which is the market leader for computer chips and microprocessors.

Figure 22-5, excerpts from a speech given by famous adman Leo Burnett, summarizes the perspective of most advertising people on the

Figure 22-5 This Message Describes the Positive Economic Effects of Advertising

> To me it means that if we believe to any degree whatsoever in the economic system under which we live, in a high standard of living and in high employment, advertising is the most efficient known way of moving goods in practically every product class.
>
> My proof is that millions of businessmen have chosen advertising over and over again in the operations of their business. Some of their decisions may have been wrong, but they must have thought they were right or they wouldn't go back to be stung twice by the same kind of bee.
>
> It's a pretty safe bet that in the next 10 years many Americans will be using products and devices that no one in this room has even heard of. Judging purely by past performance, American advertising can be relied on to make them known and accepted overnight at the lowest possible prices.
>
> Advertising, of course, makes possible our unparalleled variety of magazines, newspapers, business publications, and radio and television stations.
>
> It must be said that without advertising we would have a far different nation, and one that would be much the poorer—not merely in material commodities, but in the life of the spirit.
>
> Leo Burnett

Source: Excerpts from a speech given by Leo Burnett on the American Association of Advertising Agencies' 50th anniversary, April 20, 1967.

economic effects of advertising. Many advertising and marketing experts agree that advertising and promotion play an important role in helping to expand consumer demand for new products and services and in helping marketers differentiate their existing brands.

Summary

Advertising is a very powerful institution and has been the target of considerable criticism regarding its social and economic impact. The criticism of advertising concerns the specific techniques and methods used as well as its effect on societal values, tastes, lifestyles, and behavior. Critics argue that advertising is deceptive and untruthful; that it is often offensive, irritating, or in poor taste; and that it exploits certain groups, such as children. Many people believe advertising should be informative only and advertisers should not use subjective claims, puffery, embellishment, or persuasive techniques.

Advertising often offends consumers by the type of appeal or manner of presentation used; sexually suggestive ads and nudity receive the most criticism. Advertisers say their ads are consistent with contemporary values and lifestyles and are appropriate for the target audiences they are attempting to reach. Advertising to children is an area of particular concern, since critics argue that children lack the experience, knowledge, and ability to process and evaluate persuasive advertising messages rationally. Although an FTC proposal to severely restrict advertising to children was defeated, it remains an issue.

The pervasiveness of advertising and its prevalence in the mass media have led critics to argue that it plays a major role in influencing and transmitting social values. Advertising has been charged with encouraging materialism; manipulating consumers to buy things they do not really want or need; perpetuating stereotypes through its portrayal of certain groups such as women, minorities, and the elderly; and controlling the media.

Advertising has also been scrutinized with regard to its economic effects. The basic economic role of advertising is to give consumers information that helps them make consumption decisions. Some people view advertising as a detrimental force that has a negative effect on competition, product costs, and consumer prices. Economists' perspectives regarding the effects of advertising follow two basic schools of thought: the advertising equals market power model and the advertising equals information model. Arguments consistent with each perspective were considered in analyzing the economic effects of advertising.

Key Terms

ethics, 719
shock advertising, 724
consumer socialization process, 726
materialism, 731
Protestant ethic, 732
differentiation, 742
barrier to entry, 742
economies of scale, 743

Discussion Questions

1. The opening vignette to the chapter discusses Dove's Campaign for Real Beauty. Evaluate the "real beauty" campaign that Dove has developed to market its products from an integrated marketing communications perspective. Discuss how Dove has developed an integrated campaign around the "real beauty" concept that utilizes the various IMC tools.

2. Evaluate Dove's Campaign for Real Beauty from a social and ethical perspective giving attention to how women might respond to the use of everyday people in the ads rather than glamorous models. Do you view the campaign as movement in a positive direction with regard to the portrayal of women in advertising, or more as of a clever way for Dove to sell more beauty products? Defend your position.

3. Ethical Perspective 22-1 discusses how stealth messages and branded content are being woven into the everyday lives of consumers. Discuss why these techniques are becoming increasingly popular among marketers. Why are many watchdog groups such as Commercial Alert concerned over this trend?

4. A common criticism of advertising is that it stereotypes women. Discuss the ways this might occur. Do you think the Airwalk ad shown in Exhibit 22-5 is suggestive and symbolizes sexual submission?

5. Discuss how attitudes toward the use of sex in advertising differ between men and women. Discuss the implications of these attitudinal differences for marketers who are developing ads for each sex.

6. Ethical Perspective 22-2 discusses the clearance process used by the standards and practices department of the four major television networks. Evaluate the effectiveness of this process from the perspective of the networks as well as advertisers.

7. Ethical Perspective 22-3 discusses how the food industry is coming under attack for advertising and promoting snack food and other high caloric products to young people, which critics argue contributes to the obesity epidemic. Do you think marketers of products such as snack foods and soft drinks are responsible for the increase in obesity among young people? How should the industry respond to these criticisms and efforts to limit their advertising and promotion programs?

8. Discuss the arguments for and against advertiser influence and/or control over the media. How might a newspaper or magazine avoid being influenced by advertisers?

9. Discuss how advertising can affect product costs and the prices consumers pay for products and services.

10. Discuss the two major perspectives of the economic impact of advertising: "advertising equals market power" versus "advertising equals information."

Glossary of Advertising and Promotion Terms

Note: Numbers in parentheses after term indicate chapter(s) where term is discussed.

80/20 rule (2) The principle that 80 percent of sales volume for a product or service is generated by 20 percent of the customers.

A

absolute costs (10) The actual total cost of placing an ad in a particular media vehicle.

account executive (3) The individual who serves as the liaison between the advertising agency and the client. The account executive is responsible for managing all of the services the agency provides to the client and representing the agency's point of view to the client.

account planner (3) Advertising agency personnel who gather information that is relevant to a client's product or service and can be used in the development of the creative strategy, as well as other aspects of an IMC campaign.

account planning (8) The process of conducting research and gathering all relevant information about a client's product, service, brand, and consumers in the target audience for use in the development of creative strategy as well as other aspects of an IMC campaign.

account specific marketing (16) Development of customized promotional programs for individual retail accounts by marketers.

ad execution-related thoughts (5) A type of thought or cognitive response a message recipient has concerning factors related to the execution of the ad such as creativity, visual effects, color, and style.

adjacencies (11) Commercial spots purchased from local television stations that generally appear during the time periods adjacent to network programs.

advertising (1) Any paid form of nonpersonal communication about an organization, product, service, or idea by an identified sponsor.

advertising agency (3) A firm that specializes in the creation, production, and placement of advertising messages and may provide other services that facilitate the marketing communications process.

advertising appeal (9) The basis or approach used in an advertising message to attract the attention or interest of consumers and/or influence their feelings toward the product, service, or cause.

advertising campaign (8) A comprehensive advertising plan that consists of a series of messages in a variety of media that center on a single theme or idea.

advertising creativity (8) The ability to generate fresh, unique, and appropriate ideas that can be used as solutions to communication problems.

advertising manager (3) The individual in an organization who is responsible for the planning, coordinating, budgeting, and implementing of the advertising program.

advertising substantiation (21) A Federal Trade Commission regulatory program that requires advertisers to have documentation to support the claims made in their advertisements.

advocacy advertising (17) Advertising that is concerned with the propagation of ideas and elucidation of social issues of public importance in a manner that supports the position and interest of the sponsor.

aerial advertising (13) A form of outdoor advertising where messages appear in the sky in the form of banners pulled by airplanes, skywriting, and on blimps.

affect referral decision rule (4) A type of decision rule where selections are made on the basis of an overall impression or affective summary evaluation of the various alternatives under consideration.

affiliates (11) Local television stations that are associated with a major network. Affiliates agree to preempt time during specified hours for programming provided by the network and carry the advertising contained in the program.

affirmative disclosure (21) A Federal Trade Commission program whereby advertisers may be required to include certain types of information in their advertisements so consumers will be aware of all the consequences, conditions, and limitations associated with the use of the product or service.

affordable method (7) A method of determining the budget for advertising and promotion where all other budget areas are covered and remaining monies are available for allocation.

AIDA model (5) A model that depicts the successive stages a buyer passes through in the personal selling process including attention, interest, desire, and action.

alpha activity (19) A measure of the degree of brain activity that can be used to assess an individual's reactions to an advertisement.

alternative media (13) A term commonly used in advertising to describe support media.

animatic (8) A preliminary version of a commercial whereby a videotape of the frames of a storyboard is produced along with an audio soundtrack.

arbitrary allocation (7) A method for determining the budget for advertising and promotion based on arbitrary decisions of executives.

attitude toward the ad (5) A message recipient's affective feelings of favorability or unfavorability toward an advertisement.

attractiveness (6) A source characteristic that makes him or her appealing to a message recipient. Source attractiveness can be based on similarity, familiarity, or likability.

audimeter (11) An electric measurement device that is hooked to a television set to record when the set is turned on and the channel to which it is tuned.

audiotex (14) The use of telephone and voice information services to market, advertise, promote, entertain, and inform consumers.

average frequency (10) The number of times the average household reached by a media schedule is exposed to a media vehicle over a specified period.

average quarter-hour (AQH) figure (11) The average number of persons listening to a particular station for at least five minutes during a 15-minute period. Used by Arbitron in measuring the size of radio audiences.

average quarter-hour rating (11) The average quarter-hour figure estimate expressed as a percentage of the population being measured. Used by Arbitron in measuring the size of radio audiences.

average quarter-hour share (11) The percentage of the total listening audience tuned to each station as a percentage of the total listening audience in the survey area. Used by Arbitron in measuring the size of radio audiences.

B

balance-of-trade deficit (20) A situation where the monetary value of a country's imports exceeds its exports.

banner ad (15) An ad on a Web page that may be "hot-linked" to the advertiser's site.

barrier to entry (22) Conditions that make it difficult for a firm to enter the market in a particular industry, such as high advertising budgets.

behavioral targeting (15) A basis for target marketing based on consumers' website surfing behaviors.

behavioristic segmentation (2) A method of segmenting a market by dividing customers into groups based on their usage, loyalties, or buying responses to a product or service.

benchmark measures (7) Measures of a target audience's status concerning response hierarchy variables such as awareness, knowledge, image, attitudes, preferences, intentions, or behavior. These measures are taken at the beginning of an advertising or promotional campaign to determine the degree to which a target audience must be changed or moved by a promotional campaign.

benefit segmentation (2) A method of segmenting markets on the basis of the major benefits consumers seek in a product or service.

Better Business Bureau (BBB) (21) An organization established and funded by businesses that operates primarily at the local level to monitor activities of companies and promote fair advertising and selling practices.

billings (3) The amount of client money agencies spend on media purchases and other equivalent activities. Billings are often used as a way of measuring the size of advertising agencies.

bleed pages (12) Magazine advertisements where the printed area extends to the edge of the page, eliminating any white margin or border around the ad.

blog (15) Also known as a weblog, a blog is a Web-based publication consisting primarily of periodic articles written and provided in reverse chronological order. Blogs may reflect the writings of an individual, community political organization, or corporation.

body copy (9) The main text portion of a print ad. Also often referred to as copy.

bonus packs (16) Special packaging that provides consumers with extra quantity of merchandise at no extra charge over the regular price.

bounce-back coupon (16) A coupon offer made to consumers as an inducement to repurchase the brand.

brand development index (BDI) (10) An index that is calculated by taking the percentage of a brand's total sales that occur in a given market as compared to the percentage of the total population in the market.

brand equity (2) The intangible asset of added value or goodwill that results from the favorable image, impressions of differentiation, and/or the strength of consumer attachment of a company name, brand name, or trademark.

brand loyalty (4) Preference by a consumer for a particular brand that results in continual purchase of it.

brand manager (3) The person responsible for the planning, implementation, and control of the marketing program for an individual brand.

branded entertainment (13) The combined use of an audio-visual program (such as TV, radio, podcast, or videocast) and a brand to market a product or service. The purpose of a branded entertainment program is to entertain, while at the same time provide the opportunity for brands or products to be promoted.

buildup approach (7) A method of determining the budget for advertising and promotion by determining the specific tasks that have to be performed and estimating the costs of performing them. See objective and task method.

C

cable television (11) A form of television where signals are carried to households by wire rather than through the airways.

campaign theme (8) The central message or idea that is communicated in all advertising and other promotional activities.

carryover effect (7) A delayed or lagged effect whereby the impact of advertising on sales can occur during a subsequent time period.

category development index (CDI) (10) An index that is calculated by taking the percentage of a product category's total sales that occur in a given market area as compared to the percentage of the total population in the market.

category management system (3) An organizational system whereby managers have responsibility for the marketing programs for a particular category or line of products.

cause-related marketing (17) Image related advertising in which companies link with charities or nonprofit organizations as contributing sponsors.

cease-and-desist order (21) An action by the Federal Trade Commission that orders a company to stop engaging in a practice that is considered deceptive or misleading until a hearing is held.

Central Hudson Test (21) A four-part test used by the courts for determining restrictions on commercial speech.

central route to persuasion (5) One of two routes to persuasion recognized by the elaboration likelihood model. The central route to persuasion views a message recipient as very active and involved in the communications process and as having the ability and motivation to attend to and process a message.

centralized system (3) An organizational system whereby advertising along with other marketing activities such as sales, marketing research, and planning are divided along functional lines and are run from one central marketing department.

channel (5) The method or medium by which communication travels from a source or sender to a receiver.

Children's Online Privacy Protection Act of 1998 (21) Federal legislation which places restrictions on information collected from children via the Internet and requires that websites directed at children have a privacy policy posted on their home page and areas of the site where information is collected.

city zone (12) A category used for newspaper circulation figures that refers to a market area composed of the city where the paper is published and contiguous areas similar in character to the city.

classical conditioning (4) A learning process whereby a conditioned stimulus that elicits a response is paired with a neutral stimulus that does not elicit any particular response. Through repeated exposure, the neutral stimulus comes to elicit the same response as the conditioned stimulus.

classified advertising (12) Advertising that runs in newspapers and magazines that generally contains text only and is arranged under subheadings according to the product, service, or offering. Employment, real estate, and automotive ads are the major forms of classified advertising.

clients (3) The organizations with the products, services, or causes to be marketed and for which advertising agencies and other marketing promotional firms provide services.

clipping service (7) A service which clips competitors' advertising from local print media allowing the company to monitor the types of advertising that are running or to estimate their advertising expenditures.

close (18) Obtaining the commitment of the prospect in a personal selling transaction.

clutter (6, 11) The nonprogram material that appears in a broadcast environment, including commercials, promotional messages for shows, public service announcements, and the like.

cognitive dissonance (4) A state of psychological tension or postpurchase doubt that a consumer may experience after making a purchase decision. This tension often leads the consumer to try to reduce it by seeking supportive information.

cognitive responses (5) Thoughts that occur to a message recipient while reading, viewing, and/or hearing a communication.

collateral services (3) Companies that provide companies with specialized services such as package design, advertising production, and marketing research.

combination rates (12) A special space rate or discount offered for advertising in two or more periodicals. Combination rates are often offered by publishers who own both morning and evening editions of a newspaper in the same market.

commercial speech (21) Speech that promotes a commercial transaction.

commission system (3) A method of compensating advertising agencies whereby the agency receives a specified commission (traditionally 15 percent) from the media on any advertising time or space it purchases.

communication (5) The passing of information, exchange of ideas, or process of establishing shared meaning between a sender and a receiver.

communication objectives (1, 7) Goals that an organization seeks to achieve through its promotional program in terms of communication effects such as creating awareness, knowledge, image, attitudes, preferences, or purchase intentions.

communications task (7) Under the DAGMAR approach to setting advertising goals and objectives, something that can be performed by and attributed to advertising such as awareness, comprehension, conviction, and action.

comparative advertising (6, 9) The practice of either directly or indirectly naming one or more competitors in an advertising message and usually making a comparison on one or more specific attributes or characteristics.

competitive advantage (2) Something unique or special that a firm does or possesses that provides an advantage over its competitors.

competitive parity method (7) A method of setting the advertising and promotion budget based on matching the absolute level of percentage of sales expenditures of the competition.

compliance (6) A type of influence process where a receiver accepts the position advocated by a source to obtain favorable outcomes or to avoid punishment.

comprehension and reaction tests (19) Advertising testing to ensure receivers comprehend the message and to gauge their reaction to the same.

computer simulation models (7) Quantitative-based models that are used to determine the relative contribution of advertising expenditures on sales response.

concave-downward function model (7) An advertising/sales response function that views the incremental effects of advertising on sales as decreasing.

concentrated marketing (2) A type of marketing strategy whereby a firm chooses to focus its marketing efforts on one particular market segment.

concept testing (19) A method of pretesting alternative ideas for an advertisement or campaign by having consumers provide their responses and/or reactions to the creative concept.

conditioned response (4) In classical conditioning, a response that occurs as a result of exposure to a conditioned stimulus.

conditioned stimulus (4) In classical conditioning, a stimulus that becomes associated with an unconditioned stimulus and capable of evoking the same response or reaction as the unconditioned stimulus.

consent order (21) A settlement between a company and the Federal Trade Commission whereby an advertiser agrees to stop the advertising or practice in question. A consent order is for settlement purposes only and does not constitute an admission of guilt.

consumer behavior (4) The process and activities that people engage in when searching for, selecting, purchasing, using, evaluating, and disposing of products and services so as to satisfy their needs and desires.

consumer franchise-building promotions (16) Sales promotion activities that communicate distinctive brand attributes and contribute to the development and reinforcement of brand identity.

consumer juries (19) A method of pretesting advertisements by using a panel of consumers who are representative of the target audience and provide ratings, rankings, and/or evaluations of advertisements.

consumer-oriented sales promotion (16) Sales promotion techniques that are targeted to the ultimate consumer such as coupons, samples, contests, rebates, sweepstakes, and premium offers.

consumer socialization process (22) The process by which an individual acquires the skills needed to function in the marketplace as a consumer.

content sponsorship (15) The sponsor not only provides dollars in return for name association on the Internet but participates in the provision of content itself.

contest (16) A promotion whereby consumers compete for prizes or money on the basis of skills or ability, and winners are determined by judging the entries or ascertaining which entry comes closest to some predetermined criteria.

contextual ads (15) Internet advertising placed on the basis of the content of the Web page.

continuity (10) A media scheduling strategy where a continuous pattern of advertising is used over the time span of the advertising campaign.

contribution margin (7) The difference between the total revenue generated by a product or brand and its total variable costs.

controlled circulation basis (12) Distribution of a publication free to individuals a publisher believes are of importance and responsible for making purchase decisions or are prescreened for qualification on some other basis.

cooperative advertising (2, 16) Advertising program in which a manufacturer pays a certain percentage of the expenses a retailer or distributor incurs for advertising the manufacturer's product in a local market area.

copy platform (8) A document that specifies the basic elements of the creative strategy such as the basic problem or issue the advertising must address, the advertising and communications objectives, target audience, major selling idea or key benefits to communicate, campaign theme or appeal, and supportive information or requirements.

copywriter (3, 8) Individual who helps conceive the ideas for ads and commercials and writes the words or copy for them.

corporate advertising (17) Advertising designed to promote overall awareness of a company or enhance its image among a target audience.

corrective advertising (21) An action by the Federal Trade Commission whereby an advertiser can be required to run advertising messages designed to remedy the deception or misleading impression created by its previous advertising.

cost per order (CPO) (14) A measure used in direct marketing to determine the number of orders generated relative to the cost of running the advertisement.

cost per ratings point (10) A computation used by media buyers to compare the cost efficiency of broadcast programs that divides the cost of commercial time on a program by the audience rating.

cost per thousand (10) A computation used in evaluating the relative cost of various media vehicles that represents the cost of exposing 1,000 members of a target audience to an advertising message.

cost-plus system (3) A method of compensating advertising agencies whereby the agency receives a fee based on the cost of the work it performs plus an agreed-on amount for profit.

Council of Better Business Bureaus (21) The parent office of local offices of the Better Business Bureau. The council assists in the development of codes and standards for ethical and responsible business and advertising practices.

counterargument (5) A type of thought or cognitive response a receiver has that is counter or opposed to the position advocated in a message.

coverage (10) A measure of the potential audience that might receive an advertising message through a media vehicle.

creative boutique (3) An advertising agency that specializes in and provides only services related to the creative aspects of advertising.

creative execution style (9) The manner or way in which a particular advertising appeal is transformed into a message.

creative selling (18) A type of sales position where the primary emphasis is on generating new business.

creative strategy (8) A determination of what an advertising message will say or communicate to a target audience.

creative tactics (8) A determination of how an advertising message will be implemented so as to execute the creative strategy.

credibility (6) The extent to which a source is perceived as having knowledge, skill, or experience relevant to a communication topic and can be trusted to give an unbiased opinion or present objective information on the issue.

cross-media advertising (12) An arrangement where opportunities to advertise in several different types of media are offered by a single company or a partnership of various media providers.

cross/multimagazine deals (12) An arrangement where two or more publishers offer their magazines to an advertiser as one media package.

cross-ruff coupon (16) A coupon offer delivered on one product that is redeemable for the purchase of another product. The other product is usually one made by the same company but may involve a tie-in with another manufacturer.

cross sell (18) A term used in personal selling that refers to the sale of additional products and/or services to the same customer.

cultural values (20) Refers to beliefs and goals shared by members of a society regarding ideal end-states of life and modes of conduct.

culture (4) The complexity of learned meanings, values, norms, and customs shared by members of a society.

cume (11) A term used for cumulative audience, which is the estimated total number of different people who listened to a radio station for a minimum of five minutes during a particular daypart.

D

DAGMAR (7) An acronym that stands for defining advertising goals for measured advertising results. An approach to setting advertising goals and objectives developed by Russell Colley.

daily inch rate (10) A cost figure used in periodicals based on an advertisement placed one inch deep and one column wide (whatever the column inch).

database (14) A listing of current and/or potential customers for a company's product or service that can be used for direct-marketing purposes.

database marketing (14) The use of specific information about individual customers and/or prospects to implement more effective and efficient marketing communications.

day-after recall scores (19) A measure used in on-air testing of television commercials by various marketing research companies. The day-after recall score represents the percentage of viewers surveyed who can remember seeing a particular commercial.

dayparts (11) The time segments into which a day is divided by radio and television networks and stations for selling advertising time.

decentralized system (3) An organizational system whereby planning and decision-making responsibility for marketing, advertising, and promotion lies with a product/brand manager or management team rather than a centralized department.

deception (21) According to the Federal Trade Commission, a misrepresentation, omission, or practice that is likely to mislead the consumer acting reasonably in the circumstances to the consumer's detriment.

decoding (5) The process by which a message recipient transforms and interprets a message.

demographic segmentation (2) A method of segmenting a market based on the demographic characteristics of consumers.

departmental system (3) The organization of an advertising agency into departments based on functions such as account services, creative, media, marketing services, and administration.

derived demand (19) A situation where demand for a particular product or service results from the need for other goods and/or services. For example, demand for aluminum cans is derived from consumption of soft drinks or beer.

designated market area (DMA) (11) The geographic areas used by the Nielsen Station Index in measuring audience size. DMAs are nonoverlapping areas consisting of groups of counties from which stations attract their viewers.

differentiated marketing (2) A type of marketing strategy whereby a firm offers products or services to a number of market segments and develops separate marketing strategies for each.

differentiation (22) A situation where a particular company or brand is perceived as unique or better than its competitors.

direct broadcast satellite (DBS) (11, 20) A television signal delivery system whereby programming is beamed from satellites to special receiving dishes mounted in the home or yard.

direct channel (2) A marketing channel where a producer and ultimate consumer interact directly with one another.

direct headline (9) A headline that is very straightforward and informative in terms of the message it is presenting and the target audience it is directed toward. Direct headlines often include a specific benefit, promise, or reason for a consumer to be interested in a product or service.

direct marketing (1, 14) A system of marketing by which an organization communicates directly with customers to generate a response and/or transaction.

direct-marketing agency (3) A company that provides a variety of direct-marketing services to their clients including database management, direct mail, research, media service, creative, and production.

direct-marketing media (14) Media that are used for direct-marketing purposes including direct mail, telemarketing, print, and broadcast.

direct-response advertising (1, 14) A form of advertising for a product or service that elicits a sales response directly from the advertiser.

direct-response media (14) Media used to seek a direct response from the consumer, including direct mail, telemarketing, etc.

direct selling (14) The direct personal presentation, demonstration, and sale of products and services to consumers usually in their homes or at their jobs.

directional medium (13) Advertising media that are not used to create awareness or demand for products or services but rather to inform customers as to where purchases can be made once they have decided to buy. The Yellow Pages are an example of a directional medium.

display advertising (12) Advertising in newspapers and magazines that uses illustrations, photos, headlines, and other visual elements in addition to copy text.

dissonance/attribution model (5) A type of response hierarchy where consumers first behave, then develop attitudes or feelings as a result of that behavior, and then learn or process information that supports the attitude and behavior.

diverting (16) A practice whereby a retailer or wholesaler takes advantage of a promotional deal and then sells some of the product purchased at the low price to a store outside of their area or to a middleman who will resell it to other stores.

dyadic communication (18) A process of direct communication between two persons or groups such as a salesperson and a customer.

E

e-commerce (15) Direct selling of goods and services through the Internet.

economic infrastructure (20) A country's communications, transportation, financial, and distribution networks.

economies of scale (7, 22) A decline in costs with accumulated sales or production. In advertising, economies of scale often occur in media purchases as the relative costs of advertising time and/or space may decline as the size of the media budget increases.

effective reach (10) A measure of the percentage of a media vehicle's audience reached at each effective frequency increment.

elaboration likelihood model (ELM) (5) A model that identifies two processes by which communications can lead to persuasion—central and peripheral routes.

electrodermal response (19) A measure of the resistance the skin offers to a small amount of current passed between two electrodes. Used as a measure of consumers' reaction level to an advertisement.

electroencephalographic (EEG) measures (19) Measures of the electrical impulses in the brain that are sometimes used as a measure of reactions to advertising.

electronic teleshopping (14) Online shopping and information retrieval service that is accessed through a personal computer.

emotional appeals (6, 9) Advertising messages that appeal to consumers' feelings and emotions.

encoding (5) The process of putting thoughts, ideas, or information into a symbolic form.

ethics (22) Moral principles and values that govern the actions and decisions of an individual or group.

ethnographic research (8) A research technique that involves observing or studying consumers in their natural environment.

evaluative criteria (4) The dimensions or attributes of a product or service that are used to compare different alternatives.

event marketing (16) A type of promotion where a company or brand is linked to an event, or where a themed activity is developed for the purpose of creating experiences for consumers and promoting a product or service.

event sponsorship (16, 17) A type of promotion whereby a company develops sponsorship relations with a particular event such as a concert, sporting event, or other activity.

everyday low pricing (EDLP) (16) A pricing strategy used by retailers whereby prices are kept at a continually lower level rather than raising and lowering them during promotional periods.

exchange (1) Trade of something of value between two parties such as a product or service for money. The core phenomenon or domain for study in marketing.

exclusive (17) A public relations tactic whereby one particular medium is offered exclusive rights to a story.

external analysis (1) The phase of the promotional planning process that focuses on factors such as the characteristics of an organization's customers, market segments, positioning strategies, competitors, and marketing environment.

external audiences (17) In public relations, a term used in reference to individuals who are outside of or not closely connected to the organization such as the general public.

external audits (17) Evaluations performed by outside agencies to determine the effectiveness of an organization's public relations program.

external search (4) The search process whereby consumers seek and acquire information from external sources such as advertising, other people, or public sources.

eye tracking (19) A method for following the movement of a person's eyes as he or she views an ad or commercial. Eye tracking is used for determining which portions or sections of an ad attract a viewer's attention and/or interest.

F

failure fee (16) A trade promotion arrangement whereby a marketer agrees to pay a penalty fee if a product stocked by a retailer does not meet agreed-upon sales levels.

fear appeals (6) An advertising message that creates anxiety in a receiver by showing negative consequences that can result from engaging in (or not engaging in) a particular behavior.

Federal Trade Commission (FTC) (21) The federal agency that has the primary responsibility for protecting consumers and businesses from anticompetitive behavior and unfair and deceptive practices. The FTC regulates advertising and promotion at the federal level.

Federal Trade Commission Act (21) Federal legislation passed in 1914 that created the Federal Trade Commission and gave it the responsibility to monitor deceptive or misleading advertising and unfair business practices.

fee-commission combination (3) A type of compensation system whereby an advertising agency establishes a fixed monthly fee for its services to a client and media commissions received by the agency are credited against the fee.

feedback (5) Part of the message recipient's response that is communicated back to the sender. Feedback can take a variety of forms and provides a sender with a way of monitoring how an intended message is decoded and received.

field of experience (5) The experiences, perceptions, attitudes, and values that senders and receivers of a message bring to a communication situation.

field tests (19) Tests of consumer reactions to an advertisement that are taken under natural viewing situations rather than in a laboratory.

financial audit (3) An aspect of the advertising agency evaluation process that focuses on how the agency conducts financial affairs related to serving a client.

fixed-fee arrangement (3) A method of agency compensation whereby the agency and client agree on the work to be done and the amount of money the agency will be paid for its services.

flat rates (12) A standard newspaper advertising rate where no discounts are offered for large-quantity or repeated space buys.

Flesch formula (19) A test used to assess the difficulty level of writing based on the number of syllables and sentences per 100 words.

flighting (10) A media scheduling pattern in which periods of advertising are alternated with periods of no advertising.

focus groups (4, 8) A qualitative marketing research method whereby a group of 10 to 12 consumers from the target market are led through a discussion regarding a particular topic such as a product, service, or advertising campaign.

forward buying (16) A practice whereby retailers and wholesalers stock up on a product being offered by a manufacturer at a lower deal or off-invoice price and resell it to consumers once the marketer's promotional period has ended.

frequency (10) The number of times a target audience is exposed to a media vehicle(s) in a specified period.

frequency programs (16) A type of promotional program that rewards customers for continuing to purchase the same brand of a product or service over time (also referred to as continuity or loyalty programs).

full-service agency (3) An advertising agency that offers clients a full range of marketing and communications services including the planning, creating, producing, and placing of advertising messages and other forms of promotion.

functional consequences (4) Outcomes of product or service usage that are tangible and can be directly experienced by a consumer.

G

game (16) A promotion that is a form of sweepstakes because it has a chance element or odds of winning associated with it. Games usually involve game card devices that can be rubbed or opened to unveil a winning number or prize description.

gatefolds (12) An oversize magazine page or cover that is extended and folded over to fit into the publication. Gatefolds are used to extend the size of a magazine advertisement and are always sold at a premium.

general advertising rates (12) Rates charged by newspapers to display advertisers outside the paper's designated market areas and to any classification deemed by the publisher to be general in nature.

general preplanning input (8) Information gathering and/or market research studies on trends, developments, and happenings in the marketplace that can be used to assist in the initial stages of the creative process of advertising.

geographic segmentation (2) A method of segmenting a market on the basis of different geographic units or areas.

global advertising (20) The use of the same basic advertising message in all international markets.

global marketing (20) A strategy of using a common marketing plan and program for all countries in which a company operates, thus selling the product or services the same way everywhere in the world.

gross ratings points (GRPs) (10) A measure that represents the total delivery or weight of a media schedule during a specified time period. GRPs are calculated by multiplying the reach of the media schedule by the average frequency.

group system (3) The organization of an advertising agency by dividing it into groups consisting of specialists from various departments such as creative, media, marketing services, and other areas. These groups work together to service particular accounts.

guerrilla marketing (13) The use of nontraditional media to market one's product often employing atypical efforts, and often attempting to capitalize on competitor's promotional efforts.

H

halo effect (19) The tendency for evaluations of one attribute or aspect of a stimulus to distort reactions to its other attributes or properties.

headline (9) Words in the leading position of the advertisement; the words that will be read first or are positioned to draw the most attention.

hemisphere lateralization (19) The notion that the human brain has two relatively distinct halves or hemispheres with each being responsible for a specific type of function. The right side is responsible for visual processing while the left side conducts verbal processing.

heuristics (4) Simplified or basic decision rules that can be used by a consumer to make a purchase choice, such as buy the cheapest brand.

hierarchy of effects model (5) A model of the process by which advertising works that assumes a consumer must pass through a sequence of steps from initial awareness to eventual action. The stages include awareness, interest, evaluation, trial, and adoption.

hierarchy of needs (4) Abraham Maslow's theory that human needs are arranged in an order or hierarchy based on their importance. The need hierarchy includes physiological, safety, social/love and belonging, esteem, and self-actualization needs.

hit (15) The number of times that a specific component of a website is requested.

horizontal cooperative advertising (16) A cooperative advertising arrangement where advertising is sponsored in common by a group of retailers or other organizations providing products or services to a market.

households using television (HUT) (11) The percentage of homes in a given area that are watching television during a specific time period.

I

identification (6) The process by which an attractive source influences a message recipient. Identification occurs when the receiver is motivated to seek some type of relationship with the source and adopt a similar position in terms of beliefs, attitudes, preferences, or behavior.

image advertising (8, 17) Advertising that creates an identity for a product or service by emphasizing psychological meaning or symbolic association with certain values, lifestyles, and the like.

image transfer (11) A radio advertising technique whereby the images of a television commercial are implanted into a radio spot.

incentive-based system (3) A form of compensation whereby an advertising agency's compensation level depends on how well it meets predetermined performance goals such as sales or market share.

index numbers (10) A ratio used to describe the potential of a market. The index number is derived by dividing the percentage of users in a market segment by the percentage of population in the same segment and multiplying by 100.

indirect channel (2) A marketing channel where intermediaries such as wholesalers and retailers are utilized to make a product available to the customer.

indirect headlines (9) Headlines that are not straightforward with respect to identifying a product or service or providing information regarding the point of an advertising message.

in-flight advertising (13) A variety of advertising media targeting air travelers while they are in flight.

infomercials (14) Television commercials that are very long, ranging from several minutes to an hour. Infomercials are designed to provide consumers with detailed information about a product or service.

information processing model (5) A model of advertising effects developed by William McGuire that views the receiver of a message as an information processor and problem solver. The model views the receiver as passing through a response hierarchy that includes a series of stages including message presentation, attention, comprehension, acceptance or yielding, retention, and behavior.

informational/rational appeals (9) Advertising appeals that focus on the practical, functional, or utilitarian need for a product or service and emphasize features, benefits, or reasons for owning or using the brand.

ingredient-sponsored cooperative advertising (16) Advertising supported by raw material manufacturers with the objective being to help establish end products that include materials and/or ingredients supplied by the company.

inherent drama (8) An approach to advertising that focuses on the benefits or characteristics that lead a consumer to purchase a product or service and uses dramatic elements to emphasize them.

in-house agency (3) An advertising agency set up, owned, and operated by an advertiser that is responsible for planning and executing the company's advertising program.

ink-jet imaging (12) A printing process where a message is reproduced by projecting ink onto paper rather than mechanical plates. Ink-jet imaging is being offered by many magazines to allow advertisers to personalize their messages.

innovation adoption model (5) A model that represents the stages a consumer passes through in the adoption process for an innovation such as a new product. The series of steps includes awareness, interest, evaluation, trial, and adoption.

inquiry tests (19) Tests designed to measure advertising effectiveness on the basis of inquiries or responses generated from the ad such as requests for information, number of phone calls, or number of coupons redeemed.

inside cards (13) A form of transit advertising where messages appear on cards or boards inside of vehicles such as buses, subways, or trolleys.

instant coupon (16) Coupons attached to a package that can be removed and redeemed at the time of purchase.

in-store couponing (16) The distribution of coupons in retail stores through various methods such as tear-off pads, handouts, and on-shelf or electronic dispensers.

in-store media (13) Advertising and promotional media that are used inside of a retail store such as point-of-purchase displays, ads on shopping carts, coupon dispensers, and display boards.

integrated marketing communications (1) A strategic business process used to develop, execute, and evaluate coordinated, measurable, persuasive brand communications programs over time with consumers, customers, prospects, employees, associates, and other targeted relevant external and internal audiences. The goal is to generate both short-term financial returns and build long-term brand and shareholder value.

integrated marketing communications management (1) The process of planning, executing, evaluating, and controlling the use of various promotional mix elements to effectively communicate with a target audience.

integrated marketing communications objectives (7) Statements of what various aspects of the integrated marketing communications program will accomplish with respect to factors such as communication tasks, sales, market share, and the like.

integrated marketing communications plan (1) A document that provides the framework for developing, implementing, and controlling an organization's integrated marketing communications program.

integration processes (4) The way information such as product knowledge, meanings, and beliefs is combined to evaluate two or more alternatives.

interactive agency (3) An organization that specializes in the creation of interactive media such as CD-ROMs, kiosks, and websites.

interactive media (1, 10) A variety of media that allows the consumer to interact with the source of the message, actively receiving information and altering images, responding to questions, and so on.

interactive TV (15) Television programs that allow the viewer to interact with the program or ads.

interconnects (11) Groups of cable systems joined together for advertising purposes.

internal analysis (1) The phase of the promotional planning process that focuses on the product/service offering and the firm itself including the capabilities of the firm and its ability to develop and implement a successful integrated marketing communications program.

internal audiences (17) In public relations, a term used to refer to individuals or groups inside of the organization or with a close connection to it.

internal audits (17) Evaluations by individuals within the organization to determine the effectiveness of a public relations program.

internalization (6) The process by which a credible source influences a message recipient. Internalization occurs when the receiver is motivated to have an objectively correct position on an issue and the receiver will adopt the opinion or attitude of the credible communicator if he or she believes the information from this source represents an accurate position on the issue.

internal search (4) The process by which a consumer acquires information by accessing past experiences or knowledge stored in memory.

Internet (15) A worldwide means of exchanging information and communicating through a series of interconnected computers.

Internet Yellow Pages (13) The online version of the Yellow Pages.

interstitial (15) An advertisement that appears in a window on your computer screen while you are waiting for a Web page to load.

J

jingles (9) Songs about a brand or company that usually carry the advertising theme and a simple message.

L

laboratory tests (19) Tests of consumer reactions to advertising under controlled conditions.

Lanham Act (21) A federal law that permits a company to register a trademark for its exclusive use. The Lanham Act was amended to encompass false advertising and prohibits any false description or representation including words or other symbols tending falsely to describe or represent the same.

layout (9) The physical arrangement of the various parts of an advertisement including the headline, subheads, illustrations, body copy, and any identifying marks.

leads (18) A name given to a personal sales agent as a possible consumer.

link (15) An electronic connection between two websites.

local advertising (11) Advertising done by companies within the limited geographic area where they do business.

localized advertising strategy (20) Developing an advertising campaign specifically for a particular country or market rather than using a global approach.

low-involvement hierarchy (5) A response hierarchy whereby a message recipient is viewed as passing from cognition to behavior to attitude change.

M

magazine networks (12) A group of magazines owned by one publisher or assembled by an independent network that offers advertisers the opportunity to buy space in a variety of publications through a package deal.

mailing list (14) A type of database containing names and addresses of present and/or potential customers who can be reached through a direct-mail campaign.

major selling idea (8) The basis for the central theme or message idea in an advertising campaign.

marginal analysis (7) A principle of resource allocation that balances incremental revenues against incremental costs.

market opportunities (2) Areas where a company believes there are favorable demand trends, needs, and/or wants that are not being satisfied, and where it can compete effectively.

market segmentation (2) The process of dividing a market into distinct groups that have common needs and will respond similarly to a marketing action.

market segments (2) Identifiable groups of customers sharing similar needs, wants, or other characteristics that make them likely to respond in a similar fashion to a marketing program.

marketing (1) An organizational function and a set of processes for creating, communicating, and delivering value to customers and for managing customer relationships in ways that benefit the organization and its stakeholders.

marketing channels (2) The set of interdependent organizations involved in the process of making a product or service available to customers.

marketing mix (1, 2) The controllable elements of a marketing program including product, price, promotion, and place.

marketing objectives (1, 7) Goals to be accomplished by an organization's overall marketing program such as sales, market share, or profitability.

marketing plan (1) A written document that describes the overall marketing strategy and programs developed for an organization, a particular product line, or a brand.

marketing public relations (MPR) (17) Public relations activities designed to support marketing objectives and programs.

mass customization (1) A process whereby a company makes a product or delivers a service in response to a particular customer's needs in a cost-effective way.

mass media (5) Nonpersonal channels of communication that allow a message to be sent to many individuals at one time.

materialism (22) A preoccupation with material things rather than intellectual or spiritual concerns.

media buying services (3) Independent companies that specialize in the buying of media, particularly radio and television time.

media objectives (10) The specific goals an advertiser has for the media portion of the advertising program.

media organizations (3) One of the four major participants in the integrated marketing communications process whose function is to provide information or entertainment to subscribers, viewers, or readers while offering marketers an environment for reaching audiences with print and broadcast messages.

media planning (10) The series of decisions involved in the delivery of an advertising message to prospective purchasers and/or users of a product or service.

media strategies (10) Plans of action for achieving stated media objectives such as which media will be used for reaching a target audience, how the media budget will be allocated, and how advertisements will be scheduled.

media vehicle (10) The specific program, publication, or promotional piece used to carry an advertising message.

medium (10) The general category of communication vehicles that are available for communicating with a target audience such as broadcast, print, direct mail, and outdoor.

message (5) A communication containing information or meaning that a source wants to convey to a receiver.

missionary sales (18) A type of sales position where the emphasis is on performing supportive activities and services rather than generating or taking orders.

mnemonics (4) Basic cues such as symbols, rhymes, and associations that facilitate the learning and memory process.

mobile billboards (13) An out-of-home medium in which advertisements are able to be transported to different locations (signs painted on automobiles, trailers pulling billboards, and the like).

motivation research (4) Qualitative research designed to probe the consumer's subconscious and discover deeply rooted motives for purchasing a product.

motive (4) Something that compels or drives a consumer to take a particular action.

multiattribute attitude model (4) A model of attitudes that views an individual's evaluation of an object as being a function of the beliefs that he or she has toward the object on various attributes and the importance of these attributes.

multimagazine deals (12) Arrangements whereby two or more publishers offer advertisers the opportunity to buy space in their magazines with one single media buy.

multiplexing (11) An arrangement where multiple channels are transmitted by one cable network.

N

narrowcasting (11) The reaching of a very specialized market through programming aimed at particular target audiences. Cable television networks offer excellent opportunities for narrowcasting.

National Advertising Review Board (NARB) (21) A part of the National Advertising Division of the Council of Better Business Bureaus. The NARB is the advertising industry's primary self-regulatory body.

National Advertising Review Council (NARC) (21) An organization founded by the Council of Better Business Bureaus and various advertising industry groups to promote high standards of truth, accuracy, morality, and social responsibility in national advertising.

National Association of Attorneys General (21) An organization consisting of state attorneys general that is involved in the regulation of advertising and other business practices.

national spot advertising (11) All nonnetwork advertising done by a national advertiser in local markets.

needledrop (9) A term used in the advertising industry to refer to music that is prefabricated, multipurpose, and conventional and can be used in a commercial when a particular normative effect is desired.

negotiated commission (3) A method of compensating advertising agencies whereby the client and agency negotiate the commission structure rather than relying on the traditional 15 percent media commission.

noise (5) Extraneous factors that create unplanned distortion or interference in the communications process.

nonfranchise-building promotions (16) Sales promotion activities that are designed to accelerate the purchase decision process and generate an immediate increase in sales but do little or nothing to communicate information about a brand and contribute to its identity and image.

nonmeasured media (13) A term commonly used in the advertising industry to describe support media.

nontraditional media (13) Newer media including various forms of support media such as entertainment marketing, guerrilla marketing, product placements, and the like, as well as Internet and interactive media, such as blogs, podcasts, and more.

O

objective and task method (7) A build-up approach to budget setting involving a three-step process: (1) determining objectives, (2) determining the strategies and tasks required to attain these objectives, and (3) estimating the costs associated with these strategies and tasks.

off-invoice allowance (16) A promotional discount offered to retailers or wholesalers whereby a certain per-case amount or percentage is deducted from the invoice.

on-air tests (19) Testing the effectiveness of television commercials by inserting test ads into actual TV programs in certain test markets.

one-sided message (6) Communications in which only positive attributes or benefits of a product or service are presented.

one-step approach (14) A direct-marketing strategy in which the medium is used directly to obtain an order (for example, television direct-response ads).

open rate structure (12) A rate charged by newspapers in which discounts are available based on frequency or bulk purchases of space.

operant conditioning (instrumental conditioning) (4) A learning theory that views the probability of a behavior as being dependent on the outcomes or consequences associated with it.

order taking (18) A personal selling responsibility in which the salesperson's primary responsibility is taking the order.

out-of-home advertising (13) The variety of advertising forms including outdoor, transit, skywriting, and other media viewed outside the home.

outside posters (13) Outdoor transit posters appearing on buses, taxis, trains, subways, and trolley cars.

P

PACT (Positioning Advertising Copy Testing) (19) A set of principles endorsed by 21 of the largest U.S. ad agencies aimed at improving the research used in preparing and testing ads, providing a better creative product for clients, and controlling the cost of TV commercials.

paid search (15) Also referred to as search engine advertising in which advertisers pay only when a consumer clicks on their ad or link from a search engine page.

participations (11) The situation where several advertisers buy commercial time or spots on network television.

pass-along rate (10) An estimate of the number of readers of a magazine in addition to the original subscriber or purchaser.

pass-along readership (12) The audience that results when the primary subscriber or purchaser of a magazine gives the publication to another person to read, or when the magazine is read in places such as waiting rooms in doctors' offices.

pattern advertising (20) Advertisements that follow a basic global approach although themes, copy, and sometimes even visual elements may be adjusted.

payout plan (7) A budgeting plan that determines the investment value of the advertising and promotion appropriation.

people meter (11) An electronic device that automatically records a household's television viewing, including channels watched, number of minutes of viewing, and members of the household who are watching.

percentage charges (3) The markups charged by advertising agencies for services provided to clients.

percentage of sales method (7) A budget method in which the advertising and/or promotions budget is set based on a percentage of sales of the product.

perception (4) The process by which an individual receives, selects, organizes, and interprets information to create a meaningful picture of the world.

peripheral route to persuasion (5) In the elaboration likelihood model, one of two routes to persuasion in which the receiver is viewed as lacking the ability or motivation to process information and is not likely to be engaging in detailed cognitive processing.

personal selling (1, 10) Person-to-person communication in which the seller attempts to assist and/or persuade prospective buyers to purchase the company's product or service or to act on an idea.

personalization (15) Individuals can request that specific information they are interested in viewing be sent to their computers.

persuader stage (18) A role of personal selling that attempts to persuade market members to buy the supplier's offerings.

persuasion matrix (6) A communications planning model in which the stages of the response process (dependent variables) and the communications components (independent variables) are combined to demonstrate the likely effect that the independent variables will have on the dependent variables.

planograms (16) A planning configuration of products that occupy a shelf section in a store that is used to provide more efficient shelf space utilization.

podcasting (15) A medium using the Internet to distribute files for downloading into iPods and other MP3 players.

pop-under (15) Ads that pop-up as the user is leaving the website.

pop-ups (15) Advertisement windows on the Internet usually larger than a banner ad and smaller than a full screen.

portfolio tests (19) A laboratory methodology designed to expose a group of respondents to a portfolio consisting of both control and test print ads.

positioning (2) The art and science of fitting the product or service to one or more segments of the market in such a way as to set it meaningfully apart from competition.

posttests (19) Ad effectiveness measures that are taken after the ad has appeared in the marketplace.

preferred position rate (12) A rate charged by newspapers that ensures the advertiser the ad will appear in the position required and/or in a specific section of the newspaper.

premium (16) An offer of an item of merchandise or service either free or at a low price that is used as an extra incentive for purchasers.

preprinted inserts (12) Advertising distributed through newspapers that is not part of the newspaper itself, but is printed by the advertiser and then taken to the newspaper to be inserted.

press conference (17) The calling together of the press to announce significant news and or events.

press release (17) Factual and interesting information released to the press.

pretests (19) Advertising effectiveness measures that are taken before the implementation of the advertising campaign.

price-off deal (16) A promotional strategy in which the consumer receives a reduction in the regular price of the brand.

primacy effect (6) A theory that the first information presented in the message will be the most likely to be remembered.

primary circulation (12) The number of copies of a magazine distributed to original subscribers.

problem detection (8) A creative research approach in which consumers familiar with a product (or service) are asked to generate an exhaustive list of problems encountered in its use.

problem recognition (4) The first stage in the consumer's decision-making process in which the consumer perceives a need and becomes motivated to satisfy it.

problem-solver stage (18) A stage of personal selling in which the seller obtains the participation of buyers in identifying their problems, translates these problems into needs, and then presents a selection from the supplier's offerings that can solve those problems.

procreator stage (18) A stage of personal selling in which the seller defines the buyer's problems or needs and the solutions to those problems or needs through active buyer–seller collaboration, thus creating a market offering tailored to the customer.

product integrations (13) The act of integrating the product into television program content.

product placement (13) A form of advertising and promotion in which products are placed in television shows and/or movies to gain exposure.

product/service-specific preplanning input (8) Specific studies provided to the creative department on the product or service, the target audience, or a combination of the two.

product symbolism (2) The meaning that a product or brand has to consumers.

program rating (10, 11) The percentage of TV households in an area that are tuned to a program during a specific time period.

promotion (1) The coordination of all seller-initiated efforts to set up channels of information and persuasion to sell goods and services or to promote an idea.

promotional mix (1) The tools used to accomplish an organization's communications objective. The promotional mix includes advertising, direct marketing, sales promotion, publicity/public relations, and personal selling.

promotional products marketing (13) The advertising or promotional medium or method that uses promotional products such as ad specialties, premiums, business gifts, awards, prizes, or commemoratives.

promotional pull strategy (2) A strategy in which advertising and promotion efforts are targeted at the ultimate consumers to encourage them to purchase the manufacturer's brand.

promotional push strategy (2) A strategy in which advertising and promotional efforts are targeted to the trade to attempt to get them to promote and sell the product to the ultimate consumer.

prospecting (18) The process of seeking out prospective customers.

prospector stage (18) A selling stage in which activities include seeking out selected buyers who are perceived to have a need for the offering as well as the resources to buy it.

prospects (18) Prospective customers.

Protestant ethic (22) A perspective of life that stresses hard work and individual effort and initiative and views the accumulation of material possessions as evidence of success.

provider stage (18) A stage of personal selling in which activities are limited to accepting orders for the supplier's available offering and conveying it to the buyer.

psychoanalytic theory (4) An approach to the study of human motivations and behaviors pioneered by Sigmund Freud.

psychographic segmentation (2) Dividing the product on the basis of personality and/or lifestyles.

psychosocial consequences (4) Purchase decision consequences that are intangible, subjective, and personal.

public relations (1, 17) The management function that evaluates public attitudes, identifies the policies and procedures of an individual or organization with the public interest, and executes a program to earn public understanding and acceptance.

public relations firm (3) An organization that develops and implements programs to manage a company's publicity, image, and affairs with consumers and other relevant publics.

publicity (1, 17) Communications regarding an organization, product, service, or idea that is not directly paid for or run under identified sponsorship.

puffery (21) Advertising or other sales presentations that praise the item to be sold using subjective opinions, superlatives, or exaggerations, vaguely and generally, stating no specific facts.

pulsing (10) A media scheduling method that combines flighting and continuous scheduling.

pupillometrics (19) An advertising effectiveness methodology designed to measure dilation and constriction of the pupils of the eye in response to stimuli.

purchase intention (4) The predisposition to buy a certain brand or product.

push money (16) Cash payments made directly to the retailers' or wholesalers' sales force to encourage them to promote and sell a manufacturer's product.

push technology (15) Allows a company to "push" a message to the consumer through the Internet rather than waiting for them to find it.

Q

qualified prospects (18) Those prospects that are able to make the buying decision.

qualitative audit (3) An audit of the advertising agency's efforts in planning, developing, and implementing the client's communications programs.

qualitative media effect (6) The positive or negative influence the medium may contribute to the message.

R

ratings point (11) A measurement used to determine television viewing audiences in which one ratings point is the equivalent of 1 percent of all of the television households in a particular area tuned to a specific program.

reach (10) The number of different audience members exposed at least once to a media vehicle (or vehicles) in a given period.

readers per copy (10) A cost comparison figure used for magazines that estimates audience size based on pass-along readership.

recall tests (19) Advertising effectiveness tests designed to measure advertising recall.

receiver (5) The person or persons with whom the sender of a message shares thoughts or information.

recency effect (6) The theory that arguments presented at the end of the message are considered to be stronger and therefore are more likely to be remembered.

recognition method (19) An advertising effectiveness measure of print ads that allows the advertiser to assess the impact of an ad in a single issue of a magazine over time and/or across alternative magazines.

reference group (4) A group whose perspectives, values, or behavior is used by an individual as the basis for his or her judgments, opinions, and actions.

refund (16) An offer by a manufacturer to return a portion of a product's purchase price, usually after the consumer supplies a proof of purchase.

refutational appeal (6) A type of message in which both sides of the issue are presented in the communication, with arguments offered to refute the opposing viewpoint.

reinforcement (4) The rewards or favorable consequences associated with a particular response.

relationship marketing (1, 18) An organization's effort to develop a long-term, cost-effective link with individual customers for mutual benefit.

relative cost (10) The relationship between the price paid for advertising time or space and the size of the audience delivered; it is used to compare the prices of various media vehicles.

reminder advertising (9) Advertising designed to keep the name of the product or brand in the mind of the receiver.

repositioning (2) The changing of a product or brand's positioning.

resellers (2) Intermediaries in the marketing channel such as wholesalers, distributors, and retailers.

response (5) The set of reactions the receiver has after seeing, hearing, or reading a message.

retail advertising rates (12) Rates newspapers charge to advertisers that conduct business or sell goods and services within the paper's designated market area.

retail trading zone (12) The market outside the city zone whose residents regularly trade with merchants within the city zone.

RFM scoring method (14) The Postal Service's recommendation for scoring the value of database entries, based on recency, frequency, and monetary transactions.

rich media (15) A term for advanced technology used in Internet ads, such as a streaming video, which allows interaction and special effects.

ROI (7) Return on investment is a measure used to determine the returns received on advertising and other IMC element investments.

ROI budgeting method (return on investment) (7) A budgeting method in which advertising and promotions are considered investments, and thus measurements are made in an attempt to determine the returns achieved by these investments.

RSS (15) Really simple syndication is a specification that uses XML to organize and format Web-based content in a standard way to provide RSS feeds, which consist of titles and brief descriptions of other online articles.

run of paper (ROP) (12) A rate quoted by newspapers that allows the ad to appear on any page or in any position desired by the medium.

S

S-shaped response curve (7) A sales response model that attempts to show sales responses to various levels of advertising and promotional expenditures.

sales promotion (1, 16) Marketing activities that provide extra value or incentives to the sales force, distributors, or the ultimate consumer and can stimulate immediate sales.

sales promotion agency (3) An organization that specializes in the planning and implementation of promotional programs such as contests, sweepstakes, sampling, premiums, and incentive offers for its clients.

sales promotion trap (16) A spiral that results when a number of competitors extensively use promotions. One firm uses sales promotions to differentiate its product or service and other competitors copy the strategy, resulting in no differential advantage and a loss of profit margins to all.

salient attributes (2) Attributes considered important to consumers in the purchase decision process.

salient beliefs (4) Beliefs concerning specific attributes or consequences that are activated and form the basis of an attitude.

sampling (16) A variety of procedures whereby consumers are given some quantity of a product for no charge to induce trial.

scatter market (11) A period for purchasing television advertising time that runs throughout the TV season.

schedules of reinforcement (4) The schedule by which a behavioral response is rewarded.

script (9) A written version of the commercial that provides a detailed description of its video and audio content.

selective attention (4) A perceptual process in which consumers choose to attend to some stimuli and not others.

selective binding (12) A computerized production process that allows the creation of hundreds of copies of a magazine in one continuous sequence.

selective comprehension (4) The perceptual process whereby consumers interpret information based on their own attitudes, beliefs, motives, and experiences.

selective exposure (4) A process whereby consumers choose whether or not to make themselves available to media and message information.

selective learning (5) The process whereby consumers seek information that supports the choice made and avoid information that fails to bolster the wisdom of a purchase decision.

selective perception (4) The perceptual process involving the filtering or screening of exposure, attention, comprehension, and retention.

selective retention (4) The perceptual process whereby consumers remember some information but not all.

selectivity (12) The ability of a medium to reach a specific target audience.

self-liquidating premiums (16) Premiums that require the consumer to pay some or all of the cost of the premium plus handling and mailing costs.

self-regulation (21) The practice by the advertising industry of regulating and controlling advertising to avoid interference by outside agencies such as the government.

semiotics (5) The study of the nature of meaning.

sensation (4) The immediate and direct response of the senses (taste, smell, sight, touch, and hearing) to a stimulus such as an advertisement, package, brand name, or point-of-purchase display.

shaping (4) The reinforcement of successive acts that lead to a desired behavior pattern or response.

share of audience (11) The percentage of households watching television in a special time period that are tuned to a specific program.

shock advertising (22) Advertising in which marketers use nudity, sexual suggestiveness, or other startling images to get consumers' attention.

showing (13) The percentage of supplicated audience exposed to an outdoor poster daily.

single-source tracking (19) A research method designed to track the behaviors of consumers from the television set to the supermarket checkout counter.

situational determinants (4) Influences originating from the specific situation in which consumers are to use the product or brand.

sleeper effect (6) A phenomenon in which the persuasiveness of a message increases over time.

slotting allowance (16) Fees that must be paid to retailers to provide a "slot" or position to accommodate a new product on the store shelves.

social class (4) Relatively homogeneous divisions of society into which people are grouped based on similar lifestyles, values, norms, interests, and behaviors.

source (5, 6) The sender—person, group, or organization—of the message.

source bolsters (5) Favorable cognitive thoughts generated toward the source of a message.

source derogations (5) Negative thoughts generated about the source of a communication.

source power (6) The power of a source as a result of his or her ability to administer rewards and/or punishments to the receiver.

spam (15, 21) Unsolicited commercial e-mail.

spamming (21) The sending of unsolicited multiple commercial electronic messages.

specialized marketing communication services (3) Organizations that provide marketing communication services in their areas of expertise including direct marketing, public relations, and sales promotion firms.

specialty advertising (13) An advertising, sales promotion, and motivational communications medium that employs useful articles of merchandise imprinted with an advertiser's name, message, or logo.

split runs (12) Two or more versions of a print ad are printed in alternative copies of a particular issue of a magazine.

split run test (19) An advertising effectiveness measure in which different versions of an ad are run in alternate copies of the same newspaper and/or magazine.

sponsorship (11) When the advertiser assumes responsibility for the production and usually the content of a television program as well as the advertising that appears within it.

sponsorships (15) When advertisers sponsor content on a website, it is considered a sponsorship.

spot advertising (11) Commercials shown on local television stations, with the negotiation and purchase of time being made directly from the individual stations.

standard advertising unit (SAU) (12) A standard developed in the newspaper industry to make newspaper purchasing rates more comparable to other media that sell space and time in standard units.

standard learning model (5) Progression by the consumers through a learn-feel-do hierarchical response.

station reps (11) Individuals who act as sales representatives for a number of local stations and represent them in dealings with national advertisers.

storyboard (8) A series of drawings used to present the visual plan or layout of a proposed commercial.

strategic marketing plan (2) The planning framework for specific marketing activities.

subcultures (4) Smaller groups within a culture that possess similar beliefs, values, norms, and patterns of behavior that differentiate them from the larger cultural mainstream.

subheads (9) Secondary headlines in a print ad.

subliminal perception (4) The ability of an individual to perceive a stimulus below the level of conscious awareness.

superagencies (3) Large external agencies that offer integrated marketing communications on a worldwide basis.

superstations (11) Independent local stations that send their signals via satellite to cable operators that, in turn, make them available to subscribers (WWOR, WPIX, WGN, WSBK, WTBS).

support advertising (14) A form of direct marketing in which the ad is designed to support other forms of advertising appearing in other media.

support argument (5) Consumers' thoughts that support or affirm the claims being made by a message.

support media (13) Those media used to support or reinforce messages sent to target markets through other more "dominant" and/or more traditional media.

survey of buying power (10) An index that provides information regarding population, effective buying income, and total retail sales in an area.

sweeps periods (10, 11) The times of year in which television audience measures are taken (February, May, July, and November).

sweepstakes (16) A promotion whereby consumers submit their names for consideration in the drawing or selection of prizes and winners are determined purely by chance. Sweepstakes cannot require a proof of purchase as a condition for entry.

syndicated programs (11) Shows sold or distributed to local stations.

T

target CPM (TCPM) (10) A relative cost comparison that calculates CPMs based on the target audience as opposed to the overall audience.

target marketing (2) The process of identifying the specific needs of segments, selecting one or more of these segments as a target, and developing marketing programs directed to each.

target ratings points (TRPs) (10) The number of persons in the primary target audience that the media buy will reach—and the number of times.

team approach (17) A method of measuring the effectiveness of public relations programs whereby evaluators are actually involved in the campaign.

teaser advertising (9) An ad designed to create curiosity and build excitement and interest in a product or brand without showing it.

telemarketing (14) Selling products and services by using the telephone to contact prospective customers.

telemedia (14) The use of telephone and voice information services (800, 900, 976 numbers) to market, advertise, promote, entertain, and inform.

television households (11) The number of households in a market that own a television set.

television network (11) The provider of news and programming to a series of affiliated local television stations.

terminal posters (13) Floor displays, island showcases, electronic signs, and other forms of advertisements that appear in train or subway stations, airline terminals, and the like.

testing bias (19) A bias that occurs in advertising effectiveness measures because respondents know they are being tested and thus alter their responses.

theater testing (19) An advertising effectiveness pretest in which consumers view ads in a theater setting and evaluate these ads on a variety of dimensions.

top-down approaches (7) Budgeting approaches in which the budgetary amount is established at the executive level and monies are passed down to the various departments.

total audience (television) (11) The total number of homes viewing any five-minute part of a television program.

total audience/readership (12) A combination of the total number of primary and pass-along readers multiplied by the circulation of an average issue of a magazine.

tracking studies (19) Advertising effectiveness measures designed to assess the effects of advertising on awareness, recall, interest, and attitudes toward the ad as well as purchase intentions.

trade advertising (2) Advertising targeted to wholesalers and retailers.

trade allowance (16) A discount or deal offered to retailers or wholesalers to encourage them to stock, promote, or display a manufacturer's product.

trade-oriented sales promotion (16) A sales promotion designed to motivate distributors and retailers to carry a product and make an extra effort to promote or "push" it to their customers.

trade regulation rules (TRRs) (21) Industrywide rules that define unfair practices before they occur. Used by the Federal Trade Commission to regulate advertising and promotion.

trade show (16) A type of exhibition or forum where manufacturers can display their products to current as well as prospective buyers.

traditional media (13) Commonly thought of media that have been employed for years. These include advertising, sales promotions, public relations, and direct marketing.

transformational advertising (9) An ad that associates the experience of using the advertised brand with a unique set of psychological characteristics that would not typically be associated with the brand experience to the same degree without exposure to the advertisement.

transit advertising (13) Advertising targeted to target audiences exposed to commercial transportation facilities, including buses, taxis, trains, elevators, trolleys, airplanes, and subways.

two-sided message (6) A message in which both good and bad points about a product or claim are presented.

two-step approach (14) A direct-marketing strategy in which the first effort is designed to screen or qualify potential buyers, while the second effort has the responsibility of generating the response.

U

undifferentiated marketing (2) A strategy in which market segment differences are ignored and one product or service is offered to the entire market.

unduplicated reach (10) The number of persons reached once with a media exposure.

unfairness (21) A concept used by the Federal Trade Commission to determine unfair or deceptive advertising practices. Unfairness occurs when a trade practice causes substantial physical or economic injury to consumers, could not be avoided by consumers, and must not be outweighed by countervailing benefits to consumers or competition.

unique selling proposition (USP) (8) An advertising strategy that focuses on a product or service attribute that is distinctive to a particular brand and offers an important benefit to the customer.

up-front market (11) A buying period that takes place prior to the upcoming television season when the networks sell a large part of their commercial time.

V

value (1) The customer's perception of all of the benefits of a product or service weighed against the costs of acquiring and consuming it.

vehicle option source effect (19) The differential impact the advertising exposure will have on the same audience member if the exposure occurs in one media option rather than another.

vertical cooperative advertising (16) A cooperative arrangement under which a manufacturer pays for a portion of the advertising a retailer runs to promote the manufacturer's product and its availability in the retailer's place of business.

video news release (VNR) (17) News stories produced by publicists so that television stations may air them as news.

voiceover (9) A message or action on the screen in a commercial that is narrated or described by a narrator who is not visible.

W

want (4) A felt need shaped by a person's knowledge, culture, and personality.

waste coverage (10) A situation where the coverage of the media exceeds the target audience.

wearout (6) The tendency for a television or radio commercial to lose its effectiveness when it is seen and/or heard repeatedly.

webcasting (15) A system for pushing out site information to Web users rather than waiting for them to find the site on their own. (Often referred to as push technologies.)

website (15) The information made available to users of the Internet by the provider.

Wheeler-Lea Amendment (21) An act of Congress passed in 1938 that amended section 5 of the FTC Act to read that unfair methods of competition in commerce and unfair or deceptive acts or practices in commerce are declared unlawful.

wireless (15) A communications network that allows access, as well as transmissions to and from the Internet to travel over the air waves, rather than fixed land lines.

word-of-mouth communications (5) Social channels of communication such as friends, neighbors, associates, co-workers, or family members.

World Wide Web (WWW) (15) Commonly referred to as the Web. The commercial component of the Internet.

Y

Yellow Pages (13) A telephone directory providing names of companies that provide specific products and/or services.

Yellow Pages advertising (13) Advertisements that appear in the various Yellow Pages–type phone directories.

Z

zapping (11) The use of a remote control device to change channels and switch away from commercials.

zero-based communications planning (7) An approach to planning the integrated marketing communications program that involves determining what tasks need to be done and what marketing communication functions should be used to accomplish them and to what extent.

zipping (11) Fast-forwarding through commercials during the playback of a program previously recorded on a VCR.

Endnotes

Chapter One

1. Robert J. Coen, *Insider's Report: Robert Coen Presentation on Advertising Expenditures* (New York: Universal McCann, December 2005).
2. Ibid.
3. "AMA Board Approves New Marketing Definition," *Marketing News,* March 1, 1985, p. 1.
4. Richard P. Bagozzi, "Marketing as Exchange," *Journal of Marketing,* 39 (October 1975), pp. 32–39.
5. Lisa M. Keefe, "What Is the Meaning of 'Marketing'?" *Marketing News,* September 15, 2004, pp. 17–18.
6. Frederick E. Webster, Jr., "Defining the New Marketing Concept," *Marketing Management,* 3, no. 4 (1993), pp. 22–31.
7. Wemer Reinhartz, Manfred Krafft, and Wayne D. Hoyer, "The Customer Relationship Management Process: Its Measurement and Impact on Performance," *Journal of Marketing Research,* 41 (August 2005), pp. 293–305. Jonathan R. Capulsky and Michael J. Wolfe, "Relationship Marketing: Positioning for the Future," *Journal of Business Strategy,* July–August 1991, pp. 16–26.
8. James H. Gilmore and B. Joseph Pine II, "The Four Faces of Customization," *Harvard Business Review,* 75 (1) (January–February 1997), pp. 91–101; Robert J. Lavidge, "'Mass Customization' Is Not an Oxy-Moron," *Journal of Advertising Research,* (July–August 1999), pp. 70–72.
9. B. Joseph Pine II, Don Peppers, and Martha Rogers, "Do You Want to Keep Your Customers Forever?" *Harvard Business Review,* 73, 2, (March–April 1995), pp. 103–114.
10. Adrian Payne & Pennie Frow, "A Strategic Framework for Customer Relationship Management," *Journal of Marketing,* vol. 69 (October 2005), pp. 167–176.
11. Adrienne Ward Fawcett, "Integrated Marketing—Marketers Convinced: Its Time Has Arrived," *Advertising Age,* November 6, 1993, pp. S1–2.
12. "Do Your Ads Need a SuperAgency?" *Fortune,* April 27, 1991, pp. 81–85; Faye Rice, "A Cure for What Ails Advertising?" *Fortune,* December 16, 1991, pp. 119–22.
13. Scott Hume, "Campus Adopts 'New' Advertising," *Advertising Age,* September 23, 1991, p. 17.
14. Don E. Schultz, "Integrated Marketing Communications: Maybe Definition Is in the Point of View," *Marketing News,* January 18, 1993, p. 17.
15. Ibid.
16. Joep P. Cornelissen and Andrew R. Lock, "Theoretical Concept or Management Fashion? Examining the Significance of IMC," *Journal of Advertising Research,* (September–October 2000), pp. 7–15.
17. Philip J. Kitchen, Joanne Brignell, Tao Li and Graham Spickett Jones, "The Emergence of IMC: A Theoretical Perspective," *Journal of Advertising Research,* (March 2004), pp. 19–30.
18. Don E. Schultz, "IMC Receives More Appropriate Definition," *Marketing News,* September 15, 2004, pp. 8–9.
19. Joep P. Cornelissen and Andrew R. Lock, "Theoretical Concept or Management Fashion? Examining the Significance of IMC," *Journal of Advertising Research,* (September–October 2000), pp. 7–15.
20. Harlan E. Spotts, David R. Lambert, and Mary L. Joyce, "Marketing Déjà Vu: The Discovery of Integrated Marketing Communications," *Journal of Marketing Education,* vol. 20, (3) (December 1998), pp. 210–18.
21. Tom Duncan and Sandra E. Moriarty, "A Communication-Based Model for Managing Relationships," *Journal of Marketing* 62 (2), (April 1998), pp. 1–13.
22. Philip J. Kitchen, Joanne Brignell, Tao Li and Graham Spickett Jones, "The Emergence of IMC: A Theoretical Perspective," *Journal of Advertising Research,* (March 2004), pp. 19–30.
23. Anthony J. Tortorici, "Maximizing Marketing Communications through Horizontal and Vertical Orchestration," *Public Relations Quarterly,* vol. 36, (1) (1991), pp. 20–22.
24. Anick Jesdaun, "Broadband Is Altering Net Use in U.S. Homes," *San Diego Union-Tribune,* December 27, 2004, pp. E1, 5.
25. Meg James, "Products Are Stars in New Ad Strategy," *Los Angeles Times,* December 2, 2004, pp. C1, 10.
26. Gerry Khermouch and Jeff Green, "Buzz Marketing," *BusinessWeek,* July 30, 2001, pp. 50–56.
27. Sergio Zyman, *The End of Marketing As We Know It* (New York: HarperBusiness, 1999); Joe Cappo, "Agencies: Change or Die," *Advertising Age,* December 7, 1992, p. 26.
28. Don E. Schultz, "Be Careful Picking Database for IMC Efforts," *Marketing News,* March 11, 1996, p. 14.
29. Kevin Lane Keller, "The Brand Report Card," *Harvard Business Review,* 78 (1), (January/February 2000), pp. 3–10.
30. Kevin Lane Keller, "Conceptualizing, Measuring, and Managing Customer-Based Brand Equity," *Journal of Marketing,* vol. 57 (January 1993), pp. 1–22.
31. Michael L. Ray, *Advertising and Communication Management* (Englewood Cliffs, NJ: Prentice Hall, 1982).
32. Ralph S. Alexander, ed., *Marketing Definitions* (Chicago: American Marketing Association, 1965), p. 9.
33. Gerry Khermouch, "The Top 5 Rules of the Ad Game," *BusinessWeek,* January 20, 2003, pp. 72–73.
34. Patricia Odell, "Doritos Targets Texters in Integrated Campaign," *promomagazine.com,* March 9, 2005.
35. Kris Oser, "Sharp Touts TV in Net Mystery Adver-Blog," *Advertising Age,* November 1, 2004, p. S4.
36. Kathleen M. Joyce, "Riding the Tide: PROMO 2005 Industry Trends Report," PROMO, April 2005, pp. AR3–6.
37. Stephanie Thompson, "Food Fight Breaks Out," *Advertising Age,* January 17, 2005, pp. 1, 25.
38. Kate McArthur, "Supersized PR," *Advertising Age,* December 13, 2004, p. S6.
39. H. Frazier Moore and Bertrand R. Canfield, *Public Relations: Principles, Cases, and Problems,* 7th ed. (Burr Ridge, IL: Irwin, 1977), p. 5.
40. Paul Holmes, "Marketers See a Greater Role for Public Relations in the Marketing Mix," *Advertising Age,* January 24, 2005, pp. C4–10; Jack

Neff, "Ries' Thesis: Ads Don't Build Brands, PR Does," *Advertising Age,* July 15, 2002, pp. 14–15.

41. Stephanie Thompson, "No-Carb: Sales Fail, Trend Ends," *Advertising Age,* April 4, 2005, pp. 1, 60.

Chapter Two

1. Anita Hamilton, "Freaking for Sneakers," *Time,* March 13, 2006, p. 42; Sandra O'Loughlin, "Puma Unleashes TV To Support Growth," *Brandweek,* March 7, 2005, p. 1.
2. Stanley Holmes, "The Machine of a New Sole," *BusinessWeek,* March 14, 2005, p. 99.
3. Rich Thomaselli, "New Balance Pumps Up Ad Spend Against Nike, Reebok," www.AdAge.com, March 9, 2005, p. 1.
4. David Kiley and James R. Healey, "GM Plans To Boldly Go After Niche Markets," www.USAToday.com, February 19, 2004, pp. 1–2.
5. Kenneth Hein, "Parade of Drinks May Clog Channel," *Brandweek,* February 7, 2005, p. 4.
6. Susan M. Gianinno, "Is Populism Death for Luxury?" *Advertising Age,* October 4, 2004, p. 36.
7. Tiffany Myers, "Marketers Learn Luxury Isn't Simply for the Very Wealthy," *Advertising Age,* September 13, 2004, p. S-2.
8. Kenneth Hein, "Hallmark Heats Up WB's *Polar Express* with $70M," *Brandweek,* October 18, 2004, p. 7.
9. Roger A. Kerin, Steven W. Hartley, Eric N. Berkowitz and William Rudelius, *Marketing,* 8th ed. (Burr Ridge, IL: Irwin/McGraw-Hill, 2006).
10. Andrew M. Carlo, "The Comfort Zone," *Home Channel News,* May 24, 2004, pp. 3, 29.
11. Dale Buss, "Can Harley Ride the New Wave?" *Brandweek,* October 25, 2004, pp. 20–22.
12. Edward M. Tauber, "Research on Food Consumption Values Finds Four Market Segments: Good Taste Still Tops," *Marketing News,* May 15, 1981, p. 17; Rebecca C. Quarles, "Shopping Centers Use Fashion Lifestyle Research to Make Marketing Decisions," *Marketing News,* January 22, 1982, p. 18; and "Our Auto, Ourselves," *Consumer Reports,* June 1985, p. 375.
13. Judith Graham, "New VALS 2 Takes Psychological Route," *Advertising Age,* February 13, 1989, p. 24.
14. Stuart Elliott, "Hummer Targets 'Psychographics,'" www.NewYorkTimes.com, March 9, 2004, p. 4.
15. *Ayer's Dictionary of Advertising Terms* (Philadelphia: Ayer Press, 1976).
16. Davis A. Aaker and John G. Myers, *Advertising Management,* 3rd ed. (Englewood Cliffs, NJ: Prentice Hall, 1987), p. 125.
17. Jack Trout and Al Ries, "Positioning Cuts through Chaos in the Marketplace," *Advertising Age,* May 1, 1972, pp. 51–53.
18. Jack Trout, "Branding Can't Exist Without Positioning," *Advertising Age,* March 14, 2005, p. 28.
19. Ibid.
20. David A. Aaker and J. Gary Shansby, "Positioning Your Product," *Business Horizons,* May–June 1982, pp. 56–62.
21. Aaker and Myers, *Advertising Management.*
22. Trout and Ries, "Positioning Cuts through Chaos."
23. Tara Burghart, "Steep Slide of a Retail Giant," *San Diego Union,* November 18, 2004, pp. C1, 5.
24. Aaker and Myers, *Advertising Management.*
25. J. Paul Peter and Jerry C. Olson, *Consumer Behavior* (Burr Ridge, IL: Richard D. Irwin, 1987), p. 505.
26. Michael R. Solomon, "The Role of Products as Social Stimuli: A Symbolic Interactionism Perspective," *Journal of Consumer Research,* 10, (December 1983), pp. 319–29.
27. Don. E. Schultz, Stanley I. Tannenbaum, and Robert F. Lauterborn, *Integrated Marketing Communications* (Lincolnwood, IL: NTC Publishing Group 1993), p. 72.
28. Peter and Olson, *Consumer Behavior,* p. 571.
29. Paul W. Farris and David J. Reibstein, "How Prices, Ad Expenditures, and Profits Are Linked," *Harvard Business Review,* (November–December 1979), pp. 172–84.
30. Kerin, Hartley, Berkowitz, and Rudelius, *Marketing.*
31. David W. Stewart, Gary L. Frazier, and Ingrid Martin, "Integrated Channel Management: Merging the Communication and Distribution Functions of the Firm," in *Integrated Communication: Synergy of Persuasive Voices,* pp. 185–215, Esther Thorson & Jeri Moore (eds.), Lawrence Earlbaum Associates, 1996, Mahwah, NJ.

Chapter Three

1. Jack Neff, "P&G Redefines the Brand Manager," *Advertising Age,* October 13, 1997, pp. 1, 18, 20.
2. Thomas J. Cosse and John E. Swan, "Strategic Marketing Planning by Product Managers—Room for Improvement?" *Journal of Marketing* 47 (Summer 1983), pp. 92–102.
3. "Behind the Tumult at P&G," *Fortune,* March 7, 1994, pp. 74–82; "Category Management: New Tools Changing Life for Manufacturers, Retailers," *Marketing News,* September 25, 1989, pp. 2, 19.
4. Timothy Dewhirst and Brad Davis, "Brand Strategy and Integrated Marketing Communications," *Journal of Advertising,* vol. 34, no. 4 (Winter 2005), pp. 81–92.
5. Cosse and Swan, "Strategic Marketing Planning by Product Managers—Room for Improvement?"
6. Victor P. Buell, *Organizing for Marketing/Advertising Success,* New York: Association of National Advertisers, 1982.
7. M. Louise Ripley, "What Kind of Companies Take Their Advertising In-House?" *Journal of Advertising Research,* 31 (4), (October/November 1991), pp. 73–80.
8. Bruce Horovitz, "Some Companies Say the Best Ad Agency Is No Ad Agency at All," *Los Angeles Times,* July 19, 1989, Sec. IV, p. 5.
9. Joan Voight, "The Outsiders," *Adweek,* October 4, 2004, pp. 32–35.
10. Bradley Johnson and Alice Z. Cuneo, "Gateway 2000 Taps DMB&B," *Advertising Age,* March 24, 1997, p. 2.
11. Kate MacArthur, "Chicago Blues," *Advertising Age,* September 10, 2001, pp. 1, 12; Anthony Vagnoni, "Gotham Regains Some Lost Luster as Center of U.S. Agency Creativity," *Advertising Age,* April 12, 1999, pp. 1, 10.
12. Sally Goll Beatty, "Global Needs Challenge Midsize Agencies," *The Wall Street Journal,* December 14, 1995, p. B9.
13. R. Craig Endicott and Kenneth Wylie, "2005 Ad Age Agency Income Report," *adage.com,* May 2, 2005; Kate MacArthur and Laurel Wentz, "The Final 4: Publicis Makes Cut," *Advertising Age,* March 11, 2002, pp. 1, 43; Kathryn Kranhold, "Fallon McElligott to Be Part of Publics," *The Wall Street Journal,* February 3, 2000, p. B5.
14. Gordon Fairclough, "Pace of Ad Mergers Is Expected to Continue,"

The Wall Street Journal, April 23, 1999, p. B2.

15. Suzanne Vranica, "Ad Giant Interpublic Shops for Literacy, Talent Agencies," *The Wall Street Journal,* June 14, 2002, pp. B1, 3.
16. Bob Lammons, "A Good Account Exec Makes a Big Difference," *Marketing News,* June 3, 1996, p. 12.
17. James B. Arndorfer and Jean Halliday, "GM Signals New Marketing Era," *Advertising Age,* May 16, 2005, pp. 1, 2.
18. Anthony Vagnoni, "Small Fries," *Advertising Age,* March 4, 2002, pp. 20, 22.
19. "ANA 2004 Agency Compensation Survey Reveals Continued Client Gravitation To Fee-Based and Performance Incentive Models," Association of National Advertisers, www.ana.net/news/2004/05.
20. Kate MacArthur, "McD's Squeezes Agency Fees," November 11, 2002, *Advertising Age,* pp. 1, 45; Jack Neff, "Feeling the Squeeze," *Advertising Age,* June 4, 2001, pp. 1, 14.
21. "ANA 2004 Agency Compensation Survey Reveals Continued Client Gravitation To Fee-Based and Performance Incentive Models," Association of National Advertisers.
22. Kathryn Kranhold, "P&G Expands Its Program to Tie Agency Pay to Brand Performance," *The Wall Street Journal,* September 16, 1999, p. B12.
23. Jack Neff and Bradley Johnson, "P&G Pushes More Performance Pay," *Advertising Age,* May 10, 2004, pp. 1, 2.
24. Alice Z. Cuneo, "Nissan Ties TBWA's Pay to Car Sales," *Advertising Age,* June 7, 1999, pp. 1, 49; Jean Halliday, "GM to Scrap Agency Commissions," *Advertising Age,* November 16, 1998, pp. 1, 57.
25. Joanne Lipman, "Study Shows Clients Jump Ship Quickly," *The Wall Street Journal,* May 21, 1992, p. B6.
26. Brian Steinberg and Chad Terhune, "PepsiCo Switches Its Ad Account for Diet Pepsi to DDB Worldwide," *The Wall Street Journal,* December 7, 2004, p. B4.
27. Kathleen Sampley, "Love's Labors Lost: Behind the Breakups," *Adweek,* August 1, 2005, p. 8; Fred Beard, "Marketing Client Role Ambiguity as a Source of Dissatisfaction in Client–Ad Agency Relationships," *Journal of Advertising Research,* (September/October 1996), pp. 9–20; Paul Michell, Harold Cataquet, and Stephen Hague, "Establishing the Causes of Disaffection in Agency–Client Relations," *Journal of Advertising Research,* 32, 2, 1992, pp. 41–48; Peter Doyle, Marcel Corstiens, and Paul Michell, "Signals of Vulnerability in Agency–Client Relations," *Journal of Marketing,* 44 (Fall 1980), pp. 18–23; and Daniel B. Wackman, Charles Salmon, and Caryn C. Salmon, "Developing an Advertising Agency–Client Relationship," *Journal of Advertising Research* 26, no. 6 (December 1986/January 1987), pp. 21–29.
28. Suzanne Vranica, "Pinched Firms Woo Rivals' Happy Clients," *The Wall Street Journal,* March 4, 2002, p. B8.
29. Jennifer Comiteau, "What Agencies Think of Search Consultants," *Adweek,* August 4, 2003, pp. 14–16.
30. Fred K. Beard, "Exploring the Use of Advertising Agency Review Consultants," *Journal of Advertising Research,* 42 (1), (January/February), 2002, pp. 39–50.
31. Jack Neff, "Ries' Thesis: Ads Don't Build Brands, PR Does," *Advertising Age,* July 15, 2002, pp. 14–15; Prema Nakra, "The Changing Role of Public Relations in Marketing Communications," *Public Relations Quarterly,* 1 (1991), pp. 42–45.
32. Betsy Spathmann, "Sudden Impact," *Promo,* April 1999, pp. 42–48.
33. Quote in Laura Q. Hughes and Kate MacArthur, "Soft Boiled," *Advertising Age,* May 28, 2001, pp. 3, 54.
34. William N. Swain, "Perceptions of IMC after a Decade of Development: Who's at the Wheel and How Can We Measure Success," *Journal of Advertising Research,* March 2004, pp. 46–67; Philip J. Kitchen and Don E. Schultz, "A Multi-Country Comparison of the Drive for IMC," *Journal of Advertising Research,* January/February 1999, pp. 21–38.
35. David N. McArthur and Tom Griffin, "A Marketing Management View of Integrated Marketing Communications," *Journal of Advertising Research,* 37, no. 5 (September/October) 1997, pp. 19–26; and Adrienne Ward Fawcett, "Integrated Marketing—Marketers Convinced: Its Time Has Arrived," *Advertising Age,* November 6, 1993, pp. S1–2.
36. Claire Atkinson, "Tracking the Challenges of Integrated Marketing," *Television Weekly,* March 17, 2003, vol. 22, p. 11.

Chapter Four

1. Russell W. Belk, "Possessions and the Extended Self," *Journal of Consumer Research,* 15 (2) (September 1988), pp. 139–68.
2. Roger A. Kerin, Steven W. Hartley, Eric N. Berkowitz and William Rudelius, *Marketing,* 8th ed. (Burr Ridge, IL: Irwin/McGraw-Hill, 2006).
3. A. H. Maslow, "'Higher' and 'Lower' Needs," *Journal of Psychology* 25, (1948), pp. 433–36.
4. Morton Deutsch and Robert M. Krauss, *Theories in Social Psychology* (New York: Basic Books, 1965).
5. Dirk Zeims, "The Morphological Approach for Unconscious Consumer Motivation Research," *Journal of Advertising Research,* 44 (2), June 2004, pp. 210–215.
6. Jeffrey Ball, "But How Does It Make You Feel?" *The Wall Street Journal,* May 3, 1999, p. B1.
7. Jagdish N. Sheth, "The Role of Motivation Research in Consumer Psychology" (Faculty Working Paper, University of Illinois, Champaign: 1974); Bill Abrams, "Charles of the Ritz Discovers What Women Want," *The Wall Street Journal,* August 20, 1981, p. 29; and Ernest Dichter, *Getting Motivated* (New York: Pergamon Press, 1979).
8. Ronald Alsop, "Advertisers Put Consumers on the Couch," *The Wall Street Journal,* May 13, 1988, p. 19.
9. Ball, "But How Does It Make You Feel?"
10. For an excellent discussion of memory and consumer behavior, see James R. Betman, "Factors in Consumer Choice: A Review," *Journal of Marketing* 43 (2), (Spring 1979), pp. 37–53.
11. Gilbert Harrell, *Consumer Behavior* (San Diego: Harcourt Brace Jovanovich, 1986), p. 66.
12. Robert Lee Hotz, "Searching for the Why of Buy," *Los Angeles Times,* February 27, 2005, pp. 1, 26–27
13. J. Paul Peter and Jerry C. Olson, *Consumer Behavior,* 2nd ed. (Burr Ridge, IL: Irwin/McGraw-Hill, 1990), p. 73.
14. Gordon W. Allport, "Attitudes," in *Handbook of Social Psychology,* ed. C. M. Murchison (Winchester, MA: Clark University Press, 1935), p. 810.
15. Robert B. Zajonc and Hazel Markus, "Affective and Cognitive Factors in Preferences," *Journal of Consumer Research,* 9 (2) (June 1982), pp. 123–31.
16. Alvin Achenbaum, "Advertising Doesn't Manipulate Consumers," *Journal of Advertising Research,* (April 1970), pp. 3–13.

17. William D. Wells, "Attitudes and Behavior: Lessons from the Needham Lifestyle Study," *Journal of Advertising Research,* (February–March 1985), pp. 40–44; and Icek Ajzen and Martin Fishbein, "Attitude-Behavior Relations: A Theoretical Analysis and Review of Empirical Research," *Psychological Bulletin,* (September 1977), pp. 888–918.
18. For a review of multiattribute models, see William L. Wilkie and Edgar A. Pessemier, "Issues in Marketing's Use of Multiattribute Models," *Journal of Marketing Research,* 20 (November 1983), pp. 428–41.
19. Joel B. Cohen, Paul W. Minniard, and Peter R. Dickson, "Information Integration: An Information Processing Perspective," in *Advances in Consumer Research,* vol. 7, ed. Jerry C. Olson (Ann Arbor, MI: Association for Consumer Research, 1980), pp. 161–70.
20. Peter and Olson, *Consumer Behavior,* p. 182.
21. Peter L. Wright and Fredric Barbour, "The Relevance of Decision Process Models in Structuring Persuasive Messages," *Communications Research,* July 1975, pp. 246–59.
22. James F. Engel, "The Psychological Consequences of a Major Purchase Decision," in *Marketing in Transition,* (ed.) William S. Decker (Chicago: American Marketing Association, 1963), pp. 462–75.
23. John A. Howard and Jagdish N. Sheth, *The Theory of Consumer Behavior* (New York: John Wiley & Sons, 1969).
24. Leon G. Schiffman and Leslie Lazar Kannuk, *Consumer Behavior,* 4th ed. (Englewood Cliffs, NJ: Prentice Hall, 1991), p. 192.
25. Ivan. P. Pavlov, *Conditioned Reflexes: An Investigation of the Physiological Activity of the Cerebral Cortex,* G. V. Anrep (trans. ed.) (London: The Oxford Press, 1927).
26. Gerald J. Gorn, "The Effects of Music in Advertising on Choice: A Classical Conditioning Approach," *Journal of Marketing* 46 (Winter 1982), pp. 94–101.
27. James J. Kellaris, Anthony D. Cox, and Dena Cox, "The Effect of Background Music on Ad Processing: A Contingency Explanation," *Journal of Marketing,* vol. 57, (4) (Fall 1993), p. 114.
28. Brian C. Deslauries and Peter B. Everett, "The Effects of Intermittent and Continuous Token Reinforcement on Bus Ridership," *Journal of Applied Psychology,* 62 (August 1977), pp. 369–75.
29. Michael L. Rothschild and William C. Gaidis, "Behavioral Learning Theory: Its Relevance to Marketing and Promotions," *Journal of Marketing Research* 45, (2) (Spring 1981), pp. 70–78.
30. For an excellent discussion of social class and consumer behavior, see Richard P. Coleman, "The Continuing Significance of Social Class to Marketing," *Journal of Consumer Research* 10, (3) (December 1983), pp. 265–80.
31. Lyman E. Ostlund, "Role Theory and Group Dynamics," in *Consumer Behavior: Theoretical Sources,* ed. Scott Ward and Thomas S. Robertson (Englewood Cliffs, NJ: Prentice Hall, 1973), pp. 230–75.
32. James Stafford and Benton Cocanougher, "Reference Group Theory," in *Perspectives in Consumer Behavior,* (ed.) H. H. Kassarjian and T. S. Robertson (Glenview, IL: Scott, Foresman, 1981), pp. 329–43.
33. Jagdish N. Sheth, "A Theory of Family Buying Decisions," in *Models of Buying Behavior,* (ed.) Jagdish N. Sheth (New York: Harper & Row, 1974), pp. 17–33.
34. Russell Belk, "Situational Variables and Consumer Behavior," *Journal of Consumer Research,* (December 1975), pp. 157–64.

Chapter Five

1. Wilbur Schram, *The Process and Effects of Mass Communications* (Urbana: University of Illinois Press, 1955).
2. Ibid.
3. Joseph Ransdell, "Some Leading Ideas of Peirce's Semiotic," *Semiotica* 19 (1977), pp. 157–78.
4. Michael Solomon, *Consumer Behavior,* 6th ed. (Upper Saddle River, NJ: Pearson Prentice-Hall, 2004), pp. 73–74.
5. Nina Munk, "Levi's Ongoing Quest for Street Cred," *Fortune,* February 1, 1999, p. 40.
6. For an excellent article on the application of semiotics to consumer behavior and advertising, see David G. Mick, "Consumer Research and Semiotics: Exploring the Morphology of Signs, Symbols, and Significance," *Journal of Consumer Research* 13, no. 2 (September 1986), pp. 196–213; see also Edward F. McQuarrie and David Glen Mick, "Figures of Rhetoric in Advertising Language," *Journal of Consumer Research* 22 (4) (March 1996), pp. 424–38.
7. Robert E. Smith and Christine A. Vogt, "The Effects of Integrating Advertising and Negative Word-of-Mouth Communications on Message Processing and Response," *Journal of Consumer Psychology,* 4, no. 2 (1995), pp. 133–51; Barry L. Bayus, "Word of Mouth: The Indirect Effect of Marketing Efforts," *Journal of Advertising Research,* 25 (3) (June/July 1985), pp. 31–39; Catharine P. Taylor, "Pssst! How Do You Measure Buzz?" *Adweek,* October 24, 2005, pp. 26–28.
8. Larry Yu, "How Companies Turn Buzz Into Sales," *MIT Sloan Management Review,* (Winter 2005), pp. 5–6.
9. Quote by Gordon S. Bower in *Fortune,* October 14, 1985, p. 11.
10. Thomas V. Bonoma and Leonard C. Felder, "Nonverbal Communication in Marketing: Toward Communicational Analysis," *Journal of Marketing Research,* (May 1977), pp. 169–80.
11. Jacob Jacoby and Wayne D. Hoyer, "Viewer Miscomprehension of Televised Communication: Selected Findings," *Journal of Marketing,* 46 (4), (Fall 1982), pp. 12–26; Jacoby and Hoyer, "The Comprehension and Miscomprehension of Print Communications: An Investigation of Mass Media Magazines," *Advertising Education Foundation Study,* New York, 1987.
12. E. K. Strong, *The Psychology of Selling* (New York: McGraw-Hill, 1925), p. 9.
13. Robert J. Lavidge and Gary A. Steiner, "A Model for Predictive Measurements of Advertising Effectiveness," *Journal of Marketing* 24, (October 1961), pp. 59–62.
14. Everett M. Rogers, *Diffusion of Innovations* (New York: Free Press, 1962), pp. 79–86.
15. William J. McGuire, "An Information Processing Model of Advertising Effectiveness," in *Behavioral and Management Science in Marketing,* ed. Harry J. Davis and Alvin J. Silk (New York: Ronald Press, 1978), pp. 156–80.
16. Michael L. Ray, "Communication and the Hierarchy of Effects," in *New Models for Mass Communication Research,* ed. P. Clarke (Beverly Hills, CA: Sage, 1973), pp. 147–75.
17. Herbert E. Krugman, "The Impact of Television Advertising: Learning without Involvement," *Public Opinion Quarterly* 29 (Fall 1965), pp. 349–56.

18. Scott A. Hawkins and Stephen J. Hoch, "Low-Involvement Learning: Memory without Evaluation," *Journal of Consumer Research* 19, no. 2 (September 1992), pp. 212–25.
19. Harry W. McMahan, "Do Your Ads Have VIP?" *Advertising Age,* July 14, 1980, pp. 50–51.
20. Robert E. Smith, "Integrating Information from Advertising and Trial: Processes and Effects on Consumer Response to Product Information," *Journal of Marketing Research* 30 (May 1993), pp. 204–19.
21. DeAnna S. Kempf and Russell N. Laczniak, "Advertising's Influence on Subsequent Product Trial Processing," *Journal of Advertising,* vol. 30, no. 3, Fall 2001, pp. 27–38.
22. Harold H. Kassarjian, "Low Involvement: A Second Look," *Advances in Consumer Research,* vol. 8 (Ann Arbor: Association for Consumer Research, 1981), pp. 31–34; also see Anthony G. Greenwald and Clark Leavitt, "Audience Involvement in Advertising: Four Levels," *Journal of Consumer Research* 11, no. 1 (June 1984), pp. 581–92.
23. Judith L. Zaichkowsky, "Conceptualizing Involvement," *Journal of Advertising* 15, no. 2 (1986), pp. 4–14.
24. Richard Vaughn, "How Advertising Works: A Planning Model," *Journal of Advertising Research* 20, no. 5 (October 1980), pp. 27–33.
25. Richard Vaughn, "How Advertising Works: A Planning Model Revisited," *Journal of Advertising Research* 26, no. 1 (February/March 1986), pp. 57–66.
26. Jerry C. Olson, Daniel R. Toy, and Phillip A. Dover, "Mediating Effects of Cognitive Responses to Advertising on Cognitive Structure," in *Advances in Consumer Research,* vol. 5, ed. H. Keith Hunt (Ann Arbor, MI: Association for Consumer Research, 1978), pp. 72–78.
27. Anthony A. Greenwald, "Cognitive Learning, Cognitive Response to Persuasion and Attitude Change," in *Psychological Foundations of Attitudes,* ed. A. G. Greenwald, T. C. Brock, and T. W. Ostrom (New York: Academic Press, 1968); Peter L. Wright, "The Cognitive Processes Mediating Acceptance of Advertising," *Journal of Marketing Research* 10 (February 1973), pp. 53–62; Brian Wansink, Michael L. Ray, and Rajeev Batra, "Increasing Cognitive Response Sensitivity," *Journal of Advertising* 23, no. 2 (June 1994), pp. 65–76.
28. Peter Wright, "Message Evoked Thoughts, Persuasion Research Using Thought Verbalizations," *Journal of Consumer Research* 7, no. 2 (September 1980), pp. 151–75.
29. Scott B. Mackenzie, Richard J. Lutz, and George E. Belch, "The Role of Attitude toward the Ad as a Mediator of Advertising Effectiveness: A Test of Competing Explanations," *Journal of Marketing Research* 23 (May 1986), pp. 130–43; and Rajeev Batra and Michael L. Ray, "Affective Responses Mediating Acceptance of Advertising," *Journal of Consumer Research* 13 (September 1986), pp. 234–49; Tim Ambler and Tom Burne, "The Impact of Affect on Memory of Advertising," *Journal of Advertising Research* 29, no. 3 (March/April 1999), pp. 25–34.
30. Ronald Alsop, "TV Ads That Are Likeable Get Plus Rating for Persuasiveness," *The Wall Street Journal,* February 20, 1986, p. 23.
31. David J. Moore and William D. Harris, "Affect Intensity and the Consumer's Attitude toward High Impact Emotional Advertising Appeals," *Journal of Advertising* 25, no. 2 (Summer 1996), pp. 37–50; Andrew A. Mitchell and Jerry C. Olson, "Are Product Attribute Beliefs the Only Mediator of Advertising Effects on Brand Attitude?" *Journal of Marketing Research* 18 (August 1981), pp. 318–32.
32. David J. Moore, William D. Harris, and Hong C. Chen, "Affect Intensity: An Individual Difference Response to Advertising Appeals," *Journal of Consumer Research* 22 (September 1995), pp. 154–64; Julie Edell and Marian C. Burke, "The Power of Feelings in Understanding Advertising Effects," *Journal of Consumer Research* 14 (December 1987), pp. 421–33.
33. Richard E. Petty and John T. Cacioppo, "Central and Peripheral Routes to Persuasion: Application to Advertising," in *Advertising and Consumer Psychology,* ed. Larry Percy and Arch Woodside (Lexington, MA: Lexington Books, 1983), pp. 3–23.
34. Richard E. Petty, John T. Cacioppo, and David Schumann, "Central and Peripheral Routes to Advertising Effectiveness: The Moderating Role of Involvement," *Journal of Consumer Research* 10 (September 1983), pp. 135–46.
35. Demetrios Vakratsas and Tim Ambler, "How Advertising Works: What Do We Really Know?" *Journal of Marketing* 63 (January 1999), pp. 26–43.
36. Bruce F. Hall, "A New Model for Measuring Advertising Effects," *Journal of Advertising Research,* vol. 42, no. 2, (March/April 2002), pp. 23–31.
37. Thomas E. Barry, "In Defense of the Hierarchy of Effects: A Rejoinder to Weilbacher," *Journal of Advertising Research,* (May/June 2002), pp. 44–47.
38. William M. Weilbacher, "Point of View: Does Advertising Cause a 'Hierarchy of Effects'?" *Journal of Advertising Research,* 41, (6) (November/December 2001), pp. 19–26.

Chapter Six

1. William J. McGuire, "An Information Processing Model of Advertising Effectiveness," in *Behavioral and Management Science in Marketing,* ed. Harry J. Davis and Alvin J. Silk (New York: Ronald Press, 1978), pp. 156–80.
2. Garry Khermouch and Jeff Green, "Buzz Marketing," *BusinessWeek,* July 30, 2001, pp. 50–56; Daniel Eisenberg, "It's an Ad, Ad, Ad World," *Time,* September 2, 2002, pp. 38–41.
3. Herbert C. Kelman, "Processes of Opinion Change," *Public Opinion Quarterly* 25 (Spring 1961), pp. 57–78.
4. William J. McGuire, "The Nature of Attitudes and Attitude Change," in *Handbook of Social Psychology,* 2nd ed., ed. G. Lindzey and E. Aronson (Cambridge, MA: Addison-Wesley, 1969), pp. 135–214; Daniel J. O'Keefe, "The Persuasive Effects of Delaying Identification of High- and Low-Credibility Communicators: A Meta-Analytic Review," *Central States Speech Journal* 38 (1987), pp. 63–72.
5. Rebecca Ohanian, "The Impact of Celebrity Spokespersons' Image on Consumers' Intention to Purchase," *Journal of Advertising Research,* 21 (1) (February/March 1991), pp. 46–54.
6. David P. Hamilton, "Celebrities Help 'Educate' Public on New Drugs," *The Wall Street Journal,* April 22, 2002, p. B1.
7. James Bandler, "How Companies Pay TV Experts For On-Air Product Mentions," *The Wall Street Journal,* April 19, 2005, pp. A1, 12.
8. Karen Benezra and Jennifer Gilbert, "The CEO as Brand," *Chief Executive* www.chiefexecutive.net, vol. 174, January 2002.
9. "Business Celebrities," *BusinessWeek,* June 23, 1986, pp. 100–07.
10. Bruce Horovitz and Theresa Howard, "Wendy's Loses Its Legend," *USA TODAY,* January 9, 2002, pp. 1, 2B.

11. Frank Green, "Masters of the Pitch," *The San Diego Union-Tribune,*" January 30, 2000, pp. 1, 6.
12. Kate MacArthur, "Wendy's Set to Unveil New Brand Spokesperson," *www.adage.com,* February 18, 2004.
13. Erick Reidenback and Robert Pitts, "Not All CEOs Are Created Equal as Advertising Spokespersons: Evaluating the Effective CEO Spokesperson," *Journal of Advertising* 20, no. 3 (1986), pp. 35–50; Roger Kerin and Thomas E. Barry, "The CEO Spokesperson in Consumer Advertising: An Experimental Investigation," in *Current Issues in Research in Advertising,* ed. J. H. Leigh and C. R. Martin (Ann Arbor: University of Michigan, 1981), pp. 135–48; and J. Poindexter, "Voices of Authority," *Psychology Today,* August 1983.
14. Frank Green, "Masters of the Pitch."
15. A. Eagly and S. Chaiken, "An Attribution Analysis of the Effect of Communicator Characteristics on Opinion Change," *Journal of Personality and Social Psychology* 32 (1975), pp. 136–44.
16. For a review of these studies, see Brian Sternthal, Lynn Philips, and Ruby Dholakia, "The Persuasive Effect of Source Credibility: A Situational Analysis," *Public Opinion Quarterly* 42 (Fall 1978), pp. 285–314.
17. Brian Sternthal, Ruby Dholakia, and Clark Leavitt, "The Persuasive Effects of Source Credibility: Tests of Cognitive Response," *Journal of Consumer Research* 4, no. 4 (March 1978), pp. 252–60; and Robert R. Harmon and Kenneth A. Coney, "The Persuasive Effects of Source Credibility in Buy and Lease Situations," *Journal of Marketing Research* 19 (May 1982), pp. 255–60.
18. For a review, see Noel Capon and James Hulbert, "The Sleeper Effect: An Awakening," *Public Opinion Quarterly* 37 (1973), pp. 333–58.
19. Darlene B. Hannah and Brian Sternthal, "Detecting and Explaining the Sleeper Effect," *Journal of Consumer Research* 11, (2) (September 1984), pp. 632–42.
20. H. C. Triandis, *Attitudes and Attitude Change* (New York: Wiley, 1971).
21. J. Mills and J. Jellison, "Effect on Opinion Change Similarity between the Communicator and the Audience He Addresses," *Journal of Personality and Social Psychology* 9, no. 2 (1969), pp. 153–56.
22. Arch G. Woodside and J. William Davenport, Jr., "The Effect of Salesman Similarity and Expertise on Consumer Purchasing Behavior," *Journal of Marketing Research* 11 (May 1974), pp. 198–202; and Paul Busch and David T. Wilson, "An Experimental Analysis of a Salesman's Expert and Referent Bases of Social Power in the Buyer-Seller Dyad," *Journal of Marketing Research* 13 (February 1976), pp. 3–11.
23. Rich Thomaselli, "Searching for Michael Jordan," *Advertising Age,* September 5, 2005, p. 12.
24. Jason Stein "Inside Chrysler's Celine Dion Advertising Disaster," www.adage.com, November 24, 2003.
25. Valerie Folkes, "Recent Attribution Research in Consumer Behavior: A Review and New Directions," *Journal of Consumer Research* 14 (March 1988), pp. 548–65; John C. Mowen and Stephen W. Brown, "On Explaining and Predicting the Effectiveness of Celebrity Endorsers," in *Advances in Consumer Research,* vol. 8 (Ann Arbor, MI: Association for Consumer Research, 1981), pp. 437–41.
26. Bruce Horovitz, "Armstrong Rolls to Market Gold," *USA TODAY,* May 4, 2000, pp. 1, 2B.
27. Stephen Rae, "How Celebrities Make Killings on Commercials," *Cosmopolitan,* January 1997, pp. 164–67.
28. Chad Terhune and Brian Steinberg, "Coca-Cola Signs NBA Wunderkind," *The Wall Street Journal,* August 22, 2003, p. B5.
29. James Tenser, "Endorser Qualities Count More Than Ever," *Advertising Age,* November 8, 2004, pp. S2, 4.
30. Charles Atkin and M. Block, "Effectiveness of Celebrity Endorsers," *Journal of Advertising Research* 23, (1) (February/March 1983), pp. 57–61.
31. Ellen Neuborne, "Generation Y," *BusinessWeek,* February 15, 1999, pp. 81–88.
32. Joe Pereira, "New Balance Sneaker Ads Jab at Pro Athletes' Pretensions," *The Wall Street Journal,* March 10, 2005, p. B1.
33. Brian D. Till and Terence A. Shimp, "Endorsers in Advertising: The Case of Negative Celebrity Information," *Journal of Advertising,* 27, no. 1, Spring 1998, pp. 67–82.
34. Rich Thomaselli, "Kobe Kept on the Marketing Bench," *Advertising Age,* September 13, 2004, p. 16.
35. Stephanie Thompson, "Heroin Chic Ok, Cocaine Use Not," *Advertising Age,* September 26, 2005, pp. 3, 80.
36. James Tenser, "Endorser Qualities Count More Than Ever."
37. Betsy Cummings, "Star Power," *Sales and Marketing Management,* April 2001, pp. 52–59; Michael A. Kamins, "An Investigation into the 'Match-Up' Hypothesis in Celebrity Advertising," *Journal of Advertising* 19, no. 1 (1990), pp. 4–13.
38. Grant McCracken, "Who Is the Celebrity Endorser? Cultural Foundations of the Endorsement Process," *Journal of Consumer Research* 16, no. 3 (December 1989), pp. 310–21.
39. Ibid., p. 315.
40. B. Zafer Erdogan, Michael J. Baker and Stephen Tagg, "Selecting Celebrity Endorsers: The Practitioner's Perspective," *Journal of Advertising Research,* vol. 41, no. 43 (May/June 2001), pp. 39–48.
41. Kristina Saurwein, "Finding the Right Pitch," *Los Angeles Times,* July 20, 2002, p. B3.
42. For an excellent review of these studies, see Marilyn Y. Jones, Andrea J. S. Stanaland, and Betsy D. Gelb, "Beefcake and Cheesecake: Insights for Advertisers," *Journal of Advertising* 27, no. 2 (Summer 1998), pp. 32–51; and W. B. Joseph, "The Credibility of Physically Attractive Communicators," *Journal of Advertising* 11, no. 3 (1982), pp. 13–23.
43. Michael Solomon, Richard Ashmore, and Laura Longo, "The Beauty Match-Up Hypothesis: Congruence between Types of Beauty and Product Images in Advertising," *Journal of Advertising* 21, no. 4, pp. 23–34; M. J. Baker and Gilbert A. Churchill, Jr., "The Impact of Physically Attractive Models on Advertising Evaluations," *Journal of Marketing Research* 14 (November 1977), pp. 538–55.
44. Robert W. Chestnut, C. C. La Chance, and A. Lubitz, "The Decorative Female Model: Sexual Stimuli and the Recognition of the Advertisements," *Journal of Advertising* 6 (Fall 1977), pp. 11–14; and Leonard N. Reid and Lawrence C. Soley, "Decorative Models and Readership of Magazine Ads," *Journal of Advertising Research* 23, no. 2 (April/May 1983), pp. 27–32.
45. Amanda B. Bower, "Highly Attractive Models in Advertising and the Women Who Loathe Them: The Implications of Negative Affect for Spokesperson Effectiveness," *Journal of Advertising,* vol. 30, no. 3, (Fall 2001), pp. 51–63; Amanda B. Bower

and Stacy Landreth, "Is Beauty Best? Highly Versus Normally Attractive Models in Advertising," *Journal of Advertising,* vol. 30, no. 1, pp. 1–12.
46. Jack Neff, "In Dove Ads, Normal Is the New Beautiful," *Advertising Age,* September 27, 2004, pp. 1, 80.
47. Michelle Jeffers, "Behind Dove's 'Real Beauty,'" *Adweek,* September 12, 2005, pp. 34–35.
48. Herbert E. Krugman, "On Application of Learning Theory to TV Copy Testing," *Public Opinion Quarterly* 26 (1962), pp. 626–39.
49. C. I. Hovland and W. Mandell, "An Experimental Comparison of Conclusion Drawing by the Communicator and by the Audience," *Journal of Abnormal and Social Psychology* 47 (July 1952), pp. 581–88.
50. Alan G. Sawyer and Daniel J. Howard, "Effect of Omitting Conclusions in Advertisements to Involved and Uninvolved Audiences," *Journal of Marketing Research,* 28 (November 1991), pp. 467–74.
51. Paul Chance, "Ads without Answers Make Brain Itch," *Psychology Today* 9 (1975), p. 78.
52. Connie Pechmann, "Predicting When Two-Sided Ads Will Be More Effective Than One-Sided Ads," *Journal of Marketing Research,* 24 (November 1992), pp. 441–453; George E. Belch, "The Effects of Message Modality on One- and Two-Sided Advertising Messages," in *Advances in Consumer Research,* vol. 10, ed. Richard P. Bagozzi and Alice M. Tybout (Ann Arbor, MI: Association for Consumer Research, 1983), pp. 21–26.
53. Robert E. Settle and Linda L. Golden, "Attribution Theory and Advertiser Credibility," *Journal of Marketing Research* 11 (May 1974), pp. 181–85; and Edmund J. Faison, "Effectiveness of One-Sided and Two-Sided Mass Communications in Advertising," *Public Opinion Quarterly* 25 (Fall 1961), pp. 468–69.
54. Joel A. Baglole, "Cough Syrup Touts 'Awful Taste' in U.S.," *The Wall Street Journal,* December 15, 1999, p. B10.
55. Alan G. Sawyer, "The Effects of Repetition of Refutational and Supportive Advertising Appeals," *Journal of Marketing Research* 10 (February 1973), pp. 23–37; and George J. Szybillo and Richard Heslin, "Resistance to Persuasion: Inoculation Theory in a Marketing Context," *Journal of Marketing Research* 10 (November 1973), pp. 396–403.
56. Andrew A. Mitchell, "The Effect of Verbal and Visual Components of Advertisements on Brand Attitudes and Attitude toward the Advertisement," *Journal of Consumer Research* 13 (June 1986), pp. 12–24; and Julie A. Edell and Richard Staelin, "The Information Processing of Pictures in Advertisements," *Journal of Consumer Research* 10, no. 1 (June 1983), pp. 45–60; Elizabeth C. Hirschmann, "The Effects of Verbal and Pictorial Advertising Stimuli on Aesthetic, Utilitarian and Familiarity Perceptions," *Journal of Advertising* 15, no. 2 (1986), pp. 27–34.
57. Jolita Kisielius and Brian Sternthal, "Detecting and Explaining Vividness Effects in Attitudinal Judgments," *Journal of Marketing Research* 21, (1) (1984), pp. 54–64.
58. H. Rao Unnava and Robert E. Burnkrant, "An Imagery-Processing View of the Role of Pictures in Print Advertisements," *Journal of Marketing Research* 28 (May 1991), pp. 226–31.
59. Susan E. Heckler and Terry L. Childers, "The Role of Expectancy and Relevancy in Memory for Verbal and Visual Information: What Is Incongruency?" *Journal of Consumer Research* 18, no. 4 (March 1992), pp. 475–92.
60. Michael J. Houston, Terry L. Childers, and Susan E. Heckler, "Picture-Word Consistency and the Elaborative Processing of Advertisements," *Journal of Marketing Research,* 24 (November 1987), pp. 359–69.
61. William L. Wilkie and Paul W. Farris, "Comparative Advertising: Problems and Potential," *Journal of Marketing* 39 (1975), pp. 7–15.
62. For a review of comparative advertising studies, see Cornelia Pechmann and David W. Stewart, "The Psychology of Comparative Advertising," in *Attention, Attitude and Affect in Response to Advertising,* ed. E. M. Clark, T. C. Brock, and D. W. Stewart (Hillsdale, NJ: Lawrence Erlbaum, 1994), pp. 79–96; and Thomas S. Barry, "Comparative Advertising: What Have We Learned in Two Decades?" *Journal of Advertising Research,* (33), no. 2 (1993), pp. 19–29.
63. Patrick Meirick, "Cognitive Responses to Negative and Comparative Political Advertising," *Journal of Advertising,* vol. 31, no. 1, (Spring 2002), pp. 49–59.
64. Bruce E. Pinkleton, Nam-Hyun Um, and Erica Weintraub Austin, "An Exploration of the Effects of Negative Political Advertising on Political Decision Making," *Journal of Advertising,* 31, (1), (Spring 2002), pp. 13–25.
65. Bruce E. Pinkleton, "The Effects of Negative Comparative Political Advertising on Candidate Evaluations and Advertising Evaluations: An Exploration," *Journal of Advertising,* vol. 26, no. 1, (1997), pp. 19–29.
66. Michael L. Ray and William L. Wilkie, "Fear: The Potential of an Appeal Neglected by Marketing," *Journal of Marketing* 34 (January 1970), pp. 54–62.
67. Brian Sternthal and C. Samuel Craig, "Fear Appeals Revisited and Revised," *Journal of Consumer Research* 1 (December 1974), pp. 22–34.
68. Punam Anand Keller and Lauren Goldberg Block, "Increasing the Persuasiveness of Fear Appeals: The Effect of Arousal and Elaboration," *Journal of Consumer Research* 22, no. 4 (March 1996), pp. 448–60.
69. John F. Tanner, Jr., James B. Hunt, and David R. Eppright, "The Protection Motivation Model: A Normative Mode of Fear Appeals," *Journal of Marketing* 55 (July 1991), pp. 36–45.
70. Ibid.
71. Sternthal and Craig, "Fear Appeals Revisited and Revised."
72. Herbert Jack Rotfeld, "The Textbook Effect: Conventional Wisdom, Myth and Error in Marketing," *Journal of Marketing* 64 (April 2000), pp. 122–27.
73. For a discussion of the use of humor in advertising, see C. Samuel Craig and Brian Sternthal, "Humor in Advertising," *Journal of Marketing* 37 (October 1973), pp. 12–18.
74. Bobby J. Calder and Brian Sternthal, "A Television Commercial Wearout: An Information Processing View," *Journal of Marketing Research* 17 (May 1980), pp. 173–87.
75. Dottie Enroco, "Humorous Touch Resonates with Consumers," *USA TODAY,* May 13, 1996, p. 3B.
76. Yong Zhang, "Response to Humorous Advertising: The Moderating Effect of Need for Cognition," *Journal of Advertising* 25, no. 1 (Spring 1996), pp. 15–32; Marc G. Weinberger and Charles S. Gulas, "The Impact of Humor in Advertising: A Review," *Journal of Advertising* 21 (December 1992), pp. 35–59.
77. Marc G. Weinberger and Leland Campbell, "The Use of Humor in Radio Advertising," *Journal of*

Advertising Research 31 (December/January 1990–91), pp. 44–52.

78. Thomas J. Madden and Marc G. Weinberger, "Humor in Advertising: A Practitioner View," *Journal of Advertising Research* 24, no. 4 (August/September 1984), pp. 23–26.
79. Harold C. Cash and W. J. E. Crissy, "Comparison of Advertising and Selling: The Salesman's Role in Marketing," *Psychology of Selling,* 12 (1965), pp. 56–75.
80. Marshall McLuhan, *Understanding Media: The Extensions of Man* (New York: McGraw-Hill, 1966).
81. Marvin E. Goldberg and Gerald J. Gorn, "Happy and Sad TV Programs: How They Affect Reactions to Commercials," *Journal of Consumer Research,* 14, no. 3 (December 1987), pp. 387–403.
82. Andrew B. Aylesworth and Scott B. MacKenzie, "Context Is Key: The Effect of Program-Induced Mood on Thoughts About the Ad," *Journal of Advertising,* 27, no. 2 (Summer 1998), pp. 17–32.
83. Michael T. Elliott and Paul Surgi Speck, "Consumer Perceptions of Advertising Clutter and Its Impact across Various Media," *Journal of Advertising Research,* 38, (1) (January/February 1998), pp. 29–41; and Peter H. Webb, "Consumer Initial Processing in a Difficult Media Environment," *Journal of Consumer Research,* 6, (3) (December 1979), pp. 225–36.
84. "Record Amount of Advertising Clutter in Primetime TV," *PR Newswire,* December 15, 2003, p. 1.
85. Claire Atkinson, "Which Nets Are Kings of Clutter," *Advertising Age,* June 7, 2004, p. 53.
86. Steve McClellan, "Buyers, New Try to Skirt Clutter With Sponsor Deals," *Adweek,* October 31, 2005, p. 9.

Chapter Seven

1. Robert A. Kriegel, "How to Choose the Right Communications Objectives," *Business Marketing,* April 1986, pp. 94–106.
2. Deborah Ball, "P&G-Gillette Pushes Rivals," *The Wall Street Journal,* January 31, 2005, p. C1; Jack Neff, "P&G, Colgate Step Up Oral-Care Fight," *Advertising Age,* November 1, 2004, p. 10; Patricia Van Arnum, "Whitening Products Help to Drive Growth in Oral Care," *Chemical Market Reporter,* May 10, 2004, pp. FR10–11.
3. Laura Q. Hughes, "Measuring Up," *Advertising Age,* February 5, 2001, pp. 1, 34.
4. Debbie Howell, "Ready-To-Eat Cereal Sales Remain Soggy," *DSN Retailing Today,* January 24, 2005, p. F6.
5. Stephanie Thompson, "Kellogg Retakes Lead," *Advertising Age,* May 13, 2002, pp. 3, 73; Debbie Howell, "Cereal Selling in Need of New Promos," *DSN Retailing Today,* May 20, 2002, p. S9.
6. Stephanie Thompson, "Kellogg Roars Back with Out of Box Ads," *Advertising Age,* May 3, 2004, pp. 4–5.
7. Donald S. Tull, "The Carry-Over Effect of Advertising," *Journal of Marketing,* (April 1965), pp. 46–53.
8. Darral G. Clarke, "Econometric Measurement of the Duration of Advertising Effect on Sales," *Journal of Marketing Research,* 23 (November 1976), pp. 345–57.
9. Philip Kotler, *Marketing Decision Making: A Model Building Approach* (New York: Holt, Rinehart & Winston, 1971), Ch. 5.
10. John Gaffney, "Sweet Spot Awards," *Business 2.0,* May 2002, pp. 97–99.
11. Herb Shuldiner, "New Mini Ragtop a Big Deal," *Ward's Dealer Business,* October 2004, p. 9.
12. For a more detailed discussion of this, see William M. Weilbacher, *Advertising,* 2nd ed. (New York: Macmillan, 1984), p. 112.
13. Stephanie Thompson, "Kellogg Roars Back with Out of Box Ads."
14. Courtland I. Bovee and William F. Arens, *Advertising,* 3rd ed. (Burr Ridge, IL: Richard D. Irwin, 1989).
15. Bob Francis, "Color My World, Boise," *Brandweek,* March 18, 2002, p. R17.
16. Russell H. Colley, *Defining Advertising Goals for Measured Advertising Results* (New York: Association of National Advertisers, 1961).
17. Ibid., p. 21.
18. Don E. Schultz, Dennis Martin, and William Brown, *Strategic Advertising Campaigns,* 2nd ed. (Lincolnwood, IL: Crain Books, 1984).
19. Howard Sherman, "Positioning a Brand for Long Term Growth," in *A Celebration of Effective Advertising: 30 Years of Winning EFFIE Awards,* American Marketing Association, 1998, pp. 54–57; Andy Wood, "Campaign of the Week: Foster's Ice," *Marketing,* February 13, 1997, p. 12.
20. Michael L. Ray, "Consumer Initial Processing: Definitions, Issues, Applications," in *Buyer/Consumer Information Processing,* (ed.) G. David Hughes (Chapel Hill: University of North Carolina Press, 1974); David A. Aaker and John G. Myers, *Advertising Management,* 2nd ed. (Englewood Cliffs, NJ: Prentice Hall, 1982), pp. 122–23.
21. Sandra Ernst Moriarty, "Beyond the Hierarchy of Effects: A Conceptual Framework," in *Current Issues and Research in Advertising,* ed. Claude R. Martin, Jr., and James H. Leigh (Ann Arbor, MI: University of Michigan, 1983), pp. 45–55.
22. Aaker and Myers, *Advertising Management.*
23. Kristian S. Palda, "The Hypothesis of a Hierarchy of Effects: A Partial Evaluation," *Journal of Marketing Research* 3 (February 1966), pp. 13–24.
24. Stewart H. Britt, "Are So-Called Successful Advertising Campaigns Really Successful?" *Journal of Advertising Research* 9 (2) (1969), pp. 3–9.
25. Steven W. Hartley and Charles H. Patti, "Evaluating Business-to-Business Advertising: A Comparison of Objectives and Results," *Journal of Advertising Research* 28 (April/May 1988), pp. 21–27.
26. Ibid., p. 25.
27. Study cited in Robert F. Lauterborn, "How to Know If Your Advertising Is Working," *Journal of Advertising Research* 25 (February/March 1985), pp. RC 9–11.
28. Don E. Schultz, "Integration Helps You Plan Communications from Outside-In," *Marketing News,* March 15, 1993, p. 12.
29. Thomas R. Duncan, "To Fathom Integrated Marketing, Dive!" *Advertising Age,* October 11, 1993, p. 18.
30. Robert L. Steiner, "The Paradox of Increasing Returns to Advertising," *Journal of Advertising Research,* February/March 1987, pp. 45–53.
31. Frank M. Bass, "A Simultaneous Equation Regression Study of Advertising and Sales of Cigarettes," *Journal of Marketing Research* 6 (3) (August 1969), p. 291.
32. David A. Aaker and James M. Carman, "Are You Overadvertising?" *Journal of Advertising Research* 22 (4) (August/September 1982), pp. 57–70.
33. Julian A. Simon and Johan Arndt, "The Shape of the Advertising Response Function," *Journal of Advertising Research* 20 (4) (1980), pp. 11–28.

34. Paul B. Luchsinger, Vernan S. Mullen, and Paul T. Jannuzzo, "How Many Advertising Dollars Are Enough?" *Media Decisions* 12 (1977), p. 59.
35. Paul W. Farris, "Determinants of Advertising Intensity: A Review of the Marketing Literature," *Report no. 77–109, Marketing Science Institute,* (Cambridge, MA, 1977).
36. Jack Neff, "TV Advertising Doesn't Work for Mature Package Goods," www.AdAge.com, May 24, 2004, pp. 1–3.
37. Melvin E. Salveson, "Management's Criteria for Advertising Effectiveness," in *Proceedings 5th Annual Conference, Advertising Research Foundation,* (New York, 1959), p. 25.
38. Robert Settle and Pamela Alreck, "Positive Moves for Negative Times," *Marketing Communications,* January 1988, pp. 19–23.
39. Boonghee Yoo and Rujirutana Mandhachitara, "Estimating Advertising Effects on Sales in a Competitive Setting," *Journal of Advertising Research,* 43 (3) 2003, pp. 310–320.
40. Dan Lippe, "Media Scorecard: How ROI Adds Up," *Advertising Age,* June 20, 2005, p. S-6; 42.
41. Mike Beirne, Kenneth Hein, "Marketers' Mantra: It's ROI, or I'm Fired!" *Brandweek,* October 18, 2004, pp. 14–15.
42. Joe Mandese, "Half of Media Buys Driven by ROI, TV, Online Dominate," www.mediapost.com, April 20, 2005, pp. 1–3.
43. Wayne Friedman, "ROI Measurement Still Falls Short," *TelevisionWeek,* January 31, 2005, p. 19.
44. Hillary Chura, "Advertising ROI Still Elusive Metric," *Advertising Age,* July 26, 2004, p. 8.
45. James O. Peckham, "Can We Relate Advertising Dollars to Market Share Objectives?" in *How Much to Spend for Advertising,* ed. M. A. McNiven (New York: Association of National Advertisers, 1969), p. 30.
46. George S. Low and Jakki Mohr, "Setting Advertising and Promotion Budgets in Multi-Brand Companies," *Journal of Advertising Research,* 39 (1) (January/February 1999), pp. 667–78.
47. Ibid.
48. Bradley Johnson, "IBM Puts Squeeze on Ad Budget," *Advertising Age,* March 29, 2004, p. 1, 38.
49. Mary Welch, "Upbeat Marketers Wield Bigger Budgets, Shift Marketing Mix," *Business Marketing,* February 1993, p. 23.
50. John P. Jones, "Ad Spending: Maintaining Market Share," *Harvard Business Review,* 68 (1) (January/February 1990), pp. 38–42; and James C. Schroer, "Ad Spending: Growing Market Share," *Harvard Business Review,* 68 (1) (January/February 1990), pp. 44–48.
51. Randall S. Brown, "Estimating Advantages to Large-Scale Advertising," *Review of Economics and Statistics* 60 (August 1978), pp. 428–37.
52. Kent M. Lancaster, "Are There Scale Economies in Advertising?" *Journal of Business* 59, (3) (1986), pp. 509–26.
53. Johan Arndt and Julian Simon, "Advertising and Economics of Scale: Critical Comments on the Evidence," *Journal of Industrial Economics* 32 (2) (December 1983), pp. 229–41; Aaker and Carman, "Are You Overadvertising?"
54. George S. Low and Jakki J. Mohr, "The Budget Allocation between Advertising and Sales Promotion: Understanding the Decision Process," *AMA Educators' Proceedings, Summer 1991* (Chicago: American Marketing Association 1991), pp. 448–57.

Chapter Eight

1. Joshua Levine, "Fizz, Fizz-Plop, Plop," *Fortune,* June 21, 1993, p. 139.
2. Jean Halliday and Alice Z. Cuneo, "Nissan Reverses Course to Focus on the Product," *Advertising Age,* February 16, 1998, pp. 1, 39.
3. Jean Halliday, "Nissan Launches New Brand Campaign," August 21, 2002, http://www.adage.com/news.
4. Bob Garfield, "Award Winners' Edge: That's Entertainment," *Advertising Age,* August 3, 2004, pp. 16–17; Brent Bouchez, "Trophies Are Meaningless," *Advertising Age,* July 30, 2001, p. 16; Vanessa O'Connell, "Ad Slump Deflates Awards Show," *The Wall Street Journal,* May 21, 2002, p. B2; Jennifer Pendleton, "Awards-Creatives Defend Pursuit of Prizes," *Advertising Age,* April 25, 1988, pp. 1, 7.
5. Elizabeth C. Hirschman, "Role-Based Models of Advertising Creation and Production," *Journal of Advertising* 18, no. 4 (1989), pp. 42–53.
6. Ibid., p. 51.
7. Cyndee Miller, "Study Says 'Likability' Surfaces as Measure of TV Ad Success," *Marketing News,* January 7, 1991, pp. 6, 14; and Ronald Alsop, "TV Ads That Are Likeable Get Plus Rating for Persuasiveness," *The Wall Street Journal,* February 20, 1986, p. 23.
8. For an interesting discussion on the embellishment of advertising messages, see William M. Weilbacher, *Advertising,* 2nd ed. (New York: Macmillan, 1984), pp. 180–82.
9. David Ogilvy, *Confessions of an Advertising Man* (New York: Atheneum, 1963); and Hanley Norins, *The Compleat Copywriter* (New York: McGraw-Hill, 1966).
10. Hank Sneiden, *Advertising Pure and Simple* (New York: ANACOM, 1977).
11. Quoted in Valerie H. Free, "Absolut Original," *Marketing Insights,* Summer 1991, p. 65.
12. Jeff Jensen, "Marketer of the Year," *Advertising Age,* December 16, 1996, pp. 1, 16.
13. Cathy Taylor, "Risk Takers: Wieden & Kennedy," *Adweek's Marketing Week,* March 23, 1992, pp. 26, 27.
14. Kate MacArthur and Stephanie Thompson, "Wrigley Ads Take on Bite," *Advertising Age,* March 18, 2002, pp. 4, 70.
15. Anthony Vagnoni, "Creative Differences," *Advertising Age,* November 17, 1997, pp. 1, 28, 30.
16. Arthur J. Kover, "Copywriters' Implicit Theories of Communication: An Exploration," *Journal of Consumer Research,* vol. 21, (4) (March 1995), pp. 596–611.
17. James Webb Young, *A Technique for Producing Ideas,* 3rd ed. (Chicago: Crain Books, 1975), p. 42.
18. Debra Goldman, "Origin of the Species: Has the Planner Finally Evolved into the Agency's Most Potent Creature?" *Adweek,* April 10, 1995, pp. 28–38.
19. Jon Steel, *Truth, Lies & Advertising: The Art of Account Planning* (New York: Wiley, 1998).
20. Sandra E. Moriarty, *Creative Advertising: Theory and Practice* (Englewood Cliffs, NJ: Prentice Hall, 1986).
21. E. E. Norris, "Seek Out the Consumer's Problem," *Advertising Age,* March 17, 1975, pp. 43–44.
22. Kathryn Kranhold, "Agencies Beefing Up on Brand Research," *The Wall Street Journal,* March 9, 2000, p. B14.
23. Thomas L. Greenbaum, "Focus Groups Can Play a Part in Evaluating Ad Copy," *Marketing News,* September 13, 1993, pp. 24–25.
24. Eric J. Arnould and Melanie Wallendorf, "Market-Oriented Ethnography: Interpretation Building and Marketing Strategy Formulation," *Journal of*

Marketing Research, 31 (November 1994), pp. 388–396.

25. Gerry Khermouch, "Consumers in the Mist," *BusinessWeek,* February 26, 2001, pp. 92–94.
26. Paula Mergenhagen, "How 'Got Milk' Got Sales," *Marketing Tools,* September 1996, pp. 4–7.
27. John Sutherland, Lisa Duke and Avery Abernethy, "A Model of Marketing Information Flow," *Journal of Advertising,* vol. 22, no. 4 (Winter 2004) pp. 39–52.
28. A. Jerome Jeweler, *Creative Strategy in Advertising,* (Belmont, CA: Wadsworth, 1981).
29. John O'Toole, *The Trouble with Advertising,* 2nd ed. (New York: Random House, 1985), p. 131.
30. David Ogilvy, *Ogilvy on Advertising* (New York: Crown, 1983), p. 16.
31. Rosser Reeves, *Reality in Advertising* (New York: Knopf, 1961), pp. 47, 48.
32. Shelly Branch and Frances A. McMorris, "Irate Firms Take Comparisons to Court," *The Wall Street Journal,* December 22, 1999, p. B8.
33. Alecia Swasy, "How Innovation at P&G Restored Luster to Washed-Up Pert and Made It No. 1," *The Wall Street Journal,* December 6, 1990, p. B1.
34. Ogilvy, *Confessions.*
35. Michael McCarthy, "New Theme for Reebok," *USA TODAY,* February 10, 2005, p. 5B.
36. Martin Mayer, *Madison Avenue, U.S.A.* (New York: Pocket Books, 1958).
37. Al Ries and Jack Trout, *Positioning: The Battle for Your Mind,* New York: McGraw-Hill, 1985; "The Positioning Era Cometh," Jack Trout and Al Ries, *Advertising Age,* April 24, 1972, pp. 35–38; May 1, 1972, pp. 51–54; May 8, 1972, pp. 114–16.
38. Jack Trout, "Brands Can't Exist without Positioning," *Advertising Age,* March 14, 2005, p. 28.
39. Pamela Parker, "IBM Campaign Introduces Company's 'Other Side,'" www.clickz.com/news, April 11, 2005.
40. Jean Halliday, "Sometimes Oil and Oil Don't Mix," *Advertising Age,* March 4, 2002, pp. 4, 62.
41. Rajeev Batra, John G. Myers, and David A. Aaker, *Advertising Management,* 5th ed. (Upper Saddle River, NJ: Prentice Hall, 1996).
42. Anthony Vagnoni, "They Might Be Giants," *Advertising Age,* April 27, 1998, pp. 1, 20, 24.
43. ______, "Goodby, Silverstein Do 'Intelligent Work' with a Sales Pitch," *Advertising Age,* April 27, 1998, pp. 20, 24.
44. ______, "Having Ad Bosses Focus on the Work Key to Cult of Clow," *Advertising Age,* April 27, 1998, pp. 22, 24.

Chapter Nine

1. Sandra E. Moriarty, *Creative Advertising: Theory and Practice,* 2nd ed. (Englewood Cliffs, NJ: Prentice Hall, 1991), p. 76.
2. William M. Weilbacher, *Advertising,* 2nd ed. (New York: Macmillan, 1984), p. 197.
3. William Wells, John Burnett, and Sandra Moriarty, *Advertising* (Englewood Cliffs, NJ: Prentice Hall, 1989), p. 330.
4. Stuart J. Agres, "Emotion in Advertising: An Agency Point of View," in *Emotion in Advertising: Theoretical and Practical Explanations,* ed. Stuart J. Agres, Julie A. Edell, and Tony M. Dubitsky (Westport, CT: Quorom Books, 1991).
5. Edward Kamp and Deborah J. Macinnis, "Characteristics of Portrayed Emotions in Commercials: When Does What Is Shown in Ads Affect Viewers?" *Journal of Advertising Research,* (November/December 1995), pp. 19–28.
6. For a review of research on the effect of mood states on consumer behavior, see Meryl Paula Gardner, "Mood States and Consumer Behavior: A Critical Review," *Journal of Consumer Research* 12, no. 3 (December 1985), pp. 281–300.
7. Cathy Madison, "Researchers Work Advertising into an Emotional State," *Adweek,* November 5, 1990, p. 30.
8. Kate Macarthur, "Big Mac's Back," *Advertising Age,* March 13, 2004, pp. S1–8.
9. Christopher P. Puto and William D. Wells, "Informational and Transformational Advertising: The Different Effects of Time," in *Advances in Consumer Research,* vol. 11, ed. Thomas C. Kinnear (Ann Arbor, MI: Association for Consumer Research, 1984), p. 638.
10. Ibid.
11. David Ogilvy and Joel Raphaelson, "Research on Advertising Techniques That Work and Don't Work," *Harvard Business Review,* July/August 1982, p. 18.
12. *Topline,* no. 4 (September 1989), McCann-Erickson, New York.
13. Jean Halliday, "Porsche Plugs Upcoming SUV Online," *adage.com,* December 7, 2001.
14. Dottie Enrico, "Teaser Ads Grab Spotlight on Madison Ave.," *USA TODAY,* July 6, 1995, pp. 1, 2B.
15. Quote by Irwin Warren, cited in Enrico, "Teaser Ads Grab Spotlight."
16. Martin Mayer, *Madison Avenue, U.S.A.* (New York: Pocket Books, 1958), p. 64.
17. Sally Beatty, "P&G to Ad Agencies: Please Rewrite Our Old Formulas," *The Wall Street Journal,* November 5, 1998, pp. B1, 10; Alecia Swasy, "P&G Tries Bolder Ads—With Caution," *The Wall Street Journal,* May 7, 1990, pp. B1, 7.
18. Lynn Coleman, "Advertisers Put Fear into the Hearts of Their Prospects," *Marketing News,* August 15, 1988, p. 1.
19. Ibid.
20. Bob Garfield, "Listerine Eschews 'Creativity' for an Ad that Actually Works," *Advertising Age,* September 20, 2004, p. 57.
21. Kevin Goldman, "Chips Ahoy! Ad Uses Spin on Claymation," *The Wall Street Journal,* February 9, 1994, p. B5.
22. Barbara B. Stern, "Classical and Vignette Television Advertising: Structural Models, Formal Analysis, and Consumer Effects," *Journal of Consumer Research* 20, no. 4 (March 1994), pp. 601–15; and John Deighton, Daniel Romer, and Josh McQueen, "Using Drama to Persuade," *Journal of Consumer Research* 15, no. 3 (December 1989), pp. 335–43.
23. Moriarty, *Creative Advertising,* p. 77.
24. William F. Arens, *Contemporary Advertising,* 6th ed. (Burr Ridge, IL: Irwin/McGraw-Hill, 1998), p. 284.
25. W. Keith Hafer and Gordon E. White, *Advertising Writing,* 3rd ed. (St. Paul, MN: West Publishing, 1989), p. 98.
26. Carol Marie Cooper, "Who Says Talk Is Cheap," *New York Times,* October 22, 1998, pp. C1, 5; and Wendy Brandes, "Star Power Leaves Some Voice-Over Artists Speechless," *The Wall Street Journal,* June 2, 1995, p. B6.
27. Linda M. Scott, "Understanding Jingles and Needledrop: A Rhetorical Approach to Music in Advertising," *Journal of Consumer Research* 17, no. 2 (September 1990), pp. 223–36.
28. Ibid., p. 223.
29. Kineta Hung, "Framing Meaning Perceptions with Music: The Case of Teaser Ads," *Journal of Advertising,*

vol. 30, no. 3 (Fall 2001), pp. 39–49; Russell I. Haley, Jack Richardson, and Beth Baldwin, "The Effects of Nonverbal Communications in Television Advertising," *Journal of Advertising Research,* (July/August 1984) 24, no. 4, pp. 11–18.

30. Gerald J. Gorn, "The Effects of Music in Advertising on Choice Behavior: A Classical Conditioning Approach," *Journal of Marketing* 46 (Winter 1982), pp. 94–100.
31. Donna DeMarco, "TV Ads Go Pop: Advertisers Marry Modern Music with their Products," *Washington Times,* May 12, 2002, p. A1.
32. Todd Wasseman, "Nortel Taps Rank and File," *Brandweek,* January 3, 2000, p. 6; Stephanie N. Mehta, "Northern Telecom Plays Down Phone Roots, Embraces 'I Word,'" *The Wall Street Journal,* April 14, 1999, p. B10.
33. Chad Terhune, "To Pitch New Soda, Coke Wants the World to Sing—Again," *The Wall Street Journal,* June 13, 2005, pp. B1, 8.
34. Stephanie Thompson, "Promotions: Nostalgia Bolognese," *Brandweek,* April 14, 1997.
35. Quote from: Suzanne Vranica, " P&G Dusts Off a Familiar Tune," *The Wall Street Journal,* March 3, 2005, p. B2.
36. Ibid.
37. Eleftheria Parpis, "Creative: Best Campaign," *Adweek,* January 24, 2000, p. 1.
38. Theresa Howard, "Marketers Mine Humor from Serious Topics," *USA TODAY,* December 15, 2003, p. 10B.
39. Jack Neff, "Why P&G Won't Win Many Cannes Lions," *Advertising Age,* June 13, 2005, pp. 3, 45; Beatty, "P&G to Ad Agencies."
40. Kate MacArthur and Stephanie Thompson, "Wrigley Ads Take on Bite," *Advertising Age,* March 18, 2002, pp. 4, 70.
41. Eva Pomice, "Madison Avenue's Blind Spot," *U.S. News & World Report,* October 3, 1988, p. 49.
42. Suzanne Vranica, "Aflac Partly Muzzles Iconic Duck," *The Wall Street Journal,* December 2, 2004, p. B8.
43. Kate Macarthur, "Quizno's Axes Spongemonkey Spokesthings," *Advertising Age,* August 2, 2004, p. 6.

Chapter Ten

1. Karl Greenberg, "Auto Mobility," *Brandweek,* March 21, 2005, pp. SR1–SR 4.
2. Matthew Creamer, "Ad Groups Back Switch from 'Frequency' to 'Engagement,'" www. AdAge.com, July 21, 2005, pp. 1–3.
3. Jim Surmanek, *Advertising Media A to Z,* McGraw-Hill, 2003.
4. Chuck Ross, "Study Finds for Continuity vs. Flights," *Advertising Age,* April 19, 1999, p. 2.
5. Michael J. Naples, *Effective Frequency: The Relationship between Frequency and Advertising Effectiveness* (New York: Association of National Advertisers, 1979).
6. Joseph W. Ostrow, "Setting Frequency Levels: An Art or a Science?" *Journal of Advertising Research* 24 (August/September 1984), pp. i9–11.
7. David Berger, "How Much to Spend," *Foote, Cone & Belding Internal Report,* in Michael L. Rothschild, *Advertising* (Lexington, MA: Heath, 1987), p. 468.
8. David W. Olson, "Real World Measures of Advertising Effectiveness for New Products," *Speech to the 26th Annual Conference of the Advertising Research Foundation,* New York, March 18, 1980.
9. Naples, *Effective Frequency.*
10. Joseph W. Ostrow, "What Level Frequency?" *Advertising Age,* November 1981, pp. 13–18.
11. Jack Myers, "More Is Indeed Better," *Media Week,* September 6, 1993, pp. 14–18; and Jim Surmanek, "One-Hit or Miss: Is a Frequency of One Frequently Wrong?" *Advertising Age,* November 27, 1995, p. 46.
12. Ostrow, "What Level Frequency?"

Chapter Eleven

1. *Radio Marketing Guide and Fact Book: 2004–2005,* (New York: Radio Advertising Bureau, 2005).
2. "Nielsen Media Research Reports Universe Estimates for the 2005–2006 Television Season," www.nielsenmedia.com/newsreleases, August 25, 2005.
3. "Network Television Cost and CPM Trends," Trends in Media, Television Bureau of Advertising, New York, www.tvb.org/rcentral.
4. Lex van Meurs, "Zapp! A Study on Switching Behavior during Commercial Breaks," *Journal of Advertising Research* (January/February 1998), pp. 43–53; John J. Cronin, "In-Home Observations of Commercial Zapping Behavior," *Journal of Current Issues and Research in Advertising,* vol. 17, no. 2 (Fall 1995), pp. 69–75.
5. "Television Production Cost Survey: Report of 2004 Findings," (New York: American Association of Advertising Agencies), November 2005.
6. Brian Grow, "Hispanic Nation," *BusinessWeek,* March 15, 2004, pp. 58–70.
7. "Network Television Commercial Activity By Length of Commercial," Trends in Television, (New York: Television Bureau of Advertising), www.tvb.org/rcentral.
8. Steve McClellan "Buyers, Nets Try to Skirt Clutter With Sponsor Deals," *Adweek,* October 31, 2005, p. 9; "AAAA/ANA Annual Study Shows TV Clutter Levels Up Across Dayparts," (New York: American Association of Advertising Agencies), www.aaaa.org/news, February 14, 2002.
9. Dennis Kneal, "Zapping of TV Ads Appears Pervasive," *The Wall Street Journal,* April 25, 1988, p. 27.
10. John J. Cronin and Nancy Menelly, "Discrimination vs. Avoidance: 'Zipping' of Television Commercials," *Journal of Advertising,* vol. 21, no. 2 (June 1992), pp. 1–7.
11. John J. Cronin, "In-Home Observations of Commercial Zapping Behavior."
12. Carrie Heeter and Bradley S. Greenberg, "Profiling the Zappers," *Journal of Advertising Research,* April/May 1985, pp. 9–12; Fred S. Zufryden, James H. Pedrick, and Avu Sandaralingham, "Zapping and Its Impact on Brand Purchase Behavior," *Journal of Advertising Research,* vol. 33 (January/February 1993), pp. 58–66; and Patricia Orsini, "Zapping: A Man's World," Spring Television Report, *Adweek's Marketing Week,* April 8, 1991, p. 3.
13. Lex van Meurs, "Zapp! A Study on Switching Behavior During Commercial Breaks," *Journal of Advertising Research,* 38 (1), (January/February 1998), pp. 43–53.
14. Alan Ching Biu Tse and Rub P. W. Lee, "Zapping Behavior During Commercial Breaks," *Journal of Advertising Research,* 41 (3), (May/June 2001), pp. 25–29.
15. Anne Marie Fink, "Press Fast-Forward for TV Salvation," *Advertising Age,* June 20, 2005, p. 18.
16. Linda F. Alwitt and Paul R. Prabhaker, "Identifying Who Dislikes Television Advertising: Not by Demographics Alone," *Journal of Advertising Research,* vol. 32, no. 5 (1992), pp. 30–42.

17. Banwari Mittal, "Public Assessment of TV Advertising: Faint Praise and Harsh Criticism," *Journal of Advertising Research,* vol. 34, no. 1 (1994), pp. 35–53.
18. Lucy L. Henke, "Young Children's Perceptions of Cigarette Brand Advertising Symbols: Awareness, Affect, and Target Market Identification," *Journal of Advertising,* vol. 24, no. 4 (Winter 1995), pp. 13–28.
19. Brooks Barnes and Miram Jordan, "Big Four TV Networks Get a Wake-Up Call—in Spanish," *The Wall Street Journal,* May 2, 2005, pp. B1, 6.
20. Claire Atkinson, "TV Buyers Bow Before Fox's 'Idol,'" *Advertising Age,* September 19, 2005, pp. 1, 50.
21. Chris Pursell, "Syndicators Prepped and Stockpiling Fare," *Advertising Age,* May 14, 2001, pp. S14–16.
22. Brian Steinberg, "More Networks Are Pulling the Plugs," *The Wall Street Journal,* October 15, 2004, p. B2.
23. Ibid.
24. Sally Goll Beatty, "MSNBC Already Waging Marketing War," *The Wall Street Journal,* July 9, 1996, p. B8.
25. Joe Flint and Stefan Fatsis, "Comcast Mulls Sports Network To Rival ESPN," *The Wall Street Journal,* July 27, 2005, pp. B1, 3.
26. Eric Schmuckler, "Come Together," *Adweek,* May 30, 2005, pp. SR4, 6.
27. Leslie Cauley, "Cable-TV Firms Pledge a Tight Rein on Price Increases," *The Wall Street Journal,* April 1, 1999, p. B12.
28. Kathy Chen, "Measure to Let Satellite TV Air Network Fare," *The Wall Street Journal,* November 22, 1999, p. B8.
29. Joe Flint and Stefan Fatsis, "ESPN Snatches NFL on Monday; NBC Scores, Too," *The Wall Street Journal,* April 19, 2005, pp. B1, 9.
30. Gary Levin, "Arbitron Exits from Ratings Race," *Advertising Age,* October 25, 1993, p. 4.
31. "Nielsen Media Research Reports Universe Estimates for the 2005–2006 Television Season."
32. Suzanne Vranica and Charles Goldsmith, "Nielsen Adapts Its Methods As TV Evolves," *The Wall Street Journal,* September 20, 2003, pp. B1, 10.
33. Ibid.
34. "National People Meter Expansion Continues," www.nielsenmedia.com/newsreleases, December 15, 2005.
35. http://www.arbitron.com/portable_people_meters/home.htm; Louis Chunovic, "When Audiences Intersect," *TelevisionWeek,* June 23, 2003, p. 18; Juneg Young, "New Audience Measurement Device Tested," *Los Angeles Times,* December 26, 2001, p. C2.
36. Jim Kite, "Too Early to Think in Minutes," *Advertising Age,* February 7, 2005, p. 23.
37. Ibid.
38. "Nielsen To Deliver National TV Ratings With DVR Viewing Included," www.nielsenmedia.com/newsreleases, December 21, 2005; Hoag Levins and David Goetzl, "Nielsen Can Now Monitor TiVo," *AdAge.com,* August 7, 2002.
39. Brian Steinberg, "A Network's Dream? TV Viewers Who Recall Commercials," *The Wall Street Journal,* May 11, 2005, pp. B1, 3; Claire Atkinson, "Advertisers Press Nielsen for Spot Data," *Advertising Age,* August 2, 2004, p. 3; Dom Rossi, "Rethink 'Prime Time,'" *Advertising Age,* April 29, 2002, p. 1.
40. Cristel Russell, Andrew T. Norman, and Susan E. Heckler, "People and Their Television Shows: An Exploration Into The Construct of Audience Connectedness," *Marketing Letters,* 10 (4), pp. 387–401.
41. *Radio Marketing Guide and Fact Book: 2004–2005,* (New York: Radio Advertising Bureau, 2005).
42. Suein L. Hwang, "Old Media Get a Web Windfall," *The Wall Street Journal,* September 17, 1999, p. B1.
43. Verne Gay, "Image Transfer: Radio Ads Make Aural History," *Advertising Age,* January 24, 1985, p. 1.
44. "The Benefits of Synergy: Moving Money Into Radio," (New York: Radio Ad Effectiveness Lab, Inc.) December 2004, www.radioadlal.com.
45. Avery Abernethy, "Differences Between Advertising and Program Exposure for Car Radio Listening," *Journal of Advertising Research,* vol. 31, no. 2 (April/May 1991), pp. 33–42.
46. Martin Peers, "Radio Produces Both Gains and Skeptics," *The Wall Street Journal,* January 1, 1999, p. B6.
47. Ibid.
48. Heather Green, Tom Lowry, Catherine Young and David Kiley, "The New Radio Revolution," *BusinessWeek,* March 14, 2005, pp. 32–35.
49. Doug Young, "New Audience Measurement Device Tested."
50. Abbey Klaassen, "People Meters Shift Radio Ratings," *Advertising Age,* September 26, 2005, p. 77.

Chapter Twelve

1. Herbert E. Krugman, "The Measurement of Advertising Involvement," *Public Opinion Quarterly* 30 (Winter 1966–67), pp. 583–96.
2. *The Magazine Handbook: A Comprehensive Guide for Advertisers, Advertising Agencies and Consumer Magazine Marketers 2005/2006* (New York: Magazine Publishers of America, www.magazine.org).
3. *Samir Husni's Guide To New Magazines 2005* (Oxford, MS: Nautilus Publishing, 2005).
4. Brian Steinberg, "Gimmicky Magazine Inserts Aim to Grab Page Flippers," *The Wall Street Journal,* August 8, 2005, pp. B1, 2.
5. Scott Donaton and Pat Sloan, "Ad 'Printaculars' Under Scrutiny," *Advertising Age,* February 12, 1990, p. 3.
6. *The Magazine Handbook.*
7. Ibid.
8. Steve Fajen, "Numbers Aren't Everything," *Media Decisions* 10 (June 1975), pp. 65–69.
9. *A Study of Media Involvement,* vol. 7 (New York: Magazine Publishers of America, 1996).
10. "Magazine Industry Launches Campaign to Promote Enduring Power of Magazines to Engage Readers; Advertising Also Includes Futurist Cover Wraps and Dedicated Website," *Business Wire.* New York, February 28, 2005, p. 1.
11. Engagement: Understanding Consumers' Relationship with Media," (New York: Magazine Publishers of America, 2005), www.magazine.org/engagement.
12. *The Magazine Handbook.*
13. Sally Goll Beatty, "Philip Morris Starts Lifestyle Magazine," *The Wall Street Journal,* September 16, 1996, pp. B1, 8.
14. Jack Neff, "P&G Extends Online Custom Publishing," *Advertising Age,* March 22, 2004, pp. 24–25.
15. Jon Fine, "Audit Bureau To Change How It Counts Circulation," www.AdAge.com/news, July 17, 2001.
16. Jon Fine, "ABC Feels Heat of Circ Scandals," *Advertising Age,* January 17, 2005, pp. 1, 26.
17. Jon Fine, "ABC Intensifies Effort to Root Out Circ Fraud," *Advertising Age,* November 15, 2004, pp. 4, 49.

18. Study cited in Jim Surmanek, *Media Planning: A Practical Guide* (Lincolnwood, IL: Crain Books, 1985).
19. "How Advertising Readership Is Influenced by Ad Size," Report no. 110.1, *Cahners Advertising Research,* Newton, MA; and "Larger Advertisements Get Higher Readership," *LAP Report no. 3102,* McGraw-Hill Research, New York; "Effect of Size, Color and Position on Number of Responses to Recruitment Advertising," *LAP Report no. 3116,* McGraw-Hill Research, New York.
20. "Almost Everything You Want to Know About Positioning in Magazines," study by Roper Starch Worldwide, Inc. 1999, http://www.magazine.org/resources/research.
21. "Readership by Advertising Unit Type," *Magazine Dimensions* 2001 Media Dynamics, Inc., http://www.magazine.org/resources/fact_sheets/adv.
22. Kate Fitzgerald, "No Holding Back Rate Cuts," *Advertising Age,* March 4, 2002, p. S-2.
23. Paul D. Colford, "*YM* Magazine to Stop Publication at End of Year," *Knight Ridder Tribune Business News,* October 7, 2004, p. 1; Jon Fine, "Stop the Presses," *Advertising Age,* August 20, 2001, pp. 1, 45.
24. Seth Sutel, "*TV Guide* Makes Major Switch," *The San Diego Union Tribune,* July 27, 2005, pp. C1, 4.
25. Jenna Schnuer, "Mags in a Mail-Storm of Rate Hikes," *Advertising Age,* October 22, 2001, p. S10.
26. Larry Dobrow, "Magazine Fighting for Fair Share," *Advertising Age,* September 13, 2004, pp. S9, 11.
27. Ann Marie Kerwin, "Magazine Study Links Circ Woes to Sweepstakes Fall," *Advertising Age,* November 8, 1999, p. 3.
29. Wayne Friedman, "Cross-Platform Deals still Lacking," *Advertising Age,* April 26, 2004, p. 96; Richard Siklos and Catherine Yang, "Welcome to the 21st Century," *BusinessWeek,* January 24, 2000, pp. 37–44.
30. Junu Bryan Kim, "Cracking the Barrier of Two Dimensions," *Advertising Age,* October 6, 1991, pp. 32, 34.
31. The Source: Newspapers By The Numbers *2005* (Vienna, VA: Newspaper Association of America, 2006) www.naa.org/thesource.
32. Ann Marie Kerwin, "After a Long Lobbying Effort, 'New York Times' Wins New Ad Status," *Advertising Age,* February 22, 1999, p. 24.
33. Ann Marie Kerwin, "Big-City Dailies Eye National Stage," *Advertising Age,* February 22, 1999, p. 24.
34. Hanna Liebman, "NAA Network Ready to Roll," *Mediaweek,* December 13, 1993, p. 18.
35. David Washburn, "Union-Tribune to Offer Free Classified Ads to Individuals," *The San Diego Union Tribune,* August 8, 2005, pp. H1, 4.
36. Brian Steinberg, "Newspaper Woes Are Black and White," *The Wall Street Journal,* December 15, 2004, p. B3.
37. The Source: Newspapers By The Numbers.
38. "Brandy, Bon Jovi, Barbara Bush, Elway, Hill and Streep Return for Fourth Flight of NAA National Ad Campaign," news release, Newspaper Association of America, 1999 (http://www.naa.org).
39. Bruce Bigelow, "Newspapers Plot Ways to End Slide in Readership," *San Diego Union-Tribune,* April 27, 1999, pp. C1, 5; Newspaper Readership Initiative Information Site, http://www.naa.org/readership.
40. Ann Marie Kerwin, "Print's Power Play," *Advertising Age: The Next Century,* special issue, 1999.

Chapter Thirteen

1. *Outdoor Advertising Association,* 2006.
2. *Maritz AmeriPoll,* August 1998.
3. Denise Henry, "Appeals on Wheels," *Business 99,* April/May 1999, pp. 28–31.
4. Amanda Beeter, "New Audit Gauges Impact of Truck-Side Advertising," *Advertising Age,* January 10, 2000, p. 43.
5. David Kaplan, "Agency Offers In-Store Insight: End-Aisles, Print Surpass TV," www.mediapost.com, June 23, 2005, pp. 1–2.
6. David Kalish, "Supermarket Sweepstakes," *Marketing & Media Decisions,* November 1988, p. 34.
7. *American Public Transportation Association,* 2005.
8. *Outdoor Advertising Association,* 2006.
9. Mukesh Bhargava and Naveen Donthu, "Sales Response to Outdoor Advertising," *Journal of Advertising Research,* 39 (3), July/August 1999.
10. *American Public Transportation Association,* 2005.
11. *Promotional Products Association International,* 1996.
12. *Promotional Products Association International,* 2005.
13. *Promotional Products Association International,* 2005.
14. *Promotional Products Association International,* 2005.
15. *Yellow Pages Association,* 2005.
16. *Yellow Pages Association,* 2005.
17. *Yellow Pages Association,* 2005.
18. *Yellow Pages Association,* 2005.
19. *Yellow Pages Association,* 2005.
20. *Yellow Pages Association,* 2005.
21. *Yellow Pages Association,* 2005.
22. *Yellow Pages Association,* 2005.
23. *Yellow Pages Publishers Association,* 2002, p. 8.
24. Laura Petrecca and David Leiberman, "Film Fans Can Expect More Advertising on Big Screen," www.USAToday.com, December 6, 2005.
25. Alex Mindlin, "For Advertisers, the Silver Screen is Golden," *New York Times,* May 23, 2005, p. 1.
26. Adam Snyder, "Are Spots on Home Video Badvertising?" *Brandweek,* January 29, 1996, p. 40.
27. Ibid.
28. Hank Kim, "Regal Pre-Movie Package Boosts Recall," *Advertising Age,* June 7, 2004, p. 21.
29. *Motion Picture Association of America,* 2005.
30. Betsy Baurer, "New Quick Flicks: Ads at the Movies," *USA Today,* March 13, 1986, p. D1.
31. Michael A. Belch and Don Sciglimpaglia, "Viewers' Evaluations of Cinema Advertising," *Proceedings of the American Institute for Decision Sciences,* March 1979, pp. 39–43.
32. Snyder, "Are Spots on Home Video Badvertising?"
33. Alice Cuneo, "Now Playing: Gap, Target Take Retail to the Movies," *Advertising Age,* June 9, 1997, p. 14.
34. *Hemispheres Magazine,* 2005.
35. *Skymall,* 2005.
36. *Hemispheres Magazine,* 2005.
37. David Kaplan, "Product Placement: Well-Placed Among Consumers," www.mediapost.com, March 25, 2005, pp. 1–2; John Consoli, "ANA Survey: 63 Pct. Use Branded Entertainment," www.insidebrandedentertainment.com, March 23, 2005, p. 1.
38. *PQ Media,* February 2006.
39. David G. Kennedy, "Coming of Age in Consumerdom," *American Demographics,* April 2004, p. 14.
40. Marc Graser, "Movie Placement Creates Demand for Nonexistent Shoe," www.adage.com, January 31, 2005, pp. 1–2.

41. Jim Edwards, "Will Product Placement Get Its Own Dot-Comeuppance?" *Brandweek,* July 25, 2005, p. 13.
42. Ibid.
43. Claire Atkinson, "CBS Considers Separate Brand Integration Fees," www.AdAge.com, March 25, 2005, pp. 1–3.
44. Kennedy, "Coming of Age in Consumerdom."
45. David Kaplan, "Product Placement: Well-Placed Among Consumers."
46. Pola B. Gupta and Kenneth Lord, "Product Placement in Movies: The Effect of Prominence and Mode on Audience Recall," *Journal of Current Issues and Research in Advertising* 20, (1) (Spring 1998), pp. 1–29.
47. Gail Schiller, "Tie-Ins often Sobering for Liquor Firms," *Hollywood Reporter,* August 1, 2005, pp. 1–3, Marin Institute.org, 2006.
48. Pola B. Gupta and Stephen J. Gould, "Consumers' Perceptions of the Ethics and Acceptability of Product Placements in Movies: Product Category and Individual Differences," *Journal of Current Issues and Research in Advertising* 19, no. 1 (Spring 1997), pp. 40–49.
49. John Consoli, "80% TV Viewers Approve Product Placement," www.insidebrandedentertainment.com, March 28, 2005, p. 1.
50. Kennedy, "Coming of Age in Consumerdom."
51. Steve McClellan, "Branded Entertainment Finding Its Place(ment)," www.insidebrandedentertainment.com, March 28, 2005, pp. 1–3.
52. Gail Schiller, "Industry Seeks Formula to Value Product Integration," www.hollywoodreporter.com, December 30, 2004, pp.1–6.
53. "Consumer Products Become Movie Stars," *The Wall Street Journal,* February 29, 1988, p. 23.
54. Damon Darlin, "Highbrow Hype," *Forbes,* April 12, 1993, pp. 126–27.
55. Lorin Cipolla, "Guerilla Marketing Goes Mainstream: AMA Conference," www.promomagazine.com, February 17, 2004, p. 1.
56. Betsy Spethmann, Patrica Odell, Tim Parry, Amy Johannes, "Guerilla Marketing Grows Up," www.PROMOXtra.com, January 12, 2005, pp. 1–4.
57. Claire Atkinson, "Guerilla Marketing Tactics Detailed at NYC Conference," www.adage.com, February 16, 2004, pp 1–2.
58. ____, "Advertisers Eye Video Game Ads," www.emarketer.com, October 20, 2004, pp. 1–2.
59. Joe Mandese, "A Sense Of Place: Thomson Muscles Into Retail Media, Acquires PRN," www.mediapost.com, July 29, 2005, pp. 1–3.
60. Ira Teinowitz, "Channel One Criticized as 'Crass Commercialism,'" *Advertising Age,* May 21, 1999, p. 2.

Chapter Fourteen

1. Stan Rapp and Thomas I. Collins, *Maximarketing* (New York: McGraw-Hill, 1987).
2. Peter D. Bennett, ed., *Dictionary of Marketing Terms* (Chicago: American Marketing Association, 1988), p. 58.
3. *Direct Marketing Association Economic Impact,* 2002 (New York: Direct Marketing Association, 2002).
4. "Industry Facts and Figures, 2004," www.retailing.org, September 9, 2005, pp. 1–2; *Statistical Fact Book,* 2005, New York: Direct Marketing Association, 2005.
5. *Statistical Fact Book,* 2005, New York: Direct Marketing Association.
6. *Statistical Fact Book,* 2005, New York: Direct Marketing Association; *Thomson Media's Card Industry Directory,* 2004.
7. Jagdish N. Sheth, "Marketing Megatrends," *Journal of Consumer Marketing,* 1, (1) (June 1983), pp. 5–13.
8. *Bureau of Labor Statistics,* December 7, 2005.
9. "A 15.6 Billion Home Shopping Spree by 2006," *Response TV,* December 1997.
10. _____, "DR Industry Assists In Katrina Relief Efforts," www.responsemagazine.com, August 7, 2005, pp. 1–2.
11. Nancy Hatch Woodward, "Direct Mail Pushes the Recruiting Envelope," *HR Magazine,* May 2000, pp. 145–152.
12. "Direct Mail by the Numbers," *U.S. Postal Service,* 1999.
13. "A Potent New Tool for Selling: Database Marketing," *BusinessWeek,* September 5, 1994, pp. 56–59.
14. Herbert Kanzenstein and William S. Sachs, *Direct Marketing,* 2nd ed. (New York: Macmillan, 1992).
15. "Direct Mail by the Numbers."
16. *Statistical Fact Book,* 2005, New York: Direct Marketing Association.
17. Ibid.
18. Cleveland Horton, "Porsche 300,000: The New Elite," *Advertising Age,* February 5, 1990, p. 8.
19. David Sharp, "Catalogs Still Thrive in an Age of Growing E-Commerce," www.postgazette.com, December 2, 2004, pp. 1–2.
20. Elaine Underwood, "Is There a Future for the TV Mall?" *Brandweek,* March 25, 1996, pp. 24–26.
21. "Industry Facts and Figures, 2004," www.retailing.org, September 9, 2005, pp. 1–2; *Statistical Fact Book,* 2005, New York: Direct Marketing Association, 2005.
22. *Statistical Fact Book,* 2005, New York: Direct Marketing Association.
23. *MediaMark Research, Inc.,* 2004.
24. Marianna Morello, "Print Media + DRTV= Retail Success," *Response,* September 2002, p. 6.
25. David Kaplan, "OnStar Positions New TV Ad Format: The 'Documercial," www.mediapost, April 14, 2005, pp. 1–2.
26. Daisy Whitney, "Infomercials Get their Day, Night," *Advertising Age,* May 9, 2005, p. S-28.
27. Joe Flint, "As Seen on TV: Inside a Media Company's Bid To Make Home Shopping Chic; Scripps Tries Boutique Route Using Stars as Pitchmen and Food Network Tie-Ins; Emeril Drives a Hard Bargain," *The Wall Street Journal,* July 18, 2005, p. A.1.
28. Ibid.
29. "Industry Facts and Figures, 2004," www.retailing.org, September 9, 2005, pp. 1–2; *Statistical Fact Book,* 2005, New York: Direct Marketing Association, 2005.
30. Ibid.
31. Ibid.
32. Ibid.
33. Ibid.
34. Ibid.
35. Tom Eisenhart, "Tele-media: Marketing's New Dimension," *Business Marketing,* February 1991, pp. 50–53.
36. *Direct Selling Association,* 2005.
37. ______, "Jupiter Predicts Consumers to Receive Over 3,900 Spam E-mails Annually by 2007," www.directmag.com, September 18, 2002.
38. ______, "How HR Can Fight E-mail Spam," *HR Focus,* November, 2004, pp. 11–12.
39. *U.S. Postal Service,* Postal News, 2005.

Chapter Fifteen

1. Kevin Kelly, "We Are the Web," *Wired,* August, 2005, pp. 29–35.

2. Rick E. Bruner, "The Decade in Online Advertising," www.DoubleClick.com, April 2005, pp. 170–190.
3. ___, "Internet Usage Statistics—The Big Picture," www.internetworldstats.com, March, 2006, p. 1.
4. Jon Raj, "Visa Veers Heavily Toward Online Marketing," www.AdAge.com, April 27, 2005, pp. 1–3.
5. "The Decade in Online Advertising," p. 4.
6. ___, "The Big Battle Over Ad Budgets," www.emarketer.com, September 15, 2005, pp. 1–4.
7. Kelly, "We Are the Web," p. 31.
8. Ibid.
9. Karen Benezra, "Branding the Web," *Chief Executive,* January 2001, pp. 30–34.
10. Erwin Ephron, "Direct Response or Branding?" *Advertising Age,* November 5, 2001, p. 14.
11. Sean Callahan, "Branding: Is It Worth It?" *B to B,* August 20, 2001, p. 1, 24.
12. Wendy Davis, "E-Commerce to Surge 21 Percent," www.mediapost.com, April 20, 2005, p. 1; ___, "E-Commerce: Ten Years Later," www.emarketer.com, April 19, 2005, pp. 1–3.
13. Ibid.
14. _____, "Walmart.com 2005 Sales Top $1 Billion," www.internetretailer.com, February 15, 2006, pp. 1–2.
15. ______ "Web Ad Industry Facing Down Problems," 2002.
16. ______, "Banner Ads Are Alive—Though Not Clicking," *Marketing Week,* January 29, 2004, p. 37.
17. Tessa Wegert, "The Ad Banner Turns 10," www.clickz.com, November 4, 2004, pp. 1–2.
18. _____, "Consumers Unhappy With Web Site Simply Go Away," www.CenterforMediaResearch.com, August 23, 2005, pp. 1–2.
19. Cong Li, Robert Meeds, "Different Forced-Exposure Levels of Internet Advertising: An Experimental Study of Pop-Up Ads and Interstitials," *American Academy of Advertising Conference Proceedings,* 2005, pp. 200–208.
20. Chris Gaither, "Search-Related Ads Rely on Poetry of Words, Numbers," *Los Angeles Times,* May 29, 2005, pp. C1–C4.
21. Chris Gaither, "Yahoo to Sell 'Contextual' Website Ads," *Los Angeles Times,* August 3, 2005, p. C2.
22. www.Wikipedia.com.
23. Ian Schafer, "What Is Rich Media, Really?" www.clickz.com, September 23, 2005, p. 1.
24. Sam Whitmore, "Podcasting: Making Waves," www.Forbes.com, April 21, 2005, pp. 1–2.
25. Joel Gehman, "Podcasting Demystified," www.mediapost.com, June 6, 2005, pp. 1–2.
26. Jack Neff, "Durex Buys Condom Product Placements in Podcasts," www.AdAge.com, May 12, 2005, pp. 1–3.
27. Chris Sherman, "What Is RSS, and Why Should You Care?" www.searchenginewatch.com, August 30, 2005, pp. 1–4.
28. Amy Johannes, "Yahoo, mtvU Team for New Reality Series," www.promomagazine.com, September 26, 2005, pp. 1–2.
29. *Statistical Fact Book,* 2005, New York: Direct Marketing Association.
30. ___, "E-Mail Marketing: Alive and Well," www.eMarketer.com, April 28, 2005, pp. 1–2.
31. Chana R. Shoenberger, "Web, What Web?" *Forbes,* June 10, 2002, p. 136.
32. Wendy Davis, "E-Commerce to Surge 21 Percent," www.mediapost.com, April 20, 2005, pp. 1–2.
33. *Statistical Fact Book,* 2005, New York: Direct Marketing Association.
34. ____, "Measurement Guidelines and Measurement Certification," www.iab.net, 2006.
35. Ibid.
36. David Cohen, "Digital Media: To Compliment or Complement Traditional Media," www.clickz.com, November 24, 2004, pp. 1–4.
37. _____, "Consumers Unhappy With Web Site Simply Go Away," www.CenterforMediaResearch.com, August 23, 2005, pp. 1–2.
38. Marc Weingarten, "It's an Ad! It's a Game! It's Both!" *Business 2.0,* March 2002, p. 102.
39. ______, "New SRI Study Reveals Cloudy ITV Picture; VOD, IPG's Are Bright Spots," www.statisticalresearch.com, August 28, 2001, p. 1.
40. Theresa Howard, "Burger King to Send Extended Ad to Customers of Sprint Phone Video," www.USAToday.com, January 20, 2006, pp. 1–2.
41. Beth Snyder Bulik and Claire Atkinson, "Apple iTunes to Offer Video on Demand," www.AdAge.com, October 12, 2005, pp. 1–3.
42. ____, "Ad Execs Are Upping Online Ad Budgets," www.emarketer.com, May 5, 2005, pp. 1–2; ____, "The Big Battle Over Ad Budgets," www.emarketer.com, September 15, 2005, p. 1.
43. Geoffrey A. Fowler, "U.S. Firms Study What Flies On Hot Medium and Why—And How to Try It at Home," *The Wall Street Journal,* April 25, 2005, pp. B1, 6.
44. Shankar Gupta, "Sell Phones: U.S. Teens Already Receiving Wireless Ad Pitches, More Expected," www.mediapost.com, February 15, 2005, pp. 1–2.

Chapter Sixteen

1. Louis J. Haugh, "Defining and Redefining," *Advertising Age,* February 14, 1983, p. M44.
2. Scott A. Nielsen, John Quelch, and Caroline Henderson, "Consumer Promotions and the Acceleration of Product Purchases," in *Research on Sales Promotion: Collected Papers,* ed. Katherine E. Jocz (Cambridge, MA: Marketing Science Institute, 1984).
3. J. Jeffrey Inman and Leigh McAlister, "Do Coupon Expiration Dates Affect Consumer Behavior?" *Journal of Marketing Research,* vol. 31, August 1994, pp. 423–28.
4. "Kathleen M. Joyce, "Riding the Tide," *PROMO 2005 Industry Trends Report, PROMO,* April 2005, pp. AR3–6.
5. Ibid.
6. Betsy Spethmann, "Is Promotion a Dirty Word?" *Promo,* March 2001, pp. 64–72.
7. "Clutter: Extras, Extras!" www.promomagazine.com, August 1, 2001.
8. Ibid.
9. Betsy Spethmann, "Sudden Impact," *Promo,* April 1999, pp. 42–48; _________, "Is Advertising Dead?" *Promo,* September 1998, pp. 32–36.
10. Richard Sale, "Evaluation in Evolution," *Promo,* September 1998, pp. 79–84.
11. Matthew Boyle, "Brand Killers," *Fortune,* August 11, 2003, pp. 89–100; ______, "Attack," *Promo,* September 1999, pp. 79–84.
12. Andy Serwer, "Bruised in Bentonville," *Fortune,* April 18, 2005, pp. 84–89.
13. "The Effects of Promotion Stimuli on Consumer Purchase Behavior," (Glenview, IL: FSI Council, 1999).
14. Betsy Spethman, "Tuning in at the Shelf," *Promo 13th Annual Source Book,* 2006, pp. 22, 24.
15. Leigh McAlister, "A Model of Consumer Behavior," *Marketing Communications,* April 1987.

16. "Too Many Choices," *The Wall Street Journal,* April 20, 2001, p. B1.
17. Al Urbanski, "Techno Promo," *Promo,* August 1998, pp. 48–52, 146, 147.
18. Richard Gibson, "How Products Check Out Helps Determine Pay," *The Wall Street Journal,* August 1, 1991, p. B1.
19. Betsy Spethman, "Retail Details, *Promo 12th Annual Source Book 2005,* pp. 27–28; ____________, "Account Specific Comes Due," *Promo,* November 1996, pp. 39–48.
20. *NCH Reporter, no. 1* (Nielsen Clearing House, 1983).
21. *The Magazine Handbook,* no. 59 (New York: Magazine Publishers of America, 1991).
22. "Clutter: Extra, Extras!"
23. Judann Dagnoli, "Jordan Hits Ad Execs for Damaging Brands," *Advertising Age,* November 4, 1991, p. 47.
24. R. M. Prentice, "How to Split Your Marketing Funds Between Advertising and Promotion Dollars," *Advertising Age,* January 10, 1977, pp. 41–42, 44.
25. Betsy Spethmann, "Money and Power," *Brandweek,* March 15, 1993, p. 21.
26. Tim Parry, "Happy Customers," *Promo,* April 2005, pp. AR21–23.
27. Miller Taste Challenge, 2005 Reggie Awards—Promotion Marketing Association, www.pmalink.org/awards/reggie2005/index.
28. Evan Perez and Chad Terhune, "Today, 'Brawny' Men Help with the Kids and the Housework," *The Wall Street Journal,* October 2, 2002, p. B2.
29. "Trial and Conversion VI: Consumers' Reactions to Samples and Demonstrations," *Promotional Marketing Association, Inc.,* 2002.
30. *2004 Trend Report,* (Deerfield, IL: NCH Marketing Services).
31. J. Jeffrey Inman and Leigh McAlister, "Do Coupon Expiration Dates Affect Consumer Behavior?"
32. Jack Neff, "Coupons Get Clipped," *Advertising Age,* November 5, 2001, pp. 1, 47.
33. Karen Holt, "Coupon Crimes," *Promo,* April 2004, pp. 23–26, 70.
34. Raju Narisetti, "Many Companies Are Starting to Wean Consumers Off Coupons," *The Wall Street Journal,* January 22, 1997, pp. B1, 10.
35. Jack Neff, "Coupons Get Clipped."
36. Jack Neff, "P&G Extends Co-branded Coupons," *Advertising Age,* June 3, 1996, p. 9; Richard Sale, "Not Your Mother's Coupon," *Promo,* April 1999, pp. 56–61.
37. Survey by Oxtoby-Smith, Inc., cited in "Many Consumers View Rebates as a Bother," *The Wall Street Journal,* April 13, 1989, p. B1.
38. William R. Dean, "Irresistible but Not Free of Problems," *Advertising Age,* October 6, 1980, pp. S1–12.
39. Merissa Marr and Steven Grey, "McDonald's Woos New Partners as Disney Pact Nears End," *The Wall Street Journal,* June 6, 2005, pp. B1, 2.
40. William A. Robinson, "What Are Promos' Weak and Strong Points?" *Advertising Age,* April 7, 1980, p. 54.
41. Richard Sale, "Serving Up Sweeps," *Promo,* August 1999, pp. 70–78; "Sweepstakes Fever," *Forbes,* October 3, 1988, pp. 164–66.
42. "Next-Tech," *Promo,* July 2005, pp. 24–27.
43. Patricia Odell, "Doritos Targets Texters in Integrated Campaign," *promomagazine.com,* March 9, 2005.
44. Bob Woods, "Picking a Winner," *Promo,* August 1998, pp. 57–62.
45. Richard Sale, "Sweeping the Courts," *Promo,* May 1998, pp. 422–45, 148–52.
46. Maxine S. Lans, "Legal Hurdles Big Part of Promotions Game," *Marketing News,* October 24, 1994, pp. 15–16.
47. Survey by Oxtoby-Smith, Inc., "Many Consumers View Rebates."
48. Peter Tat, William A. Cunningham III, and Emin Babakus, "Consumer Perceptions of Rebates," *Journal of Advertising Research,* 28 (4) (August/September 1988), pp. 45–50.
49. Brian Grow, "The Great Rebate Runaround," *BusinessWeek,* December 5, 2005, pp. 34–37.
50. Edward A. Blair and E. Lair Landon, "The Effects of Reference Prices in Retail Advertisements," *Journal of Marketing,* vol. 45, no. 2 (Spring 1981), pp. 61–69.
51. Betsy Spethmann, "Switching Loyalty," *Promo,* July 2002, pp. 40–45.
52. "Calling All Shoppers," *Promo Special Report,* April 1998, pp. S5, 6.
53. R.J. Igneizi, "WD-40@50," *The San Diego Union-Tribune,* November 10, 2003, pp. D1, 4.
54. Betsy Spethmann, "Switching Loyalty."
55. Kathleen M. Joyce, "Keeping the Faith," *Promo's 12th Annual Source Book 2005,* p. 24.
56. Tim Parry, "National Impact," *Promo,* January 2005, pp. 28–30.
57. Adapted from Terrence A. Shimp, *Advertising, Promotion, and Supplemental Aspects of Integrated Marketing Communication,* Sixth Edition, (Mason, Ohio: South-Western), p. 524.
58. William L. Wilkie, Debra M. Desrochers, and Gregory T. Gundlach, "Marketing Research and Public Policy: The Case of Slotting Fees," *Journal of Marketing & Public Policy,* vol. 21, (2), (Fall 2002) pp. 275–288; Frank Green, "Battling for Shelf Control," *San Diego Union-Tribune,* November 19, 1996, pp. C1, 6, 7.
59. "Want Shelf Space at the Supermarket? Ante Up," *BusinessWeek,* August 7, 1989, pp. 60–61.
60. Ira Teinowitz, "Senators Berate Industry Abuse of Slotting Fees," *Advertising Age,* September 20, 1999, pp. 3, 66.
61. Paul N. Bloom, Gregory T. Gundlach, and Joseph P. Cannon, "Slotting Allowances and Fees: Schools of Thought and Views of Practicing Managers," *Journal of Marketing,* 64, April 2000, pp. 92–108.
62. Melissa Campanelli, "What's in Store for EDLP?" *Sales & Marketing Management,* August 1993, pp. 56–59; "Procter & Gamble Hits Back," *BusinessWeek,* July 19, 1993, pp. 20–22.
63. Janet Adamy, "Grocery Stores Cut Out the Weekly Special: Under Pressure From Discounters, Chains Lower Everyday Prices On a Range of Popular Staples," *The Wall Street Journal,* July 20, 2005, p. D1; Kerry J. Smith, "Procter Moves the Market Again," *Promo,* July 1999, p. 6; "Make It Simple," *BusinessWeek,* September 6, 1996, pp. 96–104.
64. "Crunching the Numbers," *Promo,* May 1, 2001, pp. 49–50.
65. Matthew Kinsman, "No Pain, No Gain," *Promo,* January 2002, pp. 26–28.
66. Tom Steinhagen, "Space Management Shapes Up with Planograms," *Marketing News,* November 12, 1990, p. 7.
67. Srinath Gopalakrishna, Gary L. Lilien, Jerome D. Williams, and Ian K. Sequeria, "Do Trade Shows Pay Off?" *Journal of Marketing,* vol. 59, July 1995, pp. 75–83.
68. Tobi Elkin, "Co-op Crossroads," *Advertising Age,* November 15, 1999, pp. 1, 24, 26.
69. Cynthia Rigg, "Hard Times Means Growth for Co-op Ads," *Advertising Age,* November 12, 1990, p. 24.
70. Edwin L. Artzt, "The Lifeblood of Brands," *Advertising Age,* November 4, 1991, p. 32.
71. "Everyone Is Bellying Up to This Bar," *BusinessWeek,* January 27, 1992, p. 84.

72. Jack Neff, "The New Brand Management," *Advertising Age,* November 8, 1999, pp. S2, 18; Benson P. Shapiro, "Improved Distribution with Your Promotional Mix," *Harvard Business Review,* (March/April 1977), p. 116; and Roger A. Strang, "Sales Promotion—Fast Growth, Faulty Management," *Harvard Business Review,* (July/August 1976), p. 119.
73. Quote by Thomas E. Hamilton, director of sales promotion service, William Esty Advertising, cited in Felix Kessler, "The Costly Couponing Craze," *Fortune,* June 9, 1986, p. 84.
74. Priya Raghubir and Kim Corfman, "When Do Price Promotions Affect Pretrial Brand Evaluations?" *Journal of Marketing Research* 36 (May 1999), pp. 211–22.
75. Alan G. Sawyer and Peter H. Dickson, "Psychological Perspectives on Consumer Response to Sales Promotion," in *Research on Sales Promotion: Collected Papers,* ed. Katherine E. Jocz (Cambridge, MA: Marketing Science Institute, 1984).
76. William E. Myers, "Trying to Get Out of the Discounting Box," *Adweek,* November 11, 1985, p. 2.
77. Leigh McAlister, "Managing the Dynamics of Promotional Change," in *Looking at the Retail Kaleidoscope, Forum IX* (Stamford, CT: Donnelley Marketing, April 1988).
78. "Promotions Blemish Cosmetic Industry," *Advertising Age,* May 10, 1984, pp. 22–23, 26.
79. Cliff Edwards, "Everyone Loves A Freebie—Except Dell's Rivals," *BusinessWeek,* July 22, 2002, p. 41.
80. Priya Raghubir, J. Jeffrey Inman and Hqans Gande, "The Three Faces of Consumer Promotions," *California Management Review,* vol. 465, no. 4, (Summer 2004), pp. 23–42.

Chapter Seventeen

1. Raymond Simon, *Public Relations, Concept and Practices,* 2nd ed. (Columbus, OH: Grid Publishing, 1980), p. 8.
2. Scott M. Cutlip, Allen H. Center, and Glen M. Broom, *Effective Public Relations,* 8th ed., (Upper Saddle River, NJ: Prentice Hall, 2000).
3. ______, "PR News/PRSA Survey," *PR News,* May 25, 2005, p. 1.
4. Al Ries and Laura Ries, *The Fall of Advertising and the Rise of Public Relations,* New York, Harper Collins, 2002.
5. N. Curry, "PR Isn't Marketing," *Advertising Age,* December 18, 1991, p. 18.
6. Martha M. Lauzen, "Imperialism and Encroachment in Public Relations," *Public Relations Review* 17, (3) (Fall 1991), pp. 245–55.
7. Cutlip, Center, and Broom, *Effective Public Relations.*
8. Philip Kotler and William Mindak, "Marketing and Public Relations," *Journal of Marketing* 42 (4) (October 1978), pp. 13–20.
9. Thomas L. Harris, "How MPR Adds Value to Integrated Marketing Communications," *Public Relations Quarterly,* Summer 1993, pp. 13–18.
10. Jack Neff, Cara Dipasquale, and Jean Halliday, "Ries' Thesis: Ads Don't Build Brands, PR Does," *Advertising Age,* July 15, 2002, pp. 14–15.
11. Thomas L. Harris, "Marketing PR—The Second Century," *Reputation Management,* www.prcentral.com, (January/February 1999), pp. 1–6.
12. Mark Weiner, "Marketing PR Revolution," *Communication World,* January/February 2005, pp. 1–5.
13. Simon, *Public Relations, Concepts and Practices,* p. 164.
14. Scott M. Cutlip, Allen H. Center, and Glenn M. Broom, *Effective Public Relations,* 8th ed. (Englewood Cliffs, NJ: Prentice Hall, 2000), p. 200.
15. John E. Marston, *Modern Public Relations* (New York: McGraw-Hill, 1979).
16. ______, *McDonalds Annual Report,* 2005, www.mcdonalds.com.
17. Joe Agnew, "Marketers Find the Antidrug Campaign Addictive," *Marketing News,* October 9, 1987, p. 12.
18. ______, "Pfizer Announces Improvements to Consumer Advertising for Prescription Medicines," *Pfizer News Release,* www.pfizer.com, 2005.
19. Christopher Lee, "Medicare Drug Benefit Outlined in Campaign," *Washington Post,* October 10, 2005, p. A17.
20. Edward Iwata, "U.S. Companies Step Up to Plate with Donations," *USA Today,* September 1, 2005, p. B3.
21. Tina Moore, "Pilgrim's Pride Issues Nationwide Recall of Cooked Deli Products, Largest in U.S. History," www.SFGate.com, October 15, 2002, pp. 1–3.
22. Shel Holtz, *Public Relations on the Internet* (New York: American Management Association, 1998).
23. Raymond Serafin, "Cars Squeeze Mileage from Awards," *Advertising Age,* June 4, 1990, p. 36.
24. ______, "Panera Bread Takes Top Spot In UNH Rosenberg Center Franchise 50 Index," www.unh.edu/news, June 8, 2005, p. 1–2.
25. Raymond Simon, *Public Relations, Concepts and Practices,* 3rd. ed, New York: John Wiley & Sons, 1984, p. 291.
26. Harold Mendelsohn, "Some Reasons Why Information Campaigns Can Succeed," *Public Opinion Quarterly,* Spring 1973, p. 55.
27. Weiner, "Marketing PR Revolution."
28. Walter K. Lindenmann, "An Effectiveness Yardstick to Measure Public Relations Success," *Public Relations Quarterly* 38, no. 1 (Spring 1993), pp. 7–10.
29. Deborah Holloway, "How to Select a Measurement System That's Right for You," *Public Relations Quarterly,* 37 (3) (Fall 1992), pp. 15–18.
30. Michele Gershberg, "Martha Stewart Sticks to Kinder, Gentler TV Image," www.reuters.com, September 28, 2005, pp. 1–3.
31. Jaye S. Niefeld, "Corporate Advertising," *Industrial Marketing,* July 1980, pp. 64–74.
32. Tom Garbett, "What Companies Project to Public," *Advertising Age,* July 6, 1981, p. 51.
33. _____, "Reconstructive Image Surgery, b2b Print Ads Help Bring Tyco Back From the Dead," *MIN's B 2 B,* June 6, 2005, p. 1.
34. Ed Zotti, "An Expert Weighs the Prose and Yawns," *Advertising Age,* January 24, 1983, p. M-11.
35. Jim Edwards, "Under Siege, Big Pharma Opens Image Ad Spigot," *Brandweek,* September 12, 2005, p. 9.
36. Bob Seeter, "AMA Hopes New Ads Will Cure Image Problem," *Los Angeles Times,* August 14, 1991, p. A5.
37. John Burnett, "Shopping for Sponsorships? Integration Is Paramount," *Brandweek,* February 14, 1994, p. 18.
38. Ed Zotti, "An Expert Weighs the Prose and Yawns," *Advertising Age,* January 24, 1983, p. M-11.
39. Ronald Alsop, "The Best Corporate Reputations in America," *The Wall Street Journal,* September 29, 1999, p. B1.
40. _____, *Cause Marketing Forum,* 2005.
41. David Caraviello, "Racing Fuel: Tobacco Money Makes Motorsports Go," *The Post and Courier,* May 18, 2002, p. 1A.

42. Brian Trusdell, "Will a Cigarette Ban Stall Nascar's Growth?" *Sales & Marketing Management,* February 1997, pp. 67–75.
43. David Caraviello, "Racing Fuel: Tobacco Money Makes Motorsports Go," *The Post and Courier,* May 18, 2002, p. 1A.
44. Erica Bulman, "FIA Wants Tobacco Sponsors Banned," www.dailynews.yahoo.com, November 21, 2002, pp. 1–2.
45. Theresa Howard, "Investors Can Capitalize When Companies Score Sports Sponsorships," *USA Today,* October 14, 2005, p. 5B.
46. Prakash Sethi, *Advertising and Large Corporations* (Lexington, MA: Lexington Books, 1977), pp. 7–8.
47. Janet Myers, "JWT Anti-Japan Ad Is a Bomb," *Advertising Age,* April 2, 1990, p. 4.
48. _____, Cause Marketing Forum, www.causemarketing forum.com, 2005.
49. Harvey Meyer, "When the Cause Is Just," *Journal of Business Strategy,* (November/December 1999), pp. 27–31.
50. Ibid., p. 28.
51. Ibid., p. 29.
52. Karen Benezra, "Cause and Effects Marketing," *Brandweek,* April 22, 1996, p. 38.
53. Bob Donath, "Corporate Communications," *Industrial Marketing,* July 1980, pp. 52, 53–57.
54. Janas Sinclair and Tracy Irani, "Advocacy Advertising for Biotechnology," *Journal of Advertising,* Fall 2005, pp. 59–74.
55. Donath, "Corporate Communications," p. 53.
56. Ibid., p. 52.

Chapter Eighteen

1. Ginger Conlon, "Cornering the Market," *Sales & Marketing Management,* March 1997, pp. 74–76.
2. Carl G. Stevens and David P. Keane, "How to Become a Better Sales Manager: Give Salespeople How To, Not Rah Rah," *Marketing News,* May 30, 1980, p. 1.
3. Tom Wotruba and Edwin K. Simpson, *Sales Management* (Boston: Kent Publishing, 1989).
4. Cahners Publishing Co., 2005.
5. Thomas R. Wotruba, "The Evolution of Personal Selling," *Journal of Personal Selling & Sales Management,* 11, (3) (Summer 1991), pp. 1–12.
6. James Champy, "Selling to Tomorrow's Customer," *Sales & Marketing Management,* March 1999, p. 28.
7. Kevin Hoffberg and Kevin J. Corcoran, "Selling at the Speed of Change," *Customers 2000,* pp. S22–26.
8. Jonathan R. Copulsky and Michael J. Wolf, "Relationship Marketing: Positioning for the Future," *Journal of Business Strategy,* (July/August 1990), pp. 16–20.
9. Don Pepper and Martha Rogers, "In Vendors They Trust," *Sales & Marketing Management,* November 1999, pp. 30–32.
10. Cahners Publishing Co., "Evaluating the Costs of Sales Calls in Business to Business Markets," http://www.cahners.com/research, 2002.
11. Thayer C. Taylor, "A Letup in the Rise of Sales Call Costs," *Sales & Marketing Management,* February 25, 1980, p. 24.
12. Melinda Ligos, "Gimme, Gimme, Gimme," *Sales & Marketing Management,* March 2002, pp. 32–40.
13. Erin Strout, "Spy Games," *Sales & Marketing Management,* February 2002, pp. 30–3.
14. Theodore Levitt, "Communications and Industrial Selling," *Journal of Marketing,* 31 (April 1967), pp. 15–21.
15. John E. Morrill, "Industrial Advertising Pays Off," *Harvard Business Review,* (March/April 1970), p. 4.
16. "Salespeople Contact Fewer than 10 Percent of Purchase Decision Makers over a Two-Month Period," *McGraw-Hill LAP Report no. 1029.3* (New York: McGraw-Hill, 1987).
17. *Direct Marketing Association, 2000.*
18. Peggy Moretti, "Telemarketers Serve Clients," *Business Marketing,* April 1994, pp. 27–29.
19. Rolph E. Anderson, Joseph F. Hair, and Alan J. Bush, *Professional Sales Management* (New York: McGraw-Hill 1988).

Chapter Nineteen

1. Mary Tolan, "Holidays Are Here and So Is Ad Puzzle," *Advertising Age,* November 16, 1998, p. 36.
2. Ibid.
3. _____, "Heineken to Can TV Adverts in UK," www.newsvote.bbc.co.uk, October 24, 2005, p. 1.
4. Spike Cramphorn, "What Advertising Testing Might Have Been, If We Had Only Known," *Journal of Advertising Research,* 44(2) June 2004, pp. 170–180.
5. Robyn Grenspan, "Marketers Missing Measurements," www.clickz.com, June 4, 2004, pp. 1–2.
6. Noreen O'Leary, "Does Creativity Count?" *Adweek,* December 11, 2000, pp. 30–34.
7. Barbara Lippert, "Party Pooper," *Adweek,* September 9, 2002, p. 18.
8. Laura Bird, "Loved the Ad. May (or May Not) Buy the Product," *The Wall Street Journal,* April 7, 1994, p. B1.
9. Tim Nudd, "Does Sex Really Sell?" *Adweek,* October 17, 2005, pp. 14–17.
10. Bruce Horowitz, "TV Ads the Public Will Never See," *Los Angeles Times,* August 3, 1988, p. 1.
11. *McGraw-Hill Lab Report no. 3151* (New York: McGraw-Hill, 1988); Alan D. Fletcher, *Target Marketing through the Yellow Pages* (Troy, MI: Yellow Pages Publishers Association, 1991), p. 23.
12. Personal interview with Jay Khoulos, president of World Communications, Inc., 1988.
13. David A. Aaker and John G. Myers, *Advertising Management,* 3rd edition, (Englewood Cliffs, NJ: Prentice Hall, 1987), p. 474.
14. Joel N. Axelrod, "Induced Moods and Attitudes toward Products," *Journal of Advertising Research* 3 (June 1963), pp. 19–24; Lauren E. Crane, "How Product, Appeal, and Program Affect Attitudes toward Commercials," *Journal of Advertising Research,* 4 (March 1964), p. 15.
15. Robert Settle, "Marketing in Tight Times," *Marketing Communications* 13 (1) (January 1988), pp. 19–23.
16. "What Is Good Creative?" *Topline, no. 41* (New York: McCollum Spielman Worldwide, 1994), p. 4.
17. James R. Hagerty, "Tests Lead Lowe's to Revamp Strategy," *The Wall Street Journal,* March 11, 1999, p. B18.
18. XMOS.
19. "21 Ad Agencies Endorse Copy-Testing Principles," *Marketing News* 15, (February 19, 1982), p. 1.
20. Ibid.
21. John M. Caffyn, "Telepex Testing of TV Commercials," *Journal of Advertising Research* 5 (2) (June 1965), pp. 29–37; Thomas J. Reynolds and Charles Gengler, "A Strategic Framework for Assessing Advertising: The Animatic vs. Finished Issue," *Journal of Advertising Research,* (October/November 1991), pp. 61–71; Nigel A. Brown and Ronald Gatty, "Rough vs. Finished TV Commercials in Telepex Tests," *Journal of Advertising Research,* 7 (4) (December 1967), p. 21.

22. Charles H. Sandage, Vernon Fryburger, and Kim Rotzoll, *Advertising Theory and Practice,* 10th ed. (Burr Ridge, IL: Richard D. Irwin, 1979).
23. Lyman E. Ostlund, "Advertising Copy Testing: A Review of Current Practices, Problems and Prospects," *Current Issues and Research in Advertising,* 1978, pp. 87–105.
24. Jack B. Haskins, "Factual Recall as a Measure of Advertising Effectiveness," *Journal of Advertising Research,* 4 (1)(March 1964), pp. 2–7.
25. John Philip Jones and Margaret H. Blair, "Examining 'Conventional Wisdoms' about Advertising Effects with Evidence from Independent Sources," 36 (6) *Journal of Advertising Research,* (November/December 1996), pp. 37–52.
26. Paul J. Watson and Robert J. Gatchel, "Autonomic Measures of Advertising," *Journal of Advertising Research,* 19 (1)(June 1979), pp. 15–26.
27. Priscilla A. LaBarbera and Joel D. Tucciarone, "GSR Reconsidered: A Behavior-based Approach to Evaluating and Improving the Sales Potency of Advertising," *Journal of Advertising Research,* 35 (3) (September/October 1995), pp. 33–40.
28. Flemming Hansen, "Hemispheric Lateralization: Implications for Understanding Consumer Behavior," *Journal of Consumer Research* 8 (1988), pp. 23–36.
29. Kevin Lane Keller, Susan E. Heckler, and Michael J. Houston, "The Effects of Brand Name Suggestiveness on Advertising Recall," *Journal of Marketing,* 62 (20) (January 1998), pp. 48–57.
30. Jan Stapel, "Recall and Recognition: A Very Close Relationship," *Journal of Advertising Research,* 38(1) July/August 1998, pp. 41–45.
31. Hubert A. Zielske, "Does Day-after Recall Penalize 'Feeling Ads'?" *Journal of Advertising Research,* 22, (1) (1982), pp. 19–22.
32. Arthur J. Kover, "Why Copywriters Don't Like Advertising Research—and What Kind of Research Might They Accept," *Journal of Advertising Research,* 36 (March/April 1996), pp. RC8–RC10; Gary Levin, "Emotion Guides BBDO's Ad Tests," *Advertising Age,* January 29, 1990, p. 12.
33. Terry Haller, "Day-after Recall to Persist Despite JWT Study; Other Criteria Looming," *Marketing News,* May 18, 1979, p. 4.
34 Ravi Chandiramani, "Reckitt Launches Debut iTV Campaign for Finish," *Marketing,* January 10, 2002, p. 9.
35. Kipp Cheng, "IPG Platform Gains Major Advertisers," *Adweek,* July 23, 2001, p. 5.
36. Dave Kruegel, "Television Advertising Effectiveness and Research Innovations," *Journal of Consumer Marketing,* 5 (3) (Summer 1988), pp. 43–52.
37. Gary Levin, "Tracing Ads' Impact," *Advertising Age,* November 12, 1990, p. 49.
38. John Philip Jones, "Single-source Research Begins to Fulfill Its Promise," *Journal of Advertising Research,* 35 (1) (May/June 1995), pp. 9–16.
39. Jeffrey L. Seglin, "The New Era of Ad Measurement," *Adweek's Marketing Week,* January 23, 1988, p. 24.
40. James F. Donius, "Marketing Tracking: A Strategic Reassessment and Planning Tool," *Journal of Advertising Research* 25 (1) (February/March 1985), pp. 15–19.
41. Russell I. Haley and Allan L. Baldinger, "The ARF Copy Research Validity Project," *Journal of Advertising Research,* (April/May 1991), pp. 11–32.
42. Glenn Heitsmith, "Something for Nothing," *Promo,* September 1993, pp. 30, 31, 93.
43. Ibid.
44. "Journeying Deeper into the Minds of Shoppers," *BusinessWeek,* February 4, 1991, p. 85.
45. Elizabeth Gardener and Minakshi Trivedi, "A Communications Framework to Evaluate Sales Promotion Strategies," *Journal of Advertising Research,* 38 (3) (May/June 1998), pp. 67–71.
46. David W. Schumann, Jennifer Grayson, Johanna Ault, Kerri Hargrove, Lois Hollingsworth, Russell Ruelle, and Sharon Seguin, "The Effectiveness of Shopping Cart Signage: Perceptual Measures Tell a Different Story," *Journal of Advertising Research,* 31 (February/ March 1991), pp. 17–22.
47. June Bryan Kim, "Research Makes Ski Run Easier," *Advertising Age,* August 18, 1991, p. 30.
48. Steve McClellan, "New Software to Track In-Store Radio," *Adweek,* October 10, 2005, p. 10.
49. Bettina Cornwell and Isabelle Maignan, "An International Review of Sponsorship Research," *Journal of Advertising,* 38 (1) (March 1998), pp. 1–23.
50. Michel Tuan Pham, "The Evaluation of Sponsorship Effectiveness: A Model and Some Methodological Considerations," *Gestion 2000,* pp. 47–65.

Chapter Twenty

1. David A. Aaker and Erich Joachimsthaler, "The Lure of Global Branding," *Harvard Business Review,* (November/December 1999), pp. 137–144.
2. Dana James, "Mixed Messages," *Marketing News,* July 22, 2002, pp. 1, 7–8.
3. Deborah James, "Match Game," *Marketing News,* November 11, 2002, pp. 1, 11–12; John A. Byrne, "Philip Morris: Inside America's Most Reviled Company," *BusinessWeek,* November 29, 1999, pp. 176–92.
4. Hillay Chura, "Beer Giant SAB Wins Approval for Miller Acquisition," www.AdAge.com, July 1, 2002.
5. "So Where The Bloody Hell Are You? Tourism Australia Invites the World to Australia," www.tourismaustralia.com/NewsCentre, February 27, 2006; "Drop in Travel Forces Review of Aussie Ads," *Marketing News,* September 16, 2002, p. 46.
6. Paula Lyon Andruss, "Slow Boat To China," *Marketing News,* September 10, 2001, pp. 1, 11–12; Normandy Madden, "China Ad Opportunities to Grow with WTO Deal," *Advertising Age International,* January 2000, p. 6.
7. *Colgate-Palmolive 2004 Annual Report,* www.colgatepalmolive.com.
8. Andy Serwer, "Hot Starbucks To Go," *Fortune,* January 26, 2004, pp. 61–74.
9. *General Mills 2005 Annual Report,* www.generalmills.com; Christopher Knowles, "Europe Cooks Up a Cereal Brawl," *Fortune,* June 3, 1991, pp. 175–78.
10. Robert J. Coen, *Insider's Report: Robert Coen Presentation on Advertising Expenditures* (New York: Universal McCann, December 2005).
11. Ibid.
12. R. Craig Endicott, "19th Annual Global Marketing Report," *Advertising Age,* November 14, 2005, pp. 1–53.
13. Vern Terpstra, *International Marketing,* 4th ed. (New York: Holt, Rinehart & Winston/Dryden Press, 1987), p. 427.
14. "Asian Horizons," *Sales & Marketing Management,* August 1996, pp. 64–68.
15. Marc Gunther, "MTV'S Passage To India," *Fortune,* August 9, 2004, pp. 117–125; Laurel Wentz and Charles

Newbery, "Argentina Ad Industry in Crisis," www.AdAge.com, July 29, 2002.
16. G. Pascal Zachary, "Making It In China," *Business 2.0,* August 2005, pp. 59–65.
17. Clay Chandler, "China Deluxe," *Fortune,* July 26, 2004, pp. 148–156.
18. "Spheres of Influence 2004—Global Advertising Expenditure Trends Report," *Initiative Futures Worldwide,* London, January 2004.
19. Anne Moncreiff Arrarte, "Advertisers Find Latin American Children's Media a Growing Market," *Miami Herald,* December 17, 1997.
20. Mark Lasswell, "Lost in Translation," *Business 2.0,* August 2004, pp. 68–70.
21. George E. Belch and Michael A. Belch, "Toward Development of a Model and Scale for Assessing Consumer Receptivity to Foreign Products and Global Advertising," in *European Advances in Consumer Research,* vol. 1, ed. Gary J. Bamossy and W. Fred van Raaij (Provo, UT: Association for Consumer Research, 1993), pp. 52–57.
22. Subhash Sharma, Terrence Shimp, and Jeongshin Shin, "Consumer Ethnocentrism: A Test of Antecedents and Moderators," *Journal of the Academy of Marketing Science* (Winter 1995), pp. 26–37.
23. Shelly Pannill, "The Road to Richesse," *Sales & Marketing Management,* November 1999, pp. 89–96.
24. "They All Want To Be Like Mike," *Fortune,* July 21, 1997, pp. 51–53.
25. For an excellent discussion of various elements of Japanese culture such as language and its implications for promotion, see John F. Sherry, Jr., and Eduardo G. Camargo, "May Your Life Be Marvelous: English Language Labelling and the Semiotics of Japanese Promotion," *Journal of Consumer Research,* 14 (September 1987), pp. 174–88.
26. Barbara Mueller, "Reflections on Culture: An Analysis of Japanese and American Advertising Appeals," *Journal of Advertising Research,* June/July 1987, pp. 51–59.
27. Barbara Mueller, "Standardization vs. Specialization: An Examination of Westernization in Japanese Advertising," *Journal of Advertising Research,* 31 (1) (January/February 1992), pp. 15–24; and Johny K. Johanson, "The Sense of Nonsense: Japanese TV Advertising," *Journal of Advertising,* 23, no. 1 (March 1994), pp. 17–26.
28. Michael L. Maynard and Charles R. Taylor, "Girlish Images Across Cultures: Analyzing Japanese Versus U.S. Seventeen Magazine Ads," *Journal of Advertising,* 28, no. 1 (Spring 1999), pp. 39–49.
29. John B. Ford, Patricia Kramer Voli, Earl D. Honeycutt, Jr., and Susan L. Casey, "Gender Role Portrayals in Japanese Advertising: A Magazine Content Analysis," *Journal of Advertising* 27, no. 1 (Spring 1998).
30. Francis Hsu, *Americans and Chinese: Passage to Differences,* (Honolulu, HI: University Press of Hawaii 1981).
31. Carolyn A. Lin, "Cultural Values Reflected in Chinese and American Television Advertising," *Journal of Advertising,* vol. 30, (4) pp. 83–94.
32. Don E. Schultz, "New Systems Make China Next Hot Spot," *Marketing News,* January 7, 2002, p. 5.
33. Geoffrey A. Fowler, "China Bans Nike's LeBron Ad As Offensive to Nation's Dignity," *The Wall Street Journal,* December 7, 2004, p. B4.
34. Marian Katz, "No Women, No Alcohol; Learn Saudi Taboos Before Placing Ads," *International Advertiser,* February 1986, pp. 11–12.
35. Safran S. Al-Makaty, G. Norman van Tubergen, S. Scott Whitlow, and Douglas S. Boyd, "Attitudes toward Advertising in Islam," *Journal of Advertising Research,* 36 (3) (May/June 1996), pp. 16–26.
36. Elizabeth Bryant, "P&G Pushes the Envelope in Egypt with TV Show on Feminine Hygiene," *Advertising Age International,* December 14, 1998, p. 2.
37. Dean M. Peebles and John K. Ryans, *Management of International Advertising* (Newton, MA: Allyn & Bacon, 1984).
38. "Malaysia Bans 'Sly' Tobacco Ads," *Marketing News,* September 1, 2002, p. 7.
39. Deborah James, "Match Game."
40. Simon Tegel, "Tobacco Advertising on TV to End in Mexico," www. Adageglobal.com, June 20, 2002.
41. Vanessa Fuhrmans, "In Europe, Prescription-Drug Ads Are Banned—and Health Costs Lower," *The Wall Street Journal,* March 15, 2002, pp. B1, 4.
42. Laurel Wentz, "Local Laws Keep International Marketers Hopping," *Advertising Age,* July 11, 1985, p. 20.
43. Jeremy Slate, "EC Lets Stand Toy Ad Ban," *Advertising Age International,* August 1999, pp. 1, 11.
44. Sam Loewenberg, "Effort in EU to Ban TV Ads Aimed at Kids Gains Steam," *Los Angeles Times,* July 9, 2001, p. C3.
45. Al-Makatay et al., "Attitudes Toward Advertising in Islam."
46. Naveen Donthu, "A Cross-Country Investigation of Recall of and Attitude toward Comparative Advertising," *Journal of Advertising* 27, no. 2 (Summer 1998), pp. 111–122.
47. Derek Turner, "Coke Pops Brazilian Comparative Ad," *Advertising Age,* September 9, 1991, p. 24.
48. J. Craig Andrews, Steven Lysonski, and Srinivas Durvasula, "Understanding Cross-Cultural Student Perceptions of Advertising in General: Implications for Advertising Educators and Practitioners," *Journal of Advertising,* 20, no. 2 (June 1991), pp. 15–28.
49. Jonathan Cheng, "China Demands Concrete Proof of Ad Claims," *The Wall Street Journal,* July 8, 2005, pp. B1, 4.
50. J. Boddewyn and Iris Mohr, "International Advertisers Face Government Hurdles," *Marketing News,* May 8, 1987, pp. 21–22.
51. Tze Yee-Lin, "Malaysia May Allow Foreign Commercials," *Advertising Age International,* March 1997, p. i22.
52. Matthew Rose and Leslie Chang, "Chinese Officials Force Magazines to Go without Famous Names," *The Wall Street Journal,* February 2, 2000, p. B1.
53. Sam Loewenberg, "Effort in EU to Ban TV Ads Aimed at Kids Gains Steam."
54. Ali Qassim, "U.K. Mounts Kids Advertising Program," www.adageglobal.com, April 17, 2002.
55. Stephanie Thompson, "Europe Slams Icons as Food Fights Back," *Advertising Age,* January 31, 2005, pp. 1, 38.
56. Robert D. Buzzell, "Can You Standardize Multinational Marketing?" *Harvard Business Review,* (November/December 1968), pp. 102–13; and Ralph Z. Sorenson and Ulrich E. Wiechmann, "How Multinationals View Marketing," *Harvard Business Review,* (May/June 1975), p. 38.
57. Theodore Levitt, "The Globalization of Markets," *Harvard Business Review,* (May/June 1983), pp. 92–102; and Theodore Levitt, *The Marketing Imagination* (New York: Free Press, 1986).
58. Anne B. Fisher, "The Ad Biz Gloms onto Global," *Fortune,* November 12, 1984, p. 78.
59. Maduh Agrawal, "Review of a 40-Year Debate in International Advertising," *International Marketing Review,*

vol. 12(1), pp. 26–48; William L. James and John S. Hill, "International Advertising Messages, To Adapt or Not to Adapt (That Is the Question)," *Journal of Advertising Research,* 31, June/July 1991, pp. 65–71; Keith Reinhad and W.E. Phillips, "Global Marketing: Experts Look at Both Sides," *Advertising Age,* April 15, 1988, p. 47; and Anthony Rutigliano, "The Debate Goes On: Global vs. Local Advertising," *Management Review,* June 1986, pp. 27–31.

60. Bernhard Warner, "IQ News: Gillette's Mach 3 Media Hit Hits Web: European Site Next?" *AdweekOnline,* August 24, 1998.
61. Jack Neff, "Six-Blade Blitz," *Advertising Age,* September 19, 2005, pp. 3, 53.
62. Kevin Goldman, "Professor Who Started Debate on Global Ads Still Backs Theory," *The Wall Street Journal,* October 13, 1992, p. B8.
63. Examples from speech by Eugene H. Kummel, chairman emeritus, McCann-Erickson Worldwide, and Koji Oshita, president and CEO, McCann-Erickson, Hakuhodo, Japan, in San Diego, California, October 19, 1988; Margo Sugarman, "Nescafé Israel Entry Redefines Coffee Market," *Advertising Age International,* April 1997, p. i12.
64. Joanne Lipman, "Marketers Turn Sour on Global Sales Pitch," *The Wall Street Journal,* May 12, 1988, p. 1.
65. Eric White and Jeffrey A. Trachtenberg, "One Size Doesn't Fit All," *The Wall Street Journal,* October 1, 2003, pp. B1, 2.
66. Joanne Lipman, "Marketers Turn Sour."
67. Sally Goll Beatty, "Global Needs Challenge Midsize Agencies," *The Wall Street Journal,* December 14, 1995, p. B9.
68. Criteria cited by Edward Meyer, CEO, Grey Advertising, in Rebecca Fannin, "What Agencies Really Think of Global Theory," *Marketing & Media Decisions,* December 1984, p. 74.
69. Quote cited in Reinhard and Phillips, "Global Marketing," p. 47.
70. Gregory Solman, "Mazda Goes Global for the 1st Time With Mx-5 Launch," *Adweek,* August 22, 2005, p. 7.
71. Salah S. Hassan and Lea P. Katsansis, "Identification of Global Consumer Segments: A Behavioral Framework," *Journal of International Consumer Marketing,* 3 (2), (1991) pp. 11–28.
72. Arundhati Parmar, "Global Youth United," *Marketing News,* October 28, 2002, pp. 1, 49; "Ready to Shop until They Drop," *BusinessWeek,* June 22, 1998, pp. 104–110; "Teens Seen as the First Truly Global Consumers," *Marketing News,* March 27, 1995, p. 9; Shawn Tully, "Teens: The Most Global Market of All," *Fortune,* May 16, 1994, pp. 90–97.
73. Teressa Iezzi, "Emotional Juice," *Creativity,* March 2004, pp. 10, 30–32.
74. Robert E. Hite and Cynthia L. Fraser, "International Advertising Strategies of Multinational Corporations," *Journal of Advertising Research,* 28 (4) (August/September 1988), pp. 9–17.
75. Ali Kanso, "International Advertising Strategies: Global Commitment to Local Vision," *Journal of Advertising Research,* January/February 1992, pp. 10–14.
76. Jan Jaben, "Ad Decision-Makers Favor Regional Angle, *Advertising Age International,* May 1995, pp. i3, 16.
77. Penelope Rowlands, "Global Approach Doesn't Always Make Scents," *Advertising Age International,* January 17, 1994, pp. i–1, 38.
78. Normandy Madden, "Shanghai Rises as Asia's Newest Marketing Capital," *Advertising Age,* October 14, 2002, pp. 1, 13.
79. Kevin Goldman, "Global Companies Hone Agency Rosters," *The Wall Street Journal,* July 25, 1995, p. B8.
80. Sally Goll Beatty, "Young & Rubicam Is Only One for Colgate," *The Wall Street Journal,* December 1, 1995, p. B6.
81. Beth Snyder Bulik, "Lenovo Breaks First Product Campaign Since IBM Merger," www.Adage.com, July 14, 2005.
82. Kevin Goldman, "Global Companies Hone Agency Rosters."
83. Beth Snyder Bulik and Laurel Wentz, "Samsung Review: It Wasn't California Lottery, But Almost," www.AdAge.com, November 22, 2004.
84. "Advertising Is Indeed Going Global," *Market Europe,* October 1997, pp. 8–10.
85. Anne-Marie Crawford, "Clients and Agencies Split Over Ad Superstars," www.adageglobal, May 2001, p. 16.
86. Joseph T. Plummer, "The Role of Copy Research in Multinational Advertising," *Journal of Advertising Research,* October/November 1986, p. 15.
87. Erin White, "German Ads Get More Daring, But Some Firms Aren't Pleased," *The Wall Street Journal,* November 22, 2002, p. B6.
88. Larry Speer, "French Government Attacks 'Xexist' Ads," www.adageglobal, May 2001, p. 7.
89. Normandy Madden, "Looking for the Next Brazil? Try Thailand," *Advertising Age,* April 11, 2005, p. 22.
90. Normandy Madden, "Two Chinas," *Advertising Age,* August 16, 2004, pp. 1, 22.
91. Nicola Clark, "Pay TV Doesn't Increase Viewing Time, Study Finds," *International Herald Tribune,* April 5, 2004, p. 9.
92. Mir Maqbool Alam Kahn, "TV Ad Spending Could Suffer under Pro-India Politicking," *Advertising Age International,* March 1997, p. i22.
93. Rochell Burbury, "Australia Ends Ban on Cable TV Spots," *Advertising Age International,* March 1997, p. i22.
94. Michael Laris, "China: The World's Most Populous Market," *Advertising Age,* May 15, 1996, p. 111.
95. Leslie Chang, "Cracking China's Huge TV Market," *The Wall Street Journal,* August 1, 2000, pp. B1, 4.
96. Gabriel Kahn "Chinese Puzzle: Spott Consumer Data," *The Wall Street Journal,* October 15, 2003, pp. B1, 10.
97. Chuck Ross, "Global Rules Are Proposed for Measuring TV," *Advertising Age,* August 12, 1996, pp. 3, 28.
98. Ronal Grover and Tom Lowry, "Rupert's World," *BusinessWeek,* January 19, 2004, pp. 51–60.
99. "Young Murdock's Asian Adventure," www.adageglobal.com, May 2001, pp. 30–31.
100. Leslie Chang, "A Phoenix Rises in China," *The Wall Street Journal,* May 26, 1999, pp. B1, 4.
101. Alam Khan, "TV Ad Spending Could Suffer."
102. Frank Rose, "Think Globally, Script Locally," *Fortune,* November 8, 1999, pp. 156–60.
103. Geoffrey A. Fowler and Kathy Chen, "China Blocks News Corp. Lan For TV Channel," *The Wall Street Journal,* August 21, 2005, pp. B1, 8.
104. "Over There: 'Below-the-Line' Is Coming on Strong," *Promo Magazine, Special Report,* August 1998, pp. S12–13.
105. Kamran Kashani and John A. Quelch, "Can Sales Promotion Go Global?" *Business Horizons,* May/June 1990, pp. 37–43.

106. "What You Should Know About Advertising in Japan," *Advertising World,* April 1985, pp. 18–42.
107. Lenard C. Huff and Dana L. Alden, "An Investigation of Consumer Response to Sales Promotion in Developing Markets: A Three Country Analysis," *Journal of Advertising Research,* May/June 1998, pp. 47–56.
108. Douglas J. Wood and Linda A. Goldstein, "A Lawyer's Guide to Going Global," *Promo Magazine, Special Report,* August 1998, p. S11.
109. Kashani and Quelch, "Can Sales Promotion Go Global?"
110. Andrew Tanzer, "Citibank Blitzes Asia," *Forbes,* May 6, 1995, p. 44.
111. Lisa Bertagnoli, "Selling Overseas Complex Endeavor," *Marketing News,* July 30, 2001, p. 4.
112. Ibid.
113. "Foreign Ads Go Further with PR," *International Advertiser,* December 1986, p. 30.
114. Joanna Slater, "Coca-Cola, Pepsi Pass India's Test On Pesticides," *The Wall Street Journal,* August 22, 2003, p. B5.
115. "World Internet Usage and Population Statistics," www.Internetworldstats.com, 2005.
116. Ibid.

Chapter Twenty-One

1. Fred W. Morgan and Jeffrey J. Stoltman, "Advertising and Product Liability Litigation," *Journal of Advertising,* 26, no. 2 (Summer 1997), pp. 63–75.
2. Ira Teinowitz, "Curb Proposal Raises Tobacco Markers' Ire," *Advertising Age,* March 18, 2002, p. 70; Myron Levin, "U.S. to Pursue Lawsuit to Curb Cigarette Marketing," *Los Angeles Times,* March 12, 2002, pp. C1, 15.
3. Christopher Lawton, "Beer Industry Tests FTC's Patience," *The Wall Street Journal,* February 2, 2005, p. B2; Mike Beirne, "In The Name Of Responsibility," *BrandWeek,* May 12, 2003, pp. 32–36; Joe Flint and Shelly Branch, "In Face of Widening Backlash, NBC Gives Up Plan to Run Liquor Ads," *The Wall Street Journal,* March 21, 2002, pp. B1, 4.
4. Alice Z. Cuneo, "Of Contracts and Claims; Agencies Face Liability Issues," *Advertising Age,* January 31, 2000, p. 25.
5. Steven W. Colford and Raymond Serafin, "Scali Pays for Volvo Ad: FTC," *Advertising Age,* August 26, 1991, p. 4; Alice Z. Cuneo, "Can an Agency Be Guilty of Malpractice?" *Advertising Age,* January 31, 2000, pp. 24–25.
6. Priscilla A. LaBarbera, "Analyzing and Advancing the State of the Art of Advertising Self-Regulation," *Journal of Advertising,* 9, no. 4 (1980), p. 30.
7. Ian P. Murphy, "Competitive Spirits: Liquor Industry Turns to TV Ads," *Marketing News,* December 2, 1996, pp. 1, 17.
8. John F. Archer, "Advertising of Professional Fees: Does the Consumer Have a Right to Know?" *South Dakota Law Review* 21 (Spring 1976), p. 330.
9. Bates v. State of Arizona, 97 S.Ct. 2691. 45, *U.S. Law Week* 4895, (1977).
10. Charles Laughlin, "Ads on Trial," *Link,* May 1994, pp. 18–22; and "Lawyers Learn the Hard Sell—And Companies Shudder," *BusinessWeek,* June 10, 1985, p. 70.
11. Bruce H. Allen, Richard A. Wright, and Louis E. Raho, "Physicians and Advertising," *Journal of Health Care Marketing* 5 (Fall 1985), pp. 39–49.
12. Robert E. Hite and Cynthia Fraser, "Meta-Analyses of Attitudes toward Advertising by Professionals," *Journal of Marketing* 52, no. 3 (July 1988), pp. 95–105.
13. Laughlin, "Ads on Trial."
14. Priscilla A. LaBarbera, "Analyzing and Advancing the State of the Art of Advertising Self-Regulation."
15. Shelly Branch, "Campbell Is in the Soup on V8 Ad," *The Wall Street Journal,* April 26, 2002, p. B4.
16. Jack Neff, "Household Brands Counterpunch," *Advertising Age,* November 1, 1999, p. 26.
17. Jean Halliday, "BMW to Appeal NAD Vindication of Volvo Spot," *Advertising Age,* August 19, 1996, pp. 4, 32.
18. "NAD Urges in Brawny Ads," *Advertising Age,* November 2, 1999, p. 2.
19. *NAD Case Reports, 2004 Summary* (National Advertising Division, Council of Better Business Bureaus) 33, no. 1 (January 2005), p. 2.
20. "The Electronic Retailing Self-Regulation Program: Policy and Procedures," The National Advertising Review Council, www.narcpartners.org/ersp.
21. Dorothy Cohen, "The FTC's Advertising Substantiation Program," *Journal of Marketing* 44, no. 1 (Winter 1980), pp. 26–35.
22. Eric J. Lyman, "The True Colors of Toscani," www.adageglobal, September 2001, pp. 22–23.
23. Lynda M. Maddox and Eric J. Zanot, "The Suspension of the National Association of Broadcasters' Code and Its Effects on the Regulation of Advertising," *Journalism Quarterly,* 61 (Summer 1984), pp. 125–30, 156.
24. Joe Mandese, "ABC Loosens Rules," *Advertising Age,* September 9, 1991, pp. 2, 8.
25. Avery M. Abernethy and Jan LeBlanc Wicks, "Self-Regulation and Television Advertising: A Replication and Extension," *Journal of Advertising Research,* vol. 41, (3) (May/June 2001), pp. 31–37; Eric Zanot, "Unseen but Effective Advertising Regulation: The Clearance Process," *Journal of Advertising,* vol. 14, (4) (1985), p. 48.
26. Joanne Voight and Wendy Melillo, "To See or Not To See?" *Adweek,* March 11, 2002, p. 30.
27. Mandese, "ABC Loosens Rules."
28. Steven W. Colford, "Speed Up the NAD, Industry Unit Told," *Advertising Age,* May 1, 1989, p. 3.
29. Virginia State Board of Pharmacy v. Virginia Citizens Consumer Council, 425 U.S. 748, 96 S.Ct. 1817, 48 L. Ed. 2d 346 (1976).
30. Bates v. State of Arizona.
31. Central Hudson Gas & Electric v. Public Service Commission, 447 U.S. 557,100 S. Ct. 2343, 65 L. Ed. 2d 341 (1980).
32. 44 Liquormart, Inc. v. Rhode Island, 517 U.S. 484 (1996).
33. Erik L. Collins, Lynn Zoch, and Christopher S. McDonald, "When Professional Worlds Collide: Implications of Kasky v. Nike for Corporate Reputation Management," *Public Relations Review,* vol. 30, no. 4, November 2004, pp. 411–418; Anne Gearan, "High Court Passes Up Decision on Nike Case," *The San Diego Union-Tribune,* June 27, 2003, p. C1.
34. FTC v. Raladam Co., 258 U.S. 643 (1931).
35. Edward Cox, R. Fellmeth, and J. Schultz, *The Consumer and the Federal Trade Commission* (Washington, DC: American Bar Association, 1969); and American Bar Association, *Report of the American Bar Association to Study the Federal Trade Commission* (Washington, DC: The Association, 1969).
36. *FTC Staff Report on Advertising to Children* (Washington, DC: Government Printing Office, 1978).

37. Federal Trade Commission Improvement Act of 1980, P. L., No. 96-252.
38. Bruce Silverglade, "Does FTC Have an 'Unfair' Future?" *Advertising Age,* March 26, 1994, p. 20.
39. Ivan L. Preston, *The Great American Blow-Up: Puffery in Advertising and Selling* (Madison: University of Wisconsin Press, 1975), p. 3.
40. Isabella C. M. Cunningham and William H. Cunningham, "Standards for Advertising Regulation," *Journal of Marketing* 41 (October 1977), pp. 91–97; and Herbert J. Rotfeld and Kim B. Rotzell, "Is Advertising Puffery Believed?" *Journal of Advertising,* 9 (3), (1980), pp. 16–20.
41. Herbert J. Rotfeld and Kim B. Rotzell, "Puffery vs. Fact Claims—Really Different?" in *Current Issues and Research in Advertising,* ed. James H. Leigh and Claude R. Martin, Jr. (Ann Arbor: University of Michigan, 1981), pp. 85–104.
42. Preston, *The Great American Blow-Up.*
43. Chuck Ross, "Marketers Fend Off Shift in Rules for Ad Puffery," *Advertising Age,* February 19, 1996, p. 41.
44. Federal Trade Commission, "Policy Statement on Deception," 45 ATRR 689 (October 27, 1983), p. 690.
45. For an excellent discussion and analysis of these three elements of deception, see Gary T. Ford and John E. Calfee, "Recent Developments in FTC Policy on Deception," *Journal of Marketing,* 50 no. 3 (July 1986), pp. 86–87.
46. Ray O. Werner, ed., "Legal Developments in Marketing," *Journal of Marketing* 56 (January 1992), p. 102.
47. Ira Teinowitz, "FTC Strives to Clarify 'Made in USA' Rules," *Advertising Age,* April 29, 1996, p. 12.
48. Kalpana Srinivasan, "FTC Spells Out Tough Standards for 'Made in USA,'" *Marketing News,* January 18, 1999, p. 18.
49. Cohen, "The FTC's Advertising Substantiation Program."
50. Trade Regulation Reporter, Par. 20,056 at 22,033, 1970–1973 Transfer Binder, Federal Trade Commission, July 1972.
51. John E. Califee, "FTC's Hidden Weight-Loss Ad Agenda," *Advertising Age,* October 25, 1993, p. 29.
52. Chester S. Galloway, Herbet Jack Rotfeld and Jeff I. Richards, "Holding Media Responsible For Deceptive Weight-Loss Advertising," *West Virginia Law Review,* vol. 107, no. 2, (Winter 2005), pp. 353–384; Herbet Jack Rotfeld, "Desires Versus the Reality of Self-Regulation," *The Journal of Consumer Affairs,* vol. 27, no. 2, (Winter 2003), pp. 424–427.
53. For an excellent description of the Campbell Soup corrective advertising case, see Dick Mercer, "Tempest in a Soup Can," *Advertising Age,* October 17, 1994, pp. 25, 28–29.
54. William L. Wilkie, Dennis L. McNeill, and Michael B. Mazis, "Marketing's 'Scarlet Letter': The Theory and Practice of Corrective Advertising," *Journal of Marketing* 48 (Spring 1984), pp. 11–31.
55. Warner-Lambert Co. v. Federal Trade Commission, CCH P61, 563A-D.C., August 1977 and CCH P61, 646 CA-D.C., September 1977.
56. Bruce Ingersoll, "FTC Orders Novartis to Correct Claims," *The Wall Street Journal,* May 28, 1999, p. B2; Ira Teinowitz, "Doan's Decision Worries Marketers," *Advertising Age,* May 31, 1999, p. 74.
57. Ira Teinowitz, "Doan's Decision Sets Precedent for Corrective Ads," www.AdAge.com, September 4, 2000.
58. "Deceptive Ads: The FTC's Laissez-Faire Approach Is Backfiring," *BusinessWeek,* December 2, 1985, p. 136.
59. Bruce Ingersoll, "FTC Action Snares Home Shopping, iMall," *The Wall Street Journal,* April 16, 1999, p. B2.
60. Ira Teinowitz, "Chairman Muris Promises Evolution at FTC," *Advertising Age,* June 25, 2001, pp. 3, 42.
61. Christopher Saunders, "FTC to Pursue Deceptive E-mail Advertisers," February 1, 2002, www.internetnews/IAR/article/0,,12_967151,00.html.
62. Ira Teinowitz, "Beales Makes Regulation Academic as FTC Director," *Advertising Age,* December 10, 2001, p. 66.
63. Ira Teinowitz, "FCC, FTC Vow 'Action' Against Phone Ads," *Advertising Age,* November 8, 1999, p. 129.
64. Ira Teinowitz, "Howard Stern To Abandon FM Radio," www.AdAge.com, October 6, 2004.
65. Ira Teinowitz, "Clear Channel Drops Howard Stern," www.AdAge.com, February 26, 2004.
66. Ira Teinowitz, "FCC To Probe Super Bowl Halftime Breast Incident," www.AdAge.com, February 2, 2004.
67. Ira Teinowitz and Matthew Creamer, "Fake News Videos Unmasked in FCC Crackdown," www.AdAge.com, April 18, 2005.
68. Sheryl Stolberg, "Clinton Imposes Wide Crackdown on Tobacco Firms," *Los Angeles Times,* August 24, 1996, pp. A1, 10.
69. Joy Johnson Wilson, Summary of the Attorneys General Master Tobacco Settlement Agreement, National Conference of State Legislators, www.academic.udayton.edu/health/syllabi/tobacco/summary.
70. Charles King III, and Michael Siegel, "The Master Settlement Agreement with the Tobacco Industry and Cigarette Advertising in Magazines," *The New England Journal of Medicine,* vol. 345, August 16, 2001, pp. 504–511.
71. Steven W. Colford, "$12 Million Bite," *Advertising Age,* December 2, 1991, p. 4.
72. Jan Joben, "A Setback for Competitive Ads?" *Business Marketing,* October 1992, p. 34.
73. Bruce Buchanan and Doron Goldman, "Us vs. Them: The Minefield of Comparative Ads," *Harvard Business Review,* May/June 1989, pp. 38–50.
74. Maxine Lans Retsky, "Lanham Have It: Law and Comparative Ads," *Marketing News,* November 8, 1999, p. 16.
75. Judann Pollack, "Prego Prevails in Battle Over Comparative Ad," *Advertising Age,* September 1, 1996, p. 12; Michael Fumento, "Free-a-the-Papa!" *Forbes,* February 21, 2000, p. 53.
76. Daniel Golden and Suzanne Vranica, "Duracell's Duck Will Carry Disclaimer," *The Wall Street Journal,* February 7, 2002, p. B7.
77. Michael J. Barone, Randall L. Rose, Paul W. Minniard, and Kenneth C. Manning, "Enhancing the Detection of Misleading Comparative Advertising," *Journal of Advertising Research,* 39 (5) (September/October 1999), pp. 43–50.
78. "Deceptive Ads: The FTC's Laissez-Faire Approach."
79. Jennifer Lawrence, "State Ad Rules Face Showdown," *Advertising Age,* November 28, 1988, p. 4.
80. Steven Colford, "ABA Panel Backs FTC over States," *Advertising Age,* April 10, 1994, p. 1.
81. S. J. Diamond, "New Director Putting Vigor Back into FTC," *Los Angeles Times,* March 29, 1991, pp. D1, 4.
82. Federal Trade Commission, "Trade Regulation Rule: Games of Chance in the Food Retailing and Gasoline Industries," 16 CFR, Part 419 (1982).
83. Richard Sale, "Sweeping the Courts," *Promo,* May 1998, pp. 42–45, 148–152.
84. Ira Teinowitz and Carol Krol, "Multiple States Scrutinize Sweepstakes Mailings," *Advertising Age,* February 9, 1998, p. 41.

85. Mark Pawlosky, "States Rein in Sweepstakes, Game Operators," *The Wall Street Journal,* July 3, 1995, pp. B1, 3.
86. Children Advertising Review Unit Self Regulatory Guidelines for Children's Advertising, Council of Better Business Bureaus, 2003, www.caru.org/guidelines/index.
87. Steven W. Colford, "Top Kid TV Offender: Premiums," *Advertising Age,* April 29, 1991, p. 52.
88. Federal Trade Commission, "Guides for Advertising Allowances and Other Merchandising Payments and Services," 16 CFR, Part 240 (1983).
89. William L. Wilkie, Debra M. Desrochers, and Gregory T. Gundlach, "Marketing Research and Public Policy: The Case of Slotting Fees," *Journal of Marketing & Public Policy,* vol. 21, (2), (Fall 2002), pp. 275–288.
90. Ira Teinowitz, "FTC, McCormick Reach Accord on Slotting Fees," *Advertising Age,* March 13, 2000, p. 75.
91. Federal Trade Commission, "Trade Regulation Rule: Use of Negative Option Plans by Sellers in Commerce," 16 CFR, Part 42 (1982).
92. For a more thorough discussion of legal aspects of sales promotion and mail-order practices, see Dean K. Fueroghne, *Law & Advertising* (Chicago: Copy Workshop, 1995).
93. Mary Lu Carnevale, "FTC Adopts Rules to Curb Telemarketing," *The Wall Street Journal,* September 18, 1992, pp. B1, 10.
94. Scott Hume, "900 Numbers: The Struggle for Respect," *Advertising Age,* February 18, 1991, p. S1.
95. Federal Register, "Rules and Regulations," August 9, 1993, 42364–42406.
96. "Commission to Seek Public Comment on 900-Number Rule Revisions," *Federal Trade Commission Press Release,* October 23, 1998; Russell N. Laczniak, Les Carlson, and Ann Walsh, "Antecedents of Mothers' Attitudes toward the FTC's Rule for 900-Number Advertising Directed at Children," *Journal of Current Issues and Research in Advertising* 21, no. 2 (Fall 1999) pp. 49–58.
97. "US FTC: FTC Workshop to Address Proposed Changes to its Pay-Per-Call-Rule," *M2 Presswire,* May 20, 1999.
98. Ira Teinowitz, "Congress Approves National 'Do Not Call,'" www.AdAge.com, February 13, 2003.
99. Ira Teinowitz, "'Do Not Call' Law Upheld As Constitutional," www.AdAge.com, February 17, 2004.
100. Ira Teinowitz, "'Do Not Call' Does Not Hurt Direct Marketers,"*Advertising Age,* April 11, 2005, pp. 3, 95.
101. Herbert Jack Rotfeld, "Do-Not-Call as the US Government's Improvement to Telemarketing Efficiency," *Journal of Consumer Marketing,* vol. 21, no. 4, 2004, pp. 242–244.
102. Ira Teinowitz and Jennifer Gilbert, "FTC Chairman: Stop Undisclosed Profiling on Net," *Advertising Age,* November 8, 1999, p. 2.
103. Andrea Petersen, "DoubleClick Reverses Course After Privacy Outcry," *The Wall Street Journal,* March 3, 2000, pp. B1, 6; Jennifer Gilbert and Ira Teinowitz, "Privacy Debate Continues to Rage," *Advertising Age,* February 7, 2000, pp. 44, 46.
104. "NAI Launches Privacy-Awareness Web Site," www.Adage.com, May 28, 2001; "Online Advertisers Launch Two Consumer Privacy Tools," *Network Advertising Initiative,* May 23, 2001, www.networkadvertising.org/aboutnai.
105. James Heckman, "COPPA to Bring No Surprises, Hefty Violation Fines in April," *Marketing News,* January 31, 2000, p. 6.
106. Ira Teinowitz, "FTC Proposal on Kids' Privacy Raises Ire of Watchdog Groups," www.AdAge.com, March 14, 2005.
107. Betsy Spethmann, "Private Eyes," *Promo,* January 2002, pp. 37–43.
108. "Protecting Consumers' Privacy: 2002 and Beyond," Remarks of FTC Chairman Timothy J. Muris at The Privacy 2001 Conference, Cleveland, Ohio, October 4, 2001, www.ftc.gov/speeches/muris/privisp1002.
109. Ira Teinowitz, "U.S. House Passes Anti-Spam Measure in Dawn Session," wwwAdAge.com, November 23, 2003; Spethmann, "Private Eyes;" Lisa Takeuchi Cullen, "Some More Spam, Please," *Time,* November 11, 2002, pp. 58–62.
110. Tom Zeller, Jr. "Federal Law Hasn't Curbed Junk E-mail," *The San Diego Union-Tribune,* February, 1, 2005, pp. C1, 5.

Chapter Twenty-Two

1. Robert L. Heilbroner, "Demand for the Supply Side," *New York Review of Books* 38 (June 11, 1981), p. 40.
2. David Helm, "Advertising's Overdue Revolution," speech given to the Adweek Creative Conference, October 1, 1999.
3. Joan Voight, "The Consumer Rebellion," *Adweek,* January 10, 2000, pp. 46–50.
4. Eric N. Berkowitz, Roger A. Kerin, Steven W. Hartley, William Rudelius, *Marketing,* 7th ed. (Burr Ridge, IL: Irwin/McGraw-Hill, 2003), p. 21.
5. Je Eun Lee, Meichum Kuo and Hang Lee, "College Binge Drinking in the 1990's: A Continuing Problem. Results of the Harvard School of Public Health 1999 College Alcohol Study," *Journal of American Collegiate Health,* 48 (5), 2000, pp. 199–210.
6. Jennifer Christie, Dan Fisher, John C. Kozup, Scott Smith, Scott Burton and Elizabeth H. Creyer, "The Effects of Bar-Sponsored Beverage Promotions Across Binge and Nonbinge Drinkers," *Journal of Public Policy & Marketing,* 20 (2), (Fall 2001), pp. 240–253.
7. Mike Beirne, "In The Name Of Responsibility," *BrandWeek,* May 12, 2003, pp. 32–36; Ira Teinowitz, "BoozeHounded," *Advertising Age,* March 25, 2002, pp. 1, 27.
8. Jim O'Hara, "New Study Shows Underage Youth a Target of Alcohol Marketing: Youth Are More Likely To See Alcohol Advertising Than Adults," *U.S. Newswire,* September 24, 2002.
9. Ibid.
10. Deborah Ball, "Magazines Sort Drinking-Age Readers for Ads," *The Wall Street Journal,* December 23, 2004, pp. B1, 3.
11. "Calvin's World," *Newsweek,* September 11, 1995, pp. 60–66.
12. Stephanie Bentley, "Benetton Risks Fresh Outrage," *Marketing Week,* September 13, 1996, p. 9; Gary Levin, "Benetton Ad Lays Bare the Bloody Toll of War," *Advertising Age,* February 21, 1994, p. 38.
13. Jerry Della Famina, "Benetton Ad Models Are Dressed To Kill Sales," *The Wall Street Journal,* March 20, 2000, p. A34.
14. Stephanie O'Donohoe, "Attitudes to Advertising: A Review of British and American Research," *International Journal of Advertising,* 14 (1995), pp. 245–61.
15. Banwari Mittal, "Public Assessment of TV Advertising: Faint Praise and Harsh Criticism," *Journal of Advertising Research* 34, no. 1 (January/February 1994), pp. 35–53.
16. Sharon Shavitt, Pamela Lowery, and James Haefner, "Public Attitudes toward Advertising; More Favorable Than You Might Think," *Journal of Advertising Research,* 38 (4) (July/August 1998), pp. 7–22.

17. Patricia Odell, "Consumer Feel Assaulted By Ads: Forrester," *Promo Xtra,* www.promomagazine.com/news, September 21, 2004
18. Gita Venkataramini Johar, "Consumer Involvement and Deception from Implied Advertising Claims," *Journal of Marketing Research,* 32 (August 1995), pp. 267–79; J. Edward Russo, Barbara L. Metcalf, and Debra Stephens, "Identifying Misleading Advertising," *Journal of Consumer Research,* 8 (September 1981), pp. 119–31.
19. Shelby D. Hunt, "Informational vs. Persuasive Advertising: An Appraisal," *Journal of Advertising,* Summer 1976, pp. 5–8.
20. Banwari Mittal, "Public Assessment of TV Advertising: Faint Praise and Harsh Criticism," and J. C. Andrews, "The Dimensionality of Beliefs Toward Advertising in General," *Journal of Advertising,* vol. 18, no. 1 (1989), pp. 26–35.
21. Helen Cooper, "CDC Advocates Use of Condoms in Blunt AIDS-Prevention Spots," *The Wall Street Journal,* January 5, 1994, p. B1.
22. Jack Neff, "Trojan Ads Ready for Prime Time: NBC," *Advertising Age,* May 16, 2005, p. 3.
23. David A. Aaker and Donald E. Bruzzone, "Causes of Irritation in Advertising," *Journal of Marketing,* Spring 1985, p. 47–57.
24. Stephen A. Greyser, "Irritation in Advertising," *Journal of Advertising Research* 13 (February 1973), pp. 3–10.
25. Ron Alsop, "Personal Product Ads Abound as Public Gets More Tolerant," *The Wall Street Journal,* April 14, 1986, p. 19.
26. Joan Voight and Wendy Melillo, "Rough Cut," *Adweek,* March 11, 2002, pp. 27–29; Joanne Lipman, "Censored Scenes: Why You Rarely See Some Things in Television Ads," *The Wall Street Journal,* August 17, 1987, p. 17.
27. For an interesting analysis of an interpretation of this ad from a literary theory perspective see Aaron C. Ahuvia, "Social Criticism of Advertising: On the Role of Literary Theory and the Use of Data," *Journal of Advertising,* 27, no. 1 (Spring 1998), pp. 143–62.
28. John P. Cortez and Ira Teinowitz, "More Trouble Brews for Stroh Bikini Team," *Advertising Age,* December 9, 1991, p. 45.
29. James B. Arndorfer, "Skyy Hit the Limit with Racy Ad: Critics," *Advertising Age,* February 7, 2005, p. 6.
30. Tim Nudd, "Does Sex Really Sell?" *Adweek,* October 17, 2005, pp. 14–17.
31. Hillary Chura, "Beer Exec Apologizes for Sex Show Involvement," www.AdAge.com, August 27, 2002.
32. Michael McCarthy, "Shockvertising Jolts Ad Viewers," *USA TODAY,* February 23, 2000, p. 6B.
33. Leanne Potts, "Retailers, Ads Bare Flesh for Bottom Line," *Albuquerque Journal,* December 20, 2002, p. D1.
34. Stephanie Kang, "Abercrombie & Fitch Tries to Be Less Haughty, More Nice," *The Wall Street Journal,* June 17, 2005, pp. B1, 2.
35. Rebecca Quick, "Is Ever-So-Hip Abercrombie & Fitch Losing Its Edge with Teens?" *The Wall Street Journal,* February 22, 2000, pp. B1, 4.
36. "Report of the APA Task Force on Advertising and Children," February 20, 2004 www.apa.org/releases/childrenads.html.
37. Dale Kunkel, "Children and Television Advertising," in D.G. Singer and J. L. Singer (eds.), *The Handbook of Children and Media,* (Thousand Oaks, CA.: Sage Publications, 2001), pp. 375–394.
38. Scott Ward, Daniel B. Wackman, and Ellen Wartella, *How Children Learn to Buy: The Development of Consumer Information Processing Skills* (Beverly Hills, CA: Sage, 1979).
39. Thomas S. Robertson and John R. Rossiter, "Children and Commercial Persuasion: An Attribution Theory Analysis," *Journal of Consumer Research* 1, no. 1 (June 1974), pp. 13–20; and Scott Ward and Daniel B. Wackman, "Children's Information Processing of Television Advertising," in *New Models for Communications Research,* ed. G. Kline and P. Clark (Beverly Hills, CA: Sage, 1974), pp. 81–119.
40. Merrie Brucks, Gary M. Armstrong, and Marvin E. Goldberg, "Children's Use of Cognitive Defenses against Television Advertising: A Cognitive Response Approach," *Journal of Consumer Research* 14, no. 4 (March 1988), pp. 471–82.
41. For a discussion on consumer socialization, see Scott Ward, "Consumer Socialization," *Journal of Consumer Research* 1, no. 2 (September 1974), pp. 1–14.
42. Tamara F. Mangleburg and Terry Bristol, "Socialization and Adolescents' Skepticism toward Advertising," *Journal of Advertising,* 27, no. 3 (Fall 1998), pp. 11–21.
43. *FTC Staff Report on Advertising to Children* (Washington, DC: Government Printing Office, 1978).
44. Ben M. Enis, Dale R. Spencer, and Don R. Webb, "Television Advertising and Children: Regulatory vs. Competitive Perspectives," *Journal of Advertising,* 9 no. 1 (1980), pp. 19–25.
45. Richard Zoglin, "Ms. Kidvid Calls It Quits," *Time,* January 20, 1992, p. 52.
46. Elizabeth Jensen and Albert R. Karr, "Summit on Kids' TV Yields Compromise," *The Wall Street Journal,* July 30, 1996, p. B12.
47. Sally Goll Beatty, "White House Pact on TV for Kids May Prove a Marketing Bonanza," *The Wall Street Journal,* August 2, 1996, p. B2.
48. Ronald Alsop, "Watchdogs Zealously Censor Advertising Targeted to Kids," *The Wall Street Journal*, September 5, 1985, p. 35.
49. "Report of the APA Task Force on Advertising and Children," February 20, 2004.
50. Tiffany Meyers, "Marketing to Kids Comes under Fresh Attack," *Advertising Age,* February 21, 2005, pp. S2, 8.
51. Deborah L. Vence, "Marketing to Minors Has Changed," *Marketing News,* May 22, 2002, pp. 5–6.
52. Ibid.
53. Robert E. Hite and Randy Eck, "Advertising to Children: Attitudes of Business vs. Consumers," *Journal of Advertising Research,* October/November 1987, pp. 40–53.
54. Dan Lippe, "What Children Say about Media and Advertising," www.AdAge.com, February 4, 2002.
55. Ronald Berman, *Advertising and Social Change* (Beverly Hills, CA: Sage, 1981), p. 13.
56. Quote in Joan Voight, "The Consumer Rebellion."
57. John K. Galbraith, *The New Industrial State* (Boston: Houghton Mifflin, 1967), cited in Richard W. Pollay, "The Distorted Mirror: Reflections on the Unintended Consequences of Advertising," *Journal of Marketing,* August 1986, p. 25.
58. Raymond A. Bauer and Stephen A. Greyser, "The Dialogue That Never Happens," *Harvard Business Review,* January/February 1969, pp. 122–28.
59. Morris B. Holbrook, "Mirror Mirror on the Wall, What's Unfair in the Reflections on Advertising," *Journal of Marketing,* 5 (July 1987), pp. 95–103; and

Theodore Levitt, "The Morality of Advertising," *Harvard Business Review,* July/August 1970, pp. 84–92.

60. Stephen Fox, *The Mirror Makers: A History of American Advertising and Its Creators* (New York: Morrow, 1984), p. 330.
61. Richard W. Pollay, "The Distorted Mirror: Reflections on the Unintended Consequences of Advertising," *Journal of Marketing,* 50 (April 1986), p. 33.
62. Jules Backman, "Is Advertising Wasteful?" *Journal of Marketing,* 32 (January 1968), pp. 2–8.
63. Hunt, "Informational vs. Persuasive Advertising."
64. Ibid., p. 6.
65. Basil Englis, Michael Solomon, and Richard Ashmore, "Beauty before the Eyes of Beholders: The Cultural Encoding of Beauty Types in Magazine Advertising and Music Television," *Journal of Advertising,* June 1994, pp. 49–64; Alice E. Courtney and Thomas W. Whipple, *Sex Stereotyping in Advertising* (Lexington, MA: Lexington Books, 1984).
66. Daniel J. Brett and Joanne Cantor, "The Portrayal of Men and Women in U.S. Television Commercials: A Recent Content Analysis and Trends of 15 Years," *Sex Roles* 18, no. 9/10 (1998), pp. 595–608; John B. Ford and Michael La Tour, "Contemporary Perspectives of Female Role Portrayals in Advertising," *Journal of Current Issues and Research in Advertising* 28, no. 1 (1996), pp. 81–93.
67. Beverly A. Browne, "Gender Stereotypes in Advertising on Children's Television in the 1990s: A Cross-National Analysis," *Journal of Advertising,* 27 no. 1 (Spring 1998), pp. 83–96.
68. Richard H. Kolbe, "Gender Roles in Children's Advertising: A Longitudinal Content Analysis," in *Current Issues and Research in Advertising,* ed. James H. Leigh and Claude R. Martin, Jr. (Ann Arbor: University of Michigan, 1990), pp. 197–206.
69. Debra Merskin, "Boys Will Be Boys: A Content Analysis of Gender and Race in Children's Advertisements on the Turner Cartoon Network," *Journal of Current Issues and Research in Advertising,* 24, (1), (Spring 2002), pp. 51–60.
70. Cate Terwilliger, "'Love Your Body Day' Auraria Event Takes Aim at 'Offensive' Images, Ads," *Denver Post,* September 23, 1999, p. E3.
71. Steven M. Kates and Glenda Shaw-Garlock, "The Ever Entangling Web: A Study of Ideologies and Discourses in Advertising to Women," *Journal of Advertising,* 28, no. 2 (Summer 1999), pp. 33–49.
72. Suzanne Vranica, "Stereotypes of Women Persist in Ads," *The Wall Street Journal,* October 17, 2003, p. B4.
73. Thomas H. Stevenson, "How Are Blacks Portrayed in Business Ads?" *Industrial Marketing Management* 20 (1991), pp. 193–99; Helen Czepic and J. Steven Kelly, "Analyzing Hispanic Roles in Advertising," in *Current Issues and Research in Advertising,* ed. James H. Leigh and Claude Martin (Ann Arbor: University of Michigan, 1983), pp. 219–40; R. F. Busch, Allan S. Resnik, and Bruce L. Stern, "A Content Analysis of the Portrayal of Black Models in Magazine Advertising," in *American Marketing Association Proceedings: Marketing in the 1980s,* ed. Richard P. Bagozzi (Chicago: American Marketing Association, 1980); and R. F. Busch, Allan S. Resnik, and Bruce L. Stern, "There Are More Blacks in TV Commercials," *Journal of Advertising Research,* 17 (1977), pp. 21–25.
74. James Stearns, Lynette S. Unger, and Steven G. Luebkeman, "The Portrayal of Blacks in Magazine and Television Advertising," in *AMA Educator's Proceedings,* ed. Susan P. Douglas and Michael R. Solomon (Chicago: American Marketing Association, 1987).
75. Robert E. Wilkes and Humberto Valencia, "Hispanics and Blacks in Television Commercials," *Journal of Advertising,* 18, no. 1 (1989), pp. 19–26.
76. Julia Bristor, Renee Gravois Lee, and Michelle Hunt, "Race and Ideology: African American Images in Television Advertising," *Journal of Public Policy and Marketing* 14 (Spring 1995), pp. 48–59.
77. Leon E. Wynter, "Minorities Play the Hero in More TV Ads as Clients Discover Multicultural Sells," *The Wall Street Journal,* December 24, 1993, pp. B1, 6.
78. Bob Garfield, "Ikea Again Furnishes Ad Breakthrough," *Advertising Age,* April 1, 1996, p. 61.
79. Corliss Green, "Ethnic Evaluations of Advertising: Interaction Effects of Strength of Ethnic Identification, Media Placement, and Degree of Racial Composition," *Journal of Advertising,* 28 no. 1 (Spring 1999), pp. 49–64.
80. Charles R. Taylor and Barbara B. Stern, "Asian-Americans: Television Advertising and the 'Model Minority' Stereotype," *Journal of Advertising,* 26 no. 2, (Summer 1997), pp. 47–61.
81. Jon Berry, "Think Bland," *Adweek's Marketing Week,* November 11, 1991, pp. 22–24.
82. Todd Pruzman, "Brewing New Ties with Gay Consumers," *Advertising Age,* April 8, 1996, p. 13.
83. Ronald Alsop, "Web Site Sets Gay-Themed Ad for Big, National Publications," *The Wall Street Journal,* February 17, 2000, p. B4.
84. Mike Wilke, "Commercial Closet: Millers Ads Get Gay Inclusive," www.gfn.com/archives/story.html, May 23, 2001.
85. Jeff I. Richards and John H. Murphy, II, "Economic Censorship and Free Speech: The Circle of Communication between Advertisers, Media and Consumers," *Journal of Current Issues and Research in Advertising* 18, no. 1 (Spring 1996), pp. 21–33.
86. Lawrence C. Soley and Robert L. Craig, "Advertising Pressure on Newspapers: A Survey," *Journal of Advertising,* December 1992, pp. 1–10.
87. Mark Simon, "Mercury News Ad Dispute Cooling Off: Advertisers Return While Reporters Stew," *San Francisco Business Chronicle,* July 15, 1994, p. B1.
88. Soley and Craig, "Advertising Pressure on Newspapers."
89. David Shaw, "An Uneasy Alliance of News and Ads," *Los Angeles Times,* March 29, 1998, pp. A1, 28; Steven T. Goldberg, "Do the Ads Tempt the Editors?" *Kiplinger's,* May 1996, pp. 45–49.
90. Janet Guyon, "Do Publications Avoid Anti-Cigarette Stories to Protect Ad Dollars?" *The Wall Street Journal,* November 22, 1982, pp. 1, 20; Elizabeth M. Whelan, "When Newsweek and Time Filtered Cigarette Copy," *The Wall Street Journal,* November 1, 1984, p. 3; and "RJR Swears Off Saatchi and Nabisco Is in a Sweat," *BusinessWeek,* April 18, 1988, p. 36.
91. Joanne Lipman, "Media Content Is Linked to Cigarette Ads," *The Wall Street Journal,* January 30, 1992, p. B5.
92. Laurie Freman, "Pillsbury Re-evaluates Ads on Violent Shows," *Advertising Age,* January 15, 1996, p. B6.

93. David Shaw, "An Uneasy Alliance of News and Ads," *Los Angeles Times,* March 29, 1998, pp. A1,28.
94. Steven T. Goldberg, "Do the Ads Tempt the Editors?" *Kiplingers Personal Finance,* May 1996, pp. 45–49.
95. David E. Sumner, "Who Pays for Magazines? Advertisers or Consumers?" *Journal of Advertising Research,* 41 (6), (November/December 2001), pp. 61–67.
96. Pamela Sebastian, "Boys & Girls Club Featuring Denzel Washington Is a Standout," *The Wall Street Journal,* July 8, 1996, p. B7.
97. For a discussion of monopolies in the cereal industry, see Paul N. Bloom, "The Cereal Industry: Monopolists or Super Marketers?" *MSU Business Topics,* Summer 1978, pp. 41–49.
98. Lester G. Telser, "Advertising and Competition," *Journal of Political Economy,* December 1964, pp. 537–62.
99. Robert D. Buzzell, Bradley T. Gale, and Ralph G. M. Sultan, "Market Share—A Key to Profitability," *Harvard Business Review,* (January/February 1975), pp. 97–106.
100. Beth Snyder Bulik, "LG's $100 mil charge apes Samsung Tack," *Advertising Age,* June 21, 2004, pp. 1, 33.
101. Robert D. Buzzell and Paul W. Farris, "Advertising Cost in Consumer Goods Industries," *Marketing Science Institute, Report no. 76,* August 1976, p. 111; and Paul W. Farris and David J. Reibstein, "How Prices, Ad Expenditures, and Profits Are Linked," *Harvard Business Review,* (November/December 1979), pp. 173–84.
102. Thomas M. Buron, "Reining in Drug Advertising," *The Wall Street Journal,* March 13, 2002, pp. B1, 4.
103. Paul W. Farris and Mark S. Albion, "The Impact of Advertising on the Price of Consumer Products," *Journal of Marketing,* 44 no. 3 (Summer 1980), pp. 17–35.
104. Buron, "Reining in Drug Advertising."
105. Farris and Albion, "The Impact of Advertising on the Price of Consumer Products."
106. Lee Benham, "The Effect of Advertising on the Price of Eyeglasses," *Journal of Law and Economics* 15 (October 1972), pp. 337–52.
107. Robert L. Steiner, "Does Advertising Lower Consumer Price?" *Journal of Marketing,* 37 no. 4 (October 1973), pp. 19–26.
108. Farris and Albion, "The Impact of Advertising," p. 30.
109. James M. Ferguson, "Comments on 'The Impact of Advertising on the Price of Consumer Products,'" *Journal of Marketing,* 46, no. 1 (Winter 1982), pp. 102–5.
110. Farris and Albion, "The Impact of Advertising."
111. Avery M. Abernethy and George R. Franke, "The Information Content of Advertising: A Meta-Analysis," *Journal of Advertising,* vol. 25, no. 2, (Summer 1996) pp. 1–17.
112. Cyndee Miller, "The Marketing of Advertising," *Marketing News,* December 7, 1992, pp. 1, 2.
113. "AAF's 'Great Brands' Campaign Moves to Television," press release AAF News, January 20, 2002; "Advertising. The Way Great Brands Get to Be Great Brands," *Q&A,* www.AAF.org.

Credits and Acknowledgments

Chapter 1

Photos/Exhibits

p. 3, Courtesy of the Las Vegas Convention and Visitors Authority; p. 5, Courtesy of the Las Vegas Convention and Visitors Authority; p. 6, Courtesy of Randy Snow; p. 7, Courtesy of American Red Cross; p. 8, Courtesy of NIKE, Inc.; p. 10, Courtesy of Montblanc Inc.; p. 12, Photo by David Allan Brandt. Courtesy of American; p. 16, © Viviane Moos/CORBIS; p. 18 (top), Courtesy of American Advertising Federation; p. 18 (bottom), Courtesy of Degussa Corporation; p. 20, Courtesy of Bose Corporation; p. 21 (top), Courtesy of Frito-Lay, Inc.; p. 21 (bottom), Courtesy of Sharp Electronics Corporation; p. 22, Courtesy of Chicken of the Sea International; p. 23, Courtesy of Toyota Motor North America; p. 25, AP Images; p. 27, © 2005 Starbucks Corporation. All rights reserved. Used with permission; p. 31, Courtesy of Unilever Ice Cream and CarbSmart, Inc.

Figures

p. 15, Figure 1-1, Reprinted by permission of *BusinessWeek;* p. 17, Figure 1-3, Reprinted with permission from the June 28, 2004 issue of *Advertising Age.* Copyright, Crain Communications Inc. 2004.

Chapter 2

Photos/Exhibits

p. 37, Courtesy of the San Diego Padres; p. 41, Courtesy of ASICS America Corporation; p. 42 (top), Courtesy of Pepsi-Cola North America; p. 42 (bottom), © CHANEL Inc.; p. 43, AP Images; p. 44, Courtesy of Grupo Modelo, S.A. de C.V; p. 46, Courtesy of Toyota Motor Sales, U.S.A.; p. 47 (top), Courtesy of Big Red, Incorporated; p. 47 (bottom), © 1995-2005 iVillage Inc.; p. 49 (top), Courtesy of The Home Depot; p. 49 (bottom), Courtesy of AARP; p. 50, Courtesy of GlaxoSmithKline; p. 51, Courtesy of Claritas, Inc.; p. 52 (top), Courtesy of Anheuser-Busch; p. 52 (bottom), Courtesy of Maxwell Business Systems; p. 53 (top), Courtesy of The Procter & Gamble Company; p. 53 (bottom), Reproduced with the permission of Malt-O-Meal Company, Minneapolis, Minnesota; p. 54 (top left), Courtesy of Nature's Best; p. 54 (top right), © 2002. Lands' End, Inc. Used with permission; p. 54 (bottom), Courtesy of Church & Dwight Co., Inc.; p. 55 (top), Courtesy of the California Avocado Commission; p. 55 (bottom), Courtesy of The Valvoline Company, a division of Ashland Inc.; p. 56, Courtesy of Kellogg Company; p. 57, © General Motors Corp. Used with permission, GM Media Archive; p. 59, © James Leynse/CORBIS; p. 60 (top), Courtesy of Rolex Watch U.S.A., Inc.; p. 60 (bottom), Courtesy of Pfizer Consumer Healthcare; p. 61 (top), Courtesy of P&G Prestige Products; p. 61 (bottom), M&M'S® and M&M'S MINIS® are registered trademarks of Mars, Incorporated and its affiliates. These trademarks are used with permission. Mars, Incorporated is not associated with the authors or publisher. Advertisement printed with permission of Mars, Incorporated. © Mars, Inc. 2006; p. 62, Courtesy of Etón Corporation.

Chapter 3

Photos/Exhibits

p. 67, Courtesy of MINI USA; p. 70, Courtesy of The History Channel, a programming service of A & E Television Networks; p. 73, Used with permission of The Procter & Gamble Company; p. 77, © 2005 Benetton Group SpA. Photographer David Sims; p. 76, AP Images; p. 82, Courtesy of Mentus; p. 80, © Charles O'Rear/CORBIS; p. 87 (left), Courtesy of Big Chair Creative Group; p. 87 (right), Courtesy of Initiative; p. 93 (top), DR PEPPER® is a registered trademark of Dr. Pepper/Seven Up, Inc. © 2000 Dr. Pepper/Seven Up, Inc.; p. 93 (bottom), Courtesy of Gateway, Inc.; p. 94, Tumbleweeds reprinted with special permission of NAS, Inc.; p. 95, Courtesy of International Business Machines Corporation; p. 96, Courtesy of Protocol Integrated Direct Marketing; p. 97 (top), Courtesy of Don Jagoda Associates, Inc. Melville, NY; p. 97 (bottom), Courtesy of the California Milk Advisory Board; p. 84, Courtesy of Dan Kohler.

Figures

p. 79, Figure 3-6, Reprinted with permission from the May 2, 2005 issue of *Advertising Age.* Copyright, Crain Communications Inc. 2005; p. 90, Figure 3-9, © Association of National Advertisers. Used by permission.

Chapter 4

Photos/Exhibits

p. 103, Copyright, 2005, *Los Angeles Times.* Reprinted with permission; p. 105, Courtesy of Ashworth, Inc.; p. 106, Courtesy of Toyota USA Motor Sales, Inc.; p. 107, Courtesy of Schering Corporation; p. 108, Courtesy of the California Milk Advisory Board; p. 109, Courtesy of Research in Motion; p. 110 (top), © Kimberly-Clark Worldwide, Inc. Used with permission; p. 110 (bottom), Courtesy DaimlerChrysler Corporation; p. 112, Courtesy of JOE'S; p. 113 (top), Courtesy of Tropicana Products, Inc.; p. 113 (bottom), © American Association of Advertising Agencies; p. 114, Courtesy of Alberto-Culver Company; p. 116, Courtesy of The Spokesman-Review. Ad produced by Hanna & Associates Advertising Agency; p. 117, Courtesy of PING; p. 118 (top), Courtesy of Panasonic; p. 118 (bottom), Courtesy of National Turkey Federation; p. 119, Courtesy Anheuser-Busch Companies, Inc.; p. 121, Courtesy of CDW Corporation; p. 122, Source: Fidelity Investments. Copyright 2002 FMR Corp. All rights reserved. Used with permission; p. 124, Courtesy of Lancôme, Paris; p. 125, © Eveready Battery Company, Inc. 1999. Reprinted with permission; p. 127 (left), Courtesy of The Procter & Gamble Company; p. 127 (right), Courtesy of Southwest Airlines; p. 128, Courtesy of Patrinely Group, LLC; p. 129 (left), Source: United States Navy; p. 129 (right), Courtesy of Shell Oil Company; p. 131, Courtesy of Unilever.

Chapter 5

Photos/Exhibits

p. 135, Courtesy of The Procter & Gamble Company; p. 137, Courtesy of the California Milk Advisory Board; p. 139, Courtesy of Rolex Watch U.S.A., Inc.; p. 140, Courtesy of Coach, Inc.; p. 141, © 1999 Time Inc. Reprinted by permission; p. 143, Courtesy of Anheuser-Busch; p. 147, Courtesy Johnson & Johnson Products, Inc.; p. 148, Courtesy of Zenith Electronics Corp.; p. 149, Courtesy of Subaru of America, Inc.; p. 150, Used with Permission of VISA, USA. Photography © Karen Moscowitz/Getty Images; p. 151 (top), © H.J. Heinz Company, L.P. Used with permission; p. 151 (bottom), © Eveready Battery Company, Inc. 1999. Reprinted with permission; p. 153, Courtesy of Whirlpool Corp.; p. 154, Courtesy of LG Electronics; p. 155, Used with permission of The Procter & Gamble Company; p. 158, Courtesy of Maxfli Golf.

Chapter 6

Photos/Exhibits

p. 163, Courtesy of CKE Restaurants, Inc.; p. 166, Courtesy of HEAD/Penn Racquet Sports; p. 167, Courtesy of Lever Brothers Company; p. 169, Courtesy of Wendy's International, Inc.; p. 171, Photo: P. Demarchelier for TAG Heuer; p. 173, Courtesy of New Balance Athletic Shoe, Inc.; p. 175, Courtesy of PowerBar; p. 176, Courtesy of Garmin International, Inc. 2005. All Rights Reserved; p. 178 (top), Courtesy of Unilever; p. 178 (bottom), Courtesy The Advertising Council; p. 180, Courtesy of White Wave, Inc.; p. 181 (top), Courtesy of Novartis Consumer Health Canada Inc.; p. 181 (bottom), Courtesy of The Almond Board of California; p. 182 (top), Courtesy of SOPUS Products. Image of the Acura RL is courtesy of American Honda Motor Co., Inc. Photographer, Markku Lahdesmaki, represented by @radical.media, inc.; p. 182 (bottom), Courtesy of Savin Corporation; p. 183, Courtesy of Miller Brewing Company; p. 185 (top), Courtesy of SmithKline Beecham; p. 185 (bottom), Courtesy of Wm. WRIGLEY Jr. Company; p. 187, Courtesy of Travel + Leisure. Copyright 2005 by American Express Publishing Corp.

Figures

p. 173, Figure 6-3, Reprinted with permission from the November 8, 2004 issue of *Advertising Age.* Copyright, Crain Communications Inc. 2004.

Chapter 7

Photos/Exhibits

p. 191, © age footstock/SuperStock; p. 194, Reprint of the "Safety for Everyone" ad is courtesy of American Honda Motor Co., Inc.; p. 196, Courtesy of The Gillette Company; p. 198 (top), Courtesy of MINI USA; p. 198 (bottom), Courtesy SkyTel Communications, SkyTel An MCI WorldCom Company; p. 199 (top), Courtesy of Pier 1 Imports; p. 199 (bottom), Courtesy of Philips Electronics North America Corporation; p. 204, © McGraw-Hill Companies/Jill Braaten, Photographer; p. 205, Courtesy Foster's Brewing Group; p. 209, Courtesy of the Zoological Society of San Diego; p. 211, © American Association of Advertising Agencies; p. 214, Courtesy of Philips; p. 215, Courtesy of Stokely-Van Camp, Inc.; p. 229, AP Images.

Figures

pp. 218-219, Figure 7-15, Schonfeld & Associates, Inc.; p. 227, Figure 7-23, Source: TNS Media Intelligence; p. 228, Figure 7-24, Source: TNS Media Intelligence.

Chapter 8

Photos/Exhibits

p. 235, © Justin Sullivan/Getty Images; p. 237, © 2005 BMW of North America. Used with permission. The BMW name and Logo are registered trademarks; p. 238, © 2004 Nissan. Nissan, Nissan 350Z, Nissan model names and the Nissan logo are registered trademarks of Nissan; p. 239, Courtesy of Cannes Lions International Advertising Festival; p. 241, Courtesy V&S Vin and Spirit AB. Imported by the Absolut Spirits Co., New York, NY; p. 243, Courtesy of NIKE, Inc.; p. 245, Courtesy of Wm. WRIGLEY Jr. Company; p. 244, Courtesy Norwegian Cruise Line and Goodby, Silverstein & Partners; p. 247, © Sharon Hoogstraten; p. 250, Courtesy of Little, Brown and Company; p. 249, Courtesy of the California Milk Advisory Board; p. 251, Courtesy of Skyy Spirits; p. 255, Courtesy of United Technologies; p. 256, © 2004 BMW of North America, LLC, used with permission. The BMW name and logo are registered trademarks; p. 257, Courtesy Colgate-Palmolive Company; p. 258, Courtesy of Reebok, Acamonchi, John Leguizamo; p. 259 (top), Courtesy Leo Burnett Company, Inc. as agent for Hallmark Cards, Incorporated; p. 259 (bottom), Courtesy of International Business Machines Corporation. Photography by Michele Asselin/Corbis Assignment & Representation; p. 260 (left), Courtesy of Penzoil-Quaker State Company; p. 260 (right), Courtesy of Penzoil-Quaker State Company.

Figures

p. 242, Figure 8-1, Reprinted with permission of D'Arcy, Masius, Benton & Bowles from website, © 2000; p. 253, Figure 8-3, Reprinted with permission from *Advertising Age.* Copyright, Crain Communications Inc. 2005; p. 253, Figure 8-4, From *Journal of Advertising,* vol. 33, no. 4 (Winter 2004): 42. Copyright © 2004 by American Academy of Advertising. Reprinted with permission of M.E. Sharpe, Inc.

Chapter 9

Photos/Exhibits

p. 265, Courtesy of the California Milk Advisory Board; p. 267, Courtesy of Nordica; p. 268, Courtesy of E. Hirshberg; p. 269 (left), Courtesy of MacGregor Golf; p. 269 (right), Copyright 2005 The Boeing Company; p. 270, Courtesy of Neutrogena Corporation; p. 271 (top), Courtesy of Kellogg Company; p. 271 (bottom), Courtesy of Skyy Spirits; p. 272, Courtesy of Skyy Spirits; p. 273, © American Suzuki Motor Corporation 2005. Reprinted with permission; p. 274 (top), Courtesy MasterCard International Incorporated; p. 274 (bottom), Courtesy of Wm. WRIGLEY Jr. Company; p. 275, Courtesy of Porsche Cars North America, Inc.; p. 276 (top), Courtesy of Hitachi America Ltd.; p. 276 (bottom), Courtesy of EAGLE ONE INDUSTRIES, an operating unit of VALVOLINE, a division of ASHLAND, INC. Eagle One, Nanowax and Valvoline are trademarks owned by Ashland, Inc.; p. 277 (top), Courtesy of Church & Dwight Co., Inc.; p. 277 (bottom), Courtesy of Apple Computer, Inc.; p. 278, Courtesy of Pfizer Consumer Healthcare, Pfizer Inc.; p. 279 (top), Courtesy Starkist Seafood, Pittsburgh, PA; p. 280, Courtesy of AFLAC Incorporated; p. 279 (bottom), Courtesy DaimlerChrysler Corporation; p. 281, Courtesy of bebe; p. 282, Courtesy BASF Corporation; p. 283, © 2005 Dell Inc. All Rights Reserved; p. 284 (left), Courtesy of Team One Advertising for LEXUS. Photo by Martin Oort; p. 284 (right), Courtesy of Cambridge SoundWorks; p. 285, Courtesy Sims; p. 289, Courtesy of Citigroup Inc.; p. 291, Courtesy Apple Computer, Inc.; p. 293, Eaton Corporation. All Rights Reserved 2005; Courtesy of Dr. Pepper/Seven Up, Inc. © 2005.

Chapter 10

Photos/Exhibits

p. 299, Photo by CBS/Courtesy of Getty Images; p. 301, AP Images; p. 328, Courtesy of Dyson Direct Inc.

Figures

p. 302, Figure 10-2, Reprinted with permission from the June 27, 2005 issue of *Advertising Age.* Copyright, Crain Communications Inc. 2005; p. 307, Figure 10-5, Used by pemission of Simmons Market Research Bureau, Inc.; p. 308, Figure 10-6, Mediamark Research Inc. Spring 2004. Used by permission; p. 312, Figure 10-9, The sample Oregon Survey of Buying Power data are reprinted from the 2005 Survey of Buying Power published by Sales & Marketing Management. Copyright 2005 by Claritas Inc. This information contains proprietary and confidential property of Claritas Inc. Unauthorized use, including copying of this product, is expressly prohibited; p. 316, Figure 10-15, Source: Mediamark Research Inc. Spring 2004.

Chapter 11

Photos/Exhibits

p. 335, © Harold M. Lambert/SuperStock; p. 338, Courtesy of Porsche Cars North America, Inc.; p. 340, Courtesy Comedy Central; p. 342, Courtesy Court TV; p. 343, Courtesy of TiVo Inc. © 2005 TiVo Inc. All rights reserved; p. 345, Courtesy United Paramount Network and World Wrestling Federation Entertainment, Inc.; p. 346, Courtesy of Univision; p. 348, Courtesy of Syndicated Network Television Association; p. 353 (top), Courtesy of OLN; p. 353 (bottom), Courtesy of the New York Interconnect; p. 354, © 2000 National Broadcasting Company, Inc. Used by permission. All rights reserved; p. 355, Courtesy ESPN, Inc.; p. 356, Courtesy of The History Channel, a programming service of A & E Television Networks; p. 359 (top), Courtesy of Nielsen Media Research; p. 359 (bottom), Courtesy of KFMB TV; p. 362, Courtesy Radio Advertising Bureau; p. 365, Courtesy Radio Advertising Bureau; p. 366, Courtesy Radio Advertising Bureau; p. 368, AP Images; p. 367, KCEO Radio.

Figures

p. 329, Figure 11-1, Reprinted with permission from the June 27, 2005 issue of *Advertising Age.* Copyright, Crain Communications Inc. 2005; p. 345, Figure 11-2, Reprinted with permission from the September 19, 2005 issue of *Advertising Age.* Copyright, Crain Communications Inc. 2005.

Chapter 12

Photos/Exhibits

p. 375, AP Images; p. 378, Courtesy of Virgo Publishing; p. 379 (top), Courtesy of TransWorld Media; p. 379 (bottom), Courtesy Beef Magazine; p. 380, © 2005 Samir Husni, Ph.D. – Mr. Magazine™; p. 381, Courtesy of TransWorld Media; p. 382 (top), Courtesy of Jones Agency; p. 382 (bottom), Courtesy of Time Inc.; p. 383, *Supernatural* materials courtesy of The WB Television Network TM & copyright Warner Bros. 2005; p. 384, Courtesy of WD-40 Company; p. 387 (top), Courtesy of Magazine Publishers of America; p. 386, Courtesy of Magazine Publishers of America; p. 387 (bottom), Courtesy Newsweek, Inc. All rights reserved; p. 389, Courtesy of The Procter & Gamble Company; p. 391, Reprinted by permission of the Audit Bureau of Circulation; p. 392, Courtesy of SRDS; p. 393, Courtesy of Ivy League Magazine Network; p. 394, AP Images; p. 396, Courtesy of Mother Jones; p. 397, Copyright © 2005 *The New York Times;* p. 398, Courtesy of *The Daily Aztec,* San Diego State University; p. 399 (top), Courtesy of *The San Diego Union-Tribune;* p. 399 (bottom), Courtesy of Bridgestone Golf, Inc.; p. 400 (left), Courtesy of *Chicago Tribune;* p. 400 (right), Courtesy of *The San Diego Union-Tribune;* p. 401, Courtesy of *The San Diego Union-Tribune;* p. 402, © 2005 Courtesy of Mercedes-Benz USA; p. 404, Courtesy of Newspaper National Network; p. 406, Courtesy *Miami Herald/El Nuevo Herald;* p. 407, Courtesy of *The San Diego Union-Tribune;* p. 408 (top), Courtesy *Newsweek,* Inc. All rights reserved; p. 408 (bottom), Courtesy of Newspaper Association of America; p. 410, Courtesy of *The San Diego Union-Tribune;* p. 409, © Michael Newman/Photo Edit.

Figures

p. 378, Figure 12-1, Top magazines by subscriptions and single-copy sales, Magazine Publisher of America, Fact Sheet, www.magazine.org. Used by permission; p. 388, Figure 12-3, Top 50 magazines in average paid circulation, Magazine Publisher of America, Fact Sheet, www.magazine.org. Used by

Name and Company Index

A

B

C

D

E

F

G

H

I

J

K

L

M

N

O

P

Q

R

S

T

U

V

W

X

Y

Z

Subject Index

A

B

C

D

E

F

G

H

I

J

K

L

M

N

O

P

T

U

V

W

X

Y

Z